CASE-TUTOR™ COURSEWARE FOR STUDENTS

Accompanying this textbook is an optional custom-designed supplement that you can use to help you analyze the cases.

Case-TUTOR™ contains study questions for each of the 32 cases in this book plus custom-designed case preparation exercises for 10 of the cases that walk you through the needed analysis, tutor you in appropriate use of the concepts and tools, and provide number-crunching assistance. The 10 cases for which there's a case preparation exercise on Case-TUTOR are indicated by the Case-TUTOR logo in the Table of Contents.

The study questions for each of the 32 cases serve as a guide for what to think about and what to analyze in preparing the assigned cases for class. You'll find the 10 custom-designed case preparation exercises valuable in learning how to think strategically about a company's situation, applying the tools and concepts covered in the 9 text chapters, and arriving at sound recommendations about what action management should take to improve the company's performance.

This courseware can be used with any Windows-based PC loaded with Microsoft Excel **2000, XP, and 2003.**

Case-TUTOR is **FREE** with the purchase of a new textbook when you use the unique code packaged with the book to download the software.

STRATEGY

STRATEGY
STRATEGY

STRATEGY

Winning in the Marketplace

Core Concepts • Analytical Tools • Cases

Arthur A. Thompson, Jr.
University of Alabama

John E. Gamble
University of South Alabama

A. J. Strickland III
University of Alabama

Boston   Burr Ridge, IL   Dubuque, IA   Madison, WI   New York   San Francisco   St. Louis
Bangkok   Bogotá   Caracas   Kuala Lumpur   Lisbon   London   Madrid   Mexico City
Milan   Montreal   New Delhi   Santiago   Seoul   Singapore   Sydney   Taipei   Toronto

Irwin

STRATEGY: WINNING IN THE MARKETPLACE
CORE CONCEPTS, ANALYTICAL TOOLS, CASES

Published by McGraw-Hill/Irwin, a business unit of The McGraw-Hill Companies, Inc., 1221
Avenue of the Americas, New York, NY 10020. Copyright © 2004 by The McGraw-Hill
Companies, Inc. All rights reserved. No part of this publication may be reproduced or distributed
in any form or by any means, or stored in a database or retrieval system, without the prior written
consent of The McGraw Hill Companies, Inc., including, but not limited to, in any network or
other electronic storage or transmission, or broadcast for distance learning.
Some ancillaries, including electronic and print components, may not be available to customers
outside the United States.

This book is printed on acid-free paper.

domestic   1 2 3 4 5 6 7 8 9 0 DOW/DOW 0 9 8 7 6 5 4 3
international 1 2 3 4 5 6 7 8 9 0 DOW/DOW 0 9 8 7 6 5 4 3

ISBN 0-07-284770-0

Editor-in-chief: *John E. Biernat*
Executive editor: *John Weimeister*
Managing developmental editor: *Laura Hurst Spell*
Executive marketing manager: *Ellen Cleary*
Producer, media technology: *Mark Molsky*
Lead project manager: *Mary Conzachi*
Design team leader: *Mary L. Christianson*
Photo research coordinator: *Kathy Shive*
Supplement producer: *Joyce J. Chappetto*
Senior digital content specialist: *Brian Nacik*
Cover and interior design: *Jamie O'Neal*
Cover image: *© SuperStock*
Typeface: *10.5/12 Times*
Compositor: *GAC Indianapolis*
Printer: *R. R. Donnelley*

Library of Congress Cataloging-in-Publication Data
Thompson, Arthur A., 1940-
    Strategy : winning in the marketplace : core concepts, analytical tools, cases / Arthur A.
Thompson, Jr., John E. Gamble, A. J. Strickland III – 1st ed.
        p. cm.
    Includes index.
    ISBN 0-07-284770-0 (alk. paper) — ISBN 0-07-121514-X (international : alk. paper)
    1. Strategic planning. 2. Industrial management. 3. Conglomerate
corporations—Management. 4. Strategic planning—Case studies. I. Gamble, John (John E.)
II. Strickland, A. J. (Alonzo J.) III. Title.
HD30.28.T543 2004
658.4'012—dc21
                                                                        2003048765

INTERNATIONAL EDITION ISBN 0-07-121514-X
Copyright © 2004 Exclusive rights by The McGraw-Hill Companies, Inc. for manufacture and
export. This book cannot be re-exported from the country to which it is sold by McGraw-Hill.
The International Edition is not available in North America.

www.mhhe.com

To our families and especially our wives:
Hasseline, Debra, and Kitty

About the Authors

Arthur A. Thompson, Jr., earned his BS and PhD degrees in economics from the University of Tennessee in 1961 and 1965, respectively; spent three years on the economics faculty at Virginia Tech; and served on the faculty of the University of Alabama's College of Commerce and Business Administration for 24 years. In 1974 and again in 1982, Dr. Thompson spent semester-long sabbaticals as a visiting scholar at the Harvard Business School.

His areas of specialization are business strategy, competition and market analysis, and the economics of business enterprises. He has published over 30 articles in some 25 different professional and trade publications and has authored or co-authored five textbooks and four computer-based simulation exercises.

Dr. Thompson is a frequent speaker and consultant on the strategic issues confronting the electric utility industry, particularly as concerns the challenges posed by industry restructuring, re-regulation, competition, and customers' freedom of choice. He spends much of his off-campus time giving presentations to electric utility groups and conducting management development programs for electric utility executives all over the world.

Dr. Thompson and his wife of 42 years have two daughters, two grandchildren, and a Yorkshire terrier.

John E. Gamble is currently Chairman of the Department of Management and Associate Professor of Management in the Mitchell College of Business at The University of South Alabama. His teaching specialty at USA is strategic management and he also conducts a course in strategic management in Germany through a collaborative MBA program sponsored by the University of Applied Sciences in Ludwigshafen/Worms, the State of Rhineland Westphalia, and the University of South Alabama.

Dr. Gamble's research interests center on strategic issues in entrepreneurial, health care, and manufacturing settings. His work has been published in such scholarly journals as *Journal of Business Venturing*, *Journal of Labor Research*, *Health Care Management Review*, and *Labor Studies Journal*. He is the author or co-author of more than 20 case studies published in various strategic management and strategic marketing texts. He has done consulting on industry and market analysis and strategy formulation and implementation issues with clients in public utilities, technology, non-profit, and entrepreneurial businesses.

Professor Gamble received his Ph.D. in management from the University of Alabama in 1995. Dr. Gamble also has a Bachelor of Science degree and a Master of Arts degree from The University of Alabama.

Dr. A. J. (Lonnie) Strickland, a native of North Georgia, attended the University of Georgia, where he received a bachelor of science degree in math and physics in 1965. Afterward he entered the Georgia Institute of Technology, where he received a master of science in industrial management. He earned a PhD in business administration from Georgia State University in 1969. He currently holds the title of Professor of Strategic Management in the Graduate School of Business at the University of Alabama.

Dr. Strickland's experience in consulting and executive development is in the strategic management area, with a concentration in industry and competitive analysis. He has developed strategic planning systems for such firms as the Southern Company, BellSouth, South Central Bell, American Telephone and Telegraph, Gulf States Paper, Carraway Methodist Medical Center, Delco Remy, Mark IV Industries, Amoco Oil Company, USA Group, General Motors, and Kimberly Clark Corporation (Medical Products). He is a very popular speaker on the subject of implementing strategic change and serves on several corporate boards.

He has served as director of marketing for BellSouth, where he had responsibility for $1 billion in revenues and $300 million in profits.

In the international arena, Dr. Strickland has done extensive work in Europe, the Middle East, Central America, Malaysia, Australia, and Africa. In France he developed a management simulation of corporate decision making that enables management to test various strategic alternatives.

In the area of research, he is the author of 15 books and texts. His management simulations, Tempomatic IV and Micromatic, were pioneering innovations that enjoyed prominent market success for two decades.

Recent awards for Dr. Strickland include the Outstanding Professor Award for the Graduate School of Business and the Outstanding Commitment to Teaching Award for the University of Alabama, in which he takes particular pride. He is a member of various honor leadership societies: Mortar Board, Order of Omega, Beta Gamma Sigma, Omicron Delta Kappa, and Jasons. He is past national president of Pi Kappa Phi social fraternity.

Preface

Strategy: Winning in the Marketplace is intended for core courses in strategic management or business policy at the undergraduate level. Our purpose in writing this book has been to address the frequently expressed concerns that the current array of leading introductory strategy texts contain too much detail and try to cover too much ground for a one-semester course. In talking to instructors and students, a recurring theme is that the course is overly jammed. Instructors complain about their difficulties in doing justice to 450–500 pages of text chapters and still finding enough room for such value-added assignments as cases and a substantive simulation exercise. Students complain they have trouble digesting the main elements of strategic thinking and strategic analysis given the rapid-fire pace of the course, the clutter of topics, and a sometimes intimidating or overwhelming workload.

This book endeavors to set an appealing standard for basic strategy texts. With fewer chapters and shorter cases than previous texts by two of the three co-authors, this first edition of *Strategy: Winning in the Marketplace* offers a concise, lively, and user-friendly presentation of strategic management. We have attempted to put together a book that (1) is sufficiently comprehensive in its coverage of important concepts and analytical tools; (2) has a desirable degree of depth and substance; (3) is flush with convincing examples of strategy in action; (4) maintains a straightforward, integrated flow from one chapter to the next; and (5) makes the discipline of business strategy relevant and professionally interesting to students.

But don't expect a shallow, watered-down, full-of-fluff nine-chapter treatment—the text chapters contain a *streamlined* and *substantive* 320-page presentation of core concepts and analytical techniques. And the shorter cases (spanning 590 pages and averaging about 18 pages each) are amply demanding in their analytical requirements and the need for good strategic thinking. Instructors and students alike will find plenty to chew on for a full-semester course.

On-Target Content

To have adequately on-target content, a strategy text must:

- Explain core concepts and provide examples of their relevance and use by actual companies.
- Present understandable explanations of what the essential analytical tools are, how they are used, and where they fit into the managerial process of crafting and executing strategy.
- Be up-to-date and comprehensive, with solid coverage of the landmark changes in competitive markets and company strategies being driven by globalization and Internet technology.
- Focus squarely on what every student needs to know about crafting, implementing, and executing business strategies in today's market environments.

■ Contain fresh, value-adding cases that feature interesting products and companies, illustrate the important kinds of strategic challenges managers face, embrace valuable teaching points, and spark student interest.

This textbook does all these things without being formidable for instructors to cover in one semester and without burdening students with unnecessary pages to read and absorb. Chapter discussions cut straight to the chase on what students really need to know. Our explanations of core concepts and analytical tools are, however, covered in enough depth to make them understandable and usable, the rationale being that a shallow explanation carries little punch and has almost no value. We have chosen examples that students can easily relate to. We have incorporated state-of-the-art research pertinent to a first course in strategy.

Chapter Features and Organization

The chapter presentations reflect a host of developments in the theory and practice of strategic management: the growing scope and strategic importance of collaborative alliances, the continuing march of industries and companies to wider globalization, the inclusion of the resource-based view of the firm as a standard part of strategic analysis, the spread of high-velocity change to more industries and company environments, and how implementation of Internet technology applications in companies all across the world is driving fundamental changes in both strategy and internal operations. The text chapters emphasize that a company's strategy must be matched *both* to its external market circumstances and to its internal resources and competitive capabilities. The resource-based view of the firm is prominently integrated into our coverage of crafting both single-business and multibusiness strategies; two of the three chapters on executing strategy have a strong resource-based perspective, stressing the importance of intellectual capital, core competencies, and competitive capabilities.

The following rundown summarizes the noteworthy chapter features and topical emphasis in this edition:

■ Chapter 1 introduces and defines a host of core concepts—strategy, business model, strategic visions and business missions, strategic versus financial objectives, strategic plans, strategic intent, crafting strategy, and executing strategy. Clear distinction is made between a company's strategy and its business model. A section on strategic visions and mission statements hammers home the importance of clear direction setting and a motivating strategic vision; there's an accompanying discussion of how core values and ethics tie in to a company's vision and business purpose. Emphasis is placed on why companies have to rapidly adapt strategy to newly unfolding market conditions and why strategy life cycles are often short. Following Henry Mintzberg's pioneering research, we stress how and why a company's strategy emerges from (1) the deliberate and purposeful actions of management and (2) as-needed reactions to fresh developments and changing competitive pressures. There's a section on corporate intrapreneuring to help underscore that a company's strategic plan is a collection of strategies devised by different managers at different levels in the organizational hierarchy. We've taken pains to explain why *all managers are on a company's strategy-making, strategy-implementing team*, why every manager is well advised to make the concepts and techniques of strategic management a basic part of his or her tool kit, and why the best companies want their personnel to be true students of the business. The chapter winds up with a section on corporate governance and a discussion of why strategy is important.

■ Chapter 2 sets forth the now-familiar analytical tools and concepts of industry and competitive analysis and demonstrates the importance of tailoring strategy to fit the circumstances of a company's industry and competitive environment. The standout feature of this chapter is a dramatically enhanced presentation of Michael E. Porter's "five-forces model of competition"—we think it is the clearest, most straightforward five-forces model discussion of any text in the field. Globalization and Internet technology are treated as potent driving forces capable of reshaping industry competition—their roles as change agents have become factors that most companies in most industries must reckon with in forging winning strategies.

■ Chapter 3 establishes the equal importance of doing solid company situation analysis as a basis for matching strategy to organizational resources, competencies, and competitive capabilities. The roles of core competencies and organizational resources and capabilities in creating customer value and helping build competitive advantage are *center stage* in the discussions of company resource strengths and weaknesses. SWOT analysis is cast as a simple, easy-to-use way to assess a company's resources and overall situation. There are sections describing the now-standard tools of value chain analysis, benchmarking, and competitive strength assessments—all of which, we believe, provide insight into a company's relative cost position and market standing vis-à-vis rivals. There's discussion of how company implementation of Internet technology is altering the value chain and the performance of particular value chain activities.

■ Chapter 4 deals with a company's quest for competitive advantage—the options for crafting a strategy that simultaneously hold good prospects for competitive advantage while also being well suited both to industry and competitive conditions and to its own resources and competitive circumstances. While the chapter is framed around the five generic competitive strategies—low-cost leadership, differentiation, best-cost provider, focused differentiation, and focused low-cost—it also contains important sections on what use to make of strategic alliances and collaborative partnerships; what use to make of mergers and acquisitions in strengthening the company's competitiveness; when to integrate backward or forward into more stages of the industry value chain; the merits of outsourcing certain value chain activities from outside specialists; whether and when to employ offensive and defensive moves; and the different ways a company can use the Internet as a distribution channel to position itself in the marketplace.

■ Chapter 5 explores a company's strategy options for expanding beyond its domestic boundary and competing in the markets of either a few or a great many countries—options ranging from an export strategy to licensing and franchising to multicountry strategies to global strategies to heavy reliance on strategic alliances and joint ventures. Four strategic issues unique to competing multinationally are given special attention: (1) whether to customize the company's offerings in each different country market to match the tastes and preferences of local buyers or whether to offer a mostly standardized product worldwide, (2) whether to employ essentially the same basic competitive strategy in the markets of all countries where the company operates or whether to modify the company's competitive approach country by country as needed to fit specific market conditions and competitive circumstances, (3) how to locate production facilities, distribution centers, and customer service operations to maximum competitive advantage, and (4) how to use efficient cross-border transfer of a company's resource strengths and capabilities to build competitive advantage. There's also coverage of profit sanctuaries and cross-market subsidization; the special problems associated with entry into the markets of emerging countries; and strategies that local companies in such emerging countries as India, China, Brazil, and Mexico can use to defend against the invasion of opportunity-seeking, resource-rich global giants.

▪ The treatment of diversification strategies for multibusiness enterprises in Chapter 6 lays out the various paths for becoming diversified, explains how a company can use diversification to create or compound competitive advantage for its business units, and examines the strategic options an already-diversified company has to improve its overall performance. In the last part of the chapter, the analytical spotlight is on the techniques and procedures for assessing the strategic attractiveness of a diversified company's business portfolio—the relative attractiveness of the various businesses the company has diversified into, a multi-industry company's competitive strength in each of its lines of business, and the *strategic fits* and *resource fits* among a diversified company's different businesses.

▪ The three-chapter module on executing strategy (Chapters 7–9) is anchored around a solid, compelling conceptual framework: (1) building the resource strengths and organizational capabilities needed to execute the strategy in competent fashion; (2) allocating ample resources to strategy-critical activities; (3) ensuring that policies and procedures facilitate rather than impede strategy execution; (4) instituting best practices and pushing for continuous improvement in how value chain activities are performed; (5) installing information and operating systems that enable company personnel to better carry out their strategic roles proficiently; (6) tying rewards and incentives directly to the achievement of performance targets and good strategy execution; (7) shaping the work environment and corporate culture to fit the strategy; and (8) exerting the internal leadership needed to drive execution forward. The recurring theme of these three chapters is that implementing and executing strategy entails figuring out the specific actions, behaviors, and conditions that are needed for a smooth strategy-supportive operation and then following through to get things done and deliver results—the goal here is to ensure that students understand the strategy-implementing/strategy-executing phase is a managerial exercise in making things happen and making them happen right.

Our top priority has been to ensure that the nine chapters of text hit the bull's-eye with respect to content and represent the best thinking of both academics and practitioners. But at the same time we've gone the extra mile to stay on message with clear, crisp explanations laced with enough relevant examples to make the presentation convincing, pertinent, and worthwhile to students preparing for careers in management and business. We believe our enthusiasm for the subject matter will come across to readers. And the boxed Company Spotlights and Global Spotlights in each chapter relate stories aimed at both informing students and persuading them that the discipline of strategy merits their rapt attention.

The Case Collection

The 32 cases included in this edition are the very latest and best that we could assemble; the case collection is filled with examples of strategy in action and valuable lessons for students in the art and science of crafting and executing strategy. The cases are balanced in length—close to a third of the cases are under 15 pages yet offer plenty for students to chew on; about a third are medium-length cases; and about a third are longer, detail-rich cases that call for more sweeping analysis. At least 24 of the 32 cases involve high-profile companies, products, or people that students will have heard of, know about from personal experience, or can easily identify with. There are four dot-com company cases, plus several others that will provide students with insight into the special demands of competing in industry environments where technological developments are an everyday event, product life cycles are short, and competitive maneuvering among rivals comes fast and furious. At least 21 of the cases involve situations where company resources and competitive capabilities play as large a role in the strategy-making, strategy-implementing scheme of things as industry and competitive conditions do. Scattered throughout the lineup are 13 cases concerning non-U.S. companies, globally competitive industries, and/or cross-cultural situations; these cases, in conjunction with the globalized content of the text chapters, provide ample material for linking the study of strategic management tightly to the ongoing globalization of the world economy. You'll also find 5 cases dealing with the strategic problems of family-owned or relatively small entrepreneurial businesses and 22 cases involving public companies about which students can do further research on the Internet. Eight of the cases (Whole Foods Market, Competition in the Bottled Water Industry, Callaway Golf Company, Kmart, Continental Airlines, the Transformation of BP, Southwest Airlines, and Enron) have accompanying videotape segments. We believe you will find the collection of 32 cases quite appealing, eminently teachable, and very suitable for drilling students in the use of the concepts and analytical treatments in Chapters 1 through 9. It is a case lineup that should stimulate student interest from beginning to end.

In addition, the publisher is providing website access to PDF files of five other recent cases researched and written by the authors of the text. These five "e-cases" are available to adopters and to students who purchase the text. Students who purchase new books will receive a passcode packaged with the text, allowing them to download the cases from www.mhhe.com/thompson1e/tutor. The cases and teaching notes are also available on the Instructor's Resource CD. This extends the number of cases available in the total package to 37.

The All-New Companion *GLO-BUS* Online Simulation Exercise

GLO-BUS: Developing Winning Competitive Strategies, a completely online simulation co-created by the senior author of this text with two others, is being marketed by the publisher as a companion supplement for use with this and other texts in the field. All three co-authors of this book are avid longtime simulation users. Our own experiences, together with numerous discussions with colleagues around the world, have convinced us that competition-based simulation games are *the single most effective, most stimulating exercise available* for giving students valuable practice in being active strategic thinkers and in reading the signs of industry change, reacting to the moves of competitors, evaluating strengths and weaknesses in their company's competitive position, and deciding what to do to improve a company's financial performance. The competitive circumstances of an industry simulation force participants to wrestle with charting a long-term direction for their company, setting strategic and financial objectives, and crafting strategies that produce good results and perhaps lead to competitive advantage. And by having to live with the decisions they make, players experience what it means to be accountable for their decisions and achieve satisfactory results. All this serves to drill students in responsible decision making and to improve their business acumen and managerial judgment. We think putting students through a simulation exercise helps make the strategy course a true capstone experience.

A Bird's-Eye View of *GLO-BUS*

This all-new, totally online simulation is modeled around the digital camera industry, a contemporary high-tech business students can readily identify with and understand. The market for digital cameras displays the characteristics of many globally competitive industries—fast growth, worldwide use of the product, competition among companies from several continents, production located in low-wage locations, and a marketplace where a variety of competitive approaches and business strategies can coexist. Companies design and assemble their lines of entry-level and multifeatured cameras in an Asian assembly facility and ship finished goods directly to camera retailers in North America, Asia-Pacific, Europe-Africa, and Latin America.

Competition is head-to-head—each team of students must match strategic wits against the other company teams. Depending on class size and the number of co-managers assigned to each company, an industry consists of 4, 8, or 12 competing companies. While at the beginning of the simulation each company starts off as the same overall size with the same financial condition and sells its cameras in all four geographic regions of the world market, competing companies do not begin the simulation with the same market shares in each geographic area—one-fourth of the competitors have their biggest market share in Europe-Africa, one-fourth have their biggest share in North America, and so on. As the simulation unfolds, companies can reposition themselves in the four geographic market segments and two product segments (entry-level and multifeatured cameras) however they see fit, pursuing additional sales and market share in some geographic areas and de-emphasizing or abandoning others. All companies have the flexibility to adjust their annual shipments of digital cameras to mitigate the impact of fluctuating exchange rates.

Low-cost leadership, differentiation strategies, best-cost producer strategies, and focus strategies are all viable competitive options. Company managers can try to gain an edge over rivals with more advertising, longer and more frequent promotions, longer warranties, wider product selection, or better technical support. They can have a strategy aimed at being the clear market leader in either entry-level cameras, upscale multi-featured cameras, or both. They can focus on one or two geographic regions or strive for geographic balance. They can pursue essentially the same strategy worldwide or craft slightly or very different strategies for the Europe-Africa, Asia-Pacific, Latin America, and North America markets.

Company co-managers make 44 types of decisions each period, ranging from R&D, camera components, and camera performance (10 decisions) to production operations and worker compensation (15 decisions) to pricing and marketing (15 decisions) to the financing of company operations (4 decisions). Cause–effect relationships are based on sound business and economic principles.

The *GLO-BUS* participant's guide (about 25 pages) is delivered online—students can read it on their monitors or print out a copy, as they prefer. There are built-in help screens and on-screen information that provide students with the relevant information and full instructions. Students make all *GLO-BUS* decisions online and access all the results online. While decisions are made annually, there is an option that instructors can turn on allowing students to review the results by quarter and to make changes for upcoming quarters in prices, special promotions, and production levels. Decisions are processed online automatically according to times and dates set by the instructor—nothing is required on the part of instructors beyond assigning students to teams, specifying the desired simulation schedule (done online), monitoring the results as they occur, counseling with students who may request advice about their company's performance, and deciding on a simulation grade (based on automatically calculated scores of company and individual performances using scoring weights specified by the instructor). Technical support is provided directly by the simulation co-authors and the staff at GLO-BUS.com. There is no software for students or instructors to download or install. The only requirement of players and instructors is that user PCs must be equipped with Microsoft Excel (versions 2000 or later), Internet Explorer, and have access to an Internet connection.

For more information and details, please visit www.glo-bus.com.

Instructor Support Materials

Instructor's Manual

The accompanying instructor's manual contains a section on suggestions for organizing and structuring your course, sample syllabi and course outlines, a copy of the test bank, and comprehensive teaching notes for each of the 32 cases.

Test Bank

There is a test bank prepared by the co-authors containing almost 900 multiple-choice questions and essay questions.

Computest

A computerized version of the test bank allows you to generate tests quite conveniently and to add in your own questions.

PowerPoint Slides

To facilitate preparation of your lectures and to serve as chapter outlines, you'll have access to approximately 500 colorful, professional-looking slides displaying core concepts, analytical procedures, key points, and all the figures in the text chapters. The slides are the creation of Professor Jana Kuzmicki of Troy State University.

Accompanying Case Videos

Eight of the cases—Whole Foods Market, Competition in the Bottled Water Industry, Callaway Golf Company, the Transformation of BP, Kmart, Continental Airlines, Southwest Airlines, and Enron—have accompanying videotape segments that you can show during the course of the case discussions. Suggestions for using each video are contained in the teaching note for that case.

Presentation CD-ROM

The instructor's manual, all of the PowerPoint slides, the video clips, teaching notes for the 32 cases in the text, and the five supplemental e-cases and teaching notes available with *Strategy: Winning in the Marketplace* have been installed on a CD for easy access in preparing a syllabus and daily course schedule, preparing customized lectures, and teaching the cases.

Website: www.mhhe.com/thompson1e

The instructor portion of the website contains a password-protected section that provides epilogue updates on the 32 cases contained in this text, plus an assortment of instructor's manual and other support-related materials that can be downloaded directly.

The GLO-BUS Online Simulation

The optional companion simulation of the digital camera industry is a powerful and constructive way of emotionally connecting students to the subject matter of the course. We know of no more powerful way to stimulate the competitive energy of students and prepare them for the rigors of real-world business decision making than to have them match strategic wits with classmates in running a company in head-to-head competition for global market leadership.

Student Support Materials

Chapter-End Exercises

Each chapter contains a select number of exercises, most related to research on the Internet, that reinforce key concepts and topics covered in the chapters.

Website: www.mhhe.com/thompson1e

The student portion of the website features a "Guide to Case Analysis," with special sections on what a case is, why cases are a standard part of courses in strategy, preparing a case for class discussion, doing a written case analysis, doing an oral presentation, and using financial ratio analysis to assess a company's financial condition. In addition, there are self-scoring 20-question chapter tests and a select number of Power-Point slides for each chapter.

Case-TUTOR Software

Accompanying the 32 cases is a software package containing assignment questions for all 32 cases in the text, plus analytically structured exercises for 10 of the cases that coach students in doing the strategic thinking needed to arrive at solid answers to the assignment questions for that case. Conscientious completion of the exercises helps students gain quicker command of the concepts and analytical techniques and points them toward doing good strategic analysis.

PowerWeb

With each new book, students gain access to the publisher's PowerWeb site offering current news, articles from 6,300 premium sources, a Web research guide, current readings from annual editions, and links to related sites.

Acknowledgments

We heartily acknowledge the contributions of the case researchers whose case-writing efforts appear herein and the companies whose cooperation made the cases possible. To each one goes a very special thank-you. We cannot overstate the importance of timely, carefully researched cases in contributing to a substantive study of strategic management issues and practices. From a research standpoint, strategy-related cases are invaluable in exposing the generic kinds of strategic issues that companies face, in forming hypotheses about strategic behavior, and in drawing experienced-based generalizations about the practice of strategic management. From an instructional standpoint, strategy cases give students essential practice in diagnosing and evaluating the strategic situations of companies and organizations, in applying the concepts and tools of strategic analysis, in weighing strategic options and crafting strategies, and in tackling the challenges of successful strategy execution. Without a fresh stream of well-researched, well-conceived cases, the discipline of strategic management would lose its close ties to the very institutions whose strategic actions and behavior it is aimed at explaining. There's no question, therefore, that first-class case research constitutes a valuable scholarly contribution to the theory and practice of strategic management.

In addition, a great number of colleagues and students at various universities, business acquaintances, and people at McGraw-Hill provided inspiration, encouragement, and counsel during the course of this project. Like all text authors in the strategy field, we are intellectually indebted to the many academics whose research and writing have blazed new trails and advanced the discipline of strategic management. The following reviewers provided seasoned advice and suggestions that further guided our preparation of the chapters:

Seyda Deligonul, *St. John Fisher College and Michigan State University*

David Flanagan, *Western Michigan University*

Esmeralda Garbi, *Florida Atlantic University*

Mohsin Habib, *University of Massachusetts–Boston*

Kim Hester, *Arkansas State University*

Jeffrey E. McGee, *The University of Texas at Arlington*

Diana J. Wong, *Eastern Michigan University*

As always, we value your recommendations and thoughts about the book. Your comments regarding coverage and contents will be taken to heart, and we always are grateful for the time you take to call our attention to printing errors, deficiencies, and other shortcomings. Please e-mail us at athompso@cba.ua.edu, jgamble@usouthal.edu, or astrickl@cba.ua.edu; fax us at (205) 348-6695; or write us at P.O. Box 870225, Department of Management and Marketing, The University of Alabama, Tuscaloosa, Alabama 35487-0225.

Arthur A. Thompson
John E. Gamble
A. J. Strickland

CHAPTER

1

What Is Strategy and Why Is It Important?

Unless we change our direction we are likely to end up where we are headed.
—Ancient Chinese proverb

If we can know where we are and something about how we got there, we might see where we are trending—and if the outcomes which lie naturally in our course are unacceptable, to make timely change.
—Abraham Lincoln

If you don't know where you are going, any road will take you there.
—The Koran

Without a strategy the organization is like a ship without a rudder.
—Joel Ross and Michael Kami

Each chapter begins with a series of pertinent quotes and an introductory preview of its contents.

In-depth examples—Company Spotlights and Global Spotlights—appear in boxes throughout each chapter to illustrate important chapter topics, connect the text presentation to real-world companies, and convincingly demonstrate strategy in action.

COMPANY SPOTLIGHT 1.1

A Strategy Example: Southwest Airlines

Southwest Airlines is the only major short-hop, low-fare, point-to-point carrier in the U.S. airline industry. It is one of the industry's great success stories. It is the only airline that made a profit in each of the past 25 years. In 2003, Southwest operated 375 jets to 58 airports in 30 states. The company's no-frills strategy offers passengers a single class of service at the lowest possible fares.

Aside from its low fares, which make air travel affordable to a wide segment of the U.S. population, Southwest has made friendly service a core piece of its strategy and one of its trademarks. Company personnel work hard at creating a positive, enjoyable flying experience for passengers. Gate personnel are cheery and witty, sometimes entertaining those in the gate area with trivia questions or contests. Casually dressed flight attendants warmly greet passengers coming onto planes, directing them to open seats and helping them store their bags. Southwest's attendants, all screened carefully for fun-loving and outgoing personalities, joke and chat with passengers—some even sing the announcements on take-off and landing.

Southwest's market focus is flying between pairs of cities ranging anywhere from 150 to 700 miles apart where traffic potential is high enough for Southwest to offer several daily flights. Most recently, however, Southwest has begun offering longer range flights, using its low-cost advantage to horn in on the most profitable flights of such rivals as American, United, Northwest, Delta, and US Airways. Southwest grows its business by adding more flights on existing routes and by initiating service to new airports—its objective is steady growth year after year, not rapid growth for a few years that then becomes impossible to sustain.

Recognizing that low fares necessitate zealous pursuit of low operating costs, Southwest has perfected a number of operating strategies for keeping its costs below those of rival carriers:

■ The company's aircraft fleet consists entirely of Boeing 737s, thus minimizing spare parts inventories, making it easier to train maintenance and repair personnel, improving the proficiency and speed of maintenance routines, and simplifying the task of scheduling planes for particular flights.

■ As the launch customer for Boeing's 737-300, 737-500, and 737-700 models, Southwest acquires its new aircraft at favorable prices.

■ Southwest encourages customers to make reservations and purchase tickets at the company's website. Selling a ticket on its website costs Southwest one-tenth as much as delivering a ticket through a travel agent and about

with the practice of assigning each passenger a reserved seat. Instead, passengers are given boarding passes imprinted with A, B, or C at check-in and then board in groups of 30 according to their assigned letters, sitting in whatever seat is open when they get on the plane.

■ Southwest flight attendants are responsible for cleaning up trash left by deplaning passengers

---

GLOBAL SPOTLIGHT 5.1

Microsoft, McDonald's, and Nestlé: Users of Multicountry Strategies

Microsoft's Multicountry Strategy in PC Software

In order to best serve the needs of users in foreign countries, Microsoft localizes many of its software products to reflect local languages. In France, for example, all user messages and documentation are in French and all monetary references are in euros. In the United Kingdom, monetary references are in British pounds and user messages and documentation reflect certain British conventions. Various Microsoft products have been localized into more than 30 languages.

McDonald's Multicountry Strategy in Fast Food

McDonald's has been highly successful in markets outside the United States, partly because it has been adept in altering its menu offerings to cater to local tastes. In Taiwan and Singapore, McDonald's outlets offer a bone-in fried chicken dish called Chicken McCrispy. In Great Britain, there's McChicken Tikka Naan to appeal to British cravings for Indian food. In India, McDonald's features the Maharajah Mac sandwich (an Indian version of the Big Mac); in Japan, there's the Chicken Tatsuta sandwich and a Teriyaki Burger sandwich; in Australia, there's a MeOz Burger. However, the infrastructure and operating systems that are employed in the outlets are largely the same, enabling McDonald's to achieve low-cost leadership status once it builds volume up at its outlets (sometimes a 5-year process) and once it has enough outlets operating in a country to achieve full economies of scale (sometimes a 5- to 10-year process in the largest foreign markets).

Nestlé's Multicountry Strategy in Instant Coffee

Swiss-based Nestlé, the largest food company in the world, is also the largest producer of coffee. With a total workforce of 22,541 people operating in nearly 480 factories in 100 countries, Nestlé's presence is clearly multinational. Chief executive Peter Brabeck-Letmathe advocates understanding the distinctions between the cultures in which Nestlé markets its products. "[If] you are open to new languages, you are also open to new cultures," he explains. Thus, instant coffee names like Nescafé, Taster's Choice, Ricoré, and Ricoffy line grocery shelves in various countries. If customers prefer roast or ground coffee, they can purchase Nespresso, Bonka, Zoegas, or Loumidis, depending on where they live.

Nestlé produces 200 types of instant coffee, from lighter blends for the U.S. market to dark espressos for Latin America. To keep its instant coffees matched to consumer tastes in different countries (and areas within some countries), Nestlé operates four coffee research labs that experiment with new blends in aroma, flavor, and color. The strategy is to match the blends marketed in each country to the tastes and preferences of coffee drinkers in that country, introducing new blends to develop new segments when opportunities appear and altering blends as needed to respond to changing tastes and buyer habits. In Britain, Nescafé was promoted extensively to build a wider base of instant-coffee drinkers. In Japan, where Nescafé was considered a luxury item, the company made its Japanese blends available in fancy containers suitable for gift-giving.

Sources: Nestlé website (www.nestle.com), accessed August 15, 2001; "Nestlé S.A.," Hoover's Online (www.hoovers.com), accessed August 15, 2001; Tom Mudd, "Nestlé Plays to Global Audience," *Industry Week* (www.industryweek.com), August 13, 2001; company annual reports; Shawn Tully, "Nestlé Shows How to Gobble Markets," *Fortune*, January 16, 1989, pp. 74–76; and "Nestlé: A Giant in a Hurry," *Business Week*, March 22, 1993, pp. 50–54.

---

and fresh market conditions (see Figure 1.2).[1] The biggest portion of a company's current strategy flows from previously initiated actions and business approaches that are working well enough to merit continuation and newly launched managerial initiatives to strengthen the company's overall position and performance. This part of management's game plan is deliberate and proactive, standing as the product of management's analysis and strategic thinking about the company's situation and its conclusions about how to position the company in the marketplace and tackle the task of competing for buyer patronage. But the uncertainty and unpredictability of future business conditions prevent company managers from plotting every needed strategic action in advance. A portion of a company's strategy is always developed on the fly, coming as a reasoned response to changing customer preferences, the latest strategic maneuvers of rival firms, new requirements and expectations on the part of customers, emerging technologies and market opportunities, a shifting political or economic climate, and other unforeseeable happenings. Crafting a strategy thus involves not only stitching together a comprehensive *intended strategy* but also modifying first one piece and then another as events unfold and circumstances surrounding the company's situation change (*adaptive/reactive strategy*). In short, a company's actual strategy is something managers shape and reshape as circumstances dictate and as managers learn from experience and seek out improvements.

As a rule, most multinational competitors endeavor to employ as global a strategy as customer needs permit. Philips N.V., the Netherlands-based electronics and consumer products company, operated successfully with a multicountry strategy for many years but has recently begun moving more toward a unified strategy within the European Union and within North America.[3] A global strategy can concentrate on building the resource strengths to secure a sustainable low-cost or differentiation-based competitive advantage over both domestic rivals and global rivals racing for world market leadership. Whenever country-to-country differences are small enough to be accommodated

Figures scattered throughout the chapters provide conceptual and analytical frameworks.

Margin notes define core concepts and call attention to important ideas and principles.

Key Points sections at the end of each chapter provide a handy summary of essential ideas and things to remember.

Guided Tour

Once all the higher-level strategic choices have been made, company managers can turn to the task of crafting functional and operating-level strategies to flesh out the details of the company's overall business and competitive strategy.

The timing of strategic moves also has relevance in the quest for competitive advantage. Because of the competitive importance that is sometimes associated with when a strategic move is made, company managers are obligated to carefully consider the advantages or disadvantages that attach to being a first-mover versus a fast-follower versus a wait-and-see late-mover. At the end of the day, though, the proper objective of a first-mover is that of being the first competitor to put together the precise combination of features, customer value, and sound revenue/cost/profit economics that puts it ahead of the pack in capturing an attractive market opportunity. Sometimes the company that first unlocks a profitable market opportunity is the first-mover and sometimes it is not—but the company that comes up with the key is surely the smart mover.

Exercises

1. Log on to www.business-ethics.com and review which companies are on the latest list of the 100 Best Corporate Citizens. Also review the criteria for earning a spot on this list. Are these criteria sound? Is there ample reason to believe that the 100 companies on this list pursue strategies that are ethical? Why or why not?

2. Go to www.google.com and do a search for "low-cost producer." See if you can identify five companies that are pursuing a low-cost strategy in their respective industries.

3. Using the advanced search engine function at www.google.com, enter "best-cost producer" in the exact phrase box and see if you can locate three companies that indicate they are employing a best-cost producer strategy.

Several short, mostly Internet research exercises at the end of each chapter provide a supplement to assigned cases and a further way to reinforce core concepts.

CASE 1

Whole Foods Market, Inc.

Arthur A. Thompson
The University of Alabama

Founded in 1980 as one small store in Austin, Texas, Whole Foods Market had by 2002 evolved into the world's largest retail chain of natural and organic foods supermarkets. The company had over 140 stores in the United States and Canada and sales of $2.7 billion; revenues had grown at more than 20 percent for 12 consecutive quarters. John Mackey, the company's cofounder and CEO, said that throughout its rapid growth Whole Foods Market had "remained a uniquely mission-driven company—highly selective values and stringent quality standards and co

The company's stated mission was "to i of both people and the planet"—a mission Foods, Whole People, Whole Planet" (see company's strategic plan was to continue t highest quality and most nutritious foods t to live healthier and more vital lives. Durin had been a leader in natural and organic F helping the industry gain acceptance among pany's long-term objectives were to have 4 John Mackey's vision was for Whole Foo garded as the best food retailer in every con

The Natural and Org Industry

The combined sales of natural and organic sented about 5 percent of the roughly $68. *Natural foods* are defined as foods that are r free of artificial ingredients, preservatives, cals; and as near to their whole, natural state culture's Food and Safety Inspection Ser containing no artificial ingredient or adde Sales of natural foods products had increa

Copyright © 2003 by Arthur A. Thompson. All rights res

CASE 2

mGAMES

Allen Morrison
The University of Western Ontario

Jeffrey Lopez hung up the phone, leaned forward, and buried his face in his hands. It seemed a challenge at this particular moment to try to remember why he had been so excited about his appointment as president and chief executive officer (CEO) of mGAMES (a developer of gaming software for mobile devices) just eight months ago. Lopez stood up from his large mahogany desk, walked to the window and looked out over the horizon toward Boston. It was 9:15 A.M. on Monday, July 22, 2002, and Lopez had just finished taking two telephone calls. The first had come from Benson Marks, principal shareholder and chairman of the board of mGAMES. In their call, Marks had told Lopez that he had just gotten off the phone with an old friend at Credit Suisse First Boston in New York. Specifics could not be provided, but rumors were circulating throughout the bank that a large and well-respected personal digital assistant (PDA) manufacturer was in the process of arranging financing to make a play for mGAMES. During the conversation, Marks reminded Lopez that he did not believe a takeover could be achieved without his consent—since he held 44.5 percent of mGAMES shares—but he also acknowledged that over the past year he had become increasingly concerned with the performance of mGAMES. "Now Jeff. . . you know I'm 100 percent behind you. But we've got to do something here. I need you to put a plan together and I'd like to see something within the next week."

The second call had come from Bjorger Pedersson, senior vice president of product development with a large Scandinavian telecommunications company (sales of US$23 billion). Lopez had not spoken to Pedersson since first meeting him six months earlier at an industry conference in Las Vegas, but he remembered clearly how the two of them had seemed to really click.

The 32 cases detail the strategic circumstances of actual companies and provide practice in applying the concepts and tools of strategic analysis.

IVEY

Scott Hill prepared this case under the supervision of Professor Allen Morrison solely to provide material for class discussion. The authors do not intend to illustrate either effective or ineffective handling of a managerial situation. The authors may have disguised certain names and other identifying information to protect confidentiality.

Ivey Management Services prohibits any form of reproduction, storage or transmittal without its written permission. This material is not covered under authorization from CanCopy or any reproduction rights organization. To order copies or request permission to reproduce materials, contact Ivey Publishing, Ivey Management Services, c/o Richard Ivey School of Business, The University of Western Ontario, London, Ontario, Canada, N6A 3K7; phone (519) 661-3208; fax (519) 661-3882; e-mail cases@ivey.uwo.ca.

Copyright © 2002, Ivey Management Services. One-time permission to reproduce Ivey cases granted by Ivey Management Services, January 17, 2003.

C-23

For Students: An Assortment of Support Materials

Website: www.mhhe.com/thompson1e

The student portion of the website features a "Guide to Case Analysis," with special sections on what a case is, why cases are a standard part of courses in strategy, preparing a case for class discussion, doing a written case analysis, doing an oral presentation, and using financial ratio analysis to assess a company's financial condition. In addition, there are self-scoring 20-question chapter tests and a select number of PowerPoint slides for each chapter.

Case-TUTOR Software

Accompanying the 32 cases is a software package containing assignment questions for all 32 cases in the text, plus analytically structured exercises for 10 of the cases that coach students in doing the strategic thinking needed to arrive at solid answers to the assignment questions for that case. Conscientious completion of the exercises helps students gain quicker command of the concepts and analytical techniques and points them toward doing good strategic analysis.

The *GLO-BUS* Online Simulation

This course supplement emotionally connects students to the subject matter of the course by having teams assigned to manage companies in a head-to-head contest for global market leadership in the digital camera industry. The simulation puts students in a situation where they have to make decisions relating to product design, production, workforce compensation, pricing, advertising, warranties, sales promotions, and finance. It is students' job to craft and execute a strategy for their company that is powerful enough to deliver good bottom-line performance despite the efforts of rival companies to take away the company's sales and market share. Each company competes in North America, Latin America, Europe, and Asia.

PowerWeb

With each new book, students gain access to the publisher's PowerWeb site offering current news, articles from 6,300 premium sources, a Web research guide, current readings from annual editions, and links to related sites.

Contents
in Brief

Contents

Part III Crafting the Strategy

4 Crafting a Strategy: The Quest for Competitive Advantage 108

5 Competing in Foreign Markets 160

6 Diversification: Strategies for Managing a Group of Businesses 190

Part IV Executing the Strategy

7 Building a Capable Organization 242

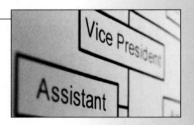

8 Managing Internal Operations: Actions That Facilitate Strategy Execution 272

9 Corporate Culture and Leadership 294

Part V Cases in Crafting and Executing Strategy

Photo Credits C-592

Indexes

STRATEGY

CHAPTER 1

What Is Strategy and Why Is It Important?

Unless we change our direction we are likely to end up where we are headed.
—Ancient Chinese proverb

If we can know where we are and something about how we got there, we might see where we are trending—and if the outcomes which lie naturally in our course are unacceptable, to make timely change.
—Abraham Lincoln

If you don't know where you are going, any road will take you there.
—The Koran

Without a strategy the organization is like a ship without a rudder.
—Joel Ross and Michael Kami

Management's job is not to see the company as it is . . . but as it can become.
—John W. Teets, former CEO Greyhound Corp.

Managers at all companies face three basic, critical questions in thinking strategically about their company's present circumstances and prospects: Where are we now? Where do we want to go? How will we get there? A probing answer to *Where are we now?* must consider the company's market position and the competitive pressures it confronts, its resource strengths and capabilities, its competitive shortcomings, the appeal its products and services have to customers, and its current performance. *Where do we want to go?* deals with the direction in which management believes the company should be headed in light of the company's present situation and the winds of market change—new markets and customer groups that the company should be positioning itself to serve, new or different capabilities the company should be adding, the improvements in competitive market position the company is aiming for, and the geographic scope and product-line makeup of the company's business in the years to come. Finally, *How will we get there?* concerns the ins and outs of crafting and executing a strategy to get the company from where it is to where it wants to go.

What Is Strategy?

The tasks of crafting and executing company strategies are the heart and soul of managing a business enterprise and winning in the marketplace. A company's **strategy** is the game plan management is using to stake out a market position, attract and please customers, compete successfully, conduct operations, and achieve organizational objectives. In crafting a strategy, management is, in effect, saying: "Among all the paths we could have chosen, we have decided to focus on these markets and customer needs, compete in this fashion, allocate our resources and energies in these ways, and use these particular approaches to doing business." A company's strategy thus indicates the choices its managers have made among alternative markets, competitive approaches, and ways of operating. It is partly the result of trial-and-error organizational learning about what worked in the past and what didn't, and partly the product of managerial analysis and strategic thinking about all the circumstances surrounding the company's situation.

> **Core Concept**
>
> A company's **strategy** consists of the combination of competitive moves and business approaches that managers employ to please customers, compete successfully, conduct operations, and achieve organizational objectives.

Striving for Competitive Advantage

The central thrust of a company's strategy is undertaking moves to strengthen the company's long-term competitive position and financial performance. Typically, a company's strategy consists of both offensive and defensive elements—some actions mount direct challenges to competitors' market positions and seek to establish a competitive edge; others aim at defending against competitive pressures, the maneuvers of rivals, and other developments that threaten the company's well-being. *What separates a powerful strategy from an ordinary or weak one is management's ability to forge a series of moves, both in the marketplace and internally, that produce sustainable competitive advantage.* With competitive advantage, a company has good prospects for winning in the marketplace and realizing above-average profitability. Without competitive advantage, a company risks being outcompeted by rivals and/or locked into mediocre financial performance.

Four of the most frequently used strategic approaches to building competitive advantage are:

1. *Striving to be the industry's low-cost provider, thereby aiming for a cost-based competitive advantage over rivals.* Wal-Mart and Southwest Airlines have earned market-leading positions because of the low-cost advantages they have achieved over their rivals.

2. *Outcompeting rivals based on such differentiating features as high quality, wide product selection, reliable performance, excellent service, attractive styling, technological superiority, or unusually good value for the money.* Successful adopters of differentiation strategies include Johnson & Johnson (product reliability), Chanel and Rolex (prestige and distinctiveness), Mercedes-Benz and BMW (engineering design and performance), L. L. Bean (good value), and Amazon.com (wide selection and convenience).

3. *Focusing on a narrow market niche and winning a competitive edge by doing a better job than rivals of satisfying the special needs and tastes of buyers comprising the niche.* Prominent companies that enjoy competitive success in a specialized market niche include eBay in online auctions, Jiffy Lube International in quick oil changes, and Whole Foods Market in natural and organic foods.

4. *Developing expertise and resource strengths that give the company competitive capabilities rivals can't easily imitate or trump with capabilities of their own.* Federal Express has superior capabilities in next-day delivery of small packages; Walt Disney has hard-to-beat capabilities in theme park management and family entertainment, and IBM has wide-ranging capabilities in supporting the information systems and information technology needs of large enterprises.

Most companies recognize that winning a durable competitive edge over rivals hinges more on building competitively valuable expertise and capabilities than it does on having superior products. Rivals can nearly always copy the attributes of a popular or innovative product. But for rivals to match experience, know-how, and specialized competitive capabilities that a company has developed and perfected over a long period of time is substantially harder to duplicate and takes much longer—Kmart, Sears, and other discount retailers and supermarket chains have found it virtually impossible to match Wal-Mart's sophisticated distribution systems and its finely honed merchandising expertise despite years of trying. Company initiatives to build competencies and capabilities that rivals don't have and cannot readily match can relate to getting innovative new products to market faster than rivals (3M Corporation), better mastery of a complex technological process (Michelin in making radial tires), expertise in defect-free manufacturing (Toyota and Honda), specialized marketing and merchandising know-how (Coca-Cola), global sales and distribution capability (Black & Decker in power tools), superior e-commerce capabilities (Dell Computer), personalized customer service (Ritz-Carlton and Four Seasons hotels), or anything else that constitutes a competitively valuable strength in creating, producing, distributing, or marketing the company's product or service.

Identifying a Company's Strategy

Except for changes that remain under wraps and in the planning stage and some about-to-be launched moves, there's usually nothing secret or mysterious about what a company's present strategy is. Its competitive approaches and actions in the marketplace

Figure 1.1   Identifying a Company's Strategy:
What to Look For

are usually visible to studious observers and, in the case of publicly owned enterprises, often have been openly discussed by company managers or summarized in press releases or other widely available company documents. Hence the content of a company's strategy can normally be deduced from its actions in the marketplace and publicly available information. Some strategy features may remain hidden for competitively sensitive or legal reasons until the company's actions become public, but to maintain the confidence of investors and Wall Street, most public companies have to be fairly open about their strategies.

Figure 1.1 depicts what to look for in identifying the substance of a company's overall strategy. To get a better grip on the content of company strategies, read the description of Southwest Airlines' strategy in Company Spotlight 1.1.

Strategy Is Partly Proactive and Partly Reactive

A company's strategy is typically a blend of (1) proactive and purposeful actions on the part of company managers and (2) as-needed reactions to unanticipated developments

A Strategy Example: Southwest Airlines

Southwest Airlines is the only major short-hop, low-fare, point-to-point carrier in the U.S. airline industry. It is one of the industry's great success stories and is the only airline that made a profit in each of the past 25 years. In 2003, Southwest operated 375 jets to 58 airports in 30 states. The company's no-frills strategy offers passengers a single class of service at the lowest possible fares.

Aside from its low fares, which make air travel affordable to a wide segment of the U.S. population, Southwest has made friendly service a core piece of its strategy and one of its trademarks. Company personnel work hard at creating a positive, enjoyable flying experience for passengers. Gate personnel are cheery and witty, sometimes entertaining those in the gate area with trivia questions or contests. Casually dressed flight attendants warmly greet passengers coming onto planes, directing them to open seats and helping them store their bags. Southwest's attendants, all screened carefully for fun-loving and outgoing personalities, joke and chat with passengers—some even sing the announcements on take-off and landing.

Southwest's market focus is flying between pairs of cities ranging anywhere from 150 to 700 miles apart where traffic potential is high enough for Southwest to offer several daily flights. Most recently, however, Southwest has begun offering longer range flights, using its low-cost advantage to horn in on the most profitable flights of such rivals as American, United, Northwest, Delta, and US Airways. Southwest grows its business by adding more flights on existing routes and by initiating service to new airports—its objective is steady growth year after year, not rapid growth for a few years that then becomes impossible to sustain.

Recognizing that low fares necessitate zealous pursuit of low operating costs, Southwest has perfected a number of operating strategies for keeping its costs below those of rival carriers:

- The company's aircraft fleet consists entirely of Boeing 737s, thus minimizing spare parts inventories, making it easier to train maintenance and repair personnel, improving the proficiency and speed of maintenance routines, and simplifying the task of scheduling planes for particular flights.

and fresh market conditions (see Figure 1.2).[1] The biggest portion of a company's current strategy flows from previously initiated actions and business approaches that are working well enough to merit continuation and newly launched managerial initiatives to strengthen the company's overall position and performance. This part of management's game plan is deliberate and proactive, standing as the product of management's analysis and strategic thinking about the company's situation and its conclusions about how to position the company in the marketplace and tackle the task of competing for buyer patronage. But the uncertainty and unpredictability of future business conditions prevent company managers from plotting every needed strategic action in advance. A portion of a company's strategy is always developed on the fly, coming as a reasoned response to changing customer preferences, the latest strategic maneuvers of rival firms, new requirements and expectations on the part of customers, emerging technologies and market opportunities, a shifting political or economic climate, and other unforeseeable happenings. Crafting a strategy thus involves not only stitching together a comprehensive *intended strategy* but also modifying first one piece and then another as events unfold and circumstances surrounding the company's situation change (*adaptive/reactive strategy*). In short, a company's actual strategy is something managers shape and reshape as circumstances dictate and as managers learn from experience and seek out improvements.

- As the launch customer for Boeing's 737-300, 737-500, and 737-700 models, Southwest acquires its new aircraft at favorable prices.

- Southwest encourages customers to make reservations and purchase tickets at the company's website. Selling a ticket on its website costs Southwest one-tenth as much as delivering a ticket through a travel agent and about one-half as much as processing a paper ticket through its own internal reservation system.

- Southwest avoids flying into congested airports, stressing instead routes between medium-sized cities and small airports close to major metropolitan areas. This improves on-time performance and reduces the fuel costs associated with planes sitting in line on crowded taxiways or circling airports waiting for clearance to land. Moreover, the company pays lower landing fees and terminal gate costs than it would at high-traffic airports like Atlanta's Hartsfield International, Chicago's O'Hare, Denver International, and Dallas–Fort Worth.

- Southwest's point-to-point route system is highly efficient, reducing both the number of aircraft and the terminal gates needed to support flight operations compared to hub-and-spoke systems of rival carriers.

- To speed the reservation process and to economize on check-in time, Southwest dispensed with the practice of assigning each passenger a reserved seat. Instead, passengers are given boarding passes imprinted with A, B, or C at check-in and then board in groups of 30 according to their assigned letters, sitting in whatever seat is open when they get on the plane.

- Southwest flight attendants are responsible for cleaning up trash left by deplaning passengers and otherwise getting the plane presentable for passengers to board for the next flight (other carriers have cleaning crews come on board to perform this function). Attendants usually have planes ready for boarding within minutes of the last passenger's exit from the plane. On occasion, pilots pitch in to facilitate turnarounds.

- Southwest has no first-class section in any of its planes, has no fancy clubs for its frequent flyers to relax in at terminals, and serves no meals on its flights (passengers are offered beverages, peanuts, and pretzel mixes only). Reprovisioning planes is simpler, faster, and cheaper when meals are not a factor.

- Southwest planes' all-leather seats are more durable and easier to maintain than cloth seats, despite higher initial costs.

- Southwest does not provide passengers with baggage transfer services to other carriers.

Source: Company documents.

Figure 1.2   A Company's Actual Strategy Is Partly Proactive and Partly Reactive to Changing Circumstances

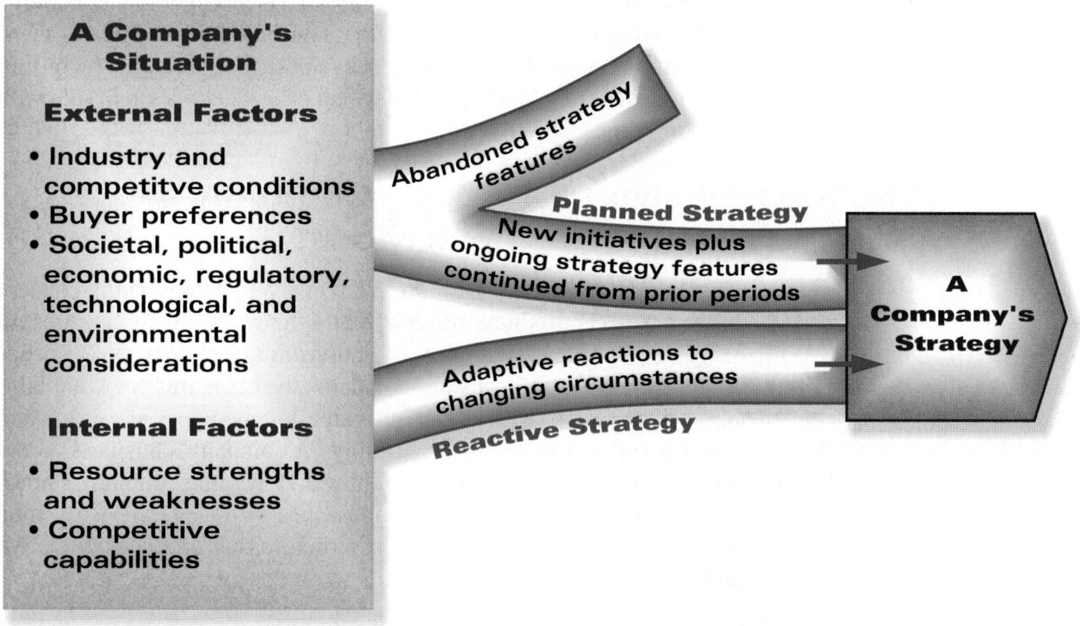

7

A Company's Strategy Evolves over Time　Because constantly developing external and internal events make it commonplace for managers to initiate fresh strategic moves and business approaches of one kind or another, *a company's strategy is a work in progress.* Most of the time a company's strategy evolves incrementally from management's ongoing efforts to fine-tune this or that piece of the strategy and to adjust certain strategy elements in response to unfolding events. Frequently making sweeping changes in strategy can be disruptive to the organization and confusing to customers—and such changes are usually unnecessary. In general, persistently tweaking a basically sound strategy to keep it freshly tuned to changing market circumstances offers greater rewards than does trying to change the basic strategy at every turn.

Nonetheless, on occasion—when a strategy is clearly failing, market conditions or buyer preferences are undergoing significant change, an opening is appearing for new strategy elements with powerful buyer appeal, competitors are doing something that demands a dramatic response, important technological breakthroughs are occurring, or the company is being hit with a major financial crisis—fine-tuning the existing strategy is not enough and major strategy shifts are called for. During periods of market turbulence (like the Internet gold rush and subsequent dot-com crash that occurred in 1997–2002), companies find it essential to revise demand forecasts, adjust key elements of their strategies, and update their financial projections at least quarterly and sometimes more frequently. At Ingram Micro, a contract manufacturer and distributor of PCs, market changes and strategic adjustments come so quickly that "rolling forecasts" of financial projections are devised for five quarters out and then updated every 60 days. Bluefly.com, a clothing e-tailer, revises its product offerings and operating budget weekly to react to daily sales patterns. Industry environments characterized by high-velocity change often require frequent shifts in strategy.[2]

> **Core Concept**
>
> Changing circumstances dictate that a company's strategy change and evolve over time—a condition that makes strategy making an ongoing process, not a one-time event.

Regardless of whether a company's strategy changes gradually or swiftly, the important point is that it is always temporary and on trial, awaiting new ideas for improvement on management's part, the appearance of new market and competitive conditions, and any other changes in the company's situation that managers believe warrant strategy adjustments. Since neither market and competitive conditions nor the company's situation stay the same for long, company managers are obligated to continually reevaluate their strategy, recrafting it as often and as extensively as they feel is needed to keep in step with changing times.

The Relationship Between a Company's Strategy and Its Business Model

> **Core Concept**
>
> A company's **business model** deals with whether the revenue/cost/profit economics of its strategy demonstrate the viability of the business enterprise as a whole.

Closely related to the concept of a company's strategy is the concept of a company's **business model.** While the word *model* conjures up images of empirical, ivory-tower relationships, such images do not apply here. A company's business model is the economic logic explaining how an enterprise can deliver value to customers at a price and cost that yields acceptable profitability.[3] A company's business model is thus management's storyline for how and why the company's product offerings and competitive approaches will generate a revenue stream and have an associated cost structure that produces attractive earnings and returns on investment.

The nitty-gritty issue surrounding a company's business model is whether the chosen strategy makes good business sense from a moneymaking perspective. The concept of a company's business model is, consequently, more narrowly focused than the concept of a company's business strategy. A company's strategy *relates broadly to its competitive initiatives and business approaches (regardless of the financial outcomes it produces), whereas its* business model *concerns whether the revenues and costs flowing from the strategy demonstrate business viability.* Companies that have been in business for a while and are making acceptable profits have a proven business model—there is clear evidence that their strategy is capable of profitability and that they have a viable enterprise. Companies that are in a start-up mode and established companies that are losing money have questionable business models: Their strategies are not producing good bottom-line results, putting their storyline about how they intend to make money and their viability as enterprises in doubt. Company Spotlight 1.2 discusses the contrasting business models of Microsoft and Red Hat Linux.

What Does the Strategy-Making, Strategy-Executing Process Entail?

The managerial process of crafting and executing a company's strategy consists of five interrelated and integrated phases:

1. *Forming a strategic vision of where the company needs to head,* a task that provides long-term direction, infuses the organization with a sense of purposeful action, and communicates to stakeholders what management's aspirations for the company are.

2. *Setting objectives* that convert the strategic vision into specific performance outcomes for the company to achieve.

3. *Crafting a strategy to achieve the objectives* and move the company toward where it wants to go.

4. *Implementing and executing the chosen strategy efficiently and effectively.*

5. *Evaluating performance and initiating corrective adjustments* in vision, long-term direction, objectives, strategy, or execution in light of actual experience, changing conditions, new ideas, and new opportunities.

Figure 1.3 displays this five-task process. Let's examine each task in enough detail to set the stage for the forthcoming chapters and give you a bird's-eye view of what this book is about.

Developing a Strategic Vision: Phase 1 of the Strategy-Making, Strategy-Executing Process

Very early in the strategy-making process, a company's senior managers need to decide what direction the company should be headed in and why such a direction makes good business sense. To draw carefully reasoned conclusions about the directional path

Microsoft and Red Hat Linux: Contrasting Business Models

Different companies have different business models and strategies, sometimes strikingly so. Consider, for example, the business models for Microsoft and Red Hat Linux in operating system (OS) software for personal computers (PCs).

Microsoft is one of the world's most successful and profitable companies, partly because of its dominant market position in OS software for PCs—first DOS, then Windows 95, Windows NT, Windows 98, Windows 2000, and Windows XP. Microsoft's business model for making money from its OS products is based on the following business logic:

- Employ a cadre of highly skilled programmers to develop proprietary Microsoft code; keep the source code hidden from users.

- Sell the resulting OS and software package to PC makers and to PC users at relatively attractive prices, and achieve large unit sales.

- Since most of Microsoft's costs are fixed (having been incurred on the front end in developing the code for the software), each copy of the software sold generates substantial margins over the variable costs of producing and packaging the CDs provided to users, which amount to only a couple of dollars per copy.

- Provide technical support to users at no cost.

Red Hat Linux, a new company formed to market the Linux OS in competition against Microsoft's Windows OS, employs a sharply different business model:

- Rely on the collaborative efforts of interested programmers from all over the world who volunteer their time and contribute bits and pieces of code to improve and polish the Linux system. Make the source code open and available to all users, allowing them to freely change the code to create a customized version of Linux. The global community of thousands of programmers who work on Linux in their spare time do what they do because they love it; because they are fervent believers that all software should be free (as in free speech); and, in some cases, because they are anti-Microsoft and want to have a part in undoing what they see as a Microsoft monopoly.

- Add value to the free, downloadable version of Linux by offering users Red Hat Linux systems containing upgraded and tested features. Linux originator Linus Torvalds and a team of more than 300 Red Hat engineers and software developers collect enhancements and new applications submitted by the "open-source" community of volunteer programmers. Thus Red Hat, unlike Microsoft, essentially has very modest up-front product development costs—all stemming from evaluating new submissions, picking and choosing which to integrate and test for performance and compatibility, and deciding which to include in new releases of Red Hat Linux.

- Charge a modest fee to those who prefer to subscribe to the Red Hat Linux version; the subscription fee includes a limited number of days of Red Hat's Web-based service and support.

- Employ a cadre of technical support personnel who provide technical support to users for a fee. Because Linux can be a bit troublesome to install and use in some multiserver, multiprocessor applications, corporate users of Linux often require technical support during start-up.

- Make as much or more money on providing technical support services, training, and consulting as on selling subscriptions to Red Hat Linux. Fees for technical support services, training, and consulting provide more than 50 percent of Red Hat's revenues.

Microsoft's business model—sell proprietary code software and give service away free—is a proven moneymaker that generates billions in profits annually. On the other hand, the jury is still out on Red Hat's business model of marketing open-source software developed mainly by volunteers and depending heavily on sales of technical support services, training, and consulting; in the early 2000s the company had less than $100 million in annual revenues and had operating losses.

Source: Company documents.

Figure 1.3   The Strategy-Making, Strategy-Executing Process

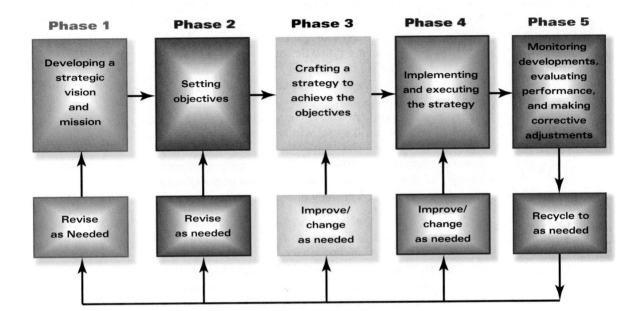

the company should take, managers must think strategically about the company's external and internal environment and answer the following direction-shaping questions:

Externally Focused Questions	Internally Focused Questions
▪ How and at what pace is the company's market environment evolving?	▪ What are our ambitions for the company? What industry standing do we want the company to have?
▪ What factors are driving market change and what impact will they have?	▪ What organizational strengths should we be trying to leverage and what weaknesses do we need to correct?
▪ What are competitors up to? In what ways are competitive conditions growing stronger or weaker?	▪ Will our present business generate adequate growth and profitability?
▪ What does the changing market and competitive landscape mean for the company's business over the next five years and beyond?	▪ What new products/services (or businesses) do we need to add?
▪ What new markets and customer groups should we be moving in position to serve? What should we abandon?	▪ What new capabilities do we need to be successful in the marketplace of the future?

> ### Core Concept
>
> A **strategic vision** is a road map of a company's future; it creates a picture of a company's destination and provides a rationale for going there.

Top management's views and conclusions about what the company's direction should be and the product-customer-market-technology focus it intends to pursue constitute a **strategic vision** for the company. A strategic vision thus delineates management's aspirations for the business, providing a panoramic view of "where are we going" and a convincing rationale for why this destination makes good business sense for the company. A strategic vision points an organization in a particular direction, charts a strategic path for it to follow, and molds organizational identity.

Well-stated visions are distinctive and specific to a particular organization; they avoid generic language like "we will become a global leader and the first choice of customers in every market we choose to serve," which could apply to scores of organizations.[4] Company Spotlight 1.3 provides examples of well-stated strategic visions developed by several prominent companies and nonprofit organizations.

According to one recent study of company vision statements:[5]

> Most visions consist of easy options like "market leadership" or "leader in quality" or "the No. 1 choice of customers." They make people feel good, require little imaginative effort, and attract consensus.
>
> Strong visions are different. They excite strong emotions. They are challenging, uncomfortable, nail biting . . . the critical mass of people who believe strongly in the vision will turn it into reality.
>
> Strong visions only emerge from organizations with demanding and determined leaders.

Visions range from strong and clear to ill-conceived and bland. A surprising number of the vision statements found on company websites and in annual reports are dull, blurry, and uninspiring, coming across as written by a committee to satisfy a variety of organizational stakeholders and public relations expectations.[6] The one-sentence vision statement a company makes available to the public, of course, provides only a glimpse of what company executives are really thinking and where the company is headed and why. A vision statement is not a panacea but rather a useful management tool for giving an organization a sense of future direction. Like any tool, it can be used properly or improperly, either strongly conveying a company's future strategic course or not.

A Strategic Vision Is Different from a Mission Statement

Whereas a strategic vision is chiefly concerned with "where we are going and why," a company mission statement usually deals with the company's *present* business scope and purpose—"who we are, what we do, and why we are here." (Many companies prefer *business purpose* to *mission statement,* but the two terms are conceptually identical and are used interchangeably.) A typical example is the mission statement of Trader Joe's, a unique grocery store chain:

> The mission of Trader Joe's is to give our customers the best food and beverage values that they can find anywhere and to provide them with the information required for informed buying decisions. We provide these with a dedication to the highest quality of customer satisfaction delivered with a sense of warmth, friendliness, fun, individual pride, and company spirit.

COMPANY SPOTLIGHT 1.3

Examples of Well-Stated Strategic Visions

Verizon Communications

To be the customer's first choice for communications and information services in every market we serve, domestic and international.

Levi Strauss & Company

We will clothe the world by marketing the most appealing and widely worn casual clothing in the world.

Microsoft Corporation

Empower people through great software—any time, any place, and on any device.

Mayo Clinic

The best care to every patient every day.

Scotland Yard

To make London the safest city in the world.

Toyota

We want to set the tone for the era . . . green and affordable . . . that means establishing a new paradigm for harmonizing personal transport with the environment. It means revolutionary cost savings in products and production processes.

Greenpeace

To halt environmental abuse and promote environmental solutions.

Intel

Our vision: Getting to a billion connected computers worldwide, millions of servers, and trillions of dollars of e-commerce. Intel's core mission is being the building-block supplier to the Internet economy and spurring efforts to make the Internet more useful. Being connected is now at the center of people's computing experience. We are helping to expand the capabilities of the PC platform and the Internet.

As we look to the future, our strategies are based on the fundamental belief that we have seen only the early stages of deployment of digital technologies. The two areas that our business focuses on, computing and communications, are the backbone of the digital infrastructure, and our products are the building blocks that make up this infrastructure.

Goldman Sachs

To be the world's premier investment bank in every sector.

General Electric

We will become number one or number two in every market we serve, and revolutionize this company to have the speed and agility of a small enterprise.

Sources: Company documents and websites and Hugh Davidson, *The Committed Enterprise* (Oxford: Butterworth Heinemann, 2002), pp. 11, 65, 91, 92.

The mission statements that appear in company annual reports or on company websites almost always stress the company's present products and services and the types of customer it serves; sometimes they indicate the company's present market standing (whether it is a market leader or the industry's fastest growing company) as well as the company's technological and business capabilities. Rarely do they say much about where the company is headed, the coming changes in its business, or its future business aspirations. Hence the conceptual distinction between a strategic vision and a mission statement is fairly clear-cut: A strategic vision portrays a company's future business scope ("where we are going"), whereas a company's mission typically describes its present business scope and business purpose ("what we do, why we are here, and where we are now").

Sometimes companies word their mission statements around "making a profit." This is misguided: Profit is more correctly an *objective* and a *result* of what a company does. Making a profit is the obvious intent of every commercial enterprise, and mission statements structured around making a profit reveal nothing valuable about a company's business or the market arena in which it operates. The valuable part of a mission statement is in distinguishing the business purpose of one profit-seeking enterprise from the business purpose of another and, further, describing the company's business in language specific enough to give the company its own identity. To learn much of value from a company's mission statement, we must know management's answer to "Making a profit doing what and for whom?"

Communicating the Strategic Vision

Effectively communicating the strategic vision down the line to lower-level managers and employees is almost as important as ensuring the strategic soundness of the organization's long-term direction and business model. Not only do people have a need to believe that the company's management knows where it's trying to take the company and what changes lie ahead both externally and internally, but if frontline employees don't know what a company's vision is, they are unlikely to be emotionally committed to making the vision a reality. Generally, a strategic vision has to be put in writing so that it can be communicated organizationwide and then evaluated and debated by organization members.

> Strategic visions become real only when the vision statement is imprinted in the minds of organization members and then translated into hard objectives and strategies.

Ideally, executives should present their vision for the company in language that reaches out and grabs people, that creates a vivid image, and that provokes emotion and enthusiasm. Expressing the strategic vision in engaging language has enormous motivational value—building a cathedral is more inspiring than laying stones. When a vision articulates a clear and compelling picture of what might be, organizational members begin to say "This is interesting. I would like to be involved and contribute to helping make it happen." In sum, a well-stated vision contains memorable language; clearly maps the company's future direction; and motivates organization members, ideally giving them the feeling their lives and their work are intertwined. If a vision doesn't move people, it is unlikely to have much beneficial organizational impact.[7]

Linking the Vision with Company Values

In the course of deciding who we are and where we are going, many companies also come up with a statement of values to guide the company's pursuit of its vision. By *values,* we mean the beliefs, business principles, and ways of doing things that are incorporated into the company's operations and the behavior of organization members. Values, good and bad, exist in every organization. They relate to such things as fairness, integrity, ethics, innovativeness, teamwork, quality, customer service, social responsibility, and community citizenship. Company values statements tend to contain between four and eight values, which, ideally, are tightly connected to and reinforce the company's vision, strategy, and operating practices. Home Depot embraces eight values (entrepreneurial spirit, excellent customer service, giving back to the community, respect for all people, doing the right thing, taking care of people, building strong relationships, and creating shareholder value) in its quest to become the world's largest home improvement retailer by operating warehouse stores filled with a wide assortment of products at the lowest prices with trained associates giving absolutely the best customer service in the industry. Du Pont stresses four values—safety, ethics, respect for people, and environmental stewardship; the first three have been in place since the company was founded 200 years ago by the Du Pont family. Loblaw, a major grocery chain in Canada, focuses on just two main values in operating its stores—competence and honesty; it expects employees to display both, and top management strives to promote only those employees who are smart and honest. At Johnson & Johnson, the two core values are teamwork and manufacturing the highest quality products.

Company managers connect values to the strategic vision in one of two ways. In companies with long-standing and deeply entrenched values, managers go to great lengths to explain how the vision matches the company's values, sometimes reinterpreting the meaning of existing values to indicate their relevance to the strategic vision. In new companies or companies having weak or incomplete sets of values, top management considers what values, beliefs, and operating principles will help drive the vision forward. Then new values that fit the vision are drafted and circulated among managers and employees for discussion and possible modification. A final values statement that connects to the vision and that reflects the beliefs and principles the company wants to uphold is then officially adopted. Some companies combine their vision and values into a single statement or document provided to all organization members and often posted on the company's website.

Of course, a wide gap sometimes opens between a company's stated values and business practices. Enron, for example, touted its four corporate values—respect, integrity, communication, and excellence—but as recent events demonstrated, some top officials did not behave in accordance with those values and the company imploded. Once one of the world's Big Five public accounting firms, Arthur Andersen was renowned for its commitment to the highest standards of audit integrity, but its high-profile audit failures at Enron, WorldCom, and other companies led to Andersen's demise.

Setting Objectives: Phase 2 of the Strategy-Making, Strategy-Executing Process

The managerial purpose of setting **objectives** is to convert the strategic vision into specific performance targets—results and outcomes the company's management wants to achieve—and then use these objectives as yardsticks for tracking the company's progress and performance. Well-stated objectives are *quantifiable,* or *measurable,* and contain a *deadline for achievement.* As Bill Hewlett, cofounder of Hewlett-Packard, shrewdly observed, "You cannot manage what you cannot measure . . . And what gets measured gets done."[8] The experiences of countless companies and managers teach that precisely spelling out *how much* of *what kind* of performance *by when* and then pressing forward with actions and incentives calculated to help achieve the targeted outcomes greatly improve a company's actual performance. It definitely beats setting vague targets like "maximize profits," "reduce costs," "become more efficient," or "increase sales" which specify neither how much nor when or else exhorting company personnel to try hard, do the best they can, and then living with whatever results they deliver.

> **Core Concept**
>
> **Objectives** are an organization's performance targets—the results and outcomes it wants to achieve. They function as yardsticks for tracking an organization's performance and progress.

Ideally, managers ought to use the objective-setting exercise as a tool for *stretching an organization to reach its full potential.* Challenging company personnel to go all out and deliver big gains in performance pushes an enterprise to be more inventive, to exhibit some urgency in improving both its financial performance and its business position, and to be more intentional and focused in its actions. Stretch objectives help

Core Concept

Financial objectives relate to the financial performance targets management has established for the organization to achieve. *Strategic objectives* relate to target outcomes that indicate a company is strengthening its market standing, competitive vitality, and future business prospects.

build a firewall against contentment with slow, incremental improvements in organizational performance. As Mitchell Leibovitz, CEO of the auto parts and service retailer Pep Boys, once said, "If you want to have ho-hum results, have ho-hum objectives."

What Kinds of Objectives to Set—The Need for a Balanced Scorecard

Two very distinct types of performance yardsticks are required: those relating to *financial performance* and those relating to *strategic performance.* Examples of commonly used financial and strategic objectives include the following:

Financial Objectives	Strategic Objectives
▨ An *x* percent increase in annual revenues.	▨ Winning additional market share (or reaching an *x* percent market share).
▨ An *x* percent increase annually in after-tax profits.	▨ Consistently getting new or improved products to market ahead of rivals.
▨ An *x* percent increase annually in earnings per share.	▨ Overtaking key competitors on product performance or quality or customer service.
▨ Regular dividend increases.	▨ Achieving lower overall costs than rivals.
▨ A larger gross profit margin.	
▨ A larger operating profit margin.	▨ Deriving *x* percent of revenues from the sale of new products introduced within the past five years.
▨ A larger net profit margin.	
▨ An *x* percent return on capital employed (ROCE).	▨ Achieving national or global market coverage for the firm's products.
▨ An *x* percent return on assets (ROA).	▨ Being a recognized technological leader.
▨ An *x* percent return on shareholder investment (ROE).	▨ Having broader or more attractive product selection than rivals.
▨ An upward-trending stock price that builds significant shareholder value over time.	▨ Deriving *x* percent of revenues from online sales.
▨ Strong bond and credit ratings.	▨ Having a better-known or more respected brand name than rivals.
▨ Reduced levels of debt.	
▨ Sufficient internal cash flows to fund new capital investment.	▨ Improving global sales and distribution capabilities.
▨ Recognition as a blue-chip company.	▨ Having a larger network of wholesale distributors and/or retail dealers than rivals.
▨ A diversified revenue base.	
▨ Stable earnings during periods of recession.	

Achieving acceptable financial results is crucial. Without adequate profitability and financial strength, a company's pursuit of its strategic vision, as well as its long-term health and ultimate survival, is jeopardized. Neither shareowners nor lenders will continue to sink additional capital into an enterprise that can't deliver satisfactory financial

Unilever *(Strategic and financial objectives)*

"Grow revenues by 5–6 percent annually; increase operating profit margins from 11 percent to 16 percent within five years; trim the company's 1,200 food, household, and personal care products down to 400 core brands; focus sales and marketing efforts on those brands with potential to become respected, market-leading global brands; and streamline the company's supply chain."

Bank One Corporation *(Strategic objective)*

"To be one of the top three banking companies in terms of market share in all significant markets we serve."

Ford Motor Company *(Strategic objectives)*

"To satisfy our customers by providing quality cars and trucks, developing new products, reducing the time it takes to bring new vehicles to market, improving the efficiency of all our plants and processes, and building on our teamwork with employees, unions, dealers, and suppliers."

Alcan Aluminum *(Strategic and financial objectives)*

"To be the lowest-cost producer of aluminum and to outperform the average return on equity of the Standard & Poor's industrial stock index."

Bristol-Myers Squibb *(Strategic objective)*

"To focus globally on those businesses in health and personal care where we can be number one or number two through delivering superior value to the customer."

3M Corporation *(Financial and strategic objectives)*

"To achieve annual growth in earnings per share of 10 percent or better, on average; a return on stockholders' equity of 20–25 percent; a return on capital employed of 27 percent or better; and have at least 30 percent of sales come from products introduced in the past four years."

Source: Company documents.

---

results. Subpar earnings and a weak balance sheet alarm creditors and shareholders, impair a company's ability to fund needed initiatives, and perhaps even put its very survival at risk (not to mention the jobs of senior executives).

But company achievement of satisfactory financial performance, by itself, is not enough. Of equal or greater importance is a company's performance on the measures of its strategic well-being—its competitiveness and market position. Unless a company's performance in the marketplace reflects improving competitive strength and market penetration, its progress is less than inspiring and its ability to continue delivering good financial performance is suspect. A company's financial performance measures are really "lagging indicators" that reflect the results of past decisions and organizational activities. The "lead indicators" of a company's future financial performance and business prospects are its current achievement of strategic targets that reflect growing competitiveness and strength in the marketplace.

A balanced scorecard for measuring company performance thus requires setting both financial objectives and strategic objectives and tracking their achievement. Unless a company is in deep financial difficulty, such that its very survival is threatened, company managers are well advised to give the achievement of strategic objectives a higher priority than the achievement of financial objectives whenever a trade-off has to be made. *The surest path to sustained future profitability quarter after quarter and year after year is to relentlessly pursue strategic outcomes that strengthen a company's business position and yield sustainable competitive advantage.* Improving competitive vitality and market position enable a company to deliver steadily improving financial results. Company Spotlight 1.4 shows selected objectives of several prominent companies.

Organizations That Use a Balanced Scorecard Approach to Objective Setting

In recent years Exxon Mobil, CIGNA, United Parcel Service, Sears, Nova Scotia Power, Duke Children's Hospital, and the City of Charlotte, North Carolina, along with numerous other organizations, have used a "balanced scorecard" approach to objective setting in all or parts of their organization. This approach, developed and fine-tuned by two Harvard professors, stems from the recognition that exclusive reliance on financial performance measures, which are lag indicators that report the consequences of past actions, induced company managers to take actions that make the company's near-term financial performance look good and to neglect the drivers, or lead indicators, of future financial performance. The solution: measure the performance of a company's strategy and make strategic objectives an integral part of a company's set of performance targets. The balanced scorecard approach to objective setting advocates using a company's strategic vision and strategy as the basis for determining what specific strategic and financial outcomes are appropriate measures of the progress the company is making. The intent is to use the balanced scorecard (containing a carefully chosen combination of strategic and financial performance indicators tailored to the company's particular business) as a tool for both managing strategy and measuring its effectiveness.

Four of the initial users of the balanced scorecard approach were money-losing operations that were trailing the industry. Each had new management teams that were implementing strategies that required market repositioning and becoming more customer-driven. All four needed to adopt a new set of cultural values and priorities, as well as to reduce costs and downsize. At these four companies, use of a balanced scorecard, consisting of both financial targets (the lag indicators) and strategic targets (the lead indicators of future financial performance), not only served as a vehicle to communicate the strategy to organization personnel but also caused the organization to become more strategy-focused.

During the last decade, growing numbers of companies have adopted a balanced scorecard approach, believing that a mix of financial and strategic performance targets is superior to a purely financial set of performance measures and that winning in the marketplace requires paying close attention to how well the company's present strategy is working.

Source: Robert S. Kaplan and David P. Norton, *The Strategy-Focused Organization: How Balanced Scorecard Companies Thrive in the New Environment* (Boston: Harvard Business School Press, 2001), Chapter 1.

As a rule, a company's set of financial and strategic objectives ought to include both near-term and longer-term performance targets. Having quarterly or annual objectives focuses attention on delivering immediate performance improvements. Targets to be achieved within three to five years prompt considerations of what to do *now* to put the company in position to perform better later. If trade-offs have to be made between achieving long-run objectives and achieving short-run objectives, the long-run objectives should generally take precedence. A company rarely prospers from repeated management actions that put better short-term performance ahead of better long-run performance.

Company Spotlight 1.5 describes why a growing number of organizations are combining the use of financial and strategic objectives to create a "balanced scorecard" approach to measuring performance.

The Concept of Strategic Intent A company's objectives sometimes play another role: Very ambitious or aggressive objectives often signal **strategic intent** to stake out a particular business position and be a winner in the marketplace, often against long odds.[9] Strategic intent can be thought of as a "big, hairy, audacious goal," or BHAG (pronounced *bee-hag*), that generally takes a long time to

> ### Core Concept
> A company exhibits **strategic intent** when it relentlessly pursues an ambitious strategic objective and concentrates its full resources and competitive actions on achieving that objective.

achieve (maybe as long as a decade or two). A company's strategic intent or BHAG can entail becoming the recognized industry leader, unseating the existing industry leader, delivering the best customer service of any company in the industry (or the world), or turning a new technology into products capable of changing the way people work and live. Ambitious companies almost invariably begin with strategic intents that are out of proportion to their immediate capabilities and market positions. But they set aggressive stretch objectives and pursue them relentlessly, sometimes even obsessively. Consider the following examples:

> Companies driving hard to achieve demanding performance targets make formidable competitors.

- In the 1960s, Komatsu, Japan's leading earth-moving equipment company, was less than one-third the size of its U.S. rival Caterpillar, had little market presence outside Japan, and depended on its small bulldozers for most of its revenue. But Komatsu's strategic intent was to eventually "encircle Caterpillar" with a broader product line and then compete globally against Caterpillar—its motivating battle cry among managers and employees was "Beat Caterpillar." By the late 1980s, Komatsu was the industry's second-ranking company, with a strong sales presence in North America, Europe, and Asia plus a product line that included industrial robots and semiconductors as well as a broad selection of earth-moving equipment.

- Nike's strategic intent during the 1960s was to overtake Adidas (which connected nicely with Nike's core purpose "to experience the emotion of competition, winning, and crushing competitors").

- Throughout the 1980s, Wal-Mart's strategic intent was to "overtake Sears" as the largest U.S. retailer (a feat accomplished in 1990).

- America Online's strategic intent is to build the strongest, most recognized brand name on the Internet.

- For some years, Toyota has been driving to overtake General Motors as the world's largest motor vehicle producer.

- When Yamaha overtook Honda in the motorcycle market, Honda responded with a warlike strategic intent: *Yamaha wo tsubusu* ("We will crush, squash, slaughter Yamaha").

Capably managed, up-and-coming enterprises with strategic intents exceeding their present reach and resources often prove to be more formidable competitors over time than larger, cash-rich rivals with modest market ambitions.

The Need for Objectives at All Organizational Levels   Objective setting should not stop with top management's establishing of companywide performance targets. Company objectives need to be broken down into performance targets for each of the organization's separate businesses, product lines, functional departments, and individual work units. Company performance can't reach full potential without each area of the organization doing its part and contributing directly to the desired companywide outcomes and results. This means setting performance targets for each organization unit that support—rather than conflict with or negate—the achievement of companywide strategic and financial objectives. The ideal situation is a team effort in which each organizational unit strives to produce results in its area of responsibility that contribute to the achievement of the company's performance targets and strategic vision. Such consistency of purpose signals that organizational units know their strategic role and are on board in helping the company move down the chosen strategic path and produce the desired results.

Crafting a Strategy: Phase 3 of the Strategy-Making, Strategy-Executing Process

Crafting strategy is partly an exercise in astute entrepreneurship—actively searching for opportunities to do new things or to do existing things in new ways. The faster a company's business environment is changing, the more critical the need for its managers to be good entrepreneurs in diagnosing the direction and force of the changes underway and in responding with timely strategic modifications.[10] Managers are always under the gun to pick up on happenings in the external environment and steer company activities in whatever new directions are dictated by shifting market conditions. This means studying market trends and the actions of competitors, listening to customers and anticipating their changing needs and expectations, scrutinizing the business possibilities that spring from new technological developments, building the firm's market position via acquisitions or new product introductions, and pursuing ways to strengthen the firm's competitive capabilities. Good strategy making is therefore inseparable from good business entrepreneurship. One cannot exist without the other.

The task of stitching a strategy together entails addressing a series of hows: *how* to grow the business, *how* to please customers, *how* to outcompete rivals, *how* to respond to changing market conditions, *how* to manage each functional piece of the business and develop needed organizational capabilities, *how* to achieve strategic and financial objectives. Companies usually have a wide degree of strategic freedom in addressing the hows of strategy. They can diversify broadly or narrowly, into related or unrelated industries, via acquisition, joint venture, strategic alliances, or internal start-up. Most industries are sufficiently diverse to offer competing companies enough strategy-making latitude to avoid carbon-copy strategies—some rivals have wide product lines, while others have narrow product lines; some target the high end of the market, while others go after the middle or low end; some strive for a competitive advantage based on lower costs than rivals, while others aim for a competitive edge based on product superiority or personalized customer service or added convenience. Some competitors position themselves in only one part of the industry's chain of production–distribution activities (preferring to be just in manufacturing or wholesale distribution or retailing), while others are integrated, with operations ranging from components production to manufacturing and assembly to wholesale distribution or company-owned retail stores. Some rivals deliberately confine their operations to local or regional markets; others opt to compete nationally, internationally (several countries), or globally (as many countries as possible). Opportunities abound for fashioning a strategy that tightly fits a company's own particular situation and that is discernibly different from the strategies of rivals.

The Ethical Component of Strategy Making

In choosing among strategic alternatives, corporate managers are well advised to embrace aboveboard actions that can pass the test of moral scrutiny. Crafting an ethical strategy means more than keeping a company's strategic actions within the bounds of what is legal. Ethical and moral standards go beyond the prohibitions of law and the language of "shall not" to the issues of *duty* and the language of "should and should not." A strategy is ethical only if all its pieces are consistent with the ethical duty management has to owners/shareholders, employees, customers, suppliers, and the community at large.

Recent headlines concerning Enron, WorldCom, Tyco, Adelphia, Dynegy, and other companies leave no room to doubt the damage that can result from ethical misconduct, corporate malfeasance, and even criminal behavior on the part of company personnel. Aside from just the embarrassment and black marks that accompany headline exposure of a company's unethical practices, the hard fact is that many customers and many suppliers are very wary of doing business with a company that engages in sleazy practices or that turns a blind eye to below-board behavior on the part of employees. They are turned off by unethical strategies or behavior and, rather than become victims or get burned themselves, wary customers will do their business elsewhere and wary suppliers will tread carefully in any business dealings they have with companies they view as unethical. Moreover, employees with character and integrity do not want to work for a company that has a shady strategy or whose executives are dishonest or unethical. There are few lasting upside benefits to unethical strategies and behavior, and the downside risks can be substantial—besides, such actions are plain wrong.

Admittedly, strategic behavior is not always easily categorized as definitely ethical or definitely unethical; many strategic actions fall in the gray zone, and whether they are ultimately deemed ethical or unethical often depends on how high one sets the bar. For example, is it ethical for a brewer of beer to advertise its products on TV at times when the ads are likely to be seen by underage viewers? Anheuser-Busch responded to concerns about the ethics of such advertising by announcing it would no longer run its beer commercials on MTV. Is it ethical for the manufacturers of firearms to encourage police departments and retired policemen to trade in or return automatic weapons whose manufacture has since been banned by Congress so they can gain access to a supply of weapons for resale? (A legal loophole allows them to traffic in weapons that were manufactured prior to the bans.) Similarly, is it ethical for firearms makers to change the designs of their automatic weapons just enough to escape the bans and prohibitions on automatic firearms instituted by Congress? Is it ethical for a meat packer to export meat products that do not meet safe standards in its home country to those countries where the safety standards are low and inspection is lax? Is it ethical for an apparel retailer attempting to keep prices attractively low to source clothing from low-cost foreign manufacturers who pay substandard wages or employ child labor?

Senior executives with strong character and ethical convictions are generally proactive in linking strategic action and ethics, forbidding the pursuit of ethically questionable business opportunities, and insisting that all aspects of company strategy reflect high ethical standards.[11] They make it clear that all company personnel are expected to act with integrity, and they put organizational systems and checks into place to monitor behavior, enforce ethical codes of conduct, and provide guidance to employees regarding any gray areas. They go beyond lip service to make a genuine commitment to conducting the company's business in an ethical manner.

Merging the Strategic Vision, Objectives, and Strategy into a Strategic Plan

Developing a strategic vision and mission, setting objectives, and crafting a strategy are basic direction-setting tasks. They map out where a company is headed, its short-range and long-range performance targets, and the competitive moves and internal action approaches to be used in achieving the targeted business results. Together, they constitute a **strategic plan** for coping with industry and competitive conditions, the expected actions of the industry's key

> **Core Concept**
>
> A company's **strategic plan** lays out its mission and future direction, performance targets, and strategy.

players, and the challenges and issues that stand as obstacles to the company's success.[12] In companies committed to regular strategy reviews and the development of explicit strategic plans, the strategic plan may take the form of a written document that is circulated to most managers and perhaps selected employees. In small, privately owned companies, strategic plans usually take the form of oral understandings and commitments among managers and key employees about where to head, what to accomplish, and how to proceed. Near-term performance targets are the part of the strategic plan most often spelled out explicitly and communicated to managers and employees. A number of companies summarize key elements of their strategic plans in the company's annual report to shareholders, in postings on their website, or in statements provided to the business media, whereas others, perhaps for reasons of competitive sensitivity, make only vague, general statements about their strategic plans that could apply to most any company.

Who Participates in Crafting a Company's Strategy?

A company's senior executives obviously have important strategy-making roles. The chief executive officer (CEO), as captain of the ship, carries the mantles of chief direction setter, chief objective setter, chief strategy maker, and chief strategy implementer for the total enterprise. Ultimate responsibility for *leading* the strategy-making, strategy-executing process rests with the CEO. In some enterprises the CEO or owner functions as strategic visionary and chief architect of strategy, personally deciding which of several strategic options to pursue, although others may well assist with data gathering and analysis and the CEO may seek the advice of other senior managers and key employees on which way to go. Such an approach to strategy development is characteristic of small owner-managed companies and sometimes large corporations that have been founded by the present CEO—Michael Dell at Dell Computer, Bill Gates at Microsoft, and Howard Schultz at Starbucks are prominent examples of corporate CEOs who maintain a heavy hand in shaping their company's strategy.

In most companies, however, the heads of business divisions and major product lines, the chief financial officer, and vice presidents for production, marketing, human resources, and other functional departments have influential strategy-making roles. Normally, a company's chief financial officer is in charge of devising and implementing an appropriate financial strategy; the production vice president takes the lead in developing and executing the company's production strategy; the marketing vice president orchestrates sales and marketing strategy; a brand manager is in charge of the strategy for a particular brand in the company's product lineup, and so on.

But it is a mistake to view strategy making as exclusively a top management function, the province of owner-entrepreneurs, CEOs, and other senior executives. The more wide-ranging a company's operations, the more that strategy making is a collaborative team effort involving managers (and sometimes key employees) down through the whole organization hierarchy. Consider Toshiba, a $43 billion corporation with 300 subsidiaries, thousands of products, and operations extending across the world. Any notion that a few senior executives in Toshiba headquarters have either the expertise or a sufficiently detailed understanding of all the relevant factors to wisely craft all the strategic initiatives taken in Toshiba's numerous and diverse organizational units is farfetched and erroneous. Rather, it takes involvement on the part of Toshiba's entire management team to

Core Concept

Every company manager has a strategy-making, strategy-executing role; viewing the tasks of managing strategy as something only high-level managers do is flawed thinking.

craft and execute the thousands of strategic initiatives that constitute the whole of Toshiba's strategy.

Major organizational units in a company—business divisions, product groups, functional departments, plants, geographic offices, distribution centers—normally have a leading or supporting role in the company's strategic game plan. Because senior executives in the corporate office seldom know enough about the situation in every geographic area and operating unit to direct every strategic move made in the field, it is common practice for top-level managers to delegate strategy-making authority to middle- and lower-echelon managers who head the organizational subunits where specific strategic results must be achieved. The more that a company's operations cut across different products, industries, and geographical areas, the more that headquarters executives are prone to delegate considerable strategy-making authority to on-the-scene personnel who have firsthand knowledge of customer requirements, can accurately evaluate market opportunities, and know how to keep the strategy responsive to changing market and competitive conditions. While managers further down in the managerial hierarchy obviously have a narrower, more specific strategy-making, strategy-executing role than managers closer to the top, the important point here is that in most of today's companies *every company manager typically has a strategy-making, strategy-executing role—ranging from major to minor—for the area he or she heads.*

Hence any notion that an organization's strategists are at the top of the management hierarchy and that midlevel and frontline managers and employees merely carry out the strategic directives of senior managers needs to be cast aside. With decentralized decision making becoming common at companies of all stripes, key pieces of a company's strategy now typically originate in a company's middle and lower ranks.[13] For example, Electronic Data Systems conducted a year-long strategy review that involved 2,500 of its 55,000 employees and was coordinated by a core of 150 managers and staffers from all over the world.[14] J. M. Smucker, well known for its jams and jellies, formed a team of 140 employees (7 percent of its 2,000-person workforce) who spent 25 percent of their time over a six-month period looking for ways to rejuvenate the company's growth; the team, which solicited input from all employees, came up with 12 initiatives to double the company's revenues over the next five years.

Involving teams of people to dissect complex situations and find market-driven, customer-driven solutions is becoming increasingly necessary in many businesses. Many strategic issues are not only too far-reaching or complex for a single manager to handle but also cross-functional and cross-departmental, thus requiring the contributions of many disciplinary experts and the collaboration of managers from different parts of the organization. A valuable strength of collaborative strategy making is that the group of people charged with crafting the strategy can easily include the very people who will also be charged with implementing it. Giving people an influential stake in crafting the strategy they must later help implement and execute builds motivation and commitment; furthermore, it allows the company to hold these people accountable for putting the strategy into place and making it work—the tired excuse of "It wasn't my idea to do this" won't fly.

In some companies, top management makes a regular practice of encouraging individuals and teams to develop and champion proposals for new product lines and new business ventures. The idea is to unleash the talents and energies of promising "corporate intrapreneurs," letting them try out untested business ideas and giving them the room to pursue new strategic initiatives. Executives judge which proposals merit support, give the chosen intrapreneurs the organizational and budgetary support they need, and let them run with the ball. Thus important pieces of company strategy originate with those intrapreneurial individuals and teams who succeed in championing a proposal through the approval stage and then end up being charged with the lead role in launching new products, overseeing the company's entry into new geographic markets, or heading up new business ventures. W. L. Gore and Associates, a privately owned company famous for its Gore-Tex waterproofing film, is an avid and highly successful practitioner of the corporate intrapreneur approach to strategy making. Gore expects all employees to initiate improvements and to display innovativeness. Each employee's intrapreneurial contributions are prime considerations in determining raises, stock option bonuses, and promotions. W. L. Gore's commitment to intrapreneurship has produced a stream of product innovations and new strategic initiatives that has kept the company vibrant and growing for nearly two decades.

A Company's Strategy-Making Hierarchy

It thus follows that *a company's overall strategy is a collection of strategic initiatives and actions* devised by managers and key employees up and down the whole organizational hierarchy. The larger and more diverse the operations of an enterprise, the more points of strategic initiative it has and the more managers and employees at more levels of management that have a relevant strategy-making role. Figure 1.4 shows who is generally responsible for devising what pieces of a company's overall strategy.

In diversified, multibusiness companies where the strategies of several different businesses have to be managed, the strategy-making task involves four distinct types or levels of strategy, each of which involves different facets of the company's overall strategy:

▪ *Corporate strategy* consists of the kinds of initiatives the company uses to establish business positions in different industries, the approaches corporate executives pursue to boost the combined performance of the set of businesses the company has diversified into, and the means of capturing cross-business synergies and turning them into competitive advantage. Senior corporate executives normally have lead responsibility for devising corporate strategy and for choosing among whatever recommended actions bubble up from the organization below. Key business-unit heads may also be influential, especially in strategic decisions affecting the businesses they head. Major strategic decisions are usually reviewed and approved by the company's board of directors. We will look deeper into the strategy-making process at diversified companies when we get to Chapter 6.

▪ *Business strategy* concerns the actions and the approaches crafted to produce successful performance in one specific line of business. The key focus is crafting responses to changing market circumstances and initiating actions to strengthen market position, build competitive advantage, and develop strong competitive capabilities. Orchestrating the development of business-level strategy is the responsibility of the manager in charge of the business. The business head has at least two other strategy-related roles: (1) seeing that lower-level strategies are well conceived, consistent, and adequately matched to the overall business strategy, and (2) getting major business-level strategic moves approved by corporate-level officers (and sometimes the board of directors) and keeping them informed of emerging strategic issues. In diversified companies, business-unit heads may have the additional obligation of making sure business-level objectives and strategy conform to corporate-level objectives and strategy themes.

Figure 1.4   A Company's Strategy-Making Hierarchy

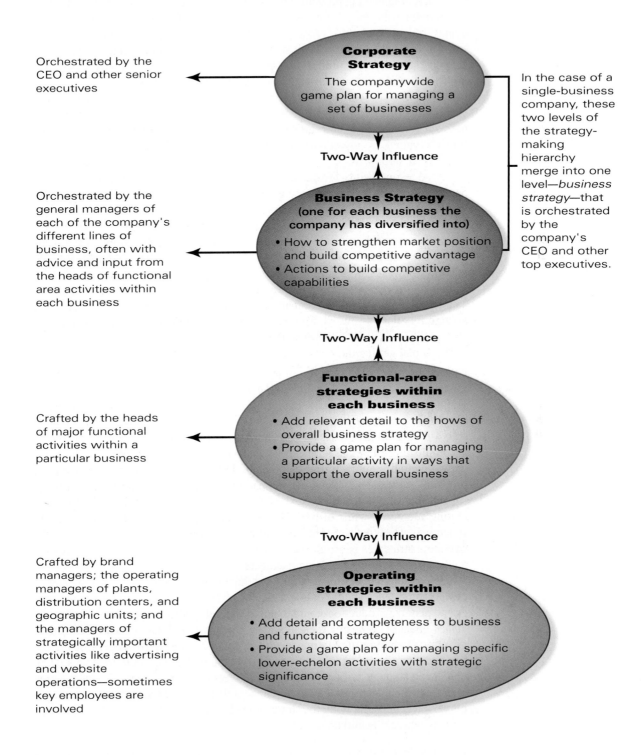

Orchestrated by the CEO and other senior executives

Corporate Strategy

The companywide game plan for managing a set of businesses

In the case of a single-business company, these two levels of the strategy-making hierarchy merge into one level—*business strategy*—that is orchestrated by the company's CEO and other top executives.

Two-Way Influence

Orchestrated by the general managers of each of the company's different lines of business, often with advice and input from the heads of functional area activities within each business

Business Strategy
(one for each business the company has diversified into)

- How to strengthen market position and build competitive advantage
- Actions to build competitive capabilities

Two-Way Influence

Crafted by the heads of major functional activities within a particular business

Functional-area strategies within each business

- Add relevant detail to the hows of overall business strategy
- Provide a game plan for managing a particular activity in ways that support the overall business

Two-Way Influence

Crafted by brand managers; the operating managers of plants, distribution centers, and geographic units; and the managers of strategically important activities like advertising and website operations—sometimes key employees are involved

Operating strategies within each business

- Add detail and completeness to business and functional strategy
- Provide a game plan for managing specific lower-echelon activities with strategic significance

▪ *Functional-area strategies* concern the actions, approaches, and practices to be employed in managing particular functions or business processes or key activities within a business. A company's marketing strategy, for example, represents the managerial game plan for running the sales and marketing part of the business. A company's product development strategy represents the managerial game plan for keeping the company's product lineup fresh and in tune with what buyers are looking for. Functional strategies add specifics to the hows of business-level strategy. Plus, they aim at establishing or strengthening a business unit's competencies and capabilities in performing strategy-critical activities so as to enhance the business's market position and standing with customers. The primary role of a functional strategy is to *support* the company's overall business strategy and competitive approach.

Lead responsibility for functional strategies within a business is normally delegated to the heads of the respective functions, with the general manager of the business having final approval and perhaps even exerting a strong influence over the content of particular pieces of the strategies. To some extent, functional managers have to collaborate and coordinate their strategy-making efforts to avoid uncoordinated or conflicting strategies. For the overall business strategy to have maximum impact, a business's marketing strategy, production strategy, finance strategy, customer service strategy, product development strategy, and human resources strategy should be compatible and mutually reinforcing rather than each serving its own narrower purposes. If inconsistent functional-area strategies are sent up the line for final approval, the business head is responsible for spotting the conflicts and getting them resolved.

▪ *Operating strategies* concern the relatively narrow strategic initiatives and approaches for managing key operating units (plants, distribution centers, geographic units) and specific operating activities with strategic significance (advertising campaigns, the management of specific brands, supply chain–related activities, and website sales and operations). A plant manager needs a strategy for accomplishing the plant's objectives, carrying out the plant's part of the company's overall manufacturing game plan, and dealing with any strategy-related problems that exist at the plant. A company's advertising manager needs a strategy for getting maximum audience exposure and sales impact from the ad budget. Operating strategies, while of limited scope, add further detail and completeness to functional strategies and to the overall business strategy. Lead responsibility for operating strategies is usually delegated to frontline managers, subject to review and approval by higher-ranking managers.

Even though operating strategy is at the bottom of the strategy-making hierarchy, its importance should not be downplayed. A major plant that fails in its strategy to achieve production volume, unit cost, and quality targets can undercut the achievement of company sales and profit objectives and wreak havoc with strategic efforts to build a quality image with customers. Frontline managers are thus an important part of an organization's strategy-making team because many operating units have strategy-critical performance targets and need to have strategic action plans in place to achieve them. One cannot reliably judge the strategic importance of a given action simply by the strategy level or location within the managerial hierarchy where it is initiated.

In single-business enterprises, the corporate and business levels of strategy-making merge into one level—business strategy—because the strategy for the whole company involves only one distinct line of business. Thus a single-business enterprise has three levels of strategy: business strategy for the company as a whole, functional-area strategies for each main area within the business, and operating strategies undertaken by lower-echelon managers to flesh out strategically significant aspects for the company's business and functional-area strategies. Proprietorships, partnerships, and owner-managed enterprises may have only one or two strategy-making levels since their strategy-making, strategy-executing process can be handled by just a few key people.

Uniting the Strategy-Making Effort   Ideally, the pieces of a company's strategy should fit together like a jigsaw puzzle. To achieve such unity, the strategizing process must generally proceed from the corporate level to the business level and then from the business level to the functional and operating levels. *Midlevel and frontline managers cannot do good strategy making without understanding the company's long-term direction and higher-level strategies.* The strategic disarray that occurs in an organization when senior managers don't exercise strong top-down direction setting and set forth a clearly articulated companywide strategy is akin to what would happen to a football team's offensive performance if the quarterback decided not to call a play for the team but instead let each

> **Core Concept**
>
> A company's strategy is at full power only when its many pieces are united.

player pick whatever play he thought would work best at his respective position. In business, as in sports, all the strategy makers in a company are on the same team and the many different pieces of the overall strategy crafted at various organizational levels need to be in sync and united. Anything less than a unified collection of strategies weakens company performance.

Achieving unity is partly a function of communicating the company's basic strategy themes effectively across the organization and establishing clear strategic principles and guidelines for lower-level strategy making. Cohesive strategy making becomes easier to achieve when company strategy is distilled into pithy, easy-to-grasp terminology that can be used to drive consistent strategic action down through the hierarchy.[15] The greater the numbers of company personnel who know, understand, and buy into the company's basic direction and strategy, the smaller the risk that people and organization units will go off in conflicting strategic directions when decision making is pushed down to frontline levels and many people are given a strategy-making role. Good communication of strategic themes and guiding principles thus serves a valuable strategy-unifying purpose.

What Makes a Strategy a Winner?

Being able to tell a winning strategy from a losing or mediocre strategy is a valuable skill. There are three tests for evaluating the merits of one strategy over another and gauging how good a company's strategy is:

The Goodness of Fit Test—To qualify as a winner, a strategy has to be well matched to industry and competitive conditions, market opportunities and threats, and other aspects of the enterprise's external environment. At the same time, it has to be tailored to company's resource strengths and weaknesses, competencies, and competitive capabilities. Unless a strategy tightly fits both the external and internal aspects of a company's overall situation, it is suspect and likely to produce less than the best possible business results.

The Competitive Advantage Test—Good strategies enable a company to build sustainable competitive advantage and then defend or protect it. The bigger the competitive edge it helps build, the more powerful and appealing the strategy is.

The Performance Test—A good strategy boosts company performance. Two kinds of performance improvement tell the most about the caliber of a company's strategy: gains in profitability and gains in the company's competitive strength and market standing.

> ### Core Concept
> A winning strategy must fit the enterprise's external and internal situation, build sustainable competitive advantage, and improve company performance.

Once a company commits to a particular strategy and enough time elapses to assess how well that strategy fits the situation and whether it is actually delivering competitive advantage and better performance, these tests can be used to determine what grade to assign the strategy. Strategies that come up short on one or more of these tests are plainly less appealing than strategies that pass all three with flying colors.

Managers can also apply the tests in picking and choosing among alternative strategic actions. A company debating which of several strategic options to employ can evaluate each for goodness of fit, competitive advantage, and performance. The strategic option with the highest prospective passing scores on all three tests can be regarded as the most attractive strategic alternative.

Other relevant criteria for judging the merits of a particular strategy include how consistent all its pieces are, what degree of risk it poses compared to alternative strategies, how adaptable it is to changing circumstances, and whether it represents a viable business model. These criteria merit consideration, but they seldom override the importance of the three tests listed above.

Implementing and Executing the Strategy: Phase 4 of the Strategy-Making, Strategy-Executing Process

Managing the implementation and execution of strategy is an operations-oriented, make-things-happen activity aimed at shaping the performance of core business activities in a strategy-supportive manner. It is easily the most demanding and time-consuming part of the strategy management process. Converting strategic plans into actions and results tests a manager's ability to direct organizational change, motivate people, build and strengthen company competencies and competitive capabilities, create a strategy-supportive work climate, and meet or beat performance targets. Initiatives have to be launched and managed on many organizational fronts.

Management's action agenda for implementing and executing the chosen strategy emerges from assessing what the company will have to do differently or better, given its particular operating practices and organizational circumstances, to execute the strategy proficiently and achieve the targeted performance. Each company manager has to think through the answer to "What has to be done in my area to execute my piece of the strategic plan, and what actions should I take to get the process under way?" How much internal change is needed depends on how much of the strategy is new, how far internal practices and competencies deviate from what the strategy requires, and how well the present work climate/culture supports good strategy execution. Depending on the amount of internal change involved, full implementation and proficient execution of company strategy (or important new pieces thereof) can take several months to several years.

In most situations, managing the strategy execution process includes the following principal aspects:

- Staffing the organization with the needed skills and expertise, consciously building and strengthening strategy-supportive competencies and competitive capabilities, and organizing the work effort.

- Developing budgets that steer ample resources into those activities critical to strategic success.

- Ensuring that policies and operating procedures facilitate rather than impede effective execution.

- Using the best-known practices to perform core business activities and pushing for continuous improvement. Organizational units have to periodically reassess how things are being done and diligently pursue useful changes and improvements.

- Installing information and operating systems that enable company personnel to better carry out their strategic roles day in and day out.

- Motivating people to pursue the target objectives energetically and, if need be, modifying their duties and job behavior to better fit the requirements of successful strategy execution.

- Tying rewards and incentives directly to the achievement of performance objectives and good strategy execution.

- Creating a company culture and work climate conducive to successful strategy implementation and execution.

- Exerting the internal leadership needed to drive implementation forward and keep improving on how the strategy is being executed. When stumbling blocks or weaknesses are encountered, management has to see that they are addressed and rectified on a timely basis.

Good strategy execution requires creating strong fits between strategy and organizational capabilities, between strategy and the reward structure, between strategy and internal operating systems, and between strategy and the organization's work climate and culture. The stronger these fits—that is, the more that the company's capabilities, reward structure, internal operating systems, and culture facilitate and promote proficient strategy execution—the better the execution and the higher the company's odds of achieving its performance targets. Furthermore, deliberately shaping the performance of core business activities around the strategy helps unite the organization.

Evaluating Performance and Initiating Corrective Adjustments: Phase 5 of the Strategy-Making, Strategy-Executing Process

The fifth phase of the strategy management process—evaluating the company's progress, assessing the impact of new external developments, and making corrective adjustments—is the trigger point for deciding whether to continue or change the company's vision, objectives, strategy, and/or strategy execution methods. So long as the company's direction and strategy seem well matched to industry and competitive conditions and performance targets are being met, company executives may well decide to stay the course. Simply fine-tuning the strategic plan and continuing with efforts to improve strategy execution are sufficient.

> **Core Concept**
>
> A company's vision, objectives, strategy, and approach to strategy execution are never final; managing strategy is an ongoing process, not a start–stop event.

But whenever a company encounters disruptive changes in its environment, questions need to be raised about the appropriateness of its direction and strategy. If a company experiences a downturn in its market position or shortfalls in performance, then company managers are obligated to ferret out the causes—do they relate to poor strategy, poor strategy execution, or both?—and take timely corrective action. A company's direction, objectives, and strategy have to be revisited anytime external or internal conditions warrant. It is to be expected that a company will modify its strategic vision, direction, objectives, and strategy over time.

Likewise, it is not unusual for a company to find that one or more aspects of its strategy implementation and execution are not going as well as intended. Proficient strategy execution is always the product of much organizational learning. It is achieved unevenly—coming quickly in some areas and proving nettlesome in others. It is both normal and desirable to periodically assess strategy execution to determine which aspects are working well and which need improving. Successful strategy execution entails vigilantly searching for ways to improve and then making corrective adjustments whenever and wherever it is useful to do so.

What Is the Role of the Board of Directors in the Strategy-Making, Strategy-Executing Process?

Since *lead responsibility* for crafting and executing strategy falls to top executives, the chief strategic role of an organization's board of directors is to exercise oversight and see that all five phases of managing the strategy-making, strategy-executing process are carried out in a manner that benefits shareholders (in the case of investor-owned enterprises) or stakeholders (in the case of not-for-profit organizations). The specter of stockholder lawsuits and the escalating costs of liability insurance for directors underscore the responsibility that corporate board members have for overseeing a company's strategic actions. Moreover, holders of large blocks of shares (mutual funds and pension funds), regulatory authorities, and the financial press consistently urge that board members, especially outside directors, be active in their oversight of company strategy and the actions and capabilities of executives.

It is standard procedure for executives to brief board members on important strategic moves and to submit the company's strategic plans to the board for official approval. But directors rarely can or should play a direct, hands-on role in crafting or executing strategy. Many outside directors, especially if they are relatively new, have limited industry-specific and company-specific knowledge. Boards of directors typically meet no more than once a month for six to eight hours. Outside board members can scarcely be expected to have detailed command of all the strategic issues or know the ins and outs of the various strategic options. They can hardly be expected to come up with compelling strategy proposals of their own to debate against those put forward by senior management. But such a hands-on role is unnecessary for good oversight. The chief task of directors is to be *inquiring critics* and *overseers,* asking probing questions and drawing on their experience and knowledge to make independent judgments about whether proposals have been adequately analyzed and whether proposed strategic actions appear to have greater promise than alternatives.[16] If executive management is bringing well-supported and reasoned strategy proposals to the board, there's little reason for board members to aggressively challenge and try to pick apart everything put before them. Asking probing questions and following up on superficial or unpersuasive answers is usually sufficient to test whether the case for the proposals is compelling and to exercise vigilant oversight. However, if the company is experiencing gradual erosion of profits and market share, and certainly when there is a precipitous collapse in profitability, board members have a duty to forcefully express their concerns about the validity of the strategy, initiate debate about the company's strategic path, hold one-on-one discussions with key executives and other board members, and perhaps directly intervene as a group to alter both the strategy and the company's executive leadership.

> **Core Concept**
>
> The central roles of a company's board of directors are (1) to critically appraise and ultimately approve strategic action plans, and (2) to evaluate the strategic leadership skills of the CEO and others in line to succeed the incumbent CEO.

Insofar as strategy is concerned, the primary hands-on role of directors is to evaluate the caliber of senior executives' strategy-making and strategy-implementing skills. The board is always responsible for determining whether the current CEO is doing a good job of strategic management (as a basis for awarding salary increases and bonuses and deciding on retention or removal). Boards must also exercise due diligence in evaluating the strategic leadership skills of other senior executives in line to succeed the CEO. When the incumbent CEO retires, the board must elect a successor, either going with an insider (frequently nominated by the retiring CEO) or deciding that an outsider is needed to perhaps radically change the company's strategic course. Board oversight and vigilance are therefore very much in play in the strategy arena, but the board's tasks seldom extend to relieving top executives of their strategy-making, strategy-implementing responsibilities and taking over these functions themselves.

Why Is Strategy Important?

Crafting and executing strategy are top-priority managerial tasks for two very big reasons. First, there is a compelling need for managers to *proactively shape* how the company's business will be conducted. A clear and reasoned strategy is management's prescription for doing business, its road map to competitive advantage, its game plan for pleasing customers and achieving performance targets. Winning in the marketplace requires a well-conceived opportunistic strategy, usually one characterized by strategic offensives to outinnovate and outmaneuver rivals and secure sustainable competitive advantage, then using this market edge to achieve superior financial performance. A powerful strategy that delivers a home run in the marketplace can propel a firm from a trailing position into one of leadership such that the firm's products/services become the industry standard. High-achieving enterprises are nearly always the product of shrewd strategy making—companies don't get to the top of the industry rankings or stay there with strategies built around timid efforts to do better. And only a handful of companies can boast of strategies that hit home runs in the marketplace due to lucky breaks or the good fortune of having stumbled into the right market at the right time with the right product. So there can be little argument that the caliber of a company's strategy matters—and matters a lot.

Second, a strategy-focused organization is more likely to be a strong bottom-line performer than an organization that views strategy as secondary and puts its priorities elsewhere. The quality of managerial strategy making and strategy execution has a highly positive impact on earnings, cash flow, and return on investment. A company that lacks clear-cut direction, has vague or undemanding objectives, has a muddled or flawed strategy, or can't seem to execute its strategy competently is a company whose financial performance is probably suffering, whose business is at long-term risk, and whose management is sorely lacking. On the other hand, when the five phases of the strategy-making, strategy-executing process drive management's whole approach to managing the company, the odds are much greater that the initiatives and activities of different divisions, departments, managers, and work groups will be unified into a *coordinated, cohesive effort*. Mobilizing the full complement of company resources in a total team effort behind good execution of the chosen strategy and achievement of the targeted performance allows a company to operate at full power. The chief executive officer of one successful company put it well when he said:

> In the main, our competitors are acquainted with the same fundamental concepts and techniques and approaches that we follow, and they are as free to pursue them as we are. More often than not, the difference between their level of success and ours lies in the relative thoroughness and self-discipline with which we and they develop and execute our strategies for the future.

Good Strategy + Good Strategy Execution = Good Management

Crafting and executing strategy are thus core management functions. Among all the things managers do, nothing affects a company's ultimate success or failure more fundamentally than how well its management team charts the company's direction, develops competitively effective strategic moves and business approaches, and pursues what needs to be done internally to produce good day-in, day-out strategy execution. Indeed, *good strategy and good strategy execution are the most trustworthy signs of good management.* Managers don't deserve a gold star for designing a potentially brilliant strategy but failing to put the organizational means in place to carry it out in high-caliber fashion; weak implementation and execution undermine the strategy's potential and pave the way for shortfalls in customer satisfaction and company performance. Competent execution of a mediocre strategy scarcely merits enthusiastic applause for management's efforts either. The rationale for using the twin standards of good strategy making and good strategy execution to determine whether a company is well managed is therefore compelling: The better conceived a company's strategy and the more competently it is executed, the more likely the company will be a standout performer in the marketplace.

Throughout the text chapters to come and the accompanying case collection, the spotlight is trained on the foremost question in running a business enterprise: What must managers do, and do well, to make a company a winner in the marketplace? The answer that emerges, and that becomes the message of this book, is that doing a good job of managing inherently requires good strategic thinking and good management

Core Concept

Excellent execution of an excellent strategy is the best test of managerial excellence—and the most reliable recipe for winning in the marketplace.

of the strategy-making, strategy-executing process. The mission of this book is to explore what "good strategic thinking" entails, to present the core concepts and tools of strategic analysis, to describe the ins and outs of crafting and executing strategy, and, through the cases that are included, to help you build your skills both in diagnosing how well the five aspects of managing strategy are being performed in actual companies and in making analysis-based recommendations for improvement. As you tackle the following pages, ponder an observation once made by Ralph Waldo Emerson: "Commerce is a game of skill which many people play, but which few play well." The overriding objective of this book is to help you become a more savvy player and equip you to succeed in business—capabilities in crafting and executing strategy are basic to managing successfully and a standard component of the managerial toolkit.

Key Points

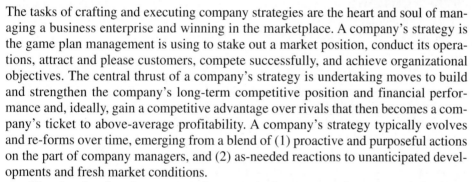

The tasks of crafting and executing company strategies are the heart and soul of managing a business enterprise and winning in the marketplace. A company's strategy is the game plan management is using to stake out a market position, conduct its operations, attract and please customers, compete successfully, and achieve organizational objectives. The central thrust of a company's strategy is undertaking moves to build and strengthen the company's long-term competitive position and financial performance and, ideally, gain a competitive advantage over rivals that then becomes a company's ticket to above-average profitability. A company's strategy typically evolves and re-forms over time, emerging from a blend of (1) proactive and purposeful actions on the part of company managers, and (2) as-needed reactions to unanticipated developments and fresh market conditions.

Closely related to the concept of strategy is the concept of a company's business model. A company's business model is management's storyline for how and why the company's product offerings and competitive approaches will generate a revenue stream and have an associated cost structure that produces attractive earnings and return on investment; in effect a company's business model sets forth the economic logic for answering the question "How do we intend to make money in this business, given our current strategy?"

The managerial process of crafting and executing a company's strategy consists of five interrelated and integrated phases:

1. *Developing a strategic vision* of where the company needs to head and what market position it is trying to stake out. This managerial step provides long-term direction, infuses the organization with a sense of purposeful action, and communicates to stakeholders what management's aspirations for the company are.

2. *Setting objectives*—managerial actions that convert the strategic vision into specific performance outcomes for the company to achieve. Objectives need to spell out *how much* of *what kind* of performance *by when* and they need to require a significant amount of organizational stretch. A balanced scorecard approach for measuring company performance entails setting both *financial objectives* and *strategic objectives.* Judging how well a company is doing by its financial performance is not enough, because financial outcomes are "lag indicators" that reflect the impacts of past decisions and organizational activities. But the "lead indicators" of a company's future financial performance are its current achievement of strategic

targets that indicate a company is strengthening its marketing standing, competitive vitality, and future business prospects.

3. *Crafting a strategy to achieve the objectives and move the company toward where it wants to go.* Crafting strategy is concerned principally with forming responses to changes under way in the external environment, devising competitive moves and market approaches aimed at producing sustainable competitive advantage, building competitively valuable competencies and capabilities, and uniting the strategic actions initiated in various parts of the company. The more wide-ranging a company's operations, the more that strategy making is a collaborative team effort involving managers (and sometimes key employees) down through the whole organization hierarchy; the overall strategy that emerges in such companies is really a collection of strategic actions and business approaches initiated partly by senior company executives, partly by the heads of major business divisions, partly by functional area managers, and partly by operating managers on the frontlines. The tests of a winning strategy are how well matched it is to the company's external and internal situation, whether it is producing sustainable competitive advantage, and whether it is boosting company performance.

4. *Implementing and executing the chosen strategy efficiently and effectively.* Managing the implementation and execution of strategy is an operations-oriented, make-things-happen activity aimed at shaping the performance of core business activities in a strategy-supportive manner. Converting a company's strategy into actions and results tests a manager's ability to direct organizational change, motivate people with a reward and incentive compensation system tied to good strategy execution and the achievement of target outcomes, build and strengthen company competencies and competitive capabilities, create a strategy-supportive work climate, and deliver the desired results. The quality of a company's operational excellence in executing the chosen strategy is a major driver of how well the company ultimately performs.

5. *Evaluating performance and initiating corrective adjustments in vision, long-term direction, objectives, strategy, or execution in* light of actual experience, changing conditions, new ideas, and new opportunities. This phase of the strategy management process is the trigger point for deciding whether to continue or change the company's vision, objectives, strategy, and/or strategy execution methods. Sometimes simply fine-tuning the strategic plan and continuing with efforts to improve strategy execution suffices. At other times, major overhauls are required.

Developing a strategic vision and mission, setting objectives, and crafting a strategy are the basic direction-setting tasks that together constitute a *strategic plan* for coping with industry and competitive conditions, the actions of rivals, and the challenges and issues that stand as obstacles to the company's success.

Crafting and executing strategy are core management functions. Whether a company wins or loses in the marketplace is directly attributable to the caliber with which it performs the five tasks that comprise the strategy-making, strategy-executing process.

Exercises

1. Go to www.redhat.com and check whether the company's business model is working. That is, is the company profitable? Is its revenue stream from selling technical support services growing or declining as a percentage of total revenues? Does your review of the company's recent financial performance suggest that its business model and strategy are changing? Explain.

2. Go to www.levistrauss.com/about/vision and read what Levi Strauss & Company says about how its corporate values of originality, empathy, integrity, and courage are connected to its vision of clothing the world by marketing the most appealing and widely worn casual clothing in the world. Do you buy what the company says, or are its statements just a bunch of nice pontifications that represent the personal values of the CEO (and make for good public relations)? Explain.

CHAPTER 2

Analyzing a Company's External Environment

Analysis is the critical starting point of strategic thinking.
—Kenichi Ohmae, consultant and author

Things are always different—the art is figuring out which differences matter.
—Laszlo Birinyi, investments manager

Competitive battles should be seen not as one-shot skirmishes but as a dynamic multiround game of moves and countermoves.
—Anil K. Gupta, Professor

Managers

are not prepared to act wisely in steering a company in a different direction or altering its strategy until they have a deep understanding of the pertinent factors surrounding the company's situation. Probing, analysis-based answers to "Where are we now and what's the situation we face?" require thinking strategically about two facets of the company's situation. One is the industry and competitive environment in which the company operates and the forces acting to reshape this environment. The other is the company's own market position and competitiveness: its resources and capabilities, its strengths and weaknesses vis-à-vis rivals, and its windows of opportunity.

A perceptive diagnosis of a company's external and internal environment is a prerequisite for managers to succeed in crafting a strategy that is an especially good fit with the company's situation, is capable of building competitive advantage, and holds good prospect for boosting company performance—the three criteria of a winning strategy. The proper sequence for managers to observe in developing company strategy begins with a strategic appraisal of the company's external and internal situation (to form a strategic vision of where the company needs to head) and moves toward an evaluation of the most promising alternative strategies and business models, and finally to a choice of strategy (see Figure 2.1).

This chapter presents the concepts and analytical tools for assessing a single-business company's external environment. Attention centers on the competitive arena in which a company operates, together with whatever other pertinent technological, societal, regulatory, or demographic influences in the larger macroenvironment are acting to reshape the company's future market arena. In Chapter 3 we explore the methods of evaluating a company's internal circumstances and competitiveness.

Figure 2.1   From Thinking Strategically to Choosing a Strategy

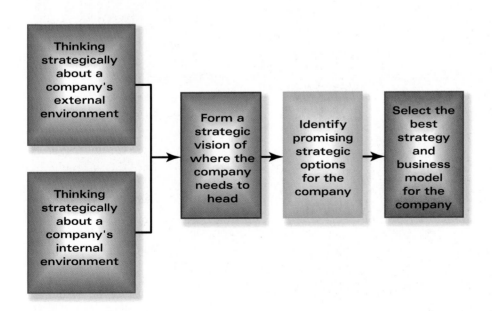

The Strategically Relevant Components of a Company's External Environment

All companies operate in a "macroenvironment" shaped by influences emanating from the economy at large; population demographics; societal values and lifestyles; governmental legislation and regulation; technological factors; and, closer to home, the industry and competitive arena in which the company operates (see Figure 2.2). Strictly speaking, a company's macroenvironment includes *all relevant factors and influences* outside the company's boundaries; by *relevant,* we mean important enough to have a bearing on the decisions the company ultimately makes about its direction, objectives,

Figure 2.2   The Components of a Company's Macroenvironment

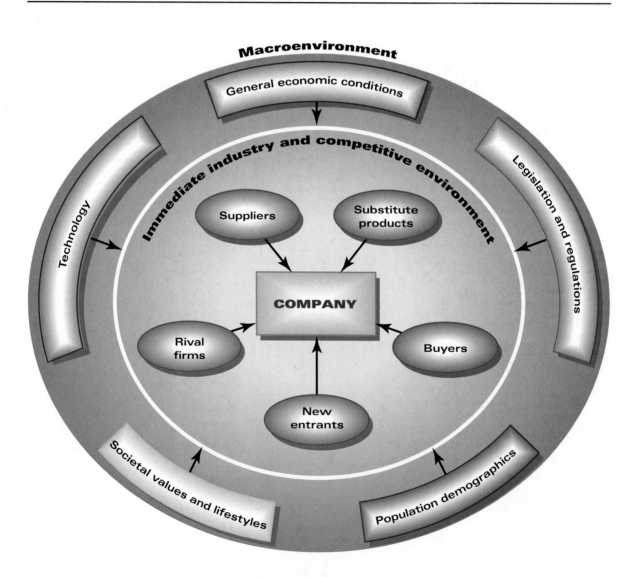

strategy, and business model. For the most part, influences coming from the outer ring of the macroenvironment have a low impact on a company's business situation and shape only the edges of the company's direction and strategy. (There are notable exceptions, though. The strategic opportunities of cigarette producers to grow their business are greatly reduced by antismoking ordinances and the growing cultural stigma attached to smoking; the market growth potential for health care and prescription drug companies is quite favorably affected by the demographics of an aging population and longer life expectancies; and companies in most all industries, seeking to capitalize on the benefits of Internet technology applications, are rushing to incorporate e-commerce elements into their strategies.) But while the strategy-shaping impact of outer-ring influences is normally low, there are enough strategically relevant trends and developments in the outer ring of the macroenvironment to justify a watchful eye. As company managers scan the external environment, they must be alert for potentially important outer-ring forces, assess their impact and influence, and adapt the company's direction and strategy as needed.

However, the factors and forces in a company's macroenvironment having the biggest strategy-shaping impact almost always pertain to the company's immediate industry and competitive environment. Consequently, it is on these factors that we concentrate our attention in this chapter.

Thinking Strategically about a Company's Industry and Competitive Environment

To gain a deep understanding of a company's industry and competitive environment, managers do not need to gather all the information they can find and spend lots of time digesting it. Rather, the task is much more focused. Thinking strategically about a company's industry and competitive environment entails using some well-defined concepts and analytical tools to get clear answers to seven questions:

1. What are the industry's strategy-shaping economic features?
2. What kinds of competitive forces are industry members facing, and how strong is each force?
3. What forces are driving changes in the industry, and what impact will these changes have on competitive intensity and industry profitability?
4. What market positions do industry rivals occupy—who is strongly positioned and who is not?
5. What strategic moves are rivals likely to make next?
6. What are the key factors for future competitive success?
7. Does the outlook for the industry present the company with sufficiently attractive prospects for profitability?

Analysis-based answers to these questions provide managers with a solid diagnosis of the industry and competitive environment. The remainder of this chapter is devoted to describing the methods of analyzing a company's industry and competitive environment.

Identifying Strategically Relevant Industry Features

Because industries differ so significantly in their basic character and structure, analyzing a company's industry and competitive environment begins with an overview of the industry's dominant economic features. The following economic features and corresponding questions need to be considered.

Economic Feature	Strategically Relevant Questions
▦ Market size and growth rate	▦ Is the industry big enough or growing fast enough to attract the attention of opportunity-seeking new entrants?
	▦ Is slowly growing buyer demand spurring increased rivalry and the acquisition or exit of weak competitors?
▦ Position in the life cycle	▦ What does the industry's position in the growth cycle (early development, rapid growth and takeoff, early maturity, maturity, saturation and stagnation, decline) indicate about the industry's growth prospects?
▦ Number of rivals	▦ Is the industry fragmented into many small companies or concentrated and dominated by a few large companies?
	▦ Is the industry going through a period of consolidation to a smaller number of competitors?
▦ Buyer needs and requirements	▦ Are buyer needs or requirements changing and, if so, what is driving the changes?
	▦ What are buyers looking for? What attributes prompt buyers to choose one brand over another?
▦ Production capacity	▦ Is a surplus of capacity pushing prices and profit margins down?
	▦ Is the industry overcrowded?
▦ Pace of technological change	▦ What role does advancing technology play in this industry?
	▦ Are ongoing upgrades of facilities/equipment essential because of rapidly advancing production process technologies?
	▦ Do most industry members have or need strong technological capabilities? Why?
▦ Vertical integration	▦ Are there important cost differences among fully integrated versus partially integrated versus nonintegrated firms?
	▦ Do fully or partially integrated firms have any competitive advantage over nonintegrated firms?

▦ Product innovation	▦ Are there opportunities to overtake key rivals by being first to market with next-generation products?
	▦ Is the industry characterized by rapid product innovation and short product life cycles?
	▦ How important is R&D and product innovation?
▦ Degree of product differentiation	▦ Are the products of rivals becoming more differentiated or less differentiated?
	▦ Are increasingly look-alike products of rivals causing heightened price competition?
▦ Scope of competitive rivalry	▦ Is the geographic area over which most companies compete local, regional, national, multinational, or global?
	▦ Is having a presence in foreign-country markets becoming more important to a company's long-term competitive success?
▦ Economies of scale	▦ Is the industry characterized by economies of scale in purchasing, manufacturing, advertising, shipping, or other activities?
	▦ Do companies with large-scale operations have an important cost advantage over small-scale firms?
▦ Experience and learning-curve effects	▦ Are certain industry activities characterized by strong learning-curve and experience ("learning by doing") effects such that unit costs decline as a company's experience in performing the activity builds?[1]
	▦ Do any companies have significant cost advantages because of their learning/experience in performing particular activities?

Identifying an industry's economic features not only sets the stage for the analysis to come but also promotes understanding of the kinds of strategic moves that industry members are likely to employ. For example, in an industry characterized by important scale economies and/or learning-experience curve effects, industry members are strongly motivated to go after increased sales volumes and capture the cost-saving economies of larger-scale operations; small-scale firms are under considerable pressure to grow sales in order to become more cost-competitive with large-volume rivals. In industries characterized by one product advance after another, companies must invest in R&D and develop strong product innovation capabilities; a strategy of continuous product innovation becomes a condition of survival. An industry that has recently passed through the rapid-growth stage and is looking at single-digit percentage increases in buyer demand is likely to be experiencing a competitive shake-out and much stronger strategic emphasis on cost reduction and improved customer service.

Analyzing the Nature and Strength of Competitive Forces

The character, mix, and subtleties of the competitive forces operating in a company's industry are never the same from one industry to another. Far and away the most powerful and widely used tool for systematically diagnosing the principal competitive pressures in a market and assessing the strength and importance of each is the *five-forces model of competition.*[2] This model, depicted in Figure 2.3, holds that the state of competition in an industry is a composite of competitive pressures operating in five areas of the overall market:

1. Competitive pressures associated with the market maneuvering and jockeying for buyer patronage that goes on among *rival sellers* in the industry.

2. Competitive pressures associated with the threat of *new entrants* into the market.

3. Competitive pressures coming from the attempts of companies in other industries to win buyers over to their own *substitute products.*

4. Competitive pressures stemming from *supplier* bargaining power and supplier–seller collaboration.

5. Competitive pressures stemming from *buyer* bargaining power and seller–buyer collaboration.

The way one uses the five-forces model to determine what competition is like in a given industry is to build the picture of competition in three steps or stages. Step 1 is to identify the specific competitive pressures associated with each of the five forces. Step 2 is to evaluate how strong the pressures comprising each of the five forces are (fierce, strong, moderate to normal, or weak). Step 3 is to consider the overall pattern of competition and the collective impact of all five forces. The analytical process is straightforward and logical.

The Rivalry among Competing Sellers

The strongest of the five competitive forces is nearly always the market maneuvering and jockeying for buyer patronage that goes on among rival sellers of a product or service. In effect, *a market is a competitive battlefield* where it is customary for rival sellers to employ whatever weapons they have in their competitive arsenal to improve their market positions and business performance. Managers have a duty to craft a competitive strategy that, at the very least, allows their company to hold its own against rivals and that, ideally, strengthens the company's standing with buyers, delivers good profitability, and *produces a competitive edge over rivals.* But when one firm makes a strategic move that produces good results, its rivals often react and respond with offensive or defensive countermoves. This pattern of action and reaction, move and countermove, is what makes competitive rivalry a combative contest. Market battles for buyer patronage are dynamic, with the competitive landscape continually changing as industry rivals initiate new rounds of market maneuvers (with some gaining and some losing momentum in the marketplace) and as their emphasis swings from one combination of product attributes, marketing tactics, and competitive capabilities to another.

> **Core Concept**
>
> Competitive jockeying among industry rivals is ever-changing, as fresh offensive and defensive moves are initiated and rivals emphasize first one mix of competitive weapons and tactics, then another.

Figure 2.3   **The Five-Forces Model of Competition:** A Key Analytical Tool

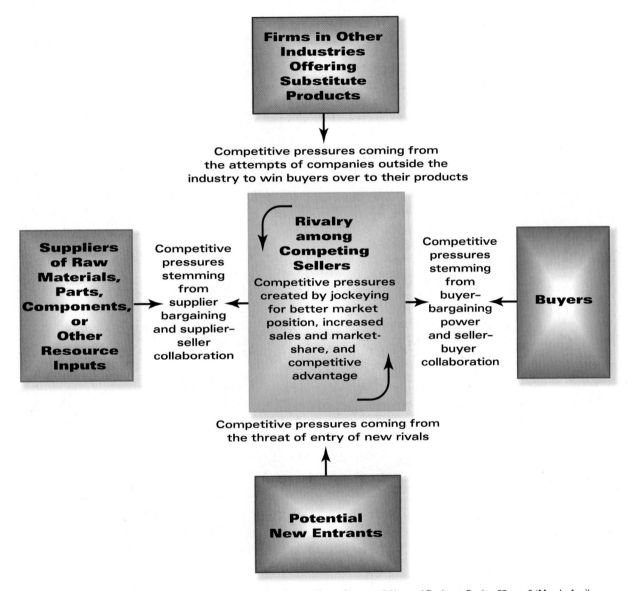

Source: Adapted from Michael E. Porter, "How Competitive Forces Shape Strategy," *Harvard Business Review* 57, no. 2 (March–April 1979), pp. 137–45.

Figure 2.4 shows a sampling of competitive weapons that firms can deploy in battling rivals and indicates the factors that influence the intensity of their rivalry. A brief discussion of some of the factors that influence the tempo of rivalry among industry competitors is in order:[3]

■ *Rivalry among competing sellers intensifies the more frequently and more aggressively that industry members undertake fresh actions to boost their market standing and performance—perhaps at the expense of rivals.* Rivalry tends to be fairly

Figure 2.4   Weapons for Competing and Factors Affecting the Strength of Rivalry

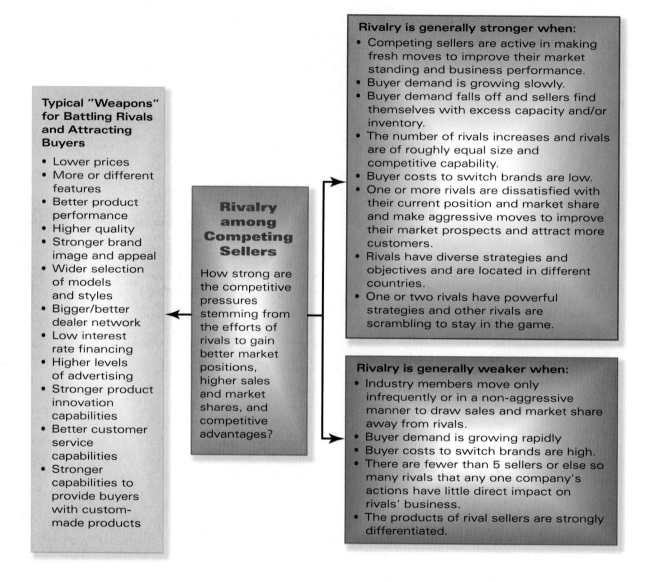

Typical "Weapons" for Battling Rivals and Attracting Buyers

- Lower prices
- More or different features
- Better product performance
- Higher quality
- Stronger brand image and appeal
- Wider selection of models and styles
- Bigger/better dealer network
- Low interest rate financing
- Higher levels of advertising
- Stronger product innovation capabilities
- Better customer service capabilities
- Stronger capabilities to provide buyers with custom-made products

Rivalry among Competing Sellers

How strong are the competitive pressures stemming from the efforts of rivals to gain better market positions, higher sales and market shares, and competitive advantages?

Rivalry is generally stronger when:

- Competing sellers are active in making fresh moves to improve their market standing and business performance.
- Buyer demand is growing slowly.
- Buyer demand falls off and sellers find themselves with excess capacity and/or inventory.
- The number of rivals increases and rivals are of roughly equal size and competitive capability.
- Buyer costs to switch brands are low.
- One or more rivals are dissatisfied with their current position and market share and make aggressive moves to improve their market prospects and attract more customers.
- Rivals have diverse strategies and objectives and are located in different countries.
- One or two rivals have powerful strategies and other rivals are scrambling to stay in the game.

Rivalry is generally weaker when:

- Industry members move only infrequently or in a non-aggressive manner to draw sales and market share away from rivals.
- Buyer demand is growing rapidly
- Buyer costs to switch brands are high.
- There are fewer than 5 sellers or else so many rivals that any one company's actions have little direct impact on rivals' business.
- The products of rival sellers are strongly differentiated.

intense whenever sellers actively engage in vigorous price competition—lively price competition pressures rival companies to aggressively pursue ways to drive costs out of the business; high-cost companies are hard-pressed to survive. Other indicators of the intensity of rivalry among industry members include:

- Whether industry members are racing to offer better performance features or higher quality or improved customer service or a wider product selection.
- How frequently rivals resort to such marketing tactics as special sales promotions, heavy advertising, rebates, or low-interest-rate financing to drum up additional sales.

- How actively industry members are pursuing efforts to build stronger dealer networks or establish positions in foreign markets or otherwise expand their distribution capabilities and market presence.

- The frequency with which rivals introduce new and improved products (and thus are competing on the basis of their product innovation capabilities).

- How hard companies are striving to gain a market edge over rivals by developing valuable expertise and capabilities.

Normally, industry members are proactive in drawing on their arsenal of competitive weapons and deploying their organizational resources in a manner calculated to strengthen their market positions and performance.

- *Rivalry intensifies as the number of competitors increases and as competitors become more equal in size and capability.* Competition is not as strong in PC operating systems, where Linux is one of the few challengers to Microsoft, as it is in fast-food restaurants, where buyers have many choices. Up to a point, the greater the number of competitors, the greater the probability of fresh, creative strategic initiatives. In addition, when rivals are nearly equal in size and capability, they can usually compete on a fairly even footing, making it harder for one or two firms to win the competitive battle and dominate the market.

- *Rivalry is usually weaker when there are fewer than five competitors or else so many rivals that the impact of any one company's actions is spread thinly across all industry members.* When an industry contains only a few rival sellers, each company tends to recognize that its actions can have immediate and significant impact on the others and, if aggressive, may provoke direct retaliation. Although occasional warfare can break out, competition among the few tends to produce a live-and-let-live approach to competing and thus a restrained use of competitive weaponry. Rivalry also tends to be weak when an industry is fragmented with so many competitors that successful moves by one have little discernible adverse impact on the others and thus may provoke no immediate response or countermove on the part of its rivals.

- *Rivalry is usually stronger in slow-growing markets and weaker in fast-growing markets.* Rapidly expanding buyer demand produces enough new business for all industry members to grow. Indeed, in a fast-growing market, a company may find itself stretched just to keep abreast of incoming orders, let alone devote resources to stealing customers away from rivals. But in markets where growth is sluggish or where buyer demand drops off unexpectedly, expansion-minded firms and/or firms with excess capacity often are quick to cut prices and initiate other sales-increasing tactics, thereby igniting a battle for market share that can result in a shake-out of weak, inefficient firms.

- *Rivalry increases as the products of rival sellers become more standardized and/or when buyer costs to switch from one brand to another are low.* When the offerings of rivals are identified it is usually easy and inexpensive for buyers to switch their purchases from one seller to another. Strongly differentiated products raise the probability that buyers will find it costly to switch brands.

- *Rivalry is more intense when industry conditions tempt competitors to use price cuts or other competitive weapons to boost unit volume.* When a product is perishable, seasonal, or costly to hold in inventory, or when demand slacks off, competitive pressures build quickly anytime one or more firms decide to cut prices and dump excess supplies on the market. Likewise, whenever fixed costs account for a large fraction of total cost so that unit costs tend to be lowest at or near full capacity, then firms come under significant pressure to cut prices or otherwise try to boost sales. Unused capacity imposes a significant cost-increasing penalty because there are fewer units over which to spread fixed costs. The pressure of high fixed costs can push rival firms into price concessions, special discounts, rebates, low-interest-rate financing, and other volume-boosting tactics.

■ *Rivalry increases when one or more competitors become dissatisfied with their market position and launch moves to bolster their standing at the expense of rivals.* Firms that are losing ground or in financial trouble often react aggressively by acquiring smaller rivals, introducing new products, boosting advertising, discounting prices, and so on. Such actions heighten rivalry and can trigger a hotly contested battle for market share. The market maneuvering among rivals usually heats up when a competitor makes new offensive moves—because it sees an opportunity to better please customers or is under pressure to improve its market share or profitability.

■ *Rivalry increases in proportion to the size of the payoff from a successful strategic move.* The greater the benefits of going after a new opportunity, the more likely it is that one or more rivals will initiate moves to capture it. Competitive pressures nearly always intensify when several rivals start pursuing the same opportunity. For example, competition in online music sales heated up with the entries of Amazon.com, Barnesandnoble.com, and Buy.com. Furthermore, the size of the strategic payoff can vary with the speed of retaliation. When competitors respond slowly (or not at all), the initiator of a fresh competitive strategy can reap benefits in the intervening period and perhaps gain a first-mover advantage that is not easily surmounted. The greater the benefits of moving first, the more likely some competitor will accept the risk and try it.

■ *Rivalry becomes more volatile and unpredictable as the diversity of competitors increases in terms of visions, strategic intents, objectives, strategies, resources, and countries of origin.* A diverse group of sellers often contains one or more mavericks willing to try novel or high-risk or rule-breaking market approaches, thus generating a livelier and less predictable competitive environment. Globally competitive markets often contain rivals with different views about where the industry is headed and a willingness to employ perhaps radically different competitive approaches. Attempts by cross-border rivals to gain stronger footholds in each other's domestic markets usually boost the intensity of rivalry, especially when the aggressors have lower costs or products with more attractive features.

■ *Rivalry increases when strong companies outside the industry acquire weak firms in the industry and launch aggressive, well-funded moves to transform their newly acquired competitors into major market contenders.* A concerted effort to turn a weak rival into a market leader nearly always entails launching well-financed strategic initiatives to dramatically improve the competitor's product offering, excite buyer interest, and win a much bigger market share—actions that, if successful, put added pressure on rivals to counter with fresh strategic moves of their own.

■ *A powerful, successful competitive strategy employed by one company greatly intensifies the competitive pressures on its rivals to develop effective strategic responses or be relegated to also-ran status.*

Rivalry can be characterized as *cutthroat* or *brutal* when competitors engage in protracted price wars or habitually employ other aggressive tactics that are mutually destructive to profitability. Rivalry can be considered *fierce* to *strong* when the battle for market share is so vigorous that the profit margins of most industry members are squeezed to bare-bones levels. Rivalry can be characterized as *moderate* or *normal* when the maneuvering among industry members, while lively and healthy, still allows most industry members to earn acceptable profits. Rivalry is *weak* when most companies in the industry are relatively well satisfied with their sales growth and market shares, rarely undertake offensives to steal customers away from one another, and have comparatively attractive earnings and returns on investment.

The Potential Entry of New Competitors

Several factors affect the strength of the competitive threat of potential entry in a particular industry (see Figure 2.5). One factor relates to the size of the pool of likely entry candidates and the resources at their command. As a rule, competitive pressures intensify the bigger the pool of entry candidates. This is especially true when some of the likely entry candidates have ample resources and the potential to become formidable contenders for market leadership. Frequently, the strongest competitive pressures associated with potential entry come not from outsiders but from current industry participants looking for growth opportunities. *Existing industry members are often strong candidates to enter market segments or geographic areas where they currently do not have a market presence.* Companies already well established in certain product categories or geographic areas often possess the resources, competencies, and competitive capabilities to hurdle the barriers of entering a different market segment or new geographic area.

A second factor concerns whether the likely entry candidates face high or low entry barriers. The most widely encountered barriers that entry candidates must hurdle include:[4]

- *The presence of sizable economies of scale in production or other areas of operation*—When incumbent companies enjoy cost advantages associated with large-scale operation, outsiders must either enter on a large scale (a costly and perhaps risky move) or accept a cost disadvantage and consequently lower profitability. Trying to overcome the disadvantages of small size by entering on a large scale at the outset can result in long-term overcapacity problems for the new entrant (until sales volume builds up), and it can so threaten the market shares of existing firms that they launch strong defensive maneuvers (price cuts, increased advertising and sales promotion, and similar blocking actions) to maintain their positions and make things hard on a newcomer.

- *Cost and resource disadvantages not related to size*—Existing firms may have low unit costs as a result of experience or learning-curve effects, key patents, partnerships with the best and cheapest suppliers of raw materials and components, proprietary technology know-how not readily available to newcomers, favorable locations, and low fixed costs (because they have older plants that have been mostly depreciated).

- *Brand preferences and customer loyalty*—In some industries, buyers are strongly attached to established brands. Japanese consumers, for example, are fiercely loyal to Japanese brands of motor vehicles, electronics products, cameras, and film. European consumers have traditionally been loyal to European brands of major household appliances. High brand loyalty means that a potential entrant must commit to spending enough money on advertising and sales promotion to overcome customer loyalties and build its own clientele. Establishing brand recognition and building customer loyalty can be a slow and costly process. In addition, if it is difficult or costly for a customer to switch to a new brand, a new entrant must persuade buyers that its brand is worth the switching costs. To overcome switching-cost barriers, new entrants may have to offer buyers a discounted price or an extra margin of quality or service. All this can mean lower expected profit margins for new entrants, which increases the risk to start-up companies dependent on sizable early profits to support their new investments.

- *Capital requirements*—The larger the total dollar investment needed to enter the market successfully, the more limited the pool of potential entrants. The most obvious capital requirements for new entrants are those associated with investing in the necessary manufacturing facilities and equipment, being able to finance the introductory advertising and sales promotion campaigns to build brand awareness and establish a clientele, securing the working capital to finance inventories and customer credit, and having sufficient cash reserves to cover start-up losses.

- *Access to distribution channels*—In consumer goods industries, a potential entrant may face the barrier of gaining adequate access to consumers. Wholesale distributors may be reluctant to take on a product that lacks buyer recognition. A network of retail dealers may have to be set up from scratch. Retailers have to be convinced to give a new brand ample display space and an adequate trial period. Entry is tough when existing producers have strong, well-functioning distributor–dealer networks and a newcomer must struggle to squeeze its way into existing distribution channels. To overcome the barrier of gaining adequate access to consumers, potential entrants may have to "buy" their way into wholesale or retail channels by cutting their prices to provide dealers and distributors with higher markups and profit margins or by giving them big advertising and promotional allowances. As a consequence, a potential entrant's own profits may be squeezed unless and until its product gains enough consumer acceptance that distributors and retailers want to carry it.

- *Regulatory policies*—Government agencies can limit or even bar entry by requiring licenses and permits. Regulated industries like cable TV, telecommunications, electric and gas utilities, radio and television broadcasting, liquor retailing, and railroads entail government-controlled entry. In international markets, host governments commonly limit foreign entry and must approve all foreign investment applications. Stringent government-mandated safety regulations and environmental pollution standards are entry barriers because they raise entry costs.

- *Tariffs and international trade restrictions*—National governments commonly use tariffs and trade restrictions (antidumping rules, local content requirements, quotas, etc.) to raise entry barriers for foreign firms and protect domestic producers from outside competition.

Whether an industry's entry barriers ought to be considered high or low and how hard it is for new entrants to compete on a level playing field depend on the resources and competencies possessed by the pool of potential entrants. Entry barriers can be formidable for newly formed enterprises that have to find some way to gain a market foothold and then over time make inroads against well-established companies. But opportunity-seeking companies in other industries, if they have suitable resources, competencies, and brand-name recognition, may be able to hurdle an industry's entry barriers rather easily. In evaluating the potential threat of entry, company managers must look at (1) how formidable the entry barriers are for each type of potential entrant—start-up enterprises, specific candidate companies in other industries, and current industry participants looking to expand their market reach—and (2) how attractive the growth and profit prospects are for new entrants. *Rapidly growing market demand and high potential profits act as magnets, motivating potential entrants to commit the resources needed to hurdle entry barriers.*[5]

Figure 2.5   **Factors Affecting the Threat of Entry**

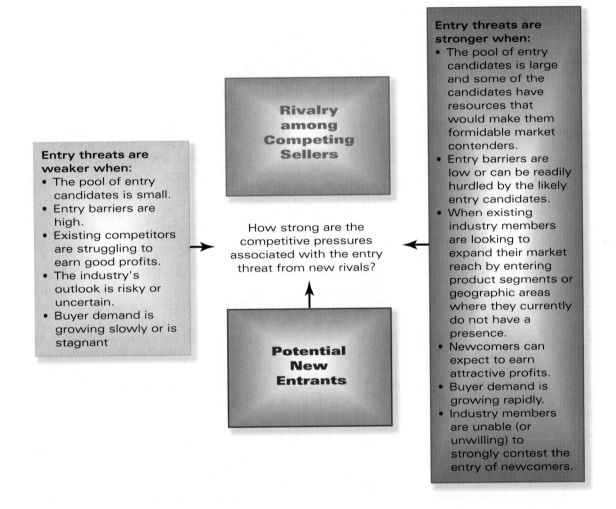

However, even if a potential entrant has or can acquire the needed competencies and resources to attempt entry, it still faces the issue of how existing firms will react.[6] Will incumbent firms offer only passive resistance, or will they aggressively defend their market positions using price cuts, increased advertising, product improvements, and whatever else they can think of to give a new entrant (as well as other rivals) a hard time? A potential entrant can have second thoughts when financially strong incumbent firms send clear signals that they will stoutly defend their market positions against newcomers. A potential entrant may also turn away when incumbent firms can leverage distributors and customers to retain their business.

> The threat of entry is stronger when entry barriers are low, when there's a sizable pool of entry candidates, when industry growth is rapid and profit potentials are high, and when incumbent firms are unable or unwilling to vigorously contest a newcomer's entry.

The best test of whether potential entry is a strong or weak competitive force in the marketplace is to ask if the industry's growth and profit prospects are strongly attractive to potential entry candidates. When the answer is no, potential entry is a weak competitive force. When the answer is yes and there are entry candidates with sufficient expertise and resources, then potential entry adds significantly to competitive pressures in the marketplace. The stronger the threat of entry, the more that incumbent firms are driven to seek ways to fortify their positions against newcomers, pursuing strategic moves not only to protect their market shares but also to make entry more costly or difficult.

One additional point: *The threat of entry changes as the industry's prospects grow brighter or dimmer and as entry barriers rise or fall.* For example, in the pharmaceutical industry the expiration of a key patent on a widely prescribed drug virtually guarantees that one or more drug makers will enter with generic offerings of their own. Use of the Internet for shopping is making it much easier for e-tailers to enter into competition against some of the best-known retail chains. In international markets, entry barriers for foreign-based firms fall as tariffs are lowered, as host governments open up their domestic markets to outsiders, as domestic wholesalers and dealers seek out lower-cost foreign-made goods, and as domestic buyers become more willing to purchase foreign brands.

Competitive Pressures from the Sellers of Substitute Products

Companies in one industry come under competitive pressure from the actions of companies in a closely adjoining industry whenever buyers view the products of the two industries as good substitutes. For instance, the producers of sugar experience competitive pressures from the sales and marketing efforts of the makers of artificial sweeteners. Similarly, the producers of eyeglasses and contact lenses are currently facing mounting competitive pressures from growing consumer interest in corrective laser surgery. Newspapers are feeling the competitive force of the general public turning to cable news channels for late-breaking news and using Internet sources to get information about sports results, stock quotes, and job opportunities.

Just how strong the competitive pressures are from the sellers of substitute products depends on three factors: (1) whether substitutes are readily available and attractively priced; (2) whether buyers view the substitutes as being comparable or better in terms of quality, performance, and other relevant attributes; and (3) how much it costs end users to switch to substitutes. Figure 2.6 lists factors affecting the strength of competitive pressures from substitute products and signs that indicate substitutes are a strong competitive force.

The presence of readily available and attractively priced substitutes creates competitive pressure by placing a ceiling on the prices industry members can charge without giving customers an incentive to switch to substitutes and risking sales erosion.[7] This price ceiling, at the same time, puts a lid on the profits that industry members can earn unless they find ways to cut costs. When substitutes are cheaper than an industry's product, industry members come under heavy competitive pressure to reduce their prices and find ways to absorb the price cuts with cost reductions.

The availability of substitutes inevitably invites customers to compare performance, features, ease of use, and other attributes as well as price. For example, ski boat manufacturers are experiencing strong competition from personal water-ski craft because water sports enthusiasts are finding that personal water skis are fun to ride and less expensive. The users of paper cartons constantly weigh the performance trade-offs with plastic containers and metal cans. Competition from good-performing substitute products pushes industry participants to incorporate new performance features and

Figure 2.6   Factors Affecting Competition from Substitute Products

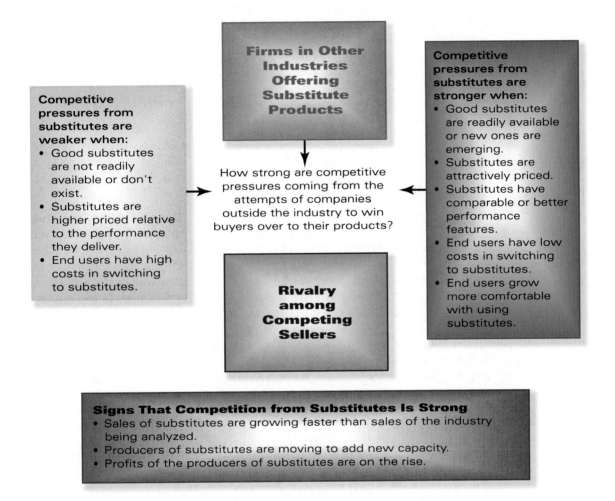

Firms in Other Industries Offering Substitute Products

How strong are competitive pressures coming from the attempts of companies outside the industry to win buyers over to their products?

Rivalry among Competing Sellers

Competitive pressures from substitutes are weaker when:
- Good substitutes are not readily available or don't exist.
- Substitutes are higher priced relative to the performance they deliver.
- End users have high costs in switching to substitutes.

Competitive pressures from substitutes are stronger when:
- Good substitutes are readily available or new ones are emerging.
- Substitutes are attractively priced.
- Substitutes have comparable or better performance features.
- End users have low costs in switching to substitutes.
- End users grow more comfortable with using substitutes.

Signs That Competition from Substitutes Is Strong
- Sales of substitutes are growing faster than sales of the industry being analyzed.
- Producers of substitutes are moving to add new capacity.
- Profits of the producers of substitutes are on the rise.

heighten efforts to convince customers their product has attributes that are superior to those of substitutes.

The strength of competition from substitutes is significantly influenced by how difficult or costly it is for the industry's customers to switch to a substitute.[8] Typical switching costs include the time and inconvenience that may be involved, the costs of additional equipment, the time and cost in testing the quality and reliability of the substitute, the psychological costs of severing old supplier relationships and establishing new ones, payments for technical help in making the changeover, and employee retraining costs. When buyers incur high costs in switching to substitutes, the competitive pressures that industry members experience from substitutes are usually lessened unless the sellers of substitutes begin offering price discounts or major performance benefits that entice the industry's customers away. When switching costs are low, it's much easier for sellers of substitutes to convince buyers to change to their products.

As a rule, then, the lower the price of substitutes, the higher their quality and performance, and the lower the user's switching costs, the more intense the competitive pressures posed by substitute products. Good indicators of the competitive strength of substitute products are the rate at which their sales and profits are growing, the market inroads they are making, and their plans for expanding production capacity.

Competitive Pressures Stemming from Supplier Bargaining Power and Supplier–Seller Collaboration

Whether supplier–seller relationships represent a weak or strong competitive force depends on (1) whether the major suppliers can exercise sufficient bargaining power to influence the terms and conditions of supply in their favor, and (2) the nature and extent of supplier–seller collaboration in the industry.

How Supplier Bargaining Power Can Create Competitive Pressures　Whenever the major suppliers to an industry have considerable leverage in determining the terms and conditions of the item they are supplying, then they are in a position to exert competitive pressure on one or more rival sellers. For instance, Microsoft and Intel, both of whom supply PC makers with products that most PC users consider essential, are known for using their dominant market status not only to charge PC makers premium prices but also to leverage PC makers in other ways. Microsoft pressures PC makers to load only Microsoft products on the PCs they ship and to position the icons for Microsoft software prominently on the screens of new computers that come with factory-loaded software. Intel pushes greater use of Intel microprocessors in PCs by granting PC makers sizable advertising allowances on PC models equipped with "Intel Inside" stickers; it also tends to give PC makers who use the biggest percentages of Intel chips in their PC models top priority in filling orders for newly introduced Intel chips. Being on Intel's list of preferred customers helps a PC maker get an allocation of the first production runs of Intel's latest and greatest chips and thus get new PC models equipped with these chips to market ahead of rivals who are heavier users of chips made by Intel's rivals. The ability of Microsoft and Intel to pressure PC makers for preferential treatment of one kind or another in turn affects competition among rival PC makers.

Several other instances of supplier bargaining power are worth citing. Small-scale retailers must often contend with the power of manufacturers whose products enjoy prestigious and well-respected brand names; when a manufacturer knows that a retailer needs to stock the manufacturer's product because consumers expect to find the product on the shelves of retail stores where they shop, the manufacturer usually has some degree of pricing power and can also push hard for favorable shelf displays. Motor vehicle manufacturers typically exert considerable power over the terms and conditions with which they supply new vehicles to their independent automobile dealerships. The operators of franchised units of such chains as Krispy Kreme Doughnuts, Burger King, Pizza Hut, and Hampton Inns must frequently agree not only to source some of their supplies from the franchisor at prices and terms favorable to that franchisor but also to operate their facilities in a manner largely dictated by the franchisor. Strong supplier bargaining power is a competitive factor in industries where unions have been able to organize the workforces of some industry members but not others; those industry members that must negotiate wages, fringe benefits, and working conditions with powerful unions (which control the supply of labor) often find themselves with higher labor costs than their competitors with nonunion labor forces. The bigger the gap between union and nonunion labor costs in an industry, the more that unionized industry members must scramble to find ways to relieve the competitive pressure associated with their disadvantage on labor costs.

The factors that determine whether any of the suppliers to an industry are in a position to exert substantial bargaining power or leverage are fairly clear-cut:[9]

- *Whether the item being supplied is a commodity that is readily available from many suppliers at the going market price.* Suppliers have little or no bargaining power or leverage whenever industry members have the ability to source their requirements at competitive prices from any of several alternative and eager suppliers, perhaps dividing their purchases among two or more suppliers to promote lively competition for orders. The suppliers of commoditylike items have market power only when supplies become quite tight and industry members are so eager to secure what they need that they agree to terms more favorable to suppliers.

- *Whether a few large suppliers are the primary sources of a particular item.* The leading suppliers may well have pricing leverage unless they are plagued with excess capacity and are scrambling to secure additional orders for their products. Major suppliers with good reputations and strong demand for the items they supply are harder to wring concessions from than struggling suppliers striving to broaden their customer base or more fully utilize their production capacity.

- *Whether it is difficult or costly for industry members to switch their purchases from one supplier to another or to switch to attractive substitute inputs.* High switching costs signal strong bargaining power on the part of suppliers, whereas low switching costs and ready availability of good substitute inputs signal weak bargaining power. Soft-drink bottlers, for example, can counter the bargaining power of aluminum can suppliers by shifting or threatening to shift to greater use of plastic containers and introducing more attractive plastic container designs.

- *Whether certain needed inputs are in short supply.* Suppliers of items in short supply have some degree of pricing power, whereas a surge in the availability of particular items greatly weakens supplier pricing power and bargaining leverage.

- *Whether certain suppliers provide a differentiated input that enhances the performance or quality of the industry's product.* The more valuable that a particular input is in terms of enhancing the performance or quality of the products of industry members or of improving the efficiency of their production processes, the more bargaining leverage its suppliers are likely to possess.

- *Whether certain suppliers provide equipment or services that deliver valuable cost-saving efficiencies to industry members in operating their production processes.* Suppliers who provide cost-saving equipment or other valuable or necessary production-related services are likely to possess bargaining leverage. Industry members that do not source from such suppliers may find themselves at a cost disadvantage and thus under competitive pressure to do so (on terms that are favorable to the suppliers).

- *Whether suppliers provide an item that accounts for a sizable fraction of the costs of the industry's product.* The bigger the cost of a particular part or component, the more opportunity for the pattern of competition in the marketplace to be affected by the actions of suppliers to raise or lower their prices.

- *Whether industry members are major customers of suppliers.* As a rule, suppliers have less bargaining leverage when their sales to members of this one industry constitute a big percentage of their total sales. In such cases, the well-being of suppliers is closely tied to the well-being of their major customers. Suppliers then have a big incentive to protect and enhance their customers' competitiveness via reasonable prices, exceptional quality, and ongoing advances in the technology of the items supplied.

■ *Whether it makes good economic sense for industry members to integrate backward and self-manufacture items they have been buying from suppliers.* The make-or-buy issue generally boils down to whether suppliers who specialize in the production of a particular part or component and make them in volume for many different customers have the expertise and scale economies to supply as good or better component at a lower cost than industry members could achieve via self-manufacture. Frequently, it is difficult for industry members to self-manufacture parts and components more economically than they can obtain them from suppliers who specialize in making such items. For instance, most producers of outdoor power equipment (lawn mowers, rotary tillers, leaf blowers, etc.) find it cheaper to source the small engines they need from outside manufacturers who specialize in small engine manufacture rather than make their own engines because the quantity of engines they need is too small to justify the investment in manufacturing facilities, master the production process, and capture scale economies. Specialists in small-engine manufacture, by supplying many kinds of engines to the whole power equipment industry, can obtain a big enough sales volume to fully realize scale economies, become proficient in all the manufacturing techniques, and keep costs low. As a rule, suppliers are safe from the threat of self-manufacture by their customers *until* the volume of parts a customer needs becomes large enough for the customer to justify backward integration into self-manufacture of the component. Suppliers also gain bargaining power when they have the resources and profit incentive to integrate forward into the business of the customers they are supplying and thus become a strong rival.

Figure 2.7 summarizes the conditions that tend to make supplier bargaining power strong or weak.

How Seller–Supplier Partnerships Can Create Competitive Pressures   In more and more industries, sellers are forging strategic partnerships with select suppliers in efforts to (1) reduce inventory and logistics costs (e.g., through just-in-time deliveries), (2) speed the availability of next-generation components, (3) enhance the quality of the parts and components being supplied and reduce defect rates, and (4) squeeze out important cost savings for both themselves and their suppliers. Numerous Internet technology applications are now available that permit real-time data sharing, eliminate paperwork, and produce cost savings all along the supply chain. The many benefits of effective seller–supplier collaboration can translate into competitive advantage for industry members who do the best job of managing supply chain relationships.

Dell Computer has used strategic partnering with key suppliers as a major element in its strategy to be the world's lowest-cost supplier of branded PCs, servers, and workstations. Because Dell has managed its supply chain relationships in ways that contribute to a low-cost, high-quality competitive edge in components supply, it has put enormous pressure on its PC rivals to try to imitate its supply chain management

Figure 2.7   Factors Affecting the Bargaining Power of Suppliers

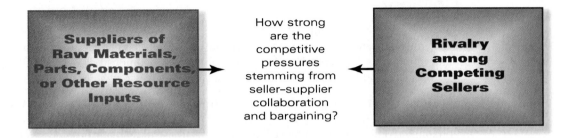

Supplier bargaining power is stronger when:
- Industry members incurs high costs in switching their purchases to alternative suppliers.
- Needed inputs are in short supply (which gives suppliers more leverage in setting prices).
- A supplier has a differentiated input that enhances the quality or performance of sellers' products or is a valuable or critical part of sellers' production process.
- There are only a few suppliers of a particular input.
- Some suppliers threaten to integrate forward into the business of industry members and perhaps become a powerful rival.

Supplier bargaining power is weaker when:
- The item being supplied is a commodity that is readily available from many suppliers at the going market price.
- Seller switching costs to alternative suppliers are low.
- Good substitute inputs exist or new ones emerge.
- There is a surge in the availability of supplies (thus greatly weakening supplier pricing power).
- Industry members account for a big fraction of suppliers' total sales and continued high volume purchases are important to the well-being of suppliers.
- Industry members are a threat to integrate backward into the business of suppliers and to self-manufacture their own requirements.
- Seller collaboration or partnering with selected suppliers provides attractive win–win opportunities.

practices. Effective partnerships with suppliers on the part of one or more industry members can thus become a major source of competitive pressure for rival firms.

The more opportunities that exist for win–win efforts between a company and its suppliers, the less their relationship is characterized by who has the upper hand in bargaining with the other. So long as the relationship is producing valuable benefits for both parties, it will last; only if a supply partner is falling behind alternative suppliers is a company likely to switch suppliers and incur the costs and trouble of building close working ties with a different supplier.

Competitive Pressures Stemming from Buyer Bargaining Power and Seller–Buyer Collaboration

Whether seller–buyer relationships represent a weak or strong competitive force depends on (1) whether some or many buyers have sufficient bargaining leverage to obtain price concessions and other favorable terms and conditions of sale, and (2) the extent and competitive importance of seller–buyer strategic partnerships in the industry.

How Buyer Bargaining Power Can Create Competitive Pressures   As with suppliers, the leverage that certain types of buyers have in negotiating favorable terms can range from weak to strong. Individual consumers, for example, rarely have much bargaining power in negotiating price concessions or other favorable terms with sellers; the primary exceptions involve situations in which price haggling is customary, such as the purchase of new and used motor vehicles, homes, and certain big-ticket items like luxury watches, jewelry, and pleasure boats. For most consumer goods and services, individual buyers have no bargaining leverage—their option is to pay the seller's posted price or take their business elsewhere.

In contrast, large retail chains like Wal-Mart, Circuit City, Target, and Home Depot typically have considerable negotiating leverage in purchasing products from manufacturers because of manufacturers' need for broad retail exposure and the most appealing shelf locations. Retailers may stock two or three competing brands of a product but rarely all competing brands, so competition among rival manufacturers for visibility on the shelves of popular multistore retailers gives such retailers significant bargaining strength. Major supermarket chains like Kroger, Safeway, and Royal Ahold, which provide access to millions of grocery shoppers, have sufficient bargaining power to demand promotional allowances and lump-sum payments (called slotting fees) from food products manufacturers in return for stocking certain brands or putting them in the best shelf locations. Motor vehicle manufacturers have strong bargaining power in negotiating to buy original equipment tires from Goodyear, Michelin, Bridgestone/Firestone, Continental, and Pirelli not only because they buy in large quantities but also because tire makers believe they gain an advantage in supplying replacement tires to vehicle owners if their tire brand is original equipment on the vehicle. "Prestige" buyers have a degree of clout in negotiating with sellers because a seller's reputation is enhanced by having prestige buyers on its customer list.

Even if buyers do not purchase in large quantities or offer a seller important market exposure or prestige, they gain a degree of bargaining leverage in the following circumstances:[10]

▪ *If buyers' costs of switching to competing brands or substitutes are relatively low*—Buyers who can readily switch brands or source from several sellers have more negotiating leverage than buyers who have high switching costs. When the products of rival sellers are virtually identical, it is relatively easy for buyers to switch from seller to seller at little or no cost and anxious sellers may be willing to make concessions to win or retain a buyer's business.

▪ *If the number of buyers is small or if a customer is particularly important to a seller*—The smaller the number of buyers, the less easy it is for sellers to find alternative buyers when a customer is lost to a competitor. The prospect of losing a customer not easily replaced often makes a seller more willing to grant concessions of one kind or another.

- *If buyer demand is weak and sellers are scrambling to secure additional sales of their products*—Weak or declining demand creates a "buyers' market"; conversely, strong or rapidly growing demand creates a "sellers' market" and shifts bargaining power to sellers.

- *If buyers are well-informed about sellers' products, prices, and costs*—The more information buyers have, the better bargaining position they are in. The mushrooming availability of product information on the Internet is giving added bargaining power to individuals. Buyers can easily use the Internet to compare prices and features of vacation packages, shop for the best interest rates on mortgages and loans, and find the best prices on big-ticket items such as digital cameras. Bargain-hunting individuals can shop around for the best deal on the Internet and use that information to negotiate a better deal from local retailers; this method is becoming commonplace in buying new and used motor vehicles. Further, the Internet has created opportunities for manufacturers, wholesalers, retailers, and sometimes individuals to join online buying groups to pool their purchasing power and approach vendors for better terms than could be gotten individually. A multinational manufacturer's geographically scattered purchasing groups can use Internet technology to pool their orders with parts and components suppliers and bargain for volume discounts. Purchasing agents at some companies are banding together at third-party websites to pool corporate purchases to get better deals or special treatment.

- *If buyers pose a credible threat of integrating backward into the business of sellers*—Companies like Anheuser-Busch, Coors, and Heinz have integrated backward into metal can manufacturing to gain bargaining power in obtaining the balance of their can requirements from otherwise powerful metal can manufacturers. Retailers gain bargaining power by stocking and promoting their own private-label brands alongside manufacturers' name brands. Wal-Mart, for example, has elected to compete against Procter & Gamble, its biggest supplier, with its own brand of laundry detergent, called Sam's American Choice, which is priced 25 to 30 percent lower than P&G's Tide.

- *If buyers have discretion in whether and when they purchase the product*—Many consumers, if they are unhappy with the present deals offered on major appliances or hot tubs or home entertainment centers, may be in a position to delay purchase until prices and financing terms improve. If business customers are not happy with the prices or security features of bill-payment software systems, they can either delay purchase until next-generation products become available or attempt to develop their own software in-house. If college students believe that the prices of new textbooks are too high, they can purchase used copies.

Figure 2.8 summarizes the circumstances that make for strong or weak bargaining power on the part of buyers.

A final point to keep in mind is that *not all buyers of an industry's product have equal degrees of bargaining power with sellers*, and some may be less sensitive than others to price, quality, or service differences. For example, independent tire retailers have less bargaining power in purchasing tires than do Honda, Ford, and Daimler-Chrysler (which buy in much larger quantities), and they are also less sensitive to quality. Motor vehicle manufacturers are very particular about tire quality and tire performance because of the effects on vehicle performance, and they drive a hard bargain with tire manufacturers on both price and quality. Apparel manufacturers confront

Figure 2.8   Factors Affecting the Bargaining Power of Buyers

Buyer bargaining power is stronger when:
- Buyer switching costs to competing brands or substitute products are low.
- Buyers are large and can demand concessions when purchasing large quantities.
- Large-volume purchases by buyers are important to sellers.
- Buyer demand is weak or declining.
- There are only a few buyers—so that each one's business is important to sellers.
- Identity of buyer adds prestige to the seller's list of customers.
- Quantity and quality of information available to buyers improves.
- Buyers have the ability to postpone purchases until later if they do not like the present deals being offered by sellers.
- Some buyers are a threat to integrate backward into the business of sellers and become an important competitor.

Buyer bargaining power is weaker when:
- Buyers purchase the item infrequently or in small quantities.
- Buyer switching costs to competing brands are high.
- There is a surge in buyer demand that creates a "sellers' market."
- A seller's brand reputation is important to a buyer.
- A particular seller's product delivers quality or performance that is very important to buyer and that is not matched in other brands.
- Buyer collaboration or partnering with selected sellers provides attractive win–win opportunities.

significant bargaining power when selling to retail chains like JCPenney, Sears, or Macy's, but they can command much better prices selling to small owner-managed apparel boutiques.

How Seller–Buyer Partnerships Can Create Competitive Pressures   Partnerships between sellers and buyers are an increasingly important element of the competitive picture in *business-to-business relationships* (as opposed to business-to-consumer relationships). Many sellers that provide items to business customers have found it in their mutual interest to collaborate closely on such matters as just-in-time deliveries, order processing, electronic invoice payments, and data sharing. Wal-Mart, for example, provides the manufacturers with whom it does business (like Procter & Gamble) with daily sales at each of its stores so that the manufacturers can maintain sufficient inventories at Wal-Mart's distribution centers to keep the shelves at each Wal-Mart store amply stocked. Dell Computer has partnered with its largest customers to create online systems for over 50,000 corporate customers, providing their employees with information on approved product configurations, global pricing, paperless purchase orders, real-time order tracking, invoicing, purchasing history, and other efficiency tools. Dell also loads a customer's software at the factory and installs asset tags so that customer setup time is minimal; it also helps customers upgrade their PC systems to next-generation hardware and software. Dell's partnerships with its corporate customers have put significant competitive pressure on other PC makers.

Determining Whether the Collective Strength of the Five Competitive Forces Is Conducive to Good Profitability

Scrutinizing each of the five competitive forces one by one provides a powerful diagnosis of what competition is like in a given market. Once the strategist has gained an understanding of the specific competitive pressures comprising each force and determined whether these pressures constitute a strong or weak competitive force, the next step is to evaluate the collective strength of the five forces and determine whether the state of competition is conducive to good profitability. Is the collective impact of the five competitive forces stronger than "normal"? Are some of the competitive forces sufficiently strong to undermine industry profitability? Can companies in this industry reasonably expect to earn decent profits in light of the prevailing competitive forces?

Is the State of Competition Conducive to Good Profitability?

As a rule, the stronger the collective impact of the five competitive forces, the lower the combined profitability of industry participants. The most extreme case of a "competitively unattractive" industry is when all five forces are producing strong competitive pressures: rivalry among sellers is vigorous, low entry barriers allow new rivals to gain a market foothold, competition from substitutes is intense, and both suppliers and customers are able to exercise considerable bargaining leverage. Fierce to strong competitive pressures coming from all five directions nearly always drive industry profitability to unacceptably low levels, frequently producing losses for many industry members and forcing some out of business. But an industry can be competitively unattractive without all five competitive forces being strong. Intense competitive pressures from just two or three of the five forces may suffice to destroy the conditions for good profitability and prompt some companies to exit the business. The manufacture of disk drives, for example, is brutally competitive; IBM recently announced the sale of its disk drive business to Hitachi, taking a loss of over $2 billion on its exit from the business. Especially intense competitive conditions seem to be the norm in tire manufacturing and apparel, two industries where profit margins have historically been thin.

> The stronger the forces of competition, the harder it becomes for industry members to earn attractive profits.

In contrast, when the collective impact of the five competitive forces is moderate to weak, an industry is competitively attractive in the sense that industry members can reasonably expect to earn good profits and a nice return on investment. The ideal competitive environment for earning superior profits is one in which both suppliers and customers are in weak bargaining positions, there are no good substitutes, high barriers block further entry, and rivalry among present sellers generates only moderate competitive pressures. Weak competition is the best of all possible worlds for also-ran companies because even they can usually eke out a decent profit—if a company can't make a decent profit when competition is weak, then its business outlook is indeed grim.

In most industries, the collective strength of the five competitive forces is somewhere near the middle of the two extremes of very intense and very weak, typically ranging from slightly stronger than normal to slightly weaker than normal and typically allowing well-managed companies with sound strategies to earn attractive profits.

Striving to Match Company Strategy to Competitive Conditions   Working through the five-forces model step by step not only aids strategy makers in assessing whether the intensity of competition allows good profitability but also promotes sound strategic thinking about how to better match company strategy to the specific competitive character of the marketplace. Effectively matching a company's strategy to the particular competitive pressures and competitive conditions that exist has two aspects:

1. Pursuing avenues that shield the firm from as many of the prevailing competitive pressures as possible.

2. Initiating actions calculated to produce sustainable competitive advantage, thereby shifting competition in the company's favor, putting added competitive pressure on rivals, and perhaps even defining the business model for the industry.

> A company's strategy is increasingly effective the more it provides some insulation from competitive pressures and shifts the competitive battle in the company's favor.

But making headway on these two fronts first requires identifying competitive pressures, gauging the relative strength of each, and gaining a deep enough understanding of the state of competition in the industry to know which strategy buttons to push.

The Drivers of Change: What Impacts Will They Have?

An industry's present conditions don't necessarily reveal much about the strategically relevant ways in which the industry environment is changing. All industries are characterized by trends and new developments that gradually or speedily produce changes important enough to require a strategic response from participating firms. The popular hypothesis that industries go through a life cycle of takeoff, rapid growth, early maturity, market saturation, and stagnation or decline helps explain industry change—but it is far from complete.[11] There are more causes of industry change than an industry's normal progression through the life cycle.

> **Core Concept**
>
> Industry conditions change because important forces are *driving* industry participants (competitors, customers, or suppliers) to alter their actions; the **driving forces** in an industry are the *major underlying causes* of changing industry and competitive conditions—some driving forces originate in the macroenvironment and some originate from within a company's immediate industry and competitive environment.

The Concept of Driving Forces

Although it is important to judge what growth stage an industry is in, there's more analytical value in identifying the specific factors causing fundamental industry and competitive adjustments. Industry and competitive conditions change because certain forces are enticing or pressuring industry participants to alter their actions.[12] **Driving forces** are those that have the biggest influence on what kinds of changes will take place in the industry's structure and competitive environment. Some driving forces originate in the company's macroenvironment;

some originate from within the company's more immediate industry and competitive environment. Driving-forces analysis has two steps: (1) identifying what the driving forces are, and (2) assessing the impact they will have on the industry.

Identifying an Industry's Driving Forces

Many events can affect an industry powerfully enough to qualify as driving forces. Some are unique and specific to a particular industry situation, but most drivers of change fall into one of the following categories:[13]

- *Growing use of the Internet and emerging new Internet technology applications—* The Internet and the adoption of Internet technology applications represent a driving force of historical and revolutionary proportions. The Internet is proving to be an important new distribution channel, allowing manufacturers to access customers directly rather than distribute exclusively through traditional wholesale and retail channels, and also making it easy for companies of all types to extend their geographic reach and vie for sales in areas where they formerly did not have a presence. Being able to reach consumers via the Internet can increase the number of rivals a company faces and escalate rivalry among sellers, sometimes pitting pure online sellers against combination brick-and-click sellers against pure brick-and-mortar sellers. The websites of rival sellers are only a few clicks apart and are "open for business" 24 hours a day every day of the year, giving buyers unprecedented ability to research the product offerings of competitors and shop the market for the best value. Companies can use the Internet to reach beyond their borders to find the best suppliers and, further, to collaborate closely with them to achieve efficiency gains and cost savings. Moreover, companies across the world are using a host of Internet technology applications to revamp internal operations and squeeze out cost savings. Internet technology has so many business applications that companies across the world are pursuing the operational benefits of Internet technology and making online systems a normal part of everyday operations. But the impacts vary from industry to industry and company to company, and the industry and competitive implications are continuously evolving. The challenges here are to assess precisely how the Internet and Internet technology applications are altering a particular industry's landscape and to factor these impacts into the strategy-making equation.

- *Increasing globalization of the industry*—Competition begins to shift from primarily a regional or national focus to an international or global focus when industry members begin seeking out customers in foreign markets or when production activities begin to migrate to countries where costs are lowest. Globalization of competition really starts to take hold when one or more ambitious companies precipitate a race for worldwide market leadership by launching initiatives to expand into more and more country markets. Globalization can also be precipitated by the blossoming of consumer demand in more and more countries and by the actions of government officials in many countries to reduce trade barriers or open up once-closed markets to foreign competitors, as is occurring in many parts of Europe, Latin America, and Asia. Significant differences in labor costs among countries give manufacturers a strong incentive to locate plants for labor-intensive products in low-wage countries and use these plants to supply market demand across the whole world. Wages in China, India, Singapore, Mexico, and Brazil, for example, are about one-fourth those in the United States, Germany, and Japan. The forces of globalization are sometimes such a strong driver that companies find it highly advantageous, if not necessary, to spread their operating reach into more and more country markets. Globalization is very much a driver of industry change in such industries as credit cards, mobile phones, motor vehicles, steel, refined petroleum products, public accounting, and textbook publishing.

- *Changes in the long-term industry growth rate*—Shifts in industry growth up or down are a driving force for industry change, affecting the balance between industry supply and buyer demand, entry and exit, and the character and strength of competition. An upsurge in buyer demand triggers a race among established firms and newcomers to capture the new sales opportunities; ambitious companies with trailing market shares may see the upturn in demand as a golden opportunity to broaden their customer base and move up several notches in the industry standings to secure a place among the market leaders. A slowdown in the rate at which demand is growing nearly always portends mounting rivalry and increased efforts by some firms to maintain their high rates of growth by taking sales and market share away from rivals. If industry sales suddenly turn flat or begin to shrink after years of rising steadily, competition is certain to intensify as industry members scramble for the available business and as mergers and acquisitions result in industry consolidation to a smaller number of competitively stronger participants. Dimming sales prospects usually prompt both competitively weak and growth-oriented companies to sell their business operations to those industry members who elect to stick it out; as demand for the industry's product continues to shrink, the remaining industry members may be forced to close inefficient plants and retrench to a smaller production base—all of which results in a much-changed competitive landscape.

- *Changes in who buys the product and how they use it*—Shifts in buyer demographics and new ways of using the product can alter the state of competition by opening the way to market an industry's product through a different mix of dealers and retail outlets; prompting producers to broaden or narrow their product lines; bringing different sales and promotion approaches into play; and forcing adjustments in customer service offerings (credit, technical assistance, maintenance and repair). The mushrooming popularity of downloading music from the Internet, storing music files on PC hard drives, and burning custom CDs has forced recording companies to reexamine their distribution strategies and raised questions about the future of traditional retail music stores; at the same time, it has stimulated sales of CD burners and blank CDs. Longer life expectancies and growing percentages of relatively well-to-do retirees are driving changes in such industries as health care, prescription drugs, recreational living, and vacation travel. The growing percentage of households with PCs and Internet access is opening opportunities for banks to expand their electronic bill-payment services and for retailers to move more of their customer services online.

- *Product innovation*—Competition in an industry is always affected by rivals racing to be first to introduce one new product or product enhancement after another. An ongoing stream of product innovations tends to alter the pattern of competition in an industry by attracting more first-time buyers, rejuvenating industry growth, and/or creating wider or narrower product differentiation among rival sellers. Successful new product introductions strengthen the market positions of the innovating companies, usually at the expense of companies that stick with their old products or are slow to follow with their own versions of the new product. Product innovation has been a key driving force in such industries as digital cameras, golf clubs, video games, toys, and prescription drugs.

■ *Technological change*—Advances in technology can dramatically alter an industry's landscape, making it possible to produce new and better products at lower cost and opening up whole new industry frontiers. Technological developments can also produce competitively significant changes in capital requirements, minimum efficient plant sizes, distribution channels and logistics, and experience or learning-curve effects. In the steel industry, ongoing advances in minimill technology (which involve recycling scrap steel to make new products) have allowed steelmakers with state-of-the-art minimills to gradually expand into the production of more and more steel products, steadily taking sales and market share from higher-cost integrated producers (which make steel from scratch using iron ore, coke, and traditional blast furnace technology). Nucor, the leader of the minimill technology revolution in the United States, came from nowhere in 1970 to emerge as the nation's biggest and the lowest-cost steel producer as of 2002, having overtaken U.S. Steel and Bethlehem Steel, both integrated producers and the longtime market leaders. In a space of 30 years, advances in minimill technology have changed the face of the steel industry worldwide.

■ *Marketing innovation*—When firms are successful in introducing new ways to market their products, they can spark a burst of buyer interest, widen industry demand, increase product differentiation, and lower unit costs—any or all of which can alter the competitive positions of rival firms and force strategy revisions. In today's world, Internet marketing is shaking up competition in such industries as electronics retailing, stock brokerage (where online brokers have taken significant business away from traditional brokers), and office supplies (where Office Depot, Staples, and Office Max are using their websites to market office supplies to corporations, small businesses, schools and universities, and government agencies).

■ *Entry or exit of major firms*—The entry of one or more foreign companies into a geographic market once dominated by domestic firms nearly always shakes up competitive conditions. Likewise, when an established domestic firm from another industry attempts entry either by acquisition or by launching its own start-up venture, it usually applies its skills and resources in some innovative fashion that pushes competition in new directions. Entry by a major firm often produces a new ballgame, not only with new key players but also with new rules for competing. Similarly, exit of a major firm changes the competitive structure by reducing the number of market leaders (perhaps increasing the dominance of the leaders who remain) and causing a rush to capture the exiting firm's customers.

■ *Diffusion of technical know-how across more companies and more countries*—As knowledge about how to perform a particular activity or execute a particular manufacturing technology spreads, the competitive advantage held by firms originally possessing this know-how erodes. Knowledge diffusion can occur through scientific journals, trade publications, on-site plant tours, word of mouth among suppliers and customers, employee migration, and Internet sources. It can also occur when those possessing technological know-how license others to use it for a royalty fee or team up with a company interested in turning the technology into a new business venture. Quite often, technological know-how can be acquired by simply buying a company that has the wanted skills, patents, or manufacturing capabilities. In recent years, rapid technology transfer across national boundaries has been a prime factor in causing industries to become more globally competitive. As companies worldwide gain access to valuable technical know-how, they upgrade their manufacturing capabilities in a long-term effort to compete head-on against established companies. Cross-border technology transfer has made the once domestic industries of automobiles, tires, consumer electronics, telecommunications, computers, and others, increasingly global.

- *Changes in cost and efficiency*—Widening or shrinking differences in the costs among key competitors tend to dramatically alter the state of competition. The low cost of e-mail and fax transmission has put mounting competitive pressure on the relatively inefficient and high-cost operations of the U.S. Postal Service—sending a one-page fax is cheaper and far quicker than sending a first-class letter; sending e-mail is faster and cheaper still. In the electric power industry, sharply lower costs to generate electricity at newly constructed combined-cycle generating plants during 1998–2001 forced older coal-fired and gas-fired plants to lower their production costs to remain competitive. Shrinking cost differences in producing multifeatured mobile phones is turning the mobile phone market into a commodity business and causing more buyers to base their purchase decisions on price.

- *Growing buyer preferences for differentiated products instead of a commodity product (or for a more standardized product instead of strongly differentiated products)*—When buyer tastes and preferences start to diverge, sellers can win a loyal following with product offerings that stand apart from those of rival sellers. In recent years, beer drinkers have grown less loyal to a single brand and have begun to drink a variety of domestic and foreign beers; as a consequence, beer manufacturers have introduced a host of new brands and malt beverages with different tastes and flavors. Buyer preferences for motor vehicles are becoming increasingly diverse, with few models generating sales of more than 250,000 units annually. When a shift from standardized to differentiated products occurs, the driver of change is the contest among rivals to cleverly outdifferentiate one another.

  On the other hand, buyers sometimes decide that a standardized, budget-priced product suits their requirements as well as or better than a premium-priced product with lots of snappy features and personalized services. Online brokers, for example, have used the lure of cheap commissions to attract many investors willing to place their own buy–sell orders via the Internet; growing acceptance of online trading has put significant competitive pressures on full-service brokers whose business model has always revolved around convincing clients of the value of asking for personalized advice from professional brokers and paying their high commission fees to make trades. Pronounced shifts toward greater product standardization usually spawn lively price competition and force rival sellers to drive down their costs to maintain profitability. The lesson here is that competition is driven partly by whether the market forces in motion are acting to increase or decrease product differentiation.

- *Reductions in uncertainty and business risk*—An emerging industry is typically characterized by much uncertainty over potential market size, how much time and money will be needed to surmount technological problems, and what distribution channels and buyer segments to emphasize. Emerging industries tend to attract only risk-taking entrepreneurial companies. Over time, however, if the business model of industry pioneers proves profitable and market demand for the product appears durable, more conservative firms are usually enticed to enter the market. Often, these later entrants are large, financially strong firms looking to invest in attractive growth industries.

  Lower business risks and less industry uncertainty also affect competition in international markets. In the early stages of a company's entry into foreign markets, conservatism prevails and firms limit their downside exposure by using less risky strategies like exporting, licensing, joint marketing agreements, or joint ventures with local companies to accomplish entry. Then, as experience accumulates and perceived risk levels decline, companies move more boldly and more independently, making acquisitions, constructing their own plants, putting in their own sales and marketing capabilities to build strong competitive positions in each country market, and beginning to link the strategies in each country to create a more globalized strategy.

- *Regulatory influences and government policy changes*—Government regulatory actions can often force significant changes in industry practices and strategic approaches. Deregulation has proved to be a potent procompetitive force in the airline, banking, natural gas, telecommunications, and electric utility industries. Government efforts to reform Medicare and health insurance have become potent driving forces in the health care industry. In international markets, host governments can drive competitive changes by opening their domestic markets to foreign participation or closing them to protect domestic companies. Note that this driving force is spawned by forces in a company's macroenvironment.

- *Changing societal concerns, attitudes, and lifestyles*—Emerging social issues and changing attitudes and lifestyles can be powerful instigators of industry change. Growing antismoking sentiment has emerged as a major driver of change in the tobacco industry; concerns about terrorism are having a big impact on the travel industry. Consumer concerns about salt, sugar, chemical additives, saturated fat, cholesterol, and nutritional value have forced food producers to revamp food-processing techniques, redirect R&D efforts into the use of healthier ingredients, and compete in developing nutritious, good-tasting products. Safety concerns have transformed the automobile, toy, and outdoor power equipment industries, to mention a few. Increased interest in physical fitness has spawned new industries in exercise equipment, mountain biking, outdoor apparel, sports gyms and recreation centers, vitamin and nutrition supplements, and medically supervised diet programs. Social concerns about air and water pollution have forced industries to incorporate expenditures for controlling pollution into their cost structures. Shifting societal concerns, attitudes, and lifestyles alter the pattern of competition, usually favoring those players that respond quickly and creatively with products targeted to the new trends and conditions. As with the preceding driving force, this driving force springs from factors at work in a company's macroenvironment.

That there are so many different *potential driving forces* explains why it is too simplistic to view industry change only in terms of the life-cycle model and why a full understanding of the *causes* underlying the emergence of new competitive conditions is a fundamental part of industry analysis. However, while many forces of change may be at work in a given industry, no more than three or four are likely to be true driving forces powerful enough to qualify as the *major determinants* of why and how the industry is changing. Thus company strategists must resist the temptation to label every change they see as a driving force; the analytical task is to evaluate the forces of industry and competitive change carefully enough to separate major factors from minor ones.

Assessing the Impact of the Driving Forces

The second phase of driving forces analysis is to determine whether the driving forces are, on the whole, acting to make the industry environment more or less attractive. Answers to three questions are needed here:

1. Are the driving forces causing demand for the industry's product to increase or decrease?

2. Are the driving forces acting to make competition more or less intense?

3. Will the driving forces lead to higher or lower industry profitability?

Getting a handle on the collective impact of the driving forces usually requires looking at the likely effects of each force separately, since the driving forces may not all be pushing change in the same direction. For example, two driving forces may be acting to spur demand for the industry's product while one driving force may be working to curtail demand. Whether the net effect on industry demand is up or down hinges on which driving forces are the more powerful. The analyst's objective here is to get a good grip on what external factors are shaping industry change and what difference these factors will make.

The Link between Driving Forces and Strategy

Sound analysis of an industry's driving forces is a prerequisite to sound strategy making. Without understanding the forces driving industry change and the impacts these forces will have on the character of the industry environment and on the company's business over the next one to three years, managers are ill-prepared to craft a strategy tightly matched to emerging conditions. Similarly, if managers are uncertain about the implications of each driving force, or if their views are incomplete or off-base, it's difficult for them to craft a strategy that is responsive to the driving forces and their consequences for the industry. So driving-forces analysis is not something to take lightly; it has practical value and is basic to the task of thinking strategically about where the industry is headed and how to prepare for the changes.

Diagnosing the Market Positions of Industry Rivals: Who is Strongly Positioned and Who Is Not?

> ### Core Concept
>
> **Strategic group mapping** is a technique for displaying the different market or competitive positions that rival firms occupy in the industry.

Since competing companies commonly sell in different price/quality ranges, emphasize different distribution channels, incorporate product features that appeal to different types of buyers, have different geographic coverage, and so on, it stands to reason that some companies enjoy stronger or more attractive market positions than other companies. Understanding which companies are strongly positioned and which are weakly positioned is an integral part of analyzing an industry's competitive structure. The best technique for revealing the market positions of industry competitors is **strategic group mapping.**[14] This analytical tool is useful for comparing the market positions of each firm separately or for grouping them into like positions when an industry has so many competitors that it is not practical to examine each one in depth.

Using Strategic Group Maps to Assess the Market Positions of Key Competitors

A **strategic group** consists of those industry members with similar competitive approaches and positions in the market.[15] Companies in the same strategic group can resemble one another in any of several ways: they may have comparable product-line breadth, sell in the same price/quality range, emphasize the same distribution channels, use essentially the same product attributes to appeal to similar types of buyers, depend on identical technological approaches, or offer buyers similar services and technical assistance.[16] An industry contains only one strategic group when all sellers pursue essentially identical strategies and have comparable market positions. At the other extreme, an industry may contain as many strategic groups as there are competitors when each rival pursues a distinctively different competitive approach and occupies a substantially different market position.

> **Core Concept**
>
> A **strategic group** is a cluster of firms in an industry with similar competitive approaches and market positions.

The procedure for constructing a *strategic group map* is straightforward:

- Identify the competitive characteristics that differentiate firms in the industry; typical variables are price/quality range (high, medium, low), geographic coverage (local, regional, national, global), degree of vertical integration (none, partial, full), product-line breadth (wide, narrow), use of distribution channels (one, some, all), and degree of service offered (no-frills, limited, full).

- Plot the firms on a two-variable map using pairs of these differentiating characteristics.

- Assign firms that fall in about the same strategy space to the same strategic group.

- Draw circles around each strategic group, making the circles proportional to the size of the group's share of total industry sales revenues.

This produces a two-dimensional diagram like the one for the retailing industry in Company Spotlight 2.1.

Several guidelines need to be observed in mapping the positions of strategic groups in the industry's overall strategy space.[17] First, the two variables selected as axes for the map should *not* be highly correlated; if they are, the circles on the map will fall along a diagonal and strategy makers will learn nothing more about the relative positions of competitors than they would by considering just one of the variables. For instance, if companies with broad product lines use multiple distribution channels while companies with narrow lines use a single distribution channel, then looking at broad versus narrow product lines reveals just as much about who is positioned where as looking at single versus multiple distribution channels; that is, one of the variables is redundant. Second, the variables chosen as axes for the map should expose big differences in how rivals position themselves to compete in the marketplace. This, of course, means analysts must identify the characteristics that differentiate rival firms and use these differences as variables for the axes and as the basis for deciding which firm belongs in which strategic group. Third, the variables used as axes don't have to be either quantitative or continuous; rather, they can be discrete variables or defined in terms of distinct classes and combinations. Fourth, drawing the sizes of the circles on the map proportional to the combined sales of the firms in each strategic group allows the map to reflect the relative sizes of each strategic group. Fifth, if more than two good competitive variables can be used as axes for the map, several maps can be drawn to give different exposures to the competitive positioning relationships present in the industry's structure. Because there is not necessarily one best map for portraying how competing firms are positioned in the market, it is advisable to experiment with different pairs of competitive variables.

COMPANY SPOTLIGHT 2.1

Comparative Market Positions of Selected Retail Chains: A Strategic Group Map Application

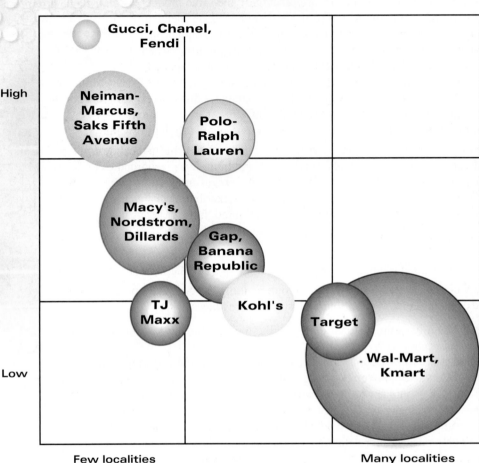

Note: Circles are drawn roughly proportional to the sizes of the chains, according to revenues.

What Can Be Learned from Strategic Group Maps

Driving forces and competitive pressures do not affect all strategic groups evenly. Profit prospects vary from group to group based on the relative attractiveness of their market positions.

One thing to look for is to what extent *industry driving forces and competitive pressures favor some strategic groups and hurt others.*[18] Firms in adversely affected strategic groups may try to shift to a more favorably situated group; how hard such a move proves to be depends on whether entry barriers for the target strategic group are high or low. Attempts by rival firms to enter a new strategic group nearly always increase competitive pressures. If certain firms are known to be trying to change their competitive positions on the map, then attaching

68

arrows to the circles showing the targeted direction helps clarify the picture of competitive maneuvering among rivals.

Another consideration is to what extent *the profit potential of different strategic groups varies due to the strengths and weaknesses in each group's market position.* Differences in profitability can occur because of differing degrees of bargaining leverage or collaboration with suppliers and/or customers, differing degrees of exposure to competition from substitute products outside the industry, differing degrees of competitive rivalry within strategic groups, and differing growth rates for the principal buyer segments served by each group.

Generally speaking, *the closer strategic groups are to each other on the map, the stronger the cross-group competitive rivalry tends to be.* Although firms in the same strategic group are the closest rivals, the next closest rivals are in the immediately adjacent groups.[19] Often, firms in strategic groups that are far apart on the map hardly compete at all. For instance, Tiffany & Co. and Wal-Mart both sell gold and silver jewelry, but their clientele and the prices and quality of their products are much too different to justify calling them competitors. For the same reason, Timex is not a meaningful competitive rival of Rolex, and Subaru is not a close competitor of Lincoln or Mercedes-Benz.

Predicting the Next Strategic Moves Rivals are Likely to Make

Unless a company pays attention to what competitors are doing and knows their strengths and weaknesses, it ends up flying blind into competitive battle. As in sports, scouting the opposition is essential. **Competitive intelligence** about rivals' strategies, their latest actions and announcements, their resource strengths and weaknesses, the efforts being made to improve their situation, and the thinking and leadership styles of their executives is valuable for predicting or

> Good scouting reports on rivals provide a valuable assist in anticipating what moves rivals are likely to make next and outmaneuvering them in the marketplace.

anticipating the strategic moves competitors are likely to make next in the marketplace. Having good information to predict the strategic direction and likely moves of key competitors allows a company to prepare defensive countermoves, to craft its own strategic moves with some confidence about what market maneuvers to expect from rivals, and to exploit any openings that arise from competitors' missteps or strategy flaws.

Identifying Competitors' Strategies and Resource Strengths and Weaknesses

Keeping close tabs on a competitor's strategy entails monitoring what the rival is doing in the marketplace, what its management is saying in company press releases, information posted on the company's website (especially press releases and the presentations management has recently made to securities analysts), and such public documents as annual reports and 10-K filings, articles in the business media, and the reports of securities analysts. (Figure 1.1 in Chapter 1 indicates what to look for in identifying a company's strategy.) Company personnel may be able to pick up useful information from a rival's exhibits at trade shows and from conversations with a rival's customers, suppliers, and former employees.[20] Many companies have a competitive intelligence unit that sifts through the available information to construct up-to-date strategic profiles of rivals—their current strategies, their resource strengths and competitive capabilities, their competitive shortcomings, and the latest pronouncements and leadership styles of their executives. Such profiles are typically updated regularly and made available to managers and other key personnel.

Those who gather competitive intelligence on rivals, however, can sometimes cross the fine line between honest inquiry and unethical or even illegal behavior. For example, calling rivals to get information about prices, the dates of new product introductions, or wage and salary levels is legal, but misrepresenting one's company affiliation during such calls is unethical. Pumping rivals' representatives at trade shows is ethical only if one wears a name tag with accurate company affiliation indicated. Avon Products at one point secured information about its biggest rival, Mary Kay Cosmetics (MKC), by having its personnel search through the garbage bins outside MKC's headquarters.[21] When MKC officials learned of the action and sued, Avon claimed it did nothing illegal, since a 1988 Supreme Court case had ruled that trash left on public property (in this case, a sidewalk) was anyone's for the taking. Avon even produced a videotape of its removal of the trash at the MKC site. Avon won the lawsuit—but Avon's action, while legal, scarcely qualifies as ethical.

In sizing up the strategies and the competitive strengths and weaknesses of competitors, it makes sense for company strategists to make three assessments:

1. Which competitor has the best strategy? Which competitors appear to have flawed or weak strategies?

2. Which competitors are poised to gain market share, and which ones seem destined to lose ground?

3. Which competitors are likely to rank among the industry leaders five years from now? Do one or more up-and-coming competitors have powerful strategies and sufficient resource capabilities to overtake the current industry leader?

The industry's *current* major players are generally easy to identify, but some of the leaders may be plagued with weaknesses that are causing them to lose ground; others may lack the resources and capabilities to remain strong contenders given the superior strategies and capabilities of up-and-coming companies. In evaluating which competitors are favorably or unfavorably positioned to gain market ground, company strategists need to focus on why there is potential for some rivals to do better or worse than other rivals. Usually, a competitor's prospects are a function of its vulnerability to driving forces and competitive pressures, whether its strategy has resulted in competitive advantage or disadvantage, and whether its resources and capabilities are well suited for competing on the road ahead.

> Today's market leaders don't automatically become tomorrow's.

Predicting Competitors' Next Moves

Predicting the next strategic moves of competitors is the hardest yet most useful part of competitor analysis. Good clues about what actions a specific company is likely to undertake can often be gleaned from how well it is faring in the marketplace, the problems or weaknesses it needs to address, and how much pressure it is under to improve its financial performance. Content rivals are likely to continue their present strategy with only minor fine-tuning. Ailing rivals can be performing so poorly that fresh strategic moves are virtually certain. Ambitious rivals looking to move up in the industry ranks are strong candidates for launching new strategic offensives to pursue emerging market opportunities and exploit the vulnerabilities of weaker rivals.

Since the moves a competitor is likely to make are generally predicated on the views their executives have about the industry's future and their beliefs about their firm's situation, it makes sense to closely scrutinize the public pronouncements of rival company executives about where the industry is headed and what it will take to be successful, what they are saying about their firm's situation, information from the grapevine about what they are doing, and their past actions and leadership styles. Other considerations in trying to predict what strategic moves rivals are likely to make next include the following:

- Which rivals badly need to increase their unit sales and market share? What strategic options are they most likely to pursue: lowering prices, adding new models and styles, expanding their dealer networks, entering additional geographic markets, boosting advertising to build better brand-name awareness, acquiring a weaker competitor, or placing more emphasis on direct sales via their website?

- Which rivals have a strong incentive, along with the resources, to make major strategic changes, perhaps moving to a different position on the strategic group map? Which rivals are probably locked in to pursuing the same basic strategy with only minor adjustments?

- Which rivals are good candidates to be acquired? Which rivals may be looking to make an acquisition and are financially able to do so?

- Which rivals are likely to enter new geographic markets?

- Which rivals are strong candidates to expand their product offerings and enter new product segments where they do not currently have a presence?

To succeed in predicting a competitor's next moves, company strategists need to have a good feel for each rival's situation, how its managers think, and what its best options are. Doing the necessary detective work can be tedious and time-consuming, but scouting competitors well enough to anticipate their next moves allows managers to prepare effective countermoves (perhaps even beat a rival to the punch) and to take rivals' probable actions into account in crafting their own best course of action.

> Managers who fail to study competitors closely risk being caught napping by the new strategic moves of rivals.

Pinpointing the Key Factors for Future Competitive Success

An industry's **key success factors (KSFs)** are those competitive factors that most affect industry members' ability to prosper in the marketplace—the particular strategy elements, product attributes, resources, competencies, competitive capabilities, and market achievements that spell the difference between being a strong competitor and a weak competitor—and sometimes between profit and loss. KSFs by their very nature are so important to future competitive success that *all firms* in the industry must pay close attention to them or risk becoming an industry also-ran. To indicate the significance of KSFs another way, how well a company's product offering, resources, and capabilities measure up against an industry's KSFs determines just how financially and competitively successful that company will be. Identifying KSFs, in light of the prevailing and anticipated industry and competitive conditions, is therefore always a

Core Concept

Key success factors are the product attributes, competencies, competitive capabilities, and market achievements with the greatest impact on future competitive success in the marketplace.

top priority analytical and strategy-making consideration. Company strategists need to understand the industry landscape well enough to separate the factors most important to competitive success from those that are less important.

In the beer industry, the KSFs are full utilization of brewing capacity (to keep manufacturing costs low), a strong network of wholesale distributors (to get the company's brand stocked and favorably displayed in retail outlets where beer is sold), and clever advertising (to induce beer drinkers to buy the company's brand and thereby pull beer sales through the established wholesale/retail channels). In apparel manufacturing, the KSFs are appealing designs and color combinations (to create buyer interest) and low-cost manufacturing efficiency (to permit attractive retail pricing and ample profit margins). In tin and aluminum cans, because the cost of shipping empty cans is substantial, one of the keys is having can-manufacturing facilities located close to end-use customers. Key success factors thus vary from industry to industry, and even from time to time within the same industry, as driving forces and competitive conditions change. Table 2.1 lists the most common types of key success factors.

An industry's key success factors can usually be deduced from what was learned from the previously described analysis of the industry and competitive environment. Which factors are most important to future competitive success flow directly from the industry's dominant characteristics, what competition is like, the impacts of the driving forces, the comparative market positions of industry members, and the likely next moves of key rivals. In addition, the answers to three questions help identify an industry's key success factors:

1. On what basis do buyers of the industry's product choose between the competing brands of sellers? That is, what product attributes are crucial?

2. Given the nature of competitive rivalry and the competitive forces prevailing in the marketplace, what resources and competitive capabilities does a company need to have to be competitively successful?

3. What shortcomings are almost certain to put a company at a significant competitive disadvantage?

Only rarely are there more than five or six key factors for future competitive success. And even among these, two or three usually outrank the others in importance. Managers should therefore bear in mind the purpose of identifying key success factors—to determine which factors are most important to future competitive success—and resist the temptation to label a factor that has only minor importance a KSF. To compile a list of every factor that matters even a little bit defeats the purpose of concentrating management attention on the factors truly critical to long-term competitive success.

Correctly diagnosing an industry's KSFs raises a company's chances of crafting a sound strategy. The goal of company strategists should be to design a strategy aimed at stacking up well on all of the industry's future KSFs and trying to be *distinctively better* than rivals on one (or possibly two) of the KSFs. Indeed, companies that stand out or excel on a particular KSF are likely to enjoy a stronger market position—*being distinctively better than rivals on one or two key success factors tends to translate into competitive advantage*. Hence, using the industry's KSFs as *cornerstones* for the company's strategy and trying to gain sustainable competitive advantage by excelling at one particular KSF is a fruitful competitive strategy approach.[22]

Core Concept

Industry key success factors need to be the cornerstones of a company's strategy.

Table 2.1   COMMON TYPES OF INDUSTRY KEY SUCCESS FACTORS

Technology-related KSFs	■ Expertise in a particular technology or in scientific research (important in pharmaceuticals, Internet applications, mobile communications, and most high-tech industries) ■ Proven ability to improve production processes (important in industries where advancing technology opens the way for higher manufacturing efficiency and lower production costs)
Manufacturing-related KSFs	■ Ability to achieve scale economies and/or capture learning-curve effects (important to achieving low production costs) ■ Quality control know-how (important in industries where customers insist on product reliability) ■ High utilization of fixed assets (important in capital-intensive/high-fixed-cost industries) ■ Access to adequate supplies of skilled labor ■ High labor productivity (important for items with high labor content) ■ Low-cost product design and engineering (reduces manufacturing costs) ■ Ability to manufacture or assemble products that are customized to buyer specifications
Distribution-related KSFs	■ A strong network of wholesale distributors/dealers ■ Strong direct sales capabilities via the Internet and/or having company-owned retail outlets ■ Ability to secure favorable display space on retailer shelves
Marketing-related KSFs	■ Breadth of product line and product selection ■ A well-known and well-respected brand name ■ Fast, accurate technical assistance ■ Courteous, personalized customer service ■ Accurate filling of buyer orders (few back orders or mistakes) ■ Customer guarantees and warranties (important in mail-order and online retailing, big-ticket purchases, new product introductions) ■ Clever advertising
Skills- and capability-related KSFs	■ A talented workforce (important in professional services like accounting and investment banking) ■ National or global distribution capabilities ■ Product innovation capabilities (important in industries where rivals are racing to be first to market with new product attributes or performance features) ■ Design expertise (important in fashion and apparel industries) ■ Short delivery time capability ■ Supply chain management capabilities ■ Strong e-commerce capabilities—a user-friendly website and/or skills in using Internet technology applications to streamline internal operations
Other types of KSFs	■ Overall low costs (not just in manufacturing) so as to be able to profitably meet low price expectations of customers ■ Convenient locations (important in many retailing businesses) ■ Ability to provide fast, convenient after-the-sale repairs and service ■ A strong balance sheet and access to financial capital (important in newly emerging industries with high degrees of business risk and in capital-intensive industries) ■ Patent protection

Deciding Whether the Industry Presents an Attractive Opportunity

The final step in evaluating the industry and competitive environment is to use the preceding analysis to decide whether the outlook for the industry presents the company with a sufficiently attractive business opportunity. The important factors on which to base such a conclusion include:

- The industry's growth potential.
- Whether powerful competitive forces are squeezing industry profitability to subpar levels and whether competition appears destined to grow stronger or weaker.
- Whether industry profitability will be favorably or unfavorably affected by the prevailing driving forces.
- The degrees of risk and uncertainty in the industry's future.
- Whether the industry as a whole confronts severe problems—regulatory or environmental issues, stagnating buyer demand, industry overcapacity, mounting competition, and so on.
- The company's competitive position in the industry vis-à-vis rivals. (Being a well-entrenched leader or strongly positioned contender in a lackluster industry may present adequate opportunity for good profitability; however, having to fight a steep uphill battle against much stronger rivals may hold little promise of eventual market success or good return on shareholder investment, even though the industry environment is attractive.)
- The company's potential to capitalize on the vulnerabilities of weaker rivals (perhaps converting a relatively unattractive *industry* situation into a potentially rewarding *company* opportunity).
- Whether the company has sufficient competitive strength to defend against or counteract the factors that make the industry unattractive.
- Whether continued participation in this industry adds importantly to the firm's ability to be successful in other industries in which it may have business interests.

As a general proposition, *if an industry's overall profit prospects are above average, the industry environment is basically attractive; if industry profit prospects are below average, conditions are unattractive.* However, it is a mistake to think of a particular industry as being equally attractive or unattractive to all industry participants and all potential entrants. Attractiveness is relative, not absolute, and conclusions one way or the other have to be drawn from the perspective of a particular company. Industries attractive to insiders may be unattractive to outsiders. Companies on the outside may look at an industry's environment and conclude that it is an unattractive business for them to get into, given the prevailing entry barriers, the difficulty of challenging current market leaders with their particular resources and competencies, and the opportunities they have elsewhere. Industry environments unattractive to weak competitors may be attractive to strong competitors. A favorably positioned company may survey a business environment and see a host of opportunities that weak competitors cannot capture.

Core Concept

The degree to which an industry is attractive or unattractive is not the same for all industry participants and all potential entrants; the opportunities an industry presents depends partly on a company's ability to capture them.

When a company decides an industry is fundamentally attractive and presents good opportunities, a strong case can be made that it should invest aggressively to capture the opportunities it sees and to improve its long-term competitive position in the business. When a strong competitor concludes an industry is relatively unattractive and lacking in opportunity, it may elect to simply protect its present position, investing cautiously if at all and looking for opportunities in other industries. A competitively weak company in an unattractive industry may see its best option as finding a buyer, perhaps a rival, to acquire its business.

Key Points

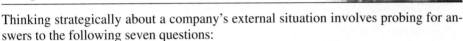

Thinking strategically about a company's external situation involves probing for answers to the following seven questions:

1. *What are the industry's strategy-shaping economic features?* Industries differ significantly on such factors as market size and growth rate, the geographic scope of competitive rivalry, the number and relative sizes of both buyers and sellers, ease of entry and exit, the extent of vertical integration, how fast basic technology is changing, the extent of scale economies and learning-curve effects, the degree of product standardization or differentiation, and overall profitability. While setting the stage for the analysis to come, identifying an industry's economic features also promotes understanding of the kinds of strategic moves that industry members are likely to employ.

2. *What kinds of competitive forces are industry members facing, and how strong is each force?* The strength of competition is a composite of five forces: the rivalry among competing sellers, the presence of attractive substitutes, the potential for new entry, the competitive pressures stemming from supplier bargaining power and supplier–seller collaboration, and the competitive pressures stemming from buyer bargaining power and seller–buyer collaboration. These five forces have to be examined one by one to identify the specific competitive pressures they each comprise and to decide whether these pressures constitute a strong or weak competitive force. The next step in competition analysis is to evaluate the collective strength of the five forces and determine whether the state of competition is conducive to good profitability. Working through the five-forces model step by step not only aids strategy makers in assessing whether the intensity of competition allows good profitability but also promotes sound strategic thinking about how to better match company strategy to the specific competitive character of the marketplace. Effectively matching a company's strategy to the particular competitive pressures and competitive conditions that exist has two aspects: (1) pursuing avenues that shield the firm from as many of the prevailing competitive pressures as possible, and (2) initiating actions calculated to produce sustainable competitive advantage, thereby shifting competition in the company's favor, putting added competitive pressure on rivals, and perhaps even defining the business model for the industry.

3. *What forces are driving changes in the industry, and what impact will these changes have on competitive intensity and industry profitability?* Industry and competitive conditions change because forces are in motion that create incentives or pressures for change. The first phase is to identify the forces that are driving

change in the industry; the most common driving forces include the Internet and Internet technology applications, globalization of competition in the industry, changes in the long-term industry growth rate, changes in buyer composition, product innovation, entry or exit of major firms, changes in cost and efficiency, changing buyer preferences for standardized versus differentiated products or services, regulatory influences and government policy changes, changing societal and lifestyle factors, and reductions in uncertainty and business risk. The second phase of driving-forces analysis is to determine whether the driving forces, taken together, are acting to make the industry environment more or less attractive. Are the driving forces causing demand for the industry's product to increase or decrease? Are the driving forces acting to make competition more or less intense? Will the driving forces lead to higher or lower industry profitability?

4. *What market positions do industry rivals occupy—who is strongly positioned and who is not?* Strategic group mapping is a valuable tool for understanding the similarities, differences, strengths, and weaknesses inherent in the market positions of rival companies. Rivals in the same or nearby strategic groups are close competitors, whereas companies in distant strategic groups usually pose little or no immediate threat. The lesson of strategic group mapping is that some positions on the map are more favorable than others. The profit potential of different strategic groups varies due to strengths and weaknesses in each group's market position. Often, industry driving forces and competitive pressures favor some strategic groups and hurt others.

5. *What strategic moves are rivals likely to make next?* This analytical step involves identifying competitors' strategies, deciding which rivals are likely to be strong contenders and which are likely to be weak, evaluating rivals' competitive options, and predicting their next moves. Scouting competitors well enough to anticipate their actions can help a company prepare effective countermoves (perhaps even beating a rival to the punch) and allows managers to take rivals' probable actions into account in designing their own company's best course of action. Managers who fail to study competitors risk being caught unprepared by the strategic moves of rivals.

6. *What are the key factors for competitive success?* An industry's key success factors (KSFs) are the particular strategy elements, product attributes, competitive capabilities, and business outcomes that spell the difference between being a strong competitor and a weak competitor—and sometimes between profit and loss. KSFs by their very nature are so important to competitive success that *all firms* in the industry must pay close attention to them or risk becoming an industry also-ran. Correctly diagnosing an industry's KSFs raises a company's chances of crafting a sound strategy. The goal of company strategists should be to design a strategy aimed at stacking up well on all of the industry KSFs and trying to be *distinctively better* than rivals on one (or possibly two) of the KSFs. Indeed, using the industry's KSFs as *cornerstones* for the company's strategy and trying to gain sustainable competitive advantage by excelling at one particular KSF is a fruitful competitive strategy approach.

7. *Does the outlook for the industry present the company with sufficiently attractive prospects for profitability?* The answer to this question is a major driver of company strategy. An assessment that the industry and competitive environment is fundamentally attractive typically suggests employing a strategy calculated to

build a stronger competitive position in the business, expanding sales efforts, and investing in additional facilities and equipment as needed. If the industry is relatively unattractive, outsiders considering entry may decide against it and look elsewhere for opportunities, weak companies in the industry may merge with or be acquired by a rival, and strong companies may restrict further investments and employ cost-reduction strategies or product innovation strategies to boost long-term competitiveness and protect their profitability. On occasion, an industry that is unattractive overall is still very attractive to a favorably situated company with the skills and resources to take business away from weaker rivals.

A competently conducted industry and competitive analysis generally tells a clear, easily understood story about the company's external environment. Different analysts can have different judgments about competitive intensity, the impacts of driving forces, how industry conditions will evolve, how good the outlook is for industry profitability, and the degree to which the industry environment offers the company an attractive business opportunity. However, while no method can guarantee a single conclusive diagnosis about the state of industry and competitive conditions and an industry's future outlook, this doesn't justify shortcutting hardnosed strategic analysis and relying instead on opinion and casual observation. Managers become better strategists when they know what questions to pose and what tools to use. This is why this chapter has concentrated on suggesting the right questions to ask, explaining concepts and analytical approaches, and indicating the kinds of things to look for. There's no substitute for staying on the cutting edge of what's happening in the industry—anything less weakens managers' ability to craft strategies that are well matched to the industry and competitive situation.

Exercises

1. As the owner of a new fast-food enterprise seeking a loan from a bank to finance the construction and operation of three new store locations, you have been asked to provide the loan officer with a brief analysis of the competitive environment in fast food. Draw a five-forces diagram for the fast-food industry, and briefly discuss the nature and strength of each of the five competitive forces in fast food.

2. Based on the strategic group map in Company Spotlight 2.1: Who are Wal-Mart's two closest competitors? Between which two strategic groups is competition the weakest? Which strategic group faces the weakest competition from the members of other strategic groups?

3. Based on your knowledge of the ice cream industry, which of the following factors might qualify as possible driving forces capable of causing fundamental change in the industry's structure and competitive environment?
   a) Increasing sales of frozen yogurt and frozen sorbets.
   b) The potential for additional makers of ice cream to enter the market.
   c) Growing consumer interest in low-calorie/low-fat dessert alternatives.
   d) A slowdown in the rate of consumer demand for ice cream products.
   e) An increase in the prices of milk and sugar.
   f) A decision by Häagen-Dazs to increase its prices by 10 percent.
   g) A decision by Ben & Jerry's to add five new flavors to its product line.
   h) A trend in ice cream manufacturers to promoting their brands on the Internet.

Figure 3.1   Identifying the Components of a Single-Business Company's Strategy

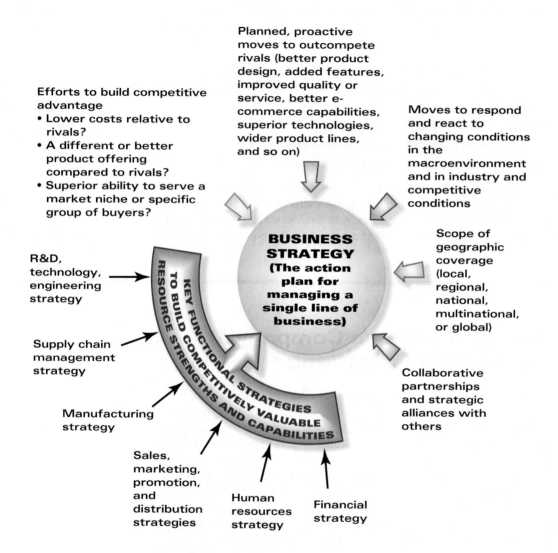

Efforts to build competitive advantage
- Lower costs relative to rivals?
- A different or better product offering compared to rivals?
- Superior ability to serve a market niche or specific group of buyers?

Planned, proactive moves to outcompete rivals (better product design, added features, improved quality or service, better e-commerce capabilities, superior technologies, wider product lines, and so on)

Moves to respond and react to changing conditions in the macroenvironment and in industry and competitive conditions

R&D, technology, engineering strategy

Supply chain management strategy

Manufacturing strategy

Sales, marketing, promotion, and distribution strategies

Human resources strategy

Financial strategy

KEY FUNCTIONAL STRATEGIES TO BUILD CONTINUAL STRATEGIES RESOURCE STRENGTHS AND CAPABILITIES COMPETITIVELY VALUABLE

BUSINESS STRATEGY (The action plan for managing a single line of business)

Scope of geographic coverage (local, regional, national, multinational, or global)

Collaborative partnerships and strategic alliances with others

poor strategy making, less-than-competent strategy execution, or both. Other indicators of how well a company's strategy is working include:

- Whether the firm's sales are growing faster, slower, or about the same pace as the market as a whole, thus resulting in a rising, eroding, or stable market share.

- Whether the company is acquiring new customers at an attractive rate as well as retaining existing customers.

- Whether the firm's profit margins are increasing or decreasing and how well its margins compare to rival firms' margins.

- Trends in the firm's net profits and return on investment and how these compare to the same trends for other companies in the industry.

- Whether the company's overall financial strength and credit rating are improving or on the decline.

- Whether the company can demonstrate continuous improvement in such internal performance measures as days of inventory, employee productivity, unit cost, defect rate, scrap rate, misfilled orders, delivery times, warranty costs, and so on.

- How shareholders view the company based on trends in the company's stock price and shareholder value (relative to the stock price trends at other companies in the industry).

- The firm's image and reputation with its customers.

- How well the company stacks up against rivals on technology, product innovation, customer service, product quality, delivery time, price, getting newly developed products to market quickly, and other relevant factors on which buyers base their choice of brands.

The stronger a company's current overall performance, the less likely the need for radical changes in strategy. The weaker a company's financial performance and market standing, the more its current strategy must be questioned. Weak performance is almost always a sign of weak strategy, weak execution, or both.

> The stronger a company's financial performance and market position, the more likely it has a well-conceived, well-executed strategy.

Sizing Up a Company's Resource Strengths and Weaknesses and Its External Opportunities and Threats

Appraising a company's resource <u>s</u>trengths and <u>w</u>eaknesses and its external <u>o</u>pportunities and <u>t</u>hreats, commonly known as **SWOT analysis,** provides a good overview of whether its overall situation is fundamentally healthy or unhealthy. Just as important, a first-rate SWOT analysis provides the basis for crafting a strategy that capitalizes on the company's resources, aims squarely at capturing the company's best opportunities, and defends against the threats to its well-being.

> **SWOT analysis** is a simple but powerful tool for sizing up a company's resource capabilities and deficiencies, its market opportunities, and the external threats to its future well-being.

Identifying Company Resource Strengths and Competitive Capabilities

A *strength* is something a company is good at doing or an attribute that enhances its competitiveness. A strength can take any of several forms:

- *A skill or important expertise*—low-cost manufacturing capabilities, strong e-commerce expertise, technological know-how, skills in improving production processes, a proven track record in defect-free manufacture, expertise in providing consistently good customer service, excellent mass merchandising skills, or unique advertising and promotional talents.

- *Valuable physical assets*—state-of-the-art plants and equipment, attractive real estate locations, worldwide distribution facilities, or ownership of valuable natural resource deposits.

- *Valuable human assets*—an experienced and capable workforce, talented employees in key areas, cutting-edge knowledge and intellectual capital, collective learning embedded in the organization and built up over time, or proven managerial know-how.[1]

- *Valuable organizational assets*—proven quality control systems, proprietary technology, key patents, mineral rights, a cadre of highly trained customer service representatives, sizable amounts of cash and marketable securities, a strong balance sheet and credit rating (thus giving the company access to additional financial capital), or a comprehensive list of customers' e-mail addresses.

- *Valuable intangible assets*—a powerful or well-known brand name, a reputation for technological leadership, or strong buyer loyalty and goodwill.

- *Competitive capabilities*—product innovation capabilities, short development times in bringing new products to market, a strong dealer network, cutting-edge supply chain management capabilities, quickness in responding to shifting market conditions and emerging opportunities, or state-of-the-art systems for doing business via the Internet.

- *An achievement or attribute that puts the company in a position of market advantage*—low overall costs relative to competitors, market share leadership, a superior product, a wider product line than rivals, wide geographic coverage, a well-known brand name, superior e-commerce capabilities, or exceptional customer service.

- *Competitively valuable alliances or cooperative ventures*—fruitful partnerships with suppliers that reduce costs and/or enhance product quality and performance; alliances or joint ventures that provide access to valuable technologies, competencies, or geographic markets.

Taken together, a company's strengths determine the complement of competitively valuable *resources* with which it competes—a company's resource strengths represent *competitive assets*. The caliber of a firm's resource strengths and competitive capabilities, along with its ability to mobilize them in the pursuit of competitive advantage, are big determinants of how well a company will perform in the marketplace.[2]

> **Core Concept**
>
> A company is better positioned to succeed if it has a competitively valuable complement of resources at its command.

Company Competencies and Competitive Capabilities   Sometimes a company's resource strengths relate to fairly specific skills and expertise (like just-in-time inventory control) and sometimes they flow from pooling the knowledge and expertise of different organizational groups to create a company competence or competitive capability. Competence or capability in continuous product innovation, for example, comes from teaming the efforts of people and groups with expertise in market research, new product R&D, design and engineering, cost-effective manufacturing, and market testing.[3] Company competencies can range from merely a competence in performing an activity to a core competence to a distinctive competence:

1. A **competence** is something an organization is good at doing. It is nearly always the product of experience, representing an accumulation of learning and the buildup of proficiency in performing an internal activity. Usually a company competence originates with deliberate efforts to develop the organizational ability to do something, however imperfectly or inefficiently. Such efforts involve selecting people with the requisite knowledge and skills, upgrading or expanding individual abilities as needed, and then molding the efforts and work products of individuals

into a cooperative group effort to create organizational ability. Then, as experience builds, such that the company gains proficiency in performing the activity consistently well and at an acceptable cost, the ability evolves into a true competence and company capability. Examples of competencies include proficiency in merchandising and product display, the capability to create attractive and easy-to-use websites, expertise in a specific technology, proven capabilities in selecting good locations for retail outlets, and a proficiency in working with customers on new applications and uses of the product.

2. A **core competence** is a proficiently performed internal activity that is *central* to a company's strategy and competitiveness. A core competence is a more valuable resource strength than a competence because of the well-performed activity's core role in the company's strategy and the contribution it makes to the company's success in the marketplace. A core competence can relate to any of several aspects of a company's business: expertise in integrating multiple technologies to create families of new products, know-how in creating and operating systems for cost-efficient supply chain management, the capability to speed new or next-generation products to market, good after-sale service capabilities, skills in manufacturing a high-quality product at a low cost, or the capability to fill customer orders accurately and swiftly. A company may have more than one core competence in its resource portfolio, but rare is the company that can legitimately claim more than two or three core competencies. Most often, *a core competence is knowledge-based, residing in people and in a company's intellectual capital and not in its assets on the balance sheet*. Moreover, a core competence is more likely to be grounded in cross-department combinations of knowledge and expertise rather than being the product of a single department or work group.

3. A **distinctive competence** is a competitively valuable activity that a company *performs better than its rivals*. A distinctive competence thus represents a *competitively superior resource strength*. A company may well perform one competitively important activity well enough to claim that activity as a core competence. But what a company does best internally doesn't translate into a distinctive competence unless the company enjoys *competitive superiority in performing that activity*. For instance, most retailers believe they have core competencies in product selection and in-store merchandising, but many retailers run into trouble in the marketplace because they encounter rivals whose core competencies in product selection and in-store merchandising are better than theirs. Consequently, *a core competence becomes a basis for competitive advantage only when it rises to the level of a distinctive competence*. Sharp Corporation's distinctive competence in flat-panel display technology has enabled it to dominate the worldwide market for liquid crystal displays (LCDs). The distinctive competencies of Toyota and Honda in low-cost, high-quality manufacturing and in short design-to-market cycles for new models have proved to be considerable competitive advantages in the global market for motor vehicles. Intel's distinctive competence in rapidly developing new generations of ever more powerful semiconductor chips for PCs and network servers has helped give the company a dominating presence in the semiconductor industry. Starbucks' distinctive competence in store ambience and innovative coffee drinks has propelled it to the forefront among coffee retailers.

> **Core Concept**
>
> A **core competence** is a competitively important activity that a company performs better than other internal activities; a **distinctive competence** is something that a company does better than its rivals.

The conceptual differences between a competence, a core competence, and a distinctive competence draw attention to the fact that competitive capabilities are not all equal. Some competencies and competitive capabilities merely enable market survival because most rivals have them—indeed, not having a competence or capability that rivals have can result in competitive disadvantage. Core competencies are *competitively* more important than competencies because they add power to the company's strategy and have a bigger positive impact on its market position and profitability. On occasion, a company may have a uniquely strong competitive capability that holds the potential for creating competitive advantage if it meets the criterion for a distinctive competence and delivers value to buyers.[4] *The importance of a distinctive competence to strategy-making rests with (1) the competitively valuable capability it gives a company, (2) its potential for being the cornerstone of strategy, and (3) the competitive edge it can produce in the marketplace.* It is always easier to build competitive advantage when a firm has a distinctive competence in performing an activity important to market success, when rival companies do not have offsetting competencies, and when it is costly and time-consuming for rivals to imitate the competence. A distinctive competence is thus potentially the mainspring of a company's success—unless it is trumped by more powerful resources of rivals.

What Is the Competitive Power of a Resource Strength?   It is not enough to simply compile a list of a company's resource strengths and competitive capabilities. What is most telling about a company's strengths, individually and collectively, is how powerful they are in the marketplace. The competitive power of a company strength is measured by how many of the following four tests it can pass:[5]

1. *Is the resource strength hard to copy?* The more difficult and more expensive it is to imitate a company's resource strength, the greater its potential competitive value. Resources tend to be difficult to copy when they are unique (a fantastic real estate location, patent protection), when they must be built over time in ways that are difficult to imitate (a brand name, mastery of a technology), and when they carry big capital requirements (a cost-effective plant to manufacture cutting-edge microprocessors). Wal-Mart's competitors have failed miserably in their attempts over the past two decades to match Wal-Mart's superefficient state-of-the-art distribution capabilities. Hard-to-copy strengths and capabilities are valuable competitive assets, adding to a company's market strength and contributing to sustained profitability.

2. *Is the resource strength durable—does it have staying power?* The longer the competitive value of a resource lasts, the greater its value. Some resources lose their clout in the marketplace quickly because of the rapid speeds at which technologies or industry conditions are moving. The value of Eastman Kodak's resources in film and film processing is rapidly being undercut by the growing popularity of digital cameras. The investments that commercial banks have made in branch offices is a rapidly depreciating asset because of growing use of direct deposits, automated teller machines, and telephone and Internet banking options.

3. *Is the resource really competitively superior?* Companies have to guard against pridefully believing that their core competences are distinctive competences or that their brand name is more powerful than the brand names of rivals. Who can really say whether Coca-Cola's consumer marketing prowess is better than Pepsi-Cola's or whether the Mercedes-Benz brand name is more powerful than that of BMW or Lexus?

4. *Can the resource strength be trumped by the different resource strengths and competitive capabilities of rivals?* Many commercial airlines (American Airlines, Delta Airlines, Continental Airlines, Singapore Airlines) have attracted large numbers of passengers because of their resources and capabilities in offering safe, convenient, reliable air transportation services and in providing an array of amenities to passengers. However, Southwest Airlines has consistently been a more profitable air carrier because it provides safe, reliable, basic services at radically lower fares. The prestigious brand names of Cadillac and Lincoln have faded in the market for luxury cars because Mercedes, BMW, Audi, and Lexus have introduced the most appealing luxury vehicles in recent years. Amazon.com is putting a big dent in the business prospects of brick-and-mortar bookstores; likewise, Wal-Mart (with its lower prices) is putting major competitive pressure on Toys "R" Us, at one time the leading toy retailer in the United States.

The vast majority of companies are not well endowed with competitively valuable resources, much less with competitively superior resources capable of passing all four tests with high marks. Most firms have a mixed bag of resources—one or two quite valuable, some good, many satisfactory to mediocre. Only a few companies, usually the strongest industry leaders or up-and-coming challengers, possess a distinctive competence or competitively superior resource.

But even if a company doesn't possess a competitively superior resource, it can still marshal potential for winning in the marketplace. Sometimes a company derives significant competitive vitality, maybe even competitive advantage, from a collection of good-to-adequate resources that collectively have competitive power in the marketplace. Toshiba's laptop computers were the market share leader throughout most of the 1990s—an indicator that Toshiba had competitively valuable resource strengths. Yet Toshiba's laptops were not demonstrably faster than rivals' laptops; nor did they have bigger screens, more memory, longer battery power, a better pointing device, or other superior performance features; nor did Toshiba provide clearly superior technical support services to buyers of its laptops. Further, Toshiba laptops were definitely not cheaper, model for model, than the comparable models of its rivals, and they seldom ranked first in the overall performance ratings done by various organizations. Rather, Toshiba's market share leadership stemmed from a *combination* of *good* resource strengths and capabilities—its strategic partnerships with suppliers of laptop components, efficient assembly capability, design expertise, skills in choosing quality components, a wide selection of models, the attractive mix of built-in performance features found in each model when balanced against price, the better-than-average reliability of its models (based on buyer ratings), and very good technical support services (based on buyer ratings). The verdict from the marketplace was that PC buyers considered Toshiba laptops as better, all things considered, than competing brands. (More recently, however, Toshiba has been overtaken by Dell Computer, the present market leader in laptop PCs.)

> Winning in the marketplace becomes more certain when a company has appropriate and ample resources with which to compete, and especially when it has strengths and capabilities with competitive advantage potential.

Identifying Company Resource Weaknesses and Competitive Deficiencies

A *weakness,* or *competitive deficiency,* is something a company lacks or does poorly (in comparison to others) or a condition that puts it at a disadvantage in the marketplace. A company's weaknesses can relate to (1) inferior or unproven skills, expertise,

Table 3.1   WHAT TO LOOK FOR IN IDENTIFYING A COMPANY'S STRENGTHS, WEAKNESSES, OPPORTUNITIES, AND THREATS

Potential Resource Strengths and Competitive Capabilities	Potential Resource Weaknesses and Competitive Deficiencies
■ A powerful strategy	■ No clear strategic direction
■ Core competencies in . . .	■ Resources that are not well matched to industry key success factors
■ A distinctive competence in . . .	■ No well-developed or proven core competencies
■ A product that is strongly differentiated from that of rivals	■ A weak balance sheet; too much debt
■ Competencies and capabilities that are well matched to industry key success factors	■ Higher overall unit costs relative to key competitors
■ A strong financial condition; ample financial resources to grow the business	■ Weak or unproven innovation capabilities
■ Strong brand-name image/company reputation	■ A product/service with ho-hum attributes or features inferior to those of rivals
■ An attractive customer base	■ Too narrow a product line relative to rivals
■ Ability to take advantage of economies of scale and/or experience and learning-curve effects	■ Weak brand image or reputation
■ Proprietary technology, superior technological skills, important patents	■ Weaker dealer network than key rivals and/or lack of adequate global distribution capability
■ Superior intellectual capital relative to key rivals	■ Behind on product quality, R&D, and/or technological know-how
■ Cost advantages	■ In the wrong strategic group
■ Strong advertising and promotion	■ Losing market share because . . .
■ Product innovation capabilities	■ Lack of management depth
■ Proven capabilities in improving production processes	■ Inferior intellectual capital relative to leading rivals
■ Good supply chain management capabilities	■ Subpar profitability because . . .
■ Good customer service capabilities	■ Plagued with internal operating problems or obsolete facilities
■ Better product quality relative to rivals	■ Behind rivals in e-commerce capabilities
■ Wide geographic coverage and/or strong global distribution capability	■ Short on financial resources to grow the business and pursue promising initiatives
■ Alliances/joint ventures with other firms that provide access to valuable technology, competencies, and/or attractive geographic markets	■ Too much underutilized plant capacity

or intellectual capital in competitively important areas of the business; (2) deficiencies in competitively important physical, organizational, or intangible assets; or (3) missing or competitively inferior capabilities in key areas. *Internal weaknesses are thus shortcomings in a company's complement of resources and represent competitive liabilities.* Nearly all companies have competitive liabilities of one kind or another. Whether a company's resource weaknesses make it competitively vulnerable depends on how much they matter in the marketplace and whether they are offset by the company's resource strengths.

Table 3.1 lists the kinds of factors to consider in compiling a company's resource strengths and weaknesses. Sizing up a company's complement of resource capabilities and deficiencies is akin to constructing a *strategic balance sheet,* on which resource strengths represent *competitive assets* and resource weaknesses represent *competitive liabilities.* Obviously, the ideal condition is for the company's competitive assets to outweigh its competitive liabilities by an ample margin—a 50–50 balance is definitely not the desired condition!

Core Concept

A company's resource strengths represent competitive assets; its resource weaknesses represent competitive liabilities.

Potential Market Opportunities	Potential External Threats to a Company's Well-Being
■ Openings to take market share away from rivals ■ Ability to grow rapidly because of sharply rising buyer demand for the industry's product ■ Serving additional customer groups or market segments ■ Expanding into new geographic markets or product segments ■ Expanding the company's product line to meet a broader range of customer needs ■ Utilizing existing company skills or technological know-how to enter new product lines or new businesses ■ Online sales via the Internet ■ Integrating forward or backward ■ Falling trade barriers in attractive foreign markets ■ Acquiring rival firms or companies with attractive technological expertise ■ Entering into alliances or joint ventures to expand the firm's market coverage or boost its competitive capability ■ Openings to exploit emerging new technologies	■ Increasing intensity of competition among industry rivals—may squeeze profit margins ■ Slowdowns in market growth ■ Likely entry of potent new competitors ■ Loss of sales to substitute products ■ Growing bargaining power of customers or suppliers ■ A shift in buyer needs and tastes away from the industry's product ■ Adverse demographic changes that threaten to curtail demand for the industry's product ■ Vulnerability to industry driving forces ■ Restrictive trade policies on the part of foreign governments that block access to attractive foreign markets ■ Costly new regulatory requirements

Identifying a Company's Market Opportunities

Market opportunity is a big factor in shaping a company's strategy. Indeed, managers can't properly tailor strategy to the company's situation without first identifying its opportunities and appraising the growth and profit potential each one holds. Depending on the prevailing circumstances, a company's opportunities can be plentiful or scarce and can range from wildly attractive (an absolute "must" to pursue) to marginally interesting (because the growth and profit potential are questionable) to unsuitable (because there's not a good match with the company's strengths and capabilities). A checklist of potential market opportunities is included in Table 3.1.

In evaluating a company's market opportunities and ranking their attractiveness, managers have to guard against viewing every *industry* opportunity as a *company* opportunity. Not every company is equipped with the resources to successfully pursue each opportunity that exists in its industry. Some companies are more capable of going after particular opportunities than others, and a few companies may be

> A company is well advised to pass on a particular market opportunity unless it has or can acquire the resources to capture it.

hopelessly outclassed. Deliberately adapting a company's resource base to put it in position to contend for attractive growth opportunities is something strategists must pay keen attention to. *The market opportunities most relevant to a company are those that match up well with the company's financial and organizational resource capabilities, offer the best growth and profitability, and present the most potential for competitive advantage.*

Identifying the Threats to a Company's Future Profitability

Often, certain factors in a company's external environment pose *threats* to its profitability and competitive well-being. Threats can stem from the emergence of cheaper or better technologies, rivals' introduction of new or improved products, the entry of lower-cost foreign competitors into a company's market stronghold, new regulations that are more burdensome to a company than to its competitors, vulnerability to a rise in interest rates, the potential of a hostile takeover, unfavorable demographic shifts, adverse changes in foreign exchange rates, political upheaval in a foreign country where the company has facilities, and the like. External threats may pose no more than a moderate degree of adversity (all companies confront some threatening elements in the course of doing business), or they may be so imposing as to make a company's situation and outlook quite tenuous. It is management's job to identify the threats to the company's future well-being and to evaluate what strategic actions can be taken to neutralize or lessen their impact.

A list of potential threats to a company's future profitability and market position is included in Table 3.1.

What Do the SWOT Listings Reveal?

Simply making lists of a company's strengths, weaknesses, opportunities, and threats is not enough; the payoff from SWOT analysis comes from the conclusions about a company's situation and the implications for strategy improvement that flow from the four lists.

SWOT analysis involves more than making four lists. The two most important parts of SWOT analysis are *drawing conclusions* from the SWOT listings about the company's overall situation, and *acting on those conclusions* to better match the company's strategy to its resource strengths and market opportunities, to correct the important weaknesses, and to defend against external threats. Figure 3.2 shows the three steps of SWOT analysis.

Just what story the SWOT listings tell about the company's overall situation is often revealed in the answers to the following sets of questions:

■   Does the company have an attractive set of resource strengths? Does it have any strong core competencies or a distinctive competence? Are the company's strengths and capabilities well matched to the industry key success factors? Do they add adequate power to the company's strategy, or are more or different strengths needed? Will the company's current strengths and capabilities matter in the future?

■   How serious are the company's weaknesses and competitive deficiencies? Are they mostly inconsequential and readily correctable, or could one or more prove fatal if not remedied soon? Are some of the company's weaknesses in areas that relate to the industry's key success factors? Are there any weaknesses that if uncorrected, would keep the company from pursuing an otherwise attractive opportunity? Does the company have important resource gaps that need to be filled for it to move up in the industry rankings and/or boost its profitability?

Figure 3.2   The Three Steps of SWOT Analysis: Identify, Draw Conclusions, Translate into Strategic Action

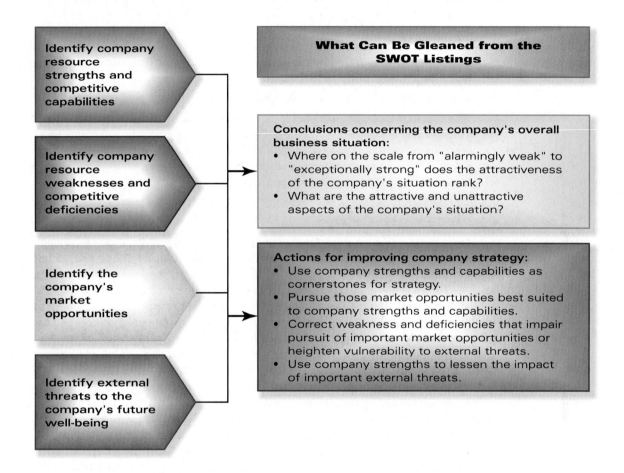

Do the company's resource strengths and competitive capabilities (its competitive assets) outweigh its resource weaknesses and competitive deficiencies (its competitive liabilities) by an attractive margin?

Does the company have attractive market opportunities that are well suited to its resource strengths and competitive capabilities? Does the company lack the resources and capabilities to pursue any of the most attractive opportunities?

Are the threats alarming, or are they something the company appears able to deal with and defend against?

All things considered, how strong is the company's overall situation? Where on a scale of 1 to 10 (where 1 is alarmingly weak and 10 is exceptionally strong) should the firm's position and overall situation be ranked? What aspects of the company's situation are particularly attractive? What aspects are of the most concern?

The final piece of SWOT analysis is to translate the diagnosis of the company's situation into actions for improving the company's strategy and business prospects. The following questions point to implications the SWOT listings have for strategic action:

▪ Which competitive capabilities need to be strengthened immediately (so as to add greater power to the company's strategy and boost sales and profitability)? Do new types of competitive capabilities need to be put in place to help the company better respond to emerging industry and competitive conditions? Which resources and capabilities need be given greater emphasis, and which merit less emphasis? Should the company emphasize leveraging its existing resource strengths and capabilities, or does it need to create new resource strengths and capabilities?

▪ What actions should be taken to reduce the company's competitive liabilities? Which weaknesses or competitive deficiencies are in urgent need of correction?

▪ Which market opportunities should be top priority in future strategic initiatives (because they are good fits with the company's resource strengths and competitive capabilities, present attractive growth and profit prospects, and/or offer the best potential for securing competitive advantage)? Which opportunities should be ignored, at least for the time being (because they offer less growth potential or are not suited to the company's resources and capabilities)?

▪ What should the company be doing to guard against the threats to its well-being?

A company's resource strengths should generally form the cornerstones of strategy because they represent the company's best chance for market success.[6] As a rule, strategies that place heavy demands on areas where the company is weakest or has unproven ability are suspect and should be avoided. If a company doesn't have the resources and competitive capabilities around which to craft an attractive strategy, managers need to take decisive remedial action either to upgrade existing organizational resources and capabilities and add others as needed or to acquire them through partnerships or strategic alliances with firms possessing the needed expertise. Plainly, managers have to look toward correcting competitive weaknesses that make the company vulnerable, hold down profitability, or disqualify it from pursuing an attractive opportunity.

At the same time, sound strategy making requires sifting through the available market opportunities and aiming strategy at capturing those that are most attractive and suited to the company's circumstances. Rarely does a company have the resource depth to pursue all available market opportunities simultaneously without spreading itself too thin. How much attention to devote to defending against external threats to the company's market position and future performance hinges on how vulnerable the company is, whether there are attractive defensive moves that can be taken to lessen their impact, and whether the costs of undertaking such moves represent the best use of company resources.

Analyzing Whether a Company's Prices and Costs Are Competitive

Company managers are often stunned when a competitor cuts its price to "unbelievably low" levels or when a new market entrant comes on strong with a very low price. The competitor may not, however, be "dumping" (an economic term for selling large amounts of goods below market price), buying market share, or waging a desperate move to gain sales; it may simply have substantially lower costs. One of the most telling signs of whether a company's business position is strong or precarious is whether its prices and costs are competitive with industry rivals. Price–cost comparisons are especially critical in a commodity-product industry where the value provided to buyers is the same from seller to seller, price competition is typically the ruling market force, and lower-cost companies have the upper hand. But even in industries where products are differentiated and competition centers on the different attributes of competing brands as much as on price, rival companies have to keep their costs *in line* and make sure that any added costs they incur, and any price premiums they charge, create ample buyer value.

For a company to compete successfully, its costs must be *in line* with those of close rivals. While some cost disparity is justified so long as the products or services of closely competing companies are sufficiently differentiated, a high-cost firm's market position becomes increasingly vulnerable the more its costs exceed those of close rivals.

Two analytical tools are particularly useful in determining whether a company's prices and costs are competitive and thus conducive to winning in the marketplace: value chain analysis and benchmarking.

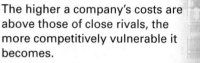

The higher a company's costs are above those of close rivals, the more competitively vulnerable it becomes.

The Concept of a Company Value Chain

Every company's business consists of a collection of activities undertaken in the course of designing, producing, marketing, delivering, and supporting its product or service. A company's **value chain** consists of the linked set of value-creating activities the company performs internally. As shown in Figure 3.3, the value chain consists of two broad categories of activities: the *primary activities* that are foremost in creating value for customers and the requisite *support activi-*

> ### Core Concept
> A company's **value chain** identifies the primary activities that create customer value and the related support activities.

ties that facilitate and enhance the performance of the primary activities.[7] The value chain includes a profit margin because a markup over the cost of performing the firm's value-creating activities is customarily part of the price (or total cost) borne by buyers—a fundamental objective of every enterprise is to create and deliver a value to buyers whose margin over cost yields an attractive profit.

Disaggregating a company's operations into primary and secondary activities exposes the major elements of the company's cost structure. Each activity in the value chain gives rise to costs and ties up assets; assigning the company's operating costs and assets to each individual activity in the chain provides cost estimates and capital requirements. Quite often, there are links between activities such that the manner in which one activity is done can affect the costs of performing other activities. For instance, Japanese producers of videocassette recorders (VCRs) were able to reduce prices from around $1,300 in 1977 to under $300 in 1984 by spotting the impact of an early step in the value chain (product design) on a later step (production) and deciding to change the product design to drastically reduce the number of parts in each VCR.[8]

The combined costs of all the various activities in a company's value chain define the company's internal cost structure. Further, the cost of each activity contributes to whether the company's overall cost position relative to rivals is favorable or unfavorable. The tasks of value chain analysis and benchmarking are to develop the data for comparing a company's costs activity by activity against the costs of key rivals and to learn which internal activities are a source of cost advantage or disadvantage. A company's relative cost position is a function of how the overall costs of the activities it performs in conducting business compare to the overall costs of the activities performed by rivals.

Figure 3.3   Representative Company Value Chain

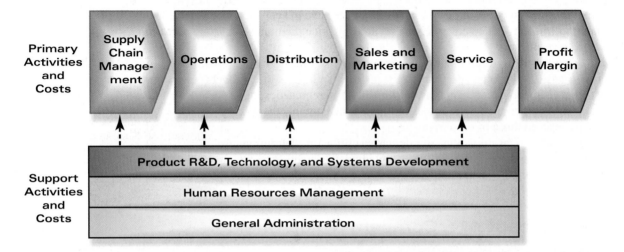

PRIMARY ACTIVITIES

- **Supply Chain Management**—Activities, costs, and assets associated with purchasing fuel, energy, raw materials, parts and components, merchandise, and consumable items from vendors; receiving, storing, and disseminating inputs from suppliers; inspection; and inventory management.

- **Operations**—Activities, costs, and assets associated with converting inputs into final product form (production, assembly, packaging, equipment maintenance, facilities, operations, quality assurance, environmental protection).

- **Distribution**—Activities, costs, and assets dealing with physically distributing the product to buyers (finished goods warehousing, order processing, order picking and packing, shipping, delivery vehicle operations, establishing and maintaining a network of dealers and distributors).

- **Sales and Marketing**—Activities, costs, and assets related to sales force efforts, advertising and promotion, market research and planning, and dealer/distributor support.

- **Service**—Activities, costs, and assets associated with providing assistance to buyers, such as installation, spare parts delivery, maintenance and repair, technical assistance, buyer inquiries, and complaints.

SUPPORT ACTIVITIES

- **Product R&D, Technology, and Systems Development**—Activities, costs, and assets relating to product R&D, process R&D, process design improvement, equipment design, computer software development, telecommunications systems, computer-assisted design and engineering, database capabilities, and development of computerized support systems.

- **Human Resources Management**—Activities, costs, and assets associated with the recruitment, hiring, training, development, and compensation of all types of personnel; labor relations activities; and development of knowledge-based skills and core competencies.

- **General Administration**—Activities, costs, and assets relating to general management, accounting and finance, legal and regulatory affairs, safety and security, management information systems, forming strategic alliances and collaborating with strategic partners, and other "overhead" functions.

Source: Adapted from Michael E. Porter, *Competitive Advantage* (New York: Free Press, 1985), pp. 37–43.

Why the Value Chains of Rival Companies Often Differ

A company's value chain and the manner in which it performs each activity reflect the evolution of its own particular business and internal operations, its strategy, the approaches it is using to execute its strategy, and the underlying economics of the activities themselves.[9] Because these factors differ from company to company, the value chains of rival companies sometimes differ substantially—a condition that complicates the task of assessing rivals' relative cost positions. For instance, competing companies may differ in their degrees of vertical integration. Comparing the value chains of a fully integrated rival and a partially integrated rival requires adjusting for differences in the scope of activities performed. Clearly the internal costs for a manufacturer that *makes* all of its own parts and components will be greater than the internal costs of a producer that *buys* the needed parts and components from outside suppliers and only performs assembly operations.

Likewise, there is legitimate reason to expect value chain and cost differences between a company that is pursuing a low-cost/low-price strategy and a rival that is positioned on the high end of the market. The costs of certain activities along the low-cost company's value chain should indeed be relatively low, whereas the high-end firm may understandably be spending relatively more to perform those activities that create the added quality and extra features of its products.

Moreover, cost and price differences among rival companies can have their origins in activities performed by suppliers or by distribution channel allies involved in getting the product to end users. Suppliers or wholesale/retail dealers may have excessively high cost structures or profit margins that jeopardize a company's cost-competitiveness even though its costs for internally performed activities are competitive. For example, when determining Michelin's cost-competitiveness vis-à-vis Goodyear and Bridgestone in supplying replacement tires to vehicle owners, we have to look at more than whether Michelin's tire manufacturing costs are above or below Goodyear's and Bridgestone's. Let's say that a buyer has to pay $400 for a set of Michelin tires and only $350 for a comparable set of Goodyear or Bridgestone tires; Michelin's $50 price disadvantage can stem not only from higher manufacturing costs (reflecting, perhaps, the added costs of Michelin's strategic efforts to build a better-quality tire with more performance features) but also from (1) differences in what the three tire makers pay their suppliers for materials and tire-making components, and (2) differences in the operating efficiencies, costs, and markups of Michelin's wholesale–retail dealer outlets versus those of Goodyear and Bridgestone. Thus, determining whether a company's prices and costs are competitive from an end user's standpoint requires looking at the activities and costs of competitively relevant suppliers and forward allies, as well as the costs of internally performed activities.

The Value Chain System for an Entire Industry

As the tire industry example makes clear, a company's value chain is embedded in a larger system of activities that includes the value chains of its suppliers and its distribution channel allies engaged in getting its product or service to end users.[10] *Accurately assessing a company's competitiveness in end-use markets requires that company managers understand the entire value chain system for delivering a product or service to end users, not just the company's own value chain.* At the very least, this means considering the value chains of suppliers and forward channel allies (if any), as shown in Figure 3.4.

Suppliers' value chains are relevant because suppliers perform activities and incur costs in creating and delivering the purchased inputs used in a company's own value chain. The costs, performance features, and quality of these inputs influence a company's own costs and product differentiation capabilities. Anything a company can do to help its suppliers' take costs out of their value chain activities or improve the quality

Figure 3.4   Representative Value Chain for an Entire Industry

Supplier-Related Value Chains	A Company's Own Value Chain	Forward Channel Value Chains	
Activities, costs, and margins of suppliers	Internally performed activities, costs, and margins	Activities, costs, and margins of forward channel allies and strategic partners	Buyer or End-user value chains

Source: Adapted from Michael E. Porter, *Competitive Advantage* (New York: Free Press, 1985), p. 35.

and performance of the items being supplied can enhance its own competitiveness—a powerful reason for working collaboratively with suppliers in managing supply chain activities.

Forward channel and customer value chains are relevant because (1) the costs and margins of a company's distribution allies are part of the price the end user pays, and (2) the activities that distribution allies perform affect the end user's satisfaction. For these reasons, companies normally work closely with their forward channel allies (who are their direct customers) to perform value chain activities in mutually beneficial ways. For instance, some aluminum can producers have constructed plants next to beer breweries and deliver cans on overhead conveyors directly to the breweries' can-filling lines; this has resulted in significant savings in production scheduling, shipping, and inventory costs for both container producers and breweries.[11] Many automotive parts suppliers have built plants near the auto assembly plants they supply to facilitate just-in-time deliveries, reduce warehousing and shipping costs, and promote close collaboration on parts design and production scheduling. Irrigation equipment companies, suppliers of grape-harvesting and winemaking equipment, and firms making barrels, wine bottles, caps, corks, and labels all have facilities in the California wine country to be close to the nearly 700 winemakers they supply.[12] The lesson here is that a company's value chain activities are often closely linked to the value chains of their suppliers and the forward allies or customers to whom they sell.

> A company's cost-competitiveness depends not only on the costs of internally performed activities (its own value chain) but also on costs in the value chain of its suppliers and forward channel allies.

Although the value chains in Figures 3-3 and 3-4 are representative, actual value chains vary by industry and by company. The primary value chain activities in the pulp and paper industry (timber farming, logging, pulp mills, and papermaking) differ from the primary value chain activities in the home appliance industry (parts and components manufacture, assembly, wholesale distribution, retail sales). The value chain for the soft-drink industry (processing of basic ingredients and syrup manufacture, bottling and can filling, wholesale distribution, advertising, and retail merchandising) differs from that for the computer software industry (programming, disk loading, marketing, distribution). A producer of bathroom and kitchen faucets depends heavily on the activities of wholesale distributors and building supply retailers in winning sales to

Table 3.2   THE DIFFERENCE BETWEEN TRADITIONAL COST ACCOUNTING AND ACTIVITY-BASED COST ACCOUNTING: A PURCHASING DEPARTMENT EXAMPLE

Traditional Cost Accounting Categories in Purchasing Department Budget		Cost of Performing Specific Purchasing Department Activities Using Activity-Based Cost Accounting	
Wages and salaries	$340,000	Evaluate supplier capabilities	$100,300
Employee benefits	95,000	Process purchase orders	82,100
Supplies	21,500	Collaborate with suppliers on just-in-time deliveries	140,200
Travel	12,400	Share data with suppliers	59,550
Depreciation	19,000	Check quality of items purchased	94,100
Other fixed charges (office space, utilities)	112,000	Check incoming deliveries against purchase orders	48,450
Miscellaneous operating expenses	40,250	Resolve disputes	15,250
		Conduct internal administration	100,200
	$640,150		$640,150

Source: Adapted from information in Terence P. Paré, "A New Tool for Managing Costs," *Fortune,* June 14, 1993, pp. 124–29.

homebuilders and do-it-yourselfers; a producer of small gasoline engines internalizes its distribution activities by selling directly to the makers of lawn and garden equipment. A wholesaler's most important activities and costs deal with purchased goods, inbound logistics, and outbound logistics. A hotel's most important activities and costs are in operations—check-in and check-out, maintenance and housekeeping, dining and room service, conventions and meetings, and accounting. Outbound logistics is a crucial activity at Domino's Pizza but comparatively insignificant at Blockbuster. Advertising and promotion are dominant activities at Anheuser-Busch but only minor activities at interstate gas pipeline companies. Consequently, generic value chains like those in Figures 3.3 and 3.4 are illustrative, not absolute, and have to be drawn to fit the activities of a particular company or industry.

Developing the Data to Measure a Company's Cost Competitiveness

Once the major value chain activities are identified, the next step in evaluating a company's cost-competitiveness involves breaking down departmental cost accounting data into the costs of performing specific activities.[13] The appropriate degree of disaggregation depends on the economics of the activities and how valuable it is to develop cross-company cost comparisons for narrowly defined activities as opposed to broadly defined activities. A good guideline is to develop separate cost estimates for activities having different economics and for activities representing a significant or growing proportion of cost.[14]

Traditional accounting identifies costs according to broad categories of expenses—wages and salaries, employee benefits, supplies, maintenance, utilities, travel, depreciation, R&D, interest, general administration, and so on. A newer method, *activity-based costing,* entails defining expense categories according to the specific activities being performed and then assigning costs to the activity responsible for creating the cost. An illustrative example is shown in Table 3.2.[15] Perhaps 25 percent of the companies that have explored the feasibility of activity-based costing have adopted

Value Chain Costs for Companies in the Business of Recording and Distributing Music CDs

The table below presents the representative costs and markups associated with producing and distributing a music CD retailing for $15.

1. Record company direct production costs		$2.40
Artists and repertoire	$0.75	
Pressing of CD and packaging	1.65	
2. Royalties		.99
3. Record company marketing expenses		1.50
4. Record company overhead		1.50
5. Total record company costs		6.39
6. Record company's operating profit		1.86
7. Record company's selling price to distributor/wholesaler		8.25
8. Average wholesale distributor markup to cover distribution activities and profit margins		1.50
9. Average wholesale price charged to retailer		9.75
10. Average retail markup over wholesale cost		5.25
11. Average price to consumer at retail		$15.00

Source: Developed from information in "Fight the Power," a case study prepared by Adrian Aleyne, Babson College, 1999.

this accounting approach. To fully understand the costs of activities all along the industry value chain, cost estimates for activities performed in the competitively relevant portions of suppliers' and customers' value chains also have to be developed—an advanced art in competitive intelligence. But despite the tediousness of developing cost estimates activity by activity and the imprecision of some of the estimates, the payoff in exposing the costs of particular activities makes activity-based costing a valuable analytical tool.[16] Company Spotlight 3.1 shows representative costs for various activities performed by the producers and marketers of music CDs.

The most important application of value chain analysis is to expose how a particular firm's cost position compares with the cost positions of its rivals. What is needed are competitor-versus-competitor cost estimates for supplying a product or service to a well-defined customer group or market segment. The size of a company's cost advantage or disadvantage can vary from item to item in the product line, from customer group to customer group (if different distribution channels are used), and from geographic market to geographic market (if cost factors vary across geographic regions).

Core Concept

Benchmarking has proved to be a potent tool for learning which companies are best at performing particular activities and then using their techniques (or "best practices") to improve the cost and effectiveness of a company's own internal activities.

Benchmarking the Costs of Key Value Chain Activities

Many companies today are **benchmarking** their costs of performing a given activity against competitors' costs (and/or against the costs of a noncompetitor in another industry that efficiently and effectively performs much the same activity). Benchmarking is a tool that allows a company to determine whether the manner in which it performs particular functions and activities represents industry "best practices" when both cost and effectiveness are taken into account.

Benchmarking entails comparing how different companies perform various value chain activities—how materials are purchased, how suppliers are paid, how inventories are managed, how products are assembled, how fast the company can get new products to market, how the quality control function is performed, how customer orders are filled and shipped, how employees are trained, how payrolls are processed, and how maintenance is performed—and then making cross-company comparisons of the costs of these activities.[17] The objectives of benchmarking are to identify the best practices in performing an activity, to learn how other companies have actually achieved lower costs or better results in performing benchmarked activities, and to take action to improve a company's competitiveness whenever benchmarking reveals that its costs and results of performing an activity do not match those of other companies (either competitors or noncompetitors).

In 1979, Xerox became an early pioneer in the use of benchmarking when Japanese manufacturers began selling midsize copiers in the United States for $9,600 each—less than Xerox's production costs.[18] Although Xerox management suspected its Japanese competitors were dumping, it sent a team of line managers to Japan, including the head of manufacturing, to study competitors' business processes and costs. Fortunately, Xerox's joint venture partner in Japan, Fuji-Xerox, knew the competitors well. The team found that Xerox's costs were excessive due to gross inefficiencies in the company's manufacturing processes and business practices; the study proved instrumental in Xerox's efforts to become cost-competitive and prompted Xerox to embark on a long-term program to benchmark 67 of its key work processes against companies identified as having the best practices in performing these processes. Xerox quickly decided not to restrict its benchmarking efforts to its office equipment rivals but to extend them to any company regarded as "world class" in performing *any activity* relevant to Xerox's business.

Thus, benchmarking has quickly come to be a tool for comparing a company against rivals not only on cost but on most any relevant activity or competitively important measure. Toyota managers got their idea for just-in-time inventory deliveries by studying how U.S. supermarkets replenished their shelves. Southwest Airlines reduced the turnaround time of its aircraft at each scheduled stop by studying pit crews on the auto racing circuit. Over 80 percent of Fortune 500 companies reportedly engage in some form of benchmarking.

The tough part of benchmarking is not whether to do it but rather how to gain access to information about other companies' practices and costs. Sometimes benchmarking can be accomplished by collecting information from published reports, trade groups, and industry research firms and by talking to knowledgeable industry analysts, customers, and suppliers. On occasion, customers, suppliers, and joint-venture partners often make willing benchmarking allies. Usually, though, benchmarking requires field trips to the facilities of competing or noncompeting companies to observe how things are done, ask questions, compare practices and processes, and perhaps exchange data on productivity, staffing levels, time requirements, and

> Benchmarking the costs of company activities against rivals provides hard evidence of a company's cost-competitiveness.

other cost components. The problem is that, because benchmarking involves competitively sensitive cost information, close rivals can't be expected to be completely open, even if they agree to host facilities tours and answer questions. Making reliable cost comparisons is complicated by the fact that participants often use different cost accounting systems.

However, the explosive interest of companies in benchmarking costs and identifying best practices has prompted consulting organizations (e.g., Accenture, A. T. Kearney, Best Practices Benchmarking & Consulting, Towers Perrin) and several newly formed councils and associations (the International Benchmarking Clearinghouse, the Strategic Planning Institute's Council on Benchmarking) to gather benchmarking data, do benchmarking studies, and distribute information about best practices without identifying the sources. Having an independent group gather the information and report it in a manner that disguises the names of individual companies permits companies to avoid having to disclose competitively sensitive data to rivals and reduces the risk of ethical problems.

Strategic Options for Remedying a Cost Disadvantage

Value chain analysis and benchmarking can reveal a great deal about a firm's cost competitiveness. Examining the costs of a company's own value chain activities and comparing them to rivals' indicates who has how much of a cost advantage or disadvantage and which cost components are responsible. Such information is vital in strategic actions to eliminate a cost disadvantage or create a cost advantage. One of the fundamental insights of value chain analysis and benchmarking is that a company's competitiveness on cost depends on how efficiently it manages its value chain activities relative to how well competitors manage theirs.[19] There are three main areas in a company's overall value chain where important differences in the costs of competing firms can occur: a company's own activity segments, suppliers' part of the industry value chain, and the forward channel portion of the industry chain.

When the source of a firm's cost disadvantage is internal, managers can use any of the following eight strategic approaches to restore cost parity:[20]

1. Implement the use of best practices throughout the company, particularly for high-cost activities.

2. Try to eliminate some cost-producing activities altogether by revamping the value chain. Examples include cutting out low-value-added activities or bypassing the value chains and associated costs of distribution allies and marketing directly to end users (the approach used by Gateway and Dell in PCs).

3. Relocate high-cost activities (such as R&D or manufacturing) to geographic areas where they can be performed more cheaply.

4. Search out activities that can be outsourced from vendors or performed by contractors more cheaply than they can be done internally.

5. Invest in productivity-enhancing, cost-saving technological improvements (robotics, flexible manufacturing techniques, state-of-the-art electronic networking).

6. Innovate around the troublesome cost components—computer chip makers regularly design around the patents held by others to avoid paying royalties; automakers have substituted lower-cost plastic and rubber for metal at many exterior body locations.

7. Simplify the product design so that it can be manufactured or assembled quickly and more economically.

Table 3.3   **OPTIONS FOR ATTACKING COST DISADVANTAGES ASSOCIATED WITH SUPPLY CHAIN ACTIVITIES OR FORWARD CHANNEL ALLIES**

Options for Attacking the High Costs of Items Purchased from Suppliers	Options for Attacking the High Costs of Forward Channel Allies
■ Negotiate more favorable prices with suppliers. ■ Work with suppliers on the design and specifications for what is being supplied to identify cost savings that will allow them to lower their prices. ■ Switch to lower-priced substitute inputs. ■ Collaborate closely with suppliers to identify mutual cost-saving opportunities. For example, just-in-time deliveries from suppliers can lower a company's inventory and internal logistics costs and may also allow its suppliers to economize on their warehousing, shipping, and production scheduling costs—a win–win outcome for both. ■ Integrate backward into the business of high-cost suppliers to gain control over the costs of purchased items—seldom an attractive option. ■ Try to make up the difference by cutting costs elsewhere in the chain—usually a last resort.	■ Push distributors and other forward channel allies to reduce their markups. ■ Work closely with forward channel allies to identify win–win opportunities to reduce costs. A chocolate manufacturer learned that by shipping its bulk chocolate in liquid form in tank cars instead of 10-pound molded bars, it could not only save its candy-bar manufacturing customers the costs associated with unpacking and melting but also eliminate its own costs of molding bars and packing them. ■ Change to a more economical distribution strategy, including switching to cheaper distribution channels (perhaps direct sales via the Internet) or perhaps integrating forward into company-owned retail outlets. ■ Try to make up the difference by cutting costs earlier in the cost chain—usually a last resort.

Source: Based in part on Michael E. Porter, *Competitive Advantage* (New York: Free Press, 1985), Chapter 3

8. Try to make up the internal cost disadvantage by achieving savings in other two parts of the value chain system—usually a last resort.

If a firm finds that it has a cost disadvantage stemming from costs in the supplier or forward channel portions of the industry value chain, then the task of reducing its costs to levels more in line with competitors usually has to extend beyond the firm's own in-house operations. Table 3.3 presents the strategy options for attacking high costs associated with supply chain activities or forward channel allies.

Translating Proficient Performance of Value Chain Activities into Competitive Advantage

A company that does a first rate job of managing its value chain activities relative to competitors stands a good chance of leveraging its competitively valuable competencies and capabilities into sustainable competitive advantage. With rare exceptions, company attempts to achieve competitive advantage with unique attributes and performance features seldom result in a durable competitive advantage. It is too easy for resourceful competitors to clone, improve on, or find an effective substitute for any unique features of a product or service.[21] A more fruitful approach to achieving and sustaining a competitive edge over rivals is for a company to develop competencies and capabilities that please buyers and that rivals don't have or can't quite match.

The process of translating proficient company performance of value chain activities into competitive advantage is shown in Figure 3.5. The road to competitive advantage begins with management efforts to build more organizational expertise in performing certain competitively important value chain activities, deliberately striving to develop competencies and capabilities that add power to its strategy

Performing value chain activities in ways that give a company the capabilities to outmatch rivals is a source of competitive advantage.

Figure 3.5   Translating Company Performance of Value Chain Activities into Competitive Advantage

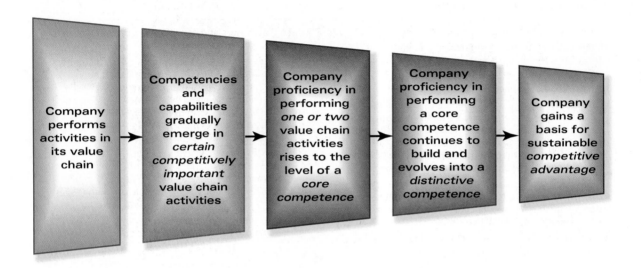

and competitiveness. If management begins to make one or two of these competencies and capabilities cornerstones of its strategy and continues to invest resources in building greater and greater proficiency in performing them, then over time one (or maybe both) of the targeted competencies/capabilities may rise to the level of a core competence. Later, following additional organizational learning and investments in gaining still greater proficiency, the core competence could evolve into a distinctive competence, giving the company superiority over rivals. Such superiority, if it gives the company significant competitive clout in the marketplace, could produce an attractive competitive edge over rivals and, more important, prove difficult for rivals to match or offset with competencies and capabilities of their own making. As a general rule, it is substantially harder for rivals to achieve "best in industry" proficiency in performing a key value chain activity than it is for them to clone the features and attributes of a hot-selling product or service. This is especially true when a company with a distinctive competence avoids becoming complacent and works diligently to maintain its industry-leading expertise and capability.

There are numerous examples of companies that have gained a competitive edge by building competencies and capabilities that outmatch those of rivals. Merck and Glaxo, two of the world's most competitively capable pharmaceutical companies, built their business positions around expert performance of a few competitively crucial activities: extensive R&D to achieve first discovery of new drugs, a carefully constructed approach to patenting, skill in gaining rapid and thorough clinical clearance through regulatory bodies, and unusually strong distribution and sales force capabilities.[22] Federal Express has linked and integrated the performance of its aircraft fleet, truck fleet, support systems, and personnel so tightly and smoothly across the company's different value chain activities that it has created the capability to provide customers with guaranteed overnight delivery services. McDonald's can turn out identical-quality fast-food items at some 25,000-plus outlets around the world—an impressive demonstration of its capability to replicate its operating systems at many locations via an omnibus manual of detailed rules and procedures for each activity and intensive training of franchise operators and outlet managers.

Assessing a Company's Competitive Strength

Using value chain analysis and benchmarking to determine a company's competitiveness on price and cost is necessary but not sufficient. A more comprehensive assessment needs to be made of the company's overall competitive strength. The answers to two questions are of particular interest: First, how does the company rank relative to competitors on each of the important factors that determine market success? Second, all things considered, does the company have a net competitive advantage or disadvantage vis-à-vis major competitors?

An easy-to-use method for answering the two questions posed above involves developing quantitative strength ratings for the company and its key competitors on each industry key success factor and each competitively decisive resource capability. Much of the information needed for doing a competitive strength assessment comes from previous analyses. Industry and competitive analysis reveals the key success factors and competitive capabilities that separate industry winners from losers. Benchmarking data and scouting key competitors provide a basis for judging the competitive strength of rivals on such factors as cost, key product attributes, customer service, image and reputation, financial strength, technological skills, distribution capability, and other competitively important resources and capabilities. SWOT analysis reveals how the company in question stacks up on these same strength measures.

Step 1 in doing a competitive strength assessment is to make a list of the industry's key success factors and most telling measures of competitive strength or weakness (6 to 10 measures usually suffice). Step 2 is to rate the firm and its rivals on each factor. Numerical rating scales (e.g., from 1 to 10) are best to use, although ratings of stronger (+), weaker (−), and about equal (=) may be appropriate when information is scanty and assigning numerical scores conveys false precision. Step 3 is to sum the strength ratings on each factor to get an overall measure of competitive strength for each company being rated. Step 4 is to use the overall strength ratings to draw conclusions about the size and extent of the company's net competitive advantage or disadvantage and to take specific note of areas of strength and weakness.

Table 3.4 provides two examples of competitive strength assessment, using the hypothetical ABC Company against four rivals. The first example employs an *unweighted rating system*. With unweighted ratings, each key success factor/competitive strength measure is assumed to be equally important (a rather dubious assumption). Whichever company has the highest strength rating on a given measure has an implied competitive edge on that factor; the size of its edge is mirrored in the margin of difference between its rating and the ratings assigned to rivals—a rating of 9 for one company versus ratings of 5, 4, and 3, respectively, for three other companies indicates a bigger advantage than a rating of 9 versus ratings of 8, 7, and 6. Summing a company's ratings on all the measures produces an overall strength rat-

High competitive strength ratings signal a strong competitive position and possession of competitive advantage; low ratings signal a weak position and competitive disadvantage.

ing. The higher a company's overall strength rating, the stronger its overall competitiveness versus rivals. The bigger the difference between a company's overall rating and the scores of *lower-rated* rivals, the greater its implied *net competitive advantage*.

Table 3.4 ILLUSTRATIONS OF UNWEIGHTED AND WEIGHTED COMPETITIVE STRENGTH ASSESSMENTS

A. Sample of an Unweighted Competitive Strength Assessment

Rating scale: 1 = Very weak; 10 = Very strong

Key Success Factor/ Strength Measure	ABC Co.	Rival 1	Rival 2	Rival 3	Rival 4
Quality/product performance	8	5	10	1	6
Reputation/image	8	7	10	1	6
Manufacturing capability	2	10	4	5	1
Technological skills	10	1	7	3	8
Dealer network/distribution capability	9	4	10	5	1
New product innovation capability	9	4	10	5	1
Financial resources	5	10	7	3	1
Relative cost position	5	10	3	1	4
Customer service capabilities	5	7	10	1	4
Unweighted overall strength rating	61	58	71	25	32

B. Sample of a Weighted Competitive Strength Assessment

Rating scale: 1 = Very weak; 10 = Very strong

Key Success Factor/ Strength Measure	Importance Weight	Ratings/Scores				
		ABC Co.	Rival 1	Rival 2	Rival 3	Rival 4
Quality/product performance	0.10	8/0.80	5/0.50	10/1.00	1/0.10	6/0.60
Reputation/image	0.10	8/0.80	7/0.70	10/1.00	1/0.10	6/0.60
Manufacturing capability	0.10	2/0.20	10/1.00	4/0.40	5/0.50	1/0.10
Technological skills	0.05	10/0.50	1/0.05	7/0.35	3/0.15	8/0.40
Dealer network/distribution capability	0.05	9/0.45	4/0.20	10/0.50	5/0.25	1/0.05
New product innovation capability	0.05	9/0.45	4/0.20	10/0.50	5/0.25	1/0.05
Financial resources	0.10	5/0.50	10/1.00	7/0.70	3/0.30	1/0.10
Relative cost position	0.30	5/1.50	10/3.00	3/0.95	1/0.30	4/1.20
Customer service capabilities	0.15	5/0.75	7/1.05	10/1.50	1/0.15	4/0.60
Sum of importance weights	1.00					
Weighted overall strength rating		5.95	7.70	6.85	2.10	3.70

Conversely, the bigger the difference between a company's overall rating and the scores of *higher-rated* rivals, the greater its implied *net competitive disadvantage*. Thus, ABC's total score of 61 (see the top half of Table 3.4) signals a much greater net competitive advantage over Rival 4 (with a score of 32) than over Rival 1 (with a score of 58) but indicates a moderate net competitive disadvantage against Rival 2 (with an overall score of 71).

However, a better method is a *weighted rating system* (shown in the bottom half of Table 3.4) because the different measures of competitive strength are unlikely to be equally important. In an industry where the products/services of rivals are virtually identical, for instance, having low unit costs relative to rivals is nearly always the most important determinant of competitive strength. In an industry with strong product differentiation, the most significant measures of competitive strength may be brand awareness, amount of advertising, product attractiveness, and distribution capability. In a weighted rating system each measure of competitive strength is assigned a weight based on its perceived importance in shaping competitive success. A weight could be as high as 0.75 (maybe even higher) in situations where one particular competitive variable is overwhelmingly decisive, or a weight could be as low as 0.20 when two or three strength measures are more important than the rest. Lesser competitive strength indicators can carry weights of 0.05 or 0.10. No matter whether the differences between the importance weights are big or little, *the sum of the weights must add up to 1.0.*

Weighted strength ratings are calculated by rating each competitor on each strength measure (using the 1 to 10 rating scale) and multiplying the assigned rating by the assigned weight (a rating of 4 times a weight of 0.20 gives a weighted rating, or score, of 0.80). Again, the company with the highest rating on a given measure has an implied competitive edge on that measure, with the size of its edge reflected in the difference between its rating and rivals' ratings. The weight attached to the measure indicates how important the edge is. Summing a company's weighted strength ratings for all the measures yields an overall strength rating. Comparisons of the weighted overall strength scores indicate which competitors are in the strongest and weakest competitive positions and who has how big a net competitive advantage over whom.

> A weighted competitive strength analysis is conceptually stronger than an unweighted analysis because of the inherent weakness in assuming that all the strength measures are equally important.

Note in Table 3.4 that the unweighted and weighted rating schemes produce different orderings of the companies. In the weighted system, ABC Company drops from second to third in strength, and Rival 1 jumps from third into first because of its high strength ratings on the two most important factors. Weighting the importance of the strength measures can thus make a significant difference in the outcome of the assessment.

Competitive strength assessments provide useful conclusions about a company's competitive situation. The ratings show how a company compares against rivals, factor by factor or capability by capability, thus revealing where it is strongest and weakest, and against whom. Moreover, the overall competitive strength scores indicate how all the different factors add up—whether the company is at a net competitive advantage or disadvantage against each rival. The firm with the largest overall competitive strength rating enjoys the strongest competitive position, with the size of its net competitive advantage reflected by how much its score exceeds the scores of rivals.

Knowing where a company is competitively strong and where it is weak in comparison to specific rivals is valuable in deciding on specific actions to strengthen its ability to compete. As a general rule, a company should try to leverage its competitive strengths (areas where it scores higher than rivals) into sustainable competitive advantage. Furthermore, it makes sense for the company to initiate actions to remedy its important competitive weaknesses (areas where its scores are below those of rivals); at the very least, it should try to narrow the gap against companies with higher strength ratings—when the leader is at 10, improving from a rating of 3 to a rating of 7 can be significant.

In addition, the competitive strength ratings point to which rival companies may be vulnerable to competitive attack and the areas where they are weakest. When a company has important competitive strengths in areas where one or more rivals are weak, it makes sense to consider offensive moves to exploit rivals' competitive weaknesses.

> High competitive strength ratings vis-à-vis competitors signal opportunity for a company to improve its long-term market position.

Identifying the Strategic Issues That Merit Managerial Attention

The final and most important analytical step is to zero in on exactly what strategic issues that company managers need to address—and resolve—for the company to be more financially and competitively successful in the years ahead. This step involves drawing on the results of both industry and competitive analysis and the evaluations of the company's own competitiveness. The task here is to get a clear fix on exactly what strategic and competitive challenges confront the company, which of the company's competitive shortcomings need fixing, what obstacles stand in the way of improving the company's competitive position in the marketplace, and what specific problems merit front-burner attention by company managers. *Pinpointing the precise things that management needs to worry about sets the agenda for deciding what actions to take next to improve the company's performance and business outlook.*

> Zeroing in on the strategic issues a company faces and compiling a "worry list" of problems and roadblocks creates a strategic agenda of problems that merit prompt managerial attention.

The "worry list" of issues and problems that have to be wrestled with can include such things as *how* to stave off market challenges from new foreign competitors, *how* to combat the price discounting of rivals, *how* to reduce the company's high costs and pave the way for price reductions, *how* to sustain the company's present rate of growth in light of slowing buyer demand, *whether* to expand the company's product line, *whether* to correct the company's competitive deficiencies by acquiring a rival company with the missing strengths, *whether* to expand into foreign markets rapidly or cautiously, *whether* to reposition the company and move to a different strategic group, *what to do* about growing buyer interest in substitute products, and *what to do* about the aging demographics of the company's customer base.

> A good strategy must contain ways to deal with all the strategic issues and obstacles that stand in the way of the company's financial and competitive success in the years ahead.

What turns up on the list of concerns about "how to . . . ," "whether to . . . ," and "what to do about . . . " signals whether the company will be able to continue the same basic strategy with minor adjustments or whether major overhaul is called for. If the worry list is relatively minor, thus suggesting the company's strategy is mostly on track and reasonably well matched to the company's overall situation, company managers seldom need to go much beyond fine-tuning of the present strategy. If, however, the issues and problems confronting the company are serious and indicate the present strategy is not well suited for the road ahead, the task of crafting a better strategy has got to go to the top of management's action agenda.

Key Points

There are five key questions to consider in analyzing a company's own particular competitive circumstances and its competitive position vis-à-vis key rivals:

1. *How well is the present strategy working?* This involves evaluating the strategy from a qualitative standpoint (completeness, internal consistency, rationale, and suitability to the situation) and also from a quantitative standpoint (the strategic and financial results the strategy is producing). The stronger a company's current

overall performance, the less likely the need for radical strategy changes. The weaker a company's performance and/or the faster the changes in its external situation (which can be gleaned from industry and competitive analysis), the more its current strategy must be questioned.

2. *What are the company's resource strengths and weaknesses, and its external opportunities and threats?* A SWOT analysis provides an overview of a firm's situation and is an essential component of crafting a strategy tightly matched to the company's situation. The two most important parts of SWOT analysis are (1) drawing conclusions about what story the compilation of strengths, weaknesses, opportunities, and threats tells about the company's overall situation, and (2) acting on those conclusions to better match the company's strategy, to its resource strengths and market opportunities, to correct the important weaknesses, and to defend against external threats. A company's resource strengths, competencies, and competitive capabilities are strategically relevant because they are the most logical and appealing building blocks for strategy; resource weaknesses are important because they may represent vulnerabilities that need correction. External opportunities and threats come into play because a good strategy necessarily aims at capturing a company's most attractive opportunities and at defending against threats to its well-being.

3. *Are the company's prices and costs competitive?* One telling sign of whether a company's situation is strong or precarious is whether its prices and costs are competitive with those of industry rivals. Value chain analysis and benchmarking are essential tools in determining whether the company is performing particular functions and activities cost-effectively, learning whether its costs are in line with competitors, and deciding which internal activities and business processes need to be scrutinized for improvement. Value chain analysis teaches that how competently a company manages its value chain activities relative to rivals is a key to building valuable competencies and competitive capabilities and then leveraging them into sustainable competitive advantage.

4. *Is the company competitively stronger or weaker than key rivals?* The key appraisals here involve how the company matches up against key rivals on industry key success factors and other chief determinants of competitive success and whether and why the company has a competitive advantage or disadvantage. Quantitative competitive strength assessments, using the method presented in Table 3.4, indicate where a company is competitively strong and weak, and provide insight into the company's ability to defend or enhance its market position. As a rule a company's competitive strategy should be built around its competitive strengths and should aim at shoring up areas where it is competitively vulnerable. Also, the areas where company strengths match up against competitor weaknesses represent the best potential for new offensive initiatives.

5. *What strategic issues and problems merit front-burner managerial attention?* This analytical step zeros in on the strategic issues and problems that stand in the way of the company's success. It involves using the results of both industry and competitive analysis and company situation analysis to identify a "worry list" of issues to be resolved for the company to be financially and competitively successful in the years ahead.

Good company situation analysis, like good industry and competitive analysis, is a valuable precondition for good strategy-making. A competently done evaluation of a company's resource capabilities and competitive strengths exposes strong and weak points in the present strategy and how attractive or unattractive the company's competitive position is and why. Managers need such understanding to craft a strategy that is well suited to the company's competitive circumstances.

Exercise

Review the information in Company Spotlight 3.1 concerning the costs of the different value chain activities associated with recording and distributing music CDs through traditional brick-and-mortar retail outlets. Then answer the following questions:

1. Does the growing popularity of downloading music from the Internet give rise to a new music industry value chain that differs considerably from the traditional value chain? Explain why or why not.

2. What costs are being cut out of the traditional value chain or bypassed as recording studios begin to sell downloadable files of artists' recordings and buyers make their own custom CDs (or play music directly from their PCs)?

3. How much more cost-effective is the value chain for selling downloadable files direct to consumers than the traditional industry value chain?

4. What do you think the growing popularity of downloading music from the Internet is doing to the competitiveness and future business prospects of brick-and-mortar retail music chains?

CHAPTER 4

Crafting a Strategy
The Quest for Competitive Advantage

Successful business strategy is about actively shaping the game you play, not just playing the game you find.
—Adam M. Brandenburger and Barry J. Nalebuff

The essence of strategy lies in creating tomorrow's competitive advantages faster than competitors mimic the ones you possess today.
—Gary Hamel and C. K. Prahalad

Competitive strategy is about being different. It means deliberately choosing to perform activities differently or to perform different activities than rivals to deliver a unique mix of value.
—Michael E. Porter

Strategies for taking the hill won't necessarily hold it.
—Amar Bhide

This chapter focuses on a company's quest for competitive advantage—the strategy options for competing successfully in a particular industry and securing an attractive market position. This chapter surveys the menu of options a company has for crafting a strategy that is well suited both to industry and competitive conditions and to its own resources and competitive circumstances and that holds good prospects for competitive advantage. We begin by describing the five *basic competitive strategy options*—which of the five to employ is a company's first and foremost choice in crafting an overall strategy. Next on a company's menu of strategic choices are the various *strategic actions* it can take to complement its choice of a basic competitive strategy:

- What use to make of strategic alliances and collaborative partnerships.
- What use to make of mergers and acquisitions.
- Whether to integrate backward or forward into more stages of the industry value chain.
- Whether to outsource certain value chain activities or perform them in-house.
- Whether and when to employ offensive and defensive moves.
- Which of several ways to use the Internet as a distribution channel in positioning the company in the marketplace.

This chapter contains sections discussing the pros and cons of each of the above complementary strategic options. The next-to-last section in the chapter discusses the need for strategic choices in each functional area of a company's business (R&D, production, sales and marketing, finance, and so on) to support its basic competitive approach and complementary strategic moves. The chapter concludes with a brief look at the competitive importance of timing strategic moves—when it is advantageous to be a first-mover and when it is better to be a fast-follower or late-mover.

Figure 4.1 shows the menu of options a company has in crafting a strategy and the order in which the choices should generally be made. It also illustrates the structure of the chapter and the topics that will be covered.

The Five Generic Competitive Strategies

A company's **competitive strategy** deals exclusively with its plans for competing successfully—its specific efforts to please customers, its offensive and defensive moves to counter the maneuvers of rivals, its responses to whatever market conditions prevail at the moment, and its initiatives to strengthen its market position. Companies the world over are imaginative in conceiving competitive strategies to win customer favor. At most companies the aim, quite simply, is to do a significantly better job than rivals of providing what buyers are looking for and thereby secure a market edge over rivals. Winning in the marketplace is nearly always a result of actions to seek and secure a sustainable competitive advantage. A company has *competitive advantage* whenever it has an edge over rivals in attracting buyers and coping with competitive forces. There are many routes to competitive advantage, but they all involve giving buyers what they

> **Core Concept**
>
> The objective of **competitive strategy** is to knock the socks off rival companies by doing a better job of providing what buyers are looking for.

Figure 4.2   The Five Generic Competitive Strategies:
Each Represents a Different Market Position

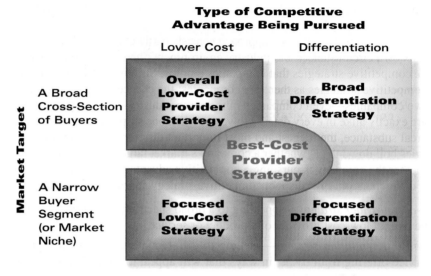

Source: Adapted from Michael E. Porter, *Competitive Strategy* (New York: Free Press, 1980), pp. 35–40.

buyers consider essential—*a product offering that is too frills-free sabotages the attractiveness of the company's product and can turn buyers off even if it is cheaper priced.* For maximum effectiveness, companies employing a low-cost provider strategy need to achieve their cost advantage in ways difficult for rivals to copy or match. If rivals find it relatively easy or inexpensive to imitate the leader's low-cost methods, then the leader's advantage will be too short-lived to yield a valuable edge in the marketplace.

A company has two options for translating a low-cost advantage over rivals into attractive profit performance. Option 1 is to use the lower-cost edge to underprice competitors and attract price-sensitive buyers in great enough numbers to increase total profits. The trick to profitably underpricing rivals is either to keep the size of the price cut smaller than the size of the firm's cost advantage (thus reaping the benefits of both a bigger profit margin per unit sold and the added profits on incremental sales) or to generate enough added volume to increase total profits despite thinner profit margins (larger volume can make up for smaller margins provided the underpricing of rivals brings in enough extra sales). Option 2 is to maintain the present price, be content with the present market share, and use the lower-cost edge to earn a higher profit margin on each unit sold, thereby raising the firm's total profits and overall return on investment.

Company Spotlight 4.1 describes Nucor Corporation's strategy for gaining low-cost leadership in manufacturing a variety of steel products.

The Two Major Avenues for Achieving a Cost Advantage   To achieve a cost advantage, a firm's cumulative costs across its overall value chain must be lower than competitors' cumulative costs. There are two ways to accomplish this:[2]

Table 4.1   DISTINGUISHING FEATURES OF THE FIVE GENERIC COMPETITIVE STRATEGIES

	Low-Cost Provider	Broad Differentiation	Best-Cost Provider	Focused Low-Cost Provider	Focused Differentiation
Strategic target	■ A broad cross-section of the market	■ A broad cross-section of the market	■ Value-conscious buyers	■ A narrow market niche where buyer needs and preferences are distinctively different	■ A narrow market niche where buyer needs and preferences are distinctively different
Basis of competitive advantage	■ Lower overall costs than competitors	■ Ability to offer buyers something attractively different from competitors	■ Ability to give customers more value for the money	■ Lower overall cost than rivals in serving niche members	■ Attributes that appeal specifically to niche members
Product line	■ A good basic product with few frills (acceptable quality and limited selection)	■ Many product variations; wide selection; emphasis on differentiating features	■ Items with appealing attributes; assorted upscale features	■ Features and attributes tailored to the tastes and requirements of niche members	■ Features and attributes tailored to the tastes and requirements of niche members
Production emphasis	■ A continuous search for cost reduction without sacrificing acceptable quality and essential features	■ Differentiating features buyers are willing to pay for; product superiority	■ Upscale features and appealing attributes at lower cost than rivals	■ A continuous search for cost reduction while incorporating features and attributes matched to niche member preferences	■ Custom-made products that match the tastes and requirements of niche members
Marketing emphasis	■ Try to make a virtue out of product features that lead to low cost	■ Tout differentiating features ■ Charge a premium price to cover the extra costs of differentiating features	■ Tout delivery of best value ■ Either deliver comparable features at a lower price than rivals or else match rivals on prices and provide better features	■ Communicate attractive features of a budget-priced product offering that fits niche buyers' expectations	■ Communicate how product offering does the best job of meeting niche buyers' expectations
Keys to sustaining the strategy	■ Economical prices/good value ■ Low costs, year after year, in every area of the business	■ Constant innovation to stay ahead of imitative competitors ■ A few key differentiating features	■ Unique expertise in simultaneously managing costs down while incorporating upscale features and attributes	■ Commitment to serving the niche at lowest overall cost; don't blur the firm's image by entering other market segments or adding other products to widen market appeal	■ Commitment to serving the niche better than rivals; don't blur the firm's image by entering other market segments or adding other products to widen market appeal

1. Outmanage rivals in the efficiency with which value chain activities are performed and in controlling the factors that drive the costs of value chain activities.

2. Revamp the firm's overall value chain to eliminate or bypass some cost-producing activities.

Let's look at each of the two approaches to securing a cost advantage.

COMPANY SPOTLIGHT 4.1

Nucor Corporation's Low-Cost Provider Strategy

Nucor Corporation is the leading minimill producer of such steel products as rolled steel, finished steel, steel joists, joist girders, steel decks, and grinding balls. It has over $4 billion in sales and produces over 10 million tons of steel annually. The company has pursued a strategy that has made it among the lowest-cost producers of steel in the world and has allowed the company to consistently outperform its rivals in terms of financial and market performance.

Nucor's low-cost strategy aims to give it a cost and pricing advantage in the commoditylike steel industry and leaves no part of the company's value chain neglected. The key elements of the strategy include the following:

■ Using electric arc furnaces where scrap steel and directly reduced iron ore are melted and then sent to a continuous caster and rolling mill to be shaped into steel products, thereby eliminating an assortment of production processes from the value chain used by traditional integrated steel mills. Nucor's minimill value chain

makes the use of coal, coke, and iron ore unnecessary; cuts investment in facilities and equipment (eliminating coke ovens, blast furnaces, basic oxygen furnaces, and ingot casters); and requires fewer employees than integrated mills.

■ Striving hard for continuous improvement in the efficiency of its plants and frequently investing in state-of-the-art equipment to reduce unit costs. Nucor is known for its technological leadership and its aggressive pursuit of innovation.

■ Carefully selecting plant sites to minimize inbound and outbound shipping costs and to take advantage of low rates for electricity (electric arc furnaces are heavy users of electricity). Nucor also avoids geographic areas where labor unions are a strong influence.

■ Hiring a nonunion workforce that uses team-based incentive compensation systems (often opposed by unions). Operating and maintenance employees and supervisors are paid weekly bonuses based on the productivity of

Controlling the Cost Drivers There are nine major cost drivers that come into play in determining a company's costs in each activity segment of the value chain:[3]

1. *Economies or diseconomies of scale*—The costs of a particular value chain activity are often subject to economies or diseconomies of scale. Economies of scale arise whenever activities can be performed more cheaply at larger volumes than smaller volumes and from the ability to spread out certain costs like R&D and advertising over a greater sales volume. Astute management of activities subject to scale economies or diseconomies can be a major source of cost savings. For example, manufacturing economies can usually be achieved by simplifying the product line, scheduling longer production runs for fewer models, and using common parts and components in different models. In global industries, making separate products for each country market instead of selling a mostly standard product worldwide tends to boost unit costs because of lost time in model changeover, shorter production runs, and inability to reach the most economic scale of production for each country model.

2. *Experience and learning-curve effects*—The cost of performing an activity can decline over time as the learning and experience of company personnel builds. Learning/experience economies can stem from debugging and mastering newly introduced technologies, finding ways to improve plant layout and work flows, making product design modifications that streamline the assembly process, and the

their work group. The size of the bonus is based on the capabilities of the equipment employed and ranges from 80 percent to 150 percent of an employee's base pay; no bonus is paid if the equipment is not operating. Nucor's compensation program has boosted the company's labor productivity to levels nearly double the industry average while rewarding productive employees with annual compensation packages that exceed what their union counterparts earn by as much as 20 percent. Nucor has been able to attract and retain highly talented, productive, and dedicated employees. In addition, the company's healthy culture and results-oriented self-managed work teams allow the company to employ fewer supervisors than what would be needed with an hourly union workforce. Nucor is proud of the more than 7,000 employees that make up the total Nucor team.

- Heavily emphasizing consistent product quality and has rigorous quality systems.

- Minimizing general and administrative expenses by maintaining a lean staff at corporate headquarters (fewer than 125 employees) and allowing only four levels of management between the CEO and production workers. Headquarters offices are modestly furnished and located in an inexpensive building. The company minimizes reports, paperwork, and meetings to keep managers focused on value-adding activities. Nucor is noted not only for its streamlined organizational structure but also its frugality in travel and entertainment expenses—the company's top managers set the example by flying coach class, avoiding pricey hotels, and refraining from taking customers out for expensive dinners.

In 2001–2002, when many U.S. producers of steel products were in dire economic straits because of weak demand for steel and deep price discounting by foreign rivals, Nucor began acquiring state-of-the-art steel making facilities from bankrupt or nearly bankrupt rivals at bargain-basement prices, often at 20 percent to 25 percent of what it cost to construct the facilities. This gave Nucor much lower depreciation costs than rivals having comparable plants.

Nucor management's outstanding execution of its low-cost strategy and its commitment to drive out non-value-adding costs throughout its value chain has allowed it to grow at a considerably faster rate than its integrated steel mill rivals and maintain high industry-relative profit margins while aggressively competing on price. In 2002, Nucor became the largest U.S. producer of steel products, overtaking U.S. Steel, the industry leader for over 70 years.

Source: Company annual reports, news releases, and website.

added speed and knowledge that accrues from repeatedly siting and building new plants, retail outlets, or distribution centers. Aggressively managed low-cost providers pay diligent attention to capturing the benefits of learning and experience and to keeping the benefits proprietary to whatever extent possible.

3. *The cost of key resource inputs*—The cost of performing value chain activities depends in part on what a firm has to pay for key resource inputs. Competitors do not all incur the same costs for items purchased from suppliers or for other resources. How well a company manages the costs of acquiring key resource inputs is often a big driver of costs. Input costs are a function of four factors:

a) *Union versus nonunion labor*—Avoiding the use of union labor is often a key to keeping labor input costs low, not just because unions demand high wages but also because union work rules can stifle productivity. Such highly regarded low-cost manufacturers as Nucor and Cooper Tire are noted for their incentive compensation systems that promote very high levels of labor productivity—at both companies, nonunion workers earn more than their unionized counterparts at rival companies but their high productivity results in lower labor costs per unit produced.

b) *Bargaining power vis-à-vis suppliers*—Many large enterprises (e.g., Wal-Mart, Home Depot, the world's major motor vehicle producers) have used their bargaining clout in purchasing large volumes to wrangle good prices on their purchases from suppliers. Having greater buying power than rivals can be an important source of cost advantage.

     c) *Locational variables*—Locations differ in their prevailing wage levels, tax rates, energy costs, inbound and outbound shipping and freight costs, and so on. Opportunities may exist for reducing costs by relocating plants, field offices, warehousing, or headquarters operations.

     d) *Supply chain management expertise*—Some companies have more efficient supply chain expertise than others and are able to squeeze out cost savings via partnerships with suppliers that lower the costs of purchased materials and components, e-procurement systems, and inbound logistics.

4. *Links with other activities in the company or industry value chain*—When the cost of one activity is affected by how other activities are performed, costs can be managed downward by making sure that linked activities are performed in cooperative and coordinated fashion. For example, when a company's materials inventory costs or warranty costs are linked to the activities of suppliers, cost savings can be achieved by working cooperatively with key suppliers on the design of parts and components, quality-assurance procedures, just-in-time delivery, and integrated materials supply. The costs of new product development can often be managed downward by having cross-functional task forces (perhaps including representatives of suppliers and key customers) jointly work on R&D, product design, manufacturing plans, and market launch. Links with forward channels tend to center on location of warehouses, materials handling, outbound shipping, and packaging. Nail manufacturers, for example, learned that delivering nails in prepackaged 1-pound, 5-pound, and 10-pound assortments instead of 100-pound bulk cartons could reduce a hardware dealer's labor costs in filling individual customer orders. The lesson here is that effective coordination of linked activities anywhere in the value chain holds potential for cost reduction.

5. *Sharing opportunities with other organizational or business units within the enterprise*—Different product lines or business units within an enterprise can often share the same order processing and customer billing systems, utilize a common sales force to call on customers, share the same warehouse and distribution facilities, or rely on a common customer service and technical support team. Such combining of like activities and sharing of resources across sister units can create significant cost savings. Furthermore, there are times when the know-how gained in one division or geographic unit can be used to help lower costs in another; sharing know-how across organizational lines has significant cost-saving potential when cross-unit value chain activities are similar and know-how is readily transferred from one unit to another.

6. *The benefits of vertical integration versus outsourcing*—Partially or fully integrating into the activities of either suppliers or distribution channel allies can allow an enterprise to detour suppliers or buyers with considerable bargaining power. Vertical integration forward or backward also has potential if there are significant cost-savings from having a single firm perform adjacent activities in the industry value chain. But more often it is cheaper to outsource certain functions and activities to outside specialists, who by virtue of their expertise and volume can perform the activity/function more cheaply.

7. *Timing considerations associated with first-mover advantages and disadvantages*—Sometimes the first major brand in the market is able to establish and maintain its brand name at a lower cost than later brand arrivals. Competitors looking to go head-to-head against such first-movers as eBay, Yahoo!, and Amazon.com have to spend heavily to come close to achieving the same brand awareness and name recognition.

On other occasions, such as when technology is developing fast, late-purchasers can benefit from waiting to install second- or third-generation equipment that is both cheaper and more efficient; first-generation users often incur added costs associated with debugging and learning how to use an immature and unperfected technology. Likewise, companies that follow rather than lead new product development efforts sometimes avoid many of the costs that pioneers incur in performing pathbreaking R&D and opening up new markets.

8. *The percentage of capacity utilization*—Capacity utilization is a big cost driver for those value chain activities associated with substantial fixed costs. Higher rates of capacity utilization allow depreciation and other fixed costs to be spread over a larger unit volume, thereby lowering fixed costs per unit. The more capital-intensive the business, or the higher the percentage of fixed costs as a percentage of total costs, the more important this cost driver becomes because there's such a stiff unit-cost penalty for underutilizing existing capacity. In such cases, finding ways to operate close to full capacity year-round can be an important source of cost advantage.

9. *Strategic choices and operating decisions*—A company's costs can be driven up or down by a fairly wide assortment of managerial decisions:

a) Adding/cutting the services provided to buyers.

b) Incorporating more/fewer performance and quality features into the product.

c) Increasing/decreasing the number of different channels utilized in distributing the firm's product.

d) Lengthening/shortening delivery times to customers.

e) Putting more/less emphasis than rivals on the use of incentive compensation, wage increases, and fringe benefits to motivate employees and boost worker productivity.

f) Raising/lowering the specifications for purchased materials.

For a company to outmanage rivals in performing value chain activities cost-effectively, its managers must possess a sophisticated understanding of the factors that drive the costs of each activity. And then they must not only use their knowledge about the cost drivers to squeeze out cost savings all along the value chain but also be so much more ingenious and committed than rivals in achieving cost-saving efficiencies that the company ends up with a sustainable cost advantage.

> Outperforming rivals in controlling the factors that drive costs is a very demanding managerial exercise.

Revamping the Value Chain Dramatic cost advantages can emerge from finding innovative ways to eliminate or bypass cost-producing value chain activities. The primary ways companies can achieve a cost advantage by reconfiguring their value chains include:

■ *Making greater use of Internet technology applications*—In recent years the Internet and Internet technology applications have become powerful and pervasive tools for reengineering company and industry value chains. For instance, Internet technology has revolutionized supply chain management. Using software packages from any of several vendors, company procurement personnel can—with only a few mouse clicks within one seamless system—check materials inventories against incoming customer orders, check suppliers' stocks, check the latest prices for parts and components at auction and e-sourcing websites, and check Federal Express delivery schedules. Electronic data interchange software permits the relevant details of incoming customer orders to be instantly shared with the suppliers of needed parts and components. All this lays the foundation for just-in-time deliveries of parts and components, and for the production of parts and components, to be matched closely to assembly plant requirements and production schedules—and such coordination produces savings for both suppliers and manufacturers. Via the Internet, manufacturers can collaborate closely with parts and components suppliers in designing new products and reducing the time it takes to get them into production. Warranty claims and product performance problems involving supplier components can be made available instantly to the relevant suppliers so that corrections can be expedited. Various e-procurement software packages streamline the purchasing process by eliminating much of the manual handling of data and by substituting electronic communication for paper documents such as requests for quotations, purchase orders, order acceptances, and shipping notices.

Manufacturers are using Internet applications to link customer orders to production at their plants and to deliveries of components from suppliers. Real-time sharing of customer orders with suppliers facilitates just-in-time deliveries of parts and slices parts inventory costs. It also allows both manufacturers and their suppliers to gear production to match demand for both components and finished goods. Online systems that monitor actual sales permit more accurate demand forecasting, thereby helping both manufacturers and their suppliers adjust their production schedules as swings in buyer demand are detected. Data sharing, starting with customer orders and going all the way back to components production, coupled with the use of enterprise resource planning (ERP) and manufacturing execution system (MES) software, can make custom manufacturing just as cheap as mass production—and sometimes cheaper. It can also greatly reduce production times and labor costs. J. D. Edwards, a specialist in ERP software, teamed with Camstar Systems, a specialist in MES software, to cut Lexmark's production time for inkjet printers from four hours to 24 minutes.

The instant communications features of the Internet, combined with all the real-time data sharing and information availability, have the further effect of breaking down corporate bureaucracies and reducing overhead costs. The whole "back-office" data management process (order processing, invoicing, customer accounting, and other kinds of transaction costs) can be handled fast, accurately, and with less paperwork and fewer personnel. The time savings and transaction cost reductions associated with doing business online can be quite significant across both company and industry value chains.

Company Spotlight 4.2 describes how one company is using Internet technology to improve both the effectiveness and the efficiency of the activities comprising its potato chip business.

▪ *Using direct-to-end-user sales and marketing approaches*—Costs in the wholesale/retail portions of the value chain frequently represent 35–50 percent of the price final consumers pay. Software developers are increasingly using the Internet to market and deliver their products directly to buyers; allowing customers to download software directly from the Internet eliminates the costs of producing and packaging CDs and cuts out the host of activities, costs, and markups associated with shipping and distributing software through wholesale and retail channels. By cutting all these costs and activities out of the value chain, software developers have the pricing room to boost their profit margins and still sell their products below levels that retailers would have to charge. The major airlines have stopped

Utz Quality Foods' Use of Internet Technology to Reengineer Value Chain Activities

Utz Quality Foods, the number three maker of salty snacks in the United States, with sales of over $200 million, recently implemented an Internet-based sales-tracking system called UtzFocus that monitors sales of the company's chips and pretzel products at each supermarket and convenience store that carries the brand. The 500 drivers/salespeople who deliver Utz snacks directly to retail stores scattered from Massachusetts to North Carolina use handheld computers to upload daily sales data (product by product and store by store) to headquarters. Managers carefully monitor the results to spot missed deliveries, pinpoint stores with lagging sales, and measure the effectiveness of special promotions.

The UtzFocus system also keeps delivery personnel up-to-date on which stores are running specials on Utz products so that drivers can make sure they have ample supplies of the right products on their trucks—and since drivers get a 10 percent commission on sales, they have a stake in making UtzFocus work. The company has also installed machines with monitoring capabilities in all of its plants, and efforts are under way to hook them up to the company's intranet to generate real-time data on the usage of ingredients, measure how close chip-slicing machines are coming to the ideal thickness of 0.057 of an inch, track how many bags of chips the main factory's seven lines are turning out, and keep inventories of ingredients and plastic bags matched to production and sales requirements. This reengineering of the value chain has produced cost-saving efficiencies, improved the effectiveness of Utz's operations, and helped boost sales.

paying commissions to travel agents on ticket sales, thereby saving hundreds of millions of dollars in commissions. Airlines now sell most of their tickets directly to passengers via their websites, ticket counter agents, and telephone reservation systems.

- *Simplifying product design*—Using computer-assisted design techniques, reducing the number of parts, standardizing parts and components across models and styles, and shifting to an easy-to-manufacture product design can all simplify the value chain.

- *Stripping away the extras*—Offering only basic products or services can help a company cut costs associated with multiple features and options. Stripping extras is a favorite technique of the no-frills airlines like Southwest Airlines.

- *Shifting to a simpler, less capital-intensive, or more streamlined or flexible technological process*—Computer-assisted design and manufacture, or other flexible manufacturing systems, can accommodate both low-cost efficiency and product customization.

- *Bypassing the use of high-cost raw materials or component parts*—High-cost raw materials and parts can be designed out of the product.

- *Relocating facilities*—Moving plants closer to suppliers, customers, or both can help curtail inbound and outbound logistics costs.

- *Dropping the "something for everyone" approach*—Pruning slow-selling items from the product lineup and being content to meet the needs of most buyers rather than all buyers can eliminate activities and costs associated with numerous product versions.

An example of accruing significant cost advantages from creating altogether new value chain systems can be found in the beef-packing industry. The traditional cost chain involved raising cattle on scattered farms and ranches, shipping them live to labor-intensive, unionized slaughtering plants, and then transporting whole sides of beef to grocery retailers whose butcher departments cut them into smaller pieces and packaged them for sale to grocery shoppers. Iowa Beef Packers revamped the traditional chain with a radically different strategy—large automated plants employing nonunion workers were built near economically transportable supplies of cattle, and the meat was partially butchered at the processing plant into small, high-yield cuts (sometimes sealed in plastic casing ready for purchase) before being boxed and shipped to retailers. Iowa Beef's inbound cattle transportation expenses, traditionally a major cost item, were cut significantly by avoiding the weight losses that occurred when live animals were shipped long distances; major outbound shipping cost savings were achieved by not having to ship whole sides of beef with their high waste factor. The company's strategy was so successful that Iowa Beef became the largest U.S. meatpacker, surpassing the former industry leaders, Swift, Wilson, and Armour.[4]

Southwest Airlines has reconfigured the traditional value chain of commercial airlines to lower costs and thereby offer dramatically lower fares to passengers. It has mastered fast turnarounds at the gates (about 25 minutes versus 45 minutes for rivals); because the short turnarounds allow the planes to fly more hours per day, Southwest can schedule more flights per day with fewer aircraft. Southwest does not offer in-flight meals, assigned seating, baggage transfer to connecting airlines, or first-class seating and service, thereby eliminating all the cost-producing activities associated with these features. The company's online reservation system and e-ticketing capability encourage customers to bypass travel agents and also reduce staffing requirements at telephone reservation centers and at check-in counters.

Dell Computer has proved a pioneer in redesigning its value chain architecture in assembling and marketing PCs. Whereas Dell's major rivals (Compaq, Hewlett-Packard, Sony, and Toshiba) produce their models in volume and sell them through independent resellers and retailers, Dell has elected to market directly to customers, building its PCs as customers order them and shipping them to customers within a few days of receiving the order. Dell's value chain approach has proved cost-effective in coping with the PC industry's blink-of-an-eye product life cycle. The build-to-order strategy enables the company to avoid misjudging buyer demand for its various models and being saddled with quickly obsolete excess components and finished-goods inventories. Also, Dell's sell-direct strategy slices reseller/retailer costs and margins out of the value chain (although some of these savings are offset by the cost of Dell's direct marketing and customer support activities—functions that would otherwise be performed by resellers and retailers). Partnerships with suppliers that facilitate just-in-time deliveries of components and minimize Dell's inventory costs, coupled with Dell's extensive use of e-commerce technologies further reduce Dell's costs. Dell's value chain approach is widely considered to have made it the global low-cost leader in the PC industry.

The Keys to Success in Achieving Low-Cost Leadership   To succeed with a low-cost-provider strategy, company managers have to scrutinize each cost-creating activity and determine what drives its cost. Then they have to use this knowledge about the cost drivers to manage the costs of each activity downward, exhaustively pursuing cost savings throughout the value chain. They have to be proactive in restructuring the value chain to eliminate nonessential work steps and low-value activities. Normally, low-cost producers work diligently to create cost-conscious corporate cultures

> Success in achieving a low-cost edge over rivals comes from exploring all the avenues for cost reduction and pressing for continuous cost reductions across all aspects of the company's value chain year after year.

that feature broad employee participation in continuous cost improvement efforts and limited perks and frills for executives. They strive to operate with exceptionally small corporate staffs to keep administrative costs to a minimum. Many successful low-cost leaders also benchmark costs against best-in-class performers of an activity to keep close tabs on how well they are doing at cost control.

But while low-cost providers are champions of frugality, they are usually aggressive in investing in resources and capabilities that promise to drive costs out of the business. Wal-Mart, one of the foremost practitioners of low-cost leadership, employs state-of-the-art technology throughout its operations—its distribution facilities are an automated showcase, it uses online systems to order goods from suppliers and manage inventories, it equips its stores with cutting-edge sales-tracking and check-out systems, and it operates a private satellite communications system that daily sends point-of-sale data to 4,000 vendors. Wal-Mart's information and communications systems and capabilities are more sophisticated than those of virtually any other retail chain in the world.

Other companies noted for their successful use of low-cost provider strategies include Lincoln Electric in arc welding equipment, Briggs & Stratton in small gasoline engines, Bic in ballpoint pens, Black & Decker in power tools, Stride Rite in footwear, Beaird-Poulan in chain saws, and General Electric and Whirlpool in major home appliances.

When a Low-Cost Provider Strategy Works Best   A competitive strategy predicated on low-cost leadership is particularly powerful when:

- *Price competition among rival sellers is especially vigorous*—Low-cost providers are in the best position to compete offensively on the basis of price, to use the appeal of lower price to grab sales (and market share) from rivals, to remain profitable in the face of strong price competition, and to survive price wars.

- *The products of rival sellers are essentially identical and supplies are readily available from any of several eager sellers*—Commoditylike products and/or ample supplies set the stage for lively price competition; in such markets, it is less efficient, higher-cost companies whose profits get squeezed the most.

- *There are few ways to achieve product differentiation that have value to buyers*—When the differences between brands do not matter much to buyers, buyers are nearly always very sensitive to price differences and shop the market for the best price.

- *Most buyers use the product in the same ways*—With common user requirements, a standardized product can satisfy the needs of buyers, in which case low selling price, not features or quality, becomes the dominant factor in causing buyers to choose one seller's product over another's.

- *Buyers incur low costs in switching their purchases from one seller to another*—Low switching costs give buyers the flexibility to shift purchases to lower-priced sellers having equally good products or to attractively priced substitute products. A low-cost leader is well positioned to use low price to induce its customers not to switch to rival brands or substitutes.

- *Buyers are large and have significant power to bargain down prices*—Low-cost providers have partial profit-margin protection in bargaining with high-volume buyers, since powerful buyers are rarely able to bargain price down past the survival level of the next most cost-efficient seller.

■ *Industry newcomers use introductory low prices to attract buyers and build a customer base*—The low-cost leader can use price cuts of its own to make it harder for a new rival to win customers; the pricing power of the low-cost provider acts as a barrier for new entrants.

As a rule, the more price-sensitive buyers are, the more appealing a low-cost strategy becomes. A low-cost company's ability to set the industry's price floor and still earn a profit erects protective barriers around its market position.

> A low-cost provider is in the best position to win the business of price-sensitive buyers, set the floor on market price, and still earn a profit.

The Pitfalls of a Low-Cost Provider Strategy   Perhaps the biggest pitfall of a low-cost provider strategy is getting carried away with overly aggressive price cutting and ending up with lower, rather than higher, profitability. A low-cost/low-price advantage results in superior profitability only if (1) prices are cut by less than the size of the cost advantage or (2) the added gains in unit sales are large enough to bring in a bigger total profit despite lower margins per unit sold. A company with a 5 percent cost advantage cannot cut prices 20 percent, end up with a volume gain of only 10 percent, and still expect to earn higher profits!

A second big pitfall is not emphasizing avenues of cost advantage that can be kept proprietary or that relegate rivals to playing catch-up. The value of a cost advantage depends on its sustainability. Sustainability, in turn, hinges on whether the company achieves its cost advantage in ways difficult for rivals to copy or match.

> A low-cost provider's product offering must always contain enough attributes to be attractive to prospective buyers—low price, by itself, is not always appealing to buyers.

A third pitfall is becoming too fixated on cost reduction. Low cost cannot be pursued so zealously that a firm's offering ends up being too features-poor to generate buyer appeal. Furthermore, a company driving hard to push its costs down has to guard against misreading or ignoring increased buyer interest in added features or service, declining buyer sensitivity to price, or new developments that start to alter how buyers use the product. A low-cost zealot risks losing market ground if buyers start opting for more upscale or features-rich products.

Even if these mistakes are avoided, a low-cost competitive approach still carries risk. Cost-saving technological breakthroughs or the emergence of still-lower-cost value chain models can nullify a low-cost leader's hard-won position. The current leader may have difficulty in shifting quickly to the new technologies or value chain approaches because heavy investments lock it in (at least temporarily) to its present value chain approach.

Differentiation Strategies

> **Core Concept**
>
> The essence of a broad differentiation strategy is to be unique in ways that are valuable to a wide range of customers.

Differentiation strategies are attractive whenever buyers' needs and preferences are too diverse to be fully satisfied by a standardized product or by sellers with identical capabilities. A company attempting to succeed through differentiation must study buyers' needs and behavior carefully to learn what buyers consider important, what they think has value, and what they are willing to pay for. Then the company has to incorporate buyer-desired attributes into its product or service offering that will clearly set it apart from rivals. Competitive advantage results once a sufficient number of buyers become strongly attached to the differentiated attributes.

Successful differentiation allows a firm to:

- Command a premium price for its product, and/or

- Increase unit sales (because additional buyers are won over by the differentiating features), and/or

- Gain buyer loyalty to its brand (because some buyers are strongly attracted to the differentiating features and bond with the company and its products).

Differentiation enhances profitability whenever the extra price the product commands outweighs the added costs of achieving the differentiation. Company differentiation strategies fail when buyers don't value the brand's uniqueness and/or when a company's approach to differentiation is easily copied or matched by its rivals.

Types of Differentiation Themes   Companies can pursue differentiation from many angles: a unique taste (Dr Pepper, Listerine); multiple features (Microsoft Windows, Microsoft Office); wide selection and one-stop shopping (Home Depot, Amazon.com); superior service (Federal Express); spare parts availability (Caterpillar guarantees 48-hour spare parts delivery to any customer anywhere in the world or else the part is furnished free); engineering design and performance (Mercedes, BMW); prestige and distinctiveness (Rolex); product reliability (Johnson & Johnson in baby products); quality manufacture (Karastan in carpets, Michelin in tires, Honda in automobiles); technological leadership (3M Corporation in bonding and coating products); a full range of services (Charles Schwab in stock brokerage); a complete line of products (Campbell's soups); and top-of-the-line image and reputation (Ralph Lauren and Starbucks).

The most appealing approaches to differentiation are those that are hard or expensive for rivals to duplicate. Indeed, resourceful competitors can, in time, clone almost any product or feature or attribute. If Coca-Cola introduces a vanilla-flavored soft drink, so can Pepsi; if Ford offers a 50,000-mile bumper-to-bumper warranty on its new vehicles, so can Volkswagen and Nissan. This is why *sustainable* differentiation usually has to be linked to core competencies, unique competitive capabilities, and superior management of value chain activities that competitors cannot readily match. As a rule, differentiation yields a longer-lasting and more profitable competitive edge when it is based on product innovation, technical superiority, product quality and reliability, comprehensive customer service, and unique competitive capabilities. Such differentiating attributes tend to be tough for rivals to copy or offset profitably, and buyers widely perceive them as having value.

> Easy-to-copy differentiating features cannot produce sustainable competitive advantage.

Where along the Value Chain to Create the Differentiating Attributes   Differentiation is not something hatched in marketing and advertising departments, nor is it limited to the catchalls of quality and service. Differentiation opportunities can exist in activities all along an industry's value chain; possibilities include the following:

- *Supply chain activities* that ultimately spill over to affect the performance or quality of the company's end product. Starbucks gets high ratings on its coffees partly because it has very strict specifications on the coffee beans purchased from suppliers.

- *Product R&D activities* that aim at improved product designs and performance features, expanded end uses and applications, more frequent first-on-the-market victories, wider product variety and selection, added user safety, greater recycling capability, or enhanced environmental protection.

▪ *Production R&D and technology-related activities* that permit custom-order manufacture at an efficient cost; make production methods safer for the environment; or improve product quality, reliability, and appearance. Many manufacturers have developed flexible manufacturing systems that allow different models to be made or different options to be added on the same assembly line. Being able to provide buyers with made-to-order products can be a potent differentiating capability.

▪ *Manufacturing activities* that reduce product defects, prevent premature product failure, extend product life, allow better warranty coverages, improve economy of use, result in more end-user convenience, or enhance product appearance. The quality edge enjoyed by Japanese automakers stems partly from their distinctive competence in performing assembly-line activities.

▪ *Outbound logistics and distribution activities* that allow for faster delivery, more accurate order filling, lower shipping costs, and fewer warehouse and on-the-shelf stockouts.

▪ *Marketing, sales, and customer service activities* that result in superior technical assistance to buyers, faster maintenance and repair services, more and better product information provided to customers, more and better training materials for end users, better credit terms, quicker order processing, or greater customer convenience.

Managers need keen understanding of the sources of differentiation and the activities that drive uniqueness to devise a sound differentiation strategy and evaluate various differentiation approaches.

Achieving a Differentiation-Based Competitive Advantage

While it is easy enough to grasp that a successful differentiation strategy must entail creating buyer value in ways unmatched by rivals, the big question is which of four basic differentiating approaches to take in delivering unique buyer value. One approach is to *incorporate product attributes and user features that lower the buyer's overall costs of using the company's product.* Making a company's product more economical for a buyer to use can be done by reducing the buyer's raw materials waste (providing cut-to-size components), reducing a buyer's inventory requirements (providing just-in-time deliveries), increasing maintenance intervals and product reliability so as to lower a buyer's repair and maintenance costs, using online systems to reduce a buyer's procurement and order processing costs, and providing free technical support.

A second approach is to *incorporate features that raise product performance.*[5] This can be accomplished with attributes that provide buyers greater reliability, durability, convenience, or ease of use. Other performance-enhancing options include making the company's product or service cleaner, safer, quieter, or more maintenance-free than rival brands. A third approach is to *incorporate features that enhance buyer satisfaction in noneconomic or intangible ways.* Goodyear's Aquatread tire design appeals to safety-conscious motorists wary of slick roads. BMW, Ralph Lauren, and Rolex have differentiation-based competitive advantages linked to buyer desires for status, image, prestige, upscale fashion, superior craftsmanship, and the finer things in life. L. L. Bean makes its mail-order customers feel secure in their purchases by providing an unconditional guarantee with no time limit: "All of our products are guaranteed to give 100 percent satisfaction in every way. Return anything purchased from us at any time if it proves otherwise. We will replace it, refund your purchase price, or credit your credit card, as you wish."

Core Concept

A differentiator's basis for competitive advantage is either a product/service offering whose attributes differ significantly from the offerings of rivals or a set of capabilities for delivering customer value that rivals don't have.

A fourth approach is to differentiate on the basis of capabilities—*to deliver value to customers via competitive capabilities that rivals don't have or can't afford to match.*[6] Japanese automakers can bring new models to market faster than American and European automakers, thereby allowing the Japanese companies to satisfy changing consumer preferences for one vehicle style versus another. CNN has the capability to cover breaking news stories faster and more completely than the major networks. Microsoft has stronger capabilities to design, create, distribute, and advertise an array of software products for PC applications than any of its rivals.

Keeping the Cost of Differentiation in Line Company efforts to achieve differentiation usually raise costs. The trick to profitable differentiation is either to keep the costs of achieving differentiation below the price premium the differentiating attributes can command in the marketplace (thus increasing the profit margin per unit sold) or to offset thinner profit margins with enough added volume to increase total profits. It usually makes sense to incorporate differentiating features that are not costly but that add to buyer satisfaction. Federal Express (FedEx) installed systems that allowed customers to track packages in transit by connecting to FedEx's website and entering the airbill number; some hotels and motels provide free continental breakfasts, exercise facilities, and in-room coffeemaking amenities; publishers are using their websites to deliver complementary educational materials to the buyers of their textbooks.

When a Differentiation Strategy Works Best Differentiation strategies tend to work best in market circumstances where:

■ *There are many ways to differentiate the product or service and many buyers perceive these differences as having value*—Unless buyers have strong preferences about certain features, profitable differentiation opportunities are very restricted.

■ *Buyer needs and uses are diverse*—The more diverse buyer preferences are, the more room firms have to pursue different approaches to differentiation.

■ *Few rival firms are following a similar differentiation approach*—There is less head-to-head rivalry when differentiating rivals go separate ways in pursuing uniqueness and try to appeal to buyers on different combinations of attributes.

■ *Technological change is fast-paced and competition revolves around rapidly evolving product features*—Rapid product innovation and frequent introductions of next-version products help maintain buyer interest and provide space for companies to pursue separate differentiating paths.

The Pitfalls of a Differentiation Strategy There are, of course, no guarantees that differentiation will produce a meaningful competitive advantage. If buyers see little value in the unique attributes or capabilities of a product, then the company's differentiation strategy will get a ho-hum market reception. In addition, attempts at differentiation are doomed to fail if competitors can quickly copy most or all of the appealing product attributes a company comes up with. Rapid imitation means that no rival achieves differentiation, since whenever one firm introduces some aspect of uniqueness that strikes the fancy of buyers, fast-following copycats quickly reestablish similarity. Thus, to build competitive advantage through differentiation a firm must search out sources of uniqueness that are time-consuming or burdensome for rivals to match. Other common pitfalls and mistakes in pursuing differentiation include:[7]

> **Core Concept**
> Any differentiating feature that works well tends to draw imitators.

- Trying to differentiate on the basis of something that does not lower a buyer's cost or enhance a buyer's well-being, as perceived by the buyer.
- Overdifferentiating so that the product quality or service level exceeds buyers' needs.
- Trying to charge too high a price premium. (The bigger the price differential, the harder it is to keep buyers from switching to lower-priced competitors.)

A low-cost provider strategy can defeat a differentiation strategy when buyers are satisfied with a basic product and don't think "extra" attributes are worth a higher price.

Best-Cost Provider Strategies

Best-cost provider strategies aim at giving customers *more value for the money.* The objective is to deliver superior value to buyers by satisfying their expectations on key quality/service/features/performance attributes and beating their expectations on price (given what rivals are charging for much the same attributes). A company achieves best-cost status from an ability to incorporate attractive attributes at a lower cost than rivals. To become a best-cost provider, a company must have the resources and capabilities to achieve good-to-excellent quality, incorporate appealing features, match product performance, and provide good-to-excellent customer service—all at a lower cost than rivals.

As Figure 4.1 indicates, best-cost provider strategies stake out a middle ground between pursuing a low-cost advantage and a differentiation advantage and between appealing to the broad market as a whole and a narrow market niche. From a competitive positioning standpoint, best-cost strategies are a *hybrid,* balancing a strategic emphasis on low cost against a strategic emphasis on differentiation (superior value). *The target market is value-conscious buyers,* perhaps a very sizable part of the overall market. *The competitive advantage of a best-cost provider is lower costs than rivals* in incorporating good-to-excellent attributes, putting the company in a position to underprice rivals whose products have similar appealing attributes.

A best-cost provider strategy is very appealing in markets where buyer diversity makes product differentiation the norm *and* where many buyers are also sensitive to price and value. This is because a best-cost provider can position itself near the middle of the market with either a medium-quality product at a below-average price or a high-quality product at an average price. Often, substantial numbers of buyers prefer midrange products rather than the cheap, basic products of low-cost producers or the expensive products of top-of-the-line differentiators. But unless a company has the resources, know-how, and capabilities to incorporate upscale product or service attributes at a lower cost than rivals, this strategy is ill-advised.

Company Spotlight 4.3 describes how Toyota has used a best-cost approach with its Lexus models.

The Big Risk of a Best-Cost Provider Strategy

The danger of a best-cost provider strategy is that a company using it will get squeezed between the strategies of firms using low-cost and differentiation strategies. Low-cost leaders may be able to siphon customers away with the appeal of a lower price. High-end differentiators may be able to steal customers away with the appeal of better product attributes. Thus, to be successful, a best-cost provider must offer buyers *significantly* better product attributes in order to justify a price above what low-cost leaders are charging. Likewise, it has to achieve significantly lower costs in providing upscale features so that it can outcompete high-end differentiators on the basis of an attractively lower price.

Toyota's Best-Cost Producer Strategy for Its Lexus Line

Toyota Motor Company is widely regarded as a low-cost producer among the world's motor vehicle manufacturers. Despite its emphasis on product quality, Toyota has achieved low-cost leadership because it has developed considerable skills in efficient supply chain management and low-cost assembly capabilities, and because its models are positioned in the low-to-medium end of the price spectrum, where high production volumes are conducive to low unit costs. But when Toyota decided to introduce its new Lexus models to compete in the luxury-car market, it employed a classic best-cost provider strategy. Toyota took the following four steps in crafting and implementing its Lexus strategy:

1. *Designing an array of high performance characteristics and upscale features into the Lexus models* so as to make them comparable in performance and luxury to other high-end models and attractive to Mercedes, BMW, Audi, Jaguar, Cadillac, and Lincoln buyers.

2. *Transferring its capabilities in making high-quality Toyota models at low cost to making premium-quality Lexus models at costs below other luxury-car makers.* Toyota's supply chain capabilities and low-cost assembly know-how allowed it to incorporate high-tech performance features and upscale quality into Lexus models at substantially less cost than Mercedes and BMW.

3. *Using its relatively lower manufacturing costs to underprice comparable Mercedes and BMW models.* Toyota believed that with its cost advantage it could price attractively equipped Lexus cars low enough to draw price-conscious buyers away from Mercedes and BMW and perhaps induce dissatisfied Lincoln and Cadillac owners to move up to a Lexus.

4. *Establishing a new network of Lexus dealers, separate from Toyota dealers, dedicated to providing a level of personalized, attentive customer service unmatched in the industry.*

Lexus models have consistently ranked among the top 10 models in the widely watched J. D. Power & Associates quality survey, and the prices of Lexus models are typically several thousand dollars below those of comparable Mercedes and BMW models—clear signals that Toyota has succeeded in becoming a best-cost producer with its Lexus brand.

Focused (or Market Niche) Strategies

What sets focused strategies apart from low-cost leadership or broad differentiation strategies is concentrated attention on a narrow piece of the total market. The target segment, or niche, can be defined by geographic uniqueness, by specialized requirements in using the product, or by special product attributes that appeal only to niche members. Examples of firms that concentrate on a well-defined market niche include eBay (in online auctions); Porsche (in sports cars); Cannondale (in top-of-the-line mountain bikes); Jiffy Lube International (a specialist in quick oil changes and simple maintenance for motor vehicles); Enterprise Rent-a-Car (specializing in providing rental cars to repair garage customers); Pottery Barn Kids (a retail chain featuring children's furniture and accessories); and Bandag (a specialist in truck tire recapping that promotes its recaps aggressively at over 1,000 truck stops). Microbreweries, local bakeries, bed-and-breakfast inns, and local owner-managed retail boutiques are all good examples of enterprises that have scaled their operations to serve narrow or local customer segments.

> Even though a focuser may be small, it still may have substantial competitive strength because of the attractiveness of its product offering and its strong expertise and capabilities in meeting the needs and expectations of niche members.

A Focused Low-Cost Strategy A focused strategy based on low cost aims at securing a competitive advantage by serving buyers in the target market niche otel 6 caters to price-conscious travelers who want a clean, no-frills place to spend the night. To be a low-cost provider of overnight lodging, Motel 6 (1) selects relatively inexpensive sites on which to construct its units (usually near interstate exits and high traffic locations but far enough away to avoid paying prime site prices); (2) builds only basic facilities (no restaurant or bar and only rarely a swimming pool); (3) relies on standard architectural designs that incorporate inexpensive materials and low-cost construction techniques; and (4) provides simple room furnishings and decorations. These approaches lower both investment costs and operating costs. Without restaurants, bars, and all kinds of guest services, a Motel 6 unit can be operated with just front-desk personnel, room cleanup crews, and skeleton building-and-grounds maintenance.

To promote the Motel 6 concept with travelers who have simple overnight requirements, the chain uses unique, recognizable radio ads done by nationally syndicated radio personality Tom Bodett; the ads describe Motel 6's clean rooms, no-frills facilities, friendly atmosphere, and dependably low rates (usually under $40 a night).

Motel 6's basis for competitive advantage is lower costs than competitors in providing basic, economical overnight accommodations to price-constrained travelers.

---

at a lower cost and lower price than rival competitors. This strategy has considerable attraction when a firm can lower costs significantly by limiting its customer base to a well-defined buyer segment. The avenues to achieving a cost advantage over rivals also serving the target market niche are the same as for low-cost leadership—outmanage rivals in controlling the factors that drive costs and reconfigure the firm's value chain in ways that yield a cost edge over rivals.

Focused low-cost strategies are fairly common. Producers of private-label goods are able to achieve low costs in product development, marketing, distribution, and advertising by concentrating on making generic items imitative of name-brand merchandise and selling directly to retail chains wanting a basic house brand to sell to price-sensitive shoppers. Several small printer-supply manufacturers have begun making low-cost clones of the premium-priced replacement ink and toner cartridges sold by Hewlett-Packard, Lexmark, Canon, and Epson; the clone manufacturers dissect the cartridges of the name-brand companies and then reengineer a similar version that won't violate patents. The components for remanufactured replacement cartridges are acquired from various outside sources, and the clones are then marketed at prices as much as 50 percent below the name-brand cartridges. Cartridge remanufacturers have been lured to focus on this market because replacement cartridges constitute a multibillion-dollar business with considerable profit potential given their low costs and the premium pricing of the name brand companies. Company Spotlight 4.4 describes how Motel 6 has kept its costs low in catering to budget-conscious travelers.

A Focused Differentiation Strategy A focused strategy based on differentiation aims at securing a competitive advantage by offering niche members a product they perceive as well suited to their own unique tastes and preferences. Successful use of a focused differentiation strategy depends on the existence of a buyer segment that is looking for special product attributes or seller capabilities and on a firm's ability to stand apart from rivals competing in the same target market niche.

Companies like Godiva Chocolates, Chanel, Rolls-Royce, Häagen-Dazs, and W. L. Gore (the maker of Gore-Tex) employ successful differentiation-based focused strategies targeted at upscale buyers wanting products and services with world-class

Ritz-Carlton's Focused Differentiation Strategy

Ritz-Carlton caters to discriminating travelers and vacationers willing and able to pay for top-of-the-line accommodations and world-class personal service. Ritz-Carlton hotels feature (1) prime locations and scenic views from many rooms; (2) custom architectural designs; (3) fine restaurants with gourmet menus prepared by accomplished chefs; (4) elegantly appointed lobbies and bar lounges; (5) swimming pools, exercise facilities, and leisure-time options; (6) upscale room accommodations; (7) an array of guest services and recreation opportunities appropriate to the location; and (8) large, well-trained professional staffs who do their utmost to make each guest's stay an enjoyable experience.

Ritz-Carlton strives to differentiate itself from other high-end lodging rivals like Four Seasons and Hyatt based on its capability to provide superior accommodations and unmatched personal service for a well-to-do clientele. Despite polar–opposite strategies, both Motel 6 and Ritz-Carlton have been able to succeed because the market for lodging consists of diverse buyer segments with diverse preferences and abilities to pay.

---

attributes. Indeed, most markets contain a buyer segment willing to pay a big price premium for the very finest items available, thus opening the strategic window for some competitors to pursue differentiation-based focused strategies aimed at the very top of the market pyramid. Another successful focused differentiator is a "fashion food retailer" called Trader Joe's, a 150-store East and West Coast chain that is a combination gourmet deli and food warehouse.[8] Customers shop Trader Joe's as much for entertainment as for conventional grocery items—the store stocks out-of-the-ordinary culinary treats like raspberry salsa, salmon burgers, and jasmine fried rice, as well as the standard goods normally found in supermarkets. What sets Trader Joe's apart is not just its unique combination of food novelties and competitively priced grocery items but also its capability to turn an otherwise mundane grocery excursion into a whimsical treasure hunt that is just plain fun. Company Spotlight 4.5 describes Ritz-Carlton's focused differentiation strategy.

When Focusing Is Attractive A focused strategy aimed at securing a competitive edge based either on low cost or differentiation becomes increasingly attractive as more of the following conditions are met:

- The target market niche is big enough to be profitable and offers good growth potential.

- Industry leaders do not see that having a presence in the niche is crucial to their own success—in which case focusers can often escape battling head-to-head against some of the industry's biggest and strongest competitors.

- It is costly or difficult for multisegment competitors to put capabilities in place to meet the specialized needs of the target market niche and at the same time satisfy the expectations of their mainstream customers.

- The industry has many different niches and segments, thereby allowing a focuser to pick a competitively attractive niche suited to its resource strengths and capabilities. Also, with more niches there is more room for focusers to avoid each other in competing for the same customers.

- Few, if any, other rivals are attempting to specialize in the same target segment—a condition that reduces the risk of segment overcrowding.

■   The focuser can compete effectively against challengers based on the capabilities and resources it has to serve the targeted niche and the customer goodwill it may have built up.

The Risks of a Focused Strategy   Focusing carries several risks. One is the chance that competitors will find effective ways to match the focused firm's capabilities in serving the target niche—perhaps by coming up with more appealing product offerings or by developing expertise and capabilities that offset the focuser's strengths. A second is the potential for the preferences and needs of niche members to shift over time toward the product attributes desired by the majority of buyers. An erosion of the differences across buyer segments lowers entry barriers into a focuser's market niche and provides an open invitation for rivals in adjacent segments to begin competing for the focuser's customers. A third risk is that the segment may become so attractive it is soon inundated with competitors, intensifying rivalry and splintering segment profits.

Strategic Alliances and Partnerships

During the past decade, companies in all types of industries and in all parts of the world have elected to form strategic alliances and partnerships to complement their own strategic initiatives and strengthen their competitiveness in domestic and international markets. This is an about-face from times past, when the vast majority of companies were content to go it alone, confident that they already had or could independently develop whatever resources and know-how were needed to be successful in their markets. But globalization of the world economy; revolutionary advances in technology across a broad front; and untapped opportunities in national markets in Asia, Latin America, and Europe that are opening up, deregulating, and/or undergoing privatization have made strategic partnerships of one kind or another integral to competing on a broad geographic scale.

Many companies now find themselves thrust into two very demanding competitive races: (1) *the global race to build a market presence in many different national markets* and join the ranks of companies recognized as global market leaders, and (2) *the race to seize opportunities on the frontiers of advancing technology* and build the resource strengths and business capabilities to compete successfully in the industries and product markets of the future.[9] Even the largest and most financially sound companies have concluded that simultaneously running the races for global market leadership and for a stake in the industries of the future requires more diverse and expansive skills, resources, technological expertise, and competitive capabilities than they can assemble and manage alone.

> Alliances and partnerships can be valuable competitive assets in racing against rivals to build a strong global presence and/or to stake out a position on new technological frontiers.

Indeed, the gaps in resources and competitive capabilities between industry rivals have become painfully apparent to disadvantaged enterprises. Allowing such gaps to go unaddressed can put a company in a precarious competitive position or even prove fatal. When rivals can develop new products faster or achieve better quality at lower cost or have more resources and know-how to exploit opportunities in attractive new market arenas, a company has little option but to try to close the resource and competency gaps quickly. Often, the fastest way to do this is to form an alliance that provides immediate access to needed capabilities and competitive strengths. In today's rapidly changing world, a company that cannot position itself quickly misses important opportunities. As a consequence, more and more enterprises, especially in fast-changing industries, are making strategic alliances a core part of their overall strategy. Alliances are so central to Corning's strategy that the company describes itself as a "network of organizations." Toyota has forged a network of long-term strategic partnerships with its suppliers of automotive parts and components. Microsoft collaborates very closely with independent software developers that create new programs to run on the next-generation versions of Windows. A recent study indicates that the average large corporation is involved in around 30 alliances today, versus fewer than 3 in the early 1990s.

Why and How Strategic Alliances Are Advantageous

Strategic alliances are cooperative agreements between firms that go beyond normal company-to-company dealings but fall short of merger or full joint venture partnership with formal ownership ties. (Some strategic alliances, however, do involve arrangements whereby one or more allies have minority ownership in certain of the other alliance members.) The value of an alliance stems not from the agreement or deal itself but rather from the capacity of the partners to defuse organizational frictions, collaborate effectively over time, and work their way through the maze of changes that lie in front of them—technological and competitive surprises, new market developments (which may come at a rapid-fire pace), and changes in their own priorities and competitive circumstances. Collaborative alliances nearly always entail an *evolving* relationship whose benefits and competitive value ultimately depend on mutual learning, cooperation, and adaptation to changing industry conditions. Competitive advantage can emerge if the combined resources and capabilities of a company and its allies give it an edge over rivals.

> **Core Concept**
>
> **Strategic alliances** are collaborative partnerships where two or more companies join forces to achieve mutually beneficial strategic outcomes.

The most common reasons why companies enter into strategic alliances are to collaborate on technology or the development of promising new products, to overcome deficits in their technical and manufacturing expertise, to acquire altogether new competencies, to improve supply chain efficiency, to gain economies of scale in production and/or marketing, and to acquire or improve market access through joint marketing agreements.[10]

A company that is racing for *global market leadership* needs alliances to:

> The best alliances are highly selective, focusing on particular value chain activities and on obtaining a particular competitive benefit. They tend to enable a firm to build on its strengths and to learn.

- Get into critical country markets quickly and accelerate the process of building a potent global market presence.

- Gain inside knowledge about unfamiliar markets and cultures through alliances with local partners. For example, U.S., European, and Japanese companies wanting to build market footholds in the fast-growing Chinese market have pursued partnership arrangements with Chinese companies to help in dealing with government regulations, to supply knowledge of local markets, to provide guidance on adapting their products to better match the buying preferences of Chinese consumers, to set up local manufacturing capabilities, and to assist in distribution, marketing, and promotional activities. The policy of the Chinese government has long been to limit foreign companies to a 50 percent ownership in local companies, making alliances with local Chinese companies a virtual necessity to gain market access.

■ Access valuable skills and competencies that are concentrated in particular geographic locations (such as software design competencies in the United States, fashion design skills in Italy, and efficient manufacturing skills in Japan).

A company that is racing to *stake out a strong position in an industry of the future* needs alliances to:

■ Establish a stronger beachhead for participating in the target industry.

■ Master new technologies and build new expertise and competencies faster than would be possible through internal efforts.

■ Open up broader opportunities in the target industry by melding the firm's own capabilities with the expertise and resources of partners.

Allies can learn much from one another in performing joint research, sharing technological know-how, and collaborating on complementary new technologies and products—sometimes enough to enable them to pursue other new opportunities on their own. Manufacturers typically pursue alliances with parts and components suppliers to gain the efficiencies of better supply chain management and to speed new products to market. By joining forces in components production and/or final assembly, companies may be able to realize cost savings not achievable with their own small volumes—Volvo, Renault, and Peugeot formed an alliance to make engines together for their large car models precisely because none of the three needed enough such engines to operate its own engine plant economically. Manufacturing allies can also learn much about how to improve their quality control and production procedures by studying one another's manufacturing methods. Often alliances are formed to utilize common dealer networks or to promote complementary products jointly, thereby mutually strengthening their access to buyers and economizing on forward channel distribution costs. United Airlines, American Airlines, Continental, Delta, and Northwest created an alliance to form Orbitz, an Internet travel site designed to compete with Expedia and Travelocity to provide consumers with low-cost airfares, rental cars, lodging, cruises, and vacation packages.

> The competitive attraction of alliances is in allowing companies to bundle competences and resources that are more valuable in a joint effort than when kept separate.

Strategic cooperation is a much-favored, indeed necessary, approach in industries where new technological developments are occurring at a furious pace along many different paths and where advances in one technology spill over to affect others (often blurring industry boundaries). Whenever industries are experiencing high-velocity technological change in many areas simultaneously, firms find it virtually essential to have cooperative relationships with other enterprises to stay on the leading edge of technology and product performance even in their own area of specialization.

Why Many Alliances Are Unstable or Break Apart   The stability of an alliance depends on how well the partners work together, their success in responding and adapting to changing internal and external conditions, and their willingness to renegotiate the bargain if circumstances so warrant. A successful alliance requires real in-the-trenches collaboration, not merely an arm's-length exchange of ideas. Unless partners place a high value on the skills, resources, and contributions each brings to the alliance and the cooperative arrangement results in valuable win–win outcomes, it is doomed. A surprisingly large number of alliances never live up to expectations. A study by Accenture, a global business consulting organization, revealed that 61 percent of alliances were either outright failures or "limping along."[11] Many alliances are dissolved after a few years. The high "divorce rate" among strategic allies has several causes—diverging objectives and priorities, an inability to work well together, changing conditions that render the purpose of the alliance obsolete, the emergence of more attractive technological paths, and marketplace rivalry between one or more allies.[12] Experience indicates that alliances stand a reasonable chance of helping a company reduce competitive disadvantage but very rarely have they proved a durable device for achieving a competitive edge over rivals.

The Strategic Dangers of Relying Heavily on Alliances and Cooperative Partnerships   The Achilles heel of alliances and cooperative strategies is the danger of becoming dependent on other companies for *essential* expertise and capabilities over the long term. To be a market leader (and perhaps even a serious market contender), a company must ultimately develop its own capabilities in areas where internal strategic control is pivotal to protecting its competitiveness and building competitive advantage. Moreover, some alliances hold only limited potential because the partner guards its most valuable skills and expertise; in such instances, acquiring or merging with a company possessing the desired resources is a better solution.

Merger and Acquisition Strategies

Mergers and acquisitions are much-used strategic options. They are especially suited for situations in which alliances and partnerships do not go far enough in providing a company with access to the needed resources and capabilities. Ownership ties are more permanent than partnership ties, allowing the operations of the merger/acquisition participants to be tightly integrated and creating more in-house control and autonomy. A *merger* is a pooling of equals, with the newly created company often taking on a new name. An *acquisition* is a combination in which one company, the acquirer, purchases and absorbs the operations of another, the acquired. The difference between a merger and an acquisition relates more to the details of ownership, management control, and financial arrangements than to strategy and competitive advantage. The resources, competencies, and competitive capabilities of the newly created enterprise end up much the same whether the combination is the result of acquisition or merger.

> No company can afford to ignore the strategic and competitive benefits of acquiring or merging with another company to strengthen its market position and open up avenues of new opportunity.

Many mergers and acquisitions are driven by strategies to achieve one of five strategic objectives:[13]

1. *To pave the way for the acquiring company to gain more market share and, further, create a more efficient operation out of the combined companies by closing high-cost plants and eliminating surplus capacity industrywide*—The merger that formed DaimlerChrysler was motivated in large part by the fact that the motor vehicle industry had far more production capacity worldwide than was needed; management at both Daimler Benz and Chrysler believed that the efficiency of the two companies could be significantly improved by shutting some plants and laying off workers; realigning which models were produced at which plants; and squeezing out efficiencies by combining supply chain activities, product design, and administration. Quite a number of acquisitions are undertaken with the objective of transforming two or more otherwise high-cost companies into one lean competitor with average or below-average costs.

2. *To expand a company's geographic coverage*—Many industries exist for a long time in a fragmented state, with local companies dominating local markets and no company having a significantly visible regional or national presence. Eventually,

though, expansion-minded companies will launch strategies to acquire local companies in adjacent territories. Over time, companies with successful growth via acquisition strategies emerge as regional market leaders and later perhaps as a company with national coverage. Often the acquiring company follows up on its acquisitions with efforts to lower the operating costs and improve the customer service capabilities of the local businesses it acquires.

3. *To extend the company's business into new product categories or international markets*—PepsiCo acquired Quaker Oats chiefly to bring Gatorade into the Pepsi family of beverages, and PepsiCo's Frito-Lay division has made a series of acquisitions of foreign-based snack foods companies to begin to establish a stronger presence in international markets. Companies like Nestlé, Kraft, Unilever, and Procter & Gamble—all racing for global market leadership—have made acquisitions an integral part of their strategies to widen their geographic reach and broaden the number of product categories in which they compete.

4. *To gain quick access to new technologies and avoid the need for a time-consuming R&D effort* (which might not succeed)—This type of acquisition strategy is a favorite of companies racing to establish attractive positions in emerging markets. Such companies need to fill in technological gaps, extend their technological capabilities along some promising new paths, and position themselves to launch next-wave products and services. Cisco Systems purchased over 75 technology companies to give it more technological reach and product breadth, thereby buttressing its standing as the world's biggest supplier of systems for building the infrastructure of the Internet. Intel has made over 300 acquisitions in the past five or so years to broaden its technological base, put it in a stronger position to be a major supplier of Internet technology, and make it less dependent on supplying microprocessors for PCs. This type of acquisition strategy enables a company to build a market position in attractive technologies quickly and serves as a substitute for extensive in-house R&D programs.

5. *To try to invent a new industry and lead the convergence of industries whose boundaries are being blurred by changing technologies and new market opportunities*—Such acquisitions are the result of a company's management betting that a new industry is on the verge of being born and deciding to establish an early position in this industry by bringing together the resources and products of several different companies. Examples include the merger of AOL and media giant Time Warner and Viacom's purchase of Paramount Pictures, CBS, and Blockbuster—both of which reflected bold strategic moves predicated on beliefs that all entertainment content will ultimately converge into a single industry and be distributed over the Internet.

In addition to the above objectives, there are instances when acquisitions are motivated by a company's desire to fill resource gaps, thus allowing the new company to do things it could not do before. Company Spotlight 4.6 describes how Clear Channel Worldwide has used mergers and acquisitions to build a leading global position in outdoor advertising and radio and TV broadcasting.

However, mergers and acquisitions do not always produce the hoped-for outcomes. Combining the operations of two companies, especially large and complex ones, often entails formidable resistance from rank-and-file organization members, hard-to-resolve conflicts in management styles and corporate cultures, and tough problems of integration. Cost savings, expertise sharing, and enhanced competitive capabilities may take substantially longer than expected to realize or, worse, may never materialize at all.

COMPANY SPOTLIGHT 4.6

How Clear Channel Has Used Mergers and Acquisitions to Become a Global Market Leader

In 2002, Clear Channel Communications was the fourth largest media company in the world behind Disney, AOL Time Warner, and Viacom/CBS. The company, founded in 1972 by Lowry Mays and Billy Joe McCombs, got its start by acquiring an unprofitable country-music radio station in San Antonio, Texas. Over the next 10 years, Mays learned the radio business and slowly bought other radio stations in a variety of states. Going public in 1984 helped the company raise the equity capital needed to fuel its strategy of expanding by acquiring radio stations in additional geographic markets.

In the late 1980s, following the decision of the Federal Communications Commission to loosen the rules regarding the ability of one company to own both radio and TV stations, Clear Channel broadened its strategy and began acquiring small, struggling TV stations. Soon thereafter, Clear Channel became affiliated with the Fox network, which was starting to build a national presence and challenge ABC, CBS, and NBC. Meanwhile, the company began selling programming services to other stations, and in some markets where it already had stations it took on the function of selling advertising for cross-town stations it did not own.

By 1998, Clear Channel had used acquisitions to build a leading position in radio and television stations. Domestically, it owned, programmed, or sold airtime for 69 AM radio stations, 135 FM stations, and 18 TV stations in 48 local markets in 24 states. The TV stations included affiliates of FOX, UPN, ABC, NBC, and CBS. Clear Channel was beginning to expand internationally. It purchased an ownership interest in a domestic Spanish-language radio broadcaster; owned two radio stations and a cable audio channel in Denmark; and acquired ownership interests in radio stations in Australia, Mexico, New Zealand, and the Czech Republic.

In 1997, Clear Channel acquired Phoenix-based Eller Media Company, an outdoor advertising company with over 100,000 billboard facings. This was quickly followed by additional acquisitions of outdoor advertising companies, the most important of which were ABC Outdoor in Milwaukee, Wisconsin; Paxton Communications (with operations in Tampa and Orlando, Florida); Universal Outdoor; and the More Group, with outdoor operations and 90,000 displays in 24 countries.

Then in October 1999, Clear Channel merged with AM-FM, Inc. After divesting some 125 properties needed to gain regulatory approval, Clear Channel Communications (the name adopted by the merged companies) operated in 32 countries and included 830 radio stations, 19 TV stations, and more than 425,000 outdoor displays.

Clear Channel's strategy was to buy radio, TV, and outdoor advertising properties with operations in many of the same local markets, share facilities and staffs to cut costs, improve programming, and sell advertising to customers in packages for all three media simultaneously. Packaging ads for two or three media allowed the company to combine its sales activities and have a common sales force for all three media, achieving significant cost savings and boosting profit margins.

Over the next four years, Clear Channel continued its strategy of growth via acquisitions. By 2002, Clear Channel Worldwide (the company's latest name) owned radio and television stations, outdoor displays, and entertainment venues in 66 countries around the world. Clear Channel operated approximately 1,225 radio and 37 television stations in the United States and had equity interests in over 240 radio stations internationally. In addition, the company operated approximately 776,000 outdoor advertising displays, including billboards, street furniture, and transit panels around the world. The company's Clear Channel Entertainment division was a leading promoter, producer, and marketer of live entertainment events and also owned leading athlete management and marketing companies.

Sources: Company documents and *Business Week,* October 19, 1999, p. 56.

Integrating the operations of two fairly large or culturally diverse companies is hard to pull off—only a few companies that use merger and acquisition strategies have proved they can consistently make good decisions about what to leave alone and what to meld into their own operations and systems. In the case of mergers between companies of roughly equal size, the management groups of the two companies frequently battle over which one is going to end up in control. A number of previously applauded mergers/acquisitions have yet to live up to expectations—the merger of AOL and Time Warner, the merger of Daimler Benz and Chrysler, the merger of J. P. Morgan and Chase Manhattan Bank, and Ford's acquisition of Jaguar. Ford paid a handsome price to acquire Jaguar but has yet to make the Jaguar brand a major factor in the luxury-car segment in competition against Mercedes, BMW, and Lexus. Novell acquired WordPerfect for $1.7 billion in stock in 1994, but the combination never generated enough punch to compete against Microsoft Word and Microsoft Office—Novell sold WordPerfect to Corel for $124 million in cash and stock less than two years later. The jury is out on whether Hewlett-Packard's acquisition of Compaq Computer will be a success.

Vertical Integration Strategies: Operating across More Stages of the Industry Value Chain

Vertical integration extends a firm's competitive and operating scope within the same industry. It involves expanding the firm's range of activities backward into sources of supply and/or forward toward end users. Thus, if a manufacturer invests in facilities to produce certain component parts that it formerly purchased from outside suppliers, it remains in essentially the same industry as before. The only change is that it has operations in two stages of the industry value chain. Similarly, if a paint manufacturer, Sherwin-Williams for example, elects to integrate forward by opening 100 retail stores to market its paint products directly to consumers, it remains in the paint business even though its competitive scope extends from manufacturing to retailing.

Vertical integration strategies can aim at *full integration* (participating in all stages of the industry value chain) or *partial integration* (building positions in selected stages of the industry's total value chain). A firm can pursue vertical integration by starting its own operations in other stages in the industry's activity chain or by acquiring a company already performing the activities it wants to bring in-house.

The Strategic Advantages of Vertical Integration

Core Concept

A vertical integration strategy has appeal *only* if it significantly strengthens a firm's competitive position.

The only good reason for investing company resources in vertical integration is to strengthen the firm's competitive position.[14] Vertical integration has no real payoff profitwise or strategywise unless it produces sufficient cost savings to justify the extra investment, adds materially to a company's technological and competitive strengths, or truly helps differentiate the company's product offering.

Integrating Backward to Achieve Greater Competitiveness Integrating backward generates cost savings only when the volume needed is big enough to capture the same scale economies suppliers have and when suppliers' production efficiency can be matched or exceeded with no dropoff in quality. The best potential for being able to reduce costs via backward integration exists in situations where suppliers have sizable profit margins, where the item being supplied is a major cost component, and where the needed technological skills are easily mastered or can be gained by acquiring a supplier with the desired technological know-how. Integrating backward can sometimes significantly enhance a company's technological capabilities and give it expertise needed to stake out positions in the industries and products of the future. Intel, Cisco, and many other Silicon Valley companies have been active in acquiring companies that will help them speed the advance of Internet technology and pave the way for next-generation families of products and services.

Backward vertical integration can produce a differentiation-based competitive advantage when a company, by performing in-house activities that were previously outsourced, ends up with a better-quality product/service offering, improves the caliber of its customer service, or in other ways enhances the performance of its final product. On occasion, integrating into more stages along the industry value chain can add to a company's differentiation capabilities by allowing it to build or strengthen its core competencies, better master key skills or strategy-critical technologies, or add features that deliver greater customer value.

Other potential advantages of backward integration include sparing a company the uncertainty of being dependent on suppliers for crucial components or support services and lessening a company's vulnerability to powerful suppliers inclined to raise prices at every opportunity. Stockpiling, contracting for fixed prices, multiple sourcing, forming long-term cooperative partnerships, and using substitute inputs are not always attractive ways for dealing with uncertain supply conditions or with economically powerful suppliers. Companies that are low on a key supplier's customer priority list can find themselves waiting on shipments every time supplies get tight. If this occurs often and wreaks havoc in a company's own production and customer relations activities, backward integration can be an advantageous strategic solution.

Integrating Forward to Enhance Competitiveness   The strategic impetus for forward integration is to gain better access to end users and better market visibility. In many industries, independent sales agents, wholesalers, and retailers handle competing brands of the same product; having no allegiance to any one company's brand, they tend to push whatever sells and earns them the biggest profits. Halfhearted commitments by distributors and retailers can frustrate a company's attempt to boost sales and market share; give rise to costly inventory pileups and frequent underutilization of capacity; and disrupt the economies of steady, near-capacity production. In such cases, it can be advantageous for a manufacturer to integrate forward into wholesaling or retailing via company-owned distributorships or a chain of retail stores. But often a company's product line is not broad enough to justify stand-alone distributorships or retail outlets. This leaves the option of integrating forward into the activity of selling directly to end users—perhaps via the Internet. Bypassing regular wholesale/retail channels in favor of direct sales and Internet retailing may lower distribution costs, produce a relative cost advantage over certain rivals, and result in lower selling prices to end users.

The Strategic Disadvantages of Vertical Integration

Vertical integration has some substantial drawbacks, however. It boosts a firm's capital investment in the industry, increasing business risk (what if industry growth and profitability go sour?) and perhaps denying financial resources to more worthwhile pursuits. A vertically integrated firm has vested interests in protecting its technology and production facilities. Because of the high costs of abandoning such investments before they are worn out, fully integrated firms tend to adopt new technologies slower than partially integrated or nonintegrated firms. Second, integrating forward or backward locks a firm into relying on its own in-house activities and sources of supply (which later may prove more costly than outsourcing) and potentially results in less flexibility in accommodating buyer demand for greater product variety. In today's world of close working relationships with suppliers and efficient supply chain management systems, very few businesses can make a case for integrating backward into the business of suppliers to ensure a reliable supply of materials and components or to reduce production costs.

Third, vertical integration poses all kinds of capacity-matching problems. In motor vehicle manufacturing, for example, the most efficient scale of operation for making axles is different from the most economic volume for radiators, and different yet again for both engines and transmissions. Building the capacity to produce just the right number of axles, radiators, engines, and transmissions in-house—and doing so at the lowest unit costs for each—is much easier said than done. If internal capacity for making transmissions is deficient, the difference has to be bought externally. Where internal capacity for radiators proves excessive, customers need to be found for the surplus. And if by-products are generated—as occurs in the processing of many chemical products—they require arrangements for disposal.

Fourth, integration forward or backward often calls for radical changes in skills and business capabilities. Parts and components manufacturing, assembly operations, wholesale distribution and retailing, and direct sales via the Internet are different businesses with different key success factors. Managers of a manufacturing company should consider carefully whether it makes good business sense to invest time and money in developing the expertise and merchandising skills to integrate forward into wholesaling and retailing. Many manufacturers learn the hard way that company-owned wholesale/retail networks present many headaches, fit poorly with what they do best, and don't always add the kind of value to their core business they thought they would. Selling to customers via the Internet poses still another set of problems—it is usually easier to use the Internet to sell to business customers than to consumers.

Integrating backward into parts and components manufacture isn't as simple or profitable as it sounds, either. Producing some or all of the parts and components needed for final assembly can reduce a company's flexibility to make desirable changes in using certain parts and components—it is one thing to design out a component made by a supplier and another to design out a component being made in-house. Companies that alter designs and models frequently in response to shifting buyer preferences often find outsourcing the needed parts and components cheaper and less complicated than making them in-house. Most of the world's automakers, despite their expertise in automotive technology and manufacturing, have concluded that purchasing many of their key parts and components from manufacturing specialists results in higher quality, lower costs, and greater design flexibility than does the vertical integration option.

Weighing the Pros and Cons of Vertical Integration   All in all, therefore, a strategy of vertical integration can have both important strengths and weaknesses. The tip of the scales depends on (1) whether vertical integration can enhance the performance of strategy-critical activities in ways that lower cost, build expertise, or increase differentiation; (2) the impact of vertical integration on investment costs, flexibility and response times, and the administrative costs of coordinating operations across more value chain activities; and (3) whether the integration substantially enhances a company's competitiveness. Vertical integration strategies have merit according to which capabilities and value-chain activities truly need to be performed in-house and which can be performed better or cheaper by outsiders. Absent solid benefits, integrating forward or backward is not likely to be an attractive competitive strategy option. In a growing number of instances, companies are proving that deintegrating (i.e., focusing on a narrower portion of the industry value chain) is a cheaper and more flexible competitive strategy.

Outsourcing Strategies: Narrowing the Boundaries of the Business

Outsourcing involves withdrawing from certain activities in the value chain and relying on outside vendors to supply the needed products, support services, or functional activities. Over the past decade, outsourcing has become increasingly popular. Some companies have found vertical integration to be so competitively burdensome that they have deintegrated and withdrawn from some stages of the industry value chain. Moreover, a number of single-business enterprises have begun outsourcing activities and concentrating their energies on a narrower portion of the value chain.

> **Core Concept**
>
> **Outsourcing** involves shifting the performance of value chain activities to outside specialists rather than performing them in-house.

Advantages of Outsourcing

Outsourcing pieces of the value chain to narrow the boundaries of a firm's business makes strategic sense whenever:

- An activity can be performed better or more cheaply by outside specialists. Many PC makers, for example, have shifted from assembling units in-house to using contract assemblers because of the sizable scale economies associated with purchasing PC components in large volumes and assembling PCs. Cisco outsources most all production and assembly of its routers and switching equipment to contract manufacturers that together operate 37 factories, all linked via the Internet.

- The activity is not crucial to the firm's ability to achieve sustainable competitive advantage and won't hollow out its core competencies, capabilities, or technical know-how. Outsourcing of maintenance services, data processing, accounting, and other administrative support activities to specialists has become commonplace. American Express, for instance, recently entered into a seven-year, $4 billion deal whereby IBM's Services division will host American Express's website, network servers, data storage, and help-desk support; American Express indicated that it would save several hundred million dollars by paying only for the services it needed when it needed them (as opposed to funding its own full-time staff).

- It reduces the company's risk exposure to changing technology and/or changing buyer preferences.

- It streamlines company operations in ways that improve organizational flexibility, cut cycle time, speed decision making, and reduce coordination costs.

- It allows a company to concentrate on its core business and do what it does best.

Often, many of the advantages of performing value chain activities in-house can be captured and many of the disadvantages avoided by forging close, long-term cooperative partnerships with key suppliers and tapping into the important competitive capabilities that able suppliers have painstakingly developed. In years past, many companies maintained arm's-length relationships with suppliers, insisting on items being made to precise specifications and negotiating long and hard over price.[15] Although a company might place orders with the same supplier repeatedly, there was no expectation that this would be the case; price usually determined which supplier was awarded an order, and companies maneuvered for leverage over suppliers to get the lowest possible prices. The threat of switching suppliers was the company's primary weapon. To make this threat credible, sourcing from several suppliers was preferred to dealing with only a single supplier.

Today, most companies are abandoning such approaches in favor of alliances and strategic partnerships with a small number of highly capable suppliers. Cooperative relationships are replacing contractual, purely price-oriented relationships. Relying on outside specialists to perform certain value chain activities offers a number of strategic advantages:[16]

- Obtaining higher quality and/or cheaper components or services than internal sources can provide.

> **Core Concept**
>
> A company should generally *not* perform any value chain activity internally that can be performed more efficiently or effectively by its outside business partners—the chief exception is when a particular activity is strategically crucial and internal control over that activity is deemed essential.

- Improving the company's ability to innovate by allying with "best-in-world" suppliers who have considerable intellectual capital and innovative capabilities of their own.

- Enhancing the firm's strategic flexibility should customer needs and market conditions suddenly shift—seeking out new suppliers with the needed capabilities already in place is frequently quicker, easier, less risky, and cheaper than hurriedly retooling internal operations to disband obsolete capabilities and put new ones in place.

- Increasing the firm's ability to assemble diverse kinds of expertise speedily and efficiently.

- Allowing the firm to concentrate its resources on performing those activities internally that it can perform better than outsiders and/or that it needs to have under its direct control.

Dell Computer's partnerships with the suppliers of PC components have allowed it to operate with fewer than four days of inventory, to realize substantial savings in inventory costs, and to get PCs equipped with next-generation components into the marketplace in less than a week after the newly upgraded components start shipping. Cisco's contract suppliers work so closely with Cisco that they can ship Cisco products to Cisco customers without a Cisco employee ever touching the gear. This system of alliances saves $500 million to $800 million annually.[17] Hewlett-Packard, IBM, Silicon Graphics (now SGI), and others have sold plants to suppliers and then contracted to purchase the output. Starbucks finds purchasing coffee beans from independent growers far more advantageous than trying to integrate backward into the coffee-growing business.

The Pitfalls of Outsourcing

The biggest danger of outsourcing is that a company will farm out too many or the wrong types of activities and thereby hollow out its own capabilities. In such cases, a company loses touch with the very activities and expertise that over the long run determine its success. Cisco guards against loss of control and protects its manufacturing expertise by designing the production methods that its contract manufacturers must use. Cisco keeps the source code for its design proprietary and is thus the source of all improvements and innovations. Further, Cisco uses the Internet to monitor the factory operations of contract manufacturers around the clock, and can therefore know immediately when problems arise and whether to get involved.

Offensive and Defensive Strategies

Competitive advantage is nearly always achieved by successful *offensive* strategic moves—initiatives calculated to yield a cost advantage, a differentiation advantage, or a resource advantage. *Defensive* strategies, in contrast, can protect competitive advantage but rarely are the basis for creating the advantage. How long it takes for a successful offensive to create an edge varies with the competitive circumstances.[18] It can be short if the requisite resources and capabilities are already in place awaiting deployment or if buyers respond immediately (as can occur with a dramatic price cut, an imaginative ad campaign, or an especially appealing new product). Securing a competitive edge can take much longer if winning consumer acceptance of an innovative product will take some time or if the firm may need several years to debug a new technology or put new network systems or production capacity in place. Ideally, an offensive move builds competitive advantage quickly; the longer it takes, the more likely it is that rivals will spot the move, see its potential, and begin a counterresponse. The size of the advantage can be large (as in pharmaceuticals, where patents on an important new drug produce a substantial advantage) or small (as in apparel, where popular new designs can be imitated quickly).

> **Core Concept**
> Competent, resourceful rivals will exert strong efforts to overcome any competitive disadvantage they face—they won't be outcompeted without a fight.

However, competent, resourceful competitors can be counted on to counterattack with initiatives to overcome any market disadvantage they face—they are not going to be outcompeted without a fight.[19] Thus, to sustain an initially won competitive advantage, a firm must come up with follow-on offensive and defensive moves. Unless the firm initiates one series of offensive and defensive moves after another to protect its market position and retain customer favor, its market advantage will erode.

Basic Types of Offensive Strategies

Most every company must at times go on the offensive to improve its market position. While offensive attacks may or may not be aimed at particular rivals, they usually are motivated by a desire to win sales and market share at the expense of other companies in the industry. Several types of strategic offensives merit consideration.[20]

Initiatives to Match or Exceed Competitor Strengths   Offensive strategies are important when a company has no choice but to try to whittle away at a strong rival's competitive advantage and when it is possible to gain profitable market share at the expense of rivals despite whatever resource strengths and capabilities they have. The classic avenue for attacking a strong rival is to offer an equally good product at a lower price.[21] This can produce market share gains if the targeted competitor has sound reasons for not resorting to price cuts of its own and if the challenger convinces buyers that its product is just as good. However, such a strategy increases total profits only if the gains in additional unit sales are enough to offset the impact of lower prices and thinner margins per unit sold. A more potent and sustainable basis for mounting a price-aggressive challenge is to *first achieve a cost advantage* and then hit

capability, much-improved performance features, an innovative new product, technological superiority, a cost advantage in manufacturing or distribution, or some kind of differentiation advantage. If the challenger's resources and competitive strengths amount to a competitive advantage over the targeted rivals, so much the better.

Defensive Strategy Options

It is just as important to discern when to fortify a company's present market position with defensive actions as it is to seize the initiative and launch strategic offensives.

In a competitive market, all firms are subject to offensive challenges from rivals. The purposes of defensive strategies are to lower the risk of being attacked, weaken the impact of any attack that occurs, and influence challengers to aim their efforts at other rivals. While defensive strategies usually don't enhance a firm's competitive advantage, they can definitely help fortify its competitive position, protect its most valuable resources and capabilities from imitation, and defend whatever competitive advantage it might have. Defensive strategies can take either of two forms: actions to block challengers and signaling the likelihood of strong retaliation.

Blocking the Avenues Open to Challengers   The most frequently employed approach to defending a company's present position involves actions that restrict a challenger's options for initiating competitive attack. There are any number of obstacles that can be put in the path of would-be challengers.[30] A defender can participate in alternative technologies to reduce the threat that rivals will attack with a better technology. A defender can introduce new features, add new models, or broaden its product line to close off gaps and vacant niches to would-be challengers. It can thwart the efforts of rivals to attack with a lower price by maintaining economy-priced options of its own. It can try to discourage buyers from trying competitors' brands by lengthening warranty coverages, offering free training and support services, developing the capability to deliver spare parts to users faster than rivals can, providing coupons and sample giveaways to buyers most prone to experiment, and making early announcements about impending new products or price changes to induce potential buyers to postpone switching, It can challenge the quality or safety of rivals' products. Finally, a defender can grant dealers and distributors volume discounts or better financing terms to discourage them from experimenting with other suppliers, or it can convince them to handle its product line *exclusively* and force competitors to use other distribution outlets.

There are many ways to throw obstacles in the path of challengers.

Signaling Challengers That Retaliation Is Likely   The goal of signaling challengers that strong retaliation is likely in the event of an attack is either to dissuade challengers from attacking at all or to divert them to less threatening options. Either goal can be achieved by letting challengers know the battle will cost more than it is worth. Would-be challengers can be signaled by:[31]

- Publicly announcing management's commitment to maintain the firm's present market share.
- Publicly committing the company to a policy of matching competitors' terms or prices.
- Maintaining a war chest of cash and marketable securities.
- Making an occasional strong counterresponse to the moves of weak competitors to enhance the firm's image as a tough defender.

Strategies for Using the Internet as a Distribution Channel

As the Internet continues to weave its way into the fabric of everyday business and personal life, and as the second wave of Internet entrepreneurship takes root, companies of all types are addressing how best to make the Internet a fundamental part of their business and their competitive strategies. Few if any businesses can escape making some effort to use Internet applications to improve their value chain activities. This much is a given—anything less risks competitive disadvantage. Companies across the world are deep into the process of implementing a variety of Internet technology applications; the chief question companies face at this point is what additional Internet technology applications to incorporate into day-to-day operations. But the larger and much tougher *strategic* issue is how to make the Internet a fundamental part of a company's competitive strategy—in particular, how much emphasis to place on the Internet as a distribution channel for accessing buyers. *Managers must decide how to use the Internet in positioning the company in the marketplace*—whether to use the Internet as *only a means of disseminating product information* (with traditional distribution channel partners making all sales to end users), as a *secondary* or *minor* channel, as *one of several important distribution channels,* as *the primary distribution channel,* or as *the exclusive channel for accessing customers.*[32] Let's look at each of these strategic options in turn.

> Companies today must wrestle with the issue of how to use the Internet in positioning themselves in the marketplace—whether to use the Internet as just a vehicle for disseminating product information, as a minor distribution channel, as one of several important distribution channels, as the primary distribution channel, or as the company's only distribution channel.

Using the Internet Just to Disseminate Product Information

Operating a website that contains extensive product information but that relies on click-throughs to the websites of distribution channel partners for sales transactions (or that informs site users where nearby retail stores are located) is an attractive market positioning option for manufacturers and/or wholesalers that already have retail dealer networks and face nettlesome channel conflict issues if they try to sell online in direct competition with their dealers. A manufacturer or wholesaler that aggressively pursues online sales to end users is signaling both a weak strategic commitment to its dealers and a willingness to cannibalize dealers' sales and growth potential. To the extent that strong partnerships with wholesale and/or retail dealers are critical to accessing end users, selling direct to end-users via the company's website is a very tricky road to negotiate. A manufacturer's efforts to use its website to sell around its dealers is certain to anger its wholesale distributors and retail dealers, who may respond by putting more effort into marketing the brands of rival manufacturers who don't sell online. In sum, the manufacturer may stand to lose more sales through its dealers than it gains from its own online sales effort. Moreover, dealers may be in better position to employ a brick-and-click strategy than a manufacturer is because dealers have a local presence to complement their online sales approach (which consumers may find appealing). Consequently, in industries where the strong support and goodwill of dealer networks is essential, manufacturers may conclude that their website should be designed to partner with dealers rather than compete with them—just as the auto manufacturers are doing with their franchised dealers.

Using the Internet as a Minor Distribution Channel

A second strategic option is to use online sales as a relatively minor distribution channel for achieving incremental sales, gaining online sales experience, and doing marketing research. If channel conflict poses a big obstacle to online sales, or if only a small fraction of buyers can be attracted to make online purchases, then companies are well advised to pursue online sales with the strategic intent of gaining experience, learning more about buyer tastes and preferences, testing reaction to new products, creating added market buzz about their products, and boosting overall sales volume a few percentage points. Nike, for example, has begun selling some of its footwear online, giving buyers the option of specifying certain colors and features. Such a strategy is unlikely to provoke much resistance from dealers and could even prove beneficial to dealers if footwear buyers become enamored with custom-made shoes that can be ordered through and/or picked up at Nike retailers. A manufacturer may be able to glean valuable marketing research data from tracking the browsing patterns of website visitors and incorporating what generates the most interest into its mainstream product offerings. The behavior and actions of Web surfers are a veritable gold mine of information for companies seeking to respond more precisely to buyer preferences.

Brick-and-Click Strategies: An Appealing Middle Ground

Employing a brick-and-click strategy to sell directly to consumers while at the same time utilizing traditional wholesale and retail channels can be an attractive market positioning option in the right circumstances. With a brick-and-click strategy, online sales at a company's website can serve as either one of several important distribution channels through which the company accesses end users or as its primary distribution channel. Software developers, for example, have come to rely on the Internet as a highly effective distribution channel to complement sales through brick-and-mortar wholesalers and retailers. Selling online directly to end users has the advantage of cutting out the costs and margins of software wholesalers and retailers (often 35 to 50 percent of the retail price). In addition, allowing customers to download their software purchases immediately via the Internet eliminates the costs of producing and packaging CDs. However, software developers are still strongly motivated to continue to distribute their products through wholesalers and retailers (to maintain broad access to existing and potential users who, for whatever reason, may be reluctant to buy online).

Despite the channel conflict that exists when a manufacturer sells directly to end users at its website in head-to-head competition with its distribution channel allies, there are three major reasons why manufacturers might want to aggressively pursue online sales and establish the Internet as an important distribution channel alongside traditional channels:

1. The manufacturer's profit margin from online sales is bigger than that from sales through wholesale/retail channels.

2. Encouraging buyers to visit the company's website helps educate them to the ease and convenience of purchasing online, thus encouraging more and more buyers to migrate to buying online (where company profit margins are greater).

3. Selling directly to end users allows a manufacturer to make greater use of build-to-order manufacturing and assembly as a basis for bypassing traditional distribution

channels entirely. Dell Computer, for instance, has used online sales to make build-to-order options a cost-effective reality. Similarly, several motor vehicle companies have initiated actions to streamline build-to-order manufacturing capabilities and reduce delivery times for custom orders from 30–60 days to as few as 5–10 days; most vehicle manufacturers already have software on their websites that permits motor vehicle shoppers to select the models, colors, and optional equipment they would like to have. In industries where build-to-order options can result in substantial cost savings along the industry value chain and permit sizable price reductions to end users, companies have to consider making build-to-order and sell-direct an integral part of their market positioning strategy. Over time, such a strategy could increase the rate at which sales migrate from distribution allies to the company's website.

A combination brick-and-click market positioning strategy is highly suitable when online sales have a good chance of *evolving* into a manufacturer's primary distribution channel. In such instances, incurring channel conflict in the short term and competing against traditional distribution allies makes good strategic sense.

Many brick-and-mortar companies can enter online retailing at relatively low cost—all they need is a Web store and systems for filling and delivering individual customer orders. Brick-and-click strategies have two big strategic appeals for wholesale and retail enterprises: They are an economic means of expanding a company's geographic reach, and they give both existing and potential customers another choice of how to communicate with the company, shop for product information, make purchases, or resolve customer service problems. Brick-and-mortar distributors and retailers (as well as manufacturers with company-owned retail stores) can shift to brick-and-click strategies by using their current distribution centers and/or retail stores for picking orders from on-hand inventories and making deliveries. Walgreen's, a leading drugstore chain, allows customers to order a prescription online and then pick it up at a local store (using the drive-through window, in some cases). In banking, a brick-and-click strategy allows customers to use local branches and ATMs for depositing checks and getting cash while using online systems to pay bills, check account balances, and transfer funds. Many industrial distributors are finding it efficient for customers to place their orders over the Web rather than phoning them in or waiting for salespeople to call in person. Company Spotlight 4.7 describes how Office Depot has successfully migrated from a traditional brick-and-mortar distribution strategy to a combination brick-and-click distribution strategy.

Strategies for Online Enterprises

A company that elects to use the Internet as its exclusive channel for accessing buyers is essentially an online business from the perspective of the customer. The Internet becomes the vehicle for transacting sales and delivering customer services; except for advertising, the Internet is the sole point of all buyer–seller contact. Many so-called pure dot-com enterprises have chosen this strategic approach—prominent examples include eBay, Amazon.com, Yahoo!, Buy.com, and Priceline.com. For a company to succeed in using the Internet as its exclusive distribution channel, its product or service must be one for which buying online holds strong appeal. Furthermore, judging from the evidence thus far, an online company's strategy must incorporate the following features:

- *The capability to deliver unique value to buyers*—Winning strategies succeed in drawing buyers because of the value being delivered. This means that online businesses must usually attract buyers on the basis of something more than just low

COMPANY SPOTLIGHT 4.7
Office Depot's Brick-and-Click Strategy

Office Depot was in the first wave of retailers to adopt a combination brick-and-click strategy. In 1996, it began allowing business customers to use the Internet to place orders. Businesses could thus avoid having to make a call, generate a purchase order, and pay an invoice—while still getting same-day or next-day delivery from one of Office Depot's local stores.

Office Depot built its Internet business around its existing network of 750 retail stores; 30 warehouses; 2,000 delivery trucks; $1.3 billion in inventories; and phone-order sales department, which handled large business customers. It already had a solid brand name and enough purchasing power with its suppliers to counter discount-minded online rivals trying to attract buyers of office supplies on the basis of superlow prices. Office Depot's incremental investment to enter the e-commerce arena was extremely low since all it needed to add was a website where customers could see pictures and descriptions of the items it carried, their prices, and in-stock availability; its marketing costs to make customers aware of its Web store option ran less than $10 million.

In setting up customized Web pages for 37,000 corporate and educational customers, Office Depot designed sites that allowed the customer's employees varying degrees of freedom to buy supplies. A clerk might be able to order only copying paper, toner cartridges, computer disks, and paper clips up to a preset dollar limit per order, while a vice president might have carte blanche to order any item Office Depot sold. Office Depot's online prices were the same as its store prices; the company's strategy was to promote Web sales on the basis of service, convenience, and lower customer costs for order processing and inventories.

In 2002, over 50 percent of Office Depot's major customers were ordering most of their supplies online because of the convenience and the savings in transactions costs. Bank of America, for example, was ordering 85 percent of its office supplies online from Office Depot.

Customers reported that using the website cut their transaction costs by up to 80 percent; plus, Office Depot's same-day or next-day delivery capability allowed them to reduce the amount of office supplies they kept in inventory.

Website sales cost Office Depot less than $1 per $100 of goods ordered, compared with about $2 for phone and fax orders. And since Web sales eliminate the need to key in transactions, order-entry errors have been virtually eliminated and product returns cut by 50 percent. Billing is handled electronically.

Office Depot's online unit accounted for $1.5 billion in sales in 2001, up sharply from $982 million in 2000. Online sales contributed 14 percent to the company's overall sales and made Office Depot the second-largest online retailer behind Amazon.com. Office Depot's online operations have been profitable from the start. Industry experts believe that Office Depot's success is based on the company's philosophy of maintaining a strong link between the Internet and its stores. "Office Depot gets it," noted one industry analyst. "It used the Net to build deeper relationships with customers."

Sources: "Office Depot's e-Diva," *Business Week Online* (www.businessweek.com), August 6, 2001; Laura Lorek, "Office Depot Site Picks Up Speed," *Interactive Week* (www.zdnet.com/intweek), June 25, 2001; "Why Office Depot Loves the Net," *Business Week*, September 27, 1999, pp. EB 66, EB 68; and *Fortune*, November 8, 1999, p. 17.

---

price—indeed, many dot-coms are already working to tilt the basis for competing away from low price and toward build-to-order systems, convenience, superior product information, attentive online service, and other ways to attract customers to buying online (as opposed to buying from offline sellers).

- *Deliberate efforts to engineer a value chain that enables differentiation, lower costs, or better value for the money*—For a company to win in the marketplace with an online-only distribution strategy, its value chain approach must hold potential for low-cost leadership, competitively valuable differentiating attributes, or a best-cost provider advantage. If a firm's strategy is to attract customers by selling at cut-rate prices, then it must possess cost advantages in those activities it performs, and it must outsource the remaining activities to low-cost specialists. If an online seller is going to differentiate itself on the basis of a superior buying experience and top-notch customer service, then it needs to concentrate on having an easy-to-navigate website, an array of functions and conveniences for customers, "Web reps" who can answer questions online, and logistical capabilities to deliver products quickly and accommodate returned merchandise. If it is going to deliver more value for the money, then it must manage value chain activities so as to deliver upscale products and services at lower costs than rivals. Absent a value chain that puts the company in an attractive position to compete head-to-head against other online and brick-and-mortar rivals, such a distribution strategy is unlikely to produce attractive profitability.

■ *An innovative, fresh, and entertaining website*—Just as successful brick-and-mortar retailers employ merchandising strategies to keep their stores fresh and interesting to shoppers, Web merchandisers must exert ongoing efforts to add innovative site features and capabilities, enhance the look and feel of their sites, heighten viewer interest with audio and video, and have fresh product offerings and special promotions. Web pages need to be easy to read and interesting, with lots of eye appeal. Website features that are distinctive, engaging, and entertaining add value to the experience of spending time at the site and are thus strong competitive assets. This generally means that the company must have strong Internet technology capabilities.

■ *A clear focus on a limited number of competencies and a relatively specialized number of value chain activities in which proprietary Internet applications and capabilities can be developed*—Low-value-added activities can be delegated to outside specialists. A strong market position is far more likely to emerge from efforts to develop proprietary Internet applications than from using third-party developers' software packages, which are also readily available to imitative rivals. Outsourcing value chain activities for which there is little potential for proprietary advantage allows an enterprise to concentrate on the ones for which it has the most expertise and through which it can gain competitive advantage.

■ *Innovative marketing techniques that are efficient in reaching the targeted audience and effective in stimulating purchases (or boosting ancillary revenue sources like advertising)*—Websites have to be cleverly marketed. Unless Web surfers hear about the site, like what they see on their first visit, and are intrigued enough to return again and again, the site will not generate enough revenue to allow the company to survive. Marketing campaigns that result only in heavy site traffic and lots of page views are seldom sufficient; the best test of effective marketing is the ratio at which page views are converted into revenues (the "look-to-buy" ratio). For example, in 2001 Yahoo!'s site traffic averaged 1.2 *billion* page views daily but generated only about $2 million in daily revenues; in contrast, the traffic at brokerage firm Charles Schwab's website averaged only 40 *million* page views per day but resulted in an average of $5 million daily in online commission revenues.

■ *Minimal reliance on ancillary revenues*—Online businesses have to charge fully for the value delivered to customers rather than subsidizing artificially low prices with revenues collected from advertising and other ancillary sources. Companies should view site-advertising revenues and other revenue extras as a way to boost the profitability of an already profitable core businesses, *not* as a means of covering core business losses.

The Issue of Broad versus Narrow Product Offerings   Given that shelf space on the Internet is unlimited, online sellers have to make shrewd decisions about how to position themselves on the spectrum of broad versus narrow product offerings. A one-stop shopping strategy like that employed by Amazon.com has the appealing economics of helping spread fixed operating costs over a wide number of items and a large customer base. Amazon has diversified its product offerings beyond books to include electronics, computers, housewares, music, DVDs, videos, cameras, toys, baby items and baby registry, software, computer and video games, cell phones and service, tools and hardware, travel services, magazine subscriptions, and outdoor-living items; it has also allowed small specialty-item e-tailers to market their products on the Amazon website. The company's tag line "Earth's Biggest Selection" seems accurate: In 2002, Amazon offered some 34 million items at its websites in the United States, Britain, France, Germany, Denmark, and Japan. Other e-tailers, such as Expedia and Hotel.com, have adopted classic focus strategies—building a website aimed at a sharply defined target audience shopping for a particular product or product category. "Focusers" seek to build customer loyalty based on attractively low prices, better value, wide selection of models and styles within the targeted category, convenient service, nifty options, or some other differentiating attribute. They pay special attention to the details that will please their narrow target audience.

The Order Fulfillment Issue   Another big strategic issue for dot-com retailers is whether to perform order fulfillment activities internally or to outsource them. Building central warehouses, stocking them with adequate inventories, and developing systems to pick, pack, and ship individual orders all require substantial start-up capital but may result in lower overall unit costs than would paying the fees of order fulfillment specialists who make a business of providing warehouse space, stocking inventories, and shipping orders for e-tailers. Outsourcing is likely to be economical unless an e-tailer has high unit volume and the capital to invest in its own order fulfillment capabilities. Buy.com, an online superstore consisting of some 30,000 items, obtains products from name-brand manufacturers and uses outsiders to stock and ship those products; thus, its focus is not on manufacturing or order fulfillment but rather on selling.

Choosing Appropriate Functional-Area Strategies

A company's strategy is not complete until company managers have made strategic choices about how the various functional parts of the business—R&D, production, human resources, sales and marketing, finance, and so on—will be managed in support of its basic competitive strategy approach and the other important competitive moves being taken. Normally, functional-area strategy choices rank third on the menu of choosing among the various strategy options, as shown in Figure 4.1. Deciding how to manage specific functions within a company's business hinges on what needs to be done in each area to support and enhance the success of the company's higher-level strategic thrusts. However, *when* functional strategies are chosen is not as important as *what* the strategies are.

Table 4.1 on page 113 indicates what the production and marketing thrusts need to be in supporting each of the five competitive strategies. Beyond these very general prescriptions, it is difficult to say just what the content of the different functional strategies should be without first knowing what higher-level strategic choices a company has made. Suffice it to say here that company personnel—both managers and employees charged with strategy-making responsibility down through the organizational hierarchy—must be told which higher-level strategies have been chosen and then must tailor the company's functional-area strategies accordingly. (To refresh your memory of what is involved here, you may want to reread the sections in Chapter 1 relating to functional-area strategies and the important role they have in a company's overall strategy—see Figure 1.4 and the subsection headed "Who Participates in Crafting a Company's Strategy?")

The Importance of Linking Strategy to Company Values and Ethical Standards

Managers do not dispassionately assess what strategic course to steer. Their choices are typically influenced by their own vision of how to compete, by their own character and ethical standards, by whether they "walk the talk" in displaying the company's stated values and exemplifying its stated business principles, and by how genuinely they strive to balance the best interests of stakeholders—employees, suppliers, customers, shareholders, and society at large. The experiences at Enron, WorldCom, Tyco, HealthSouth, Rite Aid, and several other companies illustrate that when top executives devise shady strategies or wink at unethical behavior, the impact on the company can be devastating.

But tightly linking company strategy to high ethical standards and societal acceptability goes far beyond simply avoiding a corporate black eye from the blow of public disclosure of corporate misdeeds. Ethical strategy making generally begins with two things: (1) managers who themselves have strong character (i.e., who are honest, have integrity, are ethical, and truly care about how they conduct the company's business), and (2) a set of corporate values and ethical standards that genuinely govern a company's strategy and business conduct. Many companies now have a written statement of company values and a code of ethical conduct, both of which are often posted on the company website. But there's a big difference between adopting statements and codes that serve merely as a public smoke screen and developing values and ethical standards that paint the white lines for a company's actual strategy and business conduct. Several top Enron executives made a farce of the company's stated values of "integrity, respect, communication, and excellence"—and destroyed the company in the process. Top executives, directors, and majority shareholders at Adelphia Communications ripped off the company for amounts totaling well over $1 billion and drove it into bankruptcy; their actions, which represent one of the biggest instances of corporate looting and self-dealing in American business, took place despite the company's public pontifications about the principles it would observe in trying to care for customers, employees, stockholders, and the local communities where it operated. Providian Financial Corporation, despite an otherwise glowing record of social responsibility and service to many of its stakeholders, in December 2001 paid $150 million to settle class-action lawsuits alleging that its strategy included attempts to systematically cheat credit card holders.

Boards of directors and top executives must work diligently to see that values statements and ethical codes not only are scrupulously observed in devising strategies and conducting every facet of the company's business but also become a way of life at the company. No company is protected from unethical actions on the part of executives without close monitoring by board members and strong cultural and peer pressures.

However, the recent spate of corporate scandals, which were hatched in the excesses of the late 1990s and which came home to roost in 2001–2003, has resulted in some very positive reforms. Alarmed by the public's loss of confidence in business practices and financial reporting, corporate America has moved to clean up its act (in part, no doubt, because it had little other choice). Outside auditing firms are exercising greater independence than ever before in reviewing their clients' financial statements (rather than turning a blind eye in order to win multimillion-dollar consulting contracts).

Yet it would be unfair and inaccurate to tar all companies and executives as unethical merely because of the excesses of a few that made headline news. At an important number of companies, deeply ingrained values and high ethical standards are reflected in their strategic actions. The strategy crafted by Starbucks' CEO, Howard Schultz, mirrors Schultz's insistence on customers having a very positive experience when patronizing a Starbucks store and his desire to "build a company with soul" and make Starbucks a great place to work. Deere & Company has been guided for over 165 years by four core values exhibited by its founder John Deere and long practiced by company managers and employees: quality, innovation, integrity, and commitment. Deere consistently takes top honors in *Fortune* magazine's annual listing of "America's Most Admired Companies" in the industrial and farm equipment category; in June 2002, *Crain's Chicago Business* ranked Deere & Company as the most-trusted Illinois company and gave it the top ranking for product quality. Deere's mission to "Double and Double Again the John Deere Experience of Genuine Value for Employees, Customers, and Shareholders" is pursued via a strategy aimed at rapidly expanding the company's global ability to supply customers at farmsites, worksites, homes, and turfsites with a growing line of farm, lawn and garden, golf and turf, forestry, and construction equipment products. Most companies have strategies that pass the test of being ethical, and most companies are aware that both their reputations and their long-term well-being are tied to conducting their business in a manner that wins the approval of suppliers, employees, investors, and society at large. Company Spotlight 4.8 contains an "ethics quiz" on the strategic practices of several companies—judge for yourself whether these companies measure up.

First-Mover Advantages and Disadvantages

When to make a strategic move is often as crucial as *what* move to make. Timing is especially important when *first-mover advantages* or *disadvantages* exist.[33] Being first to initiate a strategic move can have a high payoff when (1) pioneering helps build a firm's image and reputation with buyers; (2) early commitments to new technologies, new-style components, distribution channels, and so on can produce an absolute cost advantage over rivals; (3) first-time customers remain strongly loyal to pioneering firms in making repeat purchases; and (4) moving first constitutes a preemptive strike, making imitation extra hard or unlikely. The bigger the first-mover advantages, the more attractive making the first move becomes.[34] In the Internet gold-rush era, several companies that were first with a new technology, network solution, or business model enjoyed lasting first-mover advantages in gaining the visibility and reputation needed to emerge as the dominant market leader—America Online, Amazon.com, Yahoo!, eBay, and Priceline.com are cases

> **Core Concept**
>
> Because of first-mover advantages and disadvantages, competitive advantage can spring from *when* a move is made as well as from *what* move is made.

in point. But a first-mover also needs to be a fast learner (so as to sustain any advantage of being a pioneer), and it helps immensely if the first-mover has deep financial pockets, important competencies and competitive capabilities, and high-quality management. Just being a first-mover by itself is seldom enough to yield competitive advantage. The proper target in timing a strategic move is not that of being the first company to do something but rather that of being the first competitor to put together the precise combination of features, customer value, and sound revenue/cost/profit economics that gives it an edge over rivals in the battle for market leadership.[35]

However, being a fast-follower or even a wait-and-see late-mover doesn't always carry a significant or lasting competitive penalty. There are times when a first-mover's skills, know-how, and actions are easily copied or even surpassed, allowing late-movers to catch or overtake the first-mover in a relatively short period. And there are times when there are actually *advantages* to being an adept follower rather than a first-mover. Late-mover advantages (or first-mover disadvantages) arise when (1) pioneering leadership is more costly than imitating followership and only negligible experience or learning-curve benefits accrue to the leader—a condition that allows a follower to end up with lower costs than the first-mover; (2) the products of an innovator are somewhat primitive and do not live up to buyer expectations, thus allowing a clever follower to win disenchanted buyers away from the leader with better-performing products; and (3) technology is advancing rapidly, giving fast-followers the opening to leapfrog a first-mover's products with more attractive and full-featured second- and third-generation products.

In weighing the pros and cons of being a first-mover versus a fast-follower, it is important to discern when the race to market leadership in a particular industry is a marathon rather than a sprint. In marathons, a slow-mover is not unduly penalized—first-mover advantages can be fleeting, and there's ample time for fast-followers to play catch-up.[36] For instance, it took seven years for videocassette recorders to find their way into 1 million U.S. homes but only 18 months for 10 million users to sign up for Hotmail. The lesson here is that there is a market-penetration curve for every emerging opportunity; typically, the curve has an inflection point at which all the pieces of the business model fall into place, buyer demand explodes, and the market takes off. The inflection point can come early on a fast-rising curve or farther on up a slow-rising curve. Any company that seeks competitive advantage by being a first-mover should thus first pose some hard questions: Does market takeoff depend on the development of complementary products or services that currently are not available? Is new infrastructure required before buyer demand can surge? Will buyers need to learn new skills or adopt new behaviors? Will buyers encounter high switching costs? Are there influential competitors in a position to delay or derail the efforts of a first-mover? When the answers to any of these questions are yes, then a company must be careful not to pour too many resources into getting ahead of the market opportunity—the race is likely going to be more of a 10-year marathon than a 2-year sprint. But being first out of the starting block is competitively important if it produces clear and substantial benefits to buyers and competitors will be compelled to follow.

While being an adept fast-follower has the advantages of being less risky and skirting the costs of pioneering, rarely does a company have much to gain from being a slow-follower and concentrating on avoiding the "mistakes" of first-movers. Habitual late-movers, while often able to survive, are usually fighting to retain their customers and scrambling to keep pace with more progressive and innovative rivals. For a habitual late-mover to catch up, it must count on first-movers to be slow learners.

Read the brief description of what each of the following companies is doing and decide whether its strategy is ethical or not. Then ponder how you would answer the four questions that appear below.

■ Fleming Companies, the largest U.S. distributor of grocery products, has been accused by dozens of its suppliers of consistently deducting arbitrary sums (amounting to perhaps $100 million annually) from the billings they submit—the practice was said to be a part of Fleming's turnaround strategy to boost its own margins and restore profitability after five money-losing years (1996–2000). According to a food industry consultant who has worked for the company, Fleming's "relationship with vendors is ugly. They deduct and deduct until a vendor cuts them off, then they pay. Then they start deducting again." Former high-level Fleming employees claimed that the company played games with slotting fees, sometimes taking slotting fee deductions form manufacturer billings for products it never stocked in its warehouse or put on retailers' shelves. Fleming enjoys a powerful gatekeeper status because many food manufacturers use a grocery distributor to access small independent grocery chains and because many small grocers get most of their merchandise through a grocery distributor (unlike large chains like Wal-Mart and Safeway that buy directly from the manufacturers). Thus manufacturers that sell through Fleming are hesitant to cut off deliveries to Fleming or protest its deductions too vociferously because they don't have effective alternatives to getting their products to Fleming's grocery customers.

Relationships with some of Fleming's retail customers, most notably Kmart (its biggest customer) and several small independent supermarkets, were also said to be strained because of recurring service and billing issues.

■ At Salomon Smith Barney (a subsidiary of Citigroup), Credit Suisse First Boston (CSFB), and Goldman Sachs (three of the world's most prominent investment banking companies), part of the strategy for securing the investment banking business of large corporate clients (to handle the sale of new stock issues or new bond issues or advise on mergers and acquisitions) involved (1) hyping the stocks of companies that were actual or prospective customers of their investment

banking services, and (2) allocating hard-to-get shares of hot new initial public offerings (IPOs) to select executives and directors of existing and potential client companies, who then made millions of dollars in profits when the stocks went up once public trading began. Former WorldCom CEO Bernie Ebbers reportedly made more than $11 million in trading profits over a four-year period on shares of IPOs received from Salomon Smith Barney; Salomon served as WorldCom's investment banker on a variety of deals during this period. Jack Grubman, Salomon's top-paid research analyst at the time, enthusiastically touted WorldCom stock and was regarded as the company's biggest cheerleader on Wall Street.

To help draw in business from new or existing corporate clients, CSFB established brokerage accounts for corporate executives who steered their company's investment banking business to CSFB. Apparently, CSFB's strategy for acquiring more business involved promising the CEO and/or CFO of companies about to go public for the first time or needing to issue new long-term bonds that if CSFB was chosen to handle their company's new initial public offering of common stock or a new bond issue, then CSFB would ensure they would be allocated shares at the initial offering price of all subsequent IPOs in which CSFB was a participant. During 1999–2000, it was common for the stock of a hot new IPO to rise 100 to 500 percent above the initial offering price in the first few days or weeks of public trading; the shares allocated to these executives were then sold for a tidy profit over the initial offering price. According to investigative sources, CSFB increased the number of companies whose executives were allowed to participate in its IPO offerings from 26 companies in January 1999 to 160 companies in early 2000; executives received anywhere from 200 to 1,000 shares each of every IPO in which CSFB was a participant in 2000. CSFB's accounts for these executives reportedly generated profits of about $80 million for the participants. Apparently, it was CSFB's practice to curtail access to IPOs for some executives if their companies didn't come through with additional securities business for CSFB or if CSFB concluded that other securities offerings by these companies would be unlikely.

Goldman Sachs also used an IPO-allocation scheme to attract investment banking business, giving shares to executives at 21 companies—among the participants were the CEOs of eBay, Yahoo!, and Ford Motor Company. EBay's CEO was a participant in over 100 IPOs managed by Goldman during the 1996–2000 period and was on Goldman's board of directors part of this time; eBay paid Goldman Sachs $8 million in fees for services during the 1996–2001 period.

- The world's five major music recording studios—Universal, Sony, Time Warner, EMI/Virgin, and Bertlesmann—have incurred the wrath of numerous recording artists and the Recording Artists' Coalition for pursuing strategies calculated to disadvantage musicians who record for them. Most major-label record companies require artists to sign contracts committing them to do six to eight albums, an obligation that some artists say can entail an indefinite term of indentured servitude. Audits routinely detect unpaid royalties to musicians under contract; according to one music industry attorney, record companies misreport and underpay artist royalties by 10 to 40 percent and are "intentionally fraudulent." One music writer was recently quoted as saying the process was "an entrenched system whose prowess and conniving makes Enron look like amateur hour." Royalty calculations are based on complex formulas that are paid only after artists pay for recording costs and other expenses and after any advances are covered by royalty earnings. A *Baffler* magazine article outlined a hypothetical but typical record deal where a promising young band is given a $250,000 royalty advance on a new album, The album subsequently sells 250,000 copies, earning $710,000 for the record company; but the band, after repaying the record company for $264,000 in expenses ranging from recording fees and video budgets to catering, wardrobe, and bus tour costs for promotional events related to the album, ends up $14,000 in the hole, owes the record company money, and is thus paid no royalties on any of the $710,000 in revenues the recording company receives from the sale of the band's music. It is also standard practice in the music industry for recording studios to sidestep payola laws by hiring independent promoters to lobby and compensate radio stations for playing certain records. Record companies are often entitled to damages for undelivered albums if an artist leaves a recording studio for another label after seven years. Record companies also retain the copyrights in perpetuity on all music recorded under contract, a practice that artists claim is unfair. The Dixie Chicks, after a year-long feud with Sony over contract terms, ended up refusing to do another album; Sony sued for breach of contract, prompting a countersuit by the Dixie Chicks charging "systematic thievery" to cheat them out of royalties. The suits were settled out of court. One artist said, "The record companies are like cartels."

Recording studios defend their strategic practices by pointing out that fewer than 5 percent of the signed artists ever deliver a hit and that they lose money on albums that sell poorly. According to one study, only 1 of 244 contracts signed during 1994–1996 was negotiated without the artists being represented by legal counsel, and virtually all contracts renegotiated after a hit album added terms more favorable to the artist.

Some Questions for You to Consider

- Would you want to be an employee of any of the companies described above? Would you be proud of the company you worked for if you were an employee?

- Would you feel comfortable doing business with any of these companies? Why or why not?

- If you were a top executive of one of these companies, would you be proud to defend your company's actions? Would you want to step forward and take credit for having been a part of the company's strategy-making team?

- If you were a shareholder in any of these companies, would you be pleased with your company's reputation in the business world and the character of its top executives?

Sources: Ann Zimmerman, "Grocery Supplier Squeezes Suppliers at Bill-Paying Time," *The Wall Street Journal*, September 5, 2002, pp. A1, A10; Charles Gasparino, "Salomon Probe Includes Senior Executives," *The Wall Street Journal*, September 3, 2002, p. C1; Randall Smith and Susan Pulliam, "How a Star Banker Pressed for IPOs," *The Wall Street Journal*, September 4, 2002, pp. C1, C14; Randall Smith and Susan Pulliam, "How a Technology-Banking Star Doled Out Shares of Hot IPOs," *The Wall Street Journal*, September 23, 2002, pp. A1, A10; Randall Smith, "Goldman Sachs Faces Scrutiny for IPO-Allocation Practices," *The Wall Street Journal*, October 3, 2002, pp. A1, A6; Edna Gundersen, "Rights Issue Rocks the Music World," *USA Today*, September 16, 2002, pp. D1, D2.

Plus it has to hope that buyers will be slow to gravitate to the products of first-movers, again giving it time to catch up. And it has to have competencies and capabilities that are sufficiently strong to allow it to close the gap fairly quickly once it makes its move. Counting on all first-movers to stumble or otherwise be easily overtaken is usually a bad bet that puts a late-mover's competitive position at risk.

Key Points

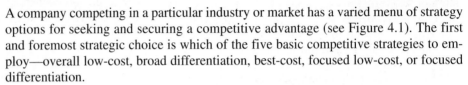

A company competing in a particular industry or market has a varied menu of strategy options for seeking and securing a competitive advantage (see Figure 4.1). The first and foremost strategic choice is which of the five basic competitive strategies to employ—overall low-cost, broad differentiation, best-cost, focused low-cost, or focused differentiation.

A strategy of trying to be the industry's low-cost provider works well in situations where:

1. The industry's product is essentially the same from seller to seller (brand differences are minor).

2. Many buyers are price-sensitive and shop for the lowest price.

3. There are only a few ways to achieve product differentiation that have much value to buyers.

4. Most buyers use the product in the same ways and thus have common user requirements.

5. Buyers' costs in switching from one seller or brand to another are low or even zero.

6. Buyers are large and have significant power to negotiate pricing terms.

To achieve a low-cost advantage, a company must become more skilled than rivals in controlling the cost drivers and/or it must find innovative ways to eliminate or bypass cost-producing activities. Successful low-cost providers usually achieve their cost advantages by imaginatively and persistently ferreting out cost savings throughout the value chain. They are good at finding ways to drive costs out of their businesses year after year after year.

Differentiation strategies seek to produce a competitive edge by incorporating attributes and features into a company's product/service offering that rivals don't have. Anything a firm can do to create buyer value represents a potential basis for differentiation. Successful differentiation is usually keyed to lowering the buyer's cost of using the item, raising the performance the buyer gets, or boosting a buyer's psychological satisfaction. To be sustainable, differentiation usually has to be linked to unique internal expertise, core competencies, and resources that translate into capabilities rivals can't easily match. Differentiation tied just to unique features seldom is lasting because resourceful competitors are adept at cloning, improving on, or finding substitutes for almost any feature that appeals to buyers.

Best-cost provider strategies combine a strategic emphasis on low cost with a strategic emphasis on more than minimal quality, service, features, or performance. The aim is to create competitive advantage by giving buyers more value for the money; this is done by matching close rivals on key quality/service/features/performance attributes and beating them on the costs of incorporating such attributes into the product or service. To be successful with a best-cost provider strategy, a company must be able to incorporate upscale product or service attributes at a lower cost than rivals. Sustaining a best-cost provider strategy generally means having the capability to simultaneously manage unit costs down and product/service caliber up.

A focus strategy delivers competitive advantage either by achieving lower costs in serving the target market niche or by developing an ability to offer niche buyers something different from rival competitors. A focused strategy based on either low cost or differentiation becomes increasingly attractive as more of the following conditions are met:

1. The target market niche is big enough to be profitable and offers good growth potential.

2. Industry leaders do not see that having a presence in the niche is crucial to their own success—in which case focusers can often escape battling head-to-head against some of the industry's biggest and strongest competitors.

3. It is costly or difficult for multisegment competitors to put capabilities in place to meet the specialized needs of the target market niche and at the same time satisfy the expectations of their mainstream customers.

4. The industry has many different niches and segments, thereby allowing a focuser to pick a competitively attractive niche suited to its resource strengths and capabilities. Also, with more niches there is more room for focusers to avoid each other in competing for the same customers.

5. Few, if any, other rivals are attempting to specialize in the same target segment—a condition that reduces the risk of segment overcrowding.

6. The focuser can compete effectively against challengers based on the capabilities and resources it has to serve the targeted niche and the customer goodwill it may have built up.

Once a company has selected which of the five basic competitive strategies to employ in its quest for competitive advantage, then it must decide whether to supplement its choice of a basic competitive strategy approach with strategic actions relating to forming alliances and collaborative partnerships, mergers and acquisitions, integration forward or backward, outsourcing certain value chain activities, offensive and defensive moves, and what use to make of the Internet in selling directly to end users, as shown in Figure 4.1.

Many companies are using strategic alliances and collaborative partnerships to help them in the race to build a global market presence and in the technology race. Even large and financially strong companies have concluded that simultaneously running both races requires more diverse and expansive skills, resources, technological expertise, and competitive capabilities than they can assemble and manage alone. Strategic alliances are an attractive, flexible, and often cost-effective means by which companies can gain access to missing technology, expertise, and business capabilities. The competitive attraction of alliances is to bundle competencies and resources that are more valuable in a joint effort than when kept separate. Competitive advantage emerges when a company acquires valuable resources and capabilities through alliances that it could not otherwise obtain on its own and that give it an edge over rivals.

Mergers and acquisitions are another attractive strategic option for strengthening a firm's competitiveness. Companies racing for global market leadership frequently make acquisitions to build a market presence in countries where they currently do not compete. Similarly, companies racing to establish attractive positions in the industries of the future merge or make acquisitions to close gaps in resources or technology, build important technological capabilities, and move into position to launch next-wave products and services. When the operations of two companies are combined via merger or acquisition, the new company's competitiveness can be enhanced in any of several ways—lower costs; stronger technological skills; more or better competitive capabilities; a more attractive lineup of products and services; wider geographic coverage; and/or greater financial resources with which to invest in R&D, add capacity, or expand into new areas.

Vertically integrating forward or backward makes strategic sense only if it strengthens a company's position via either cost reduction or creation of a differentiation-based advantage. Otherwise, the drawbacks of vertical integration (increased investment, greater business risk, increased vulnerability to technological changes, and less flexibility in making product changes) outweigh the advantages (better coordination of production flows and technological know-how from stage to stage, more specialized use of technology, greater internal control over operations, greater scale economies, and matching production with sales and marketing). Collaborative partnerships with suppliers and/or distribution allies often permit a company to achieve the advantages of vertical integration without encountering the drawbacks.

Outsourcing pieces of the value chain formerly performed in-house can enhance a company's competitiveness whenever (1) an activity can be performed better or more cheaply by outside specialists; (2) the activity is not crucial to the firm's ability to achieve sustainable competitive advantage and won't hollow out its core competencies, capabilities, or technical know-how; (3) it reduces the company's risk exposure to changing technology and/or changing buyer preferences; (4) it streamlines company operations in ways that improve organizational flexibility, cut cycle time, speed decision making, and reduce coordination costs; and/or (5) it allows a company to concentrate on its core business and do what it does best. In many situations outsourcing is a superior strategic alternative to vertical integration.

A variety of offensive strategic moves can be used to secure a competitive advantage. Strategic offensives can be aimed either at competitors' strengths or at their weaknesses; they can involve end runs or grand offensives on many fronts; they can be designed as guerrilla actions or as preemptive strikes; and the target of the offensive can be a market leader, a runner-up firm, or the smallest and/or weakest firms in the industry.

Defensive strategies to protect a company's position usually take the form of making moves that put obstacles in the path of would-be challengers and fortify the company's present position while undertaking actions to dissuade rivals from even trying to attack (by signaling that the resulting battle will be more costly to the challenger than it is worth).

One of the most pertinent strategic issues that companies face is how to use the Internet in positioning the company in the marketplace—whether to use the Internet as *only a means of disseminating product information* (with traditional distribution channel partners making all sales to end users), as a *secondary* or *minor* channel, as *one of several important* distribution channels, as the company's *primary distribution channel,* or as the company's *exclusive channel for accessing customers.*

Once all the higher-level strategic choices have been made, company managers can turn to the task of crafting functional and operating-level strategies to flesh out the details of the company's overall business and competitive strategy.

The timing of strategic moves also has relevance in the quest for competitive advantage. Because of the competitive importance that is sometimes associated with when a strategic move is made, company managers are obligated to carefully consider the advantages or disadvantages that attach to being a first-mover versus a fast-follower versus a wait-and-see late-mover. At the end of the day, though, the proper objective of a first-mover is that of being the first competitor to put together the precise combination of features, customer value, and sound revenue/cost/profit economics that puts it ahead of the pack in capturing an attractive market opportunity. Sometimes the company that first unlocks a profitable market opportunity is the first-mover and sometimes it is not—but the company that comes up with the key is surely the smart mover.

Exercises

1. Log on to www.business-ethics.com and review which companies are on the latest list of the 100 Best Corporate Citizens. Also review the criteria for earning a spot on this list. Are these criteria sound? Is there ample reason to believe that the 100 companies on this list pursue strategies that are ethical? Why or why not?

2. Go to www.google.com and do a search for "low-cost producer." See if you can identify five companies that are pursuing a low-cost strategy in their respective industries.

3. Using the advanced search engine function at www.google.com, enter "best-cost producer" in the exact phrase box and see if you can locate three companies that indicate they are employing a best-cost producer strategy.

CHAPTER

5

Competing in Foreign Markets

You have no choice but to operate in a world shaped by globalization and the information revolution. There are two options: Adapt or die.
—Andrew S. Grove, Chairman, Intel Corporation

You do not choose to become global. The market chooses for you; it forces your hand.
—Alain Gomez, CEO, Thomson, S.A.

[I]ndustries actually vary a great deal in the pressures they put on a company to sell internationally.
—Niraj Dawar and Tony Frost, Professors,
    Richard Ivey School of Business

Any company that aspires to industry leadership in the 21st century must think in terms of global, not domestic, market leadership. The world economy is globalizing at an accelerating pace as countries heretofore closed to foreign companies open up their markets; as the Internet shrinks the importance of geographic distance; and as ambitious, growth-minded companies race to build stronger competitive positions in the markets of more and more countries. Companies in industries that are already globally competitive or are in the process of globalizing are under the gun to come up with a strategy for competing successfully in foreign markets.

This chapter focuses on strategy options for expanding beyond domestic boundaries and competing in the markets of either a few or a great many countries. The spotlight will be on four strategic issues unique to competing multinationally:

1. Whether to customize the company's offerings in each different country market to match the tastes and preferences of local buyers or offer a mostly standardized product worldwide.

2. Whether to employ essentially the same basic competitive strategy in all countries or modify the strategy country by country.

3. Where to locate the company's production facilities, distribution centers, and customer service operations so as to realize the greatest locational advantages.

4. How to efficiently transfer the company's resource strengths and capabilities from one country to another in an effort to secure competitive advantage.

In the process of exploring these issues, we will introduce a number of core concepts—multicountry competition, global competition, profit sanctuaries, and cross-market subsidization. The chapter includes sections on cross-country differences in cultural, demographic, and market conditions; strategy options for entering and competing in foreign markets; the growing role of alliances with foreign partners; the importance of locating operations in the most advantageous countries; and the special circumstances of competing in such emerging markets as China, India, and Brazil.

Why Companies Expand into Foreign Markets

A company may opt to expand outside its domestic market for any of four major reasons:

1. *To gain access to new customers*—Expanding into foreign markets offers potential for increased revenues, profits, and long-term growth and becomes an especially attractive option when a company's home markets are mature. Firms like Cisco Systems, Intel, Sony, Nokia, Avon, and Toyota, which are racing for global leadership in their respective industries, are moving rapidly and aggressively to extend their market reach into all corners of the world.

2. *To achieve lower costs and enhance the firm's competitiveness*—Many companies are driven to sell in more than one country because domestic sales volume is not large enough to fully capture manufacturing economies of scale or learning-curve

effects and thereby substantially improve a firm's cost competitiveness. The relatively small size of country markets in Europe explains why companies like Michelin, BMW, and Nestlé long ago began selling their products all across Europe and then moved into markets in North America and Latin America.

3. *To capitalize on its core competencies*—A company may be able to leverage its competencies and capabilities into a position of competitive advantage in foreign markets as well as just domestic markets. Nokia's competencies and capabilities in mobile phones have propelled it to global market leadership in the wireless telecommunications business.

4. *To spread its business risk across a wider market base*—A company spreads business risk by operating in a number of different foreign countries rather than depending entirely on operations in its domestic market. Thus, if the economies of certain Asian countries turn down for a period of time, a company with operations across much of the world may be sustained by buoyant sales in Latin America or Europe.

In a few cases, companies in natural resource–based industries (e.g., oil and gas, minerals, rubber, and lumber) often find it necessary to operate in the international arena because attractive raw material supplies are located in foreign countries.

The Difference between Competing Internationally and Competing Globally

Typically, a company will *start* to compete internationally by entering just one or maybe a select few foreign markets. Competing on a truly global scale comes later, after the company has established operations on several continents and is racing against rivals for global market leadership. Thus, there is a meaningful distinction between the competitive scope of a company that operates in a select few foreign countries (with perhaps modest ambitions to expand further) and a company that markets its products in 50 to 100 countries and is expanding its operations into additional country markets annually. The former is most accurately termed an **international competitor,** while the latter qualifies as a **global competitor.** In the discussion that follows, we'll continue to make a distinction between strategies for competing internationally and strategies for competing globally.

Cross-Country Differences in Cultural, Demographic, and Market Conditions

Regardless of a company's motivation for expanding outside its domestic markets, the strategies it uses to compete in foreign markets must be *situation-driven*. Cultural, demographic, and market conditions vary significantly among the countries of the world. Cultures and lifestyles are the most obvious areas in which countries differ; market demographics are close behind. Consumers in Spain do not have the same tastes, preferences, and buying habits as consumers in Norway; buyers differ yet again in Greece, in Chile, in New Zealand, and in Taiwan. Less than 10 percent of the populations of Brazil, India, and China have annual purchasing power equivalent to $20,000. Middle-class consumers represent a much smaller portion of the population in these and other emerging countries than in North America, Japan, and much of Europe.[1] Sometimes, product designs suitable in one country are inappropriate in another—for example, in the United States electrical devices run on 110-volt electrical systems, but in some European countries the standard is a 240-volt electric system, necessitating the use of different electrical designs and components. In France consumers prefer top-loading washing machines, while in most other European countries consumers prefer front-loading machines. Northern Europeans want large refrigerators because they tend to shop once a week in supermarkets; southern Europeans can get by on small refrigerators because they shop daily. In parts of Asia refrigerators are a status symbol and may be placed in the living room, leading to preferences for stylish designs and colors—in India bright blue and red are popular colors. In other Asian countries, household space is constrained and many refrigerators are only four feet high so that the top can be used for storage. In Hong Kong the preference is for compact European-style appliances, but in Taiwan large American-style appliances are more popular.

Similarly, market growth varies from country to country. In emerging markets like India, China, Brazil, and Malaysia, market growth potential is far higher than in the more mature economies of Britain, Denmark, Canada, and Japan. In automobiles, for example, the potential for market growth is explosive in China, where sales amount to only 1 million vehicles annually in a country with 1.3 billion people. In India there are efficient, well-developed national channels for distributing trucks, scooters, farm equipment, groceries, personal care items, and other packaged products to the country's 3 million retailers, whereas in China distribution is primarily local and there is no national network for distributing most products. The marketplace is intensely competitive in some countries and only moderately contested in others. Industry driving forces may be one thing in Italy, quite another in Canada, and different yet again in Israel or Argentina or South Korea.

One of the biggest concerns of companies competing in foreign markets is whether to customize their offerings in each different country market to match the tastes and preferences of local buyers or whether to offer a mostly standardized product worldwide. While the products of a company that is responsive to local tastes will appeal to local buyers, customizing a company's products country by country *may* have the effect of raising production and distribution costs due to the greater variety of designs and components, shorter production runs, and the complications of added inventory handling and distribution logistics. Greater standardization of the company's product offering, on the other hand, can lead to scale economies and learning-curve effects, thus contributing to the achievement of a low-cost advantage. The tension between the market pressures to customize and the competitive pressures to lower costs is one of the big strategic issues that participants in foreign markets have to resolve.

Aside from the basic cultural and market differences among countries, a company also has to pay special attention to locational advantages that stem from country-to-country variations in manufacturing and distribution costs, the risks of fluctuating exchange rates, and the economic and political demands of host governments.

The Potential for Locational Advantages

Differences in wage rates, worker productivity, inflation rates, energy costs, tax rates, government regulations, and the like create sizable variations in manufacturing costs from country to country. Plants in some countries have major manufacturing cost advantages because of lower input costs (especially labor), relaxed government regulations, the proximity of suppliers, or unique natural resources. In such cases, the low-cost countries become principal production sites, with most of the output being exported to markets in other parts of the world. Companies that build production facilities in low-cost countries (or that source their products from contract manufacturers in these countries) have a competitive advantage over rivals with plants in countries where costs are higher. The competitive role of low manufacturing costs is most evident in low-wage countries like Taiwan, South Korea, China, Singapore, Malaysia, Vietnam, Mexico, and Brazil, which have become production havens for goods with high labor content. Likewise, concerns about short delivery times and low shipping costs make some countries better locations than others for establishing distribution centers.

The quality of a country's business environment also offers locational advantages—the governments of some countries are anxious to attract foreign investments and go all-out to create a business climate that outsiders will view as favorable. A good example is Ireland, which has one of the world's most pro-business environments, offering very low corporate tax rates, a government that is responsive to the needs of industry, and a policy of aggressively recruiting high-tech manufacturing facilities and multinational companies. Such policies were a significant force in making Ireland the most dynamic, fastest-growing nation in Europe during the 1990s. The single biggest foreign investment in Ireland's history is Intel's largest non-U.S. chip manufacturing plant, a $2.5 billion facility employing over 4,000 people. Another locational advantage is the clustering of suppliers of components and capital equipment; infrastructure suppliers (universities, vocational training providers, research enterprises); trade associations; and makers of complementary products in a geographic area—such clustering can be an important source of cost savings in addition to facilitating close collaboration with key suppliers.

The Risks of Adverse Exchange Rate Fluctuations

The volatility of exchange rates greatly complicates the issue of geographic cost advantages. Currency exchange rates often fluctuate 20 to 40 percent annually. Changes of this magnitude can either totally wipe out a country's low-cost advantage or transform a former high-cost location into a competitive-cost location. For instance, in the mid-1980s, when the dollar was strong relative to the Japanese yen (meaning that $1 would purchase, say, 125 yen as opposed to only 100 yen), Japanese heavy-equipment maker Komatsu was able to undercut U.S.-based Caterpillar's prices by as much as 25 percent, causing Caterpillar to lose sales and market share. But starting in 1985, when exchange rates began to shift and the dollar grew steadily weaker against the yen (meaning that $1 was worth fewer and fewer yen), Komatsu had to raise its prices six times over two years, as its yen-based costs in terms of dollars soared. Caterpillar's competitiveness against Komatsu was restored and it regained sales and lost market share. The lesson of fluctuating exchange rates is that companies that export goods to foreign countries always gain in competitiveness when the currency of the country in which the goods are manufactured is weak. Exporters are disadvantaged when the currency of the country where goods are being manufactured grows stronger. Sizable long-term shifts in exchange rates thus shuffle the global cards of which rivals have the upper hand in the marketplace and which countries represent the low-cost manufacturing location.

As a further illustration of the risks associated with fluctuating exchange rates and how they can alter the advantages of manufacturing goals in a particular country, consider the case of a U.S. company that has located manufacturing facilities in Brazil (where the currency is *reals*) and that exports most of the Brazilian-made goods to markets in European Union (where the currency is *euros*). To keep the numbers simple, assume that the exchange rate is 4 Brazilian reals for 1 euro and that the product being made in Brazil has a manufacturing cost of 4 Brazilian reals (or 1 euro). Now suppose that for some reason the exchange rate shifts from 4 reals per euro to 5 reals per euro (meaning that the real has declined in value and that the euro is stronger). Making the product in Brazil is now more cost-competitive because a Brazilian good costing 4 reals to produce has fallen to only 0.8 euros at the new exchange rate. On the other hand, if the value of the Brazilian real grows stronger in relation to the euro—resulting in an exchange rate of 3 reals to 1 euro—the same good costing 4 reals to produce now has a cost of 1.33 euros. Clearly, the attraction of manufacturing a good in Brazil and selling it in Europe is far greater when the euro is strong (an exchange rate of 1 euro for 5 Brazilian reals) than when the euro is weak and exchanges for only 3 Brazilian reals.

> Companies with manufacturing facilities in Brazil are more cost-competitive in exporting goods to world markets when the Brazilian real is weak; their competitiveness erodes when the Brazilian real grows stronger relative to the currencies of the countries where the Brazilian-made goods are being sold.

To put it another way, declines in the value of the dollar against foreign currencies reduce or eliminate whatever cost advantage foreign manufacturers might have over U.S. manufacturers and can even prompt foreign companies to establish production plants in the United States. Likewise, a weak euro enhances the cost-competitiveness of companies manufacturing goods in Europe for export to foreign markets; a strong euro versus other currencies weakens the cost-competitiveness of European plants that manufacture goods for export.

In 2002, when the Brazilian real declined in value by about 25 percent against the dollar, the euro, and several other currencies, the ability of companies with manufacturing plants in Brazil to compete in world markets was greatly enhanced—of course, in the future years this windfall gain in cost advantage might well be eroded by sustained rises in the value of the Brazilian real against these same currencies. Herein lies the risk: Currency exchange rates are rather unpredictable, swinging first one way and then another way, so the competitiveness of any company's facilities in any country is partly dependent on whether exchange rate changes over time have a favorable or unfavorable cost impact. Companies making goods in one country for export to foreign countries always gain in competitiveness as the currency of that country grows weaker. Exporters are disadvantaged when the currency of the country where goods are being manufactured grows stronger. From a different perspective, though, domestic companies that are under pressure from lower-cost imported goods gain in competitiveness when their currency grows weaker in relation to the currencies of the countries where the imported goods are made.

> **Core Concept**
>
> Fluctuating exchange rates pose significant risks to a company's competitiveness in foreign markets. Exporters win when the currency of the country where goods are being manufactured grows weaker, and they lose when the currency grows stronger. Domestic companies under pressure from lower-cost imports are benefited when their government's currency grows weaker in relation to the countries where the imported goods are being made.

Host Government Restrictions and Requirements

National governments enact all kinds of measures affecting business conditions and the operation of foreign companies in their markets. Host governments may set local content requirements on goods made inside their borders by foreign-based companies, put restrictions on exports to ensure adequate local supplies, regulate the prices of imported and locally produced goods, and impose tariffs or quotas on the imports of certain goods—until 2002, when it joined the World Trade Organization, China imposed a 100 percent tariff on motor vehicles. Governments may have burdensome tax structures or they may not. In addition, outsiders may face a web of regulations regarding technical standards, product certification, prior approval of capital spending projects, withdrawal of funds from the country, and required minority (sometimes majority) ownership of foreign company operations by local citizens. A few governments may be hostile to or suspicious of foreign companies operating within their borders. Some governments provide subsidies and low-interest loans to domestic companies to help them compete against foreign-based companies. Other governments, anxious to obtain new plants and jobs, offer foreign companies a helping hand in the form of subsidies, privileged market access, and technical assistance. All of these possibilities argue for taking a close look at a country's politics and policies toward business in general, and foreign companies in particular, in deciding which country markets to participate in and which ones to avoid.

The Concepts of Multicountry Competition and Global Competition

Core Concept

Multicountry competition exists when competition in one national market is not closely connected to competition in another national market—there is no global or world market, just a collection of self-contained country markets.

There are important differences in the patterns of international competition from industry to industry.[2] At one extreme is **multicountry competition,** in which there's so much cross-country variation in market conditions and in the companies contending for leadership that the market contest among rivals in one country is not closely connected to the market contests in other countries. The standout features of multicountry competition are that (1) buyers in different countries are attracted to different product attributes, (2) sellers vary from country to country, and (3) industry conditions and competitive forces in each national market differ in important respects. Take the banking industry in Italy, Brazil, and Japan as an example—the requirements and expectations of banking customers vary among the three countries, the lead banking competitors in Italy differ from those in Brazil or in Japan, and the competitive battle going on among the leading banks in Italy is unrelated to the rivalry taking place in Brazil or Japan. Thus, *with multicountry competition, rival firms battle for national championships and winning in one country does not necessarily signal the ability to fare well in other countries.* In multicountry competition, the power of a company's strategy and resource capabilities in one country may not enhance its competitiveness to the same degree in other countries where it operates. Moreover, any competitive advantage a company secures in one country is largely confined to that country; the spillover effects to other countries are minimal to nonexistent. Industries characterized by multicountry competition include radio and TV broadcasting; consumer banking; life insurance; apparel; metals fabrication; many types of food products (coffee, cereals, breads, canned goods, frozen foods); and retailing.

At the other extreme is **global competition,** in which prices and competitive conditions across country markets are strongly linked and the term *global* or *world market* has true meaning. In a globally competitive industry, much the same group of rival companies competes against each other in many different countries, but especially so in countries where sales volumes are large and where having a competitive presence is strategically important to building a strong global position in the industry. Thus, a company's competitive position in one country both affects and is affected by its position in other countries. In global competition, a firm's overall competitive advantage grows out of its entire worldwide operations; the competitive advantage it creates at its home base is supplemented by advantages growing out of its operations in other countries (having plants in low-wage countries, being able to transfer expertise from country to country, having the capability to serve customers who also have multinational operations, and brand-name recognition in many parts of the world). *Rival firms in globally competitive industries vie for worldwide leadership.* Global competition exists in motor vehicles, television sets, tires, mobile phones, personal computers, copiers, watches, digital cameras, bicycles, and commercial aircraft.

> ### Core Concept
> **Global competition** exists when competitive conditions across national markets are linked strongly enough to form a true international market and when leading competitors compete head to head in many different countries.

An industry can have segments that are globally competitive and segments in which competition is country by country.[3] In the hotel/motel industry, for example, the low- and medium-priced segments are characterized by multicountry competition—competitors mainly serve travelers within the same country. In the business and luxury segments, however, competition is more globalized. Companies like Nikki, Marriott, Sheraton, and Hilton have hotels at many international locations, use worldwide reservation systems, and establish common quality and service standards to gain marketing advantages in serving businesspeople and other travelers who make frequent international trips. In lubricants, the marine engine segment is globally competitive—ships move from port to port and require the same oil everywhere they stop. Brand reputations in marine lubricants have a global scope, and successful marine engine lubricant producers (Exxon Mobil, BP Amoco, and Shell) operate globally. In automotive motor oil, however, multicountry competition dominates—countries have different weather conditions and driving patterns, production of motor oil is subject to limited scale economies, shipping costs are high, and retail distribution channels differ markedly from country to country. Thus, domestic firms—like Quaker State and Pennzoil in the United States and Castrol in Great Britain—can be leaders in their home markets without competing globally.

It is also important to recognize that an industry can be in transition from multicountry competition to global competition. In a number of today's industries—beer and major home appliances are prime examples—leading domestic competitors have begun expanding into more and more foreign markets, often acquiring local companies or brands and integrating them into their operations. As some industry members start to build global brands and a global presence, other industry members find themselves pressured to follow the same strategic path—especially if establishing multinational operations results in important scale economies and a powerhouse brand name. As the industry consolidates to fewer players, such that many of the same companies find themselves in head-to-head competition in more and more country markets, global competition begins to replace multicountry competition.

At the same time, consumer tastes in a number of important product categories are converging across the world. Less diversity of tastes and preferences opens the way for companies to create global brands and sell essentially the same products in most all countries of the world. Even in industries where consumer tastes remain fairly diverse, companies are learning to use custom mass production to economically create different versions of a product and thereby satisfy the tastes of people in different countries.

In addition to noting the obvious cultural and political differences between countries, a company should shape its strategic approach to competing in foreign markets according to whether its industry is characterized by multicountry competition, global competition, or is transitioning from multicountry competition to global competition.

Strategy Options for Entering and Competing in Foreign Markets

There are a host of generic strategic options for a company that decides to expand outside its domestic market and compete internationally or globally:

1. *Maintain a national (one-country) production base and export goods to foreign markets,* using either company-owned or foreign-controlled forward distribution channels.

2. *License foreign firms to use the company's technology or to produce and distribute the company's products.*

3. *Employ a franchising strategy.*

4. *Follow a multicountry strategy,* varying the company's strategic approach (perhaps a little, perhaps a lot) from country to country in accordance with local conditions and differing buyer tastes and preferences.

5. *Follow a global strategy,* using essentially the same competitive strategy approach in all country markets where the company has a presence.

6. *Use strategic alliances or joint ventures with foreign companies as the primary vehicle for entering foreign markets* and perhaps also using them as an ongoing strategic arrangement aimed at maintaining or strengthening its competitiveness.

The following sections discuss each of these six options in more detail.

Export Strategies

Using domestic plants as a production base for exporting goods to foreign markets is an excellent *initial strategy* for pursuing international sales. It is a conservative way to test the international waters. The amount of capital needed to begin exporting is often quite minimal; existing production capacity may well be sufficient to make the goods for export. With an export strategy, a manufacturer can limit its involvement in foreign markets by contracting with foreign wholesalers experienced in importing to handle the entire distribution and marketing function in their countries or regions of the world. If it is more advantageous to maintain control over these functions, however, a manufacturer can establish its own distribution and sales organizations in some or all of the target foreign markets. Either way, a home-based production and export strategy helps the firm minimize its direct investments in foreign countries. Such strategies are commonly favored by Chinese, Korean, and Italian companies—products are designed and manufactured at home and then distributed through local channels in the importing countries; the primary functions performed abroad relate chiefly to establishing a network of distributors and perhaps conducting sales promotion and brand awareness activities.

Whether an export strategy can be pursued successfully over the long run hinges on the relative cost-competitiveness of the home-country production base. In some industries, firms gain additional scale economies and learning-curve benefits from centralizing production in one or several giant plants whose output capability exceeds demand in any one country market; obviously, to capture such economies a company must export. However, an export strategy is vulnerable when (1) manufacturing costs in the home country are substantially higher than in foreign countries where rivals have plants, (2) the costs of shipping the product to distant foreign markets are relatively high, or (3) adverse fluctuations occur in currency exchange rates. Unless an exporter can both keep its production and shipping costs competitive with rivals and successfully hedge against unfavorable changes in currency exchange rates, its success will be limited.

Licensing Strategies

Licensing makes sense when a firm with valuable technical know-how or a unique patented product has neither the internal organizational capability nor the resources to enter foreign markets. Licensing also has the advantage of avoiding the risks of committing resources to country markets that are unfamiliar, politically volatile, economically unstable, or otherwise risky. By licensing the technology or the production rights to foreign-based firms, the firm does not have to bear the costs and risks of entering foreign markets on its own, yet it is able to generate income from royalties. The big disadvantage of licensing is the risk of providing valuable technological know-how to foreign companies and thereby losing some degree of control over its use; monitoring licensees and safeguarding the company's proprietary know-how can prove quite difficult in some circumstances. But if the royalty potential is considerable and the companies to whom the licenses are being granted are both trustworthy and reputable, then licensing can be a very attractive option.

Franchising Strategies

While licensing works well for manufacturers, franchising is often better suited to the global expansion efforts of service and retailing enterprises. McDonald's, Tricon Global Restaurants (the parent of Pizza Hut, Kentucky Fried Chicken, and Taco Bell), and Hilton Hotels have all used franchising to build a presence in foreign markets. Franchising has much the same advantages as licensing. The franchisee bears most of the costs and risks of establishing foreign locations; a franchiser has to expend only the resources to recruit, train, support, and monitor franchisees. The big problem a franchiser faces is maintaining quality control; foreign franchisees do not always exhibit strong commitment to consistency and standardization, especially when the local culture does not stress the same kinds of quality concerns. Another problem that can arise is whether to allow foreign franchisees to make modifications in the franchisor's product offering so as to better satisfy the tastes and expectations of local buyers. Should McDonald's allow its franchised units in Japan to modify Big Macs slightly to suit Japanese tastes? Should the franchised Kentucky Fried Chicken units in China be permitted to substitute spices that are more appealing to Chinese consumers or should the same menu offerings be rigorously and unvaryingly required of all franchisees worldwide?

A Multicountry Strategy or a Global Strategy?

The need for a *multicountry strategy* derives from the sometimes vast differences in cultural, economic, political, and competitive conditions in different countries. The more diverse national market conditions are, the stronger the case for a multicountry strategy, in which the company tailors its strategic approach to fit each host country's market situation. Usually, but not always, companies employing a multicountry strategy use the same basic competitive theme (low-cost, differentiation, or best-cost) in each country, making whatever country-specific variations are needed to best satisfy customers and to position themselves against local rivals. They may aim at broad market targets in some countries and focus more narrowly on a particular niche in others. The bigger the country-to-country variations, the more a company's overall international strategy becomes a collection of its individual country strategies. But country to country variations still allow room to connect the strategies in different countries by making an effort to transfer ideas, technologies, competencies, and capabilities that work successfully in one country market to other fairly similar country markets. Toward this end, it is useful to view operations in each country as experiments that result in learning and in capabilities that may merit transfer to other country markets.[4]

While multicountry strategies are best suited for industries where multicountry competition dominates and a fairly high degree of local responsiveness is competitively imperative; *global strategies* are best suited for globally competitive industries.

> A multicountry strategy is appropriate for industries where multicountry competition dominates and local responsiveness is essential. A global strategy works best in markets that are globally competitive or beginning to globalize.

A global strategy is one in which the company's approach is *predominantly the same* in all countries. Although relatively *minor* country-to-country differences in a company's global strategy may be incorporated to accommodate specific situations in a few host countries, the company's fundamental competitive approach (low-cost, differentiation, best-cost, or focused) remains very much intact worldwide. Moreover, a global strategy involves (1) integrating and coordinating the company's strategic moves worldwide, and (2) selling in many if not all nations where there is significant buyer demand.

Figure 5.1 provides a point-by-point comparison of multicountry versus global strategies. *The issue of whether to employ essentially the same basic competitive strategy in the markets of all countries or whether to vary the company's competitive approach to fit specific market conditions and buyer preferences in each host country is perhaps the foremost strategic issue firms face when they compete in foreign markets.*

The strength of a multicountry strategy is that it matches the company's competitive approach to host-country circumstances and accommodates the differing tastes and expectations of buyers in each country. A multicountry strategy is essential when there are significant country-to-country differences in customers' needs and buying habits (see Global Spotlight 5.1), when buyers in a country insist on special-order or highly customized products; when host governments enact regulations requiring that products sold locally meet strict manufacturing specifications or performance standards; and when the trade restrictions of host governments are so diverse and complicated that they preclude a uniform, coordinated worldwide market approach. However, a multicountry strategy has two big drawbacks: It hinders transfer of a company's competencies and resources across country boundaries (since different competencies and capabilities may be used in different host countries), and it does not promote building a single, unified competitive advantage—especially one based on low cost. Companies employing a multicountry strategy face big hurdles in achieving low-cost leadership unless they find ways to customize their products and still be in position to capture scale economies and learning-curve effects—the capability to implement mass customization assembly at relatively low cost (as Dell and Toyota have demonstrated) greatly facilitates effective use of a multicountry approach.

Figure 5.1   How a Multicountry Strategy Differs from a Global Strategy

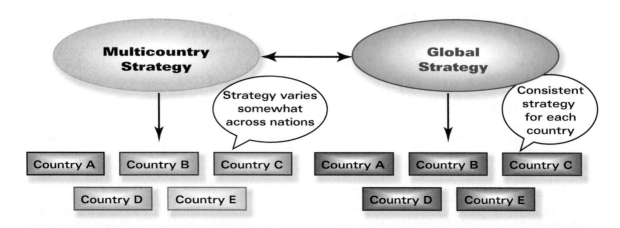

■ Customize the company's competitive approach as needed to fit market and business circumstances in each host country—strong responsiveness to local conditions.	■ Pursue same basic competitive strategy worldwide (low-cost, differentiation, best-cost, focused low-cost, focused differentiation) —with minimal responsiveness to local conditions.
■ Sell different product versions in different countries under different brand names—adapt product attributes to fit buyer tastes and preferences country by country.	■ Sell same products under same brand name worldwide.
■ Scatter plants across many host countries, each producing product versions for local markets.	■ Locate plants on basis of maximum locational advantage, usually in countries where production costs are lowest; but plants may be scattered if shipping costs are high or other locational advantages dominate.
■ Preferably use local suppliers (some local sources may be required by host government).	■ Use best suppliers from anywhere in the world.
■ Adapt marketing and distribution to local customs and cultures.	■ Coordinate marketing and distribution worldwide; make minor adaptations to local countries where needed.
■ Transfer some competencies and capabilities from country to country where feasible.	■ Compete on basis of same technologies, competencies, and capabilities worldwide; stress rapid transfer of new ideas, products, and capabilities to other countries.
■ Give country managers fairly wide strategy-making latitude and autonomy.	■ Coordinate major strategic decisions worldwide; expect local managers to stick close to global strategy.

GLOBAL SPOTLIGHT 5.1

Microsoft, McDonald's, and Nestlé: Users of Multicountry Strategies

Microsoft's Multicountry Strategy in PC Software

In order to best serve the needs of users in foreign countries, Microsoft localizes many of its software products to reflect local languages. In France, for example, all user messages and documentation are in French and all monetary references are in euros. In the United Kingdom, monetary references are in British pounds and user messages and documentation reflect certain British conventions. Various Microsoft products have been localized into more than 30 languages.

McDonald's Multicountry Strategy in Fast Food

McDonald's has been highly successful in markets outside the United States, partly because it has been adept in altering its menu offerings to cater to local tastes. In Taiwan and Singapore, McDonald's outlets offer a bone-in fried chicken dish called Chicken McCrispy. In Great Britain, there's McChicken Tikka Naan to appeal to British cravings for Indian food. In India, McDonald's features the Maharajah Mac sandwich (an Indian version of the Big Mac); in Japan, there's the Chicken Tatsuta sandwich and a Teriyaki Burger sandwich; in Australia, there's a McOz Burger. However, the infrastructure and operating systems that are employed in the outlets are largely the same, enabling McDonald's to achieve low-cost leadership status once it builds volume up at its outlets (sometimes a 5-year process) and once it has enough outlets operating in a country to achieve full economies of scale (sometimes a 5- to 10-year process in the largest foreign markets).

Nestlé's Multicountry Strategy in Instant Coffee

Swiss-based Nestlé, the largest food company in the world, is also the largest producer of coffee. With a total workforce of 22,541 people operating in nearly 480 factories in 100 countries, Nestlé's presence is clearly multinational. Chief executive Peter Brabeck-Letmathe advocates understanding the distinctions between the cultures in which Nestlé markets its products. "[If] you are open to new languages, you are also open to new cultures," he explains. Thus, instant coffee names like Nescafé, Taster's Choice, Ricore, and Ricoffy line grocery shelves in various countries. If customers prefer roast or ground coffee, they can purchase Nespresso, Bonka, Zoegas, or Loumidis, depending on where they live.

Nestlé produces 200 types of instant coffee, from lighter blends for the U.S. market to dark espressos for Latin America. To keep its instant coffees matched to consumer tastes in different countries (and areas within some countries), Nestlé operates four coffee research labs that experiment with new blends in aroma, flavor, and color. The strategy is to match the blends marketed in each country to the tastes and preferences of coffee drinkers in that country, introducing new blends to develop new segments when opportunities appear and altering blends as needed to respond to changing tastes and buyer habits. In Britain, Nescafé was promoted extensively to build a wider base of instant-coffee drinkers. In Japan, where Nescafé was considered a luxury item, the company made its Japanese blends available in fancy containers suitable for gift-giving.

Sources: Nestlé website (www.nestle.com), accessed August 15, 2001; "Nestlé S.A.," Hoover's Online (www.hoovers.com), accessed August 15, 2001; Tom Mudd, "Nestlé Plays to Global Audience," *Industry Week* (www.industryweek.com), August 13, 2001; company annual reports; Shawn Tully, "Nestlé Shows How to Gobble Markets," *Fortune,* January 16, 1989, pp. 74–78; and "Nestlé: A Giant in a Hurry," *Business Week,* March 22, 1993, pp. 50–54.

As a rule, most multinational competitors endeavor to employ as global a strategy as customer needs permit. Philips N.V., the Netherlands-based electronics and consumer products company, operated successfully with a multicountry strategy for many years but has recently begun moving more toward a unified strategy within the European Union and within North America.[5] A global strategy can concentrate on building the resource strengths to secure a sustainable low-cost or differentiation-based competitive advantage over both domestic rivals and global rivals racing for world market leadership. Whenever country-to-country differences are small enough to be accommodated within the framework of a global strategy, a global strategy is preferable to a multi-country strategy because of the value of creating both a uniform brand offering and strong competencies and capabilities not readily matched by rivals.

The Quest for Competitive Advantage in Foreign Markets

There are three ways in which a firm can gain competitive advantage (or offset domestic disadvantages) by expanding outside its domestic market.[6] One way exploits a multinational or global competitor's ability to deploy R&D, parts manufacture, assembly, distribution centers, sales and marketing, customer service centers, and other activities among various countries in a manner that lowers costs or achieves greater product differentiation. A second way involves efficient and effective transfer of competitively valuable competencies and capabilities from its domestic markets to foreign markets. A third way draws on a multinational or global competitor's ability to deepen or broaden its resource strengths and capabilities and to coordinate its dispersed activities in ways that a domestic-only competitor cannot.

Using Location to Build Competitive Advantage

To use location to build competitive advantage, a company must consider two issues: (1) whether to concentrate each activity it performs in a few select countries or to disperse performance of the activity to many nations, and (2) in which countries to locate particular activities. Companies tend to concentrate their activities in a limited number of locations in the following circumstances:

- *When the costs of manufacturing or other activities are significantly lower in some geographic locations than in others*—For example, much of the world's athletic footwear is manufactured in Asia (China and Korea) because of low labor costs; much of the production of motherboards for PCs is located in Taiwan because of both low costs and the high-caliber technical skills of the Taiwanese labor force.

> Companies can pursue competitive advantage in world markets by locating activities in the most advantageous nations; a domestic-only competitor has no such opportunities.

- *When there are significant scale economies in performing the activity*—The presence of significant economies of scale in components production or final assembly means that a company can gain major cost savings from operating a few superefficient plants as opposed to a host of small plants scattered across the world. Important marketing and distribution economies associated with multinational operations can also yield low-cost leadership. In situations where some competitors are intent on global dominance, being the worldwide low-cost provider is a powerful competitive advantage. Achieving low-cost provider status often requires a company to have the largest worldwide *manufacturing share,* with production centralized in one or a few world-scale plants in low-cost locations and often using the capacity of these plants to manufacture units sold under the brand names of rivals. Manufacturing share (as distinct from brand share or market share) is significant because it provides more certain access to production-related scale economies. Japanese makers of VCRs, microwave ovens, TVs, and DVD players have used their large manufacturing share to establish a low-cost advantage over rivals.[7]

If a firm learns how to assemble its product more efficiently at, say, its Brazilian plant, the accumulated expertise can be easily transferred via the Internet to assembly plants in other world locations. Knowledge gained in marketing a company's product in Great Britain can readily be exchanged with company personnel in New Zealand or Australia. A company can shift production from one country to another to take advantage of exchange rate fluctuations, to enhance its leverage with host country governments, and to respond to changing wage rates, components shortages, energy costs, or changes in tariffs and quotas. Production schedules can be coordinated worldwide; shipments can be diverted from one distribution center to another if sales rise unexpectedly in one place and fall in another.

Using Internet technology applications, companies can collect ideas for new and improved products from customers and sales and marketing personnel all over the world, permitting informed decisions about what can be standardized and what should be customized. Likewise, Internet technology can be used to involve the company's best design and engineering personnel (wherever they are located) in collectively coming up with next-generation products—it is becoming increasingly easy for company personnel in one location to use the Internet to collaborate closely with personnel in other locations in performing strategically relevant activities. Efficiencies can also be achieved by shifting workloads from where they are unusually heavy to locations where personnel are underutilized.

A company can enhance its brand reputation by consistently incorporating the same differentiating attributes in its products in the various worldwide markets where it competes. The reputation for quality that Honda established worldwide first in motorcycles and then in automobiles gave it competitive advantage in positioning Honda lawn mowers at the upper end of the U.S. outdoor power equipment market—the Honda name gave the company instant credibility with U.S. buyers.

Profit Sanctuaries, Cross-Market Subsidization, and Global Strategic Offensives

Profit sanctuaries are *country markets in which a company derives substantial profits because of its strong or protected market position.* Japan, for example, is a profit sanctuary for most Japanese companies because trade barriers erected around Japanese industries by the Japanese government effectively block foreign companies from competing for a large share of Japanese sales. Protected from the threat of foreign competition in their home market, Japanese companies can safely charge somewhat higher prices to their Japanese customers and thus earn attractively large profits on sales made in Japan. In most cases, a company's biggest and most strategically crucial profit sanctuary is its home market, but international and global companies may also enjoy profit sanctuary status in other nations where they have a strong competitive position, big sales volume, and attractive profit margins. Companies that compete globally are likely to have more profit sanctuaries than companies that compete in just a few country markets; a domestic-only competitor, of course, can have only one profit sanctuary (see Figure 5.2).

> **Core Concept**
>
> Companies with large, protected **profit sanctuaries** have competitive advantage over companies that don't have a protected sanctuary. Companies with multiple profit sanctuaries have a competitive advantage over companies with a single sanctuary.

Figure 5.2   Profit Sanctuary Potential of Domestic-Only, International, and Global Competitors

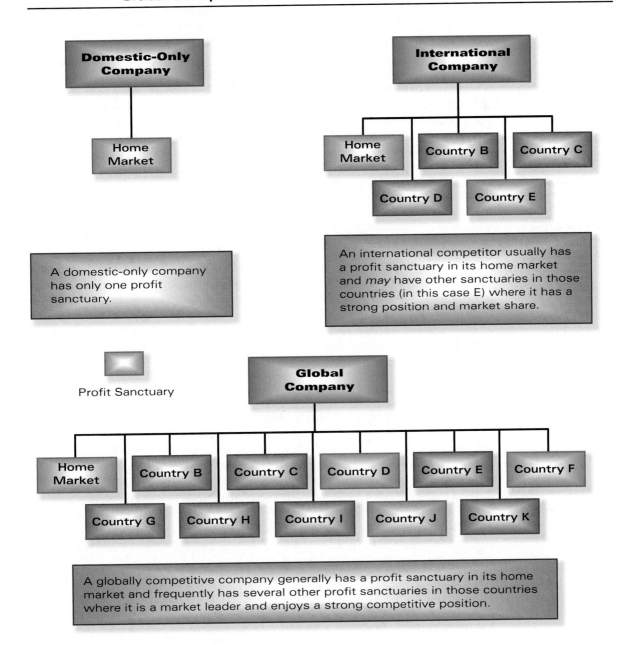

Using Cross-Market Subsidization to Wage a Strategic Offensive

Profit sanctuaries are valuable competitive assets, providing the financial strength to support strategic offensives in selected country markets and aid a company's race for global market leadership. The added financial capability afforded by multiple profit sanctuaries gives a global or multicountry competitor the financial strength to wage a market offensive against a domestic competitor whose only profit sanctuary is its home market. Consider the case of a purely domestic company in competition with a company that has multiple profit sanctuaries and that is racing for global market leadership. The global company has the flexibility of lowballing its prices in the domestic company's home market and grabbing market share at the domestic company's expense, subsidizing razor-thin margins or losses with the healthy profits earned in its sanctuaries—a practice called **cross-market subsidization.** The global company can adjust the depth of its price-cutting to move in and capture market share quickly, or it can shave prices slightly to make gradual market inroads (perhaps over a decade or more) so as not to threaten domestic firms precipitously or trigger protectionist government actions. If the domestic company retaliates with matching price cuts, it exposes its entire revenue and profit base to erosion; its profits can be squeezed substantially and its competitive strength sapped, even if it is the domestic market leader.

> **Core Concept**
>
> **Cross-market subsidization**—supporting competitive offensives in one market with resources and profits diverted from operations in other markets—is a powerful competitive weapon.

There are numerous instances across the world where domestic companies, rightly or wrongly, have accused foreign competitors of "dumping" goods at unreasonably low prices to put the domestic firms in dire financial straits or drive them out of business. Many governments have antidumping laws aimed at protecting domestic firms from unfair pricing by foreign rivals. In 2002, for example, the U.S. government imposed tariffs of up to 30 percent on selected steel products that Asian and European steel manufacturers were said to be selling at ultralow prices in the U.S. market.

Strategic Alliances and Joint Ventures with Foreign Partners

Strategic alliances and cooperative agreements of one kind or another with foreign companies are a favorite and potentially fruitful means for entering a foreign market or strengthening a firm's competitiveness in world markets. Historically, export-minded firms in industrialized nations sought alliances with firms in less-developed countries to import and market their products locally—such arrangements were often necessary to win approval for entry from the host country's government. More recently, companies from different parts of the world have formed strategic alliances and partnership arrangements to strengthen their mutual ability to serve whole continents and move toward more global market participation. Both Japanese and American companies are actively forming alliances with European companies to strengthen their ability to compete in the 15-nation European Union and to capitalize on the opening up of Eastern European markets. Many U.S. and European companies are allying with Asian companies in their efforts to enter markets in China, India, and other Asian countries.

> Strategic alliances can help companies in globally competitive industries strengthen their competitive positions while still preserving their independence.

Of late, the number of alliances, joint ventures, and other collaborative efforts has exploded. Cooperative arrangements between domestic and foreign companies have strategic appeal for reasons besides gaining wider access to attractive country markets.[9] One is to capture economies of scale in production and/or marketing—cost reduction can be the difference that allows a company to be cost-competitive. By joining forces in producing components, assembling models, and marketing their products, companies can realize cost savings not achievable with their own small volumes. A second reason is to fill gaps in technical expertise and/or knowledge of local markets (buying habits and product preferences of consumers, local customs, and so on). Allies learn much from one another in performing joint research, sharing technological know-how, studying one another's manufacturing methods, and understanding how to tailor sales and marketing approaches to fit local cultures and traditions. A third reason is to share distribution facilities and dealer networks, thus mutually strengthening their access to buyers. Fourth, allied companies can direct their competitive energies more toward mutual rivals and less toward one another; teaming up may help them close the gap on leading companies. Fifth, companies opt to form alliances with local companies (even where not legally required) because of the partner's local market knowledge and working relationships with key officials in the host country government.[10] And, finally, alliances can be a particularly useful way to gain agreement on important technical standards—they have been used to arrive at standards for videocassette recorders, assorted PC devices, Internet-related technologies, and mobile phones and other wireless communications devices.

The Risks of Strategic Alliances with Foreign Partners

Alliances and joint ventures have their pitfalls, however. Achieving effective collaboration between independent companies, each with different motives and perhaps conflicting objectives, is not easy.[11] It requires many meetings of many people working in good faith over a period of time to iron out what is to be shared, what is to remain proprietary, and how the cooperative arrangements will work. Cross-border allies typically have to overcome language and cultural barriers; the communication, trust-building, and coordination costs are high in terms of management time. Often, once the bloom is off the rose, partners with conflicting objectives and strategies discover they have deep differences of opinion about how to proceed. Tensions build up, working relationships cool, and the hoped-for benefits never materialize.[12]

Another major problem is getting alliance partners to make decisions fast enough to respond to rapidly advancing technological developments. Large telecommunications companies striving to achieve "global connectivity" have made extensive use of alliances and joint ventures with foreign counterparts, but they are encountering serious difficulty in reaching agreements on which of several technological approaches to employ and how to adapt to the swift pace at which all of the alternatives are advancing. AT&T and British Telecom, which formed a $10 billion joint venture to build an Internet-based global network linking 100 major cities, took eight months to find a CEO to head the project and even longer to come up with a name; the joint venture was abandoned in 2002.

Many times allies find it difficult to collaborate effectively in competitively sensitive areas, thus raising questions about mutual trust and forthright exchanges of information and expertise. There can also be clashes of egos and company cultures. The key people on whom success or failure depends may have little personal chemistry, be unable to work closely together or form a partnership, or be unable to come to consensus. For example, an alliance between Northwest Airlines and KLM Royal Dutch Airlines linking their hubs in Detroit and Amsterdam resulted in a bitter feud among both companies' top officials (who, according to some reports, refused to speak to each other) and precipitated a battle for control of

> Strategic alliances are more effective in helping establish a beachhead of new opportunity in world markets than in achieving and sustaining global leadership.

Northwest Airlines engineered by KLM. The dispute was rooted in a clash of business philosophies (the American way versus the European way), basic cultural differences, and an executive power struggle.[13]

Another danger of collaborative partnerships is that of becoming overly dependent on another company for essential expertise and capabilities over the long term. To be a serious market contender, a company must ultimately develop internal capabilities in all areas important to strengthening its competitive position and building a sustainable competitive advantage. When learning from allies holds only limited potential (because those allies guard their most valuable skills and expertise), acquiring or merging with a company possessing the desired know-how and resources is a better solution. If a company is aiming for global market leadership, then cross-border merger or acquisition may be a better alternative than cross-border alliances or joint ventures. Global Spotlight 5.2 relates the experiences of various companies with cross-border strategic alliances.

Making the Most of Strategic Alliances with Foreign Partners

Whether a company realizes the potential of alliances and collaborative partnerships with foreign enterprises seems to be a function of six factors:[14]

1. *Picking a good partner*—A good partner not only has the desired expertise and capabilities but also shares the company's vision about the purpose of the alliance. Experience indicates that it is generally wise to avoid partnering with foreign companies where there is strong potential of direct competition because of overlapping product lines or other conflicting interests—agreements to jointly market each other's products hold much potential for conflict unless the products are complements rather than substitutes and unless there is good chemistry among key personnel.

2. *Being sensitive to cultural differences*—Unless the outsider exhibits respect for the local culture and local business practices, productive working relationships are unlikely to emerge.

3. *Recognizing that the alliance must benefit both sides*—Information must be shared as well as gained, and the relationship must remain forthright and trustful. Many alliances fail because one or both partners grow unhappy with what they are learning. Also, if either partner plays games with information or tries to take advantage of the other, the resulting friction can quickly erode the value of further collaboration.

4. *Ensuring that both parties live up to their commitments*—Both parties have to deliver on their commitments for the alliance to produce the intended benefits. The division of work has to be perceived as fairly apportioned, and the caliber of the benefits received on both sides has to be perceived as adequate.

5. *Structuring the decision-making process so that actions can be taken swiftly when needed*—In many instances, the fast pace of technology and competitive changes dictates an equally fast decision-making process. If the parties get bogged down in discussions among themselves or in gaining internal approval from higher-ups, the alliance can turn into an anchor of delay and inaction.

6. *Managing the learning process and then adjusting the alliance agreement over time to fit new circumstances*—In today's fast-moving markets, few alliances can succeed by holding only to initial plans. One of the keys to long-lasting success is learning to adapt to change; the terms and objectives of the alliance must be adjusted as needed.

GLOBAL SPOTLIGHT 5.2

Cross-Border Strategic Alliances: The New Shape of Global Business

As the chairman of British Aerospace recently observed, a strategic alliance with a foreign company is "one of the quickest and cheapest ways to develop a global strategy." Cross-border strategic alliances are influencing competition in world markets, pitting one group of allied global companies against other groups of allied global companies. High-profile global alliances include the following:

- Airbus Industrie, one of the world's two leading makers of commercial aircraft, was formed by an alliance of aerospace companies from Britain, Spain, Germany, and France that included British Aerospace, Daimler-Benz Aerospace, and Aerospatiale. Airbus and Boeing vie for world leadership in large commercial aircraft (over 100 passengers).

- General Electric and SNECMA, a French maker of jet engines, have had a longstanding 50–50 partnership to make jet engines to power aircraft made by Boeing and Airbus Industrie. Their partnership company is called CFM International. The GE/SNECMA alliance is regarded as a model because it has enjoyed great success since the 1970s, winning market shares for aircraft with 100+ passengers of about 35 percent through the 1980s and market shares approaching 50 percent since 1995. CFM International had approximately 200 customers worldwide using its engines as of 2002.

- Two struggling auto firms, Renault of France and Nissan of Japan, formed a global partnership aimed at making them more competitive with DaimlerChrysler, General Motors, Ford, and Toyota, all of which were engaged in numerous alliances of their own. Since the early 1990s, hundreds of strategic alliances have been formed in the motor vehicle industry as both car and truck manufacturers and automotive parts suppliers moved aggressively to strengthen the ability to compete globally. Not only have there been joint production and marketing alliances between automakers strong in one region of the world and automakers strong in another region, but there have also been strategic alliances between vehicle makers and parts suppliers.

- Vodaphone AirTouch PLC and Bell Atlantic Corporation in 1999 agreed to from a partnership to create a wireless business with a single brand and common digital technology covering the entire U.S. market and to work together on global business synergies in handset and equipment purchases, global corporate account programs, global roaming agreements, and the development of new products and technologies. The new business, known as Verizon Wireless, combined the domestic U.S. operations of Bell Atlantic Mobile, AirTouch Communications, and PrimeCo Personal Communications LP. Shortly thereafter, Verizon Wireless was further strengthened by the addition of GTE's domestic wireless properties, as part of the Bell Atlantic/GTE merger. At the time of the initial partnership in 1999, Vodaphone AirTouch, based in Great Britain, was the world's largest mobile communications company, and Bell Atlantic was completing a merger with GTE to make the new company, Verizon, one of the premier telecommunications service providers in the United States and a participant in the global telecommunications market, with operations and investments in 25 countries.

- Toyota and First Automotive Works, China's biggest automaker, entered into an alliance in 2002 to make luxury sedans, sport-utility vehicles, and minivehicles for the Chinese market. The intent was to make as many as 400,000 vehicles annually by 2010, an amount equal to the number that Volkswagen, the company with the largest share of the Chinese market, was making as of 2002. The alliance envisioned a joint investment of about $1.2 billion. At the time of the announced alliance, Toyota was lagging behind Honda, General Motors, and Volkswagen in setting up production facilities in China. Capturing a bigger share of the Chinese market was seen as crucial to Toyota's success in achieving its strategic objective of having a 15 percent share of the world's automotive market by 2010.

Source: Company websites and press releases; Yves L. Doz and Gary Hamel, *Alliance Advantage: The Art of Creating Value through Partnering* (Boston, MA: Harvard Business School Press, 1998).

Most alliances with foreign companies that aim at technology-sharing or providing market access turn out to be temporary, fulfilling their purpose after a few years because the benefits of mutual learning have occurred and because the businesses of both partners have developed to the point where they are ready to go their own ways. In such cases, it is important for the company to learn thoroughly and rapidly about a partner's technology, business practices, and organizational capabilities and then transfer valuable ideas and practices into its own operations promptly. Although long-term alliances sometimes prove mutually beneficial, most partners don't hesitate to terminate the alliance and go it alone when the payoffs run out.

Alliances are more likely to be long-lasting when (1) they involve collaboration with suppliers or distribution allies and each party's contribution involves activities in different portions of the industry value chain, or (2) both parties conclude that continued collaboration is in their mutual interest, perhaps because new opportunities for learning are emerging or perhaps because further collaboration will allow each partner to extend its market reach beyond what it could accomplish on its own.

Competing in Emerging Foreign Markets

Companies racing for global leadership have to consider competing in *emerging markets* like China, India, Brazil, Indonesia, and Mexico—countries where the business risks are considerable but where the opportunities for growth are huge, especially as economies and living standards increase toward levels in the developed world.[15] With the world now comprising more than 6 billion people—fully one-third of whom are in India and China, and hundreds of millions more in other less-developed countries of Asia and Latin America—a company that aspires to world market leadership (or to sustained rapid growth) cannot ignore the market opportunities or the base of technical and managerial talent such countries offer. This is especially true given that once-high protectionist barriers in most of these countries are in the process of crumbling. Coca-Cola, for example, has predicted that its $2 billion investment in China, India, and Indonesia—which together hold 40 percent of the world's population—can produce sales in those countries that double every three years for the foreseeable future (compared to a modest 4 percent growth rate that Coca-Cola averaged in the United States during the 1990s and to only 1–2 percent U.S. growth in 2000–2002).[16]

Tailoring products for these big emerging markets often involves more than making minor product changes and becoming more familiar with their local cultures.[17] Ford's attempt to sell a Ford Escort in India at a price of $21,000—a luxury-car price, given that India's best-selling Maruti-Suzuki model sold at the time for $10,000 or less, and that fewer than 10 percent of Indian households have annual purchasing power greater than $20,000—met with a less-than-enthusiastic market response. McDonald's has had to offer vegetable burgers in parts of Asia and to rethink its prices, which are often high by local standards and affordable only by the well-to-do. Kellogg has struggled to introduce its cereals successfully because consumers in many less-developed countries do not eat cereal for breakfast—changing habits is difficult and expensive. In several emerging countries, Coca-Cola has found that advertising its world image does not strike a chord with the local populace. Single-serving packages of detergents, shampoos, pickles, cough syrup, and cooking oils are very popular in India because they allow buyers to conserve cash by purchasing only what they need immediately.

Strategy Implications   Consumers in emerging markets are highly focused on price, in many cases giving local low-cost competitors the edge. Companies wishing to succeed in these markets have to attract buyers with bargain prices as well as better products—an approach that can entail a radical departure from the strategy used in other parts of the world. If building a market for the company's products is likely to be a long-term process and involve reeducation of consumers, a company must not only be patient with regard to sizable revenues and profits but also prepared in the interim to invest sizable sums to alter buying habits and tastes. Also, specially designed or packaged products may be needed to accommodate local market circumstances. For example, when Unilever entered the market for laundry detergents in India, it realized that 80 percent of the population could not afford the brands it was selling to affluent consumers there (as well as in wealthier countries). To compete against a very low-priced detergent made by a local company, Unilever came up with a low-cost formula that was not harsh to the skin, constructed new low-cost production facilities, packaged the detergent (named Wheel) in single-use amounts so that it could be sold very cheaply, distributed the product to local merchants by hand carts, and crafted an economical marketing campaign that included painted signs on buildings and demonstrations near stores—the new brand captured $100 million in sales in a relatively short period of time. Unilever later replicated the strategy in South America with a brand named Ala.

> Profitability in emerging markets rarely comes quickly or easily—new entrants have to be very sensitive to local conditions, be willing to invest in developing the market for their products over the long term, and be patient in earning a profit.

Because managing a new venture in an emerging market requires a blend of global knowledge and local sensitivity to the culture and business practices, the management team must usually consist of a mix of expatriate and local managers. Expatriate managers are needed to transfer technology, business practices, and the corporate culture and serve as conduits for the flow of information between the corporate office and local operations; local managers bring needed understanding of the area's nuances and deep commitment to its market.

Strategies for Local Companies in Emerging Markets

If large, opportunity-seeking, resource-rich companies are looking to enter emerging markets, what strategy options can local companies use to survive? As it turns out, the prospects for local companies facing global giants are by no means grim. Their optimal strategic approach hinges on (1) whether their competitive assets are suitable only for the home market or can be transferred abroad, and (2) whether industry pressures to move toward global competition are strong or weak. The four generic options are shown in Figure 5.3.

Using Home-Field Advantages

When the pressures for global competition are low and a local firm has competitive strengths well suited to the local market, a good strategy option is to concentrate on the advantages enjoyed in the home market, cater to customers who prefer a local touch, and accept the loss of customers attracted to global brands.[18] A local company may be able to astutely exploit its local orientation—its familiarity with local preferences, its expertise in traditional products, its long-standing customer relationships. A local company, in

Figure 5.3   Strategy Options for Local Companies in Competing against Global Companies

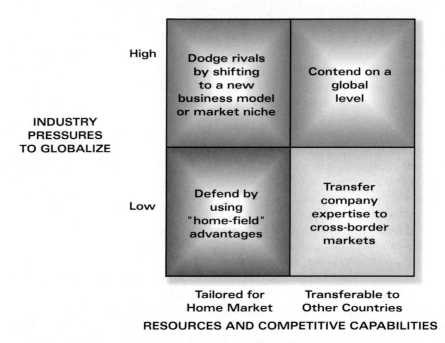

INDUSTRY
PRESSURES
TO GLOBALIZE

High

Dodge rivals
by shifting
to a new
business model
or market niche

Contend on a
global
level

Low

Defend by
using
"home-field"
advantages

Transfer
company
expertise to
cross-border
markets

Tailored for
Home Market

Transferable to
Other Countries

RESOURCES AND COMPETITIVE CAPABILITIES

Source: Adapted from Niroj Dawar & Tony Frost, "Competing with Giants: Survival Strategies for Local Companies in Emerging Markets," *Harvard Business Review* 77, no. 1 (January–February 1999), p. 122.

many cases, enjoys a significant cost advantage over global rivals (perhaps because of simpler product design, lower operating and overhead costs), allowing it to compete on the basis of a lower price. Its global competitors often aim their products at upper- and middle-income urban buyers, who tend to be more fashion-conscious, more willing to experiment with new products, and more attracted to global brands. Bajaj Auto, India's largest producer of scooters, has defended its turf against Honda (which entered the Indian market with a local joint venture partner to sell scooters, motorcycles, and other vehicles on the basis of its superior technology, quality, and brand appeal) by focusing on buyers who wanted low-cost, durable scooters and easy access to maintenance in the countryside. Bajaj designed a rugged, cheap-to-build scooter for India's rough roads, increased its investments in R&D to improve reliability and quality, and created an extensive network of distributors and roadside-mechanic stalls, a strategic approach that served it well—while Honda captured about an 11 percent market share, Bajaj maintained a share above 70 percent, close to its 77 percent share prior to Honda's entry. In the fall of 1998, Honda announced it was pulling out of its scooter manufacturing joint venture with its Indian partner.

Transferring the Company's Expertise to Cross-Border Markets

When a company has resource strengths and capabilities suitable for competing in other country markets, launching initiatives to transfer its expertise to cross-border markets becomes a viable strategic option.[19] Televisa, Mexico's largest media company, used its expertise in Spanish culture and linguistics to become the world's most prolific producer of Spanish-language soap operas. Jollibee Foods, a family-owned company with 56 percent of the fast-food business in the Philippines, combated McDonald's entry first by upgrading service and delivery standards and then by using its expertise in seasoning hamburgers with garlic and soy sauce and making noodle and rice meals with fish to open outlets catering to Asian residents in Hong Kong, the Middle East, and California.

Shifting to a New Business Model or Market Niche

When industry pressures to globalize are high, any of three options make the most sense: (1) shift the business to a piece of the industry value chain where the firm's expertise and resources provide competitive advantage, (2) enter into a joint venture with a globally competitive partner, or (3) sell out to (be acquired by) a global entrant into the home market who concludes the company would be a good entry vehicle.[20] When Microsoft entered China, local software developers shifted from cloning Windows products to developing Windows application software customized to the Chinese market. When the Russian PC market opened to IBM, Compaq, and Hewlett-Packard, local Russian PC maker Vist focused on assembling very low-cost models, marketing them through exclusive distribution agreements with selected local retailers, and opening company-owned full-service centers in dozens of Russian cities. Vist focused on providing low-cost PCs, giving lengthy warranties, and catering to buyers who felt the need for local service and support. Vist's strategy allowed it to remain the market leader, with a 20 percent share.

Contending on a Global Level

If a local company in an emerging market has transferable resources and capabilities, it can sometimes launch successful initiatives to meet the pressures for globalization head-on and start to compete on a global level itself.[21] When General Motors decided to outsource the production of radiator caps for all of its North American vehicles, Sundaram Fasteners of India pursued the opportunity; it purchased one of GM's radiator cap production lines, moved it to India, and became GM's sole supplier of radiator caps in North America—at 5 million units a year. As a participant in GM's supplier network, Sundaram learned about emerging technical standards, built its capabilities, and became one of the first Indian companies to achieve QS 9000 certification, a quality standard that GM now requires for all suppliers. Sundaram's acquired expertise in quality standards enabled it then to pursue opportunities to supply automotive parts in Japan and Europe.

Key Points

Most issues in competitive strategy are the same for domestic companies and companies that compete internationally. But there are four strategic issues unique to competing across national boundaries that merit the strategic attention of multinational companies:

1. Whether to customize the company's offerings in each different country market to match the tastes and preferences of local buyers or offer a mostly standardized product worldwide.

2. Whether to employ essentially the same basic competitive strategy in all countries or modify the strategy country by country to fit the specific market conditions and competitive circumstances it encounters.

3. Where to locate the company's production facilities, distribution centers, and customer service operations so as to realize the greatest locational advantages.

4. Whether and how to efficiently transfer the company's resource strengths and capabilities from one country to another in an effort to secure competitive advantage.

Companies opt to expand outside their domestic market for any of four major reasons: to gain access to new customers for their products or services, to achieve lower costs and become more competitive on price, to leverage their core competencies, and to spread their business risk across a wider market base. A company is an *international* or *multinational competitor* when it competes in several foreign markets; it is a *global competitor* when it has or is pursuing a market presence in virtually all of the world's major countries.

The strategies a company uses to compete in foreign markets have to be *situation-driven*—cultural, demographic, and market conditions vary significantly among the countries of the world. One of the biggest concerns of competing in foreign markets is whether to customize the company's offerings to cater to the tastes and preferences of local buyers in each different country market or whether to offer a mostly standardized product worldwide. While being responsive to local tastes makes a company's products more appealing to local buyers, customizing a company's products country by country may have the effect of raising production and distribution costs due to the greater variety of designs and components, shorter production runs, and the complications of added inventory handling and distribution logistics. Greater standardization of the company's product offering, on the other hand, enhances the capture of scale economies and experience curve effects, contributing to the achievement of a low-cost advantage. The tension between the market pressures to customize and the competitive pressures to lower costs is one of the big strategic issues that participants in foreign markets have to resolve.

Multicountry competition exists when competition in one national market is independent of competition in another national market—there is no "international market," just a collection of self-contained country markets. *Global competition* exists when competitive conditions across national markets are linked strongly enough to form a true world market and when leading competitors compete head-to-head in many different countries. A multicountry strategy is appropriate for industries where multicountry competition dominates, but a global strategy works best in markets that are globally competitive or beginning to globalize. Other strategy options for competing in world markets include maintaining a national (one-country) production base and

exporting goods to foreign markets, licensing foreign firms to use the company's technology or produce and distribute the company's products, employing a franchising
strategy, and using strategic alliances and collaborative partnerships to enter a foreign
market or strengthen a firm's competitiveness in world markets.

The number of global strategic alliances, joint ventures, and collaborative arrangements has exploded in recent years. Cooperative arrangements with foreign partners
have strategic appeal from several angles: gaining wider access to attractive country
markets, allowing capture of economies of scale in production and/or marketing, filling gaps in technical expertise and/or knowledge of local markets, saving on costs by
sharing distribution facilities and dealer networks, helping gain agreement on important technical standards, and helping combat the impact of alliances that rivals have
formed. Cross-border strategic alliances are fast reshaping competition in world markets, pitting one group of allied global companies against other groups of allied global
companies.

There are three ways in which a firm can gain competitive advantage (or offset domestic disadvantages) in global markets. One way involves locating various value
chain activities among nations in a manner that lowers costs or achieves greater product differentiation. A second way involves efficient and effective transfer of competitively valuable competencies and capabilities from its domestic markets to foreign
markets. A third way draws on a multinational or global competitor's ability to deepen
or broaden its resource strengths and capabilities and to coordinate its dispersed activities in ways that a domestic-only competitor cannot.

Profit sanctuaries are country markets in which a company derives substantial
profits because of its strong or protected market position. They are valuable competitive assets, providing the financial strength to support competitive offensives in one
market with resources and profits diverted from operations in other markets, and aid a
company's race for global market leadership. The *cross-subsidization capabilities* provided by multiple profit sanctuaries gives a global or international competitor a powerful offensive weapon. Companies with large, protected profit sanctuaries have
competitive advantage over companies that don't have a protected sanctuary. Companies with multiple profit sanctuaries have a competitive advantage over companies
with a single sanctuary.

Companies racing for global leadership have to consider competing in *emerging
markets* like China, India, Brazil, Indonesia, and Mexico—countries where the business risks are considerable but the opportunities for growth are huge. To succeed in
these markets, it is usually necessary to attract buyers with bargain prices as well as
better products—an approach that can entail a radical departure from the strategy used
in other parts of the world. Moreover, building a market for the company's products in
these markets is likely to be a long-term process, involving the investment of sizable
sums to alter buying habits and tastes and reeducate consumers. Profitability is unlikely to come quickly or easily.

The outlook for local companies in emerging markets wishing to survive against
the entry of global giants is by no means grim. The optimal strategic approach hinges
on whether a firm's competitive assets are suitable only for the home market or can be
transferred abroad and on whether industry pressures to move toward global competition are strong or weak. Local companies can compete against global newcomers by
(1) defending on the basis of home-field advantages, (2) transferring their expertise to
cross-border markets, (3) dodging large rivals by shifting to a new business model or
market niche, or (4) launching initiatives to compete on a global level themselves.

Exercises

1. Log on to www.caterpillar.com and search for information about Caterpillar's strategy in foreign markets. Is it pursuing a global strategy or a multicountry strategy? Support your answer.

2. Assume you are in charge of developing the strategy for a multinational company selling products in some 50 different countries around the world. One of the issues you face is whether to employ a multicountry strategy or a global strategy.

    (a) If your company's product is personal computers, do you think it would make better strategic sense to employ a multicountry strategy or a global strategy? Why?

    (b) If your company's product is dry soup mixes and canned soups, would a multicountry strategy seem to be more advisable than a global strategy? Why?

    (c) If your company's product is mobile phones, would it seem to make more sense to pursue a multicountry strategy or a global strategy? Why?

    (d) If your company's product is basic work tools (hammers, screwdrivers, pliers, wrenches, saws), would a multicountry strategy or a global strategy seem to have more appeal? Why?

CHAPTER 6

Diversification
Strategies for Managing a Group of Businesses

To acquire or not to acquire: that is the question.
—Robert J. Terry

Fit between a parent and its businesses is a two-edged
sword: a good fit can create value; a bad one can destroy it.
—Andrew Campbell, Michael Goold, and
   Marcus Alexander

Achieving superior performance through diversification
is largely based on relatedness.
—Philippe Very

Make winners out of every business in your company.
Don't carry losers.
—Jack Welch, former CEO, General Electric

We measure each of our businesses against strict criteria:
growth, margin, and return-on-capital hurdle rate, and
does it have the ability to become number one or two in
its industry? We are quite pragmatic. If a business does
not contribute to our overall vision, it has to go.
—Richard Wambold, CEO, Pactiv

In this chapter, we move up one level in the strategy making hierarchy, from strategy making in a single-business enterprise to strategy making in a diversified enterprise. Because a diversified company is a collection of individual businesses, the strategy-making task is a more complicated exercise than crafting strategy for a single-business enterprise. In a one-business company, managers have to contend with assessing only one industry environment and the question of how to compete successfully in it—the result is what we labeled in Chapter 1 as *business strategy* (or *business-level strategy*). But in a diversified company, the strategy making challenge involves assessing multiple industry environments and coming up with a *set* of business strategies, one for each industry arena in which the diversified company operates. And top executives at a diversified company must still go one step further and devise a companywide or *corporate strategy* for improving the attractiveness and performance of the company's overall business lineup and for making a rational business whole out of its collection of individual businesses.

In most diversified companies, corporate-level executives delegate considerable strategy-making authority to the heads of each business, usually giving them the latitude to craft a business strategy suited to their particular industry and competitive circumstances and holding them accountable for producing good results. But the task of crafting a diversified company's overall or corporate strategy falls squarely in the lap of top-level executives.

Devising a corporate strategy covering multiple businesses has four distinct facets:

1. *Picking new industries to enter and deciding on the means of entry*—The first concerns in diversifying are what new industries to get into and whether to enter by starting a new business from the ground up, acquiring a company already in the target industry, or forming a joint venture or strategic alliance with another company. A company can diversify narrowly into a few industries or broadly into many industries. The choice of whether to enter an industry via a start-up operation; a joint venture; or the acquisition of an established leader, an up-and-coming company, or a troubled company with turnaround potential shapes what position the company will initially stake out for itself.

2. *Initiating actions to boost the combined performance of the businesses the firm has entered*—As positions are created in the chosen industries, corporate strategists typically zero in on ways to strengthen the long-term competitive positions and profits of the businesses the firm has invested in. Corporate parents can help their business subsidiaries by providing financial resources, by supplying missing skills or technological know-how or managerial expertise to better perform key value chain activities, and by providing new avenues for cost reduction. They can also acquire another company in the same industry and merge the two operations into a stronger business, or acquire new businesses that strongly complement existing businesses. Typically, a company will pursue rapid-growth strategies in its most promising businesses, initiate turnaround efforts in weak-performing businesses with potential, and divest businesses that are no longer attractive or that don't fit into management's long-range plans.

3. *Pursuing opportunities to leverage cross-business value chain relationships and strategic fits into competitive advantage*—A company that diversifies into businesses with related value chain activities (pertaining to technology, supply chain logistics, production, overlapping distribution channels, or common customers) gains competitive advantage potential not open to a company that diversifies into businesses whose value chains are totally unrelated. Related diversification presents

opportunities to transfer skills, share expertise, share facilities, or share a common brand name, thereby reducing overall costs, strengthening the competitiveness of some of the company's products, and enhancing the capabilities of particular business units.

4. *Establishing investment priorities and steering corporate resources into the most attractive business units*—A diversified company's different businesses are usually not equally attractive from the standpoint of investing additional funds. It is incumbent on corporate management to (*a*) decide on the priorities for investing capital in the company's different businesses, (*b*) channel resources into areas where earnings potentials are higher and away from areas where they are lower, and (*c*) divest business units that are chronically poor performers or are in an increasingly unattractive industry. Divesting poor performers and businesses in unattractive industries frees up unproductive investments either for redeployment to promising business units or for financing attractive new acquisitions.

The demanding and time-consuming nature of these four tasks explains why corporate executives generally refrain from becoming immersed in the details of crafting and implementing business-level strategies, preferring instead to delegate lead responsibility for business strategy to the heads of each business unit.

In the first portion of this chapter we describe the various paths through which a company can become diversified and explain how a company can use diversification to create or compound competitive advantage for its business units. In the second part of the chapter, we will examine the techniques and procedures for assessing the strategic attractiveness of a diversified company's business portfolio and survey the strategic options open to already-diversified companies.

When to Diversify

So long as a company has its hands full trying to capitalize on profitable growth opportunities in its present industry, there is no urgency to pursue diversification. Companies that concentrate on a single business can achieve enviable success over many decades without relying on diversification to sustain their growth—good examples include McDonald's, Southwest Airlines, Coca-Cola, Domino's Pizza, Apple Computer, Wal-Mart, Federal Express, Hershey, Timex, Anheuser-Busch, Xerox, Gerber, and Ford Motor Company. In the nonprofit sector, continued emphasis on a single activity has proved successful for the Red Cross, the Salvation Army, the Christian Children's Fund, the Girl Scouts, Phi Beta Kappa, and the American Civil Liberties Union. Concentrating on a single line of business (totally or with a small dose of diversification) has important advantages. A single-business company has less ambiguity about who it is, what it does, and where it is headed. It can devote the full force of its resources to improving its competitiveness, expanding into geographic markets it doesn't serve, and responding to changing market conditions and evolving customer preferences. The more successful a single-business enterprise is, the more able it is to parlay its accumulated know-how, competitive capabilities, and reputation into a sustainable position as a leading firm in its industry.

The big risk of a single-business company, of course, is having all of the firm's eggs in one industry basket. If the market is eroded by the appearance of new technologies, new products, or fast-shifting buyer preferences, or if it otherwise becomes competitively unattractive, then a company's prospects can quickly dim. Consider, for example, what digital cameras are doing to the market for film and film processing, what CD and DVD technology has done to the market for cassette tapes and 3.5-inch disks, and what mobile phones are doing to the long-distance business and the need for ground-line telephones in homes. Where there are substantial risks that a single business company's market may dry up or when opportunities to grow revenues and earnings in the company's mainstay business begin to peter out, managers usually have to put diversifying into other businesses on the front-burner for consideration.

Factors That Signal It Is Time to Diversify

Diversification merits strong consideration whenever a single-business company is faced with diminishing market opportunities and stagnating sales in its principal business. But there are four other instances in which a company becomes a prime candidate for diversifying:

1. When it can expand into industries whose technologies and products complement its present business.

2. When it can leverage existing competencies and capabilities by expanding into businesses where these same resource strengths are key success factors and valuable competitive assets.

3. When diversifying into closely related businesses opens new avenues for reducing costs.

4. When it has a powerful and well-known brand name that can be transferred to the products of other businesses and thereby used as a lever for driving up the sales and profits of such businesses.

As part of the decision to diversify, the company must ask itself, "What kind and how much diversification?" The strategic possibilities are wide open. A company can diversify into closely related businesses or into totally unrelated businesses. It can diversify its present revenue and earning base to a small extent (such that new businesses account for less than 15 percent of companywide revenues and profits) or to a major extent (such that new businesses produce 30 or more percent of revenues and profits). It can move into one or two large new businesses or a greater number of small ones. It can achieve diversification by acquiring an existing company already in a business it wants to enter, starting up a new business subsidiary from scratch, or entering into a joint venture.

There's no tried-and-true method for determining when its time for a company to diversify. Judgments about the timing of a company's diversification effort are best made case by case, according to the company's own unique situation.

Building Shareholder Value: The Ultimate Justification for Diversifying

Diversification must do more for a company than simply spreading its business risk across various industries. Shareholders can easily diversify risk on their own by purchasing stock in companies in different industries or investing in mutual funds, so they don't need a company to diversify merely to spread their risk across different industries. In principle, diversification makes good strategic and business sense only if it results in added shareholder value—value that shareholders cannot capture through their ownership of different companies in different industries.

For there to be reasonable expectations that a company can produce added value for shareholders, through its own diversification efforts, a diversification move must pass three tests:[1]

1. *The industry attractiveness test*—The industry chosen for diversification must be attractive enough to yield consistently good returns on investment. Whether an industry is attractive depends chiefly on the presence of favorable competitive conditions and a market environment conducive to earning as good or better profits and return on investment than the company is earning in its present business(es). And certainly it is hard to imagine declaring an industry to be attractive if profit expectations are *lower* than in the company's present businesses.

2. *The cost-of-entry test*—The cost to enter the target industry must not be so high as to erode the potential for good profitability. A catch-22 can prevail here, however. The more attractive an industry's prospects are for growth and good long-term profitability, the more expensive it can be to get into. Entry barriers for start-up companies are likely to be high in attractive industries; were barriers low, a rush of new entrants would soon erode the potential for high profitability. And buying a well-positioned company in an appealing industry often entails a high acquisition cost. Paying too much to acquire a company in an attractive industry reduces a company's rate of return on the acquisition price and erodes the potential for enhanced shareholder value.

3. *The better-off test*—Diversifying into a new business must offer potential for the company's existing businesses and the new business to perform better together under a single corporate umbrella than they would perform operating as independent, stand-alone businesses. For example, let's say that company A diversifies by purchasing company B in another industry. If A and B's consolidated profits in the years to come prove no greater than what each could have earned on its own, then A's diversification won't provide its shareholders with added value. Company A's shareholders could have achieved the same $1 + 1 = 2$ result by merely purchasing stock in company B. Shareholder value is not created by diversification unless it produces a $1 + 1 = 3$ effect where sister businesses perform better together as part of the same firm than they could have performed as independent companies. The best chance of a $1 + 1 = 3$ outcome occurs when a company diversifies into businesses that have competitively important value chain matchups with its existing businesses—matchups that offer opportunities to reduce costs, to transfer skills or technology from one business to another, to create valuable new competencies and capabilities, or to leverage existing resources (such as brand-name reputation). Absent such strategic fits, a firm ought to be skeptical about the potential for the businesses to perform better together than apart.

Diversification moves that satisfy all three tests have the greatest potential to grow shareholder value over the long term. Diversification moves that can pass only one or two tests are suspect.

Strategies for Entering New Businesses

Entry into new businesses can take any of three forms: acquisition, internal start-up, or joint ventures/strategic partnerships.

Acquisition of an Existing Business

Acquisition is the most popular means of diversifying into another industry. Not only is it quicker than trying to launch a brand-new operation but it also offers an effective way to hurdle such entry barriers as acquiring technological know-how, establishing supplier relationships, becoming big enough to match rivals' efficiency and unit costs, having to spend large sums on introductory advertising and promotions, and securing adequate distribution. Whether friendly or hostile,[2] acquisitions allow the acquirer to move directly to the task of building a strong market position in the target industry, rather than getting bogged down in going the internal start-up route and trying to develop the knowledge, resources, scale of operation, and market reputation necessary to become an effective competitor within a few years.

However, finding the right kind of company to acquire sometimes presents a challenge.[3] The big dilemma an acquisition-minded firm faces is whether to pay a premium price for a successful company or to buy a struggling company at a bargain price. If the buying firm has little knowledge of the industry but ample capital, it is often better off purchasing a capable, strongly positioned firm—unless the price of such an acquisition is prohibitive and flunks the cost-of-entry test. However, when the acquirer sees promising ways to transform a weak firm into a strong one and has the resources, the know-how, and the patience to do it, a struggling company can be the better long-term investment.

The cost-of-entry test requires that the expected profit stream of an acquired business provide an attractive return on the total acquisition cost and on any new capital investment needed to sustain or expand its operations. A high acquisition price can make meeting that test improbable or difficult. For instance, suppose that the price to purchase a company is $3 million and that the company is earning after-tax profits of $200,000 on an equity investment of $1 million (a 20 percent annual return). Simple arithmetic requires that the profits be tripled if the purchaser (paying $3 million) is to earn the same 20 percent return. Building the acquired firm's earnings from $200,000 to $600,000 annually could take several years—and require additional investment on which the purchaser would also have to earn a 20 percent return. Since the owners of a successful and growing company usually demand a price that reflects their business's profit prospects, it's easy for such an acquisition to fail the cost-of-entry test. A would-be diversifier can't count on being able to acquire a desirable company in an appealing industry at a price that still permits attractive returns on investment.

Internal Start-Up

Achieving diversification through *internal start-up* involves building a new business subsidiary from scratch. This entry option takes longer than the acquisition option and poses some hurdles. A newly formed business unit not only has to overcome entry barriers but also has to invest in new production capacity, develop sources of supply, hire and train employees, build channels of distribution, grow a customer base, and so on. Generally, forming a start-up subsidiary to enter a new

> The biggest drawbacks to entering an industry by forming an internal start-up are the costs of overcoming entry barriers and the extra time it takes to build a strong and profitable competitive position.

business has appeal only when (1) the parent company already has in-house most or all of the skills and resources it needs to piece together a new business and compete effectively; (2) there is ample time to launch the business; (3) internal entry has lower costs than entry via acquisition; (4) the targeted industry is populated with many relatively small firms such that the new start-up does not have to compete head-to-head against larger, more powerful rivals; (5) adding new production capacity will not adversely impact the supply–demand balance in the industry; and (6) incumbent firms are likely to be slow or ineffective in responding to a new entrant's efforts to crack the market.[4]

Joint Ventures and Strategic Partnerships

Joint ventures typically entail forming a new corporate entity owned by the partners, whereas strategic partnerships represent a collaborative arrangement that usually can be terminated whenever one of the partners so chooses. Most joint ventures involve two partners and, historically, were formed to pursue opportunities that were somewhat peripheral to the strategic interests of the partners; very few companies have used joint ventures to enter new industries central to their diversification strategy. In recent years, strategic partnerships/alliances have replaced joint ventures as the favored mechanism for joining forces to pursue strategically important diversification opportunities because they can readily accommodate multiple partners and are more adaptable to rapidly changing technological and market conditions than a formal joint venture.

A strategic partnership or joint venture can be useful in at least three types of situations.[5] First, a strategic alliance/joint venture is a good way to pursue an opportunity that is too complex, uneconomical, or risky for a single organization to pursue alone. Second, strategic alliances/joint ventures make sense when the opportunities in a new industry require a broader range of competencies and know-how than any one organization can marshal. Many of the opportunities in satellite-based telecommunications, biotechnology, and network-based systems that blend hardware, software, and services call for the coordinated development of complementary innovations and integrating a host of financial, technical, political, and regulatory factors. In such cases, pooling the resources and competencies of two or more independent organizations is essential to generate the capabilities needed for success.

Third, joint ventures are sometimes the only way to gain entry into a desirable foreign market, especially when the foreign government requires companies wishing to enter the market to secure a local partner; for example, the Chinese government closed entry in the automotive industry to all but a few select automakers, and in the elevator industry it originally permitted only Otis, Schindler, and Mitsubishi to establish joint ventures with local partners. Although permission was later granted to other companies, the three early entrants were able to retain a market advantage.[6] Alliances with local partners have become a favorite mechanism for global companies not only to establish footholds in desirable foreign country markets but also to surmount tariff barriers and import quotas. Local partners offer outside companies the benefits of local knowledge about market conditions, local customs and cultural factors, and customer buying habits; they can also be a source of managerial and marketing personnel and provide access to distribution outlets. The foreign partner's role is usually to provide specialized skills, technological know-how, and other resources needed to crack the local market and serve it efficiently.

However, like alliances, joint ventures have their difficulties, often posing complicated questions about how to divide efforts among the partners and about who has effective control.[7] Conflicts between foreign and domestic partners can arise over whether to use local sourcing of components, how much production to export, whether operating procedures should conform to the local partner's or the foreign company's standards, and the extent to which the local partner is entitled to make use of the foreign partner's technology and intellectual property. As the foreign partner acquires experience and confidence in the local market, its need for the local partner typically diminishes, posing the strategic issue of whether the partnership/joint venture should be dissolved. This happens frequently in alliances between global manufacturers and local distributors.[8] Joint ventures are generally the least durable of the entry options, usually lasting only until the partners decide to go their own ways. Japanese automakers have abandoned their European distribution partners and set up their own dealer networks; BMW did the same in Japan. However, the temporary character of joint ventures is not always bad. Several ambitious local partners have used their alliances with global companies to master technologies and build key competitive skills, then capitalized on the acquired know-how to launch their own entry into the international arena. Taiwan's Acer Computer Group used its alliance with Texas Instruments as a stepping-stone for entering the world market for desktop and laptop computers.

Choosing the Diversification Path: Related versus Unrelated Businesses

Once the decision is made to pursue diversification, the firm must choose whether to diversify into **related businesses, unrelated businesses,** or some mix of both (see Figure 6.1). *Businesses are said to be related when their value chains possess competitively valuable relationships that present opportunities to transfer resources from one business to another, combine similar activities and reduce costs, share a common brand name, or create mutually useful resource strengths and capabilities.* The appeal of related diversification is exploiting these value chain matchups to realize a $1 + 1 = 3$ performance outcome and thus build shareholder value from operating separate businesses under a common corporate umbrella. *Businesses are said to be unrelated when the activities comprising their respective value chains are so dissimilar that no competitively valuable cross-business relationships are present.*

> **Core Concept**
>
> **Related businesses** possess competitively valuable cross-business value chain matchups; **unrelated businesses** have dissimilar value chains, containing no competitively useful cross-business relationships.

Most companies favor related diversification strategies because of the performance-enhancing potential of cross-business synergies. However, some companies have, for one reason or another, opted to try to build shareholder value with unrelated diversification strategies. And a few have diversified into both related and unrelated businesses. The next two sections explore the ins and outs of related and unrelated diversification.

The Case for Diversifying into Related Businesses

A related diversification strategy involves building the company around businesses whose value chains possess competitively valuable strategic fits, as shown in Figure 6.2. **Strategic fit** exists whenever one or more activities comprising the value chains

Figure 6.1   Strategy Alternatives for a Company Looking to Diversify

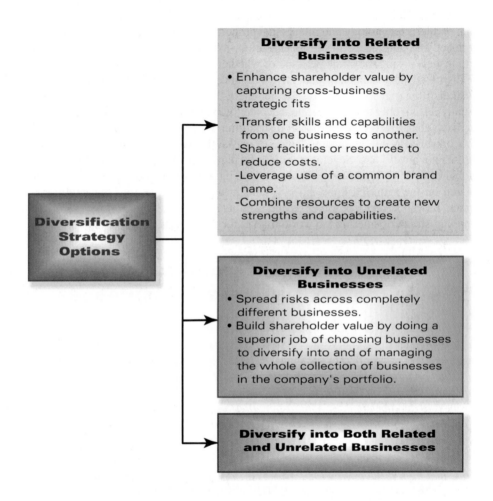

of different businesses are sufficiently similar as to present opportunities for:[9]

■ Transferring competitively valuable expertise, technological know-how, or other capabilities from one business to another.

■ Combining the related activities of separate businesses into a single operation to achieve lower costs.

■ Exploiting common use of a well-known brand name.

■ Cross-business collaboration to create competitively valuable resource strengths and capabilities.

Related diversification thus has strategic appeal from several angles. It allows a firm to reap the competitive advantage benefits of skills transfer, lower costs, common brand names, and/or stronger competitive

Figure 6.2   Related Businesses Possess Related Value Chain Activities and Competitively Valuable Strategic Fits

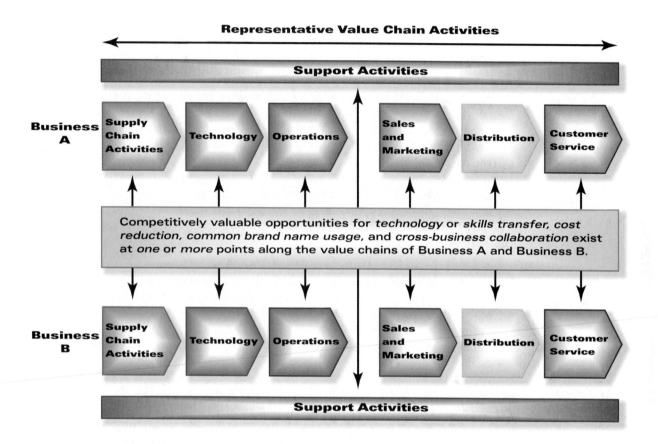

capabilities and still spread investor risks over a broad business base. Furthermore, the relatedness among the different businesses provides sharper focus for managing diversification and a useful degree of strategic unity across the company's various business activities.

Cross-Business Strategic Fits along the Value Chain

Cross-business strategic fits can exist anywhere along the value chain—in R&D and technology activities, in supply chain activities and relationships with suppliers, in manufacturing, in sales and marketing, in distribution activities, or in administrative support activities.[10]

Strategic Fits in R&D and Technology Activities   Diversifying into businesses where there is potential for sharing common technology, exploiting the full range of business opportunities associated with a particular technology and its derivatives, or transferring technological know-how from one business to another has considerable appeal. Businesses with technology-sharing benefits can perform better together than apart because of potential cost savings in R&D and potentially shorter times in getting new products to market; also, technological advances in one business can lead to increased sales for both. Technological innovations have been the driver behind the efforts of cable TV companies to diversify into high-speed Internet access (via the use of cable modems) and, further, to explore providing local and long-distance telephone service to residential and commercial customers in a single wire.

Strategic Fits in Supply Chain Activities   Businesses that have supply chain strategic fits can perform better together because of the potential for skills transfer in procuring materials, greater bargaining power in negotiating with common suppliers, the benefits of added collaboration with common supply chain partners, and/or added leverage with shippers in securing volume discounts on incoming parts and components. Dell Computer's strategic partnerships with leading suppliers of microprocessors, motherboards, disk drives, memory chips, monitors, modems, flat-panel displays, long-life batteries, and other desktop and laptop components have been an important component of the company's strategy to diversify into servers and data storage devices—products that include many components common to PCs and that can be sourced from the same strategic partners that provide Dell with PC components.

Manufacturing-Related Strategic Fits   Cross-business strategic fits in manufacturing-related activities can represent an important source of competitive advantage in situations where a diversifier's expertise in quality manufacture and cost-efficient production methods can be transferred to another business. When Emerson Electric diversified into the chain-saw business, it transferred its expertise in low-cost manufacture to its newly acquired Beaird-Poulan business division; the transfer drove Beaird-Poulan's new strategy—to be the low-cost provider of chain-saw products—and fundamentally changed the way Beaird-Poulan chain saws were designed and manufactured. Another benefit of value chain matchups in production may involve cost-saving opportunities stemming from the ability to perform manufacturing or assembly activities jointly in the same facility rather than independently, thus making it feasible to consolidate production into a smaller number of plants and significantly reduce overall production costs. When snowmobile maker Bombardier diversified into motorcycles, it was able to set up motorcycle assembly lines in the same manufacturing facility where it was assembling snowmobiles.

Distribution-Related Strategic Fits   Businesses with closely related distribution activities can perform better together than apart because of potential cost savings in sharing the same distribution facilities or using many of the same wholesale distributors and retail dealers to access customers. When Sunbeam acquired Mr. Coffee, it was able to consolidate its own distribution centers for small household appliances with those of Mr. Coffee, thereby generating considerable cost savings. Likewise, since Sunbeam products were sold to many of the same retailers as Mr. Coffee products (Wal-Mart, Kmart, department stores, home centers, hardware chains, supermarket chains, and drugstore chains), Sunbeam was able to convince many of the retailers carrying Sunbeam appliances to also take on the Mr. Coffee line and vice versa.

Strategic Fits in Sales and Marketing Activities   Various cost-saving opportunities spring from diversifying into businesses with closely related sales and marketing activities. Sales costs can often be reduced by using a single sales force for the products of both businesses rather than having separate sales forces for each business. When the products are distributed through many of the same wholesale and retail dealers or are sold directly to the same customers, it is usually feasible to give one salesperson the responsibility for handling the sales of both products (rather than have two different salespeople call on the same customer). The products of related businesses can be promoted at the same website, and included in the same media ads and sales brochures. After-sale service and repair organizations for the products of closely related businesses can often be consolidated into a single operation. There may be opportunities to reduce costs by coordinating delivery and shipping, consolidating order processing and billing, and using common promotional tie-ins (cents-off couponing, free samples and trial offers, seasonal specials, and the like). When global power-tool maker Black & Decker acquired General Electric's domestic small household appliance business, it was able to use its own global sales force and distribution facilities to sell and distribute toasters, irons, mixers, and coffeemakers because the types of customers that carried its power tools (discounters like Wal-Mart and Kmart, home centers, and hardware stores) also stocked small appliances. The economies Black & Decker achieved for both product lines were substantial.

A second category of benefits arises when different businesses use similar sales and marketing approaches; in such cases, there may be competitively valuable opportunities to transfer selling, merchandising, advertising, and product differentiation skills from one business to another. Procter & Gamble's product lineup includes Folgers coffee, Tide laundry detergent, Crest toothpaste, Ivory soap, Charmin toilet tissue, and Head & Shoulders shampoo. All of these have different competitors and different supply chain and production requirements, but they all move through the same wholesale distribution systems, are sold in common retail settings to the same shoppers, are advertised and promoted in much the same ways, and require the same marketing and merchandising skills.

A third set of benefits arises from related sales and marketing activities when a company's brand name and reputation in one business is transferable to other businesses. Honda's name in motorcycles and automobiles gave it instant credibility and recognition in entering the lawn-mower business, allowing it to achieve a significant market share without spending large sums on advertising to establish a brand identity for its lawn mowers. Canon's reputation in photographic equipment was a competitive asset that facilitated the company's diversification into copying equipment. Panasonic's name in consumer electronics (radios, TVs) was readily transferred to microwave ovens, making it easier and cheaper for Panasonic to diversify into the microwave oven market.

Strategic Fits in Managerial and Administrative Support Activities Often, different businesses require comparable types of skills, competencies, and managerial know-how, thereby allowing know-how in one line of business to be transferred to another. At General Electric (GE), managers who were involved in GE's expansion into Russia were able to expedite entry because of information gained from GE managers involved in expansions into other emerging markets. The lessons GE managers learned in China were passed along to GE managers in Russia, allowing them to anticipate that the Russian government would demand that GE build production capacity in the country rather than enter the market through exporting or licensing. In addition, GE's managers in Russia were better able to develop realistic performance expectations and make tough upfront decisions since experience in China and elsewhere warned them (1) that there would likely be increased short-term costs during the early years of start-up and (2) that if GE committed to the Russian market for the long term and aided the country's economic development it could eventually expect to be given the freedom to pursue profitable penetration of the Russian market.[11]

Likewise, different businesses sometimes use the same sorts of administrative support facilities. For instance, an electric utility that diversifies into natural gas, water, appliance sales and repair services, and home security services can use the same customer data network, the same customer call centers and local offices, the same billing and customer accounting systems, and the same customer service infrastructure to support all of its products and services.

Company Spotlight 6.1 lists the businesses of five companies that have pursued a strategy of related diversification.

Strategic Fit, Economies of Scope, and Competitive Advantage

What makes related diversification an attractive strategy is the opportunity to convert the strategic fit between the value chains of different businesses into a competitive advantage over business rivals that have not diversified or that have diversified in ways that don't give them access to such strategic-fit benefits. The greater the relatedness among the businesses of a diversified company, the greater the opportunities for skills transfer and/or combining related value chain activities to achieve lower costs and/or leveraging use of a well-respected brand name and/or collaborating to create new resource strengths and capabilities. The more competitively important the strategic fit relationships across related businesses, the bigger the window for converting strategic fits into competitive advantage over rivals lacking comparable strategic fits in their own operations.

Economies of Scope: A Path to Competitive Advantage   One of the most important competitive advantages that a related diversification strategy can produce is lower costs than competitors. Related businesses often present opportunities to consolidate certain value chain activities or use common resources, and thereby eliminate costs. Such cost savings are termed **economies of scope**—a concept distinct from *economies of scale*. Economies of *scale* are cost savings that accrue directly from a larger-sized operation; for example, unit costs may be lower in a large plant than in a small plant, lower in a large distribution center than in a small one, lower for large-volume purchases of components than for small-volume purchases. Economies of *scope*, however, stem directly from cost-saving strategic fits along the value chains of related businesses; such economies are open only to a multibusiness enterprise and are very much a phenomenon of related diversification. Most usually, economies of scope are the result of two or more businesses sharing technology, performing R&D together, using common manufacturing or distribution facilities, sharing a common sales force or distributor/dealer network, using the same established brand name, and/or sharing the same administrative infrastructure. *The greater the economies associated with cost-saving strategic fits, the greater the potential for a related diversification strategy to yield a competitive advantage based on lower costs.*

> **Core Concept**
>
> **Economies of scope** are cost reductions that flow from operating in multiple businesses; such economies stem directly from strategic fit efficiencies along the value chains of related businesses.

From Competitive Advantage to Added Profitability and Gains in Shareholder Value   Armed with the competitive advantages that come from economies of scope and the capture of other strategic-fit benefits, a company with a portfolio of related businesses is poised to achieve $1 + 1 = 3$ financial performance and the hoped-for gains in shareholder value. The strategic and business logic is compelling: A company that succeeds in capturing strategic fits along the value chains of its related businesses has a clear path to achieving competitive advantage over undiversified competitors and competitors whose own diversification efforts don't offer equivalent strategic-fit benefits. With such competitive advantage, a company then has a dependable basis for earning better-than-average profits—in particular, profits and a return on investment that exceed what the company's businesses could earn as standalone enterprises. In turn, above-average profitability is what fuels $1 + 1 = 3$ gains in

> **Core Concept**
>
> A company that leverages the strategic fit of its related businesses into competitive advantage has a clear avenue to producing gains in shareholder value.

shareholder value—the necessary outcome for satisfying the better-off test and proving the business merit of a company's diversification effort.

Consequently, a strategy of diversifying into related businesses where competitively valuable strategic fit benefits can be captured has strong potential for putting sister businesses in position to perform better financially as part of the same company than they could have performed as independent enterprises. This makes a strategy of related diversification a very appealing vehicle for building shareholder value in ways that shareholders cannot undertake by simply owning a portfolio of stocks of companies in different industries. The capture of strategic-fit benefits is possible only via a strategy of related diversification.[12]

A Word of Caution   Diversifying into related businesses is no guarantee of gains in shareholder value. Many companies have stumbled with related diversification because they overpaid for the acquired companies, failing the cost-of-entry test. And two problems commonly arise in passing the better-off test: One occurs when the likely cost savings of combining related value chain activities and capturing economies of scope are overestimated; in such cases, the realized cost savings and gains in profitability prove too small to justify the acquisition-price premium. The second occurs when transferring resources from one business to another is fraught with unforeseen obstacles that delay or diminish the strategic-fit benefits actually captured. Experience indicates that it is easy to be overly optimistic about the value of the cross-business synergies—realizing them is harder than first meets the eye.

The Case for Diversifying into Unrelated Businesses

A strategy of diversifying into unrelated businesses discounts the value and importance of the strategic-fit benefits associated with related diversification and instead focuses on building and managing a portfolio of business subsidiaries capable of delivering good financial performance in their respective industries. Companies that pursue a strategy of unrelated diversification generally exhibit a willingness to diversify into *any industry* where there's potential for a company to realize consistently good financial results. Decisions to diversify into one industry versus another are the product of an opportunistic search for good companies to acquire—*the basic premise of unrelated diversification is that any company that can be acquired on good financial terms and that has satisfactory earnings potential represents a good acquisition.* While companies pursuing unrelated diversification may well look for companies that can satisfy the industry attractiveness and cost-of-entry tests, they either disregard the better-off test or relegate it to secondary status. *A strategy of unrelated diversification involves no deliberate effort to seek out businesses having strategic fit with the firm's other businesses* (see Figure 6.3). Rather, the company spends much time and effort screening new acquisition candidates and deciding whether to keep or divest existing businesses, using such criteria as:

- Whether the business can meet corporate targets for profitability and return on investment.

- Whether the business will require substantial infusions of capital to replace out-of-date plants and equipment, fund expansion, and provide working capital.

- Whether the business is in an industry with significant growth potential.

Figure 6.3   Unrelated Businesses Have Unrelated Value Chains and No Strategic Fits

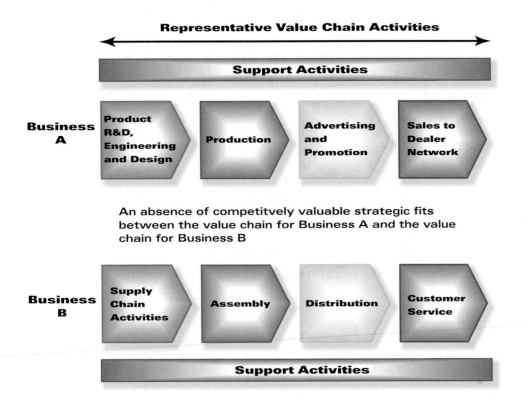

Representative Value Chain Activities

Support Activities

Business A: Product R&D, Engineering and Design → Production → Advertising and Promotion → Sales to Dealer Network

An absence of competitvely valuable strategic fits between the value chain for Business A and the value chain for Business B

Business B: Supply Chain Activities → Assembly → Distribution → Customer Service

Support Activities

- Whether the business is big enough to contribute *significantly* to the parent firm's bottom line.

- Whether there is a potential for union difficulties or adverse government regulations concerning product safety or the environment.

- Whether there is industry vulnerability to recession, inflation, high interest rates, or shifts in government policy.

Some acquisition candidates offer quick opportunities for financial gain because of their "special situation." Three types of businesses may hold such attraction:

- *Companies whose assets are undervalued*—Opportunities may exist to acquire undervalued companies and resell their assets for more than the acquisition costs.

- *Companies that are financially distressed*—Businesses in financial distress can often be purchased at a bargain price, their operations turned around with the aid of the parent company's financial resources and managerial know-how, and then either held as long-term investments in the acquirer's business portfolio (because of their strong earnings or cash flow potential) or sold at a profit, whichever is more attractive.

- *Companies that have bright growth prospects but are short on investment capital*—Cash-poor, opportunity-rich companies are usually coveted acquisition candidates for a financially strong opportunity-seeking firm.

Companies that pursue unrelated diversification nearly always enter new businesses by acquiring an established company rather than by forming a start-up subsidiary within their own corporate structures. The premise of acquisition-minded corporations is that growth by acquisition can deliver enhanced shareholder value through upward trending corporate revenues and earnings and a stock price that *on average* rises enough year after year to amply reward and please shareholders.

A key issue in unrelated diversification is how wide a net to cast in building a portfolio of unrelated businesses. In other words, should a company pursuing unrelated diversification seek to have few or many unrelated businesses? How much business diversity can corporate executives successfully manage? A reasonable way to resolve the issue of how much diversification comes from answering two questions: "What is the least diversification it will take to achieve acceptable growth and profitability?" and "What is the most diversification that can be managed, given the complexity it adds?"[13] The optimal amount of diversification usually lies between these two extremes.

Company Spotlight 6.2 lists the businesses of five companies that have pursued unrelated diversification. Such companies are frequently labeled *conglomerates* because their business interests range broadly across diverse industries.

The Merits of an Unrelated Diversification Strategy

A strategy of unrelated diversification has appeal from several angles:

1. Business risk is scattered over a set of truly *diverse* industries. In comparison to related diversification, unrelated diversification more closely approximates *pure* diversification of financial and business risk because the company's investments are spread over businesses whose technologies and value chain activities bear no close relationship and whose markets are largely disconnected.[14]

2. The company's financial resources can be employed to maximum advantage by investing in *whatever industries* offer the best profit prospects (as opposed to considering only opportunities in industries with related value chain activities). Specifically, cash flows from company businesses with lower growth and profit prospects can be diverted to acquiring and expanding businesses with higher growth and profit potentials.

3. To the extent that corporate managers are exceptionally astute at spotting bargain-priced companies with big upside profit potential, shareholder wealth can be enhanced by buying distressed businesses at a low price, turning their operations around fairly quickly with infusions of cash and managerial know-how supplied by the parent company, and then riding the crest of the profit increases generated by the newly acquired businesses.

4. Company profitability may prove somewhat more stable over the course of economic upswings and downswings because market conditions in all industries don't move upward or downward simultaneously—in a broadly diversified company, there's a chance that market downtrends in some of the company's businesses will be partially offset by cyclical upswings in its other businesses, thus producing somewhat less earnings volatility. (In actual practice, however, there's no convincing evidence that the consolidated profits of firms with unrelated diversification strategies are more stable or less subject to reversal in periods of recession and economic stress than the profits of firms with related diversification strategies.)

Five Companies That Have Diversified into Unrelated Businesses

United Technologies, Inc.

- Pratt & Whitney aircraft engines
- Carrier heating and air-conditioning equipment
- Otis elevators
- Sikorsky helicopters
- Hamilton Substrand aerospace subsystems and components

The Walt Disney Company

- Theme parks
- Disney Cruise Line
- Resort properties
- Movie, video, and theatrical productions (for both children and adults)
- Television broadcasting (ABC, Disney Channel, Toon Disney, Classic Sports Network, ESPN and ESPN2, E!, Lifetime, and A&E networks)
- Radio broadcasting (Disney Radio)
- Musical recordings and sales of animation art
- Anaheim Mighty Ducks NHL franchise
- Anaheim Angels major league baseball franchise (25 percent ownership)
- Books and magazine publishing
- Interactive software and Internet sites
- The Disney Store retail shops

Cooper Industries

- Crescent wrenches, pliers, and screwdrivers
- Nicholson files and saws
- Diamond horseshoes and farrier tools
- Lufkin measuring and layout products
- Gardner-Denver electric power tools
- Electrical construction materials
- Lighting fixtures, fuses, and circuit protection devices
- Electric utility products (transformers, relays, capacitor controls, switches)
- Emergency lighting, fire detection, and security systems

Textron, Inc.

- Bell helicopters
- Cessna Aircraft
- E-Z-Go golf carts
- Textron Automotive (instrument panels, plastic fuel tanks, plastic interior and exterior trim)
- Textron Fastening Systems (the global leader)
- Fluid and power systems
- Textron Financial Services
- Jacobsen turf care equipment
- Ransomes turf care and utility vehicles
- Tools and testing equipment for the wire and cable industry

American Standard

- Trane and American Standard furnaces, heat pumps, and air conditioners
- Plumbing products (American Standard, Ideal Standard, Standard, Porcher lavatories, toilets, bath tubs, faucets, whirlpool baths, and shower basins)
- Automotive products (commercial and utility vehicle braking and control systems)
- Medical systems (DiaSorin disease assessment and management products)

Source: Company annual reports.

Unrelated diversification can be appealing in several other circumstances. It certainly merits consideration when a firm needs to diversify away from an endangered or unattractive industry and has no distinctive competencies or capabilities it can transfer to an adjacent industry. There's also a rationale for unrelated diversification to the extent that owners have a strong preference for spreading business risks widely and not restricting themselves to investing in a family of closely related businesses.

Building Shareholder Value via Unrelated Diversification

Building shareholder value via unrelated diversification is predicated on executive skill in managing a group of unrelated businesses. For a strategy of unrelated diversification to generate gains in shareholder value, corporate-level managers must produce companywide financial results above and beyond what business-level managers could produce if the businesses operated as stand-alone entities. Corporate executives add value to a diversified enterprise by shrewdly deciding which businesses to get into and which ones to get out of, cleverly allocating the corporate parent's financial resources to businesses with the best profit potential, and consistently providing high-caliber decision-making guidance to the general managers of the company's business subsidiaries. In more specific terms, this means corporate-level executives must:

- Do a superior job of diversifying into new businesses that can produce consistently good earnings and returns on investment (thereby satisfying the attractiveness test).

- Do an excellent job of negotiating favorable acquisition prices (thereby satisfying the cost-of-entry test).

- Discern when it is the "right" time to sell a particular business (sensing when a business subsidiary is on the verge of confronting adverse industry and competitive conditions and probable declines in long-term profitability) and also selling it at the "right" price, ideally for more than the company's net investment in the business.

- Shift corporate financial resources out of businesses where profit opportunities are dim and into businesses with the potential for above-average earnings growth and returns on investment.

- Do such a good job overseeing the firm's business subsidiaries and contributing to how they are managed—by providing expert problem-solving skills, creative strategy suggestions, decision-making guidance to business-level managers, and needed infusions of investment capital—that the subsidiaries perform at a higher level than they would otherwise be able to do (a possible way to satisfy the better-off test).

To the extent that corporate executives are able to craft and execute a strategy of unrelated diversification that produces enough of the above outcomes to produce a stream of dividends and capital gains for stockholders greater than a $1 + 1 = 2$ outcome, a case can be made that shareholder value has truly been enhanced.

The Drawbacks of Unrelated Diversification

Unrelated diversification strategies have two important negatives that undercut the pluses: very demanding managerial requirements and limited competitive advantage potential.

Core Concept

The two biggest drawbacks to unrelated diversification are the difficulties of competently managing many different businesses and being without the added source of competitive advantage that cross-business strategic fit provides.

Demanding Managerial Requirements   Successfully managing a set of fundamentally different businesses operating in fundamentally different industry and competitive environments is a very challenging and exceptionally difficult proposition for corporate-level managers. It is difficult because key executives at the corporate level, while perhaps having personally worked in one or two of the company's businesses, cannot possibly have in-depth familiarity with each of the company's businesses—the prevailing competitive market conditions, driving forces, industry key success factors, each business's competitive strengths and weaknesses, and so on. The greater the number of businesses a company is in and the more diverse they are, the harder it is for corporate managers to (1) stay abreast of what's happening in each industry and each subsidiary and thus judge whether a particular business has bright prospects or is headed for trouble, (2) know enough about the issues and problems facing each subsidiary to pick business-unit heads having the requisite combination of managerial skills and know-how, (3) be able to tell the difference between those strategic proposals of business-unit managers that are prudent and those that are risky or unlikely to succeed, and (4) know what to do if a business unit stumbles and its results suddenly head downhill.[15]

In a company like Walt Disney (see Company Spotlight 6.2) or Tyco International (which acquired over 1,000 companies during the 1990–2001 period), corporate executives are constantly scrambling to stay on top of fresh industry developments and the strategic progress and plans of each subsidiary, often depending on briefings by business-level managers for many of the details. As a rule, the more unrelated businesses that a company has diversified into, the more corporate executives are reduced to "managing by the numbers"—that is, keeping a close track on the financial and operating results of each subsidiary and assuming that everything is under control in a business as long as the latest key financial and operating measures look good. Managing by the numbers can work if the heads of the various business units are quite capable, but there's still ample room for strategic issues to be glossed over and impending downturns in some of the company's key businesses to go unnoticed. Just one or two unforeseen declines or big strategic mistakes (misjudging the importance of certain competitive forces or the impact of driving forces or key success factors, encountering unexpected problems in a newly acquired business, or being too optimistic about turning around a struggling subsidiary) can cause a precipitous drop in corporate earnings and crash the parent company's stock price. As the former chairman of a Fortune 500 company advised, "Never acquire a business you don't know how to run." Because every business tends to encounter rough sledding, a good way to gauge the merits of acquiring a company in an unrelated industry is to ask, "If the business got into trouble, is corporate management likely to know how to bail it out?" When the answer is no (or even a qualified yes or maybe), growth via acquisition into unrelated businesses is a chancy strategy.[16]

Hence, while overseeing a set of widely diverse businesses may sound doable, it can turn out to be much harder than it sounds. In practice, comparatively few companies have proved that they have top management capabilities that are up to the task. There are far more companies that have tried unrelated diversification and failed than there are companies that have tried it and succeeded. It is simply very difficult for corporate executives to build shareholder value based on their expertise in (a) picking which industries to diversify into and which companies in these industries to acquire, (b) shifting resources from low-performing business into high performing businesses, and (c) giving high-caliber decision-making guidance to the general managers of their business subsidiaries. Instead of achieving $1 + 1 = 3$ gains in shareholder value, the odds are that the result of unrelated diversification will be $1 + 1 = 2$ or less.

> Relying solely on the expertise of corporate executives to wisely manage a set of unrelated businesses is *a much weaker foundation for enhancing sharehold value* than is a strategy of related diversification where corporate performance can be boosted by expert corporate-level management.

Limited Competitive Advantage Potential   The second big negative is that *unrelated diversification offers no potential for competitive advantage beyond* *that of what each individual business can generate on its own.* Unlike a related diversification strategy, there are no cross-business strategic fits to draw on for reducing costs, beneficially transferring skills and technology, leveraging use of a powerful brand name, or collaborating to build mutually beneficial competitive capabilities and thereby *adding to any competitive advantage possessed by individual businesses.* Yes, a cash-rich corporate parent can provide its subsidiaries with much-needed capital, and there are times when a corporate parent may have the managerial know-how to help resolve problems in particular business units. But, otherwise, a corporate parent pursuing unrelated diversification has little to offer in the way of enhancing the competitive strength of its individual business units. *Without the competitive advantage potential of strategic fits, consolidated performance of an unrelated group of businesses stands to be little or no better than the sum of what the individual business units could achieve if they were independent,* and it may be worse to the extent that corporate managers do a poor job of supervising certain business subsidiaries or hamstringing them with questionable corporate policies. In trying to manage a set of unrelated businesses, the value added by corporate managers depends primarily on how good they are at deciding what new businesses to add, which ones to get rid of, how best to deploy the parent company's financial resources in supporting the needs of its business units and boosting overall corporate performance, and the quality of the decision-making guidance they give to the managers of their business subsidiaries.

Combination Related–Unrelated Diversification Strategies

There's nothing to preclude a company from diversifying into both related and unrelated businesses. Indeed, in actual practice the business makeup of diversified companies varies considerably. Some diversified companies are really *dominant-business enterprises*—one major "core" business accounts for 50 to 80 percent of total revenues and a collection of small related or unrelated businesses accounts for the remainder. Some diversified companies are *narrowly diversified* around a few (two to five) related or unrelated businesses. Others are *broadly diversified* around a wide-ranging collection of related businesses, unrelated businesses, or a mixture of both. And a number of multibusiness enterprises have diversified into unrelated areas but have a collection of related businesses within each area—thus giving them a business portfolio consisting of *several unrelated groups of related businesses.* There's ample room for companies to customize their diversification strategies to incorporate elements of both related and unrelated diversification, as may suit their own risk preferences and strategic vision.

Figure 6.4 indicates what to look for in identifying the main elements of a company's diversification strategy. Having a clear fix on the company's current corporate strategy sets the stage for evaluating how good the strategy is and proposing strategic moves to boost the company's performance.

Evaluating the Strategy of a Diversified Company

Strategic analysis of diversified companies builds on the concepts and methods used for single-business companies. But there are some additional aspects to consider and a

Figure 6.4   Identifying a Diversified Company's Strategy

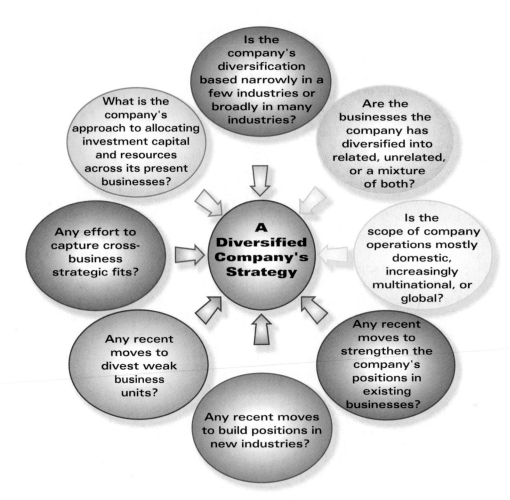

couple of new analytical tools to master. The procedure for evaluating the pluses and minuses of a diversified company's strategy and deciding what actions to take to improve the company's performance involves six steps:

1. Assessing the attractiveness of the industries the company has diversified into, both individually and as a group.

2. Assessing the competitive strength of the company's business units and determining how many are strong contenders in their respective industries.

3. Checking the competitive advantage potential of cross-business strategic fits among the company's various business units.

4. Checking whether the firm's resources fit the requirements of its present business lineup.

5. Ranking the performance prospects of the businesses from best to worst and determining what the corporate parent's priority should be in allocating resources to its various businesses.

6. Crafting new strategic moves to improve overall corporate performance.

The core concepts and analytical techniques underlying each of these steps merit further discussion.

Step 1: Evaluating Industry Attractiveness

A principal consideration in evaluating a diversified company's business makeup and the caliber of its strategy is the attractiveness of the industries in which it has business operations. Answers to several questions are required:

1. *Does each industry the company has diversified into represent a good business for the company to be in?* Ideally, each industry in which the firm operates will pass the attractiveness test.

2. *Which of the company's industries are most attractive and which are least attractive?* Comparing the attractiveness of the industries and ranking them from most to least attractive is a prerequisite to deciding how to allocate corporate resources across the various businesses.

3. *How appealing is the whole group of industries in which the company has invested?* The answer to this question points to whether the group of industries holds promise for attractive growth and profitability or whether the company may be in too many slow-growing, intensely competitive, highly cyclical businesses. A company whose revenues and profits come chiefly from businesses in relatively unattractive industries probably needs to look at building positions in additional industries that qualify as highly attractive.

The more attractive the industries (both individually and as a group) a diversified company is in, the better its prospects for good long-term performance.

Calculating Industry Attractiveness Scores for Each Industry into Which the Company Has Diversified   A simple and reliable analytical tool involves calculating quantitative industry attractiveness scores, which can then be used to gauge each industry's attractiveness, rank the industries from most to least attractive, and make judgments about the attractiveness of all the industries as a group. A sample calculation is shown in Table 6.1. The following measures of industry attractiveness are likely to come into play for most companies:

- *Market size and projected growth rate*—Big industries are more attractive than small industries, and fast-growing industries tend to be more attractive than slow-growing industries, other things being equal.

- *The intensity of competition*—Industries where competitive pressures are relatively weak are more attractive than industries where competitive pressures are strong.

- *Emerging opportunities and threats*—Industries with promising opportunities and minimal threats on the near horizon are more attractive than industries with modest opportunities and imposing threats.

- *The presence of cross-industry strategic fits*—The more the industry's value chain and resource requirements match up well with the value chain activities of other industries in which the company has operations, the more attractive the industry is to a firm pursuing related diversification. However, cross-industry strategic fits may be of no consequence to a company committed to a strategy of unrelated diversification.

Table 6.1   CALCULATING WEIGHTED INDUSTRY ATTRACTIVENESS SCORES

Industry Attractiveness Measure	Importance Weight	Industry A Rating/ Score	Industry B Rating/ Score	Industry C Rating/ Score	Industry D Rating/ Score
Market size and projected growth rate	0.10	8/0.80	5/0.50	7/0.70	3/0.30
Intensity of competition	0.25	8/2.00	7/1.75	3/0.75	2/0.50
Emerging opportunities and threats	0.10	2/0.20	9/0.90	4/0.40	5/0.50
Cross-industry strategic fits	0.20	8/1.60	4/0.80	8/1.60	2/0.40
Resource requirements	0.10	9/0.90	7/0.70	10/1.00	5/0.50
Seasonal and cyclical influences	0.05	9/0.45	8/0.40	10/0.50	5/0.25
Societal, political, regulatory, and environmental factors	0.05	10/1.00	7/0.70	7/0.70	3/0.30
Industry profitability	0.10	5/0.50	10/1.00	3/0.30	3/0.30
Industry uncertainty and business risk	0.05	5/0.25	7/0.35	10/0.50	1/0.05
Sum of the assigned weights	1.00				
Overall industry attractiveness scores		7.70	7.10	5.45	3.10

Rating scale: 1 = Very unattractive to company; 10 = Very attractive to company

- *Resource requirements*—Industries having resource requirements within the company's reach are more attractive than industries where capital and other resource requirements could strain corporate financial resources and organizational capabilities.

- *Seasonal and cyclical factors*—Industries where buyer demand is relatively steady year-round and not unduly vulnerable to economic ups and downs tend to be more attractive than industries where there are wide swings in buyer demand within or across years. However, seasonality may be a plus for a company that is in several seasonal industries, if the seasonal highs in one industry correspond to the lows in another industry, thus helping even out monthly sales levels. Likewise, cyclical market demand in one industry can be attractive if its up-cycle runs counter to the market down-cycles in another industry where the company operates, thus helping reduce revenue and earnings volatility.

- *Social, political, regulatory, and environmental factors*—Industries with significant problems in such areas as consumer health, safety, or environmental pollution or that are subject to intense regulation are less attractive than industries where such problems are not burning issues.

- *Industry profitability*—Industries with healthy profit margins and high rates of return on investment are generally more attractive than industries where profits have historically been low or unstable.

- *Industry uncertainty and business risk*—Industries with less uncertainty on the horizon and lower overall business risk are more attractive than industries whose prospects for one reason or another are quite uncertain, especially when the industry has formidable resource requirements.

After settling on a set of attractiveness measures that suit a diversified company's circumstances, each attractiveness measure is assigned a weight reflecting its relative importance in determining an industry's attractiveness—it is weak methodology to assume that the various attractiveness measures are equally important. The intensity of competition in an industry should nearly always carry a high weight (say, 0.20 to 0.30). Strategic-fit considerations should be assigned a high weight in the case of companies with related diversification strategies; but, for companies with an unrelated diversification strategy, strategic fits with other industries may be given a low weight or even dropped from the list of attractiveness measures altogether. Seasonal and cyclical factors generally are assigned a low weight (or maybe even eliminated from the analysis) unless a company has diversified into industries strongly characterized by seasonal demand and/or heavy vulnerability to cyclical upswings and downswings. The importance weights must add up to 1.0. Next, each industry is rated on each of the chosen industry attractiveness measures, using a rating scale of 1 to 10 (where a *high* rating signifies *high* attractiveness and a *low* rating signifies *low* attractiveness). Keep in mind here that the more intensely competitive an industry is, the *lower* the attractiveness rating for that industry. Likewise, the higher the capital and resource requirements associated with being in a particular industry, the lower the attractiveness rating. And an industry subject to stringent pollution control regulations or that causes societal problems (like cigarettes or alcoholic beverages) should be given a low attractiveness rating. Weighted attractiveness scores are then calculated by multiplying the industry's rating on each measure by the corresponding weight. For example, a rating of 8 times a weight of 0.25 gives a weighted attractiveness score of 2.00. The sum of the weighted scores for all the attractiveness measures provides an overall industry attractiveness score.

There are two hurdles to using this method of evaluating industry attractiveness. One is deciding on appropriate weights for the industry attractiveness measures. Not only may different analysts have different views about which weights are appropriate for the different attractiveness measures but also different weightings may be appropriate for different companies—based on their strategies, performance targets, and financial circumstances. For instance, placing a low weight on industry resource requirements may be justifiable for a cash-rich company, whereas a high weight may be more appropriate for a financially strapped company. The second hurdle is getting reliable data for use in assigning accurate and objective ratings. Without good information, the ratings necessarily become subjective, and their validity hinges on whether management has probed industry conditions sufficiently to make reliable judgments. Generally, a company can come up with the statistical data needed to compare its industries on such factors as market size, growth rate, seasonal and cyclical influences, and industry profitability. Cross-industry fits and resource requirements are also fairly easy to judge. But the attractiveness measure where judgment weighs most heavily is that of intensity of competition. It is not always easy to conclude whether competition in one industry is stronger or weaker than in another industry because of the different types of competitive influences that prevail and the differences in their relative importance. In the event that the available information is too skimpy to confidently assign a rating value to an industry on a particular attractiveness measure, then it is usually best to use a score of 5, which avoids biasing the overall attractiveness score either up or down.

Nonetheless, industry attractiveness scores are a reasonably reliable method for ranking a diversified company's industries from most to least attractive—quantitative ratings like those shown for the four industries in Table 6.1 tell a valuable story about just how and why some of the industries a company has diversified into are more attractive than others.

Interpreting the Industry Attractiveness Scores Industries with a score much below 5.0 probably do not pass the attractiveness test. If a company's industry attractiveness scores are all above 5.0, it is probably fair to conclude that the group of industries the company operates in is attractive as a whole. But the group of industries takes on a decidedly lower degree of attractiveness as the number of industries with scores below 5.0 increases, especially if industries with low scores account for a sizable fraction of the company's revenues.

For a diversified company to be a strong performer, a substantial portion of its revenues and profits must come from business units with relatively high attractiveness scores. It is particularly important that a diversified company's principal businesses be in industries with a good outlook for growth and above-average profitability. Having a big fraction of the company's revenues and profits come from industries with slow growth, low profitability, or intense competition tends to drag overall company performance down. Business units in the least attractive industries are potential candidates for divestiture, unless they are positioned strongly enough to overcome the unattractive aspects of their industry environments or they are a strategically important component of the company's business makeup.

Step 2: Evaluating Business-Unit Competitive Strength

The second step in evaluating a diversified company is to appraise how strongly positioned each of its business units are in their respective industry. Doing an appraisal of each business unit's strength and competitive position in its industry not only reveals its chances for industry success but also provides a basis for ranking the units from competitively strongest to competitively weakest and sizing up the competitive strength of all the business units as a group.

Calculating Competitive Strength Scores for Each Business Unit Quantitative measures of each business unit's competitive strength can be calculated using a procedure similar to that for measuring industry attractiveness (see Table 6.2). There are a host of measures that can be used in assessing the competitive strength of a diversified company's business subsidiaries:

- *Relative market share*—A business unit's **relative market share** is defined as the ratio of its market share to the market share held by the largest rival firm in the industry, with market share measured in unit volume, not dollars. For instance, if business A has a market-leading share of 40 percent and its largest rival has 30 percent, A's relative market share is 1.33. (Note that only business units that are market share leaders in their respective industries can have relative market shares greater then 1.0.) If business B has a 15 percent market share and B's largest rival has 30 percent, B's relative market share is 0.5. The further below 1.0 a business unit's relative market share is, the weaker its competitive strength and market position vis-à-vis rivals. *Using relative market share is analytically superior to using straight-percentage market share to measure competitive strength.* A 10 percent market share, for example, does not signal much competitive strength if the leader's share is 50 percent (a 0.20 relative market share), but a 10 percent share is actually quite strong if the leader's share is 12 percent (a 0.83 relative market share).

- *Costs relative to competitors' costs*—Business units that have low costs relative to key competitors' costs tend to be more strongly positioned in their industries than

Table 6.2   CALCULATING WEIGHTED COMPETITIVE STRENGTH SCORES FOR THE BUSINESS UNITS

Competitive Strength Measure	Importance Weight	Business A in Industry A Rating/ Score	Business B in Industry B Rating/ Score	Business C in Industry C Rating/ Score	Business D in Industry D Rating/ Score
Relative market share	0.15	10/1.50	1/0.15	6/0.90	2/0.30
Costs relative to competitors' costs	0.20	7/1.40	2/0.40	5/1.00	3/0.60
Ability to match or beat rivals on key product attributes	0.05	9/0.45	4/0.20	8/0.40	4/0.20
Ability to benefit from strategic fits with sister businesses	0.20	8/1.60	4/0.80	8/0.80	2/0.60
Bargaining leverage with suppliers/ buyers; caliber of alliances	0.05	9/0.90	3/0.30	6/0.30	2/0.10
Brand image and reputation	0.10	9/0.90	2/0.20	7/0.70	5/0.50
Competitively valuable capabilities	0.15	7/1.05	2/0.20	5/0.75	3/0.45
Profitability relative to competitors	0.10	5/0.50	1/0.10	4/0.40	4/0.40
Sum of the assigned weights	1.00				
Overall industry attractiveness scores		8.30	2.35	5.25	3.15

Rating scale: 1 = Very weak; 10 = Very strong

business units struggling to maintain cost parity with major rivals. Assuming that the prices charged by industry rivals are about the same, there's reason to expect that business units with higher relative market shares have lower unit costs than competitors with lower relative market shares because their greater unit sales volumes offer the possibility of economies from larger-scale operations and the benefits of any experience or learning-curve effects. On the other hand, a business unit with higher costs than its key rivals is likely to be competitively vulnerable unless its product is strongly differentiated from rivals and its customers are willing to pay premium prices for the differentiating features. Another indicator of low cost can be a business unit's supply chain management capabilities.

■ *Ability to match or beat rivals on key product attributes*—A company's competitiveness depends in part on being able to satisfy buyer expectations with regard to features, product performance, reliability, service, and other important attributes.

■ *Ability to benefit from strategic fits with sister businesses*—Strategic fits with other businesses within the company enhance a business unit's competitive strength and may provide a competitive edge.

■ *Ability to exercise bargaining leverage with key suppliers or customers*—Having bargaining leverage signals competitive strength and can be a source of competitive advantage.

■ *Caliber of alliances and collaborative partnerships with suppliers and/or buyers*—Well-functioning alliances and partnerships may signal a potential competitive advantage vis-à-vis rivals and thus add to a business's competitive strength. Alliances with key suppliers are often the basis for competitive strength in supply chain management.

- *Brand image and reputation*—A strong brand name is a valuable competitive asset in most industries.

- *Competitively valuable capabilities*—Business units recognized for their technological leadership, product innovation, or marketing prowess are usually strong competitors in their industry. Skills in supply chain management can generate valuable cost or product differentiation advantages. So can unique production capabilities. Sometimes a company's business units gain competitive strength because of their knowledge of customers and markets and/or their proven managerial capabilities. *An important thing to look for here is how well a business unit's competitive assets match industry key success factors.* The more a business unit's resource strengths and competitive capabilities match the industry's key success factors, the stronger its competitive position tends to be.

- *Profitability relative to competitors*—Business units that consistently earn above-average returns on investment and have bigger profit margins than their rivals usually have stronger competitive positions than business units with below-average profitability for their industry. Moreover, above-average profitability signals competitive advantage, while below-average profitability usually denotes competitive disadvantage.

After settling on a set of competitive strength measures that are well matched to the circumstances of the various business units, weights indicating each measure's importance need to be assigned. A case can be made for using different weights for different business units whenever the importance of the strength measures differs significantly from business to business, but otherwise it is simpler just to go with a single set of weights and avoid the added complication of multiple weights. As before, the importance weights must add up to 1.0. Each business unit is then rated on each of the chosen strength measures, using a rating scale of 1 to 10 (where a *high* rating signifies competitive *strength* and a *low* rating signifies competitive *weakness*). In the event that the available information is too skimpy to confidently assign a rating value to a business unit on a particular strength measure, then it is usually best to use a score of 5, which avoids biasing the overall score either up or down. Weighted strength ratings are calculated by multiplying the business unit's rating on each strength measure by the assigned weight. For example, a strength score of 6 times a weight of 0.15 gives a weighted strength rating of 0.90. The sum of weighted ratings across all the strength measures provides a quantitative measure of a business unit's overall market strength and competitive standing.

Interpreting the Competitive Strength Scores   Business units with competitive strength ratings above 6.7 (on a scale of 1 to 10) are strong market contenders in their industries. Businesses with ratings in the 3.3 to 6.7 range have moderate competitive strength vis-à-vis rivals. Businesses with ratings below 3.3 are in competitively weak market positions. If a diversified company's business units all have competitive strength scores above 5.0, it is fair to conclude that its business units are all fairly strong market contenders in their respective industries. But as the number of business units with scores below 5.0 increases, there's reason to question whether the company can perform well with so many businesses in relatively weak competitive positions. This concern takes on even more importance when business units with low scores account for a sizable fraction of the company's revenues.

Using a Nine-Cell Matrix to Simultaneously Portray Industry Attractiveness and Competitive Strength   The industry attractiveness and business strength scores can be used to portray the strategic positions of each business in a diversified company. Industry attractiveness is plotted on the vertical axis, and competitive strength on the horizontal axis. A nine-cell grid emerges from dividing the vertical axis into three regions (high, medium, and low attractiveness) and the horizontal axis into three regions (strong, average, and weak competitive strength). As shown in Figure 6.5, high attractiveness is associated with scores of 6.7 or greater on a rating scale of 1 to 10, medium attractiveness to scores of 3.3 to 6.7, and low attractiveness to scores below 3.3. Likewise, high competitive strength is defined as a score greater than 6.7, average strength as scores of 3.3 to 6.7, and low strength as scores below 3.3. *Each business unit is plotted on the nine-cell matrix according to its overall attractiveness score and strength score, and then shown as a "bubble."* The size of each bubble is scaled to what percentage of revenues the business generates relative to total corporate revenues. The bubbles in Figure 6.5 were located on the grid using the attractiveness scores from Table 6.1 and the strength scores for the four business units in Table 6.2.

The locations of the business units on the attractiveness–strength matrix provide valuable guidance in deploying corporate resources to the various business units. In general, *a diversified company's prospects for good overall performance are enhanced by concentrating corporate resources and strategic attention on those business units having the greatest competitive strength and positioned in highly attractive industries*—specifically, businesses in the three cells in the upper left portion of the attractiveness-strength matrix, where industry attractiveness and competitive strength/market position are both favorable. The general strategic prescription for businesses falling in these three cells (for instance, business A in Figure 6.5) is "grow and build," with businesses in the high–strong cell standing first in line for resource allocations by the corporate parent.

> **Core Concept**
>
> In a diversified company, businesses having the greatest competitive strength and positioned in attractive industries should generally have top priority in allocating corporate resources.

Next in priority come businesses positioned in the three diagonal cells stretching from the lower left to the upper right (businesses B and C in Figure 6.5). Such businesses usually merit medium or intermediate priority in the parent's resource allocation ranking. However, some businesses in the medium-priority diagonal cells may have brighter or dimmer prospects than others. For example, a small business in the upper right cell of the matrix (like business B), despite being in a highly attractive industry, may occupy too weak a competitive position in its industry to justify the investment and resources needed to turn it into a strong market contender and shift its position leftward in the matrix over time. If, however, a business in the upper right cell has attractive opportunities for rapid growth and a good potential for winning a much stronger market position over time, it may merit a high claim on the corporate parent's resource allocation ranking and be given the capital it needs to pursue a grow-and-build strategy—the strategic objective here would be to move the business leftward in the attractiveness–strength matrix over time.

Businesses in the three cells in the lower right corner of the matrix typically are weak performers and have the lowest claim on corporate resources. Most such

Figure 6.5   **A Nine-Cell Industry Attractiveness–Competitive Strength Matrix**

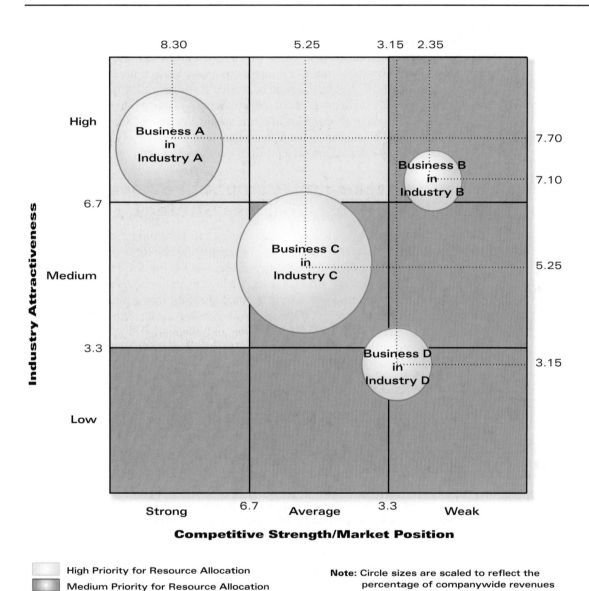

High Priority for Resource Allocation

Medium Priority for Resource Allocation

Low Priority for Resource Allocation

Note: Circle sizes are scaled to reflect the percentage of companywide revenues generated by the business unit.

businesses are good candidates for being divested (sold to other companies) or else managed in a manner calculated to squeeze out the maximum cash flows from operations—the cash flows from low-performing/low-potential businesses can then be diverted to financing expansion of business units with greater market opportunities. In exceptional cases where a business located in the three lower-right cells is nonetheless fairly profitable (which it might be if it is in the low–average cell) or has the potential for good earnings and return on investment, the business merits retention and the allocation of sufficient resources to achieve better performance.

The contribution of the nine-cell attractiveness–strength matrix is the clarity and strong logic it provides for why a diversified company needs to consider both industry attractiveness and business strength in allocating resources and investment capital to its different businesses. A good case can be made for concentrating resources in those businesses that enjoy higher degrees of attractiveness and competitive strength, being very selective in making investments in businesses with intermediate positions on the grid, and withdrawing resources from businesses that are lower in attractiveness and strength unless they offer exceptional profit or cash flow potential.

Step 3: Checking the Competitive Advantage Potential of Cross-Business Strategic Fits

A company's related diversification strategy derives its power in large part from competitively valuable strategic fits among its businesses. While step 3 in the evaluation process can be bypassed for diversified companies whose business are all unrelated (since, by design, no strategic fits are present), a high potential for converting strategic fits into competitive advantage is central to concluding just how good a company's related diversification strategy is. Checking the competitive advantage potential of cross-business strategic fits involves searching for and evaluating how much benefit a diversified company can gain from four types of value chain matchups:

1. *Opportunities to combine the performance of certain activities,* thereby reducing costs. Potential value chain matchups where economies of scope can be realized include purchasing (where combining materials purchases could lead to greater bargaining leverage with suppliers); manufacturing (where it may be possible to share manufacturing facilities); or distribution (where it may be possible to share warehousing, sales forces, distributors, dealers, online sales channels, and after-sale service activities).

2. *Opportunities to transfer skills, technology, or intellectual capital from one business to another*, thereby leveraging use of existing resources. Good candidates for transfer include speed in bringing new products to market, proven R&D skills in generating new products or improving existing technologies, organizational agility in responding to shifting market conditions and emerging opportunities, and state-of-the-art systems for doing business via the Internet.

3. *Opportunities to share use of a well-respected brand name*, thereby gaining credibility with brand-conscious buyers and perhaps commanding prominent display space with retailers.

4. *Opportunities for businesses to collaborate in creating valuable new competitive capabilities* (enhanced quality control capabilities, quicker first-to-market capabilities, greater product innovation capabilities).

Figure 6.6 illustrates the process of searching for competitively valuable cross-business strategic fits and value chain matchups. *But more than just strategic fit identification is needed. The real test is what competitive value can be generated from these fits.* To what extent can cost savings be realized? How much competitive value will come from cross-business transfer of skills, technology, or intellectual capital? Will

Figure 6.6   Identifying the Competitive Advantage Potential of Cross-Business Strategic Fits

Value Chain Activities

	Purchases from suppliers	Technology	Operations	Sales and Marketing	Distribution	Service
Business A						
Business B						
Business C						
Business D						
Business E						

Opportunity to combine purchasing activities and gain more leverage with suppliers and realize supply chain economics

Opportunity to share technology, transfer technical skills, combine R&D

Opportunity to combine sales and marketing activities, use common distribution channels, leverage use of a common brand name, and/or combine after-sale service activities

Collaboration to create new competitive capabilities

No strategic fit opportunities

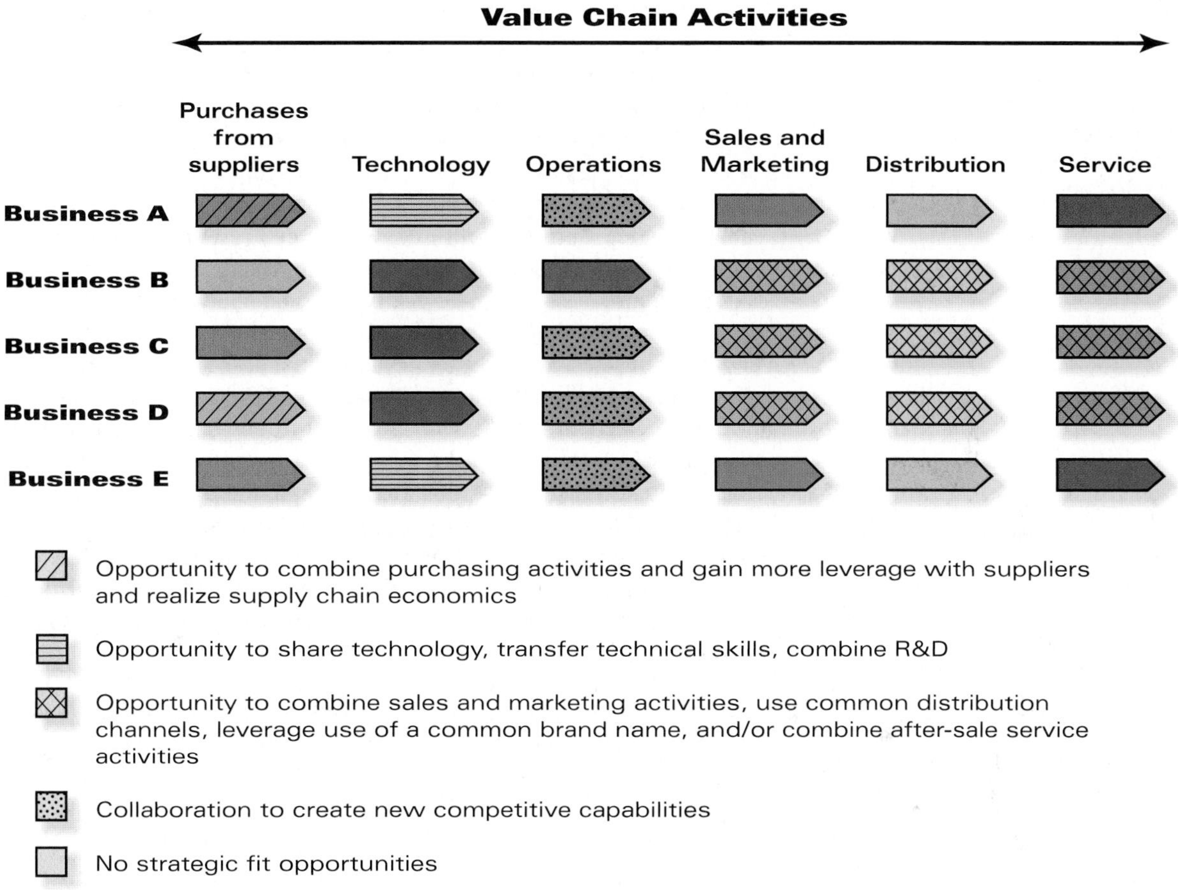

transferring a potent brand name to the products of sister businesses grow sales significantly? Will cross-business collaboration to create or strengthen competitive capabilities lead to significant gains in the marketplace or in financial performance? Absent significant strategic fits and dedicated company efforts to capture the benefits, one has to be skeptical about the potential for a diversified company's businesses to perform better together than apart.

> **Core Concept**
>
> The greater the value of cross-business strategic fits in enhancing a company's performance in the marketplace or on the bottom line, the more competitively powerful is its strategy of related diversification.

Step 4: Checking for Resource Fit

The businesses in a diversified company's lineup need to exhibit good *resource fit* as well as good strategic fit. Resource fit exists when (1) businesses add to a company's resource strengths, either financially or strategically, and (2) a company has the resources to adequately support its businesses as a group without spreading itself too thin. One important dimension of resource fit concerns whether a diversified company has the financial strength to satisfy the cash flow and investments of its different businesses.

Financial Resource Fits: Cash Cows versus Cash Hogs   Different businesses have different cash flow and investment characteristics. For example, business units in rapidly growing industries are often **cash hogs**—so labeled because the cash flows they are able to generate from internal operations aren't big enough to fund their expansion. To keep pace with rising buyer demand, rapid-growth businesses frequently need sizable annual capital investments—for new facilities and equipment, for new product development or technology improvements, and for additional working capital to support inventory expansion and a larger base of operations. A business in a fast-growing industry becomes an even bigger cash hog when it has a relatively low market share and is pursuing a strategy to become an industry leader. Because a cash hog's financial resources must be provided by the corporate parent, corporate managers have to decide whether its investment requirements are strategically and financially worthwhile.

> **Core Concept**
>
> A **cash hog** is a business whose internal cash flows are inadequate to fully fund its needs for working capital and new capital investment.

In contrast, business units with leading market positions in mature industries may, however, be **cash cows**—businesses that generate substantial cash surpluses over what is needed for capital reinvestment and competitive maneuvers to sustain their present market position. Market leaders in slow-growth industries often generate sizable positive cash flows *over and above what is needed for reinvestment in operations* because their industry-leading positions tend to give them the sales volumes and reputation to earn attractive profits and because the slow-growth nature of their industry often entails relatively modest annual investment requirements. Cash cows, though not always attractive from a growth standpoint, are valuable businesses from a financial resource perspective. The surplus cash flows they generate can be used to pay corporate dividends, finance acquisitions, and provide funds for investing in the company's promising cash hogs. It makes good financial and strategic sense for diversified companies to keep cash cows in healthy condition, fortifying and defending their market position so as to preserve their cash-generating capability over the long term and thereby have an ongoing source of financial resources to deploy elsewhere.

> **Core Concept**
>
> A **cash cow** is a business that generates cash flows over and above its internal requirements, thus providing a corporate parent with funds for investing in cash hog businesses, financing new acquisitions, or paying dividends.

Viewing a diversified group of businesses as a collection of cash flows and cash requirements (present and future) is a major step forward in understanding what the financial ramifications of diversification are and why having businesses with good financial resource fit is so important. For instance, a diversified company's businesses exhibit good financial resource fit when the excess cash generated by its cash cow businesses is sufficient to fund the investment requirements of promising cash hog businesses. Ideally, such investment over time results in growing the hogs to become self-supporting "stars" having strong or market-leading competitive positions in attractive, high-growth markets and high levels of profitability. *Star businesses* are often the cash cows of the future—when the markets of star businesses begin to mature and their growth slows, their competitive strength should produce self-generated cash flows more than sufficient to cover their investment needs. The "success sequence" is thus cash hog to young star (but perhaps still a cash hog) to self-supporting star to cash cow.

If, however, a cash hog has questionable promise (either because of low industry attractiveness or a weak competitive position), then it becomes a logical candidate for divestiture. Pursuing an aggressive invest-and-expand strategy for cash hog with an uncertain future seldom makes sense because it requires the corporate parent to keep pumping more capital into the business with only a dim hope of eventually turning the cash hog into a future star and realizing a good return on its investments. Such businesses are a financial drain and fail the resource fit test because they strain the corporate parent's ability to adequately fund its other businesses. Divesting a less attractive cash hog business is usually the best alternative unless (1) it has valuable strategic fits with other business units or (2) the capital infusions needed from the corporate parent are modest relative to the funds available and there's a decent chance of growing the business into a solid bottom-line contributor yielding a good return on invested capital.

Aside from cash flow considerations, a business has good financial fit when it contributes to the achievement of corporate performance objectives (growth in earnings per share, above-average return on investment, recognition as an industry leader, etc.) and when it materially enhances shareholder value via helping drive increases in the company's stock price. A business exhibits poor financial fit if it soaks up a disproportionate share of the company's financial resources, makes subpar or inconsistent bottom-line contributions, is unduly risky and failure would jeopardize the entire enterprise, or remains too small to make a material earnings contribution even though it performs well.

A diversified company's strategy also fails the resource fit test when its financial resources are stretched across so many businesses that its credit rating is impaired. Severe financial strain sometimes occurs when a company borrows so heavily to finance new acquisitions that it has to trim way back on capital expenditures for existing businesses and use the big majority of its financial resources to meet interest obligations and to pay down debt. Some diversified companies have found themselves so financially overextended that they have had to sell off certain businesses to raise the money to meet existing debt obligations and fund essential capital expenditures for the remaining businesses.

Competitive and Managerial Resource Fits A diversified company's strategy must aim at producing a good fit between its resource capability and the competitive and managerial requirements of its businesses.[17] Diversification is more likely to enhance shareholder value when the company has or can develop strong competitive and managerial capabilities. Sometimes the resource strengths crucial to succeeding in one particular business are a poor match with the key success factors in other businesses. For instance, BTR, a multibusiness company in Great Britain, discovered that the company's resources and managerial skills were quite well suited for parenting industrial manufacturing businesses but

> A close match between industry key success factors and company resources and capabilities is a solid sign of good resource fit.

not for parenting its distribution businesses (National Tyre Services and Texas-based Summers Group); as a consequence, BTR decided to divest its distribution businesses and focus exclusively on diversifying around small industrial manufacturing.[18] One company with businesses in restaurants and retailing decided that its resource capabilities in site selection, controlling operating costs, management selection and training, and supply chain logistics would enable it to succeed in the hotel business and in property management; but what management missed was that these businesses had some significantly different key success factors—namely, skills in controlling property development costs, maintaining low overheads, product branding (hotels), and ability to recruit a sufficient volume of business to maintain high levels of facility utilization.[19] A mismatch between the company's resource strengths and the key success factors in a particular business can be serious enough to warrant divesting an existing business or not acquiring a new business. In contrast, when a company's resources and capabilities are a good match with the key success factors of industries it is not presently in, it makes sense to take a hard look at acquiring companies in these industries and expanding the company's business lineup.

A second instance in which a diversified company can fail the resource fit test is by not having sufficient *resource depth* to support all of its businesses. A diversified company has to guard against stretching its resource base too thin and trying to do too many things. The broader the diversification, the greater the concern about whether the company has sufficient managerial depth to cope with the diverse range of operating problems its wide business lineup presents (plus those it may be contemplating getting into). The more a company's diversification strategy is tied to leveraging its resources and capabilities in new businesses, the more it has to develop a big enough and deep enough resource pool to supply these businesses with sufficient capability to create competitive advantage.[20] Otherwise its strengths end up being stretched too thin across too many businesses and the opportunity for competitive advantage is lost.

A Note of Caution   Just because a company has hit a home run in one business doesn't mean it can easily enter a new business with similar resource requirements and hit a second home run.[21] Noted British retailer Marks & Spencer, despite possessing a range of impressive resource capabilities (ability to choose excellent store locations, having a supply chain that gives it both low costs and high merchandise quality, loyal employees, an excellent reputation with consumers, and strong management expertise) that have made it one of Britain's premier retailers for 100 years, has failed repeatedly in its efforts to diversify into department store retailing in the United States. Even though Philip Morris (now named Altria) had built powerful consumer marketing capabilities in its cigarette and beer businesses, it floundered in soft drinks and ended up divesting its acquisition of 7UP after several frustrating years of competing against strongly entrenched and resource-capable rivals like Coca-Cola and PepsiCo.

Step 5: Ranking the Business Units on the Basis of Performance and Priority for Resource Allocation

Once a diversified company's strategy has been evaluated from the perspective of industry attractiveness, competitive strength, strategic fit, and resource fit, the next step is to rank the performance prospects of the businesses from best to worst and determine which businesses merit top priority for new investments by the corporate parent.

The most important considerations in judging business-unit performance are sales growth, profit growth, contribution to company earnings, and return on capital invested in the business. (As we noted in Chapter 1, more and more companies are evaluating business performance on the basis of economic value added—the return on invested capital over and above the firm's cost of capital.) Sometimes, cash flow is a big consideration. Information on each business's past performance can be gleaned from a company's financial records. While past performance is not necessarily a good predictor of future performance, it does signal whether a business is in a strong position or a weak one.

The industry attractiveness/business strength evaluations provide a basis for judging a business's prospects. Normally, strong business units in attractive industries have significantly better prospects than weak businesses in unattractive industries. And, normally, the revenue and earnings outlook for businesses in fast-growing industries is better than for businesses in slow-growing industries—one important exception is when a business has the competitive strength to draw sales and market share away from its rivals and thus achieve much faster growth than the industry as whole. As a

Figure 6.7 The Chief Strategic and Financial Options for Allocating a Diversified Company's Financial Resources

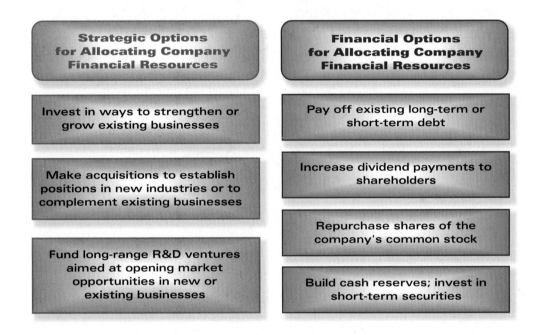

rule, the prior analyses, taken together, signal which business units are likely to be strong performers on the road ahead and which are likely to be laggards. And it is a short step from ranking the prospects of business units to drawing conclusions about whether the company as a whole is capable of strong, mediocre, or weak performance in upcoming years.

The rankings of future performance generally determine what priority the corporate parent should give to each business in terms of resource allocation. The task here is to decide which business units should have top priority for corporate resource support and new capital investment and which should carry the lowest priority. *Business subsidiaries with the brightest profit and growth prospects and solid strategic and resource fits generally should head the list for corporate resource support.* However, corporate executives need to give special attention to whether and how corporate resources and capabilities can be used to enhance the competitiveness of particular business units. Opportunities for resource transfer, activity combining, or infusions of new financial capital become especially important when improvement in some key success area could make a big difference to a particular business unit's performance.

For a company's diversification strategy to generate ever-higher levels of performance, corporate managers have to do an effective job of steering resources out of low-opportunity areas into high-opportunity areas. Divesting marginal businesses is one of the best ways of freeing unproductive assets for redeployment. Surplus funds from cash cows also add to the corporate treasury. Figure 6.7 shows the chief strategic and financial options for allocating a diversified company's financial resources. Ideally, a company will have enough funds to do what is needed, both strategically and financially. If not, strategic uses of corporate resources should usually take precedence unless there is a compelling reason to strengthen the firm's balance sheet or divert financial resources to pacify shareholders.

Step 6: Crafting New Strategic Moves to Improve Overall Corporate Performance

The diagnosis and conclusions flowing from the five preceding analytical steps set the agenda for crafting strategic moves to improve a diversified company's overall performance. The strategic options boil down to five broad categories of actions:

1. Sticking closely with the existing business lineup and pursuing the opportunities it presents.
2. Broadening the company's business scope by making new acquisitions in new industries.
3. Divesting certain businesses and retrenching to a narrower base of business operations.
4. Restructuring the company's business lineup and putting a whole new face on the company's business makeup.
5. Pursuing multinational diversification and striving to globalize the operations of several of the company's business units.

The option of sticking with the current business lineup makes sense when the company's present businesses offer attractive growth opportunities and can be counted on to generate dependable earnings and cash flows. As long as the company's set of existing businesses puts it in good position for the future and these businesses have good strategic and/or resource fits, then rocking the boat with major changes in the company's business mix is usually unnecessary. Corporate executives can concentrate their attention on getting the best performance from each of its businesses, steering corporate resources into those areas of greatest potential and profitability. The specifics of "what to do" to wring better performance from the present business lineup have to be dictated by each business's circumstances and the preceding analysis of the corporate parent's diversification strategy.

However, in the event that corporate executives are not entirely satisfied with the opportunities they see in the company's present set of businesses and conclude that changes in the company's direction and business makeup are in order, they can opt for any of the four other strategic alternatives listed above. These options are discussed in the following section.

After a Company Diversifies: The Four Main Strategy Alternatives

Diversifying is by no means the final chapter in the evolution of a company's strategy. Once a company has diversified into a collection of related or unrelated businesses and concludes that some overhaul is needed in the company's present lineup and diversification strategy, there are four main strategic paths it can pursue (see Figure 6.8). To more fully understand the strategic issues corporate managers face in the ongoing process of managing a diversified group of businesses, we need to take a brief look at the central thrust of each of the four post-diversification strategy alternatives.

Figure 6.8   A Company's Four Main Strategic Alternatives after It Diversifies

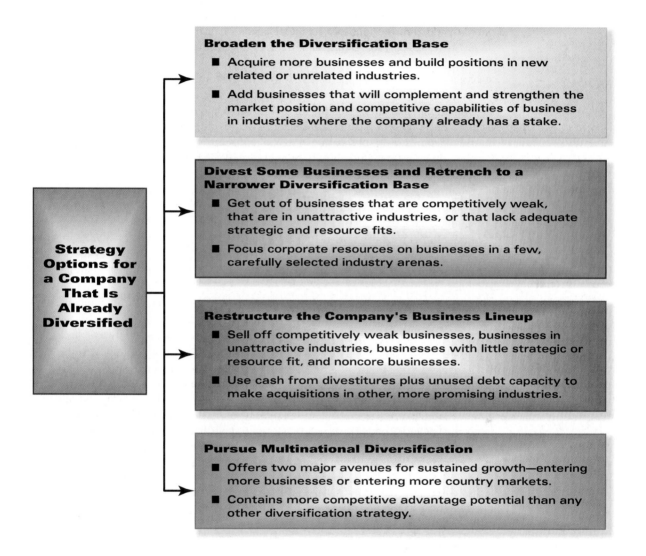

Strategies to Broaden a Diversified Company's Business Base

Diversified companies sometimes find it desirable to build positions in new industries, whether related or unrelated. There are several motivating factors. One is sluggish growth that makes the potential revenue and profit boost of a newly acquired business look attractive. A second is vulnerability to seasonal or recessionary influences or to threats from emerging new technologies. A third is the potential for transferring resources and capabilities to other related or complementary businesses. A fourth is rapidly changing conditions in one or more of a company's core businesses brought on by technological, legislative, or new product innovations that alter buyer requirements and preferences. For instance, the passage of legislation in the United States allowing banks, insurance companies, and stock brokerages to enter each other's businesses spurred a raft of acquisitions and mergers to create full-service financial enterprises capable of meeting the multiple financial needs of customers. Citigroup, already the largest U.S. bank with a global banking franchise, acquired Salomon Smith Barney to position itself in the investment banking and brokerage business and acquired insurance giant Travelers Group to enable it to offer customers insurance products.

A fifth, and often very important, motivating factor for adding new businesses is to complement and strengthen the market position and competitive capabilities of one or more of its present businesses. Viacom's acquisition of CBS strengthened and extended Viacom's reach into various media businesses—it was the parent of Paramount Pictures, an assortment of cable TV networks (UPN, MTV, Nickelodeon, VH1, Showtime, The Movie Channel, Comedy Central), Blockbuster video stores, two movie theater chains, and 19 local TV stations. Unilever, a leading maker of food and personal care products, expanded its business lineup by acquiring SlimFast, Ben & Jerry's Homemade Ice Cream, and Best Foods (whose brands included Knorr's soups, Hellman's mayonnaise, Skippy peanut butter, and Mazola cooking oils). Unilever saw these businesses as giving it more clout in competing against such other diversified food and household products companies as Nestlé, Kraft, Procter & Gamble, and Danone.

Usually, expansion into new businesses is undertaken by acquiring companies already in the target industry. Some companies depend on new acquisitions to drive a major portion of their growth in revenues and earnings, and thus are always on the acquisition trail. Cisco Systems built itself into a worldwide leader in networking systems for the Internet by making 75 technology-based acquisitions during 1993–2002 to extend its market reach from routing and switching into voice and video over Internet protocol, optical networking, wireless, storage networking, security, broadband, and content networking. Tyco International, recently beset with charges of looting on the part of several top executives, transformed itself from an obscure company in the early 1990s into a $36 billion global manufacturing enterprise with operations in over 100 countries as of 2002 by making over 1,000 acquisitions; the company's far-flung diversification includes businesses in electronics, electrical components, fire and security systems, health care products, valves, undersea telecommunications systems, plastics, and adhesives. Tyco made over 700 acquisitions of small companies in the 1999–2001 period alone.

Divestiture Strategies Aimed at Retrenching to a Narrower Diversification Base

A number of diversified firms have had difficulty managing a diverse group of businesses and have elected to get out of some of them. Retrenching to a narrower diversification base is usually undertaken when top management concludes that its diversification strategy has ranged too far afield and that the company can improve long-term performance by concentrating on building stronger positions in a smaller number of core businesses and industries. Hewlett-Packard spun off its testing and measurement businesses into a stand-alone company called Agilent Technologies so that it could better concentrate on its PC, workstation, server, printer and peripherals, and electronics businesses. PepsiCo divested its cash-hog

Focusing corporate resources on a few core and mostly related businesses avoids the mistake of diversifying so broadly that resources and management attention are stretched too thin.

group of restaurant businesses, consisting of Kentucky Fried Chicken, Pizza Hut, Taco Bell, and California Pizza Kitchens, to provide more resources for strengthening its soft-drink business (which was losing market share to Coca-Cola) and growing its more profitable Frito-Lay snack foods business. Kmart divested OfficeMax, Sports Authority, and Borders Bookstores in order to refocus management attention and all of the company's resources on restoring luster to its distressed discount retailing business, which was (and still is) being totally outclassed in the marketplace by Wal-Mart and Target.

But there are other important reasons for divesting one or more of a company's present businesses. Sometimes divesting a business has to be considered because market conditions in a once-attractive industry have badly deteriorated. A business can become a prime candidate for divestiture because it lacks adequate strategic or resource fit, because it is a cash hog with questionable long-term potential, or because it is weakly positioned in its industry with little prospect the corporate parent can realize a decent return on its investment in the business. Sometimes a company acquires businesses that, down the road, just do not work out as expected even though management has tried all it can think of to make them profitable—mistakes cannot be completely avoided because it is hard to foresee how getting into a new line of business will actually work out. Subpar performance by some business units is bound to occur, thereby raising questions of whether to divest them or keep them and attempt a turnaround. Other business units, despite adequate financial performance, may not mesh as well with the rest of the firm as was originally thought.

On occasion, a diversification move that seems sensible from a strategic-fit standpoint turns out to be a poor *cultural fit.*[22] Several pharmaceutical companies had just this experience. When they diversified into cosmetics and perfume, they discovered their personnel had little respect for the "frivolous" nature of such products compared to the far nobler task of developing miracle drugs to cure the ill. The absence of shared values and cultural compatibility between the medical research and chemical-compounding expertise of the pharmaceutical companies and the fashion/marketing orientation of the cosmetics business was the undoing of what otherwise was diversification into businesses with technology-sharing potential, product-development fit, and some overlap in distribution channels.

Recent research indicates that pruning businesses and narrowing a firm's diversification base improves corporate performance.[23] Corporate parents often end up selling off businesses too late and at too low a price, sacrificing shareholder value.[24] A useful guide to determine whether or when to divest a business subsidiary is to ask, "If we were not in this business today, would we want to get into it now?"[25] When the answer is no or probably not, divestiture should be considered. Another signal that a business should become a divestiture candidate is whether it is worth more to another company than to the present parent; in such cases, shareholders would be well served if the company sells the business and collects a premium price from the buyer for whom the business is a valuable fit.[26]

The Two Options for Divesting a Business: Selling It or Spinning It Off as an Independent Company Selling a business outright to another company is far and away the most frequently used option for divesting a business. But sometimes a business selected for divestiture has ample resource strengths to compete successfully on its own. In such cases, a corporate parent may elect to spin the unwanted business off as a financially and managerially independent company, either by selling shares to the investing public via an initial public offering or by distributing shares in the new company to existing shareholders of the corporate parent. When a corporate parent decides to spin off one of its businesses as a separate company, there's the issue of whether or not to retain partial ownership. Retaining partial ownership makes sense when the business to be divested has a hot product or technological capabilities that give it good profit prospects. When 3Com elected to divest its PalmPilot business, which investors then saw as having very promising profit potential, it elected to retain a substantial ownership interest so as to provide 3Com shareholders a way of participating in whatever future market success that PalmPilot (now Palm, Inc.) might have on its own.

Selling a business outright requires finding a buyer. This can prove hard or easy, depending on the business. As a rule, a company selling a troubled business should not ask, "How can we pawn this business off on someone, and what is the most we can get for it?"[27] Instead, it is wiser to ask, "For what sort of company would this business be a good fit, and under what conditions would it be viewed as a good deal?" Enterprises for which the business is a good fit are likely to pay the highest price. Of course, if a buyer willing to pay an acceptable price cannot be found, then a company must decide whether to keep the business until a buyer appears; spin it off as a separate company; or, in the case of a crisis-ridden business that is losing substantial sums, simply close it down and liquidate the remaining assets. Liquidation is obviously a last resort.

Strategies to Restructure a Company's Business Lineup

Restructuring strategies involve divesting some businesses and acquiring others so as to put a whole new face on the company's business lineup. Performing radical surgery on the group of businesses a company is in becomes an appealing strategy alternative when a diversified company's financial performance is being squeezed or eroded by:

> **Core Concept**
>
> **Restructuring** involves divesting some businesses and acquiring others so as to put a whole new face on the company's business lineup.

- Too many businesses in slow-growth, declining, low-margin, or otherwise unattractive industries (a condition indicated by the number and size of businesses with industry attractiveness ratings below 5 and located on the bottom half of the attractiveness–strength matrix—see Figure 6.5).
- Too many competitively weak businesses (a condition indicated by the number and size of businesses with competitive strength ratings below 5 and located on the right half of the attractiveness–strength matrix).
- Ongoing declines in the market shares of one or more major business units that are falling prey to more market-savvy competitors.
- An excessive debt burden with interest costs that eat deeply into profitability.
- Ill-chosen acquisitions that haven't lived up to expectations.

Restructuring can also be mandated by the emergence of new technologies that threaten the survival of one or more of a diversified company's important businesses or by the appointment of a new CEO who decides to redirect the company. On occasion, restructuring can be prompted by special circumstances—like when a firm has a unique opportunity to make an acquisition so big and important that it has to sell several existing business units to finance the new acquisition or when a company needs to sell off some businesses in order to raise the cash for entering a potentially big industry with wave-of-the-future technologies or products.

Candidates for divestiture in a corporate restructuring effort typically include not only weak or up-and-down performers or those in unattractive industries but also business units that lack strategic fit with the businesses to be retained, businesses that are cash hogs or that lack other types of resource fit, and businesses incompatible with the company's revised diversification strategy (even though they may be profitable or in an attractive industry). As businesses are divested, corporate restructuring generally involves aligning the remaining business units into groups with the best strategic fits and then redeploying the cash flows from the divested business to either pay down debt or make new acquisitions to strengthen the parent company's business position in the industries it has chosen to emphasize.[28]

Over the past decade, corporate restructuring has become a popular strategy at many diversified companies, especially those that had diversified broadly into many different industries and lines of business. For instance, one struggling diversified company over a two-year period divested four business units, closed down the operations of four others, and added 25 new lines of business to its portfolio (16 through acquisition and 9 through internal start-up). During Jack Welch's first four years as CEO of General Electric (GE), the company divested 117 business units, accounting for about 20 percent of GE's assets; these divestitures, coupled with several important acquisitions, provided GE with 14 major business divisions and led to Welch's challenge to the managers of GE's divisions to become number one or number two in their industry. Ten years after Welch became CEO, GE was a different company, having divested operations worth $9 billion, made new acquisitions totaling $24 billion, and cut its workforce by 100,000 people. Then, during the 1990–2001 period, GE continued to reshuffle its business lineup, acquiring over 600 new companies, including 108 in 1998 and 64 during a 90-day period in 1999. Most of the new acquisitions were in Europe, Asia, and Latin America and were aimed at transforming GE into a truly global enterprise. PerkinElmer used a series of divestitures and new acquisitions to transform itself from a supplier of low-margin services sold to the government agencies into an innovative high-tech company with operations in over 125 countries and businesses in four industry groups—life sciences (drug research and clinical screening), optoelectronics, instruments, and fluid control and containment (for customers in aerospace, power generation, and semiconductors).

Several broadly diversified companies have pursued restructuring by splitting into two or more independent companies. In 1996, AT&T divided itself into three companies—one (that retained the AT&T name) for long-distance and other telecommunications services, one (called Lucent Technologies) for manufacturing telecommunications equipment, and one (called NCR) for computer systems that essentially represented the divestiture of AT&T's earlier acquisition of National Cash Register. A few years after the split-up, AT&T acquired TCI Communications and MediaOne, both leading cable TV providers, in an attempt to restructure itself into a new-age telecommunications company offering bundled local and long-distance service, cable TV, and high-speed Internet access. In 2000, after its bundled services concept flopped and its debt had become excessive, AT&T proposed splitting itself once again, this time into four businesses—AT&T Comcast (formed by the 2002 merger of Comcast and AT&T's cable TV operations), AT&T Consumer, AT&T Business, and AT&T Wireless. Before beginning a restructuring effort in 1995, British-based Hanson PLC owned companies with more than $20 billion in revenues in industries as diverse as beer, exercise equipment, tools, construction cranes, tobacco, cement, chemicals, coal mining, electricity, hot tubs and whirlpools, cookware, rock and gravel, bricks, and asphalt. By early 1997, Hanson had restructured itself into a $3.8 billion enterprise focused more narrowly on gravel, crushed rock, cement, asphalt, bricks, and construction cranes; the remaining businesses were divided into four groups and divested.

In a study of the performance of the 200 largest U.S. corporations from 1990 to 2000, McKinsey & Company found that those companies that actively managed their business portfolios through acquisitions and divestitures created substantially more shareholder value than those that kept a fixed lineup of businesses.[29]

Multinational Diversification Strategies

The distinguishing characteristics of a multinational diversification strategy are a *diversity of businesses* and a *diversity of national markets.*[30] Such diversity makes multinational diversification a particularly challenging and complex strategy to conceive and execute. Managers have to develop business strategies for each industry (with as many multinational variations as conditions in each country market dictate). Then, they have to pursue and manage opportunities for cross-business and cross-country collaboration and strategic coordination in ways calculated to result in competitive advantage and enhanced profitability.

Moreover, the geographic operating scope of individual businesses within a diversified multinational company (DMNC) can range from one country only to several countries to many countries to global. Thus, each business unit within a DMNC often competes in a somewhat different combination of geographic markets than the other businesses do—adding another element of strategic complexity, and perhaps an element of opportunity.

Global Spotlight 6.3 shows the scope of four prominent DMNCs.

The Appeal of Multinational Diversification: More Opportunities for Sustained Growth and Maximum Competitive Advantage Potential Despite their complexity, multinational diversification strategies have great appeal. They contain *two major avenues* for growing revenues and profits: One is to grow by entering additional businesses, and the other is to grow by extending the operations of existing businesses into additional country markets. Moreover, a strategy of multinational diversification also contains six attractive paths to competitive advantage, *all of which can be pursued simultaneously*:

1. *Full capture of economies of scale and experience and learning-curve effects.* In some businesses, the volume of sales needed to realize full economies of scale and/or benefit fully from experience and learning-curve effects is rather sizable, often exceeding the volume that can be achieved operating within the boundaries of a single country market, especially a small one. *The ability to drive down unit costs by expanding sales to additional country markets is one reason why a diversified multinational may seek to acquire a business and then rapidly expand its operations into more and more foreign markets.*

2. *Opportunities to capitalize on cross-business economies of scope.* Diversifying into related businesses offering economies of scope can drive the development of a low-cost advantage over less diversified rivals. For example, a DMNC that uses mostly the same distributors and retail dealers worldwide can diversify into new businesses using these same worldwide distribution channels at relatively little incremental expense. The cost savings of piggybacking distribution activities can be substantial. Moreover, with more business selling more products in more countries, a DMNC acquires more bargaining leverage in its purchases from suppliers and more bargaining leverage with retailers in securing attractive display space for

GLOBAL SPOTLIGHT 6.3

The Global Scope of Four Prominent Diversified Multinational Corporations

Company	Global Scope	Businesses into Which the Company Has Diversified
Sony	Operations in more than 100 countries and sales offices in more than 200 countries	▪ Televisions, VCRs, DVD players, radios, CD players and home stereos, digital cameras and video equipment, PCs and Trinitron computer monitors ▪ PlayStation game consoles and video game software ▪ Columbia, Epic, and Sony Classical prerecorded music ▪ Columbia TriStar motion pictures, syndicated television programs ▪ Other businesses (insurance, financing, entertainment complexes, Internet-related businesses)
Nestlé	Operations in 70 countries and sales offices in more than 200 countries	▪ Beverages (Nescafé and Taster's Choice coffees, Nestea, Perrier, Arrowhead, & Calistoga mineral and bottled waters) ▪ Milk products (Carnation, Gloria, Neslac, Coffee Mate, Nestlé ice cream and yogurt) ▪ Pet foods (Friskies, Alpo, Fancy Feast, Mighty Dog) ▪ Contadina, Libby's, and Stouffer's food products and prepared dishes ▪ Chocolate and confectionery products (Nestlé Crunch, Smarties, Baby Ruth, Butterfinger, KitKat) ▪ Pharmaceuticals (Alcon ophthalmic products, Galderma dermatological products)
Siemens	Operations in 160 countries and sales offices in more than 190 countries	▪ Electrical power generation, transmission, and distribution equipment and products ▪ Manufacturing automation systems, industrial motors, industrial computers, industrial machinery, industrial tools, plant construction and maintenance ▪ Information and communications (solutions and services needed for corporate communication networks, telephones, PCs, mainframes, computer network products, consulting services) ▪ Mass transit and light rail systems, rail cars, locomotives ▪ Medical equipment, health care management services ▪ Semiconductors, memory components, microcontrollers, capacitors, resistors ▪ Lighting (bulbs, lamps, theater and television lighting systems) ▪ Home electronics, large home appliances, vacuum cleaners ▪ Financial services (commercial lending, pension administration, venture capital) ▪ Procurement and logistics services, business consulting services
Samsung	Operations in more than 60 countries and sales in more than 200 countries	▪ Electronics (computers, peripherals, displays, televisions, telecommunications equipment, semiconductors, memory chips, circuit boards, capacitors, information technology services, systems integration) ▪ Machinery and heavy industry (shipbuilding, oil and gas storage tank construction, marine engines, aircraft and aircraft parts, gas turbines, military hardware, industrial robots, factory automation systems) ▪ Automotive (passenger cars, commercial trucks) ▪ Chemicals (general chemicals, petrochemicals, fertilizers) ▪ Financial services (insurance, credit card services, securities trading, consumer credit services, trust management) ▪ Other affiliated companies (theme parks, hotels, medical centers, apparel, professional sports teams, film, music, and television production)

Source: Company annual reports and websites.

its products. Consider, for example, the competitive power that Sony derived from these very sorts of economies of scope when it decided to diversify into the video game business with its PlayStation product line. Sony had in-place capability to go after video game sales in all country markets where it presently did business in other product categories (TVs, computers, DVD players, VCRs, radios, CD players, and digital and video cameras). And it had the marketing clout and brand-name credibility to persuade retailers to give Sony's PlayStation products prime shelf space and visibility. These strategic-fit benefits helped Sony quickly overtake longtime industry leaders Nintendo and Sega and (so far, as of this writing) fortify its position against Microsoft's new Xbox offerings.

3. *Opportunities to transfer competitively valuable resources both from one business to another and from one country to another.* A company pursuing related diversification can gain a competitive edge over less diversified rivals by transferring competitively valuable resources from one business to another; a multinational company can gain competitive advantage over rivals with narrower geographic coverage by transferring competitively valuable resources from one country to another. But a strategy of multinational diversification enables simultaneous pursuit of both sources of competitive advantage.

4. *Ability to leverage use of a well-known and competitively powerful brand name.* Diversified multinational companies whose businesses have brand names that are well known and respected across the world possess a valuable strategic asset with competitive advantage potential. For example, Sony's well-established global brand-name recognition gives it an important marketing and advertising advantage over rivals with lesser-known brands. When Sony goes into a new marketplace with the stamp of the Sony brand on new businesses or product families, it can command prominent display space with retailers. It can expect to win sales and market share simply on the confidence that buyers place in products carrying the Sony name. While Sony may spend money to make consumers aware of the availability of its new products, it does not have to spend nearly as much on achieving brand recognition and market acceptance as would a lesser-known competitor looking at the marketing and advertising costs of entering the same new product/business/country markets and trying to go head-to-head against Sony. Further, if Sony moves into a new country market for the first time and does well selling Sony PlayStations and video games, it is easier to sell consumers in that country Sony TVs, digital cameras, PCs, and so on—plus, the related advertising costs are likely to be less than they would be without having already established the Sony brand strongly in the minds of buyers.

> **Core Concept**
>
> Transferring a powerful brand name from one product or business to another can usually be done very economically.

5. *Ability to capitalize on opportunities for cross-business and cross-country collaboration and strategic coordination.*[31] A multinational diversification strategy allows competitively valuable cross-business and cross-country coordination of certain value chain activities. For instance, by channeling corporate resources directly into a combined R&D/technology effort for all related businesses, as opposed to letting each business unit fund and direct its own R&D effort however it sees fit, a DMNC can merge its expertise and efforts *worldwide* to advance core technologies, expedite cross-business and cross-country product improvements, speed the development of new products that complement existing products, and pursue promising technological avenues to create altogether new businesses—all significant contributors to competitive advantage and better corporate performance.[32] Honda has been

very successful in building R&D expertise in gasoline engines and transferring the resulting technological advances to its businesses in automobiles, motorcycles, outboard engines, snow blowers, lawn mowers, garden tillers, and portable power generators. Further, a DMNC can reduce costs through cross-business and cross-country coordination of purchasing and procurement from suppliers, from collaborative introduction and shared use of e-commerce technologies and online sales efforts, and from coordinated product introductions and promotional campaigns. Firms that are less diversified and less global in scope have less such cross-business and cross-country collaborative opportunities.

6. *Opportunities to use cross-business or cross-country subsidization to outcompete rivals.* A financially successful DMNC has potentially valuable organizational resources and multiple profit sanctuaries in both certain country markets and certain business that it can draw on to wage a market offensive. In comparison, a one-business domestic company has only one profit sanctuary—its home market. A diversified one-country competitor may have profit sanctuaries in several businesses, but all are in the same country market. A one-business multinational company may have profit sanctuaries in several country markets, but all are in the same business. All three are vulnerable to an offensive in their more limited profit sanctuaries by an aggressive DMNC willing to lowball its prices and/or spend extravagantly on advertising to win market share at their expense. A DMNC's ability to keep hammering away at competitors with low prices year after year may reflect either a cost advantage growing out of its related diversification strategy or a willingness to accept low profits or even losses in the market being attacked because it has ample earnings from its other profit sanctuaries. For example, Sony's global-scale diversification strategy gives it unique competitive strengths in outcompeting Nintendo and Sega, neither of which are diversified. If need be, Sony can maintain low prices on its PlayStations or fund high-profile promotions for its latest video game products, using earnings from its other business lines to fund its offensive to wrest market share away from Nintendo and Sega in video games. At the same time, Sony can draw on its considerable resources in R&D, its ability to transfer electronics technology from one electronics product family to another, and its expertise in product innovation to introduce better and better video game players, perhaps players that are multifunctional and do more than just play video games. Such competitive actions not only enhance Sony's own brand image but also make it very tough for Nintendo and Sega to match Sony's prices, advertising, and product development efforts and still earn acceptable profits.

The Combined Effects of These Advantages Is Potent

A strategy of diversifying into *related* industries and then competing *globally* in each of these industries thus has great potential for being a winner in the marketplace because of the long-term growth opportunities it offers and the multiple corporate-level competitive advantage opportunities it contains. Indeed, *a strategy of multinational diversification contains more competitive advantage potential* (above and beyond what is achievable through a particular business's own competitive strategy) *than any other diversification strategy.* The strategic key to maximum competitive advantage is for a DMNC to concentrate its diversification efforts in those industries where there are resource-sharing and resource-transfer opportunities and where there are important economies of scope and brand name benefits. The more a company's diversification strategy yields these kinds

> **Core Concept**
>
> A strategy of multinational diversification has more built-in potential for competitive advantage than any other diversification strategy.

of strategic-fit benefits, the more powerful a competitor it becomes and the better its profit and growth performance is likely to be.

However, it is important to recognize that while a DMNC's cross-subsidization capabilities are a potent competitive weapon in theory, in actual practice cross-subsidization can only be used sparingly. It is one thing to *occasionally* divert a portion of the profits and cash flows from existing businesses to help fund entry into a new business or country market or wage a competitive offensive against select rivals. It is quite another thing to *regularly* use cross-subsidization tactics and thereby weaken overall company performance. A DMNC is under the same pressures as any other company to demonstrate consistently acceptable profitability across its whole operation. At some juncture, every business and every country market needs to make a profit contribution or become a candidate for abandonment. As a general rule, *cross-subsidization tactics are justified only when there is a good prospect that the short-term impairment to corporate profitability will be offset by stronger competitiveness and better overall profitability over the long term.*

> **Core Concept**
>
> Although cross-subsidization is a potent competitive weapon, it can only be used infrequently because of its adverse impact on overall corporate profitability.

Key Points

Most companies have their business roots in a single industry. Even though they may have since diversified into other industries, a substantial part of their revenues and profits still usually comes from the original or core business. Diversification becomes an attractive strategy when a company runs out of profitable growth opportunities in its original business. The purpose of diversification is to build shareholder value. Diversification builds shareholder value when a diversified group of businesses can perform better under the auspices of a single corporate parent than they would as independent, stand-alone businesses—the goal is to achieve not just a $1 + 1 = 2$ result but rather to realize important $1 + 1 = 3$ performance benefits. Whether getting into a new business has potential to enhance shareholder value hinges on whether a company's entry into that business can pass the attractiveness test, the cost-of-entry test, and the better-off test.

Entry into new businesses can take any of three forms: acquisition, internal start-up, or joint venture/strategic partnership. Each has its pros and cons, but acquisition is the most frequently used; internal start-up takes the longest to produce home-run results, and joint venture/strategic partnership, though used second most frequently, is the least durable.

There are two fundamental approaches to diversification—into related businesses and into unrelated businesses. The rationale for *related* diversification is *strategic:* Diversify into businesses with strategic fits along their respective value chains, capitalize on strategic-fit relationships to gain competitive advantage, and then use competitive advantage to achieve the desired $1 + 1 = 3$ impact on shareholder value. Businesses have strategic fit when their value chains offer potential (1) for realizing economies of scope or cost-saving efficiencies associated with sharing technology, facilities, functional activities, distribution outlets, or brand names; (2) for competitively valuable cross-business transfers of technology, skills, know-how, or other resource capabilities; (3) for leveraging use of a well-known and trusted brand name, and (4) for competitively valuable cross-business collaboration to build new or stronger resource strengths and competitive capabilities.

The basic premise of unrelated diversification is that any business that has good profit prospects and can be acquired on good financial terms is a good business to diversify into. Unrelated diversification strategies surrender the competitive advantage potential of strategic fit in return for such advantages as (1) spreading business risk over a variety of industries and (2) providing opportunities for financial gain (if candidate acquisitions have undervalued assets, are bargain-priced and have good upside potential given the right management, or need the backing of a financially strong parent to capitalize on attractive opportunities). In theory, unrelated diversification also offers greater earnings stability over the business cycle (a third advantage), but this advantage is very hard to realize in actual practice. The greater the number of businesses a conglomerate is in and the more diverse these businesses are, the harder it is for corporate executives to select capable managers to run each business, know when the major strategic proposals of business units are sound, or decide on a wise course of recovery when a business unit stumbles. Unless corporate managers are exceptionally shrewd and talented, unrelated diversification is a dubious and unreliable approach to building shareholder value when compared to related diversification.

Analyzing how good a company's diversification strategy is a six-step process:

Step 1: *Evaluate the long-term attractiveness of the industries into which the firm has diversified.* Industry attractiveness needs to be evaluated from three angles: the attractiveness of each industry on its own, the attractiveness of each industry relative to the others, and the attractiveness of all the industries as a group. Quantitative measures of industry attractiveness tell a valuable story about just how and why some of the industries a company has diversified into are more attractive than others. The two hardest parts of calculating industry attractiveness scores are deciding on appropriate weights for the industry attractiveness measures and knowing enough about each industry to assign accurate and objective ratings.

Step 2: *Evaluate the relative competitive strength of each of the company's business units.* Again, quantitative ratings of competitive strength are preferable to subjective judgments. The purpose of rating the competitive strength of each business is to gain clear understanding of which businesses are strong contenders in their industries, which are weak contenders, and the underlying reasons for their strength or weakness. The conclusions about industry attractiveness can be joined with the conclusions about competitive strength by drawing an industry attractiveness–competitive strength matrix displaying the positions of each business on a nine-cell grid. The attractiveness–strength matrix helps identify the prospects of each business and what priority each business should be given in allocating corporate resources and investment capital.

Step 3: *Check for cross-business strategic fits.* A business is more attractive strategically when it has value chain relationships with sister business units that present opportunities to transfer skills or technology, reduce overall costs, share facilities, or share a common brand name—any of which can represent a significant avenue for producing competitive advantage beyond what any one business can achieve on its own. The more businesses with competitively valuable strategic fits, the greater a diversified company's potential for achieving economies of scope, enhancing the competitive capabilities of particular business units, and/or strengthening the competitiveness of its product and business lineup, thereby realizing a combined performance greater than the units could achieve operating independently.

Step 4: *Check whether the firm's resource strengths fit the resource requirements of its present business lineup.* Resource fit exists when (1) businesses add to a company's resource strengths, either financially or strategically; (2) a company has the resources to adequately support the resource requirements of its businesses as a group without spreading itself too thin; and (3) there are close matches between a company's resources and industry key success factors. One important test of resource fit concerns whether the company's business lineup is well matched to its financial resources. Assessing the cash requirements of different businesses in a diversified company's portfolio and determining which are cash hogs and which are cash cows highlights opportunities for shifting corporate financial resources between business subsidiaries to optimize the performance of the whole corporate portfolio, explains why priorities for corporate resource allocation can differ from business to business, and provides good rationalizations for both invest-and-expand strategies and divestiture.

Step 5: *Rank the performance prospects of the businesses from best to worst and determine what the corporate parent's priority should be in allocating resources to its various businesses.* The most important considerations in judging business-unit performance are sales growth, profit growth, contribution to company earnings, and the return on capital invested in the business. Sometimes, cash flow generation is a big consideration. Normally, strong business units in attractive industries have significantly better performance prospects than weak businesses or businesses in unattractive industries. Information on each business's past performance can be gleaned from a company's financial records. While past performance is not necessarily a good predictor of future performance, it does signal which businesses have been strong performers and which have been weak performers. The industry attractiveness–competitive strength evaluations provide a basis for judging future prospects. Normally, strong business units in attractive industries have significantly better prospects than weak businesses in unattractive industries. And, normally, the revenue and earnings outlook for businesses in fast-growing industries is better than for businesses in slow-growing industries. The rankings of future performance generally determine what a business unit's priority for resource allocation by the corporate parent should be. Business subsidiaries with the brightest profit and growth prospects and solid strategic and resource fits generally should head the list for corporate resource support.

Step 6: *Crafting new strategic moves to improve overall corporate performance.* This step entails using the results of the preceding analysis as the basis for devising actions to strengthen existing businesses, make new acquisitions, divest weak-performing and unattractive businesses, restructure the company's business lineup, expand the scope of the company's geographic reach multinationally or globally, and otherwise steer corporate resources into the areas of greatest opportunity.

Once a company has diversified, corporate management's task is to manage the collection of businesses for maximum long-term performance. There are four different strategic paths for improving a diversified company's performance: (1) broadening the firm's business base by diversifying into additional businesses, (2) retrenching to a narrower diversification base by divesting some of its present businesses, (3) corporate restructuring, and (4) multinational diversification.

Broadening the diversification base is attractive when growth is sluggish and the company needs the revenue and profit boost of a newly acquired business, when it has resources and capabilities that are eminently transferable to related or complementary businesses, or when the opportunity to acquire an attractive company unexpectedly lands on its doorstep. Furthermore, there are occasions when a diversified company makes new acquisitions to complement and strengthen the market position and competitive capabilities of one or more of its present businesses.

Retrenching to a narrower diversification base is usually undertaken when corporate management concludes that the firm's diversification efforts have ranged too far afield and that the best avenue for improving long-term performance is to concentrate on building strong positions in a smaller number of businesses. Retrenchment is usually accomplished by divesting businesses that are no longer deemed suitable for the company to be in. A business can become a prime candidate for divestiture because market conditions in a once attractive industry have badly deteriorated, because it lacks adequate strategic or resource fit, because it is a cash hog with questionable long-term potential, or because it is weakly positioned in its industry with little prospect for earning a decent return on investment. Sometimes a company acquires businesses that just do not work out as expected even though management has tried all it can think of to make them profitable. Divesting such businesses frees resources that can be used to reduce debt, to support expansion of the remaining businesses, or to make acquisitions that materially strengthen the company's competitive position in one or more of the remaining core businesses. Most of the time, companies divest businesses by selling them to another company, but sometimes they spin them off as financially and managerially independent enterprises in which the parent company may or may not retain an ownership interest.

Corporate restructuring strategies involve divesting some businesses and acquiring new businesses so as to put a whole new face on the company's business makeup. Performing radical surgery on the group of businesses a company is in becomes an appealing strategy alternative when a diversified company's financial performance is being squeezed or eroded by (1) too many businesses in slow-growth or declining or low-margin or otherwise unattractive industries, (2) too many competitively weak businesses, (3) ongoing declines in the market shares of one or more major business units that are falling prey to more market-savvy competitors, (4) an excessive debt burden with interest costs that eat deeply into profitability, or (5) ill-chosen acquisitions that haven't lived up to expectations.

Multinational diversification strategies feature a diversity of businesses and a diversity of national markets. Despite the complexity of having to devise and manage so many strategies (at least one for each industry, with as many variations for country markets as may be needed), multinational diversification strategies have considerable appeal. They offer two avenues for long-term growth in revenues and profitability—one is to grow by entering additional businesses and the other is to grow by extending the operations of existing businesses into additional country markets. Moreover, multinational diversification offers six ways to build competitive advantage: (1) full capture of economies of scale and experience or learning-curve effects, (2) opportunities to capitalize on cross-business economies of scope, (3) opportunity to transfer competitively valuable resources from one business to another and from one country to another, (4) ability to leverage use of a well-known and competitively powerful brand name, (5) ability to capitalize on opportunities for cross-business and cross-country collaboration and strategic coordination, and (6) opportunities to use cross-business or cross-country subsidization to wrest sales and market share from rivals. A strategy of multinational diversification contains more competitive advantage potential than any other diversification strategy.

 ## Exercises

1. What do you see as the strategic fits that exist among the value chains of the diversified companies listed in Company Spotlight 6.1?

2. Consider the business lineup of the Walt Disney Company shown in Company Spotlight 6.2. What problems do you think the top executives at Disney would encounter in trying to stay on top of all the businesses the company is in? How might they decide the merits of adding new businesses or divesting poorly performing businesses? What types of advice might they give to the general managers of each of Disney's business units?

CHAPTER 7

Building a Capable Organization

The best game plan in the world never blocked or tackled anybody.
—Vince Lombardi

Strategies most often fail because they aren't executed well.
—Larry Bossidy, CEO Honeywell International, and
    Ram Charan, author and consultant

Organizing is what you do before you do something, so that when you do it, it is not all mixed up.
—A. A. Milne

Once managers have decided on a strategy, the emphasis turns to converting it into actions and good results. Putting the strategy into place and getting the organization to execute it well call for different sets of managerial skills. Whereas crafting strategy is largely a market-driven activity, implementing and executing strategy is primarily an operations-driven activity revolving around the management of people and business processes. Whereas successful strategy making depends on business vision, solid industry and competitive analysis, and shrewd market positioning, successful strategy execution depends on doing a good job of working with and through others, building and strengthening competitive capabilities, motivating and rewarding people in a strategy-supportive manner, and instilling a discipline of getting things done. Executing strategy is an action-oriented, make-things-happen task that tests a manager's ability to direct organizational change, achieve continuous improvement in operations and business processes, create and nurture a strategy-supportive culture, and consistently meet or beat performance targets.

Experienced managers are emphatic in declaring that it is a whole lot easier to develop a sound strategic plan than it is to execute the plan and achieve the desired outcomes. According to one executive, "It's been rather easy for us to decide where we wanted to go. The hard part is to get the organization to act on the new priorities."[1] What makes executing strategy a tougher, more time-consuming management challenge than crafting strategy is the wide array of managerial activities that have to be attended to, the many ways managers can proceed, the demanding people-management skills required, the perseverance necessary to get a variety of initiatives launched and moving, the number of bedeviling issues that must be worked out, the resistance to change that must be overcome, and the difficulties of integrating the efforts of many different work groups into a smoothly functioning whole.

Just because senior managers announce a new strategy doesn't mean that organizational members will agree with it or enthusiastically move forward in implementing it. Senior executives cannot simply tell their immediate subordinates to undertake new strategic initiatives and expect the needed actions and changes to occur in rapid-fire fashion and deliver the intended results. Some managers and employees may be skeptical about the merits of the strategy, seeing it as contrary to the organization's best interests, unlikely to succeed, or threatening to their departments or careers. Moreover, different employees may interpret the new strategy differently or have different ideas about what internal changes are needed to execute it. Long-standing attitudes, vested interests, inertia, and ingrained organizational practices don't melt away when managers decide on a new strategy and begin efforts to implement it—especially when only comparatively few people have been involved in crafting the strategy and when the rationale for strategic change has to be sold to enough organizational members to root out the status quo. It takes adept managerial leadership to convincingly communicate the new strategy and the reasons for it, overcome pockets of doubt and disagreement, secure the commitment and enthusiasm of concerned parties, identify and build consensus on all the hows of implementation and execution, and move forward to get all the pieces into place. Depending on how much consensus building, motivating, and organizational change is involved, the process of implementing strategy changes can take several months to several years.

Like crafting strategy, executing strategy is a job for the whole management team, not just a few senior managers. While an

> **Core Concept**
>
> All managers have strategy-executing responsibility in their areas of authority, and all employees are participants in the strategy execution process.

organization's chief executive officer and the heads of major units (business divisions, functional departments, and key operating units) are ultimately responsible for seeing that strategy is executed successfully, the process typically affects every part of the firm, from the biggest operating unit to the smallest frontline work group. Top-level managers have to rely on the active support and cooperation of middle and lower managers to push strategy changes into functional areas and operating units and to see that the organization actually operates in accordance with the strategy on a daily basis. Middle and lower-level managers not only are responsible for initiating and supervising the execution process in their areas of authority but also are instrumental in getting subordinates to continuously improve on how strategy-critical value chain activities are being performed and in producing the operating results that allow company performance targets to be met—their role on the company's strategy execution team is by no means minimal. *Strategy execution thus requires every manager to think through the answer to "What does my area have to do to implement its part of the strategic plan, and what should I do to get these things accomplished?"*

A Framework for Executing Strategy

Implementing and executing strategy both entail figuring out all the hows—the specific techniques, actions, and behaviors that are needed for a smooth strategy-supportive operation—and then following through to get things done and deliver results. The idea is to make things happen and make them happen right. The first step in implementing strategic changes is for management to communicate the case for organizational change so clearly and persuasively to organizational members that a determined commitment takes hold throughout the ranks to find ways to put the strategy into place, make it work, and meet performance targets. The ideal condition is for managers to arouse enough enthusiasm for the strategy to turn the implementation process into a companywide crusade. *Management's handling of the strategy implementation process can be considered successful if and when the company achieves the targeted strategic and financial performance and shows good progress in making its strategic vision a reality.*

The specific hows of executing a strategy—the exact items that need to be placed on management's action agenda—always have to be customized to fit the particulars of a company's situation. Making minor changes in an existing strategy differs from implementing radical strategy changes. The hot buttons for successfully executing a low-cost provider strategy are different from those in executing a high-end differentiation strategy. Implementing and executing a new strategy for a struggling company in the midst of a financial crisis is a different job than improving strategy execution in a company where the execution is already pretty good. Moreover, some managers are more adept than others at using this or that approach to achieving the desired kinds of organizational changes. Hence, there's no definitive 10-step checklist or managerial recipe for successful strategy execution that cuts across all company situations and all types of strategies or that works for all types of managers. The hows of implementing and executing strategy require a customized approach—one based on individual company situations and circumstances, the strategy implementer's best judgment, and the implementer's ability to use particular organizational change techniques effectively.

Figure 7.1   The Eight Components of the Strategy Execution Process

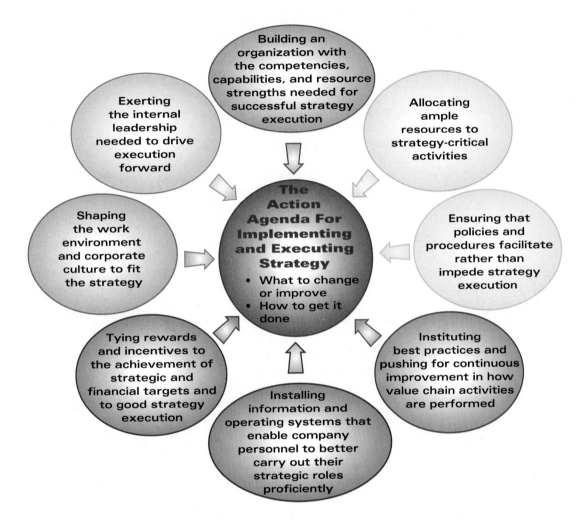

The Principal Managerial Components of the Strategy Execution Process

While a company's strategy-executing approaches always have to be tailored to the company's situation, certain managerial bases that have to be covered no matter what the circumstances. Eight managerial tasks crop up repeatedly in company efforts to execute strategy (see Figure 7.1).

1. Building an organization with the competencies, capabilities, and resource strengths to execute strategy successfully.
2. Allocating ample resources to strategy-critical activities.
3. Ensuring that policies and procedures facilitate rather than impede strategy execution.
4. Instituting best practices and pushing for continuous improvement in how value chain activities are performed.

5. Installing information and operating systems that enable company personnel to carry out their strategic roles proficiently.

6. Typing rewards directly to the achievement of strategic and financial targets and to good strategy execution.

7. Shaping the work environment and corporate culture to fit the strategy.

8. Exerting the internal leadership needed to drive implementation forward and keep improving on how the strategy is being executed.

How well managers perform these eight tasks has a decisive impact on whether the outcome is a spectacular success, a colossal failure, or something in between. Moreover, the nature of just what needs to be accomplished on these eight fronts, as determined by the particulars of a company's situation, drives the action priorities on management's agenda and shapes its implementation/execution process.

In devising an action agenda for implementing and executing strategy, the place for managers to start is with *a probing assessment of what the organization must do differently and better to carry out the strategy successfully.* They should then consider *precisely how to make the necessary internal changes* as rapidly as possible. Successful strategy implementers have a knack for diagnosing what their organizations need to do to execute the chosen strategy well and figuring out how to get things done—they are masters in promoting results-oriented behaviors on the part of company personnel and following through on making the right things happen.[2]

> When strategies fail, it is often because of poor execution—things that were supposed to get done slip through the cracks.

In big organizations with geographically scattered operating units, the action agenda of senior executives mostly involves communicating the case for change to others, building consensus for how to proceed, installing strong allies in positions where they can push implementation along in key organizational units, urging and empowering subordinates to keep the process moving, establishing measures of progress and deadlines, recognizing and rewarding those who achieve implementation milestones, directing resources to the right places, and personally leading the strategic change process. Thus, the bigger the organization, the more successful strategy execution depends on the cooperation and implementing skills of operating managers who can push needed changes at the lowest organizational levels and deliver results. In small organizations, top managers can deal directly with frontline managers and employees, personally orchestrating the action steps and implementation sequence, observing firsthand how implementation is progressing, and deciding how hard and how fast to push the process along. Regardless of the organization's size and whether implementation involves sweeping or minor changes, the most important leadership traits are a strong, confident sense of what to do and how to do it. Having a strong grip on these two things comes from understanding the circumstances of the organization and the requirements for effective strategy execution. Then it remains for those managers and company personnel in strategy-critical areas to step up to the plate and produce the desired results.

Managing the Strategy Execution Process: What's Covered in Chapters 7, 8, and 9   In the remainder of this chapter and the next two chapters, we will discuss what is involved in managing the process of implementing and executing strategy. The discussion of executing strategy in Chapters 7, 8, and 9 is framed around the eight managerial tasks shown in Figure 7.1 and the most common issues associated with each. This chapter explores building a capable organization. Chapter 8 looks at budgets, allocating establishing strategy-facilitating policies and procedures, instituting best practices, installing operating systems, and tying rewards to achievement. Chapter 9 deals with creating a strategy-supportive corporate culture and exercising appropriate strategic leadership.

Building a Capable Organization

Proficient strategy execution depends heavily on competent personnel, better-than-adequate competitive capabilities, and effective internal organization. Building a capable organization is thus always a top priority in strategy execution. As shown in Figure 7.2, three types of organization-building actions are paramount:

1. *Staffing the organization*—putting together a strong management team, and recruiting and retaining employees with the needed experience, technical skills, and intellectual capital.

2. *Building core competencies and competitive capabilities* that will enable good strategy execution and updating them as strategy and external conditions change.

3. *Structuring the organization and work effort*—organizing value chain activities and business processes and deciding how much decision-making authority to push down to lower-level managers and frontline employees.

Figure 7.2   The Three Components of Building a Capable Organization

Staffing the Organization
- Putting together a strong management team
- Recruiting and retaining talented employees

Building Core Competencies and Competitive Capabilities
- Developing a set of competencies and capabilities suited to the current strategy
- Updating and revising this set as external conditions and strategy change
- Training and retraining employees as needed to maintain skills-based competencies

Structuring the Organization and Work Effort
- Designing an organization structure that facilitates good strategy execution
- Deciding how much decision-making authority to push down to lower-level managers and front line employees

A Company with the Organizational Capability Needed for Proficient Strategy Execution

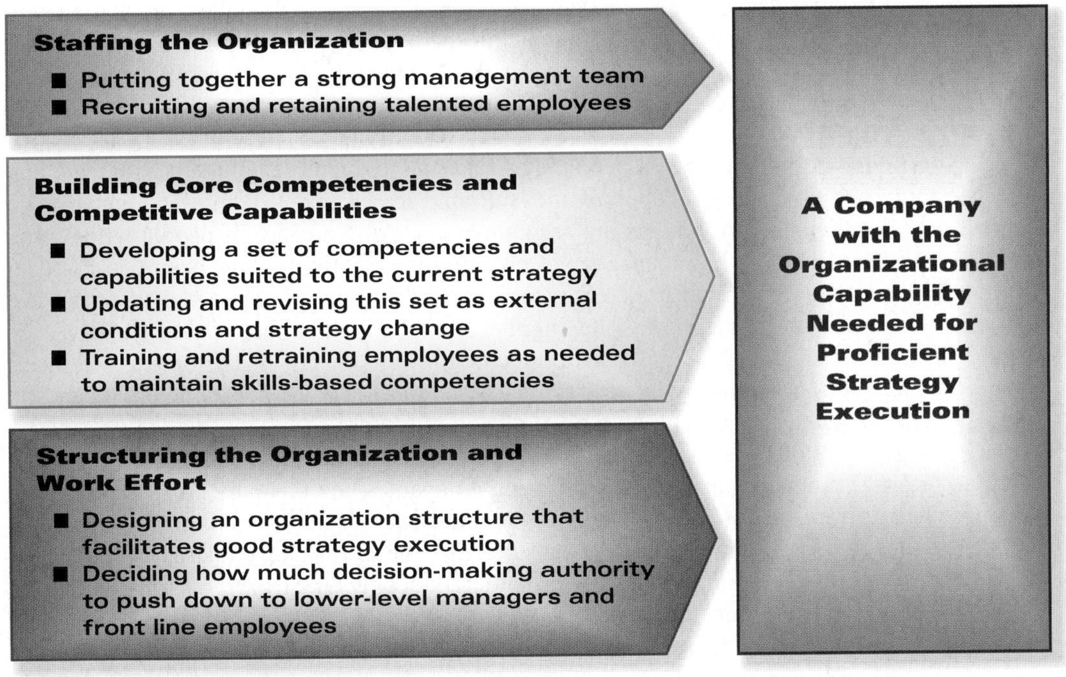

Staffing the Organization

No company can hope to perform the activities required for successful strategy execution without attracting capable managers and without employees that give it a suitable knowledge base and portfolio of intellectual capital.

Putting Together a Strong Management Team

Assembling a capable management team is a cornerstone of the organization-building task.[3] Different strategies and company circumstances often call for different mixes of backgrounds, experiences, know-how, values, beliefs, management styles, and personalities. The personal chemistry among the members of the management team needs to be right, and the talent base needs to be appropriate for the chosen strategy. But the most important condition is to fill key managerial slots with people who can be counted on to get things done; otherwise the implementation-execution process can't proceed at full speed. Sometimes the existing management team is suitable; at other times it may need to be strengthened or expanded by promoting qualified people from within or by bringing in outsiders whose experience, skills, and leadership styles better suit the situation. In turnaround and rapid-growth situations, and in instances when a company doesn't have insiders with the requisite experience or know-how, filling key management slots from the outside is a fairly standard organization-building approach. Company Spotlight 7.1 describes General Electric's widely acclaimed approach to developing a high-caliber management team.

> **Core Concept**
>
> Putting together a talented management team with the right mix of skills and experiences is one of the first strategy-implementing steps.

Recruiting and Retaining Capable Employees

Assembling a capable management team is not enough. Staffing the organization with the right kinds of people must go much deeper than managerial jobs in order to build an organization capable of effective strategy execution. Companies like Electronic Data Systems (EDS), McKinsey & Company, Cisco Systems, Southwest Airlines, Procter & Gamble, PepsiCo, Nike, Microsoft, and Intel make a concerted effort to recruit the best and brightest people they can find and then retain them with excellent compensation packages, opportunities for rapid advancement and professional growth, and challenging and interesting assignments. Having a cadre of people with strong skill sets and budding management potential is essential to their business. EDS requires college graduates to have at least a 3.5 grade point average (on a 4.0 scale) just to qualify for an interview, believing that having a high-caliber pool of employees is crucial to operating the information technology systems of its customers. Microsoft makes a point of hiring the very brightest and most talented programmers it can find and motivating them with both good monetary incentives and the challenge of working on cutting-edge software design projects. McKinsey & Company, one of the world's premier management consulting companies, recruits only cream-of-the-crop MBAs at the nation's top 10 business schools; such talent is essential to McKinsey's strategy of performing high-level consulting for the world's top corporations. The leading global accounting firms screen candidates not only on the basis of their accounting expertise but also on whether they possess the people skills needed to relate well with clients and colleagues. Southwest Airlines goes to considerable lengths to hire people who can have fun and be fun on the job; it uses special interviewing and screening

How General Electric Develops a Talented and Deep Management Team

General Electric is widely considered to be one of the best-managed companies in the world, partly because of its concerted effort to develop outstanding managers. For starters, GE strives to hire talented people with high potential for executive leadership; it then goes to great lengths to expand the leadership, business, and decision-making capabilities of all its managers. Four key elements undergird GE's efforts to build a talent-rich stable of managers:

1. GE makes a practice of transferring managers across divisional, business, or functional lines for sustained periods of time. Such transfers allow managers to develop relationships with colleagues in other parts of the company, help break down insular thinking in business "silos," and promote the sharing of cross-business ideas and best practices. There is an enormous emphasis at GE on transferring ideas and best practices from business to business and making GE a "boundaryless" company.

2. In selecting executives for key positions, GE is strongly disposed to candidates who exhibit what are called the four E's—enormous personal *energy,* the ability to motivate and *energize* others, *edge* (a GE code word for instinctive competitiveness and the ability to make tough decisions in a timely fashion, saying yes or no, and not maybe), and *execution* (the ability to carry things through to fruition).

3. All managers are expected to be proficient at what GE calls *workout*—a process in which managers and employees come together to confront issues as soon as they come up, pinpoint the root cause of the issues, and bring about quick resolutions so the business can move forward. Workout is GE's way of training its managers to diagnose what to do and how to do it.

4. Each year GE sends about 10,000 newly hired and longtime managers to its Leadership Development Center (generally regarded as one of the best corporate training centers in the world), for a three-week course on the company's six sigma quality initiative. More than 5,000 "Master Black Belt" and "Black Belt" six sigma experts have graduated from the program to drive forward thousands of quality initiatives throughout GE. Six sigma training is an ironclad requirement for promotion to any professional and managerial position and any stock option award. GE's Leadership Development Center also offers advanced courses for senior managers that may focus on a single management topic for a month. All classes involve managers from different GE businesses and different parts of the world. Some of the most valuable learning comes in between formal class sessions when GE managers from different businesses trade ideas about how to improve processes and better serve the customer. This knowledge sharing not only spreads best practices throughout the organization but also improves each GE manager's knowledge.

Each of GE's 85,000 managers and professionals is graded in an annual process that divides them into five tiers: the top 10 percent, the next 15 percent, the middle 50 percent, the next 15 percent, and the bottom 10 percent. Everyone in the top tier gets stock options, nobody in the fourth tier gets options, and most of those in the fifth tier become candidates for being weeded out. Business heads are pressured to wean out "C" players. GE's CEO personally reviews the performance of the top 3,000 managers. Senior executive compensation is heavily weighted toward six sigma commitment and producing successful business results.

According to Jack Welch, GE's CEO from 1980 to 2001, "The reality is, we simply cannot afford to field anything but teams of 'A' players."

Sources: 1998 annual report; www.ge.com; John A. Byrne, "How Jack Welch Runs GE," *Business Week,* June 8, 1998, p. 90; Miriam Leuchter, "Management Farm Teams," *Journal of Business Strategy,* May 1998, pp. 29–32; and "The House That Jack Built, *The Economist,* September 18, 1999.

methods to gauge whether applicants for customer-contact jobs have outgoing personality traits that match its strategy of creating a high-spirited, fun-loving, in-flight atmosphere for passengers; it is so selective that only about 3 percent of the people who apply are offered jobs.

In high-tech companies, the challenge is to staff work groups with gifted, imaginative, and energetic people who can bring life to new ideas quickly and inject into the organization what one Dell Computer executive calls "hum."[3] The saying "People are our most important asset" may seem hollow, but it fits high-technology companies dead-on. Besides checking closely for functional and technical skills, Dell Computer tests applicants for their tolerance of ambiguity and change, their capacity to work in teams, and their ability to learn on the fly. Companies like Amazon.com and Cisco Systems have broken new ground in recruiting, hiring, cultivating, developing, and retaining talented employees—most all of whom are in their 20s and 30s. Cisco goes after the top 10 percent, raiding other companies and endeavoring to retain key people at the companies it acquires so as to maintain a cadre of star engineers, programmers, managers, salespeople, and support personnel in executing its strategy to remain the world's leading provider of Internet infrastructure products and technology.

> **Core Concept**
>
> In many industries adding to a company's talent base and building intellectual capital is more important to good strategy execution than additional investments in capital projects.

Where intellectual capital is crucial in building a strategy-capable organization, companies have instituted a number of practices in staffing their organizations and developing a strong knowledge base:

1. Spending considerable effort in screening and evaluating job applicants, selecting only those with suitable skill sets, energy, initiative, judgment, and aptitudes for learning and adaptability to the company's work environment and culture.

2. Putting employees through training programs that continue throughout their careers.

3. Providing promising employees with challenging, interesting, and skill-stretching assignments.

4. Rotating people through jobs that not only have great content but also span functional and geographic boundaries. Providing people with opportunities to gain experience in a variety of international settings is increasingly considered an essential part of career development in multinational or global companies.

5. Encouraging employees to be creative and innovative, to challenge existing ways of doing things and offer better ways, and to submit ideas for new products or businesses. Progressive companies work hard at creating an environment in which ideas and suggestions bubble up from below rather than proceed from the top down. Employees are made to feel that their opinions count.

6. Fostering a stimulating and engaging work environment such that employees will consider the company a great place to work.

7. Exerting efforts to retain high-potential, high-performing employees with salary increases, performance bonuses, stock options and equity ownership, and other long-term incentives.

8. Coaching average performers to improve their skills and capabilities, while weeding out underperformers and benchwarmers.

Building Core Competencies and Competitive Capabilities

High among the organization-building priorities in the strategy implementing/executing process is the need to build and strengthen competitively valuable core competencies and organizational capabilities. Whereas managers identify the desired competencies and capabilities in the course of crafting strategy, good strategy execution requires putting the desired competencies and capabilities in place, upgrading them as needed, and then modifying them as market conditions evolve. Sometimes a company already has the needed competencies and capabilities, in which case managers can concentrate on nurturing them to promote better strategy execution. More usually, however, company managers have to add new competencies and capabilities to implement strategic initiatives and promote proficient strategy execution.

A number of prominent companies have succeeded in establishing core competencies and capabilities that have been instrumental in making them winners in the marketplace. Honda's core competence is its depth of expertise in gasoline engine technology and small engine design. Intel's is in the design of complex chips for personal computers. Procter & Gamble's core competencies reside in its superb marketing/distribution skills and its R&D capabilities in five core technologies—fats, oils, skin chemistry, surfactants, and emulsifiers. Sony's core competencies are its expertise in electronic technology and its ability to translate that expertise into innovative products (cutting-edge video game hardware, miniaturized radios and video cameras, TVs and DVDs with unique features, attractively designed PCs). Dell Computer has the capabilities to deliver state-of-the-art products to its customers within days of next-generation components coming available—and to do so at attractively low costs (it has leveraged its collection of competencies and capabilities into being the global low-cost leader in PCs).

The Three-Stage Process of Developing and Strengthening Competencies and Capabilities

Building core competencies and competitive capabilities is a time-consuming, managerially challenging exercise. While some organization-building assist can be gotten from discovering how best-in-industry or best-in-world companies perform a particular activity, trying to replicate and then improve on the competencies and capabilities of others is, however, much easier said than done—for the same reasons that one is unlikely to ever become a good golfer just by studying what Tiger Woods does. Putting a new capability in place is more complicated than just forming a new team or department and charging it with becoming highly competent in performing the desired activity, using whatever it can learn from other companies having similar competencies or capabilities. Rather, it takes a series of deliberate and well orchestrated organizational steps to achieve mounting proficiency in performing an activity. The capability-building process has three stages:

Stage 1—First, the organization must develop the *ability* to do something, however imperfectly or inefficiently. This entails selecting people with the requisite skills and experience, upgrading or expanding individual abilities as needed, and then molding the efforts and work products of individuals into a collaborative effort to create organizational ability.

Stage 2—As experience grows and company personnel learn how to perform the activity *consistently well and at an acceptable cost*, the ability evolves into a tried-and-true *competence* or *capability*.

Stage 3—Should the organization continue to polish and refine its know-how and otherwise sharpen its performance such that it becomes *better than rivals* at performing the activity, the core competence rises to the rank of a *distinctive competence* (or the capability becomes a competitively superior capability), thus providing a path to competitive advantage.

Many companies manage to get through stages 1 and 2 in performing a strategy-critical activity, but comparatively few achieve sufficient proficiency in performing strategy-critical activities to qualify for the third stage.

Managing the Process   Four traits concerning core competencies and competitive capabilities are important in successfully managing the organization-building process:[4]

1. *Core competencies and competitive capabilities are bundles of skills and know-how that most often grow out of the combined efforts of cross-functional work groups and departments performing complementary activities at different locations in the firm's value chain.* Rarely does a core competence or capability consist of narrow skills attached to the work efforts of a single department. For instance, a core competence in speeding new products to market involves the collaborative efforts of personnel in R&D, engineering and design, purchasing, production, marketing, and distribution. Similarly, the capability to provide superior customer service is a team effort among people in customer call centers (where orders are taken and inquiries are answered), shipping and delivery, billing and accounts receivable, and after-sale support. Complex activities (like designing and manufacturing a sports-utility vehicle or creating the capability for secure credit card transactions over the Internet) usually involve a number of component skills, technological disciplines, competencies, and capabilities—some performed inhouse and some provided by suppliers/allies. An important part of the organization-building function is to think about which activities of which groups need to be linked and made mutually reinforcing and then to forge the necessary collaboration both internally and with outside resource providers.

2. *Normally, a core competence or capability emerges incrementally* out of company efforts either to bolster skills that contributed to earlier successes or to respond to customer problems, new technological and market opportunities, and the competitive maneuverings of rivals. Migrating from the one-time ability to do something up the ladder to a core competence or competitively valuable capability is usually an organization-building process that takes months and often years to accomplish—it is definitely not an overnight event.

3. The key to leveraging a core competence into a distinctive competence (or a capability into a competitively superior capability) is *concentrating more effort and more talent than rivals on deepening and strengthening the competence or capability, so as to achieve the dominance needed for competitive advantage.* This does not necessarily mean spending more money on such activities than competitors, but it does mean consciously focusing more talent on them and striving for best-in-industry, if not best-in-world, status. To achieve dominance on lean financial resources, companies like Cray in large computers and Honda in gasoline engines have leveraged the expertise of their talent pool by frequently re-forming high-intensity teams and reusing key people on special projects. The experiences of these and other companies indicate that the usual keys to successfully building core competencies and valuable capabilities are superior employee selection, thorough training and retraining, powerful cultural influences, effective cross-functional collaboration, empowerment, motivating incentives, short deadlines, and good databases—not big operating budgets.

4. Evolving changes in customers' needs and competitive conditions often require *tweaking and adjusting a company's portfolio of competencies and intellectual capital to keep its capabilities freshly honed and on the cutting edge.* This is particularly important in high-tech industries and fast-paced markets where important developments occur weekly. As a consequence, wise company managers work at anticipating changes in customer-market requirements and staying ahead of the curve in proactively building a package of competencies and capabilities that can win out over rivals.

Managerial actions to develop core competencies and competitive capabilities generally take one of two forms: either strengthening the company's base of skills, knowledge, and intellect, or coordinating and networking the efforts of the various work groups and departments. Actions of the first sort can be undertaken at all managerial levels, but actions of the second sort are best orchestrated by senior managers who not only appreciate the strategy-executing significance of strong competencies/capabilities but also have the clout to enforce the necessary networking and cooperation among individuals, groups, departments, and external allies.

One organization-building question is whether to develop the desired competencies and capabilities internally or to outsource them by partnering with key suppliers or forming strategic alliances. The answer depends on what can be safely delegated to outside suppliers or allies versus what internal capabilities are key to the company's long-term success. Either way, though, calls for action. Outsourcing means launching initiatives to identify the most attractive providers and to establish collaborative relationships. Developing the capabilities in-house means marshaling personnel with relevant skills and experience, collaboratively networking the individual skills and related cross-functional activities to form organizational capability, and building the desired levels of proficiency through repetition (practice makes perfect).[5]

Sometimes the tediousness of internal organization building can be shortcut by buying a company that has the requisite capability and integrating its competencies into the firm's value chain. Indeed, a pressing need to acquire certain capabilities quickly is one reason to acquire another company—an acquisition aimed at building greater capability can be every bit as competitively valuable as an acquisition aimed at adding new products or services to the company's business lineup. Capabilities-motivated acquisitions are essential (1) when a market opportunity can slip by faster than a needed capability can be created internally, and (2) when industry conditions, technology, or competitors are moving at such a rapid clip that time is of the essence. But usually there's no good substitute for ongoing internal efforts to build and strengthen the company's competencies and capabilities in performing strategy-critical value chain activities.

Updating and Reshaping Competencies and Capabilities as External Conditions and Company Strategy Change   Even after core competencies and competitive capabilities are in place and functioning, company managers can't relax. Competencies and capabilities that grow stale can impair competitiveness unless they are refreshed, modified, or even phased out and replaced in response to ongoing market changes and shifts in company strategy. Indeed, the buildup of knowledge and experience over time, coupled with the imperatives of keeping capabilities in step with ongoing strategy and market changes, makes it appropriate to view a company as *a bundle of evolving competencies and capabilities.* Management's organization-building challenge is one of deciding when and how to recalibrate existing competencies and capabilities, and when and how to develop new ones. Although the task is formidable, ideally it produces a dynamic organization with "hum" and momentum as well as a distinctive competence.

From Competencies and Capabilities to Competitive Advantage

While strong core competencies and competitive capabilities are a major assist in executing strategy, they are an equally important avenue for securing a competitive edge over rivals in situations where it is relatively easy for rivals to copy smart strategies. Any time rivals can readily duplicate successful strategy features, making it difficult or impossible to outstrategize rivals and beat them in the marketplace with a superior strategy, the chief way to achieve lasting competitive advantage is to outexecute them (beat them by performing certain value chain activities in superior fashion). Building core competencies, resource strengths, and organizational capabilities that rivals can't match is thus one of the best and most reliable ways to outexecute them. Moreover, cutting-edge core competencies and organizational capabilities are not easily duplicated by rival firms; thus, any competitive edge they produce is likely to be sustainable, paving the way for above-average organizational performance.

> **Core Concept**
>
> Building competencies and capabilities has a huge payoff—improved strategy execution and a potential for competitive advantage.

The Strategic Role of Employee Training

Training and retraining are important when a company shifts to a strategy requiring different skills, competitive capabilities, managerial approaches, and operating methods. Training is also strategically important in organizational efforts to build skills-based competencies. And it is a key activity in businesses where technical know-how is changing so rapidly that a company loses its ability to compete unless its skilled people have cutting-edge knowledge and expertise. Successful strategy implementers see to it that the training function is both adequately funded and effective. If the chosen strategy calls for new skills, deeper technological capability, or building and using new capabilities, training should be placed near the top of the action agenda.

The strategic importance of training has not gone unnoticed. Over 600 companies have established internal "universities" to lead the training effort, facilitate continuous organizational learning, and help upgrade company competencies and capabilities. Many companies conduct orientation sessions for new employees, fund an assortment of competence-building training programs, and reimburse employees for tuition and other expenses associated with obtaining additional college education, attending professional development courses, and earning professional certification of one kind or another. A number of companies offer online, just-in-time training courses to employees around the clock. Increasingly, employees at all levels are expected to take an active role in their own professional development, assuming responsibility for keeping their skills and expertise up-to-date and in sync with the company's needs.

Matching Organization Structure to Strategy

There are few hard-and-fast rules for organizing the work effort to support strategy. Every firm's organization chart is partly a product of its particular situation, reflecting prior organizational patterns, varying internal circumstances, executive judgments about reporting relationships, and the politics of who gets which assignments. Moreover, every strategy is grounded in its own set of key success factors and value chain

Figure 7.3   Structuring the Work Effort to Promote Successful Strategy Execution

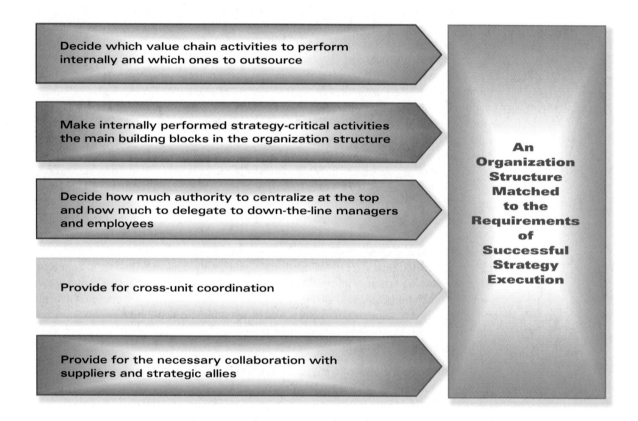

activities. But some considerations are common to all companies. These are summarized in Figure 7.3 and discussed in turn in the following sections.

Deciding Which Value Chain Activities to Perform Internally and Which to Outsource

In any business, some activities in the value chain are always more critical to strategic success and competitive advantage than others. Among the primary value chain activities are certain crucial business processes that have to be performed either exceedingly well or in closely coordinated fashion for the organization to deliver on the capabilities needed for strategic success. For instance, hotel/motel enterprises have to be good at fast check-in/check-out, room maintenance, food service, and creating a pleasant ambience. For a manufacturer of chocolate bars, buying quality cocoa beans at low prices is vital and reducing production costs by a fraction of a cent per bar can mean a seven-figure improvement in the bottom line. In discount stock brokerage, the strategy-critical activities are fast access to information, accurate order execution, efficient record keeping and transactions processing, and good customer service. In specialty chemicals, the critical activities are R&D, product innovation, getting new products onto the market quickly, effective marketing, and expertise in assisting customers. In consumer electronics, where advancing technology drives new product innovation, rapidly getting cutting-edge, next-generation products to market is a critical organizational capability.

As a general rule, strategy-critical activities need to be performed internally so that management can directly control their performance. Less important activities—like routine administrative housekeeping (doing the payroll, administering employee benefit programs, providing corporate security, managing stockholder relations, maintaining fleet vehicles) and some support functions (information technology and data processing, training, public relations, market research, legal and legislative affairs)—may be strong candidates for outsourcing. Two questions help pinpoint an organization's strategy-critical activities: "What functions or business processes have to be performed extra well or in timely fashion to achieve sustainable competitive advantage?" and "In what value chain activities would poor execution seriously impair strategic success?"[6] However, a number of companies have found ways to successfully rely on outside components suppliers, product designers, distribution channels, advertising agencies, and financial services firms to perform strategically significant value chain activities.[7] For years Polaroid Corporation bought its film from Eastman Kodak, its electronics from Texas Instruments, and its cameras from Timex and others, while it concentrated on producing its unique self-developing film packets and designing its next-generation cameras and films. Nike concentrates on design, marketing, and distribution to retailers, while outsourcing virtually all production of its shoes and sporting apparel. Likewise, a number of PC manufacturers outsource assembly, concentrating their energies instead on product design, sales and marketing, and distribution. So while performing strategy-critical activities in-house normally makes good sense, there can be times when outsourcing some of them works to good advantage.

The Merits of Outsourcing Noncritical Value Chain Activities

Managers too often spend inordinate amounts of time, mental energy, and financial resources wrestling with functional support groups and other internal bureaucracies, which diverts their attention from the company's strategy-critical activities. One way to reduce such distractions is to cut the number of internal staff support activities and instead rely on outside vendors with specialized expertise to supply such noncritical support services as website operations, data processing, fringe benefits management, and training. An outsider, by concentrating specialists and technology in its area of expertise, can frequently perform certain services as well or better, and often more cheaply, than a company that performs these services only for itself. Many mining companies outsource geological work, assaying, and drilling. E. & J. Gallo Winery outsources 95 percent of its grape production, letting farmers take on the weather and other grape-growing risks while it concentrates on wine production and sales.[8] Eastman Kodak, Ford, Exxon Mobil, Merrill Lynch, and Chevron have outsourced their data processing activities to computer service firms, believing that outside specialists can perform the needed services at lower costs and equal or better quality. A relatively large number of companies outsource the operation of their websites to Web design and hosting enterprises.

But besides less internal hassle and lower costs there are other strong reasons to consider outsourcing. Approached from a strategic point of view, outsourcing noncrucial support activities can decrease internal bureaucracies, flatten the organization structure, speed decision making, heighten the company's strategic focus, improve its innovative capacity (through interaction with best-in-world suppliers),

Core Concept

Outsourcing has many strategy-executing advantages—lower costs, less internal bureaucracy, speedier decision-making, and heightened strategic focus.

and increase competitive responsiveness.[9] Outsourcing has considerable merit when it allows a company to concentrate its own energies and resources on those value chain activities for which it can create unique value and thus become best in the industry (or, better still, best in the world). It also has merit when the company needs strategic control to build core competencies, achieve competitive advantage, and manage key customer–supplier–distributor relationships.

The Merits of Partnering with Others to Gain Added Competitive Capabilities   There is another, equally important reason to look outside for resources to compete effectively aside from just the cost savings and agility that outsourcing can permit. *Partnerships can add to a company's arsenal of capabilities and contribute to better strategy execution.* By building, continually improving, and then leveraging partnerships, a company enhances its overall organizational capabilities and builds resource strengths—strengths that deliver value to customers and consequently pave the way for competitive success.

Automobile manufacturers work closely with their suppliers to advance the design and functioning of parts and components, to incorporate new technology, to better integrate individual parts and components to form engine cooling systems, transmission systems, electrical systems, and so on—all of which helps shorten the cycle time for new models, improve the quality and performance of those models, and lower overall production costs. Prior to merging with Germany's Daimler-Benz, Chrysler transformed itself from a high-cost producer into a low-cost producer by abandoning internal production of many parts and components and instead outsourcing them from more efficient parts/components suppliers; greater reliance on outsourcing enabled Chrysler to shorten its design-to-market cycle for new models and drive down its production costs. Soft-drink and beer manufacturers all cultivate their relationships with their bottlers and distributors to strengthen access to local markets and build the loyalty, support, and commitment for corporate marketing programs, without which their own sales and growth are weakened. Similarly, fast-food enterprises like McDonald's and Taco Bell find it essential to work hand-in-hand with franchisees on outlet cleanliness, consistency of product quality, in-store ambience, courtesy and friendliness of store personnel, and other aspects of store operations. Unless franchisees continuously deliver sufficient customer satisfaction to attract repeat business, a fast-food chain's sales and competitive standing will suffer quickly. Companies like Ford, Boeing, Aerospatiale, AT&T, BMW, and Dell Computer have learned that their central R&D groups cannot begin to match the innovative capabilities of a well-managed network of supply chain partners having the ability to advance the technology, lead the development of next-generation parts and components, and supply them at a relatively low price.[10]

> **Core Concept**
> Strategic partnerships, alliances, and close collaboration with suppliers, distributors, and makers of complementary products, and even competitors all make good strategic sense whenever the result is to enhance organizational resources and capabilities.

The Dangers of Excessive Outsourcing   Critics contend that *a company can go overboard on outsourcing and so hollow out its knowledge base and capabilities as to leave itself at the mercy of outside suppliers and short of the resource strengths to be master of its own destiny.*[11] The point is well taken. Outsourcing strategy-critical activities must be done judiciously and with safeguards against losing control over the performance of key value chain activities and becoming overly dependent on outsiders. Thus, many companies refuse to source key components from a single supplier, opting to use two or three suppliers as a way of becoming overly dependent on any one supplier and giving any one supplier too much bargaining power. Moreover, they regularly evaluate their suppliers, looking not only at the supplier's overall performance but also at whether they should switch to another supplier or even bring the activity back in-house. To avoid loss of control, companies typically work closely with key suppliers, endeavoring to make sure that suppliers' activities are closely integrated with their own requirements and expectations. Most companies appear alert to the primary danger of excessive outsourcing: being caught without the internal strengths and capabilities needed to protect their well-being in the marketplace.

Making Strategy-Critical Activities the Main Building Blocks of the Organization Structure

The rationale for making strategy-critical activities the main building blocks in structuring a business is compelling: If activities crucial to strategic success are to have the resources, decision-making influence, and organizational impact they need, they have to be centerpieces in the organizational scheme. Plainly, implementing a new or changed strategy is likely to entail new or different key activities, competencies, or capabilities and therefore to require new or different organizational arrangements. If workable organizational adjustments are not forthcoming, the resulting mismatch between strategy and structure can open the door to execution and performance problems.[12] Hence, attempting to carry out a new strategy with an old organizational structure is usually unwise.

Core Concept

Just as a company's strategy evolves to stay in tune with changing external circumstances, so must an organization's structure evolve to fit shifting requirements for proficient strategy execution.

Although the stress here is on designing the organization structure around the needs of effective strategy execution, it is worth noting that structure can and does influence the choice of strategy. A good strategy must be doable. When an organization's present structure is so far out of line with the requirements of a particular strategy that the organization would have to be turned upside down to implement it, the strategy may not be doable and should not be given further consideration. In such cases, structure shapes the choice of strategy. The thing to remember, however, is that *once a strategy is chosen, structure must be modified to fit the strategy if, in fact, an approximate fit does not already exist.* Any influences of structure on strategy should, logically, come before the point of strategy selection rather than after it.

The Primary Building Blocks of the Organization Structure

The primary organizational building blocks within a business are usually *traditional functional departments* (R&D, engineering and design, production and operations, sales and marketing, information technology, finance and accounting, and human resources) and *process-complete departments* (supply chain management, filling customer orders, customer service, quality control, direct sales via the company's website).[13] In enterprises with operations in various countries around the world (or with geographically scattered organizational units within a country), the basic building blocks may also include *geographic organizational units*, each of which has profit/loss responsibility for its assigned geographic area. In vertically integrated firms, the major building blocks are *divisional units performing one or more of the major processing steps along the value chain* (raw materials production, components manufacture, assembly, wholesale distribution, retail store operations); each division in the value chain may operate as a profit center for performance measurement purposes.

The typical building blocks of a diversified company are its *individual businesses*, with each business unit usually operating as an independent profit center and with corporate headquarters performing assorted support functions for all of its business units.

Why Functional Organization Structures Often Impede Strategy Execution A big weakness of traditional functionally organized structures is that pieces of strategically relevant activities and capabilities often end up scattered across many departments, with the result that no one group or manager is accountable. Consider, for example, how a functional structure results in fragmented performance of the following strategy-critical activities:

- *Filling customer orders accurately and promptly*—a process that cuts across sales (which wins the order); finance (which may have to check credit terms or approve special financing); production (which must produce the goods and replenish warehouse inventories as needed); warehousing (which has to verify whether the items are in stock, pick the order from the warehouse, and package it for shipping); and shipping (which has to choose a carrier to deliver the goods and release the goods to the carrier).[14]

- *Fast, ongoing introduction of new products*—a cross-functional process involving personnel in R&D, engineering, purchasing, manufacturing, and sales and marketing.

- *Improving product quality*—a process that often involves the collaboration of personnel in R&D, engineering and design, components purchasing from suppliers, in-house components production, manufacturing, and assembly.

- *Supply chain management*—a collaborative process that cuts across such functional areas as purchasing, engineering and design, components purchasing, inventory management, manufacturing and assembly, and warehousing and shipping.

- *Building the capability to conduct business via the Internet*—a process that involves personnel in information technology, supply chain management, production, sales and marketing, warehousing and shipping, customer service, finance, and accounting.

- *Obtaining feedback from customers and making product modifications to meet their needs*—a process that involves personnel in customer service and after-sale support, R&D, engineering and design, components purchasing, manufacturing and assembly, and marketing research.

Handoffs from one department to another lengthen completion time and frequently drive up administrative costs, since coordinating the fragmented pieces can soak up hours of effort on the parts of many people.[15] This is not a fatal flaw of functional organization—organizing around specific functions has worked to good advantage in support activities like finance and accounting, human resource management, and engineering, and in such primary activities as R&D, manufacturing, and marketing. But fragmentation is an important weakness of functional organization, accounting for why we indicated that a company's competencies and capabilities are usually cross-functional and don't reside in the activities of a single functional department.

Increasingly during the past decade, companies have found that rather than continuing to scatter related pieces of a strategy-critical business process across several functional departments and scrambling to integrate their efforts, it is better to reengineer the

Core Concept

Business process reengineering involves pulling the pieces of a strategy-critical process out of various functional departments and integrating them into a streamlined, cohesive series of work steps performed within a single work unit.

work effort and create *process departments*. This is done by pulling the people who performed the pieces in functional departments into a group that works together to perform the whole process. Pulling the pieces of strategy-critical processes out of the functional silos and creating process departments or cross-functional work groups charged with performing all the steps needed to produce a strategy-critical result has been termed **business process reengineering.**

In the electronics industry, where product life cycles run three to six months due to the speed of advancing technology, companies have formed process departments charged with cutting the time it takes to bring new technologies and products to commercial fruition. Northwest Water, a British utility, used business process reengineering to eliminate 45 work depots that served as home bases to crews who installed and repaired water and sewage lines and equipment.[16] Now crews work directly from their vehicles, receiving assignments and reporting work completion from computer terminals in their trucks. Crew members are no longer employees but contractors to Northwest Water. These reengineering efforts not only eliminated the need for the work depots but also allowed Northwest Water to eliminate a big percentage of the bureaucratic personnel and supervisory organization that managed the crews. At acute care hospitals such as Lee Memorial in Fort Myers, Florida, and St. Vincent's in Melbourne, Australia, medical care has been reengineered so that it is delivered by interdisciplinary teams of health care professionals organized around the needs of the patients and their families rather than around functional departments within the hospital. Both hospitals created treatment-specific focused care wards within the hospital to handle most of a patient's needs, from admission to discharge. Patients are no longer wheeled from department to department for procedures and tests; instead, teams have the equipment and resources within each focused care unit to provide total care for the patient. While the hospitals had some concern about functional inefficiency in the use of some facilities, process organization has resulted in substantially lower operating costs, faster patient recovery, and greater satisfaction on the part of patients and caregivers.

Reengineering strategy-critical business processes to reduce fragmentation across traditional departmental lines and cut bureaucratic overhead has proved to be a legitimate organization design tool, not a passing fad. Process organization is every bit as valid an organizing principle as functional specialization. Strategy execution is improved when the pieces of strategy-critical activities and core business processes performed by different departments are properly integrated and coordinated.

Companies that have reengineered some of their business processes have ended up compressing formerly separate steps and tasks into jobs performed by a single person and integrating jobs into team activities. Reorganization then follows as a natural consequence of task synthesis and job redesign. When done properly, reengineering can produce dramatic gains in productivity and organizational capability. In the order-processing section of General Electric's circuit breaker division, elapsed time from order receipt to delivery was cut from three weeks to three days by consolidating six production units into one, reducing a variety of former inventory and handling steps, automating the design system to replace a human custom-design process, and cutting the organizational layers between managers and workers from three to one. Productivity rose 20 percent in one year, and unit manufacturing costs dropped 30 percent.[17]

Table 7.1   ADVANTAGES AND DISADVANTAGES OF CENTRALIZED VERSUS DECENTRALIZED DECISION-MAKING

Centralized Organizational Structures	Decentralized Organizational Structures
Basic Tenets	**Basic Tenets**
▪ Decisions on most matters of importance should be pushed to managers up the line who have the experience, expertise, and judgment to decide what is the wisest or best course of action.	▪ Decision-making authority should be put in the hands of the people closest to and most familiar with the situation, and these people should be trained to exercise good judgment.
▪ Frontline supervisors and rank-and-file employees can't be relied on to make the right decisions—because they seldom know what is best for the organization and because they do not have the time or the inclination to properly manage the tasks they are performing (letting them decide what to do is thus risky).	▪ A company that draws on the combined intellectual capital of all its employees can outperform a command-and-control company.
Chief Advantage	**Chief Advantages**
▪ Tight control from the top allows for accountability.	▪ Encourages lower-level managers and rank-and-file employees to exercise initiative and act responsibly.
Primary Disadvantages	▪ Promotes greater motivation and involvement in the business on the part of more company personnel.
▪ Slows response times because management bureaucracy must decide on a course of action.	▪ Spurs new ideas and creative thinking.
▪ Does not encourage responsibility among lower-level managers and rank-and-file employees.	▪ Allows fast response times.
▪ Discourages lower-level managers and rank-and-file employees from exercising any initiative—they are expected to wait to be told what to do.	▪ Reduces layers of management.
	Primary Disadvantages
	▪ Puts the organization at risk if many bad decisions are made at lower levels.
	▪ Impedes cross-unit coordination and capture of strategic fits.

Determining the Degree of Authority and Independence to Give Each Unit and Each Employee

In executing the strategy and conducting daily operations, companies must decide how much authority to delegate to the managers of each organization unit—especially the heads of business subsidiaries, functional and process departments, and plants, sales offices, distribution centers and other operating units—and how much decision-making latitude to give individual employees in performing their jobs. The two extremes are to *centralize decision making* at the top (the CEO and a few close lieutenants) or to *decentralize decision making* by giving managers and employees considerable decision-making latitude in their areas of responsibility. As shown in Table 7.1, the two approaches are based on sharply different underlying principles and beliefs, with each having its pros and cons.

Centralized Decision-Making   *In a highly centralized organization structure, top executives retain authority for most strategic and operating decisions and keep a tight rein on business-unit heads, department heads, and the managers of key operating units; comparatively little discretionary authority is granted to frontline supervisors and rank-and-file employees.* The command-and-control paradigm of centralized structures is based on the underlying assumption that frontline personnel have neither the time nor the inclination to direct and properly control the work they are

> There are serious disadvantages to having a small number of top-level managers micromanage the business by personally making decisions or by requiring they approve the recommendations of lower-level subordinates before actions can be taken.

performing, and that they lack the knowledge and judgment to make wise decisions about how best to do it—hence the need for managerially prescribed policies and procedures, close supervision, and tight control. The thesis underlying authoritarian structures is that strict enforcement of detailed procedures backed by rigorous managerial oversight is the most reliable way to keep the daily execution of strategy on track.

The big advantage of an authoritarian structure is tight control by the manager in charge—it is easy to know who is accountable when things do not go well. But there are some serious disadvantages. Hierarchical command-and-control structures make an organization sluggish in responding to changing conditions because of the time it takes for the review/approval process to run up all the layers of the management bureaucracy. Furthermore, to work well, centralized decision making requires top-level managers to gather and process whatever information is relevant to the decision. When the relevant knowledge resides at lower organizational levels (or is technical, detailed, or hard to express in words), it is difficult and time-consuming to get all of the facts and nuances in front of a high-level executive located far from the scene of the action—full understanding of the situation cannot be readily copied from one mind to another. Hence, centralized decision making is often impractical—the larger the company and the more scattered its operations, the more that decision-making authority has to be delegated to managers closer to the scene of the action.

Decentralized Decision-Making *In a highly decentralized organization, decision-making authority is pushed down to the lowest organizational level capable of making timely, informed, competent decisions.* The objective is to put adequate decision-making authority in the hands of the people closest to and most familiar with the situation and train them to weigh all the factors and exercise good judgment. The case for empowering down-the-line managers and employees to make decisions related to daily operations and executing the strategy is based on the belief that a company that draws on the combined intellectual capital of all its employees can outperform a command-and-control company. Decentralized decision making means, for example, that in a diversified company the various business-unit heads have broad authority to execute the agreed-on business strategy with comparatively little interference from corporate headquarters; moreover, the business-unit heads delegate considerable decision-making latitude to functional and process department heads and the heads of the various operating units (plants, distribution centers, sales offices) in implementing and executing their pieces of the strategy. In turn, work teams may be empowered to manage and improve their assigned value chain activity, and employees with customer contact may be empowered to do what it takes to please customers. At Starbucks, for example, employees are encouraged to exercise initiative in promoting customer satisfaction—there's the story of a store employee who, when the computerized cash register system went offline, enthusiastically offered free coffee to waiting customers.[18] With decentralized decision making, top management maintains control by limiting empowered managers' and employees' discretionary authority and holding people accountable for the decisions they make.

> The ultimate goal of decentralized decision making is not to push decisions down to lower levels but to put decision-making authority in the hands of those persons or teams closest to and most knowledgeable about the situation.

Decentralized organization structures have much to recommend them. Delegating greater authority to subordinate managers and employees creates a more horizontal organization structure with fewer management layers. Whereas in a centralized vertical structure managers and workers have to go up the ladder of authority for an answer, in a decentralized horizontal structure they develop their own answers and action plans—making decisions in their areas of responsibility and being accountable for results is an integral part of their job. Pushing decision-making authority down to middle and lower-level managers and then further on to work teams and individual employees shortens organizational response times and spurs new ideas, creative thinking, innovation, and greater involvement on the part of subordinate managers and employees. In worker-empowered structures, jobs can be defined more broadly, several tasks can be integrated into a single job, and people can direct their own work. Fewer managers are needed because deciding how to do things becomes part of each person's or team's job. Further, today's electronic communication systems make it easy and relatively inexpensive for people at all organizational levels to have direct access to data, other employees, managers, suppliers, and customers. They can access information quickly (via the Internet or company intranet), readily check with superiors or whomever else as needed, and take responsible action. Typically, there are genuine gains in morale and productivity when people are provided with the tools and information they need to operate in a self-directed way. Decentralized decision making can not only shorten organizational response times but also spur new ideas, creative thinking, innovation, and greater involvement on the part of subordinate managers and employees.

Insofar as all five tasks of strategic management are concerned, a decentralized approach to decision making means that the managers of each organizational unit should not only lead the crafting of their unit's strategy but also lead the decision making on how to execute it. Decentralization thus requires selecting strong managers to head each organizational unit and holding them accountable for crafting and executing appropriate strategies for their units. Managers who consistently produce unsatisfactory results have to be weeded out.

The past decade has seen a growing shift from authoritarian, multilayered hierarchical structures to flatter, more decentralized structures that stress employee empowerment. There's strong and growing consensus that authoritarian, hierarchical organization structures are not well suited to implementing and executing strategies in an era when extensive information and instant communication are the norm and when a big fraction of the organization's most valuable assets consists of intellectual capital and resides in the knowledge and capabilities of its employees. Many companies have therefore begun empowering lower-level managers and employees throughout their organizations, giving them greater discretionary authority to make strategic adjustments in their areas of responsibility and to decide what needs to be done to put new strategic initiatives into place and execute them proficiently.

Maintaining Control in a Decentralized Organization Structure Pushing decision-making authority deep down into the organization structure and empowering employees presents its own organizing challenge: *how to exercise adequate control over the actions of empowered employees so that the business is not put at risk at the same time that the benefits of empowerment are realized.*[19] Maintaining adequate organizational control over empowered employees is generally accomplished by placing limits on the authority that empowered personnel can exercise, holding people accountable for their decisions, instituting compensation incentives that reward people for doing their jobs in a manner to contributes to good company performance, and creating a corporate culture where there's strong peer pressure on individuals to act responsibly.

Capturing Strategic Fits in a Decentralized Structure   Diversified companies striving to capture cross-business strategic fits have to beware of giving business heads full rein to operate independently when cross-business collaboration is essential in order to gain strategic fit benefits. Cross-business strategic fits typically have to be captured either by enforcing close cross-business collaboration or by centralizing performance of functions having strategic fits at the corporate level.[20] For example, if businesses with overlapping process and product technologies have their own independent R&D departments—each pursuing their own priorities, projects, and strategic agendas—it's hard for the corporate parent to prevent duplication of effort, capture either economies of scale or economies of scope, or broaden the company's R&D efforts to embrace new technological paths, product families, end-use applications, and customer groups. Where cross-business R&D fits exist, the best solution is usually to centralize the R&D function and have a coordinated corporate R&D effort that serves both the interests of individual business and the company as a whole. Likewise, centralizing the related activities of separate businesses makes sense when there are opportunities to share a common sales force, use common distribution channels, rely on a common field service organization to handle customer requests for technical assistance or provide maintenance and repair services, use common e-commerce systems and approaches, and so on.

The point here is that efforts to decentralize decision making and give organizational units leeway in conducting operations have to be tempered with the need to maintain adequate control and cross-unit coordination—decentralization doesn't mean delegating authority in ways that allow organization units and individuals to do their own thing. There are numerous instances when decision-making authority must be retained at high levels in the organization and ample cross-unit coordination strictly enforced.

Providing for Internal Cross-Unit Coordination

The classic way to coordinate the activities of organizational units is to position them in the hierarchy so that the most closely related ones report to a single person (a functional department head, a process manager, a geographic area head, a senior executive). Managers higher up in the ranks generally have the clout to coordinate, integrate, and arrange for the cooperation of units under their supervision. In such structures, the chief executive officer, chief operating officer, and business-level managers end up as central points of coordination because of their positions of authority over the whole unit. When a firm is pursuing a related diversification strategy, coordinating the related activities of independent business units often requires the centralizing authority of a single corporate-level officer. Also, diversified companies commonly centralize such staff support functions as public relations, finance and accounting, employee benefits, and information technology at the corporate level both to contain the costs of support activities and to facilitate uniform and coordinated performance of such functions within each business unit.

But, as explained earlier, the functional organization structures employed in most businesses often result in fragmentation. Close cross-unit collaboration is usually needed to build core competencies and competitive capabilities in such strategically important activities as speeding new products to market and providing superior customer service. To combat fragmentation and achieve the desired degree of cross-unit cooperation and collaboration, most companies supplement their functional organization structures. Sometimes this takes the form of creating process departments to bring together the pieces of strategically important activities previously performed in

Cross-Unit Coordination on Technology at 3M Corporation

At 3M, technology experts in more than 100 laboratories around the world have come to work openly and cooperatively without resorting to turf-protection tactics or not-invented-here mindsets. 3M management has been successful in creating a collegial working environment that results in the scientists calling on one another for assistance and advice and in rapid technology transfer.

Management formed a Technical Council, composed of the heads of the major labs; the council meets monthly and has a three-day annual retreat to discuss ways to improve cross-unit transfer of technology and other issues of common interest. In addition, management created a broader-based Technical Forum, composed of scientists and technical experts chosen as representatives, to facilitate grassroots communication among employees in all the labs.

One of the forum's responsibilities is to organize employees with similar technical interests from all the labs into chapters; chapter members attend regular seminars with experts from outside the company. There's also an annual three-day technology fair at which 3M scientists showcase their latest findings for colleagues and expand their network of acquaintances.

As a result of these collaborative efforts, 3M has developed a portfolio of more than 100 technologies and created the capability to routinely use these technologies in product applications in three different divisions that each serve multiple markets.

Source: Adapted from Sumantra Ghoshal and Christopher A. Bartlett, "Changing the Role of Top Management: Beyond Structure to Process," *Harvard Business Review* 73, no. 1 (January–February 1995), pp. 93–94.

separate functional units. And sometimes the coordinating mechanisms involve the use of cross-functional task forces, dual reporting relationships, informal organizational networking, voluntary cooperation, incentive compensation tied to group performance measures, and strong executive-level insistence on teamwork and cross-department cooperation (including removal of recalcitrant managers who stonewall collaborative efforts). At one European-based company, a top executive promptly replaced the managers of several plants who were not fully committed to collaborating closely on eliminating duplication in product development and production efforts among plants in several different countries. Earlier, the executive, noting that negotiations among the managers had stalled on which labs and plants to close, had met with all the managers, asked them to cooperate to find a solution, discussed with them which options were unacceptable, and given them a deadline to find a solution. When the asked-for teamwork wasn't forthcoming, several managers were replaced.

See Company Spotlight 7.2 for how 3M Corporation puts the necessary organizational arrangements into place to create worldwide coordination on technology matters.

Providing for Collaboration with Outside Suppliers and Strategic Allies

Someone or some group must be authorized to collaborate as needed with each major outside constituency involved in strategy execution. Forming alliances and cooperative relationships presents immediate opportunities and opens the door to future possibilities, but nothing valuable is realized until the relationship grows, develops, and blossoms. Unless top management sees that constructive organizational bridge-building with strategic partners occurs and that productive working relationships emerge, the value of alliances is lost and the company's power to execute its strategy is weakened. If close working relationships with suppliers are crucial, then supply chain management must be given formal status on the company's organization chart and a significant position in the pecking order. If distributor/dealer/franchisee relationships are important, someone must be assigned the task of nurturing the relationships with forward channel allies. If working in parallel with providers of complementary products and services contributes to enhanced organizational capability, then cooperative organizational arrangements have to be put in place and managed to good effect.

Building organizational bridges with external allies can be accomplished by appointing "relationship managers" with responsibility for making particular strategic partnerships or alliances generate the intended benefits. Relationship managers have many roles and functions: getting the right people together, promoting good rapport, seeing that plans for specific activities are developed and carried out, helping adjust internal organizational procedures and communication systems, ironing out operating dissimilarities, and nurturing interpersonal cooperation. Multiple cross-organization ties have to be established and kept open to ensure proper communication and coordination.[21] There has to be enough information sharing to make the relationship work and periodic frank discussions of conflicts, trouble spots, and changing situations.[22]

Perspectives on the Organization-Building Effort

All organization designs have their strategy-related strengths and weaknesses. To do a good job of matching structure to strategy, strategy implementers first have to pick a basic design and modify it as needed to fit the company's particular business lineup.

> There is no perfect or ideal organization structure.

They must then (1) supplement the design with appropriate coordinating mechanisms (cross-functional task forces, special project teams, self-contained work teams, and so on), and (2) institute whatever networking and communication arrangements it takes to support effective execution of the firm's strategy. While companies may not set up "ideal" organizational arrangements to avoid disturbing certain existing reporting relationships or to accommodate other situational idiosyncrasies, they must work toward the goal of building a competitively capable organization.

The ways and means of developing stronger core competencies and organizational capabilities (or creating altogether new ones) have to fit a company's own circumstances. Not only do different companies and executives tackle the capabilities-building challenge in different ways, but the task of building different capabilities requires

> Organizational capabilities emerge from a process of consciously knitting together the efforts of different work groups, departments, and external allies, not from how the boxes on the organization chart are arranged.

different organizing techniques. Thus, generalizing about how to build capabilities has to be done cautiously. What can be said unequivocally is that building a capable organization entails a process of consciously knitting together the efforts of individuals and groups. Competencies and capabilities emerge from establishing and nurturing cooperative working relationships among people and groups to perform activities in a more customer-satisfying fashion, not from rearranging boxes on an organization chart. Furthermore, organization building is a task in which senior management must be deeply involved. Indeed, effectively managing both internal organization processes and external collaboration to create and develop competitively valuable competencies and capabilities is a top challenge for senior executives in today's companies.

Organizational Structures of the Future

Many of today's companies are winding up the task of remodeling their traditional hierarchical structures once built around functional specialization and centralized authority. Much of the corporate downsizing movement in the late 1980s and early 1990s was aimed at recasting authoritarian, pyramidal organizational structures into flatter, decentralized structures. The change was driven by growing realization that command-and-control hierarchies were proving a liability in businesses where customer preferences were shifting from standardized products to custom orders and special features, product life cycles were growing shorter, custom mass production methods were replacing standardized mass production techniques, customers wanted to be treated as individuals, technological change was ongoing, and market conditions were fluid. Layered management hierarchies with lots of checks and controls that required people to look upward in the organizational structure for answers and approval were failing to deliver responsive customer service and timely adaptations to changing conditions. Likewise, functional silos, task-oriented work, and fragmentation of strategy-critical activities further contributed to an erosion of competitiveness in fluid or volatile business environments.

> Revolutionary changes in how companies are organizing the work effort have been occurring since the early 1990s.

The organizational adjustments and downsizing of companies in 2001–2002 brought further refinements and changes to streamline organizational activities and shake out inefficiencies. The goals have been to make the organization leaner, flatter, and more responsive to change. Many companies are drawing on five tools of organizational design: (1) managers and workers empowered to act on their own judgments, (2) reengineered work processes, (3) self-directed work teams, (4) rapid incorporation of Internet technology applications, and (5) networking with outsiders to improve existing organization capabilities and create new ones. Considerable management attention is being devoted to building a company capable of outcompeting rivals on the basis of superior resource strengths and competitive capabilities—capabilities that are increasingly based on intellectual capital.

The organizations of the future will have several new characteristics:

- Fewer barriers between different vertical ranks, between functions and disciplines, between units in different geographic locations, and between the company and its suppliers, distributors/dealers, strategic allies, and customers.

- A capacity for change and rapid learning.

- Collaborative efforts among people in different functional specialties and geographic locations—essential to create organization competencies and capabilities.

- Extensive use of Internet technology and e-commerce business practices—real-time data and information systems, greater reliance on online systems for transacting business with suppliers and customers, and Internet-based communication and collaboration with suppliers, customers, and strategic partners.

Key Points

The job of strategy implementation and execution is to convert strategic plans into actions and good results. The test of successful strategy execution is whether actual organization performance matches or exceeds the targets spelled out in the strategic plan. Shortfalls in performance signal weak strategy, weak execution, or both.

In deciding how to implement a new or revised strategy, managers have to determine what internal conditions are needed to execute the strategic plan successfully. Then they must create these conditions as rapidly as practical. The process of implementing and executing strategy involves:

1. Building an organization with the competencies, capabilities, and resource strengths to execute strategy successfully.

2. Allocating ample resources to strategy-critical activities.

3. Ensuring that policies and procedures facilitate rather than impede strategy execution.

4. Instituting best practices and pushing for continuous improvement in how value chain activities are performed.

5. Installing information and operating systems that enable company personnel to carry out their strategic roles proficiently.

6. Tying rewards and incentives directly to the achievement of strategic and financial targets and to good strategy execution.

7. Shaping the work environment and corporate culture to fit the strategy.

8. Exerting the internal leadership needed to drive implementation forward and to keep improving on how the strategy is being executed.

The place for managers to start in implementing and executing a new or different strategy is with *a probing assessment of what the organization must do differently and better to carry out the strategy successfully.* They should then consider *precisely how to make the necessary internal changes* as rapidly as possible. Successful strategy implementers have a knack for diagnosing what their organizations need to do to execute the chosen strategy well and figuring out how to get things done—they are masters in promoting results-oriented behaviors on the part of company personnel and following through on making the right things happen.

Like crafting strategy, executing strategy is a job for a company's whole management team, not just a few senior managers. Top-level managers have to rely on the active support and cooperation of middle and lower managers to push strategy changes into functional areas and operating units and to see that the organization actually operates in accordance with the strategy on a daily basis. Middle and lower-level managers not only are responsible for initiating and supervising the execution process in their areas of authority but also are instrumental in getting subordinates to continuously improve on how strategy-critical value chain activities are being performed and in producing the operating results that allow company performance targets to be met. Thus, all managers have to consider what actions to take in their areas to achieve the intended results in executing strategy—they each need *an action agenda.*

Building a capable organization is always a top priority in strategy execution; three types of organization-building actions are paramount:

1. *Staffing the organization*—putting together a strong management team, and recruiting and retaining employees with the needed experience, technical skills, and intellectual capital.

2. *Building core competencies and competitive capabilities* that will enable good strategy execution and updating them as strategy and external conditions change.

3. *Structuring the organization and work effort*—organizing value chain activities and business processes and deciding how much decision-making authority to push down to lower-level managers and frontline employees.

Selecting able people for key positions tends to be one of the earliest strategy implementation steps. No company can hope to perform the activities required for successful strategy execution without attracting capable managers and without employees that give it a suitable knowledge base and portfolio of intellectual capital.

Building core competencies and competitive capabilities is a time-consuming, managerially challenging exercise that involves three stages: (1) developing the *ability* to do something, however imperfectly or inefficiently, by selecting people with the requisite skills and experience, upgrading or expanding individual abilities as needed, and then molding the efforts and work products of individuals into a collaborative group effort; (2) coordinating group efforts to learn how to perform the activity *consistently well and at an acceptable cost*, thereby transforming the ability into a tried-and-true *competence* or *capability*; and (3) continuing to polish and refine the organization's know-how and otherwise sharpen performance such that it becomes *better than rivals* at performing the activity, thus raising the core competence (or capability) to the rank of a *distinctive competence* (or competitively superior capability) and opening an avenue to competitive advantage. Many companies manage to get through stages 1 and 2 in performing a strategy-critical activity but comparatively few achieve sufficient proficiency in performing strategy-critical activities to qualify for the third stage.

Managerial actions to develop core competencies and competitive capabilities generally take one of two forms: either strengthening the company's base of skills, knowledge, and intellect, or coordinating and networking the efforts of the various work groups and departments. Actions of the first sort can be undertaken at all managerial levels, but actions of the second sort are best orchestrated by senior managers who not only appreciate the strategy-executing significance of strong competencies/capabilities but also have the clout to enforce the necessary networking and cooperation among individuals, groups, departments, and external allies.

Strong core competencies and competitive capabilities are an important avenue for securing a competitive edge over rivals in situations where it is relatively easy for rivals to copy smart strategies. Any time rivals can readily duplicate successful strategy features, making it difficult or impossible to outstrategize rivals and beat them in the marketplace with a superior strategy, the chief way to achieve lasting competitive advantage is to outexecute them (beat them by performing certain value chain activities in superior fashion). Building core competencies, resource strengths, and organizational capabilities that rivals can't match is one of the best and most reliable ways to outexecute them.

Structuring the organization and organizing the work effort in a strategy-supportive fashion has five aspects:

1. Deciding which value chain activities to perform internally and which ones to outsource.

2. Making internally performed strategy-critical activities the main building blocks in the organization structure.

3. Deciding how much authority to centralize at the top and how much to delegate to down-the-line managers and employees.

4. Providing for internal cross-unit coordination and collaboration to build and strengthen internal competencies/capabilities.

5. Providing for the necessary collaboration and coordination with suppliers and strategic allies.

The primary organizational building blocks within a business are usually *traditional functional departments* and *process-complete departments*. In enterprises with operations in various countries around the world (or with geographically scattered organizational units within a country), the basic building blocks may also include *geographic organizational units*, each of which has profit/loss responsibility for its assigned geographic area. In vertically integrated firms, the major building blocks are *divisional units performing one or more of the major processing steps along the value chain* (raw materials production, components manufacture, assembly, wholesale distribution, retail store operations); each division in the value chain may operate as a profit center for performance measurement purposes. The typical building blocks of a diversified company are its *individual businesses*, with each business unit usually operating as an independent profit center and with corporate headquarters performing assorted support functions for all the businesses.

Whatever basic structure is chosen, it usually has to be supplemented with interdisciplinary task forces, incentive compensation schemes tied to measures of joint performance, empowerment of cross-functional and/or self-directed work teams to perform and unify fragmented processes and strategy-critical activities, special project teams, relationship managers, and special top management efforts to knit the work of different individuals and groups into valuable competitive capabilities.

In more and more companies, efforts to match structure to strategy involve fewer layers of management authority; managers and workers are empowered to act on their own judgment; work processes are being reengineered to reduce cross-department fragmentation; collaborative partnerships exist with outsiders (suppliers, distributors/dealers, companies with complementary products/services, and even select competitors); and there's increased outsourcing of selected value chain activities, leaner staffing of internal support functions, and rapidly growing use of Internet technology applications to streamline operations and expedite cross-unit communication.

Exercise

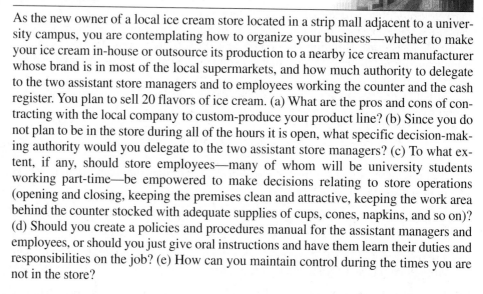

As the new owner of a local ice cream store located in a strip mall adjacent to a university campus, you are contemplating how to organize your business—whether to make your ice cream in-house or outsource its production to a nearby ice cream manufacturer whose brand is in most of the local supermarkets, and how much authority to delegate to the two assistant store managers and to employees working the counter and the cash register. You plan to sell 20 flavors of ice cream. (a) What are the pros and cons of contracting with the local company to custom-produce your product line? (b) Since you do not plan to be in the store during all of the hours it is open, what specific decision-making authority would you delegate to the two assistant store managers? (c) To what extent, if any, should store employees—many of whom will be university students working part-time—be empowered to make decisions relating to store operations (opening and closing, keeping the premises clean and attractive, keeping the work area behind the counter stocked with adequate supplies of cups, cones, napkins, and so on)? (d) Should you create a policies and procedures manual for the assistant managers and employees, or should you just give oral instructions and have them learn their duties and responsibilities on the job? (e) How can you maintain control during the times you are not in the store?

CHAPTER

8

Managing Internal Operations
Actions That Facilitate Strategy Execution

Winning companies know how to do their work better.
—Michael Hammer and James Champy

If you talk about change but don't change the reward
and recognition system, nothing changes.
—Paul Allaire, former CEO, Xerox Corporation

If you want people motivated to do a good job, give
them a good job to do.
—Frederick Herzberg

You ought to pay big bonuses for premier performance
. . . Be a top payer, not in the middle or low end of the
pack.
—Lawrence Bossidy, CEO, Honeywell International

In Chapter 7 we emphasized the importance of building organization capabilities and structuring the work effort so as to perform strategy-critical activities in a coordinated and highly competent manner. In this chapter we discuss five additional managerial actions that facilitate the success of a company's strategy execution efforts:

1. Marshaling resources to support the strategy execution effort.
2. Instituting policies and procedures that facilitate strategy execution.
3. Adopting best practices and striving for continuous improvement in how value chain activities are performed.
4. Installing information and operating systems that enable company personnel to better carry out their strategic roles proficiently.
5. Tying rewards and incentives directly to the achievement of strategic and financial targets and to good strategy execution.

Marshaling Resources to Support the Strategy Execution Effort

Early in the process of implementing and executing a new or different strategy managers need to identify the resource requirements of each new strategic initiative and then consider whether the current pattern of resource allocation and the budgets of the various subunits are suitable. Plainly, organizational units must have the budgets and resources for executing their parts of the strategic plan effectively and efficiently. Developing a strategy-driven budget requires top management to determine what funding is needed to execute new strategic initiatives and to strengthen or modify the company's competencies and capabilities. This includes careful screening of requests for more people and more or better facilities and equipment, approving those that hold promise for making a cost-justified contribution to strategy execution, and turning down those that don't. Should internal cash flows prove insufficient to fund the planned strategic initiatives, then the company must be in a financial position to raise additional funds through borrowing or selling additional shares of stock to willing investors.

A company's ability to marshal the resources needed to support new strategic initiatives and steer them to the appropriate organizational units has a major impact on the strategy execution process. Too little funding (stemming either from constrained financial resources or from sluggish management action to adequately increase the budgets of strategy-critical organizational units) slows progress and impedes the efforts of organizational units to execute their pieces of the strategic plan proficiently. Too much funding wastes organizational resources and reduces financial performance. Both outcomes argue for managers to be deeply involved in reviewing budget proposals and directing the proper kinds and amounts of resources to strategy-critical organization units.

A change in strategy nearly always calls for budget reallocations. Units important in the prior strategy but having a lesser role in the new strategy may need downsizing. Units that now have a bigger and more critical strategic role may need more people, new equipment, additional facilities, and above-average increases in their operating budgets. Strategy implementers need to be active and forceful in shifting resources, downsizing some areas and upsizing others, to not only amply fund activities with a critical role in the new strategy but also avoid inefficiency and achieve profit projections. They have to exercise their power to put enough resources behind new strategic initiatives to make things happen and make the tough decisions to kill projects and activities that are no longer justified.

Visible actions to reallocate operating funds and move people into new organizational units signal a determined commitment to strategic change and frequently are needed to catalyze the implementation process and give it credibility. Microsoft has made a practice of regularly shifting hundreds of programmers to new high-priority programming initiatives within a matter of weeks or even days. At Harris Corporation, where the strategy was to diffuse research ideas into areas that were commercially viable, top management regularly shifted groups of engineers out of government projects and into new commercial venture divisions. Fast-moving developments in many markets are prompting companies to abandon traditional annual or semiannual budgeting and resource allocation cycles in favor of cycles that match the strategy changes a company makes in response to newly developing events. Annual or semiannual budget and resource reallocation reviews do not work when companies make strategic shifts weekly. Bluefly.com, a discount Internet retailer of designer brands, revises its budgets and shifts resources weekly. Bluefly.com's CEO observed, "For us, 11 months is long-term planning."[1]

Just fine-tuning the execution of a company's existing strategy, however, seldom requires big movements of people and money from one area to another. The desired improvements can usually be accomplished through above-average budget increases to organizational units where new initiatives are contemplated and below-average increases (or even small cuts) for the remaining organizational units. The chief exception occurs where a prime ingredient of strategy is to create altogether new capabilities or to generate fresh products and business opportunities within the existing budget. Then, as proposals and business plans worth pursuing bubble up from below, managers have to decide where the needed capital expenditures, operating budgets, and personnel will come from. Companies like 3M, General Electric, and Boeing shift resources and people from area to area as needed to support the launch of new products and new business ventures. They empower "product champions" and small bands of would-be entrepreneurs by giving them financial and technical support and by setting up organizational units and programs to help new ventures blossom more quickly.

Instituting Policies and Procedures That Facilitate Strategy Execution

Changes in strategy generally call for some changes in work practices and internal operations. Asking people to alter established procedures always upsets the internal order of things. It is normal for pockets of resistance to develop and for people to exhibit some degree of stress and anxiety about how the changes will affect them, especially when the changes may eliminate jobs. Questions are also likely to arise over what activities need to be rigidly prescribed and where there ought to be leeway for independent action.

Figure 8.1   How Prescribed Policies and Procedures Facilitate Strategy Execution

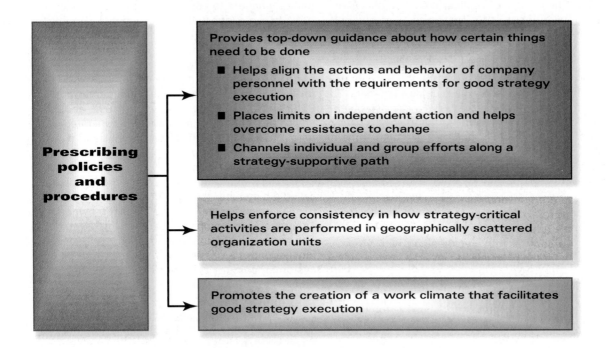

As shown in Figure 8.1, prescribing new policies and operating procedures designed to facilitate strategy execution has merit from several angles:

1. It *provides top-down guidance regarding how certain things now need to be done.* New policies and operating practices can help align actions with strategy throughout the organization, placing limits on independent behavior and channeling individual and group efforts along a path in tune with the new strategy. They also help counteract tendencies for some people to resist change—most people refrain from violating company policy or going against recommended practices and procedures without first gaining clearance or having strong justification.

2. It *helps enforce needed consistency in how particular strategy-critical activities are performed in geographically scattered operating units.* Eliminating significant differences in the operating practices of different plants, sales regions, customer service centers, or the individual outlets in a chain operation is frequently desirable to avoid sending mixed messages to internal personnel and to customers who do business with the company at multiple locations.

3. It *promotes the creation of a work climate that facilitates good strategy execution.* Because dismantling old policies and procedures and instituting new ones invariably alter the internal work climate, strategy implementers can use the policy-changing process as a powerful lever for changing the corporate culture in ways that produce a stronger fit with the new strategy.

Company managers therefore need to be inventive in devising policies and practices that can provide vital support to effective strategy implementation and execution.

Graniterock's "Short Pay" Policy: An Innovative Way to Promote Strategy Execution

In 1987, the owners of Graniterock, a 100-plus-year-old supplier of crushed gravel, sand, concrete, and asphalt in Watsonville, California, set two big, hairy, audacious goals (BHAGs) for the company: total customer satisfaction and a reputation for service that met or exceeded that of Nordstrom, the upscale department store famous for pleasing its customers. To drive the internal efforts to achieve these two objectives, top management instituted "short pay," a policy designed to signal both employees and customers that Graniterock was deadly serious about its two strategic commitments. At the bottom of every Graniterock invoice was the following statement:

> If you are not satisfied for any reason, don't pay us for it. Simply scratch out the line item, write a brief note about the problem, and return a copy of this invoice along with your check for the balance.

Customers did not have to call and complain and were not expected to return the product. They were given complete discretionary power to decide whether and how much to pay based on their satisfaction level.

The policy has worked exceptionally well, providing unmistakable feedback and spurring company managers to correct any problems quickly in order to avoid repeated short payments. Graniterock has enjoyed market share increases, while charging a 6 percent price premium for its commodity products in competition against larger rivals. Its profit margins and overall financial performance have improved. Graniterock won the prestigious Malcolm Baldrige National Quality Award in 1992, about five years after instituting the policy. *Fortune* rated Graniterock as one of the 100 best companies to work for in America in 2001 (ranked 17th) and 2002 (ranked 16th). Company employees receive an average of 43 hours of training annually. Entry-level employees, called job owners, start at $16 an hour and progress to such positions as "accomplished job owner" and "improvement champion" (base pay of $26 an hour). The company has a no-layoff policy, provides employees with 12 massages a year, and sends positive customer comments about employees home for families to read.

Source: Based on information in Jim Collins, "Turning Goals into Results: The Power of Catalytic Mechanisms," *Harvard Business Review* 77, no. 4 (July–August 1999), pp. 72–73; and Robert Levering and Milton Moskowitz, "The 100 Best Companies to Work For," *Fortune,* February 4, 2002, p. 73.

In an attempt to steer "crew members" into stronger quality and service behavior patterns, McDonald's policy manual spells out procedures in detail; for example, "Cooks must turn, never flip, hamburgers. If they haven't been purchased, Big Macs must be discarded in 10 minutes after being cooked and French fries in 7 minutes. Cashiers must make eye contact with and smile at every customer." Hewlett-Packard requires R&D people to make regular visits to customers to learn about their problems, talk about new product applications, and in general keep the company's R&D programs customer-oriented. Mrs. Fields Cookies has a policy of establishing hourly sales quotas for each store outlet; furthermore, it is company policy that cookies not sold within two hours after being baked have to be removed from the case and given to charitable organizations. Company Spotlight 8.1 describes how Graniterock's "short pay" policy spurs employee focus on providing total customer satisfaction and building the company's reputation for superior customer service.

Thus, there is a definite role for new and revised policies and procedures in the strategy implementation process. Wisely constructed policies and procedures help channel actions, behavior, decisions, and practices in directions that promote good strategy execution. When policies and practices aren't strategy-supportive, they become a barrier to the kinds of attitudinal and behavioral changes strategy implementers are trying to promote. Sometimes people hide behind or vigorously defend long-standing policies and operating procedures in an effort to stall implementation or force it along a different route. Anytime a company alters its strategy, managers should review existing policies and operating procedures, proactively revise or discard those that are out of sync, and formulate new ones to facilitate execution of new strategic initiatives.

None of this implies that companies need thick policy manuals to direct the strategy execution process and prescribe exactly how daily operations are to be conducted. Too much policy can erect as many obstacles as wrong policy or be as confusing as no policy. There is wisdom in a middle approach: *Prescribe enough policies to give organization members clear direction in implementing strategy and to place desirable boundaries on their actions; then empower them to act within these boundaries however they think makes sense.* Allowing company personnel to act anywhere between the "white lines" is especially appropriate when individual creativity and initiative are more essential to good strategy execution than standardization and strict conformity. Instituting strategy-facilitating policies can therefore mean more policies, fewer policies, or different policies. It can mean policies that require things to be done a certain way or policies that give employees leeway to do activities the way they think best.

Adopting Best Practices and Striving for Continuous Improvement

Company managers can significantly advance the cause of competent strategy execution by pushing organization units and company personnel to identify and adopt the best practices for performing value chain activities and, further, insisting on continuous improvement in how internal operations are conducted. One of the most widely used and effective tools for gauging how well a company is executing pieces of its strategy entails benchmarking a company's performance of particular activities and business processes against "best-in-industry" and "best-in-world" performers.[2] It can also be useful to look at "best-in-

> **Core Concept**
>
> Managerial efforts to identify and adopt **best practices** are a powerful tool for promoting operating excellence and better strategy execution.

company" performers of an activity if a company has a number of different organizational units performing much the same function at different locations. Identifying, analyzing, and understanding how top companies or individuals perform particular value chain activities and business processes provides useful yardsticks for judging the effectiveness and efficiency of internal operations and setting performance standards for organization units to meet or beat.

How the Process of Identifying and Incorporating Best Practices Works

A **best practice** is a technique for performing an activity or business process that at least one company has demonstrated works particularly well. To qualify as a legitimate best practice, the technique must have a proven record in significantly lowering costs, improving quality or performance, shortening time requirements, enhancing safety, or delivering some other highly positive operating outcome. Best practices thus identify a path to operating excellence. For a best practice to be valuable and transferable, it must demonstrate success over time, deliver quantifiable and highly positive results, and be repeatable.

> **Core Concept**
>
> A **best practice** is any practice that at least one company has proved works particularly well.

Benchmarking is the backbone of the process of identifying, studying, and implementing outstanding practices. A company's benchmarking effort looks outward to

Figure 8.2   From Benchmarking and Best-Practice Implementation to Operating Excellence

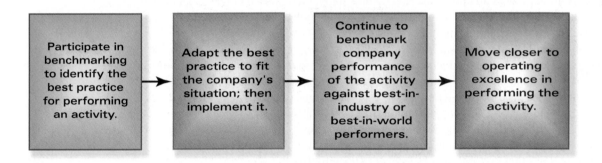

find best practice and then proceeds to develop the data for measuring how well a company's own performance of an activity stacks up against the best-practice standard. Informally, benchmarking involves being humble enough to admit that others have come up with world-class ways to perform particular activities yet wise enough to try to learn how to match, and even surpass, them at it. But, as shown in Figure 8.2, the payoff of benchmarking comes from applying the top-notch approaches pioneered by other companies in the company's own operation and thereby spurring dramatic improvements in the proficiency with which value chain tasks are performed. The goal of benchmarking is to promote the achievement of operating excellence in a variety of strategy-critical and support activities.

However, benchmarking is more complicated than simply identifying which companies are the best performers of an activity and then trying to exactly copy other companies' approaches—especially if these companies are in other industries. Normally, the outstanding practices of other organizations have to be adapted to fit the specific circumstances of a company's own business and operating requirements. Since most companies believe "our work is different" or "we are unique", the telling part of any best-practice initiative is how well the company puts its own version of the best practice into place and makes it work. Indeed, a best practice remains little more than an interesting success story unless company personnel buy into the task of translating what can be learned from other companies into real action and results. The agents of change must be frontline employees who are convinced of the need to abandon the old ways of doing things and switch to a best practice mindset. The more that organizational units utilize best practices in performing their work, the closer a company moves toward performing its value chain activities as effectively and efficiently as possible. This is what operational excellence is all about.

Legions of companies across the world now engage in benchmarking to improve their strategy execution efforts and, ideally, gain a strategic, operational, and financial advantage over rivals. A survey of over 4,000 managers in 15 countries indicated that over 85 percent were using benchmarking to measure the efficiency and effectiveness of their internal activities.[3] Since 1990, the number of companies instituting best-practice programs as an integral part of their efforts to improve strategy execution has grown significantly. Scores of trade associations and special interest organizations have undertaken efforts to collect best-practice data relevant to a particular industry or business function and make their databases available online to members. Benchmarking and best-practice implementation have clearly emerged as legitimate and valuable managerial tools for promoting operational excellence.

TQM and Six Sigma Quality Programs: Tools for Promoting Operational Excellence

Best-practice implementation has stimulated greater management awareness of the importance of business process reengineering, total quality management (TQM) programs, Six Sigma quality control techniques, and other continuous improvement methods. Indeed, quality improvement processes of one kind or another have become globally pervasive management tools for implementing strategies keyed to defect-free manufacture, superior product quality, superior customer service, and total customer satisfaction. The following paragraphs describe two specific types of programs and then discuss the difference between process reengineering and continuous improvement.

Total Quality Management Programs   *Total quality management (TQM) is a philosophy of managing a set of business practices that emphasizes continuous improvement in all phases of operations, 100 percent accuracy in performing tasks, involvement and empowerment of employees at all levels, team-based work design, benchmarking, and total customer satisfaction.*[4] While TQM concentrates on the production of quality goods and fully satisfying customer expectations, it achieves its biggest successes when it is also extended to employee efforts in *all departments*—human resources, billing, R&D, engineering, accounting and records, and information systems—that may lack pressing, customer-driven incentives to improve. It involves re-forming the corporate culture and shifting to a total quality/continuous improvement business philosophy that permeates every facet of the organization.[5] TQM aims at instilling enthusiasm and commitment to doing things right from top to bottom of the organization. It entails a restless search for continuing improvement, the little steps forward each day that the Japanese call *kaizen*. TQM is thus a race without a finish. The managerial objective is to kindle a burning desire in people to use their ingenuity and initiative to progressively improve on how tasks and value chain activities are performed. TQM doctrine preaches that there's no such thing as "good enough" and that everyone has a responsibility to participate in continuous improvement.

> **Core Concept**
> TQM entails creating a total quality culture bent on continuously improving the performance of every task and value chain activity.

Six Sigma Quality Control   *Six sigma quality control consists of a disciplined, statistics-based system aimed at producing not more than 3.4 defects per million iterations for any business process—from manufacturing to customer transactions.* The six sigma process of define, measure, analyze, improve, and control (DMAIC) is an improvement system for existing processes falling below specification and needing incremental improvement. The six sigma process of define, measure, analyze, design, and verify (DMADV) is an improvement system used to develop new processes or products at six sigma quality levels. Both six sigma processes are executed by personnel who have earned six sigma "green belts" and six sigma "black belts," and are overseen by personnel who have completed six sigma "master black belt" training. According to the Six Sigma Academy, personnel with black belts can save companies approximately $230,000 per project and can complete four to six projects a year.[6] General Electric (GE), one of the most successful companies implementing six sigma training and pursuing six sigma perfection, estimated benefits on the order of $10 billion during the first five years of implementation. GE first began six sigma in 1995 after Motorola and Allied Signal blazed the six sigma trail. Since the mid-1990s, thousands of companies around the world have discovered the far reaching benefits of six sigma. Consultants proficient in six sigma techniques have developed proprietary methodologies for implementing six sigma quality for clients, using various change management tools and applications.

The Difference between Process Reengineering and Continuous Improvement Programs   Business process reengineering and continuous improvement efforts like TQM and six sigma quality programs both aim at improved efficiency and reduced costs, better product quality, and greater customer satisfaction. The essential difference between business process reengineering and continuous improvement programs is that reengineering aims at *quantum gains* on the order of 30 to 50 percent or more whereas total quality programs stress *incremental progress*, striving for inch-by-inch gains again and again in a never-ending stream. The two approaches to improved performance of value chain activities and operating excellence are not mutually exclusive; it makes sense to use them in tandem. Reengineering can be used first to produce a good basic design that yields dramatic improvements in performing a business process fairly quickly. Total quality programs can then be used as a follow-on to reengineering and/or best-practice implementation, delivering gradual improvements by fine-tuning and honing how particular activities are performed over time. Such a two-pronged approach to implementing operational excellence is like a marathon race in which you run the first four laps as fast as you can, then gradually pick up speed the remainder of the way.

> Business process reengineering aims at one-time quantum improvement; TQM and six sigma aim at ongoing incremental improvements.

Capturing the Benefits of Best-Practice and Continuous Improvement Programs

Research indicates that some companies benefit from reengineering and continuous improvement programs (like TQM and six sigma) and some do not.[7] Usually, the biggest beneficiaries are companies that view such programs not as ends in themselves but as tools for implementing and executing company strategy more effectively. The skimpiest payoffs from best practices, TQM, six sigma, and reengineering occur when company managers seize them as something worth trying—novel ideas that could improve things. In most such instances, they result in strategy-blind efforts to simply manage better. There's an important lesson here. Best practices, TQM, six sigma quality, and reengineering all need to be seen and used as part of a bigger-picture effort to execute strategy proficiently. Only strategy can point to which value chain activities matter and what performance targets make the most sense. Absent a strategic framework, managers lack the context in which to fix things that really matter to business-unit performance and competitive success.

To get the most from programs for facilitating better strategy execution, managers have to start with a clear fix on the indicators of successful strategy execution—what specific outcomes really matter? Examples of such performance indicators include a six sigma defect rate (fewer than 3.4 defects per million), on-time delivery percentages, low overall costs relative to rivals, data indicating high percentages of pleased customers and few customer complaints, shorter cycle times, and a higher percentage of revenues coming from recently introduced products. Benchmarking best-in-industry and best-in-world performance of most or all value chain activities provides a realistic basis for setting internal performance milestones and longer-range targets.

Then comes the managerial task of building a total quality culture and instilling the necessary commitment to achieving the targets and performance measures that the strategy requires. Managers can take the following action steps to realize full value from TQM or six sigma initiatives:[8]

- Visible, unequivocal, and unyielding commitment to total quality and continuous improvement, including a quality vision and specific, measurable objectives for boosting quality and making continuous improvement.

- Nudging people toward TQM-supportive behaviors by:
  - Screening job applicants rigorously and hiring only those with attitudes and aptitudes right for quality-based performance.
  - Providing quality training for most employees.
  - Using teams and team-building exercises to reinforce and nurture individual effort (expansion of a TQM culture is facilitated when teams become more cross-functional, multitask, and increasingly self-managed).
  - Recognizing and rewarding individual and team efforts regularly and systematically.
  - Stressing prevention (doing it right the first time), not inspection (instituting ways to correct mistakes).

- Empowering employees so that authority for delivering great service or improving products is in the hands of the doers rather than the overseers.

- Using online systems to provide all relevant parties with the latest best practices and actual experiences with them, thereby speeding the diffusion and adoption of best practices throughout the organization and also allowing them to exchange data and opinions about how to upgrade the prevailing best practices.

- Preaching that performance can, and must, be improved because competitors are not resting on past laurels and customers are always looking for something better.

If the targeted performance measures are appropriate to the strategy and if all organizational members (top executives, middle managers, professional staff, and line employees) buy into the process of continuous improvement, then the work climate becomes decidedly more conducive to proficient strategy execution.

When used effectively, TQM, six sigma and other similar continuous improvement techniques can greatly enhance a company's product design, cycle time, production cost, product quality, service, customer satisfaction, and other operating capabilities—and it can even deliver competitive advantage.[9] Not only do ongoing incremental improvements add up over time and strengthen organizational capabilities but continuous improvement programs have hard-to-imitate aspects. While it is relatively easy for rivals to undertake benchmarking, process improvement, and quality training, it is much more difficult and time-consuming for them to instill a total quality culture (as occurs when TQM or six sigma techniques are religiously employed) and generate lasting management commitment to operational excellence throughout their organizations. Successfully implementing TQM or six sigma initiatives requires a substantial investment of management time and effort; some managers and employees resist such techniques, viewing them as overly ideological, burdensome, or faddish. Both TQM and six sigma are expensive in terms of training and meetings. TQM takes a fairly long time to show significant results—very little benefit emerges within the first six months. The long-term payoff of TQM, if it comes, depends heavily on management's success in implanting a culture within which TQM philosophies and practices can thrive.

Installing Information and Operating Systems

Company strategies can't be implemented or executed well without a number of internal systems for business operations. Southwest, American, Northwest, Delta, and other major airlines cannot hope to provide passenger-pleasing service without a user-friendly online reservation system, an accurate and expeditious baggage handling system, and a strict aircraft maintenance program that minimizes equipment failures requiring at-the-gate service and delaying plane departures. Federal Express (FedEx) has internal communication systems that allow it to coordinate its nearly 60,000 vehicles in handling an average of 5.2 million packages per day. Its leading-edge flight operations systems allow a single controller to direct as many as 200 of FedEx's 650-plus aircraft simultaneously, overriding their flight plans should weather or other special emergencies arise. In addition, FedEx has created a series of e-business tools for customers that allow them to ship and track packages online (either at FedEx's website or on their own company intranets or websites), create address books, review shipping history, generate custom reports, simplify customer billing, reduce internal warehousing and inventory management costs, purchase goods and services from suppliers, and respond quickly to changing customer demands. All of FedEx's systems support the company's strategy of providing businesses and individuals with a broad array of package delivery services (from premium next-day to economical five-day deliveries) and boosting its competitiveness against United Parcel Service, Airborne Express, and the U.S. Postal Service.

Otis Elevator has a 24-hour centralized communications center called OtisLine to coordinate its maintenance efforts in North America.[10] Trained operators take all trouble calls, input critical information on a computer screen, and dispatch people directly via a beeper system to the local trouble spot. Also, much of the information needed for repairs is provided directly from faulty elevators through internally installed microcomputer monitors, helping keep the outage time on Otis elevators and escalators to less than two and a half hours. From the trouble-call inputs, problem patterns across North America are identified and the information communicated to design and manufacturing personnel, allowing them to quickly alter design specifications or manufacturing procedures when needed to correct recurring problems.

Wal-Mart is generally considered to have the most sophisticated retailing systems of any company in the world. For example, Wal-Mart's computers transmit daily sales data to Wrangler, a supplier of blue jeans; Wrangler then uses a model that interprets the data, and software applications that act on these interpretations, in order to ship specific quantities of specific sizes and colors to specific stores from specific warehouses—the system lowers logistics and inventory costs and leads to fewer stockouts.[11] Domino's Pizza has computerized systems at each outlet to facilitate ordering, inventory, payroll, cash flow, and work control functions, thereby freeing managers to spend more time on supervision, customer service, and business development activities.[12] Most telephone companies, electric utilities, and TV broadcasting systems have online monitoring systems to spot transmission problems within seconds and increase the reliability of their services. At eBay, there are systems for real-time monitoring of new listings, bidding activity, website traffic, and page views. Many companies have cataloged best-practice information on their company intranets to promote faster transfer and implementation organizationwide.[13]

Well-conceived state-of-the-art operating systems not only enable better strategy execution but also strengthen organizational capabilities—perhaps enough to provide a competitive edge over rivals. For example, a company with a differentiation strategy based on superior quality has added capability if it has systems for training personnel in quality techniques, tracking product quality at each production step, and ensuring that all goods shipped meet quality standards. A company striving to be a low-cost provider is competitively stronger if it has a benchmarking system that identifies opportunities to implement best practices and drive costs out of the business. Fast-growing companies get an important assist from having capabilities in place to recruit and train new employees in large

> **Core Concept**
>
> State-of-the-art support systems can be a basis for competitive advantage if they give a firm capabilities that rivals can't match.

numbers and from investing in infrastructure that gives them the capability to handle rapid growth as it occurs. It is nearly always better to put infrastructure and support systems in place before they are actually needed than to have to scramble to catch up to customer demand. In businesses such as public accounting and management consulting, where large numbers of professional staff need cutting-edge technical know-how, companies need well-functioning systems for training and retraining employees regularly and keeping them supplied with up-to-date information. Companies that rely on empowered customer service employees to act promptly and creatively in pleasing customers need state-of-the-art information systems that put essential data in front of employees with a few keystrokes, allowing them to handle inquiries and transactions expeditiously.

Instituting Adequate Information Systems, Performance Tracking, and Controls

Accurate and timely information about daily operations is essential if managers are to gauge how well the strategy execution process is proceeding. Information systems need to cover five broad areas: (1) customer data, (2) operations data, (3) employee data, (4) supplier/partner/collaborative ally data, and (5) financial performance data. All key strategic performance indicators have to be tracked and reported as often as practical. Monthly profit-and-loss statements and monthly statistical summaries, long the norm, are fast being replaced by daily statistical updates and even up-to-the-minute performance monitoring that online technology makes possible. Many retail companies have automated online systems that generate daily sales reports for each store and maintain up-to-the-minute inventory and sales records on each item. Manufacturing plants typically generate daily production reports and track labor productivity on every shift. Many retailers and manufacturers have online data systems connecting them with their suppliers that monitor the status of inventories, track shipments and deliveries, and measure defect rates.

Real-time information systems permit company managers to stay on top of implementation initiatives and daily operations, and to intervene if things seem to be drifting off course. Tracking key performance indicators, gathering information from operating personnel, quickly identifying and diagnosing problems, and taking corrective actions are all integral pieces of the process of managing strategy implementation and execution and exercising adequate organization control. Telephone companies have elaborate information systems to measure signal quality, connection times, interrupts, wrong connections, billing errors, and other measures of reliability that affect customer service and satisfaction. To track and manage the quality of passenger service, airlines have information systems to monitor gate delays, on-time departures and arrivals, baggage handling times, lost baggage complaints, stockouts on meals and drinks, overbookings, and maintenance delays and failures. Virtually all companies now provide customer-contact personnel with computer access to customer databases so that they can respond effectively to customer inquiries and deliver personalized customer service.

Statistical information gives managers a feel for the numbers; briefings and meetings provide a feel for the latest developments and emerging issues; and personal contacts add a feel for the people dimension. All are good barometers. Managers have to identify problem areas and deviations from plan before they can take actions to get the organization back on course, either by improving the approaches to strategy execution or fine-tuning the strategy.

> **Core Concept**
>
> Having good information systems and operating data are integral to the managerial task of executing strategy successfully and achieving greater operating excellence.

Exercising Adequate Controls over Empowered Employees

Another important aspect of effectively managing and controlling the strategy execution process is monitoring the performance of empowered workers to see that they are acting within the specified limits.[14] Leaving empowered employees to their own devices in meeting performance standards without appropriate check and balances can expose an organization to excessive risk.[15] Instances abound where employees' decisions or behavior have gone awry, sometimes costing a company huge sums or producing lawsuits aside from just generating embarrassing publicity.

Managers can't devote big chunks of their time to making sure that the decisions and behavior of empowered employees are between the white lines—this would defeat the major purpose of empowerment and, in effect, lead to the reinstatement of a managerial bureaucracy engaged in constant over-the-shoulders supervision. Yet management has a clear responsibility to exercise sufficient control over empowered employees to protect the company against out-of-bounds behavior and unwelcome surprises. Management scrutiny of daily and weekly operating statistics is one of the important ways to monitor the results that flow from the actions of empowered subordinates—if the operating results flowing from the actions of empowered employees look good, then it is reasonable to assume that empowerment is working.

One of the main purposes of tracking daily operating performance is to relieve managers of the burden of constant over-the-shoulders supervision and give them time for other issues. But managerial control is only part of the answer. Another valuable lever of control in companies that rely on empowered employees, especially in those that use self-managed work groups or other such teams, is peer-based control.[16] The big majority of team members feel responsible for the success of the whole team and tend to be relatively intolerant of any team member's behavior that weakens team performance or puts team accomplishments at risk. Because peer evaluation is such a powerful control device, companies organized into teams can remove some layers of the management hierarchy. This is especially true when a company has the information systems capability to closely monitor team performance.

Tying Rewards and Incentives Directly to Good Strategy Execution

It is important for both organization subunits and individuals to be enthusiastically committed to executing strategy and achieving performance targets. Company managers typically use an assortment of motivational techniques and rewards to enlist organizationwide commitment to executing the strategic plan. A manager has to do more than just talk to everyone about how important new strategic practices and performance targets are to the organization's well-being. No matter how inspiring, talk seldom commands people's best efforts for long. *To get employees' sustained, energetic commitment, management has to be resourceful in designing and using motivational incentives—both monetary and nonmonetary.* The more a manager understands what motivates subordinates and the more he or she relies on motivational incentives as a tool for achieving the targeted strategic and financial results, the greater will be employees' commitment to good day-in, day-out execution of the company's strategic plan.

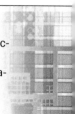

Core Concept

A properly designed reward structure is management's most powerful tool for mobilizing organizational commitment to successful strategy execution.

Strategy-Facilitating Motivational Practices

Financial incentives generally head the list of motivating tools for trying to gain wholehearted employee commitment to good strategy execution and operating excellence. Monetary rewards generally include some combination of base pay increases, performance bonuses, profit sharing plans, stock options, company contributions to employee 401(k) or retirement plans, and piecework incentives (in the case of production workers). But successful companies and managers normally make extensive use of such nonmonetary carrot-and-stick incentives as frequent words of praise (or constructive criticism), special recognition at company gatherings or in the company newsletter, more (or less) job security, stimulating assignments, opportunities to transfer to attractive locations, increased (or decreased) autonomy, and rapid promotion (or the risk of being sidelined in a routine or dead-end job). In addition, companies use a host of other motivational approaches to spur stronger employee commitment to the strategy execution process; the following are some of the most important:[17]

Core Concept

One of management's biggest strategy-executing challenges is to employ motivational techniques that build wholehearted commitment to operating excellence and winning attitudes among employees.

- *Providing attractive perks and fringe benefits*—The various options here include full coverage of health insurance premiums; full tuition reimbursement for work on college degrees; paid vacation time of three or four weeks; on-site child care at major facilities; on-site gym facilities and massage therapists; getaway opportunities at company-owned recreational facilities (beach houses, ranches, resort condos); personal concierge services; subsidized cafeterias and free lunches; casual dress every day; personal travel services; paid sabbaticals; maternity leaves; paid leaves to care for ill family members; telecommuting; compressed workweeks (four 10-hour days instead of five 8-hour days); reduced summer hours; college scholarships for children; on-the-spot bonuses for exceptional performance; and relocation services.

- *Relying on promotion from within whenever possible*—This practice helps bind workers to their employer and employers to their workers; plus, it is an incentive for good performance. Promotion from within also helps ensure that people in positions of responsibility actually know something about the business, technology, and operations they are managing.

- *Making sure that the ideas and suggestions of employees are valued and respected*—Research indicates that the moves of many companies to push decision making down the line and empower employees increases employee motivation and satisfaction, as well as boosting their productivity. The use of self-managed teams has much the same effect.

- *Creating a work atmosphere where there is genuine sincerity, caring, and mutual respect among workers and between management and employees*—A "family" work environment where people are on a first-name basis and there is strong camaraderie promotes teamwork and cross-unit collaboration.

- *Stating the strategic vision in inspirational terms that make employees feel they are a part of doing something very worthwhile in a larger social sense*—There's strong motivating power associated with giving people a chance to be part of something exciting and personally satisfying. Jobs with noble purpose tend to turn employees on. At Medtronic, Merck, and most other pharmaceutical companies, it is the notion of helping sick people get well and restoring patients to full life. At Whole Foods Market (a natural foods grocery chain), it is helping customers discover good eating habits and thus improving human health and nutrition.

- *Sharing information with employees about financial performance, strategy, operational measures, market conditions, and competitors' actions*—Broad disclosure and prompt communication send the message that managers trust their workers. Keeping employees in the dark denies them information useful to performing their job, prevents them from being "students of the business," and usually turns them off.

- *Having knockout facilities*—An impressive corporate facility for employees to work in usually has decidedly positive effects on morale and productivity.

- *Being flexible in how the company approaches people management (motivation, compensation, recognition, recruitment) in multinational, multicultural environments*—Managers and employees in countries whose customs, habits, values, and business practices vary from those at the home office often become frustrated with insistence on consistent people-management practices worldwide. But the one area where consistency is essential is conveying the message that the organization values people of all races and cultural backgrounds and that discrimination of any sort will not be tolerated.

For specific examples of the motivational tactics employed by several prominent companies, see Company Spotlight 8.2.

Striking the Right Balance between Rewards and Punishment   While most approaches to motivation, compensation, and people management accentuate the positive, companies also embellish positive rewards with the risk of punishment. At General Electric, McKinsey & Company, several global public accounting firms, and other companies that look for and expect top-notch individual performance, there's an "up-or-out" policy—managers and professionals whose performance is not good enough to warrant promotion are first denied bonuses and stock options and eventually weeded out. A number of companies deliberately give employees heavy workloads and tight deadlines—personnel are pushed hard to achieve "stretch" objectives and expected to put in long hours (nights and weekends if need be). At most companies, senior executives and key personnel in underperforming units are under the gun to boost performance to acceptable levels and keep it there or risk being replaced.

As a general rule, it is unwise to take off the pressure for good individual and group performance or play down the stress, anxiety, and adverse consequences of shortfalls in performance. There is no evidence that a no-pressure/no-adverse-consequences work environment leads to superior strategy execution or operating excellence. As the CEO of a major bank put it, "There's a deliberate policy here to create a level of anxiety. Winners usually play like they're one touchdown behind."[18] *High-performing organizations nearly always have a cadre of ambitious people who relish the opportunity to climb the ladder of success, love a challenge, thrive in a performance-oriented environment, and find some competition and pressure useful to satisfy their own drives for personal recognition, accomplishment, and self-satisfaction.*

However, if an organization's motivational approaches and reward structure induce too much stress, internal competitiveness, job insecurity, and unpleasant consequences, the impact on workforce morale and strategy execution can be counterproductive. Evidence shows that managerial initiatives to improve strategy execution should incorporate more positive than negative motivational elements because when cooperation is positively enlisted and rewarded, rather than strong-armed by orders and threats (implicit or explicit), people tend to respond with more enthusiasm, dedication, creativity, and initiative. Something of a middle ground is generally optimal—not only handing out decidedly positive rewards for meeting or beating performance targets but also imposing sufficiently negative consequences (if only withholding rewards) when actual performance falls short of the target. But the negative consequences of underachievement should never be so severe or demoralizing as to impede a renewed and determined effort to overcome existing obstacles and hit the targets in upcoming periods.

Linking the Reward System to Strategically Relevant Performance Outcomes

The most dependable way to keep people focused on strategy execution and the achievement of performance targets is to *generously* reward and recognize individuals and groups who meet or beat performance targets and deny rewards and recognition to those who don't. *The use of incentives and rewards is the single most powerful tool management has to win strong employee commitment to diligent, competent strategy execution and operating excellence.* Decisions on salary increases, incentive compensation, promotions, key assignments, and the ways and means of awarding praise and recognition are potent attention-getting, commitment-generating devices. Such decisions seldom escape the closest employee scrutiny, saying more about what is expected and who is considered to be doing a good job than any other factor. Hence, when achievement of the targeted strategic and financial outcomes become *the dominating basis* for designing incentives, evaluating individual and group efforts, and handing out rewards, company personnel quickly grasp that it is in their own self-interest to do their best in executing the strategy competently and achieving key performance targets.[19] Indeed, it is usually through the company's system of incentives and rewards that workforce members emotionally ratify their commitment to the company's strategy execution effort.

> **Core Concept**
>
> A properly designed reward system aligns the well-being of organization members with their contributions to competent strategy execution and the achievement of performance targets.

Strategy-driven performance targets need to be established for every organization unit, every manager, every team or work group, and perhaps every employee—targets that measure whether strategy execution is progressing satisfactorily. If the company's strategy is to be a low-cost provider, the incentive system must reward actions and achievements that result in lower costs. If the company has a differentiation strategy predicated on superior quality and service, the incentive system must reward such outcomes as six sigma defect rates, infrequent need for product repair, low numbers of customer complaints, and speedy order processing and delivery. If a company's growth

COMPANY SPOTLIGHT 8.2

Companies with Effective Motivation and Reward Techniques

Companies have come up with a variety of motivational and reward practices to help create a work environment that facilitates better strategy execution. Here's a glimpse of what some companies believe are best practices:

■ Several Japanese automobile producers, believing that providing employment security is a valuable contributor to worker productivity and company loyalty, elect not to lay off factory workers when business slacks off for a period but instead put them out in the field to sell vehicles. On one occasion when Mazda experienced a sales downturn and shifted unneeded factory workers to selling its models door-to-door (a common practice in Japan), its top 10 salespeople turned out to be factory workers, partly because they were able to explain the product effectively; when business picked up and the factory workers returned to the plant, their experiences in talking to customers yielded useful ideas in improving the features and styling of Mazda's product line. Southwest Airlines, FedEx, Lands' End, and Harley-Davidson (all companies that have been listed among the 100 best com-

panies to work for in America) have also instituted no-layoff policies and use employment security as both a positive motivator and a means of reinforcing good strategy execution. Top management at Southwest Airlines believes that its no-layoff policy keeps workers from fearing that by boosting their productivity they will work themselves out of their jobs.

■ Procter & Gamble, Merck, Charles Schwab, General Mills, Amgen, Tellabs, and Eli Lilly provide stock options to all employees. Having employee-owners who share in a company's success (or failure) via stock ownership is widely viewed as a way to bolster employee commitment to good strategy execution and operational excellence.

■ Nordstrom typically pays its retail salespeople an hourly wage higher than the prevailing rates paid by other department store chains; plus, it pays them a commission on each sale. Spurred by a culture that encourages salespeople to go all-out to satisfy customers, to exercise their own best judgment, and to seek out and promote new fashion ideas, Nordstrom salespeople often earn

is predicated on a strategy of new product innovation, incentives should be tied to factors such as the percentages of revenues and profits coming from newly introduced products.

Company Spotlight 8.3 provides two vivid examples of how companies have designed incentives linked directly to outcomes reflecting good strategy execution.

The Importance of Basing Incentives on Achieving Results, Not on Performing Assigned Functions To create a strategy-supportive system of rewards and incentives, a company must emphasize rewarding people for accomplishing results, not for just dutifully performing assigned functions. Focusing jobholders' attention and energy on what to *achieve* as opposed to what to *do* makes the work environment results-oriented. It is flawed management to tie incentives and rewards to satisfactory performance of duties and activities in hopes that the by-products will be the desired business outcomes and company achievements.[20] In any job, performing assigned tasks is not equivalent to achieving intended outcomes. Diligently attending to assigned duties does not, by itself, guarantee results. (As any student knows, just because an instructor teaches and students go to class doesn't mean students are learning. Teaching and going to class are activities, and learning is a result. The enterprise of education would no doubt take on a different character if teachers were rewarded for the result of student learning rather than the activity of teaching.)

> It is folly to reward one outcome in hopes of getting another outcome.

twice the average incomes of sales employees at competing stores. Nordstrom's rules for employees are simple: "Rule #1: Use your good judgment in all situations. There will be no additional rules." Nordstrom is widely regarded for its superior in-house customer service experience.

- Cisco Systems offers on-the-spot bonuses of up to $2,000 for exceptional performance; Kimberly-Clark spends about $6 million annually on events to celebrate employee successes; and FedEx gives out awards to employees whose job performance is above and beyond expectations (in 2001 the company spent over $13 million on such awards).

- Lincoln Electric, a company deservedly famous for its piecework pay scheme and incentive bonus plan, rewards individual productivity by paying workers for each nondefective piece produced. Workers have to correct quality problems on their own time—defects in products used by customers can be traced back to the worker who caused them. Lincoln's piecework plan motivates workers to pay attention to both quality and volume produced. In addition, the company sets aside a substantial portion of its profits above a specified base for worker bonuses. To determine bonus size, Lincoln Electric rates each worker on four equally important performance measures: dependability, quality, output, and ideas and cooperation. The higher a worker's merit rating, the higher the incentive bonus earned; the highest rated workers in good profit years receive bonuses of as much as 110 percent of their piecework compensation.

- Monsanto, FedEx, AT&T, Whole Foods Markets, Advanced Micro Devices, and W. L. Gore & Associates (the maker of Gore-Tex) have tapped into the motivational power of self-managed teams, recognizing that team members put considerable peer pressure on coworkers to pull their weight and help achieve team goals and expectations. At W. L. Gore (a regular member on annual listings of the 100 best companies to work for), each team member's compensation is based on other team members' rankings of his or her contribution to the enterprise.

- GE Medical Systems has a program called Quick Thanks!, in which an employee can nominate any colleague to receive a $25 gift certificate in appreciation of a job well done. Employees often hand out the award personally to deserving coworkers. In one 12-month period, over 10,000 Quick Thanks! awards were presented.

Sources: Jeffrey Pfeffer and John F. Veiga, "Putting People First for Organizational Success," *Academy of Management Executive* 13, no. 2 (May 1999), pp. 40–42; *Fortune*'s lists of the 100 best companies to work for in America—see the January 12, 1998; January 10, 2000, and February 4, 2002, issues; Jeffrey Pfeffer, "Producing Sustainable Competitive Advantage through the Effective Management of People," *Academy of Management Executive* 9, no. 1 (February 1995), pp. 59–60; and Steven Kerr, "Risky Business: The New Pay Game," *Fortune*, July 22, 1996, p. 95.

Incentive compensation for top executives is typically tied to company profitability (earnings growth, return on equity investment, return on total assets, economic value added); the company's stock price performance; and perhaps such measures as market share, product quality, or customer satisfaction. However, incentives for department heads, teams, and individual workers may be tied to performance outcomes more closely related to their strategic area of responsibility. In manufacturing, incentive compensation may be tied to unit manufacturing costs, on-time production and shipping, defect rates, the number and extent of work stoppages due to labor disagreements and equipment breakdowns, and so on. In sales and marketing, there may be incentives for achieving dollar sales or unit volume targets, market share, sales penetration of each target customer group, the fate of newly introduced products, the frequency of customer complaints, the number of new accounts acquired, and customer satisfaction. Which performance measures to base incentive compensation on depends on the situation—the priority placed on various financial and strategic objectives, the requirements for strategic and competitive success, and what specific results are needed in different facets of the business to keep strategy execution on track.

> **Core Concept**
>
> The role of the reward system is to align the well-being of organization members with realizing the company's vision, so that organization members benefit by helping the company execute its strategy competently and fully satisfy customers.

Guidelines for Designing Incentive Compensation Systems

The concepts and company experiences discussed above yield the following prescriptive

Nucor and Bank One: Two Companies That Tie Incentives Directly to Strategy Execution

The strategy at Nucor Corporation, now the biggest steel producer in the United States, is to be *the* low-cost producer of steel products. Because labor costs are a significant fraction of total cost in the steel business, successful implementation of Nucor's low-cost leadership strategy entails achieving lower labor costs per ton of steel than competitors' costs. Nucor management uses an incentive system to promote high worker productivity and drive labor costs per ton below rivals'. Each plant's workforce is organized into production teams (each assigned to perform particular functions), and weekly production targets are established for each team. Base pay scales are set at levels comparable to wages for similar manufacturing jobs in the local areas where Nucor has plants, but workers can earn a 1 percent bonus for each 1 percent that their output exceeds target levels. If a production team exceeds its weekly production target by 10 percent, team members receive a 10 percent bonus in their next paycheck; if a team exceeds its quota by 20 percent, team members earn a 20 percent bonus. Bonuses, paid every two weeks, are based on the prior two weeks' actual production levels measured against the targets.

Nucor's piece-rate incentive plan has resulted in labor productivity levels 10 to 20 percent above the average of the unionized workforces of large, integrated steel producers like U.S. Steel and Bethlehem Steel, given Nucor a cost advantage over most rivals, and made Nucor workers among the best-paid in the U.S. steel industry.

At Bank One (one of the 10 largest U.S. banks and also one of the most profitable based on return on assets), operating in a manner that produces consistently high levels of customer satisfaction makes a big competitive difference in how well the company fares against rivals; customer satisfaction ranks high on Bank One's list of strategic priorities. To enhance employee commitment to the task of pleasing customers, Bank One ties the pay scales in each branch office to that branch's customer satisfaction rating—the higher the branch's ratings, the higher that branch's pay scales. By shifting from a theme of equal pay for equal work to one of equal pay for equal performance, Bank One has focused the attention of branch employees on the task of pleasing, even delighting, their customers.

---

guidelines for creating an incentive compensation system to help drive successful strategy execution:

1. *The performance payoff must be a major, not minor, piece of the total compensation package.* Payoffs must be at least 10 to 12 percent of base salary to have much impact. Incentives that amount to 20 percent or more of total compensation are big attention-getters, likely to really drive individual or team effort; incentives amounting to less than 5 percent of total compensation have comparatively weak motivational impact. Moreover, the payoff for high-performing individuals and teams must be meaningfully greater than the payoff for average performers, and the payoff for average performers meaningfully bigger than for below-average performers.

2. *The incentive plan should extend to all managers and all workers, not just top management.* It is a gross miscalculation to expect that lower-level managers and employees will work their hardest to hit performance targets just so a few senior executives can get lucrative rewards.

3. *The reward system must be administered with scrupulous care and fairness.* If performance standards are set unrealistically high or if individual/group performance evaluations are not accurate and well documented, dissatisfaction with the system will overcome any positive benefits.

4. *The incentives should be based only on achieving performance targets spelled out in the strategic plan.* Incentives should not be linked to outcomes that get thrown in because they are thought to be nice. Performance evaluation based on factors not

tightly related to good strategy execution signal that either the strategic plan is incomplete (because important performance targets were left out) or management's real agenda is something other than the stated strategic and financial objectives.

5. *The performance targets each individual is expected to achieve should involve outcomes that the individual can personally affect.* The role of incentives is to enhance individual commitment and channel behavior in beneficial directions. This role is not well served when the performance measures by which an individual is judged are outside his or her arena of influence.

6. *Keep the time between the performance review and payment of the reward short.* A lengthy interval between review and payment breeds discontent and works against reinforcing cause and effect. Companies like Nucor and Continental Airlines have discovered that weekly or monthly payments for good performance work much better than annual payments. Nucor pays weekly bonuses based on prior-week production levels; Continental awards employees a monthly bonus for each month that on-time flight performance meets or beats a specified percentage companywide.

7. *Make liberal use of nonmonetary rewards; don't rely solely on monetary rewards.* When used properly, money is a great motivator, but there are also potent advantages to be gained from praise, special recognition, handing out plum assignments, and so on.

8. *Absolutely avoid skirting the system to find ways to reward effort rather than results.* Whenever actual performance falls short of targeted performance, there's merit in determining whether the causes are attributable to subpar individual/group performance or to circumstances beyond the control of those responsible. An argument can be made that exceptions should be made in giving rewards to people who've tried hard, gone the extra mile, yet still come up short because of circumstances beyond their control. The problem with making exceptions for unknowable, uncontrollable, or unforeseeable circumstances is that once good excuses start to creep into justifying rewards for subpar results, the door is open for all kinds of reasons why actual performance failed to match targeted performance. By and large, a "no excuses" standard is more evenhanded and certainly easier to administer.

Once the incentives are designed, they have to be communicated and explained. Everybody needs to understand how their incentive compensation is calculated and how individual/group performance targets contribute to organizational performance targets. The pressure to achieve the targeted strategic and financial performance and continuously improve on strategy execution should be unrelenting, with few (if any) loopholes for rewarding shortfalls in performance. People at all levels have to be held accountable for carrying out their assigned parts of the strategic plan, and they have to understand their rewards are based on the caliber of results that are achieved. But with the pressure to perform should come meaningful rewards. Without an ample payoff, the system breaks down, and managers are left with the less workable options of barking orders, trying to enforce compliance, and depending on the good will of employees.

Core Concept

The unwavering standard for judging whether individuals, teams, and organizational units have done a good job must be whether they achieve performance targets consistent with effective strategy execution.

Performance-Based Incentives and Rewards in Multinational Enterprises In some foreign countries, incentive pay runs counter to local customs and cultural norms. Professor Steven Kerr cites the time he lectured an executive education class on the need for more performance-based pay and a Japanese manager protested, "You shouldn't bribe your children to do their homework, you shouldn't bribe your wife to prepare dinner, and you shouldn't bribe your employees to work for the company."[21] Singling out individuals and commending them for unusually good effort can also be a problem; Japanese culture considers public praise of an individual an affront to the harmony of the group. In some countries, employees have a preference for nonmonetary rewards—more leisure time, important titles, access to vacation villages, and nontaxable perks. Thus, multinational companies have to build some degree of flexibility into the design of incentives and rewards in order to accommodate cross-cultural traditions and preferences.

Key Points

Managers implementing and executing a new or different strategy must identify the resource requirements of each new strategic initiative and then consider whether the current pattern of resource allocation and the budgets of the various subunits are suitable. Every organization unit needs to have the people, equipment, facilities, and other resources to carry out its part of the strategic plan (but no more than what it really needs). Implementing a new strategy often entails shifting resources from one area to another—downsizing units that are overstaffed and overfunded, upsizing those more critical to strategic success, and killing projects and activities that are no longer justified.

Anytime a company alters its strategy, managers should review existing policies and operating procedures, proactively revise or discard those that are out of sync, and formulate new ones to facilitate execution of new strategic initiatives. Prescribing new or freshly revised policies and operating procedures aids the task of strategy execution (1) by providing top-down guidance to operating managers, supervisory personnel, and employees regarding how certain things need to be done and what the boundaries are on independent actions and decisions; (2) by enforcing consistency in how particular strategy-critical activities are performed in geographically scattered operating units; and (3) by promoting the creation of a work climate and corporate culture that promotes good strategy execution. Thick policy manuals are usually unnecessary. Indeed, when individual creativity and initiative are more essential to good execution than standardization and conformity, it is better to give people the freedom to do things however they see fit and hold them accountable for good results rather than try to control their behavior with policies and guidelines for every situation.

Competent strategy execution entails visible, unyielding managerial commitment to best practices and continuous improvement. Benchmarking, the discovery and adoption of best practices, reengineering core business processes, and continuous improvement initiatives like total quality management (TQM) or six sigma programs, all aim at improved efficiency, lower costs, better product quality, and greater customer satisfaction. *These initiatives are important tools for learning how to execute a strategy more proficiently.* Benchmarking, part of the process of discovering best practices, provides a realistic basis for setting performance targets. Instituting "best-in-industry" or "best-in-world" operating practices in most or all value chain activities provide a means for taking strategy execution to a higher plateau of competence and nurturing a high-performance work environment. Business process reengineering is a way to make quantum progress toward becoming a world-class organization, while TQM and six sigma programs instill a commitment to continuous improvement and operating excellence. An organization bent on continuous improvement is a valuable competitive asset—one that, over time, can yield important competitive capabilities (in reducing costs, speeding new products to market, or improving product quality, service, or customer satisfaction) and be a source of competitive advantage.

Company strategies can't be implemented or executed well without a number of support systems to carry on business operations. Well-conceived state-of-the-art support systems cannot only facilitate better strategy execution but also strengthen organizational capabilities enough to provide a competitive edge over rivals. In the age of the Internet, real-time information and control systems, growing use of e-commerce technologies and business practices, company intranets, and wireless communications capabilities, companies can't hope to outexecute their competitors without cutting-edge information systems and technologically sophisticated operating capabilities that enable fast, efficient, and effective organization action.

Strategy-supportive motivational practices and reward systems are powerful management tools for gaining employee commitment. The key to creating a reward system that promotes good strategy execution is to make strategically relevant measures of performance *the dominating basis* for designing incentives, evaluating individual and group efforts, and handing out rewards. Positive motivational practices generally work better than negative ones, but there is a place for both. There's also a place for both monetary and nonmonetary incentives.

For an incentive compensation system to work well (1) the monetary payoff should be a major percentage of the compensation package, (2) the use of incentives should extend to all managers and workers, (3) the system should be administered with care and fairness, (4) the incentives should be linked to performance targets spelled out in the strategic plan, (5) each individual's performance targets should involve outcomes the person can personally affect, (6) rewards should promptly follow the determination of good performance, (7) monetary rewards should be supplemented with liberal use of nonmonetary rewards, and (8) skirting the system to reward nonperformers or subpar results should be scrupulously avoided.

Exercises

1. Go to www.google.com and, using the advanced search feature, enter "best practices." Browse through the search results to identify at least five organizations that have gathered a set of best practices and are making the best practices library they have assembled available to members. Explore at least one of the sites to get an idea of the kind of best practice information that is available.

2. Using the Internet search engine at www.google.com, do a search on "six sigma" quality programs. Browse through the search results and (*a*) identify several companies that offer six sigma training and (*b*) find lists of companies that have implemented six sigma programs in their pursuit of operational excellence. In particular, you should go to www.isixsigma.com and explore the Six Sigma Q&A menu option.

3. Using the Internet search engine at www.google.com, do a search on "total quality management." Browse through the search results and (*a*) identify companies that offer TQM training, (*b*) identify some books on TQM programs, and (*c*) find lists of companies that have implemented TQM programs in their pursuit of operational excellence.

4. Consult the latest issue of *Fortune* containing the annual "100 Best Companies to Work For" (usually a late-January or early-February issue) and identify at least 5 (preferably 10) compensation incentives that these companies use to enhance employee motivation and reward them for good strategic and financial performance.

CHAPTER 9

Corporate Culture and Leadership

An organization's capacity to execute its strategy depends on its "hard" infrastructure—its organizational structure and systems—and on its "soft" infrastructure—its culture and norms.
—Amar Bhide

Weak leadership can wreck the soundest strategy; forceful execution of even a poor plan can often bring victory.
—Sun Zi

Leadership is accomplishing something through other people that wouldn't have happened if you weren't there . . . Leadership is being able to mobilize ideas and values that energize other people . . . Leaders develop a story line that engages other people.
—Noel Tichy

The biggest levers you've got to change a company are strategy, structure, and culture. If I could pick two, I'd pick strategy and culture.
—Wayne Leonard, CEO, Entergy

In the previous two chapters we examined six of the managerial tasks that are important to good strategy execution and operating excellence—building a capable organization, marshaling the needed resources and steering them to strategy-critical operating units, establishing policies and procedures that facilitate good strategy execution, adopting best practices and pushing for continuous improvement in how value chain activities are performed, creating internal operating systems that enable better execution, and employing motivational practices and compensation incentives that gain wholehearted employee commitment to the strategy execution process. In this chapter we explore the two remaining managerial tasks that shape the outcome of efforts to execute a company's strategy: creating a strategy-supportive corporate culture and exerting the internal leadership needed to drive the implementation of strategic initiatives forward and achieve higher plateaus of operating excellence.

Building a Corporate Culture That Promotes Good Strategy Execution

Every company has its own unique culture. The character of a company's culture or work climate is a product of the core values and business principles that executives espouse, the standards of what is ethically acceptable and what is not, the behaviors that define "how we do things around here", and the stories that get told over and over to illustrate and reinforce the company's values and business practices, approach to people management, and internal politics. The meshing together of stated beliefs, business principles, style of operating, ingrained behaviors and attitudes, and work climate define a company's **corporate culture.**

> **Core Concept**
>
> **Corporate culture** refers to the character of a company's internal work climate and personality—as shaped by its core values, beliefs, business principles, traditions, ingrained behaviors, and style of operating.

The cultures of different companies vary widely. For instance, the bedrock of Wal-Mart's culture is dedication to customer satisfaction, zealous pursuit of low costs and frugal operating practices, a strong work ethic, ritualistic Saturday-morning headquarters meetings to exchange ideas and review problems, and company executives' commitment to visiting stores, listening to customers, and soliciting suggestions from employees. At Nordstrom, the corporate culture is centered on delivering exceptional service to customers; the company's motto is "Respond to unreasonable customer requests"—each out-of-the-ordinary request is seen as an opportunity for a "heroic" act by an employee that can further the company's reputation for a customer-pleasing shopping environment. Nordstrom makes a point of promoting employees noted for their heroic acts and dedication to outstanding service; the company motivates its salespeople with a commission-based compensation system that enables Nordstrom's best salespeople to earn more than double what other department stores pay. General Electric's culture is founded on a hard-driving, results-oriented atmosphere (where all of the company's business divisions are held to a standard of being number one or two in their industries as well as achieving good business results); extensive cross-business sharing of ideas, best practices, and learning; the reliance on "workout sessions" to identify, debate, and resolve burning issues; a commitment to six sigma quality; and globalization of the company. At Microsoft, there are stories of the long hours programmers put in,

The Culture at Alberto-Culver

The Alberto-Culver Company, with 2002 revenues of about $2.7 billion and over 13,000 employees worldwide, is the producer and marketer of Alberto VO5 hair care products; St. Ives skin care, hair care, and facial care products; and such brands as Molly McButter, Mrs. Dash, Consort, Just for Me, TRE-Semmé, and Static Guard. Alberto-Culver brands are sold in 120 countries. The company's Sally Beauty Company has 2,700 stores in five countries and is the world's largest distributor of professional salon products.

At the careers section of its website, the company described its culture in the following words:

> Building careers is as important to us at Alberto-Culver as building brands. We believe in a values-based workplace. We believe in the importance of families and a life/family balance. We believe in in-your-face-honesty without the taint of corporate politics. There's no talk behind your back. If there are issues you'll know, face-to-face. We believe the best ideas make their way—quickly—up an organization, not down. We believe that we should take advantage of every ounce of your talent, not just assign you to a box. We believe in celebrating our victories. We believe in open communication. We believe you can improve what you measure, so we survey and spot check all the time. For that same reason, everyone has specific goals so that their expectations are in line with their managers and the company. We believe that victory is a team accomplishment. We believe in personal development. We believe if you talk with us, you will catch our enthusiasm and want to be part of us.

Source: Alberto-Culver website, December 2, 2002.

the emotional peaks and valleys in encountering and overcoming coding problems, the exhilaration of completing a complex program on schedule, the satisfaction of working on cutting-edge projects, the rewards of being part of a team responsible for a popular new software program, and the tradition of competing aggressively. Enron's collapse in 2001 was partly the product of a flawed corporate culture—one based on the positives of product innovation, aggressive risk-taking, and a driving ambition to lead global change in the energy business but also on the negatives of arrogance, ego, greed, deliberately obscure accounting practices, and an "ends-justify-the-means" mentality in pursuing stretch revenue and profitability targets. In the end, Enron came unglued because a few top executives chose unethical and illegal paths to pursue corporate revenue and profitability targets—in a company that publicly preached integrity and other notable corporate values but was lax in making sure that key executives walked the talk.

Company Spotlight 9.1 presents Alberto-Culver's description of its corporate culture.

What to Look for in Identifying a Company's Corporate Culture

The taproot of corporate culture is the organization's beliefs and philosophy about how its affairs ought to be conducted—the reasons why it does things the way it does. A company's culture is manifested in the values and business principles that management preaches and practices, in official policies and procedures, in its revered traditions and oft-repeated stories, in the attitudes and behaviors of employees, in the peer pressures that exist to display core values, in the organization's politics, in its approaches to people management and problem solving, in its relationships with external stakeholders (particularly vendors and the communities in which it operates), and in the "chemistry" and the "personality" that permeates its work environment. Some of these sociological forces are readily apparent, and others operate quite subtly.

The values, beliefs, and practices that undergird a company's culture can come from anywhere in the organization hierarchy, sometimes representing the philosophy of an influential executive and sometimes resulting from exemplary actions on the part of a specific employee, work group, department, or division.[1] Very often, key elements of the culture originate with a founder or certain strong leaders who articulated them as a set of business principles, company policies, or ways of dealing with employees, customers, vendors, shareholders, and the communities in which it operated. Over time, these cultural underpinnings take root, become embedded in how the company conducts its business, come to be accepted and shared by company managers and employees, and then persist as new employees are encouraged to adopt and follow the professed values and practices.

The Role of Stories Frequently, a significant part of a company's culture is captured in the stories that get told over and over again to illustrate to newcomers the importance of certain values and the depth of commitment that various company personnel have displayed. One of the folktales at FedEx, world renowned for the reliability of its next-day package delivery guarantee, is about a deliveryman who had been given the wrong key to a FedEx drop box. Rather than leave the packages in the drop box until the next day when the right key was available, the deliveryman unbolted the drop box from its base, loaded it into the truck, and took it back to the station. There, the box was pried open and the contents removed and sped on their way to their destination the next day. Nordstrom keeps a scrapbook commemorating the heroic acts of its employees and uses it as a regular reminder of the above-and-beyond-the-call-of-duty behaviors that employees are encouraged to display. At Frito-Lay, there are dozens of stories about truck drivers who went to extraordinary lengths in overcoming adverse weather conditions in order to make scheduled deliveries to retail customers and keep store shelves stocked with Frito-Lay products. Such stories serve the valuable purpose of illustrating the kinds of behavior the company encourages and reveres. Moreover, each retelling of a legendary story puts a bit more peer pressure on company personnel to go an extra step when the opportunity presents itself and do their part in making company traditions live on and to display core values.

Perpetuating the Culture Once established, company cultures are perpetuated in six important ways: (1) by screening and selecting new employees that will mesh well with the culture, (2) by systematic indoctrination of new members in the culture's fundamentals, (3) by the efforts of senior group members to reiterate core values in daily conversations and pronouncements, (4) by the telling and retelling of company legends, (5) by regular ceremonies honoring members who display desired cultural behaviors, and (6) by visibly rewarding those who display cultural norms and penalizing those who don't.[2] The more that new employees are being brought into the organization the more important it becomes to screen job applicants every bit as much for how well their values, beliefs, and personalities match up with the culture as for their technical skills and experience. For example, a company that stresses operating with integrity and fairness has to hire people who themselves have integrity and place a high value on fair play. A company whose culture revolves around creativity, product innovation, and leading change has to screen new hires for their ability to think outside the box, generate new ideas, and thrive in a climate of rapid change and ambiguity. Southwest Airlines, whose two core values "LUV" and fun permeate the work environment and whose objective is to ensure that passengers have a positive and enjoyable flying experience, goes to considerable lengths to hire flight attendants and gate personnel who are witty, cheery, and outgoing and who display "whistle while you work" attitudes. Fast-growing companies risk creating a culture by chance rather than by design if they rush to hire employees mainly for their talents and credentials and neglect to screen out candidates whose values, philosophies, and personalities aren't a good fit with the organizational character, vision, and strategy being articulated by the company's senior executives.

As a rule, companies are attentive to the task of hiring people who will fit in and who will embrace the prevailing culture. And, usually, job seekers lean toward accepting jobs at companies where they feel comfortable with the atmosphere and the people they will be working with. Employees who don't hit it off at a company tend to leave quickly, while employees who thrive and are pleased with the work environment stay on, eventually moving up the ranks to positions of greater responsibility. The longer people stay at an organization, the more that they come to embrace and mirror the corporate culture—their values and beliefs tend to be molded by mentors, fellow workers, company training programs, and the reward structure. Normally, employees who have worked at a company for a long time play a major role in indoctrinating new employees into the culture.

Forces That Cause a Company's Culture to Evolve   However, even stable cultures aren't static—just like strategy and organization structure, they evolve. New challenges in the marketplace, revolutionary technologies, and shifting internal conditions—especially eroding business prospects, an internal crisis, or top executive turnover—tend to breed new ways of doing things and, in turn, cultural evolution. An incoming CEO who decides to shake up the existing business and take it in new directions often triggers a cultural shift, perhaps one of major proportions. Likewise, diversification into new businesses, expansion into foreign countries, rapid growth, an influx of new employees, and merger with or acquisition of another company can all precipitate cultural changes of one kind or another.

Company Subcultures: The Problems Posed by New Acquisitions and Multinational Operations   Although it is common to speak about corporate culture in the singular, companies typically have multiple cultures (or subcultures).[3] Values, beliefs, and practices within a company sometimes vary significantly by department, geographic location, division, or business unit. A company's subcultures can clash, or at least not mesh well, if they embrace conflicting business philosophies or operating approaches, or if key executives employ different approaches to people management or if important differences between a company's culture and those of recently acquired companies have not yet been ironed out. *Global and multinational companies tend to be at least partly multicultural* because cross-country organization units have different operating histories and work climates, as well as members who have grown up under different social customs and traditions and who have different sets of values and beliefs. The human resources manager of a global pharmaceutical company who took on an assignment in the Far East discovered, to his surprise, that one of his biggest challenges was to persuade his company's managers in China, Korea, Malaysia, and Taiwan to accept promotions—their cultural values were such that they did not believe in competing with their peers for career rewards or personal gain, nor did they relish breaking ties to their local communities to assume cross-national responsibilities.[4] Many companies that have merged with or acquired foreign companies have to deal with language- and custom-based cultural differences.

Nonetheless, the existence of subcultures does not preclude important areas of commonality and compatibility. For example, General Electric's cultural traits of boundarylessness, workout, and six sigma quality can be implanted and practiced successfully in different countries. AES, a global power company with operations in over 20 countries, has found that the four core values of integrity, fairness, fun, and social responsibility underlying its culture are readily embraced by people in most countries. Moreover, AES tries to define and practice its cultural values the same way in all of its locations while still being sensitive to differences that exist among various people groups across the world; top managers at AES express the views that people across the world are more similar than different and that the company's culture is as meaningful in Buenos Aires or Kazakhstan as in Virginia.

In today's globalizing world, multinational companies are learning how to make strategy-critical cultural traits travel across country boundaries and create a workably uniform culture worldwide. Likewise, company managements are quite alert to the importance of cultural compatibility in making acquisitions and the need to address how to merge and integrate the cultures of newly acquired companies—cultural due diligence is often as important as financial due diligence in deciding whether to go forward on an acquisition or merger. On a number of occasions, companies have decided to pass on acquiring particular companies because of culture conflicts that they believed would be hard to resolve.

Culture: Ally or Obstacle to Strategy Execution?

A company's present culture and work climate may or may not be compatible with what is needed for effective implementation and execution of the chosen strategy. *When a company's present work climate promotes attitudes and behaviors that are well suited to first-rate strategy execution, its culture functions as a valuable ally in the strategy execution process.* When the culture is in conflict with some aspect of the company's direction, performance targets, or strategy, the culture becomes a stumbling block.[5]

How Culture Can Promote Better Strategy Execution   A culture grounded in strategy-supportive values, practices, and behavioral norms adds significantly to the power and effectiveness of a company's strategy execution effort. For example, a culture where frugality and thrift are values widely shared by organizational members nurtures employee actions to identify cost-saving opportunities—the very behavior needed for successful execution of a low-cost leadership strategy. A culture built around such business principles as pleasing customers, fair treatment, operating excellence, and employee empowerment promotes employee behaviors and an esprit de corps that facilitate execution of strategies keyed to high product quality and superior customer service. A culture in which taking initiative, challenging the status quo, exhibiting creativity, embracing change, and collaborative teamwork pervade the work climate promotes creative collaboration on the part of employees and organization drive to lead market change—outcomes that are very conducive to successful execution of product innovation and technological leadership strategies.[6]

A tight culture–strategy alignment furthers a company's strategy execution effort in two ways:[7]

1. *A culture that encourages actions supportive of good strategy execution not only provides company personnel with clear guidance regarding what behaviors and results constitute good job performance but also produces significant peer pressure*

from coworkers to conform to culturally acceptable norms. The tighter the strategy–culture fit, the more that the culture pushes people to display behaviors and observe operating practices that are conducive to good strategy execution. A strategy-supportive culture thus funnels organizational energy toward getting the right things done and delivering positive organizational results. In a company where strategy and culture are misaligned, some of the very behaviors needed to execute strategy successfully run contrary to the behaviors and values imbedded in the prevailing culture. Such a clash nearly always produces resistance from employees who have strong allegiance to the present culture. Culture-bred resistance to the actions and behaviors needed for good execution, if strong and widespread, poses a formidable hurdle that has to be cleared for strategy execution to get very far.

2. *A culture imbedded with values and behaviors that facilitate strategy execution promotes strong employee identification with and commitment to the company's vision, performance targets, and strategy.* When a company's culture is grounded in many of the needed strategy-executing behaviors, employees feel genuinely better about their jobs, the company they work for, and the merits of what the company is trying to accomplish. As a consequence, company personnel are more inclined to exhibit some passion and exert their best efforts in making the strategy work, trying to achieve the targeted performance, and moving the company closer to realizing its strategic vision.

Core Concept

Because culturally approved behavior thrives, while culturally disapproved behavior gets squashed and often penalized, a culture that supports and encourages the behaviors conducive to good strategy execution is a matter that merits the full attention of company managers.

This says something important about the task of managing the strategy executing process: *Closely aligning corporate culture with the requirements for proficient strategy execution merits the full attention of senior executives.* The managerial objective is to create and nurture a work culture that mobilizes organizational energy squarely behind efforts to execute strategy. A good job of culture-building on management's part promotes can-do attitudes and acceptance of change, instills strong peer pressures for behaviors conducive to good strategy execution, and enlists more enthusiasm and dedicated effort among company personnel for achieving company objectives.

The Perils of Strategy–Culture Conflict   Conflicts between behaviors approved by the culture and behaviors needed for good strategy execution send mixed signals to organization members, forcing an undesirable choice. Should organization members be loyal to the culture and company traditions (as well as to their own personal values and beliefs, which are likely to be compatible with the culture) and thus resist or be indifferent to actions and behaviors that will promote better strategy execution? Or should they support the strategy execution effort and engage in actions and behaviors that run counter to the culture?

When a company's culture is out of sync with what is needed for strategic success, the culture has to be changed as rapidly as can be managed—this, of course, presumes that it is one or more aspects of the culture that are out of whack rather than the strategy. While correcting a strategy–culture conflict can occasionally mean revamping strategy to produce cultural fit, more usually it means revamping the mismatched cultural features to produce strategy fit. The more entrenched the mismatched aspects of the culture, the greater the difficulty of implementing new or different strategies until better strategy–culture alignment emerges. A sizable and prolonged strategy–culture conflict weakens and may even defeat managerial efforts to make the strategy work.

Strong versus Weak Cultures

Company cultures vary widely in the degree to which they are embedded in company practices and behavioral norms. Strongly embedded cultures go directly to a company's heart and soul; those with shallow roots provide little in the way of a definable corporate character.

Strong-Culture Companies   A company's culture can be strong and cohesive in the sense that the company conducts its business according to a clear and explicit set of principles and values, that management devotes considerable time to communicating these principles and values to organization members and explaining how they relate to its business environment, and that the values are shared widely across the company—by senior executives and rank-and-file employees alike.[8] Strong-culture companies have a well-defined corporate character, typically underpinned by a creed or values statement. Executives regularly stress the importance of using company values and business principles as the basis for decisions and actions taken throughout the organization. In strong-culture companies, values and behavioral norms are so deeply rooted that they don't change much when a new CEO takes over—although they can erode over time if the CEO ceases to nurture them. And they may not change much as strategy evolves and the organization acts to make strategy adjustments, either because the new strategies are compatible with the present culture or because the dominant traits of the culture are somewhat strategy-neutral and compatible with evolving versions of the company's strategy.

> In a strong-culture company, values and behavioral norms are like crabgrass: deeply rooted and hard to weed out.

Three factors contribute to the development of strong cultures: (1) a founder or strong leader who establishes values, principles, and practices that are consistent and sensible in light of customer needs, competitive conditions, and strategic requirements; (2) a sincere, long-standing company commitment to operating the business according to these established traditions, thereby creating an internal environment that supports decision making and strategies based on cultural norms; and (3) a genuine concern for the well-being of the organization's three biggest constituencies—customers, employees, and shareholders. Continuity of leadership, small group size, stable group membership, geographic concentration, and considerable organizational success all contribute to the emergence and sustainability of a strong culture.[9]

During the time a strong culture is being implanted, there's nearly always a good strategy–culture fit (which partially accounts for the organization's success). Mismatches between strategy and culture in a strong-culture company tend to occur when a company's business environment undergoes significant change, prompting a drastic strategy revision that clashes with the entrenched culture. A strategy–culture clash can also occur in a strong-culture company whose business has gradually eroded; when a new leader is brought in to revitalize the company's operations, he or she may push the company in a strategic direction that requires substantially different cultural and behavioral norms. In such cases, a major culture-changing effort has to be launched.

One of the best examples of an industry in which strategy changes have clashed with deeply implanted cultures is the electric utility industry. Most electric utility companies, long used to operating as slow-moving regulated monopolies with captive customers, are now confronting the emergence of a vigorously competitive market in wholesale power generation and growing freedom on the part of industrial, commercial, and residential customers to choose their own energy supplier (in much the same way as customers choose their long-distance telephone carriers—an industry that once was a heavily regulated market). These new market circumstances are prompting electric companies to shift away from cultures predicated on risk avoidance, centralized control of decision making, and the politics of regulatory relationships toward cultures aimed at entrepreneurial risk taking, product innovation, competitive thinking, greater attention to customer service, cost reduction, and competitive pricing.

Weak-Culture Companies   In direct contrast to strong-culture companies, weak-culture companies are fragmented in the sense that no one set of values is consistently preached or widely shared, few behavioral norms are evident in operating practices, and few traditions are widely revered or proudly nurtured by company personnel. Because top executives don't repeatedly espouse any particular business philosophy or exhibit longstanding commitment to particular values or extol particular operating practices and behavioral norms, organization members at weak-culture companies typically lack any deeply felt sense of corporate identity. While employees may have some bonds of identification with and loyalty toward their department, their colleagues, their union, or their boss, a weak company culture breeds no strong employee allegiance to what the company stands for or to operating the business in well-defined ways. Such lack of a definable corporate character results in many employees viewing their company as just a place to work and their job as just a way to make a living—there's neither passion about the company nor emotional commitment to what it is trying to accomplish. Very often, cultural weakness stems from moderately entrenched subcultures that block the emergence of a well-defined companywide work climate.

As a consequence, *weak cultures provide little or no strategy-implementing assistance* because there are no traditions, beliefs, values, common bonds, or behavioral norms that management can use as levers to mobilize commitment to executing the chosen strategy. While a weak culture does not usually pose a strong barrier to strategy execution, it also provides no support. Absent a work climate that channels organizational energy in the direction of good strategy execution, managers are left with the options of either using compensation incentives and other motivational devices to mobilize employee commitment or trying to establish cultural roots that will in time start to nurture the strategy execution process.

Unhealthy Cultures

The distinctive characteristic of an unhealthy corporate culture is the presence of counterproductive cultural traits that adversely impact the work climate and company performance.[10] The following three traits are particularly unhealthy:

1. A highly politicized internal environment in which many issues get resolved and decisions made on the basis of which individuals or groups have the most political clout to carry the day.

2. Hostility to change and a general wariness of people who champion new ways of doing things.

3. A "not-invented-here" mindset that makes company personnel averse to looking outside the company for best practices, new managerial approaches, and innovative ideas.

What makes a politicized internal environment so unhealthy is that political infighting consumes a great deal of organizational energy, often with the result that what's best for the company takes a backseat to political maneuvering. In companies where internal politics pervades the work climate, empire-building managers jealously guard their decision-making prerogatives. They have their own agendas and operate the work units under their supervision as autonomous "fiefdoms," and the positions they take on issues is usually aimed at protecting or expanding their turf. Collaboration with other organizational units is viewed with suspicion (What are "they" up to? How can "we" protect "our" flanks?), and cross-unit cooperation occurs grudgingly. When an important proposal moves to the front burner, advocates try to ram it through and opponents try to alter it in significant ways or else kill it altogether. The support or opposition of politically influential executives and/or coalitions among departments with vested interests in a particular outcome typically weigh heavily in deciding what actions the company takes. All this maneuvering takes away from efforts to execute strategy with real proficiency and frustrates company personnel who are less political and more inclined to do what is in the company's best interests.

In less-adaptive cultures where skepticism about the importance of new developments and resistance to change are the norm, managers prefer waiting until the fog of uncertainty clears before steering a new course, making fundamental adjustments to their product line, or embracing a major new technology. They believe in moving cautiously and conservatively, preferring to follow others rather than take decisive action to be in the forefront of change. Change-resistant cultures place a premium on not making mistakes, prompting managers to lean toward safe, don't-rock-the-boat options that will have only a ripple effect on the status quo, protect or advance their own careers, and guard the interests of their immediate work groups.

Change-resistant cultures encourage a number of undesirable or unhealthy behaviors—avoiding risks, not making bold proposals to pursue emerging opportunities, a lax approach to both product innovation and continuous improvement in performing value chain activities, and following rather than leading market change. In change-resistant cultures, word quickly gets around that proposals to do things differently face an uphill battle and that people who champion them may be seen as either something of a nuisance or a troublemaker. Executives who don't value managers or employees with initiative and new ideas put a damper on product innovation, experimentation, and efforts to improve. At the same time, change-resistant companies have little appetite for being first-movers or fast-followers, believing that being in the forefront of change is too risky and that acting too quickly increases vulnerability to costly mistakes. They are more inclined to adopt a wait-and-see posture, carefully analyze several alternative responses, learn from the missteps of early movers, and then move forward cautiously and conservatively with initiatives that are deemed safe. Hostility to change is most often found in companies with multilayered management bureaucracies that have enjoyed considerable market success in years past and that are wedded to the "We have done it this way for years" syndrome.

When such companies encounter business environments with accelerating change, going slow on altering traditional ways of doing things can be become a liability rather than an asset. General Motors, IBM, Sears, and Eastman Kodak are classic examples of companies whose change-resistant bureaucracies were slow to respond to fundamental changes in their markets; clinging to the cultures and traditions that made them successful, they were reluctant to alter operating practices and modify their business approaches. As strategies of gradual change won out over bold innovation and being an early mover, all four lost market share to rivals that quickly moved to institute changes more in tune with evolving market conditions and buyer preferences. These companies are now struggling to recoup lost ground with cultures and behaviors more suited to market success—the kinds of fit that caused them to succeed in the first place.

The third unhealthy cultural trait—the not-invented-here mindset—tends to develop when a company reigns as an industry leader or enjoys great market success for so long that its personnel start to believe they have all the answers or can develop them on their own. Such confidence in the correctness of how it does things and in the company's skills and capabilities breeds arrogance—there's a strong tendency for company personnel to discount the merits or significance of what outsiders are doing and what can be learned by studying best-in-class performers. Benchmarking and a search for the best practices of outsiders are seen as offering little payoff. Any market share gains on the part of up-and-coming rivals are regarded as temporary setbacks, soon to be reversed by the company's own forthcoming initiatives. Insular thinking, internally driven solutions, and a must-be-invented-here mindset come to permeate the corporate culture. An inwardly focused corporate culture gives rise to managerial inbreeding and a failure to recruit people who can offer fresh thinking and outside perspectives. The big risk of insular cultural thinking is that the company can underestimate the competencies and accomplishments of rival companies and overestimate its own progress—with a resulting loss of competitive advantage over time.

Unhealthy cultures typically impair company performance. Avon, BankAmerica, Citicorp, Coors, Ford, General Motors, Kmart, Kroger, Sears, and Xerox are examples of companies whose unhealthy cultures during the late 1970s and early 1980s contributed to ho-hum performance on the bottom line and in the marketplace.[11] General Motors, Kmart, and Sears are still struggling to uproot problematic cultural traits and replace them with behaviors having a more suitable strategy–culture fit.

Adaptive Cultures

The hallmark of adaptive corporate cultures is willingness on the part of organizational members to accept change and take on the challenge of introducing and executing new strategies.[12] Company personnel share a feeling of confidence that the organization can deal with whatever threats and opportunities come down the pike; they are receptive to risk taking, experimentation, innovation, and changing strategies and practices. In direct contrast to change-resistant cultures, adaptive cultures are very supportive of managers and employees at all ranks who propose or help initiate useful change. Internal entrepreneurship on the part of individuals and groups is encouraged and rewarded. Senior executives seek out, support, and promote individuals who exercise initiative, spot opportunities for improvement, and display the skills to implement them. Managers habitually fund product development initiatives, evaluate new ideas openly, and take prudent risks to create new business positions. As a consequence, the company exhibits a proactive approach to identifying issues, evaluating the implications and options, and implementing workable solutions. Strategies and traditional operating practices are modified as needed to adjust to or take advantage of changes in the business environment.

> **Core Concept**
>
> In adaptive cultures, there's a spirit of doing what's necessary to ensure long-term organizational success provided the new behaviors and operating practices that management is calling for are seen as legitimate and consistent with the core values and business principles underpinning the culture.

But why is change so willingly embraced in an adaptive culture? Why are organization members not fearful of how change will affect them? Why does an adaptive culture not become unglued with ongoing changes in strategy, operating practices, and behavioral norms? The answers lie in two distinctive and dominant traits of an adaptive culture: (1) Any changes in operating practices and behaviors must *not* compromise core values and long-standing business principles, and

(2) the changes that are instituted must satisfy the legitimate interests of stakeholders—customers, employees, shareowners, suppliers, and the communities where the company operates.[13] In other words, what sustains an adaptive culture is that organization members perceive the changes that management is trying to institute as legitimate and in keeping with the core values and business principles that form the heart and soul of the culture.

Thus, for an adaptive culture to remain intact over time, top management must orchestrate the responses in a manner that demonstrates genuine care for the well-being of all key constituencies and tries to satisfy all their legitimate interests simultaneously. Unless fairness to all constituencies is a decision-making principle and a commitment to doing the right thing is evident to organization members, the changes are not likely to be seen as legitimate and thus be readily accepted and implemented.[14] Making changes that will please customers and/or that protect, if not enhance, the company's long-term well-being are generally seen as legitimate and are often seen as the best way of looking out for the interests of employees, stockholders, suppliers, and communities where the company operates. At companies with adaptive cultures, management concern for the well-being of employees is nearly always a big factor in gaining employee support for change—company personnel are usually receptive to change as long as employees understand that changes in their job assignments are part of the process of adapting to new conditions and that their employment security will not be threatened unless the company's business unexpectedly reverses direction. In cases where workforce downsizing becomes necessary, management concern for employees dictates that separation be handled humanely, making employee departure as painless as possible. Management efforts to make the process of adapting to change fair and equitable for customers, employees, stockholders, suppliers, and communities where the company operates, keeping adverse impacts to a minimum insofar as possible, breeds acceptance of and support for change among all organization stakeholders.

Technology companies, software companies, and today's dot-com companies are good illustrations of organizations with adaptive cultures. Such companies thrive on change—driving it, leading it, and capitalizing on it (but sometimes also succumbing to change when they make the wrong move or are swamped by better technologies or the superior business models of rivals). Companies like Microsoft, Intel, Nokia, Amazon.com, and Dell Computer cultivate the capability to act and react rapidly. They are avid practitioners of entrepreneurship and innovation, with a demonstrated willingness to take bold risks to create altogether new products, new businesses, and new industries. To create and nurture a culture that can adapt rapidly to changing to shifting business conditions, they make a point of staffing their organizations with people who are proactive, who rise to the challenge of change, and who have an aptitude for adapting.

In fast-changing business environments, a corporate culture that is receptive to altering organizational practices and behaviors is a virtual necessity. However, adaptive cultures work to the advantage of all companies, not just those in rapid-change environments. Every company operates in a market and business climate that is changing to one degree or another and that, in turn, requires internal operating responses and new behaviors on the part of organization members. As a company's strategy evolves, an adaptive culture is a definite ally in the strategy-implementing, strategy-executing process as compared to cultures that have to be coaxed and cajoled to change. This constitutes a good argument for why managers should strive to build a strong, adaptive corporate culture.

> A good case can be made that a strongly planted, adaptive culture is the best of all corporate cultures.

Creating a Strong Fit between Strategy and Culture

It is the *strategy maker's* responsibility to select a strategy compatible with the sacred or unchangeable parts of the organization's prevailing corporate culture. It is the *strategy implementer's* task, once strategy is chosen, to change whatever facets of the corporate culture hinder effective execution.

Changing a Problem Culture   Changing a company's culture to align it with strategy is among the toughest management tasks because of the heavy anchor of deeply held values and habits—people cling emotionally to the old and familiar. It takes concerted management action over a period of time to replace an unhealthy culture with a healthy culture or to root out certain unwanted behaviors and instill ones that are more strategy-supportive. *The single most visible factor that distinguishes successful culture-change efforts from failed attempts is competent leadership at the top.* Great power is needed to force major cultural change—to overcome the springback resistance of entrenched cultures—and great power normally resides only at the top.

> Once a culture is established, it is difficult to change.

The first step in fixing a problem culture is to identify those facets of the present culture that are dysfunctional and explain why they pose obstacles to executing new strategic initiatives and achieving company performance targets. Second, managers have to clearly define the desired new behaviors and specify the key features of the culture they want to create. Third, managers have to talk openly and forthrightly to all concerned about problematic aspects of the culture and why and how new behaviors will improve company performance—the case for cultural change has to be persuasive and the benefits of a reformed culture made convincing to all concerned. Finally, and most important, the talk has to be followed swiftly by visible, aggressive actions to promote the desired new behaviors—actions that everyone will understand are intended to produce behaviors and practices conducive to good strategy execution.

The menu of actions management can take to change a problem culture includes the following:[15]

- Making a compelling case for why the company's new direction and a different cultural atmosphere are in the organization's best interests and why individuals and groups should commit themselves to making it happen despite the obstacles. Skeptics have to be convinced that all is not well with the status quo. This can be done by:
  - Challenging the status quo with very basic questions: Are we giving customers what they really need and want? Why aren't we taking more business away from rivals? Why do our rivals have lower costs than we do? How can we drive costs out of the business and be more competitive on price? Why can't design-to-market cycle time be halved? Why aren't we moving faster to make better use of the Internet and e-commerce technologies and practices? How can we grow company revenues at 15 percent instead of 10 percent? What can we do to speed up our decision making and shorten response times?
  - Creating events where everyone in management is forced to listen to angry customers, dissatisfied strategic allies, alienated employees, or disenchanted stockholders.
- Repeating at every opportunity the messages of why cultural change is good for company stakeholders (particularly customers, employees, and shareholders).

Effective culture-change leaders are good at telling stories to convey new values and connect the case for change to organization members.

- ▦ Visibly praising and generously rewarding people who display newly advocated cultural norms and who participate in implementing the desired kinds of operating practices.

- ▦ Altering incentive compensation to reward the desired cultural behavior and deny rewards to those who resist change.

- ▦ Recruiting and hiring new managers and employees who have the desired cultural values and can serve as role models for the desired cultural behavior.

- ▦ Replacing key executives who are strongly associated with the old culture.

- ▦ Revising policies and procedures in ways that will help drive cultural change.

Only with bold leadership and concerted action on many fronts can a company succeed in tackling so large and difficult a task as major cultural change. When only strategic fine-tuning is being implemented, it takes less time and effort to bring values and culture into alignment with strategy, but there is still a lead role for the manager to play in communicating the need for new cultural behaviors and personally launching actions to prod the culture into better alignment with strategy.

Symbolic Culture-Changing Actions   Managerial actions to tighten the strategy–culture fit need to be both symbolic and substantive. Symbolic actions are valuable for the signals they send about the kinds of behavior and performance strategy implementers wish to encourage. The most important symbolic actions are those that top executives take to *lead by example*. For instance, if the organization's strategy involves a drive to become the industry's low-cost producer, senior managers must display frugality in their own actions and decisions: inexpensive decorations in the executive suite, conservative expense accounts and entertainment allowances, a lean staff in the corporate office, scrutiny of budget requests, few executive perks, and so on. If the culture change imperative is to be more responsive to customers' needs and to pleasing customers, the CEO can instill greater customer awareness by requiring all officers and executives to spend a significant portion of each week talking with customers about their needs.

Another category of symbolic actions includes the ceremonial events organizations hold to designate and honor people whose actions and performance exemplify what is called for in the new culture. Many universities give outstanding teacher awards each year to symbolize their commitment to good teaching and their esteem for instructors who display exceptional classroom talents. Numerous businesses have employee-of-the-month awards. The military has a long-standing custom of awarding ribbons and medals for exemplary actions. Mary Kay Cosmetics awards an array of prizes—from ribbons to pink automobiles—to its beauty consultants for reaching various sales plateaus.

The best companies and the best executives expertly use symbols, role models, ceremonial occasions, and group gatherings to tighten the strategy–culture fit. Low-cost leaders like Wal-Mart and Nucor are renowned for their spartan facilities, executive frugality, intolerance of waste, and zealous control of costs. Nucor executives make a point of flying coach class and using taxis at airports rather than limousines. Executives sensitive to their role in promoting strategy–culture fits make a habit of appearing at ceremonial functions to praise individuals and groups that get with the program. They honor individuals who exhibit cultural norms and reward those who achieve strategic milestones. They participate in employee training programs to stress strategic priorities, values, ethical principles, and cultural norms. Every group gathering is seen as an opportunity to repeat and ingrain values, praise good deeds, reinforce cultural norms, and promote changes that assist strategy execution. Sensitive executives make sure that current decisions and policy changes will be construed by organizational members as consistent with cultural values and supportive of the company's new strategic direction.[16]

Substantive Culture-Changing Actions While symbolically leading the push for new behaviors and communicating the reasons for new approaches is crucial, strategy implementers have to convince all those concerned that the culture-changing effort is more than cosmetic. Talk and symbolism have to be complemented by substantive actions and real movement. The actions taken have to be credible, highly visible, and unmistakably indicative of the seriousness of management's commitment to new strategic initiatives and the associated cultural changes. There are several ways to accomplish this. One is to engineer some quick successes that highlight the benefits of the proposed changes, thus making enthusiasm for them contagious. However, instant results are usually not as important as having the will and patience to create a solid, competent team psychologically committed to pursuing the strategy in a superior fashion. The strongest signs that management is truly committed to creating a new culture include replacing old-culture traditionalist managers with new-breed managers, changing dysfunctional policies and operating practices, instituting new compensation incentives visibly tied to the achievement of freshly set performance targets, and making major budgetary reallocations that shift substantial resources from old-strategy projects and programs to new-strategy projects and programs.

Implanting the needed culture-building values and behavior depends on a sincere, sustained commitment by the chief executive coupled with extraordinary persistence in reinforcing the culture at every opportunity through both word and deed. Neither charisma nor personal magnetism is essential. However, personally talking to many departmental groups about the reasons for change *is* essential; organizational changes are seldom accomplished successfully from an office. Moreover, creating and sustaining a strategy-supportive culture is a job for the whole management team. Major cultural change requires many initiatives from many people. Senior officers, department heads, and middle managers have to reiterate valued behaviors and translate the organization's core values and business principles into everyday practice. In addition, for the culture-building effort to be successful, strategy implementers must enlist the support of frontline supervisors and employee opinion leaders, convincing them of the merits of practicing and enforcing cultural norms at the lowest levels in the organization. Until a big majority of employees join the new culture and share an emotional commitment to its basic values and behavioral norms, there's considerably more work to be done in both instilling the culture and tightening the strategy–culture fit.

Changing culture to support strategy is not a short-term exercise. It takes time for a new culture to emerge and prevail. Overnight transformations simply don't occur. The bigger the organization and the greater the cultural shift needed to produce a strategy–culture fit, the longer it takes. In large companies, fixing a problem culture and instilling a new set of attitudes and behaviors can take two to five years. In fact, it is usually tougher to reform an entrenched problematic culture than it is to instill a strategy-supportive culture from scratch in a brand new organization. Sometimes executives succeed in changing the values and behaviors of small groups of managers and even whole departments or divisions, only to find the changes eroded over time by the actions of the rest of the organization—what is communicated, praised, supported, and penalized by an entrenched majority undermines the new emergent culture and halts its progress. Executives, despite a series of well-intended actions to reform a problem culture, are likely to fail at weeding out embedded cultural traits when widespread employee skepticism about the company's new directions and culture-change effort spawns covert resistance to the cultural behaviors and operating practices advocated by top management. This is why management must take every opportunity to convince employees of the need for culture change and communicate to them how new attitudes, behaviors, and operating practices will benefit the interests of organizational stakeholders.

A company that has done a good job of fixing its problem culture is Alberto-Culver—see Company Spotlight 9.2.

Grounding the Culture in Core Values and Ethics

A corporate culture grounded in socially approved values and ethical business principles is a vital ingredient in a company's long-term strategic success.[17] Unless a company's executives genuinely care about how the company's business affairs are conducted, the company's reputation and ultimately its performance are put at risk. One need look no further than the scandals at companies like Enron, WorldCom, and HealthSouth to see the damage that occurs when the public spotlight is trained on a company's shady business practices and unethical behavior.

While there's no doubt that some companies and some company personnel knowingly engage in shady business practices and have little regard for ethical standards, one must be cautious about assuming that a company's core values and ethical standards are meaningless window dressing. Executives at many companies genuinely care about the values and ethical standards that company personnel exhibit in conducting the company's business; they are aware that their own reputations, as well as the company's reputation, hangs on whether outsiders see the company's actions as ethical or honest or socially acceptable. At such companies, values statements and codes of ethics matter, and they are ingrained to one degree or another in the company's culture—see Table 9.1 for the kinds of topics that are commonly found in values statements and codes of ethics.

Indeed, at companies where executives are truly committed to practicing the values and ethical standards that have been espoused, *the stated core values and ethical principles are the cornerstones of the corporate culture*. As depicted in Figure 9.1, a company that works hard at putting its stated core values and ethical principles into practice fosters a work climate where company personnel share common convictions about how the company's business is to be conducted and where they are expected to act in accord with stated values and ethical standards. By promoting behaviors that mirror the values and ethics standards, a company's stated values and ethical standards nurture the corporate culture in three highly positive ways: (1) they communicate the company's good intentions and validate the integrity and above-board character of its business principles and operating methods, (2) they steer company personnel toward both doing the right thing and doing things right, and (3) they establish a "corporate conscience" and provide yardsticks for gauging the appropriateness of particular actions, decisions, and policies (see Figure 9.2).[18]

> A company's values statement and code of ethics communicate expectations of how employees should conduct themselves in the workplace.

In 1993, Carol Bernick—vice chairperson of Alberto-Culver, president of its North American division, and daughter of the company's founders—concluded that her division's existing culture had four problems: Employees dutifully waited for marching orders from their bosses, workers put pleasing their bosses ahead of pleasing customers, some company policies were not family-friendly, and there was too much bureaucracy and paperwork. What was needed, in Bernick's opinion, was a culture in which company employees had a sense of ownership and an urgency to get things done, welcomed innovation, and were willing to taking risks.

To change the culture, Alberto-Culver's management undertook a series of actions:

- In 1993, a new position, called growth development leader (GDL), was created to help orchestrate the task of fixing the culture deep in the ranks (there were 70 GDLs in Alberto-Culver's North American division). GDLs came from all ranks of the company's managerial ladder and were handpicked for such qualities as empathy, communication skills, positive attitude, and ability to let their hair down and have fun. GDLs performed their regular jobs in addition to taking on the GDL roles; it was considered an honor to be chosen. Each GDL mentored about 12 people from both a career and a family standpoint. GDLs met with senior executives weekly, bringing forward people's questions and issues and then, afterward, sharing with their groups the topics and solutions that were discussed. GDLs brought a group member as a guest to each meeting. One meeting each year is devoted to identifying "macros and irritations"—attendees are divided into four subgroups and given 15 minutes to identify the company's four biggest challenges (the macros) and the four most annoying aspects of life at the company (the irritations); the whole group votes on which four deserve the company's attention. Those selected are then addressed, and assignments made for follow-up and results.

- Changing the culture was made an issue across the company, starting in 1995 with a two-hour State of the Company presentation to employees covering where the company was and where it wanted to be. The State of the Company address was made an annual event.

- Management created ways to measure the gains in changing the culture. One involved an annual all-employee survey to assess progress against cultural goals and to get 360-degree feedback—the 2000 survey had 180 questions, including 33 relating to the performance of each respondent's GDL. A bonfire celebration was held in the company parking lot to announce that paperwork would be cut 30 percent.

- A list of 10 cultural imperatives was formalized in 1998—honesty, ownership, trust, customer orientation, commitment, fun, innovation, risk taking, speed and urgency, and teamwork. These imperatives came to be known internally as HOT CC FIRST.

- Instituting extensive celebrations and awards programs. Most celebrations are scheduled, but some are spontaneous (an impromptu thank-you party for a good fiscal year). Business Builder Awards (initiated in 1997) are given to individuals and teams that make a significant impact on the company's growth and profitability. The best-scoring GDLs on the annual employee surveys are awarded shares of company stock. The company notes all work anniversaries and personal milestones with "Alberto-appropriate" gifts; appreciative company employees sometimes give thank-you gifts to their GDLs. According to Carol Bernick, "If you want something to grow, pour champagne on it. We've made a huge effort—maybe even an over-the-top effort—to celebrate our successes and, indeed, just about everything we'd like to see happen again."

The culture change effort at Alberto-Culver North America was viewed as a major contributor to improved performance. From 1993, when the effort first began, to 2001, the division's sales increased from just under $350 million to over $600 million and pretax profits rose from $20 million to almost $50 million.

Source: Carol Lavin Bernick, "When Your Culture Needs a Makeover," *Harvard Business Review* 79, no. 6 (June 2001), p. 61.

Table 9.1 THE CONTENT OF COMPANY VALUE STATEMENTS AND CODES OF ETHICS

Topics Commonly Appearing in Values Statements	Topics Commonly Appearing in Codes of Ethics

■ Commitment to such outcomes as customer satisfaction and customer service, quality, product innovation, and/or technological leadership
 	
■ Commitment to achievement, excellence, and results
 	
■ Importance of demonstrating such qualities as honesty, integrity, trust, fairness, quality of life, pride of workmanship, and ethics
 	
■ Importance of creativity, taking initiative, and accepting responsibility
 	
■ Importance of teamwork and a cooperative attitude
 	
■ Importance of Golden Rule behavior and respect for coworkers
 	
■ Making the company a great place to work
 	
■ Importance of having fun and creating a fun work environment
 	
■ Duty to stakeholders—customers, employees, suppliers, shareholders, communities where the company operates, and society at large
 	
■ Commitment to exercising social responsibility and being a good community citizen
 	
■ Commitment to protecting the environment
 	
■ Commitment to workforce diversity
	■ A mandate that company personnel will behave with honesty and integrity
	
	■ An expectation that all company personnel will comply fully with all laws and regulations, specifically:
	  • Antitrust laws prohibiting anticompetitive practices, conspiracies to fix prices, or attempts to monopolize
	  • Foreign Corrupt Practices Act
	  • Securities laws and prohibitions against insider trading
	  • Environmental and workplace safety regulations
	  • Discrimination and sexual harassment regulations
	
	■ Prohibitions against accepting bribes or making payments to obtain business
	
	■ Avoiding conflicts of interest
	
	■ Fairness in selling and marketing practices
	
	■ Supplier relationships and procurement practices
	
	■ Acquiring and using competitively sensitive information about rivals and others
	
	■ Political activities and lobbying
	
	■ Avoiding use of company assets, resources, and property for personal or other inappropriate purposes
	
	■ Responsibility to protect proprietary information

Figure 9.1 The Two Culture-Building Roles of a Company's Core Values and Ethical Standards

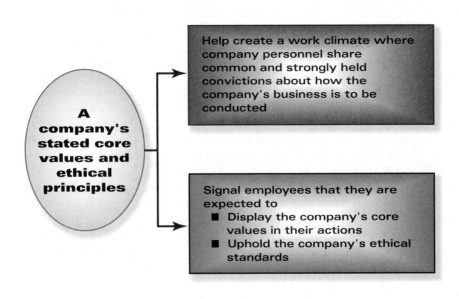

A company's stated core values and ethical principles

Help create a work climate where company personnel share common and strongly held convictions about how the company's business is to be conducted

Signal employees that they are expected to
■ Display the company's core values in their actions
■ Uphold the company's ethical standards

Figure 9.2   How the Practice of Stated Core Values and Ethical Principles Positively Impact the Corporate Culture

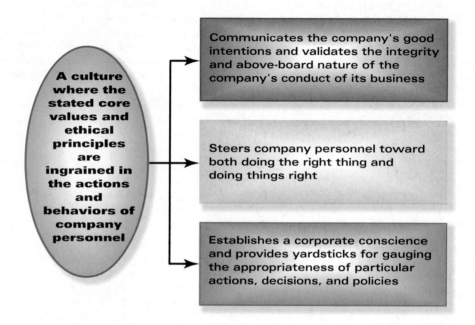

Companies ingrain their values and ethical standards in a number of different ways.[19] Tradition-steeped companies with a rich folklore rely heavily on word-of-mouth indoctrination and the power of tradition to instill values and enforce ethical conduct. But many companies today convey their values and codes of ethics to stakeholders and interested parties in their annual reports, on their websites, and in internal communications to all employees. The standards are hammered in at orientation courses for new employees and in training courses for managers and employees. The trend of making stakeholders aware of a company's commitment to core values and ethical business conduct is attributable to three factors: (1) greater management understanding of the role these statements play in culture building, (2) a renewed focus on ethical standards stemming from the corporate scandals that came to light in 2001–2002, and (3) the growing numbers of consumers who prefer to patronize ethical companies with ethical products.

However, there is a considerable difference between saying the right things (having a well-articulated corporate values statement or code of ethics) and truly managing a company in an ethical and socially responsible way. Companies that are truly committed to the stated core values and to high ethical standards make ethical behavior *a fundamental component of their corporate culture.* They put a stake in the ground, making it unequivocally clear that company personnel are expected to live up to the company's values and ethical standards—how well individuals display core values and adhere to ethical standards is often part of their job performance evaluations. Peer pressures to conform to cultural norms are quite strong, acting as an important deterrent to outside-the-lines behavior. Moreover, values statements and codes of ethical conduct are used as benchmarks for judging the appropriateness of company policies and operating practices.

At Darden Restaurants—a $4.5 billion casual dining company with over 1,200 company-owned Red Lobster, Olive Garden, Bahama Breeze, and Smokey Bones BBQ Sports Bar restaurants—the core values are operating with integrity, treating people fairly, and welcoming and celebrating workforce diversity; the company's practice of these values has been instrumental in creating a culture characterized by trust, exciting jobs and career opportunities for employees, and a passion to be the best in casual dining.[20]

Once values and ethical standards have been formally adopted, they must be institutionalized in the company's policies and practices and ingrained in the conduct of company personnel. Imbedding the values and code of ethics entails several actions:

- Incorporation of the statement of values and the code of ethics into employee training and educational programs.
- Explicit attention to values and ethics in recruiting and hiring to screen out applicants who do not exhibit compatible character traits.
- Frequent reiteration of company values and ethical principles at company events and internal communications to employees.
- Active management involvement, from the CEO down to frontline supervisors, in stressing the importance of values and ethical conduct and in overseeing the compliance process.
- Ceremonies and awards for individuals and groups who display the values.
- Instituting ethics enforcement procedures.

In the case of codes of ethics, special attention must be given to sections of the company that are particularly vulnerable—procurement, sales, and political lobbying. Employees who deal with external parties are in ethically sensitive positions and often are drawn into compromising situations. Company personnel assigned to subsidiaries in foreign countries can find themselves trapped in ethical dilemmas if bribery and corruption of public officials are common practices or if suppliers or customers are accustomed to kickbacks of one kind or another. Mandatory ethics training for such personnel is usually desirable.

As a test of your ethics, take the quiz on page 314.

Structuring the Ethics Enforcement Process   If a company's executives truly aspire for company personnel to behave ethically, then procedures for enforcing ethical standards and handling potential violations have to be developed. Even in an ethically strong company, there can be bad apples—and some of the bad apples may even rise to the executive ranks. So it is not enough to rely on an ethically-strong culture to produce ethics compliance.

The compliance effort must permeate the company, extending to every organizational unit. The attitudes, character, and work history of prospective employees must be scrutinized. Every employee must receive adequate training. Line managers at all levels must give serious and continuous attention to the task of explaining how the values and ethical code apply in their areas. In addition, they must insist that company values and ethical standards become a way of life. In general, instilling values and insisting on ethical conduct must be looked on as a continuous culture-building, culture-nurturing exercise. Whether the effort succeeds or fails depends largely on how well corporate values and ethical standards are visibly integrated into company policies, managerial practices, and actions at all levels.

A TEST OF YOUR BUSINESS ETHICS

As a gauge of your own ethical and moral standards, take the following quiz and see how you stack up against other members of your class. For the test to be valid, you need to answer the questions candidly and not on the basis of what you think the right answer is. When you finish the test, you should compare your answers to how your future employer would likely want you to answer each of these questions. Which are likely to be considered vital?

1. Is it unethical to make up data to justify the introduction of a new product if, when you start to object, your boss tells you, "Just do it"?
____Yes ____No ____Unsure (it depends) ____Need more information

2. Do you think that it is acceptable to give your boss a $100 gift to celebrate a birthday or holiday?
____Yes ____No ____Unsure (it depends) ____Need more information

3. Would it be wrong to accept a $100 gift from your boss (who is of the opposite sex) to celebrate your birthday?
____Yes ____No ____Unsure (it depends) ____Need more information

4. Is it unethical to accept an invitation from a supplier to spend a holiday weekend skiing at the supplier company's resort home in Colorado? (Would your answer be different if you were presently considering a proposal from that supplier to purchase $1 million worth of components?)
____Yes ____No ____Unsure (it depends) ____Need more information

5. Is it unethical to give a customer company's purchasing manager free tickets to the Super Bowl if he or she is looking for tickets and is likely to make a large purchase from your company?
____Yes ____No ____Unsure (it depends) ____Need more information

6. Is it unethical to use sick days provided in your company benefits plan as personal days so that you can go attend a family event or leave early for a weekend vacation?
____Yes ____No ____Unsure (it depends) ____Need more information

7. Would it be wrong to keep quiet if you, as a junior financial analyst, had just calculated that the projected return on a possible project was 18 percent and your boss (a) informed you that no project could be approved without the prospect of a 25 percent return and (b) told you to go back and redo the numbers and "get them right"?
____Yes ____No ____Unsure (it depends) ____Need more information

8. Would it be unethical to allow your supervisor to believe that you were chiefly responsible for the success of a new company initiative if it actually resulted from a team effort or major contributions by a coworker?
____Yes ____No ____Unsure (it depends) ____Need more information

9. Is it unethical to fail to come forward to support an employee wrongfully accused of misconduct if that person is a source of aggravation for you at work?
____Yes ____No ____Unsure (it depends) ____Need more information

10. Is it wrong to use your employer's staff to prepare invitations for a party that you will give when clients or customers are among those invited?
____Yes ____No ____Unsure (it depends) ____Need more information

11. Is it wrong to browse the Internet while at work if all your work is done and there is otherwise nothing you ought to be doing? (Would your answer be the same if the websites you visited were pornographic?)
____Yes ____No ____Unsure (it depends) ____Need more information

12. Is it unethical to keep quiet if you are aware that a coworker is being sexually harassed by his or her boss?
____Yes ____No ____Unsure (it depends) ____Need more information

13. Is there an ethical problem with using your employer's copier to make a small number of copies for personal use (for example, your tax returns, your child's school project, or personal correspondence)?
____Yes ____No ____Unsure (it depends) ____Need more information

14. Is it unethical to install company-owned software on your home computer without the permission of your supervisor and the software vendor?
____Yes ____No ____Unsure (it depends) ____Need more information

15. Is it unethical to okay the shipment of products to a customer that do not meet the customer's specifications without first checking with the customer?
____Yes ____No ____Unsure (it depends) ____Need more information

ANSWERS: We think a strong case can be made that the answers to questions 1, 3, 4, 5, 6, 7, 8, 9, 10, 11, 12, 13, 14, and 15 are yes and that the answer to question 2 is no. Most employers would consider the answers to questions 10 and 13 to be yes unless company policy allows personal use of company resources under certain specified conditions.

If a company is really serious about enforcing ethical behavior, it probably needs to do two things:

1. Conduct an annual audit of each manager's efforts to uphold ethical standards and require formal reports on the actions taken by managers to remedy deficient conduct.

2. Require all employees to sign a statement annually certifying that they have complied with the company's code of ethics.

While these actions may seem extreme or objectionable, they leave little room to doubt the seriousness of a company's commitment to ethics compliance. And most company personnel will think twice about knowingly engaging in unethical conduct when they know their actions will be audited and/or when they have to sign statements certifying compliance with the company's code of ethics.

Establishing a Strategy–Culture Fit in Multinational and Global Companies

In multinational and global companies, where some cross-border diversity in the corporate culture is normal, efforts to establish a tight strategy–culture fit is complicated by the diversity of societal customs and lifestyles from country to country. Company personnel in different countries sometimes fervently insist on being treated as distinctive individuals or groups, making a one-size-fits-all culture potentially inappropriate. Leading cross-border culture-change initiatives requires sensitivity to prevailing cultural differences; managers must discern when diversity has to be accommodated and when cross-border differences can be and should be narrowed.[21] Cross-country cultural diversity in a multinational enterprise is more tolerable if the company is pursuing a multicountry strategy and if the company's culture in each country is well aligned with its strategy in that country. But significant cross-country differences in a company's culture are likely to impede execution of a global strategy and have to be addressed.

As discussed earlier in this chapter, the trick to establishing a workable strategy–culture fit in multinational and global companies is to ground the culture in strategy-supportive values and operating practices that travel well across country borders and strike a chord with managers and workers in many different areas of the world, despite the diversity of local customs and traditions. A multinational enterprise with a misfit between its strategy and culture in certain countries where it operates can attack the problem by reinterpreting or deemphasizing or even abandoning those values and cultural traits which it finds inappropriate for some countries where it operates. Problematic values and operating principles can be replaced with values and operating approaches that travel well across country borders but that are still strategy supportive. Many times a company's values statement only has to be reworded so as to express existing values in ways that have more universal appeal. Sometimes certain offending operating practices can be modified to good advantage in all locations where the company operates.

Aside from trying to ground the culture in a set of core values and operating principles that have universal appeal, management can seek to minimize the existence of subcultures and cross-country cultural diversity by:

■ Instituting training programs to communicate the meaning of core values and explain the case for common operating principles and practices.

■ Drawing on the full range of motivational and compensation incentives to induce personnel to adopt and practice the desired behaviors.

■ Allowing some leeway for certain core values and principles to be interpreted and applied somewhat differently, if necessary, to accommodate local customs and traditions.

Generally, a high degree of cross-country cultural homogeneity is desirable and has to be pursued. Having too much variation in the culture from country to country not only makes it difficult to use the culture in helping drive the strategy execution process but also works against the establishment of a one-company mindset and a consistent corporate identity.

Leading the Strategy Execution Process

The litany of managing the strategy process is simple enough: Craft a sound strategic plan, implement it, execute it to the fullest, adjust it as needed, and win! But the leadership challenges are significant and diverse. Exerting take-charge leadership, being a "spark plug," ramrodding things through, and achieving results thrusts a manager into a variety of leadership roles in managing the strategy execution process: resource acquirer and allocator, capabilities builder, motivator, policymaker, policy enforcer, head cheerleader, crisis solver, decision maker, and taskmaster, to mention a few. There are times when leading the strategy execution process entails being authoritarian and hard-nosed, times when it is best to be a perceptive listener and a compromising decision maker, times when matters are best delegated to people closest to the scene of the action, and times when being a coach is the proper role. Many occasions call for the manager in charge to assume a highly visible role and put in long hours guiding the process, while others entail only a brief ceremonial performance with the details delegated to subordinates.

For the most part, leading the strategy execution process has to be top-down and driven by mandates to get things done and show good results. Just how to go about the specifics of leading organization efforts to put a strategy in place and deliver the intended results has to start with understanding the requirements for good strategy execution, followed by a diagnosis of the organization's capabilities and preparedness to execute the necessary strategic initiatives, and then decisions as to which of several ways to proceed to get things done and achieve the targeted results.[22] In general, leading the drive for good strategy execution and operating excellence calls for several actions on the part of the manager-in-charge:

1. Staying on top of what is happening, closely monitoring progress, ferreting out issues, and learning what obstacles lie in the path of good execution.
2. Putting constructive pressure on the organization to achieve good results.
3. Keeping the organization focused on operating excellence.
4. Leading the development of stronger core competencies and competitive capabilities.
5. Exercising ethics leadership and insisting that the company conduct its affairs like a model corporate citizen.
6. Pushing corrective actions to improve strategy execution and achieve the targeted results.

Staying on Top of How Well Things Are Going

To stay on top of how well the strategy execution process is going, a manager needs to develop a broad network of contacts and sources of information, both formal and informal. The regular channels include talking with key subordinates, attending presentations and meetings, reading reviews of the latest operating results, talking to customers, watching the competitive reactions of rival firms, exchanging e-mail and holding telephone conversations with people in outlying locations, making onsite visits, and listening to rank-and-file employees. However, some information is more trustworthy than the rest, and the views and perspectives offered by different people can vary widely. Presentations and briefings by subordinates may not represent the whole truth. Bad news or problems may be minimized or in some cases not reported at all as subordinates delay conveying failures and problems in hopes that they can turn things around in time. Hence, strategy managers have to make sure that they have accurate information and a feel for the existing situation. They have to confirm whether things are on track, identify problems, learn what obstacles lie in the path of good strategy execution, and develop a basis for determining what, if anything, they can personally do to move the process along.

One of the best ways for executives in charge of strategy execution to stay on top of things is by making regular visits to the field and talking with many different people at many different levels—a technique often labeled **managing by walking around (MBWA).** Wal-Mart executives have had a long-standing practice of spending two to three days every week visiting Wal-Mart's stores and talking with store managers and employees. Sam Walton, Wal-Mart's founder, insisted, "The key is to get out into the store and listen to what the associates have to say." Jack Welch, the highly effective CEO of General Electric (GE) from 1980 to 2001, not only spent several days each month personally visiting GE operations and talking with major customers but also arranged his schedule so that he could spend time exchanging information and ideas with GE

> **Core Concept**
>
> **Management by walking around (MBWA)** is one of the techniques that effective leaders use to stay informed about how well the strategy execution process is progressing.

managers from all over the world who were attending classes at the company's leadership development center near GE's headquarters. Some companies have weekly get-togethers in each division (often on Friday afternoons), attended by both executives and employees, to create a regular opportunity for tidbits of information to flow freely between down-the-line employees and executives. Many manufacturing executives make a point of strolling the factory floor to talk with workers and meeting regularly with union officials. Some managers operate out of open cubicles in big spaces populated with open cubicles for other personnel so that they can interact easily and frequently with coworkers.

Most managers rightly attach great importance to spending time with people at various company facilities and gathering information and opinions firsthand from diverse sources about how well various aspects of the strategy execution process are going. Such contacts give managers a feel for what progress is being made, what problems are being encountered, and whether additional resources or different approaches may be needed. Just as important, MBWA provides opportunities for managers to talk informally to many different people at different organizational levels, give encouragement, lift spirits, shift attention from the old to the new priorities, and create some excitement—all of which generate positive energy and help mobilize organizational efforts behind strategy execution.

Putting Constructive Pressure on the Organization to Achieve Good Results

Managers have to be out front in mobilizing organizational energy behind the drive for good strategy execution and operating excellence. Part of the leadership requirement here entails nurturing a results-oriented work climate. A culture where there's constructive pressure to achieve good results is a valuable contributor to good strategy-execution and operating excellence. Results-oriented cultures are permeated with a spirit of achievement and have a good track record in meeting or beating performance targets. If management wants to drive the strategy execution effort by instilling a results-oriented work climate, then senior executives have to take the lead in promoting certain enabling cultural drivers: a strong sense of involvement on the part of company personnel, emphasis on individual initiative and creativity, respect for the contribution of individuals and groups, and pride in doing things right.

Organizational leaders who succeed in creating a results-oriented work climate typically are intensely people-oriented, and they are skilled users of people-management practices that win the emotional commitment of company personnel and inspire them to do their best.[23] They understand that treating employees well generally leads to increased teamwork, higher morale, greater loyalty, and increased employee commitment to making a contribution. All of these foster an esprit de corps that energizes organizational members to contribute to the drive for operating excellence and proficient strategy execution.

Successfully leading the effort to instill a spirit of high achievement into the culture generally entails such leadership actions and managerial practices as:

- Treating employees with dignity and respect. This often includes a strong company commitment to training each employee thoroughly, providing attractive career opportunities, emphasizing promotion from within, and providing a high degree of job security. Some companies symbolize the value of individual employees and the importance of their contributions by referring to them as cast members (Disney), crew members (McDonald's), coworkers (Kinko's and CDW Computer Centers), job owners (Graniterock), partners (Starbucks), or associates (Wal-Mart, Lenscrafters, W. L. Gore, Edward Jones, Publix Supermarkets, and Marriott International). At a number of companies, managers at every level are held responsible for developing the people who report to them.

- Making champions out of the people who turn in winning performances—but doing so in ways that promote teamwork and cross-unit collaboration as opposed to spurring an unhealthy footrace among employees to best one another.

- Encouraging employees to use initiative and creativity in performing their work.

- Setting stretch objectives and clearly communicating an expectation that company personnel are to give their best in achieving performance targets.

- Granting employees enough autonomy to stand out, excel, and contribute.

- Using the full range of motivational techniques and compensation incentives to inspire company personnel, nurture a results-oriented work climate, and enforce high-performance standards.

- Celebrating individual, group, and company successes. Top management should miss no opportunity to express respect for individual employees and their appreciation of extraordinary individual and group effort.[24] Companies like Mary Kay Cosmetics, Tupperware, and McDonald's actively seek out reasons and opportunities to give pins, buttons, badges, and medals for good showings by average performers—the idea being to express appreciation and give a motivational boost to people who stand out in doing ordinary jobs. General Electric and 3M Corporation make a point of ceremoniously honoring individuals who believe so strongly in their ideas that they take it on themselves to hurdle the bureaucracy, maneuver their projects through the system, and turn them into improved services, new products, or even new businesses.

While leadership efforts to instill a results-oriented culture usually accentuate the positive, there are negative reinforcers too. Managers whose units consistently perform poorly have to be replaced. Low-performing workers and people who reject the results-oriented cultural emphasis have to be weeded out or at least moved to out-of-the-way positions. Average performers have to be candidly counseled that they have limited career potential unless they show more progress in the form of more effort, better skills, and ability to deliver better results.

Keeping the Internal Organization Focused on Operating Excellence

Another leadership dimension of the drive for good strategy execution is keeping the organization bubbling with fresh supplies of ideas and suggestions for improvement. Managers cannot mandate innovative improvements by simply exhorting people to "be creative," nor can they make continuous progress toward operating excellence with directives to "try harder." Rather, they have to foster a culture where innovative ideas and experimentation with new ways of doing things can blossom and thrive. There are several actions that organizational leaders can take to promote new ideas for improving the performance of value chain activities:

- *Encouraging individuals and groups to brainstorm, let their imaginations fly in all directions, and come up with proposals for improving how things are done*—Operating excellence requires that everybody be expected to contribute ideas, exercise initiative, and pursue continuous improvement. The leadership trick is to keep a sense of urgency alive in the business so that people see change and innovation as necessities. One year after taking charge at Siemens-Nixdorf Information Systems, Gerhard Schulmeyer produced the first profit in the merged company, which had been losing hundreds of millions of dollars annually since 1991; he credited the turnaround to the creation of 5,000 "change agents," almost 15 percent of the workforce, who volunteered for active roles in the company's change agenda while continuing to perform their regular jobs.

- *Taking special pains to foster, nourish, and support people who are eager for a chance to try turning their ideas into better ways of operating*—People with maverick ideas or out-of-the-ordinary proposals have to be tolerated and given room to operate. Above all, would-be champions who advocate radical or different ideas must not be looked on as disruptive or troublesome. The best champions and change agents are persistent, competitive, tenacious, committed, and fanatic about seeing their idea through to success.

- *Ensuring that the rewards for successful champions are large and visible and that people who champion an unsuccessful idea are not punished or sidelined but rather encouraged to try again*—Encouraging lots of "tries" is important since many ideas won't pan out.

- *Using all kinds of ad hoc organizational forms to support ideas and experimentation*—Venture teams, task forces, "performance shootouts" among different groups working on competing approaches, and informal "bootleg" projects composed of volunteers are just a few of the possibilities.

- *Using the tools of benchmarking, best practices, business process reengineering, TQM, and six sigma quality to focus attention on continuous improvement*—These are proven approaches to getting better operating results and facilitating better strategy execution.

Leading the Development of Better Competencies and Capabilities

A third avenue to better strategy execution and operating excellence is proactively strengthening organizational competencies and competitive capabilities. Senior management usually has to lead the strengthening of core competencies and competitive capabilities because they typically reside in the combined efforts of different work groups, departments, and strategic allies. Stronger competencies and capabilities can not only lead to better performance of value chain activities but also to a competitive edge over rivals that paves the way for better bottom-line results.

Exercising Ethics Leadership and Insisting on Good Corporate Citizenship

For an organization to avoid the pitfalls of scandal and disgrace and consistently display the intent to conduct its business in a socially acceptable manner, the CEO and those around the CEO must be openly and unequivocally committed to ethical conduct and socially redeeming business principles and values. It is never enough for senior executives to assume that all of the company's business activities are being conducted ethically, nor can it be assumed that employees understand how to handle situations that are in ethically gray areas.

Leading the enforcement of ethical behavior has four pieces. First and foremost, the CEO and other senior executives must set an excellent example in their own ethical behavior and demonstrate integrity in their actions and decisions. Company decisions have to be seen as ethical—actions speak louder than words. Second, company personnel have to be educated about what is ethical and what is not; the company may have to establish ethics training programs and discuss what to do in gray areas. Everyone must be encouraged to raise issues with ethical dimensions, and such discussions should be treated as a legitimate topic. Third, top management should regularly declare unequivocal support of the company's ethical code and take a strong stand on expecting all company personnel to conduct themselves in an ethical fashion at all times. This means iterating and reiterating to employees that it is their duty to observe the company's ethical codes. Ideally, the company's commitment to its stated values and ethical principles will instill not only a corporate conscience but also a conscience on the part of company personnel that prompts them to report possible ethical violations. While ethically conscious companies have provisions for disciplining violators, *the main purpose of enforcement is to encourage compliance rather than administer punishment.* Thus, the motive for reporting possible ethical violations is not so much to get someone in trouble as to prevent further damage and heighten awareness of operating within ethical bounds. Fourth, top management must be prepared to act as the final ar-

Lockheed Martin's Corrective Actions after Violating U.S. Antibribery Laws

Lockheed Martin Corporation is among the world's leading producers of aeronautics and space systems, with 2002 sales of $26 billion. The company designed and built the P-38 fighter, B-29 bomber, U-2 and SR-71 reconnaissance aircraft, C-130 cargo planes, F-104 Starfighter, F-16 Fighting Falcon, F-22 Raptor, and Titan and Trident missiles. It has been a major contractor on the Mercury, Gemini, Apollo, Skylab, and shuttle space programs.

Lockheed Martin's status as a U.S. government contractor was jeopardized in 1995 when company officials admitted that the company had conspired to violate U.S. antibribery laws. The infraction occurred in 1990 when Lockheed Martin paid an Egyptian lawmaker $1 million to help the company secure a contract to supply Egypt with C-130 cargo planes. The U.S. government fined Lockheed Martin $24.8 million and placed it on three-year probation during which further ethics violations could bar the company from bidding on government contracts.

After the conviction, Lockheed Martin's CEO and other senior executives put a comprehensive ethics compliance program in place to guard against subsequent violations. Completion of an online ethics training course was made mandatory for all employees; the course covered Lockheed Martin's code of ethics and business conduct. The online software system records when employees complete online sessions on such topics as sexual harassment, security, software-license compliance, labor charging, insider trading, and gratuities. It also gives the company the

capability to conduct up-to-the-minute ethics audits to determine how many hours of training have been completed by each of Lockheed Martin's 170,000 employees.

Lockheed Martin's ethics software programs provide company managers with a variety of statistics related to ethics violations that do occur at the company—like the number of detected violations of misuse of company resources, conflicts of interest, and security breaches. In addition, the system gives an accounting of the number of Lockheed Martin employees discharged, suspended, and reprimanded for ethics violations. Lockheed Martin managers and the U.S. government use the database to assess the state of business ethics at the company.

Lockheed Martin's renewed commitment to honesty, integrity, respect, trust, responsibility, and citizenship—along with its method for monitoring ethics compliance—paved the way for the company to receive the 1998 American Business Ethics Award. Upon receiving the award, the company's chairman and CEO, Vance Coffman, said, "At Lockheed Martin, we have stressed that the first and most important unifying principle guiding us is ethical conduct, every day and everywhere we do business. Receiving the American Business Ethics Award is a strong signal that we are achieving our goal of putting our Corporation on a firm ethical foundation for the challenges of the 21st century."

Sources: Lockheed Martin website and *The Wall Street Journal*, October 21, 1999, p. B1.

---

biter on hard calls; this means removing people from key positions or terminating them when they are guilty of a violation. It also means reprimanding those who have been lax in monitoring and enforcing ethical compliance. Failure to act swiftly and decisively in punishing ethical misconduct is interpreted as a lack of real commitment.

See Company Spotlight 9.3 for a discussion of the actions Lockheed Martin's top executives took when the company faced a bribery scandal.

Corporate Citizenship and Social Responsibility: Another Dimension of Model Ethical Behavior Strong enforcement of a corporate code of ethics by itself is not sufficient to make a company a good corporate citizen. Business leaders who want their companies to be regarded as exemplary corporate citizens must not only see that their companies operate ethically but also display a social conscience in decisions that affect stakeholders, especially employees, the communities in which they operate, and society at large. Corporate citizenship and socially responsible decision making are demonstrated in a number of ways: having family-friendly employment practices, operating a safe workplace, taking special pains to protect the environment (beyond what is required by law), taking an active role in community affairs, interacting with community officials to minimize the impact of layoffs or hiring large numbers of new employees (which could put a strain on local schools and utility services), and being a generous supporter of charitable causes and projects that benefit society. For example, Chick-Fil-A, an Atlanta-based fast-food chain with 700 outlets, has a charitable foundation, supports 10 foster homes and a summer camp, funds two scholarship programs, and participates in a number of one-on-one programs with children.[25] Toys "R" Us supports initiatives addressing the issues of child labor and fair labor practices around the world. Community Pride Food Stores is assisting in revitalizing the inner city of Richmond, Virginia, where the company is based. The owner of Malden Mills Industries in Malden, Massachusetts, kept employees on the company's payroll for months while a fire-razed plant was rebuilt.

What separates companies that make a sincere effort to carry their weight in being good corporate citizens from companies that are content to do only what is legally required of them are company leaders who believe strongly in good corporate citizenship. Companies with socially conscious strategy leaders and a core value of corporate social responsibility are the most likely to conduct their affairs in a manner befitting a good corporate citizen.

Leading the Process of Making Corrective Adjustments

The leadership challenge of making corrective adjustments is twofold: deciding when adjustments are needed and deciding what adjustments to make. Both decisions are a normal and necessary part of managing the strategy execution process, since no scheme for implementing and executing strategy can foresee all the events and problems that will arise. There comes a time at every company when managers have to fine-tune or overhaul the approaches to strategy execution and push for better results. Clearly, when a company's strategy execution effort is not delivering good results and making measure progress toward operating excellence, it is the leader's responsibility to step forward and push corrective actions.

The *process* of making corrective adjustments varies according to the situation. In a crisis, it is typical for leaders to have key subordinates gather information, identify and evaluate options (crunching whatever numbers may be appropriate), and perhaps prepare a preliminary set of recommended actions for consideration. The organizational leader then usually meets with key subordinates and personally presides over extended discussions of the proposed responses, trying to build a quick consensus among members of the executive inner circle. If no consensus emerges and action is required immediately, the burden falls on the manager in charge to choose the response and urge its support.

When the situation allows managers to proceed more deliberately in deciding when to make changes and what changes to make, most managers seem to prefer a process of incrementally solidifying commitment to a particular course of action.[26] The process that managers go through in deciding on corrective adjustments is essentially the same for both proactive and reactive changes: They sense needs, gather information, broaden and deepen their understanding of the situation, develop options and explore their pros and cons, put forth action proposals, generate partial (comfort-level) solutions, strive for a consensus, and finally formally adopt an agreed-on course of action.[27] The time frame for deciding what corrective changes to initiate can take a few hours, a few days, a few weeks, or even a few months if the situation is particularly complicated.

Success in initiating corrective actions usually hinges on thorough analysis of the situation, the exercise of good business judgment in deciding what actions to take, and good implementation of the corrective actions that are initiated. Successful managers are skilled in getting an organization back on track rather quickly; they (and their staffs) are good at discerning what actions to take and in ramrodding them through to a successful conclusion. Managers that struggle to show measurable progress in generating good results and improving the performance of strategy-critical value chain activities are candidates for being replaced.

The challenges of leading a successful strategy execution effort are, without question, substantial.[28] But the job is definitely doable. Because each instance of executing strategy occurs under different organizational circumstances, the managerial agenda for executing strategy always needs to be situation-specific—there's no neat generic procedure to follow. And, as we said at the beginning of Chapter 7, executing strategy is an action-oriented, make-the-right-things-happen task that challenges a manager's ability to lead and direct organizational change, create or reinvent business processes, manage and motivate people, and achieve performance targets. If you now better understand what the challenges are, what approaches are available, which issues need to be considered, and why the action agenda for implementing and executing strategy sweeps across so many aspects of administrative and managerial work, then we will look on our discussion in Chapters 7–9 as a success.

A Final Word on Managing the Process of Crafting and Executing Strategy   In practice, it is hard to separate the leadership requirements of executing strategy from the other pieces of the strategy process. As we said in Chapter 1, the job of crafting, implementing, and executing strategy is a five-task process with much looping and recycling to fine-tune and adjust strategic visions, objectives, strategies, capabilities, implementation approaches, and cultures to fit one another and to fit changing circumstances. The process is continuous, and the conceptually separate acts of crafting and executing strategy blur together in real-world situations. The best tests of good strategic leadership are whether the company has a good strategy and whether the strategy execution effort is delivering the hoped-for results. If these two conditions exist, the chances are excellent that the company has good strategic leadership.

Key Points

A company's culture is manifested in the values and business principles that management preaches and practices, in the tone and philosophy of official policies and procedures, in its revered traditions and oft-repeated stories, in the attitudes and behaviors of employees, in the peer pressures that exist to display core values, in the organization's politics, in its approaches to people management and problem solving, in its relationships with external stakeholders (particularly vendors and the communities in which it operates), and in the atmosphere that permeates its work environment. Culture thus concerns the personality a company has and the style in which it does things.

Very often, the elements of company culture originate with a founder or other early influential leaders who articulate the values, beliefs, and principles to which the company should adhere. These elements then get incorporated into company policies, a creed or values statement, strategies, and operating practices. Over time, these values and practices become shared by company employees and managers. Cultures are perpetuated as new leaders act to reinforce them, as new employees are encouraged to adopt and follow them, as stories of people and events illustrating core values and practices are told and retold, and as organization members are honored and rewarded for displaying cultural norms.

Company cultures vary widely in strength and in makeup. Some cultures are strongly embedded, while others are weak or fragmented. Some cultures are unhealthy, often dominated by self-serving politics, resistance to change, and inward focus. Un-healthy cultural traits are often precursors to declining company performance. In adap-tive cultures, the work climate is receptive to new ideas, experimentation, innovation, new strategies, and new operating practices provided the new behaviors and operating practices that management is calling for are seen as legitimate and consistent with the core values and business principles underpinning the culture. An adaptive culture is a terrific managerial ally, especially in fast-changing business environments, because company personnel are receptive to risk taking, experimentation, innovation, and changing strategies and practices—there's a feeling of confidence that the organization can deal with whatever threats and opportunities come down the pike. In direct con-trast to change-resistant cultures, adaptive cultures are very supportive of managers and employees at all ranks who propose or help initiate useful change; indeed, there's a proactive approach to identifying issues, evaluating the implications and options, and implementing workable solutions.

A culture grounded in values, practices, and behavioral norms that match what is needed for good strategy execution helps energize people throughout the company to do their jobs in a strategy-supportive manner, adding significantly to the power of a company's strategy execution effort and the chances of achieving the targeted results. But when the culture is in conflict with some aspect of the company's direction, per-formance targets, or strategy, the culture becomes a stumbling block. Thus, an impor-tant part of the managing the strategy execution process is establishing and nurturing a good fit between culture and strategy.

Changing a company's culture, especially a strong one with traits that don't fit a new strategy's requirements, is one of the toughest management challenges. Changing a culture requires competent leadership at the top. It requires symbolic actions and sub-stantive actions that unmistakably indicate serious commitment on the part of top man-agement. The more that culture-driven actions and behaviors fit what's needed for good strategy execution, the less managers have to depend on policies, rules, proce-dures, and supervision to enforce what people should and should not do.

Healthy corporate cultures are grounded in ethical business principles, socially ap-proved values, and socially responsible decision making. One has to be cautious in jumping to the conclusion that a company's stated values and ethical principles are mere window dressing. While some companies display low ethical standards, many companies are truly committed to the stated core values and to high ethical standards, and they make ethical behavior *a fundamental component of their corporate culture*. If management practices what it preaches, a company's core values and ethical standards nurture the corporate culture in three highly positive ways: (1) they communicate the company's good intentions and validate the integrity and above-board character of its business principles and operating methods, (2) they steer company personnel toward both doing the right thing and doing things right, and (3) they establish a corporate conscience that gauges the appropriateness of particular actions, decisions, and poli-cies. Companies that really care about how they conduct their business put a stake in the ground, making it unequivocally clear that company personnel are expected to live up to the company's values and ethical standards—how well individuals display core values and adhere to ethical standards is often part of the job performance evaluations. Peer pressures to conform to cultural norms are quite strong, acting as an important deterrent to outside-the-lines behavior.

To be effective, corporate ethics and values programs have to become a way of life through training, strict compliance and enforcement procedures, and reiterated management endorsements. Moreover, top managers must practice what they preach, serving as role models for ethical behavior, values-driven decision making, and a social conscience.

Successful managers have to do several things in leading the drive for good strategy execution and operating excellence. First, they stay on top of things. They keep a finger on the organization's pulse by spending considerable time outside their offices, listening and talking to organization members, coaching, cheerleading, and picking up important information. Second, they are active and visible in putting constructive pressure on the organization to achieve good results. Generally, this is best accomplished by promoting an esprit de corps that mobilizes and energizes organizational members to execute strategy in a competent fashion and deliver the targeted results. Third, they keep the organization focused on operating excellence by championing innovative ideas for improvement and promoting the use of best practices and benchmarking to measure the progress being made in performing value chain activities in first-rate fashion. Fourth, they exert their clout in developing competencies and competitive capabilities that enable better execution. Fifth, they serve as a role model in displaying high ethical standards and insist that company personnel conduct the company's business ethically and in a socially responsible manner. They demonstrate unequivocal and visible commitment to the ethics enforcement process. And, finally, when a company's strategy execution effort is not delivering good results and the organization is not making measure progress toward operating excellence, it is the leader's responsibility to step forward and push corrective actions.

Exercises

1. Go to www.hermanmiller.com and read what the company has to say about its corporate culture in the careers sections of the website. Do you think this statement is just nice window dressing, or, based on what else you can learn about the Herman Miller Company from browsing this website, is there reason to believe that management has truly built a culture that makes the stated values and principles come alive? Explain.

2. Go to the careers section at www.qualcomm.com and see what Qualcomm, one of the most prominent companies in mobile communications technology, has to say about "life at Qualcomm." Is what's on this website just recruiting propaganda, or does it convey the type of work climate that management is actually trying to create? If you were a senior executive at Qualcomm, would you see merit in building and nurturing a culture like what is described in the section on "life at Qualcomm?" Would such a culture represent a tight fit with Qualcomm's high-tech business and strategy (you can get an overview of the Qualcomm's strategy by exploring the section for investors and some of the recent press releases)? Is your answer consistent with what is presented in the "Awards and Honors" menu selection in the "About Qualcomm" portion of the website?

3. Go to www.jnj.com, the website of Johnson & Johnson and read the "J&J Credo," which sets forth the company's responsibilities to customers, employees, the community, and shareholders. Then read the "Our Company" section. Why do you think the credo has resulted in numerous awards and accolades that recognize the company as a good corporate citizen?

4. Do some research on the Internet and see if you can identify five specific examples of unethical conduct on the part of Enron personnel that contributed to the company's downfall.

5. Do a web search on Dennis Kozlowski, former CEO of Tyco International, and gather information on what unethical actions he is alleged to have engaged in during his tenure as the company's CEO. How serious do you think the alleged misconduct is? What sort of ethical climate do you think prevailed at Tyco while Kozlowski was CEO? If you had been an employee of Tyco under Kozlowski, what would your opinion be of his leadership qualities (keeping in mind that the company's financial performance during his tenure was quite good)?

Whole Foods Market, Inc.

Arthur A. Thompson
The University of Alabama

Founded in 1980 as one small store in Austin, Texas, Whole Foods Market had by 2002 evolved into the world's largest retail chain of natural and organic foods supermarkets. The company had over 140 stores in the United States and Canada and sales of $2.7 billion; revenues had grown at more than 20 percent for 12 consecutive quarters. John Mackey, the company's cofounder and CEO, said that throughout its rapid growth Whole Foods Market had "remained a uniquely mission-driven company—highly selective about what we sell, dedicated to our core values and stringent quality standards and committed to sustainable agriculture."

The company's stated mission was "to improve the health, well-being, and healing of both people and the planet"—a mission captured in the company's slogan "Whole Foods, Whole People, Whole Planet" (see Exhibit 1). In pursuit of this mission, the company's strategic plan was to continue to expand its retail operations to offer the highest quality and most nutritious foods to more and more customers, helping them to live healthier and more vital lives. During its 22-year history, Whole Foods Market had been a leader in natural and organic foods movement across the United States, helping the industry gain acceptance among growing numbers of consumers. The company's long-term objectives were to have 400 stores and sales of $10 billion by 2010. John Mackey's vision was for Whole Foods to become a national brand and be regarded as the best food retailer in every community it served.

The Natural and Organic Foods Industry

The combined sales of natural and organic foods—about $34 billion in 2001—represented about 5 percent of the roughly $685 billion in total U.S. grocery store sales. *Natural foods* are defined as foods that are minimally processed; largely or completely free of artificial ingredients, preservatives, and other non–naturally occurring chemicals; and as near to their whole, natural state as possible. The U.S. Department of Agriculture's Food and Safety Inspection Service defines *natural food* as "a product containing no artificial ingredient or added color and that is minimally processed." Sales of natural foods products had increased at double-digit rates in the 1990s, but

Exhibit 1   WHOLE FOODS MARKET'S SLOGAN: WHOLE FOODS, WHOLE PEOPLE, WHOLE PLANET

Whole Foods

We obtain our products locally and from all over the world, often from small, uniquely dedicated food artisans. We strive to offer the highest quality, least processed, most flavorful and naturally preserved foods. Why? Because food in its purest state—unadulterated by artificial additives, sweeteners, colorings and preservatives—is the best tasting and most nutritious food available.

Whole People

We recruit the best people we can to become part of our team. We empower them to make their own decisions, creating a respectful workplace where people are treated fairly and are highly motivated to succeed. We look for people who are passionate about food. Our team members are also well-rounded human beings. They play a critical role in helping build the store into a profitable and beneficial part of its community.

Whole Planet

We believe companies, like individuals, must assume their share of responsibility as tenants of Planet Earth. On a global basis we actively support organic farming—the best method for promoting sustainable agriculture and protecting the environment and the farm workers. On a local basis, we are actively involved in our communities by supporting food banks, sponsoring neighborhood events, compensating our team members for community service work, and contributing at least five percent of total net profits to not-for-profit organizations.

Source: www.wholefoodsmarket.com, December 7, 2002.

growth slowed to 8.3 percent in 2001 and was running in the single digits in 2002. Even so, this was considerably higher than the flat 1–2 percent sales growth at conventional supermarket chains. The fastest-growing categories in *Natural Foods Merchandiser*'s annual market survey were nutrition bars (21 percent); in-store food service—deli, restaurant, and juice bars (16 percent); other beverages, excluding beer, wine, coffee, tea, and dairy (12 percent); and snack foods (10 percent).

Organic foods included fresh fruits and vegetables, meats, and processed foods produced using:

■ Agricultural management practices that promoted a healthy and renewable ecosystem that used no genetically engineered seeds or crops, sewage sludge, long-lasting pesticides, herbicides, or fungicides.

■ Livestock management practices that involved organically grown feed, fresh air, and outdoor access for the animals, and no use of antibiotics or growth hormones.

■ Food processing practices that protected the integrity of the organic product and did not involve the use of radiation, genetically modified organisms, or synthetic preservatives.

In 1990, passage of the Organic Food Production Act started the process of establishing national standards for organically grown products in the United States, a movement that included farmers, food activists, conventional food producers, and consumer groups. In October 2002, the U.S. Department of Agriculture (USDA) officially established labeling standards for organic products, overriding both the patchwork of inconsistent state regulations for what could be labeled as organic and the different rules of some 43 agencies for certifying organic products. The new USDA regulations established four categories of food with organic ingredients, with varying levels of organic purity:

1. *100 percent organic products:* Such products were usually whole foods, such as fresh fruits and vegetables, grown by organic methods—which meant that the product had been grown without the use of synthetic pesticides or sewage-based fertilizers, had not been subjected to irradiation, and had not been genetically modified or injected with bioengineered organisms, growth hormones, or antibiotics. Products that were 100 percent organic could carry the green USDA organic certification seal, provided the merchant could document that the food product had been organically grown (usually by a certified organic producer).

2. *Organic products:* Such products, often processed, had to have at least 95 percent organically certified ingredients. These could also carry the green USDA organic certification seal.

3. *Made with organic ingredients:* Such products had to have at least 70 percent organic ingredients; they could be labeled "made with organic ingredients" but could not display the USDA seal.

4. *All other products with organic ingredients:* Products with less than 70 percent organic ingredients could not use the word *organic* on the front of a package, but organic ingredients could be listed among other ingredients in a less prominent part of the package.

An official with the National Organic Program, commenting on the appropriateness and need for the new USDA regulations, said, "For the first time, when consumers see the word *organic* on a package, it will have consistent meaning."[1] The new labeling program was not intended as a health or safety program (organic products have not been shown to be more nutritious than conventionally grown products, according to the American Dietetic Association), but rather as a marketing solution. An organic label has long been a selling point for shoppers wanting to avoid pesticides or to support environmentally friendly agricultural practices. However, the new regulations required additional documentation on the part of growers, processors, exporters, importers, shippers, and merchants to verify that they were certified to grow, process, or handle organic products carrying the USDA's organic seal.

Sales of organics were an estimated $9–$11 billion in 2001, up from $1 billion in 1990, and were growing at a 20–24 percent annual rate. The Organic Trade Association estimated that sales of organic food products would reach $20 billion in 2005. In 2002, organic products were sold in about 20,000 natural foods stores and about 70 percent of conventional supermarkets.

According to the USDA, 2000 was the first year in which more organic food was sold in conventional U.S. supermarkets than in the nation's 20,000 natural foods stores. In the past several years, most mainstream supermarkets had been expanding their selections of natural and organic products, which ranged from potato chips to fresh produce to wines. Fresh produce was the most popular organic product—in 2001, 5 percent of the lettuce and 3 percent of the apples produced in the United States were organically grown. Meat, dairy, and convenience foods were among the fastest growing organic product categories. A number of supermarket chains had added natural foods sections to their stores; Kroger had special sections for natural foods and organics in almost half of its 2,400 stores in 2002, and the number was growing. Wal-Mart's newest retail division, the smaller-format Neighborhood Markets, had a special "healthy-living" section that included organic foods; Costco Wholesale was experimenting with a Costco Fresh store focused on gourmet foods and wine. 7-Eleven had begun selling organic cookies at 600 stores in California. A few grocery chains, including upscale Harris Teeter in the southeastern United States and Whole Foods Market, had launched their own private-label brands of organics. Most industry observers expected that, as demand for natural and organic foods expanded, conventional supermarkets would continue to expand their offerings and selection.

Leading food processors were showing greater interest in organics as well. Heinz had recently introduced an organic ketchup and owned a 19 percent stake in Hain Celestial Group, one of the largest organic and natural foods producers. Starbucks, Green Mountain Coffee, and several other premium coffee marketers had introduced a number of organically grown coffees; Odwalla juices were organic; and Tyson Foods had introduced a line of organic chicken products. Lite House organic salad dressings had recently been added to the shelves of several mainstream supermarkets. Major food processing companies like Kraft, General Mills, Groupe Danone (the parent of Dannon Yogurt), Dean Foods, and Kellogg had all purchased organic food producers in an effort to capitalize on sales-growth opportunities for healthy foods that taste good. Dean Foods' CEO, explaining the company's acquisition of organic soy producer White Wave for $204 million in May 2002, said, "We believe that the trend toward organics is in its infancy."

Organic farmland in the United States was estimated at 2.4 million acres. An estimated 12,200 mostly small-scale farmers were growing organic products in 2002, and the number was increasing about 12 percent annually. The amount of certified organic cropland doubled between 1997 and 2001, and livestock pastures increased at an even faster rate. However, less than 1 percent of U.S. farmland was certified organic in 2002.

Several factors had combined to transform natural foods retailing, once a niche market, into the fastest-growing segment of U.S. food sales:

- Healthier eating patterns on the part of a populace that was becoming better educated about foods, nutrition, and good eating habits. Among those most interested in organic products were aging affluent people concerned about health and better-for-you foods.

- Increasing consumer concerns over the purity and safety of food due to the presence of pesticide residues, growth hormones, artificial ingredients and other chemicals, and genetically engineered ingredients.

- Environmental concerns due to the degradation of water and soil quality.

- A "wellness," or health-consciousness, trend among people of many ages and ethnic groups.

The *Nutrition Business Journal* estimated in 2001 that 0.3 percent of U.S. adults, or about 600,000 people, were heavy purchasers of organic foods, spending an average of $200 per month. Another 1.5 percent, or 3.3 million people, were light users, spending about $50 monthly. About 8 percent of American consumers bought organic products occasionally. The 90 percent of shoppers who bought no organic products at all was seen as offering excellent long-term market potential for being converted to organics, but was not viewed as the best short-term target for sales growth.

Exhibit 2 shows 2001 data for the 10 largest U.S. supermarket retailers.

Exhibit 2   TEN LARGEST U.S. SUPERMARKET CHAINS, 2001

Company	Number of Stores	2001 Sales Revenues (in billions)	Share of Total U.S. Grocery Sales ($682.3 billion)
Wal-Mart Supercenters	1,060	$65.3	9.6%
Kroger	2,392	50.1	7.3
Albertson's	2,541	37.9	5.6
Safeway	1,759	34.3	5.0
Ahold USA	1,600	23.2	3.4
Supervalu	463	21.3	3.1
Costco Wholesale	369	20.5	3.0
Sam's Clubs	500	18.4	2.7
Publix Super Markets	684	15.1	2.2
Delhaize (Food Lion, Kash 'n Karry, Hannaford Bros.)	1,461	14.9	2.2

Source: www.supermarketnews.com, December 10, 2002.

Whole Foods Market

Whole Foods Market was founded in Austin, Texas, when three local businessmen decided the natural foods industry was ready for a supermarket format. The three founders were John Mackey, owner of Safer Way Natural Foods, and Craig Weller and Mark Skiles, owners of Clarksville Natural Grocery. The original Whole Foods Market opened in 1980 with a staff of only 19. It was an immediate success. At the time, there were less than half a dozen natural foods supermarkets in the United States. By 1991, the company had 10 stores, revenues of $92.5 million, and net income of $1.6 million.

In 1997, when Whole Foods developed the "Whole Foods, Whole People, Whole Planet" slogan, John Mackey said:

> This slogan taps into perhaps the deepest purpose of Whole Foods Market. It's a purpose we seldom talk about because it seems pretentious, but a purpose nevertheless felt by many of our team members and by many of our customers (and hopefully many of our shareholders too). Our deepest purpose as an organization is helping support the health, well-being, and healing of both people (customers and Team Members) and of the planet (sustainable agriculture, organic production and environmental sensitivity). When I peel away the onion of my personal consciousness down to its core in trying to understand what has driven me to create and grow this company, I come to my desire to promote the general well-being of everyone on earth as well as the earth itself. This is my personal greater purpose with the company and the slogan perfectly reflects it.

Complementing the slogan were five core values shared by both top management and company personnel (see Exhibit 3).

Exhibit 3   WHOLE FOODS MARKET'S CORE VALUES

Our Core Values

The following list of core values reflects what is truly important to us as an organization. These are not values that change from time to time, situation to situation or person to person, but rather they are the underpinning of our company culture. Many people feel Whole Foods is an exciting company of which to be a part and a very special place to work. These core values are the primary reasons for this feeling, and they transcend our size and our growth rate. By maintaining these core values, regardless of how large a company Whole Foods becomes, we can preserve what has always been special about our company. These core values are the soul of our company.

Selling the Highest Quality Natural and Organic Products Available

- **Passion for Food**
  We appreciate and celebrate the difference natural and organic products can make in the quality of one's life.
- **Quality Standards**
  We have high standards and our goal is to sell the highest quality products we possibly can. We define quality by evaluating the ingredients, freshness, safety, taste, nutritive value and appearance of all of the products we carry. We are buying agents for our customers and not the selling agents for the manufacturers.

Satisfying and Delighting Our Customers

- **Our Customers**
  They are our most important stakeholders in our business and the lifeblood of our business. Only by satisfying our customers first do we have the opportunity to satisfy the needs of our other stakeholders.
- **Extraordinary Customer Service**
  We go to extraordinary lengths to satisfy and delight our customers. We want to meet or exceed their expectations on every shopping trip. We know that by doing so we turn customers into advocates for our business. Advocates do more than shop with us, they talk about Whole Foods to their friends and others. We want to serve our customers competently, efficiently, knowledgeably and with flair.
- **Education**
  We can generate greater appreciation and loyalty from all of our stakeholders by educating them about natural and organic foods, health, nutrition and the environment.
- **Meaningful Value**
  We offer value to our customers by providing them with high quality products, extraordinary service and a competitive price. We are constantly challenged to improve the value proposition to our customers.
- **Retail Innovation**
  We value retail experiments. Friendly competition within the company helps us to continually improve our stores. We constantly innovate and raise our retail standards and are not afraid to try new ideas and concepts.
- **Inviting Store Environments**
  We create store environments that are inviting and fun, and reflect the communities they serve. We want our stores to become community meeting places where our customers meet their friends and make new ones.

Team Member Happiness and Excellence

- **Empowering Work Environments**
  Our success is dependent upon the collective energy and intelligence of all of our Team Members. We strive to create a work environment where motivated Team Members can flourish and succeed to their highest potential. We appreciate effort and reward results.
- **Self-Responsibility**
  We take responsibility for our own success and failures. We celebrate success and see failures as opportunities for growth. We recognize that we are responsible for our own happiness and success.
- **Self-Directed Teams**
  The fundamental work unit of the company is the self- directed Team. Teams meet regularly to discuss issues, solve problems and appreciate each others' contributions. Every Team Member belongs to a Team.
- **Open & Timely Information**
  We believe knowledge is power and we support our Team Members' right to access information that impacts their jobs. Our books are open to our Team Members, including our annual individual compensation report. We also recognize everyone's right to be listened to and heard regardless of their point of view.

Exhibit 3   (continued)

- **Incremental Progress**
  Our company continually improves through unleashing the collective creativity and intelligence of all of our Team Members. We recognize that everyone has a contribution to make. We keep getting better at what we do.

- **Shared Fate**
  We recognize there is a community of interest among all of our stakeholders. There are no entitlements; we share together in our collective fate. To that end we have a salary cap that limits the compensation (wages plus profit incentive bonuses) of any Team Member to ten times the average total compensation of all full-time Team Members in the company.

Creating Wealth Through Profits & Growth

- **Stewardship**
  We are stewards of our shareholders' investments and we take that responsibility very seriously. We are committed to increasing long term shareholder value.

- **Profits**
  We earn our profits everyday through voluntary exchange with our customers. We recognize that profits are essential to creating capital for growth, prosperity, opportunity, job satisfaction and job security.

Caring About Our Communities & Our Environment

- **Sustainable Agriculture**
  We support organic farmers, growers and the environment through our commitment to sustainable agriculture and by expanding the market for organic products.

- **Wise Environmental Practices**
  We respect our environment and recycle, reuse, and reduce our waste wherever and whenever we can.

- **Community Citizenship**
  We recognize our responsibility to be active participants in our local communities. We give a minimum of 5% of our profits every year to a wide variety of community and non-profit organizations. In addition, we pay our Team Members to give of their time to community and service organizations.

- **Integrity in All Business Dealings**
  Our trade partners are our allies in serving our stakeholders. We treat them with respect, fairness and integrity at all times and expect the same in return.

Source: www.wholefoodsmarket.com, December 9, 2002.

Whole Foods Market grew at a rapid clip in the 11 years following its founding, with sales rising to $2.7 billion—a compound rate of almost 36 percent—and profits increasing to $84.5 million. Average weekly sales at the company's stores were climbing:

Fiscal Year	Average Weekly Sales
1997	$277,054
1998	293,390
1999	309,836
2000	324,710
2001	353,024
2002	392,837

The company's growth strategy was to expand via a combination of opening its own new store and acquiring existing stores. About 40 percent of the company's store base had come from acquisitions; since 1991, the company had acquired 60 stores through 13 acquisitions (see Exhibit 4). Since the natural foods industry was highly

Exhibit 4   MAJOR ACQUISITIONS BY WHOLE FOODS MARKET

Year	Company Acquired	Location	Number of Stores	Acquisition Costs
1992	Bread & Circus	Northeast United States	6	$20 million plus $6.2 million in common stock
1993	Mrs. Gooch's	Southern California	7	2,970,596 shares of common stock
1996	Fresh Fields	East Coast and Chicago area	22	4.8 million shares of stock plus options for 549,000 additional shares
1997	Merchant of Vino	Detroit area	6	Approximately 1 million shares of common stock
1999	Nature's Heartland	Boston area	4	$24.5 million
2000	Food 4 Thought (Natural Abilities, Inc.)	Sonoma County, CA	3	$25.7 million, plus assumption of certain liabilities
2001	Harry's Farmer's Market	Atlanta	3	$35 million in cash plus certain liabilities

Source: Company documents.

Exhibit 5   GROWTH IN THE NUMBER OF STORES IN THE WHOLE FOODS MARKET CHAIN

Year	Number of Stores at End of Fiscal Year	Year	Number of Stores at End of Fiscal Year
1991	10	1997	75
1992	25	1998	87
1993	42	1999	100
1994	49	2000	117
1995	61	2001	126
1996	68	2002	135

Store Counts	1997	1998	1999	2000	2001	2002
Beginning of fiscal year	68	75	87	100	117	126
New stores opened	7	9	9	17	12	11
Stores acquired	2	6	5	3	0	3
Relocations and closures	(2)	(3)	(1)	(3)	(3)	(5)
End of fiscal year	75	87	100	117	126	135

Source: Company documents.

fragmented, consisting of close to 20,000 mostly one-store operations and small and regional chains, Whole Foods' management planned to continue to pursue acquisitions of smaller chains that provided access to desirable locations and markets as well as to experienced team members. However, the company expected to grow more by opening new stores than by acquiring existing stores. Exhibit 5 summarizes the company's historical store growth.

In late November 2002, the company had 19 stores in varying stages of development, averaging 41,000 square feet. The company expected to open 6–8 stores before the end of 2002, giving it a total of more than 140 stores going into 2003.

Store Size and Product Line

The company's stores had an open format and generated average annual sales approaching $21 million. Stores more than five years old averaged about 25,000 square feet, stores less than five years old averaged about 35,000 square feet, and the company's newest stores ranged between 25,000 and 50,000 square feet (the new stores of supermarket chains like Safeway and Kroger averaged around 55,000 square feet). The company sought to locate its new stores in the upscale areas of urban metropolitan centers—95 percent were located in the top 50 statistical metropolitan areas. In 2002, Whole Foods had stores in 25 states and 33 of the top 50 U.S. metropolitan areas. In 2001, the company opened its first stores in New York City (Manhattan), Denver, Boca Raton, and St. Louis. In 2002, the company entered Portland; Albuquerque; Kansas City; Colorado Springs; and Toronto, Canada. Whole Foods Market had announced plans for a new 80,000 square-foot landmark store in Austin.

Most stores were in high-traffic shopping locations, some were freestanding, and some were in strip centers. Whole Foods had its own internally developed model to analyze potential markets according to education levels, population density, and income. After picking a target metropolitan area, the company's site consultant did a comprehensive site study and developed sales projections; potential sites had to pass certain financial hurdles. New stores opened 12 to 24 months after a lease was signed. The cash investment needed to ready a new Whole Foods Market for opening varied with the metropolitan area, site characteristics, store size, and amount of work performed by the landlord; totals ranged from as little as $2 million to as much as $16 million—the average for the past three years was $8.6 million. In addition to the cost of readying a store for operation, it took approximately $750,000 to stock the store with inventory, a portion of which was financed by vendors. Preopening expenses had averaged approximately $600,000 per store over the past three years.

Whole Foods' product line included roughly 26,000 food and nonfood items that appealed to both natural foods and gourmet shoppers:

- Fresh produce—fruits; vegetables; displays of fresh-cut fruits; and a selection of seasonal, exotic, and specialty products like cactus pears and cippolini onions.

- Meat and poultry—natural meat, turkey, and chicken products from animals raised on wholesome grains, pastureland, and well water (and not grown with the use of by-products, hormones, or steroids). There were 20 varieties of house-made sausages.

- Fresh seafood—a selection of fresh fish; shrimp; oysters; clams; mussels; homemade marinades; and exotic items like octopus, sushi, and black tip shark. A portion of the fresh fish selections at the seafood station came from the company's Pigeon Cove seafood facility and processing plant in Gloucester, Massachusetts. Seafood items coming from distant supply sources were flown in to stores to ensure maximum freshness.

- A selection of daily baked goods—breads, cakes, pies, cookies, bagels, muffins, and scones.

- Prepared foods—soups, canned and packaged goods, oven-ready meals, rotisserie meats, hearth-fired pizza, pastas, pâtés, salad bars, a sandwich station, and a selection of entrées and side foods prepared daily. Many of the prepared foods came from the company's sizable commissary operations.

- A worldwide selection of cheeses.

- Frozen foods, juices, yogurt and dairy products, smoothies, and bottled waters.

- A wide selection of bulk items in bins.

- An olive bar (with as many as 24 varieties).

- A selection of chocolates.

- Beer and wine—a wide selection of domestic and imported wines (selections varied from store to store). Organic wines were among those available.

- A coffee and tea bar. The company had its own Allegro brand of specialty and organic coffees and several of the newer stores had in-store coffee-roasting equipment that allowed customers to order any of 20 varieties roasted while they shopped. There were environmentally correct, premium exotic teas from remote forests.

- A nutrition and body care department containing vitamin supplements, herbs and teas, homeopathic remedies, soaps, natural body care and cosmetics products, yoga supplies, and aromatherapy products. All of these products were proven safe using nonanimal testing methods and contained no artificial ingredients.

- Pet products—natural pet foods (including the company's own private-label line), treats, toys, and pest control remedies.

- Grocery and household products—canned and packaged goods, pastas, soaps, cleaning products, and other conventional household items.

- A floral department with sophisticated flower bouquets.

- A "365 Every Day Value" line of private-label products that included over 360 commodity-type natural products at very competitive price points. In addition, the company had a "Whole Foods" line of best-of-class premium and superpremium organic products and an organic food product line developed for children under the "Whole Kids" label.

- Educational products (information on alternative healthcare) and books relating to healing, cookery, diet, and lifestyle. In some stores, there were cooking classes and nutrition sessions. In 2002, the company launched its own cookbook written by chef Steve Petusevsky and Whole Foods team members from across the United States; most of the 350 natural foods recipes were contributed by team members, and some were recipes for the prepared foods coming from the company's own kitchens. The cookbook, with its comprehensive glossary, healthful cooking advice, and menu planning tips, attempted to mirror the essence of Whole Foods Market.

Whole Foods stores had recently begun to stock conventional household products so as to make Whole Foods a one-stop grocery shopping destination where people could get everything on their shopping list. Perishables accounted for about 65 percent of store sales. According to one industry analyst, Whole Foods had "put together the ideal model for the foodie who's a premium gourmet and the natural foods buyer. When you walk into a Whole Foods store, you're overwhelmed by a desire to look at everything you see."[2] Prices at Whole Foods were higher than at conventional supermarkets; organics, for instance, cost 25 to 75 percent more than conventionally grown items. However, as one analyst noted, "If people believe that the food is healthier and

Exhibit 6   **WHOLE FOODS MARKET'S PRODUCT QUALITY STANDARDS AND CUSTOMER COMMITMENTS**

Our business is to sell the highest quality foods we can find at the most competitive prices possible. We evaluate quality in terms of nutrition, freshness, appearance, and taste. Our search for quality is a never-ending process involving the careful judgment of buyers throughout the company.

- We carefully evaluate each and every product we sell.
- We feature foods that are free from artificial preservatives, colors, flavors and sweeteners.
- We are passionate about great tasting food and the pleasure of sharing it with each other.
- We are committed to foods that are fresh, wholesome and safe to eat.
- We seek out and promote organically grown foods.
- We provide food and nutritional products that support health and well-being.

Source: www.wholefoodsmarket.com, December 9, 2002.

they are doing something good for themselves, they are willing to invest a bit more, particularly as they get older...It's not a fad."[3] Another grocery industry analyst noted that while Whole Foods served a growing niche, it had managed to attract a new kind of customer, one who was willing to pay a premium to dabble in health food without being totally committed to vegetarianism or an organic lifestyle.[4]

One of Whole Foods Market's foremost commitments to its customers was to sell foods that met strict standards and that were high quality in terms of nutrition, freshness, appearance, and taste. Whole Foods guaranteed 100 percent satisfaction on all items purchased and went to great lengths to live up to its core value of satisfying and delighting customers—see Exhibit 6 for the company's product quality standards.

Store Description and Site Selection

Whole Foods Market did not have a standard store design. Instead, each store's layout was customized to fit the particular site and building configuration and to best show off the particular product mix for the store's target clientele. Stores had a colorful decor, and products were attractively merchandised (see Exhibit 7). Most stores featured hand-stacked produce, in-store chefs and open kitchens, scratch bakeries, prepared foods stations, European-style charcuterie departments, sampling displays, and ever-changing selections and merchandise displays. Whole Foods got very high marks from merchandising experts and customers for its presentation—from the bright colors of the produce displays, to the quality of the foods and customer service, to the wide aisles and cleanliness. Whole Foods' merchandising skills were said to be a prime factor in its success in luring shoppers back time and again. One retailing consultant said of Whole Foods' new store in Toronto, "The visual and sensory experience is superlative. Today, food is a way of defining who we are and Whole Foods has taken it up a notch."[5] The Toronto store had biographies of farmers suspended from the ceiling on placards; a list of Whole Foods' core values and commitments to product quality greeted customers entering the store; a board calling attention to Whole Foods' "Sustainable Seafood Policy" hung on a board above the seafood station; and recipe cards were at the end of key aisles.

The company was continually experimenting with new merchandising concepts to keep stores fresh and exciting for customers. According to a Whole Foods regional manager, "We take the best ideas from each of our stores and try to incorporate them

Exhibit 7   Scenes from Whole Foods Market Stores

in all our other stores. We're constantly making our stores better."[6] The company's larger stores held expanded selections and displays of high-quality perishables—fresh produce, seafood, baked goods, and prepared foods. Management believed that the more extensive displays of high-quality perishables appealed to a broader customer base and were responsible for the larger stores showing higher performance than the smaller stores. Top management believed the acquisition of the three 70,000-square-foot Harry's Market superstores in Atlanta where 75 percent of sales were perishables would provide the company with valuable intellectual capital in all major perishables categories.

To further a sense of community and interaction with customers, stores typically included sit-down eating areas; customer comment boards; and "Take Action" centers for customers who wanted information on such topics as sustainable agriculture, organics, the sustainability of seafood supplies and overfishing problems, the environment, and similar issues. A few stores offered valet parking, home delivery, and massages. Management at Whole Foods wanted customers to view company stores as a "third place" (besides home and office) where people could gather, learn, and interact while at the same time enjoying an intriguing food-shopping and eating experience.

Marketing and Customer Service

Whole Foods spent less on advertising than conventional supermarkets, relying primarily on word-of-mouth recommendations from customers. Stores spent most of their marketing budgets on in-store signage and store events such as taste fairs, classes, and product samplings. Store personnel were encouraged to extend company efforts to encourage the adoption of a natural and organic lifestyle by going out into the community and conducting a proactive public relations campaign. Each store also had a separate budget for making contributions to philanthropic activities and community outreach programs. At the corporate level, there was a marketing initiative under way to create greater public awareness of the Whole Foods brand.

Since one of its core values was to satisfy and delight customers, Whole Foods Market strove to meet or exceed customer expectations on every shopping trip (see Exhibit 3). Competent, knowledgeable, and friendly service was a hallmark of shopping at a Whole Foods Market. The aim was to turn highly satisfied customers into advocates for Whole Foods who talked to close friends and acquaintances about their positive experiences with the company. Store personnel were personable and chatty with shoppers. Customers could get personal attention in every department of the store. When customers asked where an item was located, team members often took them to the spot, making conversation along the way and offering to answer any questions. Team members were quite knowledgeable and enthusiastic about the products in their particular department and tried to take advantage of opportunities to inform and educate customers about natural foods, organics, healthy eating, and food-related environmental issues. They took pride in helping customers navigate the extensive variety to make the best choices. Meat department personnel provided customers with custom cuts, cooking instructions, and personal recommendations.

Store Operations

Depending on store size and traffic volume, Whole Foods stores employed between 70 and 400 team members, who were organized into up to 11 teams, each led by a team leader. Each team was responsible for a different product category or aspect of store operations such as customer service and customer check-out stations. Whole Foods practiced a decentralized team approach to store operations, with many personnel, merchandising, and operating decisions made by teams at the individual store level. Management believed that the decentralized structure made it critical to have an effective store team leader. The store team leader worked with one or more associate store team leaders, as well as with all the department team leaders, to operate the store as efficiently and profitably as possible. Store team leaders were paid a salary plus a bonus based on the store's economic value added (EVA) contribution; they were also eligible to receive stock options.[7] Store team leaders reported directly to one of eight regional presidents.

Management believed its team members were inspired by the company's mission because it complemented their own views about the benefits of a natural and organic foods diet. In management's view, many Whole Foods team members felt good about their jobs because they saw themselves as contributing to the welfare of society and to the company's customers by selling clean and nutritious foods, by helping advance the cause of long-term sustainable agriculture methods, and by promoting a healthy, pesticide-free environment.

In December 2002, the company had more than 24,000 team members. None were represented by unions, although there had been a couple of unionization attempts. Whole Foods had been ranked by *Fortune* magazine for six consecutive years (1998–2003) as one of the top 100 companies to work for in America. A team member at Whole Foods' store in Austin, Texas, said, "I really feel like we're a part of making the world a better place. When I joined the company 17 years ago, we only had four stores. I have always loved—as a customer and now as a Team Member—the camaraderie, support for others, and progressive atmosphere at Whole Foods Market." According to the company's vice president of human resources, "Team members who love to take initiative, while enjoying working as part of a team and being rewarded through shared fate, thrive here."

Compensation and Incentives

Whole Foods' management strived to create a "shared-fate consciousness" on the part of team members by uniting the self-interests of team members with those of shareholders. One way management reinforced this concept was through a gain-sharing program that rewarded a store's team members according to their store's contribution to operating profit (store sales less cost of goods sold less store operating expenses). The company also encouraged stock ownership on the part of team members through three other programs:

1. *A team member stock option plan*—Team members were eligible for stock options based on seniority, promotion, or the discretion of regional or national executives.

2. *A team member stock purchase plan*—Team members could purchase a restricted number of shares at a discount from the market price through payroll deductions.

3. *A team member 401(k) plan*—Whole Foods Market stock was one of the investment options in the 401(k) plan.

Whole Foods also had a salary cap that limited the compensation (wages plus profit incentive bonuses) of any team member to 10 times the average total compensation of all full-time team members in the company—a policy mandated in the company's core values (see Exhibit 2).

The Use of Economic Value Added In 1999, Whole Foods adopted an economic value added (EVA) management and incentive system. EVA is defined as net operating profits after taxes minus a charge for the cost of capital necessary to generate that profit. Senior executives managed the company with the goal of improving EVA. According to management, stores produced a very attractive EVA on average—in the fourth quarter of fiscal 2001, after-tax return on invested capital at stores open more than a year averaged 33 percent, and stores open more than five years showed an impressive 57 percent return. In fiscal 2001, store contribution averaged 9.5 percent of sales. However, in fiscal year 2001, the company's overall EVA was a negative $30.4 million.

Management used EVA calculations to determine whether the sales and profit projections for new stores would yield a positive and large enough EVA to justify the investment; EVA was also used to guide decisions on store closings and to evaluate new acquisitions. Team members used EVA estimates to guide their decisions. Bonuses paid to team members at a store were tied to the store's EVA contribution. About 350 leaders throughout the company were on EVA-based incentive plans.

Purchasing and Distribution

Whole Foods' buyers purchased most of the items retailed in the company's stores from regional wholesale suppliers and vendors. However, store personnel sourced produce items from local organic farmers whenever possible as part of the company's commitment to promote and support organic farming methods. In recent years, the company had shifted much of the buying responsibility from the store level to the regional and national levels in order to put the company in a better position to negotiate volume discounts with major vendors and distributors. Whole Foods Market was the largest account for many suppliers of natural and organic foods. In the seafood area, company buyers were on the docks each morning to check out not only the available local and international catches coming off of dayboats fishing deep waters but also the products of environmentally responsible aquaculture farms.

The company operated eight regional distribution centers; the largest distribution center, in Austin, Texas, handled distribution of nutritional products to stores in Texas and Louisiana. In addition, the stores were supported by regional bake houses, four regional commissary kitchens that supplied many of the prepared foods, the Pigeon Cove seafood process facility in Massachusetts, a produce procurement and field inspection office, and a central coffee roasting operation.

Community Citizenship and Social Activism

Whole Foods demonstrated its community involvement in two ways: (1) by giving employees paid time off to participate in worthy community service endeavors, and (2) by donating a minimum of 5 percent of its after-tax profits in cash or products to nonprofit organizations. Further, John Mackey indicated the company was sincere in living up to its core values as they related to healthy eating habits and the environment; in the company's 2001 annual report, he stated:

> We do not carry natural and organic products to help boost our sales, we carry natural and organic products because we believe that food in its purest state—unadulterated by artificial additives, sweeteners, colorings and preservatives—is the best tasting and most nutritious food available. We actively support

Exhibit 8   WHOLE FOODS MARKET'S POSITION STATEMENT ON SEAFOOD SUSTAINABILITY

The simple fact is our oceans are soon to be in trouble. Our world's fish stocks are disappearing from our seas because they have been over fished or harvested using damaging fishing practices. To keep our favorite seafood plentiful for us to enjoy and to keep it around for future generations, we must act now.

As a shopper, you have the power to turn the tide. When you purchase seafood from fisheries using ocean-friendly methods, you reward their actions and encourage other fisheries to operate responsibly.

At Whole Foods Market, we demonstrate our long-term commitment to seafood preservation by:

- Supporting fishing practices that ensure the ecological health of the ocean and the abundance of marine life.

- Partnering with groups who encourage responsible practices and provide the public with accurate information about the issue.

- Operating our own well-managed seafood facility and processing plant, Pigeon Cove Seafood, located in Gloucester, Massachusetts.

- Helping educate our customers on the importance of practices that can make a difference now and well into the future.

- Promoting and selling the products of well-managed fisheries.

Source: www.wholefoodsmarket.com, December 9, 2002.

organic farming because we believe it is the best method for promoting sustainable agriculture as well as for protecting the environment and farm workers. It is our authenticity as a wellness lifestyle brand that is our major competitive advantage. We recognize this and are very committed long term to strengthening our brand by remaining true to our mission, core values and quality standards.

Exhibit 8 shows the company's position statement on seafood sustainability. The company had similar position statements on why genetically engineered foods were risky and why organic farming was environmentally beneficial. The company disseminated information on these and other issues in its stores and on its website; the company's website had a "legislative action center" that alerted people to pending legislation and made it easy for them to send their comments and opinions to legislators and government officials.

Whole Foods Market's Financial Performance

From 1991 to 2002, Whole Foods Market's net income rose at a compound average rate of 43.4 percent. The company's net loss of $4.8 million in 2000 was partly attributable to management's decision to dispose of the company's NatureSmart business, which manufactured and sold (via direct marketing) nutritional supplements; the assets of NatureSmart were written down by $24 million in 2000 to reflect the realizable value of the business, which subsequently was sold for $28 million in May 2001. Also in 2000, Whole Foods incurred a $14 million loss in two affiliated dot-com enterprises (gaiam.com and WholePeople.com) in which it owned a minority interest.

The company paid no dividends; 100 percent of the profits after taxes and charitable donations were reinvested in the business. Exhibits 9, 10, and 11 provide a five-year statement of operations, consolidated balance sheets, and selected cash flow data.

Exhibit 9   WHOLE FOODS MARKET, STATEMENT OF OPERATIONS, FISCAL YEARS 1998–2002 (IN THOUSANDS)

	Sept. 29, 2002	Sept. 30, 2001	Sept. 24, 2000	Sept. 26, 1999	Sept. 27, 1998
Sales	$2,690,475	$2,272,231	$1,836,630	$1,492,519	$1,308,070
Cost of goods sold and occupancy costs	1,757,213	1,482,477	1,205,096	985,000	873,088
Gross profit	933,262	789,754	633,534	507,519	434,982
Direct store expenses	675,760	574,503	460,044	363,892	313,698
Store contribution	257,502	215,251	173,490	143,627	121,284
General and administrative expenses	95,871	82,440	60,054	58,511	45,931
Goodwill amortization	—	3,129	2,246	1,198	1,153
Preopening and relocation costs	12,485	8,539	10,497	5,914	3,979
Store closure and asset disposal costs	—	9,425	—	5,940	—
Merger expenses	—	—	—	—	1,699
Operating income	149,146	111,718	100,693	72,064	68,522
Interest expense, net	(10,384)	(17,891)	(15,093)	(8,248)	(7,677)
Investment and other income (loss)	2,056	1,628	(8,015)	1,800	2,303
Income from continuing operations before income taxes	140,818	95,455	77,585	65,616	63,148
Provision for income taxes	56,327	38,182	34,584	25,590	23,454
Equity in losses of unconsolidated affiliates	—	5,626	14,074	—	—
Income from continuing operations	84,491	51,647	28,927	40,026	39,694
Discontinued operations:					
Income (loss) from discontinued operations, net of income taxes	—	—	(9,415)	—	—
Gain (loss) on asset disposal, net of income taxes	—	16,233	(23,968)	—	—
Cumulative effect of change in accounting principle, net of income taxes	—	—	(375)	—	—
Net income	$ 84,491	$ 67,880	$ (4,831)	$ 42,155	$ 45,395
Basic earnings per share	$1.50	$1.26	$(0.09)	$0.80	$0.87
Weighted average shares outstanding	56,385	53,664	52,248	52,748	52,318
Diluted earnings per share:					
Income from continuing operations	$1.40	$0.92	$ 0.53	$0.73	$0.72
Discontinued operations and effect of change in accounting principle, net of income taxes	—	0.29	(0.62)	0.04	0.10
Diluted earnings per share	1.40	1.21	(0.09)	0.77	0.82
Weighted average shares outstanding, diluted basis	63,340	56,185	54,370	54,892	55,488

Source: 2002 10K report.

Exhibit 10   WHOLE FOODS MARKET, CONSOLIDATED BALANCE SHEET, FISCAL YEARS 2001–2002 (IN THOUSANDS)

	Sept. 29, 2002	Sept. 30, 2001
Assets		
Current assets:		
Cash and cash equivalents	$ 12,646	$ 1,843
Trade accounts receivable	30,888	24,859
Merchandise inventories	108,189	98,616
Prepaid expenses and other current assets	8,950	9,151
Deferred income taxes	11,468	8,549
Total current assets	$172,141	$143,018
Property and equipment, net of accumulated depreciation and amortization	$644,688	$542,986
Long-term investments	4,426	4,706
Goodwill	80,548	67,258
Intangible assets, net of accumulated amortization	22,889	24,028
Other assets	8,159	8,513
Deferred income taxes	7,350	20,287
Net assets of discontinued operations	3,000	18,375
Total Assets	$943,201	$829,171
Liabilities and Shareholders' Equity		
Current liabilities:		
Current installments of long-term debt and capital lease obligations	$ 5,789	$ 5,944
Trade accounts payable	59,710	50,468
Accrued payroll, bonus and employee benefits	59,359	41,265
Other accrued expenses	51,440	56,237
Total current liabilities	$176,298	$153,914
Long-term debt and capital lease obligations, less current installments	161,952	250,705
Deferred rent liability	12,091	11,653
Other long-term liabilities	3,774	3,542
Total liabilities	$354,115	$419,814
Shareholders' equity: Common stock, no par value, 150,000 and 100,000 shares authorized; 57,988 and 55,114 shares issued; 57,739 and 54,770 shares outstanding	$341,940	$251,679
Common stock in treasury, at cost	—	(5,369)
Accumulated other comprehensive income	(422)	(30)
Retained earnings	247,568	163,077
Total shareholders' equity	$589,086	$409,357
Total liabilities and shareholders' equity	$943,201	$829,171

Source: Company press release, November 19, 2002, and 2002 10K report.

Exhibit 11   **WHOLE FOODS MARKET, SELECTED CASH FLOW DATA, FISCAL YEARS 1999-2002 (IN THOUSANDS)**

	1999	2000	2001	2002
Income from continuing operations	$ 40,026	$ 28,927	$ 51,647	$ 84,591
Net cash provided by operating activities	116,570	124,209	173,036	229,145
Acquisition of property and equipment	(53,496)	(41,671)	(49,009)	(61,385)
Development costs of new store locations	(80,976)	(110,864)	(103,896)	(100,000)
Payments for acquisitions, net of cash acquired	(24,500)	(25,700)	—	(35,978)
Net cash used in investing activities	(159,761)	(180,707)	(156,928)	(203,357)
Net proceeds from long-term borrowings	49,000	88,000	25,000	32,000
Payments on long-term debt and capital lease obligations	(673)	(6,625)	(78,383)	(127,956)
Proceeds from new stock issues	7,049	10,032	23,179	66,964
Net cash provided by (used in) financing activities	36,437	77,873	(30,204)	(28,992)
Cash and cash equivalents at end of year	3,582	395	1,843	12,646

Source: Company press release, November 19, 2002, and 2001 10K report.

Competitors

Whole Foods Market's two biggest competitors in the natural foods and organics segment of the food retailing industry were Wild Oats Markets and Fresh Market. Another competitor with some overlap in products and shopping ambience was Trader Joe's.

Wild Oats Markets, Inc.

Wild Oats Markets, Inc.—a 99-store natural foods chain based in Boulder, Colorado—ranked second behind Whole Foods in the natural foods and organics segment. The company's stores were in 23 states and British Columbia, Canada; stores were operated under five names: Wild Oats Natural Marketplace, Henry's Marketplace, Nature's—a Wild Oats Market, Sun Harvest, and Capers Community Markets. Founded in 1987, Wild Oats had sales of $893 million in 2001 and was projecting sales of $1.05 billion in 2003. In 1993 and 1994, Wild Oats was named one of the "500 Fastest-Growing Private Companies in America" by *Inc.* magazine. Interest quickly spread to Wall Street, and in 1996 Wild Oats became a public company traded on the NASDAQ under the symbol *OATS*. Grocery analysts believed that Wild Oats had close to a 3 percent market share of the natural and organic foods market in 2002, compared to about 9 percent for Whole Foods.

Wild Oats, under new CEO Perry Odak (formerly the CEO of Ben & Jerry's Homemade until it was acquired by Unilever in 2000), was in something of a turn-around mode in 2002. The company's prior CEO and founder, Mike Gilliland, had gone on an aggressive acquisition streak during the late 1990s to expand Wild Oats' geographic coverage; store growth peaked in 1999 with the acquisition of 47 stores. But Gilliland's acquisition binge piled up extensive debt and dropped the company into a money-losing position with too many stores, a dozen different store names, and a dozen different ways of operating. Product selection and customer service were inconsistent from one location to another.

When Odak arrived in March 2001, he began a turnaround effort: He streamlined operations, closed 28 unprofitable stores, cut prices, trimmed store staffing by 100 employees, and launched a new, smaller prototype store with a heavier emphasis on fresh food. Merchandising and marketing were revamped. The strategy was to draw in more "crossover" shoppers with lower-priced produce, meat, and seafood, along with a "Fresh Look" program stressing freshness and affordability to increase store traffic and raise the average purchase above the current $19 level. While the lower prices cut the company's gross profit margin from 30.3 percent to 29 percent, the company was trying to get the margin back over 30 percent by concentrating its purchases with fewer vendors and getting better discounts. An agreement was reached in September 2002 for Wild Oats to obtain a substantial part of its store inventories from Tree of Life, one of the leading natural foods distributors. After posting losses of $15.0 million in 2000 and $43.9 million in 2001, Wild Oats was on track to return to profitability; the company reported net earnings of $4.3 million in the first nine months of 2002.

Wild Oats' new prototype stores were 22,000 to 24,000 square feet and featured a grocery-store layout, an expanded produce section at the front of the store, a deli, a sushi bar, a juice and java bar, and a reduced selection of canned and packaged items. Wild Oats believed the smaller format was suitable for profitable entry into less-populated markets. Wild Oats had just completed arrangements to sell 4.45 million shares at $11.50 to raise capital for opening 58 stores in the next three years (13 in 2003, 20 in 2004, and 25 in 2005) and remodeling a number of existing stores. Management expected that most of the new stores would incorporate the newly developed prototype. Whole Foods was scheduled to open a number of new stores in cities where Wild Oats had stores. Wild Oats, however, was targeting city and metropolitan neighborhoods for its new stores where there were no Whole Foods stores.

Perry Odak expected that while conventional supermarkets would continue to expand their offerings of natural and organic products, the competitive threat posed by conventional supermarkets was only moderate because their selection was more limited than what Wild Oats stores offered and because they lacked the knowledge and high level of service provided by a natural foods supermarket. In his view, "they are introducing conventional shoppers to natural brands, which will benefit us in the long run." Another of Wild Oats' strategic thrusts was to drive a customer service mindset throughout the organization via training programs and enhanced employee communication. Odak wanted to position Wild Oats as a resource for value-added services and education about health and well-being.

Fresh Market

Fresh Market, headquartered in Greensboro, North Carolina, was a 34-store chain operating in seven southeastern states (Florida, Georgia, North Carolina, South Carolina, Tennessee, Virginia, and Kentucky).[8] The company was founded by Ray Berry, a former vice president with Southland Corporation who had responsibility over some 3,600 7-Eleven stores. The first Fresh Market store opened in 1982 in Greensboro. Berry borrowed ideas from stores he had seen all over the United States and, as the chain expanded, used his convenience-store experience to replicate the store format and shape the product lines. During the 1982–2000 period, Fresh Market's sales revenues grew at a 25.2 percent compound rate, reaching $193 million in 2000; revenues grew about 9.2 percent in 2001, to around $210 million. Berry believed the company's strong financial performance was due to its commitment to service and quality.

Fresh Market's concept was to offer top-quality meats, fresh fish, produce, fresh-baked goods, and specialty items, coupled with top-notch service, in neighborhood stores near educated, high-income residents. Fresh Market stores averaged 18,000 square feet and were also stocked with "upscale grocery boutique" items such as free-range chicken; pick-and-pack spices; gourmet coffees; chocolates; hard-to-get H&H bagels from New York City; Ferrara's New York cheesecake; fresh Orsini parmesan cheese; Acqua della Madonna bottled water; and an extended line of olive oils, wine, and beer. Stores also stocked a bare lineup of most general-grocery products but an expanded selection of products for cooks and entertainers, with 18 styles of designer napkins and six shelves of mustard. None of the meat and few of the deli products were prepackaged, and each department had at least one employee in the area constantly to help shoppers—the idea was to force interaction between store employees and shoppers. Fresh Market's warm lights, classical background music and terra-cotta-colored tiles made it a cozier place to shop than a typical grocery store. The average store had 75 employees, resulting in labor costs about double those of typical supermarkets.

Merchandisers at Fresh Market's headquarters selected the stores' products, but store managers placed orders directly from third-party distributors. According to Berry, Fresh Market didn't have the concentration of stores that would make running its own warehouses profitable; Berry believed some grocers' distribution operations had grown so big that they drove the retail business, rather than the other way around.

Since 2000, the company had opened three to four new stores each year and annual growth had slowed somewhat to about 10 percent. Expansion was funded by internal cash flows and bank debt. Several public companies had shown interest in buying the chain. Ray Berry, age 60, had said, "If I can get what I think the company's worth three years from now, I'll sell it. But I won't sell it for what it's worth today because I'm having too much fun." Without providing any details, Berry indicated that Fresh Market's profitability outpaced the industry average.

Trader Joe's

Based in Pasadena, California, Trader Joe's was a specialty supermarket chain with 178 stores in Arizona, California, Connecticut, Illinois, Indiana, Maryland, Massachusetts, Michigan, Nevada, New Jersey, New York, Ohio, Oregon, Pennsylvania, Virginia, and Washington. Trader Joe's was known for bringing its customers the best-quality products at the best prices. The company described its mission and business as follows:

> At Trader Joe's, our mission is to bring all our customers the best food and beverage values to be found anywhere, and the information to make informed buying decisions. There are more than 2,000 unique grocery items in our label, at prices everyone can afford. We work hard at buying things right: Our buyers travel the world searching for new items; we work with a variety of suppliers who make interesting products for us, many of them exclusive to Trader Joe's; and we make special purchases which are presented to us throughout the year. All our private label products have their own "angle," i.e., vegetarian, Kosher, organic, or just plain decadent, and all natural ingredients.
>
> Our tasting panel tastes every product before we buy it. If we don't like it, we don't buy it. If customers don't like it, they can bring it back—no questions asked!
>
> We stick to the business we know: good food at the best prices! Whenever possible we buy direct from our suppliers, in large volume. We bargain hard and manage our costs carefully. We pay in cash, and on time, so our suppliers like to do business with us.

The company stocked a variety of imported, exotic, and gourmet items, including seafood, baked goods (75 breads, muffins, and cookies from 30 bakeries), organic foods, vitamins, nuts and trail mixes, 80 cheeses from around the world, Trader Joe's whole-bean coffees, fresh produce, fresh salads and entrées, a variety of fat-free and low-fat foods, a selection of meatless entrées, pet foods, frozen entrées, snack foods and energy bars, a selection of chocolates, wine and beer, and an assortment of natural, "cruelty-free" shampoos, lotions, and body care products. Trader Joe's had recently announced that it would work with its vendors to remove genetically modified ingredients from its 800 private-label products. It had also discontinued sale of duck meat because of the cruel conditions under which ducks were grown.

Stores were open, with wide aisles and appealing displays. Because of its combination of low prices, intriguing selections, and friendly service, customers viewed shopping at Trader Joe's as an enjoyable experience. The company was able to keep the prices of its unique, exotic products attractively low (relative to those at Whole Foods, Fresh Market, and Wild Oats) partly because its buyers were always on the lookout for exotic items they could buy at a discount (all products had to pass a taste test and a cost test) and partly because most items were sold under the Trader Joe's label.

Independent Natural and Health Food Grocers

Although two vitamin/supplement chains, General Nutrition Center and Vitamin World, dominated the vitamin/supplement segment with close to 6,000 stores, in 2002 there were approximately 14,000 small, independent retailers of natural and organic foods, vitamins/supplements, and beauty and personal care products. Most were single-store, owner-managed enterprises. Combined sales of the 14,000 independents were in the range of $13 billion in 2002. Most of the independent stores had less than 2,500 square feet of retail sales space and generated revenues of less than $1 million annually, but there were roughly 1,000 natural foods and organic retailers with stores in the size range of 4,000 to 12,000 square feet and sales of between $2 million and $5 million annually.

Product lines and range of selection at the stores of independent natural and health foods retailers varied from narrow to moderately broad, depending on a store's market focus and the shopper traffic it was able to generate. Inventories at stores under 1,000 square feet could run as little as $10,000, while those at stores of 10,000 square feet or more might run $400,000. Many of the independents had some sort of deli or beverage bar, and some even had a small dine-in area with a limited health food menu. Revenues and customer traffic at most independent stores were trending upward, reflecting growing buyer interest in natural and organic products.

Endnotes

[1]As quoted in Elizabeth Lee, "National Standards Now Define Organic Food," *Atlanta Journal and Constitution,* October 21, 2002.

[2]As quoted in Marilyn Much, "Whole Foods Markets: Austin, Texas Green Grocer Relishes Atypical Sales," *Investors Business Daily,* September 10, 2002.

[3]Hollie Shaw, "Retail-Savvy Whole Foods Opens in Canada," *National Post,* May 1, 2002, p. FP9.

[4]See Karin Schill Rives, "Texas-Based Whole Foods Market Makes Changes to Cary, Charlotte, N.C., Grocery Store," *The News and Observer,* March 7, 2002.

[5]Quoted in "Produce That's Picture Perfect," *National Post,* May 9, 2002, p. AL6.

[6]Quoted in "Whole Foods Market to Open in Albuquerque, N.M.," *Santa Fe New Mexican,* September 10, 2002.

[7]EVA at the store level was based on store contribution (store revenues minus cost of goods sold minus store operating expenses) relative to store investment over and above the cost of capital.

[8]Much of the information in this section is based on M. E. Lloyd, "Specialty-Grocer Fresh Market Cultivates Upscale Consumers, Reaps Big Returns," *The Wall Street Journal,* February 20, 2001, p. B11.

mGAMES

Allen Morrison
The University of Western Ontario

Jeffrey Lopez hung up the phone, leaned forward, and buried his face in his hands. It seemed a challenge at this particular moment to try to remember why he had been so excited about his appointment as president and chief executive officer (CEO) of mGAMES (a developer of gaming software for mobile devices) just eight months ago. Lopez stood up from his large mahogany desk, walked to the window and looked out over the horizon toward Boston. It was 9:15 A.M. on Monday, July 22, 2002, and Lopez had just finished taking two telephone calls. The first had come from Benson Marks, principal shareholder and chairman of the board of mGAMES. In their call, Marks had told Lopez that he had just gotten off the phone with an old friend at Credit Suisse First Boston in New York. Specifics could not be provided, but rumors were circulating throughout the bank that a large and well-respected personal digital assistant (PDA) manufacturer was in the process of arranging financing to make a play for mGAMES. During the conversation, Marks reminded Lopez that he did not believe a takeover could be achieved without his consent—since he held 44.5 percent of mGAMES shares—but he also acknowledged that over the past year he had become increasingly concerned with the performance of mGAMES. "Now Jeff. . . you know I'm 100 percent behind you. But we've got to do something here. I need you to put a plan together and I'd like to see something within the next week."

The second call had come from Bjorger Pedersson, senior vice president of product development with a large Scandinavian telecommunications company (sales of US$23 billion). Lopez had not spoken to Pedersson since first meeting him six months earlier at an industry conference in Las Vegas, but he remembered clearly how the two of them had seemed to really click.

Pedersson was clearly excited and got right to the point:

Jeffrey, our people have been looking at your organization now for the past five months. We've been trying to identify potential strategic partners for game development, and mGAMES is No. 1 on our list. We want to work with you. In fact, we are thinking about an exclusive agreement that would essentially take up all of your capacity. We've got $70 million set aside for this to help set you up . . . and we've also already allocated some space for you in our new research facility in Menlo Park, California.

We'd like you to fly here as soon as possible to begin discussions. This could be very big. Our projections show that mobile gaming will be a $6 billion market in five years. As our exclusive partner, the upside in this deal for you guys is enormous.

I know we are jumping the gun a little. But our board wants us to move as quickly as possible, and I am looking for a partner who understands the importance of speed. I've got strict orders to have an agreement in place—with someone—within 45 days.

When the conversation with Pedersson ended, Lopez was clearly excited. However, as he looked again out the window, his ears resonated with the final words he had heard during the earlier conversation with Benson Marks: "mGAMES needs a plan that it can win with! Not only now, but for years to come."

PDAs, Mobile Phones and Handheld Gaming Devices

Beginning in the mid-1990s, handheld devices—PDAs and mobile phones—had become the largest new consumer-based technology craze worldwide. By the end of 2001, it was estimated that over 7 million mobile phones were manufactured and shipped worldwide every week. PDAs were also growing in popularity, and though at the end of 2001 only 28 million total units had been cumulatively sold, projections were that another 10 million units would be shipped during 2002.

There were some geographic differences in the adoption of various handheld units. Most Asian, European, and Middle Eastern consumers had been early to adopt mobile phones and seemed reluctant to buy into the concept of the PDAs. By 2001, mobile phones had become an essential part of their lifestyle, even to the extent that the quality of any given individual's mobile phone was often recognized as a status symbol. The weak adoption of PDAs in these parts of the world was partially due to the fact that early PDAs offered software in English only.

In contrast, North Americans were PDA-crazy, being particularly attracted to the potential for the power of PC-type functionality in the palm of their hands. Compared to Asians and Europeans, North Americans had been relatively slow to adopt mobile phones. One reason for this was because of industry restructuring following the breakup of AT&T and the repositioning of the Baby Bells. The result was not only consumer uncertainty but also a range of often confusing and expensive calling plans. Another reason for the comparatively slow adoption of cell phone technologies was the bulkiness of early mobile phones. However, by 2002, the market in North America had become essentially saturated with many wireless plans offering even lower long-distance rates than wired alternatives.

With North American cellular markets maturing and growth of PDAs accelerating, there was great uncertainty as to who would win out in the future of the handheld device business. Some observers predicted that rather than one format conquering the other, they would all add features and begin to look and perform similarly. Indeed, convergence between mobile phone and PDA technologies was occurring on all fronts. According to Phil Redman of The Gartner Group, "The handset (mobile phone) manufacturers are gunning to take on the PDAs and vice versa. Handsets are simply becoming wireless PDAs."[1]

By 2002, an increasing number of new mobile phones offered built-in personal planning software packages, and a greater number of new PDAs offered short message service (SMS), voice, and/or e-mail communication capabilities. In an exciting yet ambiguous market environment, the only certainty was that consumers were getting tired of carrying multiple devices around.

Convergence in the industry was also occurring when gaming functionality was considered. Nintendo's portable Game Boy system had long since offered personal planning and task list cartridges, and rumors were now circulating that the new Game Boy Advance system—to be released in the fall of 2002—would also offer wireless communication capability. Telecom manufacturers like Ericsson and Nokia were also reportedly engaged in the development of handheld gaming devices that had advanced gaming controls, wireless communication capability and PDA functionality. Handspring's new model had a slot to accept cartridges for playing games and running applications, and Palm had also added card slots to its latest models. David Grasior, president of wireless platform provider Synovial, asserted that "the handheld device of the future will do the things that keep you entertained when you're away from your PC and productive when you don't have a PC handy."[2]

The ongoing convergence of gaming devices, PDA and mobile phones is shown in Exhibit 1.

Competition in the emerging "handheld device industry" was fierce. Essentially, every established PC manufacturer, every telecom manufacturer, most electronics manufacturers, and many others sought to become players in this multibillion-dollar segment. New technologies and new models were constantly being released. Color capability, communication capabilities, screen size, processor speed, RAM capacity, overall size of the unit, and total functionality were all key criteria in the consumer's purchase decision.

Exhibit 1   Convergence in the Handheld Industry

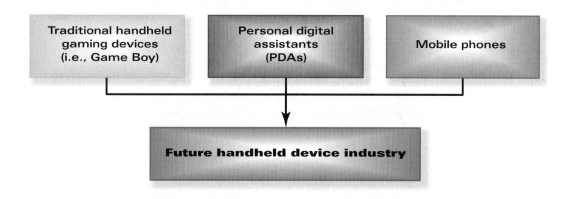

Like many others, Alex Green, vice president of business development for Motorola, believed that gaming functionality would become increasingly important in the market for handheld devices. He summarized where he saw this industry heading:

> [The future will bring us] cell phones with the power of an Xbox, PDAs on which you could play multiplayer Half-Life, with users all over the world, in real time, with real time taunting over the microphone.[3]

Mobile Gaming

Handheld gaming devices of one variety or another had been around for several decades. Electronic gaming devices were a big hit when they first arrived on the market in the mid-1970s and were fashioned so that each device was its own game. It did not take long for the major electronics manufacturers to realize the market potential for these electronic games, and soon thereafter, handheld electronic gaming became a multimillion-dollar industry. As technology evolved, more competitors entered the market. To compete, game manufacturers rolled out ever-more-complex games, leading industry sales to skyrocket. Things looked very promising for these manufacturers—until Nintendo revolutionized the market for handheld gaming devices with the launch of the cartridge-based Game Boy system in the early 1990s. The Game Boy system captivated young consumers, providing them with the new-found ability to play multiple games with advanced graphics on a single handheld gaming device. By 1995, Nintendo possessed over an 85 percent share of the handheld gaming device market.

However, like console-based gaming, the market for handheld games on the Game Boy device was somewhat fickle. Consumers constantly demanded more advanced technology, including improved performance controls, greater processor speeds, and better graphics. While new and exciting games were absolutely critical to the success of any handheld gaming device, the pattern was consistent: After a couple strong years with any particular hardware product, sales would flatten until something bigger and better was released.

In the late 1990s, the first wave of what some called "the gaming generation" arrived in the workplace, in conjunction with technology advances and the increasing popularity of mobile phones and PDAs. Game designers and manufacturers soon began to realize the huge upside potential of wireless gaming on handheld devices. In fact, many believed that with the continuous influx of the gaming generation into the working world, it would actually be wireless gaming functionality that would become the most important driver in the success of any handheld device. In 2001, Datamonitor Research projected that wireless gaming would become a $6 billion market worldwide by 2005, with four out of every five handheld device users playing wireless games.[4]

Despite the longer-term promise, in 2002, games designed for mobile phones and PDAs were a far cry from the action-packed games available on Game Boy or other handheld gaming devices. Game developers were still restricted by network and device limitations. As a result, there was some uncertainty as to which market segment would be the first to adopt the concept of wireless (interactive) gaming. When speaking about this market, the president of one mobile game development company argued:

> [The handheld segment] is not—nor will it ever be—the "gamer" market for people who play Quake, Ultima, Everquest, and Doom. It's about games that everybody already knows how to play. People think it takes complex games to

get people hooked. It doesn't. People also get hooked on very fun, simple games. Our research shows that 80 percent of people play these familiar games.[5]

Other industry insiders disagreed. They believed technology improvements within the handheld device industry would captivate even the most hard-core gamers. The president of a major wireless airtime provider commented:

Those guys still have to get up and go to the bathroom, and they have to get more Chee-tos. You don't want to lose track of the game while you're getting a Coke and a 14-pound bag of M&M's. If you play Diablo, and someone would let you do it wirelessly from a PDA, would you pay $9.95 to do it? You better believe it![6]

In short, while there were too many variables to allow an accurate assessment of how the market for wireless gaming would play itself out, those closest to the industry considered the $6 billion projection by 2005 to be conservative. Perhaps Greg Costikyan, chief design officer for unplugged Games—the individual regarded as the preeminent authority in the wireless gaming industry—summed things up best: "Someone's going to make a lot of money here."

mGAMES

The mGAMES company developed, manufactured, and distributed gaming software for various handheld and mobile devices. In 2001, net company sales reached $60.04 million and operating profits were $8.87 million. (See Exhibits 2, 3, and 4 for a review of mGAMES' financial performance.) In July 2002, mGAMES had 92 employees divided among software development, operations, marketing, sales, and service. With the exception of five regional sales managers, all employees were based at company headquarters. Just over 70 percent of company revenue came from sales in the United States and Canada, 20 percent came from Europe, and 10 percent came from Japan.

The company began operating independently in 1995 as a wholly owned affiliate of BHM Inc. BHM was a video game development company that started up in 1984 in Hastings, Massachusetts, by Benson H. Marks, using inheritance money he had

Exhibit 2   mGAMES INCOME STATEMENT, 1995–2001 (IN MILLIONS OF DOLLARS)

	1995	1996	1997	1998	1999	2000	2001
Net sales	$16.81	$22.65	$33.13	$41.09	$45.81	$55.89	$60.04
Cost of goods sold	6.40	9.33	16.84	19.74	22.96	27.50	30.12
Gross profit	10.41	13.32	16.29	21.35	22.85	28.39	29.92
Selling & admin expenses	2.31	3.11	5.22	7.94	8.23	11.07	12.26
R&D expenses	1.26	1.97	2.86	3.91	4.53	6.64	7.67
Depreciation & amortization	0.35	0.51	0.61	0.72	0.80	1.07	1.12
Operating profit	6.49	7.73	7.60	8.78	9.29	9.61	8.87
Total interest	0.12	0.29	0.38	0.43	0.48	0.70	0.76
Other income / expenses	0.21	0.46	0.89	1.13	1.27	1.43	1.50
Pretax income	6.16	6.98	6.33	7.22	7.54	7.48	6.61
After-tax income	$3.92	$5.61	$5.06	$6.35	$6.40	$6.02	$5.44

Exhibit 3   mGAMES UNIT AND DOLLAR SALES, 1995–2001

	1995	1996	1997	1998	1999	2000	2001
Unit Sales (in millions)	1.42	2.12	2.79	3.55	4.2	4.16	3.89
Dollar Sales (in millions)	$17.26	$23.45	$33.28	$41.32	$48.66	$58.13	$63.01

Exhibit 4   mGAMES 2001 BALANCE SHEET (IN MILLIONS OF DOLLARS)

Assets

Cash and equivalents	$ 0.70
Accounts receivable	4.52
Inventories	6.12
Other current assets	9.56
Total current assets	20.90
Gross plant	6.74
Accumulated depreciation	−1.75
Net plant	4.99
Deferred charges	0.46
Intangible leases	31.50
Other long-term assets	0.32
Total assets	$63.16

Liabilities and Shareholders' Equity

Notes payable	$ 1.20
Accounts payable	4.96
Accrued expenses	3.96
Taxes payable	1.81
Other current liabilities	1.21
Total current liabilities	13.14
Deferred taxes	0.90
Long-term debt	8.20
Other long-term liabilities	0.62
Total liabilities	22.86

Equity

Preferred stock	27.00
Common stock	7.00
Retained earnings	5.70
Other liabilities	0.60
Total equity	40.30
Total liabilities and equity	$63.16

received from the sale of his grandfather's extensive collection of classic cars. Marks, who in 1984 was 42 years old, held a master's degree in computer engineering from the University of Waterloo in Canada and an MBA degree from the Massachusetts Institute of Technology in Boston.

With a personal interest in video games and firsthand knowledge of the spectacular financial success realized by companies such as Commodore and Atari, Marks visualized an incredible future for the video game industry. He anticipated software would absorb the bulk of industry profits and that the greatest profits would come to firms that developed niche and game-based software. In May 1984, Marks launched BHM by hiring four graduates from MIT's combined computer science/computer engineering program. Noal Fisher, a 29-year-old computer engineer, was appointed general manager of software operations with a mandate to lead the charge in the development of video games that would, in Marks' words, "give kids something to really talk about."

From 1984 to 1994, BHM's software division experienced several ups and downs in its quest to develop hit video games. All BHM games that were deemed to have potential to become hits were sold or licensed to companies that included Nintendo and Sega. These companies would then rebrand or relabel the games for distribution under their own name. In total, BHM saw 34 of its games brought to market and it sold over 4.7 million copies worldwide in this nine-year period of time. Beginning in 1994, the company also began to market games under its own BHM brand. The advantage of self-marketing was that it allowed software companies to sell successful games (with some modifications) on multiple hardware platforms. Over time, the major hardware manufacturers also developed their own in-house software divisions to compete against the independent vendors. What emerged was a complex system whereby companies like Nintendo and Sega developed some proprietary games and contracted for the development of other games. In addition, independent companies like BHM developed and sold their own branded games and essentially worked as contractors to balance out their business portfolio.

Despite the early growth of BHM, Marks constantly wondered about the future of his business, specifically, the potential for new gaming applications. BHM's game development costs were rising year after year in the face of increased competition and more complex technologies. Along with increased development costs came bigger gambles on the next "great game." Failure could be devastating, but successful games would gush cash for the company, particularly given the low variable costs of production (less than 5 percent).

In early 1994, Marks received a call from Ichiro Hasegawa, senior vice president with a major Japanese entertainment hardware and software company. Hasegawa expressed the organization's interest to enter into an arrangement with BHM to modify a number of its games for distribution in Japan. In addition, Hasegawa indicated his company's interest in starting a mobile gaming unit that would design and manufacture handheld gaming devices. Marks handpicked five of his top software developers and announced the beginning of a new mobile gaming division and the acquisition of additional space for a small-cartridge manufacturing facility. Noal Fisher was assigned to be the division's director. From 1993 to 1994, the division modified and manufactured 26 game cartridges from the BHM library for the Japanese company, generating average annual sales of $12.1 million and pre-tax profits of $4.3 million.

With this success, in 1995, the mobile gaming division was spun off into mGAMES, a wholly owned affiliate of BHM. Fisher was appointed president and CEO, and Marks became chairman of the board. By this time, the software engineering staff had increased fivefold to 26 people. Twelve individuals were employed in manufacturing and shipping, and six more served as full-time sales and customer service representatives.

Over time, additional customers were added to mGAMES roster. In 1997, Marks took mGAMES public, selling some 55.5 percent of his shares in the process. At the time, net sales were $33.1 million and operating profits were $7.6 million. In looking back at the events surrounding the public offering, Marks commented:

> We decided to take it public because the mobile gaming industry had such a promising future. The projections I'd seen suggested that new mobile products and associated gaming applications would cause the market to grow to the billion-dollar level in the next five years. At the time of the initial offering, the stock was trading at 40 times its earnings. My other businesses weren't coming even close to doing that well. This was a hot industry and the P/E multiple was outstanding. I also thought that with publicly traded shares, it would be easier to secure financing for our long-term growth.
>
> In retrospect, the timing of the IPO might have been a mistake. Back then, Palm had sales of a couple million. Well, look at them today! Also, no one thought games would ever be played on cell phones like they are today.

In taking mGAMES public, Marks was able to maintain effective control because no other single shareholder held more than 3 percent of the stock.

Not long after the IPO, however, mGAMES' sales began to waver. Demand for its games tapered off toward the end of 1998, and management was finding it increasingly difficult to deal with customers like Nintendo and Sega. As a result, analysts had downgraded the stock to a sell rating, and Benson Marks found himself again on a quest for new gaming applications.

It was during a fall fishing trip in the Florida Keys in 1998 that Marks had the fortune of meeting Nathan Dorward, a senior executive with a major PDA manufacturer. Dorward talked about his company's forays into the development of "full-fledged computers that would rest in the palm of your hand." Dorward was also familiar with recent developments in wireless communications, and he raved to Marks about the potential for these handheld computers to "talk to one another wirelessly through the air." Soon thereafter, Marks returned to Hastings, excited about the associated potential for new gaming applications.

In early 1998, mGAMES introduced four new PDA-based games, all downloadable over the Internet. Three of the games were designed to be used on machines that used Palm-based operating systems; the fourth game was designed for a new PDA operating system being developed by Microsoft. The games generated $4.9 million in new sales and, by the end of 1999, the stock was back on track. In the year 2000, mGAMES signed development contracts with a total of five global companies interested in tapping into the PDA gaming market.

Changes in Top Management

In October of 2001, Noal Fisher announced that he would be stepping down as president of mGAMES to assume a senior executive position with a major California-based technology company. The move was a surprise to his staff who believed that Fisher had seemed happier than he had been in some time. When queried at his going-away party, his response was "The time just seems right. We are coming off some important successes and I am ready for my next big challenge. Besides, I have always wanted to get closer to 'the valley.' " Benson Marks' public statements reflected his appreciation for all that Fisher had achieved, and he offered Fisher his best wishes in his new position.

One month later, Marks appointed 39-year-old Jeffrey Lopez to the vacated position of president and CEO of mGAMES. Lopez, who was at the time serving as the vice president of sales and marketing at mGAMES, assumed his new duties on November 5, 2001.

Lopez was born in Boston and graduated from the University of Massachusetts with an undergraduate degree in computer science. After graduating, he entered the MBA program at New York University and graduated in the top 10 percent of his 1991 class. Interested in working in the computer industry, Lopez moved to Seattle to join Microsoft. Over the next several years, Lopez took on increasingly senior positions at Microsoft, including management positions in marketing, sales, and business development. Lopez was described by his friends as "very smart," "a workaholic," "driven," and "at times hot-headed."

Lopez first became acquainted with Benson Marks at a trade show in Orlando in 1993. The men kept in touch over the next three years and, in 1997, Marks asked whether Lopez would ever be interested in working for mGAMES. "He had the track record and experience to lead the company into the future of the mobile game development industry. He was my first choice for the job." One month later, Lopez joined the company in the newly created position of vice president of sales and marketing. Lopez explained his reason for joining mGAMES:

> I guess part of what intrigued me was wanting to be a big fish in a much smaller pond. I was looking for a company where I had a lot more autonomy and could have a bigger impact. I also could see that mGAMES was in a fantastic industry segment. Another reason I took the job—on top of the $150,000 signing bonus—was that I missed living in the East. My parents were in the Boston area and were getting older. I wanted to be closer to them.

The majority of mGAMES' employees were extremely pleased with the appointment. David Salt, mGAMES' chief financial officer (CFO), reported:

> I think Marks made the right decision in picking Lopez. The president needs to be someone who will move mGAMES toward the future of the mobile gaming industry. Jeff has the experience and credibility. I think he will be the guy to initiate change and listen to the ideas, not only of customers—but employees as well.

Emerging Challenges

In assuming his new position, Lopez was aware of several challenges facing the company. One problem was the escalating costs of developing new games. The company's best-selling game, Messenger of the Deep, accounted for nearly 17 percent of mGAMES' 2001 sales, representing approximately 883,000 units at $11.40 each. (More complex variations of Messenger of the Deep were also manufactured by sister company BHM for the Sony PlayStation and Nintendo 64, with an average retail price of $45.95.) While Messenger was a solid performer, it was by no means a blockbuster. True blockbuster games generated sales of over 3 million cartridges and provided enormous cash flow.

would turn it over to another company that had already expressed an interest in taking over both floors.

Weighing Options

Lopez was a believer in the future of wireless gaming. He believed in the growth projected for the industry in the next five-year period and was eager for mGAMES to become a major player in that growth. Like everyone else who worked around the industry, he was unsure how the whole technology convergence would play out. However, with the number of mobile phones that were being shipped every week, he suspected the telecom manufacturers might have the advantage in the long run. In the nearer term, however, most observers predicted that the action would most likely be focused on the new generation of gaming devices just hitting the market. Here, the market would include new cartridge-based games plus downloadable and wireless games. Several other members of the mGAMES management team, as well as two prominent members of the company's board of directors, were also extremely excited about the company's forays into wireless gaming—particularly the recent development agreements that had been signed with the PDA manufacturers.

However, Jane Parkes, mGAMES' vice president of marketing, was far less optimistic. She was concerned about the validity of the projections for the future of wireless gaming, particularly the feasibility of wireless gaming on mobile phones. Small screen size and Internet access fees were viewed as major obstacles to mobile-phone-based gaming. Lopez was aware, however, that Parkes was extremely excited about the new Game Boy Advance system and the associated new opportunities that mGAMES would expect to enjoy upon its launch. Parkes had clearly expressed her belief that mGAMES' hopes to improve upon its 7.3 percent market share in this segment would rest on the success of this launch. Any investment in new wireless technology would not only be expensive and technically risky, but would detract from the company's current focus on cartridge and downloadable games.

As Lopez stared out the window, he reflected on the road that mGAMES had traveled. He knew that the calls he had received that morning meant that mGAMES could no longer continue to cater to all the handheld device manufacturers. It was time to make some choices. He clearly understood that the organization had Nintendo and Sega to thank for its previous success, and he tried to predict the ripple effect of breaking ties with these Japanese manufacturers. While no one could be certain what the future would hold for mobile gaming, most everyone in the industry believed that the future was bright, and Lopez wanted mGAMES to play a big part in it.

Endnotes

[1] *Infoworld*, November 26, 2001, p. 1.
[2] *Computer Games Magazine*, December 6, 2001, p. 2.
[3] *Computer Games Magazine*, "Gaming Gifts on the Go," June 12, 2001, p. 2.
[4] *Wireless Review;* Overland Park, February 1, 2001; Betsy Harter, p. 1.
[5] Ibid. p. 2.
[6] Ibid. p. 3.

Sears, Roebuck and Co.

Stephen Vitucci
Tarleton Center—Central Texas

Sue A. Cullers
Tarleton State University

Sears, Roebuck and Co. traces its history to 1886, when Richard W. Sears began selling watches in Minneapolis, Minnesota. In 1887, Sears moved the business to Chicago and hired Alvah Roebuck as watchmaker. The name of the company was officially changed to Sears, Roebuck and Co. in 1893. By 1895, the business was publishing a 532-page catalog that included clothing, furniture, patent medicines, musical instruments, and many other items. Catalog retailers such as Sears and Montgomery Ward changed the face of retailing in the United States by making a wide variety of goods available at affordable prices. The early catalog merchandisers virtually killed the rural general store, which could not compete with the catalog retailer on either selection or price.

In 1906, Sears was incorporated in New York State. In the same year, it opened a 3-million-square-foot mail-order plant in Chicago, the largest business building in the world at that time. As the company continued to grow, it opened mail-order plants in other parts of the country. In 1911, Sears began extending credit to its customers, and credit has been an important part of the Sears business ever since. Through 1925, the company sold goods only via catalog, with most of its sales coming from rural areas. In response to the growth of urban areas, Sears opened its first retail store in the Chicago mail-order plant in 1925. The store was immediately successful. The company had 27 stores in operation by 1927, 400 by 1933, and more than 600 by the time the United States entered World War II in 1941. In 1931, sales from stores topped catalog sales for the first time at Sears.

Sears was exclusively a retailer until 1931, when it established Allstate Insurance Company as a wholly owned subsidiary. Allstate initially sold insurance by mail; in 1934, it began selling insurance in Sears stores. Allstate grew to be the second largest property and casualty insurer in the United States.

Sears opened its first international store in Havana, Cuba, in 1942. In 1947, it opened a store in Mexico City, and in following years expanded in Central and South America and Europe. In most of these areas, Sears had just a handful of stores. In 1953, Sears established retail operations in Canada, through what is now known as Sears Canada. The company divested itself of most of its international operations in the 1980s. After selling most of its Mexican operation in 1997, the company had international operations only in Canada, where it had more than 100 stores and a catalog business. A timeline of key company events is shown in Exhibit 1. Data for the company principal business segments are presented in Exhibit 2.

Exhibit 1   SEARS TIMELINE, 1886–2002

Year	Events
1886	Richard Sears founded watch business
1895	Sears published 532-page catalog with wide variety of merchandise
1900	Sears sales exceed those of Montgomery Ward for the first time
1925	Sears opened its first retail store
1931	Sears established Allstate Insurance Company
1942	First international Sears store opened in Havana
1970	Construction began on Sears Tower in downtown Chicago
1981	Sears acquired Dean Witter and Coldwell Banker
1985	Sears launched Discover card to compete against bank credit cards
1988	Sears acquired Western Auto Supply Company, a diversification into specialty retailing Company announced major restructuring: sale of the Sears Tower and adoption of everyday low pricing strategy
1990	Sears announced another restructuring, cutting jobs to reduce costs Wal-Mart passed Sears to become the largest retailer in the United States
1992	Company incurred the largest loss in its history Sears began to break up its financial services operations
1993	Sears discontinued all catalog operations, eliminating its "big book" and catalog stores Sears began accepting bank credit cards
1994	Sears launched Softer Side strategy
1995	Sears spun off remaining shares of Allstate, becoming almost a pure retailer
1996	Sears launched its website
1997	Bad debt expense increased substantially; company incurred a reaffirmation charge of $475 million for violation of federal bankruptcy laws
1998	Sears sold the Western Auto and Homelife furniture store chains, incurring a loss of about $350 million First The Great Indoors (TGI) store opened near Denver
1999	Sears was dropped from the Dow Jones Industrial average and competitor Home Depot was added
2000	The company began to reduce its selling space for apparel and to increase space for hard lines such as tools and appliances; Alan Lacy named CEO of Sears
2002	Sears acquired Land's End

Sears grew rapidly in the years following World War II. In 1946, Sears held a slight sales advantage over Montgomery Ward; by 1954, Sears's sales were almost three times those of Ward's. In the 1950s, recognizing the impact of widespread automobile ownership on consumers' shopping patterns, Sears expanded its retail operations into suburban shopping areas. Within 20 years, Sears had stores in many of the best malls and shopping centers in the United States. In the 1960s, Sears ruled retailing in the United States; its sales exceeded those of its four largest competitors combined. However, during the 1960s, a change in retailing occurred that was critical for Sears: the emergence and growth of discounters Kmart and Wal-Mart.

In 1970, construction began on the 110-story Sears Tower in downtown Chicago. In 1974, Sears moved its headquarters into what was then the tallest building in the world; it was to become Chicago's best-known landmark and a symbol of Sears's dominance in U.S. retailing. However, during the 1970s, Sears lost market share to Kmart and other discounters, which started to attract a large share of the mass market. Specialty stores

Exhibit 2   SEARS'S BUSINESS SEGMENTS IN 2001

Domestic Segments (including operations in the United States and Puerto Rico)

Retail

Consisted of 867 full-line stores and more than 1,300 specialty stores. Specialty stores included 248 hardware stores; 793 dealer stores; 13 The Great Indoors stores; 223 NTB National Tire and Battery Stores; and 35 outlet stores.

Services

Consisted of Sears Repair Services and Direct Response. Included service contracts, product installation and repair services, and the direct marketing of goods and services through specialty catalogs and other means.

Credit

Managed the company's credit card receivables from Sears credit cards, the Sears Gold MasterCard, and The Great Indoors Gold MasterCard.

Corporate

Included administrative activities and the Sears Online initiative.

International Segment

Operations in Canada conducted by Sears Canada Inc., a 54.4-percent-owned subsidiary. Sears Canada had 125 full-line stores, 186 specialty stores, and a general merchandise catalog.

	Operating Income by Reportable Segment (in millions)		
	2001	**2000**	**1999**
Retail and services	$1,050	$ 897	$1,170
Credit	1,366	1,522	1,347
Corporate	(266)	(354)	(322)
International	218	122	218
Total operating income	$2,368	$2,187	$2,413

	Sears Stores		
	2001	**2000**	**1999**
Number of full-line stores	867	863	858
Number of specialty stores	1,318	2,158	2,153
Sales per selling square foot	$319	$333	$327
Comparable store sales percentage increase	−2.3%	2.3%	1.7%

Source: Sears 2001 and 2000 annual reports. Number of specialty stores in 2000 and 1999 included Sears's automobile service centers, which generally were associated with a full-line store.

attracted younger and more affluent customers. Sears was perceived as old-fashioned, with a product line that was too broad and boring. Its managers were slow to react, seeming not to recognize the threat posed by specialty retailers and discounters.

Sears in the Early 1980s

In 1980, Sears was still the largest retailer in the United States, but it was losing market share to discounters (notably Wal-Mart and Kmart) and to specialty stores. The percentage of corporate profit from retailing fell from 75 percent in 1975 to 38 percent in

1980. Increasing shares of company profits came from Allstate and Sears's credit operations.

U.S. retailers in the 1980s suffered due to recession, inflation, and high interest rates. The recession hit Sears harder than any other major retailer; in the first quarter of 1980, it reported a loss from merchandising operations for the first time since the Great Depression. Sears managers concluded that the company's general merchandise retailing operation would be a slow-growth business due to changes in the marketplace, particularly the growth of discounters and specialty retailers. The company decided to try specialty retailing and to expand its financial services operations to achieve faster growth. In 1981, the company launched a chain of business machine stores, its first attempt at specialty retailing.

Sears had been a financial services company since it formed the Allstate insurance group in 1931. In October 1981, Sears announced that it was acquiring both Coldwell Banker, the largest real estate brokerage company in the country, and the stock brokerage firm Dean Witter Reynolds, at a total cost of $800 million. Still the largest retailer in the country, Sears sought to become the largest provider of consumer financial services as well. In many of its full-line stores, Sears established financial service counters staffed by Allstate, Coldwell Banker, and Dean Witter employees. It hoped that the combination of financial services and merchandising would make its stores a new kind of consumer supermarket. Sears's expansion into financial services was called a "socks and stocks" strategy by some journalists who questioned whether consumers would want to buy stocks and bonds at the same location where they bought socks and lawn mowers.

Sears managers viewed merchandising as the strength the company could leverage as it pursued other activities. As evidence of Sears's continuing commitment to retailing, the company revamped all 770 of its product lines and spent $1.7 billion to remodel its stores to reflect how customers shop. The new design, called the store of the future, featured boutiques throughout the store and improved decor.

Sears in the Late 1980s

In 1985, Sears launched a new general-purpose credit card, Discover, as a way to tie together many of the financial services it offered. Discover, intended to compete against Visa, MasterCard, and American Express, incurred pretax losses of about $400 million before becoming profitable in 1988.

Wall Street Journal analysts in 1985 concluded that the Sears financial supermarket had not yet generated the synergies and profits that the company had expected. Dean Witter had earned modest profits for Sears, but there had been disagreement over the role of Dean Witter in a retail-oriented corporation and ongoing difficulties in integrating the cultures of the two organizations.

The following year, 1986, was Sears's 100th anniversary. At its annual shareholders' meeting, planned to be a celebration, the last hour was dominated by complaints from Sears employees that the company's service was slipping. Sears announced a consolidation of merchandising operations, including the closing of four regional administrative offices. It had been consolidating operations for 10 years to reduce costs and improve profits.

In 1987, Sears set up a new unit to explore expansion into specialty merchandising. Sears considered expanding into specialty stores that wouldn't carry the Sears name or the Sears image. Given Sears's size, it would have taken many acquisitions to have much effect on the bottom line because most specialty retailers at the time had relatively few stores. Critics questioned whether increased expansion into specialty retailing would divert resources from the plan to build a consumer financial services supermarket.

Also in 1987, Sears closed 5 of its 12 national warehouses, another in a series of cost-cutting steps. Costs of its aging distribution system had contributed to Sears's trouble in competing against discount stores. In 1987, more than half of Sears' net income came from financial services operations, primarily Allstate.

In 1988, Sears acquired Western Auto Supply Company for approximately $250 million, the company's biggest move into specialty retailing. However, the Sears merchandising group continued its lackluster performance. In October 1988, Sears announced a major restructuring that included a 10 percent stock buyback, sale of its headquarters building in Chicago, introduction of everyday low pricing and an increased emphasis on national brands in retailing, and the sale of Coldwell Banker Commercial Group. The proposed sale of the Sears Tower was an embarrassing indication of how far the company had slipped in U.S. retailing. Wall Street reacted unfavorably to the restructuring; analysts had favored a more radical approach. Before Sears announced its plan, it had been advised by its investment banker that shareholders would fare better if the company was broken up. At the time the company's stock was selling for $45, and the total value per share following a breakup was estimated as high as $89. After the announcement of the restructuring, Moody's lowered Sears's debt rating by two steps, citing the company's high costs and bureaucratic structure, and predicting Sears profits would go lower in future years despite the restructuring.

Turning around Sears's retailing operations was seen as the key to its survival. In February 1989, Sears closed its stores for 42 hours to change prices to everyday low prices. New prices were to be lower than regular prices but higher than sale prices had been. Also, the company planned to run fewer sales; in 1988, Sears had made 55 percent of its sales at sale prices. One analyst said that Sears was doing the right thing but should have done it five years earlier. Two months later, Sears appeared to be continuing to run sales, an indication that management was concerned about the workability of the everyday low pricing strategy. Same-store sales declined in July, August, and September compared to the previous year, and the company eventually abandoned its everyday low pricing strategy.

For 1989, merchandising generated just 16.6 percent of Sears's profit from operating groups, compared to 41 percent five years previously. Sears merchandising had steadily lost market share throughout the 1980s. Sears had tried everyday low pricing, added national brands, and revamped displays to no avail. Discounters Wal-Mart and Kmart continued to gain momentum, and analysts speculated about when one of them would pass Sears to become the largest retailer.

Sears in the Early 1990s

Edward Brennan, Sears CEO from 1985 to 1995

Edward Brennan was described as a consummate bureaucrat, a polished organization person skilled in getting things done in a big company. His family had strong ties to Sears—his mother, father, grandfather, and two uncles had all been Sears employees. Brennan worked for Sears for 39 years, spending his entire managerial career with the company. He helped build the financial services empire in 1981 and led its dismantling more than a decade later. He was CEO during the period that the company slid from largest retailer in the United States to third largest.

Retailing

In the first quarter of 1990, Sears's profits were down 59 percent because of the performance of the company's core retail business, which reported a loss for the quarter. CEO Edward Brennan labeled the performance of the merchandising group as unsatisfactory, and the company's debt was downgraded because of continued weakness in retailing. Brennan said that the company had to get its costs under control: Operating expenses made up 30 percent of every sales dollar, compared to 23 percent at Kmart and 16 percent at Wal-Mart. Sears announced a restructuring that would eliminate thousands of jobs and reduce costs by $100 million a year. However, analysts suggested that Sears needed to reduce costs by at least $500 million to be competitive. Many of the jobs to be eliminated were nonselling retail jobs (stockers, for example), which made up a third of the workforce at Sears stores but less than a fifth at most department stores and discounters. The restructuring resulted in a charge of $155 million to the company's earnings for 1990, the second major charge for restructuring related to the poor performance of the Sears merchandising group in three years.

Sears decided that its furniture departments were too small to offer a competitive selection of furniture. Sears was the largest furniture retailer in the United States but held a market share of just 4 percent. The company opened about 200 separate Homelife furniture stores, mostly in off-mall locations. The new stores offered wider selection and mostly brand names, and moving furniture departments out of Sears stores freed up space for other merchandise, including apparel.

When Sears and Wal-Mart announced their revenues for 1990, it became clear that Wal-Mart had surpassed Sears and become the nation's largest retailer. Wal-Mart's sales for the year were $32.6 billion, and Sears's were just under $32 billion. By 1992, Kmart had become the second largest retailer, and Sears had dropped to third. The retailing industry was in the deepest recession in decades, with a record number of bankruptcy filings. Sears had been hurt by the recession more than most retailers, in part because furniture, appliances, and other durable goods accounted for two-thirds of the company's sales.

Shareholder Activism

In 1991, Sears management won a proxy fight with shareholder activist Robert A. G. Monks, who lost his bid to win a seat on Sears's board. Monks said that, if elected to the board, he would push for restructuring of the company if it continued to fall short of its performance targets. Sears had a target return on equity (ROE) of 15 percent; in 1990, its ROE was 6.8 percent. Institutional investors were pushing for a breakup of the Sears empire. In April 1991, the company's stock was selling at about $38, and the estimated breakup value of the company was $90 per share. Some analysts suggested that Sears should sell off the merchandising group and focus on its financial service operations, which were generating an increasing share of company profits.

At its May 1992 annual meeting, Sears faced a second challenge from Monks and large institutional investors, who presented five corporate governance proposals. Substantial numbers of shareholders supported the proposals, although none passed. The proposals included a resolution to have an investment banker determine whether the company should be broken up. CEO Edward Brennan argued that the company was more valuable intact than separated. In June, Sears adopted several changes in corporate governance, although they were not as sweeping as those proposed by Monks.

The Breakup of the Financial Services Supermarket

Despite Brennan's argument for keeping the company intact, Sears began to break up its financial services empire in September 1992 so it could concentrate on retailing. The board of directors approved a plan to sell Sears's remaining interest in Coldwell Banker and up to 20 percent of Allstate. The company also announced its intentions to sell 20 percent of Dean Witter Financial Services (which included the Discover card) in an initial public offering and then to spin off the balance of Dean Witter as a stock dividend to Sears stockholders.

Critics said that Sears's decision to divest its financial services companies indicated that the diversification into this area had been a failure. Also, they questioned whether the financial services operations had taken too much of top management's time and attention and contributed to the decline in retailing market share. Company managers, however, asserted that the financial services experiment had succeeded and that they had begun the divestitures to reduce Sears's debt and to distribute to shareholders a part of the value Sears had developed in the financial services companies. After the sale of Coldwell Banker and the spin-off of Dean Witter, Sears was back essentially to what it was before it acquired the companies in 1981—except that it was no longer the country's largest retailer. The decision to divest most of the financial services network appeared to have been triggered by the downgrading of Sears's debt. A few months after the announcement of the breakup, Sears's debt was again downgraded based on concerns about whether the spin-offs might leave Sears financially weakened. In 1995, Sears spun off its remaining shares of Allstate, returning to its roots as a pure retailer.

Trouble for the Big Book

The Sears catalog had been a cornerstone of the business since its beginning, but by the late 1980s, catalog operations were foundering. Wal-Mart had opened many stores in small towns, taking away traditional customers of the Sears catalog, and specialists such as Circuit City and Home Depot had taken market share in appliances and hardware. The Sears catalog had also lost market share to specialty catalog merchants. In 1990, the company decided against shutting down the catalog operation and instead tried to improve efficiency and cut costs, but the catalog continued to incur losses estimated at $150 million a year.

Arthur Martinez, Merchandising Group CEO

In August 1992, Arthur Martinez was named chairman and CEO of Sears's merchandising group. Martinez, who came to Sears from upscale Saks Fifth Avenue, was one of only a few outsiders ever to be appointed to a high-level executive position at Sears. Brennan hoped that Martinez would bring a new perspective to Sears's merchandising. The first major strategic change that Martinez introduced was a decision to begin accepting major bank credit cards. Sears had been the last big retailer that excluded all credit cards other than its own, fearing that loss of revenues by its card would exceed the benefits from accepting other credit cards.

Still, Sears incurred a loss that year of $3.9 billion, the largest in the company's history. The overall loss included a loss of $1.3 billion by the company's merchandising group. In response, Martinez announced sweeping changes: the closing of 113 poorly performing Sears stores; workforce reductions of 50,000 employees (approximately

15 percent of the merchandising group's employees); and elimination of the 96-year-old Sears catalog. Although the company stopped issuing its big book and Christmas wish book, it issued various specialty catalogs (e.g., tools and big and tall men's clothing) as a way to continue to serve its mail-order customers and to profit from its customer database. The specialty catalogs did not achieve the volume of business that the big catalog had, but they were profitable almost from the beginning. The company also began converting some of its former catalog stores into small retail stores, owned and operated by independent dealers. Most of the dealer stores were located in small towns, and they sold various hard lines: appliances, hardware, automobile tires and batteries, and lawn and garden equipment. By 2001, Sears had 793 dealer stores.

Martinez also announced a five-year, $4 billion campaign to upgrade all Sears stores, emphasizing apparel and related items. Apparel was the latest hope for turning around Sears's merchandising operations. Apparel, which offered higher margins than the hard lines for which Sears was best known (appliances and hardware), accounted for 26 percent of store sales but provided 60 percent of the merchandise group's profits. Sears joined the trend to soft goods, a move that JCPenney had made 10 years before.

A marketing study indicated that most purchasing decisions at Sears, including purchases of hard goods, were made by women. Sears identified its target customers as working women, ages 35 to 64, with family income of $16,000 to $45,000, and it sought to make its stores and merchandise selection more attractive to this target customer. The Sears strategy was to ignore discounters such as Wal-Mart and Kmart and to target JCPenney and May Department Stores. The company was trying to position itself as a mall-based department store for families with moderate incomes. For about a year, the strategy succeeded, and the company had double-digit sales growth.

Sears in the Late 1990s

Arthur Martinez, Sears CEO from 1995 to 2000

Arthur Martinez came to Sears in 1992 from Saks Fifth Avenue. He initially served as CEO of Sears's merchandising group, becoming president, chairman, and CEO of Sears in 1995. Martinez was responsible for a major reorganization of the merchandising group in 1993, which included closing 113 Sears stores and eliminating the full-line catalog. He invested billions of dollars to increase sales of apparel, advertising "Come See the Softer Side of Sears." Martinez visualized Sears as "a compelling place to shop, a compelling place to work, and a compelling place to invest."

The Full-Line Stores

Sears had a record $3.9 billion loss in 1992, but in 1993, it returned to profitability. Total revenues increased steadily from 1993 through 1997, as did revenues from merchandise sales and services. In 1994, the company adopted the advertising slogan "Come See the Softer Side of Sears" to emphasize its soft lines and to draw women shoppers to the store. Because of his success in turning around Sears's merchandising operations, Martinez was named CEO of the company as a whole in 1995.

As sales and income increased, the Softer Side strategy appeared to be paying off. However, part of Sears's sales growth was due to easy credit policies. In 1993, when Sears began accepting bank credit cards, the company had been concerned that usage of the Sears card and interest revenues would decrease. Sears adopted an aggressive policy, issuing 17 million new cards in the early 1990s. Many were issued to new card-holders who could not qualify for other credit cards. By 1997, more than one-third of personal bankruptcies in the United States included Sears as a creditor, and bad debt losses mounted.

To reduce its bad debt losses, Sears pursued reaffirmation agreements with individuals who had been granted bankruptcy. The reaffirmation agreements stated that the debtors would continue to pay on their Sears debt. By federal law, reaffirmation agreements must be filed with the bankruptcy court; however, Sears failed to file many of the agreements. A Sears subsidiary pleaded guilty to a criminal charge of bankruptcy fraud and paid a $60 million federal fine, the largest such fine in U.S. history. The scandal ultimately cost Sears about $475 million in legal fees, refunds to customers, and fines and penalties.

As Sears tightened its credit policies to control bad debts, the rapid growth in sales disappeared. Sales revenues in 1998 were $1 billion lower than in 1997. (See Exhibit 3 for Sears's income statements and Exhibit 4 for its balance sheets, 1997–2001.) Apparel sales declined; the Softer Side strategy ran out of steam. The company began to look for a new way to attract customers to the stores. In 1999 it dropped the Softer Side slogan and began to emphasize value with a new advertising slogan, "The Good Life at a Great Price. Guaranteed. Sears." Martinez had concluded that the company needed to send a stronger signal about value to its customers to compete successfully with discounters. A few months before retiring, Martinez announced that Sears, in a reversal of his previous strategy, would eliminate one-sixth of its clothing lines, decrease selling space for apparel, and increase emphasis on hard lines. Early in 2000, Sears launched a 16-store test in which most of the selling space was devoted to home decor, tools, lawn and garden, and other hard goods. Sears also tested new stores with shopping carts and centralized check-outs, similar to those at discount stores. After the test of shopping carts resulted in increased sales, the company began adding shopping carts in all of its full-line stores.

Online Activities

Sears launched its website in 1996 as an educational tool, then it moved to selling online, adding products gradually. Its first e-commerce venture was selling Craftsman tools. Then it added appliances, home services, lawn and garden, home electronics, computers and office equipment, small appliances and cookware, and baby products. Initially, the company was concerned that online sales might cannibalize in-store sales—for example, that store sales of appliances might decrease when appliances were available online. This fear did not materialize; many customers who buy in Sears stores have done research online before going to the store.

By March 2000, Sears was one of the top brick-and-click retailers in terms of visitors to its site, leading the retailing market with 1.9 million consumers logging on at least once during the month. The primary imperative for brick-and-mortar retailers selling online is the integration of multiple channels. Sears redeems online gift certificates in its stores, for example, and a product purchased online can be picked up in-store. While Sears stores were located solely in North America, the company expected its online initiatives to give it a more global profile. Also, the company hoped that e-tailing would allow it to build on its long experience with catalog and direct-mail merchandising.

Exhibit 3   CONSOLIDATED STATEMENTS OF INCOME, SEARS ROEBUCK, 1997–2001 (IN MILLIONS, EXCEPT PER COMMON SHARE DATA)

	2001	2000	1999	1998	1997
Revenues					
Merchandise sales and services	$35,843	$36,548	$35,141	$35,335	$36,371
Credit revenues	5,235	4,389	4,343	4,618	4,925
Total revenues	41,078	40,937	39,484	39,953	41,296
Costs and expenses					
Costs of sales, buying, and occupancy	26,322	26,899	25,627	25,794	26,779
Selling and administrative	8,892	8,642	8,416	8,412	8,322
Provision for uncollectible accounts	1,344	884	871	1,287	1,532
Provision for securitized receivables					
Depreciation and amortization	863	826	848	830	785
Interest	1,415	1,248	1,268	1,423	1,409
Reaffirmation charge				475	
Special charges and impairments	542	251	41	352	
Total costs and expenses	39,900	38,750	37,071	38,098	39,302
Operating income	1,178	2,187	2,413	1,855	1,994
Other income, net	45	36	6	28	144
Income before income taxes, minority interest, and extraordinary loss	1,223	2,223	2,419	1,883	2,138
Income taxes	467	831	904	766	912
Minority interest	21	49	62	45	38
Income before extraordinary loss	735	1,343	1,453	1,072	1,188
Extraordinary loss on early extinguishment of debt, net of tax				24	
Net income	$ 735	$ 1,343	$ 1,453	$ 1,048	$ 1,188
Earnings per common share—basic					
Income before extraordinary loss	$2.25	$3.89	$3.83	$2.76	$3.03
Net income	$2.25	$3.89	$3.83	$2.70	$3.03
Earnings per common share—diluted					
Income before extraordinary loss	$2.24	$3.88	$3.81	$2.74	$2.99
Net income	$2.24	$3.88	$3.81	$2.68	$2.99

Note: A change in accounting principles, in response to a Securities and Exchange Commission Staff Accounting Bulletin, causes the revenues reported here for 1998 and thereafter not to be comparable to revenues in 1997. The change does not affect the comparability of income or earnings per share for these years.

Source: Company annual reports.

Specialty Retailing

By the early 1980s, Sears had identified specialty retailing as a potential growth vehicle for the corporation. Specialty retail stores offer limited or specific lines of merchandise and frequently are located in off-mall locations, where rent and operating costs may be lower. Examples of specialty retailers include Bed, Bath & Beyond and The Gap. In the 1990s, much of the growth in retailing was in specialty retailing. Sears has made several attempts to branch out into specialty retailing, with limited success. In 1981, it launched a chain of business machine stores that initially showed promise

Exhibit 4   CONSOLIDATED BALANCE SHEETS, SEARS, ROEBUCK, 1997–2001
(IN MILLIONS, EXCEPT PER SHARE DATA)

	2001	2000	1999	1998	1997
Assets					
Current assets					
Cash and cash equivalents	$ 1,064	$ 842	$ 729	$ 495	$ 358
Retained interest in transferred credit card receivables	—	3,105	3,211	4,294	3,316
Credit card receivables	29,321	18,003	18,793	18,946	19,843
Less allowance for uncollectible accounts	1,166	686	760	974	1,113
Net credit card receivables	28,155	17,317	18,033	17,972	19,843
Other receivables	658	506	404	397	335
Merchandise inventories	4,912	5,618	5,069	4,816	5,044
Prepaid expenses and deferred charges	458	486	512	506	517
Deferred income taxes	858	920	709	791	830
Total current assets	36,105	28,794	28,667	29,271	30,243
Property and equipment					
Land	434	408	370	395	487
Buildings and improvements	6,539	6,096	5,837	5,530	5,420
Furniture, fixtures and equipment	5,620	5,559	5,209	4,871	4,919
Capitalized leases	544	522	496	530	498
Gross property and equipment	13,137	12,585	11,912	11,326	11,324
Less accumulated depreciation	6,313	5,932	5,462	4,946	4,910
Total property and equipment, net	6,824	6,653	6,450	6,380	6,414
Deferred income taxes	415	174	367	572	606
Other assets	973	1,278	1,470	1,452	1,377
Total assets	$44,317	$36,899	$36,954	$37,675	$38,700
Liabilities and shareholders' equity					
Current liabilities					
Short-term borrowings	$ 3,557	$ 4,280	$ 2,989	$ 4,624	$ 5,208
Current portion of long-term debt and capitalized lease obligations	3,157	2,560	2,165	1,414	2,561
Accounts payable and other payables	7,176	7,336	6,992	6,732	6,637
Unearned revenues	1,136	1,058	971	815	830
Other taxes	558	562	584	524	554
Total current liabilities	15,584	15,796	13,701	14,109	15,790
Long-term debt and capitalized lease obligations	18,921	11,020	12,884	13,631	13,071
Postretirement benefits	1,732	1,951	2,180	2,346	2,564
Minority interest and other liabilities	1,961	1,363	1,350	1,523	1,413
Total liabilities	38,198	30,130	30,115	31,609	32,838
Shareholders' equity					
Common shares ($.75 per share, 1,000 shares authorized)	323	323	323	323	323
Capital in excess of par value	3,500	3,538	3,554	3,583	3,598
Retained earnings	7,413	6,979	5,952	4,848	4,158
Treasury stock, at cost	(4,223)	(3,726)	(2,569)	(2,089)	(1,702)
Deferred ESOP expense	(63)	(96)	(134)	(175)	(204)
Accumulated other comprehensive loss	(831)	(249)	(287)	(424)	(311)
Total shareholders' equity	6,119	6,769	6,839	6,066	5,862
Total liabilities and shareholders' equity	$44,317	$36,899	$36,954	$37,675	$38,700

Source: Company annual reports.

and eventually expanded to 100 stores. By 1987, however, Sears began closing down the stores. In 1991, Sears started the Homelife furniture chain, eliminating the furniture departments in many of its stores. By 1996, the company stopped building the stores because of their poor performance. In November 1998, Sears sold the chain, which later filed for bankruptcy and was liquidated.

The company's biggest acquisition in specialty retailing was Western Auto, purchased in 1988. In 1997, Sears converted most of the Western Auto stores to a Parts America format, which sold auto parts but did not perform repairs, incurring a charge to earnings of $38 million. After the conversion, the chain continued to perform poorly. In November 1998, just two weeks before disposing of the Homelife chain, Sears sold 60 percent ownership interest in the 630-store Western Auto chain, incurring a pretax loss of $319 million.

Of Sears's specialty retail formats, The Great Indoors (TGI) showed perhaps the greatest potential for growth. TGI was a home decorating and remodeling store, carrying home appliances, electronics, carpeting, and decorating items. Sears intended for the quality of merchandise in the store to be "good, better, and best," carrying a wide range of prices. For example, in appliances, refrigerators ranged from $500 to $10,000. The company expected little cannibalization of Sears store sales because the TGI target demographic was wealthier than that of the typical Sears customer. In developing TGI, Sears was careful to separate its name and image from those of the new store.

The first TGI store opened in Denver in 1998. After evaluation of the performance of that store and making some changes in store design and operation, Sears opened three more stores over a two-year period. By May 2002, the TGI division had 18 units, with two more scheduled to open during 2002. However, the company did not have any store openings planned for 2003 because it was redesigning the store format. While Sears definitely planned to expand the chain further, it knew it needed to improve the units' cost control and profitability. Also, TGI had to develop an appeal to a broader segment of the market than it had yet demonstrated.

TGI stores competed against Home Depot's EXPO Design Centers, which Home Depot began opening several years earlier. Unlike general retailing, the home decorating and remodeling market, which attracted baby boomers wanting to improve their homes, had not yet reached saturation. Several other companies had also opened stores targeting this market. EXPO Design Centers and TGI carried similar merchandise. However, EXPO Design Centers catered more to customers planning a major remodeling project, while TGI had been very successful at selling "take-with" decorating items such as soap dishes and bedding.

Lacy's Leadership at Sears, 2000–Present

Alan Lacy, Named Sears CEO in 2000

Alan Lacy became the 13th CEO of Sears on October 1, 2000. Lacy, who was 46 at the time, had served as the company's senior vice president of finance, chief financial officer, and president of services. He had also been responsible for Sears's online business and for strengthening Sears's credit operations. Lacy had come to Sears in 1994 after serving as vice president for financial services and systems at Phillip Morris and senior vice president of finance and strategy at Kraft General Foods. Lacy lacked merchandising experience; his expertise was in finance, credit, and cost control.

When Alan Lacy became Sears's new president and CEO, the position was described as one of the most challenging for any executive in the United States because of the company's troubles in positioning itself and establishing a clear identity. Almost immediately, Lacy faced bad news and difficult decisions. The 2000 holiday shopping season was challenging for most retailers, and Sears had a 1.1 percent drop in comparable store sales for the period. In response, Sears announced it would close 89 underperforming stores, including four full-line department stores, and lay off 2,400 employees. Sears's fourth-quarter profit, taking into account the restructuring cost for closing the stores, was down 40.3 percent from the year before.

Lacy began a careful review of all aspects of Sears's operations and the retailing environment. Initially, Lacy identified several growth areas: the overall retail business, The Great Indoors (TGI), Sears.com, and credit operations. Lacy predicted that 2001 would be a transitional year, as Sears moved from old strategies and leadership to new. He determined that Sears's focus would continue to be its core full-line department stores, and the company began making changes in the product mix. In the second quarter of 2001, Sears closed down its cosmetics departments, which did not justify the continued investment in the business. Lacy warned that the company would exit other product lines, too, and that these decisions would cut into top-line results (revenues) and result in some loss of market share.

A *Forbes* article suggested that Sears drop apparel completely because of the company's poor performance in that area. Lacy, however, disagreed because of costs and impact on revenue and market share. In the spring of 2001, the company did open three Sears Appliance & Electronics stores in the Chicago area, testing the feasibility of stores with hard goods only.

Lacy, who had previously been in charge of credit operations, continued to expand Sears's credit portfolio. Sears began issuing a co-branded Gold MasterCard, targeting the card to customers who had inactive or low-use Sears cards. Also, Sears made arrangements for its proprietary card to be used for purchases at some businesses other than Sears—a first for private-label cards in the United States. The other businesses, in industries such as travel and entertainment, were not direct competitors with Sears. Also, cardholders could get cash advances and transfer balances from other credit cards. Sears's expansion of its credit operations brought more flexibility to cardholders and, potentially, more risk to Sears. Historically, Sears earned more from its credit card portfolio than almost any other card issuer. In 2001, Sears generated $1.37 billion in operating profits from its credit card operations.

Since the early 1980s, when Sears realized that its leadership position in retailing was in jeopardy, company CEOs had looked for a way to spur revenue growth. When Lacy began as CEO in 2000, he too launched new strategic initiatives to drive top-line growth. In October 2001, after he had been the CEO for a year, he announced a different plan and strategy. Lacy seemed to accept that Sears was a mature company and that its retailing business would grow slowly. Although still interested in revenue growth, his plan focused on controlling costs as a means to provide bottom-line (income) growth. The company began to eliminate 4,900 personnel, including 3,600 salaried positions from stores, as it sought to increase operating income by at least $1 billion by 2004.

Lacy's plan included substantial changes to differentiate the full-line stores from their competition, both discount stores and top-line department stores. In soft lines, Sears had long used a good-better-best strategy, but Lacy decided that the strategy had been too weighted on the "good" level. The company began to move away from discounters on the "good" level and away from department stores on the "best" level. Lacy described the new direction for the full-line stores as veering "from the traditional department store and toward something that resembles a discounter with better service and better merchandise." The company sought to offer an easier shopping experience for customers, remodeling some stores to provide wider aisles, centralized check-outs, and clearer signage. Most departments in the stores began to offer self-service, which customers seemed to prefer. Departments such as appliances and electronics retained their sales staffs, providing assistance in the areas where customers needed it.

In soft lines, Sears increased its emphasis on home fashions, adding new home accents and closet departments. Sweeping changes were launched in apparel departments. The first step was to dump hundreds of brands and private labels, reducing the total number of brands and labels from 1,030 to 472. Most Sears private labels were cut, as were brands also carried by discounters. The company planned to emphasize casual wear in women's apparel, de-emphasizing career wear and other dressier clothing. Sears initiated a new megabrand in apparel, Covington, which would replace some of its private labels in men's, women's, and children's clothing. Sears did retain its more important national brands, such as Levi's and Liz Claiborne.

Lacy recognized that hard goods clearly were Sears's strong suit, bringing in 60 percent of sales at Sears's mall stores. The company had three of the best-selling names in retailing: Craftsman, DieHard, and Kenmore. Sears was the number one appliance retailer in the United States, with appliance sales accounting for more than 10 percent of Sears's total business. The company had a 38 percent market share and was a destination store for appliance shopping. Sears's private label, Kenmore, was the top-selling appliance brand in the country; Sears also sold national brands such as Amana and Maytag. Appliance sales benefited Sears's bottom line through the profits made from credit and service contracts. However, Home Depot was expanding its appliance offerings and Wal-Mart had test-marketed a home appliance department. Competition in appliance sales was increasing, and Sears had the most to lose.

Sears was also the country's largest seller of tires and auto batteries. The Craftsman brand had made Sears a leader in tool sales, with a 25 to 40 percent market share; in some categories, Sears was the sales leader. Home centers generally had more space for tools than Sears, so Sears developed an expanded hardware department, Tool Territory, in its mall stores. Sears was the only retailer selling traditional tools and hardware at most shopping malls.

Lacy hoped to generate some growth from high-ticket items tied to credit and service—categories such as appliances and consumer electronics. One concern for the company was that the percentage of purchases made using Sears credit cards declined from 52.3 percent in 1998 to 47.0 percent in 2001. The company offered a wide range of services, including product installation and repair and service contracts, and it had one of the largest service organizations in the United States, with 12,000 technicians. In the mid-1990s, Sears decided that services might provide a growth mechanism for the company, and it announced a plan to grow revenues from its service business to $10 billion a year. However, the hoped-for growth in services never materialized, and services revenue in 2000 was $2.8 billion, after which the company actually scaled back some service operations. In 2000, it recognized an impairment of its investment in Sears Termite and Pest Control, and it exited this line of business.

By April 2002, Sears's most recent turnaround efforts seemed to be paying off. Sears stock hit a four-year high at $55.20 per share, and Lacy announced that he anticipated first-quarter earnings per share would be more than double those of the comparable period from 2001. However, top-line results (total sales revenue and comparable store sales) were still soft. Lacy attributed the drop in revenue to exiting certain product categories (cosmetics and flooring, among others) and said that these changes would continue to have a negative effect on sales. He highlighted Sears's strengths: continued integration of online services, the continuing strength of its hard goods, and a credit business that earned more than $5.5 billion in revenues in 2001.

In June 2002, Sears announced that it was purchasing Lands' End for $1.9 billion. Lands' End, known for the high quality of its merchandise, was a specialty apparel catalog retailer and the largest Internet apparel seller in the United States. Lands' End catalog and Internet operations would continue, and Sears planned to begin introducing Lands' End merchandise into Sears stores by the fall of 2002. Lands' End merchandise and its high-profile brand were expected to help Sears's efforts to upgrade its apparel operation. The acquisition did involve some risks: Sales in Sears stores could cannibalize Lands' End catalog sales, and the Sears image might alienate some Lands' End shoppers.

In October 2002, when Lacy had been CEO for two years, Sears's turnaround seemed well launched. The company had developed clearer strategies for both hard and soft lines and had launched new initiatives in consumer credit. However, on October 17, Sears announced that its credit division had suffered unexpected losses from delinquent cardholders that would depress earnings for the rest of the year. Earnings for the third quarter were to be 26 percent below a prediction the company had made two weeks before. For the full year, the earnings per share figure was expected to be $4.86, down from a forecast of $5.15. The company's stock posted one of its biggest one-day drops, falling by $10.80, almost 32 percent, to close at $23.15. Most of the credit trouble apparently related to the Gold MasterCard. Sears appeared to have issued MasterCards to consumers whose ability to pay was not as good as the company expected. The decrease in earnings concerned stockholders and analysts because of the importance of the credit portfolio to Sears's future profitability. Also, critics said that Sears managers should have been aware of the problems and reported them much earlier than they did. The news of lowered profits caused both stockholders and analysts to question Sears's progress in turning its operations around.

The Retailing Environment in 2001–2002

Sears, JCPenney, Montgomery Ward, Mervyn's, and Kohl's were classified as mid-tier retailers, with product quality, service, and selling prices between those of discount stores and high-end department stores such as Nordstrom's. The mid-tier had generally lost market share, especially to discount stores and specialty retailers such as Home Depot, Lowe's, Circuit City, Victoria's Secret, and Bed, Bath & Beyond.

Department Stores

In the mid-tier, only Kohl's was growing rapidly. Kohl's was a much smaller retailer than Sears, with sales of about $7 billion per year, operating 420 stores in 26 states (see Exhibit 5). Kohl's was the fastest-growing department store in the United States, pursuing consistent growth through an aggressive expansion policy. From 2000 to 2002, Kohl's added 100 new stores. When it entered a market, it entered in force, with several stores, to leverage marketing, administrative, and distribution costs. For example, in 2001, it entered the Atlanta market with 18 stores. Kohl's stores, mostly in off-mall locations, carried national-brand apparel, shoes, accessories, home furnishings, and home products at competitive prices. Sears managers viewed the growth of Kohl's as a significant competitive threat. Lacy's apparel and softline strategy for Sears appeared to emulate Kohl's merchandising strategy.

Exhibit 5   SALES AND NET INCOME OF SELECTED COMPETITORS OF SEARS, ROEBUCK, 1999–2001 (IN MILLIONS)

Company	Results for 2001	Results for 2000	Results for 1999
Wal-Mart			
Sales	$217,799	$191,329	$165,000
Net income	$ 6,671	$ 6,295	$ 5,377
Kmart			
Sales	$ 36,151	$ 37,028	$ 35,925
Net income (loss)	$ (2,418)	$ (244)	$ 403
Target Corporation			
Sales	$ 39,176	$ 36,362	$ 33,212
Net income	$ 1,368	$ 1,264	$ 1,144
JCPenney			
Sales	$ 32,004	$ 31,846	$ 31,743
Net income (loss)	$ 98	$ (705)	$ 336
Kohl's			
Sales	$ 7,489	$ 6,152	$ 4,557
Net income	$ 496	$ 372	$ 258
Home Depot			
Sales	$ 53,553	$ 45,738	$ 38,434
Net income	$ 3,044	$ 2,581	$ 2,320
Lowe's			
Sales	$ 22,111	$ 18,779	$ 15,906
Net income	$ 1,023	$ 809	$ 673

Sources: Company 10K reports for fiscal years ending closest to December 31.

JCPenney was also a mid-tier department store that competed directly with Sears. It was one of the largest retailers in the United States, operating more than 1,075 stores in all 50 states. The company sold apparel, jewelry, shoes, accessories, and home furnishings, having eliminated its hard lines in the 1980s. Like Sears, the majority of JCPenney's retailing space was found in malls. JCPenney had chosen to continue its catalog operation; catalog sales were $4.2 billion in 2000 and $3.4 billion in 2001. In 1997, JCPenney acquired the Eckerd drugstore chain, hoping through this diversification to increase both revenues and profits. JCPenney had experienced fluctuating profits for the last several years and was attempting to get its operations on track. In 2000, it decided to close 92 underperforming department stores and 279 drugstores. As a result, it incurred $488 million in restructuring costs and a net loss of $705 million for the year. In 2001, the company was marginally profitable as it began a five-year turnaround plan. Under this plan, JCPenney was offering more fashionable apparel and centralizing its decision-making process. Many retail analysts were impressed by the quality of JCPenney's management and the progress it had made in executing the turnaround strategy.

Montgomery Ward filed for bankruptcy and began liquidation in December 2000. Like Sears, Montgomery Ward had begun as a catalog company in the late 1800s. The two companies had competed directly for more than 100 years. Sears benefited when Montgomery Ward went out of business: It acquired 18 of Ward's store locations and some of the company's market share, especially in appliances. However, the failure of Montgomery Ward was a stern reminder of how unforgiving the retail environment could be, even to companies with long, illustrious histories.

Mervyn's stores were operated by Target Corporation, which also operated the discounters Target and Marshall Field's. More than 80 percent of the corporation's revenue came from Target stores, which were upscale discount stores with apparel, housewares, home furnishings, and other items. In recent years, Target had also begun opening supercenters, which included a supermarket section, deli, bakery, and various services. The Target chain was growing rapidly, opening more than 140 stores since 1999. Mervyn's, which targeted middle-income customers, had closed more than 30 stores since 1996. At the end of 2001, there were 264 Mervyn's stores, selling apparel, shoes, accessories, and softlines for the home. The Marshall Field's chain of 64 full-service department stores was located in the upper Midwest. Both Mervyn's and Marshall Field's experienced a decrease in revenues and comparable store sales in 2001.

Category Killers

Home Depot and Lowe's were category killers in home improvement products retailing. Home Depot, founded in Atlanta in 1978, was the world's largest home improvement retailer and the second largest retailer in the United States. During the 1990s, Home Depot's sales grew rapidly, primarily due to construction of new stores. In 1999, Sears was removed from the Dow Jones Industrial Average and Home Depot was added, indicating that stores such as Home Depot were perceived as the future of retailing, and Sears was not. Home Depot increased its revenues primarily through building new stores. It opened 172 new Home Depot stores in the United States during 2001, mostly by adding more stores in existing markets. At the end of 2001, it had more than 1,333 stores: 1,287 Home Depot stores in the United States, Argentina, Canada, and Mexico, and 41 EXPO Design Center stores in the United States.

Home Depot served the do-it-yourself market as well as professional builders, priding itself on the quality of service it offered to customers. It sold appliances, flooring, wall coverings, lawn and garden supplies, paint, tools, lumber, and related products, and offered installation services for many of its products. The EXPO Design Center stores, located in major metropolitan markets, offered complete home decorating and remodeling products and services, targeting middle- to upper-income customers. Home Depot started opening these stores before Sears launched The Great Indoors chain. In 2001, Home Depot opened 15 EXPO stores and expected to open at least 10 more in 2002.

Lowe's Corporation was the second largest home improvement retailer in the United States, having more than 744 stores and annual sales in excess of $22 billion. Lowe's had the largest superstores in the industry, stores with more than 150,000 square feet of selling space. Lowe's catered to the do-it-yourself market, offering more than 40,000 home improvement items. Lowe's targeted women customers because it believed that women initiate most home improvement decisions. Lowe's grew rapidly during the 1990s and added 168 stores in 2000 and 2001. Lowe's and Home Depot had taken market share from Sears in such areas as tools, appliances, and lawn and garden. In 2002, Sears began closing down the carpeting and flooring department in its stores.

Discount Retailers

Wal-Mart is the world's largest retailer, with sales double the combined sales of Sears, JCPenney, and Kmart. In 2001, Wal-Mart's sales revenue exceeded $217 billion (see

Exhibit 5). In 2002, Wal-Mart was number one in the Fortune 500, the first retailer ever to reach the top of the list. Wal-Mart had 4,400 retail stores, including discount stores, supercenters, and Sam's Club stores (members-only warehouse stores). In 1999, Wal-Mart began opening smaller stores called Neighborhood Markets; at the end of 2001, it had 34 of these units. Wal-Mart had approximately 3,300 stores located in the United States and more than 1,100 in other countries. The company was the largest retailer in Canada and Mexico and had entered South America, Asia, and Europe. Wal-Mart's rapid growth had been a dominant force in the retailing industry for the last 15 years; much of its growth came from taking market share away from mid-tier retailers. Wal-Mart was among the most innovative retailers in its use of technology. Its logistics systems and collaboration with suppliers allowed the company to maintain a competitive edge and to pass savings on to their customers. Wal-Mart had the most sophisticated management information system in retailing.

Kmart was the second largest discount retailer behind Wal-Mart, operating more than 2,100 stores in all 50 states, Guam, Puerto Rico, and the U.S. Virgin Islands. It operated discount stores and more than 100 superstores that sold garden supplies and groceries in addition to the items carried at other Kmart stores. While Kmart began growing as a discounter before Wal-Mart did, it had difficulty competing with Wal-Mart for the 10 years leading up to 2002. Kmart had incurred substantial charges to income in its efforts to revamp its stores and gain momentum in its battle against Wal-Mart. In 2001, Kmart incurred a loss of $2.4 billion, which included restructuring costs of more than $1 billion. In January 2002, Kmart filed for bankruptcy protection under Chapter 11 of the bankruptcy code, attributing the filing to a decrease in liquidity associated with sales that were lower than expected and to the intense competition in retailing. In March 2002, as part of the reorganization efforts, Kmart announced closure of 283 stores.

References and Bibliography

Appelbaum, Alec. "The Softer Side of Sears." *Money*, November 2000, p. 44.
Baeb, Eddie. "Sears' New Chief Says 'Charge It.'" *Crain's Chicago Business*, September 18, 2000, p. 1.
Bailey, Jeff. "Sears Is Discovering Discover Credit Card Isn't Hitting Pay Dirt." *Wall Street Journal*, February 10, 1988, p. 1.
———. "Moody's Lowers Sears's Rating Two Notches." *Wall Street Journal*, January 11, 1989, p. A4.
Berner, Robert, and Beth Belton. "A Change of Clothes at Sears." *Business Week*, May 27, 2002.
Buckley, Neil. "Sears Surrounded by Credit Questions." *The Financial Times*, October 17, 2002, p. 29.
Carlson, Eugene. "Upon a Little Book, Sears Built the Big Store." *Wall Street Journal*, February 21, 1989, p. B2.
Carrington, Tim. "Socks 'n' Stocks." *Wall Street Journal*, November 19, 1982, p. 1.
Catalog Age. "Sears to Convert Some Catalog Stores to Retail." July 1993, p. 21.
Chain Store Age. "Department Store Retailer of the Century: Sears, Roebuck and Co." April 2000, p. 32.
———. "Sears Charges Ahead with Co-Branded MasterCard." October 2000, p. 110.
———. "Sears Tests Hard Lines Store." June 2001.
———. "A New Plastic Side of Sears." July 2001.
———. "A Dream Grows in Brooklyn." May 2002, p. 39.
———. "Core Concept Remains as Viable as Ever," August 2002, p. 48.
Clark, Ken. "A Softer, Slimmer Side of Sears." *Chain Store Age*, December 2001.
———. "At 100, J.C. Penney Looks Ahead." *Chain Store Age*, June 2002.
Crain's Chicago Business. "Dow Disses Sears: Falling Stature of Chicago Firms." November 1, 1999, p. 12.
Curley, John. "Sears Is Opening Financial Centers In 8 Stores Today." *Wall Street Journal*, July 19, 1982, p. 21.
———. "Sears Planning Ads Touting Financial Units." *Wall Street Journal*, January 7, 1983, p. 19.
Discount Store News. "Mid-Tier Still Losing Image War." August 7, 2000, p. 51.
Dolbow, Sandra. "Mid-Tier Muddle." *Brandweek*, April 10, 2000, p. 36.
DSN Retailing Today. "Lacy Questions Corporate Direction." May 1, 2001, p. 1.
Duff, Christina. "Stockholders Send Message to Sears Board." *Wall Street Journal*, May 15, 1992, p. A2.
Edwards, Cliff. "Sears Dumps 'Softer Side,' Unveils New Ads." *Marketing News*, September 13, 1999, p. 20.
England, Robert. "Penney-wise?" *Financial World*, April 26, 1994, p. 36.
Fenley, Gareth. "A Unifying Turnaround." *Display and Design Ideas*, July 2002.
Furniture Today. "Sears, Target to Buy 53 Wards Stores." April 2, 2001.
Gallanis, Peter. "Sears to Test New Prototype." *Discount Store News*, February 7, 2000, p. 7.

———. "Lacy Identifies Agenda as New CEO of Sears." *Discount Store News,* October 2, 2000, p. 3.
Greenwald, John. "Reinventing Sears." *Time,* December 23, 1996, p. 52.
Hays, Constance L. "Sears Earnings Will Be Hurt by Credit Unit." *New York Times,* October 18, 2002, p. C1.
Heller, Laura. "Sears' Lacy Excites Wall Street with Rare Talk of Doubled Earnings." *DSN Retailing Today,* April 22, 2002.
Hilder, David, and Steve Weiner. "Big Brokerage Houses Are Problem Children for Their New Parents." *Wall Street Journal,* September 13, 1985, p. 1.
Hisey, Pete. "When the Soft Side Gets Spongy." *Retail Merchandiser,* December 2001.
———. "Harder Lines Between Mass and Mid-Tier." *Retail Merchandiser,* February 2002.
———."The Return of Sears and Penney." *Retail Merchandiser,* August 2002.
Hogsett, Don. "Sears 4Q Profits Fall 13.6%." *Home Textiles Today,* January 22, 2001.
Howell, Debbie. "Sears' Latest Openings Reveal Simpler Side of Stores." *DSN Retailing Today,* April 8, 2002.
Hutchison, Katherine. "Sears Expects Change." *DSN Retailing Today,* August 6, 2001.
———. "Sears to Eliminate Floor, Window Biz." *DSN Retailing Today,* January 21, 2002.
Houston Chronicle. "U.S. Judge Finds Sears in Contempt of Order." April 26, 1997, p. 4.
James, Frank. "Sears Sets Outlay at $1.7 Billion for Next 5 Years." *Wall Street Journal,* November 9, 1983, p. 4.
Kilman, Scott. "Sears to Bring Back Goldstein in Effort to Establish a Specialty-Store Presence." *Wall Street Journal,* February 9, 1987, p. 10.
———. "Sears to Close Five Warehouses in Move to Cut Costs, Sets $20 Million Charge." *Wall Street Journal,* March 3, 1987, p. 6.
———. "Sears Earnings Increased 37% in 2nd Quarter." *Wall Street Journal,* July 23, 1987, p. 5.
Koenig, David. "Retailers Square Off Over Home-Redesign Market." *Marketing News,* September 11, 2000, p. 42.
Kuykendall, Lavonne. "A Catalog of Reasons for Sears' Card Profits." *American Banker,* March 14, 2002.
Levin, Rich. "Retailers Find a Winning Mix." *Information Week,* September 11, 2000, p. 345.
Lillo, Andrea. "Great Indoors Keys Sears Transition." *Home Textiles Today,* March 5, 2001, p. 8.
Los Angeles Times. "Retailing: Company Said It Will Return Money, with Interest, Paid by Credit Cardholders." April 11, 1997, p. 4.
———."Sears Posts 26% Rise but Foresees Problems." October 17, 1997, p. 4.
Lueck, Thomas. "Sears to Buy Coldwell Banker in Big Expansion." *Wall Street Journal,* October 6, 1981, p. 2.
——— and Tim Carrington. "Sears Agrees to Buy Dean Witter for $607 Million in Cash and Stock." *Wall Street Journal,* October 9, 1981, p. 3.
McCoy, Charles. "Sears to Close Part of World Trade Unit, Underscoring Dismal Picture for Exports." *Wall Street Journal,* October 29, 1986, p. 2.
Patterson, Gregory. "Sears Approves Additional Powers for Shareholders." *Wall Street Journal,* June 16, 1992, p. B13.
———. "Retailing: More Stores Switch from Sales to 'Everyday Low Prices.'" *Wall Street Journal,* November 12, 1992, p. B1.
——— and Christina Duff. "Retailing: Sears Trims Operations, Ending an Era." *Wall Street Journal,* January 26, 1993, p. B1.
———. "Sears Will Re-establish Base in Malls, Target Middle-of-the-Road Merchants." *Wall Street Journal,* January 27, 1993, p. A8.
———. "Corporate Focus: 'Face Lift' Gives Sears a Fresh Look and Better Results." *Wall Street Journal,* July 20, 1993, p. B4.
Pethokoukis, James. "The Dow Dumps Its Dogs." *U.S. News & World Report,* November 8, 1999, p. 87.
Richards, Bill. "Sears Seeks to Buy Western Auto Supply as Part of Push Into Specialty Retailing." *Wall Street Journal,* March 17, 1988, p. 10.
Schwadel, Francine. "Weak Net Presses Sears to Restructure." *Wall Street Journal,* October 27, 1988, p. A8.
———. "Sears to Sell Tower, Buy 10% of Stock Back." *Wall Street Journal,* November 1, 1988, p. A3.
———. "Sears Switches Pricing Strategy to Combat Discounters." *Wall Street Journal,* November 1, 1988, p. B1.
———. "Its Expansion Lagging, Sears Now Struggles to Stay Independent." *Wall Street Journal,* November 2, 1988.
———. "The 'Sale' Is Fading as a Retailing Tactic." *Wall Street Journal,* March 1, 1989, p. B1.
———. "What Looks Like a Sale But Isn't a Sale?" *Wall Street Journal,* April 27, 1989, p. B1.
———. "Sears Dissident, Seeking Seat on Board, to Urge Restructure if Goals Aren't Met." *Wall Street Journal,* April 5, 1991, p. A51.
———. "Sears Strategy Is Large Target for Rare Gadfly." *Wall Street Journal,* May 6, 1991, p. B1.
———. "Sears Goes for Glitter in Naming Martinez to Retail Post." *Wall Street Journal,* August 11, 1992, p. B1.
Sears, Roebuck & Company. Annual reports, 1998, 1999, 2000, 2001.
———. 10K reports, 1994–2000.
Sellers, Patricia. "Sears' Big Turnaround Runs Into Big Trouble." *Fortune,* February 16, 1998, p. 34.
Sloan, Carole. "Sears Emphasizes Full-Line Stores." *Home Textiles Today,* May 14, 2001, p. 2.
———. "Softer Side of Sears to Stress Home Fashions." *Home Textiles Today,* October 29, 2001.
———. "Sears Looks to Reinvent Great Indoors Format." *Home Textiles Today,* May 13, 2002.
Souccar, Miriam Kreinin. "Challenging Banks, Sears Offering Its Card Customers a MasterCard." *American Banker,* August 31, 2000.
Sparks, Debra. "Sears: Return of the Prodigal." *Financial World,* April 11, 1995, p. 14.
Stedman, Craig. "Sears, Carrefour Plan Exchange for Retailers," *Computerworld,* March 6, 2000, p. 1.
Tatge, Mark. "The Harder Side of Sears." *Forbes,* November 13, 2000, p. 282.
Tsao, Amy. "The Ever-Changing Face of Sears." *Business Week Online.* November 7, 2001.

Wall Street Journal. "Major Retailers Had Profit Drops in Quarter, Half." August 21, 1980, p. 7.

———. "Sears Plans to Establish Company to Handle International Trading." February 26, 1982, p. 37.

———. "A Good Time Was Had by Some." May 21, 1986.

———. "Sears, Roebuck & Co." April 27, 1987, p. 17.

———. "Sears Sets Final Accord to Buy Eye Care Centers." *Wall Street Journal,* July 9, 1987, p. 34.

The Washington Post. "A New Spin in the Appliance Market; Sears Facing Competition from Wal-Mart, Home Depot." September 2, 2000, p. E1.

Weimer, De'Ann. "The Softest Side of Sears," *Business Week,* December 28, 1998, p. 60.

Weiner, Steve. "Sears Sets Early Retirement Plan to Inject Youth into Merchandising Management." *Wall Street Journal,* September 9, 1980, p. 8.

———. "Sears Finds Broadening Its Image Takes Time, Presses Staff to Adjust." *Wall Street Journal,* October 31, 1980, p. 1.

———. "Sears Will Open Business-Machine Stores in Five Test Markets Beginning This Fall." *Wall Street Journal,* January 23, 1981, p. 3.

——— and James, Frank. "Sears, a Powerhouse in Many Fields Now, Looks Into New Ones." *Wall Street Journal,* February 10, 1984, p. 1.

———. "Sears Expects Wide Acceptance for Its New Card." *Wall Street Journal,* April 25, 1985, p. 22.

CASE 4

WGirl, WBoy Calendars (A)

Kenneth G. Hardy
University of Western Ontario

In New York, on August 22, 2001, Luke Atkins sat at his desk thinking about how to raise money for charity upon his return in September to the Richard Ivey School of Business at the University of Western Ontario (Western). He thought about the potential impact of calendars featuring Western students. Before going ahead with the calendars, he wondered about the feasibility of the project and the different aspects of the marketing strategy.

Atkins was considering WBoy and WGirl calendars that would feature both male and female students at Western. Each calendar would have the same format and contents. Atkins said:

> The pictures inside will be seductive and sexy, but at the same time very classy.
> The models will have the final say, not only on their choice of clothes to wear
> in the pictures, but also on their final picture to be put in the calendar.

Atkins had some experience in the use of calendars for fund-raising purposes. While on the university rugby team, he had created a calendar featuring Western rugby players to raise money for the team. In this calendar, the players had their shirts off, and the university athletic department had rejected the calendar. Atkins changed the calendar to show action shots of the team and pictures from the team's tour of South Africa (see Exhibit 1). The calendar helped to raise almost $10,000, but he thought that this was a mere speck of what could have been raised with a more provocative calendar, namely, his original version.

Atkins was highly motivated by his new fund-raising project. He strongly believed that helping others and giving back to society were very important values. He had always been involved in charity and fund-raising activities. When he was a high school

Richard Ivey School of Business
The University of Western Ontario

Luke Atkins and Yany Grégoire prepared this case under the supervision of Professor Kenneth G. Hardy solely to provide material for class discussion. The authors do not intend to illustrate either effective or ineffective handling of a managerial situation. The authors may have disguised certain names and other identifying information to protect confidentiality.

Ivey Management Services prohibits any form of reproduction, storage or transmittal without its written permission. This material is not covered under authorization from CanCopy or any reproduction rights organization. To order copies or request permission to reproduce materials, contact Ivey Publishing, Ivey Management Services, c/o Richard Ivey School of Business, The University of Western Ontario, London, Ontario, Canada, N6A 3K7; phone (519) 661-3208; fax (519) 661-3882; e-mail cases@ivey.uwo.ca.

Exhibit 1   Format of the Rugby Calendar

University of
Western Ontario
Mustangs

May

MON	TUE	WED	THU	FRI	SAT	SUN
1	2	3	4	5	6	7
8	9	10	11	12	13	14
15	16	17	18	19	20	21
22	23	24	25	26	27	28
29	30	31				

Source: 2000 Western Rugby Calendar.

student, he had logged 300 hours of volunteering and continued his charitable work as a member of the Western rugby team. He also knew that the calendars were good fund-raising instruments, and he also wanted to demonstrate that calendars with seductive pictures could be used successfully in this context. Even if his choice of causes was not finalized yet, he was considering charities such as the Breast Cancer Society (for women) or the Jesse's Journey Foundation (for men). The Jesse's Journey Foundation was a London-based charity that funded research to find treatment and cure for neuro-muscular diseases. Atkins needed a cause that was consistent, or at least not conflicting, with his concept of calendars featuring seductive pictures. He was also exploring the idea of having men and women compete for their respective charities.

Atkins believed that the calendar market was huge. The University of Western Ontario was located in London, Ontario, with a population of 330,000, including 26,000 students who attended Western. In addition, there were more than 240,000 Western alumni across Canada and around the world.

There were many different kinds of calendars available in London, Ontario. At local stores, a student could purchase a calendar that featured models, athletes, animals, babies—the offerings were numerous. There were also free calendars given away with

Table 1   **TYPICAL CALENDAR PRICES**

Calendar	Price + Taxes
London Firefighters' calendar	$15
Sports Illustrated Swimsuit calendar	$18
Anne Geddes calendar	$18
NHL calendar	$18

Table 2   **ADVERTISING PRICES**

	Wcalendar	The Gazette
Advertisement costs	$500	$434
Exposure	WGirl calendar (monthly spread)	Quarter page (day)
	WBoy calendar ad (monthly spread)	
	Ad on back of each calendar	
	Handouts	

magazines. The London firefighters produced 10,000 copies of a calendar each year with proceeds donated to a particular charity. Also, every year Western gave first-year students free calendars that could be written on and erased, durable enough to last the rest of their university career. Most students, however, used their calendars to write down specific dates for class exams, vacations, social events and assignments. After reviewing the competition (see Table 1), Luke believed that selling a calendar for $10 to $12 would make it attractive to potential buyers. This would be at least $3 less than competing products.

By utilizing extra space on the paper, the calendars could have room for advertising that would yield funds to help cover the costs of this operation. The target segment would determine the kind of sponsors to be pursued. For example, by targeting the students, local businesses would be more likely to be interested in the project. Local businesses, however, would be less likely to be sponsors if the calendar was targeting alumni who were dispersed all over North America. (See Table 2 for suggested advertising prices and a comparison with the student newspaper, the *Gazette*.)

It might be difficult to find 12 men and 12 women models for the calendars. According to Atkins' preliminary plans, the models should be unique and represent different programs and backgrounds. The best way to recruit models was one of his major challenges. Different options were available: an ad in the student newspaper (the *Gazette*), word of mouth, Atkins' personal network and Western sport teams. Compensation for the models was also an issue. Atkins believed that he might be able to find students willing to model for free because the project was for charity. Atkins also hoped that the models would sell calendars personally, providing him with 24 sales representatives. He was willing to offer the models a commission for each calendar that was sold.

To sell the calendars to students, Atkins thought that one of the best locations would be on campus. The student union charged charitable organizations $50 per day for access to a distribution location. In order to increase students' awareness, Atkins planned to have models distribute handouts to students, and to associate sales efforts

Exhibit 2   Prototype of a Typical Page for WGirl Calendar

Source: Luke Atkins and David Raposo.

with special events held in bars in the student district. A major conference press, where all the local and national media would be invited, would also be organized to underline the launch of the calendars. For alumni and local residents, Atkins thought that the Internet was a good idea. The costs would be $350 to set up a website, $20 per month to maintain it and $20 to register the name wcalendars.com.

Also, the advertisers would be asked to use their outlets to sell calendars. Posters would be printed for the advertisers' outlets; the cost of these posters would be included in the cost of printing the calendars. Atkins set up a relationship with a new nightclub in the heart of the student entertainment district that went live-to-air on a local radio station. He thought it would be another medium to advertise his product to the greater London area before the calendars were even printed.

Atkins wanted to create a high-quality calendar. The pictures in the calendar would be the foundation for this goal. In order to more clearly communicate its vision, he built two prototypes of typical calendar pages (see Exhibits 2 and 3). After approaching professional photographers in London and Toronto, the best and least expensive solution was to have all of the pictures taken during back-to-back days. With the total photography rates averaging $5,000, the cost was still immense for this project. Each

Exhibit 3   Prototype of a Typical Page for WBoy Calendar

December

MONDAY   TUESDAY WEDNESDAY THURSDAY   FRIDAY   SATURDAY   SUNDAY

						1
2	3	4	5	6	7	8
9	10	11	12	13	14	15
16	17	18	19	20	21	22
23	24	25	26	27	28	29
30	31					

Source: Luke Atkins and David Raposo.

model needed at least an hour with the photographer, and Atkins had heard that nothing was ever finished on time in the fashion industry. Nevertheless, the price included the developing, cropping and formatting of the pictures, as well as the cost of the equipment.

Depending on the number of calendars to be printed, the number of pages and the presence of color, the cost would greatly vary (see Tables 3 and 4). At first sight, Atkins was especially interested in a calendar of 16 pages that would include 12 pages for the months, 1 cover page, 1 back page and 2 extra pages that would feature the central picture. On the other hand, his mind was not totally set on this decision. He was also considering a 28-page format, for which every month would cover 2 pages. Because Atkins was planning to print two separate calendars (i.e., one for men and one for women), two startup costs needed to be considered in the cost analysis.

Atkins wondered whether or not he should go ahead with this project. He did not have a lot of time because calendars are usually sold at the beginning of the school year. In addition, many decisions still needed to be made related to the final format of the calendar, the charity organization to approach and the marketing strategy, including market segments, product, price, distribution and advertising.

Table 3   COSTS (INCLUDING STARTUP) FOR BLACK-AND-WHITE
              CALENDARS

	1,000 Copies	2,000 Copies	3,000 Copies
16-page format	$2,500	$4,000	$ 6,000
28-page format	$5,000	$8,000	$12,500

Table 4   COSTS (INCLUDING STARTUP) FOR CALENDARS IN COLORS

	1,000 Copies	2,000 Copies	3,000 Copies
16-page format	$ 5,000	$ 7,500	$ 9,500
28-page format	$10,000	$15,000	$19,000

Competition in the Bottled Water Industry

John E. Gamble
University of South Alabama

Bottled water was among the world's most attractive beverage categories with global sales in 2001 exceeding 32 billion gallons and annual growth averaging nearly 9 percent between 1996 and 2001. Bottled water had long been a widely consumed product in Western Europe and Mexico, where annual per capita consumption averaged about 30 gallons in 2001, but until the mid-1990s bottled water had been somewhat of a novelty or prestige product in the United States. In 1990 approximately 2.2 billion gallons of bottled water were consumed in the United States and per capita consumption approximated 9 gallons. U.S. per capita consumption had grown to nearly 20 gallons a year by 2001 and was expected to grow to 26 gallons a year by 2005. The rising popularity of bottled water in the United States during the 1990s allowed the United States to become the world's largest market for bottled water by 1996 (see Exhibit 1).

Exhibit 1   LEADING COUNTRY MARKETS FOR BOTTLED WATER, 1996, 2001 (IN MILLIONS OF GALLONS)

2001 Rank	Country	1996	2001	CAGR* (1996–2001)
1	United States	3,495.1	5,425.3	9.2%
2	Mexico	2,674.2	3,496.5	5.5
3	Italy	1,923.9	2,502.6	5.4
4	Germany	2,097.6	2,336.5	2.2
5	France	1,498.9	2,064.6	6.6
6	China	565.0	2,007.8	28.9
7	Indonesia	512.1	1,352.1	21.4
8	Thailand	854.5	1,198.3	7.0
9	Brazil	475.7	1,139.6	19.1
10	Spain	884.0	1,091.4	4.3
All others		4,205.4	7,488.4	12.2
Worldwide total		21,182.4	32,104.1	8.7%

*Compound average growth rate.
Source: Beverage Marketing Corporation, as reported by *Bottled Water Reporter,* April–May 2002.

The growing popularity of bottled water in the United States was attributable to concerns over the safety of municipal drinking water, an increased focus on fitness and health, and the hectic on-the-go lifestyles of American consumers. The convenience, purity, and portability of bottled water made it the natural solution to consumers' dissatisfaction with tap water. The U.S. bottled water market, like most markets outside the United States, was characterized by fierce competitive rivalry as the world's bottled water sellers jockeyed for market share and volume gains. Both the global and U.S. bottled water markets had become dominated by a few international food and beverage producers like Coca-Cola, PepsiCo, Nestlé, and Groupe Danone, but they also included many small regional sellers that were required to develop either low-cost production and distribution capabilities or differentiation strategies keyed to some unique product attributes. At the close of 2002, industry rivals were entering new distribution channels, developing innovative product variations, entering into strategic agreements to penetrate new international markets, and acquiring smaller sellers that might hold strong positions in certain U.S. regional markets or emerging markets. Industry analysts and observers believed the recent moves undertaken by the world's largest sellers of bottled water would alter the competitive dynamics of the bottled water industry and mandate that certain players modify their current strategic approaches to competition in the industry.

Industry Conditions in 2002

Even though it was the world's largest market for bottled water, the United States remained among the faster-growing markets for bottled water since per capita consumption of bottled water fell substantially below consumption rates in Western Europe, the Middle East, and Mexico. Bottled water consumption in the United States also lagged per capita consumption of soft drinks by a wide margin. However, many U.S. consumers were making a transition from soft drinks to bottled water as the soft-drink market had grown by less than 1 percent annually between 1996 and 2001 and the market for bottled water had continued to grow at annual rates near 10 percent during the same time period. By 2002, 70 percent of U.S. households purchased bottled water at least once a year and the average water-buying household purchased 22 twelve-ounce bottles a year. Exhibits 2 through 5 illustrate the growing popularity of bottled water among U.S. consumers during the 1990s and through 2001.

Almost one-half of bottled water consumed in the United States in 1990 was bulk water delivered to homes and offices in returnable five-gallon containers and dispensed through coolers. Only 186 million gallons of water were sold in one-liter or smaller single-serving polyethylene terephthalate (PET) bottles. In 2002, bottled water sold in one-liter or smaller PET containers accounted for 36.2 percent of industry volume and 50.8 percent of dollar sales and had grown by 29.1 percent annually between 1995 and 2001. The sales of bulk water sold in 5-gallon containers or 1- or 2.5-gallon high-density polyethylene (HDPE) containers accounted for 60.9 percent of gallonage but only 43.3 percent of dollar sales. Convenience was the primary appeal of smaller, single-serving PET containers since consumers could purchase chilled water they could drink immediately. Water purchased for immediate consumption grew from 8.3 percent of industry sales volume in 1990 to 16.7 percent of sales volume in 2000. Portability also partly explained the appeal of water bottled in PET containers since the small plastic bottles were easier to carry than glasses or cups of tap water. In 2001, consumers began to prefer PET containers not only for immediate consumption but

Exhibit 2   PER CAPITA CONSUMPTION OF BOTTLED WATER BY COUNTRY MARKET, 1996, 2001

2001 Rank	Country	Per Capita Consumption (in gallons)		Compound Average Growth Rate
		1996	2001	
1	Italy	33.5	43.4	5.3%
2	France	25.7	34.7	6.2
3	Mexico	28.1	34.3	4.1
4	Belgium-Luxembourg	28.8	32.6	2.5
5	United Arab Emirates	25.7	31.3	4.0
6	Germany	25.6	28.1	1.9
7	Spain	22.3	27.3	4.1
8	Switzerland	21.1	23.8	2.4
9	Lebanon	12.7	22.5	12.1
10	Saudi Arabia	15.1	22.5	8.3
11	Austria	18.5	20.5	2.1
12	Cyprus	14.2	20.2	7.3
13	Czech Republic	12.9	19.6	8.7
14	United States	13.1	19.5	8.3
15	Thailand	14.5	19.4	6.0
Global average		3.3	4.9	8.2%

Source: Beverage Marketing Corporation, as reported by *Bottled Water Reporter,* April–May 2002.

Exhibit 3   U.S. PER CAPITA BEVERAGE CONSUMPTION, 1996 AND 2001

Beverage	Gallons per Person 1996	Gallons per Person 2001	Compound Average Growth Rate
Soft drinks	53.4	55.3	0.7%
Coffee	22.3	21.9	−0.4
Bottled water*	13.0	19.9	8.9
Milk	24.2	19.9	−3.8
Fruit beverages	15.0	15.5	0.7
Tea	9.7	9.3	−0.8
Wine	1.9	2.0	1.0
Beer and spirits	29.3	23.5	−4.3
Tap water/all other	23.2	24.5	1.1
Total	192.0	191.8	

*Note: The per capita consumption of bottled water as presented by *Beverage Aisle* varies slightly from the calculations prepared by Beverage Marketing Corporation presented in Exhibits 2 and 5.

Source: *Beverage Aisle,* August 15, 2002.

Exhibit 4   VOLUME SALES AND DOLLAR VALUE OF THE U.S. BOTTLED WATER MARKET, 1991–2001

Year	Volume Sales (in millions of gallons)	Annual Change	Industry Revenues (in millions of dollars)	Annual Change
1991	2,355.9	2.1%	$2,512.9	−0.6%
1992	2,486.6	5.5	2,658.7	5.8
1993	2,689.4	8.2	2,876.7	8.2
1994	2,966.4	10.3	3,164.3	10.0
1995	3,226.9	8.8	3,521.9	11.3
1996	3,495.1	8.3	3,835.4	8.9
1997	3,794.3	8.6	4,222.7	10.1
1998	4,130.7	8.9	4,666.1	10.5
1999	4,583.4	11.0	5,314.7	13.9
2000	4,904.4	7.0	5,809.0	9.3
2001	5,425.3	10.6	6,477.0	11.5

Source: Beverage Marketing Corporation, as reported by *Bottled Water Reporter,* April–May 2002.

Exhibit 5   U.S. PER CAPITA CONSUMPTION OF BOTTLED WATER, 1991–2001

Year	Per Capita Consumption (in gallons)	Annual Change
1991	9.3	—
1992	9.8	5.4%
1993	10.5	7.1
1994	11.5	9.5
1995	12.2	6.1
1996	13.1	7.4
1997	14.1	7.6
1998	15.3	8.5
1999	16.8	9.8
2000	17.8	6.0
2001	19.5	9.6

Source: Beverage Marketing Corporation, as reported by *Bottled Water Reporter,* April–May 2002.

also for home use as the take-home PET market for the first time exceeded the volume sales of chilled PET water sold for immediate consumption. Water packaged in PET containers sold through take-home channels accounted for 28 percent of industry sales volume in 2001 and was expected to account for more than one-half of industry growth between 2002 and 2007.

The convenience and portability of bottled water were two of a variety of reasons U.S. consumers were increasingly attracted to bottled water. An increased emphasis on healthy lifestyles and improved consumer awareness of the need for proper hydration led many consumers to shift traditional beverage preferences toward bottled water. Bottled water consumers frequently claimed drinking more water improved the appearance of their skin and gave them more energy. Bottled water analysts also believed many health-conscious consumers drank bottled water because it was a symbol to others that they were interested in health.

A certain amount of industry growth was attributable to increased concerns over the quality of tap water provided by municipal water sources. Consumers in parts of the world with inadequate water treatment facilities relied on bottled water to provide daily hydration needs, but tap water in the United States was very pure by global standards. Municipal water systems were regulated by the U.S. Environmental Protection Agency (EPA) and were required to comply with the provisions of the Safe Drinking Water Act Amendments of 2001. Consumer concerns over the quality of drinking water in the U.S. emerged in 1993 when 400,000 residents of Milwaukee, Wisconsin, became ill with flulike symptoms and almost 100 immune impaired residents died from waterborne bacterial infections. Throughout the 1990s and into the early 2000s, the media sporadically reported cases of municipal water contamination, such as in 2000 when residents of Washington, D.C., became ill after the city's water filtration process caused elevated levels of suspended materials in the water. Consumer attention to the purity of municipal water was also heightened in 2000 when the EPA proposed revising the standard for arsenic content in tap water as specified by the Safe Drinking Water Act Amendments of 1996 from 50 parts per billion (ppb) to 10 ppb. Prior to the congressional discussion of acceptable arsenic levels in drinking water, most Americans were unaware that any arsenic was present in tap water.

Even though some consumers were concerned about the purity of municipal water, most consumers' complaints with tap water centered on its chemical taste, which resulted from treatment processes that included the use of chlorine and other chemicals such as fluoride. In a tap water tasting in Atlanta hosted by *Southpoint* magazine, judges rated municipal water on taste and found some cities' waters very palatable. Water obtained from the municipal source in Memphis was said to have "a refreshing texture" and tap water from New Orleans was commended for "its neutrality." However, other municipal systems did not fare as well with the judges—some of whom suggested Houston's water tasted "like a chemistry lab," while others said Atlanta's municipal water was akin to "a gulp of swimming pool water."[1] However, there were positive attributes to the chemicals added to tap water, as chlorine was necessary to kill any bacteria in the water and fluoride had contributed greatly to improved dental health in the United States. In addition, tap water had been shown to be no less healthy than bottled water in a number of independent studies, including a study publicized in Europe that was commissioned by the World Wide Fund for Nature and conducted by researchers at the University of Geneva.

Bottled water producers in the United States were required to meet the standards of both the EPA and the U.S. Food and Drug Administration (FDA). Like all food and beverage products sold in the United States, bottled water was subject to such food safety and labeling requirements as nutritional labeling provisions and general Good Manufacturing Practices (GMPs). Bottled water GMPs were mandated under the 1962 Kefauver-Harris drug amendments to the Federal Food, Drug and Cosmetic Act of 1938 and established specifications for plant construction and design, sanitation, equipment design and construction, production and process controls, and record keeping. The FDA required bottled water producers to test for the presence of bacteria at least weekly and to test for inorganic contaminants, trace metals, minerals, pesticides, herbicides, and organic compounds annually. Bottled water was also regulated by state agencies that conducted inspections of bottling facilities and certification of testing facilities to ensure bottled water was bottled under federal GMPs and was safe to drink.

Bottled water producers were also required to comply with the FDA's Standard of Identity, which required bottlers to include source water information on their products' labels. Water labeled as "spring water" must have been captured from a borehole or natural orifice of a spring that naturally flows to the surface. "Artesian water" could be extracted from a confined aquifer (a water-bearing underground layer of rock or sand) where the water level stood above the top of the aquifer. "Sparkling water" was required to have natural carbonation as it emerged from the source, although carbonation could be added to return the carbon dioxide level to what was evident as the water emerged from the source. Even though sparkling water was very popular throughout most of Europe and the Middle East, it accounted for only 9 percent of U.S. bottled water sales in 2001.

The FDA's definition of "mineral water" stated that such water must have at least 250 parts per million of total dissolved solids and its standards required water labeled as "purified" have undergone distillation, deionization, or reverse osmosis to remove chemicals such as chlorine and fluoride. "Drinking water" required no additional processing beyond what was required for tap water but could not include flavoring or other additives that account for more than 1 percent of the product's total weight. Both "drinking water" and "purified water" had to clearly state that the water originated "from a community water system" or "from a municipal source."

Bottled water producers could also voluntarily become members of the International Bottled Water Association (IBWA) and agree to comply with its Model Code, which went beyond the standards of the EPA, FDA, or state agencies. The Model Code allowed fewer parts per million of certain organic and inorganic chemicals and microbiological contaminants than FDA, EPA, or state regulations and imposed a chlorine limitation on bottled water. Neither the FDA nor the EPA limited chlorine content. IBWA members were monitored for compliance through annual, unannounced inspections administered by an independent third-party organization.

Distribution and Sale of Bottled Water

Consumers could purchase bottled water in nearly any location in the United States where food was also sold. Supermarkets, supercenters, and wholesale clubs all stocked large inventories of bottled water, and most convenience stores dedicated at least one stand-up cooler to bottled water. Bottled water could also be purchased in most delis and many restaurants; from vending machines; and at sporting events and other special events like concerts, outdoor festivals, and carnivals. Bottled water could also be delivered directly to consumers' homes or offices.

The distribution of bottled water varied depending on the producer and the distribution channel. Typically, bottled water was distributed to large grocers and wholesale clubs directly by the bottled water producer, while most producers used third parties like beer and wine distributors or food distributors to make sales and deliveries to convenience-store buyers. Similarly, food-service distributors usually handled landing accounts with restaurants and delis and making necessary deliveries to keep the account properly stocked. Most distributors made deliveries of bottled water to convenience stores and restaurants along with their regular scheduled deliveries of other foods and beverages. Therefore, these third-party food and beverage distributors almost never made deliveries to one-time or infrequent events like art festivals or sporting events, since they were better equipped to represent a variety of food and beverage companies that wanted their products available for sale in locations where consumers made frequent food and beverage purchases. Similarly, vending machine servicing did not match the resources and competitive capabilities of most food and beverage distributors.

Because of the difficulty for food-service distributors to restock vending machines and provide bottled water to special events, Coca-Cola and PepsiCo were able to dominate such channels since they could make deliveries of bottled water along with their deliveries of other beverages. Coca-Cola and PepsiCo's vast beverage distribution systems made it easy for the two companies to make Dasani and Aquafina available anywhere Coke or Pepsi could be purchased. In addition, the two cola giants almost always negotiated contracts with sports stadiums, universities, and school systems that made one of them the exclusive supplier of all types of non-alcoholic beverages sold in the venue for some period of time. Under such circumstances, it was nearly impossible for other brands of bottled water to gain access to the account.

Coca-Cola and PepsiCo's soft-drink businesses also aided the two companies in making Aquafina and Dasani available in supermarkets, supercenters, wholesale clubs, and convenience stores. Soft-drink sales were important to all types of food stores since soft drinks made up a sizable percentage of sales and since food retailers frequently relied on soft-drink promotions to generate store traffic. Coca-Cola and PepsiCo were able to encourage their customers to purchase items across their product line to ensure prompt and complete shipment of key soft-drink products. As a diversified food products company, PepsiCo had exploited the popularity of its soft drinks, Gatorade sports drinks, Frito-Lay snack foods, and Tropicana orange juice in persuading grocery accounts to purchase not only Aquafina but also other new brands such as FruitWorks, SoBe, Lipton's iced tea, and Starbucks Frappuccino.

Since most supermarkets, supercenters, and food stores usually carried only three to five branded bottled waters plus a private-label brand, bottled water producers other than Coke and Pepsi were required to compete aggressively on price to gain access to shelf space. Market surveys indicated that wholesale prices for branded bottled water ranged between $3.50 and $7.00 per case—depending on the appeal of the product and the competitive strength of the seller. Some supermarkets and other grocery chains required bottled water suppliers to pay slotting fees in addition to offering low prices to gain shelf space. Grocers expected to pay less for private-label products and typically required private-label suppliers to prepare bids offering both purified and spring water in packaging of various sizes. Contracts were awarded to the low bidder and typically re-bid on an annual or biannual basis.

Convenience-store buyers also aggressively pressed bottled water producers and food distributors for low prices and slotting fees. Most convenience stores carried only two to four brands of bottled water beyond what was distributed by Coca-Cola and Pepsi and required bottlers to pay annual slotting fees of $300 to $400 per store in return for providing 5 to 10 bottle facings on a cooler shelf. Even though bottled water producers were responsible for paying slotting fees to gain shelf space, food-service distributors handled sales transactions with convenience stores and made all deliveries. Food and beverage distributors usually paid the bottlers of lesser-known brands $3.75 to $4.25 per case, while popular national brands commanded wholesale prices in the $5.00–$6.00 range. Typically, a distributor would represent only one or two bottled water producers and required producers to make deliveries to their warehouses. Some bottlers offered to provide retailers with rebates of approximately 25 cents per case to help secure distributors for their brand. Food distributors also asked bottled water suppliers to sponsor annual trade shows at which participating vendors (including bottled water producers) would offer discounts of approximately 25 cents per case to convenience-store customers willing to commit to large quarterly purchases. Food and beverage distributors usually allowed bottled water producers to negotiate slotting fees and rebates directly with convenience-store buyers.

There was not as much competition among bottled water producers to gain shelf space in delis and restaurants since volume was relatively low—making per unit distribution costs exceedingly high unless other beverages were delivered along with bottled water. PepsiCo and Coca-Cola were among the better-suited bottled water producers to economically distribute water to restaurants since they likely provided fountain drinks to such establishments.

Bulk water sold in returnable five-gallon containers was delivered to home and office users directly by bottled water producers. These producers usually specialized in home and office delivery, but might also sell a PET product through convenience and supermarket channels. Retail pricing to bulk water purchasers ranged between $5 and $7 per five-gallon container. Consumers of bulk water were also required to rent a cooler at $10 to $15 per month. Most bulk water sellers used a delivery route system with scheduled visits for deliveries of water and empty container pickup.

Suppliers to the Industry

The suppliers to the bottled water industry included municipal water systems; spring operators; bottling equipment manufacturers; deionization, reverse osmosis, and filtration equipment manufacturers; cooler manufacturers; sellers of racking systems; manufacturers of PET and HDPE bottles and plastic caps; label printers; and secondary packaging suppliers. Most packaging supplies needed for the production of bottled water were readily available for a large number of suppliers. Large bottlers able to commit to annual purchases of more than 5 million PET bottles could purchase bottles for as little as $0.05 per bottle, while regional bottlers purchasing smaller quantities of bottles or only making one-time purchases of bottles could expect to pay as much as $0.15 per bottle. Most PET and HDPE bottle producers preferred to reward customers choosing to develop ongoing relationships with their lowest prices. Suppliers of secondary packaging (e.g., cardboard boxes, shrink-wrap, and six-pack rings) and suppliers of printed film or paper labels were numerous and aggressively competed for the business of large bottled water producers.

Equipment used for water purification and filling bottles was manufactured and marketed by about 50 different companies in the United States. About 10 manufacturers offered a complete line of filling equipment, filtration equipment, distillation equipment, deionization equipment, bottle washers, labeling equipment, packaging equipment, and reverse osmosis equipment, with others specializing in a few equipment categories. A basic bottle-filling line could be purchased for about $125,000, while a large state-of-the-art bottling facility could require a capital investment of more than $100 million. Bottlers choosing to sell spring water could expect to invest about $300,000 for source certification, road grading, and installation of pumping equipment, fencing, holding tanks, and disinfecting equipment. Bottlers that did not own springs were also required to enter into lease agreements with spring owners that typically ranged from $20,000 to $30,000 a year. Companies selling purified water merely purchased tap water from municipal water systems at industrial rates prior to purifying and bottling the water for sale to consumers. Sellers of purified water were able not only to pay less for water they bottled, but also to avoid spring water's inbound shipping costs of $0.05 to $0.15 per gallon since water arrived at the bottling facility by pipe rather than by truck.

Key Competitive Capabilities in the Bottled Water Industry

Bottled water did not enjoy the brand loyalty of soft drinks, beer, or many other food and beverage products, but it was experiencing some increased brand loyalty with 10–25 percent of consumers looking for a specific brand and an additional two-thirds considering only a few brands acceptable. Because of the growing importance of brand recognition, successful sellers of bottled water were required to possess well-developed brand-building skills. Most of the industry's major sellers were global food companies—having built respected brands in soft drinks, dairy products, chocolates, and breakfast cereals prior to entering the bottled water industry. PepsiCo, Coca-Cola, and Nestlé were the most successful sellers at building consumer loyalty in the United States, according to a 2002 brand loyalty study conducted by NFO WorldGroup. The survey found that Aquafina consumers were rather loyal to PepsiCo's brand, as it accounted for 77 percent of regular Aquafina consumers' total bottled water purchases. Nestlé Waters' brands also commanded a 77 percent brand loyalty rating, while the Dasani brand accounted for 62 percent of bottled water consumed by frequent Dasani purchasers. Brands offered by other bottled water sellers achieved far lower levels of brand loyalty.

Bottled water sellers also needed to have efficient distribution systems to supermarket, wholesale club, and convenience store channels to be successful in the industry. It was imperative for bottled water distributors (whether direct store delivery by bottlers or delivery by third parties) to maximize the number of deliveries per driver since distribution included high fixed costs for warehouses, trucks, handheld inventory tracking devices, and labor. It was also critical for distributors and bottlers to provide on-time deliveries and offer responsive customer service to large customers in the highly price-competitive market. Price competition also mandated high utilization of large-scale plants to achieve low production costs. Volume and market share were also key factors in keeping marketing expenses at an acceptable per-unit level.

Recent Trends in the Bottled Water Industry

As the U.S. per capita consumption of bottled water grew to nearly 20 gallons in 2001, industry analysts believed the annual growth rate of bottled water sales in the U.S. would begin to slow. There was some concern among analysts that a slowing industry growth rate might set off stronger price competition in the industry. As of mid-2002, there had been some modest declines in pricing at both the retail and wholesale levels. Some of the price decline was attributable to Coca-Cola and PepsiCo's use of multi-packs in take-home PET channels, which had slightly decreased average revenue per gallon. A July 2002 pricing survey found the average retail price of bottled water sold in supermarkets had declined by 3.4 percent since July 2001, with the price of some brands down by as much as 9 percent from the previous year.

The world's largest sellers of bottled water appeared to be positioning for industry maturity by purchasing smaller regional brands, with Groupe Danone acquiring Naya for $34 million and McKesson for $1.1 billion in 2000, Suntory acquiring Great Pines Water for $19 million in 1999, and Nestlé acquiring Aberfoyle Springs in 2000 and Black Mountain and Aqua Cool in 2001. Most of the leading sellers of bottled water were making similar acquisitions worldwide. Nestlé had acquired bottled water producers in Poland, Hungary, Russia, Greece, France, and Saudi Arabia between 2000

Exhibit 6   LEADING U.S. BOTTLED WATER PRODUCERS, 2001

Rank	Company	Wholesale Sales (in millions)	Market Share	2001 Growth
1	Nestlé Waters	$2,103.3	32.5%	23.5%
2	Groupe Danone	879.9	13.6	3.3
3	PepsiCo	645.0	10.0	44.9
4	Coca-Cola	560.0	8.6	105.1
5	Suntory Water Group	507.1	7.8	−0.8
6	Crystal Geyser	235.0	3.6	27.0
7	Culligan International	155.5	2.4	41.4
8	Vermont Pure	67.1	1.0	12.6
9	Glacier Water	60.3	0.9	2.0

Source: Beverage Marketing Corporation, as reported by *Beverage Aisle,* April 15, 2002.

Exhibit 7   TOP 10 U.S. BOTTLED WATER BRANDS, 2001

Rank	Brand	Parent Company	Wholesale Sales (in millions)	Market Share	2001 Growth
1	Aquafina	PepsiCo	$645.0	10.0%	44.9%
2	Dasani	Coca-Cola	560.0	8.6	105.1
3	Poland Springs	Nestlé Waters	542.0	8.4	20.2
4	Arrowhead	Nestlé Waters	399.6	6.2	18.3
5	Sparkletts	Groupe Danone	361.8	5.6	4.1
6	Deer Park	Nestlé Waters	247.5	3.8	18.6
7	Crystal Geyser	Crystal Geyser	235.0	3.6	27.0
8	Evian	Groupe Danone	211.2	3.3	−4.0
9	Zephyrhills	Nestlé Waters	184.0	2.8	10.8
10	Ozarka	Nestlé Waters	183.9	2.8	11.7

Source: Beverage Marketing Corporation, as reported by *Beverage Aisle,* April 15, 2002.

and 2002. Groupe Danone had made a number of acquisitions in attractive global markets and had also entered into a strategic alliances and joint ventures to increase penetration of selected emerging and developed markets.

Industry consolidation created a more globally competitive environment in which the top sellers met each other in almost all of the world's markets. Danone and Nestlé had long competed against each other in most country markets, but PepsiCo and Coca-Cola were quickly becoming global sellers as they pushed Aquafina and Dasani into new international markets. In 2001, the top five sellers of bottled water accounted for 75 percent of industry sales; some industry observers believed the industry could consolidate further to three sellers accounting for 75 percent of industry sales by 2005.

Exhibit 8   COMPARISON OF PRODUCT CHARACTERISTICS OF PROMINENT ENHANCED BOTTLED WATER BRANDS

Brand	Producer	Additives	Claims to Help . . .
Aquafina Essentials	PepsiCo	Vitamins B6, B12, pantothenic acid, niacin	An active life
Dasani NutriWater	Coca-Cola	Vitamins C, B3, B6, B12	Metabolism, fighting free radicals
Glaceau Vitamin Water	Energy Brands	Guarana, ginseng	Energy level
Propel Fitness Water	PepsiCo	Vitamins B, C, and E	Energy level, fighting free radicals
Pulse Men's Health	Baxter International	Lycophene	Prostate health
Reebok Fitness Water	Clearly Canadian	Chromium	Insulin activity, cholesterol level

Source: "Enhanced Waters Pour onto Shelves," *USA Today,* August 23, 2002, p. M1.

Exhibits 6 and 7 indicate the degree of industry consolidation in the U.S. bottled water market in 2001.

The introduction of enhanced waters was the most important product innovation since bottled water gained widespread acceptance in the United States, as most sellers in 2002 were moving quickly to introduce variations of their products that included vitamins, carbohydrates, electrolytes, and other supplements. The innovation seemed to be a hit with consumers—the market for enhanced bottled waters expanded from $20 million in 2000 to $85 million in 2001 and was expected to surpass $100 million in 2002. One of the earliest enhanced waters was Energy Brands' Glaceau Vitamin Water, which was launched in 2000. In 2002, Glaceau came in 20 flavor and supplement varieties that promised mental stimulation, physical rejuvenation, and overall improved health. Glaceau was also the best-selling brand of enhanced water in late 2002, with annual sales growth of 270 percent. Glaceau retailed for about $1.49 per bottle. Baxter International was a $4.7 billion global health care company that offered three scientifically developed and tested vitamin- and nutrient-enriched waters to promote heart health, women's health, and men's health. Brands touting health benefits with wider distribution than Baxter's Pulse or Glaceau Vitamin Water included Clearly Canadian's Reebok Fitness Water, Gatorade's Propel, and PepsiCo's Aquafina Essentials.

Bottled water producers were optimistic about the prospects of selling vitamin-enhanced waters since marketing research had shown consumers (especially female baby boomers) were interested in increasing their intake of vitamins, since enhanced waters were more easily differentiated than purified or spring water, and since enhanced waters carried retail prices as much as 40 percent higher than purified water. Enhanced waters also offered higher margins than typical bottled waters. Even though enhanced waters offered potential benefits, there were some features of enhanced waters that might cause consumers to limit their consumption of such products, including the need for sweeteners to disguise the taste of added vitamins and supplements and calorie contents that ranged from 20 calories per 16-ounce serving for Propel and Reebok to 100 calories per 16-ounce serving for Glaceau. In addition, some medical researchers had suggested that consumers would need to drink approximately 10 bottles of enhanced water each day to meet minimum dietary requirements for the vitamins promoted on the waters' labels. Exhibit 8 presents a comparison of leading enhanced bottled water brands offered in late 2002.

Profiles of the Leading Bottled Water Producers

Nestlé Waters

Nestlé was Switzerland's largest industrial company and the world's largest food company, with 2001 sales of 84.7 billion Swiss francs (approximately $59 billion). The company was broadly diversified into 19 food and beverage categories that were sold in almost every country in the world under such recognizable brand names as Nescafé, Taster's Choice, Perrier, Vittel, Carnation, PowerBar, Friskies, Alpo, Nestea, Libby's, Stouffer's, and of course Nestlé. The company produced bottled water as early as 1843, but its 1992 acquisition of Perrier created the foundation of what has made Nestlé Waters the world's largest seller of bottled water, with 72 brands in 160 countries. In 2001, Nestlé recorded bottled water sales of 7.5 billion Swiss francs (approximately $5 billion) and held a 16 percent share of the global bottled water market. Nestlé's title as global leader in the bottled water industry was a result of its number one positions in the United States, Canada, Europe, and most Latin American countries. Nestlé was also aggressive in its attempts to build market-leading positions in the Middle East, Asia, and Africa through the introduction of global Nestlé products and acquisitions of established local brands in most geographic regions of the world. Nestlé acquired 11 bottled water producers in 2001 and was expected to purchase several other brands in 2002.

The company's bottled water portfolio in 2002 included 2 global brands (Nestlé Pure Life and Nestlé Aquarel), 4 international premium brands (Perrier, Vittel, Contrex, and San Pellegrino), and 66 local brands. Nestlé Pure Life was a purified water product developed in 1998 for emerging markets and in 2002 was marketed in 12 countries in Asia, Latin America, and the Middle East where safe drinking water was a primary concern. Nestlé Aquarel was developed in 2000 for the European market and was differentiated from other spring waters by its low mineral content, which was more suitable to children's taste preferences. Nestlé's other waters marketed in Europe were either spring water with a higher mineral content or sparkling waters such as Perrier and San Pellegrino. Almost all brands marketed outside of Europe were either spring water or mineral water with no carbonation.

Its brands in the United States included Arrowhead, Ice Mountain, Calistoga, Deer Park, Great Bear, Zephyrhills, Oasis, Ozarka, Poland Springs, Black Mountain, and Aqua Cool. Nestlé Waters did not market an enhanced-water product. The following table lists the 2001 wholesale sales for Nestlé's leading U.S. brands:

NESTLÉ'S LEADING U.S. BOTTLED WATER BRANDS

Brand	2001 Wholesale Sales (in millions)
Poland Springs	$542.0
Arrowhead	399.6
Deer Park	247.5
Zephyrhills	184.0
Ozarka	183.9
Ice Mountain	106.2
Aberfoyle	102.0
Perrier	85.9

Source: Beverage Marketing Corporation, as reported by *Beverage Aisle,* April 15, 2002.

**Exhibit 9   TOP 5 BRANDS OF BOTTLED WATER, BY U.S. REGIONAL MARKET
(52 WEEKS ENDING MAY 12, 2002)**

West	South Central	Mid-South	Great Lakes
1. Arrowhead	1. Ozarka	1. Aquafina	1. Aquafina
2. Aquafina	2. Dasani	2. Dasani	2. Ice Mountain
3. Private-label brand	3. Aquafina	3. Private-label brand	3. Private-label brand
4. Dasani	4. Private-label brand	4. Deer Park	4. Dasani
5. Dannon	5. Deja Blue	5. Dannon	5. Dannon

California	Southeast	Northeast	Plains
1. Arrowhead	1. Zephyrhills	1. Poland Spring	1. Aquafina
2. Crystal Geyser	2. Private-label brand	2. Private-label brand	2. Private-label brand
3. Aquafina	3. Dasani	3. Aquafina	3. Dasani
4. Private-label brand	4. Aquafina	4. Dasani	4. Dannon
5. Sparkletts	5. Dannon	5. Dannon	5. Chippewa

Source: IRI InfoScan, as reported by *National Petroleum News*, July 2002.

Nestlé's brand portfolio in the United States reflected the regional nature of the U.S. market, with most of its brands not competing against each other in specific regional markets. Dasani, Aquafina, Evian, and Perrier were among the few national brands, since most brands began as small regional sellers. For the 52 weeks ending May 12, 2002, Nestlé led most regional markets, as is demonstrated in Exhibit 9. Nestlé's market leading positions in U.S. regional markets and its competitive capabilities developed in Europe allowed it to earn the status of low-cost leader in the United States. Exhibit 10 illustrates Nestlé Waters' cost and wholesale pricing advantages relative to Coca-Cola and PepsiCo in U.S. markets. The company's $100 million bottling plant, which was under construction in Tennessee in 2002, was expected to aid Nestlé in maintaining its low-cost leadership. Nestlé Waters' management stated in mid-2002 that it expected to double the division's revenues by 2010.

Groupe Danone

Groupe Danone was established in 1966 through the merger of two of France's leading glass makers, who foresaw the oncoming acceptability of plastic as a substitute to glass containers. The management of the newly merged company believed that rather than shift its focus to the manufacture of plastic containers, the company should focus on entering markets for products typically sold in glass containers. Groupe Danone's diversification outside of glass containers began in 1969 when the company acquired Evian—France's leading brand of bottled water. Throughout the 1970s and 1980s, Groupe Danone acquired additional food and beverage companies that produced beer, pasta, baby food, cereals, sauces, confectionery, dairy products, and baked goods. In 1997, the company slimmed its portfolio of businesses to dairy products, bottled water, and a baked goods division producing cereal, cookies, and snacks. In 2002, Groupe Danone was a leading global food company, with annual sales of 44.5 billion euros, and was the world's largest producer of dairy products; the number-two producer of cereal, cookies, and baked snacks; and the largest seller of bottled water by volume. (Nestlé was the world's largest bottled water producer based on dollar sales.)

Exhibit 10   VALUE CHAIN COMPARISON FOR THE BOTTLED WATER OPERATIONS OF NESTLÉ, PEPSICO, AND COCA-COLA

	Nestlé Waters	PepsiCo	Coca-Cola
Retailer price per case	$8.44	$8.52	$8.65
Retailer margin	35.0%	17.5%	17.6%
Wholesale price per case	$5.49	$7.03	$7.13
Wholesale sales	$5.49	$7.03	$7.13
Support revenue	0.00	0.41	0.52
Total bottler revenue	$5.49	$7.44	$7.65
Expenses			
Water	$0.01	$1.67	$1.70
PET bottles	1.03	1.16	1.16
Secondary packaging	0.61	0.68	0.68
Closures	0.21	0.23	0.23
Labor/manufacturing	0.70	0.70	0.77
Depreciation	0.07	0.08	0.08
Total cost of goods sold	2.63	4.52	4.62
Gross profit	$2.86	$2.92	$3.03
Selling, general, and administrative costs	2.29	2.25	2.53
EBITA*	$0.57	$0.67	$0.50
EBITA margin	10.4%	9.0%	6.5%

*Earnings before interest, taxes, and amortization.

Source: Goldman Sachs Global Equity Research, as reported by *Beverage World,* April 2002.

The company's Aqua, Evian, and Volvic brands were three of the world's four best-selling brands of bottled water. Danone also marketed country-specific brands such as Villa del Sur in Argentina, Wahaha in China, and Dannon in the United States. In the United States, Groupe Danone also marketed the regional brands listed in the following table:

DANONE'S LEADING U.S. BOTTLED WATER BRANDS

Brand	2001 Wholesale Sales (in millions)
Sparkletts	$361.8
Evian	211.2
Dannon	112.4
Pure American	91.5
Alhambra	87.7
Volvic	7.8

Source: Beverage Marketing Corporation, as reported by *Beverage Aisle,* April 15, 2002.

Groupe Danone's strongest brands sold in the United States during 2002 were Sparkletts, which was the fifth best-selling brand in California, and Dannon, which was the fourth best-selling brand in the Plains States and the fifth best-selling brand in the West, Southeast, Northeast, Mid-South, and Great Lakes (see Exhibit 9). Evian was Danone's second best-selling bottled water brand in the United States but was not among the top five brands in any regional market.

Danone recorded worldwide bottled water sales of 3.8 billion euros in 2001 and produced an operating profit of 321 million euros from its bottled water sales that same year. The company's bottled water sales had grown at an average rate of over 8 percent between 1997 and 2001, but had declined by 8 percent between 2000 and 2001. Danone's capital investments in its bottled water business exceeded 1.4 billion euros between 1997 and 2001, and it, like Nestlé, had made a number of acquisitions of regional bottled water producers during the late 1990s and early 2000s. During 2002, Danone acquired a controlling interest in Poland's leading brand of bottled water for an undisclosed amount and purchased Canada's Sparkling Spring brand of waters for an estimated $300–$400 million. The company also entered into a joint venture with Kirin Beverage Company to strengthen its distribution network in Japan and embarked on a partnership with the Rachid Group, an Egyptian firm, to accelerate its development of market opportunities in North Africa and the Near and Middle East. Also, in mid-2002, Danone and Nestlé were bidding against each other for control of Bisleri, India's leading brand of bottled water, with about a 50 percent share of the market.

Groupe Danone's sales and market share began to decline in the United States beginning in 2000 when Coca-Cola bottlers began distributing Dasani rather than distributing only Evian and other non-Coke brands. Prior to the introduction of Dasani, about 60 percent of Evian's U.S. distribution was handled by Coca-Cola bottlers. Groupe Danone relied on Pepsi bottlers and independent bottlers for distribution to markets not handled by Coca-Cola. With Coca-Cola bottler's attention directed toward the sale of Dasani, Evian lost shelf space in many convenience stores, supermarkets, delis, restaurants, and wholesale clubs.

Groupe Danone and Coca-Cola entered into two new strategic partnerships in mid-2002 that made Coca-Cola the exclusive distributor of Evian, Dannon, and Sparkletts in the United States and Canada. The two companies entered into a distribution agreement in April 2002 whereby Coca-Cola agreed to distribute Evian along with Dasani to convenience stores, supermarkets, and other retail locations serviced by Coca-Cola's bottling operations. The two companies also began a joint venture in June 2002 that made Coke responsible for the production, marketing, and distribution of Dannon and Sparkletts in the United States. Coca-Cola provided Danone an upfront cash payment in return for 51 percent ownership of the joint venture. Danone contributed its five plants and other bottled water assets located in the United States to the joint venture. Coca-Cola also held the license for the use of the Dannon and Sparkletts brands in the United States. Danone's less popular PET brands and its home and office delivery businesses were not included in the agreement.

The Coca-Cola Company

The Coca-Cola Company was the world's leading manufacturer, marketer, and distributor of nonalcoholic beverage concentrates, with 300 brands worldwide. The company produced soft drinks, juice and juice drinks, sports drinks, water, and coffee, but it was best known for Coca-Cola, which had been called the world's most valuable brand. In 2001, the company sold more than 17.8 billion cases of beverages worldwide to record revenues of approximately $20 billion. Coca-Cola's net income for 2001 was nearly $4 billion. Sixty-two percent of Coke's revenues were generated outside of North America, with six international markets (Germany, Brazil, United Kingdom, Japan, and Mexico) each contributing more than $1 billion per year to Coca-Cola's consolidated revenues. The company also sold more than $1 billion worth of beverages in the United States each year.

Along with the universal appeal of the Coca-Cola brand, Coca-Cola's vast global distribution system that included independent bottlers, bottlers partially owned by Coca-Cola, and company-owned bottlers made Coke an almost unstoppable international powerhouse. Coca-Cola held market-leading positions in most countries in the cola segment of the soft-drink industry, and the strength of the Coca-Cola brand aided the company in gaining market share in most other soft-drink segments such as the lemon-lime and diet segments. The company had also been able to leverage Coke's appeal with consumers to gain access to retail distribution channels for new beverages included in its portfolio such as Minute Maid orange juice products, Powerade isotonic beverages, and Dasani purified water.

The Coca-Cola Company did not market and distribute its own brand of bottled water until mid-1999, when it introduced Dasani. The company created a purified water that included a combination of magnesium sulfate, potassium chloride, and salt to re-create what Coke researchers believed were the best attributes of leading spring waters from around the world. The Dasani formula was a closely guarded secret and was sold to bottlers, just as the company sold its Coke concentrate to bottlers. The Dasani name was developed by linguists who suggested the dual *a*'s gave a soothing sound to the name, the *s* conveyed crispness and freshness, and the *i* ending gave a foreign ring to the name. Dasani was supported with an estimated $15 million advertising budget during its first year on the market and was distributed through all retail channels where Coke was available. Coca-Cola's marketing expertise and vast U.S. distribution system allowed Dasani to become the second largest and fastest-growing brand of water sold in the United States by 2001. Dasani did not have significant sales outside the United States, but Coca-Cola did produce and market bottled water in foreign countries under local brand names, such as its Bonaqua brand in the Iberian market.

In late 2002, Coca-Cola was testing four varieties of enhanced bottled waters in New York, Cincinnati, and Charleston. The Dasani Nutriwater line included a lemon-tangerine flavor that promoted "bone strength" with added calcium, magnesium, and B vitamins; pear-cucumber for "balancing" that included B and C vitamins; mandarin-orange for "immunity" with vitamin C and zinc; and a multivitamin wild berry variety that included B, C, and E vitamins. Each of the varieties of Nutriwater had about 20 calories per 16-ounce serving. Coke's new product retailed for $1.19–$1.39 per 16-ounce container in test markets. Nutriwater's national rollout was expected for early 2003.

Coca-Cola's 2002 joint venture with Groupe Danone allowed Coca-Cola to jump to the rank of second largest bottled water producer in the United States. The joint venture and Evian distribution agreement provided Coke with bottled water products at all price points with Dasani positioned as an upper-mid-priced product, Evian as a premium-priced bottled water, and Sparkletts and Dannon as value-priced waters. Coke management believed the addition of Sparkletts and Dannon would allow the company to protect Dasani's near-premium pricing while gaining spring water brands that could be marketed nationally to challenge Nestlé's regional brands in the spring water segment. The editor of *Beverage Digest* noted the Coca-Cola–Groupe Danone joint venture would take Coke into several new bottled water markets, including private-label and spring water, and said the deal "has the potential of significantly altering the landscape of the bottled water business in the U.S."[2]

PepsiCo, Inc.

In 2002, PepsiCo was the world's fifth largest food and beverage company, with sales of about $27 billion. The company's brands were sold in more than 200 countries and included such well-known names as Lay's, Tostitos, Mountain Dew, Pepsi, Doritos, Lipton iced tea, Gatorade, Quaker, and Cracker Jack. PepsiCo also produced and marketed Aquafina, which in 2002 was the best-selling brand of bottled water in the United States.

PepsiCo had made attempts to enter the bottled water market in as early as 1987 when it purchased a spring water company, but its attempts were unsuccessful until its 1997 introduction of Aquafina. After experimenting with spring water and sparkling water for several years, Pepsi management believed it would be easier to produce a national brand of bottled water that could utilize its water purification facilities used in its soft-drink bottling plants. Pepsi management also believed the company could distinguish its brand of purified bottled water from competing brands by stripping all chlorine and other particles out of tap water that might impart an unpleasant taste or smell. PepsiCo began testing a filtration process for Aquafina in 1994 when it installed $3 million worth of reverse osmosis filtration equipment in its Wichita, Kansas, bottling plant to further purify municipal water used to make soft drinks. The system pushed water through a fiberglass membrane at very high pressure to remove chemicals and minerals before further purifying the water using carbon filters. The water produced by Pepsi's process was so free of chemicals that the company was required to add ozone gas to the water to prevent bacteria growth.

Pepsi sold the purification process to its bottlers who were responsible for the production and distribution of Aquafina. PepsiCo marketed the product nationally, spending about $15 million in 2000, $20 million in 2001, and $40 million in 2002 on advertising alone. PepsiCo also developed innovative supermarket displays for Aquafina, employed celebrities to endorse the product, and negotiated contracts to make Aquafina the official beverage of sports organizations such as the Professional Golfers Association of America and major league soccer.

PepsiCo was also moving into international bottled water markets, including Spain and Mexico. In late 2002, PepsiCo's bottling operations acquired Mexico's largest Pepsi bottler, Pepsi-Gemex SA de CV, for $1.26 billion. Gemex not only bottled and distributed Pepsi soft drinks in Mexico but was also Mexico's number one producer of purified water. The company's Electropura was sold only in one-gallon and larger HDPE containers, but it was expected that Pepsi management would introduce bottled water in small PET containers after it took over Gemex operations. PepsiCo also entered the bottled water market in Spain during 2002. Pepsi management supported its Spanish Aquafina launch with a $10 million advertising budget.

PepsiCo launched its Aquafina Essentials enhanced-water line in the United States during the summer of 2002. The line retailed for a suggested price of $1.49 per 20-ounce bottle and included four varieties. Multi-V was a watermelon-flavored beverage containing 25 percent of the daily requirement for vitamins B6, B12, C, E, pantothenic acid, and niacin. Daily-C was a citrus blend fortified with 100 percent of the daily requirement for Vitamin C. B-Power had a wild berry flavoring and provided 25 percent of the daily requirement of vitamins B6, B12, pantothenic acid, and niacin. Aquafina Essentials Calcium+ filled out the line and had a tangy tangerine-pineapple flavoring and provided 25 percent of the daily requirement for calcium and folic acid. The Essentials line was PepsiCo's second attempt at fortified waters. It had attempted to add calcium to Aquafina without any flavoring in 2000, but the company's director of beverage research and development said the beverage's taste was like "chewing on chalk."[3]

Suntory Water Group

Suntory Limited was a diversified Japanese consumer products company with 2001 sales of 833 billion yen (approximately $7.2 billion). The company was Japan's largest producer and distributor of alcoholic and nonalcoholic beverages and was among Japan's largest food distributors. The company also competed in the pharmaceutical and publishing industries, and operated restaurants, bars, and sports clubs in Japan. The company's businesses in the United States included independent Pepsi-Cola bottling operations, a resort management group, Suntory Pharmaceuticals, and Suntory Water Group. Suntory Water Group was the fifth largest producer and distributor of bottled water in the United States, with annual sales of $507 million in 2001. Suntory Water Group's bottled spring water was available nationwide under such regional brands as Crystal Springs, Sierra Springs, Hinckley Springs, Kentwood Springs, Belmont Springs, and Georgia Mountain. The annual sales of its best-selling brands at year-end 2001 are presented in the following table:

SUNTORY'S LEADING U.S. BRANDS

Brand	2001 Wholesale Sales (in millions)
Crystal Springs	$175.4
Sierra Springs	128.7
Hinckley Springs	95.8
Kentwood Springs	63.9

Source: Beverage Marketing Corporation, as reported by Beverage Aisle, April 15, 2002.

Suntory had made 30 acquisitions between 1999 and 2001 to increase its overall market share in the United States and to expand its home and office delivery business. In 2002, Suntory Water Group led the direct delivery bulk water segment of the U.S. bottled water industry. The company's home and office delivery business maintained delivery fleets in most parts of the United States and was supported by the company's water.com website, which allowed consumers to purchase bulk water and water bottled in PET containers for direct delivery. During 2002, Suntory introduced a calcium-enhanced bottled water and developed the first PET water package capable of being dispensed through 12-ounce can vending machines. The 11.5-ounce PET container won the Institute of Packaging Professionals' 2002 Innovation Award and would be used by all of its regional brands by early 2003.

Other Sellers

In addition to the industry's leading sellers of bottled water, there were hundreds of regional and specialty brands of bottled water in the United States. Most of these companies were privately held bottlers with distribution limited to small geographic regions that competed aggressively on price to make it onto convenience-store and supermarket shelves as third-tier brands. Many of these bottlers also sought out private-label contracts with discounters and large supermarket chains to better ensure full capacity utilization and to achieve sufficient volume to purchase bottles and other packaging at lower prices.

Another group of small bottlers, such as Penta and Trinity, used differentiating features to avoid the fierce price competition at the low end of the market and sold in the superpremium segment, where bottled water retailed from $1.50 to $2.25 per 16-ounce PET container. Penta was among the most successful superpremium brands and had differentiated itself from other brands by using a proprietary purification system that it claimed removed 100 percent of impurities from tap water. In late 2002, Penta was distributed in more than 2,700 health food stores in 48 U.S. states. The product was also available in England and Australia. The company had built brand recognition through product placements in more than 25 television series, including widely watched programs like *Friends, Scrubs,* and *The Practice.* Penta had also entered into agreements during 2002 that would place its product in four upcoming feature films. Trinity's differentiation was based on its water source, which was a 2.2-mile-deep artesian well located in the mountains of Idaho. Trinity claimed its water was incomparable in natural purity since the depth of the natural well maintained water at 138° Fahrenheit and since the water rose to the surface through crystal-lined granite faults in the mountain. Trinity was the best-selling bottled water in U.S. natural foods stores in late 2002.

Endnotes

[1] As quoted in "The Taste of Water," Bottled Water Web (www.bottledwaterweb.com/watertaste.htm).

[2] "Coca-Cola Water Deal Creates a Stir," *Atlanta Journal-Constitution,* June 18, 2002, p. 1D.

[3] "Pepsi, Coke Take Opposite Tacks in Bottled Water Marketing Battle," *The Wall Street Journal,* April 18, 2002, p. A1.

CASE 6

Dell Computer in 2003
Driving for Industry Leadership

Arthur A. Thompson
The University of Alabama

John E. Gamble
University of South Alabama

In 1984, at the age of 19, Michael Dell founded Dell Computer with a simple vision and business concept—that personal computers (PCs) could be built to order and sold directly to customers. Michael Dell believed his approach to the PC business had two advantages: (1) Bypassing distributors and retail dealers eliminated the markups of resellers, and (2) building to order greatly reduced the costs and risks associated with carrying large stocks of parts, components, and finished goods. While at times between 1986 and 1993 the company struggled to refine its strategy, build an adequate infrastructure, and establish market credibility against better-known rivals, Dell Computer's strategy started to click into full gear in the late 1990s. Going into 2003, Dell's sell-direct and build-to-order business model and strategy had provided the company with the most efficient procurement, manufacturing, and distribution capabilities in the global PC industry and given Dell a substantial cost and profit margin advantage over rival PC vendors. Dell's operating costs ran about 10 percent of revenues in 2002, compared to 21 percent of revenues at Hewlett-Packard (HP), 25 percent at Gateway, and 46 percent at Cisco Systems (considered the world's most efficient producer of networking equipment). Dell's low-cost provider status was powering its drive for market leadership in a growing number of product categories.

Dell Computer was solidly entrenched as the market leader in PC sales in the United States, with nearly a 28 percent market share in 2002, comfortably ahead of Hewlett-Packard (16.8 percent) and Gateway (5.7 percent). Dell had moved ahead of IBM into second place during 1998 and then overtaken Compaq Computer as the U.S. sales leader in the third quarter of 1999. Its market share leadership in the United States had widened every year since 2000. Worldwide, Dell Computer was in a neck-and-neck race for global market leadership with HP, which acquired Compaq Computer in May 2002. Dell was the world leader in unit sales in the first and third quarters of 2002, and HP was the sales leader in the second and fourth quarters. Dell had overtaken Compaq as the global market leader in 2001. But when HP, the third-ranking PC seller in the world, acquired Compaq, the second-ranking PC vendor, Dell found itself in a tight battle with HP for the top spot globally. Exhibit 1 shows the shifting domestic and global sales and market share rankings in PCs during the 1996–2002 period.

Since the late 1990s, Dell had also been driving for industry leadership in servers. In 2002 Dell was the number one domestic seller of entry-level servers and high-performance workstations (used for applications with demanding graphics). It was number two in the world in server shipments and within striking distance of global market leadership. In the mid-to-late 1990s, a big fraction of the servers sold were proprietary machines running on customized Unix operating systems and carrying price tags ranging from $30,000 to $1 million or more. But a seismic shift in server technology, coupled with growing cost-consciousness on the part of server users, produced a radically new server market during 1999–2002. In 2003 about 8 out of 10 servers sold were expected to carry price tags below $10,000 and to run on either Windows or the free Linux operating system rather than more costly Unix systems. The overall share of Unix-based servers shipped in 2003 was expected to be about 10 percent, down from about 18 percent in 1997. Dell's domestic and global market share in low-priced and midrange servers was climbing rapidly. Dell had over a 30 percent share of the 2002 world market for servers, up from 2 percent in 1995.

In addition, Dell was making market inroads in other product categories. Its sales of data storage devices were growing rapidly, aided by a strategic alliance with EMC, a leader in the data storage. In 2001–2002, Dell began selling low-cost, data-routing switches—a product category where Cisco Systems was the dominant global leader. In late 2002 Dell introduced a new line of handheld PCs—the Axim X5—to compete against the higher-priced products of Palm, HP, and others; the Axim offered a solid but not trendsetting design, was packed with features, and was priced roughly 50 percent below the best-selling models of rivals. Starting in 2003, Dell planned to begin marketing Dell-branded printers and printer cartridges, product categories that provided global leader HP with the lion's share of its profits. In January 2003, Dell announced that it would begin selling retail-store systems, including electronic cash registers, specialized software, services, and peripherals required to link retail-store checkout lanes to corporate information systems. Since the late 1990s, Dell had been marketing CD and DVD drives, printers, scanners, modems, monitors, digital cameras, memory cards, Zip drives, and speakers made by a variety of manufacturers.

So far, Dell's foray into new products had proved to be profitable; according to Michael Dell, "We believe that all our businesses should make money. If a business doesn't make money, if you can't figure out how to make money in that business, you shouldn't be in that business."[1] In 2002, more than half of Dell's profits came from products other than desktop computers, and the percentage from nondesktop computing was growing.

Moreover, Dell was the world's leading Internet retailer. Dell began Internet sales at its website (www.dell.com) in 1995, almost overnight achieving sales of $1 million a day. By early 2003, over 50 percent of Dell's sales were Web-enabled—and the percentage was increasing. Dell's website sales exceeded $50 million a day in 2002, up from $35 million daily in early 2000 and $5 million daily in early 1998. The company averaged over 3 million visits weekly at its 80 country-specific sites in 2002. Dell products were sold in more than 170 countries, but sales in 60 countries accounted for 97 percent of total revenues.

In its fiscal year ending January 31, 2003, Dell Computer posted revenues of $35.4 billion, up from $3.4 billion in the year ending January 29, 1995—an eight-year compound average growth rate of 34.0 percent. Over the same time period, profits were up from $140 million to $2.1 billion—a 40.5 percent compound average growth rate. A $100 investment in Dell's stock at its initial public offering in June 1988 would have been worth about $28,500 in February 2003. Dell Computer was one of the top 10 best-performing stocks on the New York Stock Exchange and the Nasdaq during the 1990s. Based on 2001 data, Dell ranked number 53 on the Fortune 500, number 131 on the Fortune Global 500, and number 23 on the Fortune Global "most admired" list.

Exhibit 1   **LEADING PC VENDORS WORLDWIDE AND IN THE UNITED STATES, BASED ON FACTORY SHIPMENTS, 1996–2002**

A. U.S. Market Shares of the Leading PC Vendors, 1998–2002

2002 Rank	Vendor	2002		2001		2000	
		Shipments (in 000s)	Market Share	Shipments (in 000s)	Market Share	Shipments (in 000s)	Market Share
1	Dell	13,324	27.9%	10,817	23.5%	9,645	19.7%
	Compaq*	—	—	5,341	11.6	7,761	15.9
2	Hewlett-Packard*	8,052	16.8	4,374	9.5	5,630	11.5
3	Gateway	2,725	5.7	3,219	7.0	4,237	8.7
4	IBM	2,531	5.3	2,461	5.3	2,668	5.5
5	Apple	1,693	3.5	1,665	3.6	n.a	n.a.
	Others	19,514	40.8	23,509	51.0	18,959	38.8
	All vendors	47,839	100.0%	46,051	100.0%	48,900	100.0%

B. Worldwide Market Shares of the Leading PC Vendors, 1996–2002[†]

2002 Rank	Vendor	2002		2001		2000	
		Shipments (in 000s)	Market Share	Shipments (in 000s)	Market Share	Shipments (in 000s)	Market Share
1	Dell	20,672	15.2%	17,231	12.9%	14,801	10.6%
	Compaq*	—	—	14,673	11.0	17,399	12.5
2	Hewlett-Packard*	18,432	13.6	9,309	7.0	10,327	7.4
3	IBM	7,996	5.9	8,292	6.2	9,308	6.7
4	Fujitsu Siemens	5,822	4.3	6,022	4.5	6,582	4.7
5	NEC	4,533	3.3	4,702	3.5	n.a.	n.a
	Others	78,567	57.8	73,237	54.9	80,640	58.0
	All vendors	136,022	100.0%	133,466	100.0%	139,057	100.0%

*Compaq was acquired by Hewlett-Packard in May 2002. The 2002 data for Hewlett-Packard include both Compaq-branded and Hewlett-Packard-branded PCs for the last three quarters of 2002, plus only Hewlett-Packard-branded PCs for Q1 2002. Compaq's worldwide PC shipments during Q1 2002 were 3,367,000; its U.S. PC shipments during Q1 2002 were 1,280,000 units.

[†]Includes branded shipments only and excludes original equipment manufacturer (OEM) sales for all manufacturers; shipments of Compaq PCs for last three quarters of 2002 are included in 2002 figures for Hewlett-Packard.

Source: International Data Corporation.

Company Background

At age 12, Michael Dell was running a mail-order stamp-trading business, complete with a national catalog, and grossing $2,000 a month. At 16 he was selling subscriptions to the *Houston Post,* and at 17 he bought his first BMW with money he had earned. He enrolled at the University of Texas in 1983 as a premed student (his parents wanted him to become a doctor), but he soon became immersed in computers and started selling PC components out of his college dormitory room. He bought random-access memory (RAM) chips and disk drives for IBM PCs at cost from IBM dealers, who at the time often had excess supplies on hand because they were required to order large monthly quotas from IBM. Dell resold the components through newspaper ads

1999		1998	
Shipments (in 000s)	Market Share	Shipments (in 000s)	Market Share
7,492	16.6%	4,799	13.2%
7,222	16.0	6,052	16.7
3,955	8.8	2,832	7.8
4,001	8.9	3,039	8.4
3,274	7.2	2,983	8.2
n.a	n.a.	n.a.	n.a.
19,248	42.6	16,549	45.6
45,192	100.0%	36,254	100.0%

1999		1998		1997		1996	
Shipments (in 000s)	Market Share	Shipments (in 000s)	Market Share	Shipments (in 000s)	Market Share	Shipments (in 000s)	Market Share
11,883	10.5%	7,770	8.5%	4,684	5.8%	2,996	4.3%
15,732	14.0	13,266	14.5	10,064	12.6	7,211	10.4
7,577	6.7	5,743	6.3	4,468	5.6	2,984	4.3
9,287	8.2	7,946	8.7	7,239	9.1	6,176	8.9
n.a	n.a.	n.a.	n.a.	n.a.	n.a.	n.a.	n.a.
5,989	5.3	5,976	6.5	4,150	5.2	4,230	6.1
62,258	55.2	50,741	55.5	49,333	61.7	45,727	66.0
112,726	100.0%	91,442	100.0%	79,938	100.0%	69,324	100.0%

(and later through ads in national computer magazines) at 10–15 percent below the regular retail price.

By April 1984 sales were running about $80,000 per month. Michael decided to drop out of college and form a company, PCs Ltd., to sell both PC components and PCs under the brand name PCs Limited. He obtained his PCs by buying retailers' surplus stocks at cost, then powering them up with graphics cards, hard disks, and memory before reselling them. His strategy was to sell directly to end users; by eliminating the retail markup, Dell's new company was able to sell IBM clones (machines that copied the functioning of IBM PCs using the same or similar components) about 40 percent below the price of IBM's best-selling PCs. The discounting strategy was successful, attracting price-conscious buyers and generating rapid revenue growth. By 1985, the company was assembling its own PC designs with a few people working on six-foot tables. The company had 40 employees, and Michael Dell worked 18-hour days, often sleeping on a cot in his office. By the end of fiscal 1986, sales had reached $33 million.

During the next several years, however, PCs Limited was hampered by growing pains—specifically, a lack of money, people, and resources. Michael Dell sought to refine the company's business model; add needed production capacity; and build a bigger, deeper management staff and corporate infrastructure while at the same time keeping costs low. The company was renamed Dell Computer in 1987, and the first international offices were opened that same year. In 1988 Dell added a sales force to serve large customers, began selling to government agencies, and became a public company—raising $34.2 million in its first offering of common stock. Sales to large customers quickly became the dominant part of Dell's business. By 1990 Dell Computer had sales of $388 million, a market share of 2–3 percent, and an R&D staff of over 150 people. Michael Dell's vision was for Dell Computer to become one of the top three PC companies.

Thinking its direct sales business would not grow fast enough, in 1990–93, the company began distributing its computer products through Soft Warehouse Superstores (now CompUSA), Staples (a leading office products chain), Wal-Mart, Sam's Club, and Price Club (now Price/Costco). Dell also sold PCs through Best Buy stores in 16 states and through Xerox in 19 Latin American countries. But when the company learned how thin its margins were in selling through such distribution channels, it realized it had made a mistake and withdrew from selling to retailers and other intermediaries in 1994 to refocus on direct sales. At the time, sales through retailers accounted for only about 2 percent of Dell's revenues.

Further problems emerged in 1993. In that year Dell reportedly had $38 million in second-quarter losses from engaging in a risky foreign-currency hedging strategy, quality difficulties arose with certain PC lines made by the company's contract manufacturers, profit margins declined, and buyers were turned off by the company's laptop PC models. To get laptop sales back on track, the company took a charge of $40 million to write off its laptop line and suspended sales of laptops until it could get redesigned models into the marketplace. The problems resulted in losses of $36 million for the company's fiscal year ending January 30, 1994.

Because of higher costs and unacceptably low profit margins in selling to individuals and households, Dell Computer did not pursue the consumer market aggressively until sales to individuals at the company's Internet site took off in 1996 and 1997. It became clear that PC-savvy individuals, who were buying their second and third computers, wanted powerful computers with multiple features; did not need much technical support; and liked the convenience of buying direct from Dell, ordering exactly what they wanted, and having it delivered to their door within a matter of days. In early 1997, Dell created an internal sales and marketing group dedicated to serving the individual consumer segment and introduced a product line designed especially for individual users.

By late 1997, Dell had become a low-cost leader among PC vendors by wringing greater and greater efficiency out of its direct sales and build-to-order business model. The company was a pioneer and an acknowledged world leader in incorporating e-commerce technology and use of the Internet into its everyday business practices. The goal was to achieve what Michael Dell called "virtual integration"—a stitching together of Dell's business with its supply partners and customers in real time such that all three appeared to be part of the same organizational team.[2] The company's mission was "to be the most successful computer company in the world at delivering the best customer experience in the markets we serve."[3]

In early 2002, Dell Computer had 34,600 employees in 34 countries, up from 16,000 at year-end 1997; approximately 42 percent of Dell's employees were located in countries outside the United States, and this percentage was growing. During fiscal years 2001 and 2002, Dell had eliminated some 5,700 employee positions worldwide to better align its cost structure with slowdowns in industrywide PC sales, business cutbacks on information technology (IT) expenditures, and stiffer competitive pressures. The company's headquarters and main office complex was in Round Rock, Texas (an Austin suburb).

Exhibits 2 through 4 provide Dell Computer's recent financial statements and geographic operating performance.

Michael Dell

Michael Dell was widely considered one of the mythic heroes within the PC industry, having been labeled "the quintessential American entrepreneur" and "the most innovative guy for marketing computers in this decade." In 1992, at the age of 27, Michael Dell became the youngest CEO ever to head a Fortune 500 company; he was a billionaire at the age of 31. Once pudgy and bespectacled, in 2003, 38-year-old Michael Dell was physically fit, considered good-looking, wore contact lenses, ate only health foods, and lived in a three-story 33,000-square-foot home on a 60-acre estate in Austin, Texas, with his wife and four children. In early 2003 Michael Dell owned about 11.8 percent of Dell Computer's common stock, worth about $8.5 billion.

In the company's early days Michael Dell hung around mostly with the company's engineers. He was so shy that some employees thought he was stuck up because he never talked to them. But people who worked with him closely described him as a likable young man who was slow to warm up to strangers.[4] He was a terrible public speaker and wasn't good at running meetings. But Lee Walker, a 51-year-old venture capitalist brought in by Michael Dell to provide much-needed managerial and financial experience during the company's organization-building years, became Michael Dell's mentor, built up his confidence, and was instrumental in turning him into a polished executive.[5] Walker served as the company's president and chief operating officer during the 1986–1990 period; he had a fatherly image, knew everyone by name, and played a key role in implementing Michael Dell's marketing ideas. Under Walker's tutelage, Michael Dell became intimately familiar with all parts of the business, overcame his shyness, learned to control his ego, and turned into a charismatic leader with an instinct for motivating people and winning their loyalty and respect. When Walker had to leave the company in 1990 because of health reasons, Dell turned to Morton Meyerson, former CEO and president of Electronic Data Systems, for advice and guidance on how to transform Dell Computer from a fast-growing medium-sized company into a billion-dollar enterprise.

Though sometimes given to displays of impatience, Michael Dell usually spoke in a quiet, reflective manner and came across as a person with maturity and seasoned judgment far beyond his age. His prowess was based more on an astute combination of technical knowledge and marketing know-how than on being a technological wizard. By the late 1990s, he was a much-sought-after speaker at industry and company conferences—he received 100 requests to speak in 1997; 800 in 1998; and over 1,200 in 1999. His views and opinions about the future of PCs, the Internet, and e-commerce practices carried considerable weight both in the PC industry and among executives

Exhibit 2   DELL COMPUTER'S CONSOLIDATED STATEMENTS OF INCOME, FISCAL YEARS 1997–2003 (IN MILLIONS, EXCEPT PER SHARE DATA)

	Fiscal Year Ended	
	January 31, 2003	February 1, 2002
Net revenue	$35,404	$31,168
Cost of revenue	29,055	25,661
Gross margin	6,349	5,507
Operating expenses:		
Selling, general and administrative	3,050	2,784
Research, development and engineering	455	452
Special charges	—	482
Total operating expenses	3,505	3,718
Operating income	2,844	1,789
Investment and other income (loss), net	183	(58)
Income before income taxes, extraordinary loss, and cumulative effect of change in accounting principle	3,027	1,731
Provision for income taxes	905	485
Income before extraordinary loss and cumulative effect of change in accounting principle	2,122	1,246
Extraordinary loss, net of taxes	—	—
Income before cumulative effect of change in accounting principle	2,122	1,246
Cumulative effect of change in accounting principle, net	—	—
Net income	$ 2,122	$ 1,246
Basic earnings per common share (in whole dollars):		
Income before extraordinary loss and cumulative effect of change in accounting principle	$0.82	$0.48
Extraordinary loss, net of taxes		—
Income before cumulative effect of change in accounting principle	$0.82	$0.48
Cumulative effect of change in accounting principle, net	—	—
Earnings per common share	$0.82	$0.48
Diluted earnings per common share (in whole dollars)	$0.80	$0.46
Weighted average shares outstanding:		
Basic	2,584	2,602
Diluted	2,644	2,726

Source: Dell Computer Corporation annual reports and press release on February 13, 2003.

worldwide. His speeches were usually full of usable information about the nuts and bolts of the Dell Computer's business model, the compelling advantages of incorporating e-commerce technology and practices into a company's operations, and developments in the IT industry.

Michael Dell was considered a very accessible CEO and a role model for young executives because he had done what many of them were trying to do. He delegated

	Fiscal Year Ended			
February 2, 2001	January 28, 2000	January 29, 1999	February 1, 1998	February 2, 1997
$31,888	$25,265	$18,243	$12,327	$7,759
25,455	20,047	14,137	9,605	6,093
6,443	5,218	4,106	2,722	1,666
3,193	2,387	1,788	1,202	826
482	374	272	204	126
105	194	—	—	—
3,780	2,955	2,060	1,406	952
2,663	2,263	2,046	1,316	714
531	188	38	52	33
3,194	2,451	2,084	1,368	747
958	785	624	424	216
2,236	1,666	1,460	944	531
—	—	—	—	(13)
2,236	1666	1,460	944	518
(59)	—	—	—	—
$ 2,177	$ 1,666	$ 1,460	$ 944	$ 518
$0.87	$0.66	$0.58	$0.36	$0.19
—	—	—	—	(0.01)
$0.87	$0.66	$0.58	$0.36	$0.18
(0.03)	—	—	—	—
$0.84	$0.66	$0.58	$0.36	$0.18
$0.79	$0.61	$0.53	$0.32	$0.17
2,582	2,536	2,531	2,631	2,838
2,746	2,728	2,772	2,952	3,126

authority to subordinates, believing that the best results came from turning "loose talented people who can be relied upon to do what they're supposed to do." Business associates viewed Michael Dell as an aggressive personality, an extremely competitive risk taker who had always played close to the edge. He spent about 30 percent of his time traveling to company operations and meeting with customers. In a typical year, he would make two or three trips to Europe and two trips to Asia.

Exhibit 3   DELL COMPUTER'S CONSOLIDATED STATEMENTS OF FINANCIAL POSITION, FISCAL YEARS 1999–2003 (IN MILLIONS OF DOLLARS)

	February 1, 2003	February 1, 2002	February 2, 2001	January 28, 2000	January 29, 1999
Assets					
Current assets:					
Cash and cash equivalents	$ 4,232	$ 3,641	$ 4,910	$ 3,809	$ 1,726
Short term investments	406	273	525	323	923
Accounts receivable, net	2,586	2,269	2,424	2,608	2,094
Inventories	306	278	400	391	273
Other	1,394	1,416	1,467	550	791
Total current assets	8,924	7,877	9,726	7,681	5,807
Property, plant and equipment, net	913	826	996	765	523
Other investments and non-current assets	5,633	4,832	2,948	3,025	547
Total assets	$15,470	$13,535	$13,670	$11,471	$ 6,877
Liabilities and Stockholders' Equity					
Current liabilities:					
Accounts payable	$ 5,989	$ 5,075	$ 4,286	$ 3,538	$ 2,397
Accrued and other	2,944	2,444	2,492	1,654	1,298
Total current liabilities	8,933	7,519	6,778	5,192	3,695
Long-term debt	506	520	509	508	512
Other	1,158	802	761	463	349
Total liabilities	10,597	8,841	8,048	6,163	4,556
Stockholders' equity:					
Preferred stock and capital in excess of $.01 par value; shares issued and outstanding: none	—	—	—	—	—
Common stock and capital in excess of $.01 par value: shares authorized: 7,000; shares issued and outstanding: 2,654, 2,601, 2,543 and 2,575, respectively	6,018	5,605	4,795	3,583	1,781
Treasury stock, at cost, 52 shares and no shares, respectively	(4,539)	(2,249)	—	—	—
Retained earnings	3,486	1,364	839	1,260	606
Other	(92)	(26)	(12)	465	(66)
Total stockholders' equity	4,873	4,694	5,622	5,308	2,321
Total liabilities and stockholders' equity	$15,470	$13,535	$13,670	$11,471	$ 6,877

Source: Dell Computer Corporation annual reports and press release, February 13, 2003.

Exhibit 4 GEOGRAPHIC AREA INFORMATION, DELL COMPUTER, FISCAL 2000–2003 (IN MILLIONS OF DOLLARS)

	Fiscal Year Ended			
	January 31, 2003	February 1, 2002	February 2, 2001	January 28, 2000
Net revenues				
Americas				
Business	$19,394	$17,275	$18,969	$15,160
U.S. Consumer	5,653	4,485	3,902	2,719
Total Americas	25,047	21,760	22,871	17,879
Europe	6,912	6,429	6,399	5,590
Asia-Pacific-Japan	3,445	2,979	2,618	1,796
Total net revenues	$35,404	$31,168	$31,888	$25,265
Operating income				
Americas				
Business	$ 1,945	$ 1,482	$ 1,999	$ 1,800
U.S. Consumer	308	260	253	204
Total Americas	2,253	1,742	2,252	2,004
Europe	388	377	347	359
Asia-Pacific-Japan	203	152	169	94
Special charges	—	(482)	(105)	(194)
Total operating income	$ 2,844	$ 1,789	$ 2,663	$ 2,263

Source: Dell Computer Corporation annual reports.

Dell Computer's Strategy

The core of Dell Computer's strategy in 2002–2003 was to use its strong capabilities in supply chain management, low-cost manufacturing, and direct sales capabilities to expand into product categories where it could provide added value to its customers in the form of lower prices. Its standard pattern of attack was to identify an IT product with good margins; figure out how to build it (or else have it built by others) cheaply enough to be able to significantly under price-competitive products; market the new product to Dell's steadily growing customer base; and then watch the market share points, incremental revenues, and incremental profits pile up.

Dell management believed it had the industry's most efficient business model. The company's strategy was built around a number of core elements: a cost-efficient approach to build-to-order manufacturing, partnerships with suppliers aimed at squeezing cost savings out of the supply chain, direct sales to customers, award-winning customer service and technical support, pioneering use of the Internet and e-commerce technology, and product-line expansion aimed at capturing a bigger share of the dollars its customers spent for IT products and services.

Cost-Efficient Build-to-Order Manufacturing

Dell built its computers, workstations, and servers to order; none were produced for inventory. Dell customers could order custom-equipped servers and workstations based on the needs of their applications. Desktop and laptop customers ordered whatever configuration of microprocessor speed, random-access memory, hard disk capacity, CD or DVD drives, fax/modem/wireless capabilities, graphics cards, monitor size, speakers, and other accessories they preferred. The orders were directed to the nearest factory. In 2003 Dell had assembly plants in Austin, Texas; Nashville, Tennessee; Limerick, Ireland; Xiamen, China; Penang, Malaysia; and El Dorado do Sul, Brazil. At all locations, the company had the capability to assemble PCs, workstations, and servers; Dell assembled its data storage products at its Austin, Limerick, and Penang plants. In 2002, typical orders were built and delivered in three to five days.

Until 1997, Dell operated its assembly lines in traditional fashion with workers performing a single operation. An order form accompanied each metal chassis across the production floor; drives, chips, and ancillary items were installed to match customer specifications. As a partly assembled PC arrived at a new workstation, the operator, standing beside a tall steel rack with drawers full of components, was instructed what to do by little red and green lights flashing beside the drawers. When the operator was finished, the drawers containing the used components were automatically replenished from the other side, and the PC chassis glided down the line to the next workstation. However, Dell had reorganized its plants in 1997, shifting to "cell manufacturing" techniques whereby a team of workers operating at a group workstation (or cell) assembled an entire PC according to customer specifications. The shift to cell manufacturing reduced Dell's assembly times by 75 percent and doubled productivity per square foot of assembly space. Assembled computers were first tested and then loaded with the desired software, shipped, and typically delivered five to six business days after the order was placed.

At Dell's newest plant in Austin, the cell manufacturing approach had been abandoned in favor of an even more efficient assembly-line approach. Workers at the new plant in 2002 could turn out about 700 desktop PCs per hour on three assembly lines than took half the floor space of the now-closed cell manufacturing plant in Austin, where production had run about 120 units per hour. Although the new Austin plant was designed for production of 400 units per hour, management believed that it would be able to improve operations enough to boost hourly production from the current 700 units to 1,000 units per hour. The gains in productivity had been achieved partly by redesigning the PCs to permit easier and faster assembly and partly by innovations in the assembly process, and partly by reducing the number of times a computer was touched by workers during assembly and shipping by 50 percent. At both Dell's Austin plant and its plant in Ireland, workers could assemble a PC in two to three minutes. Moreover, just-in-time inventory practices that left pallets of parts sitting around everywhere had been tweaked to just-in-the-nick-of-time delivery by suppliers of the exact parts needed every couple of hours; double-decker conveyor belts moved parts and components to designated assembly points. Newly assembled PCs were routed on conveyors to shipping, where they were boxed and shipped to customers the same day.

Dell was regarded as a world-class manufacturing innovator and a pioneer in how to mass-produce a customized product—its methods were routinely studied in business schools worldwide. Most of Dell's PC rivals—notably, IBM and HP/Compaq—had given up on trying to produce their own PCs as cheaply as Dell and shifted to outsourcing their PCs from contract manufacturers. Dell management believed that its in-house manufacturing delivered about a 6 percent cost advantage versus outsourcing.

Exhibit 5   Comparative Value Chain Models of PC Vendors

Traditional Build-to-Stock Value Chain Used by Hewlett-Packard, IBM, Sony, and Most Others

Manufacture and delivery of PC parts and components by suppliers	Assembly of PCs as needed to fill orders from distributors and retailers	Sales and marketing activities of PC vendors to build a brand image and establish a network of resellers	Sales and marketing activities of resellers	Purchases by PC users	Service and support activities provided to PC users by resellers (and some PC vendors)

Build-to-Order, Sell-Direct Value Chain Developed by Dell Computer

Manufacture and delivery of PC parts and components by supply partners	Custom assembly of PCs as orders are received from PC buyers	Sales and marketing activities of PC vendor to build brand image and secure orders from PC buyers	Purchases by PC users	Service and support activities provided to PC users by Dell or contract providers

Close collaboration and real-time data-sharing to drive down costs of supply chain activities, minimize inventories, keep assembly costs low, and respond quickly to changes in the makeup of customer orders

Dell's build-to-order strategy meant that it had no in-house stock of finished goods inventories and that, unlike competitors using the traditional value chain model, it did not have to wait for resellers to clear out their own inventories before it could push new models into the marketplace—resellers typically operated with 30 to 60 days inventory of prebuilt models (see Exhibit 5). Equally important was the fact that customers who bought from Dell got the satisfaction of having their computers customized to their particular liking and pocketbook.

Quality Control

All assembly plants had the capability to run testing and quality control processes on components, parts, and subassemblies obtained from suppliers, as well as on the finished products Dell assembled. Suppliers were urged to participate in a quality certification program that committed them to achieving defined quality specifications. Quality control activities were undertaken at various stages in the assembly process. In addition, Dell's quality control program included testing of completed units after assembly, ongoing production reliability audits, failure tracking for early identification of problems associated with new models shipped to customers, and information obtained from customers through its service and technical support programs. All of the company's plants had been certified as meeting ISO 9002 quality standards.

Partnerships with Suppliers

Michael Dell believed that it made much better sense for Dell Computer to partner with reputable suppliers of PC parts and components than to integrate backward and get into parts and components manufacturing on its own. He explained why:

> If you've got a race with 20 players all vying to make the fastest graphics chip in the world, do you want to be the twenty-first horse, or do you want to evaluate the field of 20 and pick the best one?[6]

Dell evaluated the various makers of each component; picked the best one or two as suppliers; and then stuck with them as long as they maintained their leadership in technology, performance, quality, and cost. Management believed that long-term partnerships with reputable suppliers had at least five advantages. First, using name-brand processors, disk drives, modems, speakers, and multimedia components enhanced the quality and performance of Dell's PCs. Because of varying performance among different brands of components, the brand of the components was quite important to customers concerned about performance and reliability. Second, because Dell partnered with suppliers for the long term and because it committed to purchase a specified percentage of its requirements from each supplier, Dell was assured of getting the volume of components it needed on a timely basis even when overall market demand for a particular component temporarily exceeded the overall market supply. Third, Dell's long-run commitment to its suppliers made it feasible for suppliers to locate their plants or distribution centers within a few miles of Dell assembly plants, putting them in position to make deliveries daily or every few hours, as needed. Dell supplied data on inventories and replenishment needs to its suppliers at least once a day—hourly in the case of components being delivered several times daily from nearby sources.

Fourth, long-term supply partnerships facilitated having some of the supplier's engineers assigned to Dell's product design teams and being treated as part of Dell. When new products were launched, suppliers' engineers were stationed in Dell's plants; if early buyers called with a problem related to design, further assembly and shipments were halted while the supplier's engineers and Dell personnel corrected the flaw on the spot.[7] Fifth, long-term partnerships enlisted greater cooperation on the part of suppliers to seek new ways to drive costs out of the supply chain. Dell openly shared its daily production schedules, sales forecasts, and new model introduction plans with vendors. Dell also did a three-year plan with each of its key suppliers and worked with suppliers to minimize the number of different stock-keeping units of parts and components in its products and to identify ways to drive costs down.

Commitment to Just-in-Time Inventory Practices

Dell's just-in-time inventory emphasis yielded major cost advantages and shortened the time it took for Dell to get new generations of its computer models into the marketplace. New advances were coming so fast in certain computer parts and components (particularly microprocessors, disk drives, and wireless devices) that any given item in inventory was obsolete in a matter of months, sometimes quicker. Moreover, rapid-fire reductions in the prices of components were not unusual—for example, Intel regularly cut the prices on its older chips when it introduced newer chips, and it introduced new chip generations about every three months. Michael Dell explained the dramatic economics of minimal component inventories as follows:

> If I've got 11 days of inventory and my competitor has 80 and Intel comes out with a new chip, that means I'm going to get to market 69 days sooner.
>
> In the computer industry, inventory can be a pretty massive risk because if the cost of materials is going down 50 percent a year and you have two or three months of inventory versus eleven days, you've got a big cost disadvantage. And you're vulnerable to product transitions, when you can get stuck with obsolete inventory.[8]

For a growing number of parts and components, Dell's close partnership with suppliers was allowing it to operate with no more than two hours of inventory.

Dell's supplier of monitors was Sony. Because the monitors Sony supplied with the Dell name already imprinted were of dependably high quality (a defect rate of fewer than 1,000 per million), Dell didn't even open up the monitor boxes to test them at its Reno, Nevada, monitor distribution center.[9] Utilizing sophisticated data exchange systems, Dell arranged for its shippers (Airborne Express and United Parcel Service) to pick up computers at U.S. assembly plants, then pick up the accompanying monitors at its Reno distribution center and deliver both to the customer simultaneously. The savings in time and cost were significant.

Dell had been working hard for the past several years to refine and improve its relationships with suppliers and its procedures for operating with smaller inventories. In fiscal year 1995, Dell averaged an inventory turn cycle of 32 days. By the end of fiscal 1997 (January 1997), the average was down to 13 days. The following year, it was 7 days, which compared very favorably with Gateway's 14-day average, Compaq's 23-day average, and the estimated industrywide average of over 50 days. In fiscal year 1999 and 2000, Dell operated with an average of six days' supply in inventory; the average dropped to five days' supply in fiscal year 2001 and to four days' supply in 2002 and 2003.

Dell's Direct Sales Strategy and Marketing Efforts

With thousands of phone, fax, and Internet orders daily and ongoing field sales force contact with customers, the company kept its finger on the market pulse, quickly detecting shifts in sales trends, design problems, and quality glitches. If the company got more than a few of the same complaints, the information was relayed immediately to design engineers who checked out the problem. When design flaws or components defects were found, the factory was notified and the problem corrected within a few days. Management believed Dell's ability to respond quickly gave it a significant advantage over PC makers that operated on the basis of large production runs of variously configured and equipped PCs and sold them through retail channels. Dell saw its direct sales approach as a totally customer-driven system, with the flexibility to transition quickly to new generations of components and PC models.

Dell's Customer-Based Sales and Marketing Focus   Unlike technology companies that organized their sales and marketing efforts around product lines, Dell was organized around customer groups. Dell had placed managers in charge of developing sales and service programs appropriate to the needs and expectations of each customer group. Up until the early 1990s, Dell operated with sales and service programs aimed at just two market segments—high-volume corporate and governmental buyers and low-volume business and individual buyers. But as sales took off in 1995–97, these segments were subdivided into finer, more homogeneous categories that by 2000 included global enterprise accounts, large and midsize companies (over 400 employees), small companies (under 400 employees), health care businesses (over 400 employees), federal government agencies, state and local government agencies, educational institutions, and individual consumers. Many of these customer segments were further subdivided—for instance, within the federal category, Dell had formed separate sales forces and marketing programs for the army, navy, and air force; in education, there were separate sales and marketing programs for K–12 schools; higher education institutions; and personal-use purchases by faculty, staff, and students. Dell's largest global enterprise accounts were assigned their own dedicated sales force—for example, Dell had a sales force of 150 people dedicated to meeting the needs of General Electric's facilities and personnel scattered across the world.

Dell's sales to individuals and small businesses were made by telephone, fax, and the Internet. It had call centers in the United States, Europe, and Asia with toll-free lines; customers could talk with a sales representative about specific models, get information faxed or mailed to them, place an order, and pay by credit card. The Asian and European call centers were equipped with technology that routed calls from a particular country to a particular call center. Thus, for example, a customer calling from Lisbon, Portugal, was automatically directed to a Portuguese-speaking sales rep at the call center in Montpelier, France.

Dell in Japan   While NEC, Toshiba, Fujitsu, and Hitachi had the leading shares of the $20 billion PC market in Japan for 2002, Dell was fifth, with a 7.7 percent dollar share, and IBM ranked sixth. Other competitors included Sony, Sharp, and Matshusita. Counting units sold, however, Dell was number one in business desktop computers and was number two in entry-level and midrange servers, with a 19.1 percent share in mid-2002. Dell's 2002 sales in Japan were up about 20 percent, in a market where overall sales were flat. Dell's technical and customer support was ranked the best in Japan in 2002 by *Nikkei PC,* an industry trade magazine. Dell had 200 full-time personnel at its call center in Japan and was tracking Japanese buying habits and preferences with its proprietary software. The head of Dell's consumer PC sales group in Japan had installed 34 kiosks in leading electronics stores around Japan, allowing shoppers to test Dell computers, ask questions of staff, and place orders—about half the sales were to people who did not know about Dell prior to visiting the kiosk.

Dell believed that it was more profitable than any other PC-server vendor selling in the Japanese market. Dell's profit margins in Japan were higher than those in the U.S. market, and sales were rising briskly. Dell overtook NEC in servers to become the second-ranking seller of servers in the fourth quarter of 2002. Japan ranked 20th worldwide in personal computers per capita, with a rate of 31.5 computers per 100 people; the United States ranked 1st, with 58.5 computers per 100 people.[10]

Dell in China   Dell Computer entered China in 1998 and achieved faster growth there than in any other foreign market it had entered. The market for PCs in China was the third largest in the world, behind the United States and Japan, and was on the verge of being the second largest. Unit volume was expanding 20–30 percent annually and with a population of 1.4 billion people (of which some 400 million lived in metropolitan areas where computer use was growing rapidly), the Chinese market for PCs was expected to become the largest in the world by 2010. The market leader in China was Legend, a local company; other major local PC producers were Founder and Great Wall. IBM, Hewlett-Packard, Dell, Toshiba, Acer, and NEC Japan were among the top 10 market share leaders in China. All of the major contenders except Dell relied on resellers to handle sales and service; Dell sold directly to customers in China just as it did elsewhere.

Dell's primary target market in China consisted of large corporate accounts. Management believed that many Chinese companies would find the savings from direct sales appealing, that they would like the idea of having Dell build PCs and servers to their requirements and specifications, and that—once they became a Dell customer—they would like the convenience of Internet purchases and the company's growing array of products and services. Dell recognized that its direct sales approach put it at a short-term disadvantage in appealing to small business customers and individual consumers. According to an executive from rival Legend, "It takes two years of a person's savings to buy a PC in China. And when two years of savings is at stake, the whole family wants to come out to a store to touch and try the machine."[11] But Dell believed that over time, as Chinese consumers became more familiar with PCs and more comfortable with making online purchases, it would be able to attract growing numbers of small business customers and consumers through Internet and telephone sales. In 2002, about 40 percent of Dell's sales in China were over the Internet.

Dell's sales in Asia were expected to surpass those in Europe by year-end 2003 and to become Dell's biggest region outside the United States by 2005.

Dell in Latin America   In 2002 PC sales in Latin America exceeded 5 million units. Latin America had a population of 450 million people. Dell management believed that in the next few years PC use in Latin America would reach 1 for every 30 people (one-tenth the penetration in the United States), pushing annual sales up to 15 million units. The company's plant in Brazil, the largest market in Latin America, was opened to produce, sell, and provide service and technical support for customers in Brazil, Argentina, Chile, Uruguay, and Paraguay.

Using Dell Direct Store Kiosks to Access Individual Consumers   In 2002 Dell began installing Dell Direct Store kiosks in a variety of retail settings. The kiosks did not carry inventory, but customers could talk face-to-face with a knowledgeable Dell sales representative, inspect Dell's products, and order them on the Internet while at the kiosk. The idea for using kiosks had begun in Japan, where Dell sales reps were encountering resistance to Dell's direct sales approach from individual buyers—Japanese consumers were noted for wanting to touch and feel a product before committing to purchase it. When kiosks were installed in Japanese retail settings, they proved quite popular and helped generate a big boost in Dell's share of PC sales to consumers in Japan. The success of kiosks in Japan had inspired Dell to try them in the United States. About 60 kiosks were in place at U.S. locations during the 2002 holiday sales season. In January 2003, Dell announced that it would begin placing Dell Direct Store kiosks in selected Wal-Mart and Sears stores.

Customer Service and Technical Support

Service became a feature of Dell's strategy in 1986 when the company began providing a year's free on-site service with most of its PCs after users complained about having to ship their PCs back to Austin for repairs. Dell contracted with local service providers to handle customer requests for repairs; on-site service was provided on a next-day basis.

Dell also provided its customers with technical support via a toll-free phone number and e-mail. Dell received close to 40,000 e-mail messages monthly requesting service and support. Bundled service policies were a major selling point for winning corporate accounts. If customers preferred to work with their own service provider, Dell supplied the provider of choice with training and spare parts needed to service customers' equipment. Recently, Dell had instituted a First Call Resolution initiative to strengthen its capabilities to resolve customer inquiries or difficulties on the first call; first call resolution percentages were made an important measure in evaluating the company's technical support performance.

Value-Added Services   Dell kept close track of the purchases of its large global customers, country by country and department by department—and customers themselves found this purchase information valuable. Dell's sales and support personnel used their knowledge about a particular customer's needs to help that customer plan PC purchases, to configure the customer's PC networks, and to provide value-added services. For example, for its large customers Dell loaded software and placed ID tags on newly ordered PCs at the factory, thereby eliminating the need for the customer's IT personnel to unpack the PC, deliver it to an employee's desk, hook it up, place asset tags on the PC, and load the needed software from an assortment of CD-ROMs and diskettes—a process that could take several hours and cost $200–$300.[12] While Dell charged an extra $15 or $20 for the software-loading and asset-tagging services, the savings to customers were still considerable—one large customer reported savings of $500,000 annually from this service.[13]

Premier Pages   Dell had developed customized, password-protected websites called Premier Pages for over 40,000 corporate, governmental, and institutional customers worldwide. These Premier Pages gave customers' personnel online access to information about all Dell products and configurations the company had purchased or that were currently authorized for purchase. Employees could use Premier Pages to (1) obtain customer-specific pricing for whatever machines and options the employee wanted to consider, (2) place an order online that would be electronically routed to higher-level managers for approval and then on to Dell for assembly and delivery, and (3) seek advanced help desk support. Customers could also search and sort all invoices and obtain purchase histories. These features eliminated paper invoices, cut ordering time, and reduced the internal labor customers needed to staff corporate purchasing and accounting functions. Customer use of Premier Pages had boosted the productivity of Dell salespeople assigned to these accounts by 50 percent. Dell was providing Premier Page service to thousands of additional customers annually and adding more features to further improve functionality.

www.dell.com   At the company's website, which underwent a global redesign in late 1999 and had 50 country-specific sites in local languages and currencies, prospective buyers could review Dell's entire product line in detail, configure and price customized PCs, place orders, and track orders from manufacturing through shipping. The closing rate on sales at Dell's website was 20 percent higher than that on sales inquiries received via telephone. The company was adding Web-based customer service and support tools to make a customer's online experience pleasant and satisfying.

In February 2003, over 50 percent of Dell's technical support activities were being conducted via the Internet. Dell was aggressively pursuing initiatives to enhance its online technical support tools and reduce the number and cost of telephone support calls (which totaled about 8 million in 2000). Management believed that enhancing www.dell.com to shrink transaction and order fulfillment times, increase accuracy, and provide more personalized content resulted in a higher degree of "e-loyalty" than traditional attributes like price and product selection.

On-Site Services   Corporate customers paid Dell fees to provide technical support, on-site service, and help with migrating to new IT technologies. Services were one of the fastest growing part of Dell, accounting for almost $4 billion in sales in 2002. Dell's service business was split about 50–50 between what Michael Dell called close-to-the-box services and management and professional services—but the latter were growing faster, at close to 25 percent annually. Dell estimated that close-to-the-box support services for Dell products represented about a $50 billion market, whereas the market for management and professional services (IT life-cycle services, deployment of new technology, and solutions for greater IT productivity) was about $90 billion. IT consulting services were becoming more standardized, driven primarily by growing hardware and software standardization, reduction in on-site service requirements (partly because of online diagnostic and support tools, growing ease of repair and maintenance, increased customer knowledge, and increased remote management capabilities), and declines in the skills and know-how that were required to perform service tasks on standardized equipment and install new, more standardized systems.

In a fall 2002 speech, Michael Dell explained the company's move into services:

> We developed a couple of years ago an organization we originally called Dell Technology Consulting, and what they do is the kind of technical consulting, the SAN [storage area network] installation and design, the Microsoft Exchange implementation, the Oracle 9i rack, the cluster installation and design. Last year we did about 2000 engagements with Dell Technology Consulting.
>
> We acquired a company called Plural, which is totally focused on the Microsoft application environment, and have combined those resources together to create what we now call Dell Professional Services . . . Our focus here is, first and foremost, to support our thrust into enterprise products. And we know that as customers require those products, you can't have a 70 percent increase in SAN shipments year over year, you can't have a billion dollar external storage business unless you can design and install those products.[14]

Dell's strategy in services, like its strategy in hardware products, was to bring down the cost of IT consulting services for its large enterprise customers. The providers of on-site service, technical support, and other types of IT consulting typically charged premium prices and realized hefty profits for their efforts. During 2001–2002, according to Michael Dell, customers who bought the services being provided by Dell saved 40 to 50 percent over what they would have paid other providers of IT services. Going into 2003, Dell had some 8,000 employees in its services group and top management foresaw services as playing an expanding role in the company's growth. Kevin Rollins, Dell's president, indicated the company's business model "isn't just about making cheap boxes, it's also about freeing customers from overpriced relationships" with such vendors as IBM, Sun Microsystems, and Hewlett-Packard.[15]

While a number of Dell's corporate accounts were large enough to justify dedicated on-site teams of Dell support personnel, Dell generally contracted with third-party providers to make the necessary on-site service calls. Customers notified Dell when they had problems; such notices triggered two electronic dispatches—one to ship replacement parts from Dell's factory to the customer sites and one to notify the contract service provider to prepare to make the needed repairs as soon as the parts arrived.[16] Bad parts were returned so that Dell could determine what went wrong and how to prevent such problems from happening again. Problems relating to faulty components or flawed components design were promptly passed along to the relevant supplier for correction.

Customer Forums   In addition to using its sales and support mechanisms to stay close to customers, Dell periodically held regional forums for its best customers. The company formed Platinum and Gold Councils composed of its largest customers in the United States, Europe, Japan, and the Asia-Pacific region; regional meetings were held every six to nine months.[17] Some regions had two meetings—one for chief information officers and one for technical personnel. At the meetings, which frequently included a presentation by Michael Dell, Dell's senior technologists shared their views on the direction of the latest technological developments, what the flow of technology really meant for customers, and Dell's plans for introducing new and upgraded products over the next two years. There were also breakout sessions on topics of current interest. Dell found that the information gleaned from customers at these meetings assisted the company in forecasting demand for its products.

Pioneering Leadership in Use of the Internet and E-Commerce Technology

Dell Computer was a leader in using the Internet and e-commerce technologies to squeeze greater efficiency out of its supply chain activities, to streamline the order-to-delivery process, to encourage greater customer use of its website, and to gather and utilize all types of information. In a 1999 speech to 1,200 customers, Michael Dell said:

> The world will be changed forever by the Internet . . . The Internet will be your business. If your business isn't enabled by providing customers and suppliers with more information, you're probably already in trouble. The Internet provides a dramatic reduction in the cost of transactions and the cost of interaction among people and businesses, and it creates dramatic new opportunities and destroys old competitive advantages. The Internet is like a weapon sitting on a table ready to be picked up by either you or your competitors.[18]

Dell Computer's use of its website and various Internet technology applications had proved instrumental in helping the company become the industry's low-cost provider and drive costs out of its business. Internet technology applications were a cornerstone of Dell's collaborative efforts with suppliers. The company provided order-status information quickly and conveniently over the Internet, thereby eliminating tens of thousands of order-status inquiries coming in by phone. It used its website as a powerful sales and technical support tool. Few companies could match Dell's competencies and capabilities in the use of Internet technology to improve operating efficiency and gain new sales in a cost-efficient manner.

Expansion into New Products

Dell's recent expansion into data storage hardware, switches, handheld PCs, printers, and printer cartridges represented an effort to diversify the company's product base and to use its competitive capabilities in PCs and servers to pursue revenue growth opportunities. Dell had expanded its product line to include storage devices designed to handle a variety of customers' needs for high-speed data storage and retrieval; management saw storage devices as a growth opportunity because the computing systems of corporate and institutional customers were making increasing use of high-speed data storage and retrieval devices. Dell's PowerVault line of storage products had data protection and recovery features that made it easy for customers to add and manage storage and simplify consolidation. Because it relied on standardized technology and components (which were considerably cheaper than customized ones) as building blocks for its storage products, Dell had been able to drive down storage prices for its customers by about 50 percent during 2001–2002.

Dell began selling its own data-routing switches in 2001. As sales of these switches accelerated and as Dell mulled whether to expand into other networking products and Internet gear, Cisco elected to discontinue supplying its switches to Dell for resell as of October 2002. Dell's family of PowerConnect switches—simple commodity-like products generally referred to as layer 2 switches in the industry—carried a price of $20 per port, versus $70–$100 for comparable Cisco switches and $38 for comparable 3Com switches. Most of Dell's sales of switches were to customers who were in the process of buying Dell servers. Michael Dell used Dell's entry into data networking switches to explain the logic behind the company's strategy to expand into products and services that complemented its sales of PCs, workstations, and servers:

> In the United States, Dell has about a 46 percent share of the market for small computer systems sold to large corporations, which does not mean that we sell to 46 percent of corporations; it means we sell to about 90 percent of corporations and one out of two of the products they buy is Dell. So we have pretty profound access and coverage within large corporations.
>
> Every computer that we sell to businesses is attached to a network. So you buy a PC, you buy a server, you attach them with switches, layer 2 and layer 3, into a WAN [wide-area network], into some fiber optic backbone or something that connects out to the broader Internet or intranet or whatever the network may be.
>
> So it's a fairly logical adjacency to say, okay, you're buying PCs from Dell, how about switches from Dell. And it turns out that that's a fairly easy thing for us to sell.[19]

Some observers saw Dell's 2003 entry into the printer market as another deliberate attack on Hewlett-Packard—going after HP's biggest and most profitable business segment at a time when HP management was busy tackling the challenges of merging its operations with those of Compaq and trying to make its acquisition a success. Dell's Axim line of handheld PCs was priced at about 50 percent less than HP's popular iPaq line of handhelds, and Dell's storage and networking products also carried lower prices than comparable HP products. Dell management, however, indicated the company's entry into the printer market was driven by a desire to add value for its customers. Michael Dell explained, "We think we can drive down the entire cost of owning and using printing products. If you look at any other market Dell has gone into, we have been able to significantly save money for customers. We know we can do that in printers; we have looked at the supply chain all the way through its various cycles and we know there are inefficiencies there. I think the price of the total offering when we include the printer and the supplies . . . can come down quite considerably."[20]

When Dell announced it had contracted with Lexmark to make printers and printer and toner cartridges for sale under the Dell label beginning in 2003, HP immediately discontinued supplying HP printers to Dell for resale at Dell's website. Dell had been selling Lexmark printers for two years and since 2000 had resold about 4 million printers made by such vendors as HP, Lexmark, and other vendors to its customers.

Lexmark designed and made critical parts for its printers but used offshore contract manufacturers for assembly. Gross profit margins on printers (sales minus cost of goods sold) were said to be in single digits in late 2002, but the gross margins on printer supplies were in the 50–60 percent range—brand-name ink cartridges for printers typically ran $25 to $35.

Dell's Entry into the White-Box PC Segment

In 2002 Dell announced it would begin making so-called white-box (i.e., unbranded) PCs for resale under the private labels of retailers. PC dealers that supplied white-box PCs to small businesses and price-conscious individuals under the dealer's own brand name accounted for about one-third of total PC sales and about 50 percent of sales to small businesses. According to one industry analyst, "Increasingly, Dell's biggest competitor these days isn't big brand-name companies like IBM or HP, it's white-box vendors." Dell's thinking in entering the white-box PC segment was that it was cheaper to reach many small businesses through the white-box dealers that already served them than by using its own sales force and support groups to sell and service businesses with fewer than 100 employees. Dell believed its low-cost supply chain and assembly capabilities would allow it to build generic machines cheaper than white-box resellers could buy components and assemble a customized machine. Management expected that Dell would achieve $380 million in sales of white-box PCs in 2003 and would generate profit margins equal to those on Dell-branded PCs. Some industry analysts were skeptical of Dell's move into white-box PCs because they expected white-box dealers to be reluctant to buy their PCs from a company that had a history of taking their clients. Others believed this was a test effort by Dell to develop the capabilities to take on white-box dealers in Asia and especially in China, where the sellers of generic PCs were particularly strong.

Going into 2003, Dell Computer had a war chest of over $9 billion in cash and liquid investments that it could deploy in its pursuit of attractive revenue growth opportunities. Management had expressed a desire to grow the company revenues to around $60 or $65 billion annually by 2006. The company wanted such products as servers, storage devices, switches and routers, printers, and other peripherals to account for 50 percent of revenues within four or five years. According to Michael Dell, whereas Dell's unit shipments, revenues, and profits were all up at double-digit rates in the second quarter of 2002, "on average, the rest of the industry was down 4 percent in shipments, down 10 percent in revenue and lost money."[21]

Other Elements of Dell's Business Strategy

Dell's strategy had two other elements that assisted the company's drive for industry leadership: R&D and advertising.

Research and Development   Dell's R&D focus was to track and test new developments in components and software, ascertain which ones would prove most useful and cost-effective for customers, and then design them into Dell products. Management's philosophy was it was Dell's job on behalf of its customers to sort out all the new technology coming into the marketplace and help steer customers to options and solutions most relevant to their needs. The company talked to its customers frequently about "relevant technology," listening carefully to customers' needs and problems and endeavoring to identify the most cost-effective solutions.

Dell was a strong advocate of incorporating standardized components in its products so as not to tie either it or its customers to one company's proprietary technology and components, which almost always carried a price premium and increased costs for its customers. Dell actively promoted the use of industrywide standards and regularly pressed its suppliers of a particular part or component to agree on common standards. Michael Dell and other company officials saw standardized technology as beginning to take over the largest part of the $875 billion spent annually on IT—standardization was very much evident in the areas of servers, storage, networking, and high-performance computing. One example of the impact of standardized technology was at the University of Buffalo, where Dell had installed a 5.6 teraflop cluster of about 2,000 Dell servers containing 4,000 microprocessors that was being used to decode the human genome. The cluster of servers, which were the same as those Dell sold to its business customers, had been installed in about 60 days at a cost of a few million dollars and represented the third most powerful supercomputer in the world. High-performance clusters of PCs and servers were replacing mainframe computers and custom-designed supercomputers because of their much lower cost. Amerada Hess, attracted by Dell's use of standardized and upgradable parts and components, installed a cluster of several hundred Dell workstations and allocated about $300,000 a year to upgrade and maintain it; the cluster had replaced an IBM supercomputer that cost $1.5 million a year to lease and operate. Studies conducted by Dell indicated that, over time, products incorporating standardized technology delivered about twice the performance per dollar of cost as products based on proprietary technology.

Dell's R&D group included over 3,000 engineers, and its annual R&D budget was $450 to $500 million. The company's R&D unit also studied and implemented ways to control quality and to streamline the assembly process. About 15 percent of Dell's 800 U.S. patents were ranked "elite."

Advertising   Michael Dell was a strong believer in the power of advertising and frequently espoused its importance in the company's strategy. His competitive zeal resulted in the company's being the first to use comparative ads, throwing barbs at Compaq's higher prices. Although Compaq won a lawsuit against Dell for making false comparisons, Michael Dell was unapologetic, arguing that the ads were very effective: "We were able to increase customer awareness about value."[22] Dell insisted that the company's ads be communicative and forceful, not soft and fuzzy.

The company regularly had prominent ads describing its products and prices in such leading computer publications as *PC Magazine* and *PC World,* as well as in *USA Today, The Wall Street Journal,* and other business publications. In the spring of 1998, the company debuted a major multiyear, worldwide TV campaign to strengthen its brand image using the theme "Be Direct." Most recently, Dell had been successful in gaining sales to consumers with a popular ad campaign featuring Steven, the "Dude, You're Gettin' a Dell" guy, enthusiastically pitching Dell products. A second popular campaign featured a group of young Dell interns working their way through Dell's operations and talking with workers about their jobs.

Dell's Performance in 2002 and Early 2003

In 2001–2002 Dell added about 16,000 new business customers in North and South America alone—in the United States, Dell had gained about 1,500 new business customers each quarter since mid-2001. In its largest accounts, the portion of revenue coming from new customers had increased 50 percent above 2001 levels, and revenues from existing corporate accounts were up by about 20 percent. The company believed that close to $6 billion of its fiscal 2003 revenues could be attributed to market share gains in the past eight quarters. Management believed that its strategy to acquire new customers, keep its customers satisfied, and sell them a growing array of IT products and services was working well.

According to data compiled by Dell management, in the second quarter of 2002, Dell generated operating income of $75,000 per employee, versus $15,000 for Hewlett-Packard, $10,000 for IBM, and −$1,000 for Sun Microsystems. Whereas Dell's revenues were running close to or above record levels on a quarterly basis in mid-2002, the revenues of its chief competitors were averaging about 62 percent of their all-time peak-quarter revenues—and most were not expected to exceed their previous quarterly peak for at least two years. From the third quarter of 1997 through the first quarter of 2002, Dell's unit worldwide market share had risen 158 percent; during the same period, HP's worldwide unit market share had dropped by 23 percent and IBM's unit share was down 19 percent. From 1998 through the second quarter of 2002, Dell had increased its U.S. share of entry-level and midrange servers from about 12 percent to an industry-leading 29.9 percent, edging out Hewlett-Packard, whose share had dropped from 43 percent in 1998 to 29.8 percent in mid-2002; third-ranked IBM's share had remained relatively constant at around 11 percent. Dell's market share in fiscal 2003 was higher than in fiscal 2002 in all regions of the world.

Dell's strategy was also generating good cash flows. Statistics compiled by Dell indicated that its free cash flow (defined as cash flow from operations minus capital expenditures) had averaged just over 12 percent of revenues during 1997–2002; this compared very favorably with free cash flows at Sun Microsystems (about 9 percent), IBM (about 6 percent), and Hewlett-Packard (nearly 3 percent). Going into 2003, Dell had $9.9 billion in cash and investments, a company record.

During the November 2002–January 2003 period (the fourth quarter of Dell's 2003 fiscal year), the company posted its best-ever quarterly product shipments, revenues, and operating profits. Management indicated that Dell's global market share in PCs in the last quarter of fiscal 2003 was almost 3 points higher than in its fiscal 2002 fourth quarter, and its U.S. share was 5 points higher—in servers, Dell's market share was over 3 points higher. Unit shipments were up 25 percent, and shipments in China, France, Germany, and Japan increased a combined 39 percent, with server sales in those countries up 47 percent. Despite steadily eroding average selling prices of $1,640 in fiscal 2003; $1,700 in 2002; $2,050 in 2001; $2,250 in 2000; and $2,600 in 1998, Dell's revenues were climbing as the company gained volume and market share in virtually all product categories and geographic areas where it competed.

Market Conditions in the Information Technology Industry in Early 2003

Analysts expected the $875 billion worldwide IT industry to grow roughly 5 percent in 2003, following a 2.3 percent decline in 2002 and close to a 1 percent decline in 2001—corporate spending for IT products accounted for about 45 percent of all capital expenditures of U.S. businesses. From 1980 to 2000, IT spending had grown at an average annual rate of 12 percent and then flattened. The recent slowdown in IT spending

Exhibit 6   **ACTUAL AND PROJECTED WORLDWIDE SHIPMENTS OF PCS, 1980–2004**

Year	Volume of PC Shipments (millions)
1980	1
1985	11
1990	24
1995	58
1996	69
1997	80
1998	91
1999	112
2000	140
2001	134
2002	136
2003	147*
2004	164*

*Forecast.

Source: International Data Corporation.

reflected a combination of factors: sluggish economic growth worldwide that was prompting businesses to delay upgrades and hold on to aging equipment longer; over-investment in IT in the 1995–99 period; declining unit prices for many IT products (especially PCs and servers); and a growing preference for lower-priced, standard-component hardware that was good enough to perform a variety of functions using off-the-shelf Windows or Linux operating systems (as opposed to relying on propri-etary hardware and customized Unix software). The selling points that appealed most to customers were standardization, flexibility, modularity, simplicity, economy of use, and value.

Exhibit 6 shows actual and projected PC sales for 1980–2004 as compiled by in-dustry researcher International Data Corporation. According to Gartner Research, the billionth PC was shipped sometime in July 2002; of the billion, an estimated 550 mil-lion were still in use. Nearly 82 percent of the 1 billion PCs that had been shipped were desktops, and 75 percent were sold to businesses. With a world population of 6 billion, most industry participants believed there was ample opportunity for further growth in the PC market. Computer usage in Europe was half of that in the United States, even though the combined economies of the European countries were a bit larger than the U.S. economy. Growth potential for PCs was seen as particularly strong in China, In-dia, several other Asian countries, and portions of Latin America. Many industry ex-perts foresaw a time when the installed base of PCs would exceed 1 billion units, and some believed the total would eventually reach 1.5 billion—a ratio of one PC to every four people in the world.

Forecasters also predicted that there would be a strong built-in PC replacement de-mand as microprocessor speeds continued to escalate. A microprocessor operating at 450 megahertz could process 600 million instructions per second (MIPS); Intel had forecast that it would be able to produce microprocessors capable of 100,000 MIPS by 2011. Such speeds were expected to spawn massive increases in computing functionality and altogether new uses and applications not only for PCs but also for computing devices of all types. At the same time, forecasters expected full global buildout of the Internet, which would entail the installation of millions of servers.

Currently, there was growing interest in notebook computers; many businesses were turning to notebooks equipped with wireless data communications capability to improve worker productivity and keep workers connected to important information. The emergence of Wireless Fidelity (Wi-Fi) networking technology was fueling the trend—Wi-Fi systems were being used in businesses, on college campuses, in airports, and other locations to link users to the Internet and to private networks. Another next-generation PC, the tablet PC, used a penlike stylus for writing notes on text documents and e-books. The media center PC combined a full-function PC with such consumer electronic devices as a DVD player, music jukebox, and personal video recorder. Two other devices—flat-panel LCD monitors and DVD recorder drives—were also stimulating sales of new PCs.

The Server Market

In the server market, a sea-change shift from proprietary servers running Unix operating systems to much lower-cost Intel/Windows/Linux server technologies was generating a slowdown in dollar revenues from server sales despite rapidly increasing unit volume. Dell was the market leader in the number of low-end and midrange servers shipped but because of its low prices trailed far behind Hewlett-Packard, IBM, and Sun Microsystems in total revenues from server sales. The rapid inroads that Dell was making into the server market had greatly intensified competition in servers in the past three years. In late 2002, HP, IBM, and Sun were in a dead heat for market share leadership based on dollar volume.[23] In the third quarter of 2002, IBM overtook HP as the overall revenue leader in servers, with 30.0 percent of the market versus HP's 27.2 percent. However, HP edged out Sun for the lead in Unix-based servers, with a revenue share of 32.9 percent versus Sun's 30.4 percent.

The Unix share of the server operating system market (based on unit shipments) was said to have decreased by 50 percent over the past five years compared to Windows and Linux, which had almost tripled in use—Dell estimated that Unix-based servers accounted for about 17 percent of unit volume and 55 percent of dollar volume in mid-2002. A number of industry observers believed that Linux was the "new Unix" and that the days of using expensive, proprietary Unix systems were numbered.

Competing Value Chain Models in the Global PC Industry

When the personal computer industry first began to take shape in the early 1980s, the founding companies manufactured many of the components themselves—disk drives, memory chips, graphics chips, microprocessors, motherboards, and software. Subscribing to a philosophy that mandated in-house development of key components, they built expertise in a variety of PC-related technologies and created organizational units to produce components as well as handle final assembly. While certain noncritical items were typically outsourced, if a computer maker was not at least partially vertically integrated and an assembler of some components, then it was not taken seriously as a manufacturer.

But as the industry grew, technology advanced quickly in so many directions on so many parts and components that the early personal computer manufacturers could not keep pace as experts on all fronts. There were too many technological innovations in components to pursue and too many manufacturing intricacies to master for a vertically integrated manufacturer to keep its products on the cutting edge. As a consequence, companies emerged that specialized in making particular components. Specialists could marshal enough R&D capability and resources to either lead the technological developments in their area of specialization or else quickly match the advances made by their competitors. Moreover, specialist firms could mass-produce the component and supply it to several computer manufacturers far cheaper than any one manufacturer could fund the needed component R&D and then make only whatever smaller volume of components it needed for assembling its own brand of PCs.

Thus, in the early 1990s, computer makers began to abandon vertical integration in favor of a strategy of outsourcing most components from specialists and concentrating on efficient assembly and marketing their brand of computers. Recall Exhibit 5, which shows the value chain model that such manufacturers as Compaq Computer, IBM, Hewlett-Packard, Sony, Toshiba, and Fujitsu-Siemens used in the 1990s. It featured arm's-length transactions between specialist suppliers, manufacturer/assemblers, distributors and retailers, and end users. However, Dell, Gateway, and Micron Electronics employed a shorter value chain model, selling directly to customers and eliminating the time and costs associated with distributing through independent resellers. Building to order avoided (1) having to keep many differently equipped models on retailers' shelves to fill buyer requests for one or another configuration of options and components, and (2) having to clear out slow-selling models at a discount before introducing new generations of PCs. Direct sales eliminated retailer costs and markups (retail dealer margins were typically in the range of 4 to 10 percent).

Because of Dell's success in using its business model and strategy to become the low-cost leader, most other PC makers in 2003 were endeavoring to emulate various aspects of Dell's strategy, but with little notable success. Nearly all vendors were trying to cut days of inventory out of their supply chains and reduce their costs of goods sold and operating expenses to levels that would make them more competitive with Dell. In an effort to cut their assembly costs, several of the leading PC makers (including IBM and Hewlett Packard) had begun outsourcing assembly to contract manufacturers and refocused their internal efforts on product design and marketing. Virtually all vendors were trying to minimize the amount of finished goods in dealer/distributor inventories and shorten the time it took to replenish dealer stocks. Collaboration with contract manufacturers was increasing to develop the capabilities to use a build-to-order model and be able to deliver orders to customers in 7 to 14 days, but this was complicated by the use of offshore contract manufacturers.

While most PC vendors would have liked to adopt Dell's sell-direct strategy for at least some of their sales, they were reluctant to push direct sales hard for fear of alienating the dealers on whom they depended for the bulk of their sales. Dealers saw sell-direct efforts on the part of a manufacturer whose brand they represented as a move to cannibalize their business and to compete against them. So far, other than Dell and Gateway, the remaining PC vendors had elected, for the most part, to market their products through independent dealers who were responsible for handling sales and service to customers. However, Dell's success in gaining large enterprise customers with its direct sales force had forced growing numbers of PC vendors to supplement the efforts of their independent dealers with direct sales and service efforts of their own. Going into 2003, several of Dell's rivals were selling 15 to 25 percent of their products direct.

Exhibit 7　DELL'S PRINCIPAL COMPETITORS AND DELL'S MARKET SHARE, BY PRODUCT CATEGORY, 2002

Product Category	Dell's Principal Competitors	Estimated Worldwide Market Size in 2003	Dell's Worldwide Share, 2002
PCs and workstations	Hewlett-Packard (maker of both Compaq and HP brands), IBM, Gateway, Apple, Acer, Sony, Fujitsu-Siemens (in Europe and Japan), Legend (in China)	$162 billion	~16%
Servers	Hewlett-Packard, IBM, Sun Microsystems, Fujitsu	$50 billion	~9%
Data storage devices	Hewlett-Packard, IBM, EMC, Hitachi	$31 billion	~6%
Networking switches and related equipment	Cisco Systems, Enterasys, Nortel, 3Com	$58 billion	<1%
Handheld PCs	Palm, Sony, Hewlett-Packard, Toshiba, Casio	$4 billion	<1%
Printers and printer cartridges	Hewlett-Packard, Lexmark, Canon, Epson	$35–45 billion	0
Cash register systems	IBM, NCR, Wincor Nixdorf, Hewlett-Packard, Sun Microsystems	$4 billion (in North America)	0
Services	Accenture, IBM, Hewlett-Packard, many others	$350 billion	~2%

Source: Compiled by the case authors from a variety of sources, including International Data Corporation and www.dell.com.

Profiles of Selected Competitors in the PC Industry

This section presents brief profiles of four of Dell's principal competitors. Exhibit 7 summarizes Dell's principal competitors in the various product categories where it competed and the sizes of these product markets.

Hewlett-Packard

In one of the most contentious and controversial acquisitions in U.S. history, Hewlett-Packard shareholders voted by a narrow margin in early 2002 to approve the company's acquisition of Compaq Computer, the world's second largest full-service global computing company (behind IBM) and a company with 2001 revenues of $33.6 billion and a net loss of $785 million. Compaq had passed IBM to become the world leader in PCs in 1995 and remained in first place until it was overtaken by Dell in late 1999. Compaq acquired Tandem Computer in 1997 and Digital Equipment Corporation in 1998 to give it capabilities, products, and service offerings that allowed it to compete in every sector of the computer industry.[24] When Compaq purchased it, Digital was a troubled company with high operating costs, an inability to maintain technological leadership in high-end computing, and a nine-year string of having either lost money or barely broken even.[25] The acquisitions gave Compaq a product line that included PCs, servers, workstations, mainframes, peripherals, and such services as business and e-commerce solutions, hardware and software support, systems integration, and technology consulting. In 2000, Compaq spent $370 million to acquire certain assets of Inacom Corporation that management believed would help Compaq reduce inventories, speed cycle time, and enhance its capabilities to do business with customers via the Internet.

Carly Fiorina, who became HP's CEO in 1999, explained why the acquisition of Compaq was strategically sound:

With Compaq, we become No. 1 in Windows, No. 1 in Linux and No. 1 in UNIX . . . with our combined market position in servers, we will be able to engage the software community in building the applications that will drive demand for [Intel's] Itanium systems.

Compaq is the leading provider of storage systems in the world on a revenue basis. With Compaq, we become the No. 1 player in storage, and the leader in the fastest growing segment of the storage market—storage area networks.

With Compaq, we double our service and support capacity in the area of mission-critical infrastructure design, outsourcing and support. And while support is frequently considered the boring part of the services business, it produces mid-teens operating margins quarter after quarter. It's like the supplies business—more is better.

Compaq is No. 1 today in high-performance computing as a result of their Tandem acquisition. Between Himalaya, their fault-tolerant computing systems, and our own super-fast Superdome, we will have an incredibly powerful position at the high end of the server market. And we gain access to new customers and markets where fault-tolerant computing is required: national security, the military and the world's largest stock exchanges, for example.

Let's talk about PCs . . . Compaq has been able to improve their turns in that business from 23 turns of inventory per year to 62—100 percent improvement year over year—and they are coming close to doing as well as Dell does. They've reduced operating expenses by $130 million, improved gross margins by three points, reduced channel inventory by more than $800 million. They ship about 70 percent of their commercial volume through their direct channel, comparable to Dell. We will combine our successful retail PC business model with their commercial business model and achieve much more together than we could alone.

With Compaq, we will double the size of our sales force to 15,000 strong. We will build our R&D budget to more than $4 billion a year, and add important capabilities to HP Labs. We will become the No. 1 player in a whole host of countries around the world—HP operates in more than 160 countries, with well over 60 percent of our revenues coming from outside the U.S. The new HP will be the No. 1 player in the consumer and small- and medium-business segments. And in the enterprise space, this company will be able to compete for every single customer's business.

We have estimated cost synergies of $2.5 billion by 2004 . . . By 2003, the PC and personal devices business will earn 3 percent operating margin, which more than returns its cost of capital and generates substantial cash. Our enterprise business will earn 9 percent, and our services business will earn 14 percent. All in all, the company will generate $1.5 billion of cash flow net of capital expenditures every quarter.

It is a rare opportunity when a technology company can advance its market position substantially and reduce its cost structure substantially at the same time. And this is possible because Compaq and HP are in the same businesses, pursuing the same strategies, in the same markets, with complementary capabilities.

However, HP's acquisition of Compaq was met with considerable skepticism from both industry analysts and investors. Opponents pointed out that no large mergers of technology companies had proved successful and delivered the promised benefits. The

Exhibit 8   PERFORMANCE OF HEWLETT-PACKARD'S FOUR MAJOR BUSINESS GROUPS, FISCAL YEARS 2000–2002 (IN BILLIONS OF DOLLARS)

	Printing and Imaging	Personal Computing Systems*	Enterprise Systems†	HP Services
2002 (fiscal year ending October 31)				
Net revenue	$20,324	$14,733	$11,400	$9,095
Operating income (loss)	3,249	(401)	(968)	1,022
Inventories	3,136	843	1,188	629
2001 (fiscal year ending October 31)				
Net revenue	$19,426	$10,117	$ 8,395	$6,124
Operating income (loss)	1,849	(412)	(291)	647
Inventories	3,433	602	843	342
2000 (fiscal year ending October 31)				
Net revenue	$20,346	$12,008	$ 9,628	$5,730
Operating income (loss)	2,523	335	660	578
Inventories	3,475	685	1,080	337

*Includes desktop and notebook PCs, workstations, handheld PCs, and DVD drives.
†Primarily composed of servers and storage devices.
Note: The figures for 2002 include data for Compaq Computer only for the period May 3 through October 31, 2002, the end of HP's fiscal year.
Source: HP's 2002 10K report.

PC businesses of both companies were unprofitable, and skeptics doubted that combining the two would produce a profitable business capable of competing effectively with Dell. In 2001–2002, Compaq was struggling to make a success of several prior acquisitions and was losing market share in many market categories—its revenues in 2001 were almost $9 billion below revenues in 2000. Many also saw the merger as likely to divert management attention and resources away from HP's core imaging and printing business, which generated the bulk of HP's profits.

HP completed its acquisition of Compaq on May 3, 2002, producing a company with combined annual revenues close to $82 billion and transforming HP into a company with four major business groups: imaging and printing; personal computing systems (desktop and notebook PCs, workstations, handheld PCs, and DVD drives); enterprise systems (composed primarily of servers and storage devices); and IT services—see Exhibit 8 for the performance of these four segments. As of December 2002, HP management had moved aggressively to cut the size of the combined workforces by 17,900 employees (versus a previously announced cut of 15,000) and expected to achieve cost savings of $3 billion in 2003, a year ahead of initial plans. Going into 2003, HP management believed the integration was solidly on track, beating or meeting all its integration milestones to date. Outsiders, however, had heard anecdotal reports of infighting among the various camps in the new company.[26]

HP reported total revenues of $56.6 billion and losses of $903 million for fiscal 2002, versus revenues of $45.2 billion and net profits of $408 million for fiscal 2001. HP had sales of $48.9 billion and net profits of $3.9 billion in 2000. The combined revenues of HP and Compaq in 2002, however, were running close to 10 percent below comparable 2001 levels, indicating that HP and Compaq products were losing ground in the marketplace.

In the fourth quarter of 2002, HP had an estimated 16.1 percent worldwide share of PC sales, versus 15.7 percent for Dell, 5.8 percent for third-place IBM, 4.3 percent for Fujitsu Siemens, and 3.3 percent for NEC. In the United States, HP had a 20.8 percent share, versus 29.2 percent for Dell. Analysts believed that HP retook the top spot in the 2002 fourth quarter because HP's strong presence in retail stores gave it an advantage over Dell in selling to holiday shoppers and because it had aggressive promotions and price cuts. An HP marketing official said, "HP is attacking Dell on price and beating them with new and innovative products. We're growing faster than the market and gaining share across all regions and categories. [Dell] can no longer claim price as a competitive advantage. The momentum is clearly with HP."[27]

While it was true that HP's performance in the fourth quarter of 2002 was better than in the third quarter and might reflect growing momentum on HP's part, its fourth-quarter 2002 revenues for its Personal Computing Systems group were still about 8 percent below what HP and Compaq had achieved in the fourth quarter of 2001. Statistics released by both International Data Corporation and Gartner Research showed HP losing market share in the fourth quarter of 2002 compared to what HP and Compaq enjoyed in the fourth quarter of 2001, with Dell's fourth-quarter 2002 share about 20 percent higher than its fourth-quarter 2001 share. What was most encouraging about HP's fourth-quarter performance was management's report that the company had been able to narrow its losses in Personal Computing Systems by year-end 2002 to a −1.7 percent operating margin, reduce total channel inventories to 4.3 weeks, and improve distribution efficiency.

Going into 2003, Hewlett-Packard was

- Number one globally in imaging and printing.

- Number one globally in personal computers (based on fourth-quarter 2002 statistics reported by Gartner Research).

- Number one globally in Unix, Windows, and Linux servers.

- Number one globally in enterprise storage (with revenues about 35 percent greater than the number two vendor as of mid-2002).

- Number one globally in management software.

- Number three globally in IT services.

HP management saw IBM, not Dell, as its biggest competitor.

In an effort to gain market momentum and prove that the Compaq acquisition was going to prove successful, HP had recently introduced a number of new products, including a tablet PC, a media center PC, new iPAQ Pocket PC designs, new monitors, a first-ever mobile workstation, and two Intel Itanium 2–based workstations that would support Unix, Windows, and Linux.

In January 2003, Carly Fiorina provided her take on developments in the world IT market and HP's future strategy and prospects:

> The value proposition for IT has to change. . . . This industry has been focused on a cyclical economic environment. And we all know that the cyclical economic environment means that there have been substantial declines in growth rates; that smaller start-up players have been struggling to survive; and that in fact, consolidation in the IT industry is happening.
>
> . . . The market trends that we are seeing today are not being driven by cyclical economics, although clearly that's going on. I believe what we're really seeing in the IT industry today is being driven as much by changes in customer

requirements . . . customer requirements are no longer simply about the fastest, hottest box. Customer requirements are no longer simply about the latest killer app. They are no longer about what's the next big thing, or the next coolest piece of technology. Customers are focused on something much more fundamental and much more practical, and that is: How do I get a better return on my technology investment? How do I get real value? How do I make sure that I can live with, not only the initial costs, but the ongoing costs of owning and operating technology?

And just as important, you want to know: do I as a customer, have freedom? Can I choose the pieces I want? Can I make sure that I stay in control of my environment and in control of my investment? How do I stay in control of what is core to my business, because in fact the last thing I want to do as a customer is to hand the keys of the kingdom over to someone else? How do I make sure I have freedom of choice?

So, in the midst of all this change, and in the face of those fundamental, practical, and profound requirements, what is it that HP is focused on?

Our strategy—our investment—our commitment, are focused around four fundamental principles; first, that we will be the company that provides the best return on information technology (RoIT). And by the best return on information technology, we deliver on that commitment through our products, our people, our services, and importantly, our partners. And by return on information technology, what we mean is lowest total cost of ownership, improved productivity, better manageability, better interoperability, reduced complexity, improved reliability, and security.

And we think we come to the table with a portfolio that differentiates us from our competitors and uniquely positions us to meet those goals. Today, we [are] the number one company in supercomputing; number one in network management capability through our OpenView platform and professional services; number one in servers—in Windows and Linux and UNIX; number one in storage; number one in imaging and printing at a time when imaging and printing are critical to [customers'] infrastructure as [they] digitize [their] processes; number one in laptops and PCs; and a leader in IT services.

Our portfolio today runs from desktop to print shop; from palmtop to nonstop computing systems; from printers that sell for $49.99—and by the way, those $49.99 printers have 100 patents associated with them and drop 18 million drops of ink a second, proving that hi-tech and low cost can go together—everything from $49.99 printers to multimillion dollar commercial publishing systems.

That portfolio has helped us become the number one consumer IT company in the world; the number one small- and medium-business technology company in the world; and the number one or two enterprise IT technology company in the world—depending on how you count . . . We believe it is factually accurate to say that we are the leading technology company in the world.

For a company that does 60 percent of its business outside the United States . . . we believe it is an advantage for our partners and for our customers that we have capabilities in 160 countries, that we do business in 43 currencies and 15 languages around the world . . . More than one billion people around the world use HP technology every day.

For our consumer customers, as our second principle, we're focused on providing what we would call simple, rewarding experiences—technology and solutions that are simple to own, simple to buy, simple to operate, and provide rewarding experiences that make consumers' lives more productive, more communicative, more fun, and more valuable.

Our third principle is to deliver world-class cost structures and world-class capabilities. We believe we are the company that provides the best technology at the lowest cost with the best total customer experience.

. . . In the last six months of 2002, we introduced more than one hundred new products and added 1,400 patents, bringing our patent portfolio to over 17,000 worldwide. This happens to be the fastest rate of innovation as measured by product introduction and patent generation in HP history.

We believe that open, standards-based modular building blocks are the surest way to lower acquisition costs. And that is why you have seen us—and will continue to see us—invest heavily to make sure that our product line is the most modular, the most standards-based in the industry, because we think modularity and openness gives you flexibility and choice.

You'll also see us stick to an engineering paradigm that bets on heterogeneity and a diverse technology environment . . . [Customers] are going to see us continue to invest in being the leading platform provider for NT, for UNIX and Linux platforms. Because we think all three are critical in building out an IT infrastructure.

We . . . have a standards-based building block approach to systems design in engineering—again, in everything from computing to storage.

We're focused on providing the best price/performance curve—hi-tech, low cost.

HP ships more Linux servers than anyone else in the world. Our Linux business is now a $2 billion business annually inside HP. We partner with Oracle as well as SAP on Linux. And we think we have a lead in Linux for sure in the high-performance technical computing realm. Importantly, we have the most comprehensive set of service offerings in Linux, and frankly, we think it is the service offerings as well as our technology that set us apart when we are competing on Linux opportunities. We don't see a company like Dell, for example, in the competition really at all because of the importance of the service and support offerings.

. . . We have been a leader in standards for many, many years, and have about 700 people who work in about 300 different standards organizations around the world, and we think we clearly have one of the largest and most effective standards programs in the industry. We are really focusing our standards efforts and the participation in these standards bodies in areas like improved compatibility and interoperability, because it is compatibility and interoperability that is critical to giving you the flexibility and adaptability and economic benefit that you're looking for.

We at HP are very excited about where we are today. Fundamentally, we think we have a very different set of investments and approaches to the marketplace than our competitors, and we believe that freedom of choice, adaptability, and the best return on information technology is what [customers] want and where we have an advantage.

We want to be the company that gives [customers] the best technology, at the lowest cost with the best total customer experience. That is the strategy that HP is focused on. That is the value we are delivering today in the marketplace.

Exhibit 9   IBM'S PERFORMANCE BY BUSINESS SEGMENT, 2001–2002 (IN BILLIONS OF DOLLARS)

Business Segment	External Revenues	Pretax Income (Loss) from Continuing Operations
2002		
Global services	$36,360	$3,657
Enterprise systems	12,646	1,561
Personal and printing systems	11,049	57
Technology	3,935	(1,057)
Software	13,074	3,556
Global financing	3,203	955
Enterprise investments	1,022	(293)
2001		
Global services	$34,956	$5,161
Enterprise systems	13,743	1,830
Personal and printing systems	11,982	(153)
Technology	5,149	177
Software	12,939	3,168
Global financing	3,407	1,143
Enterprise investments	1,118	(317)

Source: IBM press release, January 16, 2003.

IBM

IBM was seen as a "computer solutions" company and had the broadest and deepest capabilities in customer service, technical support, and systems integration of any company in the world. IBM's Global Services business group was the world's largest information technology services provider. IBM had 2002 sales of $81.2 billion and earnings of $3.6 billion versus 2001 revenues of $83.1 billion and profits of $7.7 billion. Its two biggest and best performing businesses were software and services (see Exhibit 9). Once the world's undisputed king of computing and information processing, IBM was struggling to remain a potent contender in PCs, servers, storage products, and other hardware-related products. Since the early 1990s, IBM had been steadily losing ground to competitors in product categories it had formerly dominated. Its recognized strengths—a potent brand name, global distribution capabilities, a position as the longtime global leader in mainframe computers, and strong capabilities in IT consulting services and systems integration—had proved insufficient in overcoming buyer resistance to IBM's premium prices. Many of its former customers had turned to lower-priced vendors—the old adage "No one ever got fired for selecting IBM products" no longer applied. IBM's revenues had been essentially flat to down for the past five years.

Believing that open architectures and common standards were inevitable in the years to come, IBM management had begun turning the company away from dependence on its proprietary products and technology, where it had made its name and reputation, and toward standardized products and technologies in the mid-1990s. Even so, no cohesive strategic theme really stood out at IBM during the 1995–2002 period beyond that of growing its revenues from services and software as the company's business in hardware products eroded. To offset its declining share of PC and server sales, in 1998 and 1999 IBM moved to boost its R&D and manufacturing efforts to become a leading global supplier of computing components (hard drives and storage devices) and microelectronics products. It signed a long-term agreement with Dell to supply over $7 billion in components in 1999 and had increased its sales of parts and components to other PC makers as well.

IBM's Troubles in PCs   IBM's market share in PCs was in a death spiral—it had lost more market share in the 1990s than any other PC maker. Once the dominant global and U.S. market leader, with a market share exceeding 50 percent in the late 1980s and early 1990s, IBM was fast becoming an also-ran in PCs, with a global market share under 6 percent in 2002. Its last stronghold in PCs was in laptop computers, where its ThinkPad line was a consistent award winner on performance, features, and reliability. The vast majority of IBM's laptop and desktop sales were to large enterprises that had IBM mainframe computers and had been long-standing IBM customers. IBM's PC group had higher costs than rivals, making it virtually impossible to match rivals on price and make a profit.

IBM distributed its PCs, workstations, and servers through reseller partners, but used its own sales force to market to large enterprises. IBM competed against rival hardware vendors by emphasizing confidence in the IBM brand and the company's long-standing strengths in software applications, IT services and support, and systems integration capabilities. IBM had responded to the direct sales inroads Dell had made in the corporate market by allowing some of its resellers to economize on costs by custom-assembling IBM PCs to buyer specifications.

Gateway

Gateway, a San Diego–based company (recently relocated from South Dakota), had 2002 revenues of $4.2 billion (down from $6.1 billion in 2001) and a net loss of $309 million (an improvement over the loss of $1.03 billion in 2001). Gateway's all-time peak revenues were $9.6 billion in 2000 and its peak-year profits were $428 million. Founder, chairman, and CEO Ted Waitt, 41, owned over 30 percent of the company. Waitt had dropped out of college in 1985 to go to work for a computer retailer in Des Moines, Iowa; after nine months, he quit to form his own company. The company, operating out of a barn on his father's cattle ranch, sold add-on parts by phone for Texas Instruments' PCs. In 1987, the company, using its own PC design, started selling fully equipped PCs at a price near that of other PC makers. Sales took off, and in 1991 Gateway topped the list of *Inc.* magazine's list of the nation's fastest-growing private companies. The company went public in 1993, achieving sales of $1.7 billion and earnings of $151 million. The company had differentiated itself from rivals with eye-catching ads; some featured black-and-white-spotted cows, while others featured company employees (including one with Waitt dressed as Robin Hood). Gateway, like Dell, built to order and sold direct.

Gateway entered the server segment in 1997. In 1999, the company became the first PC maker to bundle its own Internet service with its PCs. To promote the Gateway name in the retail marketplace, the company had opened 280 Gateway Country Stores—227 in the United States, 27 in Europe, and 26 in the Asia-Pacific region—that stocked Gateway PCs and peripheral products and that conducted classes for individuals and businesses on the use of PCs. It had also launched an online software and peripheral Web store with more than 30,000 products.

Gateway's strength had traditionally been in the consumer segment. Going into 2000, Gateway was the number one seller of PCs to consumers, but it lost its lead over the next two years to Dell Computer. In 2001–2002, Gateway's top management began a series of initiatives to reverse the company's deteriorating market position; the company had:

- Closed its retail stores in Canada, Europe, the Middle East, Africa, and the Asia-Pacific region, along with 70 underperforming U.S. retail locations.

- Combined its consumer and business sales organization into a single unit.

- Focused its sales and marketing efforts on consumers, small and medium-sized businesses, educational institutions, and government.

- Consolidated its manufacturing operations and call center operations, paving the way for a 50 percent cutback in its workforce in 2001. Manufacturing operations in Ireland and Malaysia were closed, and all production was moved to the company's two existing plants in South Dakota and Virginia. Further cutbacks to reduce the workforce from 14,000 to 11,500 employees were announced in early 2002.

- Supplemented its sell-direct distribution strategy by stocking a limited inventory of prebuilt Gateway PCs in its retail stores that customers could take home immediately.

- Improved its offering of digital cameras, music, and videos and actively marketed broadband Internet services to its customers via alliances with a number of cable broadband Internet access providers.

- Worked with third-party financing partners to provide financing for businesses and consumers to purchase gateway PCs.

- Introduced a sleek new line of desktop and notebook PCs with industry-leading features. Gateway's notebook sales in 2002 outpaced the U.S. market, growing by approximately 16 percent. Gateway's desktop PCs earned numerous awards, including *Computer Shopper*'s "Best PC Line of the Year" in 2002 for the Gateway 700 Series, *PC World*'s "Best Buy" in the office PCs value category for the Gateway 500S, and *PC Magazine*'s "Editor's Choice" in a round-up of value PCs for the Gateway 300S Value.

- Refreshed its spotted-cow box logo used since 1998.

- Expanded and improved its e-support, local support, and call centers—moves that boosted the company's already leading customer satisfaction rankings by 5 percentage points, according to Alliance Research.

- Started selling consumer electronics products made by other manufacturers in its retail stores, including digital cameras, MP3 players, and high-end plasma-screen TVs.

Going into 2003, it was unclear whether Gateway could become a strong contender in the domestic PC market. Its fourth-quarter 2002 results were disappointing: revenues of $1.06 billion (versus a best-case scenario of $1.2 billion) and shipments of only 720,000 PCs despite heavy advertising and aggressive pricing during a holiday-season quarter when its sales had typically been highest (Gateway had shipped 729,000 units in the traditionally weaker third quarter). Analysts believed that the company's retail stores were a "relatively expensive channel" that added about 10 percent to the company's cost structure.

Sun Microsystems

Sun's strength was in technical computing—it was the leader in high-end workstations and high-performance servers. But the Silicon Valley company, headed by pugnacious chairman and CEO Scott McNealy, was mired in difficulty in early 2003. Sales had nose-dived to $12.5 billion in fiscal 2002 (ending June 30) from an all-time high of $18.3 billion in fiscal 2001, and gross profit margins had dropped 20 percent. Fiscal 2002 losses were $587 million, down from record profits of $1.85 billion in fiscal 2000; in the first six months of fiscal 2003, Sun reported net losses of nearly $2.3 billion, partly due to write-offs and restructuring charges. Sun's stock price had fallen from its all-time high of $64 to around $3 per share in February 2003. According to a *Business Week* article:

> A fearsome posse of competitors, from Dell Computer to Microsoft and Intel, is battering its way into Sun's core market for computer servers, selling low-cost machines at a fraction of Sun's price. A few years ago, servers powered by Microsoft Windows software and Intel chips couldn't perform in the same league with Sun. Now they can. Worse, Linux's open-source software is making inroads into McNealy's market. It's created by legions of volunteers, and it's free—a price that's hard to beat. McNealy finds himself selling the tech equivalent of a Mercedes in a market of Honda buyers.[28]

Sun customer E*Trade Group had recently replaced 60 Sun servers costing $250,000 each with 80 Intel-powered Dell servers running Linux that cost $4,000 each.

Sun designed its own chips and wrote its own server software (called Solaris). It spent close to 18 percent of revenues on R&D, aiming at outcompeting rivals by having Sun servers and Sun software run superefficient networks better than rival brands of servers and software. It had cash and cash equivalents of close to $5 billion and had recently bought back $500 million worth of common stock, paid down its debt by $200 million (leaving it with long-term debt of $1.5 billion), and shaved about $600 million out of its supply chain (boosting its gross margins by about 5 percent). It had also begun outsourcing servers that ran on Linux, which Sun was selling at prices starting about $2,700. McNealy's goal was for Sun to have a 30 percent share of what was expected to be a $6.5 billion market for Linux-based servers in 2004. Sun's strategy was also to move bigger into services; the company had tripled the size of its service staff to 13,000 employees. In January and February 2003, Sun announced a blitz of new, high-performing server products at very competitive prices.

Michael Dell's View of Dell Computer's Prospects and Challenges

In a February 2003 article in *Business 2.0,* Michael Dell said, "The best way to describe us now is as a broad computer systems and services company. We have a pretty simple system. The most important thing is to satisfy our customers. The second most important thing is to be profitable. If we don't do the first one well, the second one won't happen."[29] For the most part, Michael Dell was not particularly concerned about the efforts of competitors to copy many aspects of Dell's build-to-order, sell-direct strategy. He explained why:

> The competition started copying us seven years ago. That's when we were a $1 billion business. Now we're [$36] billion. And they haven't made much progress to be honest with you. The learning curve for them is difficult. It's like going from baseball to soccer.[30]

> I think a lot of people have analyzed our business model, a lot of people have written about it and tried to understand it. This is an 18½ year process . . . It comes from many, many cycles of learning . . . It's very, very different than designing products to be built to stock . . . Our whole company is oriented around a very different way of operating . . . I don't, for any second, believe that they are not trying to catch up. But it is also safe to assume that Dell is not staying in the same place. You know, this past year we've driven a billion dollars of cost out of our supply chain, and certainly next year we plan to drive quite a bit of cost out as well.[31]

In a presentation at the University of Florida in the fall of 2002, Michael Dell explained how the company decided to move into new areas, usually in an effort to get a bigger share of its customer's expenditures on IT:

> We tend to look at what is the next big opportunity all the time. We can't take on too many of these at once, because it kind of overloads the system. But we believe fundamentally that if you think about the whole market, it's about an $800 billion market, all areas of technology over time go through a process of standardization or commoditization. And we try to look at those, anticipate what's happening, and develop strategies that will allow us to get into those markets. In the server market in 1995 we had a 2 percent market share, today we have over a 30 percent share, we're number 1 in the U.S. How did that happen? Well, first of all it happened because we started to have a high market share for desktops and notebooks. Then customers said, oh yes, we know Dell, those are the guys who have really good desktops and notebooks. So they have servers, yes, we'll test those, we'll test them around the periphery, maybe not in the most critical applications at first, but well test them here. [Then they discover] these are really good and Dell provides great support . . . and I think to some extent we've benefited from the fact that our competitors have underestimated the importance of value, and the power of the relationship and the service that we can create with the customer.
>
> And, also, as a product tends to standardize there's not an elimination of the requirement for custom services, there's a reduction of it. So by offering some services, but not the services of the traditional proprietary computer company, we've been able to increase our share. And, in fact, what tends to happen is customers embrace the standards, because they know that's going to save them costs. Let me give you an example . . . about a year ago we entered into the data networking market. So we have Ethernet switches, layer 2 switches. So if you have PCs and servers, you need switches; every PC attaches to a switch, every server attaches to a switch. It's a pretty easy sale, switches go along with computer systems. We looked at this market and were able to come up with products that are priced about 2½ times less than the market leader today, Cisco, and as a result the business has grown very, very quickly. We shipped 1.8 million switch ports in a period of about a year, when most people would have said that's not going to work and come up with all kinds of reasons why we can't succeed.[32]

On another occasion, Michael Dell spoke about the size of the company's future opportunities:

> When technologies begin to standardize or commoditize, the game starts to change. Markets open up to be volume markets and this is very much where

Dell has made its mark—first in the PC market in desktops and notebooks and then in the server market and the storage market and services and data networking. We continue to expand the array of products that we sell, the array of services and, of course, expand on a geographic basis.

The way we think about it is that there are all of these various technologies out there . . . What we have been able to do is build a business system that takes those technological ingredients, translates them into products and services and gets them to the customer more efficiently than any company around.

We only have about a 3 percent market share in the $800 billion-plus IT market, so we think . . . we've got a lot more opportunity going forward . . . It's a pretty exciting time to be in our industry and the opportunities are pretty awesome.[33]

Endnotes

[1]Quoted in "Dell Puts Happy Customers First," *Nikkei Weekly,* December 16, 2002.

[2]This was the term Michael Dell used in an interview published in the *Harvard Business Review.* See Joan Magretta, "The Power of Virtual Integration: An Interview with Dell Computer's Michael Dell," *Harvard Business Review,* March–April 1998, p. 75.

[3]Information posted on www.dell.com, February 1, 2000.

[4]"Michael Dell: On Managing Growth," *MIS Week,* September 5, 1988, p. 1.

[5]"The Education of Michael Dell," *Business Week,* March 22, 1993, p. 86.

[6]Quoted in Magretta, "The Power of Virtual Integration," p. 74.

[7]Magretta, "The Power of Virtual Integration," p. 75.

[8]Ibid., p. 76.

[9]Ibid.

[10]According to figures cited in Ken Belson, "How Dell Is Defying an Industry's Gravity in Japan," *New York Times,* December 8, 2002, Section 3, p. 4.

[11]Quoted in Neel Chowdhury, "Dell Cracks China," *Fortune,* June 21, 1999, p. 121.

[12]Magretta, "The Power of Virtual Integration," p. 79.

[13]"Michael Dell Rocks," *Fortune,* May 11, 1998, p. 61.

[14]Speech to Gartner Fall Symposium, Orlando, FL, October 9, 2002.

[15]Quoted in Kathryn Jones, "The Dell Way," *Business 2.0,* February 2003.

[16]Kevin Rollins, "Using Information to Speed Execution," *Harvard Business Review,* March–April, 1998, p. 81.

[17]Magretta, "The Power of Virtual Integration," p. 80.

[18]Keynote speech given on August 25, 1999, in Austin, Texas, at Dell's DirectConnect Conference.

[19]Remarks by Michael Dell, MIT Sloan School of Management, September 26, 2002; posted at www.dell.com.

[20]Quoted in the *Financial Times* Global News Wire, October 10, 2002.

[21]Quoted in *Investor's Business Daily,* September 6, 2002.

[22]"The Education of Michael Dell," p. 85.

[23]Based on data compiled and reported by International Data Corporation.

[24]"Can Compaq Catch Up?" *Business Week,* May 3, 1999, p. 163.

[25]More information on Digital's competitive position can be found in "Compaq-Digital: Let the Slimming Begin," *Business Week,* June 22, 1998.

[26]"HP Blames Economy, Not Merger, for Its Soft Sales," *Houston Chronicle,* August 28, 2002, Business section, p. 1.

[27]Quoted in *Investor's Business Daily,* January 17, 2003, p. A1.

[28]"Will Sun Rise Again?" *Business Week,* November 25, 2002, p. 120.

[29]Kathryn Jones, "The Dell Way," *Business 2.0,* February 2003; posted at www.business2.com.

[30]Comments made to students at the University of North Carolina and reported in the *Raleigh News & Observer,* November 16, 1999.

[31]Remarks by Michael Dell, Gartner Fall Symposium, Orlando, Florida, October 9, 2002; posted at www.dell.com.

[32]Ibid.

[33]Remarks by Michael Dell, MIT Sloan School of Management, September 26, 2002, and posted at www.dell.com.

Green Mountain Coffee Roasters, Inc.

Keith F. Moody
Pace University

Alan B. Eisner
Pace University

Green

Mountain Coffee Roasters, Inc., began selling coffee by the cup in 1981. As demand for its coffees grew, Green Mountain expanded into whole-bean sales via mail order and increased its number of retail cafés. By 1997, Green Mountain was operating 12 outlets in Vermont, Connecticut, Illinois, Maine, Massachusetts, and New York, which accounted for 10 percent of Green Mountain's revenue. In May 1998, Green Mountain announced it would close its company-owned coffee shops and focus its resources on developing its much-faster-growing wholesale business. While the retail coffee shops often helped stimulate consumers who tried and liked the coffees to subsequently purchase Green Mountain's brands at local supermarkets, the company felt that the sales and profits prospects at its retail stores made exit from retail distribution a wise course of action. Looking for a different way to stimulate consumer demand for its brand in supermarket channels, Green Mountain acquired 41 percent of Keurig, Inc., for approximately $14.4 million in April 2002; Keurig manufactured innovative one-cup brewing systems that were used primarily in providing coffee in business offices.

In announcing the results for fiscal year 2002, Robert P. Stiller, chairman, president, and chief executive officer of Green Mountain, said:

> While I am disappointed in our fourth-quarter and full-year results for fiscal 2002, I believe we have initiatives in place to return to double-digit growth in fiscal 2003. We have distinguished ourselves with our focus on both superior execution and being a responsible corporate citizen, and can now leverage these positions to competitive advantage. I am excited about our recent customer acquisitions. They solidify our plans to grow sales between 10 and 15 percent in fiscal 2003.

William G. Hogan, Green Mountain's chief financial officer, elaborated on the company's near-term prospects:

> In fiscal year 2003, we anticipate growth in coffee pounds shipped and dollar sales in the range of 10 to 15 percent. Earnings per share growth expectations also are expected to be in the range of 10 to 15 percent, prior to the noncash loss of our equity investment in Keurig, Incorporated. Based on newly received information from Keurig management, we now anticipate a full-year non cash loss in the range of $0.10 to $0.14 on our equity investment in Keurig, as compared

to our earlier expectation that the impact would be in the range of $0.07 to $0.10 for the year. We continue to believe in the strategic value and compelling potential of our investment in Keurig over the long term, despite this disappointing near-term setback, which is related primarily to higher than originally expected expenses in entering the home brewer market.

Company Background

In 1981, Green Mountain Coffee Roasters hung its shingle on the front of a small café in Waitsfield, Vermont. The company roasted and served premium coffee on the premises. The demand for Green Mountain's high-quality, freshly roasted coffee soon grew beyond the café's walls as restaurants and inns in the area asked for coffee and coffeemaking equipment. Green Mountain Coffee Roasters was soon in the business of wholesaling its coffees to restaurants and then grocers. Before long, out-of-state skiers at local ski resorts began asking if the café could send Green Mountain coffee to their homes in New York, Connecticut, Pennsylvania, and Florida; these requests spurred the company's entry into the mail-order business.

In 2003, Green Mountain was one of the leading U.S. specialty coffee companies, with sales of $100 million—see Exhibit 1 for a summary of the company's recent performance. It roasted 90 varieties and blends of high-quality arabica coffees, which it sold through a catalog mailed nationally; at the company's website (www.greenmountaincoffee.com); and at wholesale to some 6,700 customer accounts that included supermarkets, specialty food stores, convenience stores, hotels, restaurants, universities, travel and office coffee-service customers, and food-service companies. Sales were concentrated in New England, but the company was expanding its geographic

Exhibit 1   SUMMARY OF GREEN MOUNTAIN COFFEE'S PERFORMANCE, 1998–2002 (IN THOUSANDS, EXCEPT PER SHARE DATA)[a]

	2002	2001	2000[d]	1999	1998
Coffee pounds shipped[b]	13,504	12,408	10,871	9,004	7,739
Pound growth over prior year[b]	8.8%	14.1%	20.7%	16.3%	24.0%
Net revenues[b]	$100,000	$95,576	$84,001	$64,881	$55,825
Revenue growth[b]	4.6%	13.8%	29.5%	16.2%	30.1%
Income, continuing operations[b]	$5,970	$5,782	$4,153	$2,247	$340
Earnings per share (diluted)[b c]	$0.82	$0.80	$0.59	$0.32	$0.05
Total assets	$54,687	$34,496	$27,174	$23,878	$24,563
Total liabilities	$27,622	$15,896	$17,157	$12,196	$15,095
Debt/equity ratio	1.02:1	0.85:1	1.71:1	1.04:1	1.59:1
Equity	$27,065	$18,600	$10,017	$11,682	$9,468
Book value per share[c]	$3.97	$2.79	$1.61	$1.66	$1.34
Return on equity (TTM)[b]	26.1%	40.4%	38.3%	21.2%	3.4%

[a]Fiscal years end on the last Saturday in September.

[b]During fiscal 1998 the company discontinued its company-owned retail store operation. The above figures were restated to reflect results from continued operations.

[c]Prior years' results were restated to reflect 2-for-1 stock split effective January 11, 2001.

[d]The fiscal year ended September 30, 2000, was a 53-week year. All other fiscal years presented are 52-week years.

Exhibit 2   GREEN MOUNTAIN COFFEE'S PERCENTAGE OF SALES BY GEOGRAPHIC REGION, FISCAL YEARS 2001 AND 2002

Region	52 wks ended September 28, 2002	52 wks ended September 29, 2001	Full-Year Increase (in pounds)	Full-Year Percentage Increase
Northern New England (ME, NH, & VT)	29.5%	30.7%	149,000	4.0%
Southern New England (MA, CT, & RI)	22.4	23.9	37,000	1.3
Mid-Atlantic (NY, NJ, & PA)	24.4	21.7	558,000	21.2
South Atlantic	7.9	8.0	72,000	7.4
South Central	3.5	3.4	66,000	16.5
Midwest	2.2	2.3	8,000	2.9
West	2.6	2.1	86,000	34.1
Multi–regional	6.7	6.9	49,000	5.9
International	0.8	1.0	(37,000)	−26.6
Totals	13,097,000 pounds	12,109,000 pounds	988,000	8.2%

Note 1: Excludes coffee pounds shipped in the Consumer Direct Channel.

Note 2: The allocation by region of coffee pounds shipped to certain McLane Company, Inc., warehouses for distribution to convenience stores has been estimated. Since the second quarter of 2002, these estimates have been based on actual shipment patterns from each McLane warehouse to convenience stores.

Source: Green Mountain Coffee Roasters, Inc., 2002 annual report.

reach (see Exhibit 2). Green Mountain's wholesale customers resold the coffee in whole-bean or ground form for home consumption and/or brewed and sold coffee beverages at their place of business. Green Mountain's coffee products included single-origin, estate, certified organic, Fair Trade, flavored, and proprietary blends of coffee sold under the Green Mountain Coffee Roasters and Newman's Own Organics brands. Green Mountain purchased approximately 34 percent of its coffee from specifically identified farms, estates, cooperatives, and cooperative groups in fiscal 2002, and expected to increase this amount to as much as 40 percent in fiscal 2003.

The company carefully selected its coffee beans and then roasted the beans in small batches to ensure consistency and to maximize their taste and flavor differences. The company had developed specific roasting programs for each bean type to establish a Green Mountain "signature" for that bean type, which the company called its "appropriate roast." Management believed that the company's distinctive convection air roasting methods further enabled it to more exactly duplicate specific roasts, ensuring Green Mountain's ability to provide consistent taste profiles and to distinguish its coffees from those of other specialty coffee companies. Green Mountain nitrogen-flushed its packaged coffee and employed one-way valve bag packaging technology that provided a minimum shelf life of six months; this technology enabled Green Mountain to expand its distribution while maintaining its high standards for quality and freshness. The company's attention to quality control and distinctive flavors had resulted in strong customer loyalty to the Green Mountain brand. Green Mountain coffee was sold in a variety of packages, including whole-bean, fractional, and one-cup Keurig portions; the packaging equipment for Keurig K-Cup portion packs was owned by Green Mountain, and the company paid a royalty to Keurig for each K-Cup sold.

Exhibit 3   GREEN MOUNTAIN COFFEE ROASTERS' CORE VALUES AND BELIEFS

- **A passion for coffee**—We love great coffee, we make great coffees, and we work hard to ensure people have an outstanding coffee experience—anytime and anywhere they buy Green Mountain.
- **Performance**—We manage the business to create value for our customers and for our stockholders, and to build financial strength.
- **A destination workplace**—We strive to create an atmosphere that fosters teamwork, personal growth and a healthy work–life balance.
- **Social responsibility**—We share a commitment to improve the environment and to make our local and global communities better.
- **Ethics**—We act with honesty and integrity in all our actions and relationships.

Source: www.greenmountaincoffee.com, January 3, 2003.

Management described its commitment to customers in the following terms:

At Green Mountain Coffee, we are dedicated to providing the richest aroma and flavor, for the highest quality coffee experience. We travel the globe to purchase the finest coffees, small batch roast them to peak flavor, and vacuum package them fresh for your enjoyment.

We take our time . . . and taking our time has its own reward . . . perfect coffee. The company's strategic intent was "to be the leading specialty coffee company by providing the highest quality coffee and having the largest market share in its targeted markets while maximizing Company value." Green Mountain intended to achieve this objective by differentiating and reinforcing the Green Mountain brand and engendering a high degree of customer and consumer loyalty. Green Mountain's core values and beliefs are shown in Exhibit 3.

In October 2002, *Forbes* named Green Mountain as one of the "200 best small companies in America" for the third consecutive year. For 2002, Green Mountain was ranked 62nd overall, 27th by five-year average return on equity, and 13th by five-year earnings per share growth. To be included in the *Forbes* listing, companies had to have a five-year average return on equity of 5 percent or more, a minimum stock price of $5 per share, and a net profit of 5 percent or greater, excluding extraordinary and nonrecurring items.

Headquartered in Waterbury, Vermont, Green Mountain went public in September 1993 and was listed on the NASDAQ National Market under the stock symbol GMCR. Exhibits 4 and 5 present the company's financial statements. In 1999–2002, about 95 percent of Green Mountain's revenues were derived from its wholesale operations. Green Mountain had never paid a cash dividend on its common stock; top management anticipated that for the foreseeable future earnings would be reinvested in growing the business.

Retail Operations

In fiscal 1997, Green Mountain Coffee Roasters was operating 12 company-owned stores in Vermont, Connecticut, Illinois, Maine, Massachusetts, New Hampshire and New York, which made up approximately 10 percent of total revenues. However, by April of 1998, store sales were only 6 percent of total net sales companywide due to

Exhibit 4   GREEN MOUNTAIN COFFEE CONSOLIDATED BALANCE SHEETS, 2001–2002 (DOLLARS IN THOUSANDS)

	September 28, 2002	September 29, 2001
Assets		
Current assets:		
Cash and cash equivalents	$ 800	$ 979
Receivables, less allowances of $351 and $492 at September 28, 2002, and September 29, 2001, respectively	9,132	9,142
Inventories	5,876	5,876
Other current assets	789	707
Income taxes receivable	528	743
Deferred income taxes, net	546	738
Total current assets	17,671	18,185
Fixed assets, net	20,834	14,397
Investment in Keurig, Incorporated	14,491	151
Goodwill and other intangibles	1,465	1,546
Other long-term assets	226	144
Deferred income taxes, net	—	73
Total assets	$54,687	$34,496
Liabilities and Stockholders' Equity		
Current liabilities:		
Current portion of long-term debt	$ 3,193	$ 195
Accounts payable	6,271	6,099
Accrued compensation costs	1,031	1,682
Accrued expenses	1,271	1,664
Total current liabilities	11,766	9,640
Long-term debt	12,079	256
Long-term line of credit	3,130	6,000
Deferred tax liability	647	—
Commitments and contingencies		
Stockholders' equity:		
Common stock, $0.10 par value: Authorized 20,000,000 shares; issued 7,956,872 and 7,804,647 shares at September 28, 2002, and September 29, 2001, respectively	795	780
Additional paid-in capital	19,793	18,390
Retained earnings	14,648	8,678
Accumulated other comprehensive (loss)	(12)	(219)
ESOP unallocated shares, at cost—40,941 and 73,800 shares at September 28, 2002, and September 29, 2001, respectively	(1,109)	(2,000)
Treasury shares, at cost—1,138,273 and 1,137,506 shares at September 28, 2002, and September 29, 2001, respectively	(7,050)	7,029)
Total stockholders' equity	27,065	18,600
Total liabilities stockholders' equity	$54,687	$34,496

Source: Green Mountain Coffee Roasters' 2002 10K report.

Exhibit 5   GREEN MOUNTAIN COFFEE, CONSOLIDATED STATEMENT OF OPERATIONS, 2000-2002 (DOLLARS IN THOUSANDS EXCEPT PER SHARE DATA)

	Year Ended		
	September 28, 2002	September 29, 2001	September 30, 2000
Net sales	$100,000	$95,576	$84,001
Cost of sales	56,785	55,205	50,835
Gross profit	43,215	40,371	33,166
Selling and operating expenses	25,045	23,278	20,377
General and administrative expenses	7,490	6,972	5,887
Loss on abandonment of equipment	—	—	135
Operating income	10,680	10,121	6,767
Other (expense) income	(30)	39	48
Interest expense	(280)	(533)	(583)
Income before income taxes	10,370	9,627	6,232
Income tax expense	(4,138)	(3,845)	(2,079)
Income before equity in net earnings of Keurig, Inc.	6,232	5,782	4,153
Equity in net earnings of Keurig, Inc.	(262)	—	—
Income from continuing operations	5,970	5,782	4,153
Discontinued operations:			
Income on disposal of retail stores, net of income tax expense of $81 and $40 for the years ended September 29, 2001, and September 30, 2000, respectively	—	118	60
Net income	$ 5,970	$ 5,900	$ 4,213
Basic income per share:			
Weighted average shares outstanding	6,677,394	6,398,577	6,586,844
Income from continuing operations	$0.89	$0.90	$0.63
Income from discontinued operations	$0.00	$0.02	$0.01
Net income	$0.89	$0.92	$0.64
Diluted income per share:			
Weighted average shares outstanding	7,264,310	7,196,740	6,979,244
Income from continuing operations	$0.82	$0.80	$0.59
Income from discontinued operations	$0.00	$0.02	$0.01
Net income	$0.82	$0.82	$0.60

Source: Green Mountain Coffee Roasters' 2002 10K report.

elimination of the Plattsburgh, New York, store (for which the lease had expired); the temporary closing of two stores due to relocation; and flat sales at the remaining stores. Furthermore, the company's coffee-retailing operations were losing money and were a cash drain. Management opted to exit this part of its business, even though the stores had long been viewed as an important vehicle for getting consumers to sample Green Mountain coffee by the cup.

Growth Strategy

Green Mountain was focused on building awareness of its brands and profitably growing its business. Going into 2003, management believed the company could grow sales over the next few years in the range of 15 to 20 percent annually by increasing market share in existing markets, expanding into new geographic markets, and selectively pursuing other opportunities, including acquisitions. In recent years, the primary growth in the coffee industry had come from the specialty coffee category, driven by the wider availability of high-quality coffee, the emergence of upscale coffee shops throughout the country, and the general level of consumer knowledge of and appreciation for coffee quality—trends that benefited Green Mountain. The company also participated in special events to provide sampling opportunities to potential buyers and give its Green Mountain brand more visibility. A key component of management's growth strategy was to make Green Mountain coffees readily convenient and available for consumer trial by the cup at convenience stores, office coffee services, and food-service establishments, thereby spurring sales of Green Mountain coffees in supermarkets and specialty food stores. The National Coffee Association, in a study of its national coffee-drinking trends through 2002, stated that "79 percent of coffee drinkers drink coffee at home." In addition to its efforts to boost sales in its core geographic markets, the company was also introducing Green Mountain coffee in selected new markets across the United States, principally through office, convenience-store, and supermarket channels.

To promote catalog sales, Green Mountain focused solicitations on catalog customers who bought regularly, especially members of the company's "Coffee Club" who had customized standing orders for automatic reshipment. Recently, the company had begun pursuing ways to increase traffic on its website both to build brand awareness nationwide and boost direct sales to consumers where the company had a limited presence in supermarkets and specialty food stores.

Customers And Customer Service

Green Mountain had a strong regional presence in the Northeast and was gaining market share in other areas of the country. Major wholesale customers included the American Skiing Company alpine resorts, Amtrak, ARAMARK, ExxonMobil convenience stores (almost 2,000 locations), Fred Meyer Stores, Hannaford Bros. Supermarkets, Kash n' Karry food stores, Kings supermarkets, Nestlé Waters of North America, Price Chopper, Shaw's supermarkets, Sodexho, and Wild Oats (see Exhibit 6). Acquiring additional flagship customers was viewed as key to the company's geographic expansion strategy because such customers provided great visibility and sampling opportunities. Exhibit 7 shows the percentage of coffee shipments by sales channel.

Green Mountain primarily used in-house sales people to establish and service its wholesale accounts. There were 27 area sales managers and 6 regional sales managers assigned to geographic territories, reporting to a national sales manager. The wholesale territories were concentrated in the northeastern and mid-Atlantic states, as well as Florida, Illinois, and Michigan. In addition to geographic sales personnel, Green Mountain had a sales staff of 12 people focused on supermarket accounts, a sales group of 11 individuals dedicated to office coffee-service accounts, a national convenience-stores sales manager, an international sales account manager, and a national food-service manager. However, in the office coffee-service and food-service

Exhibit 6   GREEN MOUNTAIN COFFEE'S CHIEF WHOLESALE ACCOUNTS, 2002

Convenience Stores	Restaurants	Supermarkets	Office Coffee Services	Other Food Services
Mirabito Fuel Group dba Quickway	Aureole Restaurant, NYC	Fred Meyer— 130 stores	Allied Office Products	Amtrak, Northeast corridor
RL Vallee, Inc., dba Maplefields	The Culinary Institute of America	Hannaford Bros. —142 stores	ARAMARK Refreshment Services	American Skiing Company
TETCO	New England Culinary Institute	Kash n' Karry— 141 stores	BostonbeaN Coffee Company	Columbia University
Uni-Marts	The Harvard Club, NYC	Kings Super Markets—27 stores	Corporate Coffee Systems	Delta Express and Delta Shuttle
	Trapp Family Lodge	Price Chopper— 31 stores	Crystal Rock/ Vermont Pure Springs	New Jersey State Aquarium
		Roche Bros.— 13 stores	Perrier's Poland Springs	Stowe Mountain Resort
		Stop & Shop—322 stores (primarily coffee by the cup)	U.S. Coffee	
		Shaw's/Star Market—152 stores		

Source: Green Mountain Coffee's 10K report.

Exhibit 7   GREEN MOUNTAIN COFFEE, POUNDS SHIPPED (WHOLE BEAN AND GROUND), BY SALES CHANNEL, 2001-2002

Sales Channel	53 wks ended September 28, 2002	52 wks ended September 29, 2001	Full-Year Increase (in pounds)	Full-Year Percentage Increase
Supermarkets	27.2%	24.7%	603,000	19.7%
Convenience stores	29.6	29.0	400,000	11.1
Other retail	1.9	2.0	7,000	2.8
Restaurants	8.5	9.3	(3,000)	−0.3
Other coffee service distributors	22.4	24.2	24,000	0.8
Other food service	7.4	8.4	(43,000)	−4.1
Consumer direct	3.0	2.4	108,000	36.1
	100.0%	100.0%		
Total Pounds Shipped	13,504,000	12,408,000	1,096,000	8.8%

Note 1: Certain prior-year customer channel classifications were reclassified to conform to current year classifications
Note 2: Coffee pounds shipped to several of the former Frontier distributors have been reclassified from Other Retail and Other Food Service to the Supermarket channel to reflect the fact that most of the sales are to natural foods grocery stores.
Source: Green Mountain Coffee Roaster's 2002 10K report.

sectors, the company used the services of independent distributors who purchased coffee from Green Mountain for resale to wholesale customers. Management believed the use of such distributors provided access to those customers whose size or geographic location made servicing them directly economically inefficient.

Green Mountain generally provided wholesale customers with brewing, grinding, and related equipment and product displays at no charge; this "loaner equipment" was usually installed on the customer's premises by the company's internal or contracted service personnel. A customer also was assigned a service technician who serviced, repaired, and provided preventive maintenance and emergency service on such equipment. Additionally, for supermarket customers, Green Mountain employed a team of merchandisers to ensure that supermarket displays were clean and appropriately stocked. Most of Green Mountain's competitors did not provide such high levels of sales and equipment service support.

To support efforts to be responsive to customer needs and expectations, Green Mountain had established regional distribution centers to handle the dispatch of customer service calls and to supply coffee to its wholesale customers. Green Mountain had also established relationships with some of its vendors to drop-ship items directly from the vendor to the customer, thereby significantly decreasing shipping times and costs. The company had an online inventory system for its central and regional distribution centers to expedite customer service and improve its direct-store-delivery process and capability. Green Mountain attempted to maintain adequate inventory to satisfy customer demand and avoid backorders. Its online ordering application on its website was fully integrated with its enterprise resource planning system so that customers received instantaneous, electronic shipping confirmations for all online orders.

Green Mountain sought to educate its wholesale customers, employees, and vendor partners about the origin and preparation of coffee through a course comprised of a series of on-site training programs, tours, manuals, and hands-on learning experiences known as "Coffee College." The training effort covered growing and harvesting; coffee tasting and cupping; grinding, filtering, and brewing; roasting and packaging; and preparing coffee beverages. Over 500 employees of Green Mountain's customers attended Coffee College in fiscal 2002, primarily at the company's Java University located at the Waterbury, Vermont, headquarters. In addition, Green Mountain's catalog and website provided customers with an overview of the unique qualities of the different coffees from around the world and the various degrees of roast. They also provided updates on the current coffee crisis and its impact on coffee-farming communities.

Socially Responsible Business Practices

Green Mountain Coffee Roasters was dedicated to conducting business in a manner that balanced economic goals with environmental and social impacts on the local and global communities. The company believed that doing well financially went hand in hand with giving back to the community and protecting the environment. The company strived to make a positive difference in the communities where it operated and did business, contributing at least 5 percent of its pretax profit annually to support socially responsible initiatives, many of which it had supported for over 10 years.

In 1989, Green Mountain established an environmental committee composed of employees to explore how the company's commitment to "to actions consistent with an environmental conscience" should affect its business practices and to supervise the company's extensive on-site recycling program. In 1992, Green Mountain launched its line of Stewardship coffees, which were grown and harvested with proper care and respect for the land and the workers. Green Mountain employees traveled to coffee farms to evaluate the farm management and quality of the coffee; strong relations had been established with the growers of six Stewardship coffees in Hawaii, Mexico, Costa Rica, Peru, Guatemala, and Sumatra. In 1997 Green Mountain funded construction of a beneficio and hydro plant for 16 coffee-farming families in Peru. In the Oaxaca region of

Mexico, where the company's Organic Mexican Select coffee was grown, the company funded a Coffee Kids microlending project and a women's health care project for the early detection of cervical cancer. In 2001, Green Mountain provided support to the Productores de Cafe La Trinidad cooperative for construction of coffee-washing stations and an educational seminar for farmers.

The company was an active participant in a program whereby Fair Trade (certified by TransFairUSA) established price guarantees ensuring that the small-scale farmers who grew and processed these beans received a fair price for their efforts and were thus better able to care for themselves, their families, and their communities while reinvesting in the care and quality of their coffee. Fair Trade coffees accounted for 7.2 percent of the company's total coffee pounds shipped in fiscal 2002, up 22 percent from the previous year. Most of the Fair Trade coffees Green Mountain purchased from growers were certified as organic—this meant they were cultivated with natural gardening techniques like composting and terracing; grown entirely without pesticides, herbicides, or chemical fertilizers; and were almost always "shade grown" (interspersed with other plants) to preserve vanishing wildlife habitat and discourage erosion. Green Mountain also supported other efforts to improve the quality of life in coffee-producing countries. In the Aceh region of Indonesia, for example, Green Mountain provided seed funding to Gayo Organic Coffee Farmer's Association, which produced the company's Organic Sumatran Reserve coffee. This project was started in partnership with ForesTrade, a Vermont-based supplier of organic oils and spices. In fiscal 2001, Green Mountain committed funding for land purchase and construction of a community center. In addition to local quality-of-life improvements, these programs helped ensure that a stable supply of quality organic coffees would be available to Green Mountain to satisfy growing consumer demand.

Approximately 1,600 not-for-profit organizations in the United States benefited from the company's cash or coffee product donations in fiscal 2002. Under a program called Community Action for Employees (CAFE), Green Mountain encouraged its employees to perform volunteer work for nonprofit and community-based organizations on company time. In fiscal 2002, the company reimbursed 38 percent of its employees for 2,226 hours of community volunteer time, a 46 percent increase in participation compared to 2001.

Employee Development

Green Mountain Coffee Roasters strived to be a destination workplace for its employees. Management believed that dedication to employee training and development, as well as a highly inclusive and collaborative work environment, was vital to attracting and retaining the most highly performing, qualified, and motivated employees. The company offered numerous educational workshops and professional seminars; a leadership development program; a series of coffee-knowledge classes; other personal and professional development opportunities, including David Allen's GettingThingsDone; and personal financial planning.

An employee stock purchase plan was introduced in 2000. In conjunction with the introduction of this plan, Green Mountain initiated a series of business literacy trainings for all its employee-owners. The first three sessions concentrated on fundamental business concepts and how they applied to the coffee business, along with learning to understand financial statements. More recently, the company had rolled out Committed Engaged Owners (CEO) training to its managers and supervisors that focused on advanced financial statement literacy for non financial managers. In addition, there were staff development programs to provide employees with the motivation and ability to offer Green Mountain customers the very best quality in service, thereby fostering long-term relationships. The company also offered an educational assistance plan providing financial support to employees seeking to improve their skills through continuing education.

As of September 28, 2002, Green Mountain had 474 full-time employees and 55 part-time employees. It supplemented its workforce with temporary workers from time to time, especially during the peak November–December holiday season to service increased customer and consumer demand.

The Coffee Industry

Sales in the U.S. coffee market in 2002 were flat, despite growing popularity of specialty and premium-priced coffees. Regions with the fastest growth included Europe and Asia (particularly Japan). The United States, responsible for up to 80 percent of world coffee consumption during World War II, accounted for only 20 percent of world consumption in 2001—mainly because of rapid growth in coffee consumption in other parts of the world. Brazil had emerged as the second largest consuming country after the United States. In 1997 the total number of pounds of coffee consumed worldwide was more than double the level at the end of World War II.

According to marketing consultants Adrian Slywotzky and Kevin Mundt:

> What occurred was value migration . . . The majors' business designs—their customer selection, resource allocation, and growth strategies—were marred by an overly categorical definition of products and benefits, a limited field of competitive vision, and an obsolete view of the customer. New innovators implemented business designs that anticipated shifts in customer priorities ahead of the established three.
>
> Value migration occurred rapidly. The three majors held nearly 90% of the multi-billion-dollar retail market in 1987. Within six years, the gourmet, whole-bean roasters, Starbucks, and other regional cafés had collectively created nearly $1 billion in shareholder value, and together obtained 22% of the coffee market share. By the end of 1993, the approximate market value of the majors was $4 billion, down $1 billion from 1988. The majors failed to create a new design for their coffee business to respond to the trend. Instead, they reverted to price-cutting and coupons.[1]

During the 1980s and most of the 1990s, the three largest coffee marketers—Procter & Gamble, Phillip Morris/Kraft, and Nestlé—paid scant attention to the new specialty roasters and instead spent millions on advertising to maintain their brand shares in what proved to be a declining segment of the market. Discounting (and millions of coupons) did nothing to raise the prestige of their brands (see Exhibit 8). Despite constant price promotion, traditional coffee brands like Folger's and Maxwell House were supermarket loss leaders. The Big Three showed little signs of being threatened by the growing host of regional whole-bean roasters who were marketing their premium brands in supermarkets and specialty stores. Although the newly introduced premium-priced, gourmet regional and local brands (like Green Mountain) were experiencing double-digit growth rates, to the majors their total sales were minuscule

Exhibit 8   PROFILES OF THE BIG THREE COFFEE MARKETERS

Company	Market Share/Revenue	Brands
Procter & Gamble	35% of U.S. coffee market 4% of revenue from coffee sales $1.5 billion revenue from coffee in 1996	Folgers, High Point, Millstone, Brothers
Kraft	30% of the U.S. coffee market 2% of revenue from coffee $1.2 billion revenue from coffee in 1996	Maxim, Maxwell House, Brim, Sanka, Chase & Sanborn, Gevalia, General Foods International Coffees
Nestlé SA	10% of the U.S. Coffee market 0.9% of revenue from U.S. coffee sales $400 million revenue from U.S. coffee sales Largest coffee marketer in the world	Hills Bros, MJB, Nescafé, Taster's Choice

in what was a $5 billion industry. Having made several failed attempts at marketing gourmet coffee, the brand leaders assumed that gourmet coffee was a passing fad.[2]

In the United States, and increasingly abroad, the specialty coffee industry continued to grow in the 1990–2002 period. In 1998, industry sources estimated that total retail sales of specialty coffee would reach $5.0 billion in 2000, up from $1.5 billion in 1990. According to the Specialty Coffee Association of America (SCAA), sales of brewed, whole-bean, and ground specialty coffee totaled approximately $7.5 billion in 1999. In the United States, this new segment of the coffee industry accounted for 5 percent of the world's coffee output—diverting some fine coffees from European markets that were accustomed to high-quality beans.

An important aspect of the specialty coffee industry was its relative decommodification of coffee. Whereas the Big Three coffee marketers had focused their attention on attractive pricing and consistency of flavor and taste, companies in the gourmet coffee segment paid close attention to origin, quality, processing, and cultivation methods as relevant qualities of the bean. Gourmet coffee marketers had also broadened their offerings to include different roasts and grinds, thus creating a much richer, personal coffee landscape for premium coffee lovers.

As specialty coffee continues to grow in popularity and develop a bigger presence on retailer shelves, many regional companies were looking for expansion opportunities. According to one analyst, "Everyone's looking to see what company is going to be number two to Starbucks."[3] The major marketers like Procter & Gamble, Kraft, and Nestlé, recognizing finally that the gourmet segment was more than a fad, had introduced premium and gourmet versions of Folger's, Maxwell House, and Nescafé coffee brands—Green Mountain competed with the marketers of these brands in trying to "upsell" coffee drinkers to the specialty coffee segment. Procter & Gamble had also begun pushing its Millstone and Brothers brands (both gourmet whole-bean supermarket entries) and Quickava drive-throughs. Kraft had acquired General Foods International Coffees and Gevalia, the world's largest mail-order coffee business, with annual revenues of more than $100 million.

The Specialty Coffee Segment

Most specialty or gourmet coffees used mainly high-quality arabica beans. The arabica bean was widely considered superior to its counterpart, the robusta bean, which was used mainly in regular coffee. High quality arabica beans usually grew at high elevations, absorbed little moisture, and matured slowly. These factors resulted in beans with a mild aroma and a bright, pleasing flavor that was suitable for premium coffees.

The specialty coffee segment consisted of two distinct subsegments: whole-bean and ground coffee sold in packages for home, office, and restaurant consumption and fresh-brewed coffee sold by the cup in coffee bars like Starbucks, Seattle's Best Coffee shops, and hundreds of other coffeehouses that had sprung up in the last decade. Rapid growth in the patronage of specialty coffeehouses, which grew from 500 units in 1991 to over 12,000 outlets in 2000, was the primary driver of growing demand for gourmet coffees, which often retailed for $8 to $12 per pound. Mounting willingness on the part of affluent coffee drinkers to pay premium prices for top-notch coffees, both in packages and by the cup, had stopped a 30-year slide in overall coffee consumption in the United States. In 1998, 5 million more Americans reported drinking coffee than in 1997—almost half of all Americans reported drinking a specialty coffee drink in 1998. While the overall U.S. coffee market was stagnant, the specialty segment grew by 8 percent annually in the 1990s.

Whole-bean coffee had grown in popularity because coffee connoisseurs believed that grinding the beans at home and brewing freshly ground coffee resulted in better taste and flavor. According to the 1999 Gallup Survey on Coffee Consumption, nearly 36 percent of all coffee drinkers had purchased specialty whole-bean coffee for home consumption at least once in the three months prior to the survey. In the same survey, consumers stated that 33 percent of those whole-bean purchases were made at a retail price per pound of over $7.00. Most whole-bean specialty coffees for home consumption were purchased in supermarkets or neighborhood grocery stores. According to the 1999 Gallup survey, 61 percent of those consumers who had purchased such products did so most frequently in a supermarket or grocery store; other important purchase locations included specialty coffee stores (14 percent), mail-order catalogs or clubs (4 percent), and gourmet food stores (2 percent).

The specialty coffee industry was regarded as having significant profit potential. Specialty beans that retailed for up to $12 a pound could be purchased from growers in green or unroasted form for about $2 per pound in years when crop yields were good. However, adverse weather and growing conditions could produce sharp upward spikes in prices of coffee beans, especially premium and relatively scarce varieties. In recent years, green coffee prices had been under considerable downward pressures due to oversupply; Green Mountain executives believed this situation was likely to persist in the short term although they expected higher bean prices in 2003 and beyond than the record lows set earlier in 2002. The low coffee price ranges generally experienced in recent years were not considered high enough to support proper farming and processing practices for top-grade coffees, potentially endangering supplies of premium-grade beans. To protect their access to supplies of top-grade beans, many specialty coffee companies, including Green Mountain, had entered into long-term contracts to purchase needed supplies from the growers of high-quality beans. In addition, companies from time to time purchased coffee futures contracts and coffee options to provide additional protection when they were unable to enter into coffee purchase commitments or when the price of a significant portion of their committed contracts were not fixed.

The whole-bean specialty coffee category was highly fragmented on the supply side, with a host of new brands appearing on the market during the 1990s. Green Mountain's primary competitors in whole-bean specialty coffee sales included Gevalia, Illy Café, Millstone, Peet's Coffee & Tea, Seattle's Best, and Starbucks. In 2002, there were an estimated 500 smaller and regional brands that also competed in this category.

Starbucks: Green Mountain's Chief Competitor in Specialty Coffee

Starbucks had sales of $2.6 billion in fiscal 2001 and $3.3 billion in fiscal 2002 (ending September 29, 2002); net earnings in fiscal 2002 were $215.1 million, up from $181.2 million in 2001. Going into 2003, Starbucks was the leading retailer, roaster, and brand of specialty coffee in the world, with more than 6,200 retail locations in North America, Latin America, Europe, the Middle East, and the Pacific Rim. In addition to the coffees and coffee merchandise sold at its retail locations, Starbucks produced and sold bottled Frappuccino coffee drinks (through a joint venture with PepsiCo), Starbucks DoubleShot coffee drinks, a line of innovative Tazo brand premium teas, several flavors of superpremium coffee ice creams (distributed through a joint venture partnership with Dreyer's), whole-bean and ground packaged Starbucks coffees (distributed through an arrangement with Maxwell House and sold in supermarkets), and a line of music CDs. Sales at company-operated retail stores accounted for approximately 84 percent of revenues in both 2001 and 2002, with most of the remainder coming from sales of Starbucks coffees in supermarkets and grocery stores.

Starbucks' primary strategic objective was to establish Starbucks as the most recognized and respected brand in the world. The strategy was to achieve this objective by rapidly expanding the company's retail operations domestically and internationally, growing sales of Starbucks products distributed by its various strategic partners, and selectively pursuing opportunities to leverage the Starbucks brand through the introduction of new products and the development of new distribution channels. Starbucks' performance targets for fiscal 2003 were:

- To open at least 1,200 new stores in fiscal 2003.
- To grow sales 3 to 7 percent at its existing stores.
- To increase total revenues by approximately 20 percent.

For the next three to five years, the company was targeting revenue growth of approximately 20 percent per year, earnings per share growth of approximately 20 to 25 percent per year, and 10,000 stores worldwide in 60 countries by the end of fiscal 2005. Starbucks had a long-term global store target of at least 25,000 stores worldwide.

Starbucks began selling its whole-bean and ground coffees in vacuum packages in supermarkets and other grocery outlets in 1998 via a long-term licensing agreement with Kraft Foods, the parent of Maxwell House; Kraft managed all distribution, marketing, advertising and promotion for Starbucks Coffee in grocery, warehouse club, and mass merchandise stores. At year-end 2002, Starbucks Coffee was available in 18,000 supermarkets throughout the United States; it also had more than 5,600 institutional food-service accounts in business offices, educational institutions, and health care facilities.

Starbucks spent very little money on advertising, opting to build the brand "cup by cup" with customers and depending on word of mouth, the appeal of its retail stores, distinctive packaging, and prominent supermarket displays. It was the only marketer of gourmet coffees with national market coverage and was well on its way to becoming a global company. Starbucks' vision was to become the most recognized and respected brand of coffee in the world. To achieve this vision, the company's founder and CEO, Howard Schultz, believed the company had to challenge the status quo, be innovative, and take risks.

Recent Developments at Green Mountain Coffee

Green Mountain management believed that competition in the specialty coffee segment would intensify in upcoming years, especially in supermarket channels. To strengthen the company's position, management was aggressively pursuing new accounts and upgrading its product line. The company had recently signed a 10-year agreement to be the exclusive roaster, seller, and distributor of Newman's Own Organics Fair Trade Certified coffees. Six original coffees had been created, including a rare *flavored* Fair Trade organic coffee, Café Almond Biscotti; each was roasted from the finest organic arabica beans. The coffees were currently available to consumers via the company's catalog and Web store, and were scheduled for introduction in selected supermarkets nationwide beginning in early 2003. The addition of this line gave Green Mountain the broadest selection of Fair Trade organic coffees in the industry.

In the fall of 2002, Green Mountain formed a partnership with Wild Oats Markets, a leading national natural and organic foods retailer, to exclusively sell Green Mountain's 22 varieties of double-certified organic and Fair Trade coffee in its 73 nationwide Wild Oats and Nature's Stores' bulk coffee and coffee bar departments. The agreement made Wild Oats the leading organic Fair Trade coffee retailer in the United States.

Faced with flat sales of coffee in the office coffee-service (OCS) channel, Green Mountain in fall 2002 expanded its relationship with ARAMARK, a leading distributor in the OCS market, giving ARAMARK the right to distribute Green Mountain coffee to ARAMARK customers throughout North America. ARAMARK's Refreshment Services division provided more than 1 billion cups of coffee annually to customers at over 60,000 U.S. locations. Under the new agreement ARAMARK became an authorized distributor of the Keurig Premium Coffee Systems, with Green Mountain providing both K-Cups and Green Mountain coffee packets to ARAMARK for use in brewing machines that Green Mountain distributed nationwide. A K-Cup was a pre-portioned single-serve coffee cartridge used in conjunction with the Keurig coffee brewer to brew a cup of coffee in 30 seconds. The agreement made Green Mountain coffee the only branded coffee in ARAMARK's multi national distribution system that was available in both a single-cup portion pack system and in foil-sealed packets of ground coffee for use in conventional drip brewers. Green Mountain was one of four coffee roasters that manufactured and distributed the K-Cups used in Keurig coffee brewers—Keurig's core business was licensing OCS distributors to sell and distribute K-Cups and brewers to offices both nationally and internationally. Green Mountain was also supporting the testing of the Keurig single-cup brewer for the home market. Management viewed the company's partnership with Keurig as an important growth driver, accounting for the company's recent purchase of a 41 percent ownership stake.

In November 2002, Green Mountain's CEO, Robert Stiller, announced that Daniel R. Martin would join Green Mountain as vice president of sales and marketing in mid-December. At the time, Martin was vice president of marketing services at the Great Atlantic & Pacific Tea Company (A&P) and previously had been the General Manager of A&P's Eight O'Clock Coffee Company division from February 2001 until August 2002. From July 1988 to February 2001, Martin held roles in sales and brand management at Kraft Foods, including positions in the Maxwell House and Gevalia coffee divisions. Martin had served on the board of directors of the National Coffee Association and had an MBA from the Harvard Business School.

Endnotes

[1]Adrian J. Slwotzky and Kevin Mundt, "Hold the Sugar: Starbucks Corp.'s Business Success," *Across the Board* 33, no. 8 (September 1996), p. 39.

[2]Ibid., p. 39.

[3]Carl Peel, "Los Angeles, a Microcosm of the Country," *Tea and Coffee Trade Journal* 169, no. 4 (April 1997), pp. 16–28.

Ocean Spray Cranberries in 2003
At the Crossroads

Vincent Amanor-Boadu
Kansas State University

Michael Boland
Kansas State University

David Barton
Kansas State University

In late February 2003, Northland Cranberries, Inc., (NCI) made an $800 million offer to acquire Ocean Spray Cranberries (OSC), the market leader in the cranberry industry. Furthermore, a group of OSC grower–members won a lawsuit that enabled them to propose a new slate of directors that would be voted on at the March 8, 2003, annual meeting. The need to communicate a strategy for addressing the industry's profitability problem had become increasingly necessary in the last few years because of declining cranberry prices to levels not seen in the industry's recent history, and a mounting disaffection among OSC's grower–members. Despite OSC's desire to enhance its marketing efforts and balance fruit supply and demand, prices were still dismal as the 2003 winter came to an end and the disaffection among grower–members seemed to be increasing. Ocean Spray Cranberries was in a unique position of "working for its grower–members" in deciding to take steps to address the company's marketing difficulties and simultaneously ease the price pressure confronting its grower–members.

The Cranberry Industry

The Cranberry Marketing Committee (CMC), under Chapter IX, Title 7 of the Code of Federal Regulations, referred to as the Federal Cranberry Marketing Order, which was part of the Agricultural Marketing Agreement Act of 1937, was responsible for both regulating cranberry production to ensure stability in the industry and conducting cranberry promotions in several countries. The CMC regulated production in all 10 states in which cranberries were produced and handled, allotting production quotas to approximately 1,200 producers who sold to approximately 18 handlers and/or processors each year to manage supply and demand. The 10-state production area covered cranberries grown in Connecticut, Massachusetts, Michigan, Minnesota, New Jersey, Oregon, Rhode Island, Washington, Wisconsin, and Long Island in the state of New York.

Juice consumption had been increasing over time due to the introduction of new products and changes in consumer preferences. Although the cranberry industry was unique at the production level, its products competed in the marketplace with many

Exhibit 1   PER CAPITA CONSUMPTION OF FRESH CRANBERRIES AND CRANBERRY JUICE IN THE U.S., 1989 TO 2000 (IN POUNDS OF FRESH WEIGHT EQUIVALENT)

Year	Fresh	Juice	Total
1989	0.07	1.33	1.39
1990	0.05	1.27	1.32
1991	0.07	1.54	1.61
1992	0.07	1.50	1.57
1993	0.07	1.35	1.42
1994	0.08	1.70	1.77
1995	0.08	1.49	1.57
1996	0.08	1.59	1.67
1997	0.07	1.82	1.90
1998	0.08	1.88	1.96
1999	0.11	2.12	2.23
2000	0.14	1.78	1.91

Note: The pounds of fresh weight equivalent multiplied by 8.8 equals the number of gallons consumed per capita.
Source: Putnam and Allshouse.

other products, from beverages to confectionery ingredients. Beverage was the dominant product for the cranberry industry, but sauces and jellies were also important products and their challenges were no different from those confronting the beverage products (see Exhibit 1). The market was competitive, and cranberry products did not exhibit any uniquely advantageous characteristics over their competitors except during the holiday season, when cranberry sauce became a favorite. Thus, after more than three decades of active promotion and advertising, cranberry sauce and jelly were still not daily household food items. They were still in the same psychographic space as horse radish, spiced apples, and mint jelly (i.e., holiday items). As noted in research conducted for OSC in 1972, these products were "tradition-bound, almost synonymous with Thanksgiving and turkey."

Consumption of non citrus juices such as grape, apple, and cranberry had increased from 1989 to 2001, while that of pineapple had declined (see Exhibit 2). In general, however, non citrus juice consumption had remained flat during this time period. Citrus juices such as orange and grapefruit had seen increases in consumption over time.

There were three key components in understanding the cranberry industry: production, processing, and marketing and distribution. Events at each of these levels interacted to influence conditions in the whole industry. This case discusses each separately while looking at the broader industry structure.

Cranberry Production

Although cranberries were produced in 10 states, the concentration of production was in five states: Massachusetts, New Jersey, Oregon, Washington, and Wisconsin. Wisconsin dominated cranberry production, accounting for about 51 percent of average production between 1999 and 2001 (see Exhibit 3). Massachusetts and New Jersey together accounted for an average of 40 percent, with the remaining production in the Pacific Northwest states of Washington and Oregon. Despite the CMC's supply controls, the industry had been going through some tough times in the past decade. For

Exhibit 2   PER CAPITA FRUIT JUICE CONSUMPTION, 1989/90 TO 2000/01
MARKETING YEARS (IN POUNDS OF FRESH WEIGHT EQUIVALENT)

	Grape	Apple	Cranberry	Orange	Grapefruit	Prune	Pineapple	Total
1989/90	0.31	1.45	0.15	4.20	0.62	0.04	0.44	7.37
1990/91	0.28	1.72	0.14	4.65	0.41	0.04	0.50	7.89
1991/92	0.36	1.52	0.17	4.29	0.40	0.03	0.50	7.40
1992/93	0.38	1.57	0.17	5.19	0.59	0.04	0.48	8.60
1993/94	0.35	1.79	0.15	5.06	0.54	0.04	0.42	8.54
1994/95	0.29	1.79	0.19	5.38	0.64	0.04	0.35	8.82
1995/96	0.46	1.60	0.17	5.27	0.69	0.03	0.39	8.79
1996/97	0.39	1.72	0.18	5.38	0.62	0.03	0.39	8.89
1997/98	0.41	1.57	0.20	5.59	0.57	0.03	0.35	8.85
1998/99	0.28	1.83	0.21	5.26	0.61	0.03	0.29	8.64
1999/00	0.45	1.82	0.24	5.83	0.66	0.02	0.33	9.53
2000/01	0.35	1.85	0.20	5.25	0.68	0.02	0.31	8.89

Source: Putnam and Allshouse.

Exhibit 3   BARRELS OF CRANBERRY PRODUCTION BY STATE, 1993 TO 2002
(1 BARREL = 100 POUNDS)

	Massachusetts	New Jersey	Oregon	Washington	Wisconsin	Total
1993	1,880,000	386,000	156,000	137,000	1,360,000	3,919,000
1994	1,952,000	558,000	330,000	202,000	1,640,000	4,682,000
1995	1,592,000	454,000	170,000	177,000	1,800,000	4,193,000
1996	1,722,000	467,000	312,000	180,000	1,990,000	4,671,000
1997	2,100,000	580,000	350,000	165,000	2,339,000	5,534,000
1998	1,872,000	521,000	355,000	168,000	2,540,000	5,456,000
1999	1,875,000	700,000	328,000	147,000	3,307,000	6,357,000
2000	1,953,000	489,000	398,000	180,000	2,692,000	5,712,000
2001	1,416,000	566,000	365,000	142,000	2,840,000	5,329,000
2002	1,780,000	410,000	455,000	168,000	2,907,000	5,720,000

Source: USDA National Agricultural Statistics Service, Cranberries Report.

example, cranberry prices peaked in 1996, averaging about $65.90 per barrel, after being relatively stable through the first half of the 1990s (see Exhibit 4). Since 1996, average industry prices had fallen precipitously, reaching a low of $17.80 per barrel in 1999.

The source of the price pressure had been attributed to rapid production expansion by existing producers and new entrants attracted to the industry at a time when other crops were experiencing significant difficulties, as well as increasing productivity on cranberry lands (see Exhibit 5). Thus, unlike the mid-1990s when cranberry production was increasing and cranberry products' sales were increasing even faster, the late 1990s presented a situation where production was growing much faster than demand. Production expenses averaged about $35 a barrel.

Exhibit 4 AVERAGE CRANBERRY PRICE AND BARRELS OF PRODUCTION, 1993 TO 2001 (1 BARREL = 100 POUNDS)

	Price	Production
1993	$50.20 per barrel	3,919,000 barrels
1994	49.30	4,682,000
1995	53.40	4,193,000
1996	65.90	4,671,000
1997	63.70	5,534,000
1998	36.60	5,456,000
1999	17.80	6,357,000
2000	19.60	5,712,000
2001	22.90	5,329,000

Source: USDA National Agricultural Statistics Service, Cranberries Report.

Exhibit 5 AVERAGE HARVESTED ACRES OF CRANBERRIES AND YIELDS, 1993 TO 2001 (1 BARREL = 100 POUNDS)

	Acres of Cranberries Produced	Yield in Barrels per Acre
1993	29,400	133.3
1994	31,100	150.5
1995	32,800	127.8
1996	34,000	137.4
1997	35,700	155.9
1998	36,600	149.1
1999	37,500	169.5
2000	36,600	156.1
2001	34,200	155.8

Source: USDA National Agricultural Statistics Service, Cranberries Report.

With cranberry prices hovering at all-time lows and well below cost of production, the CMC decided to cut production by about 27 percent, from 6.3 million barrels in 1999 to 4.6 million barrels for 2001. To achieve this objective, the CMC allocated to growers only 65 percent of their historic sales, which was defined as the best four years out of the last seven (1994 to 2000). The production prevailing limits in 2000 and 2001 helped boost prices (see Exhibit 4). There were no production restrictions imposed in 2002 and cranberry prices fell once again.

Several years of low prices had created significant anxiety in the cranberry industry. In an industry where a marketing board controlled supply, many producers were unhappy with the way that supply controls had worked and had directed their anger at those organizations that purchased, processed, and marketed the cranberries. At the height of the crisis in 1999, the Associated Press reported Niles Porter, age 57, of Grayland, Washington, as saying, "It's going to weed out everybody if they don't do something about it real fast." Mr. Porter, who had been an OSC member for more than 14 years, lamented that "Ocean Spray told us all along that its growers would be protected from any downfalls that were created in prices, and we'd be all right. The independents would be the ones that would suffer."[1] Other processors and handlers had been accused of putting undue pressure on producers by reducing prices in the middle of contracted delivery periods. Several of these accusations led to lawsuits, some of which resulted in substantial settlements, confirming growers' belief that they lacked bargaining power in the current structure of the industry.

The increasing recognition of lack of negotiating leverage when entering into contracts with processors and handlers led some growers to break away from existing farmer-owned cooperatives such as OSC and form new cooperatives. For example, the Wisconsin Cranberry Cooperative (WCC), formed in 2001 with 70 growers, aimed to develop "strategic options to save the family-scale cranberry farms" by (1) raising industry prices and returning a larger share of margin dollars to growers; (2) creating a collective bargaining agency; and (3) potentially developing high-value cranberry products in niches ignored by the large processors.[2] Other producers exited the industry, transforming their "bogs into fish farms." Finally, some producers began to more fully understand the marketing strategies of their cooperative-owned processing companies and how they affected their own financial performance.[3] Still other producers expanded in an attempt to make up for lower prices with volume. In short, the cranberry industry was undergoing significant changes as producers dealt with the industry pressure on profit margins.

Cranberry Processors

There were two distinct markets for cranberries: fresh and processed. The fresh market comprised cranberries sold directly to consumers for consumption without processing and was not subject to most of the CMC's supply restrictions. The processed cranberry market included juice, powdered, dried, and sliced cranberries, as well as sauces and jellies (see Exhibit 6). Exhibit 7 shows the major cranberry processors and their product groups. With the exception of American Cranberry Company, a New Jersey–based company that was involved only in fresh and frozen cranberries, all other companies were involved in three or more categories of products. Ocean Spray, for example, participated in 9 of the 10 products, the exception being dried unsweetened, while Northland Cranberries, based in Wisconsin, was involved in six product groups.

Since OSC was the dominant player in the industry, controlling more than 50 percent of the U.S. cranberry beverage market, it had been held responsible by many for the industry's production-price crisis. This criticism may have been unfounded since OSC had tried to control production in the early 1990s and its efforts had been thwarted by independent handlers in the industry who saw an opportunity to increase their market share. Some paid premiums of 20 to 30 cents per pound over OSC's price, attracting production and causing some growers to sever their relationships with OSC. The result of this competition was a reduction in OSC's share of the production market, from 85 percent to 43 percent, in a very short time. The loss of market share for OSC contributed to a loss of the production stability that had prevailed in the industry for much of its history.

Although these processors competed in moving their products through retail and distribution, they collaborated to enhance the competitive position of the cranberry category against other products such as beverages, jellies, or sauces. This collaboration was done through the marketing efforts of the CMC. For example, in its April 2002 international market report, the CMC's German agency illustrated the generic promotion of U.S. cranberries in Germany, from newspaper interviews of experts promoting

Exhibit 6   Major Cranberry Product Categories

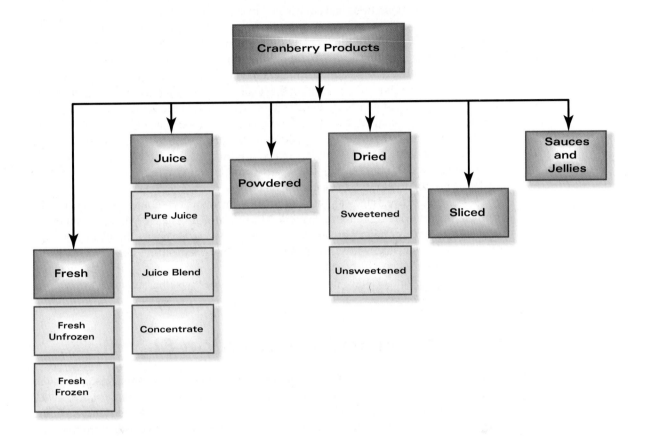

Exhibit 7   MAJOR CRANBERRY PROCESSING COMPANIES AND THE PRODUCT CATEGORIES IN WHICH THEY PARTICIPATED

Cranberry Processing Companies	Fresh	Frozen	Juice	Juice Blends	Juice Concentrates	Powdered	Dried Sweetened	Dried Unsweetened	Sliced	Sauce
American Cranberry Company	•	•								
Clement Pappas Company, Inc.	•		•	•						•
Cliffstar Corporation			•	•	•	•				
Decas Cranberry Sales	•	•			•	•	•		•	
Halls Cape Cod Cranberries	•	•						•		
Northland Cranberries, Inc.	•	•	•	•	•					•
Ocean Spray Cranberries, Inc.	•	•	•	•	•	•	•		•	•
Oregon Cranberry Company	•	•								
Urban Processing						•	•	•	•	
Welch Foods, Inc.			•	•						
Wisconsin Cranberry Cooperative	•	•					•			•

"U.S. cranberry juice" consumption to address urinary tract infections to sending samples of dried sweetened cranberries to "test kitchens" of women's magazines.

The market conditions had contributed to significant competition among the major processors in the domestic market. Ocean Spray and Northland Cranberries, Inc., the only publicly traded cranberry processor, accounted for more than 80 percent of raw cranberry intake. In the late 1990s, OSC had lost market share to Northland in the juice category. In 1999, at the height of the cranberry supply glut and seeking to take advantage of research results indicating the health benefits of cranberries, Northland introduced 27 percent cranberry juice content across all its blends. It also introduced a seal to promote its new formulation. It was thought that OSC would follow suit to contribute to increased cranberry utilization to reduce inventory and address the price problem. However, Donald Hatton, then board chair of OSC, noted that the Northland experiment was not as "successful as we would have expected," intimating that the surplus had led to a price war within the industry.

The general feeling was that the processing industry should focus on moving products—introducing innovative products and packaging, and creating consumer interest in cranberry juice, blends, and other products. This was the challenge confronting the industry, whose long-run success depended on the ability of its major processors to successfully deal with its long-running malaise. The challenge was daunting, given the changes that were occurring in the consumer marketplace vis-à-vis competitor products.

The Retail and Distribution Sector

Food retailers sought to maximize sales revenue per linear foot of shelf space. Products that generated high revenues per foot of shelf space were allocated more space. Moreover, the merchandising strategy of most retailers was to minimize product-sourcing costs and maximize product turnover. Minimizing procurement costs had led many retailers to develop specific alliances with various suppliers, and suppliers with multi-product lines had consistently maintained competitive advantage in these alliances. Thus, suppliers that could promise a "one-stop shopping experience" for retailers held an advantage over single-line suppliers. From that perspective, the ability of a food processor to have a varied product line and to gain shelf space for its products in many retail outlets was critical for success.

Although carbonated soft drinks dominated the beverage market, accounting for almost twice the share of fruit juices and drinks, the general consensus among industry watchers was that the growth area was in fruit juices. Cranberry products, especially juice and juice blends, competed for shelf space with various products in the carbonated and non carbonated soft-drink categories (see Exhibits 8 and 9). But while fruit juices enjoyed a niche for a long time as healthy and wholesome, a growing number of new and innovative products had emerged in the market, ranging from organic to "energy" drinks aimed at a youthful and health-conscious population. In the beverage supply industry, consolidation had achieved a mutual benefit for both the acquiring and the acquired companies: improved product slate and improved access. The major beverage companies such as Coca-Cola, PepsiCo, and Cadbury Schweppes developed strong multi product lines, including fruit juices, primarily through acquisitions.

Cadbury Schweppes acquired Snapple Beverage Group from Triarc for $1.45 billion in 2000, offering it increased access to the U.S. market and the non carbonated beverage market. It also acquired Nantucket Allserve, Inc., a leading fruit-content juice

Exhibit 8   MARKET SHARES OF TOP 10 U.S. NON CARBONATED BEVERAGE COMPANIES IN 2000

Company	Market Share
Coca-Cola	25.5%
Gatorade	20.0
PepsiCo	16.0
Triarc	7.9
Cadbury Schweppes	5.9
Arizona Tea	2.8
Ocean Spray	2.3
SoBe	2.0
Procter & Gamble	1.9
Veryfine	1.3

Exhibit 9   COMPARATIVE MARKET SHARES OF RETAIL BEVERAGES, 2000

Category	Market Share
Carbonated soft drink	38.9%
Non carbonated soft drink	8.2
Milk	23.8
Bottled water	6.7
Beer	5.5
Liquid tea	1.0
Liquid coffee	1.0
Fruit juice drink	15.9

producer. John Sunderland, CEO of Schweppes, commented on the acquisition as supporting "our strategy of participating in the high growth premium beverage market" and broadening "our portfolio of strong branded products."[4] Coca-Cola marketed Powerade, Fruitopia, and Minute Maid, all strong non-carbonated drink brands targeting different market segments.

PepsiCo acquired South Beach Beverage Company, manufacturer of the teen-focused SoBe fruit-flavored energy drinks. It had recently acquired Quaker Foods and Beverages, which owned the Gatorade line and brand, giving it increased complementarity in its beverage business. In addition, PepsiCo had acquired Tropicana Pure Premium, the third largest brand, after Coca-Cola Classic and Pepsi-Cola, from Seagrams. It also marketed Lipton ready-to-drink tea, Aquafina bottled water, and Fruitworks.

PepsiCo, since 1992, had been OSC's exclusive distributor for its single-serve (less than 20-ounce) products and by 1997, it was generating about $225 million in sales for OSC. The arrangement resulted in PepsiCo company-owned bottlers ceasing to handle juices of competing companies such as Welch's and Mott's. OSC also benefitted from the associated promotion, shelf space purchasing, and other services developed by PepsiCo. PepsiCo was exclusive distributor for OSC juice products until early 2001, when that relationship was terminated. This action had a dramatic effect on the fortunes of OSC.

The Company

Ocean Spray Cranberries was founded in 1930 when three producers joined forces to enhance their marketing activities. It was incorporated as an agricultural cooperative and focused on developing innovative cranberry products. Since its inception, the company had been active in developing and introducing new cranberry products. For example, it introduced Cranberry Juice Cocktail in 1930, becoming the first producer of cranberry juice drinks. In 1963, it introduced the first juice blend, Cran·Apple. The success of the juice blend led to the development of new flavors in OSC's product line. In 2001, it introduced white cranberry juice drinks and added two new flavors of Craisins (sweetened dried cranberries), a product introduced in 1995 that had enjoyed sustained success.

OSC diversified its membership to include grapefruit growers from Florida's Indian River region in 1976. The rationale for this expansion was to gain access to grapefruit for processing and increase OSC's ability to develop and market new and innovative juice blends. Ocean Spray grapefruit juice quickly became one of the leading bottled grapefruit juices in the country, as did Ocean Spray pink grapefruit juice cocktail, the very first citrus blend of its kind. Ocean Spray ruby red grapefruit juice drink was introduced in 1991, becoming the most successful product introduction in OSC history to that point. Following that, Ocean Spray introduced grapefruit juice drinks blended with strawberries, tangerines, and mangos, as well as a premium 100 percent ruby red grapefruit juice.

The company in 2002 accounted for more than 70 percent of cranberry production and processing in North America, with about 900 cranberry grower-owners (750 cranberry growers and 150 citrus growers), and 100 in Canada. Ocean Spray also had made investments in Cranberries Austral, SA, a small Chilean company, thereby expanding its reach in its bid to maintain leadership in cranberry procurement, processing, and marketing. The largest 50 growers produced almost 65 percent of OSC's cranberries.

OSC employed 2,000 people worldwide. This was relatively fewer than the number of employees it had before it started rationalizing its workforce in 1999. Sales per employee were estimated at about $565,000 on a gross basis, which compared with Coca-Cola's $544,500 and was more than twice PepsiCo's sales per employee of $200,000.[5] OSC had eight plants across the United States, seven of which processed cranberries and one (in Vero Beach, Florida) that processed grapefruit. The seven cranberry processing facilities' locations and principal activities were as follows: Middleboro, Massachusetts (juice concentrate, flavored drinks, fresh fruit packaging, and distribution); Carver, Massachusetts (receiving plant); Bordentown, New Jersey (flavored drinks, bottling, and distribution); Henderson, Nevada (flavored drinks, bottling, and distribution); Sulphur Springs, Texas (flavored drinks, bottling, and distribution); Kenosha, Wisconsin (juice concentrate, fresh fruit receiving); and Markham, Washington (juice concentrate, flavored drinks, and fresh fruit packaging).

The Kenosha plant was processing the white cranberry juice introduced by the company in 2001 and had also benefited from a $7 million expansion to facilitate its processing capacity for white cranberries. The Kenosha warehouse had increased its efficiency significantly through investments in information technology to help with inventory management and traceability. With the elimination of manual recording of code dates on the cases and the introduction of wireless technology, cases per labor hour increased from 451 to 550 and volume shipped increased by 1.8 million cases a year with 2,200 fewer labor hours.[6] The Kenosha warehouse also experienced improved inventory management, leading to the elimination of its dependence on a third-party warehouse that had been used to house an overrun of 10,000 pallet loads.

Ocean Spray Cranberries Operates as a Cooperative

Ocean Spray processed and sold the cranberries and citrus grown by its producer-members, who were required to deliver the fruit to OCS for processing and handling. It returned to the shareholders their proportional share of pooled net revenue obtained from the sale of the fruit less administrative and sales expenses. Because cranberry and citrus concentrate could be stored in barrels, the total value of an individual year's crop might take several years to determine. Thus, producers paid their production expenses, gave their fruit to OSC, and waited for their revenues after the citrus or cranberries had been sold. The agreement was called a cooperative marketing agreement.

Many of OSC's members were small and operated third- or fourth-generation cranberry farms. One characteristic unique to OSC was that it required producers to plant their predetermined quota every year. This agreement was called a common stock equity quota. If a producer did not plant its quota, OSC could redeem the producer's equity shares at a price below their actual worth and reallocate the quota. This was different from most businesses that operated as a cooperative.

The par value of OSC's stock was $25 per share, and one share equaled one barrel of juice. If a grower did not deliver a crop for three years, its shares would all be redeemed at the $25 per barrel price along with any accumulated allocated earnings. In recent years, the asset value of OSC's shares had been estimated at 10 times their $25 per share price. OSC had a 24-member board of directors until 2001, when the board was reduced to 15 members. The present board consisted of 11 growers, the CEO, and three outside directors unaffiliated with OSC.

Organizational Changes

Since the beginning of 1999, Ocean Spray's management had been reorganized, with about 100 executives either having their jobs eliminated or moving to new positions. These changes culminated in the retirement of its veteran president/chief executive officer, Tom Bullock, in December 1999, one day after an advisory committee of co-op grower-members voiced a complaint of no confidence.[7] A relatively complete overhaul in management occurred, and Robert Hawthorne, who had 24 years of experience at General Mills and Pillsbury, took over as CEO in January 2000. Randy Papadelis, known for his marketing and sales performance at Welch Foods, joined in July 2000 as the president and chief operating officer. Timothy Chan, formerly with Pillsbury Brands Group and the grocery division of Campbell Soup Company, was hired as the chief financial officer. The top executives making up the new management team all had strong backgrounds in marketing and sales. The focus of the new management team was on boosting the sales of cranberry products chiefly via product innovation.

The new executive team developed new strategies aimed at improving OSC's financial performance (see Exhibits 10 and 11). The company had a good year in 2001, posting a 95 percent increase in net earnings, a 62 percent decrease in selling, general, and administrative expenses, and a $108 million increase in free cash flow. It was also able to reverse the decline in sales of 64-ounce beverages and regain market share in this product category. The new management team also introduced 42 new product versions in its first year and launched the white cranberry juice drinks in both the United States and Canada, committing $30 million to its marketing and promotion and using all media including TV, which was something OSC had not done for a number of years. The team also invigorated the declining Ocean Spray light juice drinks by reformulating and repositioning them, resulting in a growth rate of 60 percent by the end of the year and reversing sales declines of 40 percent a year earlier.

The new executive management team improved OSC's international business, expanding the company's presence in China and increasing international sales to $211 million, or 16 percent of total sales in 2001. On the technology front, the company improved its enterprisewide resource planning system, significantly boosting on-time delivery and order fill rates while minimizing inventories.

Exhibit 10 INCOME STATEMENT DATA, OCEAN SPRAY CRANBERRIES, 1995–2001
(IN THOUSANDS OF $)

	2001	2000	1999	1998	1997	1996	1995
Revenue	$1,103,841	$1,381,951	$1,338,476	$1,445,905	$1,402,796	$1,400,275	$1,328,068
Cost of goods sold	712,390	750,821	727,229	711,306	720,931	748,084	684,937
Gross profit	391,451	631,130	611,247	734,599	681,865	652,191	643,131
SG&A expense	174,235	455,779	384,089	374,561	328,177	328,644	298,011
Operating income	194,954	125,147	165,680	301,779	300,715	273,736	297,389
Total net income	142,954	73,487	134,894	280,041	273,251	249,612	276,382

Source: OSC annual reports.

Exhibit 11 BALANCE SHEET DATA, OCEAN SPRAY CRANBERRIES, 1996–2001
(IN THOUSANDS OF $)

	2001	2000	1999	1998	1997	1996
Cash	$ 29,438	$ 11,040	$ 13,559	$ 5,057	$ 8,023	$ 6,285
Net receivables	147,413	128,715	186,555	194,495	167,582	166,684
Inventories	226,038	254,558	220,815	222,954	185,430	184,921
Prepaid expenses	5,483	7,373	15,077	7,023	5,443	4,262
Deferred income taxes	9,185	6,716	3,709	676	1,676	2,315
Total current assets	417,557	408,402	439,715	430,205	368,154	364,467
Total assets	$893,233	$927,728	$959,058	$927,907	$778,160	$743,948
Total current liabilities	$210,229	270,512	270,207	327,595	244,817	248,170
Long-term debt	349,802	332,225	337,008	378,710	288,988	244,054
Total liabilities	560,031	602,737	607,215	706,305	533,805	492,224
Total equity	333,202	324,991	351,843	221,602	244,355	251,724
Total liabilities and equity	$893,233	$927,728	$959,058	$927,907	$778,160	$743,948

Source: OSC annual reports.

Marketing and Distribution

Ocean Spray's marketing was reorganized into three divisions, each focusing on a well-defined customer or market segment: technology, food service, and international.

OSC's Ingredient Technology Group was organized as a product development resource for the food industry and other commercial clients. Its principal goal was to work with clients in the development and testing of recipes and products, and its principal resource was the more than 50 years of experience and knowledge generated from testing thousands of ideas for the use of fruit in food product and recipe development. Its clients include such companies as Kellogg, Campbell Soup, General Mills, and Pepperidge Farms. The Ingredient Technology Group sought to increase the use of cranberries and cranberry products in food and beverage innovations undertaken by the food industry.

OSC's Foodservice Division provided service and recipe innovation ideas to the food-service industry, ranging from dispensing fountains to working with restaurants to develop new drinks and mixes. Supplying mixes in branded containers instead of generic containers was seen as a potential growth market by OSC management.

Ocean Spray Worldwide oversaw the distribution of Ocean Spray's products throughout the United States, Canada, and the rest of the world. The division was organized into five groups: (1) United States; (2) Canada; (3) Europe/Middle East/Africa; (4) Asia/Pacific, and (5) Latin America and the Caribbean. Each of these groups had a central point of contact to facilitate effective information and product movement. The division also oversaw product promotion and advertising in the different regions, ensuring that advertising messages and promotional relationships were structured to deliver the expected results of improved sales and increased profitability.

With the retail market being mostly saturated with juice drinks, OSC's strategy was built around a new marketing campaign for its cranberry juices, mixes, and blends. It was also looking at possible opportunities in other categories such as snacks, fruit roll-ups, and desserts. Management was planning to launch 34 new products in 2002 and 38 more in 2003. Additionally, it was seeking to enhance OSC's competitiveness through innovation in containers. For example, a new Ripple Grip™ rectangular bottle for the 64-ounce juice and juice drink lines was introduced in August 2002. The new bottles were easier to hold and pour from, and fit better on grocery store shelves and in refrigerator doors. OSC expected to convert the entire 64-ounce juice line to the new Ripple Grip rectangular bottle by the end of 2002.

OSC entered into a strategic alliance with Nestlé in early 2002 to capture economies of scale in processing, logistics, and raw material and packaging purchasing. The Nestlé alliance involved shifting Nestlé's manufacturing of its Libby's Juicy Juice and Libby's Kerns Nectars to OSC facilities. Additionally, the companies were also to pursue collaborative procurement of common raw and packaging materials, and common operating supplies, as well as to share logistics to increase process efficiency throughout their supply chains. This alliance was important because it gave OSC access to a major food processor's capabilities and potentially opened the door to Nestlé's distribution channels in the future. Given the definition of the problem at OSC—moving products through effective marketing and in so doing managing down the inventory in the cranberry industry—a strong distribution relationship was almost imperative for the company to achieve its turnaround objective.

Challenges in the 1990s

Northland Cranberries, Inc., and OSC were the two major firms operating in the cranberry processing industry as of 2002–2003. Northland was formed in 1987 when five individual grower limited partnerships were consolidated into Northland, which secured a contract with OSC to purchase its cranberries, and Northland went public on NASDAQ. In 1988, using the proceeds from its stock offering, Northland purchased more growing facilities to become the largest cranberry grower in Wisconsin. By 1993, Northland had acquired several other competitors to become the single largest grower in OSC. It then elected to leave OSC, become a processor, and assume the responsibility of selling its own cranberries. Northland constructed a $5 million receiving, processing, storage, and packaging facility in Wisconsin Rapids, Wisconsin. It introduced its Northland brand of fresh cranberries to supermarkets across the country and started building brand equity.

In 1995, it introduced Northland 100 percent juice cranberry blends in Wisconsin—cranberry raspberry, cranberry apple, cranberry grape, cranberry cherry, and cranberry strawberry—which made it a fully integrated cooperative. In 1998, it acquired Minot Food Packers and the juice division of Seneca Foods Corporation. The Seneca deal offered Northland significant access to regional brands and distribution channels. A year later its national supermarket market share was estimated at double digits. It then reformulated Northland 100 percent juice cranberry blends to achieve 27 percent juice content across the entire line in accordance with studies showing health benefits from cranberry juice. It sold its private-label juice business to Cliffstar Corporation and consolidated manufacturing operations.

In the early and mid-1990s, OSC was a very profitable company due to its branded cranberry products, which had little or no competition at a time when cranberry juice consumption was increasing. Producers received $55 per barrel of cranberry juice in 1994, 1995, and 1997 and a $60 per barrel price in 1996. In the mid-1990s, OSC encouraged new producers to join the company and existing growers to expand production in anticipation of growth in demand. Since then prices had plummeted as acreage expanded and new cranberry processors as well as competing fruit juices entered the industry.

In February 1999, OSC announced at its annual meeting that the 1998 price per barrel was anticipated to be in the mid-$50s. Within days of the annual meeting, producer shareholders were informed that the price would be $42 to $48 per barrel, and ultimately a $29 price was given to producers ($8 of which would ultimately be retained by OSC as an overpayment due to higher inventories). In April 2000, the estimated returns for the 1999 crop were $10.75 per barrel. Management also indicated that it would likely be another five years before prices were $35 a barrel again. Many of OSC's members were small producers that could not sustain several years of prices below production costs. Furthermore, they were obligated to continue producing their quota even though the prices they would receive for their crop were far below their production costs.

In 2000, OSC and others lobbied to get the CMC to adopt a 35 percent reduction in supply through controls on acreage. The CMC authorized a 15 percent reduction, but this was still not enough to stabilize the industry. In 2001, the U.S. Department of Agriculture set up a marketing order on behalf of cranberry members nationwide that established an allotment percentage of 65 percent. The order also established a quota for cranberry production at 4.6 million barrels. Fresh cranberries were exempted because their sales were small and they could not easily be converted for use in juices.

In 1999, producer shareholders in OSC began to lobby for management to consider (1) selling assets (specifically spinning off the branded juice operations), (2) merging with another firm, or (3) liquidating the company. This would allow the proceeds to benefit the existing shareholders equally. Three consultants were hired: a Harvard Business School professor, a financial consultant, and an investment banker. The professor advised management to "run, not walk," to talk to a strong buyer or merger partner. The financial consultant advised that a sale was advisable and appropriate because the juice operations had synergistic potential with potential buyers. The investment banker recommended that a sale or merger be pursued. It also indicated that OSC could expect $350 per share ($270 after debt payment) for the $25 par value stock. The investment banker identified 13 potential buyers and indicated that a high degree of interest existed among them. Several of these firms then contacted OSC about the possibility of acquiring the fruit juice business. The firm's value was estimated to be $1.6 to $1.8 billion at that time.

Ocean Spray's board of directors voted 13 to 11 in November 1999 in favor of a resolution to not sell the branded fruit juice business and designated the consultant's reports as confidential. An OSC grower surveyed members and found that 64 percent of the respondents favored some form of strategic merger for the branded juice business. A follow-up survey commissioned by OSC in early 2000 was conducted by a Cornell University economist. This survey found that many growers were critical of management and some favored a merger, but the results were criticized because producers were not told the information on the value of the company as estimated by the consultants.

The board of directors then decided to propose a resolution that would reduce the number of directors to no more than 15 (to essentially remove the directors in favor of a merger or sale of assets) and another resolution that would enable the board to remove a director without cause (to remove a director who was strongly in favor of the sale or merger of the company). At this point, several directors resigned. At the 2000 annual meeting, the members voted on two sets of directors and the two resolutions proposed by the board. One set of directors was nominated by the traditional nominating committee while another set of directors included some of the former board members that had resigned. Both resolutions passed, and the nominating committee directors were elected. The new directors included several of OSC's largest members. Management then announced that the 1998 and 1999 prices would be less than $20 a barrel. In August 2000, the board again announced that a sale or merger was not going to be pursued.

Meanwhile, strategic initiatives of the major players in the beverage marketplace had significant competitive implications for OSC in the rapidly growing noncarbonated beverage segment. In 2000, PepsiCo bought Tropicana and its line of juices. The distribution agreement with OSC included a no compete clause. The acquisition of Tropicana meant that PepsiCo no longer needed OSC and it terminated the distribution agreement. For OSC, the loss of the distribution relationship with PepsiCo technically presented a major loss of cheap access to retail distribution channels and placed it in direct competition with PepsiCo in the fruit juice and juice blend markets. With its control of South Beach Beverage Company and Tropicana (the No. 1 producer of chilled orange juice), PepsiCo now had products that it could push directly against OSC in the distribution channels.

The 2001 Annual Meeting

Shareholders, including the third largest grower in OSC, attempted to initiate resolutions with the board that would enable the shareholders to vote on whether to sell or merge OSC. The board announced that such resolutions were outside the scope of actions that could be initiated by shareholders. Several shareholders then requested copies of the consultants' reports so they could be shown to the members, who could then make an informed choice about whether to proceed with the resolutions. The board then decided to not use the traditional regional nomination of directors and to choose a slate of directors themselves. A lawsuit filed by the shareholders forced OSC to make the consultants' information public at the annual meeting and allow the resolutions to be voted on by OSC members.

At the 70th annual meeting in San Diego, California, in January 2001, the grower-owners rejected resolutions calling for the company's board to explore a sale opportunity by a 2:1 margin. The plaintiffs accused the board, most of whom were among OSC's top 50 growers, of creating "a privileged class of shareholder," able to weather

Pacific Cataract and Laser Institute

Competing in the LASIK Eye Surgery Market

John J. Lawrence,
University of Idaho

Linda J. Morris,
University of Idaho

Dr. Mark Everett, clinic coordinator and optometric physician (OP) of the Pacific Cataract and Laser Institute (PCLI) office in Spokane, Washington, looked at the ad that Vancouver, Canada–based Lexington Laser Vision (LLV) had been running in the Spokane papers and shook his head. This was neither the first nor the only clinic advertising low-priced laser-assisted in situ keratomileusis (LASIK) eye surgeries. Dr. Everett just could not believe that doctors would advertise and sell laser eye surgery based on low price as if it were a stereo or a used car. The fact that they were advertising based on price was bad enough, but the price they were promoting—$900 for both eyes—was ridiculous. PCLI and its cooperating optometric physicians would not even cover their variable cost if they performed the surgery at that price. A typical PCLI customer paid between $1,750 and $2,000 per eye for corrective laser surgery. While Dr. Everett knew that firms in Canada had several inherent cost advantages, including a favorable exchange rate and regulatory environment, he could not understand how they could undercut PCLI's price so much without compromising service quality.

PCLI was a privately held company that operated a total of 11 clinics throughout the northwestern United States and provided a range of medical and surgical eye treatments including laser vision correction. Responding to the challenge of the Canadian competitors was one of the points that would be discussed when Dr. Everett and the other clinic coordinators and surgeons who ran PCLI met next month to discuss policies and strategy. Dr. Everett strongly believed that the organization's success was based on surgical excellence and compassionate concern for its patients and the doctors who referred them. PCLI strived to provide the ultimate in patient care and consideration. Dr. Everett had joined PCLI in 1993 in large part because of how impressed he had been by how PCLI treated its patients, and he remained committed to this patient-focused value.

He was concerned, however, about his organization's ability to attract laser vision correction patients. He knew that many prospective PCLI customers would be swayed by the low prices and would travel to Canada to have the procedure performed, especially

The authors thank Dr. Mark Everett for his cooperation and assistance with this project. The authors also thank the anonymous *Case Research Journal* reviewers and the anonymous North American Case Research Association 2000 annual meeting reviewers for their valuable input and suggestions. An earlier version of this case received the Cooper Award as the best case in health care presented at the NACRA 2000 Annual Meeting.

Exhibit 1   **Map Showing PCLI Clinic Locations** [Clinics designated by a ◆; Anchorage, AK, clinic not shown]

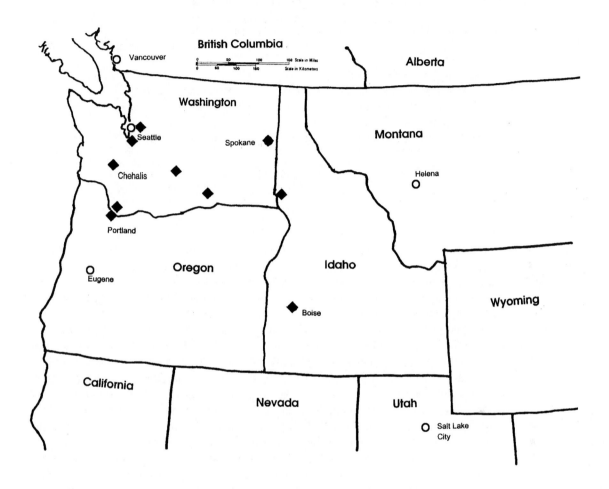

since most medical insurance programs covered only a small portion of the cost of this procedure. Dr. Everett believed strongly that PCLI achieved better results and provided a higher-quality service experience than the clinics in Canada offering low-priced LASIK procedures. He also felt PCLI did a much better job of helping potential customers determine which of several procedures, if any, best met the customers' long-term vision needs. Dr. Everett wondered what PCLI should do to win over these potential customers—both for the good of the customers and for the good of PCLI.

Pacific Cataract and Laser Institute

Pacific Cataract and Laser Institute (PCLI) was founded in 1985 by Dr. Robert Ford and specialized in medical and surgical eye treatment. The company was headquartered in Chehalis, Washington, and operated clinics in Washington, Oregon, Idaho, and Alaska (see Exhibit 1 for a map of PCLI locations). In addition to laser vision correction, PCLI provided cataract surgery, glaucoma consultation and surgery, corneal transplants,

Exhibit 2   PACIFIC CATARACT AND LASER INSTITUTE'S CORE VALUES

- We believe patients' families and friends provide important support and we encourage them to be as involved as possible in our care of their loved ones.
- We believe patients and their families have a right to honest and forthright medical information presented in a manner they can understand.
- We believe that a calm, caring, and cheerful environment minimizes patient stress and the need for artificial sedation.
- We believe that all our actions should be guided by integrity, honesty, and courage.
- We believe that true success comes from doing the right things for the right reasons.
- We believe that efficient, quality eye care is provided best by professionals practicing at the highest level of their expertise.
- We believe that communicating openly and sharing knowledge with our optometric colleagues is crucial to providing outstanding patient care.
- We believe that the ultimate measure of our success is the complete satisfaction of the doctors who entrust us with the care of their patients.

retinal care and surgery, and eyelid surgery. Dr. Ford founded PCLI on the principle that doctors must go beyond science and technology to practice the art of healing through the Christian principles of love, kindness, and compassion. The organization had defined eight core values that were based on these principles. These core values, shown in Exhibit 2, guided PCLI's decision making as it attempted to fulfill its stated mission of providing the best possible co-managed services to the profession of optometry.

Co-management involved PCLI working closely with a patient's doctor of optometry (OD). In co-managed eye care, family ODs were the primary care eye doctors who diagnosed, treated, and managed certain diseases of the eye that did not require surgery. When surgery was needed, the family OD referred patients to ophthalmologists (e.g., PCLI's eye surgeons) for specialized treatment and surgery. Successful co-management, according to PCLI, depended on a relationship of mutual trust and respect built through shared learning, constant communication, and commitment to providing quality patient care. PCLI's co-management arrangements did not restrict ODs to working with just PCLI, although PCLI sought out ODs who would use PCLI as their primary surgery partner and who shared PCLI's values. Many ODs did work exclusively with PCLI unless a specific patient requested otherwise. PCLI-Spokane had developed a network of 150 family ODs in its region.

PCLI operated its 11 clinics in a very coordinated manner. It had seven surgeons that specialized in the various forms of eye surgery. These surgeons, each accompanied by several surgical assistants, traveled from center to center to perform specific surgeries. The company owned two aircraft that were used to fly the surgical teams between the centers. Each clinic had a resident optometric physician who served as that clinic's coordinator and essentially managed the day-to-day operations of the clinic. Each clinic also employed its own office support staff. PCLI's main office in Chehalis, Washington, also employed patient counselors who worked with the referring family ODs for scheduling the patient's surgery and a finance team to help patients with medical insurance claims and any financing arrangements (which were made through third-party sources). Dr. Everett was the Spokane clinic's resident optometric physician and managed the day-to-day activities at that clinic. Actual surgeries were performed in the Spokane clinic only one or two days a week, depending on demand and the surgeons' availability.

Laser Eye Surgery and LASIK

Laser eye surgery was performed on the eye to create better focus and lessen the patient's dependence on glasses and contact lenses. Excimer lasers were the main means of performing this type of surgery. Although research on the excimer laser began in 1973, it was not until 1985 that excimer lasers were introduced to the ophthalmology community in the United States. The U.S. Food and Drug Administration (FDA) approved the use of excimer lasers for photorefractive keratectomy (PRK) in October 1995, for the purpose of correcting nearsightedness. PRK entailed using computer-controlled beams of laser light to permanently resculpt the curvature of the eye by selectively removing a small portion on the outer top surface of the cornea called the epithelium. The epithelium naturally regenerated itself, although eye medication was required for three to four months after the procedure.

In the late 1990s, laser-assisted in situ keratomileusis (LASIK) replaced PRK as the preferred method to correct or reduce moderate to high levels of nearsightedness (i.e., myopia). The procedure required the surgeon to create a flap in the cornea using a surgical instrument called a microkeratome. This instrument used vacuum suction to hold and position the cornea and a motorized cutting blade to make the necessary incision. The surgeon then used an excimer laser to remove a micro-thin layer of tissue from the exposed, interior corneal surface (as opposed to removing a thin layer of tissue on the outer surface of the cornea as was the case with PRK). The excimer laser released a precisely focused beam of invisible low-temperature light. Each laser pulse removed less than 0.000001 inch. After the cornea had been reshaped, the flap was replaced. The actual surgical procedure took only about five minutes per eye. LASIK surgery allowed a patient to eliminate the regular use of glasses or contact lenses, although many patients still required reading glasses.

While LASIK used the same excimer laser that had been approved for other eye surgeries in the United States by the Ophthalmic Devices Panel of the FDA, it was not an approved procedure in the United States but was under study. LASIK was offered by U.S. clinics but was considered an off-label use of the laser. *Off-label* was a term given to medical services and supplies that had not been thoroughly tested by the FDA but that the FDA permitted to be performed and provided by a licensed medical professional. Prescribing aspirin as a blood thinner to reduce the risk of stroke was another example of an off-label use of a medical product—the prescribing of aspirin for this purpose did not have formal FDA approval but was permitted by the FDA.

The LASIK procedure was not without some risks. Complications arose in about 5 percent of all cases, although experienced surgeons had complication rates of less than 2 percent. According to the American Academy of Ophthalmology, complications and side effects included irregular astigmatism, resulting in a decrease in best corrected vision; glare; corneal haze; over correction; under correction; inability to wear contact lenses; loss of the corneal cap, requiring a corneal graft; corneal scarring and infection; and in an extremely rare number of cases, loss of vision. If lasering was not perfect, a patient might develop haze in the cornea. This could make it impossible to achieve 20/20 vision, even with glasses. The flap could also heal improperly, causing fuzzy vision. Infections were also occasionally an issue.

While PRK and LASIK were the main types of eye surgery currently performed to reduce a patient's dependence on glasses or contact lenses, there were new surgical procedures and technologies that were in the test stage that could receive approval in the United States within the next 3 to 10 years. These included intraocular lenses that were implanted behind a patient's cornea; laser thermokeratoplasty (LTK) and conductive keratoplasty (CK), which used heat to reshape the cornea; and custom LASIK technologies that could better measure and correct the total optics of the eye. These newer methods had the potential to improve vision even more than LASIK, and some of these new processes also might allow additional corrections to be made to the eye as the patient aged. Intraocular lenses were already widely available in Europe.

LASIK Market Potential

The market potential for LASIK procedures was very significant, and the market was just beginning to take off. According to officials of the American Academy of Ophthalmology, over 150 million people wore glasses or contact lenses in the United States. About 12 million of these people were candidates for current forms of refractive surgery. As procedures were refined to cover a wider range of vision conditions, and as the FDA approved new procedures, the number of people who could have their vision improved surgically was expected to grow to over 60 million. As many as 1.7 million people in the United States were expected to have some form of laser eye surgery during 2000, compared to 500,000 in 1999 and 250,000 in 1998. Laser eye repair was the most frequently performed surgery in all of medicine.

Referrals were increasingly playing a key role in the industry's growth. Surgeons estimated that the typical patient referred five friends, and that as many as 75 percent of new patients had been referred by a friend. A few employers were also beginning to offer laser eye surgery benefits through managed care vision plans. These plans offered discounts from list prices of participating surgeons and clinics to employees. The partners of Vision Service Plan (VSP), for example, gave such discounts and guaranteed a maximum price of $1,800 per eye for VSP members. The number of people eligible for such benefits was expected to grow significantly in the coming years. PCLI did not participate in these plans and did not offer such discounts.

LASIK at PCLI

The process of providing LASIK surgery to patients at PCLI began with the partnering OD. The OD provided the patient with information about LASIK and PCLI, reviewed the treatment options available, and answered any questions the patient might have concerning LASIK or PCLI. If a patient was interested in having the surgery performed, the OD performed a pre-exam to make sure the patient was a suitable candidate for the surgery. Assuming the patient was able to have the surgery, the OD made an appointment for the patient with PCLI and forwarded the results of the pre-exam to Dr. Everett. PCLI had a standard surgical fee of $1,400 per eye for LASIK. Each family OD added on additional fees for pre- and postoperative exams depending on the number of visits per patient and the OD's costs. Most of the ODs charged $700 to $1,200, making the total price of laser surgery to the patient between $3,500 and $4,000. This total price was presented to the patient rather than two separate service fees.

Once a patient arrived at PCLI, an ophthalmic assistant measured the patient's range of vision and took a topographical reading of the eyes. Dr. Everett would then explain the entire process to the patient, discuss the possible risks, and have the patient read and sign an informed consent form. The patient would then meet the surgeon and have any final questions answered. The meeting with the surgeon was also intended to reduce any anxiety that the patient might have regarding the procedure. The surgical procedure itself took less than 15 minutes to perform. After the surgery was completed, the patient was told to rest his or her eyes for a few hours and was given dark glasses and eyedrops. The patient was required to return either to PCLI or to his or her family OD 24 hours after their surgery for a follow-up exam. Additional follow-up exams were required at one week, one month, three months, six months, and one year to make sure the eyes healed properly and that any problems were caught quickly. The patient's family OD performed all of these follow-up exams.

Three of PCLI's seven surgeons specialized in LASIK and related procedures. The company's founder, Dr. Robert Ford, had performed over 16,000 LASIK procedures during his career, more than any other surgeon in the Northwest. His early training was as a physicist, and he was very interested in and knowledgeable about the laser technology used to perform LASIK procedures. Because of this interest and understanding, Dr. Ford was an industry innovator and had developed a number of procedural enhancements that were unique to PCLI. Dr. Ford had developed an enhanced software calibration system for PCLI's lasers that was better than the system provided by the laser manufacturers.

More significantly, Dr. Ford had also developed a system to track eye movements. Using superimposed live and saved computer images of the eye, PCLI surgeons could achieve improved eye alignment to provide more accurate laser resculpting of the eye. Dr. Ford was working with Laser Sight, a laser equipment manufacturer developing what PCLI and many others viewed as the next big technological step in corrective eye surgery—custom LASIK. Custom LASIK involved developing more detailed corneal maps and then using special software to convert these maps into a program that would run a spot laser to achieve theoretically perfect corrections of the cornea. This technology was currently in clinical trials in an effort to gain FDA approval of the technology, and Dr. Ford and PCLI were participating in these trials. Although Dr. Ford was on the leading edge of technology and had vast LASIK surgical experience, very few of PCLI's patients were aware of his achievements.

Competition

PCLI in Spokane faced stiff competition from clinics in both the United States and Canada. There were basically three types of competitors. There were general ophthalmology practices that also provided LASIK surgeries, surgery centers like PCLI that provided a range of eye surgeries, and specialized LASIK clinics that focused solely on LASIK surgeries.

General ophthalmology practices provided a range of services covering a patient's basic eye care needs. They performed general eye exams, monitored the health of patients' eyes, and wrote prescriptions for glasses and contact lenses. Most general ophthalmology practices did not perform LASIK surgeries (or any other types of surgeries) because of the high cost of the equipment and the special training needed to perform the surgery, but a few did. These clinics were able to offer patients a continuity of care that surgery centers and centers specializing solely in LASIK surgeries could not. Customers could have all pre- and postoperative exams performed at the same location by the same doctor. In the Spokane market, a clinic called Eye Consultants was the most aggressive competitor of this type. This organization advertised heavily in the local newspaper, promoting an $1,195 per eye price (see Exhibit 3). The current newspaper

Exhibit 3   Eye Consultant's Advertisement

LASIK

Special Offer

$1195 PER EYE *

INCLUDING pre- and post operative care!

WHEN: Thursday
          June 4
          6:00 p.m.
WHERE: Clear Vision
          Laser Center
          Quail Run Office Park
          2200 E. 29th Avenue
          Suite 110
            CALL TODAY
          Seating is Limited

See LASIK Live!

Come to this free LIVE LASIK seminar
to receive this special offer.

*ONLY for seminar attendees who
schedule a procedure within 90 days!

Compare our Quality ~ Compare our Price
Save $600 on Both Eyes!

EYE CONSULTANTS
David Cohen, M.D.
Chris Sturbaum, M.D.

The Doctors You Trust
For Excellence
In Local Eye Care

CALL XXX-XXXX

promotion invited potential customers to a free LASIK seminar put on by the clinic's staff, and seminar attendees who chose to have the procedure qualified for the $1,195 per eye price, which was a $300 per eye discount from the clinic's regular price.

Surgery centers did not provide for patient's basic eye care needs but rather specialized in performing eye surgeries. These centers provided a variety of eye surgeries, including such procedures as cataract surgeries and LASIK surgeries in addition to other specialty eye surgeries. PCLI was this type of clinic. The other surgery center of this type in the Spokane area was Empire Eye. PCLI viewed Empire Eye as its most formidable competitor in the immediate geographic area. Empire Eye operated in a similar way as PCLI. It relied heavily on referrals from independent optometric physicians, did not advertise aggressively, and did not attempt to win customers with low prices. It did employ a locally based surgeon who performed its LASIK procedures, although this surgeon was not nearly as experienced as Dr. Ford at PCLI.

LASIK clinics provided only LASIK or LASIK/PRK procedures. They did not provide for general eye care needs, nor did they provide a range of eye surgeries as surgery centers did. These clinics generally had much higher volumes of LASIK patients than general ophthalmology or surgery centers, allowing them to achieve much higher utilization of the expensive capital equipment required to perform the surgeries. The capital cost of the equipment to perform the LASIK procedure was about U.S.$500,000.

The largest of these firms specializing in LASIK surgeries was TLC Laser Eye Centers, Inc. TLC was based in Mississauga, Ontario, and had 56 clinics in the United States and 7 in Canada. During the first quarter of 2000, TLC generated revenues of U.S.$49.3 million by performing 33,000 surgeries. This compared with first quarter of 1999, when the company had revenues of U.S.$41.4 million on 25,600 procedures. TLC was the largest LASIK eye surgery company in North America and performed more LASIK surgeries in the United States than any other company. The closest TLC centers to Spokane were in Seattle, Washington, and Vancouver, British Columbia. The second largest provider of LASIK surgeries in the United States was Laser Vision Centers (LVC), based in St. Louis, Missouri. Its closest center to Spokane was also in Seattle.

Almost all of the Canadian competitors that had been successful at attracting U.S. customers were clinics specializing solely in LASIK surgeries. The largest Canadian competitor was Lasik Vision Corporation (LVC), based in Vancouver, British Columbia. LVC operated 15 clinics in Canada and 14 in the United States, and was growing rapidly. LVC had plans to add another 21 clinics by the end of 2000. During the first quarter of 2000, LVC generated revenues of U.S.$20.1 million by performing 26,673 procedures. This compared to first quarter of 1999, when the company had revenues of only U.S.$4.3 million on 6,300 procedures.

In total, there were 13 companies specializing in providing LASIK surgeries in British Columbia, mostly in the Vancouver area. One of the British Columbia firms that advertised most aggressively in the Spokane area was Lexington Laser Vision (LLV). LLV operated a single clinic staffed by nine surgeons and equipped with four lasers. The clinic scheduled surgeries six days a week and typically had a two-month wait for an appointment.

The service design process at LLV was designed to accommodate many patients and differed significantly from PCLI's service process. To begin the process, a patient simply called a toll-free number for LLV to schedule a time to have the surgery performed. Once the patient arrived at the LLV clinic he or she received a preoperative examination to assess the patient's current vision and to scan the topography of the patient's eyes. The next day the patient returned to the clinic for the scheduled surgery. The typical sequence was to first meet with a patient counselor who reviewed with the patient all pages of a LASIK information booklet that was sent to the patient following the scheduled surgery date. The patient counselor answered any questions the patient had regarding the information in the booklet and ensured that the patient signed all necessary surgical consent forms. Following this step, a medical assistant surgically prepped the patient and explained the postcare treatment of the eyes. After this preparation, the surgeon greeted the patient, reviewed the topographical eye charts with the patient, explained the recommended eye adjustments for the patient, and reiterated the surgical procedure once again. The patient would then be transferred to the surgery room, where two surgical assistants were available to help the doctor with the 5- to 10-minute operation. Once the surgery was completed, a surgical assistant led the patient to a dark, unlit room so that the patient's eyes could adjust. After a 15-minute waiting period, the surgical assistant checked the patient for any discomfort and repeated the instructions for postcare treatment. Barring problems or discomfort, the surgical assistant would hand the patient a pair of dark wrap around sunglasses with instructions to avoid bright lights for the next 24 hours. At the scheduled post operative exam the next day, a medical technician measured the patient's corrected vision and scheduled any additional post operative exams. If desired, the patient could return to the clinic for the one-week, one-month, and three-month postoperative exams at either the LLV clinic or one of the U.S.-based partner clinics of LLV. In some cases, the patient opted to have these post-operative exams performed by his or her family OD.

U.S. patients traveling to LLV or the other clinics in British Columbia to have the surgery performed needed to allow for three days and two nights for the surgery. A pre-exam to ensure that the patient was a suitable candidate for the surgery was performed the first day, the surgery itself was performed the second day, and the 24-hour post-exam was performed on the third day. Two nights in a hotel near LLV cost approximately U.S.$100 and airfare to Vancouver cost approximately U.S.$150 from Spokane. Lexington Laser Vision had a sister clinic in the Seattle area where patients could go for postoperative exams. LLV requested patients undergo follow-up exams at one week, one month, and three months. These exams were included in the price as long as the patient came to either the Seattle or the Vancouver clinic. Some patients outside of the Seattle/Vancouver area arranged with their family ODs to perform these follow-ups at their own expense to avoid the time and cost of traveling.

A breakdown of the estimated cost structure for each of these different competitors is shown in Exhibit 4. Dr. Everett believed that both Eye Consultants and LLV were probably incurring losses. Both were believed to be offering below-cost pricing in response to the significant price competition going on in the industry. Eye Consultants was also believed to be offering below-cost pricing in order to build volume and gain surgeon experience. PCLI's own cost structure was fairly similar to Empire Eye's cost structure, as both operated in a similar fashion.

The Canadian Advantage

LASIK clinics operating in Canada had a number of advantages that allowed them to charge significantly less than competitors in the United States. First, the Canadian dollar had been relatively weak compared to the U.S. dollar for some time, fluctuating between C$1.45 and C$1.50 per U.S. dollar. This exchange rate compared to rates in the early 1990s, which fluctuated between C$1.15 and C$1.20 per U.S. dollar. On top of this, the inflation rate in Canada averaged only 1.5 percent during the 1990s compared to 2.5 percent in the United States. This dual effect of a weakened Canadian dollar combined with somewhat higher inflation in the United States meant that Canadian providers had, over time, acquired a significant exchange rate cost advantage.

Exhibit 4   **LASIK-RELATED REVENUE AND COST ESTIMATES FOR PCLI'S COMPETITORS (ALL FIGURES ARE IN U.S.$)[1]**

	Eye Consultants	Empire Eye	TLC Clinic	Lexington Laser Vision[2]
Type of operation	General ophthalmology practice	Eye surgery center	Specialized LASIK clinic	Specialized LASIK clinic
Location of operation	Spokane, Washington	Spokane, Washington	Seattle, Washington	Vancouver, British Columbia
Number of procedures/year	~600	~1,000	~4,000	~10,000
Price to customer, per eye	$1,195	$1,900	$1,600	$500
Estimated revenues	$717,000	$1,900,000	$6,400,000	$5,000,000
Estimated expenses				
Payments for pre- and post operative care[3]	$120,000	450,000	1,400,000	1,500,000
Royalties	150,000	250,000	1,000,000	0
Surgeon's Fees/Salary	120,000	300,000	1,200,000	1,500,000
Medical Supplies	30,000	50,000	200,000	500,000
Laser Service	100,000	100,000	200,000	400,000
Depreciation	125,000	125,000	250,000	500,000
Marketing	75,000	75,000	400,000	500,000
Overhead	200,000	350,000	500,000	600,000
Total annual expenses	$920,000	$1,700,000	$5,150,000	$5,500,000

[1]This table was developed from a variety of public sources relating to both the LASIK industry in general and individual competitors. In a number of cases, the figures represent aggregated "estimates" of data from several sources. Estimated expenses are based largely, but not entirely, on discussion of the LASIK industry cost structure provided in James Pethokoukis, "Eyeing the Bottom Line: Just Who Profits from Your Laser Eye Surgery May Surprise You", *U.S. News and World Report,* March 30, 1998, pp. 80-82.

[2]This cost structure was thought to be typical of all of the specialized LASIK clinics located in British Columbia, Canada, that competed with PCLI.

[3]In some cases, these costs are paid directly by the patient to the postoperative care provider; they have been included here because they represent a part of the total price paid by the customer.

Second, laser surgery equipment manufacturers charged a $250 patent royalty fee for each surgery (i.e., each eye) performed in the United States. The legal system in Canada prevented equipment manufacturers from charging such a royalty every time a surgery was performed, amounting to a $500 cost savings per patient for Canadian clinics. Competitive pressure among surgery equipment manufacturers had caused this fee to drop in recent months to as low as $100 for certain procedures performed on some older equipment in the United States, giving U.S. clinics some hope that this cost disadvantage might decrease over time.

Third, clinics in the United States generally paid higher salaries and/or fees to surgeons and support staff than did their Canadian rivals. The nationalized health system in Canada tended to limit what doctors in Canada could earn compared to their U.S. peers. LASIK clinics themselves were not part of the Canadian national health system because they represented elective surgeries. However, Canadian LASIK clinics could pay their surgeons a large premium over what they could make in the nationalized system, but this was still significantly less than a comparable surgeon's earnings in the United States. This cost differential extended to the referring optometrists who provided pre- and post operative exams and whose fees were typically included in the price quoted to customers. Many Canadian clinics relied more heavily on advertising and word-of-mouth customer referral rather than referrals from optometrists and de-emphasized pre- and postoperative exams.

Fourth, there was some speculation among U.S. clinics that some low-priced Canadian clinics were making a variety of care-compromising quality trade-offs, such as not performing equipment calibration and maintenance as frequently as recommended by the equipment manufacturers and reusing the microkeratome blades used to make the initial incision in the cornea. Canadian clinics denied that the choices that they made compromised the quality of care received by the patient. Finally, it seemed clear to Dr. Everett that Canadian providers were in the midst of a price war and that at least some of the clinics were not generating any profit at the prices they were charging.

Canadian providers also had significant noncost advantages. Because of differences in the approval process of medical equipment and procedures, laser eye surgery technologies were often available in Canada before they became readily available in the United States. Approval of new medical technologies in Canada was often based on evidence from other countries that the technology was safe, whereas approval of new medical technologies in the United States required equipment manufacturers to start from scratch with a series of studies. As a result of this, and combined with the volume that the Canadian clinics' low prices generated, many Canadian clinics had more experience with laser eye surgery than comparable U.S. clinics. Experience was a critical factor in a clinic or specific surgeon having low rates of complications. Further, the differences in the approval processes between the countries allowed Canadian providers the ability to offer advanced equipment not yet available in the United States. For example, the FDA approved the first generation of excimer laser for use in the United States in October 1995. No centers in Canada, however, had purchased this particular laser since 1995 because more advanced versions of the technology had become available for use in Canada. While some of these equipment advances had minimal impact on the results for the average patient, they had, at the very least, provided Canadian clinics a marketing advantage.

U.S. Competitors' Responses to the Canadian Challenge

The surgeons and staff at PCLI knew from reading a variety of sources and from following changes in the industry that most U.S.-based clinics were experiencing some loss of customers to Canadian competitors. These companies were responding in a variety of ways in an attempt to keep more patients in the United States. One company in the industry, LCA, had created a low-priced subsidiary, LasikPlus, as a way to compete with lower-priced competitors in Canada. LasikPlus had facilities in Maryland and California and charged $2,995, compared to the $5,000 price charged by the parent company's LCA Vision Centers. One way that the LasikPlus subsidiary had cut costs was by employing its own surgeons. Regular LCA Vision Centers provided only the facilities and equipment, and contracted out with independent surgeons to perform the procedures.

Another strategy that U.S. firms were using to compete was to partner with managed care vision benefits firms, health maintenance organizations (HMOs), and large businesses. TLC Laser Eye Centers had been the most aggressive at using this strategy. It had partnered with Vision Service Plan (VSP) to provide the surgery to VSP members at a $600 discount, and had partnered with HMO Kaiser Permanente to provide

Kaiser members a $200 discount. TLC was also attempting to get employers to cover part of the cost for their employees, and was letting participating companies offer a $200 discount on the procedure to their employees. Over 40 businesses had signed up by late 1999, including Southern California Edison, Ernst & Young, and Office Depot. TLC was not the only provider pursuing this strategy. LCA Vision centers had partnered with Cole Managed Vision to provide the surgery to Cole members at a 15 percent discount.

One of the significant advantages that U.S. providers had over their Canadian competitors was convenience, since patients did not have to travel to Canada to have the procedure performed. Most facilities providing the surgery in the United States, however, were located in major metropolitan areas, which may not be seen as being all that much more convenient for potential patients living in smaller communities and rural areas. One competitor had taken this convenience a step further. Laser Vision Centers was using mobile lasers to bring greater convenience to patients living in these smaller communities. It used a patented cart to transport the laser to ophthalmologists' offices, where it could be used for a day or two by local surgeons. LVC could also provide a surgery team in locations where no surgeons were qualified to perform the procedure. The company was serving patients in over 100 locations in this manner and was expanding its efforts.

Technological or procedural advances offered clinics another basis on which to compete. For example, during the summer of 1999, Dr. Barrie Soloway's clinic was the first in the United States to get an Autonomous laser. This laser was designed to overcome a major problem in eye surgery, the tendency for the eye to move while the procedure was being performed. In an interview with *Fortune* magazine, Autonomous's founder, Randy Frey, described the advantages of this new technology:

> At present, doctors stabilize the eye merely by asking the patient to stare at a blinking red light. But, says Frey, aiming a laser at the eye is "a very precise thing. I couldn't imagine that you could make optics for the human eye while the eye was moving." The eye, he explains, makes barely perceptible, involuntary movements about five times a second. This "saccadic" motion can make it difficult to get a perfectly smooth correction. "The doctor can compensate for the big, noticeable movements," Frey says, "but not the little ones.". . .
>
> Frey's machine uses radar to check the position of the eye 4,000 times a second. He's coupled this with an excimer laser whose beam is less than one millimeter in diameter, vs. six millimeters for the standard beam. Guided by the tracker, this laser ablates the cornea in a pattern of small overlapping dots.

There were a number of technological advances under development like the Autonomous laser system that could have a significant impact on this industry. With approvals for new procedures generally coming quicker in Canada than in the United States, however, it was unclear whether technological advances could help U.S. providers differentiate themselves from their Canadian competitors.

The Upcoming Strategy and Policy Meeting

Every time Dr. Everett saw an exuberant patient after surgery, or read a letter of gratitude from a patient, he knew in his heart that he and his colleagues were doing something

Exhibit 5   Pacific Cataract and Laser Institute Advertisement

Thinking About LASIK?

Ask your optometrist first.

The reason is simple. Excellent visual results are highly dependent on the skill of the surgeon you select.

Optometrists – also known as optometric physicians – do not perform surgery. However, these doctors provide most of the after-surgery care. This gives them the unique opportunity to see first hand the good and not-so-good outcomes of numerous surgeons.

Your optometrist can guide you to a surgeon who consistently obtains excellent results and is appropriate for your type of correction.

The question I asked my eye doctor was "Who would you trust to treat your eyes?"

The results of surgery last a lifetime. See your optometric physician!

LASER VISION CORRECTION
PACIFIC CATARACT and LASER INSTITUTE

www.pcli.com
(509) XXX-XXXX
(800) XXX-XXXX

SPOKANE   YAKIMA   KENNEWICK   TACOMA   BELLEVUE   CHEHALIS   VANCOUVER, WA   BOISE   LEWISTON   PORTLAND   ANCHORAGE

special. He was energized by the fact that the laser vision corrections they were performing were changing peoples' lives. He was also proud of the fact that they continued to treat all of their customers as special guests. But he knew that for every LASIK patient they saw at PCLI, there was another potential PCLI patient who went to Canada to have the surgery performed. PCLI had the capacity to do more laser vision correction surgeries in Spokane than they were presently doing, and he wanted to make use of that capacity. He felt that both PCLI and prospective patients from Spokane and the surrounding communities would be better off if more of these patients chose PCLI for laser vision correction surgeries.

But Dr. Everett was not sure what, if anything, should change at PCLI to attract these potential customers. PCLI had already begun to advertise. Advertising, in general, was not a commonly used practice in the U.S. medical community, and some in the medical profession considered much of the existing advertising in the industry to be ethically questionable. While Dr. Everett was comfortable with the advertisements PCLI had started running three months ago (see Exhibit 5), he was still unsure whether PCLI should be advertising at all. More important, he felt that advertising represented only a partial solution, at best. What was needed was a clear strategic focus for the organization that would help it respond to the Canadian challenge.

One obvious answer was to also compete on price. But he simply could not conceive of PCLI treating eye surgery like a commodity and competing solely on price. Such a strategy seemed inconsistent with PCLI's core values, unwise from a business standpoint since PCLI's operating costs were much higher than its Canadian competitors, and simply wrong from an ethical standpoint. The problem was, he was not sure what strategic focus PCLI should pursue in order to retain its strong position in the Pacific Northwest LASIK market. What he did know was that whatever this strategy was to be, it needed to emerge from next month's meeting, and he wanted to be prepared to help make that happen. He wanted to have a clear plan to bring to the table at this meeting to share with his colleagues, even if it was simply a reaffirmation to continue doing what they were presently doing.

Valassis Communications

Deborah R. Ettington
Eastern Michigan University

"Valassis will be the leader in online promotions."[1]
—Alan F. Schultz, chairman, president, and CEO

In May 2000 Valassis Communications, Inc., was an $800 million company headquartered in Livonia, Michigan, a suburb of Detroit. Its primary business was printing freestanding inserts (FSIs), the four-color booklets of coupons and other promotions inserted in Sunday newspapers throughout the United States. However, with rapid growth of the Internet, CEO Alan Schultz had led the company into a number of new ventures to take advantage of opportunities in an online world.

Schultz, 41, was elected CEO and president in June 1998, and appointed chairman of the board of directors in December 1998. Previously he had served as executive vice president and chief operating officer (1996–98) and executive vice president of sales and marketing (1992–96.) He joined Valassis in 1984 when it merged with his previous employer, Inserts. Schultz replaced long-term CEO David Brandon, who left to become president and CEO of nearby Domino's Pizza.

Schultz spent a total of $10.6 million cash on strategic acquisitions and equity investments in 1999 and had just announced another alliance in April 2000. These investments were intended to support a three-pronged e-commerce strategy:

1. Attract revenues from growing e-commerce media sales.

2. Build a significant Web presence with an online coupon service and eventually with other Internet products and services.

3. Capitalize on the growth of the online grocery business.[2]

To support this strategy, Schultz announced in June 1999 that Suzanne C. Brown would fill the newly created position of vice president of Internet and e-commerce services. Brown was formerly vice president of western sales, where she had been leading the company's Internet efforts since January 1999. Prior to joining Valassis in 1984, Brown worked for Procter & Gamble, a leading consumer packaged goods manufacturer. She left Valassis in 1994 to work for ADVO, a competitor, but returned in 1996.

Brown described her perspective on the new position:

> Just as the marketing environment has evolved over the years, so has Valassis. It's amazing to have witnessed our company quickly changing from an FSI provider to a full-service solution provider, including technology and Internet-related products and services. There are tremendous opportunities awaiting

---

**Exhibit 1   Valassis Communications, Stock Price
              Performance, 1992–May 2000**

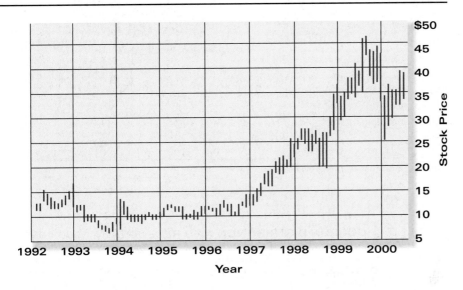

Valassis in the realm of the Internet, and I'm thrilled to be driving such forward-thinking initiatives.[3]

Schultz was optimistic when he announced 1999's financial results:

> With another record year behind us, our focus is on the future. The long-term outlook is exceptionally promising: The FSI industry is strong, our core businesses are meeting or beating annual expectations, and our new ventures are building momentum.[4]

Yet, despite these initiatives, in May 2000 the company's stock was trading in the mid-$30s, well below its high of $47 in the third quarter of 1999. (Exhibit 1 shows stock price history.) What would it take to convince investors of the promising future foreseen by management? Was the company moving fast enough to exploit the growth potential of the Internet? Or was it moving too fast and jeopardizing its strong position in the paper coupon industry?

The U.S. Coupon Industry

The History of Couponing

The first discount coupon was attributed to Asa Candler, the druggist who bought the formula for Coca-Cola. In 1894, Candler gave out handwritten tickets for a free glass of his new drink. C. W. Post distributed the first grocery coupon, worth one cent toward a purchase of Grape Nuts, in 1895. Coupons increased in popularity during the Great Depression as households struggled to save money on their grocery bills. By 1965, one-half of Americans were coupon users; that total increased to 65 percent in 1975 and 81 percent in 1998.[5]

In the 1970s, about 70 percent of coupons were distributed on run-of-press (ROP) newspaper pages, with only about 7 percent running in FSIs. During the 1980s, packaged

Exhibit 2   DISTRIBUTION OF COUPONS BY MEDIA TYPE, 1997

Distribution Medium	% of Total
Freestanding insert	80.5
Handout	8.7
In/on package	3.3
Magazine	3.2
Direct mail	2.6
Newspaper	1.3
Other (including Internet)	0.4
Total	100.0

Source: *Brandmarketing* 5, no. 4 (April 1998), p. 12.

Exhibit 3   COUPON DISTRIBUTION AND REDEMPTION, 1990–1999

Year	Coupons Distributed (billions)	Coupons Redeemed (billions)	Redemption Rates (%)	Time to Expiration (months)
1990	279.4	7.1	2.5%	4.9
1991	292.0	7.5	2.6	4.4
1992	310.0	7.7	2.5	4.0
1993	298.5	6.8	2.3	3.1
1994	309.7	6.2	2.0	3.4
1995	291.9	5.8	2.0	3.3
1996	268.5	5.3	2.0	3.0
1997	250.2	4.9	2.0	3.1
1998	249.0	4.8	1.9	3.1
1999	256.0	4.7	1.8	3.2

Source: NCH NuWorld Marketing, "Worldwide Coupon Distribution and Redemption Trends."

goods manufacturers shifted their ads to FSIs so that, by 1991, 80 percent of coupons ran in FSIs. Other distribution methods included handouts, attachment to the package, magazines, direct mail, and newspapers. (Exhibit 2 shows distribution by media type in 1997.) Coupon distribution peaked in 1994 at over 300 billion coupons and declined or remained steady through 1998. Redemption rates also declined during this period. (Exhibit 3 contains coupon distribution and redemption rates for 1990–99.)

Differing Views of the Value of Couponing

The coupon industry was often criticized for high costs and ineffectiveness. For example, one industry observer complained in *Discount Store News* about the use of doubled coupons by retailers:

> Sure, I know it helps build traffic in stores, spike sales, squeeze the competition and move merchandise through the pipeline. But in the final analysis, I believe excessive couponing hurts retailers, suppliers, and consumers and damages the

spirit of partnership. It does not single-handedly improve profitability or enhance image.

It also annoys, alienates, and confuses consumers and does little to encourage store loyalty. It creates long lines that most retailers can't handle; it creates out-of-stocks, which force rain checks that in turn create other fulfillment issues. And it creates price wars that few retailers can win.[6]

One leading coupon distributor, Procter & Gamble (P&G), even experimented with dropping coupons completely in three New York markets in 1996. Angry consumers wrote letters to the editor, picketed, boycotted, and petitioned to get their coupons back.[7] P&G restored the coupons. In October 1997, P&G, nine other consumer products firms, and Wegmans Food Market Inc., without admitting guilt, agreed to pay a total of $4.2 million to settle state antitrust charges that they had colluded to reduce the number of shopping coupons distributed in western New York.[8]

Manufacturers also reduced the number of coupons by trying multibrand coupons, and by using more targeted promotions. One approach offered by Catalina Marketing's Checkout Coupons used consumer purchases to trigger coupons distributed at the checkout register. The redemption rate for Checkout Coupons in 1996 was 9 percent, compared to an average redemption rate of about 3 percent.[9] David Diamond, executive vice president for marketing and new applications, explained Catalina Marketing's appeal:

> Fundamentally, it is both more effective and efficient to target. You are not chopping down trees and sending lots of FSIs for dog food to people who don't own dogs. And you can personalize communication based on the buying habits of the person.[10]

However, the industry emphasized research indicating that consumers were still attracted by discount offerings. Some industry experts agreed, arguing that brand marketers and consumers actually liked coupons. For example, Joan Johnson, president of Punch Marketing, a marketing communications company located in Clemmons, North Carolina, said:

> It is amazing and somewhat laughable that a consumer promotion that has so much consumer loyalty is being vilified. It is largely coming because retailers have to bear the administrative logistics and they are tired of that. To think that a consumer is never going to be interested in saving money again is ridiculous. It is simply not human nature.[11]

When a customer purchased a product using a coupon, the retailer discounted the customer's bill and transmitted the coupon to a clearinghouse. The clearinghouse sorted the coupons and billed the manufacturers, who reimbursed the retailers for the face value of the coupon, plus a handling fee.

The industry had cooperated to address high costs of redemption. In January 1998, the Grocery Manufacturers of America (GMA) and the Joint Industry Coupon Committee (JICC) released a report titled "Coupons: A Complete Guide." The purpose of the report was to offer best practices for most efficient use of coupons, including use of more sophisticated bar codes, scanning devices, and elimination of unclear coupons that were hard to handle at the register.[12]

Couponing Rebounds in 1999

Coupon distribution was back up in 1999, increasing 3 percent over 1998,[13] with 92 percent of coupons distributed by FSIs, down slightly from 1998.[14] Consumer packaged

Exhibit 4   BREAKDOWN OF COUPON SPENDING, 1999 (IN BILLIONS)

Total spending	$6.153	
Face value	3.6	(59%)
Distribution	2.0	(32%)
Processing, handling, & other	0.5	(9%)

Source: NCH NuWorld Marketing.

Exhibit 5   DEMOGRAPHICS OF COUPON USERS, 1998

Age	% Using Coupons	Income	% Using Coupons
18–24	74	<$15,000	74
25–34	82	$15–25,000	83
35–44	83	$25–50,000	76
45–54	82	$50,000+	83
55–64	81		
65+	82		

Source: NCH NuWorld Marketing Limited, reprinted at www.couponmonth.com.

goods manufacturers spent more than $6 billion on coupons.[15] (Exhibit 4 shows the breakdown of this spending.) Electronic distribution methods grew by 20–30 percent but still accounted for less than half a share point of total coupon distribution. The average FSI redemption rate decreased slightly, to 1.1 percent, while redemption rates for other methods increased. Early evidence of electronic coupon usage showed much higher redemption rates, ranging from 20 percent to as high as 50 percent for personalized coupon packages. (Exhibit 5 shows the demographics of coupon users in 1998.)

From the manufacturer's perspective, coupons remained an important marketing tool. Wally Marx, president of Wallace Marx & Associates, an Edina, Minnesota, marketing consulting firm, explained in a *Brandmarketing* interview:

> The bottom line is, coupons are alive, well, and healthy—an essential part of the marketing mix. They are a very effective way to introduce new brands, gain trial and encourage pantry loading, and are probably the lowest-cost sampling method. Marketers are learning to use coupons more efficiently and more effectively, better targeting markets, better valuing their coupons by using high values in markets with high potentials, and tightening purchase requirements and expiration dates.[16]

Internet Shopping and Coupon Use

NPD Group, a marketing research firm, reported in May 1999 that 49 percent of Web-surfing respondents were aware of Web-based coupons, and 87 percent of these intended to either begin using them or increase the frequency with which they used them. Online coupon users were typically between the ages of 25 and 44.[17] A third of them had annual household incomes exceeding $75,000, versus 23 percent of the U.S. population in that income range.[18]

Forrester Research, Inc., a leading technology research firm, predicted in May 2000 that the number of households shopping online would nearly double, to 38 million, in the next two years. A study by the Boston Consulting Group, a prominent management consultancy, indicated that the demographic profile of new Internet users was changing to look more like the general population. New Internet users over the past year were 53 percent female, versus 42 percent for those using the Internet for three years or more. Half of new users had household incomes below $50,000, versus 34 percent of experienced users. New users included 35 percent with a high school education or less, compared to 17 percent of experienced users. Another research firm, Jupiter Communications, estimated that 42 percent of the U.S. population would be online by the end of 2000, compared to 14 percent in 1996.[19]

Company History

George F. Valassis incorporated Valassis Communications in 1970 as a sales agent for printing companies. In 1972, the company pioneered freestanding inserts (FSIs). George Valassis sold the company to Australia-based Consolidated Press Holdings (CPH) in 1986 for $365 million. CPH sold half its interest for nearly $1 billion when Valassis went public in 1992.[20] The company used much of the proceeds from the initial public offering to pay CPH a large dividend, leaving the company with about $550 million in debt and a shareholders' equity deficit of about $400 million.[21] CPH sold the remainder of its interest in the company in a secondary offering completed in July 1997.

After earning $82 million in 1993, Valassis experienced double trouble in 1994. A new competitor, Sullivan Graphics Inc., entered the FSI business, triggering a price war, followed soon by a paper price increase of 65 percent. Valassis lost $400,000 in 1994. Sullivan exited the business after less than a year, selling out to News America, the only other competitor in the FSI business. Valassis's financial performance improved steadily after 1995. By 1999 revenues were $795 million, with net income of $114 million. (Exhibits 6 through 9 contain financial data.)

Valassis Communications' Products and Services

Valassis described its product portfolio in its 1999 annual report as follows:

> Valassis Communications, Inc., leads the marketing services industry by providing a wide range of strategic marketing solutions for manufacturers and retailers. The company's products and services meet a variety of marketing objectives by delivering the right communications to the right consumers at the right time through the right media. From mass to one-to-one marketing, Valassis' strategic solutions include newspaper-delivered co-op and specialty inserts, advertising, product sampling, direct mail, and e-commerce solutions, as well as consulting services.

Three business divisions (Free-Standing Inserts, Valassis Impact Promotions, Targeted Marketing Services) comprised most of Valassis's revenue. An equity investment in the

Exhibit 6   VALASSIS COMMUNICATIONS, INCOME STATEMENTS, 1995–99 ($ MILLIONS)

	1999	1998	1997	1996	1995
Revenue					
FSI	$586.7	$567.7	$521.3	$504.1	$480.7
VIP	118.1	103.1	89.2	89.4	76.8
TMS	69.0	48.4	41.0	N/A	N/A
Other	20.8	22.2	24.0	N/A	N/A
Total revenue	$794.6	$741.4	$675.5	$659.1	$613.8
Cost of products sold	$491.6	$485.1	$436.2	$473.1	$466.1
SG&A	83.1	77.2	77.4	67.1	59.5
Amortization	5.2	8.1	8.6	8.2	9.6
Restatement[1]	0.0	0.0	0.0	3.1	(3.1)
Operating earnings	214.7	171.0	153.3	107.6	81.7
Minority interests	0.0	0.0	0.0	0.0	(1.4)
Writedowns/sale of business	0.0	0.0	0.0	0.0	16.9
Interest expense	26.0	34.5	38.3	39.6	40.5
Income taxes	67.5	52.2	45.1	28.2	13.0
Income before extraordinary loss	121.1	84.3	69.9	39.8	12.7
Extraordinary loss (net of taxes)[2]	6.9	13.6	0.0	0.0	0.0
Net income	$114.2	$ 70.7	$ 69.9	$ 39.8	$ 12.7

[1]Restated in 1998 due to change from LIFO to FIFO inventory valuation.

[2]Results for the following years include:

1998: A one-time charge of $3.7 million, net of tax, for expenses related to the early retirement and resulting amendment to the employment contract of the former CEO, as well as an extraordinary loss of $13.6 million, net of tax, due to the early extinguishment of debt.

1999: An extraordinary loss of $6.9 million, net of tax, due to early extinguishment of debt, as well as a tax benefit, net of associated close-down costs related to Valassis of Canada, of $2.7 million.

Source: Annual reports and 10K reports.

Customer Relationship Marketing Group represented a new business area. (Exhibits 10 and 11 contain financial performance by segment.)

Freestanding Inserts (FSIs)

Almost three-quarters of Valassis's revenue ($587 million) came from freestanding inserts (FSIs). FSIs were referred to as co-op promotions because they contained promotions from a number of companies in different product categories (versus solo inserts, which featured only one company's products). Valassis's FSIs were delivered to over 58 million households across the United States (61 percent of total U.S. households) 43 times a year through over 530 Sunday newspaper editions. Its FSI business held approximately a 50 percent market share.

Valassis also offered an FSI program for smaller counties not efficiently covered by national FSI programs. This C&D County Supercenter Program was started in 1995 to meet the needs of customers interested in targeting Wal-Mart grocery shoppers and was distributed to over 5 million households. In Canada, Valassis published Shop & Save FSI, distributed to approximately 5 million households (45 percent of Canadian households).

Exhibit 7   VALASSIS COMMUNICATIONS, CONSOLIDATED BALANCE SHEETS AT DECEMBER 31, 1995–99 ($ MILLIONS)

	1999	1998	1997	1996	1995
Assets					
Current assets:					
Cash and equivalents	$ 11.1	$ 6.9	$ 35.4	$ 60.2	$ 34.4
Accounts receivable	94.1	95.4	81.7	92.8	84.4
Raw material inventory	11.7	11.8	11.0	6.1	13.8
Work in progress inventory	17.5	20.1	15.7	14.7	14.3
Prepaid expenses & other	6.0	5.8	4.5	1.9	3.7
Deferred income taxes	1.5	1.8	2.0	2.1	4.3
Refundable income taxes	0.4	1.2	0.8	—	0.1
Total current assets	142.3	143.1	151.1	177.8	155.0
Net property, plant, and equipment	52.8	46.4	40.2	34.8	34.9
Net intangible assets	40.1	41.2	47.3	55.9	64.1
Equity investments and advances to investees	9.6	—	—	—	—
Other assets	2.4	1.4	2.3	5.2	4.9
Total assets	$247.2	$232.0	$240.9	$273.7	$258.9
Liabilities and stockholders' deficit					
Current liabilities:					
Accounts payable	$ 77.7	$ 69.1	$ 59.2	$ 67.3	$ 72.0
Accrued interest	3.6	4.5	5.1	6.1	6.4
Accrued expenses	30.5	26.3	25.9	22.4	21.2
Progress billings	57.7	58.6	58.2	57.2	49.2
Current portion, long-term debt	—	—	—	7.3	—
Income taxes payable	—	—	—	1.1	—
Total current liabilities	169.6	158.6	148.4	161.4	148.8
Long-term debt	291.4	340.5	367.1	395.9	416.0
Deferred income taxes	1.9	1.5	2.3	2.6	3.0
Total debt	462.9	500.6	517.8	559.9	567.8
Minority interests	—	—	—	0.4	0.4
Stockholders' deficit:					
Common stock	0.6	0.6	0.4	0.4	0.4
Additional paid-in capital	76.9	69.4	72.4	41.3	39.6
Accumulated deficit	(51.7)	(165.9)	(236.6)	(306.5)	(349.5)
Foreign currency translations	(0.5)	(0.3)	(0.1)	(0.3)	0.2
Treasury stock, at cost	(240.9)	(172.3)	(113.0)	(21.5)	—
Total stockholders' deficit	(215.6)	(268.5)	(276.9)	(286.6)	(309.3)
Total liabilities and stockholders' deficit	$247.2	$232.0	$240.9	$273.7	$258.9

Source: Annual reports and 10K reports.

Exhibit 8   VALASSIS COMMUNICATIONS, CONSOLIDATED STATEMENTS OF CASH FLOW, 1997–1999 ($ MILLIONS)

	Years Ended December 31		
	1999	1998	1997
Cash flow from operating activities			
Net earnings	$ 114.2	$ 70.7	$ 69.9
Adjustments:			
Depreciation	7.7	7.6	6.8
Amortization	5.2	8.2	8.8
Provision for losses on A/R	1.9	0.9	0.9
Stock-based compensation	2.2	2.7	1.4
(Gain)/loss on sale of property, plant and equipment	(0.1)	0.0	(0.2)
Deferred income taxes	0.7	(0.6)	(0.1)
Minority interest	0.0	0.0	(0.5)
Changes in assets & liabilities			
Total adjustments	32.5	17.3	20.6
Net cash provided by operations	$ 146.7	$ 87.9	$ 90.5
Cash flow from investments:			
Additions to property, plant and equipment	$ (14.3)	$ (13.4)	$ (13.0)
Proceeds from sale of property, plant and equipment	0.2	0.1	1.0
Investments and acquisitions	(10.7)	(0.5)	0.0
Other	(0.2)	(0.2)	0.1
Net cash used in investments	$ (24.9)	$ (13.9)	$ (11.9)
Cash flow from financing:			
Issuance of common stock	$ 11.9	$ 30.0	$ 17.1
Purchase of treasury shares	(80.5)	(105.7)	(91.5)
Repayment of long-term debt	(219.7)	(153.7)	(36.2)
Borrowings of long-term debt	99.7	127.0	0.0
Capital contribution	0.0	0.0	7.3
Revolving line of credit	70.9	0.0	0.0
Net cash used in financing	$(117.7)	$(102.5)	$(103.3)
Net (decrease)/increase in cash and equivalents	$ 4.2	$ (28.5)	$ (24.7)
Cash and equivalents at beginning of year	6.9	35.4	60.2
Cash and equivalents at end of year	11.1	6.9	35.4

Source: Annual reports and 10K reports.

Exhibit 9   VALASSIS COMMUNICATIONS, REVENUE BY GEOGRAPHIC LOCATION, 1997–99 ($ MILLIONS)

	1999	1998	1997
United States	$774.0	$721.1	$657.2
Canada	20.6	20.3	18.3
Total	$794.6	$741.4	$675.5

Source: 10K reports.

Exhibit 10 VALASSIS COMMUNICATIONS, REVENUE AND PROFIT BY BUSINESS SEGMENT, 1997–99 ($ MILLIONS)

	1999	1998	1997
Free-Standing Inserts (FSI)			
Revenues from external customers	$585.4	$567.7	$521.3
Intersegment revenue	6.1	4.4	0.6
Depreciation/amortization	11.0	13.2	12.6
Segment profit	161.8	121.5	99.8
Valassis Impact Promotions (VIP)			
Revenues from external customers	$118.1	$103.1	$ 89.2
Intersegment revenue	—	—	—
Depreciation/amortization	1.8	2.2	2.1
Segment profit	12.2	9.0	9.8
All Others			
Revenues from external customers	$ 90.9	$ 69.4	$ 62.7
Intersegment revenue	—	—	—
Depreciation/amortization	0.1	0.3	0.7
Segment profit	14.5	4.8	3.1

Source: 10K reports.

Exhibit 11 VALASSIS COMMUNICATIONS, OPERATING DIVISION DATA

	1999 Revenues ($ millions)	2000 Growth Forecast	Top 10 Customers % of Sales
Free-Standing Inserts (FSI)	585	4 to 6%	24%
Valassis Impact Promotions (VIP)	118	15%	54%
Targeted Marketing Services (TMS)	69	N/A	N/A
Product Sampling & Advertising	N/A	20%	50%
Run-of-Press (ROP)	N/A	0	93%
Promotion Watch	N/A	0	N/A
Customer Relationship Marketing Group (CRMG)	0	N/A*	N/A
Other revenue	22	N/A	N/A

*CRMG was expected to begin reporting revenue in the second half of 2000.
Source: Annual reports and 10K reports.

FSI promotions could be tailored to particular markets by varying coupon values, promotion copy, and terms of the offer. To increase the value of coupons for its customers, Valassis offered Horizons Coding. This bar coding on the FSI coupons allowed brand marketers to track redemption rates better by individual newspapers, coupon style, and format.

FSIs were particularly popular with consumer packaged goods manufacturers and franchise retailers. No single customer accounted for more than 10 percent of FSI sales.

Valassis Impact Promotions (VIP)

Valassis Impact Promotions (VIP) offered specialty promotions in a variety of shapes, sizes, and formats such as inserts featuring a single customer (solos), die-cuts, door hangers, box toppers, posters, calendars, and magnets. Promotions could be delivered through newspapers and direct mail. VIP promotions could be run any day of the year in any U.S. newspaper, allowing orders to be placed on a national, regional, or local basis.

Traditional customers were food-service franchises and retailers, while new customers were in such categories as telecommunications and computer hardware.

Targeted Marketing Services (TMS)

Targeted Marketing Services (TMS) included sampling, on-page newspaper promotion and advertising, and Promotion Watch, a security consulting business for implementing sweepstakes contests. TMS products included:

- Newspac, a sample attached to a brochure inserted into the newspaper.
- Newspouch, a product sample inside a newspaper delivery bag.
- Direct mail sampling.
- Brand Bag and Brand Bag+, advertisements printed on newspaper delivery bags that could include an attached coupon.
- Targeted FSIs for individual customers.
- Targeted solo inserts that promoted manufacturers' products in conjunction with specific retail locations.

Valassis also helped customers with different packaging options for samples. Customers could target their promotional programs based on demographics, geography, retail locations, or competitive users.

Promotion Watch provided promotion security consulting services, including execution of sweepstakes and contests. Valassis helped customers with the entire process, from preliminary planning through the writing of official rules, overseeing the printing and placement of winning pieces, and conducting background investigations of winners.

Traditional customers were consumer packaged goods companies, with new customers in the categories of e-commerce, mass merchandisers, telecommunications, financial institutions, and automotive.

Customer Relationship Marketing Group (CRMG)

In 1999, Valassis purchased a 30 percent equity stake in Relationship Marketing Group (RMG), a company that provided grocery retail frequent shopper data. RMG, founded in 1995, brought relationships with over 1,500 grocery retail outlets nationwide. The purpose of the new Customer Relationship Marketing Group (CRMG) was to build long-term relationships with retailers by helping them target promotions.

Suzanne E. Griffin, vice president and general manager of CRMG, explained the purpose of the program:

> It will allow retailers to reach the right consumers, with the right offer, at the right time, in the specific promotional medium that the individual consumer will respond to. This will be accomplished through a proprietary system which collects, integrates, analyzes and applies customer data.[22]

CRMG was expected to begin reporting revenue in the second half of 2000.

Other Marketing Services

Valassis also offered services to assist customers in planning, executing and evaluating the success of their promotions. Research Services obtained and provided industry research on coupon distribution and redemption trends and competitive activity. TACTest was a program allowing quick testing of multiple promotion options using split market runs in nine test markets. Media Services provided analysis of current market coverage, competitive activity, and high opportunity areas.

Discontinued Operations

Effective January 2000, Valassis closed Carole Martin Gifts, an unprofitable Canadian mail-order business, part of a 1995 acquisition. Two previous divestitures, both in 1997, were a discontinued joint venture called Valassis de Mexico and Valassis France.

Valassis Operations

Production and Procurement

Valassis printed its own FSIs at three facilities located in Livonia, Michigan (225,000 square feet); Wichita, Kansas (138,000 square feet); and Durham, North Carolina (110,000 square feet). The company believed that in-house printing provided an advantage in quality control. Pre-press operations (preparing customers' materials for printing) were located in Plymouth, Michigan, near the Livonia facility.

Valassis claimed to be the low-cost producer in the industry, due to its efforts to lower the three largest components of cost of goods sold:

1. Paper (41 percent).
2. Media—fees paid to newspapers to insert coupons (36 percent).
3. Printing (23 percent).

Valassis purchased primarily one type of paper (coated groundwood No. 5 sheet) from three primary suppliers. During 1999, Valassis negotiated multiple-year contracts for 75 percent of paper requirements, preventing prices from varying more than 6–10 percent in a 12-month period; remaining paper requirements were purchased on 3–6 month contracts. On average, the company maintained less than 30 days' paper inventory.[23]

In 1995 and 1996, paper prices fluctuated dramatically, increasing nearly 70 percent in 1995, before returning in early 1997 to 1994 levels. Prices increased less dramatically in 1997 and the first half of 1998, and decreased during the second half of 1998 and throughout 1999. Management expected flat paper prices in the first half of 2000 due to favorable supply conditions.

Media costs were driven by the size of FSI and contract terms. The average size of FSI booklets increased in 1998 and 1999, reducing the cost per coupon due to distribution efficiencies. Valassis was the sixth largest buyer of newspaper space in the United States. This position helped the company negotiate lower contract prices. FSIs were estimated to represent 5 to 8 percent of newspaper revenue and were an important reason consumers subscribed to Sunday newspapers.[24]

Valassis had decreased printing costs annually for 11 years through investment in new technology that also improved customer service. For example, in October 1999 the company produced its first variable data printing job on a web printing press for T.G.I. Friday's Restaurant System. The variable data using Valassis's proprietary Aztec scanner code included the customer's address, address of the closest restaurant, the customer's dining points, and a promotional offer. The company reported that very few U.S. printers used a web press system for this type of application. Ron Goolsby, vice president of Livonia Printing Division, explained:

> Providing more valuable products and services to our clients is always one of our goals at Valassis. With this upgrade in printing technology, we have the capability to shorten the make ready and production time of a 750,000-piece job, from three weeks to just 24 hours.[25]

The pre-press operation was in the process of converting to a full digital workflow, using state-of-the-art computer-to-plate technology. This technology enabled increased efficiency, sharper images, and reduced turnaround time. The company planned to spend approximately $15 million each year for the next three to five years to increase printing capacity and replace or rebuild equipment as required.

Sales

Valassis operated regional sales offices in 10 cities: Atlanta; Boston; Chicago; Dallas; Livonia; Los Angeles; Minneapolis; Montreal; Toronto; and Wilton, Connecticut. Account managers from various product lines served customers in teams, using a consultative selling approach, helping customers choose the right markets, media, and designs to meet their marketing objectives. A significant portion of revenue was from repeat business.

FSI customers were billed 75 percent of each order 8 weeks before publication, and the balance immediately prior to publication. These progress billings were shown on the balance sheet as a current liability and recognized as revenue when published.

Finance

Valassis did not pay cash dividends but was actively repurchasing common stock. The firm had recently announced a third consecutive 5-million-share common stock repurchase program and planned to allocate at least half of future cash flow to share repurchases. Schultz explained the rationale for this program:

> Repurchasing our stock has been an excellent investment and has enhanced shareholder value. We continue to believe share repurchase is one of the most efficient uses of our substantial cash flow. The new authorization also demonstrates our strong confidence in the future.[26]

The company also restructured long-term debt in 1999, lowering interest expense by approximately $8 million. Over the past four years, the firm expended a total of $426 million on share repurchase and debt reduction.

The company completed a 3-for-2 stock split effective May 13, 1999, in the form of a 50 percent stock dividend. (See the stock price history in Exhibit 1.) Schultz explained the rationale for a stock split:

> The board of directors has determined that a desirable trading range for our stock is between $30 and $50 per share. Based on the consumer orientation of our products, we want our stock to be a reasonable purchase for individual investors.[27]

Exhibit 12   VALASSIS COMMUNICATIONS BOARD OF DIRECTORS, 2000

Director/Affiliation	Age	Date Appointed to Directorship
Alan F. Schultz Chairman, president, and CEO of Valassis Communications, Inc.	41	December 1995
Richard N. Anderson Executive vice president of manufacturing and purchasing, Valassis Communications, Inc.	54	December 1998
Patrick F. Brennan Retired president and CEO of Consolidated Papers, Inc. (paper manufacturer)	68	August 1998
Seth Goldstein Entrepreneur-in-residence and principal of Flatiron Partners (an Internet venture capital firm)	29	March 1999
Brian J. Husselbee President and CEO of NCH NuWorld Marketing Limited (coupon clearinghouse)	48	August 1998
Joseph E. Laird Jr. Cofounder, chairman, and CEO of Laird Squared, LLC (investment bank specializing in database information industry)	54	June 1999
Robert L. Recchia Executive vice president and chief financial officer of Valassis Communications, Inc.	43	October 1991
Marcella A. Sampson Retired dean of students and director of career services at Central State University, Ohio	69	August 1998
Ambassador Faith Whittlesey Chairman and president of American Swiss Foundation; president of Maybrook Associates, Inc.; Former U.S. Ambassador to Switzerland and member of Senior White House Staff	61	January 1992

Source: Proxy statement, April 12, 2000; and 1999 annual report.

On September 2, 1999, the company adopted a shareholder rights plan. The plan involved declaring a dividend of one preferred stock purchase right for each outstanding share of the company's common stock. The rights would be exercisable only if a person or group not approved by the board of directors acquired 15 percent or more of Valassis's common stock or announced a tender offer for 15 percent or more of the common stock. (Exhibit 12 contains board composition.) Schultz explained the purpose of the plan:

> The rights are intended to enable all of our shareholders to realize the long-term value of their investment in Valassis. The rights do not prevent a proxy contest or a takeover, but should encourage anyone seeking to acquire Valassis to negotiate with the board prior to attempting a takeover.[28]

Exhibit 13   VALASSIS COMMUNICATIONS RANKING ON *FORTUNE*'S LIST OF "100 BEST COMPANIES TO WORK FOR"

Year	Position in Ranking	Number of Employees (U.S./ outside U.S.)	Percent Women	Percent Minorities	Job Growth	Voluntary Turnover (previous year)	Average Training (hours/ year/ employee)
1999	26	1,357/69	51%	11%	15%	5%	58
1998	37	1,274/221	49	9	4	8	58
1997	67	1,182/56	47	8	(8)	10	53

Source: *Fortune,* January 10, 2000; January 11, 1999; January 12, 1998.

Human Resource Management

Valassis employed over 1,600 employees across the United States and Canada. The majority of employees were involved in manufacturing (64 percent), with the rest in sales and marketing (23 percent), and management information systems and administration (12 percent). None of the employees were represented by unions (unusual in southeast Michigan). In 1999, Valassis was named one of *Fortune* magazine's "100 Best Companies to Work for in America" for the fourth consecutive year, moving to the number 26 position from number 37 in 1998 (see Exhibit 13). *Working Mother* magazine also named Valassis to its 1999 list of "100 Best Companies for Working Mothers," and *Crain's Detroit Business* identified Valassis as one of the "Best Places to Work in Southeast Michigan."

Valassis offered a number of programs to help employees balance home and work. Some of the more unusual programs included paid paternity leave, back-up child care, Gourmet to Go (meals ordered by 10:00 AM, delivered by 4:00 PM), Wheels on Loan (for when personal vehicles were being repaired), employee discounts for household cleaning services, and dry cleaning and hair salon on site. Marcia Hyde, vice president of human resources, emphasized the value of the company's focus on work/life balance issues:

> Our employee work/life balance program is a win–win situation. Employees are at their most innovative and productive when they aren't feeling pulled from their families due to the pressures of everyday life. We go the extra mile to make their lives simpler, and the pay-off is happier employees who stay with Valassis for long, full careers.[29]

Another area where Valassis continued to invest was employee education. The Valassis Learning Network included training programs for new employee orientation, understanding the business, personal productivity, leadership development, and life management development. Family members could also take courses ranging from baby-sitting skills to interviewing techniques and public speaking. Employees' children received high school graduation gifts from the company.[30]

In the area of health and wellness programs, the company provided on-site fitness facilities, an on-site doctor, a "Doctor On-Line" to answer medical questions, and a resource and referral service.[31]

Compensation included profit sharing and team achievement bonus plans covering all salaried and hourly employees.

Exhibit 14   SELECTED DATA FOR VALASSIS COMMUNICATIONS' COMPETITORS ($ MILLIONS)

Company	Ownership	Year Founded	1999 Revenue	1999 Net Income	1998 Revenue	1998 Net Income
News Corp. Ltd.[1]	Public	1997[1]	$13,585	$678	$12,641	$1,140
Cox Enterprises Inc.	Family	1898	3,378	N/A	3,130	N/A
International Data	Private	1964	2,560	N/A	2,060	N/A
Big Flower Holdings	Public/Private[2]	1992[3]	1,800	N/A	1,740	38
ADVO, Inc.	Public	1929	1,040	39	1,047	36
Valassis	Public	1970	795	114	741	71
Catalina Marketing Corp.	Public	1983	265	37	217	33
Sunflower Group	Private	1964	80*	N/A	67*	N/A

*Estimated

N/A = Not available

[1]Parent of News America. News America Marketing was created in 1997 by combining News Corp.'s existing FSI business with ACTMEDIA. Magazines/inserts business was 10% of News Corp. revenue in 1999.

[2]BFG was acquired by Vertis, Inc., a private investor group in 2000.

[3]BFG was founded in 1992/93 to acquire Treasure Chest Advertising, founded in 1967.

Sources: www.sec.gov (EDGAR online); www.newscorp.com; www.coxenterprises.com; *Printing News,* June 19, 2000 (www.printingnews.com/pages/issues/2000); www.datatrak.com/BGFDatat.pdf; forbes.com (Forbes 500 Largest Private Companies, 1998, 1999); www.transnationale.org; www.hoovers.com; www.sunflowergroup.com; and M. Cohen, S. Durchslag, and L. Goldstein, "Valassis: Sunflower in Discovery," *Promo,* August 1999.

Exhibit 15   U.S. ADVERTISING BY MEDIUM, 1999 ($ MILLIONS)

Medium	Expenditures
Magazine	$15,529.9
Sunday magazine	1,111.4
Newspaper	17,844.1
National newspaper	3,332.2
Outdoor	1,993.8
Network TV	18,003.1
Spot TV	15,387.0
Syndicated TV	2,996.2
Cable TV	8,754.6
Network radio	463.5
Spot radio	2,373.2
Internet	1,940.0
Yellow Pages	12,652.0
Total measured	$102,381.0
Total unmeasured*	$112,920.1
Total advertising	$215,301.1

*Unmeasured media include direct mail, promotion, co-op, couponing, catalogs, business and farm publications, special events, and other.

Source: *Advertising Age,* September 25, 2000, p. S4.

Competitors

Valassis shared the FSI market evenly with one direct competitor, News America Marketing. Other competitors included companies that distributed coupons in other ways, for example by direct mail (Val-Pak Direct Marketing Systems), in-store at checkout or at the shelf (Catalina Marketing), and over the Internet. (Exhibit 14 contains information about major competitors.) Valassis also competed with all other media for the advertising and promotion budgets of manufacturers and retailers. (Exhibit 15 shows 1999 advertising expenditures by media.)

News America

News America was the U.S. operating division of News Corporation Ltd., Rupert Murdoch's huge media and entertainment conglomerate. News Corp.'s empire encompassed newspapers, magazines, book publishers, paper manufacturing, television broadcasting, movie production, TV and cable stations, and the Los Angeles Dodgers.[32] News America's portfolio of products sharing the SmartSource brand included FSIs, in-store advertising, at-shelf couponing, sampling, and demonstration events. News America had recently announced minority investments in Planet U (expert in Internet electronic couponing,) and SoftCard Systems (provider of incentive programs aimed at frequent shoppers.)[33]

Sullivan Marketing, Inc., had attempted unsuccessfully to enter the FSI market in November 1993. Sullivan claimed that Valassis and News America violated antitrust laws by operating as a duopoly from 1988 until 1992. In February 1994, Sullivan exited the market by transferring its contracts and sales agreements to News America.

Cox Enterprises

Cox Enterprises, Inc., was another media conglomerate containing businesses that competed with Valassis. These included Carol Wright, Val-Pak Direct Marketing Systems (direct mail coupons), and Cox Sampling (solo direct mail sampling).[34] Val-Pak launched its own website in 1999, using its database of over 30,000 coupons. Shoppers could print coupons for selected areas off the website, or they could register for e-mail delivery of coupons in selected categories.[35] Val-Pak had recently announced an alliance with Catalina Marketing's Supermarkets Online to provide co-branded web pages. This alliance promised consumers easy access to local and national coupon offers.[36] Cox Enterprises also comprised newspapers, book publishing, telecommunications, television and radio, and auctions, among other businesses.

Catalina Marketing

Catalina Marketing Services, a unit of Catalina Marketing Corporation, marketed Checkout Coupon and other electronic marketing programs to supermarkets and mass merchandisers. Its scanner coupons cost about $90 per thousand people reached (versus $6–$7 per thousand for FSI coupons) but prompted redemption rates of 9 percent (versus 3 percent for FSIs).[37] In 2000, Catalina had over 13,500 U.S. stores in its network, plus over 2,000 in Europe and almost 400 through a Japanese joint venture.

Due to its extensive store network, Catalina's Supermarkets Online was the leader in Internet couponing. ValuePage was accepted in over 11,500 supermarkets within the Catalina Marketing Network. Coupons were provided by e-mail, based on consumer buying preferences, and manufacturers were charged only for redeemed coupons, at a lower price than Catalina's scanner coupons. However, Supermarkets Online was not yet profitable.[38]

Catalina was pursuing other alliances besides the one with Val-Pak. It entered a joint venture with ACNielsen to combine Catalina's frequent shopper data and Nielsen's consumer data to provide information to manufacturers and retailers. In March 2000, it announced an alliance with MyPoints.com, a provider of Internet direct marketing services to jointly market online direct marketing and loyalty solutions. PCData Online ranked MyPoints a top 10 Internet shopping site in January 2000.[39]

Other Competitors

Valassis competed with numerous other companies in specific segments of its business. ADVO, Inc., provided direct mail services such as ShopWise and the Missing Child card program. Sunflower Group specialized in sampling. Big Flower Holdings included Treasure Chest Advertising, the nation's largest printer of advertising circulars and inserts, plus TV listings and Sunday comics.[40] International Data provided consumer promotions management services including promotion analysis, coupon processing and redemption, direct mail and sampling. Its online database, BrandData, offered information about the success rates of coupons and competitors' coupons.[41]

Valassis was also facing new market entry via forward and backward integration. For example, in January 2000, Kraft Foods announced an alliance with Meredith Corporation, a large magazine publisher, and News America Corp. The alliance would produce "Food & Family," a custom-published insert to replace Kraft's spending on co-op FSIs. The publication was planned to appear monthly, through newspaper distribution, and include articles and recipes in addition to coupons for Kraft brands.[42] Another example was NCH NuWorld Marketing Ltd., primarily a provider of coupon processing and marketing information services. However, in August 1999, NCH announced a license agreement with Evolve Products, Inc., a producer of handheld display remote controls, to develop in-home coupon distribution through cable television.[43] Newspapers were also getting into the online coupon business. For example, Nando Media, a division of McClatchy Newspapers, had allied with NetValue Inc. to offer major retailers online coupons.[44]

Valassis Communications' E-Commerce Strategy

Valassis responded to the growth of Internet usage and increased competition in the coupon industry by developing a three-pronged e-commerce strategy:

1. Selling traditional media products to Internet companies.
2. Delivering coupons online.
3. Investing in the online grocery business.

Selling to Internet Companies

The first part of Valassis's e-commerce strategy was to sell its traditional offline media (e.g., FSIs and sampling) to online companies. The company's research indicated that 56 percent of FSI readers used the Internet and 63 percent of "wired" FSI readers had visited a website that they had seen listed in print advertising such as a magazine or newspaper. One example of this approach was "Surf and Save," a special FSI section featuring e-commerce companies. Suzanne Brown explained the potential for this segment:

> These rapidly emerging companies are looking for effective tools to increase web traffic. Our products, such as the FSI, and our targeted marketing services provide effective and efficient new ways for e-commerce marketers to get in front of millions of consumers every week. With the introduction of so many e-commerce sites, it's incredibly important for them to differentiate themselves and gain critical mass in their respective categories. Even the most fabulous online shopping experience can't be successful if nobody knows where to find it.[45]

In October, 1999, Valassis added to its own Surf and Save product by acquiring The Net's Best (TNB), LLC, for $3.9 million, net of cash acquired, plus future payments contingent on performance. The Net's Best, started a year earlier with a $1 million venture capital investment, maintained a website designed for Internet shoppers and produced a newspaper-delivered FSI sold to companies doing business on the Internet.[46] Valassis intended to maintain the name, The Net's Best, while merging the acquired company's six employees with Valassis's FSI operations. In 2000 Valassis planned to publish 12 co-op e-commerce inserts and 12 targeted solo e-commerce inserts, reaching 29 million households. Brown explained the objective of the acquisition:

> This acquisition will allow us to expedite our growth plans. Valassis will complement the TNB FSI with our co-op FSI, polybag advertising, direct mail, and other media capabilities. Our goal is to be the premier provider of marketing services to the Internet and e-commerce industries, and this acquisition brings us that much closer to the goal.[47]

Delivering Coupons Online

The second part of Valassis's e-commerce strategy was to expand into online coupons. It implemented this strategy through strategic investments and alliances. The first move in 1999 was to purchase 51 percent of Merge, LLC, renamed Save.com, an online coupon and promotion network.

Save.com was a network approach to online couponing, where coupons could be delivered to consumers at their favorite websites as well as on the Save.com site. The software would also permit delivery through CD-ROMs, and installation on original computer equipment. A proprietary scanner code (Aztec) provided security and maintained consumer profile data.

After a successful pilot test in September 1999, Valassis planned a national rollout in the second quarter of 2000. The test ran in two markets on seven participating websites, featuring over 130 national brands. Of all coupons viewed, 30 percent were selected (the "click" rate) compared to an industry average rate for banner advertisements of only 0.4 percent. Of those coupons clicked, 69 percent were printed.[48] Suzanne Brown was pleased with the results and optimistic about the future of online coupons:

> The high level of registration and downloads attests, once again, to consumers' insatiable appetite for value, particularly when it's this easy to do. As more and more families become wired, Save.com will become a daily tradition, just as Sunday freestanding inserts have been a weekly American tradition for decades.[49]

In May 2000, Save.com purchased two websites, MyCoupons.com and Direct-Coupons.com, from DirectStuff.com for an undisclosed amount of cash and a two-year marketing alliance. Valassis estimated the value of the total deal at $23 million. As part of the marketing alliance, DirectStuff.com would continue to manage both sites, as well as Save.com's website. MyCoupons.com was a consumer site that provided coupons, and DirectCoupons.com was a weekly e-mail publication with 450,000 subscribers. DirectStuff.com was started in 1994, and offered its first coupon website in 1995. By 2000, the company had 22 employees and three divisions, Advertising Network (online advertising), Publications Network (e-mail publications for coupons and recipes) and Gift Certificate Network.[50]

In addition to the Save.com equity investment, in April 2000 Valassis announced a strategic alliance with Coupons.com, a privately held company that delivered coupons directly to consumers over the Internet.[51]

Investing in Online Groceries

The third part of Valassis's e-commerce strategy was to participate in the growth of the online grocery business. It implemented this strategy through a strategic investment by acquiring 54 percent of Independent Delivery Services (IDS), a subsidiary of Dawick Enterprises, in 1999. IDS provided the technology for existing supermarkets to enter the online grocery business. Alan Schultz, Valassis's president, discussed the rationale for this investment:

> The potential for this service is huge. We believe that the traditional grocery store, who already has a relationship with the consumer, will ultimately win the battle for online grocery shoppers. The IDS service is what traditional grocery chains need to successfully migrate into Internet selling and compete with start-up e-commerce grocery companies. It is our intention to provide grocery retailers with a variety of products and services to build customer loyalty. The investment in IDS helps put Valassis in direct contact with retailers, who play a critical role in one-to-one relationship marketing. Not only does this investment move forward our Internet initiatives, it is also another step toward a comprehensive customer attainment and retention system.[52]

One example of an enhanced service was a recent partnership between IDS and BeeLineShopper.com to help consumers with special diet or nutritional needs develop their shopping lists. Dawn Dawick, president and CEO of IDS, was also enthusiastic about the partnership:

> IDS's market leadership and retail relationships, combined with Valassis's marketing expertise and relationships with major consumer package goods companies, will allow us to create WIN-WIN-WIN all the way down the channel.[53]

Valassis also sought synergies across its online and offline businesses. For example, it had recently announced the intention to use the small white space at the top of each page of FSIs to deliver banner messages promoting the company's online products and services. The IDS investment was expected to enhance the retailer relationships being developed by the Customer Relationship Marketing Group (CRMG.)

Valassis reported $4.4 million in e-sales during the first quarter of 2000 and predicted a total for the year of $20 million. Schultz and Brown were pleased with their results so far. But had they gone far enough to compete in an online world and meet the expectations of their customers and investors? Or were they moving too quickly, investing in areas with unknown profit potential? What challenges did their e-commerce strategy pose for their bread-and-butter FSI business? Was the organization equipped to handle the revolution under way?

Endnotes

[1]Company news release, April 26, 2000.

[2]1999 annual report.

[3]Company news release, June 21, 1999.

[4]Company news release, February 24, 2000.

[5]Coupon Council at www.couponmonth.com/pages/allabout.htm, accessed May 21, 2000.

[6]T. Lisanti, "The Almighty Coupon, Redux," *Discount Store News* 37, no. 18 (September 21, 1998), p. 13.

[7]A. A. Love, "Companies Want to Cut Coupons, but Consumers Demand Bargains." *Marketing News* 3, no. 10 (May 12, 1997), p. 15.

[8]"N.Y. Coupon Antitrust Case Settled for $4.2m," *Supermarket Business* 52, no. 10 (October 1997), p. 9

[9]V. Alonzo, "The Future of Couponing Is Still Debatable," *Incentive* 170, no. 9 (September 1996), p. 8.

[10]R. Turesik, "Sticking with Coupons," *Supermarket News,* BrandMarketing supplement, 5, no. 4 (April 1998), p. 12.

[11]Ibid.

[12]www.gmabrands.com/news/docs/newsrelease.cfm?docid=133, accessed May 21, 2000.

[13]www.couponpros.com/shouldNCHtrends.htm, accessed May 21, 2000.

[14]www.couponpros.com/shouldCMS1999trends.htm, accessed May 21, 2000 and www.nuworld.com/us/news/article, accessed May 21, 2000.

[15]www.prnewswire.com, accessed April 13, 2000.

[16]N. Brumback, "Coupon Comeback," *Brandmarketing* 6, no. 9 (October 1999), p. 24.

[17]"Couponing Jumps Online," *Potentials* 32, no. 5 (May 1999), pp. 16–17.

[18]U.S. Census Bureau, Current Population Reports, pp. 60–209. *Money Income in the U.S.: 1999* (Washington DC: Government Printing Office, 2000).

[19]W. Zellner, "Wooing the Newbies," *Business Week, E-Biz,* May 15, 2000, pp. EB116–EB120.

[20]George Hunter, "Shopping: Valassis Ready to Roll," *The Detroit News,* May 29, 1997, D1.

[21]T. Pratt, "Street jumps on Salomon for pricing of tough IPO," *Investment Dealers Digest* 58, no. 11 (March 16, 1992), p. 16.

[22]Company news release, October 7, 1999.

[23]Ibid., April 20, 1999.

[24]B. Cohen, & R. Settles, "Free Standing Coupon Inserts: Walking or Running to Electronic Channels?" posted February 2001 to www.digitaledge.org/monthly/2001_02/coupons/coupons101.html. Accessed at www.kan-non.com/work/articles_pdf/freestanding_coupon_inserts.pdf on May 1, 2002.

[25]Company news release, October 25, 1999.

[26]Ibid., January 10, 2000.

[27]Ibid., April 5, 1999.

[28]Ibid., September 2, 1999.

[29]Ibid., July 21, 1999.

[30]Ibid., July 28, 1999.

[31]Ibid., August 5, 1999.

[32]www.hoovers.com/co/capsule/6/0,2163,41816,00.html, accessed May 19, 2000.

[33]www.newscorp.com/report99/mag1.html, accessed May 19, 2000.

[34]www.coxdirect.com/corporate.html, accessed May 18, 2000.

[35]"Val-Pak Launches World's Largest Coupon Site," *Direct Marketing* 61, no. 9 (January 1999), p. 7.

[36]www.prnewswire.com/02-24-2000, accessed May 18, 2000.

[37]P. Thomas, "Web Trade-Off: Personal Profile for Market Savings; Coupons Tailored to Family Shopper," *The Arizona Republic,* June 23, 1998, p. E4.

[38]www.prnewswire.com, accessed May 18, 2000.

[39]Ibid.

[40]www.hoovers.com/co/capsule/3/0,2163,41633,00.html and 7/0,2163,46937,00.html, accessed May 19, 2000.

[41]"International Data LLC launches on-line coupon redemption database," *Direct Marketing* 61, no. 9 (January 1999), p. 12.

[42]S. Thompson, "Kraft, Meredith Team to Deliver Custom Insert," *Advertising Age* 71, no. 5 (January 31, 2000), pp. 2, 92.

[43]www.nuworld.com/us/news/articles, accessed May 21, 2000.

[44]J. L. Phipps, "The cyberclip," *Editor & Publisher,* Mediainfo.com Supplement, April 1999, pp. 32–33.

[45]Company news release, August 23, 1999.

[46]M. Ballon, "Valassis Acquires Producer of Newspaper Circulars," *Los Angeles Times,* October 21, 1999, p. C3.

[47]Ibid., October 18, 1999.

[48]Ibid., February 24, 2000.

[49]Ibid., February 15, 2000, and June 15, 1999.

[50]www.prnewswire.com, accessed May 15, 2000.

[51]"Insert Company Strikes Deal with Coupons.com," *iMarketing News* 2, no. 17 (May 1, 2000), p. 7.

[52]Company news release, September 2, 1999.

[53]Ibid.

Artemis Images
Providing Content in the Digital Age

Joseph R. Bell
University of Northern Colorado

Joan Winn
University of Denver

Christine
Nazarenus tried to retain her optimism. Thirteen had always been a lucky number for her, but Friday, July 13, 2001, had the earmarks of being the unluckiest day of her life. She was more than disappointed. She was shattered. Yet she knew that she had hard facts, not just gut feel, that offering images and products on the World Wide Web was the wave of the future. She was sure that the management team she had put together had the creativity and skills to turn her vision into reality. Managing her own company had seemed the obvious solution, but she hadn't counted on how overwhelming the start-up process would be. Now, two years later, she was trying to figure out what went wrong and if the company could survive.

It had been so clear on day one. Archived photographs and images had tremendous value if they could be efficiently digitized and cataloged. Sports promoters and publishers had stores of archived information, most of it inaccessible to those who wanted it. Owners and fans represented only part of the untapped markets that the Internet and digital technology could serve. She had conceived a simple business model: Digitize documents using the latest technology, tag them with easy-to-read labels, and link them to search engines for easy retrieval and widespread use. But over the ensuing months so many factors affected the look, feel, and substance of the company that Artemis Images would become.

So many things seemed outside her control that she wondered how she could have been so sure of herself back in February of 1999. Enthusiastically, Chris had approached a number of friends and acquaintances to help in the formation of a new dot-com company that seemed a sure bet. Frank Costanzo, a former colleague from Applied Graphics Technologies (AGT), shared Chris's enthusiasm, as did longtime friend George Dickert. George, in turn, contacted Greg Hughes, who was enrolled in a business planning course. Grateful for the opportunity to help launch a real company, Greg took the idea and honed it as part of a class assignment. The plan was a confirmation of Chris's confidence in the venture. But as she looked over the original plan, she knew there was a lot of work yet to do. Greg understood the business idea, but he didn't understand the work involved to actually run a business. George and Frank understood digital technology and project management but, like Chris, had never launched, much less worked for, a start-up company. Chris knew that she had the technology and talent she needed and felt confident that the four friends could construct a business model that would put Artemis ahead of the current image providers. Greg's business plan looked like the perfect vehicle to appeal to investors for the funds they needed to proceed.

The Business Idea

In 1999, Chris had been working for three years as vice president of sales out of the Colorado office of AGT, a media management company that provided digital imaging management and archiving services for some of the largest publishers and advertisers in the world. AGT had sent Chris to Indianapolis to present a content management technology solution to the Indianapolis Motor Speedway Corporation (IMSC) as it prepared marketing materials for the 2001 Indy 500. IMSC is the host of the 80-plus-year-old Indy 500, the largest single-day sporting event in the world; NASCAR's Brickyard 400, the second largest single-day sporting event in the world; and other events staged at the track. Chris's original assignment was a clear one: IMSC needed to protect its archive of photographs, many of which had begun to decay with age. The archive included 5–7 million photographs and dynamically rich multimedia formats of video, audio, and in-car camera footage.

Chris discovered that the photo archives at IMSC were deluged with requests (personally or via letters) from fans for images. She was amazed that a relatively unknown archive had generated nearly $500,000 in revenues in 1999 alone. Further discussions with IMSC researchers revealed that requests often took up to two weeks to research and resulted in a sale of only $60–$100. However, IMSC was not in a position, strategically or financially, to acquire a system to digitize and preserve these archives. Not willing to leave the opportunity on the table, Chris asked herself, "What is the value of these assets for e-commerce and retail opportunities?" Without a doubt, IMSC and some of her other clients (Condé Nast, BBC, National Motor Museum) would be prime customers for digitization and content management of their collections.

Chris knew that selling photos on the Internet could generate substantial revenue. She conceived of a business model where the system would be financed through revenue sharing, rather than the standard model where the organization paid for the system up-front. IMSC was interested in this arrangement, but it was outside the normal business practices of AGT. AGT wanted to sell systems, not give them away. They couldn't see the value of managing other organizations' content.

As Chris told the story, her visit to the archives at IMSC was her *Jerry Maguire* experience. In the movie, Jerry is sitting on the bed when everything suddenly becomes clear and now he must pursue his dream. Like Jerry, Chris believed so passionately that her idea would bear fruit that, when AGT turned down Chris's request for the third time, she quit her job to start Artemis Images on her own.

Building a Team

When AGT was not interested in Chris's idea of on-site digitization and sale of IMSC's photo archives, Chris was not willing to walk away from what she saw as a gold mine. She contacted her friends and colleagues from AGT. Swept up in the dot-com mania,

Exhibit 1 ARTEMIS IMAGES' MANAGEMENT TEAM, 1999–2000

- Christine Nazarenus, 34, was formerly vice president of national accounts for AGT, one of the top three content management system providers in the world, securing million-dollar deals for this $500 million company. She is an expert in creating digital workflow strategies and has designed and implemented content management solutions for some of the largest corporations in the world, including Sears, Condé Nast, Spiegel, Vio, State Farm, and Pillsbury. Ms. Nazarenus has extensive general management experience and has managed a division of over 100 people. Chris holds a BA in communications from the University of Puget Sound.

- George Dickert, 32, most recently worked as a project manager for the Hibbert Group, a marketing materials distribution company. He has experience with e-commerce, Web-enabled fulfillment, domestic and international shipping, call centers, and CD-ROM. He has overseen the implementation of a million-dollar account, has managed over $20 million in sales, and has worked with large companies, including Hitachi, Motorola, ON Semiconductor, and Lucent Technologies. Mr. Dickert has an MBA from the University of Colorado. George and Christine have been friends since high school.

- Frank Costanzo, 40, is currently a senior vice president at Petersons.com. Petersons.com has consistently been ranked as one of the top 100 sites worldwide. Mr. Costanzo is an expert in content management technology and strategy and was previously a vice president at AGT. Mr. Costanzo has done in-depth business analysis and created on-site service solutions in the content management industry. He has worked on content management solutions for the world's top corporations, including General Motors, Hasbro, Bristol-Meyers Squibb, and Sears.

- Greg Hughes, 32, is currently a senior sales executive with one of the largest commercial printers in the world. Mr. Hughes has 10 years' sales experience and has sold million-dollar projects to companies like US West, AT&T, R. R. Donnelly, and MCI. His functional expertise includes financial and operational analysis, strategic marketing, fulfillment strategies, and the evaluation of start-to-finish marketing campaigns. Mr. Hughes has an MBA from the University of Colorado.

Chris named her company e-Catalyst and incorporated it as an S-corporation on May 3, 1999, with four owners: Christine Nazarenus, George Dickert, Frank Costanzo, and Greg Hughes. (See Exhibit 1 for profiles of these partners.) Expecting that they would each contribute equally, each partner was given a 25 percent interest in the company. Chris fully expected them to work as a team, so no formal titles were assigned, largely as a statement to investors that key additions to the team might be needed and welcomed. As another appeal to potential investors—and to broaden the team's expertise—Chris and George put together a roster of experts with content management, systems and technology experience as their first advisory board. Greg's professor and several local business professionals agreed to serve on the board of advisers, along with an Indy 500–winning driver-turned-entrepreneur, and Krista Elliott Riley, president of Elliott Riley, the marketing and public relations agency that represented Indy 500 and Le Mans Sports Car teams and drivers. Chris felt confident that her team had the expertise she needed to launch a truly world-class company.

Chris and George quit their jobs and took the challenge of building a company seriously. They contacted one of the Rocky Mountain region's oldest and most respected law firms for legal advice. They worked with two lawyers, one who specialized in representing Internet companies as general counsel and one who specialized in intellectual property rights. With leads from her many contacts at AGT, Chris contacted venture capitalists to raise money for the hardware, software licensing, and personnel costs of launching the business.

The dot-com bust of 2000 did not make things easy. Not wanting to look like yet another dot-com in search of money to throw to the wind, Chris and her team changed their name to Artemis Images. Artemis, the Greek goddess of the hunt, had been the name of Chris's first horse as well as her first company, Artemis Graphics Greeting Cards, her first entrepreneurial dabble at the age of 16. Chris had always been enthralled with beautiful images.

Artemis Images' Niche

In her work at AGT, Chris had observed that many organizations had vast stores of intellectual property (photos, videos, sounds, and text), valuable assets often underutilized because they existed in analog form and could deteriorate over time. Chris's vision was to preserve and enable the past using digital technology and the transportability of the World Wide Web. Chris envisioned a company that would create a digitized collection of image, audio, and video content that she could sell to companies interested in turning their intellectual property into a source of revenue.

Publishers and sports promoters were among the many organizations with large collections of archived photos and videos. Companies like Boeing, General Motors, and IMSC are in the business of producing planes, cars, or sporting events, not selling memorabilia. However, airplane, car, and sports fans are a ready market for photos of their favorite vehicle or videos of their favorite sports event.

Proper storage and categorization of archived photos and videos is complex and expensive. In 2000, the two common solutions were to sell the assets outright or to set up an in-house division devoted to managing and marketing them. Most organizations were unwilling to sell their assets, as they represented their priceless brand and heritage. Purchasing software and hiring specialized personnel to digitize and properly archive their assets was a costly proposition that lay beyond the core competence of most companies. Chris's work with AGT convinced her that there were literally thousands of companies with millions of assets that would be interested in a company that would digitize and manage their photo and video archives.

Chris understood a company's resistance to selling its archives, and the high cost of obtaining and scanning select images for sale. However, she also understood the value to an organization of having its entire inventory digitized, thus creating a permanent history for the organization. She proposed a revenue-sharing model whereby Artemis Images would digitize a client's archives but would not take ownership. Instead, her company would secure exclusive license to the archive, with 85 percent of all revenue retained by Artemis Images, and 15 percent paid to the archive owner. She expected that the presence of viewable archives on the Artemis Images website would lure buyers to the site for subsequent purchases.

The original business model was a business-to-consumer (B2C) model. Starting with the IMSC contract, Artemis Images would work with IMSC to promote the Indy 500 and draw the Indy race fans to the Artemis Images website. Photos of the current-year Indy 500 participants—and historical photos including past Indy participants, winners, entertainers, celebrities (e.g., Arnold Palmer on the Indy golf course)—would be added to IMSC's archived images and sold for $20–$150 apiece to loyal fans. A customer could review a variety of photo options on the Artemis website, then select and order a high-resolution image. The order would be secured through the Web with a credit card, the image transferred to the fulfillment provider, and a hard copy mailed to the eager recipient. The website was sure to generate revenue easier than IMSC's traditional sales model of the past.

Having established the model with IMSC content in the auto racing market, Chris and George built the business plan around obvious market possibilities that might appeal to a wider range of consumers and create a comprehensive resource for stock photography. Since the Artemis Images team had prior business dealings with two of the three largest publishers in the world, publishing was the obvious target for future contracts. Future markets would be chosen similarly, where the Artemis team had established relationships. These markets would be able to build on the archive already created and would bring both consumer-oriented content and salable stock images. Greg made a list of examples of some industries and the content that they owned:

- Sports: images of wrestling, soccer, basketball, bodybuilding, football, extreme sports.
- Entertainment: recording artists, the art from their CDs, movie stars, pictures of events, pictures from movie sets.
- Museums: paintings, images of sculpture, photos, events.
- Corporations: images of food, fishing, planes, trains, automobiles.
- Government: coins, stamps, galaxies, satellite imaging.

As Chris and George worked with Greg to put together the business plan, they began to see other revenue-generating opportunities for their virtual-archive company. Customers going to IMSC or any other Artemis client's website would be linked to Artemis Images's website for purchase of photos or videos. Customer satisfaction with image sales would provide opportunities to sell merchandise targeted to specific markets and to syndicate content to other websites. For motorsports, obvious merchandise opportunities would include T-shirts, hats, and model cars. For landscapes it might be travel packages or hiking gear. Corporate customers might be interested in software, design services, or office supplies. Unique content on Artemis Images' website could be used to draw traffic to other companies' sites. Chris and her team planned to license the content on an annual basis to these sites, creating reach and revenues for Artemis Images.

Another potential market for Artemis Images lay in the unrealized value of the billions of images kept by consumers worldwide in their closets and drawers. These images were treasured family heirlooms that typically sat unprotected and underutilized. Consumers could offer their photographs for sale or simply pay for digitization services for their own use. If just 10 percent of the U.S. population were to allow Artemis Images to digitize their archive and half of these people ordered just one 8-by-10-inch print, Artemis Images could create a list of 25 million consumers and generate revenues of approximately $250 million. Because images suffer no language barriers, the worldwide reach of the Internet and the popularity of photography suggested potential revenues in the billions.

Working together on the business plan, the Artemis team brainstormed ways they could attract customers to the Artemis Images site by providing unique content and customer experiences. A study by Forrester Research analyzed the key factors driving repeat site visits and found that high-quality content was cited by 75 percent of consumers as the number one reason they would return to a site. The Artemis team wanted to create a community of loyal customers through additional unique content created by the customers themselves. This would include the critical chats and bulletin boards that are the cornerstone of any community-building program. Artemis Images could continuously monitor this portion of the site to add new fan experiences to keep the experience fresh. Communities would be developed based on customer interests.

As the company gained clients and rights to sell their archived photos and videos, Artemis would move toward a business-to-business (B2B) model. Chris and George knew marketing managers at National Geographic, CMG World Wide, the BBC, Haymarket Publishing (which included the Formula 1 archive), Condé Nast, and International Publishing Corporation. These large publishers controlled and solicited a wide range of subject matter (fashion, nature, travel, hobbies, etc.) yet often had little idea of what existed in their own archives, or had difficulty in getting access to it. Finding new images was usually an expensive and time-consuming proposition. Artemis Images could provide the solution. For example, Condé Nast (publisher of *Vogue, Bon Appetit, Condé Nast Traveler, House & Garden,* and *Vanity Fair*) might like a photo for its travel magazine from the National Geographic archives. They would be willing to pay top dollar for classic stock images, given the number of viewers who would see the image. Price per image was typically calculated on circulation volume, much like royalty fees on copyrighted materials. Similarly, advertising agencies use hundreds of images in customer mockups. For example, an agency may desire an image of a Pacific island. If Artemis Images held the rights to Condé Nast and National Geographic, there might be hundreds of Pacific island photos from which to choose. As with the B2C concept, a copy of the image would be transferred through the Web with a credit card or on account, if adequate bandwidth were available (only low-resolution images would be available to view initially), or via overnight mail in hard copy or on disk.

The transition from B2C to B2B seemed a logical progression, one that would amass a large inventory of salable prints and, at the same time, draw in larger per-unit sales. The basic business model was the same. Artemis would archive photos and videos that could be sold to other companies for publication and promotion brochures. Chris and George expected that this model could be replicated for other vertical markets, including other sports, nature, entertainment, and education.

While the refocus on the B2B market seemed a surer long-term revenue stream for the company, both B2B and B2C were losing favor with the investing community. Chris and George refocused the business plan as an application service provider (ASP). With the ASP designation, Artemis Images could position itself as a software company, generating revenue from the licensing of its software processes. In 2000, ASPs were still in favor with investors.

Artemis Images' revenue would come from three streams: (1) sales of images to businesses and consumers, (2) syndication of content, and (3) sales of merchandise. Projected sales were expected to exceed $100 million within the first four years, with breakeven occurring in year 3. (See Exhibits 2, 3, and 4 for projected volume and revenues.)

To implement this strategy, Artemis Images needed an initial investment of $500,000 to begin operations, hire the team, and sign four additional content agreements. A second round of $1.5 million and a third round of $3 million to $8 million (depending on number of contracts) were planned, to scale the concept to 28 archives and over $100 million in assets by 2004. (See Exhibit 5 for the funding and ownership plan.)

The Content Management Industry

According to GISTICS, the trade organization for digital asset management, the content management market (including the labor, software, hardware, and physical assets necessary to manage the billions of digital images) was projected to be a $2 trillion market worldwide in the year 2000 (1999 Market Report). Content could include images, video, text, and sound. Artemis Images intended to pursue two subsets of the content management market. The first was the existing stock photo market, a business-to-business market where rights to images were sold for limited use in publications like magazines, books, and websites. Deutsche Bank's Alex Brown estimated this to be a $1.5 billion market in 2000. Corbis, one of the two major competitors in the digital imaging industry, estimated it to be a $5 billion market by 2000.

Commercially produced images were also in demand by consumers. Industry insiders believed that this market was poised for explosive growth in 2000, as Web-enabled technology facilitated display and transmission of images directly from their owners to individual consumers. The archives from the Indianapolis Motor Speedway was an example of this business-to-consumer model. Historically, consumers who bought from the archive had to visit the museum at IMSC or write a letter to the staff. Retrieval and fulfillment of images then required a manual search of a physical inventory, a process that could take as long as two weeks. Web-based digitization and search engines would reduce the search time and personnel needed for order fulfillment, and allow customers the convenience of selecting products and placing orders online. The *Daily Mirror,* a newspaper in London, had displayed its archived images on its own website and had generated over $30,000 in sales to consumers in its first month of availability. IMG, a sports marketing group, placed a value of $10 million on the IMSC contract.

Competition

There were a variety of stock and consumer photo sites, ranging from those that served only the business-to-business stock photo market to amateur photographers posting their pictures. Most sites did not offer a "community" (the Internet vehicle for consumer comments and discussion), a powerful search engine, and ways to repurpose the content (e-greeting cards, prints, photo mugs, calendars, etc.). In addition, the archives available in digital form were limited because other content providers worked from the virtual world to the physical world versus the Artemis Images model of working from the physical world to the virtual world. Competitors had problems with integrated digital workflows and knowing where the original asset resided due to the distributed nature of their archives. They scanned images on demand, which severely limited the content available to be searched on their websites.

Chris and Greg evaluated the six major competitors for their business plan:

1. www.corbis.com: Owned by Bill Gates, Corbis had an archive of over 65 million images, only 650,000 of which were available on the Web to be accessed by consumers for Web distribution (e-greeting cards, screen savers, etc.). About 350,000 images were available for purchase as prints. The site was well designed and the search features were good, but there was no community on the site. The niche Corbis pursued was outright ownership of archives and scanning on demand. Corbis had recently acquired the Louvre archive, for a reported purchase price of over $30 million.

2. www.getty-images.com: An archive of over 70 million images. In 1999, this site was only a source to link to their other wholly owned subsidiaries, including Art.com. There were no search capabilities, no community. This website functioned

Exhibit 2   ARTEMIS IMAGES, ANTICIPATED SALES VOLUME AND ON-SITE OPERATIONS, 2001–2003

	Volumes 2001				
	Jan-01	Feb-01	Mar-01	Apr-01	May-01
Consumer photos	0	0	7,500	7,500	27,000
Stock photos	0	0	0	3,750	4,500
Subtotal	0	0	7,500	11,250	31,500
Licensing deals	0	0	0	0	0
Merchandise orders	0	0	6,000	6,000	21,600

	Volumes 2002				
	Jan-02	Feb-02	Mar-02	Apr-02	May-02
Consumer photos	12,000	15,000	15,000	15,000	54,000
Stock photos	6,000	7,500	9,000	10,500	12,000
Subtotal	18,000	22,500	24,000	25,500	66,000
Licensing deals	8	9	10	11	12
Merchandise orders	9,600	12,000	12,000	12,000	43,200

	Volumes 2003				
	Jan-03	Feb-03	Mar-03	Apr-03	May-03
Consumer photos	24,800	31,000	31,000	31,000	111,600
Stock photos	17,000	21,250	25,500	29,750	34,000
Subtotal	41,800	52,250	56,500	60,750	145,600
Licensing deals	16	16	16	16	16
Merchandise orders	15,600	19,500	19,500	19,500	70,200

	Onsite Operations (by quarters)				
	2000	2001			
	Qtr 4	Qtr 1	Qtr 2	Qtr 3	Qtr 4
Onsites (cumulative)	1	4	4	7	10

Source: e-Catalyst Business Plan, February 28, 2000.

only as a brochure for the company. Like Corbis, Getty was focused on owning content and then scanning on demand.

3. www.art.com: A good site in design and navigation, this site was a wholly owned subsidiary of Getty and was positioned as the consumer window to a portion of the Getty archive. As with Corbis, customers were able to buy prints, send e-greeting cards, and so on. Despite the breadth of the Getty archive, this site had a limited number of digitized images available.

4. www.mediaexchange.com: Strictly a stock photo site targeted toward news sources, the site was largely reliant on text. It was difficult to navigate and had an unattractive graphical user interface.

| Volumes 2001 | | | | | | | |
Jun-01	Jul-01	Aug-01	Sep-01	Oct-01	Nov-01	Dec-01	Total
9,000	9,000	22,500	18,000	9,000	4,500	22,500	136,500
5,250	6,750	7,500	9,000	9,750	10,500	11,250	68,250
14,250	15,750	30,000	27,000	18,750	15,000	33,750	204,750
1	1	2	4	5	6	7	26
7,200	7,200	18,000	14,400	7,200	3,600	18,000	109,200

| Volumes 2002 | | | | | | | |
Jun-02	Jul-02	Aug-02	Sep-02	Oct-02	Nov-02	Dec-02	Total
18,000	18,000	45,000	36,000	18,000	9,000	45,000	300,000
15,000	15,000	15,000	15,000	15,000	15,000	15,000	150,000
33,000	33,000	60,000	51,000	33,000	24,000	60,000	450,000
13	14	15	16	16	16	16	156
14,400	14,400	36,000	28,800	14,400	7,200	36,000	240,000

| Volumes 2003 | | | | | | | |
Jun-03	Jul-03	Aug-03	Sep-03	Oct-03	Nov-03	Dec-03	Total
37,200	37,200	93,000	74,400	37,200	18,600	93,000	620,000
42,500	42,500	42,500	42,500	42,500	42,500	42,500	425,000
79,700	79,700	135,500	116,900	79,700	61,100	135,500	1,045,000
16	16	16	16	16	16	16	192
23,400	23,400	58,500	46,800	23,400	11,700	58,500	390,000

| Onsite Operations (by quarters) | | | | | | | |
| 2002 | | | | 2003 | | | |
Qtr 1	Qtr 2	Qtr 3	Qtr 4	Qtr 1	Qtr 2	Qtr 3	Qtr 4
13	13	16	19	22	25	28	28

5. www.thepicturecollection.com: Strictly a stock site offering the *Time* photo archive, this site was well designed with good search capabilities. Searches yielded not only a thumbnail image but also a display of the attached locator tags, or metadata.

6. www.ditto.com: The world's leading visual search engine, Ditto.com enabled people to navigate the Web through pictures. The premise was twofold: deliver highly relevant thumbnail images and link to relevant websites underlying these images. By 2000, Ditto.com had developed the largest searchable index of visual content on the Internet.

Exhibit 3   PROJECTED MONTHLY REVENUE STREAM FOR ARTEMIS IMAGES, 2001–2003

	Revenues 2001				
	Jan-01	Feb-01	Mar-01	Apr-01	May-01
Consumer photos	$0	$0	$149,925	$149,925	$ 539,730
Stock photos	0	0	0	562,500	675,000
Subtotal	0	0	149,925	712,425	1,214,730
Syndication	0	0	0	0	0
Merchandise	0	0	45,000	45,000	162,000
Total	$0	$0	$194,925	$757,425	$1,376,730

	Revenues 2002				
	Jan-02	Feb-02	Mar-02	Apr-02	May-02
Consumer photos	$ 239,880	$ 299,850	$ 299,850	$ 299,850	$1,079,460
Stock photos	900,000	1,125,000	1,350,000	1,575,000	1,800,000
Subtotal	1,139,880	1,424,850	1,649,850	1,874,850	2,879,460
Syndication	283,333	358,333	441,667	533,333	633,333
Merchandise	72,000	90,000	90,000	90,000	324,000
Total	$1,495,213	$1,873,183	$2,181,517	$2,498,183	$3,836,793

	Revenues 2003				
	Jan-03	Feb-03	Mar-03	Apr-03	May-03
Consumer photos	$ 495,752	$ 619,690	$ 619,690	$ 619,690	$ 2,230,884
Stock photos	2,550,000	3,187,500	3,825,000	4,462,500	5,100,000
Subtotal	3,045,752	3,807,190	4,444,690	5,082,190	7,330,884
Syndication	1,650,000	1,783,333	1,916,667	2,050,000	2,183,333
Merchandise	117,000	146,250	146,250	146,250	526,500
Total	$4,812,752	$5,736,773	$6,507,607	$7,278,440	$10,040,717

Source: e-Catalyst Business Plan, February 28, 2000.

Exhibit 6 shows a comparison of Artemis Images to the two major players in the stock photography market, Getty and Corbis. This table illustrates only revenues from stock photo sales and does not include potential revenue from consumer sales, merchandise, advertising or other potential revenue sources.

According to its marketing director, Corbis intended to digitize its entire archive, and was in the process of converting analog images into digital images, with 63 million images yet to be converted. While Getty and Corbis were established players in the content industry, they were just recently feeling the effects of e-commerce:

- In 1999, Corbis generated 80 percent of its revenues from the Web versus none in 1996.
- Getty's e-commerce sales were up 160 percent between 1998 and 1999.
- In 1999, 34 percent of Getty's revenues came from e-commerce versus 17 percent in 1998.

| Revenues 2001 | | | | | | | |
Jun-01	Jul-01	Aug-01	Sep-01	Oct-01	Nov-01	Dec-01	Total
$ 179,910	$ 179,910	$ 449,775	$ 359,820	$ 179,910	$ 89,955	$ 449,775	$ 2,728,635
787,500	1,012,500	1,125,000	1,350,000	1,462,500	1,575,000	1,687,500	10,237,500
967,410	1,192,410	1,574,775	1,709,820	1,642,410	1,664,955	2,137,275	12,966,135
8,333	16,667	33,333	66,667	108,333	158,333	216,667	608,333
54,000	54,000	135,000	108,000	54,000	27,000	135,000	819,000
$1,029,743	$1,263,077	$1,743,108	$1,884,487	$1,804,743	$1,850,288	$2,488,942	$14,393,468

| Revenues 2002 | | | | | | | |
Jun-02	Jul-02	Aug-02	Sep-02	Oct-02	Nov-02	Dec-02	Total
$ 359,820	$ 359,820	$ 899,550	$ 719,640	$ 359,820	$ 179,910	$ 899,550	$ 5,997,000
2,250,000	2,250,000	2,250,000	2,250,000	2,250,000	2,250,000	2,250,000	22,500,000
2,609,820	2,609,820	3,149,550	2,969,640	2,609,820	2,429,910	3,149,550	28,497,000
741,667	858,333	983,333	1,116,667	1,250,000	1,383,333	1,516,667	10,100,000
108,000	108,000	270,000	216,000	108,000	54,000	270,000	1,800,000
$3,459,487	$3,576,153	$4,402,883	$4,302,307	$3,967,820	$3,867,243	$4,936,217	$40,397,000

| Revenues 2003 | | | | | | | |
Jun-03	Jul-03	Aug-03	Sep-03	Oct-03	Nov-03	Dec-03	Total
$ 743,628	$ 743,628	$ 1,859,070	$ 1,487,256	$ 743,628	$ 371,814	$ 1,859,070	$ 12,393,800
6,375,000	6,375,000	6,375,000	6,375,000	6,375,000	6,375,000	6,375,000	63,750,000
7,118,628	7,118,628	8,234,070	7,862,256	7,118,628	6,746,814	8,234,070	76,143,800
2,316,667	2,450,000	2,583,333	2,716,667	2,850,000	2,983,333	3,116,667	28,600,000
175,500	175,500	438,750	351,000	175,500	87,750	438,750	2,925,000
$9,610,795	$9,744,128	$11,256,153	$10,929,923	$10,144,128	$9,817,897	$11,789,487	$107,668,800

Strategy

Artemis Images intended to provide digitization and archive management by employing a professional staff who would work within each client-company's organization, rather than in an off-site facility of its own. Chris's model was to provide digitized archive services in exchange for (1) exclusive rights to market the content on the Internet, (2) merchandising rights and (3) promotion of Artemis Images' uniform resource locator (URL), effectively co-branding Artemis Images with each client-partner. Chris envisioned a software process that would be owned or licensed by Artemis, and that could be used for digitizing different archive media, such as photos, videos, and text.

Chris and George expected Artemis Images to partner with existing sellers of stock photography and trade digitizing services for promotion through their sales channels. Artemis Images would pursue these relationships with traditional sales and marketing

Exhibit 4   ARTEMIS IMAGES, PRO FORMA FINANCIAL SUMMARY 2000

	Summary Profit and Loss Statement				
	2000	2001	2002	2003	Total
Revenues	$ 0	$14,393,468	$40,397,000	$107,668,800	$162,459,268
Cost of sales	0	5,186,454	11,398,800	30,457,520	47,042,774
Gross profit	0	9,207,014	28,998,200	77,211,280	115,416,494
Operations	439,847	13,623,571	27,109,143	47,078,657	88,251,217
Net income before tax	(439,847)	(4,416,556)	1,889,057	30,132,623	27,165,277
Taxes (38%)	0	0	0	10,322,805	10,322,805
Net income	($439,847)	($ 4,416,556)	$ 1,889,057	$ 19,809,818	$ 16,842,472

	Summary Balance Sheet			
	2000	2001	2002	2003
Assets				
Cash and equivalents	$428,020	$4,490,768	$4,958,270	$21,508,477
Accounts receivable	0	2,488,942	4,936,217	11,789,487
Inventories	0	0	0	0
Prepaid expenses	0	0	0	0
Depreciable assets	0	0	0	0
Other depreciable assets	0	0	0	0
Depreciation	0	0	0	0
Net depreciable assets	0	0	0	0
Total assets	$428,020	$6,979,710	$9,894,487	$33,297,964
Liabilities and capital				
Accounts payable	$367,867	$ 1,836,113	$ 2,861,833	$ 5,589,379
Accrued income taxes	0	0	0	866,113
Accrued payroll taxes	0	0	0	0
Total liabilities	$367,867	$ 1,836,113	$ 2,861,833	6,455,492
Capital contribution	500,000	10,000,000	10,000,000	10,000,000
Stockholders' equity	0	0	0	0
Retained earnings	(439,847)	(4,856,403)	(2,967,346)	16,842,472
Net capital	60,153	5,143,597	7,032,654	26,842,472
Total liabilities and capital	$428,020	$ 6,979,710	$ 9,894,487	$33,297,964

Source: e-Catalyst Business Plan, February 28, 2000.

techniques. Salespeople would call on the major players and targeted direct mail, trade magazine advertising, and public relations would be used to reach the huge audience of smaller players. In addition, content partners were expected to become customers, as they were all users of stock photography.

As Artemis Images gained clients, the company would have access to some of the finest and most desirable content in the world. Chris knew that the workflow expertise of the management team would put them in a good position to provide better quality more consistently than either Corbis or Getty. This same expertise would allow

Exhibit 5   ARTEMIS IMAGES' ORIGINAL FUNDING PLAN

	Round 1	Round 2	Round 3	Round 4	Exit
Financing assumptions					
2003 revenues	$110,000,000				
2003 EBITDA	$ 30,000,000				
2003 revenue growth rate	40%				
2003 valuation	$440,000,000				
Valuation/revenue	4				
Valuation/EBITDA	14.67				
Round 1 financing	$ 500,000				
Round 2 financing	$ 1,500,000				
Round 3 financing	$ 3,000,000				
Round 4 financing	$ 5,000,000				

	Round 1 Oct-00	Round 2 1-Jan	Round 3 1-Mar	Round 4 1-Jun	Exit 3-Dec
Number of shares outstanding					
Total number of shares outstanding prior to financing	6,000,000	7,200,000	9,000,000	11,250,000	11,250,000
Shares issues this round	1,200,000	1,800,000	2,250,000	1,406,250	1,406,250
Total number shares outstanding after financing	7,200,000	9,000,000	11,250,000	12,656,250	12,656,250
Valuations					
Pre-money valuation	$2,500,000	$6,000,000	$12,000,000	$40,000,000	$440,000,000
Amount of financing	500,000	1,500,000	3,000,000	5,000,000	0
Post-money valuation	$3,000,000	$7,500,000	$15,000,000	$45,000,000	$440,000,000
Price per share	$0.42	$0.83	$1.33	$3.56	$34.77
Resulting ownership					
Founders	83.33%	66.67%	53.33%	47.41%	47.41%
Round 1 investors	16.67	13.33	10.67	9.48	9.48
Round 2 investors	0.00	20.00	16.00	14.22	14.22
Round 3 investors	0.00	0.00	20.00	17.78	17.78
Round 4 investors	0.00	0.00	0.00	11.11	11.11
Total	100.00%	100.00%	100.00%	100.00%	100.00%
Value of ownership					
Founders	$2,500,000	$5,000,000	$ 8,000,000	$21,333,333	$208,592,593
Round 1 investors	500,000	1,000,000	1,600,000	4,266,667	41,718,519
Round 2 investors	0	1,500,000	2,400,000	6,400,000	62,577,778
Round 3 investors	0	0	3,000,000	8,000,000	78,222,222
Round 4 investors	0	0	0	5,000,000	48,888,889
Total	$3,000,000	$7,500,000	$15,000,000	$40,000,000	$440,000,000

	Round 1	Round 2	Round 3	Round 4	
Payback to investors					
Holding period (years)	3.25	3.00	2.75	2.50	
Times money back	83.44	41.72	26.07	9.78	
Internal rate of return (IRR)	290%	247%	227%	149%	

Source: e-Catalyst Business Plan, February 28, 2000.

Exhibit 6   COMPARATIVE DATA FOR ARTEMIS IMAGES AND SELECT COMPETITORS

	Stock Photo Market					
	Artemis Images	Artemis Images	Artemis Images	Artemis Images	Getty	Corbis
	Indy Archive 2000[a]	2000	2001	2002	1999	1999
Archive size	5,000,000	5,000,000	50,000,000	95,000,000	70,000,000	65,000,000
Cumulative number of images digitized	345,600	345,600	6,796,800	21,542,400	1,200,000	2,100,000
% Digitized[b]	7%	7%	14%	23%	1.71%	3.2%
# of image sales needed to hit revenue target	0	0	151,484	623,493	1,646,667	666,666
% of archive that must be sold to hit revenue target[c]	0	0	0.30%	0.16%	2.35%	1.00%
Revenues[d]	0	0	$22,722,600	$93,523,950	$247,000,000	$100,000,000
Revenue per image in archive	0	0	$0.45	$0.98	$3.53	$1.54
Revenue per digitized image	0	0	$3.25	$4.30	$205.83	$47.62

[a]Artemis Images had already secured an exclusive content agreement from the Indianapolis Motor Speedway Corporation.

[b]Estimates based on scanning 1,920 images a day per scanner, 2 scanners per archive. As scanning technologies improve the throughput numbers were expected to go up.

[c]The percentage of the Artemis Images archive that needed to be sold to hit revenues projections varied between 0.03% and 0.22% as compared to an actual 2.35% for Getty and to 0.6% for Corbis.

[d]The Artemis Images revenue numbers were based on selling a certain number of images at $150 per image. $150 was the minimum average price paid for stock photographs. Corbis was privately held; this figure was an estimate.

Artemis to have a much larger digital selection, with a website design that would be easily navigable for customers to find what they needed.

Using on-site equipment, the client's content would be digitized, annotated (by attaching digital information tags, or metadata), and uploaded to the corporate hub site. Metadata would allow the content to be located by the search engine and thus viewed by the consumer. For example, a photo of Eddie Cheever winning the Indy 500 would have tags like Indy 500, Eddie Cheever, win photo, 1998, and so on. Therefore, a customer going to the website and searching for "Eddie Cheever" would find this specific photo, along with the hundreds of other photos associated with him. The Artemis corporate database was intended to serve as the repository for search and retrieval from the website.

The traditional content management strategy forced organizations to purchase technology and expertise. Artemis Images' model intended to alleviate this burden by exchanging technology and expertise for exclusive web distribution rights and a share of revenues. The operational strategy was to create an infrastructure based on installing and operating digital asset management systems at their customers' facilities to create a global digital archive of images, video, sound, and text. This would serve to lock Artemis Images into long-term relationships with these organizations and ensure that

Artemis Images would have both the best historical and the most up-to-date content. Artemis Images would own and operate the content management technology, with all other operational needs outsourced, including Web development, Web hosting, consumer data collection, and warehousing and fulfillment of merchandise (printing and mailing posters or prints). Artemis Images would scan thousands of images per day, driving down the cost per image to less than $2, versus the Corbis and Getty model of scan-on-demand, where the cost per image was approximately $40. The equipment needed for both the content management and photo production would be leased to minimize start-up costs and ensure greater flexibility in the system's configuration.

The original plan was to purchase and install software and hardware at their main office in Denver, Colorado, contract with a Web development partner, and set up the first on-site facility at Indianapolis Motor Speedway Corporation. The Denver facility would serve as a development lab, to create a standard set of metadata to be used by all of their partners' content. This consistency of annotation information was intended to allow for consistent search and retrieval of content. Artemis Images' goal was to build a world-class infrastructure to handle content management, consumer data collection, and e-commerce. This infrastructure would allow them to amass a large content and transaction volume by expanding to other market segments. Developing their own structure would ensure standardization of content and reduced implementation time. Outreach for news coverage and the development of community features would be negotiated concurrently. The time line in Exhibit 7 illustrates the Artemis Images' development plan.

Financial Projections

Revenues were expected to come from four primary sources:

1. **Consumer photos:** IMSC's archive sold approximately 53,000 photos in 1999 to a market limited to consumers who visited the archive or wrote to its staff. Artemis Images based its projected sales on an average of 15,000 images sold per archive in 2001, increasing to 20,000 images per archive in 2003. Price: $19.99 for an 8-by-10-inch photo.

2. **Stock photos:** Stock photos ranged in price from $150 to $100,000, depending on the uniqueness of the photo. Competitors Getty and Corbis, two of the leaders in this market, sold 2.35 percent and 0.6 percent of their archive, respectively. Based on an average selling price of $150, Getty generated approximately $6.00 in revenue for each image in its archive; Corbis generated approximately $1.85. Artemis Images constructed financial projections based on sales of 0.30 percent of its archive in 2001 and 0.16 percent of its archive in 2002. Artemis Images' margin was based on a return of $0.20 per image in its archive for 2001, increasing to $0.60 per image in 2003.

3. **Syndication:** The team's dot-com experience led them to believe that websites with exclusive content were able to syndicate their content to other websites. They anticipated that Artemis Images would generate revenues of $100,000 per year from each contract for content supplied as marketing tools on websites. Existing companies with strong content had been able to negotiate five new agreements per week for potential annual revenues of $5 million.

4. **Merchandise:** According to America Online/Roper Starch Worldwide, approximately 30 percent of Internet users regularly made purchases. Artemis Images

Exhibit 7   Artemis Images' Development Time Line

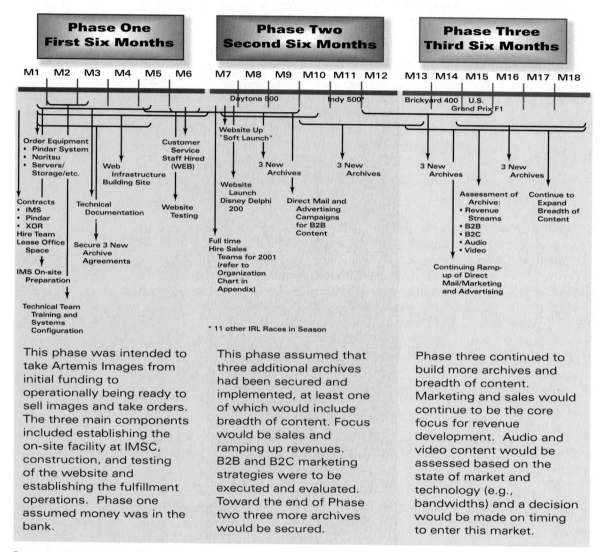

Source: e-Catalyst Business Plan, February 28, 2000.

used a more conservative assumption that only 1 percent of unique visitors would make a purchase. Estimates of the average purchase online varied widely, ranging from Wharton's estimate of $86.13 to eMarketers' estimate of $219. The Artemis Images team viewed $50 per purchase as a conservative figure.

Chris and George felt confident that Artemis Images would be able to reach the revenue projections for number of photos sold. IMSC's archive had sold approximately 53,000 photos in 1999, an increase of 33 percent over 1998. These sales had been generated solely by consumers who had visited the archive in person, estimated at 1 million people. In other words, 1 out of every 28 possible consumers actually purchased an image. Chris and George assumed that if even 1 out of 160 unique visitors to the website purchased a photo, the Artemis website would generate 42 percent more than IMSC's 1999 figures (see Exhibit 6 for projected sales volume). Chris and George believed that this projection was reasonable in light of the fact that IMSC did not market its archive and significant publicity and advertising would accompany Artemis Images' handling of the archive. As breadth of content and reach of the Web increased, 2002 revenues should easily be double those of 2001.

Since the team previously had configured and sold content management systems, they were familiar with the costs associated with this process, including both equipment and personnel. They carefully conducted research to stay abreast of recent improvements in technology and intended to be on the lookout for cost reductions and process improvements.

The Launch: Problems from the Start

Chris dove into the Artemis Images project with a vengeance. Having secured a five-year contract for exclusive rights and access to the IMSC archive, she found a dependable technician who was eager to relocate to Indianapolis to start the scanning and digitizing process. A reputable, independent photo lab agreed to handle printing and order fulfillment. Chris's visit to the Indy 500 in May 2000 was a wonderful networking opportunity. She met executives from large companies and got leads for investors and clients. She secured an agreement with a Web-design company to build the Artemis Images site, careful to retain ownership of the design. She contacted over 100 potential venture capitalists and angel investors.

Personally, she was on a roll. Financially, she was rapidly going into debt. Frank and Greg, legal owners of the company, had long since contributed ideas, contacts, or legwork to the Artemis Images launch. While confident that his work on the business plan would appeal to investors, Greg viewed the start-up company as a risk to which he was unwilling to commit. Likewise, Frank decided to hold on to his job at Petersons.com, a unit of Thompson Learning, until the first round of investor funding had been secured. Frank continued to offer advice, but he had a wife and two preschool children to support.

Each meeting with a potential funder resulted in a suggestion on how to make the business more attractive for investment. Sometimes they helped, sometimes they just added to Chris's and George's frustration. Beating the bushes for money over two years was exhausting, to say the least. The lack of funds impacted the look and feel of the business, and severely strained relationships among the founding partners. Heated discussions ensued as to the roles that each was expected to play, the reallocation of equity ownership in the company, and the immediate cash needed to maintain the Indianapolis apartment and pay the scanning technician and Web developers, not to mention out-of-pocket expenses needed to manage and market the business.

Chris and George appealed to their families for help. George's father contributed $5,000. Chris's mother tapped into her retirement, mostly to pay Chris's mortgage and to fund Chris's trips to potential clients and investors in London, New York, and Boston. By May 2001, Chris's mother's contribution had exceeded $200,000. A $50,000 loan from a supportive racing enthusiast provided the impetus for Artemis Images to reorganize as a C corporation. All four original partners had stock in the new

Exhibit 8   REVISED PRO FORMA FINANCIAL SUMMARY, 2001

	Summary Profit and Loss Statement				
	2001	2002	2003	2004	Total
Revenues	$ 5,312*	$373,779	$2,294,116	$4,735,400	$7,408,607
Cost of sales	1,700	43,368	265,312	564,480	874,860
Gross profit	3,612	330,411	2,028,804	4,170,920	6,533,747
Operations	52,499	328,550	1,235,363	2,035,430	3,651,842
Net income before tax	(48,887)	1,861	793,441	2,135,490	2,881,905
Taxes (38%)	0	0	283,638	811,486	1,095,124
Net income	($48,887)	$ 1,861	$ 509,803	$1,324,004	$1,786,781

	Summary Balance Sheet			
	2001	2002	2003	2004
Assets				
Cash and equivalents	$45,113	$ 78,260	$675,347	$2,615,573
Accounts receivable	0	13,610	222,950	462,200
Inventories	0	0	0	0
Prepaid expenses	0	0	0	0
Depreciable assets	0	0	0	0
Other depreciable assets	0	0	0	0
Depreciation	0	0	0	0
Net depreciable assets	0	0	0	0
Total assets	$45,113	$ 40,574	$898,297	$3,077,773
Liabilities and Capital				
Accounts payable	$ 4,000	$ 12,355	$ 61,882	$ 105,868
Accrued income taxes	0	0	283,638	1,095,124
Accrued payroll taxes	0	0	0	0
Total liabilities	$ 4,000	$ 12,355	$345,520	$1,200,992
Capital contribution	90,000†	90,000	90,000	90,000
Stockholders' equity	0	0	0	0
Retained earnings	(48,887)	(61,781)	462,777	1,786,781
Net capital	41,113	28,219	552,777	1,876,781
Total liabilities and capital	$45,113	$ 40,574	$898,287	$3,077,773

*Approximately two-thirds of these transactions were executed by Artemis staff and friends to test the website.
†Chris's mother's contribution to her daughter for mortgage and living expenses is not included.

company, but Chris held the majority share (66 percent), George held 30 percent, and Frank's and Greg's shares were each reduced to 2 percent. Financial projections were revised downward (see Exhibit 8).

The site was officially launched on May 18, 2001. It was beautiful. Chris held her breath as she put in her credit card late that evening when the site went live. The shopping cart failed and the order could not be processed. Chris knew she was in trouble.

The Crash

From the first, the website had problems. The Web development contract stipulated that the website for the Indy 500 would go live by May 8, 2001, to coincide with the monthlong series of events held at the Indianapolis Motor Speedway leading up to the Indy 500 on May 27. However, the Web development took longer than anticipated, and the site was first operational on May 18. The developers neglected to test the Web interface properly, and serious failures were encountered when the site was activated. The site went down for 24 hours, only to face similar problems throughout the following week, again shutting down on May 27. More technical difficulties delayed the reactivation of the site until May 31, after the Indy racing series had ended.

Throughout June, consumer traffic was far less than originally anticipated. The site was not easily navigable. The shopping cart didn't work. Yet the Web builder demanded more money. Fearful of a possible lawsuit, investors stayed away. The crash of the dot-coms added kindling to the woodpile. Chris and George started to rethink their original business model. They were held hostage, as they owned no tangible assets.

Website tracking data indicated that between May and July there had been at least $40,000 worth of attempted purchases. Chris read through hundreds of angry e-mails, and tried manually to process orders. Orders that were successfully executed resulted in spotty fulfillment. Many photos ordered were never shipped, were duplicated, or were incorrectly billed. At the same time, she tried to negotiate with the software developers' demand for payment and keep alive a $250,000 investment prospect.

On July 9, 2001, the Web development company threatened an all-or-nothing settlement. They wanted payment in full for the balance of the contract even though the site didn't work. Absent full payment, they would shut down the site within the week. The investor offered to put up 80 percent of the balance owed on the full contract to acquire the code to fix it. The company refused. On Friday, July 13, Chris had to tell IMSC that in less than 48 hours the site would be shut down. The investor took his $250,000 elsewhere.

On Tuesday, July 17, Chris called an emergency meeting with George. George had had enough. The stress was affecting his health, his relationships, and his lifestyle. He believed that his family had already contributed more money than he had a right to ask. He was putting in long hours with no money to show for his efforts. His girlfriend had been putting pressure on George to quit for some time. Now he had run out of reasons to stay.

Chris was devastated. How could she face the people in Indianapolis? It was hard for her to come to grips with having let them down. Having put so much of herself into this venture, she wasn't sure she could let go. At the same time, she wasn't sure how to go on.

Chris reflected, "At one time, I defined success by my title, my salary, and my possessions. Working for AGT, I had it all. I started Artemis Images because I really cared about IMSC and making the Indy motorsports images available to its fans. Now, I realize that there is a profound satisfaction in building a company. I can see my future so clearly, but living day to day now is so hard. And I'm still enthralled with beautiful images."

Callaway Golf Company
Sustaining Advantage in a Changing Industry

John E. Gamble
University of South Alabama

As Annika Sorenstam walked from the 18th green after posting scores of 67–70–70–68 to win the 2002 ADT Championship by three strokes, Callaway Golf Company's director of tour development looked on and thought of how Sorenstam's success aided the company in its development of new products for recreational golfers. Members of Callaway Golf's tour development staff had been in West Palm Beach during the late-November 2002 tournament's practice rounds to help Sorenstam, a Callaway Golf touring professional staff member, prepare for the tournament. Callaway's manufacturers' representatives and other staff members were on hand to help Sorenstam decide whether any turf, weather, and ground conditions might require the use of a special club and to make any necessary modifications to Sorenstam's 11 Callaway clubs, which included Steelhead X-14 irons, an Odyssey White Hot 2-Ball putter, and the company's new Great Big Bertha II titanium driver. The staff also had a supply of Callaway HX Red golf balls, which Sorenstam would use in the tournament.

Annika Sorenstam was among Callaway Golf Company's most notable touring professionals, with 13 tournament wins in 2002, 42 tour victories since turning professional in 1993, and the lowest score ever posted during a Ladies Professional Golf Association (LPGA) tournament (59). Sorenstam's 13 worldwide wins and 11 LPGA Tour wins during 2002 were the most wins recorded by a woman golfer in one season since Mickey Wright's 13 wins in 1964. Professional golfers like Annika Sorenstam or Charles Howell III of the PGA Tour were essential to new product development since Callaway's staff could not only observe how their prototypes of new products performed in tournament play but also gain the insight of touring professionals during prototype development. Sorenstam had visited Callaway Golf Company's Helmstetter Test Center many times between tournaments to hit balls with the company's new prototypes and give the company's R&D staff feedback on the performance and feel of new clubs. Annika began using the prototype of Callaway Golf's Great Big Bertha II in September 2002, when she won the Williams Championship in Tulsa. After using the new driver in tournament play, Sorenstam called the Great Big Bertha II "the greatest driver Callaway Golf has ever made" and asserted: "It's given me some extra distance . . . I'm probably carrying it at least 10 yards further—I mean, this week I had some drives that I just couldn't believe."[1] Sorenstam's average drive during the tournament of 284.5 yards represented an improvement of 22 yards over her previous average driving distance, and she went on to win five of the season's final eight tournaments with the new Great Big Bertha II driver.

As Callaway Golf Company entered 2003, CEO Ron Drapeau was pleased that the new club was on the market, since the company's sales of drivers and fairway woods had declined by 21 percent during 2002. Callaway Golf's declining sales of drivers reflected the industry's maturity and overall stagnant demand for drivers, but the golf equipment industry's leader in the sales of drivers and fairway woods, irons, and putters also faced other issues, such as the entry of aggressive new rivals and performance restrictions placed on golf clubs by the sport's governing body. Drapeau, who had been quickly installed as CEO in May 2001 after founder Ely Callaway was diagnosed with cancer, had called key managers to review the company's situation to better ensure its strategies would sustain Callaway Golf's number one ranking in the golf equipment industry. A review of Callaway Golf Company's financial performance between 1989 and 2002 is presented in Exhibit 1.

Company History

Callaway Golf Company began to take form in 1983 when Ely Reeves Callaway Jr. purchased a 50 percent interest in a Temecula, California, manufacturer and marketer of hickory-shafted wedges and putters for $400,000. Upon acquiring an interest in Hickory Stick USA, Ely Callaway became the company's president and CEO and soon began to transform the little-known maker of reproductions of antique clubs into the world's largest producer of golf clubs. Ely Callaway, a native of Georgia and distant cousin of golfing legend Bobby Jones, was an avid golfer and successful businessman. After graduating from Emory University in 1940, Callaway spent most of his career in the textile industry where his gracious and open style of dealing with almost everyone he met helped him gain promotion after promotion until he became president and director of Burlington Industries in 1968.

Callaway retired from Burlington Industries in 1973 and in the following year established a 150-acre vineyard in the valley outside of San Diego amid a chortle emanating from northern California skeptics who believed fine wines could not be produced in southern California. Callaway proved his critics wrong when the winery's first vintage won numerous awards and was selected for Queen Elizabeth II's bicentennial luncheon in New York at the Waldorf Astoria. By the end of the 1970s, Callaway had put Temecula, California, on the map as a bona fide wine-producing area. In 1981 he sold the company to Hiram Walker & Sons for more than $14 million—earning a $9 million profit.

Callaway wasted little time before venturing into the golf equipment industry with his 1983 purchase of 50 percent of Hickory Stick USA. He knew from the outset that the company's prospects for outstanding profits were limited as long as its product line was restricted to hickory-shafted clubs. Callaway noticed that most golf equipment had changed very little since the 1920s and believed that, due to the difficulty of the game of golf (there was so much room for variation in each swing of the club and for off-center contact with the ball), recreational golfers would be willing to invest in high-tech, premium-priced clubs if such clubs could improve their game by being more forgiving of a less-than-optimum swing. Ely Callaway's vision was at odds with that of Hickory Stick's founders, and the conflict eventually resulted in Callaway's outright purchase of the company. In 1985 Callaway hired Richard C. Helmstetter as the company's chief club designer; Helmstetter was aided by a team of five aerospace and metallurgical engineers in developing what Callaway termed a "demonstrably superior and pleasingly different" line of clubs that was set apart from competing brands by its technological innovation. Helmstetter and his team introduced the company's S2H2 (short,

Exhibit 1   CALLAWAY GOLF COMPANY, FINANCIAL SUMMARY, 1989–2002 (IN THOUSANDS, EXCEPT PER SHARE AMOUNTS)

	2002	2001	2000	1999	1998
Net sales	$792,064	$ 816,163	$ 837,627	$ 719,038	$703,060
Pretax income	111,671	98,192	128,365	85,497	(38,899)
Pretax income as a percent of sales	14%	12%	15%	12%	−6%
Net income	$69,446	$58,375	$80,999	$55,322	$(25,564)
Net income as a percent of sales	9%	7%	10%	8%	−4%
Fully diluted earnings per share[c]	$1.03	$0.82	$1.16	$0.78	$(0.38)
Shareholders' equity	$543,387	$514,349	$511,744	$499,934	$453,096
Market capitalization at Dec. 31	$788,256	$1,489,012	$1,380,926	$1,349,595	$769,725

[a]The company was not public until February 1992.
[b]Includes cumulative effect of an accounting change of $1,658,000.
[c]Adjusted for all stock splits through February 10, 1995; not adjusted for February 10, 1995 stock split.
Source: Callaway Golf Company annual reports.

straight, hollow hosel) line of irons in 1988 and an S2H2 line of metal woods in 1989. The 1988 S2H2 launch was accompanied by a name change—Callaway Hickory Stick USA became Callaway Golf Company. The S2H2 line of clubs was well received by professional and recreational golfers alike and became the number one driver on the Senior PGA Tour by year-end 1989.

The company's engineers followed up the successful S2H2 line in 1991 by launching the Big Bertha—named by Callaway after the World War I German long-distance cannon. The Big Bertha was revolutionary in that it was much larger than conventional woods and lacked a hosel (the socket in the head of the club into which the shaft is inserted) so that the weight could be better distributed throughout the head. This innovative design gave the clubhead a larger sweet spot, which allowed a player to strike the golf ball off-center and not suffer much loss of distance or accuracy. By 1992 Big Bertha drivers were number one on the Senior PGA, LPGA, and Hogan Tours. Callaway Golf Company became a public company on February 28, 1992. By year-end 1992 its annual revenues had doubled to $132 million, and by 1996 it had become the world's largest manufacturer and marketer of golf clubs, with annual sales of more than $683 million.

Ely Callaway's 1996 Retirement and the Formation of the Callaway Golf Ball Company

Callaway Golf continued to lead the golf equipment industry through the mid-1990s with innovative new lines of clubs. The company also introduced a line of golf apparel in 1996 that was available to golfers through an exclusive licensing agreement with Nordstrom. In May 1996 Ely Callaway announced he would retire as CEO and focus on the company's diversification into golf balls through a new subsidiary. Callaway believed that the company possessed the technological expertise to develop superior-performing golf balls and that the addition of golf balls was a natural fit with the company's golf club business. In announcing his retirement and the creation of the new golf ball subsidiary, Callaway commented, "We believe that there is a good and reasonable opportunity for Callaway Golf Ball Company, in due time, to create, produce and merchandise a golf ball that will be demonstrably superior to, and pleasingly different

1997	1996	1995	1994	1993	1992	1991[a]	1990[a]	1989[a]
$848,941	$683,536	$557,048	$451,779	$256,376	$132,956	$54,753	$21,518	$10,380
213,765	195,595	158,401	129,405	69,600	33,175	10,771	2,185	329
25%	29%	29%	29%	27%	25%	20%	10%	3%
$132,704	$122,337	$97,736	$78,022	$42,862[b]	$19,280	$6,416	$1,842	$329
16%	18%	18%	17%	17%[b]	15%	12%	9%	3%
$1.85	$1.73	$1.40	$1.07	$0.62	$0.32	$0.11	$0.04	$0.01
$481,425	$362,267	$224,934	$186,414	$116,577	$49,750	$15,227	$8,718	$6,424
$2,120,813	$2,094,588	$1,604,741	$1,127,823	$901,910	$245,254	—	—	—

from, any other golf ball we know of."[2] Upon the launch of the company's first golf ball in early 2000, Ely Callaway pointed out, "We have 7 million people out there playing our products, and 80% of them think they're the best clubs in the world—we have almost a guaranteed 'try' on our new products."[3]

Callaway Golf Company's 1998 Performance and the Return of Ely Callaway as CEO

A variety of events occurred shortly after Ely Callaway's retirement that resulted in both Callaway Golf's loss of market share in fairway woods and poor financial and market performance in 1998. The U.S. and international markets for golf clubs moved from rapid growth to maturity during 1997 and 1998 as the growth in the number of golfers began to level off and a large percentage of avid golfers who had purchased titanium drivers saw little reason to upgrade again until dramatic innovations were available. Global market maturity was compounded by the Asian financial crisis that began in late 1997 and made the export of U.S.-made products, especially expensive luxury goods like Callaway golf clubs, unaffordable for many Asian consumers. In addition, many club manufacturers believed that discussions at the United States Golf Association (USGA) during 1998 to limit innovations in golf club design caused many golfers to postpone club purchases.

The emergence of shallow-faced fairway woods had as much to do with Callaway's downturn as any other single event. Callaway had dominated the market for fairway woods since the early 1990s, when the Big Bertha line gained in popularity. By 1996 no other manufacturer came close to Callaway in building a loyal following among fairway woods customers. However, Callaway's dominance in fairway woods was severely challenged in 1997 when relatively unknown golf manufacturers Adams Golf and Orlimar Golf each heavily promoted a line of shallow-faced fairway woods that they claimed made it easier for golfers to hit a ball off the fairway or from a poor lie. Adams's and Orlimar's success came more or less directly at the expense of Callaway since no other golf club manufacturer sold large volumes of fairway woods.

Callaway's new CEO, Donald Dye, took much of the blame for Callaway's failure to predict the popularity of shallow-faced woods and was ultimately responsible for initiatives that took management's focus off golf clubs. Under Dye, Callaway Golf began new ventures in golf course and driving range management, opened interactive golf sites, and launched a golf publishing business. After a record year in 1997, the company's financial and market performance suffered immensely during 1998. In October 1998, Dye resigned as Callaway's CEO and Ely Callaway returned to rebuild the company.

Ely Callaway's first efforts upon his return to active management at Callaway Golf were to "direct [the company's] resources—talent, energy, and money—in an ever-increasing degree toward the creation, design, production, sale and service of new and better products."[4] As part of his turnaround strategy Ely Callaway also initiated a $54.2 million restructuring program that involved a number of cost-reduction actions and operational improvements. Callaway's strategies allowed the company to regain its technological leadership with the introduction of Callaway Golf Company's low-center-of-gravity Steelhead line of metal woods in 1998, the ERC Forged Titanium Driver in 1999, and variable face thickness X-14 irons and the ERC II Forged Titanium Driver in 2000. In February 2000 a survey of golf equipment company executives voted Callaway's Big Bertha driver the best golf product of the century by a two-to-one margin. The same group of executives called Ely Callaway the most influential golf trade person of the 1990s.

Ely Callaway stepped down as president and CEO of the company on May 15, 2001, after being diagnosed with pancreatic cancer. He was replaced by the company's senior executive vice president of manufacturing, Ron Drapeau, and passed away at his home in Rancho Santa Fe, California, on July 5, 2001. Drapeau had begun his employment with Callaway Golf in late 1996 and had headed the company's Odyssey Golf unit for 18 months before becoming responsible for all of the company's manufacturing operations as vice president of manufacturing in February 1999.

A time line of Callaway Golf Company's key dates and product launches is presented in Exhibit 2. Its income statements for 1999 through 2002 are presented in Exhibit 3. Exhibit 4 presents the company's balance sheets for 2000–2002. The performance of the company's stock price is graphed in Exhibit 5.

Callaway's Approach to Building Competitively Important Resources and Capabilities

Under both Ely Callaway and Ron Drapeau, Callaway Golf Company's ability to develop "demonstrably superior and pleasingly different" golf clubs was a result of activities performed by the company throughout its value chain. Callaway's differentiation was achieved through its exploitation of unique resource strengths and competitive capabilities that were unmatched by many of its rivals in the industry.

Product Development and the Helmstetter Test Center

When Ely Callaway purchased Hickory Stick USA, he believed strongly that developing "demonstrably superior and pleasingly different" golf clubs would result from a physics-oriented R&D effort rather than a focus on cosmetics. Richard Helmstetter and his engineering team were critical to the execution of Callaway Golf's competitive strategy. Throughout the company's history, Callaway Golf had consistently outspent

Exhibit 2   TIMELINE OF CALLAWAY GOLF COMPANY'S KEY DATES AND MAJOR
PRODUCT LAUNCHES, 1982–2002

1982
Hickory Stick
USA is
founded in
Temecula,
California.

1983
Ely Callaway
purchases
an interest in
Hickory Stick
USA.

1985
Richard
Helmstetter
is hired as a
consultant—
soon
becomes the
company's
chief club
designer.

1989
S2H2
stainless
steel woods
are
introduced.

Callaway
Golf is the
No. 1 driver
on the
Senior PGA
Tour.

1991
The Big
Bertha
driver is
launched.

1992
Callaway
Golf begins
trading on
the NYSE
under the
ticker
symbol ELY.

1994
Original Big
Bertha irons
are
introduced.

1995
The Titanium
Great Big
Bertha
driver is
launched.

Callaway
Golf drivers
become
number one
on all major
professional
tours.

1996
Callaway
becomes the
world's
largest
manufacturer
of golf clubs.

Callaway
Golf Ball
Company
formed.

1997
Callaway
Golf acquires
Odyssey
Sports, Inc.,
maker of
Odyssey
putters.

Great Big
Bertha
tungsten-
titanium
irons are
introduced.

1999
ERC forged
titanium
drivers are
introduced in
Europe and
Asia.

Great Big
Bertha
Hawk Eye
tungsten-
injected
irons are
introduced.

2000
Rule 35
golf ball
launched.

Odyssey
White Hot
putters are
introduced.

Steelhead
Plus drivers,
fairway
woods are
introduced.

X-14 irons
are
introduced.

2001
ERC II forged titanium
driver is launched.

Hawk Eye VFT titanium
drivers and fairway
woods are launched.

Odyssey Tri-Hot putter
with tungsten weight
flange is introduced.

CB1 and CTU 30 golf
balls is introduced.

Odyssey White Hot
2-Ball putter is
introduced.

Ely Callaway passes
away at age 82.

2002
HX golf ball is
introduced.

C4 driver is introduced.

Big Bertha III Steelhead
drivers and fairway
woods are introduced.

ERC forged titanium
fairway woods are
introduced.

New Big Bertha irons
are launched.

Great Big Bertha II
titanium driver and
fairway woods are
launched.

X-16 irons are
introduced.

Roger Cleveland-
designed forged wedges
are introduced.

Warbird golf balls are
introduced.

**Exhibit 3   CALLAWAY GOLF COMPANY, INCOME STATEMENTS, 1999–2002
(IN THOUSANDS, EXCEPT PER SHARE AMOUNTS)**

	2002	2001	2000	1999
Net sales	$792,064	$816,163	$837,627	$719,038
Cost of sales	393,068	411,585	440,119	384,265
Gross profit	398,996	404,578	397,508	334,773
Selling expenses	200,153	188,306	170,541	128,565
General and administrative expenses	56,580	71,058	70,333	92,478
Research and development expenses	32,182	32,697	34,579	34,002
Restructuring credits	—	—	—	−5,894
Sumitomo transition expenses	—	—	—	5,713
Income from operations	110,081	112,517	122,055	79,909
Interest and other income, net	1,590	7,149	8,791	9,182
Interest expense	—	−1,552	−1,524	−3,594
Unrealized energy derivative losses	—	−19,922	—	—
Income before income taxes and cumulative effect of accounting change	111,671	98,192	129,322	85,497
Income taxes	42,225	39,817	47,366	30,175
Income before cumulative effect of accounting change	69,446	58,375	81,956	55,322
Cumulative effect of accounting change	—	—	−957	—
Net income	$ 69,446	$ 58,375	$ 80,999	$ 55,322
Earnings per common share:				
Basic				
Income before cumulative effect of accounting change	$1.04	$0.84	$1.17	$0.79
Cumulative effect of accounting change	—	—	−0.01	—
	$1.04	$0.84	$1.16	$0.79
Diluted				
Income before cumulative effect of accounting change	$1.03	$0.82	$1.14	$0.78
Cumulative effect of accounting change	—	—	−0.01	—
	$1.03	$0.82	$1.13	$0.78
Common equivalent shares:				
Basic	66,517	69,809	69,946	70,397
Diluted	67,274	71,314	71,412	71,214

Source: Callaway Golf Company annual reports.

its rivals in the industry on R&D. Between 1999 and 2002, the company's research and development budget averaged more than $33 million annually—more than most of its key rivals' combined R&D budgets. The company's R&D efforts allowed it to continually beat its competitors to the market with new innovations. Callaway's engineers were the first to develop an oversize driver in 1990, were the first to make clubheads even larger by using titanium in 1995, were the first to use a combination of materials

Exhibit 4   CALLAWAY GOLF COMPANY, BALANCE SHEETS, 2000–2002 (IN THOUSANDS)

	2002	2001	2000
Assets			
Current assets:			
Cash and cash equivalents	$108,452	$ 84,263	$102,596
Marketable securities	—	6,422	—
Accounts receivable, net	63,867	48,653	58,836
Inventories, net	151,760	167,760	133,962
Current deferred taxes	34,519	27,266	29,354
Other current assets	10,429	20,327	17,721
Total current assets	$369,027	$354,691	$342,469
Property, plant and equipment, net	167,340	133,250	134,712
Intangible assets, net	121,317	121,313	113,760
Deferred taxes	—	20,282	23,332
Other assets	—	18,066	16,661
Total assets	$679,845	$647,602	$630,934
Liabilities and Shareholders' Equity			
Current liabilities:			
Accounts payable and accrued expenses	$ 61,720	$ 38,261	$ 44,173
Accrued employee compensation and benefits	23,168	25,301	22,574
Accrued warranty expense	13,464	34,864	39,363
Note payable, current portion	3,160	2,374	—
Income taxes payable	7,649	1,074	3,196
Total current liabilities	109,161	101,874	109,306
Long-term liabilities:			
Deferred compensation	7,375	8,297	9,884
Energy derivative valuation account	19,922	19,922	—
Note payable, net of current portion	—	3,160	—
Commitments and contingencies			
Shareholders' equity:			
Preferred Stock, $.01 par value, 3,000,000 shares authorized, none issued and outstanding at December 31, 2002, 2001, and 2000	—	—	—
Common Stock, $.01 par value, 240,000,000 shares authorized, 82,694,173 shares and 78,958,963 shares issued at December 31, 2001 and 2002, respectively	836	827	790
Paid-in capital	371,496	419,541	347,765
Unearned compensation	−15	−211	−1,214
Retained earnings	439,454	388,609	349,681
Accumulated other comprehensive loss	−3,847	−4,399	−6,096
Less: Grantor Stock Trust held at market value, 10,764,690 shares and 5,300,000 shares at December 31, 2001 and 2000, respectively	−134,206	−206,144	−98,713
	673,718	598,223	592,213
Less: Common Stock held in treasury, at cost, 4,939,000 shares and 4,815,241 shares at December 31, 2001 and 2000, respectively	−130,331	−83,874	−80,469
Total shareholders' equity	543,387	514,349	511,744
Total liabilities and shareholders' equity	$679,387	$647,602	$630,934

Source: Callaway Golf Company annual reports.

**Exhibit 5   Monthly Performance of Callaway Golf
                 Company's Stock Price, 1992–February 2003**

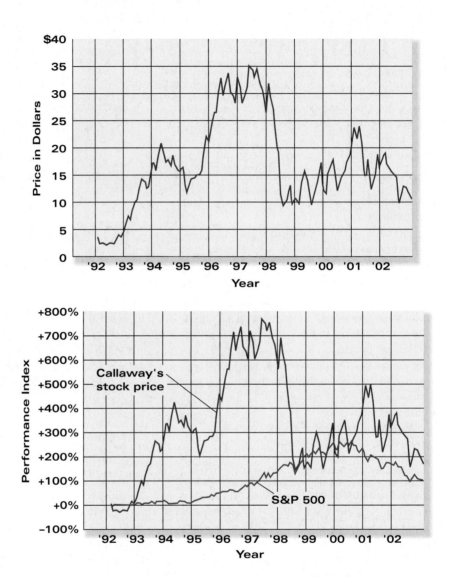

(titanium and tungsten) in clubhead design in 1997, and in 1999 became the first to introduce a forged titanium driver. In 2002 Callaway Golf Company had been granted more than 500 golf-related patents worldwide and had an additional 500 patent applications pending.

Callaway Golf opened the Richard C. Helmstetter Test Center in 1994 to house its research and product development efforts. Located about a mile away from Callaway's main campus, the test center included a laboratory and a golfing area. The test center laboratory was home to Helmstetter's engineers, who worked both on teams and individually to develop new models of clubheads and shafts. Callaway's products were designed on powerful workstations running computer-aided design (CAD) software similar to that used in the aerospace industry. The CAD software allowed engineers to not only design new clubheads and shafts but also conduct aerodynamic and strength testing in a simulated environment. Richard Helmstetter believed that not only did the process of designing golf clubs closely follow the design of aircraft but so did the selection of materials. In a live online chat hosted from the 2000 Masters Golf Tournament in Augusta, Georgia, Helmstetter noted, "Golf clubs seem to follow advances in aircraft. The Wright Brothers made their airplanes out of wood and canvas, and the golf clubs at the time were wood and canvas. Then came advances in metals and stainless steel, and in recent times high-strength lightweight materials like titanium and graphite have been used. I am not sure what the next advance in materials is going to be, but whatever they are making the next space shuttle out of is probably a good place to look."[5]

The Helmstetter Center also included a club fitting and club specifications area that utilized the company's Carlsbad Performance Center to match equipment to a golfer's swing characteristics. The internally developed proprietary video and computer system used stereo imaging techniques to capture a sequence of eight multiple exposures of the clubhead and ball at various time intervals immediately before and after a golfer hit a ball into a net approximately 10 feet from where it was struck. Callaway's proprietary computer software analyzed the video images of the clubhead's approach to the ball and the ball's rotational patterns over its first few feet of flight to make a variety of calculations needed to project the ball's ultimate path. The projected path was displayed on a six-foot video screen that showed the ball's simulated flight along the 18th fairway at Pebble Beach. The computer system also recorded the clubhead speed, ball velocity, side spin, back spin, attack angle, and launch angle to calculate efficiency rating, carry, roll, total distance, and dispersion (deviation from a straight path). All of these statistics were projected on the screen, along with the image of the ball's flight down the fairway. The equipment allowed the company to build a set of clubs for the touring professional that had the perfect swing weight, frequency, loft, lie, and length to maximize distance and accuracy.

Recreational golfers were also allowed to visit the Carlsbad Center for custom-fitting sessions with Callaway's research staff. In 2002 the company launched its Callaway Golf Performance Center Trailer—a truck-based mobile performance center that traveled across the United States since appointments for custom-fitting sessions performed at the company's Carlsbad, California, headquarters required up to a one-year wait. Callaway Golf also opened two corporate performance centers—one in London and one in Tokyo—and authorized three retailers to operate performance centers in golf shops located in Boston, Las Vegas, and Indian Wells, California. Callaway Golf also created a portable Custom Fitting Solution powered by an IBM Thinkpad; retailers in all 50 states could use this program to best match Callaway's clubs to the swing characteristics of retail customers shopping in their stores.

The Helmstetter Test Center had two primary uses: It provided an ideal place to custom-fit clubs for the touring pros who used Callaway equipment, and it allowed Callaway R&D staff to test new products in the developmental stage. Once a professional's new clubs were fitted using the video and computer capabilities of the Callaway Performance Analysis System, the touring pro could then use the center's eight-acre outdoor testing facility to hit balls and fine-tune his or her clubs by requesting minor modifications to the clubhead or shaft. Callaway included nontouring professionals in addition to engineers among its R&D staff. The golfing staff was critical to the product development process since engineers were able to refine new prototypes based on the feedback and recommendations of Callaway's R&D staff golfers. Callaway's engineers also tested prototypes with robots to evaluate the distance and accuracy of the club, but only a human could evaluate the feel of a golf club striking a ball.

Callaway's Purchasing and Production Processes

Once its clubheads were designed on a CAD system and tested in the Helmstetter Center, stainless-steel master plates were cut by Callaway to the exact specifications called for by the CAD program using computer numerical control (CNC) milling equipment. Each clubhead mold was made by pouring liquid wax between the stainless-steel master plates. The wax clubheads were removed from the master plates and sprayed with a mixture of highly heat-resistant material. The wax was melted out of these heat-resistant molds, leaving a hollow core. The hollow molds were then sent to an investment casting house and filled with either stainless steel or titanium. The casting house then broke away the mold and welded, sanded, and painted the clubheads before sending them to Callaway for further assembly.

Callaway Golf used five investment casting houses that underwent extensive screening and were closely monitored during the casting process. Company management believed that it was particularly important to supervise the casting process since poor casting could produce clubhead inconsistencies that could lead to poor performance or product failures. Even though Callaway Golf was certain it would obtain high-quality clubheads through its sourcing agreements, it made daily inspections of incoming clubhead shipments using the materials analysis and durability testing capabilities of the Helmstetter Center.

Like its clubheads, all of Callaway's shafts were designed and tested at the Helmstetter Center. Callaway manufactured all prototype shafts by hand at the testing center but contracted shaft production out to independent shaft manufacturers once specifications were established for the various graphite shafts used in its product line. As with clubheads, shafts were drawn from incoming shipments and tested at the company's R&D facility. Steel shafts were contracted out and inspected in a similar fashion. Callaway had produced as much as 50 percent of its graphite shafts internally during the late 1990s but outsourced 100 percent of its shaft requirements in 2003.

Callaway Golf's cell manufacturing process allowed the company to include quality control inspections throughout each club's assembly. In addition, the assembly plant was highly automated, with all processes requiring very tight tolerances performed by computer-controlled machinery. For example, drilling necessary to produce Callaway's tapered bore-through hosels was done by a series of precision drill presses that ensured that each hosel was drilled at the correct angle. Once the hosel had been drilled through, the clubhead moved to a production station that checked the lie and loft angles of the club and made any necessary corrections by slightly bending the clubhead to the proper angle.

Each shaft was inspected for fractures prior to insertion into the clubhead, and then the entire assembled club was weighed to assess the swing weight. Callaway production workers could choose between four different medallions bearing the Callaway name to bring a finished iron to the exact specified swing weight. Once the proper medallion was selected, it was permanently affixed to the back of the clubhead with a press. Swing weights for assembled woods were brought to their specifications by filling the clubhead with epoxy through a small hole in the rear of the clubhead.

After a baking process that dried the glue used to attach the shaft to the clubhead, each club was fitted with a grip using a laser alignment device, airbrushed to add details like the club number and Callaway trademarks, and then visually inspected for blemishes or other imperfections. Each finished club was individually wrapped by hand to protect its finish during shipping.

Sales and Customer Service

New product development at Callaway Golf Company was a cross-functional effort that included not only the R&D staff but also the company's sales and advertising staffs. Callaway sales and advertising personnel would evaluate new designs created by the company's aerospace engineers and recommend design changes based on their knowledge of the market. Once a new design was settled on, Callaway's sales force and its internal advertising staff would create a name for the new product line, an advertising campaign, and promotional materials that would accompany the launch of the new generations of clubs in tandem with the R&D staff's developmental and testing processes.

Callaway's customer service department was viewed as a critical component of the company's overall level of differentiation. Callaway's customer service staff was made up of experienced employees who were offered a generous compensation package that included commissions for superior performance in meeting the needs of Callaway's retailers and consumers. Many of Callaway's rivals viewed customer service as a low-value-adding activity and typically made customer service a place for entry-level employees to become acquainted with the business. Each Callaway Golf's customer service representative received eight weeks of training before being allowed to handle a customer service inquiry. No other company in the industry provided more than three weeks of training to its customer service personnel. In addition to training, Callaway promoted a team-oriented atmosphere where the company's knowledge base could expand through the mentoring of newer employees by longtime customer service employees. Callaway Golf's customer service was also enhanced by its Callaway Connect e-business solution, which allowed retailers and sales staff to enter orders, check order status, and check inventory availability via an Internet connection.

The entire customer service staff was empowered to make a final decision regarding a consumer or retailer complaint or warranty claim. Callaway customer service personnel were allowed to make decisions that might be pushed to the CEO at some other golf equipment companies. For example, if a golfer was vacationing and had a problem with a club, Callaway customer service staff could overnight a new club to the customer. Callaway customer service staff members were also known to send a gift to club owners who had experienced problems with Callaway equipment. Callaway offered a two-year warranty on all of its products that entitled the owner to replace any defective product with a new product rather than return the product for a repair. In addition, Callaway generally chose to replace defective or broken clubs for the life of the club rather than stick to its two-year warranty period. A Callaway sales executive remarked, "A bad experience with a Callaway product usually winds up making someone a Callaway customer for life."

Callaway Golf's Product Line in 2003

Drivers and Fairway Woods

Callaway Golf's line of drivers and fairway woods in 2003 included the 380 cubic centimeter Great Big Bertha II forged titanium driver, Great Big Bertha II titanium fairway woods and Big Bertha Steelhead III stainless-steel drivers and fairway woods. The

Exhibit 6   GOLF EQUIPMENT MARKET SIZE AND CALLAWAY GOLF COMPANY MARKET SHARE, 1999–2002

	Market Size (thousands of units)			
	1999	2000	2001	2002
Drivers and fairway woods	2,906	2,939	2,990	3,087
Irons	6,967	7,140	7,170	7,420
Putters	1,683	1,673	1,649	1,655
Golf balls*	20,463	20,796	21,320	20,812
	Callaway Golf's Market Share			
	1999	2000	2001	2002
Drivers and fairway woods	30.9%	28.6%	24.7%	21.6%
Irons	14.4%	15.9%	15.8%	16.1%
Putters	30.7%	30.6%	30.3%	40.2%
Golf balls	—	2.3%	4.3%	5.7%

*In thousands of dozens
Source: Golf Datatech, LLC.

company's forged titanium products were Callaway's most innovative drivers and fairway woods and therefore carried the highest price points. All Callaway drivers and fairway woods were available in a variety of lofts and could be equipped with shafts of varying stiffness. Callaway was the market leader in driver and fairway wood sales and was the most-used brand of drivers and fairway woods in professional tournaments. Exhibit 6 provides market shares for Callaway Golf's various product lines between 1999 and 2002. The exhibit also presents industry sales for woods, irons, putters, and golf balls for the 1999–2002 period.

Irons

Callaway Golf was also the market leader in iron sales in 2003. Its line of irons included Hawk Eye VFT tungsten-injected titanium irons that included a proprietary "tungsten weight matrix" that lowered the clubs' center of gravity, Big Bertha stainless-steel irons, and newly launched Big Bertha Steelhead X-16 stainless-steel irons. The X-16 line was a redesign of the company's X-14 irons that were introduced in 2000 and became Callaway Golf's best-selling irons ever. The X-14 and X-16 irons were widely used by recreational golfers and by professional golfers on the LPGA and Senior PGA (see Exhibit 6).

Putters

Callaway Golf Company developed Callaway-branded putter lines in the early 1990s that sold moderately well, but it became the leading manufacturer and marketer of putters with its 1997 acquisition of Odyssey Golf. Odyssey became known as an innovator in putters when it popularized polymer clubface inserts. Many golfers preferred putters with an insert since the material created a softer noise and provided more feel when putting a ball. Callaway's Odyssey putters remained the industry's leading brand of putters in 2003 and were available in four basic designs. Its White Hot 2-Ball putter became the industry's best-selling product soon after its 2001 launch. In both 2001 and 2002, Odyssey led the world's six major professional tours combined in wins, and its White Hot 2-Ball putter had been used to win more than 12 tournaments since its introduction.

Wedges

In mid-2002, Callaway Golf introduced a line of forged steel wedges designed by Roger Cleveland, founder of Cleveland Golf and creator of the most popular wedges with professionals and serious recreational golfers. Roger Cleveland sold his interest in Cleveland Golf in 1990 to Skis Rossignol SA of France and began working with Callaway Golf in 1996 as the company's chief golf club designer. Cleveland's wedge designs introduced in 2002 were a significant departure from previous Callaway wedges since Cleveland's traditionally styled wedges featured a hosel and were made from forged carbon steel rather than cast stainless steel. Upon the announcement of the new line, Roger Cleveland discussed how Callaway's technological expertise aided in the development of wedge designs that, he believed, were superior to his previous designs:

> I wanted to create a "new classic" wedge design that tour pros and top amateurs would instantly feel comfortable with, but with features that live up to the Callaway Golf standard of being demonstrably superior and pleasingly different for golfers of all skill levels. That's where we started. What I didn't want to do was make wedges that were exactly like what I've designed in the past. Maybe that would have been the safest and most conventional route, but I wanted to see if we could take wedge design someplace better. Most of my previous wedge designs have been cast from 8620 stainless steel, mainly because shape and design could be maintained because minimum weight would be removed during the process. Forging at that time was inconsistent. But Callaway Golf's expertise in club production gave me the opportunity to forge these wedges out of soft 1020 carbon steel. This makes for a unique structural difference that adds to the quality and versatility of these wedges. We start with a red-hot cylinder of 1020 carbon steel and pound it into the shape we want. This process yields a near net shape with minimal weight removal required, therefore not compromising the design. Then we mill the face and the grooves using a computerized process for the kind of precision you want from clubs you rely upon for scoring and accuracy. Forging also makes our wedges easy to adjust. Wedges cast in either 8620 or 17-4 steel have different chemistries than forged 1020 carbon steel, which can be bent to any spec without difficulty.[6]

Golf Balls

Callaway Golf spent three years between 1997 and 2000 developing in parallel its new golf ball and its state-of-the-art production facility. The company's entry into the market represented a $170 million investment in the research and development of the ball, construction of the new 225,000-square-foot production facility, and development and purchase of special manufacturing equipment. Callaway's manufacturing facility and its equipment were designed specifically for the unique production requirements for the new ball.

Ely Callaway believed that the company's new custom-designed manufacturing equipment and facility would contribute to the company's competitive strength and the ball's success. "No one else has the collection of late '90s equipment that we have, everything you need to make a better ball. No one has put it together and purchased it all the way we have. Some of the companies, because of the age of some of their equipment, just can't utilize the latest equipment without going outside."[7] Callaway's competitors were so interested in the company's new golf ball facility that they took aerial photographs of the plant's foundation as it was under construction.

Callaway Golf Ball Company engineers recruited from DuPont and Boeing used aerodynamic computer programs first used by Boeing and General Electric to evaluate more than 300 dimple patterns and more than 1,000 variations of ball cores, boundary layers, and cover materials to create the company's first new golf balls. Once designed, the company's production process used computers to mill the rubber core, control injection molding of a boundary layer, and deposit a proprietary urethane coating to golf balls as they were assembled. The golf balls then moved through a transparent tube to a battery of diagnostic machines that ensured that each ball was exactly the same. A laser was then used to twice measure the depth of each of the ball's 382 dimples, and an electrical process was used to securely and evenly bond paint to the ball. Each ball was then X-rayed and machine-inspected before being packed or rejected. Callaway's production process included 16,000 quality assurance checkpoints, and Callaway employees were allowed to stop the flow of balls at the first sign of defects.

Even though the industry had long been dominated by Titleist and Spalding, many analysts believed that Callaway's ability to develop technologically advanced products, its marketing expertise, and its established retailer network would allow the company to quickly gain a 2–3 percent share of the market. It was also expected that Callaway's golf ball operations would considerably impact the company's net profit since profit margins in the premium segment of the golf ball market ranged between 60 and 75 percent. In addition, golf ball sales were less seasonal since they were consumable items that were purchased throughout the year. Also, unlike a $400 driver, golfers could not delay the purchase of golf balls until they felt financially ready to make a large purchase. The company's objective for its golf ball business was to capture a 10 percent share of the market within two years and ultimately become one of the two top brands of golf balls.

In 2003 Callaway Golf's line of golf balls included two premium-priced models (HX and CTU 30) that matched Titleist's highest price point and a midprice ball (CB1). In late 2002 Callaway introduced a new sub-brand of golf balls focused on the value segment of the industry. Callaway believed that its Warbird sub-brand would appeal to higher handicap golfers, whose purchases made up about 40 percent of the industry's unit volume. The new value-priced golf balls were produced in Callaway's Carlsbad golf ball plant to boost the plant's capacity utilization. Marketing for the Warbird golf balls emphasized the distance capability and durability of the balls and proclaimed Warbird was "powered by Callaway Golf."

Apparel and Accessories

Callaway Golf Company complemented its lines of golf clubs and golf balls with an extensive line of golf accessories that included golf bags, golf gloves, golf caps and hats, travel bags and covers, golf towels, and golf umbrellas. Between 1996 and 2001, Callaway also received royalty payments from the sale of Callaway Golf licensed apparel in Nordstrom's 80 department stores. Nordstrom's annual sales of Callaway golf shirts

Exhibit 7

Product Group	2002	2001	2000	1999
Woods	$310.0	$392.9	$403.0	$429.0
Irons	243.5	248.9	299.9	221.3
Balls	66.0	54.9	34.0	—
Putters, accessories, and other	172.6	119.5	100.8	68.7
Net sales	$792.1	$816.2	$837.6	$719.0

Source: Callaway Golf Company annual reports.

ranged between $20 and $30 million. The two companies mutually terminated their licensing agreement at year-end 2001 to allow Callaway to enter a more lucrative apparel licensing agreement with Ashworth, Inc.—the leading producer and distributor of golf apparel. Ashworth designed two lines of golf shirts, vests, and pants that were launched during the fall of 2002. The Callaway Sport line ($39–$59) and Callaway Collection ($60–$100) lines were distributed to most off-course golf shops and department stores throughout the United States, Canada, Europe, Australia, New Zealand, and South Africa. Callaway Golf entered into a similar licensing agreement with Sanei International to create and sell golf apparel in Japan. Analysts expected Ashworth's sales of Callaway Golf apparel to reach $100 million by 2005. A Callaway Golf vice president suggested that the licensing agreement might prove to be an important part of Callaway's business considering the success of other sporting goods manufacturers that had entered the apparel industry: "Do you know how much of Nike's sales are in apparel? The risk would be not getting involved and exploring an opportunity with our brand that makes a lot of sense."[8] Callaway Golf also entered into a licensing agreement with Tour Golf Group in January 2003 that would allow the company to produce and sell Callaway Golf men's and women's footwear collections that would become available in retail golf shops in the United States and Canada in March 2003.

Callaway Golf Company's sales by product line between 1999 and 2002 (in millions of dollars) are presented in Exhibit 7.

Player Development and Endorsements and Use of Callaway Products by Golf Professionals

Callaway Golf Company's golf clubs and golf balls were endorsed by the professional golfers shown in Exhibit 8, but many more professional golfers chose to use the company's equipment—even without compensation. In some instances, non-Callaway Golf staff players using Callaway Golf equipment might indirectly pay to use the company's products since all manufacturers except Callaway Golf Company paid "tee up fees" to golfers willing to use their brand of clubs for a single tournament. Manufacturers were motivated to pay such fees to improve their count for the week as recorded by the Darrell Survey. (Manufacturers frequently touted Darrell Survey counts in their ads.)

In assembling a professional staff to endorse the company's products and test prototypes of new equipment, Ely Callaway had preferred that the company build long-term relationships with players who shared his views of loyalty and the importance of

Exhibit 8   CALLAWAY GOLF COMPANY STAFF PROFESSIONALS, 2003

PGA Tour				
Golf Clubs and Golf Balls		**Golf Balls Only**		
Ben Crane	Stephen Ames	Brian Gay	Mark Wiebe	Phil Tataurangi
Brian Henninger	Jim Carter	Carl Paulson	Rich Beem	Scott Simpson
Carlos Franco	Rocco Mediate	Chris Perry	Chris Perry	Boo Weekley
Charles Howell III	Olin Browne	Fred Funk	Peter Lonard	Brian Gay
Jeff Julian	Ty Tryon	Lee Janzen	Eduardo Herrera	Tripp Isenhour
Per-Ulrik Johansson		Mark Calcavecchia	K. J. Choi	

LPGA Tour				
Golf Clubs and Golf Balls		**Golf Balls Only**		
Jane Geddes	Kristi Albers	Jackie	Amy Fruwirth	Pearl Sinn
Jill McGill	Cindy Schreyer	Gallagher-Smith	Mitzi Edge	Sally Dee
Kelli Kuehne	Laurie Rinker-Graham	Becky Iverson	Sherri Turner	Vicki Fergon
Emilee Klein	Beth Bauer	Betsy King	Tammie Green	Helen Alfredsson
Rachel Teske	Donna Andrews	Charlotta Sorenstam	Wendy Ward	Sherri Steinhauer
Annika Sorenstam	Michelle Ellis	Cristie Kerr	Lorie Kane	Susan Parry
Liselotte Neumann	Becky Iverson	Fiona Pike	Maggie Will	Vicki Goetze-Ackerman
Leta Lindley	Leslie Spalding	Jan Stephenson	Marisa Baena	Janice Moodie
Rosie Jones	Ashli Bunch	Jennifer Hubbard	Maggie Will	Catriona Matthew
	Cindy Flom	Jeong Jang	Candi Kung	Alison Nicholas

PGA European Tour				
Golf Clubs and Golf Balls		**Golf Balls Only**		
Alastair Forsyth	Paul Lawrie	Ignacio Garrido	Padraig Harrington	Peter Baker
Niclas Fasth	Pierre Fulke	Chris Gane	Olle Karlsson	Malcolm Mackenzie
Colin Montgomerie	Tony Johnstone	Darren Fichardt	Peter Hanson	Richard Green
Eduardo Romero	Seve Ballesteros	Graham Fox	Raphael Jacquelin	Santiago Luna
Nick Dougherty	Bernard Gallacher	Malcolm Mackenzie	Sam Walker	Soren Kjeldsen
Barry Lane	Phillip Price	Mark James	Soren Hansen	Rolf Muntz
Mark McNulty		Mikko Ilonen	Tom Gillis	Bradley Dredge
		Marc Farry	Paul Eales	Constantino Rocca
		Miguel Angel Martin	Stuart Little	Gary Clark
		Michele Reale	Kenneth Ferrie	Carl Suneson

character. Callaway Golf also required its professional staff to carry a minimum of 10 Callaway clubs to be on its staff, while other manufacturers required golfers to carry only one of their clubs while signed to an endorsement contract. As a result, most of Callaway Golf's professional staff had been with the company for many years, if not their entire professional career.

Callaway's player development staff also looked for individuals with worldwide appeal since nearly 50 percent of its sales were to consumers outside the United States.

Exhibit 8   Continued

Champions Tour

Golf Clubs and Golf Balls		Golf Balls Only		
Andy North	Arnold Palmer	Bob Eastwood	Leonard Thompson	Mark McCumber
Terry Mauney	Bob Murphy	Butch Sheehan	DeWittt Weaver	Rocky Thompson
Walter Morgan	Danny Edwards	Jerry McGee	Tommy Aaron	Don Pooley
David Graham	Mark Pfeil	Don Bies	Walter Hall	Larry Nelson
Orville Moody	Gary Player	George Archer	Gibby Gilbert	
Stewart Ginn	Rodger Davis			
Jim Dent	Jim Thorpe			
Dave Eichelberger	John Mahaffey			
Jim Colbert	Bruce Fleisher			
Bob Charles				

Japan Golf Tour Organization

Golf Clubs and Golf Balls	Golf Balls Only			
Dean Wilson	Christian Pena	Gregory Meyer	Ryuichi Oda	Satoshi Ishigaki
Eiji Mizoguchi	Eijiro Koyama	Kazuhiro Kinjo	Seiji Iwadate	Shoichi Yamamoto
Mitsutaka Kusakabe	Hiroshi Makino	Go Higaki	Takenori Hiraishi	Takuya Ogawa
Kenichi Kuboya	Jun Kikuchi	Hisashi Sawada	Tatsuo Takasaki	Tatsuya Shiraishi
Kodai Ichihara	Keng-Chi Lin	Jeev Milkha Singh	Terry Price	Un Ho Park
Prayad Marksaeng	Kosaka Makisaka	Rick Gibson	Tsutomu Ide	TC Chen
Tohru Taniguchi	Manabu Taguchi	Mitsugu Kawai	Satoshi Oide	Tomonori Takahashi
	Brad Andrews	Naoki Hattori	Takeashi Kanemoto	Yutaka Horinouchi
	Nobuhito Sato	Peter Teravainen	Takuya Sugaya	Naoki Hattori
	Richard Backwell	Kunichika Iha	Mitsuhiro Tateyama	

Nationwide Tour

Golf Clubs and Golf Balls	Golf Balls Only			
Jeff Quinney	Ahmad Bateman	Dave Rummells	Ken Green	Mike Springer
Steve Scott	Craig Kanada	Gene Sauers	Mike Sullivan	Richard Johnson
	Gary Hallberg	John Adams	Scott Gump	Jeff Hart
	Brian Claar	Ken Green	Marco Dawson	Eric Meeks
	John Restino	Vic Wilk	Rich Barcelo	
	Billy Judah	Victor Schwamkrug	Stiles Mitchell	

Source: Callaway Golf Company website.

In many ways, Annika Sorenstam was the prototypical professional staff member for Callaway Golf—she had never endorsed any other golf equipment manufacturer's products, was among the best in her field, was disciplined in her personal life, and was immensely popular in Asia and Europe as well as in the United States. Callaway had recently signed five of golf's "young guns"—Charles Howell III (joined PGA Tour at 21), Jeff Quinney (turned professional at 21), Steve Scott (joined Buy.com tour at 22),

Exhibit 9   OVERVIEW OF THE GOLF EQUIPMENT INDUSTRY IN 2002

Industry Characteristics	Competitive Rivalry
■ In 2002 approximately 25.4 million Americans played golf. The number of U.S. golfers had increased only slightly from about 25 million in 1995. Similarly, the number of golfers in Asia and Europe had remained stable between the 1990s and 2002 at about 16 million and 2 million golfers, respectively. ■ Women accounted for 25% of all golfers in the United States. Seventeen percent of golfers were juniors aged 5 to 17, and 10% of golfers represented a racial minority. ■ The wholesale value of golf equipment sales in the United States had declined from $2.7 billion in 1999 to $2.5 billion in 2001. Most manufacturers believed that industry growth had been limited by slow economic conditions; USGA restrictions on clubhead performance; and the difficulty of the game, which resulted in many golfers giving up the game each year. ■ Most golfers were rather limited in their golfing abilities. A 2001 National Golf Foundation survey of recreational golfers found that the average golf score for men was 97 and 114 for women and less than 2% of golfers held single-digit handicaps. In addition, a Golf 20/20 Foundation survey found that the sensation of a well-struck ball was the number one reason recreational golfers enjoy the game—three times more important to such golfers than achieving a low score. ■ In 2001 the wholesale value of the international golf ball market was estimated at $1.5 billion, and that of the U.S. golf ball market at $650 million.	■ Competitive rivalry in the industry centered on technological innovation in clubhead and shaft design, product performance, company image and tour exposure, and point-of-sale merchandising. ■ The pace of technological innovation had increased rapidly during the late 1990s and early 2000s as industry leaders, Callaway Golf, Ping Golf, Taylor Made Golf, and Titleist each attempted to beat the other to market with clubs touting unique performance characteristics. ■ Similarly, the manufacturers of golf balls introduced new products at 12–18-month intervals to keep the interest of golfers who were looking for products that included new innovations and improved performance. ■ Golf club manufacturers relied greatly on endorsements from touring professionals to gain recognition in the industry. Titleist, long known for its golf balls and irons, burst onto the market for drivers in 2000 with its 975D driver that was used by Tiger Woods in professional tournaments. Nike hoped for a similar benefit as it entered the golf equipment industry in 2002.

Nick Dougherty (turned professional at 19), and Ty Tryon (joined PGA Tour at 17)—in the belief that these young golfers might ultimately exhibit the appeal and success in men's golf that Annika had achieved in women's golf. At season-end 2002, Howell recorded one tournament win and a second-place finish in the tour championship. Howell also made the cut to the final tournament rounds in 27 out of 32 events entered during 2002 and earned more than $2.5 million during the year. Quinney had made two of five cuts on the nationwide tour during the first months of the 2003 season, Scott had won the Texas Classic while playing on the Canadian tour, and Nick Dougherty was named the 2002 European PGA Rookie of the Year. Ty Tryon, who was still enrolled in high school while playing on the PGA Tour, received a medical exemption for most of 2002 after suffering from tonsillitis and mononucleosis and failing to make a cut in the five of six events he entered in 2002. Callaway Golf did not limit its search for new staff members to younger golfers, with Arnold Palmer and Gary Player joining the staff in 2000 and 2001, respectively.

Supplier–Seller Relationships	Seller–Buyer Relationships
■ Most club makers' manufacturing activities were restricted to club assembly since clubhead production was contracted out to investment casting houses and shafts and grips were usually purchased from third-party suppliers. ■ Companies like Callaway Golf independently designed their shafts, while others collaborated with shaft manufacturers to develop proprietary graphite shafts and still others purchased standard graphite shafts from shaft manufacturers.	■ Most pro-line or high-quality golf equipment manufacturers distributed their products through on-course pro shops and a select number of off-course pro shops, such as Edwin Watts and Nevada Bob's. The off-course pro shops accounted for the largest portion of retail golf club sales because they carried a wider variety of brands and marketed more aggressively than on-course shops. Most on-course pro shops sold only to members and carried few clubs since their members purchased golf clubs less frequently than apparel and footwear. ■ Pro-line manufacturers limited their channels of distribution to on-course and off-course pro shops because they believed that PGA professionals had the training necessary to properly match equipment to the customer. ■ Custom-fitting was offered by some manufacturers and large off-course pro shops with the use of specialized computer equipment. Common swing variables recorded and evaluated in determining the proper clubs for golfers included clubhead speed and path, club face angle at impact, ball position, the golfer's weight distribution, ball flight pattern, and ball flight distance. ■ Pro shops generally chose to stock only pro-line equipment and did not carry less expensive, less technologically advanced equipment. Low-end manufacturers sold their products mainly through discounters, mass merchandisers, and large sporting goods stores. These retailers had no custom-fitting capabilities and rarely had sales personnel knowledgeable about the performance features of the different brands and models of golf equipment carried in the store. The appeal of such retail outlets was low price, and they mainly attracted beginning golfers and occasional golfers who were unwilling to invest in more expensive equipment.

Challenges Confronting Callaway Golf Company in 2003

When Ron Drapeau became Callaway Golf Company's CEO in May 2001, he promised employees he would not stray from Ely Callaway's mission "to develop 'demonstrably superior and pleasingly different' products for the average golfer." He also offered them assurance: "This will not change. We will continue to invest in research and development to introduce exciting new clubs and balls that occasionally bring a little more enjoyment to the millions of average golfers who have become devoted believers in our company and our products."[9] Even though Callaway Golf's vision and competitive strategy seemed to fit its industry situation well in 2003, Callaway Golf Company was confronted by a number of issues, including a softening economy in most major markets for golf clubs, declining industry growth rate, the entry of new rivals into the industry, and onerous regulations limiting golf club performance. Exhibit 9 discusses the state of the golf equipment industry in the early 2000s.

Slowing Growth in Demand for Golf Equipment

The soft global economy and recessions in many key markets for premium golf clubs had decreased demand for such products since layoffs by major corporations between 2000 and 2002 affected more than 1 million U.S. workers and since many employed consumers were limiting spending on premium-priced products. Uncertain economic conditions also created revenue shortfalls for Callaway Golf and other producers of premium golf equipment since volatile exchange rates either artificially raised the cost of such products to export consumers or made it difficult to repatriate profits from foreign subsidiaries. Ron Drapeau explained in an August 2002 *Smart Money* interview how the economic situation in Japan alone had a considerable effect on the company's earnings: "The uncertainty in Japan is the biggest variable [in our 2002 earnings outlook]. Japan accounts for 16 percent of sales and is our second-largest market. Because of the soft economy and the banking crisis, there is less golf being played for business and less gift giving. When people have concerns about discretionary spending, they cut back on golf."[10] The following table illustrates the importance of international markets to Callaway Golf Company's financial performance between 1999 and 2002:

Geographic Market	2002	2001	2000	1999
United States	$438.7	$444.1	$451.2	418.4
Japan	136.9	130.7	122.0	55.9
Europe	102.6	118.4	125.5	115.7
Rest of Asia	58.0	63.9	82.4	73.1
Rest of World	55.9	59.1	56.5	55.9
Net Sales	$792.1	$816.2	$837.6	$719.0

Source: Callaway Golf Company annual reports.

The lack of growth in the number of new golfers was also a concern for Callaway Golf and its rivals in the golf equipment industry. Golf had seemingly reached maturity as a sport, with the number of new participants each year barely exceeding the number who were giving up the sport. There had been some hope among industry executives that Tiger Woods's universal popularity would help grow the game of golf by creating interest in the sport among youth and minorities. Woods's inclusion in the field of touring professionals had benefited television networks, with TV ratings soaring during tournaments where Tiger was contending for a championship, but as of 2002 Woods's presence had done little to bring new participants to the sport. In an interview with *Smart Money,* Ron Drapeau said, "Tiger has helped television ratings, but that hasn't translated into more players. We need to find ways to introduce young people to golf. Secondly, the cost of golf is a concern: We need to see more affordable municipal-type golf courses, including alternative facilities; 9-hole courses, pitch-and-putt and par 3 courses. The time it takes to play is also an issue."[11]

Nike's Entry into the Golf Equipment Industry

Nike management was among those who believed that Tiger Woods could not only generate interest in golf but also help generate substantial revenues for a golf equipment company. Upon his professional debut in 1996, Tiger Woods signed a $40 million five-year contract to endorse Nike shoes and apparel. In 1999 Woods extended the contract for an additional five years for $90 million to endorse Nike's new golf ball and forthcoming golf clubs. As with its apparel and footwear, Nike outsourced the production of its golf balls (in this instance to Bridgestone), while it hired a custom-club designer to design and lead its new golf club business. Nike's new driver, irons, and wedges were introduced during the 2002 PGA Merchandise Show. The company's 2002 line of golf clubs achieved only modest success and an improved line, including a 400 cubic centimeter forged titanium driver, was introduced during the 2003 PGA Merchandise Show. Tiger Woods began endorsing the company's golf ball in 2000 and began using its driver and irons in 2002. Nike had also signed an endorsement agreement with PGA professional David Duval to use the company's golf balls, driver, and irons in tournament play. When asked how the company would respond to Nike's entry into the golf equipment industry, Ron Drapeau suggested, "We're going to continue to do what we do: invest heavily in R&D and bring innovative products to market. Nike will sell clubs; they will get some market share. We're going to try to make sure it's not out of our share—let them get it from some of our competitors. But they have a great marketing organization, and they have the best athlete in the world. So they're going to sell product. How successful they are will depend on how good the product is."[12]

The USGA's Coefficient of Restitution Measurement

In 2001 the Big Bertha ERC II forged titanium driver was Callaway's best-performing and most innovative driver. The driver was technologically superior to any driver offered by Callaway's key rivals, but did not conform to the coefficient of restitution (COR) limitation established by the United States Golf Association (USGA). As a nonconforming club, the ERC II was barred from use by recreational or professional golfers in the United States, Canada, and Mexico who intended to play by the USGA's Rules of Golf. The USGA refused to calculate handicaps for golfers who had used the ERC II or other nonconforming equipment but did not attempt to restrict the club's usage among players who did not choose to establish or maintain handicaps. The Callaway Big Bertha ERC II did, however, conform to the Rules of Golf as published by the Royal and Ancient (R&A) Golf Club of St. Andrews, Scotland, which governed play in most countries outside of North America.

The discrepancy between USGA and R&A club specifications arose in 1998 when the USGA, having observed the rapid technological advances in golf equipment made by Callaway Golf and other leading golf equipment manufacturers, established a performance threshold for all new golf equipment. In order to prevent manufacturers from developing clubs with a so-called springlike effect, the USGA limited the COR of new golf equipment to 0.83. The COR was calculated by firing a golf ball at a driver out of a cannonlike machine at 109 miles per hour. The speed that the ball returned to the cannon could not exceed 83 percent of its initial speed (90.47 miles per hour). The USGA called the ratio of incoming to outgoing velocity the coefficient of restitution (COR). The intent of the USGA COR threshold was to limit the distance that golf balls could be hit since studies indicated that every 0.01 increase in COR resulted in two extra yards of carry. USGA officials had cited the added distance achieved by PGA professionals while hitting from the tee had caused some courses to lengthen certain holes and had stated that excessive technological advances resulting in a springlike or trampoline effect ultimately threatened the integrity of the game of golf.

During the 2000 Masters Tournament in Augusta, Georgia, Richard Helmstetter challenged the suggestion that clubs with a high COR could produce a springlike effect:

> We do a great deal of research at Callaway Golf and I think we are the most technologically advanced golf company in the world. We have been unable to find any evidence at all that a club face, no matter how thin, plays a role like a trampoline in striking the ball. We do think that certain kinds of construction and materials will reduce the loss of energy in the golf ball at impact and give the golfer longer drives, but this is quite different from a trampoline. The club face vibrates during impact at a speed so high that it cannot be timed, we believe, to the compression and release of a golf ball. Consequently, we think that trampoline effect is a misnomer, if not a myth entirely.[13]

Callaway challenged the USGA's ruling with its October 2000 introduction of the ERC II since its management believed that the 6–10 additional yards of carry achieved by recreational golfers using the ERC II posed no threat to the game of golf. Callaway Golf executives did concede that equipment limitations might be set for professional golfers but saw no need to limit the performance of equipment used by recreational golfers who might gain more pleasure from hitting longer drives. Ely Callaway suggested there were "two games of golf—tournament golf and recreational golf, and the two games differ in many respects. . . . We believe that recreational golfers should not be denied the benefits of modern technology that can bring them added enjoyment that comes from occasionally hitting the ball a little bit further."[14]

Upon the announcement that Callaway Golf would make the club available to golfers in the United States, Arnold Palmer supported the company's decision by saying, "I think what Callaway is doing is just right. I have given a lot of thought to conforming and non-conforming clubs. If my daughter, who is a 100s shooter can shoot 90 with a non-conforming driver, I can't imagine that there would be anything wrong with that."[15]

The USGA and the R&A developed a compromise proposal on COR and driving clubs in May 2002 that would make all existing clubs legal for recreational play by raising the COR to 0.86, effective January 1, 2003. The effect of high-COR clubs on golfers' handicaps would be evaluated for five years, at which point a decision would be made to revert to the 0.83 standard or to retain the 0.86 COR threshold. Under the agreement, touring professionals engaged in competitive events in North America would be required to use equipment meeting the 0.83 COR limitation. Other tours were free to adopt the 0.83 COR standard or continue with no COR limitations in tournament golf. On August 6, 2002, the USGA unexpectedly retreated from its proposed agreement with the R&A on global COR standards and returned to its previous position of requiring all golfers wishing to post a score to use equipment that met its 0.83 COR restriction. Callaway Golf's Great Big Bertha II, introduced in late 2002, conformed to the USGA's 0.83 COR restriction. The company did produce Great Big Bertha II+ drivers that exceeded the 0.83 COR limitation for golf markets outside the United States and other countries where golf was governed by USGA rules.

Declining Innovation Gap between Callaway Golf and Its Traditional Rivals

Callaway's ERC II driver, introduced in 2001, had been the company's most innovative driver developed, but it was rejected by the USGA because of its potential springlike effect. Callaway Golf answered the complaints of the USGA with the development of the Great Big Bertha II, which offered the best of Callaway's research and development capabilities while not exceeding a COR of 0.83. However, in early 2003, most of Callaway Golf's key rivals also had products that pushed the USGA's 0.83 COR limitation. Cobra Golf offered a 427 cubic centimeter (cc) deep face driver with a COR of 0.828; Cleveland Golf had introduced a 400 cc deep face driver with a COR of 0.83; Taylor Made Golf's three 500 series drivers ranged in size from 310 cc to 400 cc, and all approached the 0.83 COR restriction; and both Titleist and Ping were testing high-COR drivers on the PGA Tour that were scheduled for release to consumers by the spring of 2003. Titleist's new 983K 312 cc prototype driver had generated considerable interest from recreational golfers after Titleist staff player Ernie Els won the first two tournaments of the 2003 PGA Tour while using the new driver and became first on the PGA Tour in driving distance with an average drive of 319.6 yards.

Callaway's Performance Going into 2003

As Callaway Golf Company entered fiscal 2003, Ron Drapeau had much to be pleased with. The company's 2002 net income had increased by 19 percent to $69.5 million although its net sales of $792.1 million had declined by about 2.5 percent from the $816.1 million recorded in 2001. The company's sales of putters and accessories grew by 45 percent between year-end 2001 and year-end 2002, and the company's golf ball was quickly moving toward Callaway's sales targets with sales of $66.0 million, which represented a 20 percent improvement from fiscal 2001. However, the company's sales of drivers and fairway woods had declined by 21 percent between year-end 2001 and year-end 2002, and iron sales had declined by 2 percent during 2002.

Much of Callaway's improvement in golf ball sales could be attributed to the performance of Callaway's HX and CTU 30 golf balls on the world's major professional tours. At the conclusion of the 2002 season, Callaway Golf balls had been used to win 69 times across the world's six major professional tours, including Rich Beem's 2002 PGA Championship victory, for which he used the Callaway Golf CTU 30 golf ball. Callaway Golf balls recorded five victories among the 12 major championships across the PGA, Senior PGA, and LPGA Tours in 2002—more than any other brand of ball. In addition, in late 2002 Callaway became the only golf ball manufacturer to ever beat Titleist in the Darrell Survey golf ball usage count during a professional tournament.

Drapeau could also be pleased with the tour exposure of the company's other products, with Odyssey putters accounting for 92 wins across the six major professional tours during 2002, Callaway Golf fairway woods recording 94 wins, and Callaway's Great Big Bertha II driver accounting for 10 wins in the first 16 weeks it was available for tour usage. Callaway Golf also had completed a successful 2003 PGA Merchandise Show where the Great Big Bertha II and X-16 irons were showcased along with the company's new apparel collection, new versions of the Odyssey 2-Ball putter, and new models of forged wedges. Ron Drapeau and Callaway Golf's other chief managers hoped the new lines and models would prove popular with recreational golfers and that golfers might consider the purchase of a Great Big Bertha II, despite its performance limitation as a USGA-conforming club and the availability of similar-performing drivers offered by other equipment manufacturers.

Endnotes

[1]Callaway Golf Company press release, September 9, 2002.

[2]"Donald H. Dye Given CEO Duties at Callaway Golf Company," *Two-Ten Communications*, 1996.

[3]"Callaway Enters the Ball Game," *Show News*, February 5, 2000.

[4]Callaway Golf Company 1998 annual report.

[5]Quoted in *The Callaway Connection*, Summer 2000.

[6]Callaway Golf press release, July 15, 2002.

[7]"Long on Promises, Short on Explanation," *Golfweek*, February 5, 2000.

[8]Quoted in "Shirtmaker Creating New Callaway lines," *San Diego Union-Tribune*, October 13, 2001, p. C1.

[9]Quoted in *The Callaway Connection*, Summer 2001, p. 3.

[10]Quoted in *Smart Money*, August 2002, p. 34.

[11]Ibid.

[12]Ibid.

[13]Quoted in *The Callaway Connection*, Spring 2000, p. 7.

[14]Quoted in "Callaway Golf Introduced ERC II Forged Titanium Driver—Its Hottest and Most Forgiving Driver Ever," *PR Newswire*, October 24, 2000.

[15]Ibid.

Microsoft's Xbox

Joshua J. Kittner
New York University

Melissa A. Schilling
New York University

Stephen Karl
New York University

In the fall of 1999, Microsoft announced to the world that it would enter the videogame console business with its own technologically advanced game console, the Xbox. The Xbox was targeted at males ages 18 to 34, making it positioned directly against Sony's PlayStation2. By the time the Xbox hit the market, PlayStation2 (PS2) would already have a significant lead in installed base and availability of games (there were more than 300 PS2 game titles available at the end of 2001), but Microsoft was counting on the technological advantages offered by the Xbox to tip consumer preferences. The Xbox operating system ran on a 733 megahertz (MHz) microprocessor from Intel, which was more than twice as fast as the processors used in any other game console on the market—including the Toshiba 300 MHz microprocessor supplied in the PlayStation2. The Xbox had 64 megabytes of memory and a data rate of 400 megabits per second per pin with 6.4 gigabytes (GB) per second bandwidth, enabling more information to be processed faster. The Xbox memory chip would give game developers nearly twice the memory offered in other game consoles. The Xbox also offered a 10-gigabyte hard drive, enabling gamers to save a virtually unlimited number of games. Customers also did not have to trade off technological advantages against price: The Xbox launched at a retail price of $299, significantly less than its production costs (it was estimated that Microsoft lost between $100 and $125 per unit).

Both the Xbox and Nintendo's GameCube were launched in November of 2001 (in time for the extremely important Christmas season) and sold briskly. By the year's end, it was estimated that 1.3 million GameCube units and 1.5 million Xbox units had been sold.[1] However, both of the new consoles were outrun by PS2, which sold approximately 2 million units in December 2001 alone. By the end of 2001, PS2 had a worldwide installed base of over 20 million units. (See Exhibit 1 for comparative specifications for PS2 and Xbox.) While some analysts considered this evidence that Microsoft stood a poor chance of overtaking Sony's position in the gaming market, others were wary of discounting Microsoft too soon. It was, after all, the company that had defined many of the rules of competition in high-technology industries where complementary goods (such as software or games) were important. Would Microsoft be able to capture and dominate the videogame industry as it had done in personal computer operating systems and several software applications markets? Unlike Sony, Microsoft had almost no experience in designing and manufacturing hardware. Microsoft also

Exhibit 1   COMPARISON OF XBOX TO PLAYSTATION2

	Xbox	PlayStation 2
Central processing unit	733 MHz Intel	300 MHz
Graphics processor	300 MHz custom-designed X-Chip, developed by Microsoft and nVidia	150 MHz Sony GS
Total memory	64 MB	38 MB
Memory bandwidth	6.4 GB/sec	3.2 GB/sec
Polygon performance	300 M/sec	66 M/sec
Sustained polygon performance (full features)	100+ M/sec	20 M/sec
Micropolygons/particles per second	300 M/sec	Not supported
Particle performance	300 M/sec	150 M/sec
Simultaneous textures	4	1
Pixel fill rate—no texture	4.8 G/Sec (anti-aliased)	2.4 G/sec
Pixel fill rate—1 texture	4.8 G/Sec (anti-aliased)	1.2 G/Sec
Compressed textures	Yes (8:1)	No
Full scene anti-alias	Yes	No
Micro polygon support	Yes	No
Storage medium	4x DVD, 8 GB hard disk, 8 MB memory card	2x DVD, 8 MB memory card
I/O	4x DVD 8GB hard disk 8MB memory card	2x DVD 8MB memory card
Audio channels	64	48
3D audio support	Yes	No
MIDI DLS2 support	Yes	No
AC3 encoded game audio	Yes	No
Broadband enabled	Yes	Future upgrade
Modem enabled	Future upgrade	Yes
DVD movie playback	Built in	Utility required to be on memory card
Game pad included	No	Yes
Maximum resolution	1920 × 1080	1280 × 1024
Maximum resolution (2 × 32 bpp frame buffers +Z)	1920 × 1080	540 × 480
HDTV Support	Yes	Limited
Launch date	Fall 2001	Fall 2000

Source: www.webdesk.com.

did not have the consumer electronics brand equity of Sony. Many industry observers wondered why Microsoft, which had come to rely almost wholly on original equipment manufacturer (OEM) agreements and licensing for its revenue, would choose to enter such a completely different market. Did Microsoft consider the videogame console to be a threat to its PC operating system business? Or was Microsoft just looking for a new and exciting market in which to extend its reach?

Microsoft's History[2]

Childhood friends Bill Gates and Paul Allen shared a fascination for computers throughout their early lives. As teens, Gates and Allen worked together for several years helping local Seattle businesses, such as Information Sciences Inc., develop programs and locate bugs in existing computer systems. Along the way, Gates and Allen developed valuable programming knowledge. In 1973 Gates left Seattle to begin studies at Harvard University. However, following MIPS' 1974 introduction of the Altair, arguably the first personal computer,[3] Allen convinced Gates to drop out of school and develop a software program for the Altair. The program enabled basic operating directions to be read into the machine using paper tape. With this, Microsoft was born.

Microsoft's big break came when it licensed an operating system program, MS-DOS (a clone of CP/M, the dominant operating system software for the proliferation of personal computers based on Intel microprocessors), to IBM in 1980. Following a fallout with IBM, Microsoft began work on a graphical user interface, called Windows, to make MS-DOS more user friendly. Notably, the Windows program (introduced in 1984) was remarkably similar in appearance and function to Apple's graphical Macintosh operating system introduced in 1983. Microsoft developed several updated versions of Windows, and by 1993 a million copies of Windows were being sold every month. By 1995 the company held roughly 80 percent of the personal computer operating system market. The company eventually branched out into other areas of consumer and business software and, by anchoring all of its applications to the dominance of Windows, gained tremendous market share in several computer software categories, including word processing, spreadsheet applications, database applications, presentation software, utility software (such as disk compression and memory management), and eventually Web server software and browsers.[4]

In the fall of 1999, Microsoft announced its intention to enter the videogame console industry. Microsoft had neither the arcade experience possessed by Nintendo and Sega nor the extensive consumer electronics experience of Sony. However, Microsoft did have some experience and brand image in the computer gaming industry. Microsoft had been successful developing games, such as Flight Simulator and the Age of Empires series. Microsoft had also been successful in offering online gaming. The Microsoft Gaming Zone, which allowed for multiplayer gaming, had over 12 million registered members as of 2001 and was considered by many to be the precursor for multiplayer gaming on the Xbox.[5]

The Videogame Industry: Seven Generations

Generation One

The birth of the videogame industry can be traced to Ralph Baer and Sanders Associates, a military electronics consulting firm. The Pentagon came to Sanders in 1965 with a need for computer simulations to help increase soldiers' strategical thinking skills and improve their reflexes.[6] The Pentagon also wanted a system that could be used on inexpensive equipment, such as a television monitor. In the past, games such as Spacewars could be played only on $40,000 terminals.

Baer and a team of engineers, including Bill Harrison and Bill Rusch, worked over the course of the year to produce a working prototype of a videogame console. In 1966, the team displayed their work to a Pentagon review board. The Pentagon was unimpressed with the system but allowed research to continue. At this meeting, Baer gave his opinion that video games could be a profitable form of personal entertainment. Baer's superiors, however, believed that the military would benefit from gaming technology more than civilians, and kept the project top secret.[7]

Eventually, the Pentagon became disenfranchised with the videogame idea, and Baer was granted the right to commercially produce his product. Baer signed on with Magnavox, and the Odyssey was born in 1972, becoming the first home videogame system. In its first year the Odyssey sold 100,000 units at a price of $100.[8] However, the Odyssey would soon come to an end.

In 1971, Nolan Busnell and Al Alcorn had created the arcade game Pong. The team decided to transform the arcade hit into a home version, entitled Atari Pong. The home version of Pong was a single unit with built-in paddles and speakers. Though the Atari could only play Pong (unlike the Odyssey, which could play 12 games), most customers were unwilling to pay more for the Odyssey because the multiple-game system only had a few desirable games.[9] Pong, and over 60 similar knockoffs, would soon flood the market because of the creation of large-scale integrated (LSI) circuits, which allowed the systems to be priced low. Pong dominated the market until 1977 and the introduction of the Atari VCS/2600, the leader of the second generation of video games.[10]

Generation Two

The second generation of systems saw the implementation of a microprocessor, first in the Fairchild Channel F system, then in other systems. The microprocessor allowed for better graphics and sound, as well as more complex games. Atari was still the leader in the industry, but the advancements of other companies, such as Fairchild, led Bushnell to press for the development of a new system using the microprocessor and allowing for multiple games. This system, called the VCS/2600, sold for $200, with games selling for between $20 and $40. Atari sold over $5 billion worth of 2600 systems and products over a five-year period. The height of this generation saw yearly sales of $3 billion in the United States alone.[11]

Generation Three

The third generation of videogame systems, 1981–84, was a brief and dark episode in the history of video games. Though this generation saw the introduction of several new systems, including the Atari 5200 and 7800, and Coleco's ColecoVision, it ended in a crash that many observers thought the industry would not survive. In 1985, sales of videogame systems amounted to only $100 million worldwide, and analysts were proclaiming the videogame industry dead. Speculation about the reasons for the crash included a noticeable difference between the quality of arcade games and home games, and oversaturation of the market by lackluster game titles. Game titles for the Atari system had been rapidly produced both by Atari's licensees and by unlicensed developers, resulting in a proliferation of dubious-quality games. Distributors and retailers that had stocked the titles ended up with large amounts of worthless inventory.

Generation Four

The fourth generation, 1985–89, saw the rebirth of the home videogame industry. The reduction in cost of dynamic RAM chips, which allowed for greater memory storage and faster access of data, coupled with the introduction of higher-powered eight-bit processors, allowed home gaming systems to compete with arcade games. Companies that dominated previous generations, such as Atari and Magnavox, released updated versions of their older systems. However, two new companies from Japan, Sega and Nintendo, which also produced arcade games, achieved the greatest success.[12]

In 1984, Sega was the first of the Japanese companies to introduce a new console, called the Master System, to the market. The strong initial sales of the Master System were an indicator that the videogame market was growing again. Realizing this, Nintendo's Hiroshi Yamamuchi pressed his engineers to design their own home console. The Nintendo Entertainment System (NES) was released only six months after Sega's product.

The Master System seemingly was poised to be the leader of the market, with a technologically superior product. The Master System had two cartridge ports, one for playing normal cartridges and the other smaller port for playing games that required less memory. Sega also used this smaller port to develop 3D technology. Players could plug 3D glasses with small LCD displays into this port, and images would flash on the LCD screens in conjunction with the primary image on the television to produce a 3D effect.

Nintendo's early deliveries of its system were filled with defects, angering retailers and consumers. However, Nintendo's executives used almost all of the company's financial resources for advertising. Nintendo also focused on the establishment of quality games and characters, and was able to produce more games than those available for the Master System.

The Master System went on to sell 2 million units and at times held an 11 percent market share. The NES sold 19 million units by 1990 and could be found in more than a third of the households in America and Japan.[13] Nintendo's Super Mario Brother's 3 grossed over $500 million in America in 1989, selling 7 million copies in the United States and 4 million in Japan. By 1990 Nintendo passed Toyota as Japan's most successful company.

Sega, however, was able to stay afloat based on the success of its arcade games and was working to transform its arcade architecture for home system use. Nintendo was not concerned. Bill White, a Nintendo executive, said "[Our players] are extremely happy with the existing system. . . . We haven't maxed out our eight-bit system yet."[14]

Generation Five

In 1989 Sega released the Genesis, a 16-bit system with a 7.6 MHz processor. NEC, another large Japanese gaming company, had released its 16-bit system, the Turbo-Graphix 16, six months earlier. However, Sega had a large catalog of arcade games for the new system while NEC's system did not. Nintendo tried to form an alliance with NEC to use the TurboGraphix 16 as its new system, but this union ultimately fell through. The summer of 1990 saw the Genesis take more than 55 percent of new system sales and 20 percent of the gaming market from Nintendo. Many of the third-party games developers dropped their Nintendo accounts to begin working with Sega.

In response, Nintendo engineers began working on a new 16-bit system. Released in 1991, the Super Nintendo Entertainment System (SNES) had a better graphics processor, could produce more screen colors, and had better audio output than the Genesis. The SNES, however, only had a 3.58 MHz processor, and Sega highlighted this fact. Both companies would continue to upgrade their systems, but neither would achieve true market dominance. In 1992, Nintendo had controlled 80 percent of the videogame market based on combined 8-bit and 16-bit sales, but in 1994 and 1995, Sega was the market leader.[15]

Generation Six

The sixth generation of video games began with a dispute between Sony and Nintendo, concerning a CD peripheral that the companies were jointly developing. The basis of the disagreement was that Sony's legal staff had skillfully written an agreement that would give Sony publishing profits from SNES CD-based games. Nintendo, however, wanted to keep these royalties. Thus Nintendo went to Philips Electronics to create a CD-ROM that would work with the CD-interactive, Philips new gaming/home entertainment product. Sony, which had a prototype finished, began to work on a CD-only (as opposed to game-cartridge-based) 32-bit machine, which came to be known as the PlayStation.

Atari also made a startling reentry to the videogame industry, by introducing its 64-bit Jaguar (actually two 32-bit chips working in tandem). It had a 13.3 MHz clock speed and was technically equivalent to a 32-bit system. However, game developers had lost confidence in Atari, and the resulting lack of game support led to the failure of the system. Sega had also begun to work on a 32-bit system, named the Saturn.

Sega and Sony released their new entrants into the market in 1995. Sega announced that it would release the Saturn on September 2, but it ended up releasing it in early May at $400. Sales were low and few titles were initially available because game developers were caught off-guard by the early release. By contrast, Sony launched the PlayStation at $300, $100 less than expected, with a large catalog of games and rave reviews.

Nintendo did not respond to the moves of its competitors until 1996 (after more than two years of preannouncements), when it introduced the Nintendo 64, a cartridge-based system.[16] Nintendo sold over 1.7 million units in three months, despite the fact that there were only two software titles available at the console's release (one being Super Mario). Nintendo claimed that it could have sold 2.5 million units during the holiday season if it could have produced that many.

In April of 1997, Sony announced that it had sold 11 million PlayStations in Japan, the United States, and Europe.[17] Four months later this number had almost doubled at 20 million. Later in the year Sega began to develop a new 128-bit system named Dreamcast, which was based on Microsoft's Windows CE operating system. Shortly after this, Sony began working on the successor to the PlayStation. In 1999, Nintendo announced it was planning on releasing a new system called the GameCube[18] using an IBM processor, and later that year Microsoft announced that it would be entering the videogame industry with the release of the Xbox.[19] The seventh generation had arrived.[20]

The Videogame Industry: Competitive Environment

Market and Demographics

In 1999, sales of videogame hardware, software, and other accessories exceeded $7 billion, with software sales alone of $3.3 billion.[21] Ninety-three million players bought software for their Sony PlayStation, Nintendo 64 or PC.[22] Children's leisure software for the PC topped $17.5 billion, with 77 million units sold in 1999. The Yankee Group predicted that by the end of 2003, 43.5 million homes in the United States would have a videogame console, up from 35.9 million in 1998. The seventh-generation consoles, such as the PS2, GameCube, Xbox and Dreamcast, would account for 85 percent of this installed base.

Many homes also had multiple consoles; in 2001, 23 percent of console households had two or more systems and 20 percent had three or more systems. Furthermore, the demographics of video games appeared to be changing. Whereas the arcade games on which video games had initially been based primarily targeted adolescents, in 2001 over 40 percent of videogame players were over 18 in console households, and 41 percent were over 18 in PC-based households.[23] Female players were also becoming a growing constituency, accounting for 15 percent of the videogame market by the spring of 2000.[24]

With the exception of the GameCube, the seventh generation had moved toward becoming home entertainment systems rather than just dedicated gaming systems.[25] The systems incorporated functions such as the ability to play DVDs and CDs, send e-mail, and surf the Web. The impact these systems would have on other platforms, such as the PC, was uncertain. However, 23 percent of home PC users said the primary function of the PC was for playing games, while 21 percent said game playing was the second most frequent activity on the computer.[26]

Suppliers

Microsoft developed the operating system for the Xbox in-house. Microsoft gained experience in this area when it developed the operating platform for Sega's Dreamcast. George T. Chronis, executive editor of the videogame trade magazine *Games Business,* pointed to that angle: "Microsoft has learned a lot helping Sega create a competitive console. . . . They've taken that and they're going to apply it to their own piece of hardware."[27] The operating system would use a simple stripped-down version of Windows. The development costs of the operating system were minimal due to Microsoft's previous experience and expertise in operating system design.

The Xbox operating system would run on a 733 MHz microprocessor that would be supplied by Intel. The estimated price for the microprocessor was $425, which was more than the targeted retail price of the whole console at $300.[28] This processor would be more than twice as fast as any current game console processor on the market, including Toshiba's 300 MHz processor in the Sony PS2. Originally Microsoft was going to be supplied by Advanced Micro Devices (AMD) but later chose Intel based on its past relations with the company.

Another major component was the memory system. Microsoft signed Micron to a six-year contract to supply the majority of the SDRAM chips. The Xbox would have 64 megabytes of memory and a data rate of 400 megabits per second (Mbps) per pin with 6.4 GB per second bandwidth. This meant that more information, in larger chunks, could be processed faster. The Xbox memory chip gave game developers nearly twice the memory offered in other game consoles. Robert Bach, chief Xbox officer, described the benefit of working with Micron: "Working with Micron to pack this amount of memory into Xbox will liberate game developers to produce more exhilarating, imaginative, and immersive game play for gamers."[29]

Microsoft would incorporate its DirectX interface technology that it used in its PC systems through the nVidia graphic chip and Wolfson Microelectronics audio chip. This technology allowed it to improve graphics, audio, and multimedia integration in games. The 300 MHz 3D nVidia graphic chip processes more than 1 trillion operations per second, which allows sharper images for high-resolution graphics because colors and shapes are changing at a faster rate. The system can support 1920 × 1080 pixels. This means that images, such as a character's face, would be able to be seen in more detail, due to a larger amount of pixels being used. The Wolfson chip had the ability to send six-speaker Dolby encoding through 256 channels to stereo speakers, allowing the games to be heard in surround sound. NVidia would also provide the 10/100 Mbps for DSL or cable connection for online game playing. Other suppliers included Seagate, which would provide the hard drive; Integrated Circuit Systems, which would provide the connections, wiring, and timing between the hardware components; and Applied Microsystems, which would supply the technology for the DVD aspect.

Despite all the advanced technology, many consumers worried about the reliability of the game console, noting the propensity of Microsoft-based systems to crash. To reassure customers of the game system's reliability, Microsoft pointed out that the Xbox would operate its games from a DVD to avoid hard drive failures. In addition, Microsoft noted that the Xbox had only one function to perform, whereas PC systems crash due to the large number of applications vying for operating system resources.[30]

Microsoft outsourced assembly of the Xbox to Flextronics. Flextronics was one of the world's largest contract electronics manufacturers, and Microsoft believed that using Flextronics would help ensure quality assembly and a smooth launch. Additionally, in 2001, Flextronics was already acting as the OEM for all of Microsoft's other hardware products. Flextronics' nine worldwide production centers allowed for quick market reaction and the capacity to meet demand on the launch date. (Problems with meeting launch and demand targets had plagued Sony on the release of its PS2 in October, 2000, causing many customers to opt for different consoles.) Flextronics' main North American productions would be staged in Mexico. Microsoft would also be the only producer to set up locations in Europe with its Hungary location. The Hungarian facilities had cost $110 million and would employ 10,000 workers. Microsoft predicted that its $3 billion contract would result in 6–7 percent of GDP for the Hungarian nation, and be the ninth largest employer.[31]

Microsoft has had tense relationships with suppliers in the past. Suppliers often questioned Microsoft's dedication to projects, and many times it was the suppliers who bore the financial brunt of unsuccessful projects. For example, Microsoft entered the handheld computer market with its Windows-based personal digital assistant (PDA) in the early 1990s. Unfortunately, Microsoft did not meet its sales forecast. While Microsoft's development costs had been minimized by building the handheld's system based on Windows and its other applications, other suppliers were left with large amounts of inventory, sunk development costs, and binding contracts.[32]

Competitors

Going into 2001, the market leaders in the gaming industry were Sony, Sega, and Nintendo. The industry practice of subsidizing console production with game royalties had made it difficult for smaller competitors to enter. A company had to be able to bear substantial early losses to accumulate a sufficient installed base to reap the benefits of game licensing. Only then could a company hope to recoup its high production and R&D costs.

Sega   Founded in 1951 by David Rosen, Sega began as an art export company that moved into photograph booths. In the 1960s Sega (*Service Games*) began making

Exhibit 2   SEGA FINANCIALS, 1999–2001 ($ MILLIONS, EXCEPT PER SHARE AMOUNTS)

	2001	2000	1999
Income Statement Data			
Revenue	$1,922.9	$3,213.6	$2,234.9
Cost of goods sold	1,727.5	2,753.3	1,694.4
Gross profit	195.4	460.3	540.5
Gross profit margin	10.2%	14.3%	24.2%
SG&A expense	$ 607.1	$ 842.8	$ 522.9
Operating income	(411.8)	(382.5)	17.5
Operating profit margin	−21.4%	−11.9%	0.8%
Net income	$ (409.5)	$ (406.4)	$ (360.0)
Net profit margin	−21.3%	−12.6%	−16.1%
Balance Sheet Data			
Cash	$ 297.9	$ 890.1	$ 845.5
Net receivables	164.9	356.8	358.4
Inventories	131.6	403.7	517.0
Total current assets	766.7	2,003.4	2,148.2
Total assets	2,251.8	3,557.5	3,573.3
Short-term debt	716.7	199.1	390.7
Total current liabilities	1,227.8	1,863.2	1,046.2
Long-term debt	234.2	310.6	1,802.3
Total liabilities	1,519.8	2,792.3	2,895.0
Total equity	732.1	765.1	678.3

Note: Some figures may not add up due to rounding.
Source: Hoover's.

coin-operated games. In 2001, this division remained along with its Amusement Park Division (which only operated in Japan) and the Home Entertainment Division.

Sega had a history of technologically sound but poorly received systems, including the Master System in the mid-1980s and Saturn in 1995. However, its Genesis system in 1989 was a success and a leading competitor of the Nintendo system. Sega's seventh-generation system, the Dreamcast, was released in early 2000. Prior to the Dreamcast's release, Sega was suffering from its lowest market share in years—12 percent. Fortunately, Sega was able to beat competition to the market with the Dreamcast (the Dreamcast was the first 128-bit system to market) and was able to climb to 25 percent market share by the fall of 2000. Sega's success turned out to be shortlived after Sony released the much-anticipated PlayStation2. Despite 25 percent price cuts, the Dreamcast was crushed in the holiday sales season.

At year-end 2000, Sega issued a press release that changed its previous estimates from a $14 million profit to a $200 million loss, giving it a fourth straight losing quarter. (See Exhibit 2 for full financials.)[33] Sega also released its future business plan. Sega decided to license out its Dreamcast platform and exit console production. These announcements caused Sega's stock price to plummet and made Sega a possible

Exhibit 3   NINTENDO FINANCIALS, 1999–2001 ($ MILLIONS, EXCEPT PER SHARE AMOUNTS)

	2001	2000	1999
Income Statement Data			
Revenue	$3,661.2	$5,279.4	$4,806.0
Cost of goods sold	2,204.3	2,745.2	2,609.6
Gross profit	1,456.9	2,534.2	2,196.3
Gross profit margin	39.8%	48.0%	45.7%
SG&A expense	$ 786.4	$1,557.3	$ 927.9
Operating income	670.5	976.9	1,268.4
Operating profit margin	18.3%	18.5%	26.4%
Net income	$ 764.7	$ 531.3	$ 720.5
Net profit margin	20.9%	10.1%	15.0%
Diluted earnings per share ($)	$ 5.40	$ 3.75	n.a.
Balance Sheet Data			
Cash	$6,530.2	$5,630.5	$5,361.3
Net receivables	433.1	680.6	523.4
Inventories	178.6	287.5	269.8
Total current assets	7,585.5	7,675.5	6,794.6
Total assets	8,458.8	8,846.5	7,500.4
Short-term debt	0.0	0.0	0.0
Total current liabilities	1,779.1	1,603.8	1,586.2
Long-term debt	0.0	0.0	0.0
Total liabilities	1,826.8	1,667.4	1,621.0
Total shareholders' equity	6,632.0	7,179.1	5,879.4

Note: Some figures may not add up due to rounding.
Source: Hoover's.

takeover candidate. In early January 2001, the *New York Times* reported that Nintendo was interested in purchasing Sega for $2 billion in order to gain its game development expertise. However on March 30, 2001, Sega announced it had different plans: it would be signing a long-term alliance with Microsoft. The companies would kick off the relationship by releasing 11 of Sega's upcoming games on the Xbox platform.

Nintendo   Originally founded in 1889 as a producer of playing cards, Nintendo blossomed into a multibillion-dollar company. It was the leader in the 1980s with the Nintendo Entertainment System (NES) and was a major contender in the late 1990s with the Nintendo 64. Nintendo was also one of the first handheld game producers. In handheld games, it controlled 90 percent of the Japanese market and 99 percent of the North American and European markets.[34] Its dominance in this industry had allowed Nintendo's business to remain profitable despite stiff competition in console gaming systems. (See Exhibit 3 for full financial reports.)

Of the competitors vying for the market in 2001, Nintendo would be the last company to come out with a seventh-generation console that could compete with the PlayStation2, Dreamcast, or Xbox. The arrival of the GameCube was delayed because of Nintendo's tardiness in sending development kits that were essential to developers to produce games. Analysts saw Nintendo's late arrival as costly to market share.

Despite this weakness, one of Nintendo's greatest strengths was its game development. It produced 80 percent of its games in-house and continually had three to five games on the top 10 sellers list year after year. In addition, the majority of other top sellers were also available on the Nintendo system as well. It had been especially strong in marketing to younger users with Mario Brothers, Donkey Kong, and Poké-mon. In 2000, Zachary Liggett, an analyst with WestLB Panmure in Tokyo, noted: "They still have a huge hold on the little kiddie market."[35] Nintendo hoped that its success with children's games would enable it to be successful with the GameCube.

Sony   The Sony Company began in a bombed-out building in Tokyo in 1946 after World War II. Masaru Ibuka, an engineer, and Akio Morita, a physicist, invested the equivalent of $1,500 to start a company with 20 employees repairing electrical equipment and attempting to build its own products. Focusing on innovation, Sony would grow into a company that would ultimately invent the Trinitron TV, the Walkman, the floppy disk, the CD, and PlayStation.

Sony first entered the game console market when Nintendo asked it to develop a new platform in 1992. Sony hoped to leverage its new SuperDisc audio disk that it had developed with Philips in the gaming platform. After several contract disputes with Nintendo and Philips, it ceased the relationship with Nintendo and commenced development of its own console. It was well publicized that Sony had spent over $500 million in developing the PlayStation. From the time it launched the product in 1995 to 1998 it sold nearly 40 million consoles worldwide. As of 2001, Sony Computer Entertainment, led by CEO Ken Kutaragi, was providing 40 percent of parent Sony Corporation's profit. (See Exhibit 4 for full financial reports.)

By the end of 1999, the PlayStation controlled about 75 percent of the game console market, and it planned to defend against competition from Nintendo's Nintendo 64 and Sega's Saturn by introducing an even more advanced console, the PlayStation2. PS2 was launched in early November of 2000, but shipments were slowed by a shortage of supply and faulty systems, creating obstacles for the crucial holiday retailing season. There was speculation that Sony intentionally short-supplied the market to create hype and increase demand. This speculation was at its height when several news sources reported that Saddam Hussein had smuggled 4,000 PlayStation2 units into Iraq with the presumed intention of using them for military purposes. Some experts estimated that an integrated bundle of 12–15 PlayStation2s could provide enough computer power to control Iraqi unmanned aerial vehicles. (The United Nations forbade computer hardware from being sold or transferred to Iraq.)[36]

In the 2000 holiday season, sales of the original PlayStation (with redesigned looks under the name PSOne) were twice those of the new PlayStation2. Sony came under Wall Street criticism for releasing the revamped PSOne so close to the release of the PS2. The slowing in the economy made the PSOne, priced at $100, seem more attractive than the $300 priced PS2. One game analyst noted, "I think some parents thought they could get the PS2 for their kids. Now they see they can't, and the PSOne looks like a pretty good deal."[37] The PS2 accounted for only 6 percent of console sales during the holiday while Sony's PSOne accounted for 61 percent, surpassing Sega's 17 percent with the Dreamcast and Nintendo 64's 15 percent. Sony was able to regain its lost market share but was unable to establish PlayStation2 as the dominant game console.

Some analysts speculated that Microsoft would be unable to compete against Sony in the videogame console market. For example, Motoharu Sone, an analyst at Universal

Exhibit 4   SONY FINANCIALS, 1999–2001 ($ MILLIONS, EXCEPT PER SHARE AMOUNTS)

	2001	2000	1999
Income Statement Data			
Revenue	$58,518.0	$63,082.0	$57,109.0
Cost of goods sold	38,901.0	43,849.0	39,066.0
Gross profit	19,617.0	19,233.0	18,043.0
Gross profit margin	33.5%	30.5%	31.6%
SG&A expense	$13,071.0	$14,071.0	$12,615.0
Depreciation & amortization	4,743.0	2,892.0	2,582.0
Operating income	1,803.0	2,270.0	2,846.0
Operating profit margin	3.1%	3.6%	5.0%
Net income	$ 134.0	$ 1,149.0	$ 1,505.0
Net profit margin	0.2%	1.8%	2.6%
Diluted earnings per share ($)	$0.15	$1.24	$1.65
Balance Sheet Data			
Cash	$ 4,858.0	$ 5,906.0	$ 4,978.0
Net receivables	10,362.0	9,957.0	8,519.0
Inventories	7,543.0	8,106.0	7,379.0
Total current assets	27,820.0	29,572.0	25,798.0
Total assets	62,624.0	64,219.0	52,944.0
Short-term debt	10,251.0	9,679.0	7,156.0
Total current liabilities	21,174.0	20,381.0	16,327.0
Long-term debt	6,749.0	7,678.0	8,720.0
Total liabilities	44,100.0	43,626.0	37,617.0
Total equity	18,524.0	20,593.0	15,328.0
Shares outstanding (millions)	919.6	907.3	819.9

Note: Some figures may not add up due to rounding.
Source: Hoover's.

Securities, noted, "Its [Sony's] hardware specifications are second to none, and it's perhaps hard to catch up, particularly in terms of graphics. It already has 70 million original PS users, and many of them would shift to buy PS2 because games are compatible. These two factors will likely keep Sony from losing dominance."[38]

Videogame Developers

The success of a game console relied heavily on the availability of popular games for the system. The larger the number of popular games available for a system, the more attractive it became to potential customers. In turn, the more customers who adopted a particular system, the more attractive that system became to potential game developers. Thus, a self-reinforcing cycle could propel a particular system to an extremely powerful position if that system could attain an advantage in either the availability of complementary goods, the size of its installed base, or both. This cycle, known as a network externalities effect, was common in industries in which standards, compatibility, and complementary goods (such as games) were important.[39] By 2001, Microsoft was well established as a leader in developing PC games (see Exhibit 5). It

Exhibit 5   TOP-SELLING PC TITLES (AS OF MAY 2000)

Title	Developer	Category	Price
1. Who Wants to Be a Millionaire	Disney	Family Entertainment	$19
2. The Sims	Electronic Arts	Strategy	42
3. Roller Coaster Tycoon	Hasbro	Strategy	27
4. Age of Empire II	Microsoft	Strategy	44
5. Roller Coaster Tycoon Expansion	Hasbro	Strategy	19
6. Sim City 3000	Electronic Arts	Strategy	39
7. Unreal Tournament	Infogrames	Action	43
8. Half-Life	Havas	Action	32
9. Rainbow Six Gold	Red Storm	Strategy	28
10. Who Wants to Be a Millionaire, 2nd	Disney	Family Entertainment	18

Source: PC Data.

Exhibit 6   TOP-SELLING GAME CONSOLE TITLES (AS OF MAY 2000)

Title	Developer	Platform	Category	Price
1. Pokémon Stadium	Nintendo	Nintendo 64	Action	$60
2. Pokémon Yellow	Nintendo	Game Boy	Adventure	26
3. WWF	THQ Inc.	PlayStation	Sports	41
4. Gran Turismo 2	Sony	PlayStation	Simulation	40
5. Pokémon Trading Card	Nintendo	Game Boy	Action	25
6. Syphon Filter 2	989 Studio	PlayStation	Action	41
7. Pokémon Blue	Nintendo	Game Boy	Adventure	25
8. Pokémon Red	Nintendo	Game boy	Adventure	26
9. Crazy Taxi	Sega	Dreamcast	Simulation	50
10. Mario Party 2	Nintendo	Nintendo 64	Family Entertainment	50

Source: PC Data.

would try to leverage those strengths in developing console games. However, there were fairly significant differences in game development between the platforms. As noted by Don Coyner, director of marketing at Microsoft's Games division, "Each has a very distinct audience. . . . PC games are more cerebral, while console games are more visceral. If you look at the top 10 games lists for these two platforms, you'll see that they don't really match up."[40] (See Exhibits 5, 6, and 7.) Microsoft would now be making a whole new style of game. In order to make this transition, Microsoft acquired a few small-name developers such as Bungie. In addition, it would only produce 30–40 percent of the games in-house, while relying on third-party developers to produce the majority of games, similar to Sony's strategy (see Exhibit 8).

To attract third-party developers, a company needed to be able to convince the market that its console would be successful, and supply effective development kits that facilitated programming for the operating system of the console. Microsoft's brand name enabled the company to enlist most of the major third-party game developers to produce games for the Xbox (see Exhibit 9). Microsoft also got rave reviews from developers for the simplicity with which games could be programmed for the Xbox. Because Microsoft leveraged its user-friendly DirectX technology, PC game developers

Exhibit 7   COMPARISON OF PROFIT MARGINS BY CATEGORY
(AS OF MAY 2000)

	Console Profit Margin	PC Profit Margin
Action	35.4%	12.6%
Adventure	19.7	12.3
Arcade	2.7	2.6
Children	3.3	6.9
Family Entertainment	1.6	14.8
Simulation	13.6	11.6
Sports	19.1	8.8
Strategy	4.0	28.5
Other	0.5	1.9

Source: PC Data.

were already familiar with the technology, enabling an easy transition from PC to console. Furthermore, since DirectX was a commonly used tool among amateur game developers, Microsoft allowed online Xbox applications development for a small fee.

Microsoft's major disadvantage in the videogame industry was its inexperience in developing characters to attract the younger portion of the market. Characters such as Sonic the Hedgehog, Mario, Solid Snake, and Pokémon had proved crucial in the success of Nintendo and Sega. To combat this, Microsoft announced that it would team up with the Danish company Lego to build brand image among the younger generation. Corey Wade, an analyst at Alexander & Associates, which studied home entertainment trends, criticized Microsoft: "I don't think they have a clue now how to come up with a Nintendo-style game aimed at a 12-year-old."[41] In 2001, Nintendo had approximately a 15 percent market share, and that was expected to grow with its release of the GameCube. Microsoft appeared better positioned to battle Sony for the remaining market share—that of males in their teens and 20s.

Microsoft's Strategy

Though producing consumer electronics hardware did not seem an obvious fit with Microsoft's product portfolio, many industry observers speculated that Microsoft had begun to see the videogame console industry as a threat to its dominance in PC operating systems. Sony, Nintendo, and Sega were all producing consoles that would enable gamers to access the Internet. This idea had been pioneered by Nintendo in 1989, when it formed a joint venture with AT&T to network NES households and allow downloading of games and videogame chat lines. This venture never fully materialized, and the idea was scrapped; however, the Dreamcast and PS2 resurrected the idea and provided modems for online access. Rumors also circulated that Sony planned to incorporate a Linux port on the Sony PlayStation2—a move that would understandably raise some concerns at Microsoft, since Linux was an alternative to Microsoft's Windows operating system. Should the gaming console prove to become a primary portal to the Internet, it posed a real competitive threat to the PC industry.

Exhibit 8 TITLES SCHEDULED FOR RELEASE ON LAUNCH DATE

Title	Developer	Genre
1906: Arctic Odyssey	DarkWorks	Other
Amped: Snowboarding	Microsoft	Racing
Arctic Thunder	Midway Home Ent.	Racing
Azurik: Rise of Perathia	Adrenium Games	Action
Battlefield 1942	Digital Illusions	Action
Black and White	Lionhead Studios	Action
Bounty Hunter	Warthog PLC	Action
Breed	Brat Designs	Action
Brute Force	Acclaim	Other
Call of the Dragonfly	Lost Boys Interactive	Other
Codename: Gotham	Bizarre Creations	Racing
Crash Bandicoot X	Konami Corporation	Action
Crimson Skies	Microsoft	Sims
Dead or Alive 3	Tecmo, LTD.	Action
Defender of the Crown	Cinemaware Inc.	Other
Divine Divinity	Larian Studios	RPG*
Dragons Lair 3D	Blue Byte Software	Action
Dreadnoughts	Xenopi	Action
Druid King	Sidhe Interactive	RPG
Earth and Beyond	Westwood Studios	Action
Engalus	Crytek Studios	Other
eRacer	Rage	Racing
F1 World Grand Prix 3	Hasbro Interactive	Racing
Fuzion Frenzy	Blitz Games Ltd	Other
Giants	Interplay Ent.	Strategy
Halo	Bungie	Shooters
Harry Potter	Electronic Arts	Other
Heaven and Hell	MadCat Interactive	RPG
Internal Affairs	Attention to Detail	Other
Jurassic Park X	Konami Corporation	Other
Knockout Kings	Electronic Arts	Sports
Madden NFL 2002	Electronic Arts	Sports
Malice	Argonaut Games	Other
Max Payne	Remedy Entertainment	Shooters
Mechwarrior X	Microsoft	Shooters
Medal of Honor:	2015	Strategy
Metal Dungeon	Panther Software	RPG
Metal Gear Solid X	Konami Corporation	Shooters
New Legends	THQ	Action
Nightcaster	VR-1 Entertainment	RPG
Munch's Oddysee	Oddworld Inhabitants	Other
Project K-X	Dream Factory	Other
Psychotoxic	NuClearVision Ent.	Shooters

continued

Exhibit 8   Continued

Title	Developer	Genre
NFL Fever 2002	Microsoft	Sports
Republic	Eidos interactive	Other
Salt Lake City	Attention to Detail	Sims
Seraphim	Valkyrie Studios	Action
Urban Warfare	Zombie VR Studios	Shooters
Silent Hill X	Konami Corp	Other
Silent Space	Crytek Studios	Strategy
Ski-Doo X Racing	Daydream Software	Racing
Soldier of Fortune	Majesco Inc.	Shooters
SRC	Criterion Software	Other
SSX Snowboarding	Electronic Arts	Sports
Stunt Driver	Climax Ltd. Co.	Sports
Tetris World	THQ	Other
The Sims	Electronic Arts	Sims
The Thing	Konami Corp	Other
Title Defense	Climax Ltd. Co.	Sports
Tony Hawk 2	Activision, Inc.	Sports
Tour De France	Konami Corp	Other
V.I.P.	Ubi Soft Ent	Other
Virtual Velocity	Ubi Soft Ent	Other
Warcaster	Tremor Ent.	Other
Warzone Online	Paradox Ent.	Other
Wiggles	Innonics	Strategy
WWF Raw Is War	THQ	Other
X-Isle	Crytek Studios	Other
Yager	Yager Development	Action

*RPG = Role-playing game.

Organizational Structure

To manage the development and deployment of the new game console, Microsoft established a new division that would be led by a chief Xbox officer, Robert Bach, who would report directly to Bill Gates. The Xbox division would be highly autonomous, with its own branches for marketing, operations, and technical development. In general Microsoft was known to use very flexible structures and frequent reorganization. Some analysts saw this as an indication of instability and evidence of poor management. There were also high reorganization costs involved in the constant change. A Microsoft spokesperson played down such criticisms, noting that Microsoft "continually makes adjustments to the organization to meet the changing nature of needs."[42]

Exhibit 9   GAME DEVELOPERS FOR THE XBOX

Acclaim	DarkWorks	Imagineer Co. Ltd.	Over Works Inc.	Takuyo Kougyo Co., Ltd.
Activision, Inc.	Datam Polystar	Incredible Tech.	Pacific Coast P&L	TDK Mediactive, Inc.
Adrenium Games	Daydream Software	Infogrames	Panther Software	Tecmo, LTD.
Aki Corp.	Deep Red Games	Innonics	Panther Software Inc.	Telenet Japan Co., LTD.
Alfa System Co. Ltd.	Digital Anvil	Interplay Ent.	Papyrus	Terminal Reality
ALTAR Interactive	Digital Illusions	Jaleco Ltd.	Paradigm Studios	The Codemasters
Anchor Inc.	Digital Rim	Kaboom Studios	Paradox Entertainment	The Collective, Inc.
Angel Studios Inc.	DigitalWare Inc.	Kalisto Ent.	Pipe Dream Interactive	The LEGO Company
Arc System Works	Dma Design Ltd.	Kemco / Kotobuki	Qube	The Pitbull Syndicate
Argonaut Games	Dream Factory	Kodiak Interactive	R A C	The Whole Experience
Arika Co. Ltd.	DreamCatcher	Koei Co. Ltd.	Radical	THQ
Artdink Corp	DreamForge	Konami Corporation	Rage	Titus
Artoon Co. Ltd.	Dwango Co., Ltd.	Kool Kizz	Rainbow Studios	TopWare Interactive
Ask Co. Ltd.	Dynamix	Kuju Entertainment	Raven Software	Totally Games
Atlus Co. Ltd.	Edge of Reality	Larian Studios	Red Storm	Treasure, Inc.
Attention to Detail	Eidos interactive	Legend Ent.	Reflections Interactive	Tremor Entertainment
Awesome Dev.	Electronic Arts	LightWeight Co. Ltd.	Remedy Entertainment	Ubi Soft Entertainment
bam! Entertainment	Empire Interactive	Lionhead Studios	Revolution Software	Valkyrie Studios
Bandai Co. Ltd.	Eon Digital Ent.	Lost Boys Interactive	Ripcord Games	Valve, LLC
Barking Dog Studios	Epic Games	MadCat Interactive	Riverhillsoft Inc	Victor Interactive
Bethesda Softworks	Escape Factory	Majesco Inc.	Rockstar Games	Video System Co., Ltd.
BioWare Corp.	Fox Interactive	Mass Media Inc.	Saffire Corporation	Virgin Interactive
Bizarre Creations	From Software	Max-International Inc.	SCi Entertainment Group	VIS entertainment PLC
Blitz Games Ltd	Funcom	MGM Interactive	Shoeisha Co., Ltd.	Volition, Inc.
Blue Byte Software	Gameplay	Microids	Sidhe Interactive	VR-1 Ent.
Blue Shift, Inc.	Gathering	Microsoft	Sierra	Warthog PLC
Brat Designs	Genki Co. Ltd.	Midas Interactive	Silicon Dreams Studio Ltd.	Westwood Studios
Bungie	Global A Ent.	Midway Home	Simon & Schuster Interactive	XeNN inc.
Bunkasha Publishing	h.a.n.d. inc.	Monolith Productions	Sky.Co., Ltd.	Xenopi
Capcom Co. Ltd.	H.I.C. Co. Ltd.	Monster Games Inc.	SouthPeak Interactive	Yager
Charybdis Limited	Hasbro Interactive	Mythos Games Ltd	Spike Co., Ltd.	Yuki Enterprise
Cinemaware Inc.	Havas Interactive	Nagi Corporation	Starbreeze Studios	Zombie VR
Climax Ltd. Co.	Headlock Inc.	Namco Limited	Stormfront Studios	Zono, Inc.
Conspiracy Ent.	Heavy Iron Studios	Nest Corporation	T&E Soft, Inc.	
Core Design Ltd.	Housemarque	Neversoft Ent.	Taito Corporation	
Crave Entertainment	Hudson Soft	Nihilistic Software Inc.	Takara Co., LTD.	
Criterion Software	Humongous Ent.	Nihon Create Inc.	Take-Two Interactive	
Cryo	id Software, Inc.	NovaLogic Inc		
Crystal Dynamics	I-Imagine Interactive	NuClearVision		
Crytek Studios	Image Corporation	Oddworld Inhabitants		

Exhibit 10   MICROSOFT FINANCIALS, 1999–2001 ($ MILLIONS, EXCEPT PER SHARE AMOUNTS)

	2001	2000	1999
Income Statement Data			
Revenue	$25,296.0	$22,956.0	$19,747.0
Cost of goods sold	1,919.0	2,254.0	1,804.0
Gross profit	23,377.0	20,702.0	17,943.0
Gross profit margin	92.4%	90.2%	90.9%
SG&A expense	$10,121.0	$ 8,925.0	$ 6,890.0
Depreciation & amortization	1,536.0	748.0	1,010.0
Operating income	11,720.0	11,029.0	10,043.0
Operating profit margin	46.3%	48.0%	50.9%
Net income	$ 7,346.0	$ 9,421.0	$ 7,785.0
Net profit margin	29.0%	41.0%	39.4%
Diluted earnings per share ($)	$1.32	$1.70	$1.42
Balance Sheet Data			
Cash and short-term investments	$31,600.0	$23,798.0	$17,236.0
Net receivables	3,671.0	3,250.0	2,245.0
Inventories	0.0	0.0	0.0
Total current assets	39,637.0	30,308.0	20,233.0
Total assets	59,257.0	52,150.0	37,156.0
Short-term debt	0.0	0.0	0.0
Total current liabilities	11,132.0	9,755.0	8,718.0
Long-term debt	0.0	0.0	0.0
Total liabilities	11,968.0	10,782.0	8,718.0
Total equity	47,289.0	41,368.0	28,438.0
Shares outstanding (millions)	5,383.0	5,283.0	5,109.0

Note: Some figures may not add up due to rounding.
Source: Hoover's.

Marketing

Microsoft planned a marketing budget for the Xbox of $500 million to be spent over a span of 18 months, the biggest launch in the company's history.[43] (See Exhibit 10 for company financials.) The budget would include funding for in-store merchandising, promotion, retailer incentives, events, sponsorships, and traditional advertising. Promotional partners in the fast-food, beverage and sports industries were expected to share the expenses. Microsoft planned on using broad consumer media (television, radio, the Internet, and business publications) and trade publications. In addition, Microsoft reimbursed qualified resellers and original equipment manufacturers (OEMs) for certain advertising expenditures.

McCannErickson Worldwide, an advertising agency based in New York, would handle the $150 million Xbox advertising account. The focus of the advertising campaign was expected to be a sense of passion and exhilaration. Microsoft would also continue to tout the technological superiority of the Xbox in comparison to the PlayStation2 and GameCube. The gaming division's marketing department had the goal of making the Xbox one of the top five consumer brands worldwide. To help accomplish this, John O'Rourke, vice president of marketing for the Xbox, employed an experienced staff that included (among others) Don Coyner (director of marketing, Games Division), who had spent seven years at Nintendo, and Jennifer Booth (marketing director, research), who had launched Sony's original PlayStation in 1995.[44]

Research and Development

In 1991, Microsoft established its own computer science research organization, Microsoft Research, after it saw a need to support long-range research that would be the foundation for future products. Microsoft spent $250 million a year on its four research labs, part of a $4 billion research and development budget, which was, among large technology companies, one of the highest ratios of investment to revenue.

Microsoft Research committed time and money to research in graphics, such as animation, multiresolution geometry, and layered-depth images; audio; and artificial intelligence. All of these areas were vital in the development of the Xbox and games produced by Microsoft.[45]

While in general Microsoft's corporate research labs focused on goals extending 5 to 10 years beyond current product cycles, their close interaction with the rest of the company allowed for short-term results with the various product development groups. For example, some CD-ROM game titles used technology or tools created by Microsoft Research.

The neXt Box?

Microsoft was a very large, well-known company with tremendous capital to access and unsurpassed brand recognition. Microsoft had also demonstrated repeatedly its mastery of strategically developing and deploying technology in industries characterized by network externalities, in which standards and complementary goods played crucial roles. Such industries had a tendency to select one or a few winners and exclude all other would-be competitors. Microsoft's reputation for dominance in such industries likely played a significant role in its ability to attract game developers, and in industry analysts' perceptions of the firm's likelihood of success.

However, it was also impossible to overlook the fact that Microsoft's dominance had always been in software. The production of hardware—especially consumer electronics—posed very different requirements for inventory, manufacturing, and distribution. Furthermore, Microsoft's success in many of its software categories could be traced to its dominance in PC operating systems; however, the market share of Windows would likely prove to be of little use in the game console market. Finally, Microsoft would be marketing to new types of customers, both in terms of distributors and end consumers. Though it would likely sell the Xbox through some of the same distributors with which it had relationships for selling software, it would now need much greater penetration into distributors such as Toys "R" Us, Babbages, and Circuit City. It would also need to cultivate a radically different brand image in the game console market than the one it had achieved in the software market, and to make much greater use of marketing channels such as television advertising and gaming magazines.

Overall, the videogame console market represented a fundamentally different kind of business for Microsoft, and it would be battling very large, well-established

Exhibit 11 Pictures of Products

Microsoft's Xbox

Sony's PlayStation One
(PSOne)

Sony's PlayStation One
(PSOne Mobile)

Sony's PlayStation2
(PS2)

Sega's Dreamcast

Nintendo's GameCube

Source: www.xbox.com, www.sega.com, www.nintendo.com, www.sony.com.

Exhibit 12 COMPETITIVE SUMMARY OF THE 128-BIT U.S. VIDEOGAME CONSOLE MARKET

Competitors	Sony PlayStation2	Microsoft Xbox	Nintendo GameCube
Introduction	March 2000	November 2001	November 2001
Price	$299	$299	$199
Technological functionality	CD/DVD based	CD/DVD based	Mini-disc based
	128 bits	128 bits	128 bits
	300 MHz clock speed	733 MHz clock speed	485 MHz clock speed
	32 MB RAM	64 MB RAM	40 MB RAM
	Broadband compatible	Broadband compatible	
Backward compatibility	Yes	Not applicable	No
Developers	Internal and external; 40% of games produced in-house	Internal and external; 40% of games produced in-house	Internal and external; 80% of games produced in-house
Game titles	About 300 by December 2001; 483 by March 2002	About 40 by December 2001; 205 in March 2002	About 20 by December 2001; 117 in March 2002

competitors. Not everyone was sure it was a battle it would win. Would the Xbox's technological advantages be able to attract gamers away from the game consoles of Nintendo and Sony? Though Microsoft had legions of third-party developers signed up for game licensing, such agreements often did not translate into actual game titles. After all, 3DO, a company that had launched a videogame system in 1993, had signed on

300 game developers at its launch, but those license arrangements translated into only five actual game titles by March of 1994. It seemed clear that PC game developers would embrace the Xbox, but Microsoft's intention was not to simply attract current PC gamers to the platform—its intention was to battle for a share of Sony and Nintendo's market of console gamers. (See Exhibit 11 for pictures of the competing game systems and Exhibit 12 for a competitive summary of 128-bit systems.)

Endnotes

[1]D. Frankel, "Videogame Business Boffo on Big Launches," *Video Business,* December 31, 2001, p. 38.
[2]www.allsands.com.
[3]The Altair was a kit that included an Intel microprocessor and enough hardware to assemble a box with toggle switches and lights, but no terminal, keyboard, or software. It was essentially useless, but it inspired the imaginations of thousands of young computer hobbyists who could, for the first time, own their own computer.
[4]Microsoft leveraged its control in the operating system market into the applications markets in a number of ways, including bundling arrangements (whereby a copy of a particular application was included in the Windows purchase) and giving its internal applications developers priority access to the Windows code, making it possible for them to develop programs that worked better with Windows and came out sooner than applications developed by competitors such as Lotus.
[5]www.planetxbox.com.
[6]S. Hart, "Guns, Games, and Glory: The Birth of Home Videogames," www.geekcomix.com/vgh.
[7]S. Hart, "A Brief History of Videogames," www.geekcomix.com/vgh.
[8]www.geekcomix.com/vgh.
[9]Ibid.
[10]S. Cohen, *Zap! The Rise and Fall of ATARI* (New York: McGraw-Hill, 1984), p. 46.
[11]E. Provenzo, *Videokids* (Cambridge, MA: Harvard University Press, 1991), p. 10.
[12]www.videotopia.com.
[13]D. Sheff, *Game Over: How Nintendo Zapped an American Industry, Captured Your Dollars and Enslaved Your Children* (New York, NY: Random House, 1993), preface.
[14]"Nintendo's Show of Strength," *Dealerscope Merchandising,* February 1991, p. 15.
[15]A. Brandenberger, "Power Play (B): Sega in 16-Bit Video Games," *Harvard Business School Case,* #9-795-103, 1995.
[16]www.nintendo.com.
[17]www.sony.com.
[18]Yuri Kageyama, "Nintendo Unveils New Videogame Console," *Associated Press,* August 24, 2000.
[19]www.microsoft.com.
[20]www.videogames.com.
[21]www.pcdata.com.
[22]www.tdctrade.com.
[23]www8.techmall.com.
[24]www.gametrends.com.
[25]*DVD for Games Machines* (London: Miller Freeman, 2000).
[26]www.gametrends.com.
[27]T. Ham, and J. Gaudiosi, "Microsoft and Sony Prepare for Mortal Combat," *Washington Post,* March 10, 2000, p. E11.
[28]N'Gai Croal, "How to Be a Player," *Newsweek* 135, no. 12 (2000), p. 62.
[29]Microsoft press release, June 12, 2000.
[30]Dean Takahashi, "Microsoft Goes Gaming," *Electronic Business* 26, no. 5 (2000), p. 44.
[31]MTI Econews.
[32]Nicholas Weaver, "Why the Xbox Could Easily Fail and Why Microsoft So Greatly Desires a Success," www.cs.berkeley.edu.
[33]Timna Tanners, "Game Developers See Sega as Both Boon and Threat," *Reuters News,* February 7, 2001.
[34]B. Fulford, "Super Hiroshi-san," *Forbes,* May 1, 2000, p. 90.
[35]Yuri Kageyama, "Nintendo Unveils New Videogame Console," *Associated Press,* August 24, 2000.
[36]N. McDowell, "Saddam At It Again," www.sonyweb.com/news, December 19, 2000.
[37]www.yahoo.cnet.com.
[38]T. Ham, and J. Gaudiosi, "Microsoft and Sony Prepare for Mortal Combat," *Washington Post,* March 10, 2000, p. E11.
[39]Network externalities are *positive consumption externalities* that occur when the user of a good derives more benefit from that good the more other users there are of the same (or similar) good.
[40]Microsoft press release, "Xbox to Deliver Ultimate Console Gaming Experience," www.gamerevolution.com, 2000.
[41]Ham and Gaudiosi, "Microsoft and Sony Prepare for Mortal Combat."
[42]James Niccolai, and Clare Haney, www.thestandard.com, March 12, 1999.
[43]T. Elkin, "Gearing Up for Xbox Launch," *Advertising Age* 71, no. 48 (2000), p. 16.
[44]www.gamingmaxx.com.
[45]www.research.microsoft.com.

The U.S. Publishing Industry in 2001 (A)

Industry Dynamics

Karel Cool
INSEAD

Petros Paranikas
INSEAD

During the 1980s and 1990s, the U.S. publishing industry went through massive consolidation that left it dominated by five publishing groups: Random House, Penguin Putnam, HarperCollins, Simon & Schuster, and Time Warner. The consolidation process was far from over, however. The Internet had opened up many opportunities for the publishing world with authors, printers, wholesalers, retailers, and publishers all announcing their intentions to participate one way or another in electronic publishing. It was a complex scenario—new companies were constantly being created, alliances were continually being formed, standards had not been agreed on, and profits remained on the distant horizon. Both established companies and start-ups were trying to anticipate how the publishing industry would change and what strategies would be successful.

This case provides an overview of the publishing market in the United States at the beginning of 2001, the industry value chain, and the major competitors. The companion case, "The U.S. Publishing Industry in 2001 (B): eBooks and ePublishing," describes the e-initiatives and strategies of established players and newcomers in the publishing industry.

The U.S. Market for Books

In 2000, net sales in the U.S. book publishing industry reached $25 billion, up from $17 billion in 1992. (See Exhibits 1 and 2 for sales data.) With sales in 2000 of $6.5 billion, down 3.7 percent from 1999, trade books formed the largest market segment, encompassing adult and juvenile, fiction and nonfiction titles in hardbound and paperbound formats. The second largest segment was professional books, with 2000 sales of $5.1 billion, up from $4.7 billion in 1999. It included business, law, medical, and technical titles. The only market segment to shrink between 1992 and 2000 was mail order, which dropped from $630 million to $432 million, a decline attributable to the expansion of superstores, price clubs, and Internet retailers. The U.S. publishing industry was expected to grow in constant dollars at 2 percent until 2004. Export sales were also

This case was written by Karel Cool, BP Professor of European Competitiveness at INSEAD and Petros Paranikas, MBA INSEAD, 2000. It is intended to be used as a basis for classroom discussion rather than to illustrate either effective or ineffective handling of an administrative situation. We would like to thank the Boston Consulting Group for sponsoring the case and assisting in the data collection and analysis. Copyright © 2002 INSEAD, Fontainebleau, France. Used with permission.

Exhibit 1 U.S. NET SALES OF BOOKS, BY MARKET SEGMENT, 1987–2000 ($ MILLIONS)

	Sales						% of Total Sales $	Compound Annual Growth Rate (%)			
	1987	1992	1997	1998	1999	2000		1987–2000	1992–2000	1998–1999	1999–2000
Adult hardbound	$1,351	$2,223	$2,664	$2,752	$3,037	$2,686	10.60%	5.40%	2.40%	10.40%	−11.60%
Adult paperbound	727	1,262	1,732	1,908	2,047	1,901	7.50	7.70	5.30	7.30	−7.20
Juvenile hardbound	479	851	909	954	1,061	1,201	4.70	7.30	4.40	11.30	13.20
Juvenile paperbound	157	327	470	535	647	753	3.00	12.80	11.00	20.90	16.40
Trade	2,713	4,662	5,774	6,149	6,792	6,541	25.80%	7.00%	4.30%	10.50%	−3.70%
Bibles	178	260	285	296	310	323	1.30	4.70	2.80	4.70	4.30
Other	461	647	847	882	907	924	3.60	5.50	4.50	2.80	1.80
Religious	639	907	1,133	1,178	1,217	1,247	4.90%	5.30%	4.10%	3.30%	2.50%
Business	389	490	768	852	910	N/A	N/A	N/A	N/A	N/A	N/A
Law	780	1,128	1,503	1,592	1,727	N/A	N/A	N/A	N/A	N/A	N/A
Medical	407	623	857	919	983	N/A	N/A	N/A	N/A	N/A	N/A
Technical	632	866	1,029	1,056	1,101	N/A	N/A	N/A	N/A	N/A	N/A
Professional	2,207	3,107	4,156	4,419	4,720	5,130	20.20%	6.70%	6.50%	6.80%	8.70%
Book clubs	679	742	1,143	1,209	1,272	1,292	5.10	5.10	7.20	5.20	1.50
Mail order	658	630	512	471	413	432	1.70	−3.20	−4.60	−12.30	4.60
Paperbacks	914	1,264	1,434	1,514	1,552	1,599	6.30	4.40	3.00	2.50	3.00
University press	171	280	368	392	412	402	1.60	6.80	4.60	5.10	−2.40
K–12 education	1,696	2,081	3,005	3,315	3,416	3,881	15.30	6.60	8.10	3.00	13.60
Higher education	1,550	2,084	2,670	2,889	3,129	3,237	12.80	5.80	5.70	8.30	3.50
Tests	104	140	191	205	219	234	0.90	6.40	6.60	6.90	7.00
Subscription reference	438	572	737	767	789	809	3.20	4.80	4.40	2.80	2.60
Other	424	449	510	526	542	559	2.20	2.20	2.80	2.90	3.30
Other	6,631	8,243	10,570	11,288	11,742	12,446	49.10%	5.00%	5.30%	4.00%	6.00%
Total/ overall average	$12,190	$16,918	$21,633	$23,033	$24,472	$25,363	100.00%	5.80%	5.20%	6.20%	3.60%

Source: Association of American Publishers.

Exhibit 2   Between 1992 and 2000 Juvenile Paperbound and K–12 Were Fastest Growing Segments

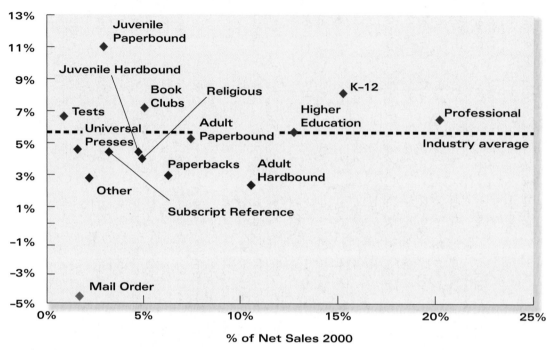

Source: Association of American Publishers.

expected to continue to rise, driven by the increased use of English at an international level, the global use of the Internet for purchasing books and the positive economic outlook for Canada and the European Union (which accounted for 66 percent of U.S. book exports). Exhibit 3 gives the value of imports and exports of books to and from the United States in 1998.

While books appealed to consumers of all ages, older consumer groups tended to buy more books. Consumers 55 years and older accounted for 34 percent of adult book purchases, while those under 34 accounted for 19 percent.[1] Consumers aged between 45 and 54 had the highest book-purchasing propensity, followed by consumers above 55. (See Exhibits 4 and 5.) Households with an income of $59,999 or less accounted for 61 percent of adult book purchasers in 1999. Households within higher income brackets demonstrated an above-average propensity to purchase books and accounted for the remaining sales. Households with two members demonstrated the highest interest in book purchasing, accounting for 44 percent of adult book purchases in 1999, while single-member households accounted for 19 percent of sales. Distribution of sales and propensity to purchase adult books by household income are presented in Exhibits 6 and 7. Exhibits 8 and 9 show the distribution of purchases and propensity to purchase adult books by household size. Exhibits 10 and 11 show distribution relative to the education level of the head of household.

Exhibit 3   U.S. TRADE PATTERNS IN PRINTING AND PUBLISHING IN 1998 ($ MILLIONS)

Regions	Exports		Regions	Imports	
	Value	Share		Value*	Share
NAFTA	$2,369	50%	NAFTA	$1,130	34%
Latin America	286	6	Latin America	42	1
Western Europe	997	21	Western Europe	1,046	31
Japan/Chinese Economic Area	455	10	Japan/Chinese Economic Area	833	25
Other Asia	188	4	Other Asia	221	7
Rest of world	427	9	Rest of world	54	2
World	$4,722		World	$3,325	

Top Five Countries	Value	Share	Top Five Countries	Value	Share
Canada	$2,018	43%	Canada	$975	29%
United Kingdom	478	10	United Kingdom	474	14
Mexico	351	7	China	376	11
Japan	279	6	Hong Kong	269	8
Australia	221	5	Italy	174	5

*Values do not sum to total due to rounding.
Source: U.S. Industry & Trade Outlook 2000, p. 25-2.

Exhibit 4   Distribution of Adult Book Purchases in 1999 by Age of Consumer

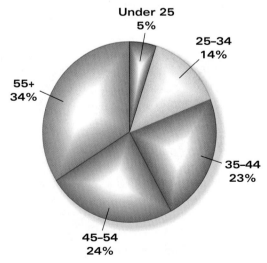

Source: BISG 1999 Consumer Research Study on Book Purchasing, Adult Book Industry Overview, 2000, p. II-4.

Exhibit 5   Propensity to Purchase Adult Books by Consumer Age

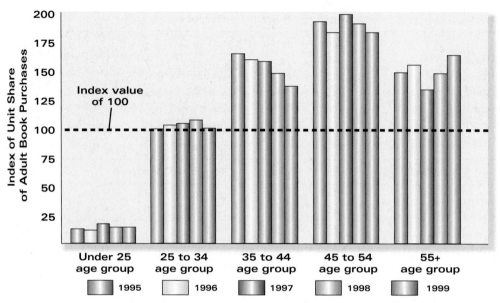

Note: Index based on Distribution of Unit Book Sales/Distribution of Consumer Age. Index value greater than 100 identifies above average book purchase group.

Source: BISG 1999 Consumer Research Study on Book Purchasing, Adult Book Industry Overview, 2000, p. AD 2. U.S. Census Bureau, Statistical Abstract of the United States, 2000, Table 12.

Exhibit 6   Distribution of Adult Book Purchases in 1999 by Household Income

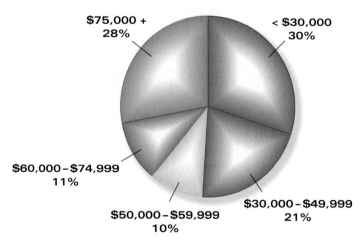

Source: BISG 1999 Consumer Research Study on Book Purchasing, Adult Book Industry Overview, 2000, p. II-4.

Exhibit 7   **Propensity to Purchase Adult Books by Household Income**

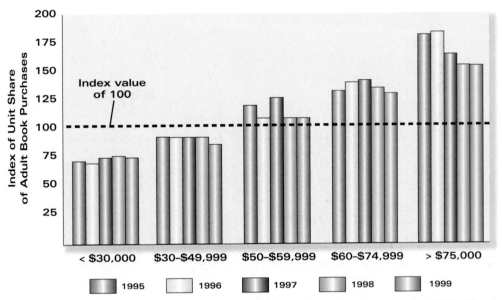

Note: Index based on Distribution of Unit Book Sales/Distribution of Consumer Age. Index value greater than 100 identifies above average book purchase group.

Source: BISG 1999 Consumer Research Study on Book Purchasing, Adult Book Industry Overview, 2000, p. AD 2.

Exhibit 8   **Distribution of Adult Book Purchases in 1999 by Household Size**

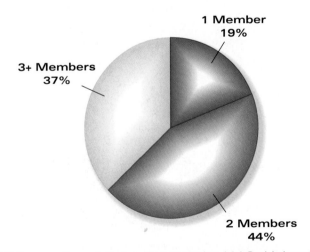

Source: BISG 1999 Consumer Research Study on Book Purchasing, Adult Book Industry Overview, 2000, p. II-4.

Exhibit 9   Propensity to Purchase Adult Books by Household Size

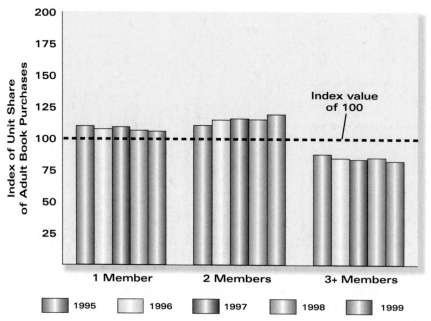

Note: Index based on Distribution of Unit Book Sales/Distribution of Consumer Age. Index value greater than 100 identifies above average book purchase group.

Source: BISG 1999 Consumer Research Study on Book Purchasing, Adult Book Industry Overview, 2000, p. AD 2.

Exhibit 10   Distribution of Adult Book Purchases in 1999 by Education of Household Head

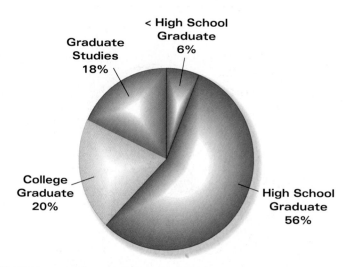

Source: BISG 1999 Consumer Research Study on Book Purchasing, Adult Book Industry Overview, 2000, p. II-4.

Exhibit 11   Propensity to Purchase Adult Books by Education of Household Head

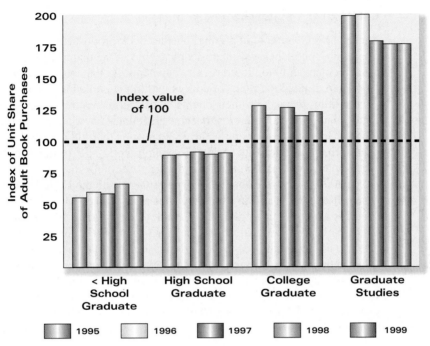

Note: Index based on Distribution of Unit Book Sales/Distribution of Consumer Age. Index value greater than 100 identifies above average book purchase group.

Source: BISG 1999 Consumer Research Study on Book Purchasing, Adult Book Industry Overview, 2000, p. AD 2.

The Publishing Industry Value Chain

Authors

Although 50,000 new titles were published in the United States every year, new authors found it difficult to get published. Industry consolidation had made publishers focus on titles with best-seller potential, making it harder for new authors to break in. As Cord Harper, a new author, put it, "You don't get looked at unless you're well-known. It's a Catch-22."[2] Those who managed to break through received an advance against royalties of $5,000 to $15,000, as well as a royalty rate of 10 to 15 percent on the hardcover sales of their book.[3] As publishers focused their marketing efforts on promoting established writers, most new authors never earned out their advances.[4] New authors who failed to succeed commercially after two books usually had to find a new publisher.

The fixation with best-sellers prompted the rise of "mega-authors" who dominated the best-seller charts. Six authors (Steele, King, Clancy, Grisham, Crichton, and Koontz) wrote 63 of the 100 best-selling books between 1986 and 1996. They used their market power to negotiate higher advances and royalty rates in multibook deals. For example, Tom Clancy received $45 million from Penguin Putnam for two books, while HarperCollins paid $40 million to publish the next two titles by Michael Crichton.

Simon & Schuster was paying Stephen King 50 percent of net revenues generated from the sale of his books.

Literary Agents

Agents assisted authors in putting together book proposals for submission to publishers. When a publisher was interested in acquiring the manuscript, the agent negotiated the agreement and monitored royalty payments. As the consolidation of the 1980s and 1990s had thinned the ranks of editors within the publishing houses, some agents offered editing services to their clients. Most publishers refused to consider unrepresented manuscripts. It therefore became essential for new authors to find an agent. Yet, in 2000, less than 2 percent of the 383 agencies that did not charge fees for reading manuscripts were actively seeking to submit work; and, of these, only one had managed to place books with publishers during 1999.

In 2000, there were about 1,000 literary agents in the United States. Thirty percent were self-employed and an additional 35 percent worked for agencies employing fewer than five agents. A handful of firms employed more than 10 agents, and the high end of the market was dominated by three mega-agencies (William Morris, Creative Artists Agency, and International Creative Management) that catered to the needs of established authors. Once an agent agreed to represent an author, an agreement of fixed duration was signed stipulating the terms of their cooperation.[5] Agents usually were paid 10 to 15 percent of the authors' royalties from U.S. sales, 20 to 30 percent from foreign sales and 10 to 15 percent from film commissions.[6] Some best-selling authors preferred to be represented by specialized attorneys at law who charged hourly fees.

Printers

In 1997 the U.S. book printing market was a $5.5 billion business, growing by 3.2 percent annually since 1992. Although more than 40,000 printing presses operated in the United States, there were only about 700 book printers due to the significant capital expenditure involved: the cost of a single four-color, roll-fed 35″ × 23″ offset press could exceed $1 million, while a fully outfitted printing line could exceed $5 million. The leaders in the U.S. book printing market were R. R. Donnelley, Quebecor World (USA) Inc., and Banta.

According to a Standard & Poor's DRI study commissioned by Printing Industries of America, U.S. printed sales would grow until 2006 at a rate lower than U.S. gross domestic product. While trade publishers remained focused on printed media, increased importance would be given to multichannel publishing, enabling publishers to convert content into a number of revenue-generating products (print, Web pages, or e-books). The three leading companies had expanded into digitization of content, online services, and logistics. Exhibit 12 presents selected financial data for R. R. Donnelley, Quebecor (USA), and Banta.

Wholesalers

While there were many specialized wholesalers in the United States, the industry was dominated by Ingram Books, a company belonging to the family-controlled Ingram Industries group. In 2000, Ingram Books distributed approximately 175 million titles, generating over $1 billion in revenues. The company's eight distribution centers delivered 95 percent of all orders within 48 hours, giving it a substantial advantage over publishers whose delivery times ranged from three to five working days.

Running out of warehouse space, in 1997 Ingram Books established Lightning Source, a print-on-demand (POD) subsidiary that filled orders for out-of-stock titles. Ingram counted on Lightning Source to shield it from the threat of disintermediation. In 2000, Lightning Source agreed to digitize books for Penguin Putnam, Simon & Schuster, and Microsoft. In addition it provided POD services for Amazon.com, Barnesandnoble.com, and numerous electronic publishers.

Exhibit 12   SELECTED FINANCIAL DATA FOR R. R. DONNELLEY, QUEBECOR WORLD INC., AND BANTA CORPORATION, 1997–1999 (IN MILLIONS OF $)

Income Statement Data	R. R. Donnelley			Quebecor World Inc.			Banta Corporation		
	1997	1998	1999	1997	1998	1999	1997	1998	1999
Sales	$4,850.03	$5,018.44	$5,183.41	$3,483.20	$3,808.16	$4,952.54	$1,202.48	$1,335.80	$1,278.28
Cost of sales	3,571.66	3,642.81	3,701.39	2,756.91	3,004.44	3,861.65	901.81	1,003.46	943.70
Gross profit	1,278.38	1,375.63	1,482.02	726.29	803.71	1,090.88	300.67	332.34	334.57
SG&A	511.12	524.78	628.58	268.24	301.11	347.89	145.52	167.93	162.99
EBITDA	767.26	850.85	853.44	458.05	502.60	742.99	155.15	164.41	171.58
Depreciation	327.77	317.43	323.01	190.68	214.20	299.90	62.11	66.86	68.21
EBIT	439.49	533.42	530.43	267.37	288.39	443.10	93.04	97.55	103.37
Interest expense	100.72	83.16	95.18	71.19	72.94	126.74	12.01	11.76	13.10
Nonoperating income/expense	41.70	19.21	29.44	5.38	8.64	4.56	3.29	(0.57)	(0.66)
Special items	(70.70)	43.84	42.84	—	13.49	(180.00)	(13.50)	0.87	(55.00)
Pretax income	309.77	513.31	507.53	201.56	237.59	140.92	70.82	86.09	34.61
Total taxes	97.24	214.73	195.01	69.11	74.83	48.16	27.50	33.15	18.60
Minority interest	6.00	4.00	1.00	2.01	3.20	12.70	—	—	—
Net income	$ 206.53	$ 294.58	$ 311.52	$ 130.44	$ 159.56	$ 80.06	$ 43.32	$ 52.94	$ 16.01
Balance Sheet Data									
Assets									
Cash	$ 47.81	$ 66.23	$ 41.87	$ 0.38	$ 0.31	$ 3.61	$ 16.43	$ 26.58	$ 27.65
Receivables	814.66	843.09	941.88	683.84	695.87	743.31	228.48	233.20	218.05
Inventory	201.40	182.93	194.31	253.23	233.02	486.23	95.34	74.72	86.09
Other current assets	82.69	52.74	51.78	20.91	25.04	27.83	25.42	20.11	24.07
Total current assets	1,146.57	1,144.99	1,229.85	958.36	954.23	1,260.98	365.68	354.62	355.86
Property, plant, and equipment	1,788.12	1,700.93	1,710.67	2,044.38	2,210.96	2,881.11	338.36	318.64	327.35
Other non-current assets	1,199.48	941.90	912.95	472.80	676.92	2,614.17	77.18	96.71	90.13
Total assets	$4,134.17	$3,787.82	$3,853.46	$3,475.54	$3,842.12	$6,756.25	$781.22	$769.97	$773.34

continued

Exhibit 12   Continued

Balance Sheet Data

	R. R. Donnelley			Quebecor World Inc.			Banta Corporation		
	1997	1998	1999	1997	1998	1999	1997	1998	1999
Liabilities and Shareholders' Equity									
Total current liabilities	$ 812.62	$ 898.30	$1,203.46	$ 739.05	$ 710.12	$1,221.29	$ 200.37	$ 196.49	$ 245.35
Total noncurrent liabilities	1,730.05	1,588.64	1,511.74	1,300.15	1,567.49	3,214.08	166.75	163.54	174.22
Total liabilities	2,542.67	2,486.94	2,715.21	2,039.20	2,277.61	4,435.37	367.11	360.04	419.57
Shareholders' equity									
Preferred stock—total	—	—	—	212.48	212.48	212.48	—	—	—
Common stock	1,591.50	1,300.88	1,138.26	1,223.86	1,352.02	2,108.40	414.10	409.93	353.78
Total shareholders' equity	1,591.50	1,300.88	1,138.26	1,436.34	1,564.50	2,320.88	414.10	409.93	353.78
Total liabilities and shareholders' equity	$4,134.17	$3,787.82	$3,853.46	$3,475.54	$3,842.12	$6,756.25	$ 781.22	$ 769.97	$ 773.34

Source: CompuStat.

Exhibit 13   Average Price Paid per Adult Book Purchased in 1999

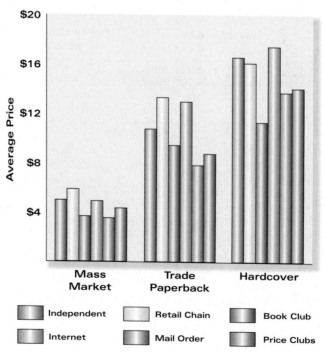

Source: BISG 1999 Consumer Research Study on Book Purchasing, Adult Book Industry Overview, 2000, p. III-13.

Exhibit 14   SELECTED FINANCIAL DATA FOR INGRAM INDUSTRIES & BAKER & TAYLOR, 1995–1999

Ingram Industries					
	1995	1996	1997	1998	1999
Sales ($ million)	$11,000	$1,463	$1,796	$2,000	$2,032
Net income ($ million)	NA	NA	NA	NA	NA
Income as % of sales	NA	NA	NA	NA	NA
Employees	13,000	5,300	6,362	6,500	6,500

Source: Hoover's Company Profiles.

Baker & Taylor					
	1995	1996	1997	1998	1999
Sales ($ million)	$783.5	$751.3	$828.8	$883.2	$1,021.4
Net income ($ million)*	$(3.2)	$(3.0)	$24.0	$22.0	$22.0
Income as % of sales	(0.41%)	(0.39%)	2.89%	2.49%	2.15%
Employees	NA	NA	NA	NA	2,500

*Net Income from Operations before Extraordinary Items.
Source: Baker & Taylor S1 SEC Filing, July 23, 1999.

Baker & Taylor, the second largest book distributor in the United States, stocked approximately 250,000 book titles and fulfilled 90 percent of orders within 48 hours. In 1999 the company rationalized its distribution centers, shutting down smaller facilities and expanding the remaining centers to a total shipping capacity of 166 million units.

Wholesalers attracted retailers through free shipments, speedy deliveries, and volume discounts. In addition, both Ingram Books and Baker & Taylor had created "vendor of record" programs, encouraging retailers to purchase all their books from them. Despite their efforts, the wholesalers' market share declined as publishers lured retailers with increased discounts and the market share of independent retailers—a traditional stronghold of wholesalers—continued to shrink.[7] Average 1999 adult book purchase prices by distribution channel are presented in Exhibit 13. Exhibit 14 presents selected financial data for Ingram Industries and Baker & Taylor.

Retailers

The dominance of independent retailers, which had been challenged by mall-based bookstores in the 1980s, came to an end in the 1990s as superstores took the U.S. market by storm. Compared to traditional bookstores that stocked 15,000 titles in 2,500 square feet, superstores offered 150,000 titles in 30,000 square feet and remained open from 9 AM to 11 PM, seven days a week. In addition, they typically offered customers a comfortable environment to encourage browsing, including a café, children's section, music department, and magazine section. Superstores often hosted special events ranging from author signings and book club meetings to children's activities. Prices were very competitive, with discounts of up to 40 percent off suggested retail prices for hardback best-sellers.

Barnes & Noble and Borders had pioneered the superstore concept. By 1999, Barnes & Noble operated 542 superstores and 400 bookstores in the United States, with a turnover of $3 billion, up 9.6 percent from 1998. It planned to introduce additional superstores and entertainment software stores, while accelerating the closure of unprofitable mall bookstores. Seeking to diversify its activities, Barnes & Noble paid $208 million in 1999 to acquire Babbage's Etc., a videogame retailer with a network of 526 stores. In addition, the company established a production facility in the Philippines, where it digitized titles on behalf of publishers and converted them into POD titles or e-books. The company promised to introduce music POD technology in its stores in 2001 and planned to have book POD presses installed by 2003. During 2000, its share price increased by 28.5 percent.

In 1999, Borders operated 294 superstores and 904 mall-based bookstores, generating $2.8 billion of revenue, up 14 percent from 1998. Borders planned to continue expanding its superstore network while opening mall-based bookstores on an opportunistic basis.[8] As the company failed to meet analysts' expectations in 2000, its share price fell by 28.1 percent from its December 31, 1999, value. Trying to improve in-store performance, Borders announced at the beginning of 2001 that it would curtail its superstore expansion program. Between 30 and 40 mall-based bookstores would be eliminated, while the product mix of the remaining stores would expand to include music and gifts. The company would look for "any and all ways" to cut its losses without hurting Borders' in-store online activities that were profitable.[9] Exhibit 15 presents selected financial data on Barnes & Noble and Borders.

The advent of superstores and the inroads made by online retailing had reduced the market share of independent booksellers from 32 percent in 1991 to 17 percent in 1999. The American Booksellers Association (ABA) saw its membership decline from 5,200 members in 1992 to 3,300 in 1999.[10] Exhibit 16 shows the market share of distribution channels from 1995 to 1999.

A major change in book retailing in the 1990s was the birth of online bookselling. According to a survey carried out on behalf of the ABA, online book sales were the fastest-growing segment of the book retailing industry in the United States, accounting for 5.4 percent of adult book purchases in 1999, up from 1.9 percent in 1998.[11] With 1999 sales of $1.6 billion (up from $610 million in 1998) Amazon.com dominated online book sales in the United States.[12] Launched in July 1995, Amazon offered users access to an unprecedented range of titles (virtually all titles stocked by wholesalers and publishers) and 24-hour hassle-free shopping and home delivery. The company quickly became known for its excellent customer service and utilized cutting-edge technology to offer a seamless shopping experience: customer reviews, e-mail order verification, customized recommendations, and one-click shopping were all pioneered by Amazon. Books were usually shipped within two to five days of the date of order, and customers paid delivery charges.

In 1997, the company went through a successful initial public offering, and a year later it opened its music and video stores, while expanding through acquisitions in the United Kingdom and Germany. Threatened by the potential acquisition of Ingram Books by Barnes & Noble, in 1998 Amazon started building its own distribution network. Having successfully completed a $1.25 billion bond offering in 1999, the company embarked on an ambitious acquisition spree that included Drugstore.com, HomeGrocer.com, Pets.com, Gear.com, and Della.com, a wedding gift registry. In addition, the company expanded its distribution capacity, adding eight distribution centers to its network.[13]

Exhibit 15   SELECTED FINANCIAL DATA FOR BARNES & NOBLES INC. AND THE BORDERS GROUP

	Barnes & Noble Inc.			Borders Group Inc.		
	1997	**1998**	**1999**	**1997**	**1998**	**1999**
Income Statement ($ millions)						
Sales	$2,796.85	$3,005.61	$3,486.04	$2,266.00	$2,595.00	$2,999.20
Cost of sales	2,019.29	2,142.72	2,483.73	1,581.10	1,795.60	2,067.00
Gross profit	777.56	862.89	1,002.31	684.90	799.40	932.20
SG&A	553.34	585.99	672.04	492.10	565.40	675.80
EBITDA	224.22	276.90	330.27	192.80	234.00	256.40
Depreciation	76.95	88.35	112.30	54.80	66.70	84.70
EBIT	147.27	188.56	217.97	138.00	167.30	171.70
Interest expense	38.11	25.39	25.21	7.20	16.20	17.90
Nonop income/expense	0.45	(70.36)	(41.59)	—	—	—
Special items	—	63.76	67.47	—	—	(5.50)
Pretax income	109.60	156.57	218.64	130.80	151.10	148.30
Total taxes	44.94	64.19	89.64	50.60	59.00	58.00
Net income	$ 64.67	$ 92.38	$ 129.00	$ 80.20	$ 92.10	$ 90.30
Balance Sheet ($ Millions)						
Assets						
Cash	$ 12.70	$ 31.08	$ 24.25	$ 65.10	$ 42.80	$ 41.60
Receivables	43.86	57.52	58.24	59.50	62.90	68.90
Inventory	852.11	945.07	1,102.45	879.10	1,019.60	1,077.70
Other current assets	68.90	54.63	56.58	14.70	8.00	10.00
Total current assets	977.56	1,088.31	1,241.52	1,018.40	1,133.30	1,198.20
PP&E	482.13	510.35	568.05	373.70	493.80	558.20
Other noncurrent assets	131.48	208.94	604.22	142.80	139.50	158.40
Total assets	$1,591.17	$1,807.60	$2,413.79	$1,534.90	$1,766.60	$1,914.80
Liabilities and Shareholders' Equity						
Liabilities						
Total current liabilities	$ 712.85	$ 772.32	$ 922.85	$ 881.40	$ 988.80	$1,027.90
Total non-current liabilities	346.57	356.49	644.58	55.40	62.70	84.30
Total liabilities	1,059.42	1,128.81	1,567.43	936.80	1,051.50	1,112.20
Shareholders' equity						
Preferred stock—total	—	—	—	—	—	—
Common stock	531.76	678.79	846.36	598.10	715.10	802.60
Total shareholders' equity	531.76	678.79	846.36	598.10	715.10	802.60
Total liabilities and shareholders' equity	$1,591.17	$1,807.60	$2,413.79	$1,534.90	$1,766.60	$1,914.80

Source: CompuStat.

Exhibit 16   Distribution Channel Market Share of Adult Book Purchases

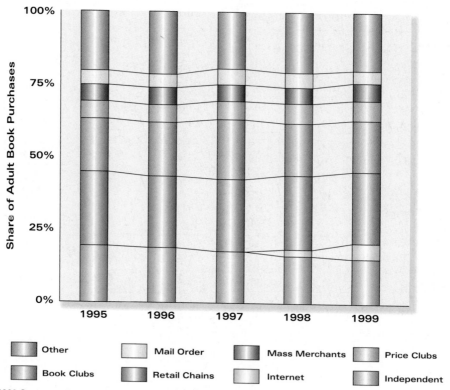

Source: BISG, 1999 Consumer Research Study on Book Purchasing, 2000, p. II-8.

In 2000, Amazon continued its aggressive expansion by signing a 10-year agreement to set up a co-branded store with Toysrus.com and opening online stores in France and Japan. Drugstore.com agreed to pay Amazon $100 million in exchange for a link in its home page, while Greenlight.com paid $15 million for the right to sell cars for two years through the Amazon website.

However, Amazon did not escape the decline of the Nasdaq in 2000: By the end of the year, the company's share price had plunged from $76.13 to $15.56. In an effort to improve its bottom line, Amazon quietly raised its book prices during the summer by 10 percent[14] but saw the growth of its core business slow to 11 percent between Q3 and Q4. Amid growing investor concern about the viability of the company,[15] CEO Jeff Bezos pledged that by the end of 2001 the company would be profitable.

With 1999 sales of $202 million, up from $62 million in 1998, Barnesandnoble.com was the second largest Internet bookseller in the United States. Barnesandnoble.com was launched in 1997 as a separate entity because Barnes & Noble wanted to minimize sales cannibalization and avoid charging sales tax on Internet sales. Despite using Firefly collaborative filtering technology to provide customized recommendations, Barnesandnoble.com failed to differentiate itself sufficiently from Amazon and was forced to compete primarily on price.[16]

In 1998, Barnesandnoble.com partnered with Enews.com to offer magazine subscriptions and launched a dedicated e-book store. During the same year, German media conglomerate Bertelsmann AG acquired 40 percent of the company by paying Barnes & Noble $75 million, making a $150 million cash contribution to the online bookstore and pledging an additional $50 million for working capital.

In 1999, barnesandnoble.com went public raising $468 million and changed its uniform resource locator (URL) to the shorter bn.com. In early 2000, bnRadio was launched, allowing users to listen to songs and audio books excerpts. Also in 2000, the company invested $20 million in electronic publisher MightyWords.com in exchange for a 25 percent equity stake[17] and acquired Fatbrain.com, the third largest online bookseller in the United States.[18]

In the second half of 2000, the company intensified its efforts to improve its profitability by eliminating deep discounts on New York Times best-sellers, purchasing more books directly from publishers and leveraging the Barnes & Noble bookstores to reduce customer acquisition costs.[19] Barnesandnoble.com installed Internet service counters within bookstores, enabling customers to order items from its website and have them delivered either in-store or at home. In addition it introduced a loyalty program that enabled customers paying a flat annual fee of $25 to enjoy a discount of 10 percent in bookstores and 5 percent on website purchases.[20]

Despite its efforts, the company failed to meet analysts' expectations and saw its share price plummet from $14.19 at the end of 1999 to $2.12 at the beginning of 2001.[21] To regain investor confidence, Barnesandnoble.com slashed 16 percent of its workforce. Analysts wondered whether bn.com might be reintegrated within Barnes & Noble, as Bertelsmann AG was reportedly unhappy with its investment in the company.[22] Exhibit 17 presents selected financial data for Amazon.com and Barnesandnoble.com, while Exhibit 18 presents the evolution of year-on-year growth of sales of Amazon.com.

Publishers

In 1997, there were an estimated 53,000 book publishers in the United States.[23] Yet the market was dominated by a handful of houses that had grown by acquisition. In 2000, the top five publishers—Random House, Penguin Putnam, HarperCollins, Simon & Schuster, and Time Warner—had 83.5 percent of *Publishers Weekly* best-selling hardcover charts and 78.9 percent of the paperback charts. Adding the next five players within each category led to a market share of 91.9 percent in the hardcover charts and 95.2 percent in paperback charts.[24] Exhibit 19 presents the breakdown of hardcover and paperback best-sellers by publisher in 2000.

Consolidation in the 1990s had numerous drivers. Seeking to take advantage of media convergence, publishers tried to reposition themselves by gaining access to a wider range of titles. In addition, size would enable publishers to reap economies of scale and act as a counterbalance to the increasing power of retail chains. Finally, as foreign media conglomerates were not allowed to purchase broadcasting stations, the acquisition of U.S. publishers provided them with access to the world's largest media market.

As some deals were financed by debt, publishing companies shifted their attention to improving their bottom lines. Literary editors, who had traditionally focused on the quality of the books they edited, became profit-and-loss centers, many of them focusing their attention on the discovery of the next John Grisham. At the same time, publishers extended profitability analysis from book categories to individual titles and eventually started eliminating unprofitable titles.

Exhibit 17   SELECTED FINANCIAL DATA FOR AMAZON.COM AND BARNESANDNOBLE.COM

	Amazon.com Inc.				Barnes&Noble.com Inc.			
	1997	1998	1999	2000	1997	1998	1999	2000
Income Statement ($ millions)								
Sales	$147.76	$ 610.00	$1,639.84	$ 2,761.98	$ 11.95	$ 61.83	$202.57	$ 320.12
Cost of sales	115.56	466.46	1,312.39	2,021.75	7.84	40.75	146.09	261.80
Gross profit	32.20	143.53	327.45	740.24	4.11	21.09	56.48	58.31
SG&A	58.02	195.63	673.63	997.57	15.38	98.12	165.27	215.91
EBITDA	(25.82)	(52.10)	(346.18)	(257.34)	(11.27)	(77.03)	(108.80)	(157.59)
Depreciation	3.39	52.29	251.50	406.23	2.28	6.82	13.85	36.09
EBIT	(29.21)	(104.39)	(597.68)	(663.57)	(13.55)	(83.86)	(122.64)	(193.68)
Interest expense	0.28	26.64	87.97	130.92	—	—	—	—
Nonop income/expense	1.90	6.48	(34.32)	(416.47)	—	0.71	20.24	(6.99)
Special items	—	—	—	(200.31)	—	—	—	(75.05)
Pretax income	(27.59)	(124.55)	(719.97)	(1,411.27)	(13.55)	(83.15)	(102.41)	(275.72)
Total taxes	—	—	—	—	—	—	—	—
Minority interest	—	—	—	—	—	—	(54.25)	(146.39)
Net income	$ (27.59)	$(124.55)	$ (719.97)	$(1,411.27)	$(13.55)	$ (83.15)	$ (48.15)	$(129.33)
Balance Sheet ($ millions)								
Assets								
Cash	$125.07	$373.45	$ 706.19	$1,100.52	$ —	$ 96.94	$478.05	$ 212.30
Receivables	—	—	—	—	0.43	2.39	15.52	26.13
Inventory	8.97	29.50	220.65	174.56	0.62	1.58	3.89	48.22
Other current assets	3.30	21.31	85.34	86.04	9.25	10.77	8.16	5.98
Total current assets	137.34	424.25	1,012.18	1,361.13	10.29	111.68	505.61	292.64
PP&E	9.27	29.79	317.61	366.42	15.95	39.77	97.85	150.50
Other noncurrent assets	2.41	194.42	1,141.76	407.62	0.08	50.70	76.05	85.76
Total assets	$149.01	$648.46	$2,471.55	$2,135.17	$ 26.33	$202.14	$679.52	$ 528.90
Liabilities and Shareholders' Equity								
Liabilities								
Total current liabilities	$ 43.82	$161.58	$ 738.94	$ 974.96	$ 7.11	$ 33.00	$ 75.94	$ 135.99
Total noncurrent liabilities	76.70	348.14	1,466.34	2,127.46	—	—	482.90	282.80
Total liabilities	120.52	509.72	2,205.27	3,102.42	7.11	33.00	558.84	418.79
Shareholders' equity								
Preferred stock—total	—	—	—	—	—	—	—	—
Common stock	28.49	138.75	266.28	(967.25)	19.21	169.15	120.68	110.11
Total shareholders' equity	28.49	138.75	266.28	(967.25)	19.21	169.15	120.68	110.11
Total liabilities and shareholders' equity	$149.01	$648.46	$2,471.55	$2,135.17	$ 26.33	$202.14	$679.52	$ 528.90

Source: Company annual reports.

Exhibit 18   Amazon.com Sales Growth on a Year-on-Year Basis

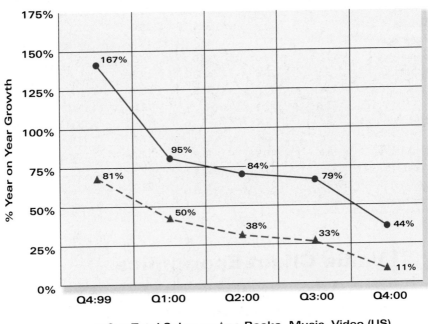

Source: Robertson Stephens, Amazon.com, Inc., January 31, 2001, p. 4.

Exhibit 19   BEST-SELLERS BY PUBLISHER IN 2000, *PUBLISHERS WEEKLY* CHARTS

Company	Hardcover				Paperback			
	Number of Books	Number of Weeks	Share (%)*	Change from Prior Year (%)	Number of Books	Number of Weeks	Share (%)*	Change from Prior Year (%)
Random House Inc.	69	505	33.00	(5.90)	55	377	24.60	(8.70)
Penguin Putnam Inc.	39	269	17.60	3.70	49	266	17.40	4.90
HarperCollins	29	196	12.80	3.50	29	216	14.10	(1.30)
Simon & Schuster	29	166	10.80	(2.50)	31	196	12.80	(0.05)
Time Warner	19	143	9.30	0.10	15	153	10.00	(3.20)
Von Holtzbrinck	13	57	3.70	(0.40)	9	77	5.00	3.10
Hyperion	7	53	3.50	(0.40)	4	35	2.30	—
Tyndale	3	19	2.50	(0.20)	4	39	2.50	1.10
Health Communications	—	—	—	—	12	63	4.10	(0.09)
Silhouette	—	—	—	—	9	37	2.40	1.20

*Share represents publisher's share of the 1,530 hardcover or 1,530 paperback best-seller positions during 2000.

Source: D. Maryles, "Who's Topping the Charts?" *Publishers Weekly*, January 8, 2001.

Exhibit 20   BOOK RETURNS AS PERCENTAGE OF GROSS SALES, 1993–1999

	1993	1994	1995	1996	1997	1998	1999
Adult trade hardcover	28.3%	27.6%	32.3%	35.1%	36.3%	31.5%	30.8%
Adult trade paperback	21.7	20.2	23.5	25.0	23.6	23.6	22.7
Juvenile trade hardcover	20.0	18.1	17.1	18.7	17.3	16.9	15.6
Juvenile trade paperback	16.8	12.5	15.0	18.9	26.4	21.1	24.5
Mass-market paperback	39.6	39.6	42.3	43.5	46.4	43.5	43.5
Mail order	18.4	19.6	21.8	20.7	25.2	24.7	26.4
Book clubs	21.2	21.4	—	19.6	20.0	19.6	20.5
Bibles and testaments	7.7	7.1	7.7	10.9	13.6	—	—
Professional	13.7	13.1	15.1	17.2	15.5	15.1	16.2
University press hardcover	16.6	16.3	16.8	19.1	17.6	16.8	18.5
University press paperback	20.7	19.0	19.5	22.9	20.3	21.4	20.9
College	22.5	23.2	21.6	23.1	23.2	23.6	22.8

Source: BISG, *Book Industry Trends 2000*, 2000, p. 2-187.

Value Chain Economics

Publishers sold most books either to wholesalers or retailers. Retailers received volume-based discounts of 44 to 55 percent off the retail price, while wholesalers received an additional discount of 1 to 2 percent. Although the terms under which publishers traded were outlined in the ABA's buyer guide, independent retailers filed a complaint with the Federal Trade Commission claiming that publishers offered preferential terms to large retailers. In 1997, Penguin settled with the ABA, paying $25 million for having violated a consent decree it had signed in 1995. In 1998, the ABA and some of its members sued Barnes & Noble, Borders, Amazon.com, and Barnesandnoble.com claiming these sellers had used their clout to secure preferential treatment from publishing houses. The litigation was still pending at the beginning of 2001.

Due to the uncertainty surrounding the commercial potential of new authors, retailers had been unwilling to stock their books without indemnity from the publishers. Since the Depression era, books had been sold on a consignment basis, enabling retailers to return them for full credit to be applied against future purchases. Returned books were either destroyed or sold at a discount through alternative distribution channels.

In the 1990s, book returns had increased, reaching 36.3 percent of hardcover sales in 1997. Seeking to address the problem, publishers contemplated offering additional discounts to retailers that waived their right of return or instituting year-end bonuses that were inversely related to the levels of returns generated by a retailer. In addition, publishers considered reducing the size of print runs. The risk of stockouts would be mitigated by the installation of inventory management systems utilizing point-of-sales data, coupled with increased use of POD systems. Exhibit 20 presents returns as a percentage of publishers' gross sales from 1993 to 1999.

Based on data collected by Veronis & Suhler in 1993, the costs of paper, printing, and binding were 34 percent of publishers' net sales, while author royalties amounted to 16 percent. Marketing consumed 13 percent, editing cost 5 percent and general administrative expenses were 9 percent of net sales. Adding fulfilment costs (shipping) of 7 percent and depreciation charges of 3 percent left publishers with an average operating income of approximately 13 percent.[25]

Traditional Competitors

Random House

With 2000 sales of $2 billion,[26] Random House was the biggest trade publisher in the United States, encompassing a wide array of imprints that included Ballantine Books (hardcover, trade paperback, and mass-market paperback books); Bantam (adult fiction and nonfiction); Dell (popular culture titles); and Crown (popular fiction and nonfiction).[27] An estimated 20 percent of revenues stemmed from sales outside the United States.

The origins of Random House could be traced to 1925, when Bennett Cerf and Donald Klopfer purchased from their employer, publisher Horace Liveright, the Modern Library imprint. Random House was founded two years later and went public in 1959. In 1960, the company purchased publisher Alfred A. Knopf. RCA bought Random House in 1965 and eight years later expanded the publisher through the acquisition of Ballantine Books.

In 1980, RCA sold Random House to Advance Publications, which belonged to billionaires Si and Donald Newhouse, for $60 million. Under Si Newhouse, Random House's imprints were allowed to bid for titles against each other, while editors were encouraged to acquire titles written by celebrity authors. Pursuing an aggressive expansion strategy, Newhouse acquired Fawcett Books in 1982, Times Books in 1984, Fodor's Travel Guides in 1986, Crown Publishing in 1988, and the electronic publishing division of Bantam Doubleday Dell in 1993. Disappointed by the modest profitability of the company, Newhouse sold Random House in 1998 for $1.2 billion to the German media conglomerate Bertelsmann AG, which combined it with Bantam Doubleday Dell.

With 2000 sales of $16.5 billion,[28] Bertelsmann AG was the third largest media company in the world. Founded in 1835 in Germany, the company evolved from a religious publisher to a multinational conglomerate with interests in 600 companies in more than 50 countries.

Bertelsmann AG was engaged in publishing, music (BMG Entertainment), magazines (75 percent of Gruner + Jahr), and TV and radio (67 percent of European broadcaster RTL Group)[29] as well as print services. The company had significant Internet holdings including e-tailers Bol.com and CDnow.com, a 40 percent equity stake in Barnesandnoble.com, and a $20 million investment in Napster.com. Bertelsmann AG was controlled by a foundation directed by Bertelsmann executives and the Mohn family.

Bertelsmann expected the company to deliver a 15 percent return on assets. However, the company's profitability in 1997 had plummeted to 0.1 percent. Peter Olson, an American lawyer who had started his career in publishing in 1992 as the chief operating officer of Bantam Doubleday Dell, was appointed as the new CEO of Random House.[30] To restore the profitability of the company, Olson pursued a number of initiatives: Imprints were consolidated within publishing groups, and editors were prohibited from bidding against each other for the acquisition of manuscripts unless a third publisher was involved. To streamline distribution, Olson expanded Random House's distribution center in Westminster, Maryland, and shut down the Bantam Doubleday Dell warehouse in Des Plaines, Illinois. The merger of sales forces, coupled with a reduction of overhead, eliminated 7 percent of the workforce.

In the summer of 1999, Olson's efforts seemed to be paying off, as during his first year at the helm, the combined entity placed a record-breaking 157 books on the bestseller list, generated revenues of $1.6 billion and achieved a return on assets of approximately 15 percent. In 2000, the integration process continued.

Exhibit 21   SELECTED FINANCIAL DATA FOR BERTELSMANN AG, PEARSON PLC, AND NEWS CORPORATION, 1997–2000

Income Statement ($ millions)	Bertelsmann AG			Pearson PLC			News Corporation Ltd.			
	1997	1998	1999	1997	1998	1999	1997	1998	1999	2000
Sales	$10,910.01	$11,174.81	$12,651.12	$3,424.74	$3,982.41	$5,381.18	$11,216.00	$12,842.00	$14,394.79	$13,400.72
Cost of sales	NA	NA	NA	1,664.06	1,784.18	2,151.18	9,642.00	10,767.00	12,238.28	11,497.76
Gross profit	NA	NA	NA	1,760.69	2,198.22	3,230.00	1,574.00	2,075.00	2,156.51	1,902.96
SG&A	NA	NA	NA	1,289.04	1,558.04	2,335.29	TBC	TBC	TBC	TBC
EBITDA	1,198.87	1,217.36	1,462.68	471.65	640.18	894.71	1,574.00	2,075.00	2,156.51	1,902.96
Depreciation	430.29	408.38	542.73	97.38	109.75	342.38	249.00	282.00	337.16	335.57
EBIT	768.58	808.98	919.96	374.27	530.43	552.33	1,325.00	1,793.00	1,819.35	1,567.39
Interest expense	94.92	88.59	171.82	114.70	149.65	300.39	695.00	788.00	840.26	648.45
Nonop income/expense	74.47	78.85	106.11	(164.88)	864.66	676.69	519.00	396.00	232.71	110.46
Special items	—	—	—	97.38	(199.54)	(153.43)	—	—	—	—
Pretax income	748.13	799.24	854.25	192.06	1,045.90	775.20	1,149.00	1,401.00	1,211.80	1,029.40
Total taxes	250.68	253.11	411.30	132.32	312.61	290.70	103.00	176.00	189.74	195.85
Minority interest	—	—	—	NA	6.65	9.69	37.00	5.00	49.58	81.80
Net income	$ 497.46	$ 546.13	$ 442.94	$ 59.74	$ 726.64	$ 474.81	$ 1,009.00	$ 1,220.00	$ 972.48	$ 751.75

Balance Sheet
($ millions)

Assets										
Cash	$ 180.58	$ 207.84	$ 190.32	$ 320.80	$ 573.67	$ 529.72	$ 2,712.00	$ 2,614.00	$ 4,947.01	$ 2,769.35
Receivables	2,400.16	2,610.44	3,257.33	832.92	1,686.08	1,686.06	2,561.00	2,814.00	2,605.40	3,183.14
Inventory	643.48	622.07	763.71	566.48	1,020.96	1,115.97	439.00	474.00	1,157.59	1,579.93
Other current assets	72.04	72.04	96.38	384.13	442.30	148.58	962.00	871.00	251.22	305.71
Total current assets	3,296.27	3,512.39	4,307.74	2,104.34	3,723.01	3,480.33	6,674.00	6,773.00	8,961.21	7,838.13
PP&E	2,367.55	2,217.15	3,714.88	755.71	723.32	654.08	3,970.00	4,404.00	4,993.29	3,551.55
Other noncurrent assets	934.56	973.50	1,564.41	504.65	4,394.78	4,505.85	20,375.00	21,835.00	21,726.39	27,771.12
Total Assets	$ 6,598.38	$ 6,703.03	$ 9,587.03	$3,364.71	$8,841.11	$8,640.25	$31,019.00	$33,012.00	$35,680.89	$39,160.81
Liabilities and Shareholders' Equity										
Liabilities										
Total current liabilities	$ 1,567.34	$ 1,493.84	$2,203.03	$1,839.25	$2,251.43	$2,403.12	$ 3,963.00	$ 5,075.00	$4,923.21	$5,379.27
Total noncurrent liabilities	2,991.57	2,970.15	4,781.35	1,297.70	4,847.06	4,103.72	11,509.00	11,484.00	14,383.55	15,940.78
Total liabilities	4,558.90	4,463.98	6,984.38	3,136.95	7,098.49	6,506.84	15,472.00	16,559.00	19,306.76	21,320.06
Shareholders' equity										
Preferred stock—total	—	—	—	—	—	—	953.00	860.00	3,562.01	3,922.95
Common stock	2,039.48	2,239.05	2,602.65	227.76	1,742.61	2,133.42	14,594.00	15,593.00	12,812.12	13,917.80
Total shareholders' equity	2,039.48	2,239.05	2,602.65	227.76	1,742.61	2,133.42	15,547.00	16,453.00	16,374.13	17,840.75
Total liabilities and shareholders' equity	$ 6,598.38	$ 6,703.03	$9,587.03	$3,364.71	$8,841.11	$8,640.25	$31,019.00	$33,012.00	$35,680.89	$39,160.81

Source: Company financial statements.

Pearson PLC

With 2000 revenues of $1.2 billion, the Penguin Group was the second largest trade publisher in the United States. The company belonged to Pearson PLC, a UK-based media conglomerate, which had acquired Penguin in 1971 and Putnam Berkeley in 1996. Penguin's trade publishing division benefited from the Putnam acquisition, as the latter's bottom-line-oriented culture prevailed,[31] leading to substantial increases in sales ($871 million in 1997, up 38 percent from 1996) and profits ($95 million in 1997, up 126 percent from 1996). In 1999, sales growth declined to 5 percent, but Penguin still increased its operating margin from 12 percent to 14 percent.[32] In 2000, Penguin completed the acquisition of troubled UK publisher Dorling Kindersley for $500 million. The company expected to reap additional cost savings through the integration of its warehouse operations in the spring.[33]

HarperCollins

With 2000 sales topping $1 billion[34] (up from $764 million in 1999), HarperCollins Publishers was the third largest trade publisher in the United States. Having gone through a successful turnaround in the mid-1990s, HarperCollins consisted of 21 imprints, including HarperPerennial, Regan Books, HarperCollins UK, and Zondervan. In 1987, Rupert Murdoch's News Corporation acquired the company, and in 1989 it merged with publisher William Collins creating HarperCollins.[35] In 1994, HarperCollins Interactive was launched to develop CD-ROM titles, and a year later the company announced plans to digitize over 10,000 books from its backlist and sell them through the online bookstore of Delphi, an online service provider owned by Murdoch.

Poor operating results by HarperCollins led Murdoch in 1996 to sell the company's U.S. educational publishing division to Pearson and appoint Jane Friedman, a former Random House executive, as CEO of the company. Seeking to improve profitability, in 1997 Friedman canceled 100 planned titles and News Corporation took a $270 million restructuring charge. Aggressive reduction of overheads eliminated $25 million of annual expenses while the introduction of a computerized shipping system reduced returns from 40 percent in 1997 to 28 percent in 1998.

Encouraged by the company's turnaround and seeking to capture economies of scale, News Corp. spent $180 million in 1998 to acquire Hearst Corporation's book operations, which included the Avon Books and William Morrow & Company imprints. The expansion of HarperCollins continued in 1999 through the acquisition of Ecco and Amistad, two smaller presses. Exhibit 21 presents selected financial data on Bertelsmann AG, Pearson PLC, and News Corporation.

Having restructured their companies and the industry, the three leading firms readied themselves for the next battle: e-publishing. They knew a new breed of competitors was seeking to challenge their hard-won competitive positions.

Endnotes

[1] See *1999 Consumer Research Study on Book Purchasing* (BISG, 2000), p. II-4.

[2] See C. Leonard, "Online Publishing Companies Give Authors Chance to See Work in Print," *Columbia Daily Tribune*, August 30, 2000.

[3] If a book was published in paperback format, the author received royalties ranging between 6 and 7.5 percent for trade paperback sales and 6 and 10 percent for mass-market paperback sales.

[4] See L. Perkins, *The Insider's Guide to Getting an Agent*, (Writer's Digest Books, 1999), p. 117.

[5] Ibid., p. 86.

[6] A. N. Greco, *The Book Publishing Industry* (Allyn & Bacon, 1996), p. 142. See also Perkins, *The Insider's Guide to Getting an Agent*, p. 86.

[7] See D. Carvajal, "Independent Booksellers Plan to Open On-line Store," *New York Times*, March 15, 1999.

[8] See SEC 10K filing, April 24, 2000.

[9] J. Milliot, "Borders Looks for Earnings Gain in Fiscal 2002," *Publishers Weekly*, February 12, 2001.

[10] Carvajal, "Independent Booksellers."

[11] "Online Book Sales Skyrocketed In '99" Associated Press, June 2, 2000.

[12] D. Brady, "How Barnes & Noble Misread the Web," *Business Week*, February 7, 2000.

[13] "Amazon.com, Inc. Overview," Hoover's Company Profiles, January 2, 2001.

[14] D. Kirkpatrick, "Quietly, Booksellers Are Putting an End to the Discount Era," *New York Times*, October 19, 2000.

[15] G. Morgenson, "Market Place: A No-Nonsense Portrait of Amazon," *New York Times*, February 7, 2001.

[16] Brady, "How Barnes & Noble Misread the Web."

[17] "Fatbrain.com Closes $36 Mn. Investment in MightyWords Subsidiary," *Business Wire*, June 6, 2000.

[18] J. Mutter and C. Reid, "Barnes&Noble.com to Buy Fatbrain.com for $64 M," *Publishers Weekly*, September 18, 2000.

[19] C. Guglielmo, "Don't Write Off Barnes & Noble," *Upside Magazine*, April 21, 2000.

[20] J. Milliot, "B&N, bn.com Launch Joint Programs," *Publishers Weekly*, October 30, 2000.

[21] J. Blair, "Bookseller on ohe Web to Cut Staff," *New York Times*, February 8, 2001.

[22] "Major Internet Custom Press Announced It Will Soon Stop Offering Free Basic Service," Associated Press, February 15, 2001.

[23] Book Industry Study Group, "The Rest of Us: The First Study of America's 53,000 Independent, Smaller Book Publishers," 2000.

[24] D. Maryles, "Who's Topping the Charts?" *Publishers Weekly*, January 8, 2001.

[25] Greco, *The Book Publishing Industry*, p. 97.

[26] J. Milliot, "The Land of the Giants," *Publishers Weekly*, January 1, 2001.

[27] Bertelsmann annual report, 1998–99, p. 27.

[28] H. Lottman, "Bertlesmann Revenues Up 25%; Looks to More U.S. Buys," *Publishers Weekly*, September 18, 2000.

[29] J. Ewing, "We're in the Driver's Seat", *Business Week*, February 19, 2001, p. 21.

[30] D. Carvajal, "Responsible Party: Peter Olson; Your $40 Pledge, Her $3 Tote Bag Turning a Page on Salaries," *New York Times*, May 21, 2000.

[31] J. Lorinc, "Random's New Era: With Executives in Place, the Merged Trade Giant Takes Its First Steps," *Quill & Quire*, March 1, 1999.

[32] J. Milliot and C. Reid, "Pearson Book Sales Topped $3 b. in 1999," *Publishers Weekly*, March 13, 2000.

[33] J. Milliot, "Pearson Makes Big Buy as Revenues Rise," *Publishers Weekly*, August 7, 2000.

[34] J. F. Baker, "Harper Breaks the Billion. Mark," *Publishers Weekly*, August 21, 2000.

[35] "HarperCollins, Inc.," Hoover's Company Profiles, January 2, 2001.

The US Publishing Industry in 2001 (B)

E-Books and E-Publishing

Karel Cool
INSEAD

Petros Paranikas
INSEAD

There was nothing random about the way CEO Peter Olson had transformed Random House during his three years at the helm of the company. Under his leadership, the company had completed its integration with Bantam Doubleday Dell ahead of schedule and significantly improved its profitability. Now that the operations of its core businesses were streamlined, Olson felt it was time to develop a comprehensive e-book strategy that would enable the company to compete effectively against traditional and electronic publishers.

Meanwhile Craig MacAskill, CEO of electronic publisher MightyWords, had just completed a radical repositioning of the company. Not only had he slashed the number of titles offered by MightyWords from 10,000 to 2,500, but he had also asked the remaining authors to accept royalty rate reductions of 40 percent. MightyWords also had abandoned its direct-to-consumer strategy in favor of the creation of a distribution network. MacAskill hoped that these actions would enable the company to compete against other electronic publishers.

This case provides an overview of the market for e-books as well as the various initiatives and the strategies competitors appeared to be pursing in early 2001. The companion case, "The U.S. Publishing Industry in 2001 (A): Industry Dynamics," provides an overview of the publishing market in the United States at the beginning of 2001, as well as the industry value chain and the major competitors.

The Advent of E-books

Dedicated Devices

The origins of digital paper can be traced to Xerox PARC, where in 1978 Nicholas Sheridon, a young physicist, patented the Twisting Ball Panel Display, a flexible sheet that could be "printed" with an electrostatic charge.[1] While Xerox failed to commercialize the display, SoftBook Press, a California start-up, launched in 1997 the first commercial e-book reader. The SoftBook reader was capable of displaying one full

This case was written by Karel Cool, BP Professor of European Competitiveness at INSEAD and Petros Paranikas, MBA INSEAD, 2000. It is intended to be used as a basis for classroom discussion rather than to illustrate either effective or ineffective handling of an administrative situation. We would like to thank the Boston Consulting Group for sponsoring the case and assisting in the data collection and analysis. Copyright © 2002 INSEAD, Fontainebleau, France. Used with permission.

page of text and could download content through a built-in modem from SoftBook's servers. However, the unit was bulky, weighed more than three pounds, and cost $599.

A year later, NuvoMedia, another California start-up, launched the Rocket eBook at a price of $499.[2] The Rocket eBook was smaller than the SoftBook but weighed more and did not incorporate a modem. Users had to download e-books from their PC and transfer them to the device. Content could be purchased from Barnesandnoble.com at prices equal to or higher than the price of a hard copy. Both ventures turned out to be less than successful. At the beginning of 2000, each company had sold only 10,000 units and both were acquired by Gemstar International, the publisher of *TV Guide*.

Gemstar improved the original technology—adding embedded copyright protection, easier-to-read screens, and long-lasting batteries— and introduced the REB 1100 and 1200 in October 2000.[3] The units, priced between $299 and $699, were available in the United States through retailers Best Buy, Circuit City, and OfficeMax. Industry observers pointed out that the prices remained high and the units were less versatile than the devices they replaced. Added David Dyer, publisher of Renaissance E Books: "At U.S.$300, I don't think the REBs are going to sell as well as Gemstar is promising because it appears they not only cost more but don't do as much as the old device did. But the jury is still out."[4] Gemstar promised to reduce prices significantly by the end of 2001 as it anticipated costs to fall by 50 percent within six months.[5] MP3 support would be offered as an after-market add-on, while a self-publishing utility would be available as soon as the company felt it presented no piracy risk. Gemstar planned to generate revenues by selling e-books at a price equal to 15 to 20 percent of the price of a printed version.

In its efforts to develop REB-compatible content, Gemstar expected to be supported by News Corporation, which owned 43 percent of the company and had announced its intention to acquire a controlling interest. To spark consumer interest, Gemstar asked trade publishers to exclusively introduce some of their upcoming titles on the REB format for a limited time. While publishers publicly applauded the efforts to develop the e-book market, they proved reluctant to provide REB-compatible content. Finally, Penguin Putnam, Simon & Schuster, St. Martin's Press, Warner Books, and Harlequin agreed to offer six titles on an exclusive basis of 90 days. In January 2001, 5 of the 15 titles on the *New York Times* best-seller list of December 2000 had been introduced in REB format. Users could purchase REB titles from the Gemstar website or any authorized bookseller. Seeking to contain the risk of piracy, Gemstar prevented users from downloading titles to their computers and then transferring them to their REBs. Gemstar supported the launch of the products with a $100 million consumer awareness campaign, which resulted in Oprah Winfrey's TV show featuring the REB 1100. Exhibit 1 presents the multitude of options Gemstar faced in positioning itself in the e-book publishing value chain.

Software-Based Readers

Dedicated e-book readers faced competition from software applications that ran on personal digital assistants (PDAs) and computers. Claiming that by 2003, e-books would generate more than $1 billion of revenues,[6] Microsoft introduced *MS Reader*, a software-based e-book reader that improved the on-screen reading experience through Microsoft's ClearType technology. MS Reader could run on PocketPC PDAs; PCs running Windows OS; the forthcoming Microsoft Tablet; and the eBookman, a low-cost PDA alternative offered by Franklin Electronic Publishers. A Macintosh-compatible version was under development while the company was evaluating the possibility of introducing the MS Reader for alternative operating systems.

Exhibit 1   Gemstar's Options in the Publishing Value Chain

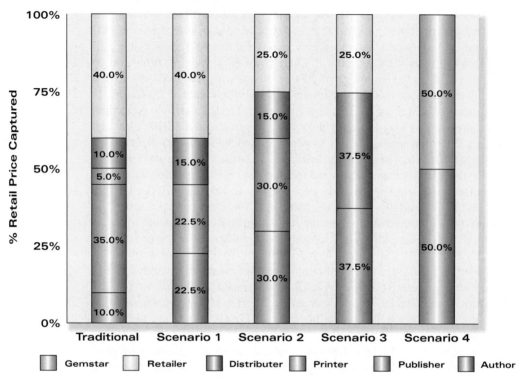

Note: Traditional scenario depicts current industry structure; Scenarios 1 and 4 depict potential evolution of Gemstar's position according to Robertson Stephens; Scenarios 2 & 4 developed by case writer on the basis of reduced retailer margins; Scenarios 1,2,3 & 4 have been updated to reflect 50% author's eBook royalties.

Source: Robertson Stephens, Gemstar, May 4, 2000, p. 3; case writer analysis.

To support its launch, Microsoft closed several content agreements. R. R. Donnelley and Lightning Source agreed to convert print-based titles to the MS Reader format. Amazon.com and Barnesandnoble.com launched e-book stores selling converted titles. Amazon initially carried only MS Reader–compatible titles, while Barnesandnoble.com included titles in alternative formats.[7] While both the MS Reader and the Gemstar REBs supported the Open eBook (OEB) specification, titles digitized for one platform were incompatible with the other.[8]

Seeking to alleviate publishers' concerns about piracy, Microsoft equipped MS Reader with three levels of encryption. At the lowest level ("sealed"), the title was encrypted to prevent users from tampering with it, but could be transmitted freely. The middle level of security ("inscribed") incorporated within the file some personalized information related to the owner of the book, who could still pass it on. At the highest level of security (owner exclusive), users were prevented from passing on the title or reading it on unauthorized devices.[9]

In spite of Microsoft's concerted effort to push its e-book software solution, Adobe Inc., a software company that specialized in desktop publishing software and electronic document solutions, decided to challenge Microsoft. At the heart of Adobe's strategy was its Portable Document Format (PDF), which had become the de facto standard in electronic document delivery with over 180 million downloads of the free

Exhibit 2   COMPARING THE FEATURES OF THE PDF AND OEB STANDARDS

	PDF	OEB
Open specification	Yes	Yes
Proprietary	Yes	No
Layout separate from content	No	Yes
Based on XML	No	Yes
Text, graphics, fonts in one file	Yes	No
Scales to fit screen size	No	Yes
Dedicated devices available now	No	Yes
Built-in digital-rights management	Yes	No
Enhanced display technology	No*	Yes
Ability to print	Yes	No
Windows OS version	Yes	Yes
Mac OS version	Yes	No†
Unix/Linux OS version	Yes	No
Palm OS version	Yes	No
Pocket PC/Windows CE version	No	Yes

*CoolType technology to be included in future version of eBook Reader.

†Microsoft has announced that it is developing a Mac OS compatible version of MS Reader.

Source: M. Frauenfelder, "Digital Publishing: An Open E-Book," *The Industry Standard*, July 31, 2001.

Acrobat Reader software. PDF enjoyed an additional advantage as it enabled publishers to convert effortlessly Adobe Postscript files, in which they stored their titles, into PDF files.[10] Trying to make PDF the standard for e-book readers, Adobe introduced in 2000 the Acrobat *eBook Reader* and the Adobe Content Server, a software system facilitating the transformation of PDF files into eBook Reader files.[11]

The eBook Reader was based on a reader developed by GlassBook, which had been acquired by Adobe in September 2000. Although the eBook Reader initially ran only on Wintel computers, Adobe was preparing versions for the Mac, Linux, and Palm operating systems. Strong copyright protection enabled publishers to define parameters, including how many copies a user could make, if the title could be loaned, and whether the book would expire after a certain period.[12] The next version of the program would incorporate CoolType, Adobe's answer to Microsoft's ClearType technology. And unlike the MS Reader, the eBook Reader enabled users to print the titles they purchased.

While Microsoft focused on the consumer market, Adobe believed that the educational and the professional markets held more promise. Thus, the company negotiated with publishers to produce reference material for the eBook Reader. Lightning Source and Barnesandnoble.com would digitize books in this format, which could then be purchased through Barnesandnoble.com or Adobe's website. Both Adobe and Microsoft planned to generate revenues by charging a 3 percent fee on each e-book sale, as well as licensing their server solutions. A comparison of the features of the PDF and OEB formats is presented in Exhibit 2.

An alternative format for PDAs running the Palm, PocketPC, and Windows CE Operating Systems was provided by Peanut Press, which had been acquired in February 2000 by netLibrary. NetLibrary focused on providing libraries with content in digital format and would use the Peanut Reader to enable library patrons to "borrow" any of its 13,000 titles, download it on their PDAs, and browse it offline.[13] Peanut Reader books were encrypted and required a password to be unlocked. Peanut Press had digitization agreements with numerous trade publishers, including Random House and Time Warner. NetLibrary focused on reference and business title publishers, having digitization agreements with publishers such as Oxford University Press and Harvard Business School Publishing. Titles in the Peanut Reader format could be purchased from the Peanut Press or the netLibrary websites. In March 2001, netLibrary sold Peanut Press for an undisclosed sum to Palm Inc., which changed the company's name to Palm Digital Media. The Peanut Press Reader—which is now called Palm Reader—and two e-books would be bundled with all new Palm devices.[14]

E-Publishing

These initiatives in the e-book market were very closely monitored by the entire publishing industry. E-Publishing appeared to offer new opportunities to many. Said Mark Smith, CEO of Spirit Virtual Books, an electronic publisher: "Prior to the evolution of the Internet as an alternative distribution channel . . . your chance of being published was as good as spotting the next Elvis."[15] Electronic publishers (e-publishers) changed this, providing authors with the opportunity to reach a wider audience. Self-publishing, known as vanity press, had been an option before. However, it usually had been unsuccessful because self-published authors lacked the resources and capabilities to market and distribute their work.[16]

Publication by an e-publisher could be online, via traditional retail channels, or via a combination of the two. If an author elected to make a book available only online, the e-publisher would convert the book to an e-book format and make it available for sale via their own website as well as affiliated sites. If the author opted for a hardcover or a paperback version, the e-publisher registered the book with the catalogs of wholesalers and booksellers and satisfied orders print-on-demand (POD) systems. Processing of payments was handled by the e-publisher, which offered additional services such as editing, graphic design, or marketing at an extra charge. For their basic services, e-publishers usually charged a flat fee plus a percentage of the cover price ranging between 25 and 50 percent.

E-Publishers: Main Competitors

While the landscape of online publishing evolved continuously, a small number of companies seemed to have established themselves.

MightyWords   MightyWords was established in March 2000 as a subsidiary of Fatbrain.com. Chris MacAskill and Kim Orumchian had launched Fatbrain in 1995, working out of MacAskill's garage.[17] Fatbrain initially focused on technical publishing but quickly expanded into setting up intranet-based corporate bookstores. Since launching its first custom online store in February 1996, Fatbrain had generated total online revenues of $42.5 million, making it the third largest online bookseller in the United States. Its online customer base had grown from 1,600 in January 1997 to 246,000 in January 2000, with repeat purchases accounting for approximately 58 percent of its online revenues in 2000.[18]

Fatbrain completed a successful initial public offering in 1998 and in April 1999 expanded into the e-book market through its eMatter initiative. While most e-publishers focused on book-length titles, eMatter specialized in titles between 10 and 100 pages, which had been plagued by a dearth of distribution channels. Forgoing setup fees, the company charged authors $1 per month for each title placed on its website. Prices were set by authors, who received a royalty of 50 percent on each sale and retained copyright and distribution rights. Titles were offered in secure PDF format and sold through Fatbrain's website. Individual authors did not receive marketing or editorial support. Although the market for e-books had yet to be proved, MacAskill had high aspirations for eMatter: "The day a big-name author sells a million copies on eMatter, we will have created a new marketplace. The day a new, undiscovered author sells a million copies we will have changed the world."[19]

Authors responded enthusiastically and within six weeks eMatter's catalog had grown to 3,000 titles.[20] Although the influx continued—by March 2000 the catalog had reached 7,000 titles—eMatter was plagued by high marketing costs, lower than expected revenues, and a lack of compelling content. In addition, going through the Fatbrain website alienated some authors. According to Judy Kirkpatrick, marketing vice president: "What we were finding was that the better-known writers would go to the eMatter site, see that it was connected to the bookstore and that searches brought up all this technical information, and say 'What am I doing here?'"[21]

Believing in eMatter's potential, in March 2000 MacAskill decided to launch MightyWords, a Fatbrain subsidiary that would focus on the publication of original content from known and unknown authors.[22] Seeking to improve the quality of content offered, Fatbrain contacted literary agents asking them to submit previously unpublished work of their clients. Agents reacted favorably as MightyWords provided their clients with an alternative distribution channel. Publishers proved less receptive: When Fatbrain approached Stephen King's agent to discuss the possibility of publishing "Riding the Bullet" exclusively through Fatbrain, Simon & Schuster was irked and subsequently banned Fatbrain and MightyWords from offering the story. In addition, Simon & Schuster asked Fatbrain to refrain from negotiating with its authors in the future, unless it obtained the publisher's permission in advance.

MightyWords offered authors similar terms to eMatter. Posting a title cost $1 per month; authors set prices, assumed responsibility for marketing their books, received royalties of 50 percent, and retained all intellectual property rights. In addition, they had access to MightyWord's online community, which enabled them to interact directly with their readers. Titles posted were available for sale in secure PDF format via the MightyWords website.

To promote its website, MightyWords agreed with 10 celebrities to pen personal stories related to the U.S. Constitution's Bill of Rights and made the essays available free of charge from the site. The company also launched the American Perspectives Writing Competition, inviting authors to share their perspectives on what the Bill of Rights meant to them, with two grand prizes of $15,000. Additionally, the company planned a marketing campaign to include advertisements in the *New Yorker* and the *New York Times*.

In July 2000, MightyWords modified its distribution strategy, establishing partnerships with sites that would offer its 10,000 titles for sale. The first distribution agreement was signed with Fatbrain, while Barnesandnoble.com followed shortly thereafter. As part of its revamped distribution strategy, MightyWords started offering its titles in both PDF and MS Reader formats.[23] At the same time, MightyWords completed its first round of financing, receiving $36 million. Interestingly, $20 million came from Barnesandnoble.com[24] in exchange for a 25 percent equity stake. Two months later, Barnesandnoble.com acquired Fatbrain for $64 million and became the largest shareholder of MightyWords.

Seeking to improve its profitability, MightyWords analyzed readers' purchasing patterns and determined that they preferred brand-name business, technical, health and fiction titles from well-known authors.[25] In November 2000, the company eliminated 75 percent of the titles and 50 percent of the authors in its catalogue. Eliminated authors were encouraged to either resubmit their books in paper format or to publish in 1stBooks, a competitor of MightyWords.[26]

Moving forward, the company decided to edit titles professionally and shoulder the marketing responsibility. Given the increased involvement of MightyWords with each title, the company reduced royalty rates to 30 percent. Explaining the rationale behind the changes, Kirkpatrick said: "We are interested in building a company that is here for the long term. What we are doing is fine-tuning a sustainable business model. So many authors were frustrated that we weren't giving them any marketing help when that just isn't what we are set up to do. We think they will be best served by other companies that help in that area."[27]

The business model of the company evolved further with the introduction of the Mighty Network in December 2000. While MightyWords' original distribution strategy focused on reaching consumers directly, by the end of 2000 the company had realized the importance of branding content. According to MacAskill: "It is the highly branded, highly credible, high-quality stuff that sells. Writing is hard. We are technologists who approached this and were perhaps a little naive about that."[28]

The Mighty Network enabled distributors to select specific MightyWords titles or collections and offer them via their site. Stores were automatically built and hosted by MightyWords with no engineering resources expended by the distributors, who had access to real time status reports evaluating revenues and users' buying patterns. In addition, third party content providers were encouraged to upload their content to the network, making it immediately available to all existing distributors. Exhibit 3 presents selected financial data for Fatbrain.com.

1st Books   1stBooks was established in 1997 by Tim Jacobs when he was unable to find a publisher for books he had written. In four years the company created a catalogue of 4,500 e-books. Its 2000 turnover was estimated to be $5 million, with profits of approximately $1 million. Most titles came from previously unpublished authors. The company supported a wide array of formats including hardcover, paperback, audio, PDF and the Rocket eBook. Titles were available for sale on the company's website as well as on Barnesandnoble.com, Amazon.com and retailers supplied by Ingram Books. As printing took place on a POD basis, 1stBooks carried no inventory. Pricing was determined by 1stBooks, but authors retained the copyright to their work and were free to publish elsewhere at any time. Every six months the company's three best-selling authors split an award of $35,000.

The cost of using 1stBooks was driven by the publishing format: For online books an author had to pay $459 while a paperback edition would cost an additional $400. The initial fee included a set of basic marketing services; an in-depth package was available at extra cost. Author royalties varied widely based on sales volumes and formats: Until an e-book generated sales of $300, author royalties were 100 percent; thereafter they declined to 40 percent. Rocket eBooks and audio books generated royalties of 50 percent, while paperbacks had royalties of 30 percent.[29]

Xlibris.com   Also founded in 1997, Xlibris focused on POD publishing, as John Feldcamp, founder and CEO of the company believed e-books had been overhyped: "Only eight people in the country are buying e-books and they're all the CEOs of e-

Exhibit 3   SELECTED FINANCIAL DATA FOR FATBRAIN INC., 1998–2000
(IN THOUSANDS OF $)

	1998	1999	2000
Income Statement Data			
Revenues			
Online	$ 3,021	$10,662	$ 28,776
Retail and other	7,927	9,118	6,562
Cost of revenues			
Online	2,189	$ 8,433	$ 23,191
Retail and other	5,216	5,967	4,286
Gross Profit	3,543	5,380	7,861
Operating expenses			
Research and development	860	2,858	6,598
Sales and marketing	4,192	9,918	25,121
General and administrative	1,674	2,909	7,354
Other	—	—	—
Total operating expenses	6,726	15,685	39,073
Operating Income	(3,183)	(10,305)	(31,212)
Total net nonoperating income	(7)	366	943
Income before income taxes	(3,190)	(9,939)	(30,269)
Income tax provision	—	—	—
Net income	$ (3,190)	$ (9,939)	$(30,269)
Balance Sheet Data			
Assets			
Cash and equivalents	$ 4,974	$14,685	$ 20,842
Accounts receivable, net	153	1,268	3,027
Inventories	3,683	3,204	5,798
Other current assets	440	1,068	3,471
Total current assets	9,250	20,225	33,138
Noncurrent assets	4,348	19,389	15,327
Total Assets	$13,598	$39,614	$ 48,465
Liabilities and Shareholders' Equity			
Liabilities			
Total current liabilities	$ 3,620	$ 3,083	$ 11,336
Total noncurrent liabilities	53	35	12
Total liabilities	3,673	3,118	11,348
Stockholders' equity			
Common stock	7	11	13
Paid-in capital	13,764	50,270	75,909
Warrants	12	12	5,261
Accumulated loss on investments	—	(47)	(25)
Accumulated deficit	(3,858)	(13,750)	(44,041)
Total stockholders' equity	9,925	36,496	37,117
Total liabilities and & shareholders' equity	$13,598	$39,614	$ 48,465

Source: Fatbrain's SEC filings.

book companies."[30] From its inception until the spring of 2000 the company had published approximately 700 titles. In April 2000 it secured a multimillion-dollar investment by Random House Ventures in exchange for a 49 percent equity stake.[31]

Prior to the Random House investment, Xlibris charged authors fees that ranged from $450 to $1,200 to publish their work in hardcover or paperback formats.[32] Fees depended on the technical complexity of a book and the amount of personal attention the author wished to receive. A starter and an advanced marketing starter kit were provided at an additional charge of $125 and $350, respectively.

Books were available for sale via the Xlibris website, Barnes & Noble, Borders, Amazon.com, Barnesandnoble.com as well as retailers supplied by Ingram Books. Xlibris set prices at $8 for e-books, $16 for paperbacks and $25 for hardcover books. Royalties for paperbacks and hardcover books were 10 percent if sold via a retailer, 25 percent if sold via Xlibris. E-book royalties were 25 percent if the book was sold via a retailer or 50 percent if it was sold via the Xlibris website.[33] Authors retained all rights to their work and were free to seek an alternate publisher—two of Xlibris's most successful authors had already moved to Random House.

Random House funding enabled Xlibris to stop charging for its core services, leading to a significant increase in the number of manuscripts submitted: by the beginning of 2001 Xlibris's catalogue had 4,000 titles.[34] The company announced plans to expand internationally in Germany, the United Kingdom, and Japan. Despite its expanded catalogue, Xlibris remained unprofitable and in March 2001 started charging $200 for its core and $1,600 for its premium services. At the same time, the company curtailed its plans for international expansion and announced layoffs.[35]

The Reaction of Publishers and Online Retailers

Publishers   Although Random House had started digitizing its backlist in 1998, it had refrained from entering the e-book market until 2000. In April the company acquired through Random House Ventures a 49 percent equity stake in Xlibris.[36] Four months later, the company launched its first digital imprint, @Random, which promised to publish 20 original titles per year, focusing on shorter, informative works.[37] Titles would be initially published in digital format at a price of $9.95; paperback editions would follow for $15 to $23.[38] At the same time, the Modern Library imprint announced the release of e-book editions of 100 best-selling classic titles used as standard academic texts.[39] E-books would be available in multiple formats from online retailers.

In November 2000, Random House eliminated a major source of friction with authors by becoming the first major trade publisher to offer a 50 percent royalty rate on e-book sales. In February 2001, the company also filed a lawsuit, possibly with far-reaching implications: Random House sued RosettaBooks, an electronic publisher, for selling without its permission e-book versions of eight books that were originally published by Random House. Although RosettaBooks claimed that authors had transferred their electronic publishing rights to it, the court would have to decide whether these rights belonged to Random House in the first place.[40] An overview of the e-book related holdings of Bertelsmann AG, the parent company of Random House, is presented in Exhibit 4.

Other publishers also quickly launched e-book initiatives. In 2000, Penguin Putnam reached an agreement with Lightning Source to digitize its backlist and provide digital rights management and e-book fulfilment services.[41] In addition, the company would continue offering Dorling Kindersley content free online to promote its book

Exhibit 4   E-Book-Related Holdings of Bertelsmann AG in the U.S. Publishing Industry, with Ownership Percentages

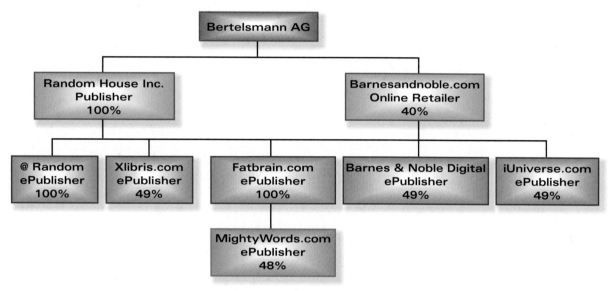

Source: Press search; case writer analysis.

offerings. HarperCollins followed with PerfectBound, its digital imprint, at the beginning of 2001. PerfectBound would initially focus on existing titles and introduce eight e-books per month.[42] Its e-books would incorporate additional features, such as author's interviews or speeches,[43] and would be available in multiple formats from online retailers.

Retailers   Signaling its commitment to the e-book market, at the beginning of 2001 Barnesandnoble.com formed Barnes & Noble Digital to function as its electronic publishing imprint. Pursuing the same editorial strategy as PerfectBound, Barnes & Noble Digital began by focusing on existing titles. Lacking an established author base, the imprint tried to lure published authors offering higher royalties, up-to-date sales information, and the ability to sell both e-books and out-of-print titles through www.bn.com. Royalties offered by Barnes & Noble Digital were 35 percent of the retail price if a book was sold via www.bn.com and 25 percent if it was sold by a third-party retailer. To stimulate demand, prices would be lower than other imprints, ranging from $5.95 to $7.95 per title. The first book to be published, in the spring of 2001, *The Book of Counted Sorrows*, was by best-selling author Dean Koontz.[44]

Outlook

Expert opinions varied widely regarding the potential of the e-book market. Andersen Consulting (now Accenture), in a report commissioned by the Association of American Publishers, predicted that by 2005 there would be 28 million e-book devices available with e-book content revenues reaching $2.3 billion, approximately 10 percent of the total consumer book market. Andersen's forecast depended on the adoption of an e-book standard, the proliferation of e-book content, and the improvement of e-book devices as well as success in creating increased consumer awareness.[45]

Exhibit 5   Forrester Research Projection for E-Book Market

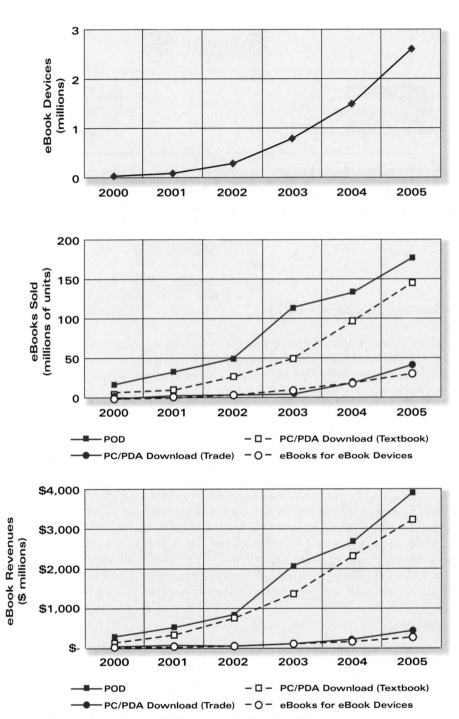

Source: D. O'Brien, Books Unbound, Forrester Research, December 2000.

Exhibit 6   *THE PLANT* **INCOME/EXPENSE REPORT THROUGH DECEMBER 31, 2000**

Deposits to plittrum (Income/revenue)	$712,448.61
Expenses	
Compositing and design services	14,000.00
Advertising:	
Print ads	139,616.75
Ad design	1,150.00
	140,766.75
Web hosting and maintenance	102,849.59
Total expenses	$257,616.34
Net profit*	$463,832.27

*Net profit not equal to revenues minus costs, which equal $454,832.
Source: www.stephenking.com.

Jupiter Research's predictions were more conservative: By 2005 it expected 6.5 million dedicated e-book devices to be used, generating annual e-book sales of $125 million.[46] Forrester Research forecast that 2.6 million e-book devices would be in use, generating online trade publishing sales of $73 million.[47] Finally, according to Veronis & Suhler, it was questionable whether consumer interest in e-books would generate enough new readers to provide a meaningful boost in overall end-user spending in the consumer market until 2004.[48] Exhibit 5 presents Forrester Research's projections for the penetration and sales of e-book devices.

Yet some authors had not hesitated to take the plunge. In 2000, Stephen King had tested the market, publishing the short story "Riding the Bullet" on the Internet for $2.50. Scribner, a Simon & Schuster imprint, coordinated the effort, which succeeded beyond all expectations, reaching 500,000 downloads within 48 hours.[49] Intrigued by his success, King went one step further, posting the novel *The Plant* in serialized installments on his website. Readers could download each installment free of charge, but the project would fold unless at least 75 percent of them paid $1 per installment. While Simon & Schuster dismissed *The Plant* as a reflection of King's endless capacity to innovate and experiment,[50] King held a different view: "My friends," he wrote on his site, "we have the chance to become Big Publishing's worst nightmare."[51] King shelved the project after the sixth installment, when the portion of paying readers sank to 46 percent. *The Plant*, however, not only turned once more the spotlight on the e-book market but also generated a profit of $463,000, legitimizing self-publishing as an alternative to traditional first serial rights distribution channels. Exhibit 6 depicts the profit and loss statement of *The Plant*.

All players in the publishing industry knew there were many opportunities and that the time was now if they wanted to make a move. The industry, however, was changing very rapidly, and old and new competitors had not finalized their strategies. CEO Olsen of Random House wondered how his company could maintain its preeminence in the 21st century, just as CEO MacAskill of MightyWords was planning to upstage the established players.

Endnotes

[1]P. Kunkel, "Scrap the Presses—Print and the Web Are Racing toward the Biggest Media Merger in History," *Wired*, August 8, 2001.

[2]J. Greene, "eBooks' Brass Band," www.businessweek.com, April 3, 2000.

[3]J. Greenstein, "Reading Addicts to Get New E-fix," *The Industry Standard*, October 12, 2000.

[4]M. J. Rose, "At What Cost, eBooks?" www.wired.com, October 17, 2000.

[5]P. Kafka, "Horror Story," *Forbes*, August 21, 2000.

[6]D. Hawkins, "Electronic Books: A Major Publishing Revolution," *Online Magazine*, September 1, 2000.

[7]E. Nawotka and C. Reid, "Dealing at Seybold," *Publishers Weekly*, September 4, 2000.

[8]A number of publishers in conjunction with Microsoft and Gemstar participated in the Open eBook Forum, which developed the Open eBook (OEB) File Format for the digital transmission of e-books. Unfortunately the OEB standard did not extend to the display of e-books on computer devices; as a result, titles developed for the MS Reader were incompatible with Gemstar reading devices. See M. Frauenfelder, "Digital Publishing: An Open E-Book," *The Industry Standard*, July 31, 2000.

[9]M. Letts & M. Walter, "Spotlight—Microsoft Cranks Up Its Wide-Ranging EBook Program; Company Business and Marketing," *Seybold Report on Internet Publishing*, July 1, 2000.

[10]Frauenfelder, "Digital Publishing."

[11]I. Austen, "New Electronic Book Software Makes Lending Out Impossible," *New York Times On The Web*, February 22, 2001.

[12]K. Mayfield, "Adobe's Novel Approach to E-Books," www.wired.com, January 29, 2000.

[13]Peanut Press press release, "Netlibrary to Acquire peanutpress.com," February 9, 2000.

[14]F. Paul, "Palm Unveils New PDAs, Acquires eBook Outfit," Reuters, March 19, 2001.

[15]J. Swartz, "Digital Books Could Be Your Big Break," *San Francisco Chronicle*, November 12, 1998.

[16]N. Negroponte, "Negroponte: Message 19," *Wired*, January 1995.

[17]CEO Profile, www.mightywords.com.

[18]SEC 10KSB filing, April 25, 2000.

[19]MightyWords press release, "MightyWords Launches New Digital Marketplace for the Written Word," March 16, 2000.

[20]M. Adams, "E-books: The Companies, the Hype, the Costs, the Reality," *Foreword*, January 1, 2000.

[21]M. Lindi, "Fatbrain.com Launches Mass Market Website," *Foreword*, March 1, 2000.

[22]S. Zeitchik, "From Fatbrain to MightyWords," www.publishersweekly.com, March 20, 2000.

[23]P. Hilts, "MightyWords Titles to Be Offered at bn.com," www.publishersweekly.com, November 6, 2000.

[24]"Barnes & Noble.com Invests In MightyWords," *Online Reporter*, July 12, 2000.

[25]E. Nawotka, "MightyWords Slashes Self-publishing Program," *Publishers Weekly*, November 20, 2000.

[26]M. J. Rose, "A Bad Ending For E-authors," www.wired.com, November 11, 2000.

[27]Ibid.

[28]E. White, "MightyWords Will Syndicate Its Texts to Other Web Sites, Stop Direct Sales," *Wall Street Journal*, December 13, 2000

[29]www.1stBooks.com.

[30]C. Reid, "Xlibris Names Senior Executives," *Publishers Weekly*, August 21, 2000.

[31]M. Letts and M. Walter, "Profile—Xlibris: Building an Isp for Budding Authors; Company Business and Marketing; Company Profile," *Seybold Report on Internet Publishing*, August 1, 2000.

[32]"Major Internet Custom Press Announced It Will Soon Stop Offering Free Basic Service," Associated Press, February 15, 2001.

[33]Xlibris press release, "Xlibris Adds E-book Format to Product Line; Over 3,000 Titles Are Available For Sale," October 9, 2001.

[34]Ibid.

[35]"Major Internet Custom Press."

[36]"Random House, Inc., Purchases Minority Stake in Publishing Service Provider Xlibris," PRNewswire, April 3, 2000.

[37]B. Minzesheimer, "E-books Attract Literary Superstars Niche Grows Beyond Marketing Tool," *USA Today*, February 8, 2001.

[38]G. Mariano, "Random House Turns to Niche eBook Sales," www.cnet.com, January 22, 2001.

[39]C. Reid, "Random House, Modern Library to Offer E-books," *Publishers Weekly*, August 7, 2000.

[40]D. Kirkpatrick, "Random House Sues Over Rights to Publishing E-books," *New York Times*, February 28, 2001.

[41]E. Nawotka, "Lightning Source Adds Penguin Putnam," *Publishers Weekly*, August 28, 2000.

[42]P. Colford, "HarperCollins to Release Up to 100 Electronic Books This Year," *Daily News*, February 21, 2001.

[43]"New Imprint to Feature eBooks," Associated Press, February 20, 2001.

[44]C. Reid, "bn.com Launches eBook Imprint," *Publishers Weekly*, January 8, 2001.

[45]"Reading in the New Millenium," Andersen Consulting, March 22, 2000.

[46]M. Frauenfelder, "Digital Publishing: An Open E-Book," *The Industry Standard*, July 31, 2000.

[47]D. O'Brien, "Books Unbound," Forrester Research Inc., December 2000.

[48]Veronis Suhler, *Communications Industry Forecast*, 2000, p. 250.

[49]C. Johnson, "Simon & Schuster's eBook Scores an Indirect Hit," *Forrester Brief*, April 26, 2000.

[50]M. J. Rose, "King's Fans Want New eBook," www.wired.com, January 15, 2000.

[51]Bob Minzesheimer, "King's eBook a Retail Nightmare?" *USA Today*, July 20, 2000.

Alltrista Corporation's Entry into the Home Canning Market in Hungary

Woody D. Richardson
Ball State University

Ray V. Montagno
Ball State University

William L. Skinner
Ball State University

As Bill Skinner hung up the phone his words seemed to hang in the air: "Jack, I know the sales figures are disappointing, but this is a great potential market and we need to give the test market more time!" Bill was senior vice president of administration and corporate development and a concept champion for Alltrista's entry into the home canning market in Eastern Europe. As president of the Consumer Products Division, Jack Metz was ultimately responsible for the evaluation of Alltrista's test market. Since getting the go-ahead to begin the market research in January 1998, Bill had accomplished a great deal in the ensuing 18 months. Still, the test market sales for the first summer (1999) were disappointing, and Bill wasn't sure whether Jack would give the project the time it needed, much less a second year. Of course, the final decision would be made at the next meeting of the group-level vice presidents where the president and CEO, Thomas Clark, would hear from the divisions in the Metals Products Group and Plastic Products Group of Alltrista.

Origins of Alltrista Corporation

Alltrista Corporation (www.alltrista.com) began as a spin-off from Ball Corporation (http://ballcorp.com). Ball Corporation was founded by five brothers—Edmund, Frank, George, Lucius, and William Ball—to make tin-jacketed, glass-lined containers in the 1880s. In 1884, the Ball Brothers Glass Manufacturing Company began manufacturing the home canning jar. Through the years Ball Corporation diversified into plastics, cans, and aerospace. In March 1993, Ball underwent a restructuring that spun off seven divisions to form Alltrista Corporation. Alltrista consisted of consumer products (jars), metal services, zinc products, Unimark plastics, industrial plastics, plastic packaging, and the LumenX Company. The newly formed company began trading on the Nasdaq exchange using the symbol JARS, but it later moved to the New York Stock Exchange and changed its trading symbol to ALC.

Alltrista's Development

Since becoming an independent company, Alltrista had made several alterations to its corporate holdings. Plant closings and consolidations, asset sales, and purchases were initiated as the company sought acquisitions to strengthen some aspects of its business while at the same time divesting itself of noncore businesses. Alltrista's acquisitions included the Bernandin and Fruit Fresh brands (1994), the Kerr brand (1996), and Triangle Plastics (1999). Alltrista's divestitures included its Metal Services business (1996), LumenX (1998), and the Plastic Products Company (1999). By 1999 the company consisted of a Metals Products Group and the Plastics Products Group. The metal products group included the Consumer Products Company (Ball, Kerr, Bernandin, and Fruit Fresh brands) and the Zinc Products Company (maker of coin blanks for production of U.S. and Canadian pennies and anticorrosion zinc products sold under the Lifejacket brand) and accounted for 53 percent of Alltrista's sales. In plastic products, Alltrista was the largest industrial plastics thermoformer in North America. The Plastics Group supplied components to companies in agriculture (John Deere); appliances (Whirlpool); heavy trucks (Peterbilt, Kenworth, Freightliner and Navistar); manufactured housing (Fleetwood and Champion); personal products (Gillette); and health care (Johnson & Johnson). The Plastics Group constituted 47% of Alltrista's sales.

Financials

In 1997, Alltrista established a goal to achieve $500 million in sales and $50 million in operating profit by 2002. The 1999 milestones targeted were $330 million in sales and operating profits of $33 million. The executive team felt confident of reaching or exceeding its goals. Additional financial information on Alltrista is presented in Exhibit 1.

Home Canning

Canning is a process of preserving food by heating and sealing it in airtight containers. Nicolas Appert, a French confectioner, invented the process in 1809. Food cooked in open kettles was placed in glass jars and sealed with corks held in place by wire. The jars were then submersed in boiling water.

Home canning became an important way to preserve food when an American, John L. Mason, patented a two-piece screw-on lid that created a tight seal. Although the material components have changed, the process has remained virtually unchanged through the years. For an explanation of the various processes and equipment used in home canning see http://homecanning.com; http://extension.usu.edu/publica/foodpubs/canguide/canguil.pdf; or any federal, state, or county extension service website.

Home Canning Potential in Hungary

On a train ride through Austria and Hungary in February 1998, Bill Skinner was struck by the number of gardens he saw. A cursory investigation led him to believe that the home canning market in Eastern Europe was not being met by the branded jars available in Western Europe. Eastern European households relied on reusing pickle jars as a home canning device. This knowledge, coupled with the fact that most Eastern

Exhibit 1   FIVE-YEAR REVIEW OF SELECTED FINANCIAL DATA FOR ALLTRISTA CORP. ($ THOUSANDS, EXCEPT PER SHARE AMOUNTS)

	Year Ended December 31				
	1999	**1998**	**1997**	**1996**	**1995**
Income Statement Data					
Net sales	$353,521	$252,464	$247,225	$215,574	$206,959
Operating earnings before depreciation & amortization	56,179	40,752	40,485	38,372	36,834
Operating earnings	38,482	30,204	30,100	27,803	24,018
Income from continuing operations	30,307	17,597	17,241	15,504	12,623
Loss from discontinued operations	(87)	(1,870)	(2,404)	(894)	(1,124)
Extraordinary loss from early extinguishment of debt (net of income taxes)	(1,028)	—	—	—	—
Net income	$ 29,192	$ 15,727	$ 14,837	$ 14,510	$ 11,499
Basic earnings per share:					
Cash operating earnings	$8.34	$5.76	$5.46	$4.96	$4.72
Income from continuing operations	4.50	2.48	2.33	1.99	1.62
Loss from continuing operations	(.01)	(.26)	(.33)	(.11)	(.15)
Extraordinary loss from early extinguishment of debt (net of income taxes)	(.15)	—	—	—	—
	$4.34	$2.22	$2.00	$1.88	$1.47
Balance Sheet Data					
Total assets	$338,751	$165,831	$166,577	$154,079	$162,650
Property, plant, and equipment, net	89,866	46,856	45,010	45,660	56,083
Goodwill, net	115,276	24,548	24,947	20,549	7,534
Long-term debt	121,060	21,429	25,714	30,000	30,000
Stock Price Data					
High price	$34.00	$29.25	$29.75	$26.13	$24.50
Low price	19.44	19.00	20.50	18.00	17.75
Year-end price	22.13	24.00	28.38	25.75	18.00

Source: Company annual reports.

European households maintained vegetable gardens, led Bill to conduct more formal market research into the opportunity. From his time spent in Eastern Europe, Bill knew that home canning techniques were passed from generation to generation with a heavy reliance on preservatives. As the economic conditions of a country improved and fresh fruits and vegetables became more accessible, the drudgery of home canning became less desirable. However, family ties were very strong and the older family members depended on the younger ones to provide reusable pickle jars to preserve food, while the younger members were all too willing to accept the food preserved by their parents and grandparents.

Market Research

In mid-1998, Alltrista commissioned a Hungarian firm to conduct research on the home canning market. Hungary was chosen for several reasons. First, the country was representative of other Eastern European nations (Poland, Ukraine, and the Czech Republic). Its population of approximately 10 million people—comparable to Indiana, Alltrista's home state—made it manageable. Finally, the Hungarian economy was improving with a lot of inward investment and a pro-business government. Family incomes in Hungary were about $600 per month on average—higher in Budapest and western Hungary and much lower east of the Danube.

The research conducted included focus groups, home testing of the product, mall intercepts, and door-to-door canvassing. Alltrista supplied jars and lids from its Canadian facility but at the same time began the process of locating and reviewing potential suppliers in Hungary. The research confirmed Bill's anecdotal evidence. Home canning was integral to the Hungarian lifestyle. The average family had approximately 200 jars of preserved food in its pantry. On average each household consumed 150 jars each year and replaced about 10 percent of its inventory each year due to breakage or loss. Hungary had about 2.9 million households. If each averaged 200 jars, then 580 million jars would be in use with 58 million (10 percent) being replaced each year. Some of the participants in the research admitted buying new jars each year, with the balance coming from new pickle jars or from family and friends. The research firm estimated that only half of the replacement jars were purchased, resulting in a total market potential of 29 million.

In the summer of 1998 two groups were selected to test Alltrista's home canning system. Half of the families were located in Budapest and half in Derecske, about 200 kilometers east of Budapest. Each group actively practiced home canning and expressed an interest in participating in the test. After a training session, each group was given 120 jars and lids. Throughout the summer, each family's canning activity was monitored, photographs were taken, and debriefings were held in October. Families expressed the belief that the food preserved using Alltrista's jars and lids tasted better than food canned in other jars. The pickle jars used by most families required used lids that did not seal as well as Alltrista's. The sealing problem required the use of preservatives that affected the flavor of the food. The families felt that the food preserved in its own natural juices without preservatives made the Alltrista canned food more flavorful.

The market research also collected information on prices, common jar sizes, and the most common fruits and vegetables preserved. The most desirable jar sizes, frequency of use, and target price points are listed in Exhibit 2.

In 1998–99, the Hungarian forint was valued at 220 per U.S. dollar. The price targets listed in Exhibit 2 were tested in mall intercepts and included all intermediary markups and the 25 percent value added tax. The research also indicated that, for ease of handling at the hypermarkets, 250, 500, and 1,000 milliliter jars should be packaged 12 per tray and the 2000 milliliter jars packaged 6 per tray.

Competition consisted of the used pickle or jam jar that had a lug cap closure. Alltrista did not make lug caps, but it did consider buying or producing lug caps for the market. On a visit to a store in Budapest during the research, Bill noticed a bushel basket of empty pickle jars with new lids in an adjacent basket. Bill tried matching the lids to the jars, but none would fit. Ultimately, the number of different pickle and jam jar designs and sizes made it impractical to enter the market with lids only.

Exhibit 2   JAR INFORMATION

Jar Size (ml)	Ratio of Use	Price (Hungarian forints)
250	10%	225
500	20	250
1,000	50	300
2,000	20	400

The Test Market

Based on the market research, Bill requested that the project move into the test market phase. Bill spent the last two months of 1998 searching for a qualified glass supplier, packaging company, distributor, and advertising agency to expedite the move to the test market pending the evaluation of the market research by Alltrista. Each of the identified partners was eager to begin, but Bill asked them to wait until January 1999 when a decision from Alltrista would be forthcoming.

In January the word from corporate was *go*. A flurry of activity ensued. Glass molds were made, jars produced, cartons designed and produced, and advertising developed. Additionally, lids were imported from Alltrista's facility in Canada, and the products were assembled. After over 100 years in the home canning market in the United States, Alltrista was turning its attention to Eastern Europe.

Basically the pricing for the test market stayed at the targeted price points except for some isolated trials in selected stores. Replacement 720 milliliter empty pickle jars (overruns from the glass companies) were available in some stores for 60 forints (27 cents) and lids of a proper size might be found for 35 forints (15 cents). Branded jars from Western Europe were found in the marketplace but were scarce and were priced above the Alltrista target prices.

The products were distributed to 3,500 retail establishments throughout Hungary. The outlets ranged from hypermarkets to the small mom-and-pop stores that accounted for over 40 percent of the retail outlets in Hungary. Distribution was accomplished by an exclusive agent who sold the jars to the trade, picked them up at the assembly operation (located near the glass container plant), and delivered them either directly to the stores or to the retailer's warehouse. The agent/distributor was already selling consumer products to the retail trade, and this product line was unique and was additive for him. The product was in the markets by April.

Television advertising began in March 1999 with a 30-second commercial and a 10-second spot running on selected channels and programs in Hungary. Saatchi & Saatchi was the agency. Print advertising and infomercials were begun about the same time. A kick-off party was held for food editors at one of the most exclusive restaurants in Budapest where 45 of the 60 editors invited actually showed up. For the year, Alltrista spent close to $1 million on advertising.

Instructions were included in each jar so that the homemaker could follow the methods recommended by the experienced home economists from the United States, and some specific recipes based on local Hungarian tastes were included with the instructions.

Bill's goal was to acquire 20 percent (6 million jars) of the annual market of 29 million jars that had been determined by the market research. During the first year of the test market, he felt that achieving 30–50 percent of the goal could be considered a success. It was expensive to establish a glass container production plant, but after the line was running the unit costs dropped drastically. The glass containers were storable by design, and Bill anticipated future sales to other Eastern European countries. For the test market, Alltrista contracted with suppliers rather than setting up manufacturing operations. Because of these factors 7.5 million jars were produced. At the end of the summer of 1999, only 300,000 jars had been sold, leaving an inventory of 7.2 million jars.

Additional Opportunities

Basic research into the market potential of Poland and the Czech Republic had been conducted simultaneously with the Hungarian test market. Owing to lifestyle similarities, The potential for these two countries, per household, was similar to that of Hungary. The prospect of these additional sales coupled with the experience from the Hungarian test market bolstered Bill's confidence regarding continuing the test market despite the disappointing first-year sales. However, Bill knew the decision to continue would be no slam dunk back at headquarters. As Bill packed his bag to head to the meeting, he wondered what type of reception he would receive. He was sure that some vice presidents had designs on the budget allocation for this project, despite its modest size. He also knew that all the vice presidents and especially the CEO would require a compelling case for continuing Alltrista's home canning test market in Eastern Europe.

Global Market Opportunity in the Olive Oil Industry
The Case of Baser Food

Ven Sriram
University of Baltimore

As Altay Ayhan gazed out of his Istanbul office window in early January 2002, the snow was falling slowly onto the streets below. As sales and marketing director for Baser Food, a wholly owned subsidiary of Baser Holding, a major industrial group in Turkey, Ayhan was responsible for determining the future strategic direction of the company's olive oil business. He had a meeting in two weeks with his boss, Mehmet Baser, and was expected to present his recommendations regarding growth strategies for packaged olive oil.

There were several options that occurred to Ayhan, each offering prospects for growth but with varying levels of risk. A fundamental question to be answered was whether the company should focus on its domestic market or seek to expand its operations in its existing export markets. Since 1998, the company had embarked on an ambitious export effort—exporting its branded olive oils to the United States, Russia, and several other countries. This was due both to Ayhan's own efforts and the commitment of Mehmet Baser, who saw enormous potential in global markets. Alternatively, Ayhan could recommend a strategy of identifying potential new markets. Countries such as China and India, with their large populations, were attractive, although their unfamiliarity with the product meant that a major marketing campaign would have to be developed in order to change deeply held food habits. He could also focus on the major olive oil producing and consuming countries such as Italy, Spain, and Greece, with whose brands Baser already competed in the U.S. and other markets. Ayhan anticipated that if he pursued the latter strategy, he would have an uphill struggle, as the local producers would fight hard to protect their home turf. Also, the prolonged economic crisis that Turkey was in from early 2001 was a factor to be considered. With a high annual inflation rate and a resulting drop in real incomes, many consumers were switching to cheaper edible oils such as sunflower oil and corn oil. Ayhan realized that he was in for a difficult two weeks while he weighed his options and made his decision.

Industry Background

Edible Oils

Edible oils, also called pourable oils, included all liquid oils and formed a part of most diets around the world. Taste preferences varied regionally depending on the climate

Reprinted by permission from the *Case Research Journal,* volume 22 issue 4. Copyright © 2002 by Ven Sriram and the North American Case Research Association. The author acknowledges Mr. Altay Ayhan and Mr. Mehmet Baser for their valuable help in preparing this case.

and availability of suitable seeds and vegetables. For instance, coconut oil was used in many parts of Southeast Asia, whereas in some African countries, cottonseed, peanut, and palm seed oils formed a part of the diet. Similarly mustard, sesame, sunflower, corn, and soybean oils were also processed in different areas. Olive oil was an integral part of the cuisine in the Mediterranean region, and its use was spreading to other parts of the world as well. Most olive trees were to be found in the Mediterranean region, although other places with a similar climate—such as California in the United States and countries such as Australia and South Africa—also had olive groves. Olive oil was the only edible oil produced from a fresh fruit and was therefore not considered a vegetable oil.

Olive Oil

Olive trees grow best in warm climates with the right soil conditions. Each tree yields on average about 15 to 20 kilograms (kg) of olives a year—or about three to four liters of olive oil.[1] The world's major olive-growing countries—Spain, France, Italy, Greece, and Turkey in Europe; Syria, Lebanon, and Israel in the Middle East; Morocco, Tunisia, and Algeria in Africa; Cyprus in the Mediterranean Sea; California in the United States—reflected these climatic conditions. In Turkey, olive trees grew primarily along the southern coast of the Marmara Sea and along the Aegean coast.

Environmental and other conditions had a significant impact on olive trees and hence on oil production. Olive flies harmed the trees and decreased olive growth rates. In the years when the climatic conditions were mild, the output was high. In high-productivity seasons and years, European buyers tried to cut the price.[2]

Olive output was also affected by agricultural conditions, which changed frequently from one year to the next. This was especially so in countries such as Turkey, where olives were not picked by machine. Instead, branches were hit with sticks in order to dislodge the fruit. It took at least a year for the damaged branches to regenerate and become productive again. Therefore, years with low volumes of production often followed high-productivity years. In Turkey, climatic conditions had improved over the last five years, new olive trees had been planted, and growers had been encouraged to increase olive production and had been trained in the care and watering of trees. The result had been higher production volumes.[3]

Production Process

Unlike vegetable and seed-based oils, olive oil was not commonly seen as a commodity, for two major reasons. First, as with wine, the weather, soil, and other conditions determined the taste and flavor of the fruit and, as a result, the oil. Customers, particularly in the Mediterranean, had thus developed preferences for olives from specific regions. In fact, in countries such as Turkey, producers of packaged olives and olive oil frequently stated the place of origin on their labels. Second, olive oils were categorized according to taste, aroma, and color. The best-quality olives were crushed and pressed to yield oil, which, after filtration, was then ready for consumption. Extra-virgin (called *sizma* in Turkey) and virgin (called *naturel* in Turkey) olive oils were processed mechanically or manually and did not involve any chemical processing. Extra-virgin oil had an acidity level of less than 1.0 percent and was a premium product that commanded the highest prices and margins, whereas virgin had an acidity level of 1–2 percent. In the case of light olive oil (called *rafine* or *kizartmalik* in Turkey), the product was refined, since the olives used would not be appropriate for consumption by merely crushing and pressing. A mixture of 85–90 percent refined olive oil and 10–15 percent extra-virgin olive oil was called pure (*riviera* in Turkey).[4] Pomace (*pirina* in Turkey) was the lowest-quality olive oil, with a natural acidity level of over 2 percent; it was refined, deodorized, and bleached to reduce its acidity level. In most markets, it was not usually used for cooking but rather for other purposes such as in the manufacture of soaps and animal feed.

Olive Oil and Health

Olive oil consumption had been increasing even in countries where it was not traditionally used. A major reason for its popularity was its health benefits. In countries like the United States, where there was a growing health-consciousness among some segments of the society, the industry had done a good job promoting the product's benefits: its effectiveness in the lowering of LDL cholesterol and raising HDL cholesterol, the fact that it was natural and rich in vitamins, and so on. It was used both in cooking and as a salad dressing.[5]

Olive oil provided the basic fatty acids necessary for the body and also had a high caloric value; besides, some basic vitamins such as A, D, E, and K could be dissolved only in oil. Olive oil was the only natural fruit oil that, because of its natural odor, taste, and color could be consumed directly, like fruit juice. Besides its health benefits, olive oil was believed to contribute to a soft, healthy, young-looking skin.[6]

The Olive Oil Industry in Turkey

Market Conditions

Since November 2000, Turkey had been going through the worst recession in its history. The economic crises of November 2000 and February 2001 had shown the weaknesses of the Turkish economy, and budget deficits had continued in a highly inflationary environment. In 2000, the wholesale price index rose by 51.4 percent and the consumer price index by 54.9 percent. In 2001, inflation rates were reportedly 88.6 percent for wholesale goods and 68.5 percent for consumer goods.[7]

The economy was highly unstable even after a year of attempts to stabilize it. Energy costs were increasing as a result of high taxes applied by the government, and the prices of crude olive oil had gone up—both of which facts affected the structure of production costs negatively. The overall domestic market shrank by almost 10 percent in 2001.

Edible Oil Sector

For the olive oil sector, huge export opportunities existed in the Middle East and Turkic Republics. Lack of governmental support for the sector was a setback for Turkish olive oil exports in the year 2000.[8]

Ayhan estimated the annual volume of domestic consumption of vegetable oils (e.g., sunflower, corn, cottonseed, and soybean) to be around 1 to 1.2 million tons. The annual vegetable oil consumption was 17 kilograms (kg) per capita, whereas around 1 kg of olive oil per person was consumed annually in Turkey. This contrasted with an annual per capita consumption in the European Union (EU) of almost 4 kg. However, the EU figures masked the fact that per capita consumption in Mediterranean member countries such as Greece, Italy, and Spain was well over 10 kg annually. A comparison

Exhibit 1   TURKEY'S OLIVE OIL EXPORTS BY TYPE (IN MILLIONS)

Types	1997		1998		1999		2000	
	Tons	Value	Tons	Value	Tons	Value	Tons	Value
Extra Virgin	4,684	$10,523	9,660	$15,977	22,630	$ 41,528	5,081	$ 9,627
Virgin	4,362	8,797	3,755	5,966	11,819	16,243	1,453	2,587
Refined	23,980	47,592	14,751	22,420	26,144	44,143	1,844	3,747
Pure	6,636	14,775	18,096	27,845	36,291	64,066	6,250	13,077
Other	8,639	5,654	2,018	1,463	6,209	4,070	1,786	1,369
Total	48,328	$87,341	49,016	$75,386	103,093	$170,050	16,414	$30,407

Source: Foreign Trade Department, www.igeme.org.tr.

of the consumption of corn oil to sunflower oil revealed that the market share of corn oil had increased while the market share of sunflower oil was decreasing. This was partly due to the price difference resulting from the different rates of customs duties— 38 percent for sunflower oil and 12 percent for corn oil.[9] Ayhan's data showed that by volume, sunflower oil accounted for 81 percent of all edible oil consumption in Turkey in 2000, followed by olive oil with 10 percent and corn oil with 9 percent. By value, sunflower oil's share was 66 percent, followed by olive oil with 25 percent and corn oil with 8 percent. These differences in volume and value shares indicated that olive oil was more expensive than the other edible oils in Turkey.

In the period 1990–91 to 1994–95 an average of 81,000 tons of olive oil was produced, and in the period 1995–96 to 1999–00, olive oil production averaged 100,000 tons.[10]

Turkey's Exports and Imports of Olive Oil

Turkey's olive oil exports reflected some dramatic fluctuations from year to year (see Exhibit 1). The reasons behind this were agricultural problems with olive growth and, as a result, olive oil production. Other important factors influencing olive oil exports of Turkey were problems regarding the production techniques, marketing policy development, and the fluctuations in the supply of olive oil from other producing countries. The increase in exports was partly due to the dry weather and resulting drop in production in Italy and Spain during the last five seasons.

As a result of the increase in consumption and demand for olive oil in the world, new export market opportunities for Turkey had emerged. In total, Turkey exported olive oil to about 70 countries. The major importers of Turkish olive oil are listed in Exhibit 2.

Countries like Spain and Italy, which were also producers and exporters of olive oil, had a 55 percent share in Turkish olive oil exports between 1996 and 2000. Turkey's exports to these countries were affected by the production level and demand structure in these countries. In that respect, EU countries were important export markets for Turkey. However, Turkey faced a dilemma in her relations with these countries. Since the exports were unbranded and in bulk form, the demand was high in periods when these countries were faced with agricultural problems and their own processing volumes were low. Olive oil imported from Turkey was then processed and

Exhibit 2   TURKISH OLIVE OIL EXPORTS, BY COUNTRY, 1996–2000

Country	1996-2000	2000
United States	23.0%	36.0%
Italy	31.0	6.0
Spain	24.0	14.0
Saudi Arabia	3.0	9.0
Switzerland	2.0	—
Argentina	—	8.0
United Arab Emirates	—	4.0
All others	17.0	23.0
Total	100.0%	100.0%

Source: Foreign Trade Department, www.igeme.org.tr.

sold in these markets and re-exported to other export markets under Spanish or Italian brand names. This meant that Turkish firms then were faced with competition from their own olive oil branded by re-exporters from other countries.

Although Turkey was self-sufficient in terms of olive oil processing to meet the domestic demand, there was also a small amount (1,088 tons, worth $2.06 million in 2000) of olive oil imports. Imports took place in seasons where the domestic production was insufficient. The basic exporters to Turkey were Tunisia, Italy, Saudi Arabia, and Egypt.

Competition

Although Turkey was a major olive oil producer, olive oil accounted for only a small share of the total liquid oil market. While there were unbranded and unpackaged products, almost all branded sales went through supermarkets. The major brands were Komili (a Unilever Turkey brand); Taris (a government cooperative); and others such as Kristal, Bizim, and Luna. Ayhan estimated that Komili and Taris together accounted for about 60 percent of the market by value. Komili positioned its brand as part of a modern lifestyle and emphasized its health benefits, while Taris was a more economically priced brand. Both had ongoing media campaigns and, as a result, enjoyed some brand loyalty. However, partly as a result of Turkey's economic crisis, consumers had been switching to cheaper brands (Taris's market share had been increasing while Komili's had been declining) and some were consuming less expensive cooking oils such as sunflower and corn oils. The high inflation rate was also a factor in making consumers more price-sensitive and less brand-loyal.

The World of Olive Oil

Production

Although olives could be grown in many parts of the world with the right temperature, soil, and climatic conditions, the bulk of world olive oil production was still concentrated in the traditional olive-growing region, the Mediterranean rim. The EU and six other countries (Turkey, Syria, Morocco, United States, Argentina, and Egypt) accounted for

Exhibit 3   WORLD OLIVE OIL PRODUCTION (000 TONS)

	1995–96	1996–97	1997–98	1998–99	1999–00	2000–01
Algeria	51.5	50.5	15.0	54.5	33.5	50.0
Argentina	11.0	11.5	8.0	6.5	11.0	3.0
European Union*	1,403.5	1,754.5	2,116.5	1,707.0	1,878.5	1,919.5
Jordan	14.0	23.0	14.0	21.5	6.5	27.0
Morocco	35.0	110.0	70.0	65.0	40.0	35.0
Palestine	12.0	12.0	9.0	5.5	2.0	20.0
Syria	76.0	125.0	70.0	115.0	81.0	165.0
Tunisia	60.0	270.0	93.0	215.0	210.0	130.0
Turkey	40.0	200.0	40.0	170.0	70.0	200.0
Others	32.5	38.5	30.0	40.5	41.5	41.0
Total	1,735.5	2,595.0	2,465.5	2,400.5	2,374.0	2,590.5

*Spain, Italy, and Greece accounted for virtually all of the olive oil produced within the European Union.
Note: 2000–01 data are provisional.
Source: www.internationaloliveoil.org/eng/Eco-OliveOilProduction.html.

almost 90 percent of world table olive production and almost all of world exports according to provisional 2000–01 data.[11] In the EU, the major producing countries were Spain, Italy, and Greece.

Not surprisingly, the countries that were the largest olive growers were also the largest producers of olive oil (Exhibit 3). The average annual olive oil production between 1990–91 and 1997–98 was 1.992 million tons.[12] Of the EU total, Spain, Italy, and Greece accounted for almost the entire production. The other olive oil producers included Israel, Lebanon, Cyprus, Iran, and Egypt. These production figures also clearly showed the phenomenon mentioned earlier—that is, years where the olive, and consequently olive oil, yield was high were frequently followed by years with much lower production volumes.

Consumption

As can be seen from Exhibit 4, world consumption of olive oil had been increasing steadily. Interestingly, however, the major producing countries were also the major consuming ones, and this made Ayhan wonder whether the cooking and eating habits could be changed so that consumers in other countries would switch to using olive oil, as they appeared to be doing in the United States.

Based on some internal company data from the mid-1990s, Ayhan could see that per capita consumption figures (Exhibit 5) from selected countries showed that olive oil consumption was very small relative to vegetable oils both globally and in each of the major markets. It was highest in the EU, where the 3.9 kg/year represented an almost 20 percent share of edible oil consumption compared to olive oil's 3.6 percent share globally. However, given the increase in global olive oil consumption, Ayhan was sure that olive oil now accounted for a higher percentage of vegetable oil consumption, particularly in countries where segments of the population were health-conscious.

Exhibit 4   WORLD OLIVE OIL CONSUMPTION (IN THOUSANDS OF TONS)

	1995–96	1996–97	1997–98	1998–99	1999–00	2000–01
Algeria	36.0	50.0	31.5	44.0	42.0	45.0
European Union	1,387.0	1,566.5	1,705.5	1,709.0	1,731.0	1,776.5
Israel	7.5	7.5	6.5	9.5	12.5	13.0
Jordan	16.0	22.0	19.0	19.0	9.0	23.0
Morocco	25.0	50.0	55.0	55.0	55.0	47.0
Syria	78.0	85.0	95.0	88.0	90.0	110.0
Tunisia	34.5	70.0	52.0	49.0	60.0	60.0
Turkey	63.0	75.0	85.0	85.0	60.0	75.0
Australia	16.5	21.5	17.5	24.0	25.5	31.0
Brazil	23.0	21.5	27.5	23.5	32.0	35.0
Libya	5.0	10.0	7.0	16.0	11.0	12.0
United States	101.0	130.5	142.5	151.0	169.0	190.5
Canada	14.0	19.0	17.5	18.5	23.0	25.0
Japan	16.5	26.0	34.0	28.5	27.0	29.0
Other	24.5	84.0	84.5	93.0	75.0	108.5
Total	1,892.5	2,238.5	2,380.0	2,413.0	2,422.0	2,580.5

Note: 2000–01 data are provisional.
Source: www.internationaloliveoil.org/eng/Eco-OliveOilConsumption.html.

Exhibit 5   PER CAPITA ANNUAL EDIBLE OIL CONSUMPTION

	Olive Oil (kg)	Vegetable Oil (kg)	Olive Oil Share (%)
Argentina	0.1	15.8	0.4%
Australia	0.9	11.9	7.3
Brazil	0.1	13.0	1.1
Canada	0.5	17.4	2.9
Japan	0.1	12.5	1.1
United States	0.4	24.0	1.6
European Union	3.9	19.5	19.8
Rest of world	0.3	9.5	3.6

Source: Internal company data, 1995.

World Exports and Imports

As stated earlier, the Mediterranean countries accounted for the majority of global exports of olive oil (Exhibit 6). Given the importance of olive exports to the economies of these countries, they, particularly the EU, had been engaged in promotion programs in order to increase global olive oil import and consumption. In the 1998–99 season, Spain exported 275,000 tons, and Italy and Greece 180,000 tons each. (Note: These numbers add up to more than the EU's export volume stated in the table because all the EU figures in the case refer only to EU trade with non-EU countries, whereas figures for individual countries reflect their total trade.)

Exhibit 6   WORLD OLIVE OIL EXPORTS, 1995–2001 (IN THOUSANDS OF TONS)

	1995–96	1996–97	1997–98	1998–99	1999–00	2000–01
Argentina	4.5	6.0	7.5	6.0	6.0	4.0
European Union	165.0	220.0	227.0	208.5	298.5	305.0
Morocco	11.5	35.0	7.5	15.5	0.0	0.0
Syria	11.0	6.0	3.0	4.0	2.5	10.0
Tunisia	26.5	115.0	117.0	175.0	112.0	108.0
Turkey	19.0	40.5	35.0	86.0	16.6	85.0
United States	9.0	8.0	4.5	6.0	5.5	6.0
Other	10.0	7.5	5.5	5.0	3.4	5.0
Total	256.5	438.0	407.0	506.0	444.5	523.0

Note: 2000–01 data is provisional.
Source: www.internationaloliveoil.org/eng/Eco-OliveOilExports.html.

Exhibit 7   WORLD OLIVE OIL IMPORTS, 1995-2001 (IN THOUSANDS OF TONS)

	1995–96	1996–97	1997–98	1998–99	1999–00	2000–01
Argentina	0.5	6.5	7.0	3.5	2.0	7.5
European Union	73.5	145.5	118.0	225.5	116.5	107.5
Australia	16.0	21.5	17.5	23.5	25.0	30.0
Brazil	23.0	21.5	27.5	23.5	32.0	35.0
United States	105.0	140.0	144.0	155.0	175.0	198.0
Canada	14.0	19.0	17.5	18.5	23.0	25.5
Japan	16.5	26.0	34.0	28.5	27.0	29.0
Switzerland	3.5	5.0	5.5	6.0	8.0	8.0
Other	40.5	49.5	50.0	67.0	59.5	77.0
Total	292.5	434.5	421.0	551.0	486.0	517.5

Note: 2000–01 data is provisional.
Source: www.internationaloliveoil.org/eng/Eco-OliveOilImports.html

As can be seen from Exhibit 7, since 1995–1996 there had been impressive increases in olive oil imports, even in nontraditional olive oil importing and consuming countries. The health and other benefits of olive oil was believed to have contributed to increased olive oil consumption in these countries. It is interesting to note that many of the producing countries were not major importers, indicating that a large portion of their consumption came from their own domestic production.

Baser Food

History

Baser Food was a wholly owned subsidiary company of Baser Holding, one of the leading industrial, commercial, and financial groups in Turkey. Baser started its operations in 1973 in chemicals and extended its operations into plastics, packaging, textiles, food, foreign trade, and finance. The group was successful in different sectors. For example, Baser Chemicals operated a joint venture with Colgate-Palmolive in which the Baser family was the majority shareholder. Baser Food was a 100 percent family-owned company. Both Mehmet Baser and Altay Ayhan worked for years for Colgate-Palmolive in Turkey and were experienced brand managers in the fast-moving consumer goods sector.

Corporate Vision and Mission

Baser Food's vision was to produce the highest quality olive oil for customers in all world markets. The basic aim of the company was to introduce and promote its branded Turkish olive oil into world markets. Hence, Ayhan's major focus was on sales and marketing activities for olive oil in accordance with the needs and wants of the customers in both the domestic and international markets, and to assure a global brand presence. Baser and Ayhan were committed to making the company's flagship olive oil brand (Cavallo d'Oro) a global one. However, given the high cost of global expansion, they were very careful in selecting export markets. They intended to focus primarily on countries with per capita incomes over $2,000 and some low-income countries with large populations since the higher socioeconomic classes in these countries were likely to be more willing to change cooking and eating habits and could afford olive oil.

Product Lines and the Production

Baser Food specialized in the production of olive oil and was among the major olive oil producers in Turkey. Olive oil production, filling, and packaging activities took place in the factory located in Mugla/Yatagan, on Turkey's Aegean coast. The factory employed the most recent technologies for the production of olive oil in accordance with the standards set by the International Olive Oil Council (IOOC) and regulations of the U.S. Food and Drug Administration. The processing, filling and packaging capacity of the plant in Mugla was around 3,000 tons per month.[13] The company was the only major Turkish olive oil producer that did not manufacture any products other than olive oil. In high-yield years, the plant operated at approximately 80 percent of capacity; this fell to 40 percent during years when olive oil production declined.

The company had an annual sales turnover of about $25 million and employed approximately 50 people. Of its volume, $20 million was exported and the remainder was sold in Turkey both as a private label ($4 million) and under the company's brand, Cavallo d'Oro ($1 million). Private-label brands included department store brands such as Migros and Metro in Turkey and Quality, Tip, and Aro in other European countries. Distributor brands such as Sclafani, Aurora, and Roland were used in the United States and Canada. Of the export volume, $12 million was unbranded bulk exports, primarily to importers in Italy and Spain, where it was then repackaged and sold under the importers' brands. In many countries these exports were labeled as Italian or Spanish olive oil even though the contents were Turkish. U.S. regulations now required that such products had to be labeled as being imported from Turkey and to state the source country(ies) of the olive oil, although the label could indicate that the contents had been packed in Italy or Spain. Exports under the Cavallo d'Oro and MedOlive brand names accounted for $3 million of export volume, and the balance was private-label export such as the distributor brands mentioned earlier. Domestic sales growth had averaged a steady 10–15 percent over the last few years, whereas exports had doubled over the past year. Margins were approximately 15 percent.

Exhibit 8   CAVALLO D'ORO STRATEGY SUMMARY

Brand:	Cavallo d'Oro
Primary positioning	Cavallo d'Oro branded olive oil contains only the best selected olives from the Ayvalik region of Western Turkey to give a delightfully aromatic taste to healthy meals: "The finest olive oil."
Objectives	Brand awareness and trial in the short run
	To be a strong brand in the long run (one year)
Types	Extra-virgin olive oil; pure olive oil; refined olive oil (light)
Competitors	Spanish, Italian, and Greek brands
Source of business	Sunflower oil, corn oil, soybean oil, and margarine users, as well as users of other olive oil brands on the market
Target market	Health- and taste-conscious people
Physical benefits	Provides nutrition and good health. Helps control cholesterol level, renovate cells, and delay aging and heart disease. Helps muscle growth in children. Improves calcium in bones of older people.
Emotional benefits	Feeling of heath and confidence
Reason to buy	Top-quality olive oil from the best olives of western Turkey
Brand character	Natural, pure, tasty, authentic
Pricing strategy	85–90% of market leader
Promotions	Taste approval through sampling by taste panels, sachets and on-pack promotions
Sizes	250-milliliter, 500-milliliter, 1-liter glass bottles
	250-milliliter, 500-milliliter, 1-liter plastic bottles
	3-liter, 5-liter tins

Brands

The key brand of the firm was Cavallo d'Oro. This brand was highly valued in the many world markets where it had been introduced, due to its quality, packaging, and label. This brand had also been launched in the Turkish domestic market as well as in retail chains such as Carrefour. Exhibit 8 summarizes the strategy for the Cavallo d'Oro brand.

In certain foreign markets, such as Hungary and Israel, the company also used other brands such as MedOlive because the company used multiple distributors and each asked for a separate brand. So whereas Cavallo d'Oro was Baser's main brand, its secondary brands could be found on store shelves in these markets as well. Baser felt that since many consumers in the United States and elsewhere had strong favorable perceptions about Italian olive oil, it was to the company's advantage to use Italian rather than Turkish-sounding brand names.

International Operations

Baser Food was also a member of the North American Olive Oil Association (NAOOA). The firm started to export Cavallo d'Oro by the end of 1999 and became the largest Turkish-branded olive oil exporter in 2000. Thinking back over the past year's operations, Ayhan leaned back in his armchair and felt very proud of the accomplishments of Baser Food. For the period November 1999 to September 2000, Ayhan estimated that his company now accounted for 37 percent of the total packaged olive oil exports of Turkey. And now in 2002, the company operated in about 20 international markets.[14] The main export market for Cavallo d'Oro was the United States, where the product was offered for sale in major chain stores in 15 states. In addition, Baser Food also marketed its olive oil brands in such countries as Spain, Italy, Germany, Taiwan, Venezuela, Russia, Poland, Bulgaria, Georgia, Azerbaijan, South Korea, Malaysia, Canada, Romania, Saudi Arabia, and Ukraine.

In most foreign markets, Baser employed exclusive distributors who were not permitted to represent other companies' products. However, one of the two U.S. distributors also distributed Spanish olive oil as well as other canned food products such as fruits, tuna, and tomato paste. In managing the export activity, two managers (one with a degree in international trade and the other with a degree in economics/business administration) and two support staff assisted Ayhan at the Istanbul headquarters of Baser Food, although most market visits and distributor contacts overseas were handled by Ayhan. The assistants monitored and followed up the company's plans and represented Baser Food in the many international food shows the company participated in.

Since both Mehmet Baser and Ayhan traveled regularly to foreign markets and developed global strategic plans, they understood the need for patience when it came to international markets. Their experience with Colgate-Palmolive, Polgat of Israel, and the sister company Baser Chemicals' operations in Ukraine had created a atmosphere in Baser Food that was strong in its international focus. The liaison offices in Russia and Kazakhstan were signs of the company's commitment to global business. Since Baser was an exporter, it faced little asset risk overseas, but there were risks involved in the collection of accounts receivable. The use of a factoring payment system and insurance reduced the risk, but Ayhan recognized that some risk was unavoidable.

Future Objectives

Recently, the firm had begun to enter markets in the Pacific Rim, including Japan, Australia, Taiwan, and Malaysia. Mehmet Baser and Ayhan were very optimistic about the market opportunities in this part of the world. However, China, with its 1.3 billion people, only imported 2,000 tons of olive oil annually (pure and extra-virgin accounted for 40 percent each, and pomace, because of its low price, the other 20 percent), highlighting the task that lay ahead if a strategy of growth from nontraditional markets was to be pursued. At this point, the focus was to gain distribution access and shelf space, particularly in supermarkets that stocked and sold international foods.

Potential Markets

There were several foreign markets into which Baser Food had entered and others where olive oil consumption was expected to increase due to the promotional efforts of the IOOC.[15] Of course, the domestic market was important, but Ayhan had to weigh the risks and opportunities of focusing on Turkey versus pursuing expansion in those country markets Baser had already entered versus entering additional country markets. He could certainly pursue growth opportunities in a number of different country markets, but resource constraints were forcing him to prioritize and focus on those export markets that would ultimately matter most to the company's future success.

Exhibit 9   U.S. POURABLE OILS, PERCENT VOLUME SALES BY TYPE, 1995–2000

Type of Oil	1995	1996	1997	1998	1999	2000
Canola	22.9%	23.2%	23.0%	26.1%	25.7%	25.4%
Corn	20.4	20.7	19.6	18.5	18.2	17.5
Vegetable	47.0	46.9	47.0	44.5	45.2	44.4
Olive	7.7	7.0	8.0	8.4	8.3	9.6
Others	2.0	2.2	2.4	2.5	2.6	3.1
	100.1%	100.0%	100.0%	100.0%	100.0%	100.0%
Total (millions of pounds)	1,157	1,184	1,192	1,182	1,200	1,211

Source: ACNielsen (quoted in NAOOC chairman's report, midyear meeting, January 2001).

United States

Ayhan attended the midyear 2001 meeting of the NAOOA in San Diego, California. At this meeting, the association's chairman presented the following key data on the U.S. retail market (based on ACNielsen and U.S. Department of Commerce data):

- Nearly 50 new brands of olive oil had appeared in the U.S. market in 2000.

- Import volume for 2000 grew by 15 percent, with extra-virgin accounting for 45 percent of imports, up from 28 percent in 1991. At the retail level, extra-virgin accounted for 37 percent of sales volume, up from 26 percent in 1996 and 47 percent by value, up from 35 percent in 1996.

- Olive oil accounted for almost 10 percent of all pourable oil retail sales by volume, and the category grew by over 16 percent in 2000. In terms of dollar sales, olive oil represented 32 percent of the value, making it first, and sales were estimated at $370 million.

- Household penetration was almost 30 percent.

- Most olive oil purchases were made in households with annual family incomes greater than $70,000, with a concentration on the East Coast. The New York metropolitan area accounted for over 33 percent of U.S. olive oil sales.

The growing trend in U.S. olive oil consumption can be seen in Exhibits 9 and 10. Household consumption had increased partly due to the health benefits of the product and the growing interest in Mediterranean food (particularly Italian and Greek) and incorporating this cuisine as a way of staying healthy. The success of Italian food chains had meant that olive oil sales had increased in the food service sector as well since in many of these restaurants olive oil was used in the cooking and was often served as an accompaniment to bread. ConAgra hoped to tap into this trend by launching Fleischmann's Premium Blend spread made with olive oil.[16] Also, the efforts of industry associations such as the NAOOA (www.naooa.org) and the California Olive Oil Council (COOC) (www.cooc.com) helped increase the awareness and usage of olive oil in the United States, although the efforts of the COOC to promote U.S.-produced olive oils could hurt exporters like Baser.

While the U.S. market undoubtedly represented huge growth potential, the high costs and low margins concerned Ayhan. Because of the fierce competition, and relative lack of brand loyalty, chain store retailers were able to negotiate aggressively with

Exhibit 10   U.S. POURABLE OILS, PERCENT VALUE SALES BY TYPE, 1995–2000

Type of Oil	1995	1996	1997	1998	1999	2000
Canola	20.4%	18.8%	18.1%	20.9%	20.5%	19.3%
Corn	17.0	15.7	14.9	14.6	14.4	13.0
Vegetable	36.4	34.6	33.7	33.0	33.1	31.0
Olive	22.7	27.1	29.1	27.5	27.8	32.0
Others	3.6	3.8	4.0	4.0	4.2	4.6
	100.1%	100.0%	99.8%	100.0%	100.0%	99.9%
Total (in millions)	$1,037	$1,236	$1,221	$1,179	$1,158	$1,158

Source: ACNielsen (quoted in NAOOC chairman's report, midyear meeting, January 2001).

manufacturers both in terms of prices and access to shelf space. Ayhan estimated margins for Baser to be 10–15 percent and slotting fees to be between $25,000 and $50,000 for each stock-keeping unit (SKU) for the chain stores. Almost the entire $500,000 annual marketing budget of Baser Foods was being spent on below-the-line trade promotion in order to gain access to retail shelf space. Ayhan also estimated that $2 million would be required to implement a TV and radio campaign to build the brand. In 2000, Hormel Foods launched the Italian olive oil brand Carapelli in the U.S. market with a $13 million TV and print campaign (compared to $8.5 million in total media expenditure for the entire category in 1999). Carapelli became the third largest brand in the United States, with annual sales of $31 million; Unilever's Bertolli brand led the market with $128 million in sales.[17]

The growth trend was also supported by ACNielsen household panel data that showed a penetration of 29.8 percent for olive oil, up from 26.2 percent in 1997. At the retail level, olive oil sales had increased from $259 million in 1995 to $370 million in 2000. Canola oil continued to be popular because it was two to three times less expensive than olive oil. Also, some U.S. companies imported canola oil from Canada and extra-virgin olive oil from Turkey and elsewhere, blended the two, packaged the blend in the United States, and retailed it for a price lower than olive oil.

One trend in U.S. imports was that virgin olive oil consumption, and therefore imports, was increasing, possibly due to its perceived health benefits and the industry's promotion efforts (see Exhibit 11).

Australia

Australia was another country Ayhan was seriously considering as part of his expansion plans. Several factors made Australia an attractive potential market:

- Its relatively high per capita income.
- Political and economic stability.
- Familiarity with Mediterranean cuisine as a result of immigrants from Italy, Greece, and other countries in the region.
- Australians' general concern with health and their diets—olive oil imports were growing at an average of 15 percent per year over the past several years.

Exhibit 11   VALUE OF U.S. OLIVE OIL IMPORTS BY COUNTRY, WITH PERCENTAGE BEING VIRGIN OIL ($ THOUSANDS)

	1995	1996	1997	1998
Italy	$248,929 (39%)	$341,937 (39%)	$313,140 (45%)	$243,350 (48%)
Spain	46,265 (59%)	63,996 (65%)	53,782 (65%)	53,349 (66%)
Turkey	28,611 (23%)	23,944 (23%)	26,871 (40%)	16,679 (31%)
Portugal	2,076 (4%)	2,936 (2%)	2,805 (6%)	3,320 (22%)
Greece	9,500 (48%)	12,584 (69%)	13,098 (74%)	9,981 (77%)
Morocco	1,416 (28%)	8,873 (65%)	5,939 (52%)	4,551 (84%)
Tunisia	4,920 (81%)	n.a.	2,876 (99%)	3,511 (88%)
Other	4,255	14,042	6,403	4,595
Total	$345,972 (41%)	$468,312 (44%)	$424,914 (49%)	$339,336 (52%)

Note: The figures in parentheses represent the percentage share which was virgin olive oil. For instance, 39% of U.S. olive oil imports from Italy in 1995 were virgin oil.

Source: Compiled from Goksu, Caglar (2000). Olive Oil Export Market Research, IGEME.

Exhibit 12   AUSTRALIA'S OLIVE OIL IMPORTS BY COUNTRY (IN TONS)

	1995–96	1996–97	1997–98	1998–99 (est.)
Spain	9,550	10,882	12,097	9,384
Italy	4,505	4,883	6,085	4,714
Greece	1,628	1,565	1,387	1,049
Turkey	0	21	227	258
Other	182	357	433	74
Total	15,865	17,687	20,002	15,479

Source: Compiled from Goksu, Caglar (2000). Olive Oil Export Market Research, IGEME.

- High consumption rates of imported olive oil—although there was some domestic production, over 95 percent of olive oil consumed was imported, valued at close to $100 million annually.
- High per capita consumption among the nontraditional olive oil consuming countries (Exhibit 5).

As can be seen from Exhibit 12, there was a steady increase in import volume, suggesting a growing acceptance of the product among Australian consumers. The olive oil market was less price competitive than the US and this enabled Baser Food to enjoy margins of 25–30%. Also, Ayhan believed that an initial investment of $100,000, which local distributors would be willing to share, would be sufficient to enter the market. Based on IOOC and Australian customs statistics for 1999–2000, Ayhan estimated 25% of these imports to be virgin/extra virgin, 74% pure and the remainder, pomace.

Others

The IOOC had identified several countries in addition to the United States and Australia that they felt represented potentially viable markets: Brazil, Canada, China, Japan, Taiwan and Thailand. As a result of the IOOC's promotional efforts and the increasing popularity of the Mediterranean diet emphasized by the EU promotional campaigns, olive oil consumption had begun to spread into these nontraditional markets.[18] However, there was some instability because for the majority of the consumers in these markets, olive oil was still a nonessential product and the demand was therefore both more price- and income-elastic than in the traditional consuming countries such as Spain, Italy or Greece. Another means of approaching these markets would be by the major Turkish producers creating a joint fund, with some support from the Turkish government perhaps, to stimulate primary demand in these new markets. But Mehmet Baser felt that this was not likely in the near future and any demand stimulation would have to be done by Baser Food alone. However, this could prove to be very expensive.

Ayhan had very limited information about these markets but knew that some behavioral change would be necessary in consumers' dietary habits in order for olive oil sales to increase significantly. This would clearly require heavy promotion to create awareness of the product and its health and other benefits before consumer acceptance could be achieved. For China, Ayhan estimated that it would cost $1 million to properly launch Cavallo d'Oro in the Shanghai region alone. In many ways it was easier to grow from markets where the product was accepted and the category was already represented on supermarket shelves rather than to develop the entire category single-handedly. In other potential markets like Eastern Europe, Baser played the role of the follower, allowing large companies from Italy and elsewhere to bear the high costs of gaining product acceptance and distribution. As a result, Baser spent just $200,000, shared with the distributor, to gain entry into Poland, for example.

On the other hand, there were likely some first-mover advantages, despite the high initial entry costs, to entering these countries before the competitors did. Mehmet Baser was also of the view that some of the emerging markets were easier to penetrate because they had very few established competitors and the resource requirements needed to gain brand awareness and retail presence would be lower than in the more established olive-oil-consuming countries. Ayhan recognized that the choice of market was very critical for a small emerging-market multinational like Baser Food to be successful globally, particularly when the competition was companies such as Unilever Bestfoods and its powerful Bertolli brand.

Endnotes

[1]Nilay Kirmanli, "Zeytin-Zeytinyagi Sektor Arastirmasi" (Olive–Olive Oil Sector Study), ITO, Yayinlari December 22, 2000.

[2]Sektor Dosyasi, "Kati ve Sivi Yaglar" (Sector Report—Fat and Oil), *GIDA* November 6, 2000.

[3]www.igeme.org.tr.

[4]Kirmanli, "Zeytin-Zeytinyagi"; Sabahat Akcay Tuna, "Zeytin Agaci, Zeytin, Zeytinyagi" (Olive Tree, Olive, Olive Oil), 1997; and interview with Altay Ayhan, April 15, 2002.

[5]Akcay Tuna, "Zeytin Agaci."

[6]Publio Viola, "Olive Oil and Health," International Olive Oil Council, Spain, State Institute of Statistics—National Accounts, 1997.

[7]www.die.gov.tr/seed/nation/page12.html.

[8]Taskin Tuglular, "Bitkisel Yag Sektoru," *GIDA,* November 2000, p. 42.

[9]Ibid.

[10]Kirmanli, "Zeytin-Zetinyagi."

[11]www.internationaloliveoil.org.

[12]Caglar Goksu, "Olive Oil Export Market Research," IGEME; Aegean Olive and Olive Oil Exporters Union, Working Report 2000–01, 2000.

[13]www.Baserfood.com.

[14]Interview with Altay Ayhan, December 2001 and January 2002.

[15]www.internationaloliveoil.org.

[16]Stephanie Thompson, "Spreading Out into Olive Oil," *Advertising Age* 72, no. 34 (August 20, 2001), p. 39.

[17]Ibid.

[18]G. Quaranta, and V. Rotundo, "Economic and Commercial Prospects for Olive Oil in View of the Changes in the Common Market Organization (CMO)—Part One," *OLIVÆ* 91 (April 2002), pp. 20–24.

The Earth-Moving Equipment Industry in 2000

Piero Morosini
International Institute for Management Development

Hans Huber
International Institute for Management Development

The earth-moving equipment industry was part of the construction equipment industry. Earth-moving equipment consisted of the following product groups: off-highway and dump trucks; wheel and crawler loaders; motor graders; excavators (either on wheels or crawler based); bulldozers; asphalt finishers; mini excavators; skid steer loaders (see Exhibit 1 for the most common product lines). It did not include items such as cranes, forestry equipment, or special-purpose machinery in the broader construction equipment category. List prices of earth-moving machines differed widely, depending on size and performance capabilities. For example, new skid steer loaders sold for as little as $25,000, whereas medium-sized crawler excavators could sell for $250,000 or more. In addition, all major players in the industry offered used equipment or rental solutions to customers.

In 2000 the global market for earth-moving equipment alone was estimated to be worth around $40 billion (see Exhibit 2). Major players in the industry had, however, diversified into related industries—such as agricultural equipment—and a significant part of their revenues came from such products. In the late 1980s and early 1990s, the market for earth-moving equipment experienced a significant drop in units sold and from then on it tended to grow slowly, with many product groups stagnating (see Exhibit 3).

Building construction—residential, commercial, industrial and governmental—represented the major source of demand for such equipment. Other important uses were in larger public projects, such as road and dam building, surface mining, mass transit construction, infrastructure repair and maintenance, and waste site management.

Traditionally, market demand was extremely sensitive to the general macroeconomic indicators of interest rates and inflation, which were key drivers for construction spending (see Exhibits 4 and 5 for U.S. data). Buyers of earth-moving equipment included construction companies, large and small contractors, state and local governments, mining and industrial concerns, logging companies, and farmers. There were few global clients in the construction business. These rare large clients tended to be loyal to particular brands and concentrated their operations in one region more than others. Key elements in the decision to purchase were performance/price characteristics of the product, service capability of manufacturers and their distributors, availability of rental and financing programs, delivery within a short time, and general product reputation.

Exhibit 1   Some Common Lines of Earth-Moving Equipment

Backhoe loader

Wheel dozer

Handlers

Scrapers

Excavators

Telehandlers

Off-highway trucks

Track loaders

Skidders

Motor graders

Skid steer loaders

Wheel loaders

Source: www.caterpillar.com, September 2001.

Exhibit 2   Estimated Distribution of Worldwide Market for Earth-Moving Equipment 2000 ($ billion)

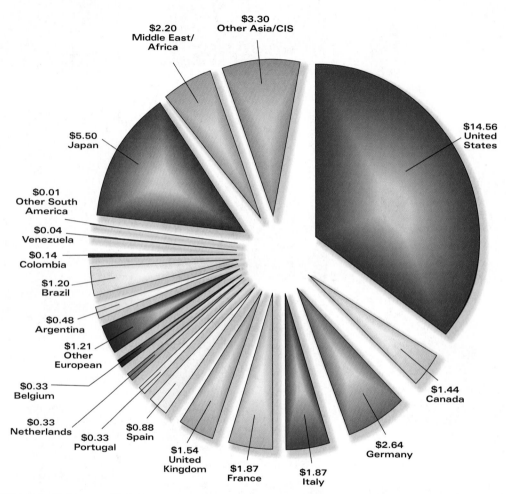

Source: Salomon Smith Barney and industry sources.

The use of specific kinds of construction equipment varied according to cultural and climatic conditions. Whereas the same type of truck could be sold worldwide, the choice of excavators was somewhat culturally conditioned. For example, Japanese construction companies preferred crawler excavators, but the German market demanded mostly rubber wheels.

A market segment that experienced spectacular growth in this otherwise mature industry was the rental market. Worldwide purchases of construction equipment for rental had risen from around $6 billion in 1990 to $24 billion by 2000 (see Exhibit 6).

The earth-moving equipment industry was highly competitive and relatively concentrated. In 1960 eight companies accounted for 40 percent of worldwide sales. According to industry surveys, there were five companies with 65 percent of worldwide sales during 2000. The increasing concentration in the industry was not caused by

Exhibit 3   **Earth-Moving Equipment Sold Worldwide (units)**

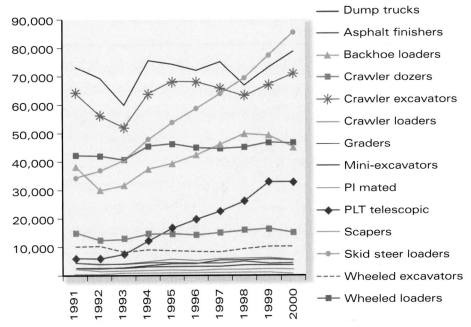

- Dump trucks
- Asphalt finishers
- Backhoe loaders
- Crawler dozers
- Crawler excavators
- Crawler loaders
- Graders
- Mini-excavators
- PI mated
- PLT telescopic
- Scapers
- Skid steer loaders
- Wheeled excavators
- Wheeled loaders

Source: Salomon Smith Barney.

Exhibit 4   **Construction Spending in the United States ($ billion)**

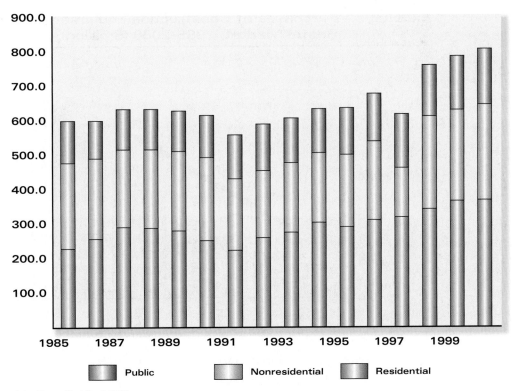

Public   Nonresidential   Residential

Source: John Deere Fact Book 2000.

Exhibit 5   **Mortgage Rates in the United States, 1985–2000**

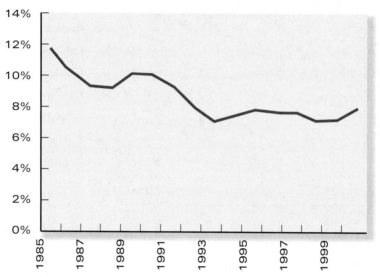

Source: John Deere Fact Book 2000.

Exhibit 6   **Purchases of Construction Equipment for the Rental Market, 1985–2000 ($ billion)**

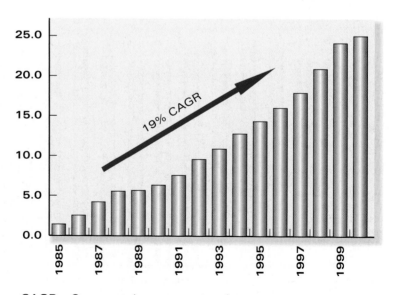

CAGR = Compound average growth rate.

Source: Terex Analyst presentation August 2001.

**Exhibit 7   WORLDWIDE MARKET SHARES FOR EARTH-MOVING
EQUIPMENT (% BASED ON UNITS)**

	1984	2000
Caterpillar	34%	31%
Komatsu	14	15
J. I. Case/CNH	6	7
Deere & Co.	6	6
Volvo	6	6
Dresser Industries	4	Merged with Komatsu
Fiat-Allis	3	Merged into CNH
All others	27%	35%

Source: Salomon Smith Barney, IMD research.

leading players gaining market share, but rather by mergers between firms that lost market share and apparently experienced difficulties (see Exhibit 7). In general, the high levels of capital investment required for this industry meant high barriers to exit, which, during weak periods of demand, made pricing extremely competitive. To be less exposed to currency fluctuations worldwide, manufacturers with aspirations to become global players set up manufacturing facilities around the world.

Product Portfolio

Generally, producers of earth-moving equipment could be positioned on a two-by-two matrix, according to geographic scope and product offering. Only Caterpillar, Komatsu, Volvo, and CNH offered a full line of products all over the world. Other companies either had a more restricted product range or were more limited in their geographic scope, or both (see Exhibit 8). Exhibit 9 shows key product groups with which different players chose to compete.

During the late 1980s and early 1990s both market demand and expansion into the United States required firms to include heavy crawler-based excavators in their product ranges. By the late 1990s, the market had turned to compact machines, such as mini excavators and skid steer loaders. This did not mean that smaller equipment had replaced heavy machinery, but market growth and demand for new equipment was much stronger in these categories. In 1998 Caterpillar, for example, used its plant at Desford, United Kingdom, for the European launch of a new class of "compact" machines costing as little as £15,000 ($25,000) per unit. Although the firm was best known for its large diggers and earth movers that sold for over £300,000 ($500,000), the new machines were an essential part of Caterpillar's strategy to grow sales.

In the mid-1990s, several manufacturers invested in forklift products to grow their businesses. In 1997 Mitsubishi and Caterpillar integrated their operations in a forklift joint venture (JV) in Almere, near Amsterdam. Output of electric and internal combustion lifting trucks rose from 1,000 units before the JV to over 10,000, worth $280 million in revenues per year. These forklifts were sold in Europe, the Middle East, and Africa. In the same year, British manufacturer JCB promised a full frontal assault on

Exhibit 8   Product/Geography Matrix of Earth-Moving Equipment Manufacturers in 2000

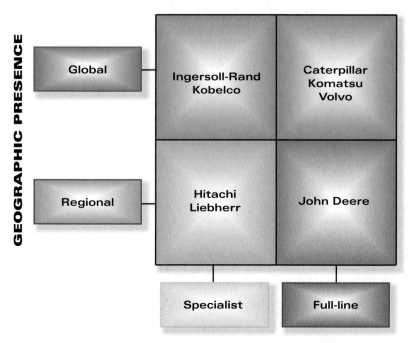

Source: IMD research, interviews with CNH.

Exhibit 9   PRODUCT RANGES OF DIFFERENT MANUFACTURERS

	Caterpillar	Komatsu	CNH	Volvo	JCB	Deere
Dump trucks	X	X		X	X	X
Backhoe loaders	X	X	X		X	X
Crawler dozers		X	X			X
Crawler excavators	X	X	X	X	X	X
Crawler loaders	X		X	X		X
Graders	X	X	X	X		X
Mini-excavators	X	X		X	X	X
Telescopic handlers	X		X		X	
Scrapers	X					X
Skid steer loaders	X	X	X		X	
Wheeled excavators		X	X	X	X	
Wheeled loaders	X	X	X	X	X	X
Directional drills		X	X			
Integrated toolcarriers	X					
Forklifts	X		X		X	X

Source: IMD research.

Exhibit 10   FINANCIAL RESULTS OF THE BIGGER PLAYERS

	CNH Global	Caterpillar†	Komatsu	Deere & Co.
	2000	**2000**	**2001**	**Fiscal 2001**
Revenue	$9,337.0	$18,913.0	$8,945.1	$13,136.8
Cost of goods sold	7,820.0	14,497.0	6,386.5	8,936.1
R&D	338.0	649.0	359.4	542.1
SG&A expenses	1,007.0	2,099.0	2,094.1	1,504.9
Income before taxes	−540.0	1,250.0	159.2	777.5
Net income	$−381.0	$ 1,053.0	$ 54.9	$ 485.5
	1999*	**1999**	**2000**	**Fiscal 2000**
Revenue	$9,929.0	$18,559.0	$10,535.6	$11,750.9
Cost of goods sold	8,320.0	14,481.0	7,552.8	8,177.5
R&D	357.0	626.0	402.5	458.4
SG&A expenses	1,173.0	2,079.0	2,289.3	1,362.1
Income before taxes	−349.0	1,170.0	183.8	365.1
Net income	$−188.0	$ 946.0	$ 127.0	$ 239.2

*Pro forma.
†Machinery and engines.
Source: Companies' annual reports.

the world's $10-billion-a-year lift truck market. Its innovative Teletruk used a telescopic arm, rather than a platform, to hoist loads. JCB aimed to capture 10 percent of the European market for lift trucks by 2000, which would have meant selling about $300 million worth of lift trucks a year, putting JCB among the top five makers in Europe. In 1998 JCB lift truck products had estimated revenues of $275 million, placing the company at number 15 in the world and number 6 in Europe. The world leader in that segment remained German Linde AG, with sales of $2.5 billion in 1998.

Any company with the key technology and the development and manufacturing capabilities to respond to new trends in construction activity would be in a position to reap above average benefits.

Financial Performance

After accumulating losses of $953 million in the mid-1980s and further losses in the early 1990s, Caterpillar downsized extensively and fundamentally adapted its cost structure and operations. By 2000 Caterpillar was clearly in a league of its own, with revenues almost twice those of its two closest competitors, CNH and Komatsu (see Exhibit 10). (John Deere & Co. was more focused on agricultural machinery and did not really compete globally against the Big Three.)

Other manufacturers of construction equipment that did not necessarily offer a full product range or have a global presence were also successful. Specialist, or niche, players such as JCB and Liebherr, among others, regularly produced solid results. For 2000, privately owned JCB announced net profits of £41.6 million ($62.1 million) on record revenues of £889.4 million ($1.3 billion). The company derived 74 percent of

Exhibit 11   Revenues from Construction Equipment ($ million) and Percentage of Group Revenue in 2000

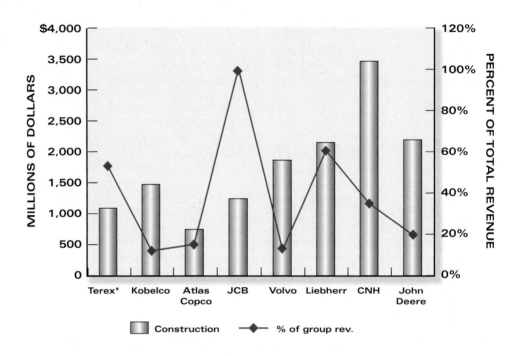

*Earth-moving equipment only.

Source: IMD research, company annual reports.

its revenues from exports. Liebherr had net revenues of Swiss francs (SFr) 5.7 billion ($3.6 billion) in 1999, yielding net earnings of SFr 197 million ($123 million). In 2000 revenues increased to SFr 6.2 billion ($3.8 billion). The company was the world leader in cranes for the construction industry.

Specialist Producers

Within the construction equipment industry, some firms were leaders in relatively narrow product domains, for example, Linde for forklifts or Liebherr for cranes. This specialization also applied to many manufacturers of earth-moving equipment. One of the Japanese company Kobelco's business units produced only small and medium-sized excavators in addition to cranes; the Swedish firm Atlas Copco concentrated its construction and mining business on rock drilling and breaker equipment. In general, these specialist manufacturers were part of more diversified larger groups of companies. Exhibit 11 shows the revenues these specialist manufacturers generated with construction equipment. It also shows the percentage of sales realized in 2000 compared with total sales of the group.

The specialist manufacturer Terex operated two major business units: for earth-moving equipment and lifting. The company aimed to produce at lower cost, especially

Exhibit 12   TEREX'S RECENT EARTH-MOVING EQUIPMENT ACQUISITIONS

Company	Acquisition Date	Product Focus
Payhauler	January 1998	Dump haulers, off-highway trucks
O&K Mining	March 1998	Large hydraulic excavators
Powerscreen	July 1999	Washing systems, screens, trommels
Cedarapids	August 1999	Asphalt mixing plants
Re-Tech	September 1999	Trommels, recycling units
Fermec	December 2000	Loader backhoes
Jacques	January 2001	Screens, feeders, crushers

Source: www.terex.com, September 2001.

with lower overhead, than the competition. It had a tradition of acquiring smaller specialist firms with strong products that could gain substantial market share by being leveraged through the company's more extensive distribution network. (See Exhibit 12 for Terex's acquisitions in its earth-moving unit.)

Liebherr produced mostly medium-sized excavators and wheeled loaders for earth moving. Other manufacturers, such as JCB and Volvo, had greater variety in selected ranges of products (mostly excavators and articulated loaders); the same applied to John Deere in the U.S. market. These three companies (JCB, Volvo and John Deere) were increasingly investing in broadening their product range and moving toward becoming full-line players. All of these specialist companies operated within an established, but somewhat mature, customer base in their home countries, as well as with fully owned subsidiaries in the United States. The only exception was John Deere, which remained focused only on North America and, to a lesser extent, South America.

Local Presence

The few global full-line players maintained strong positions in the geographic regions where they had first grown. Caterpillar was clearly number one in North America. It had also made more inroads into the still fragmented European market than its competitors, although European companies, i.e. CNH and Volvo were number two and number three there. Komatsu dominated the southeastern Asian markets, with a market share "at home" in Japan of around 40 percent (see Exhibit 13).

International sales were followed by capital investments abroad. Global players set up manufacturing facilities in countries that were targeted for sales growth. In the late 1990s and 2000, the biggest competitors, Caterpillar and Komatsu, both tried to expand further into the southeastern Asian markets, particularly China, but also Indonesia, India and Russia. Frequently these investments were made in the form of JVs with local businesses, combining foreign technological expertise and manufacturing skills with local labor and market access. Exhibit 14 shows that even in international operations, there was a specialization of skills around product lines in different manufacturing facilities.

Exhibit 13   Market Shares of Global Manufacturers in 2000 by Region

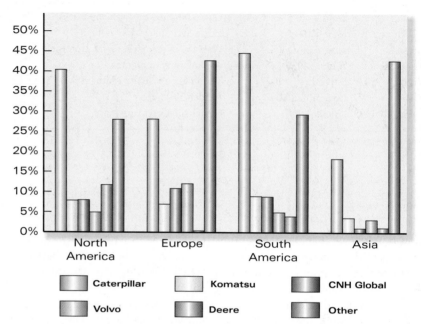

Source: Salomon Smith Barney, IMD research.

Supplier Relationships

The level of manufacturing in many companies producing construction equipment was low: Instead, these firms preferred to outsource many of their components. Competition among such suppliers was intense, and the most common components became heavily standardized. As a result, the same piece of equipment could often be sourced from different suppliers at very low prices.

The basic components could be divided into the following categories:

- *Microcomponents:* As in the automotive industry, instrumentation inside the vehicle, the lighting system, steering wheel, and so on were outsourced. Due to the heavy-duty use of construction equipment, the specifications for such components were often more rigorous than for those in the automotive industry.

- *Equipment attachments:* These included components such as an excavator bucket or hammer. The wide variety of such attachments and their different sizes required specialized suppliers. As an exception, Ingersoll-Rand performed these activities in-house as a way to further differentiate itself from the competition.

- *Metal fitting:* The fitting together of different subcomponents into larger pieces was considered a low-value-added activity and was outsourced in most instances.

▓ *Driveline:* Fierce competition and rapid innovation marked this activity. The aim was to enhance the performance and flexibility of the equipment's mobility, either on tracks or on wheels. More and more electronic components became part of the driveline.

Major suppliers in the industry were, for example, Zahnradfabrik Friedrichshafen (ZF); with total revenues of euros 6.5 billion in 2000. It was estimated that about 7 percent of its revenues were linked to construction equipment. Carraro (revenues of euros) 169.4 million had acquired O&K Antriebstechnik from CNH in 2000 and specialized in producing axles and reduction gears. Industry specialists expected the company to reach exclusive supplier relationships with Caterpillar for a selected product range, including compact wheel loaders, backhoe loaders, and telehandlers. Another supplier, Berco, was part of German firm Thyssen Krupp. Berco's main activities were in the components forming the undercarriage of equipment. Cummins was an important supplier of diesel engines, and Caterpillar had bought Perkins, another diesel engine producer, in the late 1990s (see Exhibit 15). Although mergers, takeovers and management buy-outs were common among suppliers, the market structure was still fairly fragmented, with the purchasing power mostly residing with the buyer (i.e., the manufacturer of the earth-moving equipment).

Dealer Distribution Network

In general, manufacturers relied on independent distributors to sell their equipment. These distributors operated their own networks of branches within confined regional sales territories and typically contracted as exclusive dealers; that is, they committed to selling one single brand of products for a given product segment. The pivotal role of these exclusive distributors was beyond doubt. For Caterpillar alone, the global network of dealers included 90,179 employees operating throughout 643 rental stores. The net value of these dealers (in December 2000) was estimated at around $7.14 billion, compared with Caterpillar's market capitalization of around $15 billion.

However, there were many small and medium-sized dealers that did not have exclusive franchises and were free to sell any brand of equipment. They often responded to local needs and derived most of their revenues from the sale of used equipment or from rentals. In fact, they were often true boutiques, offering a more or less comprehensive choice of products from different manufacturers (see Exhibit 16 for an example) depending on the local availability of used equipment or products to be rented. As manufacturers progressively became more concentrated, dealers realized the advantages of dealing with only one supplier ("one-stop shopping"). Shopping around for different products from different manufacturers became less interesting for the dealer, since it was able to source extensive product ranges from the smaller number of manufacturers in the market.

Manufacturers expanding into new markets had to choose the right distributor partnerships. When Caterpillar aimed to enter the German excavator market in the late 1980s, it knew that local needs were already being served by established brands such as Sennebogen, Zettelmeyer, Eder, Zeppelin, Hanomag, O&K, and Liebherr. These manufacturers regularly sold directly to the end customers, most of them construction companies. Independent dealers were the exception not the rule in this manufacturer-dominated environment. How should Caterpillar enter such a market?

Exhibit 14   INTERNATIONAL SCOPE OF MANUFACTURING OF THE MAJOR GLOBAL PLAYERS, 2000

	North America	Europe	South America
Caterpillar	United States: 26 manufacturing locations Canada: 2 manufacturing locations	Manufacturing locations in: Belgium: 1 France: 3 Germany: 4 Hungary: Ireland: 3 Italy: 8 The Netherlands: 1 Poland: 1 Sweden: 1 United Kingdom: 14	Brazil: motor graders, wheel type loaders, scrapers Mexico: 5 manufacturing locations
Komatsu (construction)	Tennessee: hydraulic excavators, wheel loaders, motor graders, cranes Quebec: hydraulic excavators, wheel loaders, motor graders, cranes Illinois: large wheel loaders, large dump trucks Indiana: diesel engines Kentucky: remanufactured products Texas: buckets, teeth, adapters	United Kingdom: hydraulic excavators Germany: wheel loaders, compactors Italy: mini and small hydraulic excavators, backhoe loaders, skid steer loaders Germany: super large hydraulic excavators	Mexico: small presses, attachments for construction equipment Brazil: hydraulic excavators, bulldozers, wheel loaders
CNH Global	United States: construction equipment, hay tools United States: construction equipment United States: construction equipment, tractors, planters, air seeders United States: construction equipment United States (JV): hydraulic crawler excavators United States (JV): low-cost diesel engines	Belgium: components France: construction equipment France: components Germany: construction equipment Italy: 3 construction equipment plants Italy: components Italy Fiat-Hitachi (JV): excavators United Kingdom (JV): low emission engines	Brazil: 2 construction equipment plants

Source: Company annual reports and websites.

With a more complete product range than the local specialist manufacturers, Caterpillar formed a JV in 1990. Its partners were Eder, which would concentrate on manufacturing (outsourcing some products to Sennebogen), and Zeppelin, which would become a sole distributor. Everyone was able to concentrate on the activities that it performed best, and all parties appeared to benefit from this win–win situation.

However, for Eder the JV turned into a disaster, since it was completely dependent on orders coming through Zeppelin and it had to make capital investments in order to be

Rest of the World	Japan
China (4xJVs): hydraulic excavators, construction machinery components, diesel engines, moving undercarriage and castings Australia: 2 locations, equipment customization, motor graders, replacement parts Manufacturing locations in: Russia: 1 Indonesia: 1 India: 4 South Africa: 1	Japan (JV): 2 manufacturing locations
Russia (JV): metal works for hydraulic excavators Indonesia: hydraulic excavators, bulldozers, wheel loaders, motor graders, dump trucks Indonesia: crawler components and spare parts China (JV): wheel loaders, motor graders, hydraulic excavators China: iron castings and parts for construction equipment and industrial vehicles, foundry molds China (JV): hydraulic excavators Thailand: hydraulic excavators	Japan: small and medium bulldozers, small hydraulic excavators, minimal rear-swing radius hydraulic excavators, mini hydraulic excavators, mini wheel loaders, small and medium wheel loaders, crawler carriers, transmissions, torque converters Japan: large bulldozers, medium and large hydraulic excavators, mobile crushers, mobile soil improvers, mobile tub grinders Japan: engines for constr. machinery and industrial vehicles, diesel generators, marine engines, rolling stock engines, hydraulics Japan: rough terrain cranes, dump trucks, large wheel loaders, motor graders, road construction machinery, towing tractors Japan: mini hydraulic excavators, skid steer loaders, mini agricultural and forestry equipment, general purpose engines, hydraulic equipment Japan: diesel engines
India (JV): loader backhoes, vibratory compactors	

able to manufacture new products developed by Caterpillar. In 1994 Eder decided to quit the JV, and its once important excavator business disappeared from the German market in the space of a couple of years. By 2001 Zeppelin was one of Caterpillar's biggest exclusive distributors worldwide, but its main emphasis was on the German market. Sennebogen was 92 percent owned by Caterpillar and produced specialist products such as telescopic handlers and cranes under its own brand. In contrast with the decline and concentration among German manufacturers, independent dealerships have increased.

Exhibit 15   SOME REPRESENTATIVE DATA ON COMPONENT SUPPLIERS IN 2000

Supplier	Product Focus	2000 Revenues	1999/2000 Net profit	1999/2000 Net cash flow
Carraro	Axles (Agricultural & construction equipment components)	€169.4m (52%)	3.2%/0.8%	€30.7m/€18.28m
ZF	(Driveline & axle)	€6,164m (939m)	7.3%/2.9%	€640m/€501m
O&K Antriebs-technik	Reduction gears, axles & drivelines	€56.3m	Acquired by Carraro in 2000	
Cummins	Diesel engines (Engine part of business)	$6,597m (61%)	2.4%/0.1% (4%/0.4%)	$388m/$307m
Berco	Track chains & rollers, undercarriage components	NA (2,965 employees)	NA	NA
Kayaba	Hydraulic components	$1,631m	−1.1%/−3.8%	NA

Source: IMD Internet research.

Exhibit 16   EXAMPLE OF A BOUTIQUE DEALER IN EUROPE BEFORE MARKET CONCENTRATION

Product	Brands Offered
Grader	Caterpillar, Faun-Frisch
Excavator	Caterpillar, Komatsu, O&K, Hanix
Wheel loader	Caterpillar, Liebherr, Hanomag, O&K, Samsung, Kramer, Volvo
Wheeled excavator	Komatsu, Liebherr, O&K
Backhoe loader	JCB
Mini excavator	PEL, Schaeffer
Skid steer loader	Bobcat, Caterpillar
Telescopic handler	Sennebogen

Source: Sample dealer in Germany, found on the Internet.

Distributors wielded significant negotiating power over manufacturers. Dealerships discovered they could add real value to the end customer by helping to solve problems. In fact, the relationship between the end customer and the dealer became increasingly strong and came to be the dealer's key asset. Whenever something went wrong with the equipment, the dealer was contacted first. The local dealer also provided maintenance and spare parts, as well as explaining the various product features to the customer and helping him choose the best product for his specific construction needs. The close personal relationship between the dealer and the end customer was also illustrated by the fact that many sales contracts were signed over the lunch table.

This market intelligence also proved extremely valuable for the manufacturer, allowing it to develop more differentiated products and thus to capture more market

Exhibit 17   RDO EQUIPMENT: JOHN DEERE'S BIGGEST DISTRIBUTOR

Revenue Data	
Total revenues	$680,378,000
Construction revenue	$316,577,000
Equipment sales	68.8%
Parts and service	30.1%
Rental	1.1%

Source: RDO annual report, 2000.

share at higher prices. It was common for distributors to organize monthly meetings with manufacturers to allow them to demonstrate new products and train sales staff.

The strong relationship between dealers and customers and the potential to add value through technical expertise induced dealers to offer more comprehensive product ranges. Although many construction jobs could be accomplished with more universal and less differentiated equipment, it was easier for the dealer to discriminate between applications and customer groups if the product was differentiated as well. The economies gained by sourcing from one manufacturer instead of several were significant. In particular, a dealer's growing bargaining power could be focused on one manufacturer.

The market power of these dealers vis-à-vis certain manufacturers increased as dealerships consolidated as well. John Deere, for example, had long encouraged consolidation among its network of 90 dealers, which accounted for about 80 percent of sales in 2000. (The remaining sales were handled by Deere directly.) In 1999 the company sponsored a buy-out venture in which it acquired eight dealerships through partnerships dubbed Nortrax and Nortrax II. Credit Suisse, the partner in this buy-out venture, committed $3.6 billion to the Nortrax projects. John Deere's biggest dealer was RDO Equipment, with 48 locations in nine states and around $680 million in revenues in 2000 (refer to Exhibit 17). RDO Equipment had planned to expand further to control 15 percent or more of John Deere's construction equipment market share in the United States, but was blocked from further acquisitions by the manufacturer.

The traditional concept of using distributors to sell equipment to end customers was challenged by several factors. During the 1990s, the shift from purchasing equipment toward renting opened alternative sales channels for manufacturers: When Tadano, a Japanese crane manufacturer, entered the United States by distributing through rental houses, industry experts had overwhelmingly considered it a strategic mistake. But since then, market pressures have forced distributors to offer rental services as well, as they came to realize that putting assets to work was good for lowering inventory costs as well as for promoting equipment.

Another conceivable threat came from the Internet. The possibility of buying, selling, and leasing equipment over the Internet would allow for disintermediation of the distributor. Very soon, however, distributors integrated such business-to-business (B2B) ventures into their own operations. TradeYard.com, an Internet-based marketplace for new and used construction equipment, for instance, was selected as the exclusive online partner of Associate Equipment Distributors, the trade association of U.S. distributors.

The Global Full-Line Players

Caterpillar

Headquartered in Peoria, Illinois, Caterpillar was the world's largest and most globally present producer of earth-moving machinery. It was also among the world's largest producers of diesel engines and occupied a second-tier position in the forklift truck market.

In 2000 the company generated revenues from machinery of $11.9 billion, from engines of $7.1 billion, and from financial services of $1.5 billion. Replacement parts accounted for a significant portion of the company's sales and earnings, with gross margins on parts being estimated at a stable 40 percent over the years. Back in the late 1980s the company had faced probably the most severe and long-lasting crisis in its history—for three years it had been losing approximately $1 million per day. In an effort to downsize and ultimately make the firm's cost structure more flexible, Caterpillar's bosses took on the United Auto Workers (UAW) union, which led to a strike that started in 1991 and continued sporadically until the end of 1995. In March of that year the company eventually got the flexible seven-year deal that it wanted with the UAW; in return, wages and conditions were improved and the strikers were employed again.

Over the years the company has produced only heavy machinery and engines and has steadfastly avoided diversification beyond these lines. Its management also believed that Caterpillar should compete in the all-important national market segments with its products, not only as a global profit seeker but also to ensure that local producers would find it difficult to grow into world-class competitors. Rapid capital-intensive expansion within Europe was one example of such pre-emptive behavior. Product standardization and interchangeability of components were key factors for success, essential to achieve efficiencies with regard to manufacturing costs and internationalization. At the same time, productivity increased tremendously: It used to take 6,000 workers 25 days to get one big back loader through the plant; in the late 1990s 3,000 workers achieved the same work in 6 days. These improvements were mainly due to redesigning production flows and higher degrees of automation. New product design and launch could be done in as little as 27 months, while the same job 15 years earlier would probably have taken up to 10 years.

Most of Caterpillar's research money was targeted directly at product development, product improvement, and applied research. The company undertook "pure" research only in exceptional circumstances, for example, when it needed new materials or components that its suppliers could not provide.

Caterpillar's ability to sell and service its machinery depended on a large and financially strong network of independent dealers. In 2000 this network consisted of 63 dealers in the United States and 157 abroad. In total, these dealers operated 1,844 branch stores and 643 rental stores, of which 517 branch stores and 244 rental stores were in the United States. The price premiums that Caterpillar equipment usually commanded above that of competitors were partially attributed to the excellent service provided in these dealerships. On bids for larger projects or in markets where Caterpillar did not have dealer backup, the price premiums were much smaller (not more than 10 percent). Setting up international dealership networks provided a distribution outlet and allowed Caterpillar to assess demand in newly entered markets. Only if demand was considered sufficient would the company proceed with setting up manufacturing facilities as well.

Komatsu

Established in 1921 as a specialist producer of mining equipment, Komatsu expanded into agricultural machinery during the 1930s and, during World War II, into military equipment. The heavy machinery expertise the company had developed positioned it well to expand into producing the earth-moving equipment needed for postwar reconstruction. Soon, construction equipment dominated Komatsu's sales.

Starting in the 1970s, Komatsu's strategy was simply "to catch up and overtake Caterpillar." As part of this strategy the company had focused on some key products, such as the bulldozer, and sold them more cheaply than Caterpillar. In general, list prices were between 10 and 15 percent lower than Caterpillar's, but sometimes its equipment was sold for 30 percent less than its rival's. In that period Komatsu's products were widely considered of lower quality than Caterpillar's.

During the late 1980s the company's president, Masao Tanaka, started to pursue internationalization more aggressively than his predecessor had done. Tanaka wished to establish autonomous bases with regional capabilities in manufacturing, sales and finance in the three core markets: Japan, the United States, and Europe. This change in strategy was mostly driven by the high value of the yen at the time, which made Japanese products less competitive abroad, and by the stagnant construction equipment market in Japan.

For the European market, the company produced wheel loaders in its UK plant. It sourced mini-excavators from the Italian company FAI, using engines made by Perkins, a British diesel manufacturer. It also sourced articulated dump trucks from Brown in the UK and vibratory rollers from ABG Werke (Germany), marketing them around the world under its own name. It even imported backhoe loaders from FAI into Japan.

In the United States, Komatsu entered into a 50/50 JV with Dresser, the American oil services company, in late 1988. The new $1.4 billion company, Komatsu Dresser Corporation (KDC), combined the U.S.-based finance, engineering, and manufacturing operations of both companies, while maintaining separate sales and marketing organizations. Using all four of the two parent companies' plants in the United States and Brazil, the JV produced most major construction products including hydraulic excavators, bulldozers, wheel loaders, and dump trucks. In 1996 Komatsu Dresser became Komatsu America International.

In the early 1990s, as it failed to gain market share abroad and domestic demand shifted to smaller and lighter equipment, the company started questioning its long-established strategy of catching up with Caterpillar. It came up with a new slogan of the three G's: Growth, Global, Groupwide. To communicate the vision, new company president Tetsuya Katada began referring to the company not as a construction equipment manufacturer but as a "total technology enterprise." This meant that Komatsu had to reduce its dependence on its traditional business and grow businesses such as electronics, robotics, and plastics so that by the mid-1990s the nonconstruction part of Komatsu would account for 50 percent of its sales.

By 2001 this goal had clearly not been achieved: 65.5 percent of Komatsu's sales came from construction and mining equipment, 10.7 percent from electronics-related businesses, and 23.8 percent from other sales. Its revised midrange strategy for the 21st century "reconfirmed the significance of Komatsu's construction and mining equipment business as a core operation." The new growth strategy for the construction equipment business consisted of four key elements:

1. *Expansion of sales in overseas markets:* 53.5 percent of total sales of all business operations were still generated in Japan (as of 2001). For the future, the company aimed to become a more customer-driven organization abroad, adapting its product range and overall marketing more to the local needs.

2. *Product differentiation and full-line offerings:* Strategic alliances with other companies were being sought in order to benefit from products with high potential for growth that were not in the company's own product range.

3. *Environment-related businesses:* This meant developing less polluting, low emission engines. Komatsu also identified growing environmental awareness as a source of important business opportunities.

4. *Solution-based services:* The company would expand sales and profits by targeting after-market businesses, ranging from lease and rental, parts and service, and used equipment sales to logistics and insurance.

The company distributed its products through its own subsidiaries, JV partners, and independent dealers worldwide. In Japan most of Komatsu's sales were made directly by operating units or by company-owned distributors. Outside Japan the company depended mostly on independent distributors but also sometimes used JV or subsidiary units. For example, in Germany Komatsu was represented through 52 dealer stores, among them Komatsu Hanomag, a fully owned specialist manufacturer. In the United States, the company was represented at 250 locations. In California, for example, the company worked through two independent distributors, the bigger with seven branch stores. In Korea, Komatsu formed an alliance with Daewoo Heavy Industries that sold through Daewoo's network of 24 outlets nationwide. For 2000 the alliance had set itself a target to sell 60 units of machinery; the target for the following year was double—120 units.

CNH Global

CNH Global was firmly embedded in the Fiat Group. Historically, Fiat had started experiments with machinery for agricultural use about 100 years ago, when it constructed its first harvesters.

An important date was 1972, when Fiat established a JV with Allis, a U.S.-based company with a strong presence in the agricultural equipment business. As part of this JV, Fiat-Allis had built a manufacturing plant in the United States for the agricultural and construction equipment businesses. However, the JV was not a success and Fiat pulled out of the North American market.

In the late 1980s and early 1990s, when the industry cycle for construction equipment was at a low, the company seriously questioned whether it should stay in the construction business: Although Fiat then had 40 percent of the Italian market for construction equipment, it remained a small player on the European scale, not to mention worldwide. In addition to this geographical weakness, the company lacked important products and technologies. Without access to the crucial hydraulics technology, the company could not produce excavators, and excavators then represented 40 to 50 percent of the construction vehicles market.

To gain access to this hydraulics technology, Fiat entered talks with Hitachi and John Deere in 1991. When John Deere dropped out, Fiat finalized a JV with Hitachi in late 1993. The JV was aimed to develop, manufacture, distribute, and sell medium to heavy excavators in Europe. Back in 1991 Fiat had acquired Ford New Holland, a specialist manufacturer of agricultural machinery. In November 1998 Fiat bought part of

Exhibit 18   CNH'S NET SALES BY GEOGRAPHIC AREA IN 2000 ($ MILLION)

Net Sales	Agricultural and Construction Equipment and Financial Services	Construction Equipment
Western Europe	3,613	1,432
North America	4,072	1,562
South America	633	220
Rest of world	1,019	246
Total net sales	9,337	3,460

Source: CNH annual report, 2000.

O&K's construction vehicles activities. This acquisition allowed Fiat to access the United States through alternative hydraulics technology without violating the venture with Hitachi that restricted operations to Europe.

Fiat continued to produce all of O&K's lines of excavators at its Berlin manufacturing plant. However, it sold the output in different ways and different regions of the world. In Europe the company continued selling the O&K brand through the same distribution channels as before. However, for the U.S. market, the company customized the O&K excavator and sold it under the New Holland brand. This allowed Fiat to offer a complete range of construction equipment in the U.S. market, which had been sourced from different manufacturing sites worldwide.

On November 12, 1999, New Holland acquired Case in a business merger for $4.6 billion in cash. Case Corporation was North America's number two maker of farm machinery and the world's largest maker of small to medium-sized construction equipment. The new company was called CNH and included all acquisitions, JVs, and other operations in both the agricultural and the construction businesses (see Exhibit 18 for financial information). In 2000 the new company decided on its global strategy for the construction business. There were several key elements, each of which is discussed in the following paragraphs.

Multibrand and Multichannel   CNH's strategy was aimed to be fundamentally different from that of its competitors, for example, Volvo, Caterpillar, Komatsu, and JCB, which all sold under a single brand through relatively uniform sales channels. CNH intended to sell under the Case and New Holland brands in the United States, under the Fiat-Hitachi, O&K, New Holland Light, and Case brands in the European Union, and under both the Case and the New Holland–Allis brands in South America. The company also sold equipment under the brands of Case Poclain, Link-Belt, and Fiat-Allis.

These established brands were expected to retain dealer and customer loyalty and help to better segment the market by customer and region. The brand would help to differentiate the product, which would then be sold through different channels. These different channels would remain with the independent distributors and dealers that had already handled the various brands before consolidation under CNH. The only notable exceptions to this model of independent distributors were Germany, Denmark, Austria, and Switzerland, where manufacturers traditionally worked through proprietary distribution channels. CNH aimed to gradually introduce more independent dealers in these countries as well.

revenues through its Caterpillar rental stores by providing more machines, tools and engines than any of its competitors.

E-Business

One obvious possibility for e-commerce was the purchase of new construction equipment and spare parts via the Web. For example, Liftme.com, an e-business started in 1998, aimed to bring crane buyers and sellers together. The business had between 200 and 300 cranes on its books at any one time. These virtual middlemen—which did not even own the cranes—threatened to alter the role of independent distributors. However, despite all the opportunities through e-business, e-relationships were not expected to undermine the importance of a physical presence. This was probably why the websites of all major manufacturers referred to their dealerships. In terms of procurement, Komatsu offered a Web page inviting tenders for basic parts.

Another extension of the product-centered value chain through added service was with remote machine monitoring and tracking—satellite-based systems allowed equipment owners to track the location and condition of machines in their fleet. Each machine was equipped with a black box that collected status and condition data from the engine, hydraulic, and other diagnostic systems. Then, at preprogrammed intervals, the box transmitted the data to a low orbit satellite network, which relayed it back to an Earth-based receiving station. There it was stored in a powerful database, which could display a variety of machine and fleet reports via a password-protected website.

Smucker's Acquisitions of Jif and Crisco

John E. Gamble
University of South Alabama

In mid-2002, the J. M. Smucker Company was the leading producer and marketer of jams, jellies, and preserves in the United States, Canada, and Australia but was quickly becoming less relevant within the global processed foods industry. The company's 2001 annual sales of $651 million paled in comparison to the 2001 revenues of such food industry giants as Nestlé, with revenues of 84.7 billion Swiss francs ($61.3 billion); Unilever, with sales of 51.5 billion euros ($49.1 billion); and Kraft Foods, with revenues of $33.8 billion. In addition, the company's small size and limited product line—which included fruit spreads, natural and organic beverages, ice cream toppings, natural peanut butters, and a few specialty items—put it at a bargaining disadvantage with grocery retailers, which were becoming fewer in number and larger in size as a wave of consolidation had resulted in the top five supermarket chains accounting for 40 percent of all U.S. grocery sales in 2002. Smucker had little ability to bargain for price increases or demand better in-store product placement with chains like Kroger and Wal-Mart, whose annual grocery sales each reached nearly $50 billion, or with other leading chains, whose annual sales reached $20 billion or more.

The larger food producers like Nestlé, Kraft Foods, General Mills, and Campbell Soup had begun acquiring smaller food companies and sometimes merging with equally large food companies to broaden their product lines and strengthen their hand in negotiating favorable shelf space with increasingly powerful supermarket chains. A record number of mergers and acquisitions occurred in the processed food industry between 2000 and 2002, with some mergers involving cash and stock transactions as large as $19 billion.

Smucker's fourth generation of family management fully understood that the company would need to pursue its own acquisitions to survive as an independent food company in a rapidly consolidating industry. In 2001, the company identified two business lines owned by Procter & Gamble that were slated for divestiture that it believed would fit within its range of management skills and would allow it to become a larger, stronger competitor in the food industry: Jif and Crisco. The acquisition was completed in June 2002 in an $810 million stock swap that resulted in the creation of a new J. M. Smucker with a wider range of products and a new class of stock. Going into fiscal 2003, brothers and co-CEOs Tim and Richard Smucker said the acquisitions of the two brands gave the J. M. Smucker Company three American icon brands and seven brands with number one positions in their respective categories. Further, it would allow the

Exhibit 1   J. M. SMUCKER'S BUSINESS PORTFOLIO PRIOR TO ITS ACQUISITIONS OF JIF AND CRISCO

Product Category	Brands and Products
Fruit spreads	Smucker's jams, jellies, and preserves; Smucker's low-sugar and sugar-free preserves; Smucker's Simply 100% Fruit; Smucker's cider apple butter; Smucker's peach butter; Lost Acres preserves; Dickinson's preserves; Glen Ewin fruit spreads (Australia); Allowrie fruit spreads (Australia); Double Fruit spreads (Canada); IXL fruit spreads (Australia); Good Morning fruit spreads (Canada); Shirriff fruit spreads (Canada)
Peanut butter	Smucker's natural peanut butter, Smucker's Goober PB&J, Laura Scudder peanut butter, Adam's peanut butter
Snacks and sandwiches	Smucker's Snackers, Smucker's Uncrustables
Ice cream toppings	Smucker's Magic Shell, Smucker's Microwaveable Ice Cream Topping, Smucker's Spoonable Ice Cream Topping, Smucker's Sugar Free Ice Cream Topping, Smucker's Sundae Syrup, Smucker's Dove Dark Chocolate Ice Cream Topping, Smucker's Dulce de Leche Milk Caramel Ice Cream Topping
Specialty items	Smucker's fruit syrup; Smucker's Plate Scraper Dessert Topping; Smucker's sugar-free breakfast syrup; Smucker's strawberry pie glaze; Smucker's tomato ketchup; Taylor's sauces, marinades, and salad dressings (Australia)
Beverages	R. W. Knudsen Family natural fruit beverages, spritzers, celebratory beverages, and sports drinks; Santa Cruz certified organic beverages; After The Fall natural fruit drinks, spritzers, and celebratory beverages; Rocket Juice herbal fruit drinks

Source: J. M. Smucker Company website.

company to record 2003 sales in excess of $1.3 billion and double its profits and cash flows. In addition, Tim and Richard Smucker believed the merger would allow J. M. Smucker to ultimately grow to $3 billion through a "three-legged" growth strategy that included organic sales growth of existing brands, new product introductions, and further strategic acquisitions that fit within the company's vision of owning and marketing number one, "center-of-store" food brands, with an emphasis on North America.

J. M. Smucker's product line and business portfolio prior to its acquisitions of Jif and Crisco are presented in Exhibit 1. Exhibit 2 provides a financial summary for the J. M. Smucker Company between 1993 and 2002.

Company History

The J. M. Smucker Company was founded in 1879 when Jerome Monroe Smucker built a steam-powered cider mill in Orrville, Ohio. Finding that his state-of-the-art mill could produce far more apple cider than he could sell, Smucker used a family recipe for apple butter to expand his product line rather than waste the excess cider. Smucker's apple butter became a hit within the local community and by 1920 the company began building a complete line of jams, jellies, and preserves to capitalize on the success of its initial product. The J. M. Smucker Company began to distribute its products nationally in 1942 and expanded its product line again to include ice cream toppings in 1948. The

Exhibit 2   FINANCIAL SUMMARY FOR THE J. M. SMUCKER COMPANY, 1993–2002 (IN THOUSANDS, EXCEPT PER SHARE AMOUNTS)

	2002	2001	2000	1999	1998	1997	1996	1995	1994	1993
Net sales	$687,148	$651,242	$641,885	$612,662	$574,855	$542,602	$528,576	$510,888	$478,228	$462,160
Income before cumulative effect of change in accounting method [a][b][c]	30,851	28,198	26,273	38,233	34,771	30,935	29,453	32,461	31,931	37,399
Cumulative effect of change in accounting method [d][e]	—	(992)	—	—	(2,958)	—	—	—	—	—
Income from continuing operations	30,851	27,206	26,273	38,233	31,813	30,935	29,453	32,461	31,931	32,945
(Loss) Income from discontinued operations [f]	—	—	—	—	—	—	(140)	3,842	(1,433)	—
Net income	$ 30,851	$ 27,206	$ 26,273	$ 38,233	$ 31,813	$ 30,935	$ 29,313	$ 36,303	$ 30,498	$ 32,945
Financial Position										
Long-term debt	$135,000	$135,000	$ 75,000	$ —	$ —	$ —	$ 60,800	$ 67,100	$ 48,558	$ 887
Total assets	524,892	479,104	477,698	437,657	410,695	384,773	424,952	405,995	362,851	294,811
Other Data										
Earnings per common share										
Income before cumulative effect of change in accounting method [a][b][c]	$1.26	$1.11	$0.92	$1.32	$1.20	$1.06	$1.01	$1.11	$1.10	$1.27
Cumulative effect of change in accounting method [d][e]	—	(0.04)	—	—	(0.10)	—	—	—	—	—
Income from continuing operations	1.26	1.07	0.92	1.32	1.10	1.06	1.01	1.11	1.1	1.27
(Loss) Income from discontinued operations [f]	—	—	—	—	—	—	—	0.14	-0.05	—
Net income	$1.26	$1.07	$0.92	$1.32	$1.10	$1.06	$1.01	$1.25	$1.05	$1.27
Dividends declared per common share	$0.64	$0.64	$0.61	$0.57	$0.53	$0.52	$0.52	$0.51	$0.47	$0.43

[a] Includes, in 2002, merger and integration costs of $5,031 ($3,160 after tax), or $0.13 per share, related to the Jif and Crisco transaction.

[b] Includes in 2001 a nonrecurring charge of $2,152 ($1,313 after tax), or $0.05 per share, relating to the sale of real estate, and in 2000 nonrecurring charges of $14,492 ($9,626 after tax), or $0.34 per share, relating to the impairment of certain long-lived assets.

[c] Includes, in 1993, the cumulative effect of adopting the provisions of Statement of Financial Accounting Standards No. 106, *Employer's Accounting for Postretirement Benefits Other Than Pensions.*

[d] Reflects, in 2001, the impact of adopting the provisions of the Securities and Exchange Commission's Staff Accounting Bulletin No. 101, *Revenue Recognition in Financial Statements* (SAB 101). Had SAB 101 been retroactively applied to all periods presented, earnings per common share would have been $0.01 lower in 1999.

[e] Reflects, in 1998, the cumulative effect of adopting the provisions of the Emerging Issues Task Force of the Financial Accounting Standards Board Issue No. 97-13, *Accounting for Costs Incurred in Connection with a Consulting Contract That Combines Business Process Reengineering and Information Technology Transformation* (EITF 97-13).

[f] Represents Mrs. Smith's.

company prided itself on meeting or exceeding consumer expectations and introduced reduced-calorie fruit spreads in 1958 as Americans began to become more aware of caloric intake. J. M. Smucker Company went public in 1959 and grew rapidly under the direction of Jerome Smucker's grandson, Paul Smucker, who oversaw the introduction of tomato ketchup in 1963, the sale of Smucker's fruit spreads to Kellogg's for Pop-Tarts filling in 1964, the introduction of peanut butter in 1965, and the introduction of Smucker's Goober, a striped peanut-butter-and-jelly product, in 1968.

Paul Smucker also led the company to introduce fruit-flavored breakfast syrups, low-sugar preserves, and natural peanut butters during the 1970s and began acquiring other food companies to broaden J. M. Smucker Company's product line and diversify beyond spreads, peanut butter, and condiments in the 1980s. The company acquired Magic Shell (the maker of an ice cream topping that hardened as soon as it was cooled by the ice cream) in 1982 and Knudsen & Sons (a leading producer of fruit and vegetable juices) in 1984. When Paul Smucker retired from active management of the company in 1987, his two sons, Tim Smucker and Richard Smucker, became responsible for the company's day-to-day operations. The two brothers represented the fourth generation of Smucker family management and carried out the acquisitions of Good Morning in 1988 and Henry Jones Foods in 1989. Good Morning was a producer of marmalade and dessert toppings sold in Canada, and Henry Jones was the leading manufacturer and marketer of jams and jellies in Australia. The company introduced Simply 100% Fruit in 1987 and Smucker's Light Preserves in 1990. Laura Scudder peanut butter and After The Fall fruit juices were acquired in 1994, while Adams peanut butter was acquired in 1997. The company introduced Smucker's Snackers (prepackaged cracker snack kits) in 1997 and Smucker's Uncrustables (crustless prepared peanut-butter-and-jelly sandwiches) in 2000. Smucker had acquired the Mrs. Smith's business unit from Philip Morris/Kraft in 1997, but divested it two years later. In 2001, Smucker acquired the formulated fruit and vegetable preparation businesses of International Flavors and Fragrances to expand its industrial fruit-fillings business, which was among its fastest-growing businesses during the early 2000s. J. M. Smucker Company was listed in the top quartile of *Fortune*'s "100 Best Companies to Work For" every year since the magazine created the ranking in 1997.

The Creation of the "New" J. M. Smucker Company

In June 2002, Timothy and Richard Smucker finalized the boldest expansion plan in the J. M. Smucker Company's history by acquiring the Jif and Crisco brands from Procter & Gamble in an $810 million stock swap. The Jif and Crisco acquisitions would transform J. M. Smucker from a company where jams, jellies, and preserves historically made up more than 50 percent of the company's sales to a more broadly diversified food products company with approximately 25 percent of its revenues coming from the sale of fruit spreads; 25 percent coming from peanut butter sales; 25 percent coming from the sale of shortening and edible oils; and the remaining 25 percent being accounted for by the sale of natural beverages, condiments, ice cream toppings, and snacks and sandwiches.

Procter & Gamble (P&G) had identified Jif and Crisco as divestiture candidates in the early 2000s (along with many other brands, including Comet, Prell, and

Chloraseptic) as its corporate strategy shifted to an emphasis on its star brands such as Tide detergent, Downy fabric conditioner, Bounty paper towels, Charmin bathroom tissue, and Folgers coffee. P&G management also believed that greater growth rates were possible in skin care, health care, feminine care, and baby care categories than in food staples such as peanut butter and shortening. The Smucker Company had long desired Jif, with Paul Smucker having told P&G management during the 1970s to call him first if it ever chose to sell the leading brand of peanut butter. In fact, Smucker's preparations for the merger began in early 2000 when Tim and Richard Smucker asked the company's board to consider a proposal to eliminate the Smucker Company's two-tiered voting rights structure that gave the Smucker family 75 percent of voting rights even though they held only 34 percent of outstanding shares. The proposal was approved by shareholders in August 2000 and was necessary since the company intended to issue up to $1 billion worth of shares to acquire Jif and Crisco. The issue would involve a change to the company's charter, and under such circumstances Wall Street investors would have been able to call for the company to adopt "one share/one vote" voting rights. The new voting rights structure did leave intact a super voting power clause that gave the Smucker family 10-to-1 voting rights in the event of extraordinary situations such as a potential sale of the company.

To avoid taxation on the sale of the two brands to Smucker, P&G executed a Revised Morris Trust spin-off format that called for the assets of Jif and Crisco to be spun off into a new company, whose shares were immediately exchanged for Smucker shares. A traditional spin-off or sale of assets would have left P&G and its shareholders exposed to considerable taxation since its cost basis in Crisco and Jif would be based on investments dating from 1911 in Crisco's case and 1955 in the case of Jif. The innovativeness of the transaction was recognized by *Investment Dealers Digest,* which honored the engineers of the merger with its 2002 Best Overall Deal and 2002 M&A Breakthrough Deal awards. Once the transaction was completed on June 1, 2002, each P&G shareholder received 1 share of the new J. M. Smucker Company stock for every 50 shares of P&G held. Smucker shareholders received 0.9451 of a share of the new J. M. Smucker for every 1 Smucker share held on May 31, 2002.

The Smucker family and the company's top management team expected the merger to boost the company's 2003 revenues to $1.3 billion, improve its earnings before interest, taxes, depreciation, and amortization (EBITDA) from $91 million to $190–$200 million, improve net income from $34 million to $88–$93 million, and improve free cash flow by $80 million, even after proposed capital expenditures of $55 million. The company believed the addition of Jif and Crisco would allow the company's revenues to ultimately grow to $3 billion, while the upper bound of long-term revenues would have been approximately $1 billion without the acquisitions. Many investment analysts agreed with Smucker management's expectations, noting Jif was a natural fit within Smucker's portfolio and suggesting that even though integrating Crisco into the portfolio might prove challenging, it was a one-of-a-kind product. An analyst from the Fourteen Research Corporation suggested that demand for the product should be steady because "you either use butter, margarine, oil or Crisco."[1]

The new J. M. Smucker Company shares began trading on June 3, 2002. Exhibit 3 presents the performance of the new J. M. Smucker Company's stock from the date of the company's change in its charter through December 2002.

Exhibit 3   **Weekly Performance of J. M. Smucker Company's Stock Price, September 2000–December 2002**

(a) Trend in J. M. Smucker Company's Common Stock Price after the adoption of new voting rights

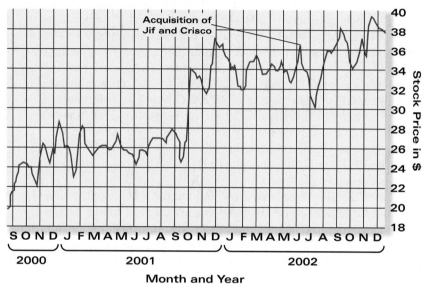

(b) Performance of J. M. Smucker Company's Stock Price versus the S&P 500 Index

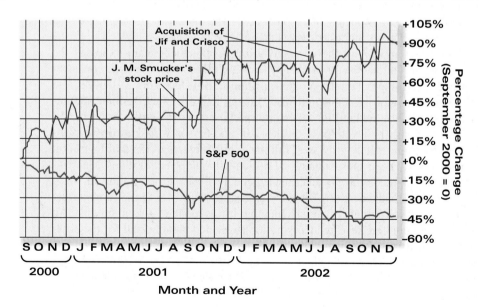

Overview of the Processed Foods Industry

The processed food industry was composed of many subsectors, each with differing growth expectations, profit margins, competitive intensity, and business risks. Industry participants were constantly challenged to respond to changing consumer preferences and to fend off maneuvers from rival firms to gain market share. Competitive success started with creating a portfolio of attractive products and brands; from there, success depended largely on the ability to achieve organic sales growth for existing brands and improve profit margins and on product line growth through acquisitions (it was generally considered cheaper to buy a successful brand than to build and grow a new one from scratch). Advertising and promotions were considered a key to increasing unit volume and helping drive consumers toward higher margin products; sustained volume growth also usually entailed gaining increased international exposure for a company's brands. Improving a company's profit margins included not only shifting sales to products with higher margins but also boosting efficiency and driving down unit costs.

Between 2000 and 2002, there was a wave of megamergers involving high-profile food and household products companies (see Exhibit 4). Three factors were driving consolidation pressures in the food industry—slower growth rates in the food sector, rapid consolidation in retail grocery chains (which enhanced the buying power of supermarket chains and enhanced their ability to demand and receive "slotting fees" for allocating manufacturers favorable shelf space on their grocery aisles), and fierce competition between branded food manufacturers and private-label manufacturers.

The earnings growth picture for many food companies had been bleak for several years, and the trend was expected to continue. In the United States, for example, sales of food and household products were, on average, growing 1–2 percent, slightly higher than the 1 percent population growth. More women working outside the home, decreasing household sizes, and greater numbers of single-person and one-parent households were causing a shift of food and beverage dollars from at-home outlays to away-from-home outlays. As a result of changing food consumption patterns, restaurants' share of the food dollar had grown from 33 percent in 1980 to 46 percent in 2001. Americans were projected to spend 53 percent of their food dollars in restaurants by 2010. A Prudential analyst explained the growth in the number of meals eaten away from home by stating simply, "Women have stopped cooking, and men haven't started."[2] The growth rate for food and household products across the industrialized countries of Europe was in the 2 percent range, with many of the same growth-slowing factors at work as in the United States. Food industry growth rates in emerging or less-developed countries were more attractive—in the 3–4 percent range, prompting most growth-minded food companies to focus their efforts on markets in Latin America, Asia, Eastern Europe, and Africa.

The consolidation of the U.S. supermarket industry resulted in nearly 40 percent of industry sales being accounted for by Kroger, Wal-Mart, Albertson's, Safeway, and Ahold USA in 2001. In 1995 the top five supermarket companies had accounted for just over 25 percent of industry sales. Between 1997 and 2001 there were approximately 75 mergers and acquisitions in the supermarket industry, with much of the merger activity occurring as a result of traditional supermarket companies' attempts to better compete with Wal-Mart. Wal-Mart did not enter the grocery industry until 1988,

Exhibit 4   MERGERS AND ACQUISITIONS AMONG FOOD COMPANIES, 2000–2002

Companies Involved	Transaction Date	Value of Deal	Brand Portfolio of Acquiring Company	Brand Portfolio of Company Being Acquired
Nestlé acquired a majority control of Dreyer's Grand Ice Cream, Inc.	2002	$2.4 billion in stock	*Nestlé brands:* chocolates and candies (Nestlé, Crunch, KitKat, Smarties, Butterfinger, Cailler, Frigor, Chokito, Galak/Milkybar, Yes, Quality Street, Baci, After Eight, Baby Ruth, Lion, Nuts, Rolo, Aero, Polo); dairy (Carnation, Milkmaid, Nespray, Nido, Neslac, Gloria, Bärenmarke); coffee (Nescafé, Taster's Choice, Bonka, Zoegas, Ricoffy, Loumidis, Coffee-mate); beverages (Nesquik, Nestea, Carnation, Libby's, Perrier, San Pellegrino, Poland Spring, Calistoga, Vittel, Valvert, Arrowhead, Buxton, Vera); frozen foods (Stouffer's, Maggi, Buitoni); culinary products (Maggi, Libby's, Crosse & Blackwell, Buitoni); ice cream (Nestlé, Häagen-Dazs, Frisco, Dairy Farm); pet care (Friskies, Fancy Feast, Alpo, Mighty Dog, Gourmet); others (Power Bar, Nestlé cereal, Alcon eye care products)	Dreyer's ice creams and sherbets
Del Monte Foods acquired the pet foods, tuna, soup, and infant feeding businesses of the H. J. Heinz Company	2002	$2.8 billion in stock	Del Monte canned fruits and vegetables, Contadina canned tomato products, S&W canned fruits and vegetables	Heinz steak sauces and other condiments; Ore Ida potatoes; Wyler's bouillon and soup mixes; Weight Watchers dinners; StarKist tuna; pet foods (9 Lives, Kibbles and Bits, Meaty Bone, Skippy); baby foods (Heinz, Nature's Goodness, Plasmon, Farley's, tinytums)
Nestlé acquired Chef America	2002	$2.6 billion in cash	See above	Chef America frozen stuffed sandwiches
Associated British Foods PLC acquired 19 brands, including Mazola cooking oil, Argo and Kingsford's cornstarches, Karo and Golden Griddle syrups, Henri's salad dressing, and a number of related Canadian brands from Unilever.	2002	$360 million in cash	*Associated British Foods* brands: Silver Spoon sweeteners (UK); Allinsons, Kingsmill, Ryvita, and Speedibake breads (UK); Ovomaltine malt beverage (Europe, China, Thailand); Twinings and Jackson of Piccadilly teas.	*Unilever brands:* spreads (I Can't Believe It's Not Butter, Country Crock, Imperial, Promise); olive oil (Bertolli and Puget); Breyer's ice cream, Popsicle, and Good Humor; Lipton; Ragú; Wishbone; fragrances Lagerfeld, (Calvin Kline; Vera Wang, Nautica); personal care products (Dove, AquaNet, Pond's, Vaseline, Q-Tips; detergents (Wisk, Surf, Snuggle); shampoos (ThermaSilk, Suave, Finesse, Organics); toothpastes (Aim, Pepsodent, Close-Up).

Description	Year	Brands	Additional brands
Sara Lee acquired Earthgrains Company	2001	$1.8 billion in cash	*Sara Lee brands*: Sara Lee (Deli lunch meats, sliced and packaged meats, fresh and frozen bakery products, frozen foods); coffee and coffee systems (Douwe Egberts and Superior); meats (Hillshire Farms, Aoste, Bryan, Ball Park, Jimmy Dean); Kiwi shoe products; apparel (Champion, Playtex, Hanes, DIM, Wonderbra, Loveable, Bali, Just My Size, Nurdie, L'eggs)	Earth Grains, IronKids, Rainbo, Colonial, and Grant's Farms breads
George Weston Limited (a Canadian baked goods company) acquired Bestfoods Baking Company from Unilever	2001	$1.8 billion in cash	*George Weston brands*: Weston, Maplehurst, Stroehmann, Interbake Foods, Arnie's breads and pastries, Heritage Salmon	*Unilever brands*: See above
Campbell Soup acquired several European soups and sauces businesses from Unilever	2001	$900 million in cash	*Campbell Soup brands*: soups (Campbell's, Healthy Request, Simply Home, Swanson's broth, Liebeg, Erasco, Homepride, Stock Pot); bakery (Pepperidge Farm, Arnott's); culinary (Pace, V8, Prego, Swanson's, Franco-American, Homepride Pasta Bake, Kimball sauces); chocolates (Godiva)	*Unilever brands*: See above
Nestlé acquired Ralston Purina Company	2001	$10.3 billion in cash	See listing of Nestlé brands, above	*Ralston Purina pet food and pet care brands*: Purina Dog Chow, Purina Puppy Chow, Felix, Purina One, T Bonz, Beggin' Strips, Pro Plan, Puppy Chow, Tidy Cats, Tender Vittles
General Mills acquired the Pillsbury unit of Diageo (a UK-based company with a wide-ranging portfolio of alcoholic beverage brands and the parent of Burger King and Pillsbury)	2000	$10.5 billion in cash	*General Mills brands*: Big G cereals (Wheaties, Cheerios, Total, Lucky Charms, Trix, Chex, Golden Grahams); Betty Crocker desserts and side dishes; Gold Medal flours; Bisquick; Hamburger Helper; Lloyd's; Yoplait and Colombo yogurts; Pop Secret; Chex Mix snacks; Nature Valley; Bugles	*Pillsbury brands*: Pillsbury and Martha White flours, baking mixes, and baking products; Häagen-Dazs ice cream and frozen yogurt; Green Giant frozen and canned vegetables, Old El Paso Mexican foods, Totino's and Jeno's pizzas, Progresso, and Hungry Jack
Philip Morris (the parent of Kraft Foods prior to Kraft's 2001 IPO) acquired Nabisco	2000	$19 billion in cash, stock, and debt	*Kraft Foods brands*: Kraft cheeses, mayonnaise, salad dressings, barbeque sauces, and dinners; Post cereals; Jell-O; Velveeta; Cheez Whiz; Cracker Barrel, Di Giorgo and Hoffman's cheeses; Claussen pickles; Maxwell House, Yuban, and Sanka coffees; Minute Rice; Tobler and Toblerone chocolates; Louis Rich and Oscar Mayer meats; Miracle Whip; Shake 'N Bake; Breakstone; Cool Whip; Planters; Kool-Aid; Stove Top; Altoids	*Nabisco brands*: Nabisco cookies, crackers, and snacks; Grey Poupon French mustards

continued

Exhibit 4   Continued

Companies Involved	Transaction Date	Value of Deal	Brand Portfolio of Acquiring Company	Brand Portfolio of Company Being Acquired
Kellogg's acquired Keebler	2000	$4.4 billion	*Kellogg's brands:* Kellogg's cereals, Eggo, Nutri-Grain, Pop-Tarts, Kashi cereal and breakfast bars, Rice Crispies Treats, Snack'Ums	*Keebler brands:* Keebler cookies; Murray cookies; Keebler snack foods (Cheez-It, Wheatables, Toasteds, Munch'ems, Harvest Bakery, Snax Stix); Krispy and Zesta saltine crackers; Club crackers; Hi-Ho crackers; Golden Vanilla Wafers; Ready Crust pie shells
ConAgra acquired International Home Foods	2000	$2.9 billion	*ConAgra brands:* Armour, Banquet, Butterball, Blue Bonnet and Parkay margarines, Chun King, La Choy, Orville Redenbacher's and Act II popcorns, Peter Pan, County Line cheeses, Morton prepared foods, Eckrich meats, Fleischmann's, Egg Beaters, Healthy Choice, Hunt's	*International Home Foods brands:* Chef Boyardee, Pam cooking spray, Louis Kemp/Bumblebee seafood products, Libbey's canned meats, Gulden's mustard
PepsiCo acquired Quaker Oats	2000	$12.4 billion in cash and stock	*PepsiCo brands:* Pepsi soft drinks, Mountain Dew, Frito-Lay snack foods, Tropicana juices	*Quaker brands:* Gatorade, Quaker Oats cereals, Rice-a-Roni, Aunt Jemima, Near East, Golden Grain–Mission pastas
Cadbury Schweppes acquired the Snapple Beverage Group from Triarc, Inc.	2000	$1.45 billion	*Cadbury Schweppes brands:* Schweppes and Canada Dry tonics, sodas, and ginger ales; 7UP, Dr Pepper, and A&W sodas; Mott's apple juices; Clamato juices; Cadbury chocolates and confectionery items; and Trebor, Pascall, Cadbury Éclair, and Bassett candies	*Snapple brands:* Snapple ready-to-drink teas and beverages

Exhibit 5   ESTIMATED SALES AND NUMBER OF SUPERMARKET LOCATIONS FOR THE TOP 15 U.S. GROCERS, YEAR-END 2001

Rank	Company	Estimated Sales (in billions)	Number of Supermarket Locations (Store sales of $2 million or greater)
1	The Kroger Co.*	$46.7	2,429
2	Safeway	31.5	1,568
3	Albertson's	30.2	1,713
4	Wal-Mart*,†	28.2	1,103
5	Ahold USA	24.1	1,245
6	Food Lion/Delhaize	15.2	1,464
7	Publix	14.6	687
8	Winn-Dixie	13.0	1,141
9	Great A&P Tea	8.5	519
10	Supervalue*	7.4	550
11	H-E-B Grocery Co.	7.1	278
12	Shaw's	4.3	187
13	Meijer*	3.9	153
14	Pathmark	3.9	142
15	Military Commissary	3.6	196

*Supercenter statistics reduced to include only traditional supermarket items.

†Warehouse clubs such as Sam's Club and Costco represent a substantial volume of food sales, but they have been omitted from the Progressive Grocer ranking because of sales to businesses and institutions in institutional packaging not directly competitive with supermarkets. It is estimated that the 501 Sam's Clubs would add $18.5 billion of supermarket equivalent sales to Wal-Mart total, lifting total sales to $46.7 billion, a virtual tie with number one Kroger.

Source: "The Super 50," *Progressive Grocer,* April 15, 2002.

with the opening of its first Supercenter, but became the co-leader of the supermarket industry in 2001 when its annual grocery sales reached $46.7 billion. Competition in the industry was expected to intensify further with Wal-Mart's annual addition of 150–175 new Supercenters and 15–20 smaller Neighborhood Markets to expand its chain of more than 1,500 stores. The industry's other leading grocery companies believed that mergers between the larger chains and acquisitions of smaller chains would provide greater purchasing power to meet Wal-Mart's discount pricing. A portfolio manager for a capital management firm explained how consolidation in the supermarket industry and the increasing competitive strength of retailers fueled consolidation in the processed foods industry. "The only way these food companies can improve their margins and strike better deals with supermarkets is to add scale. Otherwise, the chains can just about dictate what they want to pay."[3] Exhibit 5 presents estimated sales and number of stores with annual sales exceeding $2 million for the top 15 U.S. grocers.

Since 1985 the share of private-label food and beverages sold in the United States had risen steadily, accounting for roughly 25 percent of total grocery sales in 2000, up from 19 percent in 1992. Growing shopper confidence in the leading supermarket chains and other food retailers like Wal-Mart had opened the way for retail chains to effectively market their own house-brand versions of name-brand products—provided the house-brand was priced attractively below the competing name brands. Indeed, with the aid of checkout scanners and computerized inventory systems, retailers knew as well or better (and more quickly) than manufacturers what customers were buying and what price differential it took to induce shoppers to switch from name brands to private-label brands. These developments tilted the balance of power firmly toward retailers. Thus, competition between private-label goods and name-brand goods in supermarkets was escalating rapidly, since retailers' margins on private-label goods often exceeded those on name-brand goods. The battle for market share between private-label and name-brand goods was expected to continue as private-label manufacturers improved their capabilities to match the quality of name-brand products while also gaining the scale economies afforded by a growing market share.

Branded manufacturers were trying to counteract the bargaining power of large supermarket chains and the growth of private-label sales by building a wide-ranging portfolio of strong brands—the thesis being that retailers, fearful of irritating shoppers by not carrying well-known brands, would be forced to stock all of the manufacturer's name-brand products and, in many cases, award them favorable shelf space. At the same time, because they faced pressures on profit margins in negotiating with retailers and combating the competition from rival brands (both name-brand rivals and private-label rivals), manufacturers were trying to squeeze out costs, weed out weak brands, focus their efforts on those items they believed they could develop into global brands, and reduce the number of versions of a product they manufactured wherever local market conditions allowed (to help gain scale economies in production).

Exhibit 6 provides a brief profile of selected competitors of The J. M. Smucker Company. Other competitors included Sara Lee, H. J. Heinz, ConAgra, Kellogg's, and well over 100 regional and local food products companies around the world. Many of the leading food products companies had a food-service division that marketed company products to restaurants, cafeterias, and institutions (e.g., schools, hospitals, college student centers, private country clubs, corporate facilities) to gain access to the growing away-from-home segment of the food market.

J. M. Smucker's Approach to Building Shareholder Value in the Processed Foods Industry

The J. M. Smucker Company's corporate strategy was comprised of three main components: (1) growing the market share of its existing brands, (2) introducing new products, and (3) making strategic acquisitions. In 2002, the company was the market leader in seven food categories, including fruit spreads, with a 40.6 percent market share; dessert toppings, with a 61.3 percent market share; health and natural beverages, with a 54.0 percent market share; and natural peanut butter, with a 66.5 percent market share. The market share of Smucker's core U.S. fruit spreads business had grown from 20 percent since 1977 through the company's commitment to its "With a name like Smucker's, it has to be good" advertising campaign and carefully selected sponsorships. The company spent about $10 to $15 million annually promoting its jams, jellies, and preserves in television and print ads and had been a longtime sponsor of Willard Scott's birthday segment on NBC's *Today* show. During 2002, the company also sponsored Walt Disney World Resorts' "100 Years of Magic" Celebration, the World Figure Skating Championships, and other skating specials aired on NBC such as "Smucker's Stars on Ice."

J. M. Smucker management intended to utilize similar marketing strategies to improve the market leading positions of Jif and Crisco. Smucker managers also intended to explore co-branding opportunities between Smucker's fruit spreads and Jif peanut

Exhibit 6   PROFILE OF SELECTED J. M. SMUCKER COMPETITORS

Company (Headquarters)	Product Categories/Brands	Sales	Profits	Key Facts
Nestlé (Swiss)	■ Chocolates and candies (Nestlé, Crunch, KitKat, Smarties, Butterfinger, Cailler, Frigor, Chokito, Galak/Milkybar, Yes, Quality Street, Baci, After Eight, Baby Ruth, Lion, Nuts, Rolo, Aero, Polo)	2001: SFr 84.7 billion	2001: SFr 6.68 billion	World's largest food company with sales in almost every country of the world; 509 factories; 231,000 employees
	■ Dairy (Carnation, Milkmaid, Nespray, Nido, Neslac, Gloria, B‰renmarke)	2000: SFr 81.4	2000: SFr 5.76	
	■ Coffee (Nescafé, Taster's Choice, Bonka, Zoegas, Ricoffy, Loumidis, Coffee-mate	1999: SFr 74.7	1999: SFr 4.72	
	■ Beverages (Nesquik, Nestea, Carnation, Libby's, Perrier, San Pellegrino, Poland Spring, Calistoga, Vittel, Valvert, Arrow-head, Buxton, Vera)	1998: SFr 71.7	1998: SFr 4.20	
	■ Frozen Foods (Stouffer's, Maggi, Buitoni)	1997: SFr 70.0	1997: SFr 4.18	
	■ Culinary products (Maggi, Libby's, Crosse & Blackwell, Buitoni)	1996: SFr 60.5	1996: SFr 3.59	
	■ Ice Cream (Nestlé, Frisco, Dairy Farm)			
	■ Pet care (Friskies, Fancy Feast, Alpo, Mighty Dog, Gourmet, Ralston Purina)			
	■ Cosmetics (L'Oréal)			
	■ Others—PowerBar, Nestlé cereal, Alcon eye care products			
	■ Food services			

continued

Exhibit 6   Continued

Company (Headquarters)	Product Categories/Brands	Sales	Profits	Key Facts
Unilever (Dutch, British)	■ Margarines, spreads, and cooking oils (I Can't Believe It's Not Butter, Country Crock, Imperial, Take Control, and Promise spreads; Brummel & Brown; Bertolli and Puget olive oils; Flora/Becel spreads and cooking products) ■ Frozen foods (Birds Eye frozen foods (UK), Iglo frozen foods, Gorton's frozen seafood products, Findus pan-prepared meals, and Quattro Stelle meal solutions) ■ Ice cream and frozen novelties (Breyer's, Magnum, Solero, Walt's, Langnese, Ola, Algida, Cornetto, Viennetta, Pinguino, Carte d'Or, Klondike, Popsicle, Good-Humor) ■ Tea-based beverages (Lipton, Brooke Bond, and Beseda) ■ Culinary products (Ragú and Five Brothers pasta and pizza sauces, Colman's mustard and sauces; Amora and Maille mustards, ketchup, and dressings; Lawry's seasonings; Upron Spices and seasonings; Wishbone and Calvè salad dressings; Calvè peanut butter; Slotts and Klocken mustards, ketchup, and seasonings; Sizzle & Stir sauces; Wishbone salad dressings; Oxo stock cubes; Cup-A-Soup; Recipe; McDonnell's; Bla Band; Lipton soups) ■ Desserts (Carte de'Or) ■ Bakery products (Bread and confectionery mixes, baking ingredients, frozen bakery products such as Danish pastries, muffins, and croissants) ■ Fragrances and toiletry items (Calvin Klein, Chloè, Cerruti, Valentino, Lagerfeld, Nautica, Vera Wang, Rexona/Sure, Axe/Lynx, Dove, Degree, Brut, Suave, Impulse) ■ Hair care products (ThermaSilk, Sunsilk, mod's hair [Japan], Finesse, Suave, Caress, Dove, Salon Selectives, Timotei, and Organics shampoos; AquaNet and Rave hair care products) ■ Oral care products (Aim, Pepsodent, Mentadent, and Close-up [Asia, Pacific, United States], Signal [Europe], Zhonghua [China] toothpastes; Signal and Mentadent chewing gums) ■ Soaps, lotions, and skin care (Dove, Lux, Degree, Caress, Lever 2000, Lifebuoy, and Shield's soap bars; Pond's, Vaseline, and Fair & Lovely skin care products; Hazeline shampoos and skin care products [sold in China]; Q-Tips cotton swabs and balls) ■ Laundry detergents (Wisk, Oxo, Omo, Surf, Ala, Persil, All, and Skip detergents; Snuggle, Cajoline, and Comfort fabric conditioners) ■ Household cleaning products (Domestos surface cleaners, Cif household cleaners, Sunlight dish detergents, and Solvol [a heavy duty hand cleaner marketed in Australia and New Zealand]) ■ Diagnostics (Unipath pregnancy tests)	2001: €51.5 billion 2000: €47.6 1999: €41.0 1998: €40.4 1997: €42.9	2001: €1.84 billion 2000: €1.11 1999: €2.77 1998: €2.94 1997: €4.96	Among world's largest food companies with sales of €52.2 billion and 265,000 employees in 2001. More than one-half of the company's sales are generated by its foods division brands. Initiated a Path to Growth strategy in 2000 that would reduce the size of the company's portfolio of 1,600 brands, concentrate R&D and advertising on the company's leading brands, divest a number of underperforming brands and businesses, boost product innovation, make new acquisitions, and achieving faster growth in sales and earnings. The world leader in margarine and related spreads and olive oil, with sales in more than 50 countries. Lipton was the world's most popular tea brand. One of the largest fragrance businesses in the world. Dove was the world's number one brand of soap.

Company	Products	Revenues	Net Income	Highlights
Procter & Gamble (U.S.)	■ Baby care (Pampers, Luvs) ■ Laundry products (Tide, Cheer, Downy, Bounce, Bold, Dreft, Era, Gain, Ivory Snow, Ariel) ■ Household cleaners (Joy, Cascade, Dawn, Comet, Mr. Clean/Top Job) ■ Food/Beverage (Folgers, Jif, Crisco, Pringles, Sunny-Delight, Millstone) ■ Health and oral care (Crest, Pepto-Bismol, Metamucil, Vicks, Nyquil) ■ Feminine care (Always, Tampax) ■ Paper products (Bounty, Charmin, Puffs) ■ Personal care (Ivory, Camay, Safeguard, Zest, Secret, Old Spice, Cover Girl, Max Factor, Head & Shoulders, Olay, Pert, Vidal Sassoon, Pantene, Physique, Noxema, Hugo Boss) ■ Pet care (Iams)	2002: $40.2b billion 2001: $39.2 2000: $40.0 1999: $38.1 1998: $37.2 1997: $35.8 1996: $35.3	2002: $4.35 billion 2001: $2.92 2000: $3.54 1999: $3.76 1998: $3.78 1997: $3.42 1996: $3.05	Sales in over 140 countries; on-the-ground operations in more than 70 countries, 110,000 employees; and 300 brands. Tide's market share was over four times larger than its nearest competitor; Ariel laundry detergent was sold in 115 countries (with the highest or second highest share in 25 countries). Tide and Ariel had combined sales greater than any other P&G brand.
Kraft Foods (U.S.)	■ Chocolates and candies (Life Savers, Creme Savers, Altoids and Gummi Savers; Cote d'Or, Terry's, Gallito, Milka, and Toblerone chocolate and confectionery products; and Jell-O ready-to-eat refrigerated desserts. ■ Snacks and crackers (Nabisco, Oreo, Chips Ahoy!, SnackWells cookies; Ritz, Premium, Triscuit, Wheat Thins, Cheese Nips; Planters nuts; Balance Bar nutrition and energy snacks; Lyux salty snacks; Terrabusi, Canale, Club Social, Cerealitas, Trakinas, and Lucky biscuits) ■ Meats (Oscar Mayer and Louis Rich cold cuts, hot dogs, and bacon; Boca Burger soy-based meat alternatives; and Simmenthal meats in Italy) ■ Cereals (Post Raisin Bran, Grape-Nuts and other ready-to-eat cereals; Cream of Wheat and Cream of Rice) ■ Culinary products (Jell-O, Cool Whip frozen whipped topping; Miracle Whip; Kraft and Good Seasons salad dressings; A-1 steak sauce; Kraft and Bull's-Eye barbecue sauces; Grey Poupon premium mustards; Claussen pickles; Royal dry packaged desserts and baking powder; Kraft and ETA peanut butter; Vegemite yeast spread; Miracoli pasta dinners and sauces; Shake'N Bake coatings. ■ Convenient meals (DiGiorno, Tombstone, Jack's, and Delissio frozen pizzas; Kraft macaroni & cheese dinners; Minute Rice, Stove Top meal kits; Lunchables)	2001: $33.8 billion 2000: $26.5 1999: $26.8 1998: $27.3 1997: $27.7 1996: $27.9	2001: $1.88 billion 2000: $4.62 1999: $4.25 1998: $4.18 1997: $4.20 1996: $3.36	International sales accounted for about 35% of the total; Kraft had 228 manufacturing plants (147 outside the United States) and 550 distribution centers and depots (176 outside the United States); in the United States, Kraft brands had number one market share ranking based on dollar volume in 23 grocery and food categories; in international markets, Kraft brands were number one based on unit volume in one or more countries in 10 product categories.

continued

Exhibit 6   Continued

Company (Headquarters)	Product Categories/Brands	Sales	Profits	Key Facts
Kraft Foods (U.S.) (continued)	■ Beverages (Maxwell House, General Foods International Coffees, Yuban, Jacobs, Gevalia, Carte Noire, Jacques Vabre, Kaffe, HAG, Grand' Mere, Kenco, Saimaza, and Dadak coffees; Capri Sun, Tang, Crystal Light, Country Time, Royal, Verao, Fresh, Frisco, Q-Refres-Ko, and Ki-Suco powdered soft drinks; Suchard Express, O'Boy, Milka and Kaba chocolate drinks) ■ Cheeses (Kraft, Velveeta, Cracker Barrel, Eden, and Dairylea cheeses; Philadelphia cream cheese, Cheez Whiz process cheese sauce; Knudsen and Breakstone's cottage cheese and sour cream)			
Groupe Danone (France)	■ Dairy (Danone and Dannon yogurts, cream cheese, yogurt-style cheeses, and fresh dairy desserts, Actimel, Galbani, La Serenisima) ■ Bottled water (Evian, Volvic, Aqua, Boario, Crystal Springs, Ferrarelle) ■ Biscuits and crackers (LU, Bagley, Danone, Opavia, Bolshevik, Jacobs, Saiwa, Britannia, Griffin's, several others) ■ Culinary (Lea & Perrins, HP steak sauce, Amoy Asian products) ■ Baby foods (Blédini—France) ■ Cheese (Galbani—Italy)	2001: €14.5 billion 2000: €14.3 1999: €12.9 1998: €13.5 1997: €12.8 1996: €12.1	2001: €132 million 2000: €721 1999: €598 1998: €559 1997: €506 1996: €325	World leader in fresh dairy products (15.1% share worldwide); bottled waters have a #1 market share in several countries and a 10.8% share worldwide; LU crackers was the #1 brand in several countries in Asia-Pacific region; had a 9% market share in biscuits/crackers worldwide. Sales in 120 countries (38% outside the European Union); 148 production plants, 86,000 employees

General Mills/Pillsbury (U.S.)	▪ Flours and baking mixes (Pillsbury, Martha White, Gold Medal, Bisquick, Robin Hood) ▪ Snacks and beverages ▪ Ice cream and dairy (Häagen-Dazs, Yoplait and Trix yogurts) ▪ Desserts (Betty Crocker) ▪ Cereals (Cheerios, Wheaties, Total, Lucky Charms, Trix, Cocoa Puffs, many others) ▪ Frozen and refrigerated foods (Green Giant, Totino's, Pillsbury, Jeno's) ▪ Dinner mixes (Betty Crocker, Hamburger Helper, Farmhouse) ▪ Culinary (Progresso soups, Old El Paso Mexican foods, Green Giant) ▪ Snacks (Chex mix, Nature Valley, Pop Secret) ▪ Foodservice	2002: $7.95 billion 2001: $5.45 2000: $6.70 1999: $6.25 1998: $6.03 1997: $5.61 1996: $5.42	2002: $458 million 2001: $665 2000: $614 1999: $535 1998: $422 1997: $445 1996: $476	The acquisition of Pillsbury in 2001 made General Mills a $13 billion company with a wider and stronger product/brand portfolio; still, about 95% of sales were in the United States.

*Operating earnings—Philip Morris did not report net income separately for its business divisions. Kraft Foods became an independent company through a $5 billion IPO in March 2001.

Source: Compiled by the case researcher from company websites and company documents.

butter to improve the sales of both brands. Back-to-school promotions were also expected to increase the sales of Jif, as were fall bake promotions thought to lead to increases in Crisco's sales. The market shares of Jif peanut butter and Crisco oils along with the shares of their major competitors are presented in the following tables. Crisco held a 65.2 percent share of the shortening market.

PEANUT BUTTER

Brand	Share
Jif	34.9%
Skippy	22.9
Peter Pan	14.5
Private label	17.9
Rest of market	9.8
Total	100.0%

Source: IRI, 52 weeks ending July 2002 (does not include Wal-Mart or club store data).

EDIBLE OILS

Brand	Share
Private label	33.0%
Crisco	22.0
Wesson	20.3
Mazola	15.0
Rest of market	9.7
Total	100.0%

Source: IRI, 52 weeks ending July 2002 (does not include Wal-Mart or club store data).

The company was able to grow the market share of its Smucker-branded products through advertising and other marketing tactics and because of the commitment to those brands by the Smucker family and the company's managers. Whereas larger food companies might be tempted to neglect a brand that, while a market leader, might be a minor contributor to the portfolio's overall performance, Smucker's focused portfolio forced its managers to grow the share of every brand and afforded managers the time to do so. The company's utilization of food brokers to distribute Smucker products to supermarket chains, independent grocers, and wholesale clubs also helped it maintain and grow sales in each category. Smucker's limited portfolio precluded the use of a dedicated sales force to make sales calls to supermarket buyers and to check for proper shelf placement in stores, but food brokers were able to cost-effectively provide superior service to Smucker along with other food companies that they might represent. Smucker maintained similar relationships with brokers selling to food-service channels such as hotels, restaurants, and schools. Most of Smucker's products sold in food-service channels were small, individually sized packs of fruit spreads used to control diners' portions. Brokers were also used when Smucker products were sold to other food companies as fillings or flavorings and helped the company grow market share in such industry segments.

J. M. Smucker's market share growth and sales growth were also aided by the introductions of such products as Simply 100% Fruit in 1987 and Smucker's Light

Preserves in 1990, but Smucker's Uncrustables was the company's most notable new product introduction during the early 2000s. The frozen crustless peanut-butter-and-jelly sandwiches had allowed the company's food-service business unit to grow sales by $16 million during fiscal 2002 as school systems saw the sandwiches as a protein-rich menu item that would be readily accepted by children. The company expected further growth from Uncrustables sales since even though the sandwiches were sold to school systems in 40 states in 2002, a relatively low percentage of school districts in each state purchased the product. Smucker also intended to make Uncrustables available in 55 percent of U.S. retail grocery stores through its food broker distributors in 2003. The company also planned to launch a grilled-cheese version of Smucker's Uncrustables in 2003. Other new products driving revenue growth at Smucker in 2002 were its sugar-free fruit spreads and natural peanut butter products; Twix Magic Shell and Milky Way spoonable ice cream toppings; and Plate Scrapers decorative dessert toppings, which were primarily sold to restaurants. Smucker's jellies, jams, and preserves packaged in squeeze containers had test-marketed well during 2002 and were to be distributed to an expanded market in 2003.

Recent acquisitions also contributed to companywide sales growth with Smucker's three health and natural food brands—R. W. Knudsen Family, Santa Cruz Organic, and After The Fall—experiencing sales increases as the U.S. market for natural and organic products had grown to $28 billion in 2002. The Mrs. Smith's pie business acquired from Philip Morris/Kraft Foods in 1997 was among the Smucker Company's few acquisition failures. Smucker management suggested that the acquisition's lack of success was rooted in the seasonal nature of the pie business (about 80 percent of all pies were purchased in November and December) and the business's outdated manufacturing facilities acquired from Philip Morris. Smucker management chose to divest the business in 1999 after concluding the plants would have required considerable capital investments to adequately improve efficiency and that pie manufacturing varied from fruit spread production and packaging to an extent that would prevent Mrs. Smith's pies from being produced in existing Smucker's plants. For the most part, Smucker management had been very successful in blending the manufacturing operations of its acquisitions with the operations of its various business segments. Exhibit 7 presents a list of Smucker manufacturing facilities in 2002 and products produced at each plant. The Jif and Crisco acquisitions added two facilities to the list—Jif's peanut butter plant in Lexington, Kentucky, and Crisco's oil and shortening plant in Cincinnati, Ohio.

The company's acquisition of International Flavors and Fragrances' formulated fruit and ingredient businesses in 2001 added $15 million to Smucker's 2002 sales and bolstered the company's competitive position in the food ingredients industry, where it supplied fruit filling to such companies as Kellogg's and Groupe Danone, the producer of Dannon yogurts. In 2002, Smucker eliminated low-margin ingredient contracts with food manufacturers that would reduce sales during 2003 and 2004 by $40 to $50 million. The elimination of the less profitable accounts was expected to reduce the industrial segment's earnings by less than $1 million, even though revenues would decrease by as much as $50 million. Acquisitions also aided Smucker's international business unit with the addition of IXL and Allowrie, making Smucker the largest manufacturer of fruit spreads in Australia. Australia and Canada were Smucker's two largest international markets, but the company had achieved some success in Latin America and Mexico, with a 22 percent sales increase in those markets in 2002 alone. At the beginning of 2003, Smucker's products were distributed in more than 45 countries located in Europe, Asia/Pacific, and Latin America.

Exhibit 7   J. M. SMUCKER COMPANY'S PROCESSING AND MANUFACTURING LOCATIONS PRIOR TO ITS ACQUISITIONS OF JIF AND CRISCO

Domestic Manufacturing Locations	Products Produced
Orrville, Ohio	Fruit spreads, toppings, industrial fruit products, Smucker's Snackers
Salinas, California	Fruit spreads, toppings, syrups
Memphis, Tennessee	Fruit spreads, toppings
Ripon, Wisconsin	Fruit spreads, toppings, condiments, industrial fruit products
New Bethlehem, Pennsylvania	Peanut butter and Goober products
Chico, California	Fruit and vegetable juices, beverages
Havre de Grace, Maryland	Fruit and vegetable juices, beverages
West Fargo, North Dakota	Frozen peanut-butter-and-jelly Uncrustable sandwiches

Domestic Fruit Processing Locations	Fruit Processed
Watsonville, California	Strawberries, oranges, apples, peaches, apricots (also produces industrial fruit products and frozen peanut-butter-and-jelly sandwiches)
Woodburn, Oregon	Strawberries, raspberries, blackberries, blueberries (also, produces industrial fruit products)
Grandview, Washington	Grapes, cherries, strawberries, cranberries, apples, boysenberries, blackberries, red raspberries, red currants, and pears
Oxnard, California	Strawberries

International Manufacturing Locations	Products Produced
Ste-Marie, Quebec, Canada	Fruit spreads, sweet spreads, industrial products
Kyabram, Victoria, Australia	Fruit spreads, toppings, fruit pulps, fruit bars
Livingston, Scotland	Industrial fruit products
São José do Rio Pardo, Brazil	Industrial fruit products

Source: J. M. Smucker Company 2002 10 K report.

Selected financial statistics for the company's domestic and international operations are presented in Exhibit 8. The company's sales contribution by product line between 2000 and 2002 is presented in the following table:

Product Category	2002	2001	2000
Fruit spreads	37%	38%	39%
Industrial ingredients	16	15	15
Portion control/food service	11	12	12
Juices and beverages	10	10	10
Toppings and syrups	8	9	9
Peanut butter	7	7	7
Other	11	9	8
Total	100%	100%	100%

Source: J. M. Smucker Company 2002 10 K report.

**Exhibit 8   SELECTED FINANCIAL STATISTICS FOR J. M. SMUCKER COMPANY'S
DOMESTIC AND INTERNATIONAL SEGMENTS, 2000–2002 (IN THOUSANDS)**

	Year Ended April 30		
	2002	2001	2000
Net sales			
Domestic	$590,327	$557,921	$551,324
International	96,821	93,321	90,561
Total net sales	$687,148	$651,242	$641,885
Depreciation			
Domestic	$ 21,838	$ 20,484	$ 19,789
International	2,094	2,037	1,885
Total depreciation	$ 23,932	$ 22,521	$ 21,674
Segment profit			
Domestic	$101,530	$ 87,276	$ 89,570
International	9,949	8,415	10,387
Total segment profit	$111,479	$ 95,691	$ 99,957
Interest income	$ 2,181	$ 2,918	$ 2,706
Interest expense	(9,207)	(7,787)	(3,111)
Amortization expense	(4,625)	(4,400)	(4,524)
Nonrecurring charge	—	−2,152	−14,492
Corporate administrative expenses	(46,681)	(39,443)	(39,371)
Merger and integration costs	(5,031)	—	—
Other unallocated income (expenses)	2,082	−335	234
Income before income taxes and cumulative effect of change in accounting method	$ 50,198	$ 44,492	$ 41,399
Assets			
Domestic	$438,644	$402,021	$399,237
International	86,248	77,083	78,461
Total assets	$524,892	$479,104	$477,698
Long-lived assets			
Domestic	$211,380	$210,222	$207,478
International	33,699	33,640	38,774
Total long-lived assets	$245,079	$243,862	$246,252
Expenditures for additions to long-lived assets			
Domestic	$ 26,371	$ 27,714	$ 26,012
International	2,682	1,671	13,824
Total expenditures for additions to long lived assets	$ 29,053	$ 29,385	$ 39,836
Current assets and liabilities included in businesses acquired, net of cash acquired	125	—	1,460
Total of additions to property, plant, and equipment and businesses acquired, net of cash acquired	$ 29,178	$ 29,385	$ 41,296

Source: J. M. Smucker Company 2002 10 K report.

The addition of Jif and Crisco was expected to change the sales contribution mix of the portfolio as follows:

Product Category	Projected Fiscal Year 2003 Sales Contribution
Fruit spreads	26%
Peanut butter	26
Edible oils/shortening	23
Formulated products	8
Beverages	5
Toppings/syrups	5
Snacks	3
Other	4
Total	100%

Source: J. M. Smucker Company Investor Presentation, September 4, 2002.

The "New" J. M. Smucker Company's Performance during Fiscal 2003

The Jif and Crisco acquisitions created new opportunities for J. M. Smucker, but they also created specific issues that Smucker management was required to address to ensure the smooth integration of the new brands into Smucker's portfolio. During early fiscal 2003, the company had been able to leverage its existing broker network to provide in-store marketing support and to distribute Jif and Crisco to supermarkets. Smucker's managers had also focused on the integration of the Jif and Crisco manufacturing facilities, especially so with Crisco, a very different product than what the company had produced before. The company was still examining ways to leverage raw material synergies between brands in Smucker's expanded portfolio into 2003.

The results of the new J. M. Smucker Company looked promising through the first six months of fiscal 2003. Its revenues had improved by 87 percent, to $641.9 million versus $342.6 million for the first six months of fiscal 2002. Jif and Crisco contributed $260.4 million to the company's revenue increase, but the sale of the company's traditional brands had also grown by 11 percent between second-quarter 2002 and second-quarter 2003. Sales of Smucker's fruit spreads increased by 7 percent during the second quarter 2003, Uncrustables sales were up 16 percent, portion control food-service products were up 10 percent, natural beverages improved nearly 17 percent, international sales had grown by 33 percent, and Jif sales increased by 6 percent during the quarter. The only disappointment was a 2 percent sales decline for Crisco oils and shortening products.

Excluding the costs of the merger, Smucker's net income during its first six months of fiscal year 2003 had grown to $45.1 from $16.3 million during the first six months of fiscal year 2002. The cost of the merger was expected to approximate $10 million in 2003 and $15 million in total. Tim Smucker summed up the company's expected performance for midway through 2003 by stating, "Our goals for the Jif and Crisco businesses during this period were to make sure that we achieved a smooth

Exhibit 9   J. M. SMUCKER COMPANY CONSOLIDATED STATEMENTS OF INCOME, 2000–2002 (IN THOUSANDS, EXCEPT PER SHARE AMOUNTS)

	Year Ended April 30		
	2002	2001	2000
Net sales	$687,148	$651,242	$641,885
Cost of products sold	462,157	443,948	432,993
Gross profit	$224,991	$207,294	$208,892
Selling, distribution, and administrative expenses	$165,172	$155,973	$153,297
Merger and integration costs	5,031	—	—
Nonrecurring charge	—	2,152	14,492
Operating Income	$ 54,788	$ 49,169	$ 41,103
Interest income	2,181	2,918	2,706
Interest expense	(9,207)	(7,787)	(3,111)
Other income—net	2,436	192	701
Income before income taxes and cumulative effect of change in accounting method	$ 50,198	$ 44,492	$ 41,399
Income taxes	19,347	16,294	15,126
Income before cumulative effect of change in accounting method	$ 30,851	$ 28,198	$ 26,273
Cumulative effect of change in accounting method, net of tax benefit of $572	—	(992)	—
Net income	$ 30,851	$ 27,206	$ 26,273
Earnings per common share:			
Income before cumulative effect of change in accounting method	$1.26	$1.11	$0.92
Cumulative effect of change in accounting method	—	(0.04)	—
Net income per common share	$1.26	$1.07	$0.92
Earnings per common share—assuming dilution:			
Income before cumulative effect of change in accounting method	$1.24	$1.10	$0.91
Cumulative effect of change in accounting method	—	(0.04)	—
Net income per common share—assuming dilution	$1.24	$1.06	$0.91

Source: J. M. Smucker Company 2002 10 K report.

integration and then concentrate on stabilizing the businesses and beginning to make the investments needed for future growth. We are doing the right things to help these brands grow steadily and profitably in the long term, including providing greater brand support and consumer marketing, ensuring better retail coverage, and working more closely with our customers."[4]

Income statements, balance sheets, and statements of cash flow for Smucker in 2000–2002 are presented in Exhibits 9 through 11.

Exhibit 10   J. M. SMUCKER COMPANY'S BALANCE SHEETS, 2001—
2002 (IN THOUSANDS)

	April 30,	
	2002	**2001**
Assets		
Current assets		
Cash and cash equivalents	$ 91,914	$ 51,125
Trade receivables, less allowance for doubtful accounts	57,371	55,986
Inventories:		
Finished products	52,817	54,614
Raw materials, containers, and supplies	63,722	59,561
	116,539	114,175
Other current assets	13,989	13,956
Total current assets	$279,813	$235,242
Property, plant, and equipment		
Land and land improvements	$ 16,911	$ 17,684
Buildings and fixtures	87,126	79,862
Machinery and equipment	242,590	247,235
Construction in progress	7,504	17,072
	354,131	361,853
Accumulated depreciation	(191,342)	(190,283)
Total property, plant, and equipment	$162,789	$171,570
Other noncurrent assets		
Goodwill	33,510	33,788
Other intangible assets	14,825	11,848
Other assets	33,955	26,656
Total other noncurrent assets	82,290	72,292
Total assets	$524,892	$479,104

Exhibit 10   Continued

	April 30	
	2002	**2001**
Liabilities and Shareholders' Equity		
Current liabilities		
Accounts payable	$ 32,390	$ 29,967
Salaries, wages, and additional compensation	22,866	15,250
Accrued marketing and merchandising	11,563	8,559
Income taxes	2,078	2,916
Dividends payable	3,979	3,897
Other current liabilities	7,555	7,473
Total current liabilities	$ 80,431	$ 68,062
Noncurrent liabilities		
Long-term debt	$135,000	$135,000
Postretirement benefits other than pensions	14,913	14,224
Deferred income taxes	4,105	4,981
Other noncurrent liabilities	10,299	6,052
Total noncurrent liabilities	$164,317	$160,257
Shareholders' equity		
Serial preferred shares—no par value:		
Authorized—3,000,000 shares; outstanding–none	—	—
Common Shares—no par value:		
Authorized—70,000,000 shares; outstanding—24,869,463 in 2002 and 24,359,281 in 2001 (net of 7,555,113 and 8,065,295 treasury shares, respectively), at stated value	6,217	6,090
Additional capital	33,184	19,278
Retained income	267,793	253,226
Less:		
Deferred compensation	(2,725)	(2,248)
Amount due from ESOP Trust	(8,562)	(8,926)
Accumulated other comprehensive loss	(15,763)	(16,635)
Total shareholders' equity	280,144	250,785
Total liabilities and shareholders' equity	$524,892	$479,104

Source: J. M. Smucker Company 2002 10 K report.

Exhibit 11   J. M. SMUCKER COMPANY'S STATEMENTS OF CONSOLIDATED CASH FLOWS, 2000–2002 (IN THOUSANDS)

	Year Ended April 30		
	2002	**2001**	**2000**
Operating Activities			
Net income	$ 30,851	$ 27,206	$ 26,273
Adjustments to reconcile net income to net cash provided by operating activities:			
Depreciation	23,932	22,521	21,674
Amortization	4,625	4,400	4,524
Nonrecurring charge, net of tax benefit	—	1,313	9,626
Cumulative effect of change in accounting method, net of tax benefit	—	992	—
Deferred income tax expense (benefit)	1,545	2,040	−3,872
Changes in assets and liabilities, net of effect from business acquisitions:			
Trade receivables	(1,217)	5,196	(11,678)
Inventories	(2,063)	17,326	(6,792)
Other current assets	(11)	3,830	(733)
Accounts payable and accrued items	12,483	10,558	(9,174)
Income taxes	25	(1,084)	2,580
Other—net	(3,170)	(6,102)	(157)
Net cash provided by operating activities	$ 67,000	$ 88,196	$ 32,271
Investing Activities			
Additions to property, plant, and equipment	$(23,464)	$(29,385)	$(32,240)
Businesses acquired, net of cash acquired	(5,714)	—	(9,056)
Disposal of property, plant, and equipment	7,060	278	91
Other—net	1,608	1,495	1,387
Net cash used for investing activities	$(20,510)	$(27,612)	$(39,818)
Financing Activities			
Proceeds from long-term debt	—	$ 60,000	$ 75,000
Repayment of short-term debt—net	—	—	(8,966)
Purchase of treasury shares	$ (1,128)	(80,964)	(17,654)
Dividends paid	(15,568)	(16,686)	(17,212)
Net amount received from ESOP trust	364	297	303
Other—net	10,524	5,028	(217)
Net cash (used for) provided by financing activities	(5,808)	(32,325)	31,254
Effect of exchange rate changes on cash	107	(907)	(615)
Net increase in cash and cash equivalents	40,789	27,352	23,092
Cash and cash equivalents at beginning of year	51,125	23,773	681
Cash and cash equivalents at end of year	$ 91,914	$ 51,125	$ 23,773

( ) Denotes use of cash.
Source: J. M. Smucker Company 2002 10 K report.

Endnotes

[1]"Orrville, Ohio, Jelly Maker's Peanut Butter Buy Proves Tasty," *Investor's Business Daily,* January 16, 2002.
[2]Ibid.
[3]"Jif and Crisco to Join Smucker," *Mergers and Acquisitions Journal,* December 1, 2001.
[4]J. M. Smucker Company press release, November 15, 2002.

Diageo, PLC

Armand Gilinsky Jr.
Sonoma State University

Richard Castaldi
San Francisco State University

Wine is a small percentage of our sales, the growth rates are very exciting, and Sterling [Vineyards] will give us a sound platform. But wine is capital intensive and we must be confident we can maximize capital investment and drive an appropriate return for our shareholders.

—Paul Walsh, Chief Executive Officer, Diageo PLC

As a company, if you're looking to invest in spirits or wine, it's spirits every time. I hugely admire what companies like Southcorp are doing, but let me tell you: if they had a decent portfolio of spirits brands, they wouldn't be bothering.

—Jack Keenan, President, United Distillers and Vintners, Diageo PLC

Wine is a very dynamic and attractive segment to Diageo. The premium end of the business is still growing at double-digit rates. There is a lot of demand out there for premium wine, and we expect demand for these wines will continue to be very strong.

—Ray Chadwick, President, Diageo Chateau and Estate Wines

In April 2002, Diageo PLC announced its intent to sell its Glen Ellen and MG Vallejo wine subsidiaries to the Wine Group for $83 million. The sale was to include the Glen Ellen and MG Vallejo brand names and all existing inventory but not the vineyards/facilities of the two wineries. Glen Ellen and MG Vallejo wines typically sold for about $5 to $7 a bottle. These brands did not fit into Diageo's increasing emphasis on marketing premium wine brands that sold for $10 to $15 a bottle and higher. Wine industry observers viewed the sale of Glen Ellen and MG Vallejo as a move toward brand rationalization, that is, allowing Diageo to concentrate its marketing efforts on a smaller number of more upscale brands.

Six months later, in October 2002, Ray Chadwick, president of Diageo Chateau & Estate Wines, reviewed his company's remaining wine portfolio. Diageo Chateau & Estate Wines was based in Napa, California. Chadwick was pondering which, if any, further changes to the portfolio should be made:

The authors were assisted by researchers Dan Dhruva and James Cavanagh, MBA students at San Francisco State University, in preparing the case. The authors gratefully acknowledge a Business and International Education (BIE) grant from the U.S. Department of Education and a matching grant from the College of Business at San Francisco State University in support of this research.

We understand and pay attention to the desires of our consumers. We're constantly evaluating our business. We own over 2,000 acres in the Napa Valley. We have long-term leases on over 300 acres in Napa. That makes us the largest grape grower in the Napa Valley. We are still open to acquiring new vineyards if we can do so at a price that makes sense. The economics have to be right. We are currently looking at several vineyard opportunities in the Napa Valley. I can tell you that we have no plans to sell any of our vineyards at this time. We have a very large vineyard operation in Monterey County, Paris Valley Ranch (approximately 1,500 acres). We have in addition to that probably another 700 acres or so of coastal vineyards in the south coast [of California].

To justify his evaluation and recommendations, Chadwick needed to determine which, if any, synergies could be achieved between his division's premium wine holdings in California and Diageo's holdings of some of the most highly recognized spirits and beer brands in the world. Diageo also owned 34 percent of Moët Hennessy, the wine and spirits unit of French luxury goods maker Moët Hennessy Louis Vuitton (LVMH).

Cost synergy appeared to have become the main driver of growth at Diageo. In 2001 Diageo had sold its Guinness World Records business to a media company, Gullane Entertainment, for $63 million. In a rebranding move to emphasize the Diageo name, the company scrapped its Guinness/UDV unit and folded those operations into a new premium drinks division. Diageo also decided to sell its Pillsbury unit to General Mills for $10.5 billion as part of the company's effort to focus on its spirits, wine, and beer businesses and to shed less profitable operations. The Pillsbury divestiture gave Diageo a 33 percent stake in General Mills.

Diageo's stock price began to rise in response, reaching a 52-week high on the New York Stock Exchange of $55.40 on May 3, 2002. Yet securities analysts over the summer and early fall of 2002 had been progressively downgrading their recommendations on Diageo's stock from "strong buy" to "underperforming, medium risk." See Exhibit 1 for Diageo's stock price chart, 1997–2002, and analysts' forecasts.

Diageo subsequently announced that it has gone back to the drawing board in an attempt to unload its Burger King business (the number two burger chain, after McDonald's, with more than 11,300 locations). Diageo's July 2002 agreement to sell Burger King for $2.26 billion unraveled after a group composed of Texas Pacific Group, Bain Capital, and Goldman Sachs Capital Partners backed out of the deal in November. New suitors reportedly interested in Burger King included Warren Buffett's Berkshire Hathaway, owner of Dairy Queen, although Buffett publicly denied he had an interest in buying Burger King.

Almost one year earlier, Diageo had finally acquired the beverage assets of the Canada-based Joseph E. Seagram Company (Seagram's) in a hotly contested bidding war with rival Allied-Domecq. Following the acquisition of Seagram's liquor and wine portfolio, Diageo became the largest spirits and wine holding company in the world. The acquisition included two major California brands, Sterling Vineyards and Beaulieu Vineyards, as well as importing rights and/or partial ownership in about 200 French wines and champagne, including many estate-bottled French Burgundies; wines from Barton & Guestier (Bordeaux, France); and F. E. Trimbach wines (Alsace, France).

Exhibit 1   Diageo's Stock Price Movements, 1998–2002

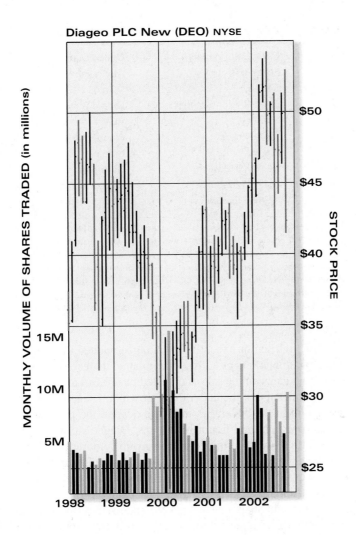

Diageo PLC New (DEO) NYSE

Diageo (NYSE:DEO)	2000	2001	2002E	2003E
P/E ratio	19.9x	17.3x	17.0x	14.3x
Dividend yield	2.8%	3.0%	3.2%	3.4%
ROI	19.3%	20.1%	18.4%	20.7%
Core EPS growth	8.5%	15.1%	1.6%	14.5%

Sources: www.StockCharts.com, accessed October 28, 2002; Diageo company reports, and Salomon Smith Barney estimates as of October 25, 2002.

Exhibit 2   WORLD'S BIGGEST WINEMAKERS, RANKED BY SALES IN CALENDAR YEAR 2000 ($ MILLIONS)

Rank	Company[a]	Country	Wine Sales in 2000
1.	E.&J. Gallo Winery[b]	United States	$1,500
2.	Foster's Group[c]	Australia	818
3.	Seagram[d]	Canada	800
4.	Constellation Brands[e]	United States	712
5.	Southcorp	Australia	662
6.	Castel Frères	France	625
7.	Diageo[f]	Britain	590
8.	Henkell & Sonlein	Germany	528
9.	Robert Mondavi	United States	481
10.	Kendall-Jackson	United States	366

[a]List excludes France's LVMH, which earned more than 75% of its $1.6 billion wine sales in champagne.
[b]Includes Gallo of Sonoma (Healdsburg, CA) with estimated sales of $190 million.
[c]Includes Beringer Blass Wine Estates (Napa, CA) with estimated sales of $440 million.
[d]Includes Seagram Chateau & Estates (Napa, CA) with estimated sales of $273 million.
[e]Includes Franciscan Estates (Rutherford, CA) with estimated sales of $200 million.
[f]Includes Guinness (Rutherford, CA) with estimated sales of $303 million.
Sources: *Business Week*, September 3, 2001, p. 57; *North Bay Business Journal* estimates (June 11, 2001).

Although senior executives at Diageo wanted the conglomerate to be viewed by the financial markets as a growth company, its recent growth in profits had primarily come from gains on the sale of divested businesses and cost savings. Some security analysts predicted that the underlying growth at Diageo would remain low relative to its peer group in the beverages industry, despite the promise of its new ready-to-drink brands based on malt liquor beverages. Diageo's clout in global drinks markets had been continually undermined by the group's poorer performing regional brands. Diageo appeared extremely reluctant to bite the bullet and dispose of these poor-quality assets. For these reasons and others, Diageo's stock price performance had not yet met investors' and investment analysts' expectations.

Diageo and Seagram Chateau & Estate Wines (the acquired Seagram wine brands) had combined estimated wine revenues of nearly $600 million. However, its rivals in the wine industry were ahead or in close pursuit: E.&J. Gallo Winery held the number one position at an estimated $1.5 billion in sales. Other rivals included Foster's Group (Beringer Blass Wine Estates) at $818 million in sales, Constellation Brands at $712 million, Robert Mondavi at $481 million, and Kendall-Jackson Wine Estates at $366 million. See Exhibit 2 for a comparison of the world's largest winemakers, ranked by sales.

Company Background

Based in London, England, Diageo was created in 1997 through the merger of two British companies, Grand Metropolitan PLC and Guinness PLC. Diageo—from the Latin word for "day" and the Greek word for "world"—competed in the food, alcoholic beverages, and fast-food restaurants sectors, although it had publicly stated its intention to exit from all sectors except the beverage industry.

Prior to their 1997 merger, Scottish-based Guinness/United Distillers (Guinness) and London-based Grand Metropolitan (GrandMet) owned beer and hard liquor (spirits) brands. Guinness had well-known beer (Guinness Stout, Bass Ale, and Harp Lager) and spirit brands and experience with distributing products in emerging markets such as Asia and Latin America. Guinness, through its United Distillers (UD) division, also owned whiskey (Johnnie Walker, Bell's), gin (Gordon's, Tanqueray), and various other alcohol brands. GrandMet, through its International Distillers and Vintners (IDV) division, was a holding company with vodka (Smirnoff), liqueur (Bailey's), rum (Malibu), and tequila (through its partnership with the José Cuervo) brands. GrandMet also owned Pillsbury Foods and the Burger King fast-food restaurant chain, enabling it to maintain a sizable presence in the American market.

Both holding companies expected that a consolidation of competing companies in the spirits/beer industry would soon occur and sought acquisitions of related lines of business. In April 1997, George Bull, chairman of GrandMet, and Tony Greener, chairman of Guinness, met in London and reached a tentative agreement to merge the two companies.

Publicly, both companies gave a number of reasons for the merger. The merger would create one of the largest providers of branded food and beverages in the world. The major reason for the merger, though, was the specific benefits, or synergies, to be realized from combining the premium spirits brands of Guinness and GrandMet. Both companies had extensive experience selling and distributing internationally and the combined portfolio of brands covered the entire spirits spectrum. At the time it was consummated, the merger was expected to save £175 million (roughly $263 million at an exchange rate of £1 = $1.50), although this total was later estimated to be £290 (about $435 million). One of the first consequences of the merger was that the spirits divisions were combined to form a new division called United Distillers and Vintners (UDV). Under the new Diageo holding company corporate structure, Guinness Brewing became one division, UDV became another, and Pillsbury and Burger King were combined into a separate food division.

From 1997 to the year 2000, the merger was not received as favorably by the investment community as Diageo had originally hoped. During this period, Diageo's stock price lagged behind the London Stock Index by 20 percent. By 2000, its food division, which had been facing intense price competition, contributed about 35 percent of total company operating profits. The Guinness and UDV divisions contributed the remaining 65 percent of group operating profits. Exhibits 3 through 6 present 1998–2002 financial statements and ratios. Exhibit 7 presents 2000–2002 company segment information by line of business and by geographical region.

Hired two years after the merger, Paul Walsh, Diageo's CEO, stated his intention to focus on the drinks business. See Exhibit 8 for a list of Diageo's portfolio of beverage brands. In 2000, Walsh merged Guinness Brewing with United Distillers and Vintners to create a more focused core of beverages businesses (now named Guinness UDV) upon which to build future earnings growth.

In 2000, Seagram Corporation was in the process of being acquired by Vivendi Corporation. Vivendi was interested in Seagram's entertainment-related assets and made public its plan to sell off Seagram's numerous liquor brands. At this juncture, Diageo already owned 12 of the top 100 spirits brands in the world. In seeking Seagram's liquor brands, CEO Walsh was moving Diageo further along the spirits-oriented strategy.

Meanwhile, Allied Domecq, another British alcoholic beverages conglomerate, joined the chase for ownership of Seagram's valuable drinks brands. Allied Domecq, the number two distiller of alcohol in the world behind Diageo, had already entered

Exhibit 3   DIAGEO PLC, SUMMARY STATEMENTS OF INCOME AND EXPENSES, 1998–2002*

	Fiscal Year Ending June 30				
	2002	**2001**	**2000**	**1999**	**1998**
Turnover (revenues)—continuing operations	$14,741	$12,933	—	$18,716	$29,229
Turnover (revenues)—discontinued operations	2,183	6,299			176
Total turnover (revenues)	16,924	$19,232	$18,010	18,716	29,405
Operating costs	14,444	16,422	15,307	16,309	25,803
Operating profit	2,480	2,810	2,704	2,407	3,602
Share of profits of associates	424	305	296	286	452
Trading profit	2,904	3,115	3,000	2,693	4,054
Disposal of fixed assets	−33	29	8	−16	−3
Sale of businesses—continuing operations	749	42	−255	165	869
Merger expenses	—	—	—	—	141
Sale of businesses—discontinued operations	483	(77)	—	—	452
Utilization of provision	—	—	—	—	415
Total				149	688
Interest payable (net)	599	495	551	514	807
Profit on ordinary activities before tax	3,504	2,584	2,202	2,328	3,934
Taxation on profit on ordinary activities	949	653	608	698	1,510
Profit on ordinary activities after tax	2,555	$ 1,980	$ 1,593	$ 1,630	$ 2,424
Minority interests—equity	−74	$ 65	$ −56	$ −78	$ −111
Minority interests—nonequity	−57	55	−56	−57	−90
Profit for the period	2,426	1,880	1,481	1,495	2,223
Dividends	1,151	1,136	1,082		
Transferred to reserves	1,275	684	399		
Average ordinary shares outstanding—basic		4,779	5,148	5,606	6,447
Average ordinary shares outstanding—diluted		4,784	5,156	5,633	6,598
Year end ordinary shares outstanding		4,828	5,192	5,440	5,938
Earnings per share—basic	$ 0.73	$ 0.54	$ 0.44	$ 0.42	$ 0.57
Earnings per share—diluted	$ 0.73	$ 0.54	$ 0.44	$ 0.42	$ 0.57

Note: Entries for 2001 and 2002 have been restated to account for goodwill from the acquisition of Seagram's drink businesses.

*All quantities converted from £ sterling to dollar amounts in millions except per share amounts.

Source: Diageo annual reports.

into negotiations with Seagram to purchase the Captain Morgan's rum brand. Allied Domecq was consolidating alcohol brands under one corporate umbrella and had already begun to shed some of its core nondrinks businesses, including a doughnut chain in Spain and its pub operations in the United Kingdom.

Exhibit 4   DIAGEO PLC, CONSOLIDATED BALANCE SHEETS, 1998–2002*

	Fiscal Year Ending June 30				
	2002	2001	2000	1999	1998
Intangible assets	$ 8,151	$ 8,028	$8,025	$ 8,232	$ 7,854
Tangible assets, gross	n.a.	7,290	7,231	7,917	7,650
Less: Accumulated depreciation	n.a.	2,795	2,561	2,874	2,655
Tangible assets, net	3,818	4,495	4,670	5,043	4,994
Investments	4,775	2,085	2,270	2,149	2,067
Inventory stocks	3,474	3,348	3,246	3,494	3,715
Debtors due within one year	3,314	2,948	2,799	3,064	3,384
Debtors due after one year	1,815	1,926	1,801	2,047	1,660
Debtors subject to financing arrangements	—	—	59	60	30
Investments					804
Cash at bank and in hand	2,394	2,607	1,613	1,741	4,159
Total current assets	10,997	10,347	9,518	10,406	13,752
Borrowings	5,577	5,098	4,652	6,196	7,849
Other creditors	5,468	4,946	4,969	5,605	5,855
Creditors due within one year	11,045	10,044	9,621	11,801	13,704
Borrowings	5,567	5,651	5,638	5,387	4,808
Other creditors	−74	136	152	159	404
Creditors due after one year	5,640	5,787	5,790	5,546	5,212
Provision for liabilities and charges	1,221	924	1,053		1,171
Minority interest—equity	276	293	256	284	281
Minority interest—nonequity	557	565	615	616	608
Total minority interests	n.a.	858	871	900	889
Called up share capital	1,395	1,481	1,502	1,574	1,892
Share premium account	1,986	1,971	1,950	2,012	1,863
Revaluation reserve	194	206	209	275	316
Capital redemption reserve	4,518	4,431	4,475	4,659	4,772
Profit and loss account	—	−404	−988	−2,131	−1,151
Reserves attributable to equity shareholders	7,607	6,204	5,646	4,814	5,799
Shareholders' funds before minority interest	9,002	7,685	7,148	6,388	7,691
Total capital and reserves	$ 9,834	$ 8,584	$8,019	$ 7,288	$ 8,580

n.a. = not available due to reclassification and reporting of balance sheet entries.

*All quantities converted from £ sterling to dollar amounts in millions.

Source: Diageo annual reports.

Diageo prevailed in the battle for Seagram's, and in December 2000, Diageo and the French company Pernod Ricard agreed to jointly purchase Seagram's alcohol assets and divide them between the two companies. Diageo paid $5 billion, while Pernod Richard contributed $3.15 billion to the deal. Diageo stood to gain the Seagram whiskey brand (Seven Crown) and Seagram wine assets. These wine assets included Sterling Vineyards (Napa Valley), Monterey Vineyard, and Mumm Cuvée Napa. It also

Exhibit 5   DIAGEO PLC, CONSOLIDATED CASH FLOWS, 1998–2002

	Fiscal Year Ending June 30				
	2002	2001	2000	1999	1998
Net operating cash flow	$3,012.0	$3,414.0	$2,108.0	$ 589.0	$3,201.7
Net investing cash flow	2,262.0	(785.0)	(59.0)	191.0	1,498.4
Net financing cash flow	(2,676.0)	(1,435.0)	(2256.0)	(552.0)	(4071.7)
Net change in cash	(253.0)	150.0	(208.0)	227.0	628.3
Depreciation and amortization	459.0	573.0	553.0	535.0	806.7
Capital expenditures	878.0	(659.0)	(1059.0)	(599.0)	(953.4)
Cash dividends paid	(1,157.0)	(1,088.0)	(1,036.0)	(1,054.0)	(1,813.4)

*All quantities converted from £ sterling to dollar amounts in millions.
Source: Diageo annual reports and 10K reports.

Exhibit 6   DIAGEO PLC, SELECTED FINANCIAL RATIOS, FISCAL YEARS 1998–2001

	2001	2000	1999	1998
Profitability				
Return on total equity (%)	25.61	25.11	20.55	13.22
Return on assets (%)	9.13	8.03	7.02	6.64
Return on invested capital (%)	12.15	10.92	9.45	8.90
Cash earnings return on equity (%)	36.66	38.05	21.36	21.66
Cost of goods sold to sales (%)	75.05	70.67	66.24	59.72
Gross profit margin (%)	20.29	26.12	30.34	36.53
Operating profit margin (%)	19.64	16.20	18.49	18.50
Pretax margin (%)	13.88	10.61	12.88	14.05
Net margin (%)	11.18	8.22	9.49	9.03
Activity				
Assets per employee ($)	$344,496	$333,540	$350,909	$381,522
Assets turnover (x)	0.64	0.78	0.64	0.57
Inventory turnover (x)	3.72	3.97	3.00	2.56
Net sales to gross fixed assets (x)	2.18	2.61	2.07	2.12
Capital expenditures percent sales (%)	4.00	4.61	5.38	6.42
Leverage				
Total debt percent common equity (%)	152.17	149.29	187.77	169.56
Long-term debt percent common equity (%)	80.29	82.10	87.74	64.76
Long-term debt percent total capital (%)	41.74	42.17	43.38	36.19
Equity percent total capital (%)	51.98	51.37	49.44	55.89
Total debt percent total assets (%)	43.83	42.82	45.65	44.41
Total capital percent total assets (%)	55.41	55.83	49.17	46.86
Liquidity				
Quick ratio (x)	0.50	0.43	0.39	0.56
Current ratio (x)	0.85	0.80	0.71	0.88
Cash ratio (x)	30.54	20.90	20.82	41.04
Receivables percent current assets (%)	28.85	32.17	33.81	22.00
Inventories percent current assets (%)	37.01	42.06	41.80	30.72
Inventories days held (days)	96.71	90.78	120.16	140.58

Source: Diageo annual reports.

Exhibit 7   DIAGEO PLC. SEGMENT ANALYSIS, 2002, 2001, AND 2000 (MILLIONS, BRITISH £ STERLING)

	Fiscal Year 2002			Fiscal Year 2001			Fiscal Year 2000		
	Revenue	Operating Profit	Total Assets	Revenue	Operating Profit	Total Assets	Revenue	Operating Profit	Total Assets
Line of Business									
Premium drinks	£ 8,704 77%	£1,768 83%	£8,275 85%	£ 7,580 59%	£1,432 67%	£ 5,123 48%	£ 7,117 60%	£1,286 65%	£ 4,972 49%
Quick-service restaurant	1,123 10	160 8	1,430 15	1,042 8	177 8	1,432 13	941 8	202 10	1,356 13
Packaged food*	1,455 13	190 9	— —	4,199 33	518 24	4,077 38	3,812 32	492 25	3,734 37
Total	£11,282 100%	£2,118 100%	£9,705 100%	£12,821 100%	£2,127 100%	£10,632 100%	£11,870 100%	£1,980 100%	£10,062 100%
Geographical Area									
Europe	£ 4,204 37%	£ 679 32%	£3,886 40%	£ 4,073 32%	£ 614 29%	£ 3,763 35%	£ 4,181 35%	£ 585 30%	£ 3,804 38%
North America	4,717 42	866 41	4,705 48	6,401 50	1,001 47	6,193 58	5,639 48	956 48	5,696 57
Asia Pacific	1,001 9	231 11	726 7	990 8	206 10	246 2	886 7	170 9	183 2
Latin America	639 6	193 9	134 1	776 6	188 9	216 2	697 6	165 8	252 3
Rest of world	721 6	149 7	254 3	581 5	118 6	214 2	467 4	104 5	127 1
Total	£11,282 100%	£2,118 100%	£9,705 99%	£12,821 100%	£2,127 100%	£10,632 100%	£11,870 100%	£1,980 100%	£10,062 100%

*Discontinued operations in 2002.

Note: Percentages may not add up to 100% due to rounding.

Source: Diageo annual reports.

Exhibit 8   DIAGEO'S PORTFOLIO OF DRINKS BUSINESSES AND PRIORITY BRANDS

Global Priority Brands in 2002	
Brand	**Recent News**
Johnnie Walker	Net sales up 4%
Baileys	Volume up 10%
J&B	Volume up 5% in Spain
Tanqueray	Relaunched with marketing spend up 11%
Smirnoff Red	Volume up 7%
Smirnoff flavours	Now 1 million cases; Ice up 98%
Cuervo	U.S. market share up 1.1%
Guinness	Creating a platform for future growth
Captain Morgan	Growing volume and market share in the United States

Local Priority Brands in 2002 and 2003			
Brand	**Market**	**Brand**	**Market**
Archers	Great Britain	Dimple/Pinch	Korea
Beaulieu Wines	United States	Goldschlager	United States
Bells	Great Britain	Gordons gin	Great Britain
Bells	South Africa	Gordons gin	United States
Buchanan's	United States	Harp	Ireland
Buchanan's	Venezuela	Old Parr	Japan
Budweiser	Ireland	Red Stripe	Jamaica
Bundaberg rum	Australia	Romana Sambuca	United States
Cardhu	Spain	Rumple Minze	United States
Carlsberg	Ireland	Smithwicks	Ireland

Added for 2003			
Brand	**Market**	**Brand**	**Market**
Cacique	Spain	Seagram's 7	United States
Crown Royal	United States	Seagram's VO	United States
Malta	Africa	Sterling Vineyards	United States
Myers's Rum	United States	Tusker	Kenya
Pilsner	Kenya	Windsor Premier	Korea

Source: Diageo's presentation to Securities' Analysts and Investors, London, September 5, 2002.

included numerous wine brands with which Seagram had import agreements, such as Barton & Guestier (France) and San Telmo (Argentina). Industry analysts predicted that many of Seagram's remaining smaller brands would then be divested.

A large stumbling block to completing the deal was the U.S. Federal Trade Commission (FTC). Even though regulators in Europe and Canada (Seagram's home country) had approved the deal, the FTC was concerned that Diageo would have a monopoly over the U.S. rum market if the deal went through. On October 23, 2001, the members of the FTC voted to seek a preliminary injunction to block the sale. Joe Simmons, the director of the FTC's bureau of competition, said at the time, "This will create a dangerous likelihood of reduced competition and higher prices for consumers of rum." The FTC's reasoning was that Diageo would own the second largest rum producer in the United States (Seagram's Captain Morgan brand) and the third largest (Diageo's Malibu brand). The FTC indicated that Diageo would probably have to sell one of its rum brands in order to finalize the Seagram purchase. In a press release following the FTC announcement, Paul Walsh stated, "We are encouraged by the FTC's willingness to have further discussions."

In late October 2001, Diageo completed the sale of its Pillsbury unit to General Mills, and plans were already under way to spin off its Burger King unit by summer 2002. Diageo received a 33 percent minority stake in the newly merged General Mills and Pillsbury as well as $4.5 billion in cash. Despite intense focus on what it now called its "global priority" brands, Diageo had not yet succeeded in mitigating its high (relative to the industry) financial and operating leverage, vestiges of the 1997 merger. However, some industry analysts remained skeptical that Diageo wasn't yet completely drinks/alcohol focused. After the Pillsbury deal was announced, Morgan Stanley Dean Witter beverage analyst Alexandra Oldroyd remarked, "People are disappointed that [Diageo] didn't get out of the food [sector] altogether." Walsh rebutted Oldroyd's criticism by pointing out that the General Mills cash-and-stock deal was the only one available since "not many companies have $10.5 billion in cash."

On December 21, 2001, the FTC gave its final approval to Diageo to complete the Seagram deal, based on Diageo's promise to sell its Malibu Rum brand. Commenting on the FTC's decision, Paul Walsh said, "Last summer we announced Diageo's strategic realignment behind premium drinks. Our strategy is to focus on our priority brands in their most important markets." In February of 2002 Diageo sold Malibu rum to its rival, Allied Domecq, for $795 million. Diageo also sold one of Seagram's wine brands, Mumm Cuvée Napa, to Allied Domecq for $39 million. By the end of the wheeling and dealing, Diageo had strengthened its position in the rum market and had also procured significant wine assets in terms of wineries, brands, and export rights.

Overview of the Wine Industry

Wine, the German poet Goethe once wrote, "rejoices the heart of men, and joy is the mother of virtue." Wine has been a part of civilization for thousands of years. One legend that is believed to have arisen in 3500 B.C. described how a tasting of accidentally fermented grape juices turned King Jamshid of Sumer and thus the entire kingdom into wine lovers. Regardless of the validity of legends concerning the origins of wine, grape growing and winemaking were essentially the same in 2002 as they had become by the time of the Roman Empire (220 A.D.). Selected vines were planted and cared for, grapes harvested and crushed, and grape juice transformed into wine through the process of fermentation and then blending, bottling, and labeling. Over the centuries, grape growers and winemakers developed small refinements and improvements in the procedure so as to help the natural process along.

Wine is a complex beverage. It contains so many natural substances that scientists are still discovering new facts about it (including the purported health benefits of red wine with regard to preventing heart disease, known as the French paradox). Its complexity has accounted for the vast number of producers in the United States and around the world, and the great variety of wines found in the marketplace. According to the *Adams Wine Handbook,* there are more producers of wine than any other beverage product.

Unlike the production of beer or spirits beverages (e.g., whiskey, vodka, rum, gin), wine production is primarily an agricultural pursuit. A winemaker could really only further improve the quality of the wine by using better-quality grapes. A bad grape crop (e.g., due to weather or pest infestation) could result in a shortage of supply and inconsistent quality in the year-to-year vintages. On the other hand, a glut of grapes due to a bountiful harvest would alleviate supply shortages but not always guarantee consistency of quality.

Spirits and beer production were mostly process-related. A better technical process in the efficiency of distilling, for example, could lead to larger quantities being produced as well as improved taste and perceived quality of the final product. Supply and demand imbalances in raw materials and ingredients had little effect on quality and quantity of production, due to the longer shelf lives of both raw materials inputs (e.g., grains, yeast, water) and production outputs (e.g., beer, whisky, gin).

The nature and circumstances of wine, spirits, and beer consumption could be varied as well. Wine consumption was historically part of daily life in Mediterranean countries. Wine was consumed with the cuisine of the area, and the two complemented each other. In other countries, however, wine was seldom a part of mainstream culture. The markets of Japan, East Asia, and India consumed little wine, and future consumption in those areas was confounded by the fact that traditional wine varieties were not known to be well suited to the diverse cuisines of those regions. Hard liquor (whiskies) and beer dominated alcohol consumption in the United States. In the United States in particular, a strong lobby of anti-alcohol groups, along with other publicity regarding the effects of alcohol on health and public safety, were considered by some industry observers to have had a lasting negative impact on the sale and consumption of wine, beer, and spirits. Anti-alcohol groups advocated stringent labeling and distribution requirements for all alcoholic beverages.

The U.S. Wine Industry

The U.S. wine industry was composed of approximately 1,500 wineries in all 50 states; however, it was highly concentrated, with the top 10 wineries accounting for 70 percent (by volume) of U.S. production, according to the 1999 *Adams Wine Handbook*. California dominated the U.S. wine industry with over 800 wineries, which accounted for more than 90 percent of the wine produced in and exported by the United States. Washington, Oregon, and Idaho, had attracted approximately 200 wineries and were developing an export presence and a reputation for quality wines.

During the 1990s several major trends emerged in the U.S. wine industry: (1) consolidation of the industry's "three-tier" distribution network (winery–wholesaler–retailer); (2) market segmentation due to consumers' "trading up" from inexpensive jug wines to premium-priced "varietal" wines, such as Chardonnay, Merlot, and Cabernet Sauvignon;[1] and (3) the emergence of global markets for wines, notably the increasing share of foreign imports.

Distribution Channels

Wine was sold through a three-tier distribution system. Wineries (the first tier) or importers sold wine to wholesalers (the second tier), who provided legal fulfillment of wine products to local retail businesses (the third tier) within a certain state. Wine was a controlled substance, and laws in each state differed regarding how wine could be sold. Typically, wine passed through the second tier via wholesalers and distributors, making direct shipping to retailers or selling wine through the Internet and wine-buying clubs difficult or impossible in all but 13 states. Thus, access to wholesale distribution channels was considered by wineries to be critical. Meanwhile, second-tier distribution channels were consolidating due to the advantages of scale and scope afforded to larger distributors, and due to the fact that there was similar consolidation under way in the third tier, primarily on the retail (off-premises) side.

The third tier of the distribution system consisted of retail and nonretail outlets. According to *Adams Wine Handbook,* supermarkets, convenience stores, club stores, mail-order and Internet retailers, specialty stores, and wine clubs accounted for 78 percent of total sales volume. Supermarkets alone accounted for 41 percent of retail wine sales and were very influential in wine distribution. They were dominant in food and drink retailing and made one-stop shopping an appealing concept for consumers. Furthermore, supermarkets had considerable bargaining leverage with wholesalers. The role of specialty stores in wine distribution diminished due to the increasing power of supermarkets. Specialty stores' share of retail wine sales was about 23 percent in 1998. Nevertheless, specialty stores were not likely to disappear soon because they provided superior customer service. Moreover, their sales staff had extensive knowledge of wines. Specialty stores also carried specialty brands and limited production labels, attracting wine connoisseurs and enthusiasts. On-premises sales via nonretail outlets such as restaurants, hotels, and airlines accounted for the remaining 22 percent of wine volume in the United States, according to *Adams Wine Handbook.* See Exhibit 9 for an estimated breakdown of percentage sales for each distribution channel by country.

Market Segmentation

"Table" wines were those with 7–14 percent alcohol content by volume and were traditionally consumed with food. This was in contrast to other wine products such as sparkling wines (champagnes), wine coolers, and fortified wines, which were typically consumed as stand-alone beverages. Table wines that retailed at less than $3.00 per 750-milliliter bottle were generally considered to be generic or "jug" wines, while those selling for more than $3.00 per bottle were considered "premium" wines.

Premium wines generally had a vintage date on their labels. This meant that the product was made with at least 95 percent of grapes harvested, crushed, and fermented in the calendar year shown on the label and used grapes from an appellation of origin (e.g., Napa Valley, Sonoma Valley, Central Coast).[2] Within the premium table wine category, a number of market segments emerged, based on retail price points. "Popular premium" wines generally fell into the range of $3.00–$7.00 per bottle, while "premium" wines retailed for $7.00–$10.00 and "superpremium" wines retailed for $10.00–$15.00. The "ultrapremium" category sold for $15.00–$30.00 per bottle. Any retail price above $30.00 per bottle was considered "luxury premium." See Exhibit 10 for wine market segmentation by price point.

The Wine Institute estimated that 1999 U.S. wine market retail sales had reached $18 billion, growing from $11.7 billion in 1990. The U.S. wine market ranked 3rd in the world behind France and Italy. However, the United States ranked 30th in the world in per capita consumption of wine in 1999. The greatest concentration of table wine consumers was in the 35-to-55 age bracket. About the same proportion of men and women consumed wine. While all income levels consumed wine, higher income was associated with greater wine consumption. In 1998, adults in families earning over $75,000 annually represented 18.7 percent of the population and 31.4 percent of the

Exhibit 9   PERCENTAGE OF WINE MOVING THROUGH VARIOUS DISTRIBUTION CHANNELS IN 2000

	HORECA*	Supermarkets	Specialists	Other†
Western Europe				
Austria	26%	41%	4%	30%
Belgium	44	39	7	10
France	28	38	19	14
Greece	30	36	20	14
Germany	20	43	7	30
Italy	14	34	8	44
Netherlands	12	62	21	5
Portugal	10	81	5	6
Spain	57	33	7	4
United Kingdom	20	59	18	2
Americas				
Argentina	15	10	2	75
Canada	24	5	65	6
Chile	45	26	14	14
United States	22	41	23	14
Other				
South Africa	34	28	34	3
Australia	57	15	19	9
Japan	61	7	17	15

*HORECA = Hotels, restaurants, and cafés.
†Other includes direct sales, mail orders, corner and food shops.
Source: *Euromonitor.*

Exhibit 10   U.S. CONSUMERS' WINE PURCHASES IN FOOD STORES IN 2000

ACNielsen/Adams Category	Volume Share	Case Volume Change (000)	Volume % Change	Revenue % Change
Total wine	100%	1,266	3%	10%
Up to $3	39	−920	−4	−4
$3 to $7	41	539	3	3
$7 up to $10	13	1,298	22	24
$10 up to $14	5	468	23	25
$14 and over	2	146	18	24

Sources: Gomberg-Fredrikson & Associates' data, compiled from ACNielsen/Adams.

domestic table wine consumption. Still, according to the *Adams Wine Handbook,* barely more than 10 percent of the adults in the United States consumed 86 percent of all wine sold. See Exhibit 11 for wine consumption patterns in the United States by year, 1981–2000, and Exhibit 12 for a table comparing wine consumption in the top 10 wine-consuming nations in 2000.

Exhibit 11   U.S. WINE CONSUMPTION, 1981–2000

Year	Total Wine per Resident	Total Wine, Millions of Gallons	Total Table Wine, Millions of Gallons
2000	2.01 gallons	565	505
1999	2.02	551	482
1998	1.95	526	466
1997	1.94	520	461
1996	1.89	500	439
1995	1.77	464	404
1994	1.77	459	395
1993	1.74	449	381
1992	1.87	476	405
1991	1.85	466	394
1990	2.05	509	423
1989	2.11	524	432
1988	2.24	551	457
1987	2.39	581	481
1986	2.43	587	487
1985	2.43	580	378
1984	2.34	555	401
1983	2.25	528	402
1982	2.22	514	397
1981	2.20	506	387

Source: www.wineinstitute.org.

Exhibit 12   TOP 10 WINE-CONSUMING NATIONS, 2000

Country	Wine Consumption (million liters)	Share of World Consumption
France	3,290	15.0%
Italy	3,080	14.0
USA	2,140	9.8
Germany	1,956	8.9
Spain	1,450	6.6
Argentina	1,276	5.8
United Kingdom	915	4.2
China (inc. Taiwan)	553	2.5
Russia	550	2.5
Romania	521	2.5

Source: G. Dutruc-Rosset, extracted from the *Report on World Vitiviniculture*. Presented at the World Congress of the OIV in Adelaide, October 12, 2001.

Global Markets

By 2000, the United States had become the second largest market for exported wine and the fourth leading producer of wine in the world. In 2000, U.S. wine exports to 164

Exhibit 13   TOP 10 GRAPE-PRODUCING NATIONS, RANKED BY GRAPE
             PRODUCTION, 2000

Country	Grape Production (million tons)	Share of World Production
Italy	8,871	14.2%
France	7,627	12.2
United States	6,792	10.9
Spain	6,641	10.6
Turkey	3,400	5.4
China (including Taiwan)	3,013	4.8
Iran	2,300	3.8
Argentina	2,191	3.5
Chile	1,900	3.0
Germany	1,408	2.5
Rest of world	18,266	29.1
World total	62,409	100.0%

Note: percentages may not add up to 100% due to rounding.

Source: G. Dutruc-Rosset, extracted from the *Report on World Vitiviniculture.* Presented at the World Congress of the OIV in Adelaide, October 12, 2001.

countries totaled $560 million, of which more than 90 percent came from California. Wine was produced commercially in over 60 countries, with 23 percent (by volume) of the wine produced in the world being exported to international markets, according to *Wines & Vines.* Leading wine producers included the Old World wineries in France, Italy, and Spain, which were also the leading exporters. So-called New World producers—such as the United States, Australia, Chile, Argentina, and South Africa—had been making both production and export inroads globally over the past few decades. For example, France, Italy, and Spain all exported more than 25 percent of the wine they produced; Australia exported over 40 percent, and Chile exported over 80 percent of its production. Many observers attributed Australia and Chile's high rates of growth in exports to the comparatively smaller size of their home markets. See Exhibits 13, 14, and 15 for year-2000 comparisons among wine-producing nations, ranked by grapes produced, volume of wine produced, and volume of wine exported.

Until the mid-1990s, the U.S. wine market remained largely a domestic industry, with some imports from France, Italy, and Spain competing with U.S. wineries. By 1999, however, imports had risen to 20 percent of the U.S. market, seven percentage points above 1995, according to *Wine Business Monthly.* Australian and Chilean wines began making rapid inroads into the U.S. market. For example, from 1995 to 1999, Australia increased the value of its exports to the United States by 243 percent and Chile by 152 percent. Since 1995, the unfavorable balance of trade for wine in the United States had increased by 78 percent. Tariffs and trade barriers played a pivotal role in obstructing U.S. wineries' access to various country markets.

Wine exports from the United States nevertheless grew consistently, from a base of $137 million in 1990 to $548 million in 1999, according to the U.S. Department of Commerce. Also, the U.S. wine industry enjoyed the highest rate of increased wine exports (19.3 percent) in 1998, among the major wine producing countries listed in the *2000 World Vineyard, Grape, and Wine Report.* At the same time, U.S. wineries also

Exhibit 14   WORLD'S TOP 10 WINE-PRODUCING NATIONS, RANKED BY
             VOLUME, 2000

Country	Wine Production (million liters)	Share of World Production
France	5,754	20.9%
Italy	5,162	18.8
Spain	4,113	15.0
United States	2,210	8.0
Argentina	1,254	4.6
Germany	985	3.6
Australia	859	3.1
South Africa	695	2.4
Portugal	669	2.4
Chile	667	2.4
Rest of world	5,123	18.8
World	27,491	100.0%

Note: percentages may not add up to 100% due to rounding.
Source: G. Dutruc-Rosset, extracted from the *Report on World Vitiviniculture*. Presented at the World Congress of the OIV in Adelaide, October 12, 2001.

Exhibit 15   TOP 10 EXPORTERS OF WINE IN THE WORLD, 2000

Country	Wine Exports (million liters)	Share of World Exports
Italy	1,780	27.5%
France	1,508	23.3
Spain	865	13.4
United States	297	4.6
Australia	285	4.4
Chile	270	4.2
Germany	254	3.9
Portugal	210	3.2
Moldavia	152	2.3
South Africa	139	2.1
Rest of world	714	11.0
World	6,474	100.0%

Note: percentages may not add up to 100% due to rounding.
Source: G. Dutruc-Rosset, extracted from the *Report on World Vitiviniculture*. Presented at the World Congress of the OIV in Adelaide, October 12, 2001.

faced increasing threats to their domestic market share due to globalization in the wine industry. *Wines & Vines* reported in 1999 that the United States had only 4.2 percent (by volume) of the world export wine market, while producing 8 percent (by volume) of the wine produced in the world. The U.S. wine industry exported only 13 percent of the wine it produced, while other countries had more intensely developed their export markets. Ten U.S. wineries accounted for more than 89 percent of exports. Nearly 50 percent of U.S. wineries exported their products.

The leading U.S. exporter by volume was E.&J. Gallo, accounting for about half of U.S. exports and more than four times the volume of its nearest export competitor. E.&J. Gallo exported approximately 13 percent of its total production. U.S. wineries typically exported only a small percentage of their production. Wente Vineyards was a notable exception. Wente had made exports a cornerstone of its long-term strategy, as 60 percent of its annual case sales were in 147 different country markets.

By 2001, the superpremium and ultrapremium market segments had become highly fragmented, composed of hundreds of individual, small to large wine-producing operations, all competing to produce the most acclaimed wines each year. Although the largest among these producers held advantages in scale and capital, the smallest were able to compete by consistently producing high-quality wines in limited quantities (known in the industry as "on-allocation"). On-allocation wines often gained critical acclaim from wine enthusiasts, in part because of their scarcity. Smaller wine producers, however, remained at a disadvantage when trying to compete for grape sources against larger, better-financed competitors, such as Foster Group's Beringer Blass Wine Estates, Robert Mondavi Corporation, Kendall-Jackson, Sebastiani Vineyards, E.&J. Gallo, and Constellation Brands' Canandaigua division. Many of these rival firms owned portfolios of brands; invested in winemaking facilities and vineyards across California and abroad; and produced wines across the price spectrum of the premium, superpremium, and ultrapremium market segments. The ability of a winery to produce brands in multiple segments appealed to distributors and retailers, who were in turn hoping to sell broad product lines to consumers.

Due to the globalization of markets and the creation of the European Union, trade barriers were falling worldwide. The worldwide consolidation trend accelerated among wineries and distributors. For example, Allied Domecq (United Kingdom), BRL Hardy (Australia), Brown Forman Corporation (United States), Constellation Brands (United States), Fosters Group (Australia), and Southcorp (Australia) had all courted larger premium wineries in Northern California, such as Buena Vista and Kendall-Jackson, for acquisitions. Wine industry analysts anticipated further consolidation in the wine industry as large wine and alcoholic beverage conglomerates continued to acquire smaller winery operations across national borders, in order to gain access to premium and ultrapremium brands, as well as access to the growing markets for those brands.

Competition

Diageo Chateau & Estates Wines competed with two major types of businesses: stand-alone wineries and conglomerates. Diageo's primary stand-alone winery competitors in the United States included publicly traded Robert Mondavi and the privately held Kendall-Jackson, E.&J. Gallo, and a host of small to medium-sized wineries primarily based in Northern California. Large conglomerate competitors included Allied Domecq, Brown-Forman's Wine Estates division, Constellation Brands' Canandigua division, Fortune Brands, Foster's Group's Beringer Blass Wine Estates division, Moët Hennessy Louis Vuitton (LVMH), Southcorp, and UST (formerly known as U.S. Tobacco). Comparative historical financial data for many of Diageo's publicly traded competitors in the alcoholic beverages industry are shown in Exhibits 16 and 17.

Since the end of Prohibition in 1933, the jug wine segment had been almost completely dominated in both the U.S. and global markets by E.&J. Gallo, a family-owned

Exhibit 16 SELECTED FINANCIAL AND OPERATING HIGHLIGHTS OF GLOBAL ALCOHOL AND BEVERAGE CONGLOMERATES, 1999–2001

Company	Headquarters Location	Sales ($ millions) 2001	2000	1999	Net Income ($ millions) 2001	2000	1999	ROE 2001	2000	ROA 2001	2000
Allied-Domecq[a]	Bristol, England	$4,318	$6,154	$ 3,948	$516	$476	$114	117.7%	N/A	12.7%	N/A
Brown-Forman	Louisville, KY	2,180	2,009	2,134	233	202	218	19.6	20.8%	19.3	19.3%
Constellation Brands, Inc.	Fairport, NY	3,154	2,340	1,497	136	97.3	77.4	14.4	15.8	3.9	3.3
Fortune Brands	Lincolnshire, IL	5,678	5,579	5,844	385	(891)	(138)	18.9	−6.2	7.5	−2.3
Foster's Group[b]	Australia	2,244	1,874	1,656	256	236	203	12.2	18.5	9.0	12.8
Moët Hennessy Louis Vuitton (LVMH)[c]	Paris, France	1,168	8,589	10,909	10	696	680	0.2	10.3	2.0	8.4
Southcorp[b]	Australia	1,375	1,441	1,554	118	168	11	15.2	N/A	N/A	N/A
UST	Greenwich, CT	1,670	1,548	1,512	492	442	469	84.6	163.3	24.4	26.8

N/A = Not available.

[a]Converted from British £ sterling to U.S. dollars at a rate of £1 = U.S. $1.50.

[b]Converted from Australian dollars to U.S. dollars at a rate of $1 Australian = U.S. $0.55.

[c]Converted from euros to U.S. dollars at a rate of €1 = U.S. $0.95.

Sources: Company reports; *Value Line*; and www.WSRN.com, accessed October 25, 2002.

Exhibit 17 SELECTED STOCK PRICE AND FINANCIAL DATA FOR PUBLICLY TRADED U.S. ALCOHOL BEVERAGE COMPANIES, 2002

Stock	Ticker Symbol	Recent Stock Price	Price/ Earnings Ratio (×)	12-Month Earnings Per Share	30-Day Price Change	1-Year Price Change	Beta	Dividend Yield	Stock Market Capital- ization ($ million)	Return on Equity	Pretax Margin	Long- term Debt to Capital
Brown-Forman Corporation	BF.B	$75.00	23	$3.29	13%	23%	0.44	1.9%	$ 2,963	18.3%	17.8%	2.8%
Chalone Wine Group	CHLN	8.65	62	0.14	8	−10	0.25	Nil	104	2.8	6.5	38.6
Constellation Brands	STZ	25.50	14	1.82	0	19	0.30	Nil	1,994	17.5	8.2	53.6
Diageo PLC (ADS)	DEO	46.14	15	2.98	−8	15	0.39	3.1	39,346	24.8	13.4	40.5
Robert Mondavi Corporation	MOND	31.86	14	2.21	6	−1	0.82	Nil	305	6.1	9.3	41.0

Source: Compiled by casewriters in October 2002 from statistics prepared by Richard Joy, *Standard & Poor's Rankings*.

wine business. However, during the 1980s, large alcoholic beverage companies, such as Canandaigua and the Wine Group, entered and competed with E.&J. Gallo in the jug wine market segment. Although Modesto, California-based E.&J. Gallo was still the single largest wine producer in the world, accounting for about 45 percent of California wine sales, it had failed to capitalize on changes in consumer demand toward a preference for premium wines. In recent years, E.&J. Gallo, like many other jug wine producers, had put increasing strategic emphasis on the premium wine market, opting to develop and launch new E.&J. Gallo brands with grapes grown on its 2,300 acres of prime vineyards in Sonoma County, acreage acquired to supply the development of new premium and ultrapremium brands.

Besides the wine companies, several large food and beverage conglomerates, such as Nestlé, Pillsbury, Suntory, PepsiCo, and Coca Cola, entered the premium market by acquiring premium to ultrapremium wineries in the 1970s. However, during the 1980s, each of these food and beverage companies divested their wine holdings, choosing instead to focus on their core businesses. The beneficiaries of these divestitures were the wine and alcoholic beverage companies that continued to build their portfolios of wine brands. For example, while Diageo and Allied Domecq owned a host of other diversified businesses, Constellation/Canandigua focused primarily on alcoholic beverages and related products such as bottled water. All three firms, however, were firmly rooted in distilled spirits, and continued to expand their wine businesses.

Diageo's Chateau & Estates division faced intense global competition in the premium and ultrapremium wine segments. Rival beverage conglomerates such as Brown-Forman, Foster's Group, and Constellation/Canandaigua were expanding their wine portfolios through acquisitions and partnership arrangements. Diageo's multibrand rivals had historically expanded their wine portfolios through acquisitions of independent wineries as well as purchases of and majority interests in the beverage divisions of other conglomerates. In 2000 and 2001, several rivals began divesting those satellite businesses that diverted resources from their core beverage businesses; for instance, Allied Domecq sold the majority of its food operations. Exhibit 18 presents a comparison of portfolios and recent strategic moves by several major competitors in the wine industry.

At the wine industry's annual trade conference in Sacramento, California, in January 2002, several industry experts predicted that the wine industry would continue to grow despite the challenges of economic uncertainty, consolidation, and oversupply of grapes. The experts opined that the accelerating trend of worldwide consolidation in the producer and trade segments would be more than offset by several factors. These included the continuing increase in the number of small wineries, a fundamental increase in consumer demand, the increasing affluence of the wine-buying public, and the results of decade-long efforts directed toward improving quality in production, sales, and service. Vic Motto, of Motto Kryla, Fisher, a wine industry consultant, remarked:

> Globalization has created a world market with a trend towards worldwide normalization of taste and stylistic standards. Global communication networks have also created the potential for small brands to access the same consumers as large ones. However, no one has succeeded in building a global brand—yet.

Exhibit 18 BRAND PORTFOLIOS AND RECENT STRATEGIC MOVES OF DIAGEO'S MAJOR WINE INDUSTRY COMPETITORS

Company	Portfolio Brands—Wine	Other Portfolio Brands	Annual Wine Production	Recent Strategic Moves
Allied Domecq	Clos du Bois, Callaway Coastal, Atlas Peak, William Hill, Bodegas Balbi, Graffigna & Ste Sylvie, Montana, Marques de Arienzo, Harveys, Cockburn's, La Ina, Mumm and Perrier-Jouet.	*Spirits:* Ballantine's, Beefeater, Kahlua, Sauza, Stolichnaya, Tia Maria, Maker's Mark, Courvoisier Canadian Club *Fast food:* Dunkin' Donuts, Baskin-Robbins and Togo's	Atlas Peak: 40,000 cases; 500 acres owned Callaway: 340,000 cases; 40 acres owned, 605 leased or controlled Clos du Bois: 1.4 million cases; 640 acres owned, 160 leased or controlled	Unsuccessfully bid to acquire Seagram's drinks businesses assets in 2001.
Constellation (Canandaigua)	Almaden, Arbor Mist, Franciscan Oakville Estate, Simi, Estancia, Talus, Taylor, Vendange	*Spirits and beer:* Paul Masson brandy, Corona Extra, Modelo Especial, St. Pauli Girl, Alice White, Black Velvet, Fleischmann's, Schenley, Ten High, Stowells of Chelsea	30 million cases; 765 acres owned, 2,600 leased or controlled.	Acquired Ravenswood Estates (Sonoma, CA) for $148 million in cash and assumed debt in July 2001.
E.&J. Gallo	E.&J. Gallo (Modesto, CA): Gallo, Thunderbird, Carol Rossi, Bartles & Jaymes Gallo of Sonoma (Healdsburg, CA): E.&J. Gallo Estate, Gallo of Sonoma, Anapamu, Marcelina, Rancho Zabacho, Indigo Hills	None	E.&J. Gallo (Modesto, CA): 90 million cases (est.) Gallo of Sonoma (Healdsburg, CA): 1 million cases (est.); 3,000 acres	Is world's largest wine producer and leading U.S. wine exporter, selling in 85 countries; wines also account for over 25% of all U.S. wine sales; exports one million bottles annually to the French market; plans to create first-mover advantage in the Indian wine market.
Kendall-Jackson	Kendall-Jackson, Pepi, La Crema, Edmeades Estate, Camelot, Tapiz, Villa Arceno, Calina	None	4 million cases; 12, 000 acres	Launched new Australian line, Yangarra Park in 2001; in May 2001, rejected several takeover bids, including one by BFC; also lost five-year battle with Gallo over alleged theft of trade secrets.
Robert Mondavi	Robert Mondavi Winery, Robert Mondavi Coastal, Woodbridge, La Famiglia de Robert Mondavi, Byron, Arrowood, Vichon Mediterranean, Opus One, Caliterra, Luce	None	Case volume unknown; 7,730 acres	Formed joint ventures with producers in France, Chile, and Italy; created a $10 million wine country attraction in 2001 at Disney's California Adventure theme park; began shift from vineyard development to production—internal grape supply expected to rise from 7% to 20% by 2004.

Sources: Dow Jones Interactive Online, accessed October 25, 2002, and *Wines and Vines' 2001 Annual Buyers' Guide.*

Exhibit 19 RAY CHADWICK'S BIOGRAPHY

Ray Chadwick

President, Diageo Chateau & Estates

Chadwick was appointed president of Diageo's wine operations in December 2001. At that time he assumed responsibility for the integrated wine operations of Guinness North America and Seagram Chateau & Estate Wines. Previously, Chadwick served as Executive Vice President and Chief Financial Officer of the Seagram Chateau & Estate Wines Company, where his responsibilities included the overall direction of the finance function, long range and strategic planning, international sales, business development, information services, and environmental affairs. Chadwick served concurrently as Managing Director of Barton & Guestier, S.A., and had functional responsibility for the finance function at the Seagram Beverage Company. Chadwick first joined Seagram in 1974 and has worked in a variety of roles, including market research, sales and finance. He also spent time in London in an international marketing role for Brown-Forman. Chadwick served as integration leader when The Seagram Classics Wine Company and Seagram Chateau and Estate Wines Company were merged in 1996. He served as co-integration leader during the merger of Diageo and Seagram wine operations in 2001, which led to the formation of Diageo Chateau & Estate Wines. Chadwick holds Bachelor of Arts and Master of Arts degrees from the University of Virginia, as well as an M.B.A. from the University of Chicago. He also studied in France for several years, including a year in Bordeaux under the auspices of the Fulbright program. He currently serves on the Board of Directors of the Wine Institute.

Source: www.aboutwines.com.

Future Uncertainties

At the time of Ray Chadwick's promotion in December 2001 to president of the Chateau & Estates wine division, another Diageo executive had said publicly:

> With Ray Chadwick's rich and long history in the wine business, he will bring a thorough understanding of what it takes to be successful in a competitive industry. Additionally, Ray has a command of the intricate financial issues, as well as the strategic vision critical to leading a portfolio that will contain some of the finest wines in the world. Key to being successful in the wine industry is how well you build and maintain relationships.

As Chadwick considered changes in the portfolio for his Chateau & Estates wine division, many observers still questioned Diageo's wisdom of entering the wine industry at all, with its lower profit margins (compared to spirits and beer) and the industry's increased reliance on an uncertain grape supply and consumer demand. Exhibit 19 presents Chadwick's biography.

In a January 2002 interview with a reporter at *Wine Business Insider*, Chadwick spoke of Diageo's philosophy behind entering the wine business:

> Wines are a very attractive consumer segment with a strong growth potential. Wine is definitely a complement to Diageo's strategy to be a total beverage alcohol company. Diageo is very focused on the consumer and we think about "consumer need" states and what types of beverage alcohol consumers tend to drink in these various need states. There's one need state which is the dinner table: wine tends to be the choice when people choose to consume beverage alcohol. When people sit at the table and they eat, they tend to use wine.

Still, some observers argued that the wine market required a completely different set of skills from Diageo's other beverages brand businesses, and that wine was more about vintage than brand, so there would be little transfer of skills in the Seagram acquisition. An anonymous critic, quoted in *Marketing Week,* said:

> I would question the long-term growth potential of a company that moves from being a conglomerate with lots of diverse interests to being a business focused purely on high-value drinks. The alcoholic drinks market is not a high growth industry—the only way to grow is to take market share from someone else.

However, other observers believed that global trends favored Diageo. As beverages analyst Alan Gray of ING Barings Charterhouse Securities pointed out in the same *Marketing Week* article, "There are growth and cost benefits to come—Diageo can sell the acquired brands through its own distribution network."

In an interview with *Wine Business Insider* in January 2002, Chadwick commented on Diageo's future relationships with its distributors:

> Let me address this very directly. [We want] to develop a more efficient and effective way of bringing [our] total portfolio of products—including wines—to market. We want to create a new way of working with our distributors and brokers. Over the coming months we will begin a process with our distributors and brokers to develop this new kind of relationship. And we can foresee the possibility of adjustments to our distributor network in the next year or eighteen months, but that process is just beginning. In broad strokes, the new relationship will be more collaborative, more fact-based, more long-term, and more focused on delivering greater value to consumers and customers: understanding the consumer better, understanding customers and consumers better, for example, working with our distributors to really fine tune our channel strategy. I can honestly say to you that no decisions have been made yet.

Despite all the economic, social and political turmoil that marked 2001, global retail dollars from the sale of wine, beer and diversified spirits increased approximately 3.5 percent to $127.3 billion (from $122.8 billion in 2000), according to *Beverage Dynamics.* Spirits retail sales increased 2.9 percent, from approximately $37.3 billion to more than $38.4 billion. Wine retail sales grew about 4.4 percent, from $18.1 billion to just under $19.0 billion. Beer dollar volume sales also rose, up 3.7 percent from $67.4 billion in 2000 to almost $70.0 billion in 2001. Although the percentage gains over the previous year were smaller in 2001 than in 2000, consumption trends favored higher-end products.

A few months before the 2002 sale of the Glen Ellen brand to the Wine Group, Chadwick explained the segmentation of Diageo's wine brands to *Wine Business Insider:*

> Super-premium wines are growing really well. The $12–$15 category continues to be a really attractive category for us. The economy and the events of September 11 have caused some business to shift from on-premise to off-premise. People are staying home but they're still drinking wine at home with friends at the table. The off-premise sector has been strong. On-premise was relatively weak for a while and has begun to come back in many areas. There's no doubt that the low end of the business has been soft, but again, that $12–$15 category—where we've got some really good brands—continues to be very strong. BV [Beaulieu Vineyards] and Sterling are two of the great Napa Valley brands. We've got a stable of other California brands: Glen Ellen, the Monterey Vineyard, Blossom Hill, Mumm Cuvée Napa. On the European side, we have a world-renowned collection of great labels from Bordeaux and Burgundy, and

we also have B&G French wines. And our other French relationships—most notably Trimbach from Alsace—we expect will continue to grow.

Question marks still remained regarding Diageo's future in a global market where economic uncertainties increased the difficulty of forecasting and planning future growth. Much of the Chateau & Estates division's success would depend on the basic skills of marketing: well-timed innovation, informed analysis of social and demographic trends, and leveraging strong distribution, particularly in the United States. Chadwick wondered how to manage the wine brands more profitably, leveraging Diageo's formidable resources and history of successfully marketing other beverages. In the January 2002 *Wine Business Insider* interview, Chadwick discussed the future of his portfolio of wine brands:

> BV will remain BV and Sterling will remain Sterling. Each will operate independently and each will retain their unique character. Within our portfolio, they complement each other. BV was founded 100 years ago, it is high end in certain appellations, notably Carneros and Rutherford. Georges de Latour (the late founder) is an icon in the industry. Sterling was the first Napa Valley Winery to bottle a vintage-dated varietal—Merlot—again, it has a unique set of vineyards. Our plan is to have a focused wine division with dedicated sales and marketing teams. We're also going to have dedicated finance, human resources and operations departments within the wine division. Any overlap is minimal. As you may be aware, Guinness UDV markets wines together with spirits. And those individuals that focused on wines are being considered for opportunities within Chateau & Estates. We're still putting the company together, but we intend to have a very, very strong and large organization. We are very alert to opportunities to expand our current business, but the economics have to be right. We have to provide returns to our shareholders.

Still, Chadwick wondered, should Diageo lead or follow its chief rivals into further diversification outside of its current French and U.S. wine holdings?

Endnotes

[1]In 1983, laws in the United States had taken effect controlling what wineries could put on their labels. The term *varietal wine* meant one variety of grape—the name of a single grape could be used if not less than 75 percent of the wine was derived from grapes of that variety, the entire 75 percent of which was grown in the labeled appellation of origin.

[2]*Appelation of origin* was a general term for the label designations that indicated geographic origins of bottled wines that met specific legal requirements. Any wine, at least 75 percent of which was made of grapes grown in the area designated on its label and that conformed to the laws and regulations relevant there, was entitled to a country, state, or county appellation. *§ Title 27 Part 4 of the Code of Federal Regulations. Washington, DC: Bureau of Alcohol, Tobacco and Firearms, Regulatory Agency, United States Department of the Treasury.*

Bibliography

"2000 California Wine Sales Up—For Seventh Consecutive Year." www.thewineman.com, March 15, 2001.
ABC News Radio. "Foster's to Expand Its Wine Arm," August 29, 2001. *Adams Wine Handbook.* New York: Adams Business Media, 1999.
"All Merge: Consolidation Strikes the Australian Wine Industry." www.industrysearch.com, October 5, 2000.
"Allied Domecq PLC." www.hoovers.com, accessed February 15, 2002.
Brandes, R. "Growth Brands," *Beverage Dynamics* 114, no. 2 (March 2002), pp. 14–23.
"Care to See the Wine List? Global Drinks Firms Ready to Buy." www.industrysearch.com/, May 28, 2001.
De Luca, J. "The outlook for the California wine industry in 2002," Presentation to the North Bay Economic Outlook conference, Rohnert Park. CA, February 2002.
"Diageo Confirms Pillsbury Sale." http://news.bbc.co.uk, July 17, 2000.
"Diageo Plans Napa HQ," *North Bay Business Journal,* March 17, 2002, p. 1.
Echikson, W., et. al. "Wine War." *Business Week,* September 3, 2001, pp. 54–60.
Fish, T., and J. Gaffney. "Sale of Seagram's Wines & Spirits Blocked by U.S. Regulators." www.winespectator.com, October 24, 2001.
Foster's Group Inc. Annual reports 2000 and 2001.

"Foster's Group Limited." www.hoovers.com, accessed February 15, 2002.

Gaffney, J. "Diageo Sells Glen Ellen for $83 Million." www.winespectator.com, March 18. 2002.

"Globalization, Who's Leading the Way?" *Wines & Vines,* April 2002.

Gomberg-Fredrikson. *1999 Annual Wine Industry Review.* Gomberg, Fredrikson & Associates, 703 Market Street, Suite 1602, San Francisco, CA 94103.

Lamb, R., and E. Mittleberger. *In Celebration of Wine and Life.* New York: Drake, 1984.

Lucas, G. "Small Wine Merchants Uncork Anger." *San Francisco Chronicle,* April 16, 2002, p. A13.

Mansson, P-H. "Who Really Controls the Vineyards of France." *Wine Spectator,* November 30, 2001, pp. 89–92.

Manuel, D. "What's a Premium Wine?" www.supermarketguru.com, November 19, 2001.

Motto Kryla Fisher. "High-End California Wine Sales Increase 10% in 2001," Unified Grape Symposium, Sacramento, CA, January 2002.

"Q&A with Diageo Chateau & Estates President Raymond Chadwick," *Wine Business Insider,* January 2002.

Quackenbush, J. "Diageo Plans Napa HQ." *North Bay Business Journal,* January 7, 2002, p. 1.

Rachman, G. "The Globe in a Glass." *The Economist,* December 18, 1999, pp. 91–105.

Radio National. "The Business Report: Fosters' Wine on the March," January 2001.

"Regional Spotlight: Australia." www.winepros.com, accessed February 15, 2002.

Robert Mondavi, Inc., press release, July 25, 2001.

Simon, A. *The Noble Grapes and the Great Wines of France.* New York: McGraw-Hill, 1957.

Standard & Poor's. *Industry Surveys: Alcoholic Beverages & Tobacco,* March 1, 2001.

"The Brave New World of Wine" http://www.itsfood.com/, accessed January 15, 2002.

"Topsy-Turvy Down Under." http://WineSquire.com, accessed February 15, 2002.

"Turning to the Bottle." *Marketing Week,* November 1, 2001, p. 25.

"US Clears $8 Billion Seagram Deal." http://news.bbc.co.uk, December 19, 2001.

LVMH's Diversification Strategy into Luxury Goods

John E. Gamble
University of South Alabama

In 2002, Moët Hennessy Louis Vuitton (LVMH) was the world's largest luxury products company, with annual sales of 12.2 billion euros (€) and a business portfolio that included some of the most prestigious brand names in wines and champagnes, fashion, watches and jewelry, and perfumes and cosmetics. The French conglomerate's business portfolio also included two prestigious Parisian department stores, two chains of duty-free shops, a retail cosmetics chain, e-commerce businesses, and a variety of French media properties. Even though no one "needed" LVMH's products—a magnum of its 1985 Dom Pérignon Rose champagne retailed for $925, its Givenchy gowns could exceed $15,000, and the finest TAG Heuer watch carried a retail price of about $58,000—the company's products were desired by millions across the world. CEO Bernard Arnault suggested that desire for the company's products "in some way, fulfills a fantasy. You feel as if you must buy it, in fact, or else you won't be in the moment. You will be left behind."[1]

The company's business portfolio began to take shape in 1987 when Louis Vuitton, known worldwide for its purses and luggage, merged with the maker of Moët & Chandon champagne and Hennessy cognac. LVMH's present lineup of star luxury brands was forged by Bernard Arnault, who became CEO of the company in 1989 and promptly set about acquiring such names as Christian Dior, Fendi, Donna Karan, Givenchy, Celine, Christian Lacroix, and Marc Jacobs in fashion and leather goods; TAG Heuer and Ebel in watches; and Le Bon Marche and Sephora in retailing. By 2002 Arnault had assembled a portfolio of nearly 50 luxury brands, which he categorized as a collection of star brands and rising stars—brands that Arnault believed "speak to the ages" but, at the same time, feel intensely modern.[2] Arnault suggested that star brands were not only timeless and modern but also highly profitable and rapidly growing. He portrayed star brands as illogical since, in most cases, the quality of timelessness was in conflict with innovation, and rapid growth usually was at odds with high profits. When asked about the managerial challenges of developing star brands, Arnault stated, "Mastering the paradox of star brands is very difficult and rare—fortunately. In my opinion, there are fewer than ten star brands in the luxury world."[3]

Arnault believed LVMH's collection of star brands such as Moët & Chandon, Krug, Louis Vuitton, Givenchy, and Parfums Christian Dior and its rising stars like Donna Karan, Christian Lacroix, and Kenzo would lead to long-term corporate advantage since star brands had staying power. "The brand is built, if you wish, for eternity. It has been around for a long time; it has become an institution. Dom Pérignon is a perfect example. I can guarantee that people will be drinking it in the next century. It was created 250 years ago, but it will be relevant and desired for another century and beyond that."[4]

Arnault's rapidly growing portfolio had allowed LVMH to grow from approximately €2.5 billion in 1990 to €12.2 billion in 2001. However, the company's sales growth slowed in late 2001 and early 2002 as the effects of the September 11, 2001, terrorist attacks on New York City and Washington, D.C., and a lingering global recession contributed to a worldwide decline in the purchase of luxury goods. In addition, LVMH management issued three profit warnings during its fourth quarter 2001 prior to announcing a net income of €10 million for fiscal 2001. As LVMH's stock price reflected the company's slowing sales growth and weak profitability, its investors began to call for Arnault to evaluate the company's portfolio for possible restructuring. A summary of LVMH's financial performance between 1993 and 2001 is presented in Exhibit 1. A time line of its brands is presented in Exhibit 2.

Company History

LVMH's history as an enterprise is traced to 1743 when Moët & Chandon was established in the Champagne Province in northeastern France. Moët & Chandon not only became among France's premier brands of champagne but was also sought after outside of France, with exports accounting for a large percentage of its sales by the 20th century. The company first diversified in 1968 when it acquired Parfums Christian Dior and a 1971 merger between Moët & Chandon and Champagne Mercier combined France's two best-selling brands of champagne. The company changed its name to Moët-Hennessy when it again merged in 1971; this time with Jas Hennessy & Company, the world's second largest producer of cognac.

The company diversified further in 1987 as the French government launched into an era of privatization to promote economic growth and reduce the country's excessively high unemployment rate. The families who controlled Moët-Hennessy and leather goods designer Louis Vuitton saw a merger between their two companies as their best strategy to prevent the companies from becoming takeover targets of large international corporations making investments in France. The $4 billion merger that created LVMH allowed the heirs of the two companies' founders to retain control of the new entity with a combined ownership of 50 percent of outstanding shares. The new ownership structure also placed Hennessy heir and chairman Alain Chevalier in the position of chairman of LVMH, while Vuitton family member and company president Henry Racamier became LVMH's director general.

The new company became France's 40th largest company, with total revenues in 1987 of FF 13.1 billion ($2.1 billion) and a portfolio of such well-known luxury brands as Veuve Clicquot, Moët & Chandon, and Dom Pérignon champagnes; Canard-Duchêne wines; Hennessy cognac; Christian Dior and Givenchy perfumes and cosmetics; Georges Delbard (France's leading grower of roses); and Louis Vuitton leather handbags and luggage. On the day the merger was consummated, LVMH chairman Alain Chevalier also signed an international distribution agreement with British brewer Guinness PLC to improve the distribution of the company's champagne and cognac brands in Asia and the United States. The joint venture with Guinness called for both firms to acquire interlocking interests of about 10 percent of each company's shares

Exhibit 1   SUMMARY OF LVMH'S FINANCIAL PERFORMANCE, 1993–2001 (IN MILLIONS OF EUROS, EXCEPT PER SHARE AMOUNTS)

	2001	2000	1999	1998*	1997*	1996*	1995*	1994*	1993*
Net sales	€12,229	€11,581	€8,547	€6,936	€7,322	€4,748	€4,539	€4,264	€3,630
Income from operations	1,560	1,959	1,547	1,184	1,269	1,071	1,111	1,037	856
Operating margin	12.8%	16.9%	18.1%	17.1%	17.3%	22.6%	24.5%	24.3%	23.6%
Net income before amortization of goodwill and unusual items	€ 334	€ 846	€ 738	€ 525	€ 742	€ 679	€ 640	€ 559	€ 453
Earnings per share before amortization of goodwill and unusual items	€ 0.68	€ 1.75	€ 1.53	€ 1.07	€ 1.52	€ 1.39	€ 1.31	€ 1.16	€ 0.99
Net income	€ 10	€ 722	€ 693	€ 267	€ 690	€ 563	€ 617	€ 979	€ 545
Net income per share	€ 0.02	€ 1.49	€ 1.44	€ 0.55	€ 1.41	€ 1.16	€ 1.26	€ 2.03	€ 1.18
Dividend per share including tax credit	€ 1.13	€ 1.13	€ 1.02	€0.927	€0.927	€0.828	€0.782	€0.711	€0.542
Cash flow from operations	€ 919	€ 1,214	€1,051	€ 571	€1,163	€ 851	€ 904	€ 935	€ 700
Capital expenditures	984	857	574	381	310	n.a.	n.a.		
Stockholders' equity	8,701	8,512	7,781	6,316	6,179	5,486	4725	4,625	3,567
Long-term debt	5,402	3,498	3,085	1,425	1,382	675	573	794	1,180

n.a. = Not available.

*French franc to euro conversion rate at 6.5595.

Source: LVMH annual reports.

Exhibit 2   HISTORY OF LVMH BRANDS

16th Century

1593	Château d'Yquem champagne

18th Century

1729	Ruinart champagne
1743	Moët & Chandon champagne
1763	Hine cognac
1765	Hennessy cognac
1772	Veuve Clicquot champagne
1780	Chaumet watches and jewelry

19th Century

1828	Guerlain perfumes
1843	Krug champagne
1846	Loewe leather goods
1852	Le Bon Marché department store
1854	Louis Vuitton leather goods
1858	Mercier champagne
1860	Heuer watches
1865	Zenith watches
1868	Canard Duchêne champagne
1870	La Cote Desfossés publications
1870	La Samaritaine department store
1895	Berluti leather goods

20th Century

1911	Ebel watches
1925	Fendi fashion and furs
1925	Omas writing instruments
1930	Acqua di Parma perfumes
1936	Dom Pérignon champagne
1936	Fred fashion
1945	Celine fashion
1947	Parfums Christian Dior perfumes
1948	Emilio Pucci fashion
1952	Connaissance des Arts magazine
1952	Givenchy fashion

1957	Parfums Givenchy perfumes
1960	DFS duty free shoppers
1963	Miami Cruiseline Services duty free shoppers
1970	Etude Tajan fine art auction house
1970	Kenzo fashion
1972	Mount Adam wine
1973	Domaine Chandon champagne
1973	Sephora cosmetics retailing
1974	Investir magazine
1976	Cape Mentelle wine
1979	Art & Auction magazine
1983	Radio Classique radio network
1984	Donna Karan fashion
1984	Marc Jacobs fashion
1984	Newton wine
1984	Thomas Pink fashion
1985	Benedom–CD Montres watches
1985	Cloudy Bay wine
1985	La Tribune de l'Economie magazine
1987	Christian Lacroix fashion
1987	Kenzo Parfums perfumes
1987	Laflachère toiletries/household items
1989	Make Up For Ever cosmetics
1991	Fresh cosmetics
1991	StefanoBi leather goods
1995	Hard Candy cosmetics
1995	BeneFit Cosmetics
1996	Bliss cosmetics and spas
1996	Urban Decay cosmetics
1997	Chandon Estates wine
2000	eLuxury Internet luxury retailer

21st Century

2001	LVMH/De Beers joint venture diamond retail stores

Source: LVMH website.

and accounted for nearly one-fourth of LVMH and Guinness profits within the joint venture's first year.

The success of the LVMH-Guinness joint venture led Alain Chevalier to propose that Guinness purchase an additional 10 percent interest in LVMH to further protect the company from possible foreign raiders. The growing relative importance of the company's wine, champagne, and spirits businesses and the proposal for increased ownership of LVMH shares by Guinness became worrisome to Racamier and other Vuitton family members who believed the company's core business should center on fashion and leather goods. To fortify the company's focus on haute couture, Racamier in mid-1988 asked Bernard Arnault (the owner of the Christian Dior, Celine, and Christian Lacroix brands) to purchase shares of LVMH and join forces with Vuitton heirs in their disagreement with Chevalier.

Thirty-nine-year-old Bernard Arnault had only recently become known among France's business elite, since only four years before he was building condominiums in Florida for his family's modest real estate and construction firm. Arnault returned to France in 1984 and purchased nearly bankrupt Agache-Willot-Boussac—a state-owned conglomerate of retailing, fashion, and manufacturing. The French government sold Arnault the business at far below book value in expectation that privatization would bring an entrepreneurial spirit to the company's collection of businesses and ultimately expand employment by Agache-Willot-Boussac. Arnault saw his mission differently than the French government and sold the assets of Agache-Willot-Boussac's poor-performing businesses and retained its profitable businesses, of which Christian Dior was the most notable. Within three years of the company's acquisition by Arnault, Agache-Willot-Boussac (renamed Financiere Agache by Arnault) had earned $112 million on revenues of $1.9 billion. In 1987, Arnault leveraged Financiere Agache's cash flow from operations and liquidated assets to expand its presence in the fashion industry with the purchase of Celine, a fashion and leather goods company, and the launch of a new fashion brand headed by France's hottest young designer, Christian Lacroix.

After meeting with LVMH's director general, Henry Racamier, Arnault also met with the company's chairman, Alain Chevalier, before forming a joint venture with Guinness PLC to purchase 37 percent of LVMH's shares. Guinness was receptive to Arnault's proposal to form the joint venture since it assured the British company's management that its highly profitable distribution agreement with LVMH would remain intact, despite the feud between the Hennessy and Vuitton clans. Financiere Agache held a 60 percent interest in the joint venture, while Guinness held 40 percent. The controlling interest in the Guinness-Agache joint venture made Bernard Arnault the largest shareholder of LVMH by November 1988 and gave him a blocking minority of shares. After becoming LVMH's largest shareholder and asked of his intentions to bring about management changes at the company, Bernard Arnault commented that he approved of Chevalier's strategies, but added: "His problem is that he is not a major shareholder. In the businesses I manage, I'm the principal shareholder; and that helps me control the situation."[5]

Bernard Arnault became LVMH's president in January 1989 and chairman in mid-1990 after prevailing in an 18-month legal battle with Henry Racamier, who had petitioned the court to invalidate a portion of Arnault's stake in LVMH. Upon becoming chairman, Arnault launched an aggressive plan to transform LVMH into France's largest company. Arnault dismissed LVMH's top management, folded Agache's brands and assets into LVMH, and began making rapid acquisitions to expand the company's portfolio of luxury brands. Many French executives resented Arnault's business tactics and questioned his motives in becoming the head of LVMH. An ex-LVMH officer called Arnault "an asset shuffler, a raider, a French Donald Trump," and after a meeting with Arnault, the chairman of Yves Saint Laurent characterized the LVMH chief as "friendly—like a bird of prey that might want to devour you."[6] Bernard Arnault dismissed such criticism by asserting, "I'm going to run LVMH for the long term. We'll become an even stronger No. 1. My image will change."[7]

LVMH under Bernard Arnault

When Bernard Arnault became president of LVMH in January 1989, the company was the world's leading luxury products group with revenues of FF 16.4 billion (approximately €2.5 billion) and net income of FF 2.0 billion (approximately €300 million) in 1988. The company's business portfolio included champagnes and wines, cognac and spirits, luggage, leather goods and accessories, perfumes and beauty products, and horticulture. The 1988 revenue and operating income contributions and capital expenditures for each business unit are presented in the following table. The table also presents each business unit's percentage of sales to countries outside of France.

	Champagne and Wines	Cognac and Spirits	Luggage, Leather Goods and Accessories	Perfumes and Beauty Products	Horticulture
Sales (in millions)	FF 4,876	FF 4,083	FF 3,530	FF 3,735	FF 218
% from outside France	72%	98%	84%	74%	40%
Income from operations (in millions)	FF 1,042	FF 1,348	FF 1,458	FF 594	FF (202)
Capital expenditures (in millions)	FF 272	FF 114	FF 214	FF 170	N/A

N/A = Not available.
Source: LVMH 1988 annual report.

LVMH's champagne and wines business unit was the global leader in premium champagnes, with some of the oldest and most prestigious brands in the world. Dom Pérignon was arguably the best-known brand of champagne, Ruinart was the world's oldest champagne company, and Mercier was France's best-selling brand of champagne. Moët & Chandon, Canard-Duchêne, Veuve Clicquot Ponsardin, and Henriot rounded out LVMH's portfolio of centuries-old champagne brands. LVMH's champagne and wine division also included the respected Napa Valley sparkling wine producer Domaine Chandon. LVMH's cognac and spirits business, like its champagne and wine business unit, possessed two of the most prestigious brands worldwide with Hennessy and Hine—both founded in the mid-1700s and consistently recognized by connoisseurs for quality.

Louis Vuitton accounted for the largest share of LVMH's luggage, leather goods, and accessories division's sales, with market leading positions in luggage and travel accessories worldwide. Louis Vuitton's luggage had been popular since the mid-1800s, when Vuitton's monogrammed products first became available to affluent travelers who visited his Paris store. In 1988 Louis Vuitton leather products were available in 118 fine department stores in Europe, the United States, and Asia. Loewe was a prestigious Spanish brand that earned the distinction of Supplier to the Royal Household in

1905 and had since become noted for fine ready-to-wear leather and textile apparel, handbags, and travel accessories. Loewe also marketed a fragrance line in 1988.

LVMH's perfumes and beauty products division was composed of three different houses: Parfums Christian Dior was internationally renowned for its quality, innovation, and prestige and was the leading prestige brand of fragrance in France; the brand was also among the fastest growing in the United States and held the number one position in Western Europe. Parfums Givenchy was among the most successful prestige brands in the United States and had extended its product line to include cosmetics in 1988. RoC specialized in hypoallergenic cosmetics and was endorsed by dermatologists in Europe and the United States. RoC was the number one hypoallergenic cosmetic brand in Europe and was expected to increase sales both in Europe and the United States as LVMH expanded its distribution beyond pharmacy channels.

LVMH's horticulture group held a majority interest in Georges Delbard—one of the world's most respected producers of high-quality rose bushes and fruit trees. The company utilized a direct sales force to market its plants to horticulture professions and operated 12 Jardineries Delbard retail stores to make its products available to consumers in France.

LVMH's Rapid Growth under Bernard Arnault

LVMH's rapid portfolio diversification began shortly after Arnault gained a controlling percentage of company shares when it acquired Givenchy Couture haute couture, men's and women's ready-to-wear fashions, and accessories in November 1988. LVMH's management had been working to unite its Parfums Givenchy with Givenchy Couture since 1987 and agreed on terms with Hubert de Givenchy just prior to Arnault's becoming president of LVMH in January 1989. In 1990 Arnault purchased an additional interest in Loewe and purchased all assets of Pommery—the largest vineyard in the Champagne Province and producer of champagnes since 1860. Arnault's most ambitious target during 1990 was Guinness PLC. Arnault increased LVMH's share in Guinness from about 12 percent to 24 percent in what was suggested by outsiders as an attempt to make LVMH the world's largest alcoholic beverage seller with more than $5.5 billion in sales and a vast international distribution network.

Arnault abandoned his quest to gain a controlling stake in Guinness in 1994 when Guinness management agreed to a stock swap between LVMH and the British brewer that netted LVMH $1.9 billion in cash. Arnault had initiated a few small acquisitions of fashion and spirits businesses between 1990 and 1994, but the $1.9 billion cash infusion that resulted from the company's Guinness stock swap allowed Arnault to pursue his pledge to shareholders that LVMH was going to buy more luxury companies in cosmetics, perfume, fashion, and retailing.[8] Arnault initially focused on L'Oréal, a leading manufacturer and marketer of cosmetics with 1993 sales of $6 billion, and French drug manufacturer Sanofi, which bought Yves Saint Laurent in 1993. However, neither company was acquired by LVMH. Arnault brought additional fashion and fragrance brands to the company's portfolio and diversified outside of luxury goods with the purchase of three of France's leading financial and business publications—*Investir, La Tribune Desfosses,* and *L'Agefi.* Arnault also used the company's cash reserves to expand the number of company-owned retail stores where its Louis Vuitton and Loewe leather goods and Celine, Christian Dior, and Givenchy haute couture and ready-to-wear fashions could be found.

Bernard Arnault believed that LVMH control of the retail channels where its products were sold was critical to the success of luxury brands. The use of company-owned retail locations allowed LVMH not only to make certain its products were of the highest quality and most elegant but also to ensure that its products were sold by retailers offering the highest level of customer service. Arnault believed that ultimately the finer points of retailing impacted the overall image of luxury products as much as the products' attributes. This belief drove the company's moves into vertical integration into the operation of Louis Vuitton, Christian Dior, and other designer-label stores in Paris, New York, Beverly Hills, and other locations and also led to the $2.5 billion acquisition of Duty Free Shoppers (DFS) in 1996. San Francisco–based DFS operated a chain of 180 duty-free boutiques in Asia and various international airports. Arnault saw DFS as an ideal acquisition candidate since the chain specialized in the sale of luxury goods to affluent international travelers and since its stores were concentrated in Asia. Asia was among LVMH's best geographic markets, accounting for as much as two-thirds of the sales of such products as Louis Vuitton luggage.

Arnault expanded further into retailing in 1997 with the acquisition of French cosmetics retailer Sephora and the purchase of a 30 percent interest in Douglas International, a German beauty-goods retailer with 190 stores in Europe and the United States. LVMH also expanded its line of fine champagnes in 1997 with the acquisition of Château d'Yquem—a brand produced with such care and under such exacting standards that each vine yielded just one glass of champagne. Arnault again made an attempt to have LVMH become the world's largest wine and spirits producer and distributor when he spent $2.3 billion in 1997 to purchase 11 percent of Grand Metropolitan PLC—a British food conglomerate with $1.5 billion in annual wine and spirits sales. Arnault used the ownership position in Grand Met to insert himself into merger negotiations that were under way between Guinness and Grand Met. Arnault proposed an alternate merger scenario that would combine Guinness, Grand Met, and LVMH and make LVMH the controlling entity with a 35 percent stake in the three-way merger. Guinness and Grand Met shareholders rejected the proposal but provided Arnault with a $400 million payoff to allow the two-way merger to proceed, an 11 percent interest in the new company, and a seat on its board of directors.

Arnault expanded LVMH's retailing operations beyond specialty retailing in 1998 with the acquisition of famous Parisian department stores La Belle Jardiniere and Le Bon Marché. Arnault also added Laflachère—France's leading producer of hygiene, beauty, and household cleaning products—and Marie-Jeanne Godard, a fine fragrance line, to LVMH's portfolio in 1998, but his boldest acquisition spree occurred during 1999 and 2000. During that two-year period, Arnault created a new watch and jewelry division with the purchase of TAG Heuer, Ebel, Chaumet, and Zenith; pushed the company into makeup-artist-quality cosmetics with the purchase of Bliss, BeneFit, Hard Candy, Make Up for Ever, Fresh, and Urban Decay; and entered the fine art and collectible auction industry with the acquisition of famous auction houses Phillips, de Pury & Luxembourg, and L'Etude Tajan.

Arnault's buying binge broadened the company's media operations via the addition of a French radio network and magazines targeted to music aficionados and art connoisseurs. Other business additions included (a) New World wine producers located in the United States and Australia; (b) new retail outlets in the form of an Italian cosmetics retailing chain and Miami Cruiseline Services, which offered duty-free shopping aboard 100 cruise ships sailing in the Caribbean and elsewhere; (c) an enhanced line of champagnes with Krug, the producer of some of the world's most expensive champagnes; and (d) the fashion houses of Emilio Pucci, Thomas Pink, and Fendi.

Arnault had attempted to add Gucci to the company's impressive lineup of designer brands by purchasing more than 34 percent of the Italian fashion label's shares but was thwarted by rival French conglomerate Pinault-Printemps-Redout (PPR) when it acquired 42 percent of Gucci shares. The battle for control of Gucci pitted France's two wealthiest men, LVMH's Arnault and PPR's Francois Pinault, against each other in a battle that would eventually be won by Pinault but would provide LVMH with more than $1.8 billion for its stake in Gucci. LVMH's most notable acquisitions in 2001 included Donna Karan International and La Samaritaine, the largest department store in Paris. A complete list of LVMH's acquisitions and divestitures is presented in Exhibit 3.

LVMH's Approach to Building Shareholder Value in Luxury Products Businesses

LVMH's corporate strategy under Bernard Arnault included diversification into a wide variety of luxury products. The company's wines, champagnes, haute couture and ready-to-wear fashions, cosmetics, fragrances, writing instruments, watches, and jewelry were among the most innovative, prestigious, elegant, and expensive produced. The company's retailing division focused on the sale of luxury items—whether LVMH products or brands offered by rival producers. The company's media division, for the most part, published periodicals of interest to the financial and art communities and its auction house specialized in the sale of fine art. LVMH's broad collection of businesses was grouped into six business units. Exhibit 4 presents LVMH's business portfolio in 2002.

Wine and Spirits

The production of extraordinary class wine and champagne required considerable attention to detail and decades-long commitment to quality. For example, Château d'Yquem's vineyards were cultivated over generations and were made up of vines grown from individually selected seeds. Also, on nine occasions during the 20th century the winery rejected an entire harvest, viewing all grapes from the season as unworthy of the brand. Wine production also required technical expertise to develop techniques to improve the immune systems of vines to prevent grape diseases and the skills of master blenders, who selected combinations of grapes that would result in exceptional vintages. Not any less important was the time required to produce fine wines and champagnes, some of which were aged for several years prior to distribution. Distribution from production facilities to retail outlets was typically handled by either a subsidiary, a joint venture, or a third party.

In 2002 LVMH was the world's leading champagne producer, with a 22 percent global market share and a 2001 sales volume of 49.8 million bottles. The company was also number one in the global cognac market, with a 36 percent market share and a 2001 sales volume of 40.1 million bottles. Eighty-nine percent of LVMH's wine and spirits were sold outside of France. LVMH's still wine sales were becoming stronger as Newton's California wines and MountAdam's Australian wines benefited from Moët Hennessy's international distribution network and began to gain praise from connoisseurs beyond their domestic markets. The company's champagne sales declined by

Exhibit 3 LVMH ACQUISITIONS AND DIVESTITURES

LVMH Acquisitions		
Year Company Acquired	Principal Business	Acquisition Cost
1987 Hine	Cognac production	Not disclosed
1988 Givenchy	Haute couture, ready-to-wear fashions	FF 225 million
1990 11.4% of Guinness PLC (United Kingdom)	Brewing and spirits production and distribution	FF 8.2 billion
10.75% of Loewe SA (Spain)	Leather goods, fashion	Not disclosed
Pommery	Champagne production	Not disclosed
1991 67.5% of Asbach Brandy (Germany)	Brandy production	Not disclosed
Morris E Curiel Distributing (Venezuela)	Beer distributing	Not disclosed
Pampero (Venezuela)	Spirits production	Not disclosed
70% of Union Cervecera (Spain)	Brewing	Not disclosed
1993 Christian Lacroix	Haute couture, ready-to-wear fashions	FF 80 million
Kenzo	Haute couture, ready-to-wear fashions/ fragrances	FF 483 million
55% of Desfosses International	Media production, magazines, radio	FF 126 million
1994 Outstanding 50% of *Investir*	Financial magazine	Not disclosed
49.99% of Djedi Holding (Guerlain)	Fragrances	Not disclosed
1995 An additional 41% of Fred Joaillier	Haute couture, ready-to-wear fashions	Not disclosed
44% of Desfosses International	Media production, magazines, radio	Not disclosed
1996 An additional 76% of Loewe SA (Spain)	Leather goods, fashion	€120 million
Outstanding interest in Djedi Holding (Guerlain)	Fragrances	Not disclosed
Outstanding 41% of Djedi Holding (Guerlain)	Fragrances	Not disclosed
54% of Celine SA	Haute couture, ready-to-wear fashions	Not disclosed
Remaining interest in Fred Joaillier	Haute couture, ready-to-wear fashions	Not disclosed
58.75% of DFS (USA)	Duty-free retail shops in Asia/Pacific, airports	$2.6 billion
Remaining 46% of Celine	Haute couture, ready-to-wear fashions	Not disclosed
1997 51% of Château d'Yquem	Champagne production	Not disclosed
Sephora	Cosmetics retailing	FF 1.6 billion
30% stake in Douglas International (Germany)	Cosmetics retailing	Not disclosed
1998 An additional 37% of Château d'Yquem	Champagne production	FF 111 million
Marie-Jeanne Godard	Fragrances	€118 million
Le Bon Marché	Department store in Paris	1,343,150 shares
99% of La Belle Jardiniere	Retailer in Paris	Not disclosed
Interest in Cie Financiere Laflachere	Household items, toiletries	Not disclosed
1999 Krug	Champagne production	FF 1 billion
Increased interest to 52% in Cie Financiere Laflachere	Household items, toiletries	Not disclosed
Increased interest in Gucci from 4.8% to 34.4%	Haute couture, ready-to-wear fashions	FF 7 billion
70% of Bliss (USA)	Cosmetics production, health spas	Not disclosed
BeneFit (USA)	Cosmetics production	Not disclosed
Increased interest to 64% in Château d'Yquem	Champagne production	Not disclosed

continued

Exhibit 3 Continued

LVMH Acquisitions

Year	Company Acquired	Principal Business	Acquisition Cost
	Hard Candy (USA)	Cosmetics production	Not disclosed
	TAG Heuer (Switzerland)	Watch design and assembly	SFr 1.15 billion
	70% of Thomas Pink (United Kingdom)	Haute couture, ready-to-wear fashions	£42 million
	Ebel (Switzerland)	Watch design and assembly	Not disclosed
	Chaumet	Watch design and assembly	Not disclosed
	Majority interest in Make Up For Ever (USA)	Cosmetics producer	Not disclosed
	Zenith (Switzerland)	Watch design and assembly, mechanism production	Not disclosed
	Radio Classique & SID Editions	French radio stations, media	Not disclosed
	5% of Oxygen Media (USA)	U.S. television and Internet media	Not disclosed
	72.5% interest in Phillips, de Pury & Luxembourg	Fine art auctioning	€90 million
2000	Miami Cruiseline Services (USA)	Duty free cruiseline retailing	€361 million
	67% of Emilio Pucci (Italy)	Haute couture, ready-to-wear fashions	Not disclosed
	Urban Decay (USA)	Cosmetics production	Not disclosed
	Omas (Italy)	Writing instrument production	Not disclosed
	25.50% of Fendi (Italy)	Haute couture, ready-to-wear fashions, furs	€295 million
	65% of Fresh Inc (USA)	Cosmetics production	Not disclosed
	Control of Boidi (Italy)	Cosmetics retailing	Not disclosed
	60% of Newton Vineyards (USA)	Winery and vineyards	$45 million
	An additional 5% of Oxygen Media (USA)	U.S. television and Internet media	Not disclosed
	MountAdam Vineyards (Australia)	Winery and vineyards	Included w/Newton
	L'Etude Tajan	Fine art auctioning	Not disclosed
	Micromania	Videogame retailing	Not disclosed
	Art & Auction, Connaissance des Arts	Art magazines	Not disclosed
2001	Majority interest in La Samaritaine	Parisian department store	Not disclosed
	Donna Karan International (USA)	Haute couture, ready-to-wear fashions	$243 million
	Morellato (Italy)	Watch bracelet producer	Not disclosed
	50% interest in Acqua di Parma (Italy)	Fragrances	Not disclosed

LVMH Divestitures

Year	Company Divested	Principal Business	Sales Price
1993	RoC Group	Cosmetics producer	FF 1,314 million
1997	9.43% of Guinness PLC	Brewing and spirits producer and distributor	FF 7,989 million
	50% of Christian Dior Perfumes Inc (USA)	Fragrances	Not disclosed
	Delbard Group	Roses and fruit tree producer	Not disclosed
1999	Simi Winery (USA)	Winery	Not disclosed
2001	34.4% interest in Gucci	Haute Couture, ready-to-wear fashions	$806.5 million
2002	Pommery	Champagne producer	€230 million
	45% interest in Phillips, de Pury & Luxembourg	Fine art auctioning	Not disclosed

Source: Extel Financial Limited Annual Card, April 24, 2002.

Exhibit 4   LVMH'S BUSINESS PORTFOLIO IN 2002

Wines and Spirits	Fashion and Leather Goods	Perfumes and Cosmetics	Watches and Jewelry	Selective Retailing	Media and Other Businesses
Moët & Chandon	Louis Vuitton	Parfums Christian Dior	TAG Heuer	Duty Free Shoppers (DFS)	L'Etrude Tajan
Dom Pérignon	Loewe	Guerlain	Ebel	Miami Cruiseline	Advertising agency
Veuve Clicquot	Celine	Parfums Givenchy	Zenith	Sephora	Press agency
Krug	Berluti	Kenzo Parfums	Benedom—CD Montres	Le Bon Marché	Radio Classique
Mercier	Kenzo	Bliss	Fred	La Samaritaine	*La Tribune*
Ruinart	Givenchy	Hard Candy	Chaumet		*Investir*
Canard-Duchêne	Christian Lacroix	BeneFit Cosmetics	Omas		*Jazzman*
Château d'Yquem	Marc Jacobs	Urban Decay	LVMH/De Beers		*Le Monde de la Musique*
Chandon Estates	Fendi	Fresh	joint venture		*Défis*
Cloudy Bay	StefanoBi	Make Up For Ever			*SID Editions*
Cape Mentelle	Emilio Pucci	Laflachère			*Salon des Entrepreneurs*
Hennessy	Thomas Pink	Acqua di Parma			5 news-related Internet sites
Hine	Donna Karan				*Connaissance des Arts*
Newton					*Art and Auction*
MountAdam					Sephora.com
					eLUXURY.com

Source: LVMH website.

7 percent in 2001 as retailers continued to reduce inventories built up prior to 1999's millennium celebrations and as demand for champagne in the United States fell by 29 percent after the September 11, 2001, terrorist attacks on Washington, D.C., and New York City. The sales of Hennessy and Hine expanded by 6 percent as the cognac market continued to grow in the United States and Asia.

Fashion and Leather Goods

The fashion and leather industry entailed the recruitment of highly talented and creative designers who were able to create a line of apparel or accessories that appealed to some segment of consumers. Designers had a great deal of leeway with the direction of their designs since individual tastes and preferences varied considerably among consumers. For example, whereas Ralph Lauren designs tended to reflect elements of men's and women's fashion that had been popular for decades, other designers such as LVMH's John Galliano (chief designer at Christian Dior) had caught the attention of the fashion world with a line of women's wear created from newspaper. Other important elements of creating high-end apparel and leather goods included the selection of fabrics or leather and the quality of construction. LVMH's Louis Vuitton products were all hand-assembled by craftsmen who had trained for years perfecting their talents. Apparel and leather goods were distributed to either third-party retailers or company-owned retail locations.

LVMH's Louis Vuitton was the world's leading luxury brand and the foundation of LVMH's Fashion and Leather Goods division, which had increased both sales and operating income by more than 100 percent between 1998 and 2001. LVMH's Fashion and Leather Goods division also included such prestigious brands as Kezno, Christian Lacroix, Marc Jacobs, Berlucci, Thomas Pink, Donna Karan, Emilio Pucci, Givenchy, Celine, and Fendi. In 2001, Louis Vuitton grew by 9 percent, while the entire division grew by 13 percent. The group outpaced its key rivals by a notable margin as Prada Group's sales increased by 5 percent (the sales of the Prada brand grew by 1 percent), Hermes' sales grew by 6 percent, and Groupe Gucci's sales increased by 1 percent, while the Gucci brand grew by 4 percent. France accounted for 11 percent of the division's sales.

Perfumes and Cosmetics

Success in the global cosmetics, fragrance, and toiletry (CFT) industry was largely attributable to the ability of producers to develop new combinations of chemicals and natural ingredients to create innovative and unique fragrances and develop cosmetics that boasted product benefits beyond cleansing and moisturizing to anti-aging, antipollution, firming, and sebum regulation. The industry was highly fragmented, with various distribution channels and multiple subcategories existing within each product category. For example, within the color cosmetics category, products like eyeliner, mascara, foundation, concealer, nail polish, and lipstick could be purchased from supermarkets, drugstores, discounters, specialty retailers, department stores, or direct sellers such as Mary Kay or Avon. In addition, the sales growth rates for the subcategories of beauty products could also vary greatly. For example, between 2000 and 2001, the U.S. sales of eye shadow increased by nearly 14 percent, while the sales of foundation declined by 2 percent. The market for beauty products was also segmented by consumer demographics and by geography. Teen consumers tended to look for specific product characteristics that were very different from what was expected by baby

boomers. Country-specific differences in consumer preferences and complexions further fragmented the global CFT industry, while market penetration rate created varying growth opportunities across the world.

LVMH's perfumes and cosmetics business led the European luxury segment and had outpaced industry growth by 18.0 percent in 1999, 17.5 percent in 2000, and 5.0 percent in 2001 to reach sales of 2.2 billion euros at year-end 2001. The company's growth was attributed to its strong brands, new product introductions that included Flower by Kenzo, J'adore by Christian Dior, Hot Couture by Givenchy, and Michael by Michael Kors; the addition of new American cosmetics brands such as BeneFit, Fresh, Urban Decay, and Make Up For Ever; and the success of its Sephora retail cosmetics operations. Sephora's network of stores located in Europe, the United States, and Japan carried LVMH's perfumes and cosmetics brands, which were also sold by prestigious retailers around the world. The division also included Laflachère—France's leading brand of hygiene, beauty, and household cleaning products. Even though LVHM's perfumes and cosmetics division had recorded impressive growth rates, its sales ranked it seventh in the industry and were only about one-sixth that of industry leader L'Oréal. Approximately 80 percent of the division's sales were outside of France.

Watches and Jewelry

The watch and jewelry industry was much like the fashion and CFT industries in that it was highly fragmented with multiple product categories and wide-ranging price points. The upscale segment of the industry also reflected the fashion industry's demand for quality and creative or distinctive designs. The producers of many exquisite timepieces such as Rolex, Cartier, and Patek Phillipe maintained long-established lines known not only for style but also for craftsmanship and accuracy. Most manufacturers of upmarket watches also added new models from time to time that were consistent with the company's tradition, history, and style. Watch production involved the development and production of the movement (although many watch manufacturers purchased movements from third-party suppliers), case design and fabrication, and assembly. Watches were rarely sold by manufacturers directly to consumers but rather were usually distributed to independent jewelers or large upscale department stores.

LVMH's watch and jewelry division was established in 1999 with the acquisitions of TAG Heuer, Ebel, Chaumet, Benedom-Christian Dior, and Zenith. The Omas line of Italian pens was added in 2000. The company's most popular watches included TAG Heuer's Kirium F1 and Monza lines, Christian Dior's Chris 47, and Ebel Beluga and Classic Wave. Zenith was the only Swiss watchmaker to produce chronographs without outsourcing the movement. The automatic chronograph movement utilized in its El Primero also equipped the Rolex Daytona and other fine Swiss chronographs. New watch and jewelry lines by Ebel, Christian Dior Watches, Chaumet, and Fred were scheduled for release in 2002.

The division experienced a sales decline of 11 percent during 2001 as it withdrew from contract manufacturing for third-party brands. LVMH acquired the supplier of its TAG Heuer watch bracelets and opened a TAG Heuer boutique in London in 2001. The division also opened new Fred jewelry stores in Paris, London, and Tokyo during 2001. LVMH planned to open an Omas shop in Milan and its first De Beers jewelry store during 2002. The first De Beers store would be located in London and was to be part of a worldwide chain of jewelry stores that would be operated as a joint venture between LVMH and De Beers Centenary AG, the world's largest producers of diamonds. Only 7 percent of LVMH's sales of watches and jewelry originated from France.

Exhibit 5   LVMH's Global Network of Retail Stores, 2000 and 2001

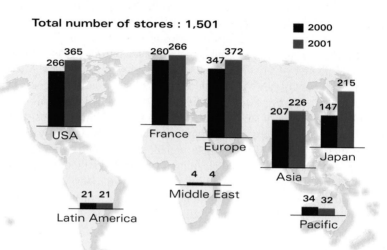

Source: LVMH 2001 Annual Results Presentation.

Selective Retailing

LVMH's selective retailing division was made up of DFS and Miami Cruiseline duty-free stores, Le Bon Marché and La Samaritaine department stores, and Sephora cosmetics stores. The division also operated upscale Galleria shopping malls located in downtown areas of major air destinations in the Asia-Pacific region and the United States. LVMH's Gallerias featured DFS stores, Sephora, and designer boutiques such as Louis Vuitton, Hermes, Chanel, Prada, Fendi, Celine, Bulgari, and Tiffany. LVMH opened two new Gallerias in 2001—one located in Hawaii and the other in Hollywood, California.

Le Bon Marché was Paris's most exclusive department store, and La Samaritaine—the city's largest department store—was being repositioned with an emphasis on upscale fashion and accessories. Sephora was the leading retail beauty chain in France and the United States, and the second largest beauty chain in Europe. In 2001 Sephora operated more than 225 stores in Europe and more than 80 stores in the United States, all of which carried LVMH's products and other prestigious brands of cosmetics, fragrances, and skin care products, including Chanel, Dolce and Gabbana, Elizabeth Arden, Hugo Boss, Naomi Campbell, Gianni Versace, and Burberry. Sephora had operated seven stores in Japan, but withdrew from that market and from Germany in 2001. A change in strategy initiated in 2001 called for the chain to focus on country markets where it could achieve profitable growth, such as the United States, Italy, France, and Greece. LVMH believed that developing countries such as Poland and Romania also presented profitable growth opportunities for Sephora.

The division's 2001 sales grew by 6 percent even though the sales of DFS fell by 10 percent after tourism in the Asia–Pacific region fell by more than 50 percent after the September 11, 2001, terrorist attacks on the United States. Sephora's sales increased 23 percent during 2001 with its strongest performance coming in the United States,

Portugal, Italy, France, and the United Kingdom. Exhibit 5 depicts LVMH's global network of company-owned fashion, watch and jewelry, and selective retail stores by geographic region.

Other Businesses

LVMH also maintained a business unit made up of media, art auction, and e-commerce businesses. Media operations included six print publications sold in France, two art-related publications marketed to the international art market, business newsletters, and a French radio network. The division's other media businesses included an advertising sales company, an audiovisual press agency, and four news-related Internet sites. The most prominent businesses of LVMH's media sector were *Investir,* France's leading online and print daily investment publication; Radio Classique's network of radio stations across France, which attracted 600,000 listeners a day; *Connaissance des Arts* and *Art & Auction,* which were benchmark art publications with monthly circulations of 40,000 and 17,500, respectively; and *Jazzman* and *Le Monde de la Musique,* two leading French music publications.

The company held an interest in Phillips, de Pury & Luxembourg, the world's third largest auction house specializing in fine art and antiquities, and owned L'Etrude Tajan, the leading fine art auction house in France. The group's eLUXURY website was launched in June 2000 and offered more than 50 of the world's most exclusive brands, including LVMH's Louis Vuitton, Dior, Fred, Guerlain, and Celine and a number of non-LVMH luxury brands. Sephora.com offered the largest and most diverse selection of beauty products on the Internet with over 11,000 products and more than 230 brands. The division's operating loss of 372 million euros in 2001 was largely attributable to Internet development costs and expansion costs at Phillips, de Pury & Luxembourg.

LVMH's performance by business group for 1999–2001 is presented in Exhibit 6.

LVMH's Corporate Strategy

Although much of LVMH's growth was attributable to the acquisition of new businesses, Arnault placed an emphasis on internal growth by exploiting common strategies and capturing strategic-fit benefits across the portfolio. Arnault based the company's strategies on a set of core values that were essential to the success of each business unit. Arnault demanded that each of the corporation's businesses demonstrate commitment to creativity, innovation, and product excellence. The long-term success of LVMH's brands, in Arnault's view, was largely a function of artistic creativity, technological innovation, and the closest attention to every detail of the production process. Innovation and creativity contributed to internal growth among LVMH's businesses, with new products accounting for more than 18 percent of Louis Vuitton's 2001 sales and more than 20 percent of LVMH's cosmetics and fragrance sales in 2001. LVMH management believed that by 2005 more than 10 percent of the company's champagne sales would be generated by 15 new cuvées introduced in 1998.

The image and reputation of the company's products were seen as equal to the creativity and craftsmanship employed during the development and production of LVMH luxury goods since image was a product dimension that defied logic but caused consumers to have strong desires for a particular brand. Arnault believed that image was priceless and irreplaceable, and that it required stringent management control over every element of a brand's image, including advertisements, corporate announcements, and speeches by management and designers.

Exhibit 6   **LVMH'S PERFORMANCE BY BUSINESS GROUP, 1999–2001 (IN MILLIONS OF EUROS)**

	2001	2000	1999
Sales			
Wine and Spirits	€ 2,232	€ 2,336	€2,240
Fashion and Leather Goods	3,612	3,202	2,295
Perfumes and Cosmetics	2,231	2,072	1,703
Watches and Jewelry	548	614	135
Selective Retailing	3,475	3,287	2,162
Other businesses and eliminations	131	70	12
Total	€12,229	€11,581	€8,547
Operating Profit			
Wine and Spirits	€ 676	€ 716	€ 655
Fashion and Leather Goods	1,274	1,169	826
Perfumes and Cosmetics	149	184	146
Watches and Jewelry	27	59	5
Selective Retailing	(194)	(2)	(2)
Other businesses and eliminations	(372)	(167)	(83)
Total	€ 1,560	€ 1,959	€1,547
Capital Expenditures			
Wine and Spirits	€ 61	€ 66	€ 52
Fashion and Leather Goods	210	194	155
Perfumes and Cosmetics	90	83	68
Watches and Jewelry	26	16	9
Selective Retailing	205	294	266
Other businesses and eliminations	392	204	24
Total	€ 984	€ 857	€ 574

Source: LVMH 2001 annual report.

The final element of LVMH's corporate strategy—control over the distribution and sale of its products—allowed its divisions to listen to customer needs, better understand their tastes, and anticipate their desires. LVMH's ownership of more than 1,500 retail locations in developed countries throughout the world also allowed the company to refine its brands' images with controlled store aesthetics, a consistent retailing approach, and irreproachable customer service.

Bernard Arnault discussed LVMH's strategic approach to managing its portfolio of star brands in an October 2001 *Harvard Business Review* interview:

Product Quality

The problem is that the quality of timelessness takes years to develop, even decades. You cannot just decree it. A brand has to pay its dues—it has to come to stand for something in the eyes of the world. But you can, as a manager, enhance timelessness—that is, create the impression of timelessness sooner rather than later. And you do that with uncompromising quality.

A lot of companies talk about quality, but if you want your brand to be timeless, you have to be a fanatic about it. Before we launch a Louis Vuitton suitcase, for example, we put it in a torture machine, where it is opened and closed five times per minute for three weeks. And that is not all—it is thrown, and shaken, and crushed. You would laugh if you saw what we do, but that is how you build something that becomes an heirloom. By the way, we put some of our competitors' products through the same tests, and they come out like bouillie—the mush babies eat.

Quality also comes from hiring very dedicated people and then keeping them for a long time. We try to keep the people at the brands, especially the artisans—the seamstresses and other people who make the products—because they have the brand in their bones—its history, its meaning. At the stores, too, many of the salespeople have the brand in their bones. Most companies clean house when they acquire a new brand. We don't do that because we have found it hurts quality terribly. When you clean house, you usher out the people who respect the brand the most and who contribute to its longevity, its timelessness, its authenticity.

Innovation
Fashion, of course, comes from innovation—the creativity of the designers. That is sometimes harder to guarantee than quality, which you can actually build in to a product, but just as important. The hard truth is, you must be old and new at once. In a star brand you honor your past and invent your future at the same time. It is a subtle balance.

If you think and act like a typical manager around creative people—with rules, policies, data on customer preferences, and so forth—you will quickly kill their talent. Our whole business is based on giving our artists and designers complete freedom to invent without limits.

Our philosophy is quite simple, really. If you look over a creative person's shoulder, he will stop doing great work. Wouldn't you, if some manager were watching your every move, clutching a calculator in his hand? So that is why LVMH is, as a company, so decentralized. Each brand very much runs itself, headed by its own artistic director. Central headquarters in Paris is very small, especially for a company with 54,000 employees and 1,300 stores around the world. There are only 250 of us, and I assure you, we do not lurk around every corner, questioning every creative decision.

The most successful creative people want to see their creations in the street. They don't invent just to invent. Yes, they come up with many exciting ideas, and many of these ideas shock; they look crazy at first, completely crazy. But the true artists that make LVMH a success, they don't want the process to end there. They want people to wear their dresses, or spray their perfume, or carry the luggage they have designed.

The responsibility of the manager in a company dependent on innovation, then, very much becomes picking the right creative people—the ones who want to see their designs on the street. And that desire inside them is something that you, as a leader of a company, can only sense. After all, most artists don't go around proclaiming, "I want to be a commercial success." They would actually hate to say that. And frankly, if you asked them, they would say they don't actually care one way or another if people buy their products. But they do care. It's just buried in their DNA, and as a manager, you have to be able to see it there. I know you are going to ask, "How can I see into a person's DNA, to know if he is an artist with commercial instincts?" So I will answer, it just takes experience. Years of practice—trial and error—and you learn.

And just as important, to allow creativity to happen, a company has to be filled with managers who have a certain love of artists and designers—or whatever kind of creative person you have in your company, if you deeply appreciate and love what creative people do and how they think, which is usually in unpredictable and irrational ways, then you can start to understand them. And finally, you can see inside their minds and DNA.

Image

Without growth, it is not a star brand, as far as I am concerned. In 2000, Louis Vuitton, which is by far the largest luxury brand in the world, had 40% growth in sales, which makes it a superstar, no? Growth shows the shareholders that you have struck the right balance between timelessness and fashion and that you have been able to charge a premium price because of that correct balance.

Now, growth is not just a function of high price. You also grow when you move into new markets, such as those in developing countries. But mainly, growth is a function of high desire. Customers must want the product. That sounds simple, I am sure, but to get advertising right is very, very difficult—it's difficult to get advertising to represent the true brand. Most companies think it is enough to use advertising to present a picture of the product. That's not enough. You need to project the image of the brand itself.

The latest Dior ad campaign is a perfect example of how to do this right. [A Parfums Christian Dior J'adore advertisement is presented in Exhibit 7.] You would know this was an ad for a Dior product even without the name of the company there. You cannot mistake it for anything else. You know this is Dior because the model projects the image of the brand—very sexy and modern, very feminine and energetic.

The last thing you should do is assign advertising to your marketing department. If you do that, you lose the proximity between the designers and the message to the marketplace. At LVMH, we keep the advertising right inside the design team. With the Dior campaign, John Galliano (chief designer) himself did the makeup on the model. He posed her. The only thing Galliano did not do himself was snap the photo.

Craftsmanship and the Production Process

It is true that the front end of a star brand—the innovation, supporting the creative process, the advertising, and so on—is very, very expensive. High profitability comes at the back end of the process, and behind the scenes.

It comes in the atelier—the factory. Our products have unbelievably high quality; they have to. But their production is organized in such a way that we also have unbelievably high productivity. The atelier is a place of amazing discipline and rigor. Every single motion, every step of every process, is carefully planned with the most modern and complete engineering technology. It's not unlike how cars are made in the most modern factories. We analyze how to make each part of the product, where to buy each component, where to find the best leather at the best price, what treatment it should receive. A single purse can have up to 1,000 manufacturing tasks, and we plan each and every one. In that way, the LVMH production process is the exact opposite of its creative process, which is so freewheeling and chaotic.

If you walk into a Vuitton factory, you will see very few machines. Almost every piece is made by hand. Usually, piecework is the most inefficient operating system in the world, but for us it is different because we give our craftsmen and craftswomen fantastic training. They are trained for months before they touch the products, and then, every task they do has been studied and refined for many years, so we know precisely how to arrange the atelier. No motion is wasted there. And that allows us to offer a very high quality product at a cost that makes our business very profitable.

The one catch to this system is that it takes time. You cannot rush the training of the artisans or the planning of the atelier to make a product at maximum efficiency. When we come up with a new purse, for instance, it takes months to plan a process for producing it so that it will be profitable. So sometimes customers have to wait because output is so limited. Which is why you get long lines outside your stores. And actually, that is not such a bad thing sometimes, because those lines have a way of increasing demand even further. But the main reason for the lines of customers is the combination of exceptional quality and craftsmanship at a good price.

Risk Tolerance

We don't like failures. We try to avoid them. That is why, with many of our new products, we make a limited number. We do not put the entire company at risk by introducing all new products all the time. In any given year, in fact, only 15% of our business comes from the new; the rest comes from traditional, proven products—the classics.

Vuitton is a perfect example. This year, Marc Jacobs came up with the graffiti design, and it was a big departure for the line. Did you see it? It is beautiful and crazy, right? It does not look like Vuitton at first glance; who would have thought of that on suitcases? But we only had that on several items—for which, by the way, there is now a waiting list worldwide. The rest of the products were Vuitton that you could have bought last year, or five years ago, or ten years from now. They are legacy pieces.

We will use the same approach with the new Dior handbag. It is very exciting, very expensive. You will see it in all the ads and want to buy it. I assure you we will be out of stock fast. But it is very expensive: $1,800. We will make only several thousand of them. The rest of the line will reflect some ideas of that new purse—the same shape—but will be less radical in terms of fabrics and design. We will make more of those and sell them for less. That way, we can have our creativity but also minimize risk.

Of course, with some businesses, you cannot avoid risk, and sometimes you do not succeed. And so you learn. With still other businesses, you cannot say they are outright failures or learning experiences, just that their success is taking time. That is the case with Christian Lacroix.

At the beginning, we thought, "Okay, we have a genius here with Christian Lacroix," but we learned that genius is not enough to succeed. It was something of a shock, to be honest, to discover that even great talent could not launch a brand from zero. A brand must have a heritage; there are no shortcuts.

The fact is, star brands take time to grow. Take some of the small makeup companies we have acquired recently, like Bliss and Urban Decay. When we bought them, they were little start-ups run by their founders—very simple businesses, but with a lot of originality in the products. So now we know we must nurture them until they have some history. But even if it takes ten or 15 years for them to become stars, that has been an amazing investment, right?

Exhibit 7   Advertisement for Parfums Christian Dior J'adore

Source: Parfums Christian Dior website.

Capturing Synergies between Business Units

LVMH management had identified a variety of opportunities for its portfolio of businesses to share best practices, leverage competencies and skills, and combine common activities to reduce expenses. In 1999, the company created its training institute, LVMH House, in London to allow managers from different businesses, job classifications, or geographic regions to discuss such issues as leadership, technological innovation, design innovation, and operating efficiency and share their personal knowledge and experiences. By year-end 2001, more than 600 LVMH managers had attended LVMH House forums. The interactions between managers from different divisions had spawned continuing discussions of strategy and operations via the company's Intranet and had initiated several intercompany projects.

Much of LVMH's Internet strategy resulted from forums held at LVMH House between May and October 2001. The theme of forum sessions focused on business-to-business, business-to-enterprise, and business-to-consumer opportunities and resulted in the formulation of strategies used in the development of LVMH's 50-plus brand websites and e-commerce activities at ThomasPink.com, eLUXURY.com, and Sephora.com. The forums also helped the company implement online information exchange systems between some LVMH businesses and their suppliers and distributors. The company had successfully instituted the e-procurement of office supplies at Moët

& Chandon and had created a common internal communications system called LVMH pl@net that allowed its businesses to share information through company intranets.

Among the most important competencies that LVMH management had hoped to transfer between businesses was its approach to customer relationship management. LVMH management believed that its ability to develop richer, deeper ties with a targeted group of customers was essential to building customer loyalty for its prestigious luxury brands. Relationship management entailed maintaining personal communications with customers through mail, e-mail, Internet sites, or in-store systems to transform an initial impulse purchase into more frequent purchases for larger amounts. LVMH's president of Parfums Christian Dior suggested, "The better you know your customers, the better you can define messages and actions that will trigger their desire to purchase products."[9]

Customer relationship management also allowed LVMH to pursue cross-selling opportunities between product lines. A Louis Vuitton executive explained, "A customer who bought a trendy leather goods item like a Monogram Graffiti bag is likely to be interested in our ready-to-wear lines, and should be on the list to receive special communications on our latest collection."[10] In 2001, Parfums Christian Dior had conducted joint promotions with Christian Dior Couture in major department stores to introduce fragrance customers to Dior fashions. LVMH's Moët & Chandon also conducted joint promotions with the company's fashion businesses to promote its name among established purchasers of LVMH fashions by creating the Moët & Chandon Fashion Awards and the Moët Fashion Debut.

LVMH had achieved cost savings through the development of a common research and development group for its variety of fragrance and cosmetics brands. Beginning in 2000, LVMH Laboratories' 220 researchers developed beauty care, makeup, and fragrance solutions for Dior, Guerlain, and Givenchy and conducted development work for Kenzo Parfums and its U.S. cosmetics brands (BeneFit, Bliss, Urban Decay, Hard Candy, and Fresh). The development of LVMH Laboratories not only allowed competencies and resources to be shared between the company's cosmetics and fragrance brands but also created a single office responsible for toxicology research and regulatory affairs.

LVMH also began implementing a common supply chain management system in its perfumes and cosmetics business in 2001 that would allow its brands to manage orders, production, purchasing, accounting, finance, and inventories. The new enterprise resource planning (ERP) system had been partially employed at Parfums Christian Dior and was expected to lead eventually to substantial improvements in margins and cash flow, out-of-stock rates, obsolescence costs, and product freshness and availability since the CFT industry required product lines that might include thousands of products. Efficient inventory management was also critical to success in the CFT industry since items were very expensive and fragile and since retailers demanded quick renewal rates.

LVMH in 2002: Luxury Products and Global Economic Uncertainty

LVMH's slowing sales growth and declining profitability was, in some part, a function of declining demand for luxury goods. Its dilemma was not unlike that of other luxury goods producers like Prada, Richemont, Gucci, and Bulgari, which had all issued profit warnings in 2001. Beginning in 2000, most developed countries had experienced some economic slowdown, which was compounded by the effects of the September 11, 2001, terrorist attacks on the United States. The threat of terrorism had contributed to a decline in international travel during late 2001 and had created an emotional climate where champagne, designer fashions, and expensive timepieces seemed less important than during the boom years of the late 1990s. For example, the global sales of champagne declined by 20 percent during 2001 and the men's apparel industry declined 7 percent—falling from $60.9 billion in 2000 to $54.7 billion in 2001. The chief executive of Richemont, owner of Cartier, Dunhill, and Montblanc brands, explained the state of the luxury goods industry by suggesting, "We sell the feelgood factor and there are few people in the world that feel good, especially after 11 September."[11]

Some analysts and investors believed that LVMH's problems ran deeper than a cyclical move away from spending on big-ticket luxury items. Arnault had been criticized for his purchase of Phillips, de Pury & Luxembourg in 1999 and his subsequent attempts to unseat incumbents Sotheby's and Christie's as the world's two leaders among fine art auctioning. Some believed the move was part of an ongoing personal rivalry between Arnault and Pinault-Printemps-Redoute chairman Francois Pinault, who had purchased Christie's in 1998. Arnault had attempted to acquire Sotheby's after Pinault's acquisition of Christie's but was unable to agree on a price.

Under Arnault, Phillips, de Pury & Luxembourg undertook aggressive strategies to make a name for itself in the art auction industry such as offering generous guarantees to win prestigious consignments. However, Phillips's auctions frequently failed to meet the guarantees, leaving the art auction house liable for the shortfall. It was estimated that Phillips, de Pury & Luxembourg lost $80 million on one auction alone. Phillips's management justified the guarantees, claiming that the tactics would allow the auction house to build market share. However, analysts questioned the overall strategy to overtake either Sotheby's or Christie's, arguing that there was not room in the fine art market for three auction houses since there were only about 50 private collectors who bought works of art for $20 million or more. Among others, a J. P. Morgan analyst claimed, "The deal didn't make any sense to begin with. Auction houses are not luxury goods, so why bother with that?"[12] LVMH's art auction house recorded a net loss of approximately $150 million in fiscal 2001.

Analysts and investors also questioned the company's acquisition of Donna Karan, claiming the brand did not meet Arnault's star brand criteria. Donna Karan became known worldwide during the late 1980s as her sophisticated business suits became a hit with executive women and her DKNY casual wear obtained a dedicated following among urban women for after-business attire. However, beginning in 1996, Donna Karan International began to lose favor with upscale consumers as Karan's designs strayed from her traditional roots into a hodgepodge of unrelated styles. Donna Karan also pushed the company into financial distress as she spent lavishly on a New York flagship store and designs that never made it to the runway. The brand was tarnished further when Donna Karan signed licensing agreements that allowed Haggar to produce and distribute Donna Karan branded men's slacks and Van Heusen to produce and sell Donna Karan shirts. In addition, Donna Karan lost prestigious retail accounts like Neiman Marcus when DKNY liquidated its growing inventories to discounter T. J.

Maxx. Arnault justified the acquisition, claiming that "what appealed to us is the fact that [Donna Karan] is one of the best-known brand names in the world."[13]

Investors also called for Arnault to examine the worth of LVMH's selective retailing businesses. DFS and Sephora had each lost approximately $100 million during 2001, and the company's department stores in Paris required considerable capital investments and carried brands outside of LVMH's portfolio. A Merrill Lynch analyst suggested that LVMH "should focus on high-end luxury brands and not pour more money into low-margin and capital-intensive retailing."[14] LVMH's head of its perfume and cosmetics business supported concerns of investors by stating, "The fact that LVMH owns DFS and Sephora is entirely neutral to my business. To be successful they have to treat competitors as they treat me. There is no synergy from having these two businesses."[15]

Bernard Arnault began restructuring LVMH's portfolio during the first six months of 2002, divesting more than €800 million worth of assets that included a portion of its stake in Phillips, de Pury & Luxembourg; Pommery Champagne; and certain real estate properties. LVMH's sale of Pommery Champagne for approximately €230 million allowed it to retain the world's fifth largest champagne producer's 470 hectares of vineyards. The sales price of Phillips, de Pury & Luxembourg was not disclosed but was suggested by insiders to be less than LVMH's original €90 million investment. Arnault dismissed reports claiming that the company was considering the sale of DFS, Miami Cruiseline, Le Bon Marché, La Samaritaine, and Sephora by stating, "I do not plan to sell them in this current market—so they are not for sale"; he acknowledged, however, that "these retailing businesses are loss-making. We do not like businesses that lose money, but we know why they are losing money and we will fix them."[16] Arnault also denied reports that LVMH was considering the sale of Loewe.

With Arnault controlling 48 percent of LVMH shares and a majority of shareholder votes, many analysts believed that portfolio restructuring would come slowly at LVMH. A Merrill Lynch luxury goods analyst likened Arnault's penchant for acquisitions to that of a collector of fine art (which Bernard Arnault was) observing, "Arnault has rarely sold anything."[17] An ABN Ambro analyst characterized Arnault as "not a man who likes to admit he has been wrong on a number of occasions . . . so the disposal process may be slow."[18] Arnault hinted that he might divest LVMH's selective retailing businesses in the future when he stated that "retailing is not a core business for LVMH" and suggested that the company would not "expand further in retailing beyond our existing plans."[19] There was also some belief that, rather than retrench, Arnault might like to expand the portfolio further, with Giorgio Armani, Tiffany & Company, and Bulgari named as potential acquisition candidates.

LVMH's stock performance between 1994 and May 2002 is tracked in Exhibit 8. The company's consolidated statements of income and balance sheets for 1999 through 2001 are presented in Exhibits 9 and 10, respectively. The company's first-quarter 2002 sales of wines and spirits increased 19 percent over those of first quarter 2001. Its first-quarter 2002 fashion and leather goods sales increased 22 percent over the same period in 2001, while the sales of its selective retailing division declined by 5 percent. The company's sales of watches, jewelry, perfumes, and cosmetics remained nearly unchanged between the first quarter of 2001 and the first quarter of 2002.

Exhibit 8   Market Performance of LVMH's Common Stock, by Quarter, 1994–May 2002

(a) Trend in LVMH's Common Stock Price

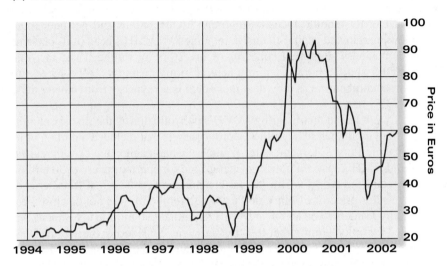

(b) Performance of LVMH's Stock Price versus the Paris Stock Exchange

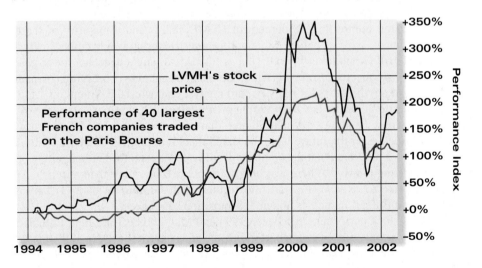

Exhibit 9   **LVMH'S STATEMENTS OF INCOME, 1999–2001 (IN MILLIONS OF EUROS, EXCEPT PER SHARE AMOUNTS)**

	2001	2000	1999
Net sales	€12,229	€11,581	€8,547
Cost of sales	4,654	4,221	3,132
Gross margin	7,575	7,360	5,415
Marketing and selling expenses	4,568	4,206	2,964
General and administrative expenses	1,447	1,195	904
Income from operations	1,560	1,959	1,547
Financial expense—net	459	421	227
Dividends from non-consolidated investments	21	45	97
Other income or expense—net*	(455)	109	18
Income before income taxes	667	1,692	1,435
Income taxes	192	633	554
Income (loss) from investments accounted for using the equity method	(42)	(34)	(6)
Net income before amortization of goodwill, minority interests, and unusual items	433	1,025	875
Amortization of goodwill	168	141	102
Net income before minority interests and unusual items	265	884	773
Minority interests	(99)	(179)	(137)
Net income before unusual items	166	705	636
Unusual items†	(156)	17	57
Net income	€ 10	€ 722	€ 693
Earnings per share before amortization of goodwill, minority interests, and unusual items	€0.89	€2.11	€1.81
Fully diluted earnings per share before amortization of goodwill, minority interests, and unusual items	€0.89	€2.11	€1.81
Earnings per share	€0.02	€1.49	€1.43
Fully diluted earnings per share	€0.02	€1.49	€1.43
Average number of common shares outstanding during the year	488,064,659	484,800,930	483,157,146
Number of common shares and share equivalents after dilution	488,072,374	484,886,474	483,445,278

*Other income and expenses include the results linked to LVMH's treasury shares; in 2001, this item included 39 million euros of realized capital gains and a 343 million euro provision for depreciation of the shares held at year-end. For 2000, LVMH recorded 115 million euros of capital gains from the sales of its treasury shares. In 2001, this item also includes various asset write-offs, notably for unconsolidated equity investments.

†Unusual items include €864 million of proceeds from Gucci, which include €774 million in capital gains from the disposal of these shares and €90 million for an exceptional dividend received in the fourth quarter. Unusual charges included €446 million in restructuring provisions, €385 million of which was for Selective Retailing in order to lower the break-even point of these companies, which are very sensitive to economic fluctuations. Exceptional asset depreciation totaling €480 million was also recorded. This figure includes €323 million for DFS goodwill, €83 million on the Bouygues equity stake and €60 million on the Group's unconsolidated equity investments in the new technologies business. Lastly, the balance includes notably a charge for the sale of LVMH's controlling stake in Phillips, de Pury & Luxembourg to its current principals at December 31, 2001, including a full write-off of goodwill. Unusual items are disclosed net of a €71 million positive tax effect. The €57 million unusual income item for 1999 reflects the €315 million gain realized as a result of the Diageo share buy-back program, to which LVMH tendered 143 million shares. This was partly offset by indirect charges related to the acquisition of equity interests; by a provision related to the residual interest in Diageo; by reorganization costs related to Fashion activities and logistics; and by asset depreciations, primarily related to intangible assets.

Source: LVMH 2001 annual report.

Exhibit 10   LVMH'S BALANCE SHEETS, 1999–2001 (IN MILLIONS OF EUROS)

	2001	2000	1999
Assets			
Current assets			
Cash and cash equivalents	€ 795	€ 695	€ 546
Short-term investments	622	1,326	183
Treasury shares	1,046	1,289	853
Trade accounts receivable	1,538	1,638	1,442
Deferred income taxes	544	266	273
Inventories	3,655	3,382	2,943
Prepaid expenses and other current assets	1,352	1,596	1,500
Total current assets	9,552	10,192	7,740
Investments and other assets circulant			
Investments accounted for using the equity method	77	21	10
Unconsolidated investments and other investments	1,386	1,892	3,959
Treasury shares	318	156	210
Other noncurrent assets	467	307	251
Property, plant and equipment, net	4,208	3,367	2,856
Brands & other intangible assets, net	4,308	3,415	2,527
Goodwill, net	3,516	3,842	3,181
Total, other assets	14,280	13,000	12,994
Total assets	€23,832	€23,192	€20,734
Liabilities and Stockholders' Equity			
Current liabilities			
Short-term borrowings	€ 3,765	€ 5,333	€ 4,439
Accounts payable	1,401	1,305	1,087
Accrued expenses and other current liabilities	2,622	2,371	2,548
Income taxes	—	318	139
Current portion of long-term debt	238	235	161
Total current liabilities	8,026	9,562	8,374
Net deferred income taxes	169	110	167
Long-term liabilities			
Long-term debt, less current portion	5,402	3,498	3,085
Other long-term liabilities	1,250	1,164	921
Repackaged notes	284	346	406
Total long-term liabilities	6,936	5,008	4,412
Minority interests in subsidiaries	1,800	1,481	1,077
Stockholders' equity			
Common stock	147	147	147
Additional paid-in capital and retained earnings	6,894	7,017	6,679
Cumulative translation adjustment	(140)	(133)	(122)
Total stockholders' equity	6,901	7,031	6,704
Stockholders' equity and minority interests	8,701	8,512	7,781
Total liabilities and stockholders' equity	€23,832	€23,192	€20,734

Source: LVMH 2001 annual report.

Endnotes

[1]Quoted in "The Perfect Paradox of Star Brands: An Interview with Bernard Arnault of LVMH," *Harvard Business Review,* 79, no. 9 (October 2001), p. 116.

[2]Ibid.

[3]Ibid.

[4]Ibid.

[5]Quoted in "Pivotal Figure Emerges in Moët-Vuitton Feud," *New York Times,* September 19, 1988, p. D1.

[6]Both quotes from "Bernard Arnault Is Building a Huge Empire—But Can He Manage It?" *Business Week,* July 30, 1990, p. 48.

[7]Ibid.

[8]Quoted in "Arnault Is Shopping," *Business Week,* February 7, 1994, p. 44.

[9]Quoted in "Focus on Customer Relationship Management," www.lvmh.com.

[10]Quoted in "Special Report: Internet at the Heart of Customer Relationship Management," www.lvmh.com.

[11]Quoted in "Fading Feelgood Factor Leaves Luxury Labels Tarnished," *Independent*, November 18, 2001, p. B5.

[12]Quoted in "Luxury Conglomerate Sells Its Art Auction House," *New York Times,* February 20, 2002, p. C1.

[13]Quoted in *The Business,* April 7, 2002.

[14]Quoted in "A Veteran Dealmaker Chews Over His Core," *Financial Times,* November 21, 2001, p. 16.

[15]Ibid.

[16]Quoted in "Retailing Is 'Non-core' for LVMH, Says Arnault," *Financial Times,* November 21, 2001, p. 30.

[17]Ibid.

[18]Quoted in "LVMH's Auction House Sale Reflects Troubles," *Daily Deal,* February 21, 2001.

[19]Quoted in "A Veteran Dealmaker Chews Over His Core."

Robin Hood

Joseph Lampel
New York University

It was in the spring of the second year of his insurrection against the High Sheriff of Nottingham that Robin Hood took a walk in Sherwood Forest. As he walked he pondered the progress of the campaign, the disposition of his forces, the Sheriff's recent moves, and the options that confronted him.

The revolt against the Sheriff had begun as a personal crusade. It erupted out of Robin's conflict with the Sheriff and his administration. However, alone Robin Hood could do little. He therefore sought allies, men with grievances and a deep sense of justice. Later he welcomed all who came, asking few questions and demanding only a willingness to serve. Strength, he believed, lay in numbers.

He spent the first year forging the group into a disciplined band, united in enmity against the Sheriff and willing to live outside the law. The band's organization was simple. Robin ruled supreme, making all important decisions. He delegated specific tasks to his lieutenants. Will Scarlett was in charge of intelligence and scouting. His main job was to shadow the Sheriff and his men, always alert to their next move. He also collected information on the travel plans of rich merchants and tax collectors. Little John kept discipline among the men and saw to it that their archery was at the high peak that their profession demanded. Scarlock took care of the finances, converting loot to cash, paying shares of the take, and finding suitable hiding places for the surplus. Finally, Much the Miller's son had the difficult task of provisioning the ever-increasing band of Merrymen.

The increasing size of the band was a source of satisfaction for Robin, but also a source of concern. The fame of his Merrymen was spreading, and new recruits were pouring in from every corner of England. As the band grew larger, their small bivouac became a major encampment. Between raids the men milled about, talking and playing games. Vigilance was in decline, and discipline was becoming harder to enforce. "Why," Robin reflected, "I don't know half the men I run into these days."

The growing band was also beginning to exceed the food capacity of the forest. Game was becoming scarce, and supplies had to be obtained from outlying villages. The cost of buying food was beginning to drain the band's financial reserves at the very moment when revenues were in decline. Travelers, especially those with the most to lose, were now giving the forest a wide berth. This was costly and inconvenient to them, but it was preferable to having all their goods confiscated.

Robin believed that the time had come for the Merrymen to change their policy of outright confiscation of goods to one of a fixed transit tax. His lieutenants strongly resisted this idea. They were proud of the Merrymen's famous motto: "Rob the rich and give to the poor." "The farmers and the townspeople," they argued, "are our most important allies. How can we tax them, and still hope for their help in our fight against the Sheriff?"

Robin wondered how long the Merrymen could keep to the ways and methods of their early days. The Sheriff was growing stronger and becoming better organized. He now had the money and the men and was beginning to harass the band, probing for its weaknesses. The tide of events was beginning to turn against the Merrymen. Robin felt that the campaign must be decisively concluded before the Sheriff had a chance to deliver a mortal blow. "But how," he wondered, "could this be done?"

Robin had often entertained the possibility of killing the Sheriff, but the chances for this seemed increasingly remote. Besides, killing the Sheriff might satisfy his personal thirst for revenge, but it would not improve the situation. Robin had hoped that the perpetual state of unrest, and the Sheriff's failure to collect taxes, would lead to his removal from office. Instead, the Sheriff used his political connections to obtain reinforcement. He had powerful friends at court and was well regarded by the regent, Prince John.

Prince John was vicious and volatile. He was consumed by his unpopularity among the people, who wanted the imprisoned King Richard back. He also lived in constant fear of the barons, who had first given him the regency but were now beginning to dispute his claim to the throne. Several of these barons had set out to collect the ransom that would release King Richard the Lionheart from his jail in Austria. Robin was invited to join the conspiracy in return for future amnesty. It was a dangerous proposition. Provincial banditry was one thing, court intrigue another. Prince John had spies everywhere, and he was known for his vindictiveness. If the conspirators' plan failed, the pursuit would be relentless, and retributions swift.

The sound of the supper horn startled Robin from his thoughts. There was the smell of roasting venison in the air. Nothing was resolved or settled. Robin headed for camp promising himself that he would give these problems his utmost attention after tomorrow's raid.

Howard Distribution Company
Turmoil at the Top

Daniel F. Jennings
Texas A&M University

Slowly rising from his chair in his plush fourth-floor office overlooking Savannah Bay in Savannah, Georgia, Harry Stone, president of Howard Distribution Company (HDC) greeted Clark Greene, vice president and general manager of HDC's Southern Region, and invited him to sit down.

"Clark, I believe that something has gone wrong," Stone stated as Greene remained standing. "You have many excellent qualities. In fact, I recognized them when I promoted you to vice president/general manager. But after reviewing the progress of the Southern Region over the past six months, I see that the results are below our expectations."

Greene moved to a large window in Stone's office and watched the July vacationers enjoying themselves on the bay this midmorning. His pulse quickened as he waited for Stone to continue.

Stone said, "Costs in the Southern Region are higher than budgeted, your branch managers are unhappy with your leadership, and the morale of your people is low. I'm also concerned with how you have failed to cooperate with Bill Williams."

Greene became angry at the mention of Williams, a young and aggressive individual with an executive MBA from the University of Texas. Williams was new to HDC, but Greene knew that senior management was pleased with his performance.

Stone continued, "Clark, last week in Atlanta I was speaking with one of our suppliers. He indicated that your dealings with his company were not entirely clean. He intimated that you were after kickbacks. That comment really hurt me. HDC has always been ethical in its dealings with suppliers. I know, however, that you are 52, that your two children are in college, and that your wife has been ill."

Greene continued to look out the window as Stone concluded, "Clark, I know that you have spent nearly all of your life in Georgia, most of it Savannah. It will be difficult for you to move away and even harder for you to find a similar position in Savannah. It pains me to do this, but I have to ask for your resignation. I will do my best to help you find a suitable position."

Turning slowly from the window with his face flushed, Greene finally replied to Stone, "Harry, I can't believe this is taking place. It's all wrong. I've worked for this company for 15 years. I built the Southern Region. Granted, the results of this year haven't met expectations, but the Southern Region has been the largest contributor to the company's bottom line this year as well as in past years. I bet that your boy

Williams has been telling you about the supplier deals. He won't stop at anything to build himself up and to discredit me. Whatever he says is a lie, and I'm not going to let him get me. I won't take it."

A period of silence followed in which Stone and Greene merely looked at one another. Suddenly, Greene said, "I won't resign," and immediately left Stone's office, his heart pounding.

Stone sat motionless as he watched the door close. He was uncertain about his next course of action. He never expected that Greene would refuse to resign. After a time of reflection, Stone decided to continue with his plan, with one modification.

"Sandy, please come in and take a memo," Stone said to his secretary over the intercom. Stone then dictated a letter to Clark Greene informing him that his employment with HDC had ended effective that afternoon, July 10, 2001. Later that same day, Stone issued a general memorandum informing senior management that Greene had resigned and that Robert Wright, corporate manager of quality assurance, would be the acting general manager of the Southern Region. Stone also had his secretary schedule a meeting that night in Atlanta with the nine branch managers of the Southern Region so that he could personally tell them about the change and their new acting general manager.

While Stone was preparing his memos and developing his plan of action, Greene was in the process of contacting his old friend and former boss Wallace Davis regarding the events that had taken place. Davis was a past president of HDC and an influential member of HDC's board of directors and its powerful executive committee. Greene intended to have Davis take his termination to the board for deliberation.

History of Howard Distribution Company

Two brothers, Clovis and Marvin Howard, started Howard Distribution Company in 1912. Prior to the start-up, Clovis had worked as a general sales manager for a large manufacturing firm and later became an independent selling agent representing several manufacturing firms with complementary products. Marvin was a certified public accountant who owned his own accounting firm. Very successful as a sales agent, Clovis added several employees and finally asked Marvin to join him in 1912. Since the 1912 start-up, HDC had been headquartered in Savannah and had evolved into an industrial distributor with sales of $400 million. The company's product line included abrasives, fasteners, fluid power equipment, hand and power tools, industrial rubber products, pipe valves and fittings, safety supplies, power transmission equipment, pumps, brushes, lubricants, gloves, precision measuring tools, hoists and cranes, shelving and racks, cordage, paint supplies, janitorial supplies, an assortment of electrical products, and industrial paper products.

Clovis and Marvin Howard, now both deceased, had been succeeded by Clovis's two sons, Hunt and Jason. Hunt Howard became president and guided HDC into its present position. In 1988 Hunt Howard died suddenly while playing tennis. Jason Howard was concerned about his ability to properly manage the company and took a number of steps to remove himself from certain management responsibilities. First, he named Wallace Davis as president of HDC and created an executive committee composed of himself and two other board members. The executive committee addressed certain strategic and tactical issues facing the company and presented recommendations to the full board. The executive committee met as needed, whereas the full board had regularly scheduled meetings. Exhibit 1 provides selected information about HDC's board of directors.

Exhibit 1 BACKGROUND INFORMATION ON HDC'S BOARD OF DIRECTORS

Name	Age, Place Where Most of Life Spent	Education	Current Activity	Position on the Board and Executive Committee	Association with HDC	
					Employee	Board Member
Wallace Davis	65, Georgia	BS (Marketing) University of Georgia	Retired	Board member, executive committee member	33	16
Jason Howard	68, Georgia	No academic degree	Retired finance director	Chairman of the board, chairman of the executive committee	35	21
Lane Jefferson	70, Georgia	JD (Law) University of Georgia	Retired attorney	Board member	0	12
Donald Meechan	55, Georgia	BS (Civil Engineering) University of Georgia	President, Meechan Construction	Board member	0	7
Louis Nelson	58, Georgia	MS (Accounting) Georgia State University	Vice president of finance, HDC	Board member	32	6
Harry Stone	50, New York City	BA (History) Hamilton College (NY)	President, HDC	Board member, executive committee member	6	6
Richard Tanner	56, Georgia	Ph.D. (Marketing) Stanford University	Dean, College of Business, University of Georgia	Board member	0	20

Exhibit 2   OWNERSHIP OF HOWARD DISTRIBUTION COMPANY, 2001

Owners	Ownership (%)
Jason Howard	52%
Remaining members of the Howard family	23
Wallace Davis	15
Remaining members of the board of directors	10
	100%

Presently, HDC was privately owned. Exhibit 2 details the ownership of HDC.

Present Structure of HDC

HDC was organized into two regions, Southern and Southwest. The Southern Region had nine branches located in North and South Carolina, Georgia, Alabama, and Tennessee with the regional vice president and general manager located in a large regional distribution center in Atlanta, Georgia. The Southwest Region had six branches located in Texas, Louisiana, and Oklahoma with the vice president and general manager located in a large regional distribution center in Houston, Texas. Exhibit 3 depicts HDC's skeletal organizational structure.

The president, Harry Stone, reported to the board of directors. Another HDC executive, Louis Nelson, the vice president of finance, was also a member of the board. Both Stone and Nelson regularly attended monthly board meetings. From time to time, other senior managers attended board meetings to keep the board informed of matters of importance in their area of specialty. According to Jason Howard, chairman of the board of directors, "This practice gives us an opportunity to know what is really going on in the company."

In addition to managing the company and attending to his normal duties as president, Harry Stone took a special interest in negotiations involving integrated supply contracts with customers and certain other contracts concerning suppliers. It was not uncommon for Louis Nelson to become involved in these negotiations as well.

Harry Stone, HDC's President

Harry Stone had replaced Wallace Davis as president of HDC on January 1, 1995, after Davis resigned to accept a position as executive vice president of a manufacturing company headquartered in a foreign country that had been an HDC supplier. During the seven years Davis was president, HDC had prospered and expanded into the Southwest. Davis had been a member of HDC's board of directors since 1985 and became a member of the executive committee in 1999 after retiring from the manufacturing company.

Davis recommended Stone to Jason Howard after a fruitless search for a candidate within the company and the industry. HDC's board of directors agreed to hire Stone, then the executive director of a trade association located in New York City; Stone came to be regarded by board members as a person of integrity, dedication, and charm. Even

Exhibit 3   Howard Distribution Company's Organizational Structure in 2001

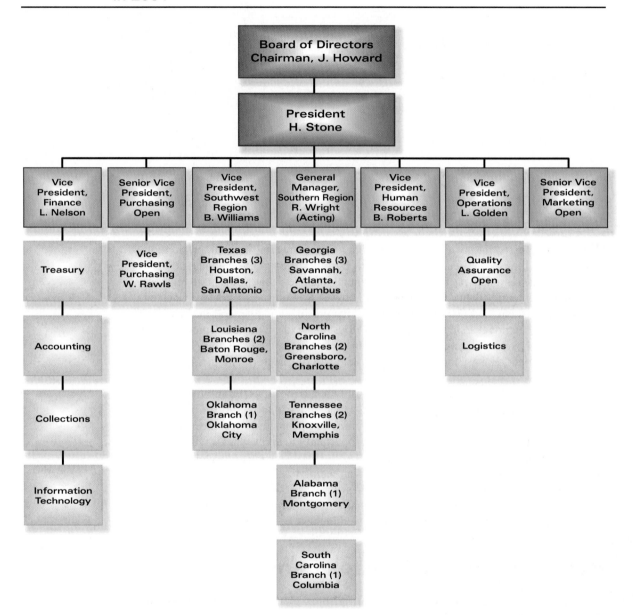

though the tight-knit business community in Savannah in 1995 was nearly impervious to outsiders, Stone was immediately admitted and was well liked. During the early months of Stone's presidency at HDC, morale soared because, as his employees stated, Stone was both extraordinarily hardworking (he worked 75-hour weeks) and "human." Stone was also one of Savannah's best fund-raisers for community projects and, though not an alumnus of the University of Georgia, had raised over $1 million to support the business school.

However, HDC had not performed well financially under Stone's leadership. Rising costs and fierce competition had put severe pressure on HDC's profit margins. In an attempt to offset the decline in margins, Stone began to make changes in personnel during 2000.

In September 2000, Joe Ireland, vice president and general manager of the Southern Region, accepted a position with another company. Ireland told HDC's board he was leaving because Stone had expected the impossible and had made life miserable for him and his family. Ireland told the board that he had planned for over a year to take his daughter to Europe after her graduation from college, but that Stone had forced him to not go because of an "important" meeting that had developed unexpectedly. Ireland's wife and daughter left without him and Ireland told the board that the "important" meeting never materialized. After Ireland left HDC, Stone promoted Clark Greene, who had nearly 15 years' experience with HDC, to vice president and general manager of the Southern Region.

In October 2000, Bill Williams was promoted to vice president and general manager of the Southwest Region, replacing Dale Scott. In early 1999, Stone created a new position of senior vice president for marketing and brought in his old friend Bill Williams, whom he hoped could develop marketing strategies for HDC. Williams had been a general sales manager with a manufacturing firm that supplied products to HDC and had lived in New York City. Williams and Stone frequently played golf together and told many people within HDC that they had done so while they both lived in New York. When Williams was promoted to vice president and general manager of the Southwest Region, Scott, who had 28 years' experience with HDC, was assigned to Williams's former position of senior vice president for marketing. Although Scott retained the base salary as a vice president and general manager in his new job, he was not allowed to participate in certain incentive programs and had to give up certain perks. Scott told a board member that he felt he had been demoted and that his pay had definitely been cut. Scott discussed his reassignment with the executive committee and was advised to lodge a formal complaint before the full board. Scott, however, chose not to do so. In April 2000, Scott resigned from HDC and was now employed as a sales manager with a building materials distributor at a lower salary than he earned while employed with HDC.

In November 2000, Stone asked Don Allen, senior vice president for purchasing, to resign. Stone stated that Allen, with 30 years at HDC, "lacked the ability to negotiate with key suppliers." Before Allen was asked to resign, the executive committee developed a severance package for him that was approved by the full board. Allen refused to resign and argued that he was being treated unfairly in that he did not have the final say in supplier negotiations because of the involvement of Stone and Nelson. Allen brought his grievance to the full board, which rejected his appeal. Allen, aged 54 at the time, was visibly shaken by the board's decision and was now a purchasing agent for a local firm at 30 percent of his former salary. Allen was the first longtime employee to be terminated by HDC and the first employee to receive such a severance. After the Allen episode, one board member stated, "The event was very painful; it left a lot of questions with us about Stone's leadership."

Meeting at the Country Club

Clark Greene leaned across the table in the restaurant of Savannah's most exclusive country club. The man across from him was Wallace Davis, his old friend and mentor.

"Wallace, thanks for meeting with me today. I know that you are very busy. I have to talk with you. Something has happened that you should know about. I'll try to be brief. Harry and I met this morning in his office, and he asked for my resignation. I refused. Before he left his office to go to Atlanta to meet with my people, he terminated my employment with HDC, effective this afternoon."

Davis showed no emotion as Greene continued.

"I control HDC's four largest customers and I can easily take them to a competitor. But Stone had the gall to accuse me of soliciting kickbacks from a supplier. He has absolutely no proof of any wrongdoing on my part. I believe that Williams put Stone up to it. He's been charging a substantial portion of his region's expenses to my region. I've been arguing with him about these expenses for the past several weeks and told him that I was going to talk with Nelson and have him straighten things out. Williams told me that he would have my head if I went to either Nelson or Stone about the matter. Williams told me that someone in his accounting department had probably made a mistake and, if that was the case, he didn't want to reverse any charges from my region to his region. He told me that I should just suck it up and that my region could afford a few extra charges."

Fingering the handle of his coffee cup, Davis stated, "This is a surprise to me. I'm very sorry that this has happened to you. Something strange is occurring. Last week the executive committee met to discuss certain items. Stone was at the meeting, but he didn't say anything about your situation."

"I don't know what to do. How long will the board allow Stone to destroy the very people who have built HDC?" asked Greene.

"The full board has its regular monthly meeting next week. I can't call another meeting of the executive committee to investigate this because Jason is out of town. It is too sensitive to discuss by telephone. It needs to be discussed face-to-face," replied Davis.

"Well," said Greene, "I just hope that the board takes this as an opportunity to straighten out HDC. There are serious problems regarding the manner in which responsibility is delegated and the criteria that are used to evaluate employees. Too many things are unclear since Ireland, Scott, and Allen have been forced out of HDC. The morale of the top management team is very low. Earnings are not improving. Everyone is concerned about saving his own skin. Who will be axed next?"

Stone's Trip to Atlanta

Stone was deeply shaken over Greene's refusal to resign. On the plane to Atlanta he tried to analyze the situation. He realized he had made a mistake in promoting Greene to vice president and general manager, although Greene had performed well in his previous assignments and had scored well on the battery of tests that were administered to all HDC executives.

"I must stick to my guns," thought Stone. "I will refuse to be blackmailed by the four powerful customers Clark Greene has in his pocket. I can't allow my authority to be challenged, especially by a man I believe has taken kickbacks."

After a sleepless night, Stone telephoned Jason Howard, who was on vacation, to inform him of Greene's "resignation."

"I'm surprised and concerned. This is a sad occasion. Clark Greene was a valuable employee. Frankly, Harry, I'm concerned—but you are the boss. We'll try to handle the matter appropriately at the board meeting next week," responded Howard.

As he returned the telephone receiver to its cradle, Howard became quite pensive. For the first time since he had become associated with HDC, he felt that a problem existed in how affairs of the company were being managed—they were not being handled as he believed they should be.

Jason Howard had never missed a board meeting, and his deep concern for HDC was reflected in how he usually helped in HDC's decision-making process—being careful after long consideration and debate. He had discussed Allen's resignation privately with Stone first, then with the executive committee, and then with the full board. Although Howard had supported Stone in the Allen matter, he was not fully convinced that Allen should have left HDC. Howard reflected on the long hours he had spent on deciding Stone's appointment as president of HDC and the many private discussions he had with each board member. He considered the thorough manner in which both Mr. and Mrs. Stone were interviewed and the procedures used to investigate Stone before the board selected him for the presidency of HDC.

The Board Meeting

The board of directors of HDC met at 8:00 A.M. on July 18, 2001. The meeting promptly came to order. The agenda items included HDC's second-quarter financial performance; a long-term lease on an additional building for the regional distribution center in Houston, Texas; the anticipated state of the national economy for the reminder of the year; a new request from a charity in San Antonio, Texas, for contributions; and a personnel announcement from Stone.

The last item covered in the meeting was Stone's announcement.

"Mr. Chairman, members of the board," Stone began, "I regret to inform you that effective July 10, 2001, Mr. Clark Greene has resigned from our company . . . "

CASE 24

The Transformation of BP

Michelle Rogan
London Business School

Lynda Gratton
London Business School

Sumantra Ghoshal
London Business School

On June 25, 1992, the board of BP, the United Kingdom's largest industrial enterprise, cut its dividend and removed its chief executive, Robert Horton. The move came as the company sought to overcome a series of interlinked challenges—the transition to private-sector ownership, which had coincided with the stock market collapse in 1987; the fall in oil prices after the Gulf War; and rising debts and increasing unit costs.

Within a decade the company was leading the restructuring of the sector, had reduced costs and debt, and was earning after-tax income of over $1 billion a month. By 2001 BP was generating annual revenues of $120 billion, employing 100,000 people in over 100 countries, and had taken its place as one of the three supermajors in the oil industry (see financials in Exhibit 1).

Within the oil industry and beyond, BP had become a model of both financial performance and corporate social responsibility, breaking rank by accepting that the risks of climate change were too dangerous to ignore and by refusing to accept the long-entrenched trade-off between environmental protection and increased energy consumption that many had come to take for granted.

This study looks at how that transformation was achieved, and in particular at the way in which changes in the management of the company influenced both performance and reputation.

Building the Platform for Superior Performance

In retrospect it is possible to see that a number of the changes necessary to achieve the transformation of BP had begun before 1992.

As chairman and chief executive, Robert Horton had begun a process of "cultural change," shaking up BP's entrenched bureaucracies and reducing staff numbers. Sir John Browne, chief executive of BP Exploration from 1989 to 1995 and subsequently chief executive of BP as a whole, had initiated radical steps in 1989 to focus exploration spending on a limited number of the best prospects around and to reduce costs.

The real impact of such developments became apparent, however, only after 1992 under the leadership of Horton's successor David Simon (later to become a minister in Tony Blair's first government as Lord Simon of Highbury). Simon stabilized the

BP Amoco Statement of Financial Position

	1991	1992	1993	1994	1995	1996	1997	1998	1999
Assets									
Cash and equivalents	$ 1,340.79	$ 377.50	$ 310.28	$ 293.28	$ 616.20	$ 258.57	$ 275.56	$ 875.00	$ 1,551.00
Receivables	7,954.98	6,979.22	5,245.13	6,639.36	7,141.68	8,740.68	7,005.20	6,835.00	10,488.00
Inventories	5,596.91	5,102.29	3,941.97	4,302.48	4,389.84	5,085.21	4,284.46	3,642.00	5,124.00
Prepaid expenses	2,141.15	1,901.09	1,613.43	1,703.52	2,031.12	2,540.07	2,704.14	3,508.00	4,230.00
Current assets—other	1,568.93	1,550.77	1,168.70	940.68	1,020.24	1,546.35	1,822.68	2,366.00	2,084.00
Total current assets	18,602.76	15,910.87	12,279.50	13,879.32	15,199.08	18,170.88	16,092.04	17,226.00	23,477.00
Plant, property, and equipment (gross)	64,571.10	61,390.56	59,623.04	63,034.92	66,856.92	69,587.44	71,811.60	120,820.00	121,925.00
Accumulated depreciation	27,642.34	28,320.05	29,149.60	31,749.12	35,160.84	36,343.45	37,482.80	63,469.00	66,242.00
Plant, property, and equipment (net)	36,928.76	33,070.51	30,473.44	31,285.80	31,696.08	33,243.99	34,328.80	57,351.00	55,683.00
Investments at equity	2,131.80	2,429.59	2,433.44	2,669.16	3,263.52	3,302.26	3,570.66	4,162.00	4,334.00
Investments and advances—other	1,335.18	747.45	484.62	525.72	157.56	157.17	117.86	5,121.00	5,319.00
Intangibles	452.54	374.48	156.62	137.28	152.88	157.17	147.74	151.00	292.00
Deferred charges	0.00	0.00	0.00	0.00	0.00	0.00	0.00	0.00	0.00
Assets—other	0.00	0.00	0.00	0.00	0.00	15.21	318.72	489.00	456.00
Total Assets	$59,451.04	$52,532.90	$45,827.62	$48,497.28	$50,469.12	$55,046.68	$54,575.82	$84,500.00	$89,561.00
Liabilities									
Accounts payable	$ 5,873.67	$ 5,278.96	$ 4,476.83	$ 5,959.20	$ 6,809.40	$ 7,843.29	$ 6,407.60	$ 5,450.00	$ 8,680.00
Notes payable	2,008.38	2,450.73	1,009.13	787.80	965.64	1,235.39	1,093.94	1,659.00	3,809.00
Accrued expenses	3,857.81	3,405.05	2,309.33	2,375.88	2,717.52	2,638.09	2,631.10	2,897.00	4,041.00
Taxes payable	1,277.21	1,254.81	1,155.41	1,054.56	1,725.36	2,055.04	2,353.88	2,395.00	2,558.00
Debt (long-term) due in one year	1,071.51	1,221.59	817.06	837.72	185.64	552.63	793.48	1,178.00	1,091.00
Other current liabilities	3,683.90	3,178.55	2,579.72	2,383.68	2,730.00	3,618.29	3,514.22	4,587.00	3,096.00
Total current liabilities	17,772.48	16,789.69	12,347.47	13,398.84	15,133.56	17,942.73	16,794.22	18,166.00	23,275.00
Long-term debt	12,168.09	11,667.77	10,555.26	8,899.80	7,425.60	5,871.06	5,330.26	10,918.00	9,644.00
Deferred taxes	755.48	619.10	366.42	444.60	586.56	684.45	647.40	1,632.00	1,783.00

continued

Exhibit 1 Continued

BP Amoco Statement of Financial Position

	1991	1992	1993	1994	1995	1996	1997	1998	1999
Investment tax credit	0.00	0.00	0.00	0.00	0.00	0.00	0.00	0.00	0.00
Minority interest	561.00	385.05	147.75	170.04	168.48	184.21	92.96	1,072.00	1,061.00
Liabilities—other	8,271.01	8,003.00	8,008.05	8,335.08	8,725.08	8,740.68	8,285.06	10,926.00	10,517.00
Total liabilities	39,528.06	37,464.61	31,424.95	31,248.36	32,039.28	33,423.13	31,149.90	42,714.00	46,280.00
Shareholders' Equity									
Preferred stock	22.44	18.12	17.73	18.72	18.72	20.28	19.92	21.00	21.00
Common stock	2,520.76	2,046.05	2,013.83	2,146.56	2,174.64	2,387.97	2,392.06	4,842.00	4,871.00
Capital surplus	3,925.13	3,251.03	2,968.30	3,244.80	3,347.76	3,733.21	3,776.50	3,056.00	3,684.00
Retained earnings (net other)	13,454.65	9,753.09	9,402.81	11,838.84	12,888.72	15,482.09	17,237.44	33,867.00	34,705.00
Total shareholders' equity	19,922.98	15,068.29	14,402.67	17,248.92	18,429.84	21,623.55	23,425.92	41,786.00	43,281.00
Total liabilities and equity	$59,451.04	$52,532.90	$45,827.62	$48,497.28	$50,469.12	$55,046.68	$54,575.82	$84,500.00	$89,561.00

BP Amoco Income Statement

	1991	1992	1993	1994	1995	1996	1997	1998	1999
Sales (net)	$57,725.01	$58,852.50	$51,638.63	$50,667.48	$57,047.48	$69,780.36	$71,274.40	$68,304.00	$83,566.00
Cost of goods sold	43,140.21	45,612.90	39,116.81	39,076.20	43,950.86	55,305.12	56,424.20	53,059.00	65,995.00
Gross profit	14,584.80	13,239.60	12,521.81	11,591.28	13,096.62	14,475.24	14,850.20	15,245.00	17,571.00
Selling, general, and administrative expenses	6,637.50	6,984.42	5,664.74	4,680.27	5,389.38	5,277.48	5,546.48	5,609.00	5,541.00
Operating income before depreciation	7,947.30	6,255.18	6,857.08	6,911.01	7,707.24	9,197.76	9,303.72	9,636.00	12,030.00
Depreciation, depletion, and amortization	4,403.76	3,927.63	3,856.28	3,333.87	3,220.04	3,463.20	3,047.12	5,255.00	4,708.00
Operating income after depreciation	3,543.54	2,327.55	3,000.80	3,577.14	4,487.20	5,734.56	6,256.60	4,381.00	7,322.00
Interest expense	1,407.15	1,355.82	1,085.96	872.10	837.40	700.44	577.28	1,172.00	1,359.00
Nonoperating income/expense	(7.08)	985.89	363.47	729.81	954.32	1,491.36	401.80	784.00	3,343.00

Special items	(2,280.00)	850.00	(101.68)	(804.96)	(1,529.44)	55.08	(354.60)	(1,759.38)	0.00
Pretax income	7,026.00	4,843.00	5,979.44	5,720.52	3,074.68	3,489.93	1,923.71	198.24	2,129.31
Income taxes—total	1,880.00	1,520.00	1,915.52	1,726.92	1,309.82	1,058.76	1,012.09	1,000.05	1,451.40
Minority interest	138.00	63.00	13.12	12.48	(7.90)	18.36	2.96	8.85	(56.64)
Income before extraordinary items and discontinued operations (EI&DO)	5,006.00	3,258.35	4,049.16	3,979.56	1,771.18	2,411.28	907.19	(812.43)	732.78
Net income (loss)	5,008.00	3,260.00	4050.80	3,981.12	1,772.76	2,412.81	908.66	(810.66)	734.55
Preferred dividends	2.00	1.65	1.64	1.56	1.58	1.53	1.48	1.77	1.77
Net income available for common stock	$5,006.00	$3,258.35	$4,049.16	$3,979.56	$1,771.18	$2,411.28	$907.19	$(812.43)	$732.78
Earnings per Share									
Primary	$1.55	$2.04	$4.26	$8.52	$3.83	$5.29	$2.00	$(1.80)	$1.68
Fully diluted	1.54	2.04	4.26	8.52	3.83	5.29	2.00	(1.80)	1.68
Common Shares									
For primary EPS calculation (millions)	3,231.00	1,606.33	950.30	467.75	461.50	456.17	452.92	450.42	448.25
For fully diluted EPS calculation (millions)	3,249.50	1,606.33	—	—	—	—	—	—	—
Outstanding at fiscal year-end	3,247.34	1,613.84	960.43	470.85	464.61	458.55	454.26	451.55	449.41

Source: Compustat, accessed February 14, 2001.

company, increasing revenues and reducing costs and laid the foundation for the process of transformation, which can be dated from 1995 when Browne, backed by his deputy Rodney Chase, took over the reins of the business.

Nick Butler, policy adviser to Browne and his top team throughout the period, described what followed as "Act I, taking the steps to create a high-grade business portfolio and human capital. Creating the base for something interesting."

Ralph Alexander, one of BP's group vice presidents, recalled:

> When Browne stepped in as CEO in 1995, we knew we had to create something different. We looked at the ROACE [return on average capital employed]; we were all operating within a limited space. We realized that to break out we had to redefine ourselves. It was not about beating Exxon, but how to beat the ROACE of Microsoft. We wanted to create a company with sufficient scale to take regional shocks and with enough reach to thrive in almost any circumstances.

Thus began a series of mergers and acquisitions that would put BP in the superweight category. Browne led BP through two critical and successful mergers totaling $120 billion, first with Amoco in 1998 and then with ARCO in 1999. BP had become the third largest company in the oil industry, trailing behind only Royal Dutch Shell and Exxon Mobil. With its acquisition of Burmah Castrol in July 2000, BP had become a combined group with a market value of more than $200 billion. BP's goals moving forward from the three mergers were to lop $4 billion off its annual costs worldwide, to sell assets of $10 billion, and to boost capital spending to a total of $26 billion over the three years to the end of 2001.

While achieving scale, these mergers also created a large, fragmented company. By 2000, the company consisted of three camps, divided by their very different heritages: approximately 60,000 from BP, 40,000 from Amoco, and 20,000 from ARCO. BP's management had to decide how to bring together the diverse strengths of the three different heritage companies into a single new business. Though unifying the company would be a challenge, management believed a single global brand supported by an integrated global organization was the best way forward.

Sir John Browne explained the core premises on which the management of BP based its responses to this challenge:

> The organization that we evolved from 1995 onwards was founded on several simple concepts. Number one was our observation that people work better in smaller units, because the closer you can identify people to objectives and targets, the better things happen. So we started off with what we came to call the Atomic Structure, so that the big, long-term targets of the company could be divided up and deployed into smaller units that could take full ownership of these targets . . .
>
> . . . The second premise was contradictory to that, and that was our observation that any organization of scale could create proprietary knowledge through learning . . . so the question was how could you get independent atomic units to work together to share information, to learn and to retain that learning . . .
>
> . . . The third theme we observed was the very different interaction between people of equal standing, if you will, when they reviewed each other's work, than there was when a superior reviewed the work of a subordinate. We concluded that the way to get the best answers would be to get peers to challenge and support each other, than to have a hierarchical challenge process.

. . . The fourth organizational element was very much oriented towards the strategic and operating foundation of the company, in a pure business sense. You could have strategic aims for each business segment and it could all be translated into targets, but there had to be more to it. That more had to do with the company, as a whole, so we focused on something called reputation.

Creating Performance Leaders: The Atomic Organization

A cornerstone of Act I was an increasing emphasis on leadership development and deployment. To quote Nick Butler:

> Ten or 12 years ago, BP was a collection of fiefdoms. These fiefdoms were extremely separate: They lived in separate buildings and had separate management systems and different philosophies. The fiefdoms did not mix, and the people barely came together at the top. John's fundamental philosophy was that to succeed, these disparate parts had to be brought together as one company with a coherent overall strategic direction, one share price, and one set of metrics. That was the only way to extract the benefits of the synergies and to make the whole something more than the parts.

At the center of this integration were the 400 men and women who collectively led the enterprise. Leading this group were the six managing directors, who had total, collective responsibility for the policy of the enterprise. This group formally met in weekly meetings to review and gather experiences. They also used these meetings as an opportunity to discuss the movement of people within the top 300. A separate committee met as needed to allocate capital. The team met in away days twice a year—once with the full main board, including the nonexecs—to consider longer-term strategy. Informal dialogue within the team was high. As Nick Butler explained,

> Initially the different businesses were located in separate buildings and only met at formal meetings. The first step was to move into the same building. At first they were on separate floors in the same building, but they were still not really meeting. So the process took another step forward. The whole management team was integrated; they were located on the same floor in the same building. That produced real change—real cooperation and a close association across the boundary lines.

This close association was further bonded through their respective chiefs of staff, who met to discuss agendas and schedules, and to make sure that all the links were working.

Browne and his team believed the primary task of the top management was to focus on strategic issues: about reputation, economic shifts, societal shifts, and strategic-issue-based governance. To achieve this, the board rarely used any operational reports. As Chase commented, "If you preoccupy your management with operational, not strategic issues, you never get to this position. We have chosen a form of organization that has given almost the entirety of operational delivery to some very young men and women of fantastic talent around the world. We preoccupy ourselves strategically."

Next came the 40 group vice presidents, who oversaw large pieces of the business. Until the reorganization of 2001, this group did not have individual accountability for specific business areas, but shared collective responsibility for the total operation.

Their primary roles were to coach the business unit leaders, to manage the succession process and to make sure that each business unit head had a performance contract that was both achievable and a stretch.

This group of vice presidents was also the primary feed for top management succession. In Browne's words: "This is the group from which the top six (the managing directors of the future) will be identified. It means that at any one time there are about 15 who could be my successor, and that in turn means that we have a sufficient pool of talent both to manage a company of this size and to ensure that there is no complacency."

At the base, and core, of BP's organization, below the level of the group vice presidents, lay a relatively simple architecture of 150 business units, each led by its own business unit leader. While the top team managed the external relations of the firm, particularly with the governments, and engaged in debate regarding long-term strategic meaning and purpose, the business unit leaders focused on the delivery of operating performance.

Chase described the business unit structure of BP as "an extraordinarily flat, dispersed, decentralized process of delivery." A business unit could be an oil field, a gas field, a refinery, a chemical plant, or a regional marketing area. As Chase explained, "The reason we selected 150 was that each had to be potentially material to the rest of the group. If there wasn't potential to build a billion-dollar business, we would not make it a business unit." The dismantling of the hierarchical, functionally based company had begun in 1990 when CEO Robert Horton launched Project 1990, which included a large scale restructuring of BP and the removal of many management layers. David Simon, who assumed the role of CEO in 1992, continued this decomposition by further breaking down the functional walls and restructuring the company into 90 different business units. Browne and his team continued this process, and by 2000 the company consisted of 150 separate business units held together by strong performance management processes.

Horizontally, the 150 business units were further organized into 15 peer groups. The peer groups consisted of a network of related business units within a particular business stream—essentially those in a similar business, facing similar challenges.

Setting the Targets: The Performance Contract

Driving down vertically through the business was the performance contract process, designed to create a clear "line of sight" for individual business unit leaders and the collective corporate business goals (see Exhibit 2). As Chase described, "We run our businesses with very tightly defined key performance indicators. Some are financial. Others relate to our commitment to be a force for good. We use exactly the same process—define the goal, define the input to achieve the goal, and then start monitoring."

David Watson, group vice president of business information, described the performance management process as a "structure for having conversations." The performance contract was the product of a series of such conversations—within the business unit, within the peer group, and with the top management team. In an annual process, business unit leaders worked with their teams to identify their unit's goals for the year—financial, social and environmental—and documented them in the performance contract. Next they met with their business unit peer group to align each unit's targets

Exhibit 2   Performance Management Process

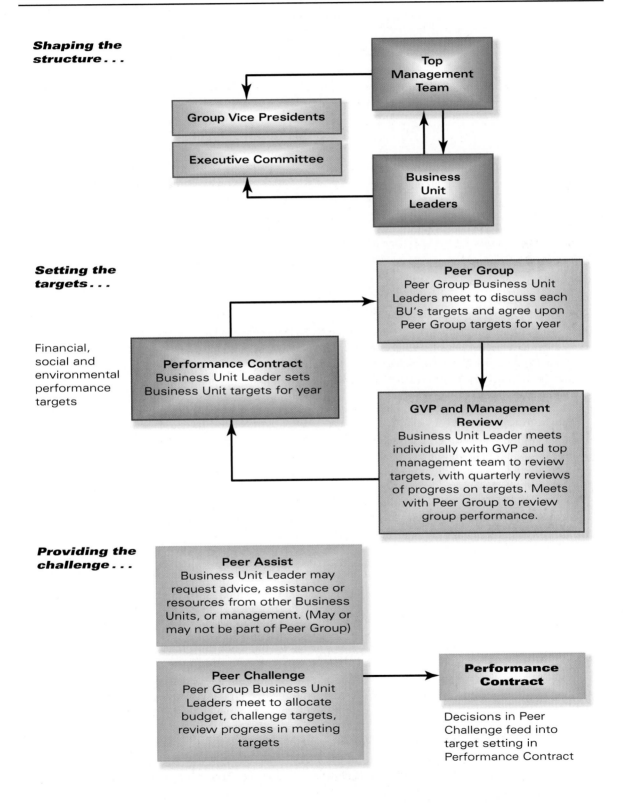

Shaping the structure . . .

Top Management Team

Group Vice Presidents

Executive Committee

Business Unit Leaders

Setting the targets . . .

Financial, social and environmental performance targets

Performance Contract
Business Unit Leader sets Business Unit targets for year

Peer Group
Peer Group Business Unit Leaders meet to discuss each BU's targets and agree upon Peer Group targets for year

GVP and Management Review
Business Unit Leader meets individually with GVP and top management team to review targets, with quarterly reviews of progress on targets. Meets with Peer Group to review group performance.

Providing the challenge . . .

Peer Assist
Business Unit Leader may request advice, assistance or resources from other Business Units, or management. (May or may not be part of Peer Group)

Peer Challenge
Peer Group Business Unit Leaders meet to allocate budget, challenge targets, review progress in meeting targets

Performance Contract

Decisions in Peer Challenge feed into target setting in Performance Contract

Exhibit 3   Performance Contract

1999 Business Unit Performance Contract				
Financial	**1998 Baseline**	**1998 Actual**	**1999 Contract**	**1999 Stretch**
Net income				
Income improvement*				
Net cash flow				
Prize delivery†				
Net investment				

CREATING A SAFETY CULTURE

Develop and implement Poland Safety Contract to Employees and Contractors.

Implement employee near-miss program achieving 300 near miss reports in 1999.

PEOPLE BASICS

100% BP Staff employees receive appraisals for their 1998 performance.

100% BP Staff employees engage in a career development discussion with their Team Leader.

100% BP Team Leaders receive upward feedback.

OTHER

Establish Poland As a Business Unit

Establish comprehensive safety programme—2Q

- Institute assurance programme—3Q (planned for September 15)

Establish Management information processes to ensure reliable and timely reporting—3Q

Manage lobby plan with values tied to each category and 100% deliverables with 1999 key contacts plan.

Manage Volume Growth and Protect Market Share

- Balance growth, market share and profitability. Considering this balance, ensure operational processes are in place to achieve 1999 volume increases of xx in LPG and xx in retail

Rebase Costs for Current Environment

Identify levers to re-base costs to achieve 10% ROACE by 2002—1Q

Improve Capital Efficiency and Decapitalize As Suitable

Deliver 30% capital efficiency improvement in new builds and complete **full cost** builds for xx million per site

Develop decapitalization options & landbank strategy—2Q

Develop Retail strategy to support consideration for further investment with Financial Memorandum to CAC in 2Q.

with those of the collective peer group. The final conversation was with the top management team. (See Exhibit 3 for an example of a performance contract.)

"The actual contract is relatively simple," said Chase. "A few financial goals—profit before tax, cash flow, investment, return on invested capital—I have never seen more than four. Then there are two or three high-level nonfinancial targets. Once the contract is decided, people are free to achieve them in whatever way they find appropriate."

Quarterly, the top team met with the business unit leaders to review progress toward the goals. Failure to meet the terms of the contract was a serious matter and at times meant reassignment of the business unit leader. "There is an understanding here . . . that

Exhibit 3   Continued

Leading Indicators of Progress					
PRIZE/KEY ACTIVITY SET	1Q	2Q	3Q	4Q	Yr

New Build start-ups
Specific divestments ($6 million)
Additional divestments ($4 million)
LPG Slawkow terminal on-line

Management Information improved processes
and streamline transaction accounting

KPIs	1998 Actual	1999 Plan	1999 Latest Estimate	1999 Stretch	PG5 Range	PG3 CoCo Average
Fuel margin (cpl)						
Retail volume growth						
Retail MSC like-for-like growth						
MSC/onsite costs (incl. depr)						
CoCo onsite costs ($k/site)						
Offsite costs ($million)						
Onsite costs/GP						
Offsite costs/SOC						
SOC/$ invested (CoCo)						

	1998 Actual	1999 Plan	1999 Latest Estimate	1999 Stretch	PG5 BM	LPG PG Average
LPG volume						
LPG bulk installations (#)						
LPG unit margin ($/tonne)						
LPG debtor days (end-year)						
LPG fixed cost cover						
S&D retail added value (cpl)						
Supply LPG added value ($/ton)						
Filling plants ($million)						
Transport cylinder ($/ton)						
Transport bulk ($/ton)						

*99 Income (including prize) less delta margin less delta forex less delta tax rate less 98 income.

†No prize delivery until Income improvement = Target improvement − Prize

this is a performance culture and either you deliver or you don't," explained Richard Newton, group vice president. Chase commented, "You deliver what you promise—that is our performance mantra. If you do not believe you can deliver, do not make the promise." What if someone does not deliver? "We start from the assumption that if you can't cut it in a particular job you might be able to somewhere else. You are given one or two options to perform somewhere else."

Providing the Stretch: the Peer Challenge

Performance contracts set the unit's targets, but peer groups provided the challenge and stretch to each unit. The peer group played three roles in the challenge. First, business goals were discussed within the peer groups prior to the finalization of the performance contract. Second, peer groups were a key mechanism for determining resource allocation. Finally, they were the primary means of knowledge sharing. One executive described peer groups as "the forum in which business units must fight their corner, justify their promises to their closest colleagues and prove they deserve the resources they seek in competition with other business units."

"The Peer Challenge," Polly Flinn, business unit head and vice president of retail marketing, explained, "was about convincing people in similar positions to support your investment proposal knowing they could invest that same capital [elsewhere] and going eyeball to eyeball with them—and then having to reaffirm whether you have made it or not over the coming months or quarters."

The key for the peer group process to reach its full potential was an obligation for every high-performing business unit to assist and improve the underperforming units. Chase summarized the reasons why the peer group structure worked for BP:

> One of the things we find when we talk to other companies is that they disbelieve us when we say that our performance units have a high capacity and bias to improve one another. The point is they have to do that or they can't meet their goals, because they have performance outputs for the whole peer group. Today the top three business units in the peer group are responsible for the improvement of the bottom three. That's how they work in a structural sense. They are measured for it.

The performance measurement associated with the peer group processes forced the business unit leaders to "grab good ideas from one another and to impose their good ideas on one another," added Chase. This motivation was built into the bonus structure. Fifty percent of a business unit leader's bonus was based on peer group performance, and 50 percent on business unit performance.

Integration through Collective Learning

If performance management was the foundation of Act I, then relentless collective learning was the leverage point.

"In order to generate extraordinary value for shareholders, a company has to learn better than its competitors and apply that knowledge throughout its business faster and more widely than they do," said Sir John Browne. "Any organization that thinks it does everything the best and that it need not learn from others is incredibly arrogant and foolish." This commitment to knowledge and insight was deeply ingrained in BP. John Manzoni, head of BP's gas, renewables, and power business, explained:

> I always say to people, your seat at the table inside BP depends on your level of insight, it does not depend on the position where you sit in the organization. And you find all over the place that people get to sit at important tables and have important conversations and the reason that they are there is because they bring insight.

Four factors converged to help BP become a learning organization: the intellectual curiosity of the top management team, the firmwide attention to relentlessly building human capital, the "Peer Assist" process, and the depth and quality of conversations. Together they ensured that insights were leveraged across the company.

Intellectual Curiosity at the Top

Balancing the competitive nature of the performance-driven side of BP's culture was the intellectual curiosity and openness to knowledge sharing of the people in the company, especially evident in the top team. Browne and his colleagues were described by a *Financial Times* journalist as "an unusually active and well-financed university faculty—earnest, morally engaged and careful of other's sensibilities."[1] Strategic thinking and deep questioning of business purpose were the normal way of operating. In Sir John Browne's words,

> This company is founded on a deep belief in intellectual rigor. In my experience, unless you can lay out rational arguments as the foundation of what you do, nothing happens. Rigor implies that you understand the assumptions you have made . . . assumptions about the state of the world, of what you can do, and how your competitors will interact with it, and how the policy of the world will or will not allow you to do something.

While Browne's appetite for knowledge was insatiable, he himself was a creator of knowledge—a sort of theory builder. As theory builder he relentlessly engaged his top team in discussions around ideas. The resulting intellectual, strategic focus of the team was extraordinary. Asked about the genesis of the strategic nature of the senior team, Chase had this to say:

> We are a deeply questioning team; we constantly inspect what we do to find out whether it is in fact the exercise of laziness or prejudice. We do it in every area; we do it behaviorally, in business process terms, and in operational delivery . . . It helps if your CEO is a very strategic thinker. John is not only a strategic thinker by predisposition but by intellectual learning and a constant search for strategic improvement. He is a continuous researcher for new ideas. He is an unusual CEO; he constantly surrounds himself with strategic stimuli.

Asked to describe some of the strategic issues discussed in the top management team, John Browne elaborated:

> We look at economic history, the rate of change in capital intensive industries, and we ask ourselves how we think the oil industry will change as a result of transportation changes . . . based on what happened, for instance, when canals were put in the UK in the late 18th century. We think about these long-term trends, and what are the consequences of doing the business we are doing, and how we can manage these consequences. Those consequences matter. Environmental questions related to burning oil and gas influence supply and demand parameters of oil and gas because if people worry about that, then they inevitably change their attitude about how they get their energy . . . We test our assumptions . . . What is really going to happen. Could the price of oil drop below $10 a barrel over the medium term? Unlikely, but what happens if it does? We think about how technological substitution in the short term will work . . .

the main point is that all these things we keep interrogating and asking ourselves how dependent are we on one or the other of these factors.

This openness to questioning and learning extended beyond the boundaries of the enterprise. The members of the top team had also established networks of talking partners across industry. Sir John Browne's membership of the boards of Intel and Goldman Sachs provided added insights into industry models. As Nick Butler explained,

> Membership of the board of Intel has been critical to him. About 18 months ago people thought that established businesses like BP would be destroyed by IT, there would be no need for intermediaries. What he had seen at Intel convinced him that this was not the case, there was some potential in B2B, but very little in B2C. The insights from Intel averted risks of overinvestment even though we looked old-fashioned at the time.

The team was also involved with Cambridge University, having set up a multidisciplinary institute on fluid flow analysis that brought together chemists, engineers, physicists, and academic staff.

Members of the top team visited the institute four or five times a year and maintained contacts with numerous faculties not just in Cambridge but also at Stanford, Yale, and a wide range of other very high-quality academic institutions around the world. As Nick Butler, who held many of these links on behalf of Browne, explained, "The process keeps us in touch with people who know more than we do. It is a daily reminder that we are only one relatively small part of a complex world. It is a reminder of all things we do not know."

Relentlessly Building Human Capital

The intellectual curiosity of the top team provided a model for the company. Seeking those within the company who had the insight necessary to run the business was an obsession. The focus on the development of individual talent began from the top with the profound obligation the top team felt to the long-term intellectual health of BP. Much of their time on a day-to-day basis was spent coaching the talented men and women in the organization. Each member typically coached and mentored cohorts of 7 to 10 group vice presidents. Chase described how he saw this role:

> I gossip with them about what is really going on within the inner cabinet, I share confidences, I tell them about my discussions with John Browne. I build trust with them. I agree with them what their weaknesses are, and agree to work with them. You have to take the time to engage them with examples that will make them broader and wiser. To develop their sense of responsibility for the firm; who are they developing. The greatest pleasure I get is from this development of talent.

In turn, the group vice presidents coached the business unit heads. A subgroup also sat on the Learning and Development Committee. The committee met monthly to discuss the long-term development of key talent. As David Watson, a member of the committee, explained, "We are experimenting with a new learning model based on reflection. Each committee meeting is two days of deep, meaningful dialogue." Watson continued, "The whole way we are thinking about learning and development is starting with the brand values: the possibility that actually what we should be developing for future leadership is people with the brand values deeply embedded, not just people who know how to run a part of the business."

BP's management also created forums for the development and expression of its collective intellect through university-based education programs for executives. In a special program developed at Cambridge University, BP executives debated issues such as the social impact of business, the future of international society, valuing nature and ethics. At Stanford and Harvard they used case studies to hone their knowledge of globalization and sources of competitive advantage, and their skills in country risk analysis. The themes of all the programs had a common thread summed up in the name of the Cambridge program, "Thinking into the Future—Learning from the Past." The programs represented a new orientation of the company toward society, its customers, and its employees.

Through formal processes, high-potential individuals had the option to enter the Group Development Program (GDP). This program was a combination of skill assessment, training and development, and career progression. A subset of those individuals in the GDP was selected to serve as "turtles" or personal assistants.[2] As a turtle, the executive would become a shadow to Chase, Browne, or another top team member and be involved in all conversations, all meetings, and all discussions of the top management. "They come with us around the world. They sit in all our executive meetings," explained Chase. "It is a 15-hour-a-day job and they do it for about 12 months. But in return they see everything."

Turtles and the GDP were examples of the "stretch" that was part of a career at BP. Manzoni, who was the first personal assistant to Browne even before the word *turtle* was used, explained, "I have had tremendous opportunities for learning because I have had no bloody idea how to do the job that I have been put into almost every single time." Those that succeeded were rewarded with rapid advancement in their careers at BP.

But this relentless building of human capital was not simply limited to those on the Group Development Program or the turtles. From the end of 1999 onward the company had put substantial resources behind stitching together the 275 human resource intranet systems it had developed and inherited. As Dave Latin, who managed the project, commented, "Following the mergers we saw this as an opportunity to simplify. What got the board excited was the aspiration that e-HR could touch each of the 100,000 employees and cause a shift in behavior." Over the following two years an ever-increasing portfolio of intranet-based developmental tools was rolled out across the world.

"Competencies Online" enabled individuals to assess their current skills and development needs by seeking e-enabled feedback from their peers and colleagues; individuals profiled and communicated their competencies and job aspirations on myProfile, whilst myAgent continuously scouted and reported back job and project vacancies with similar competency needs. Managers who posted the competency profiles of the job and project vacancies in their team using myJobMarket automatically received matched information from the many thousands of online résumés. Within a year BP had created a vibrant and transparent internal labor market, with over 17,000 logging in every week to the myCareer portal. The goal was to get to a situation, by the end of 2001, when all BP employees would use the portal to profile their skills, find job matches, identify their development needs and access learning and development opportunities.

Leveraging through Peer Assist

Performance contracts and Peer Challenge were the backbone of the performance management process. However, the heart of the collective intellectual and social capital of the organization was most evident in Peer Assists. Business unit leaders regularly provided help to one another—to help identify the best strategy, to learn more about a new area of work, or to give validation to a decision—in the form of advice or actual resources through a Peer Assist. Peer Assists spanned peer group boundaries, often requiring the involvement of people in multiple divisions of the company.

Polly Flinn, former Amoco employee and vice president of retail marketing, learned quickly at BP that federal behavior was the norm. While serving as the retail business unit lead in Poland in 1999, Flinn asked for assistance from four leaders at BP who came together in a Peer Assist team to look at the Poland strategy and give Flinn their advice. After Flinn implemented the advice from the Peer Assist, the retail marketing business in Poland became profitable for the first time. In 1998, the business unit lost $20 million; in 2000 it earned $6 million. "This was BP at its best," recalled Flinn. When Flinn was faced with the near impossible task of masterminding the development and rollout of BP's new retail offering, BP Connect, she called on the Peer Assist process once again, but this time on a much grander scale. "The BP Connect Peer Assist was Poland times 30," recalled Flinn. "Of the 300 people involved, only 10 percent actually had Performance Contract goals related to BP Connect, yet because of their desire to share their skills and their expectations of federal behavior, people contributed."

Leaders at BP viewed participation in a Peer Assist as having mutual benefits for both parties. "First, the team that has asked for the Peer Assist obtains strategic and operational insight from the most respected experts in BP," explained Flinn. "Secondly, it is a development opportunity for the people who participate. People want to do it." Top management also participated in Peer Assists, especially regarding strategic issues. Chase, deputy CEO, visited the prototype BP Connect in Atlanta and "became in effect the brand champion for this offer in terms of explaining it to other businesses in BP. He helped to build support for the retail network," said Flinn.

Creating Purposeful Conversations

People learn and share learning through conversations. At BP, management explicitly focused on enhancing the depth, breadth, and quality of conversations at all levels, as a means to supporting organization-wide learning. As Rodney Chase described,

> One of the most pressing reasons to create a dialogue . . . has been the rise of connectivity within the space in which BP operates. There are people who by dint of communications, flexibility and immediacy have the capacity to find things out and transmit the information instantaneously. . . . It is palpable, it is very real and it is expressed with great frequency. It is on my screen now everyday.

"There's no point in just changing a process," explained Watson. "It has to start with changing the fabric—the information. If it is the same information, we'll get the same conversations, so we have to provide different information for different conversations." The source of the information that fueled the conversations had shifted—no longer were communications primarily a top down process. There was a growing recognition that the information for dialogue and conversation came from many sources including families and young employees.

"This organization does not work as a series of instructions—it works by conversations and consensus. It takes longer to get there, but once you do, the whole organization moves," Manzoni explained.

Beyond enhancing the richness and diversity of information, the company made an effort to improve and sharpen the quality of conversations through two means: linking conversations to purpose, and legitimizing dissent and challenge.

According to John Browne, "People do not learn, at least in a corporate environment, without a target. You can implore people to learn, and they will to some extent. But if you say 'Look the learning is necessary in order to cut the cost of drilling a well by 10 percent,' then they will learn with a purpose." This philosophy was built into BP by linking as many conversation processes as possible to tangible and concrete goals. Peer assists and peer reviews. performance contracts—they were all primarily aimed at developing intense, purposeful conversations, driven by concrete goals and targets.

The other basis of enhancing the learning value of conversations was to legitimize dissent and challenge. Again in the words of John Browne:

> People are challenged the whole time. "Just run that by me one more time" is the mildish challenge. "I don't understand it" to "surely you've got this wrong" to "no, that is far too conventional and we have to think of a different way"— the discussions, debates, and challenges happen everywhere. I participate in it; everyone participates in it. If you were sitting in the management committee, sometimes it gets very hot indeed. "No it doesn't make sense"—"Well, make it make sense!" The questions are continuously around . . . For example, Rodney and I have worked together since 1984, and we have worked close up through the ranks and it is a very close relationship. You would think we would be so familiar with each other that we would know the way each other thinks, but it is actually the reverse. We challenge each other very hard, in a very appropriate way, but it is the purpose of the relationship to get a better result, and we do that. And that, in turn, encourages others to do that.

Deep inside the organization, conversations and dialogue occurred in forums such as Performance Contract discussions or message boards on the intranet. Use of the intranet was not limited to young hires. Rodney Chase, a 30-year veteran of BP, checked the message boards daily and was actively engaged in the communication. Chase saw dialogue with employees and stakeholders as essential to operating as a business in society:

> For a global institution we are very nimble. When we want something to happen around the world, we can get all the swallows in our worldwide organization to flip like that. They can go in this direction, they can go in that direction. How does it happen? I have no idea. It is some combination of informal word of mouth, networks, which are encouraged, informal networks based on career friendships, or based on professional groupings, or based on clubs on the intranet. If you've got an important message that needs to get out in the firm, it will happen in 24 hours. And you can be certain that every thinker in the organization will have heard about it and will be thinking about it. It means that the forces for inertia have been largely swept away.

Aligning Organizational and Individual Values

When John Browne and Rodney Chase joined what was then British Petroleum as young graduates, they were joining one of the United Kingdom's most prestigious branded companies. But over time the relationship between the oil industry and society had become increasingly tense. While society demanded the products of energy—heat, light, and mobility—it also demanded that the production of these things be done harmlessly. When accidents occurred, public outrage was the result. In 1989, the Exxon *Valdez* oil spill in Alaska was one such accident. Later in 1995, the Shell Brent Spar incident was another.[3] The two major points of tension were the societal impact of the extraction of oil and the environmental impact of emissions during refining and consumption of fuel.

This tension came to a head for BP in 1997 when a nongovernmental organization, Amnesty International, accused BP of funding private armies in Colombia. A team of BP engineers had discovered what they soon realized to be the largest oil reservoir in the western hemisphere. The oil find had attracted merchants and investors, laborers and contractors, the army, and the guerrillas who wanted to extract their own political rent from the process. The team was in the middle of a region of underdeveloped infrastructure, complex social problems, and a government fighting a 35-year civil war. Upon setting up exploration operations, BP was accused by Amnesty International of providing lethal training to the Colombian security forces through the services of a British-owned private security firm. The Amnesty International news release asserted that these "Colombian security forces have been responsible for widespread extrajudicial executions, torture and 'disappearances' of civilians." BP's reputation was badly tarnished. Though BP denied the accusation, the management realized that a change in the way that BP worked with local communities needed to occur.

Awakening of a Force for Good

The question "What is your personal Colombia?" echoed in the minds of all BP's executives. Memories of the incident affected every decision made by an executive and shaped a new outlook regarding BP's role as a business. Edwards explained, "When we talked to the outside world, the oil industry was seen as big, powerful, dirty, secretive, gray—and we didn't want that. We didn't want to be an unknown player in a big sector not known for goodness or as a force for goodness." Chase described the formation of the concept of force for good:

> We now have a century of dealing with nations with the fundamental task of the search for and extraction of energy raw materials. It is very much out of that history that the commitment to becoming a force for good was born . . . It's not enough for us simply to find the resources and create for the host nations the wealth extraction from the release of those resources. It is not seen either by them or us as a sufficient force for good. We have to recognize and plan more specifically other goals which are not so obviously the role of the commercial enterprise.

John Browne personally saw the company's efforts at being a force of good more in terms of building reputation—the last of the core premises of organizational design he had enumerated. "There is, I believe, no conflict between investing in reputation and creating long-term shareholder value," he said. The primary benefit of reputation, however, lay in building the emotional strength of the organization. As he described:

> The interesting thing about the behaviour of this firm is that we always start with the foundation of rationality but we recognize that that in itself will not take you far. What you have to apply on top of it is an emotional state . . .
>
> It is easy to detach the employees from a company. A company is pretty impersonal and artificial, and it produces continuous contradictions which have to be resolved. We have the contradiction that we produce oil and gas, and we want to reduce the impact of that on the environment. The question to us is how do you genuinely allow people to transform all their individuality into the company, because if they can do that then people will begin to think and behave in a way that is aligned to the goals of the company.
>
> To build the reputation, we picked four areas. First, safety: when you invite someone to come and work, you should send them home in the same shape as when they arrived—that is a minimum requirement for respect of a person, and you have to take that terribly seriously. Second, you have to take care of the natural environment. It is important because people do not want companies to make a mess and leave them behind. Third, everyone wants a place in the ideal which is free of all discrimination; it doesn't matter what you stand for in terms of your race, gender, sexual orientation or religious beliefs. All that matters is merit. Fourth, the company has to invest in the community from which the people have come, so as to narrow the gap between life within the company and life outside the company.

In a show of commitment to these goals, Browne took an unusual and risky stand in a speech regarding climate change at Stanford University. He admitted that global climate change was a problem that BP could no longer ignore and outlined BP's plans for addressing the problem:

> The time to consider the policy dimensions of climate change is not when the link between greenhouse gases and climate change is conclusively proven but when the possibility cannot be discounted and is taken seriously by the society of which we are part. We in BP have reached that point . . . To be absolutely clear—we must now focus on what can and what should be done, not because we can be certain climate change is happening, but because the possibility can't be ignored. If we are all to take responsibility for the future of our planet, then it falls to us to begin to take precautionary action now.[4]

The steps Browne outlined were to control BP's emissions, to fund continuing scientific research, to take initiatives for joint implementation, to develop alternative fuels for the long term, and to contribute to the public policy debate in search of the wider global answers to the problem. In an industry characterized by an old-boys' network spanning the major oil companies, this move was met with surprise and hostility. "Some of the skeptics and the press said, 'He has left the church. He is no longer with the industry,'" recalled Edwards, "But as soon as [Browne] made this speech, the internal feedback was unbelievable—from children of employees, spouses." BP officially removed itself from the Global Climate Coalition, a lobbying and public relations organization based in Washington, D.C., which opposed government intervention with regard to the climate. Browne was, in fact, responding to internal pressures to leave the coalition. BP's employees felt that what the coalition was arguing for was "intellectually unjustifiable" because credible scientists were finding the opposite—that gas emissions were contributing to global warming.

A year later, in April 1998, BP began to receive recognition for its bold moves. *Oil & Gas Journal* highlighted BP in a review of financial strategies of the top oil and gas companies:

> Within the top 10, there is one striking example of a company being driven by a different vision. BP has designated corporate citizenship and being "forward-thinking about the environment, human rights, and dealing with people and ethics" as "the new fulcrum of competition between oil companies in the late 1990s." Several of the other leading companies have adopted parts of this approach, with Shell probably going the furthest. But none has been as explicit or committed as BP.[5]

The stand that Browne took placed BP in a distinctive position in its industry. As an example, following the Stanford speech, BP struck up an agreement with the Environmental Defense Fund to design a system for trading greenhouse gas emissions within BP. In this system, revenues and costs of carbon trades were treated like actual cash flows, which allowed BP to measure environmental performance as financial performance. These actions were part of the company's increasing concern with being progressive and green—in other words being a force for good. Being a force for good was about having "goals that are worth pursuing for everyone; that have to do with making society better as result of our participation than if we had not been there," remarked Chase.

From Act I to Act II: The Challenges and Questions

In July 2000, after a wide-ranging exercise involving staff throughout the company as well as external specialists, BP launched a new corporate branding designed to project both the changes that had taken place and the company's aspirations for the future.

The company would be known simply as BP, with the familiar BP shield and Amoco torch replaced by a fresh new symbol depicting a vibrant sunburst of green, white, and yellow. Named the Helios mark after the sun god of ancient Greece, the new logo was intended to exemplify dynamic energy—in all its forms, from oil and gas to solar—that the company delivered to its 10 million daily customers around the world. The attributes of the brand—progressive, green, innovative, and performance-driven—were the values that would shape BP's future.

At a press conference, the launch of the new brand, under the provocative slogan "Beyond Petroleum" was described by one analyst as "a sunrise brand for a sunset company." Though the company had made great progress on many fronts, BP clearly needed to produce final proof that it could achieve long-term growth with short-term returns.

BP's financial situation, relative to that of the other supermajors, Exxon Mobil and Royal Dutch Shell, added to the challenge of achieving long-term growth. Over 90 percent of BP's 500,000 shareholders were individual investors. As of the end of the third quarter of 2000, its net debt-to-capital ratio was 25 percent, increased from 19 percent in the previous quarter and well above Exxon Mobil's 9.5 percent and Royal Dutch's 1.7 percent.[6] Although BP's return on capital employed (ROCE), at 19.7 percent, was

Exhibit 4   BP, Royal Dutch Shell (RD), Exxon Mobil (XOM), and S&P 500 Index Share Price Comparison

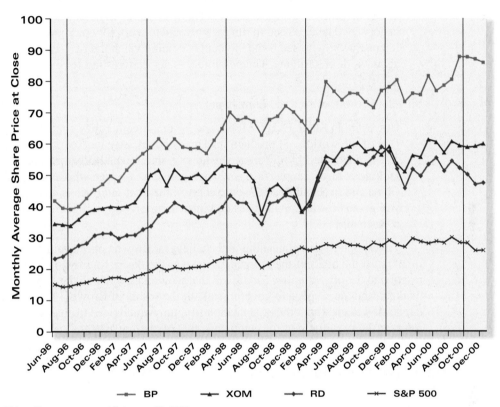

Source: Yahoo Finance, accessed February 19, 2001.

the highest of the international majors in 2000,[7] its stock was trading at a discount to Exxon Mobil (see Exhibit 4 for comparison).[8] Alexander, as the voice of concern of BP's management, explained the challenge the company faced: "We cannot deliver what our brand means unless we can grow ROCE and the top line at the same time. We have built ROCE [by cost cutting], but we have not grown the top line."

Those on the outside were skeptical of BP's growth strategy. A financial analyst expressed doubt of BP's possible success.

> BP is coming to the end of its restructuring and acquisition phase. It is now signaling a return to an organic growth oriented strategy . . . We are skeptical that BP can sustain its target of 10 percent annual earnings growth . . . Our view is supported by history, which shows that few companies are able to grow capital employed organically and cut costs at the same time. If BP does manage to deliver underlying earnings growth of over 10 percent annually it will be a major achievement.[9]

But beyond these issues was a broader question of the role of public and private sector companies in the energy field. As Nick Butler reflected:

I believe that over the last century the world has been artificially divided into the public and the private sectors. The private sector has been seen as exploitative, narrow, and self-interested. The public world has been seen as representing the interests of the whole community. This dichotomy has been established and underpins the political debate. This was not always the case in economic history . . . The two used to run together and to work for common purpose. It is interesting now to see if the moment is coming when the two sectors can once again work in harmony. The possibility is very interesting for a company such as BP.

Sir John Browne echoed the same issue:

However big Shell, Exxon Mobil, and BP are, together they control only 9 percent of the world's oil production. This is not exactly market dominance. The rest is controlled by different versions of state-owned organizations. We are looking at how the interface is changing, and as you see what is happening in China and in Saudi Arabia, you recognize that that interface is changing. Who will get to do what? Will states do things themselves or will there be some new partnership?

To respond to these questions and challenges, Browne once again reorganized BP in 2001. At the heart of the reorganization was the desire to grow organically, and to respond to the opportunities for growth that would largely lie in the hands of different markets, and the respective governments. In the words of Browne, "As we set up the targets, it was clear that the organization structure would need to change in order to be right for the next phase of the company—that of organic growth."

The Reorganization of 2001

One change was to consolidate the business units, thus reducing their total number. "We had created too many components," said Browne "and with growing scale, that had led to too much complexity, too many interactions. We had to balance complexity against ownership."

For example, the company consolidated its four business units in Alaska into one. They shared drilling capacity, operated in a single taxation environment, and single reputational environment. While consolidating the units, decentralization was maintained, perhaps enhanced, by delegating accountability down from the business unit leaders to the next level of managers.

The role and deployment of the group vice presidents were also changed. Instead of being jointly responsible for performance, they were made personally accountable for the performance of the sum of their business units. Previously, in order to integrate the leadership cadre, they had all been located in London. "That worked," said Browne, "but actually in a decentralized model, the senior managers of the company should be out there with the business units to build relationships." So he distributed the group vice presidents around the world—as presidents or regional directors in the United States, Asia, Latin America, and so on. "Now they have both business and regional accountability," he said. "They have a specific remit, and they are the face of the company."

At the heart of this change was an acknowledgment of the regional role as an enabler of organic growth. "It is not completely clear to me," said Browne, in a marvelous example of British understatement, "that the business goals of the corporation and the goals of the government are automatically aligned without a lot of effort . . . You can say to them you want them to work five times harder and they will say, 'Why? So that you can bring in imported equipment and take out the money?' " He continued:

> Take the case of Trinidad. I have heard this time and again from prime ministers and presidents there. They used to be a big producer of sugar, and they couldn't afford to buy the boiled sweets that were made in the UK . . . We have a gigantic amount of gas in Trinidad, and we have to think and we have to do several things. We have to work with the government to build capacity. Our role is very much recruitment and training of people—we are less good at doing what governments should be doing such as building roads. Number two, we need to work with them to expand the number of small and medium enterprises in the country . . . build things with other people who will use some of that gas . . . We are going to be a part of all that investment, not exclusively, but our reputation and the fact that we will be there and making sure the project works will allow other people to come in and invest. This is good news for us, because they will use the gas, and it is good news for the government. We have to build this mutuality.

To build this mutuality, BP needed strong local relationships. Browne said, "It would be extraordinarily unwise to continuously go to a government, flying in from London, saying I need the following things. You need someone who can set it in the context and say the company is doing this, and this is where the mutual advantage is." This was the enhanced role for the group vice presidents—thereby opening doors for the business units so that they could effectively do their work to grow the business.

The third element of the 2001 reorganization was a consolidation and strengthening of the functional competencies of BP. Browne explained: "We believed that greater emphasis was needed for enhancing our marketing skills, and understanding the differences between marketing and sales. That difference is now put in real organizational terms, so for the first time in the company's history, we have a marketing director and she is in charge of the strategic side." Similarly, the technology group was given full accountability for the strategic goals and targets in the areas of technology development, and for deployment of people. "We have to focus heavily not only on how we retain and deploy people in this area, but how we continuously renew the quality of people because this is a very fundamental part of our functional capability," said Browne.

Similarly, the highly fragmented internal supply and trading organization was consolidated into one entity, with the goal of stopping internal transactions and to leverage scale. In the words of Browne: "It is certainly true that returns to supply and trading increase with scale—they just do, and you can prove it—and we have reached such a scale that we had to consider that benefit. But, equally, your reputation is highly dependent on how you use that scale, especially in unregulated markets, and that worries us a lot. In unregulated markets, these decisions of judgment are critical to the reputation of the firm, and that is something that has to be done in one place."

While describing these organizational changes, Browne emphasized BP's fundamental philosophy about organizing:

> The thing about organization is nothing is ever fixed, at least in BP, and we renew ourselves by learning what is good about the past and changing all things that are not so good. They are behaviour dependent. Grouping the group vice presidents in London to make them into a team so that they knew each other,

and could interact among themselves in a way that made the peer groups effective—that worked. I believe that investment will endure, and now we can send them outside London. In three or five years time, we may have to change again because it might become silo-like, and we might think that the best way would be to bring them all back to London or New York, or try something completely different.

Was this reorganization enough, or even right, as a response to the challenges and questions? Sir John Browne was slightly philosophical in his reply:

> Some of our competitors do not have a good reputation. Yet they trade at a higher multiple than BP. Does reputation matter? If you are from Mars, would you not say that those with worse reputations are valued more highly? . . . This debate which still goes on is about deep-seated values. Recruitment, motivation, great place to work . . . these should all in theory be expressed in market value at the end, but in practice may take more than one period to do so. But, in the end, I firmly believe that the more a company reflects the values of the society from which its people are drawn, the better the company is.

Endnotes

[1]John Lloyd, "Company Law," *Business Financial Times Weekend Magazine,* September 9, 2000.
[2]Derived from Teenage Mutant Ninja Turtles, adventure cartoon characters popular in the 1980s, the term *turtle* was used to describe a person who is able to do "high-energy, surprising things and appear to be normal," explained Lee Edwards, former turtle to CEO Sir John Browne.
[3]Shell in 1995 planned to dispose of the Brent Spar, an offshore loading buoy, by scuttling it in deep water off the northwestern coast of Britain. Environmentalists were outraged, and a consumer boycott ensued. Shell stations were vandalized, some of them firebombed, or shot at with automatic weapons. Finally Shell brought the buoy to a Norwegian port and eventually dismantled it.
[4]Sir John Browne in a speech at Stanford University, California, May 19, 1997.
[5]"Common Financial Strategies Found among Top 10 Oil and Gas Firms," *Oil & Gas Journal,* April 20, 1998.
[6]Salomon Smith Barney Equity Research Report, November 13, 2000.
[7]Ibid.
[8]UBS Warburg Global Equity Research Report, November 9, 2000.
[9]Commerzbank Securities Research Report, September 22, 2000.

Maple Leaf Foods
Leading Six Sigma Change

Brian Golden
University of Western Ontario

It was the spring of 2001 and Bruce Miyashita, vice-president (VP) Six Sigma of Maple Leaf Foods, was reflecting on Maple Leaf's Six Sigma experiences to date. A year after its launch, Six Sigma had been rolled out to three of the 10 Independent Operating Companies (IOCs) at Toronto-based Maple Leaf Foods (MLF). It was a project that was off the ground but was not yet completed. Several questions were going through Miyashita's head: "What was and was not working?" "What should we have done differently?" "Have we pushed the program hard enough and fast enough?" "Should we be satisfied?"

Overview of Maple Leaf Foods

MLF was a leading global food processing company, based in Toronto, Canada. Employing more than 12,000 people at operations across Canada, the United States, Europe, and Asia, the Maple Leaf brand had been introduced more than 100 years ago. Currently known as Maple Leaf Foods, the company was the result of a merger of Maple Leaf Mills Limited and Canada Packers, the most recent of numerous transformations during the company's history. Among its 11 IOCs were Maple Leaf Pork, Maple Leaf Poultry, Canada Bread, Maple Leaf Consumer Foods, Shur-Gain, and Landmark.

Its present incarnation was incorporated in 1990, and began operations in 1995 under the control of the McCain Capital Corporation and the Ontario Teachers' Pension Plan Board. MLF common shares traded on the Toronto Stock Exchange under the symbol "MFI." In 2000, MLF reported sales of about Cdn$4 billion, up from Cdn$3.5 billion in 1999. Net earnings were Cdn$90 million, down from Cdn$147 million in

1999. This drop in earnings was expected, due to increasing hog prices and the start-up costs of MLF's new Brandon plant, the largest pork processing plant in Canada. MLF was expecting to report healthy profits by the second quarter of 2001.

From leadership and human resource decisions, to relations with customers, to market-entry decisions, MLF prided itself as being guided by six fundamental values:

- Do what's right
- Be performance driven
- Have a bias for action
- Continuously improve
- Be externally focused
- Dare to be transparent

At the strategic level, MLF was driven by its seven core strategic principles:

- Build High Performance Leadership
- Focus on Markets and Categories Where We Can Lead
- Develop Brand Equity
- Offer the Best Quality Products
- Be the Lowest Cost Producer
- Execute with Precision and Continuous Improvement
- Think Global

The Introduction of Six Sigma

Six Sigma was a disciplined, data-driven approach and methodology for eliminating defects in any process. The name "Six Sigma" was also a metric referring to the achievement of only 3.4 defective parts per million. The fundamental objective of the Six Sigma methodology was the implementation of a measurements-based strategy that focused on process improvement and variation reduction through the application of Six Sigma improvement projects. This was accomplished through the use of two Six Sigma sub-methodologies: define, measure, analyze, improve, control (DMAIC) and define, measure, analyze, design, verify (DMADV). The Six Sigma DMAIC process was an improvement system for existing processes falling below specification and looking for incremental improvement. The Six Sigma DMADV process was an improvement system used to develop new processes or products at Six Sigma quality levels.

MLF embraced Six Sigma as the essential discipline to achieve and maintain what was known internally as the "Leadership Edge." The term "Leadership Edge" at MLF signified two things: competitive edge through leadership, and the competitive edge of its leaders.

Michael McCain, the 42-year-old president and chief executive officer (CEO), believed that the personal success of the employees was highly integrated with the continuous success of the business. This belief led MLF to establish an array of processes to support the internal development of leaders. MLF used these processes to aim the spotlight on values, accomplishments, potential, and goals. Thus, senior management worked with employees to plan specific development actions to ensure the employees' continued growth and progression as business leaders. McCain explained:

When we created MLF, our predecessor companies had a history of continuous improvement—it was an improved version of TQM (Total Quality Management). I wanted to build a culture around continuous improvement, but in 1995, we agreed that the organization needed to be ready to accept part of this process. This reorganization included restructuring and stabilization, which were huge issues in terms of management changes, etc. We used that period to consider what foundation to build.

We decided to go with continuous improvement in some form, recognizing that this was a journey, not a one-off program. For me, it was almost a personal life decision because the leader of a business can only champion a small set of things. And two of the central pieces in MLF I was championing were Six Sigma and Leadership Edge.

Our values and principles define the type of people and the culture in which they work. And Six Sigma defines the way they work—having a tight linkage between leadership and culture.

What makes our situation different from others is that I am a CEO who is not just here for a short time. We're owner-operators and Six Sigma has been endorsed by our board of directors.[1] This is not just another job for us and we're going to be here long-term.

The Five Dimensions of Six Sigma

Philosophy

At MLF, the Six Sigma philosophy—doing the right things right—meant quantitatively understanding and consistently meeting critical customer needs with minimal waste throughout the entire value chain. This was tied to MLF's core values, and was an approach to be applied to all business and to every kind of business process. In the manufacturing area, for example, one Six Sigma project addressed customer complaints by reducing defects incurred while processing bacon. Another project decreased the work needed to clean chicken thighs that had gone through the deboning machine. In the service area, a project was initiated to improve the office communications with Japanese customers.

Metric

The sigma metric (which measured variation relative to customer expectations) helped MLF to quantify quality, to benchmark every one of its products and processes, and to establish measurable stretch goals. As the capability of business process increased (as measured through the sigma metric), costs decreased, cycle time was reduced and customer satisfaction increased.

The difference between 99 percent effectiveness and almost 100 percent effectiveness can be illustrated as follows:

> Ninety-nine percent is roughly 3.8 sigma. A 3.8 sigma or 99 percent capability is like going without electricity for seven hours per month, while Six Sigma is seven seconds per month without electricity.

Miyashita regularly recounted this imagery in his communication efforts to make the Six Sigma metric tangible to employees.

Exhibit 2   Six Sigma Misconceptions

Six Sigma Is Just for Manufacturing

Six Sigma is appropriate for any business process, whether it's a factory making something out of metal, transforming something (like turning pulp into paper), or processing something like poultry or pork, or whether it's a paper factory, that is, a factory that processes documents or forms.

Sigma Quality Costs Too Much

The old belief in industry was that Four Sigma was the optimum quality level. To improve beyond Four Sigma was unprofitable because, the thinking went, the cost of detecting and fixing defects rose faster than the benefits. This is true if you reduce defects through inspection. If, on the other hand, you use tools to prevent defects through better process setup, operation, and product/process design, the cost of reducing defects is more than offset by the benefits. Also, as defects become rarer and rarer, a company can radically change how it does business. People can be redeployed to do value-added work rather than fighting fires or finding and fixing defects.

Ninety-nine Percent Is Good Enough

Ninety-nine percent is roughly 3.8 sigma. A 3.8 sigma or 99 percent capability is like going without electricity for seven hours per month, while Six Sigma is seven seconds a month without electricity.

About Product Quality

Six Sigma is focused on the quality of processes and understanding what root causes affect the ability of business processes to work consistently. Six Sigma is not about inspection or rework. While Six Sigma is concerned about the end results of a process, the focus of Six Sigma is, first, to ensure we precisely quantify the customer's needs, and second, to improve the ability of business processes to consistently deliver the required results with a minimum of waste. When we focus only on product or service quality, we tend to have a mindset of inspection. When we focus on the process, we take on a mindset of defect prevention.

About Product Quality—Part 2

The Six Sigma focus on process quality is important because you can have a situation where the end product has no defects, but there is a huge "hidden" factory to find and fix defects. The goal is to have no defects in the end product without the hidden factory.

It's Just TQM

TQM or Total Quality Management has many positive aspects. But as implemented by the vast majority of organizations, it suffers from three things that the Six Sigma approach, as described here, avoids. First, most organizations approached TQM and "quality" as primarily an issue of people's attitudes. While this is important, it ignores the need to demonstrate real bottom-line financial results. Money is the reason we do Six Sigma. Defect elimination is how we make the money. Second, most TQM efforts, despite the rhetoric of management, was something delegated down. Quality was of concern to the "technical people or the workforce." The Six Sigma philosophy is that while we must achieve buy-in at all levels of the company, direction and ownership must flow from the top. Third, while TQM uses some statistical and other advanced tools, the Six Sigma toolkit embraces a wider spectrum of tools, ranging from the basic to the advanced.

About Technical Stuff

While statistics and other improvement tools are important to Six Sigma, at least 80 percent of the challenge of Six Sigma is about change and leadership. Continually striving for Six Sigma performance in an organization presents enormous change challenges. Entire ways of thinking about the business are questioned. People who have vested interests in the status quo are threatened. People must learn new things and assume new roles. Better metrics reveals gaps we never saw before. In short, truly pursuing Six Sigma unleashes tremendous forces, and unless the management of a company takes on the task of leading Six Sigma, not just managing it, the result will be some money-saving projects, but not a sustained competitive and strategic improvement.

fully voluntary. Maple Leaf's management wanted to encourage interested individuals to step forward and apply for black belt training.[3] Other personnel could attend a five-day "green belt" education course that provided both awareness in Six Sigma and a grounding in some basic tools.

Exhibit 2   Continued

People Have To Be Perfect

A Six Sigma level of performance is 99.9997 percent right. How is it possible to have this level of performance in businesses that are people intensive? Maybe this is possible with an automated assembly line, but not when a lot of human beings are involved. First, Six Sigma focuses on the process, not the personalities. It says: let's better understand how this process works. Let's use various tools and techniques to eliminate or make it very difficult for defects to occur, even when a lot of people are involved, by better process design and setup. Second, the Six Sigma methodology spends a lot of time making sure we understand what is truly critical to the customer and translating those needs to something we can quantify. Many times a process is making defects because of the way we interpreted the customers' needs. Often, we misinterpret the needs, assume we know what they are, don't update the specifications, or react to one person's idea of what the needs are, rather than understanding what others are saying. In short, a "defect" might not really be a defect, depending on how well the customer's needs are defined. Third, with the use of various tools, we can often achieve high sigma performance by making processes robust to the variability of inputs and environmental factors.

Just Cost Reduction

Six Sigma is focused on bottom-line results. But these results don't come just from direct cost savings from less inspection, rework, and scrap. They can come from reducing cycle times and, therefore, helping to reduce the raw material and work-in-progress inventories, which cost us money. It can come from the reduction of warranty and other customer claims. It also comes from market share benefits of better product and service quality that enhances our brand.

By systematically driving down defects throughout the business system, Six Sigma helps improve not only costs but also cycle time and, therefore, working and fixed capital requirements. Fewer defects means less rework, scrap, or down-graded product. It also frees up capacity, often reducing the need for capital expansion. Fewer defects reduce the number of inspections. The reduction of defects in the system reduces the quantity of escaping defects, defects that make it through inspections. These defects drive repair, claims, and warranty costs. They also hurt customer satisfaction.

Longer cycle times hurt our ability to consistently meet delivery requirements. Increased costs make it harder for us to profitably compete on lower costs. Lower product and service quality hurts our costs as well as our brand.

"Doing Some Projects"

While it's understood that Six Sigma requires buy-in from all levels, and that senior management must let others take the initiative, the fact remains that if the executives and senior management of a company view Six Sigma as low priority for their time and attention, Six Sigma will languish and achieve only a fraction of its full bottom-line potential. When practices, policies, and behaviors are questioned as they are questioned by Six Sigma, there can be no gap between the philosophy of Six Sigma and the actions of senior management, otherwise Six Sigma will be just another flavor-of-the-month program.

Six Sigma Is a Program

Six Sigma is definitely not a program. Programs begin and end. While the start-up of a Six Sigma effort does require resources to get it going, the end state of Six Sigma is a never-ending performance mindset. The goal is to move from Six Sigma as a new concept to "this is the way we do things around here."

Source: Company files.

The ideal black belts were smart, mature people intrigued by processes, with, on average, five to six years of work experience at MLF or another organization. This afforded them a realistic view of work situations and allowed the candidates to not be too frustrated by initial inertia. They had to be "people persons" since they served as consultants to line managers and teams, lacking formal authority to implement programs. As another attribute, McCain and Miyashita wanted level-headed people with no ego problems. These black belt trainees had to be confident in their abilities and had to be able to share project successes.

Miyashita and technical consultants began schooling green belts and by July 2000, the first class of black belts was five months old. Miyashita noticed that although the

Exhibit 3   SIX SIGMA ROLES AND RESPONSIBILITIES

Profile Summary	Who?	What Do They Do?	How Many?
Executive Group	■ Business unit executives; also known as "quality council" in some companies	■ Approve Six Sigma policy ■ Set goals ■ Commit resources; select black belts ■ Own the results ■ Create the vision of Six Sigma ■ Approve projects	■ Executive group as a whole
Six Sigma Champion	■ Champion is an executive or senior manager who provides day-to-day implementation leadership ■ Experienced line executive who knows the business and is respected	■ Change agent ■ Link between vision and strategy of Six Sigma ■ Formulate Six Sigma policy with corporate ■ Help define projects ■ Help select black belts ■ Set up business unit infrastructure (e.g., project tracking) ■ Coordinate deployment in business unit	■ One full-time executive per business unit
Business Unit Core Team	■ Led by Six Sigma champion ■ Reps from line management and support functions (HR, Finance, IT) (part time) ■ Black Belts	■ Help formulate Six Sigma policy ■ Coordinate their functions' support of Six Sigma	■ One core team for each major business unit (e.g., where you have a president), and/or one at a corporate level ■ Part-time
Process Owners	■ The person responsible for all aspects of a process's performance ■ The process owner might also be the project owner	■ Measure process performance ■ Improve process performance through such actions as application of Six Sigma methodology and tools in a project ■ Ensure improvements are implemented and sustained	■ All managers own one or more processes ■ Processes exist in levels or tiers
Project Champion (Sponsor)	■ The person responsible for all aspects of a project's success ■ The project owner might also be the process owner or champion	■ Ensure the right resources are on the team/available to the team ■ Ensure project is implemented ■ Provide day-to-day support ■ Ensure process owner is on board	■ Each project has one accountable Project Owner (no committees!)

All employees	■ Any employee from the president to the most recent new hire	■ Walk the talk of Six Sigma philosophy and principles in their job —What and how they measure things —Supporting project teams —Helping to sustain the improvements ■ Help others understand the goals and methods of Six Sigma ■ Apply Six Sigma training in their area (e.g., might receive black belt or green belt training and apply on their job)	■ Whole organization
Project Team Members	■ Salary and/or hourly employees ■ Work in the process, understand the process, or understand the customer ■ Could include customer and/or suppliers	■ Identify the root causes of the problem and find solutions ■ Implement the change with the process owner ■ People from the process to sustain the gains	■ Most projects have anywhere from 3 to 10 people—it depends on the project ■ Most are part-time; some might be full-time for a few days or weeks—depends
Black Belts (BBs)	■ Full-time project team leaders	■ Lead project teams through the Six Sigma methodology to solve the program defined in the project charter ■ Provide problem solving/analytical support to the organization ■ Train project team members ■ Work closely with the project owner to ensure implementation	■ Typically one or two black belts per 100 employees, often more as justified by the payback (this is in addition to people who receive black belt training and apply on-the-job)
Master Black Belts (MBBs)	■ Experts in tools and methods of Six Sigma ■ Full-time coaches and trainers ■ Have gone through black belt training ■ Strong teaching/communication skills ■ Long-term career path	■ Provide coaching and training to the organization (technical and change management) ■ Provide regular (e.g., weekly) technical advice to black belts and the project teams ■ Participate on core team to create Six Sigma infrastructure (e.g., project database, training curriculum)	■ Usually one master black belt per 20 to 30 black belts, depending on factors such as geography

Source: Company files.

program had sufficient numbers of interested trainees, it was not drawing the appropriate numbers of women. He explained:

> We've had significant problems attracting women. My pet theory is that all things being equal, women make better black belts. One common stereotype for men recounts that men do not like to look at road maps. We need black belts to be very good at networking and getting coaching. The vast majority of coaching comes from me right now and I notice that some people are very eager to learn. I think guys feel bad asking what they perceive as "silly" questions.

Over the next few months, however, the number of external candidates (including a substantial portion of women), had grown, as MLF was able to use the profile of its Six Sigma program to attract new candidates.

Black belts signed up for 25 days of training and a minimum of two years in that role—there was no limit on maximum length. MLF had 16 black belts currently, targeting to add at least 24 to 34 new black belts per year. Miyashita aimed to produce 120 to 150 black belts by 2003. It cost MLF approximately Cdn$140,000 to train each black belt, including salary and training costs. He thought that they would perform between 1.5 to 2.0 projects per year, saving MLF at least Cdn$100,000 per project annually.

Miyashita noted that at his previous role at Bombardier, the attrition rate for black belts was 18 percent. In reality, if the numbers of people lured away to other companies was subtracted, the attrition rate was only 4 percent.

Initial Challenges and Preemptive Measures

Early on in the process, Miyashita was aware that many employees were wondering how Six Sigma would affect their lives on a day-to-day basis, and also over the long term. In anticipation of this possible reaction, Miyashita crafted a message that identified the benefits to employees (and not just MLF) from Six Sigma. The benefits he often spoke of included the following:

- I'll be more marketable internally and externally because of the training I've received
- I'll have time for training
- I'll have time to make improvements
- There'll be less firefighting
- I'll understand other parts of the business better
- I'll have power over numbers
- I'll be focusing on the process that creates a product or service; I'll see more of the whole process
- Defects or problems will be things to learn from

McCain also recounted some initial resistance to Six Sigma:

> People would say: "I don't like it, and I won't do it" "If I put my head down long enough, this too will pass." Yes, if someone else owned MLF, perhaps that would be the case. But this is not so—people should realize that we're here for the long term. Six Sigma is championed by the board of directors and shareholders, and is the fundamental way that we're doing things.

In 1998, I told them that we would be starting a program in a year. Six months later, I reminded them that July 1999 would see the kickoff of an improvement process. Even when we announced Six Sigma, half the people in the room thought that I was crazy.

They said, "3.4 defective parts per million is impossible." People who say that have not gone through the program.[4] They also said "Six Sigma only applies to metal benders—in food, we have natural causes that are God-given and we can't control them."

In addition, some plant managers were embarrassed that Six Sigma was able to diagnose quality problems that had been previously undetected. Other managers were not pleased that they were not seen as the "heroes"—that a green belt or black belt was necessary to help them improve their own business. Miyashita lamented that this was an indication that Six Sigma was not implemented as well as possible. One of the objectives of the change management training was to stress the importance of sharing success.

An anticipated issue was low statistical literacy among employees, delaying black belts at the pre-project level. To counteract this, the black belts were trained to educate employees as necessary, in the course of project design and implementation. Relevant statistical terms would then be put in context and explained to the employees. A frequent example was the need for black belts to explain the requirement to monitor variance from the mean, rather than relying solely on the mean.

Another concern was MLF's bias to action—a core value. MLF faced a long history of "shoot first, ask questions later." With Six Sigma, employees had to do research prior to prescribing solutions. Thus, this cultural bias to action was seen as an impediment to Six Sigma. The challenge was how to get people to value "looking before leaping."

In addition, succession planning was a constant issue. As one manager in the International IOC commented:

If someone moves from green to black belt, we need to backfill that person in the IOC. There can be fallout since the new person (replacing the new black belt) needs to be able to step in and fill the gap. It might take some time for them to be able to do that, and if a bottleneck is created because of the time to get up to speed, Six Sigma gets blamed. We weren't given any additional resources when we lost the IOC member to his black belt role, so Six Sigma can actually make my life harder, not easier.

It was ironic then that many newly minted black belts and green belts, full of excitement about the new skill sets they had developed, had no immediate post-training projects on which to work. According to one manager, "Some people were trained 14 months ago, and if these are concepts that you don't deal with every day and were new to begin with, I don't know how helpful they will be." In other cases, the projects were perceived as make-work projects just so a new green belt could "tick off the box and say they completed a project." Over time, as interest in Six Sigma began to build, it was expected that the supply and demand of important projects would reach an equilibrium.

Finally, Six Sigma was not, strictly speaking, necessary for MLF's success; MLF had performed well without Six Sigma. Thus, a challenge for McCain and Miyashita was to create dissatisfaction with the status quo. It was one thing to espouse the MLF value of continual improvement; it was another to create the impetus for change (with the risk of failure) when business was good (and rewards were tied to performance). To address this challenge, Miyashita's "Why Six Sigma?" publication and the presentations provided numerous examples of well-performing companies (e.g., GE, Motorola, Mazda) that were able to markedly improve performance through Six Sigma.

The First Project at Poultry

Located at the Toronto facility, already considered to be the benchmark plant in MLF, the first Six Sigma project involved deboning chicken thighs. Jim Long, black belt at Poultry, was in charge of this "boneless chicken thigh process." Employees had been spending an inordinate amount of time performing inspections and compensating for machines that were not producing optimal output. At the start, 6 out of every 10 thighs to arrive at the trim table still had excess skin or bone that had not been removed by the equipment. A design experiment was created and carried out, resulting in an increase of 15 percent to 16 percent in the output per employee, per hour.

Brock Furlong, president of Poultry, one of the first three IOCs selected for Six Sigma implementation, explained that there were initial challenges. First, there was the issue of being first—he did not have anyone to turn to for implementation plans. There were no benchmarks to go by, as Poultry was a unique IOC in the Food Division. There were also no detailed process outlines or maps and this hampered the division's ability to implement the first projects quickly.

Cultural issues also came into play because decision-making at Poultry had been top-down. But Six Sigma calls for implementation at the ground level. Part of that previous culture of top-down decision-making had a strong bottom-line focus, and Six Sigma was a significant investment in time, energy and resources at the lower and middle levels. Furlong concluded, "Many people in our IOC were sitting back and saying 'Prove it.'"

The Bacon Plant

For months, Maple Leaf Food's bacon plant, located in Manitoba, had been receiving a high number of customer complaints because of defective products. Its unionized workforce was constantly reminded by plant supervisors that bacon yield had to improve, leading to a high degree of frustration during work hours. In addition, because they were not achieving their bacon yield numbers, employees were not receiving performance bonuses.

Louann Hulsman, black belt trainee at MLF Consumer Foods, recounted her initial project experience:

Consumer complaints about bacon had started to climb in 1999 (prior to Miyashita's arrival) and we had to go in and try to fix the issues at our bacon plant. We inspected-out the defects so that the products coming out were of higher quality. But that increased the cost of production to the plant. We found a bottleneck in the flow, and the result was that we had created a holding spot for work-in-progress. This became a scheduling nightmare for a while, and we were looking for a solution.

As soon as Six Sigma resources were available, we grabbed them, pulled them in and said, "Let's go!" Some employees even said, "I don't understand what you want me to do, but if you're telling me that it will reduce my frustration, improve my processes, then let's go." The employees gave us 120 percent support, to the point that we were fully staffed with volunteers to schedule experiments and monitor results. We had sign-up sheets and people were signing up for two to three steps each!

Originally, we were at about 3,000 defects per million, and now we're at 1,400 defects per million. Complaints have come down from 50 per million pieces to less than 20 per million. But that came at a cost—we could not make our standard yield of product per pound of raw material. Then we found factors and levels that could increase first grade yield by another 10 percent.

Fundamentally, the people did not want to come to work to make bad finished products and have supervisors yelling at them. It worked and the team at North Battleford is amazing. There was someone in the plant almost 24 hours a day and all the people on the floor were interested in the project, giving us suggestions and moral support.

When we first started, we figured that poor quality of raw materials was the source of the problem. But we've made improvements without changing raw material quality, increasing our first grade yields. The line workers could really see the difference. They'd say, "We want this kind of bacon because this is the best." In my mind, the projects are working when people on the job notice the difference.

Long-Term Management Commitment

McCain recounted:

Most people can tell if the CEO is championing the project. I tell people that I am the champion for it. In my opinion, Bruce Miyashita has executed Six Sigma brilliantly—he overcame such objections as "We're doing so many things besides Six Sigma," getting people to cough up their best people for black belt training.

We've got to be committed to this as a 5- to 10-year process. It is a cultural revolution. And people might not fundamentally appreciate what it takes to embark on that. There will be people deselected because they don't buy in. We did three IOCs in our first year. Our management informed everybody that we were not mandating when they jumped on the train—if they did not feel ready, they did not have to do that immediately. But it's not a question of if, it's when.

For the first 18 months, we started with more Six Sigma resources than demand. But now we've got more demand than resources. We've told people that unless they are at the top of their game, Six Sigma will not work. You will only get it if you're good. And, it matters—25 percent of an IOC president's short-term bonus is based on Six Sigma implementation.

We've told them how well the three IOCs are doing. We've spread the stories of initial success. We've got tangible victories, but if the baseball game analogy could be used, we're in the first inning of a nine-inning game.

Miyashita was also doing his part to publicize Six Sigma to MLF management. In addition to the work he performed with the black belts, he was a regular speaker on the Leadership Edge Foundations Program (which trained the top 500 MLF managers). This program, designed and delivered by a leading business school, provided another opportunity for McCain and Miyashita to stress the importance of Six Sigma and to broadcast ongoing successes.

The Future

As demand for Six Sigma resources outstripped supply, Miyashita wanted Six Sigma documents available online and the new black belts shouldering more of the training load. In addition, he wanted the program institutionalized with a more robust project tracking system. Also, he wanted to train or hire a couple dozen more black belts in order to achieve critical mass for Six Sigma resources. Last, he wanted to promote a black belt to master black belt. He knew that McCain's commitment was vital.

Miyashita concluded:

> McCain is preaching it. Given the limitations of a CEO's time, he does enough. He'll go to the shop floor and ask "What's the sigma of that hog?" That floors people, because he *really* expects you to give him the answer. McCain understands this stuff and, along with me, preaches it every day.
>
> The jury is out as to whether this will be successful. But honestly, only time will tell. What can I do to increase the odds of success? If you think about it, the odds are stacked against us. Many companies have tried and failed. Within MLF, if we do not resolve all the tiny issues as soon as they arise, we also run the risk of failure.
>
> Are we being aggressive enough? We know that we have a thin bench of players, but are we pushing hard enough, being disruptive enough? Maybe we should've launched the IOCs all at once, instead of going in with our contained approach. It's a legitimate question. Some of it is irreversible and we'll have to deal with what we have done. I agree with McCain that we're in the first inning of a nine-inning ball game . . . in a 162-game season.

Endnotes

[1] Family members owned approximately one-third of MLF's equity. McCain's father, Wallace McCain, was chairman of MLF and McCain's brother, Scott McCain, was the president of the agribusiness IOCs.

[2] McCain believed that an IOC had to achieve stability before Six Sigma could be of any use. He stressed that if an IOC were involved with "putting out fires"—in a state of flux—attempting to implement Six Sigma would certainly be an exercise in failure. He stated, "Unless you're at the top of your game, Six Sigma will not work."

[3] "Master black belt" is the industry term for the people who train and coach the black belts.

[4] McCain elaborated that Six Sigma was not a goal but a philosophy of constant improvement. He invited dissenters to improve their processes to the point of diminishing returns, stating that if that level of quality could be achieved across the company, Maple Leaf Foods would be peerless.

Kmart
Striving for a Comeback

John E. Gamble
University of South Alabama

In March 2003 Kmart Corporation was entering what its management hoped would be the last two months of bankruptcy protection that had allowed it to continue its operations even though it had been delinquent on obligations of more than $4.7 billion owed to creditors, vendors, and leaseholders. The bankruptcy, which was filed in January 2002, was the largest bankruptcy in U.S. retailing history and was the culmination of decades of poor strategy execution that resulted in an overall deterioration of Kmart's competitive position in the discount retail industry and a roller-coaster earnings history.

Specific problems that contributed to Kmart's bankruptcy were poor supply chain management, poor customer service, frequent stockouts of popular items, excessive inventory of slow-selling items, poor store housekeeping, unsound pricing strategies, and too many deteriorating stores built in the 1960s and 1970s. To make matters worse, as Kmart committed blunder after blunder in strategy execution during the 1980s and 1990s, Wal-Mart's distribution efficiency was becoming the global benchmark across all industries and the department store operator Dayton Hudson was perfecting its strategy for its Target stores that made designer-inspired apparel and housewares available at discount prices. Kmart's problems and competitive liabilities had long been obvious not only to industry insiders but also to the company's board of directors, employees, and customers, but the problems had been unresolved throughout a series of five executive regime changes dating to the late 1980s—three of which had occurred between June 2000 and January 2003.

Kmart's most recent CEO, Julian Day, who was installed in January 2003, began his tenure with the company in March 2002, when as chief operating officer he aided outgoing CEO James Adamson in the implementation of Kmart's restructuring plan. The reorganization plan, which focused on improving the company's weak competitive position and restoring financial solvency, included the closure of 600 stores and elimination of 52,000 employees, the restructuring of Kmart's supply chain, the elimination of slow-moving inventory, and the development of new private-label soft goods licensed from Disney and Joe Boxer that might compete with more expensive branded apparel. Upon his acceptance of the new position, Day stated the company would emerge from bankruptcy by April 30, 2003, and was poised to be a contender in the U.S. discount retail industry as it had achieved "a discernible shift in the company's internal culture, . . . repositioned itself as a high/low retailer of exclusive proprietary brands, . . . and restructured the store base and distribution network to protect and strengthen Kmart's competitive position in key markets."[1]

When the company closed out its fiscal 2002 books on January 31, 2003, the plan had yet to achieve any great successes with Kmart Corporation recording a net loss of $3.2 billion for the year and experiencing a sales decline of 18.5 percent during the fourth quarter of 2002 while rivals Wal-Mart and Target achieved sales growth of 12.3 percent and 9.0 percent, respectively, during the quarter. In addition, Kmart's sales per square foot (a key performance measure in retailing) of $212 during 2002 trailed Wal-Mart's sales per square foot of $404 and Target's sales per square foot of $263 by an unacceptable margin. Exhibit 1 presents a summary of Kmart's financial performance between 1992 and 2002. The company's common shares were delisted by the New York Stock Exchange in December 2002.

Company History and Background

Kmart's roots in the discount retail industry can be traced to 1899 when Sebastian S. Kresge opened a five-and-dime store in downtown Detroit, Michigan. Kresge's 5- and 10-cent pricing strategy appealed to turn-of-the-century working families and allowed him to expand the S. S. Kresge Company chain to 85 stores with $10 million in sales by 1912. Kresge was known for his bold and innovative strategies, which included expansion into Canada in 1929, the development of a mall-based store concept in the first suburban shopping center in 1937, the use of newspaper advertising circulars in the 1940s, and the introduction of checkout lines in the 1950s. When Sebastian Kresge retired as CEO of the company in 1959, his successor, Harry Cunningham, began to investigate new store concepts that included a wider variety of household items and apparel than what was found in five-and-dimes. Cunningham opened the first Kmart full-line discount store in Garden City, Michigan, in 1962. The new store concept was an instant hit with consumers, and Cunningham responded by opening an average of about three new Kmart stores each month over the next four years. At the time of Sebastian Kresge's death in 1966, the S. S. Kresge Company operated 753 Kresge variety stores and 162 Kmart full-line discount stores with combined annual sales of over $1 billion.

Throughout the remainder of the 1960s and 1970s, Kresge management continued to increase the number of Kmart stores and replaced existing Kresge stores with Kmart stores. In 1976, the S. S. Kresge Company opened 271 stores and thus became the only retailer to ever open 17 million square feet of retailing space in one year. By year-end 1976, Kresge operated 1,206 Kmart stores and 441 Kresge five-and-dime stores. The company changed its name to Kmart Corporation in early 1977 since its Kmart stores had generated nearly 95 percent of the company's 1976 domestic revenues. In 1981 the company opened its 2,000th Kmart location.

During the 1980s and early 1990s Kmart management diversified the company into additional retailing businesses rather than rely only on new Kmart store openings to generate revenue growth. In 1984 Kmart acquired Builders Square (a chain of warehouse-style home centers) and Walden Book Company, which operated Waldenbooks stores in all 50 states. PayLess Drug Stores, Inc., and Bargain Harold's Discount Outlets (a Canadian retailer) were acquired in 1985. In 1988 three start-up businesses—American Fare hypermarts (giant stores carrying a huge variety of household, apparel, and supermarket merchandise), Pace Membership warehouse clubs, and Office Square warehouse-style office supply stores—were added to the corporation's portfolio of retail businesses.

Exhibit 1   SELECTED FINANCIAL AND OPERATING STATISTICS, KMART CORPORATION, 1992–2002
(DOLLARS IN MILLIONS, EXCEPT PER SHARE DATA)

	2002	2001	2000	1999	1998	1997	1996	1995	1994	1993	1992
Summary of Operations											
Total sales	$30,762	$36,151	$37,028	$35,925	$33,674	$32,183	$31,437	$31,713	$29,563	$28,039	$26,470
Cost of sales, buying and occupancy	26,258	29,853	29,732	28,161	26,357	25,167	24,390	24,675	22,331	20,732	19,087
Selling, general and administrative expenses	6,544	7,588	7,366	6,569	6,288	6,174	6,274	6,876	6,651	6,241	5,830
Restructuring, impairment and other charges	705	1,091	—	—	19	114	—	—	—	—	—
Interest expense, net	155	344	287	280	293	363	453	434	479	467	411
Continuing income (loss) before income taxes, preferred dividend, and reorganization items	(2,900)	(2,725)	(370)	959	755	407	330	(313)	102	(306)	1,142
Chapter 11 reorganization items, net	(362)	183	—	—	—	—	—	—	—	—	—
Net income (loss) from continuing operations	(3,262)	(2,612)	(268)	594	491	242	231	–230	96	(179)	745
Discontinued operations, net	43	166	—	(230)	—	—	(451)	(341)	200	(795)	196
Net income (loss)	($ 3,219)	($ 2,446)	($ 268)	$ 364	$ 491	$ 242	($ 220)	($ 571)	$ 296	($ 974)	$ 941
Per Share of Common Stock											
Basic:											
Continuing income (loss)	($6.44)	($5.29)	($ 0.53)	$ 1.21	$ 1.00	$ 0.50	$ 0.48	($ 0.51)	$ 0.19	($ 0.41)	$ 1.63
Discontinued operations	$0.08	$0.34	$ —	($ 0.47)	$ —	$ —	($ 0.93)	($ 0.74)	$ 0.44	($ 1.74)	$ 0.43
Net income (loss)	($6.36)	($4.95)	($ 0.53)	$ 0.74	$ 1.00	$ 0.50	($ 0.45)	($ 1.24)	$ 0.65	($ 2.13)	$ 2.06
Book value	($0.59)	$6.42	$12.09	$12.73	$11.84	$10.89	$10.51	$10.99	$13.15	$13.39	$16.64
Financial Data											
Total assets	$11,238	$14,183	$14,815	$15,192	$14,238	$13,614	$14,286	$15,033	$16,085	$15,875	$16,769
Liabilities subject to compromise	7,969	8,093	—	—	—	—	—	—	—	—	—
Long-term debt	623	330	2,084	1,759	1,538	1,725	2,121	3,922	1,989	2,209	2,995
Long-term capital lease obligations	—	857	943	1,014	1,091	1,179	1,478	1,586	1,666	1,609	1,612
Capital expenditures	252	1,385	1,089	1,277	981	678	343	540	1,021	793	1,187
Depreciation and amortization	737	824	777	770	671	660	654	685	639	650	566
Basic weighted average shares outstanding (millions)	506	494	483	492	492	487	486	460	457	457	456
Number of stores	1,829	2,114	2,105	2,171	2,161	2,136	2,261	2,310	2,481	2,486	2,435
U.S. Kmart store sales per comparable selling square footage	$212	$235	$236	$233	$222	$211	$201	$195	$181	$160	$152
U.S. Kmart total selling square footage (millions)	139	154	153	155	154	151	156	160	166	182	181

Source: Kmart Corporation annual reports.

The Sports Authority (a 10-store chain of sporting goods superstores) was acquired in 1990 to complement and strengthen Kmart's own Sports Giant stores started in 1989; the Sports Giant stores were subsequently renamed and integrated into the Sports Authority chain. Kmart also acquired a 22 percent interest in OfficeMax office supply superstores in 1990 and increased its interest in the business to over 90 percent in 1991. In 1992, Kmart management acquired Borders, Inc. (a chain of 22 book superstores in the midwestern and northeastern United States); purchased a chain of 13 discount stores in the Czech Republic and Slovakia; acquired Bizmart (a 105-store chain of office supply stores); and announced that it would open up to 100 Kmart stores in Mexico in a 50–50 joint venture with Mexican retailer El Puerto de Liverpool. The company also entered into a joint venture with Metro Limited to open discount stores in Singapore in 1994.

The following year, Kmart's board brought in new executive management after concluding the company's diversification moves had done little to improve revenues and had actually damaged earnings by distracting management's attention from the company's core discount store business. With its sales growing at an annual rate of only 7.7 percent between 1980 and 1990, Kmart Corporation lost its position as the world's largest discount chain in 1990 to Wal-Mart. Kmart's position had weakened further by 1995, following annual sales rate growth of only 1.2 percent between 1990 and 1995. Wal-Mart's sales, by comparison, had grown at annual rates of 34.8 percent and 23.5 percent over the same respective periods. Exhibit 2 presents a financial comparison of Kmart Corporation, Target, and Wal-Mart Stores for selected years between 1980 and 2002.

Kmart under Joseph Antonini, 1987–1995

Kmart's strategy of growth via diversification into a variety of retail businesses was initiated by Bernard Fauber, the company's chief executive officer from 1980 to 1987. However, most of Kmart's acquisitions were orchestrated by Joseph Antonini, who succeeded Fauber as Kmart's chairman, CEO, and president in 1987. Both Fauber and Antonini believed that entry into specialty retail stores would provide the company with greater growth opportunities than would be possible with only the Kmart chain of discount stores. The move to expand Kmart's scope of retail operations was intended to position the company in such fast-growing product categories as drugstore merchandise, office supplies, books, building materials, and sporting goods. Antonini also believed it made good strategic sense for Kmart to be involved in warehouse clubs and hypermarts because such stores were simply a larger-scale and slightly modified retailing format of the traditional discount stores that Kmart was already operating. Antonini saw the purchase of the discount stores in the Czech Republic and Slovakia and the joint ventures in Mexico and Singapore as valuable ways to begin positioning Kmart more aggressively in international retail markets.

Antonini's second strategic initiative to stimulate revenue growth focused on a $3.5 billion "renewal" program in 1991 to modernize, expand, or relocate Kmart's 2,435 discount stores. Most of these stores were built during the company's dramatic growth period in the 1960s and 1970s and had undergone little or no remodeling or renovation since they were constructed. Antonini wanted to increase the size of Kmart stores from a typical 80,000 square feet to about 100,000 square feet so that a wider

Exhibit 2   COMPARATIVE FINANCIAL PERFORMANCE OF TARGET, KMART, AND WAL-MART, 1980, 1990, 1995-2002

Year	Sales* (in millions of dollars)			Operating Profit* (in millions of dollars)			Operating Profit as a Percent of Sales			Net Income* (in millions of dollars)			Net Income as a Percentage of Sales		
	Target	Kmart	Wal-Mart	Target	Kmart	Wal-Mart	Target	Kmart	Wal-Mart	Target†	Kmart	Wal-Mart	Target†	Kmart	Wal-Mart
1980	$ 1,531	$14,118	$ 1,643	$ 91	n.a	n.a	5.9%	n.a	n.a	n.a.	$ 429	$ 56	n.a.	3.0%	3.4%
1990	8,175	29,775	32,602	466	1,151	2,212	5.7	3.9%	6.8%	n.a.	756	1,291	n.a.	2.5	4.0
1995	15,807	31,713	93,627	721	162	5,247	4.6	0.5	5.6	n.a.	(571)	2,740	n.a.	-1.8	2.9
1996	17,853	31,437	104,859	1,048	773	5,722	5.9	2.5	5.5	n.a.	(220)	3,056	n.a.	-0.7	2.9
1997	20,368	32,183	117,558	1,287	728	6,503	6.3	2.3	5.5	n.a.	242	3,526	n.a.	0.8	3.0
1998	23,014	33,674	137,634	1,578	1,010	8,120	6.9	3.0	5.9	n.a.	491	4,430	n.a.	1.5	3.2
1999	26,080	35,925	165,013	2,022	1,239	10,105	7.8	3.4	6.1	n.a.	364	5,377	n.a.	1.0	3.3
2000	29,278	37,028	191,329	2,223	(83)	11,490	7.6	-0.2	6.0	n.a.	(268)	6,295	n.a.	-0.7	3.3
2001	32,588	36,151	217,799	2,546	(2,381)	12,077	7.8	-6.6	5.5	n.a.	(2,446)	6,671	n.a.	-6.8	3.1
2002	36,917	30,762	246,525	3,088	(2,745)	13,644	8.4	-8.9	5.5	n.a.	(3,219)	8,039	n.a.	-10.5	3.3

n.a. = not available.

*The fiscal year end for all three retailers occurs on or near January 31 of each year. In Wal-Mart's case, data for the period January 31, 1979 through January 31, 1980 are reported in Wal-Mart's annual report as 1980 results. Because the company's fiscal year results really cover 11 months of the previous calendar year, this exhibit shows Wal-Mart's 1996 fiscal results in the 1995 row, its 1997 fiscal results in the 1996 row, and so on. This adjustment makes Wal-Mart's figures correspond more to the same time frame as the calendar year data for Kmart and Target, which both report results as if the 11-month period dictated the year rather than the closing month.

†Net income is not reported for Target Corporation's Target stores. The company's retail chains include Mervyn's, Marshall Field's, and Target. The company does not make net income figures available for its different chains.

Source: Company annual reports.

variety of merchandise could be offered to consumers. The modernized Kmart stores provided brighter lighting, wider aisles, more modern and colorful interior signs, and more attractive merchandise displays. In 1992 he announced that the company would launch as many as 500 Super Kmart Centers that, like American Fare, would include both a discount store and a grocery store in a 160,000–180,000 square foot building. By 1994 the sales of the renovated and new Super Kmart Centers were 23 percent above the sales of the chain's older, unrefurbished stores.

Antonini also initiated efforts to increase the volume of apparel sold in Kmart stores. He believed that increased sales of high-margin apparel would provide the stores with better operating margins and allow the company to offer lower everyday pricing on nonapparel items, like household items and health and beauty products. The company improved the styling and quality of its private-label apparel and began to include more natural fibers and less polyester in its garments. Kmart used endorsements from Jaclyn Smith and Kathy Ireland to create private-label branded lines of apparel to appeal to fashion-conscious and designer-conscious shoppers. Antonini also added national brands of apparel and footwear like Wrangler, Hanes, L.A. Gear, and Brittania to the company's merchandise mix.

Attempts to Cure Kmart's Longstanding Inventory Management Problems

Joseph Antonini also believed that the company needed to correct its long-running inability to maintain proper inventory levels in its stores. Kmart had been confronted with this problem for years, but the company had never really been able to resolve it. Most Kmart stores either frequently stocked out of popular items and/or were burdened with excess stocks of slow-moving items that eventually had to be marked down significantly. Antonini believed that Kmart's decentralized buying and merchandising process was at the root of the company's poor inventory management practices. Typically, Kmart buyers negotiated purchases with manufacturers, distribution people shipped products to stores, advertising specialists coordinated the company's advertising, and a separate marketing staff was responsible for promotions. Additionally, the company's store managers were authorized to purchase merchandise specific to their geographic locale and to place special ads in local area newspapers.

Antonini and Kmart's chief information officer, David Carlson, implemented a number of state-of-the-art information systems to correct the inventory management problems in the company's 2,000+ stores. In 1990 Kmart launched a GTE Spacenet satellite-based network that linked individual Kmart stores with the Kmart corporate office in Troy, Michigan, and some suppliers. The system allowed Kmart management to eliminate its traditional decentralized inventory management process and adopt a centralized process that was intended to reduce escalating inventory costs while meeting local preferences and price sensitivities. The GTE Spacenet communication system allowed management to implement its Central Merchandising Automated Replenishment (CMAR) system that was jointly developed by Kmart's information systems staff and Electronic Data Systems, a leading supplier of data processing services. The CMAR system allowed Kmart's corporate office to keep track of every sale in each store. All scanner data were transmitted via a local area network to a Unix server in the back room of each individual store. At the end of every day, the server transmitted sales data to the corporate headquarters via the GTE Spacenet satellite.

The next morning Kmart product category managers studied the sales data from each store; later in the day they placed orders with vendors to replenish each store's inventory. Vendors that were members of Kmart's Partners in Merchandise Flow program were allowed to monitor the scanner data themselves and ship to Kmart distribution centers when they determined it was necessary to maintain Kmart's desired inventory levels. The distribution centers used a cross-docking system that helped keep inventory levels at the distribution center to a minimum. A senior executive at Kmart explained how centralized category management allowed the company to reduce expenses and keep products that consumers wanted on the shelves:

> Category management has been very successful for us. It's shifted our entire focus to the front door. Years ago we were busy with shipments—looking at what was coming in the back door from our suppliers. Today we have a front-door focus in that we are focusing on the consumer and what the register tape tells us she's taking out the front door. We've seen dramatic improvements in turnover. In fact, we used to call our distribution centers "warehouses" because products would come in and sometimes just sit there. Now they are truly distribution centers with goods flowing in and right out, often within a day or two.[2]

Kmart identified about 1,500 hard-line categories and several hundred soft-line categories and selected managers to make all buying and merchandising decisions—including pricing, assortments, and promotions—for their assigned category of products. Each category manager used the scanner data available from CMAR and demographic profiles and consumer purchasing behavior data provided by third parties such as Nielsen Marketing Research to make their purchasing decisions. Each category manager was required to develop a sales plan, a gross margin plan, and a turnover plan that was presented to the senior marketing executives at the beginning of the financial year.

Kmart spent about $160 million annually to create and implement information systems like CMAR technology and other state-of-the art computer systems during Antonini's tenure as Kmart's top executive. The company implemented electronic data interchange (EDI) systems with some suppliers that attempted to reduce the company's dependence on paper-based transaction processing. The company also developed the ShopperTrack system, which used backroom computers and ceiling-mounted sensors to monitor how many customers were in each department throughout the day. The system used the tracking data to project store and department customer counts at 15-minute intervals. Store managers were instructed to use this information to schedule employee staffing at the store's checkout stations and merchandise departments.

Difficulties in Implementing and Executing Antonini's Strategy

At the outset, both Wall Street and Kmart investors reacted favorably to Antonini's moves to diversify the corporation into a number of attractive discount retail segments, to renovate and enlarge Kmart stores, to improve merchandise selection, quality and availability, and to improve information systems. The consensus was that these moves would allow the company to grow faster and to compete more effectively against its major rivals. However, as efforts to implement the strategy continued to unfold, events made it increasingly clear that Kmart was being outmaneuvered by its rivals; Wal-Mart, in particular, was leaving Kmart far behind (see Exhibit 2). Kmart's sales per store continued to run near $180 per square foot in 1994, despite the merchandising efforts initiated by Antonini and other Kmart executives. Also, Kmart's pricing continued to average 10 to 15 percent above its chief competitors, as Kmart sought to boost its subpar store margins and make up for the higher selling, general, and administrative expenses brought on by relatively low sales volumes per square foot of selling space.

Moreover, while Fauber and Antonini built Kmart's retailing portfolio far beyond its core discount store base, Kmart management never was able to transform any of its acquisitions into enterprises able to compete successfully against key segment rivals in terms of sales, net income, or efficient inventory management. In almost every retailing business that Kmart diversified into, it trailed the industry leader by a considerable distance. Sales volumes at Builders Square stores were only one-third of those at industry leader Home Depot. The company's Pace warehouse clubs never were able to match the selection and pricing of Sam's Clubs and, in the end, many of Pace's store locations were eventually sold to Wal-Mart.

Knowledgeable retail analysts attributed the failure of Kmart's American Fare stores in part to poor store design and poor store management. PayLess Drugs, Waldenbooks, and OfficeMax were all weak-performing businesses under Kmart's management, posting either operating losses or minimal operating profits.

Joseph Antonini attributed some of Kmart's difficulties in the apparel segment of its core retail discount business to rapidly shifting market conditions rather than weak strategy on Kmart's part. For example, although the Kathy Ireland and Jaclyn Smith apparel lines were successfully positioned as national brands in the minds of shoppers, as the company had planned, the initial success proved short-lived. By 1994, sales of the two apparel lines were sagging because of changing buyer preferences. Antonini, whose background and experience had been largely in apparel and soft lines, explained the reasons for the downturn: "Substantial shifts are taking place. For example, clothes just don't mean as much as they did five years ago, focus groups tell us. Designer names are not driving shoppers to stores, but in many ways have the opposite effect. Today, Mom is usually the last family member to get a new outfit. She is sacrificing for her family."[3] Antonini, in a 1994 *Forbes* interview, said that the U.S. economy played a role in undermining some of Kmart's merchandising efforts: "The economy is hurting, disposable income is down, and people are spending money only on essential products. The fringe items—and I consider apparel to be a fringe item—aren't selling anywhere across the country like they used to."[4]

Antonini's expectation that sales of higher-margin apparel items would allow the company to offer lower prices on thousands of other items sold in Kmart stores didn't pan out either. As it turned out, Kmart was at a cost disadvantage relative to Wal-Mart and was not able to meet Wal-Mart's pricing on many items. In addition, Wal-Mart management was intent on being the low-price leader and chose not to allow competitors to price popular items below what Wal-Mart charged. A Wal-Mart executive gave the following explanation of the importance of the company's five-point operating cost advantage in setting its pricing strategy: "It's very simple. We're not going to be undersold. What that means is, that in an all-out price war, [our competitors] will go broke 5% before we will."[5]

When asked about Wal-Mart's meteoric climb to the top of the full-line discount industry, Antonini stated that Wal-Mart managers, whom he at times referred to as "snake oil salesmen,"[6] came across as successful largely because Wal-Mart was new to the industry and consumers were inclined to try out a new store. In 1994 he commented, "They have enjoyed the advantage of being the new show in town in many of our markets."[7] Antonini suggested that Wal-Mart's newcomer advantage was very similar to the new retail shopping excitement that Kmart was able to create during its period of rapid growth in the 1960s and 1970s.

Kmart's Image with Consumers   Surveys of U.S. discount store shoppers commissioned by *Chain Store Age Executive* found three consistent negative images that customers attributed to Kmart: out-of-stock merchandise, poor housekeeping, and indifferent service. Additionally, the consumers surveyed found Wal-Mart's locations more convenient and believed that Wal-Mart offered better pricing and product selection than Kmart. Antonini's store renovation and remodeling strategy was directed at eliminating Wal-Mart's pricing and selection advantage. However, in 1995—the company's fourth year into its renovation, relocation, and remodeling strategy—sales per square foot at Kmart remained flat at around $195, resulting in selling, general, and administrative expense ratios that were far above Wal-Mart's because the typical Wal-Mart store had sales per square foot of over $370. The higher expense ratios kept Kmart's bottom-line performance from materially improving.

Kmart's Store Renovation and Renewal Program   Wall Street analysts were very critical of Kmart's efforts to upgrade its stores. Many investors were displeased with Kmart management's use of the proceeds of a $1 billion equity issue in 1991. At the time the new shares of stock were sold, management had indicated that the capital was to be used to renovate and refurbish older Kmart stores and build new Super Kmart Centers. As it turned out, a big portion of the money spent in its "renewal" program went into acquiring new specialty retail stores rather than renovating older Kmart stores. Wall Street analysts made the following comments about Kmart's store renewal efforts.

> They aren't doing full renovations, just repainting or putting in new linoleum instead of gutting the stores entirely and redesigning them. And that has hurt them. It's back to the old Kmart culture where it's better to spend money on new stores and expand the chain.
>
> Even Betty Crocker got a new hairdo. I just drove by a Kmart store sign and it looked like a Howard Johnson should be next to it, circa 1957. They have a long way to go before getting rid of the popcorn smell when you walk in the door.[8]

Some shareholders and industry analysts suggested that the lack of management commitment to the store renewal program was a result of the company's past strategies. Kmart had achieved great success during the 1960s and 1970s as a result of its rapid addition of stores. The company's stock jumped from $0.50 per share when the first Kmart store was opened in 1962 to $32 in 1972. Some investors believed that the era of store growth at Kmart helped mold a managerial mind-set that favored putting more emphasis on store expansion than on proper management of existing stores and on merchandising efforts to boost annual sales at each existing store.

Continuing Inventory Problems   Even though Kmart had invested far more than its industry rivals on developing systems and procedures to correct its inventory-related problems, the problems still existed. Kmart stores still were faced with frequent stockouts of merchandise, and some of Kmart's vendors had criticized Kmart's buying procedures, stating that the corporate office frequently placed orders for merchandise and then later canceled the orders. A Kmart executive explained the difficulties of implementing its centralized merchandising strategy:

Bringing this decision-making power to the desktop is a hurdle. Category management evolved with computer systems, but it's still a challenge to get these high-powered PCs on everyone's desktops and to have them linked together via local area networks. Furthermore, some buyers may not be computer literate or used to dealing with scanner and syndicated data. So it can be an educational process as well as a hardware installation process. Most of our buyers started out as store managers, so to them it's attractive to think, "Oh, I'll call my old store to see how this product is doing." We have to get them additionally looking at and relying on this internal computer data, syndicated third party data, and quantitative information. It also takes a certain kind of person, someone who knows merchandising, who knows computer processing, who knows about financing, who knows a little about advertising—someone who knows enough about everything, as opposed to being a specialist in just one area. The information and the software available are just tools. You still need an experienced person who can tie it all together.[9]

In a January 28, 2002, interview published in *Crain's Detroit Business,* David Carlson, Kmart's chief information officer between 1984 and 1995, provided further understanding of why Antonini's efforts to cure Kmart's inventory management problems failed:

One of the core problems was that there was just way too much merchandise, and the stores didn't have adequate volume to justify the assortment. I produced reports that showed our inventory turns in the fishing rod category were abysmal. But the merchants were never able to move in the right direction of editing what was carried in the stores to ensure higher-moving items were in stock. The number of items just kept growing. Too often customers would go to Kmart and stores would be out of stock, or shelves would be full of the wrong products. If headquarters said you had to carry 13 toasters, you carried 13 toasters. Never mind the fact that the bottom-five were each selling one or less a year.

Customer Service Problems   Some Kmart stores were plagued with unresponsive customer service. A 1994 *Forbes* article cited customer complaints of indifferent Kmart employees who, when asked for a specific item in the store, would wave their hand in a general direction. One disgruntled shopper complained, "At the superstores in Farmington Hills or Southfield, the help is surly and uncooperative and you can never find the products that you need and have to have."[10]

Floyd Hall's Turnaround Efforts, 1995–2000

Kmart's board of directors appointed Floyd Hall as the company's new chairman, chief executive officer, and president in June 1995. Hall, who was recruited from Grand Union Supermarkets, had engineered Target's growth during the 1980s and had more recently gotten Grand Union back on track. Floyd Hall accepted the position with the intention of turning around Kmart within three years and then moving on to other ventures. He said, "I'm just trying to build a team . . . get a good succession plan and new policies and practices in place."[11] Hall and the board quickly assembled a new top-level management team—with 12 new vice presidents in marketing, product development, strategic planning, finance, administration, merchandising, information systems, and other key areas. The 12 new vice presidents had an average of 27 years of retail experience. When Hall asked his new management team to review and evaluate Kmart's competitive position, he found that Kmart trailed Wal-Mart by a considerable distance on every key performance indicator. Wal-Mart's customers averaged 32 store visits per year, while Kmart's customers averaged 15 visits per year. Kmart's sales per square foot in 1994 were $185, compared to Wal-Mart's $379 and Target's $282. Only 19 percent of Kmart shoppers considered themselves loyal to the chain, while 46 percent of Wal-Mart shoppers considered themselves loyal Wal-Mart shoppers. Hall stated, "The most devastating news I saw in all the research was that 49% of Wal-Mart's shoppers drive past a Kmart to get to Wal-Mart."[12]

Hall believed that Kmart must be fixed "department by department" and that management must not try to "put a Band-Aid on our problems. This requires surgery."[13] Hall's first priority was to close nearly 400 Kmart stores and divest all noncore businesses from the company's portfolio between 1995 and 1997. Hall also initiated over $900 million in cost reductions during 1995 and 1996 by consolidating the company's Canadian operations with its U.S. operations, clearing out $700 million in old inventory, and using the company's volume buying power to reduce the cost of benefits for its 300,000 employees.

Some of the portfolio restructuring actually had taken place in the months just before Antonini's departure. Kmart sold PayLess Drug Stores in 1993 and spun off OfficeMax and Sports Authority as independent, stand-alone companies in late 1994. The initial public offerings of stock in OfficeMax and in Sports Authority were completed in December 1994, with Kmart retaining a 25 percent equity ownership in OfficeMax and a 30 percent equity ownership in Sports Authority. In addition, the company's 21.5 percent interest in Cole Myer, an Australian retailer, was sold in 1994.

In 1995 and 1996, Hall and Kmart's new management team sold the company's Czech and Slovak stores for $115 million; completed public offerings of stock to divest the company's remaining interests in OfficeMax and Sports Authority (netting the company an after-tax gain of $155 million); sold the assets of the Kmart auto centers to Penske for $84 million; completed a public stock offering of Borders Bookstores group (which resulted in an after-tax loss of $185 million); and sold the Rite Aid drugstore chain for $257 million. The company also discontinued its joint ventures in Singapore and Mexico in 1996 and divested its 162-store Builders Square home improvement chain for a mere $10 million in 1997.

A Near Bankruptcy as Floyd Hall Begins a Turnaround

Floyd Hall and the other members of Kmart's top management team were confronted with a potentially devastating financial crisis during the last half of 1995 that was a result of Kmart's poor cash flow and the financial decisions made by previous Kmart management. As was common with most retailers, Kmart management had a long-standing preference of financing new store construction off the company's balance sheet. Groups of newly constructed stores were sold to pension funds, insurance companies, and other such organizations, who then leased the stores back to Kmart on long-term lease agreements. This was a hidden financial obligation, since long-term lease payment obligations were not required, under accounting rules then prevailing, to be shown as a long-term liability on Kmart's balance sheet; the company had only to report current-year lease payments as an operating expense on its annual income statement.

In the early 1990s, Kmart's financial officers had agreed to special "put provisions" in a number of Kmart's store leasing agreements in exchange for better lease terms from the financing organizations. The put provisions stipulated that if Kmart's bond rating was downgraded to junk-bond status, then Kmart would immediately be obligated to buy back the leased stores from the lease owner. Kmart's contingent liability under the put provisions amounted to about $600 million. In July 1995—just one month after Hall became Kmart's CEO—Kmart was placed on credit watch by various credit rating agencies as an indication that they were considering downgrading Kmart's bond rating. The credit watch placement prevented Kmart from borrowing on 30–60-day commercial paper over the October–November period to pay suppliers for shipping the volume of goods needed to build its Christmas inventory. In order to have ample inventories for the Christmas season, Kmart was forced to activate a $2 billion backup revolving line of credit, adding interest costs and further straining Kmart's already precariously thin profit margins and cash flows. To make matters worse, the covenants of Kmart's $2 billion revolving line of credit stated that if the leaseholders exercised their put options, any borrowings under the line of credit would immediately become due and payable. Kmart's accounts payable to its vendors already exceeded $3.5 billion for its purchases for Christmas inventory. The potential for Kmart to be faced with obligations to its vendors and creditors totaling $6 billion, compounded by swirling rumors, drove the company's stock price down to $5¾ per share—50 percent of its book value.

As Wall Street rumors predicted, Kmart's long-term debt was downgraded to junk bond status in January 1996. Hall and Kmart financial officers had already visited with the leaseholders in late December of 1995 and negotiated an agreement for them not to immediately exercise the put options and demand payment. With temporary agreements in place, Hall and Kmart financial executives used the company's available cash to pay vendors in a manner sufficiently timely to ensure continued shipments of merchandise. As Kmart paid its suppliers, management continued talks with the 70 banks that funded Kmart's line of credit. Kmart's creditors agreed to allow the company to suspend principal payments on its debt for 18 months while Hall and Kmart's financial officers negotiated a new financing proposal with a consortium of banks led by Chemical Bank. Chemical Bank agreed to put a consortium of lenders together to provide Kmart with $3.7 billion to refinance its obligations under the revolving line of credit and the leased-store debt associated with put options—contingent on the company's ability to raise $750 million through an equity issue. The close call with bankruptcy came to an end in June 1996, when Kmart issued $1 billion in convertible preferred shares and signed a new $3.7 billion financing agreement with Chemical Bank.

Attracting Customers to Kmart

Floyd Hall and his new management team developed a combination of new strategies and improved implementation techniques to better compete with low-cost leader Wal-Mart and rapidly growing Target.

A New Merchandising and Distribution Strategy   Kmart had been confronted with serious inventory management problems as far back as the early 1980s, and the new management team saw inventory management as the single biggest problem that had to be corrected. A big part of the solution, they believed, lay in eliminating many slow-selling items and unpopular brands and reducing the number of vendors. Under Antonini's centralized merchandising strategy, Kmart carried one or two national brands, an assortment of second- and third-tier brands, and some private-label brands. The new top management team found that many of the second- and third-tier brands cluttered store shelves and frequently did not sell without deep markdowns. Kmart's new merchandising executives eliminated some second-tier brands and most third-tier brands and began to develop its private-label brands to fill the gaps in its merchandise mix left by the removal of the lesser-known brands.

Kmart also completely redesigned the Martha Stewart Everyday bed and bath collection and relaunched the brand in 1997. The Martha Stewart private-label line of linens, towels, and other bed and bath products had been created during the Antonini era; however, under Antonini, the brand had not done particularly well because of inadequate promotion and a limited product line. The reintroduced Martha Stewart bed and bath collection included a wider variety of products—linens, bath towels, beach towels, draperies, pillows, blankets, lawn and garden products, baby products, and paint.

Company management took a series of steps to improve its working relationships with suppliers, to correct stockouts, and to reduce its distribution costs. Kmart began a Collaborative Forecasting and Replenishment program with vendors that shared Kmart's customer and product information with its suppliers over the Internet. The company also upgraded its IBM Inventory Forecasting and Replenishment Modules system to shorten its replenishment cycle by a full day. Kmart's chief information officer, Donald Norman, said that the company had reduced the amount of time to replenish some merchandise from 40 hours to 18 hours.

Improving Kmart's Store Productivity and Relative Cost Position   Despite the efforts of Kmart executives, at year-end 1996 Kmart's store productivity still trailed Wal-Mart's by a wide margin. Kmart had sales of $201 per square foot of retail space, compared to sales of $379 per square foot for Wal-Mart. While Kmart's new superstores achieved higher sales volumes than the company's older stores, they did not attract customers in sufficient volume to come close to matching sales per square foot at Wal-Mart. Kmart executives saw increased store traffic as the key to improving store productivity and lowering prices.

Hall developed and rolled out a redesign of existing stores that was intended to attract more customers to Kmart stores. The company tested its high-frequency Pantry concept during 1995 in selected stores and announced in 1997 that it would expand the Pantry concept to as many as 1,800 stores during the next three years. The Pantry concept was a redesign of existing stores that took items typically found in a convenience store and placed them in the front of Kmart stores. Merchandise that was already sold in Kmart stores—diapers, paper towels, bread, milk, dog food, beverages, snack foods, and so on—was gathered and placed in one department, then supplemented by additional dry grocery items. Kmart rearranged remaining store merchandise so that frequently purchased items like small appliances and soft lines (underwear, T-shirts, socks, and fleece products) were placed near the Pantry area. The cost to convert an existing Kmart store to the new Pantry concept was $600,000 versus $10 million for a new 100,000-square-foot Kmart store or $20 million for a new 180,000 Super Kmart Center.

Changes in Structure, Communications, Culture, and Rewards   Concerned that the attitudes and performance of Kmart store managers and associates were adversely impacting shopper visits and loyalty, Hall brought all Kmart store managers together in 1996 for the company's first-ever store managers' meeting.

At the meeting, the executive team explained the company's mission and strategy and what individual store managers' roles were in implementing the strategy. The executive team also made it clear that they intended to end Kmart's historically insular, turf-wary organizational culture and adopt a more team-oriented atmosphere at both corporate headquarters and in the stores. The company also announced its new management development program to help the company develop future store-level and corporate-level managers from within its ranks.

Kmart corporate management also unveiled a new organizational structure during the conference that reduced the number of stores that each district manager was responsible for from 28 to 14. This reduction was intended to allow district managers to have the time necessary to visit every store in their districts more frequently and to provide better coaching to store managers. Within the stores, associates no longer had at-large responsibility but instead were assigned to departments. Kmart executives believed that giving associates defined areas of responsibility would create a feeling of ownership within their department and encourage employees to offer better service.

A new incentive compensation plan for store managers was developed to replace Kmart's old managerial pay plan. Previously, Kmart managers were paid a salary plus a bonus based on store sales. Under the new compensation plan, store managers were eligible for both bonuses and stock options. The new bonus plan tied 50 percent of a store manager's bonus to meeting the store's budget objectives for the year and 50 percent to the store's customer satisfaction rating. The customer satisfaction rating was determined by the results of independent mystery shoppers who visited each store 28 times per year.

Hall's Success in Getting Kmart on Track   By 1999, Floyd Hall's turnaround efforts were showing signs of success: More than 1,600 Kmart stores had been remodeled with wider aisles, brighter lighting, and lower shelving; the Martha Stewart line accounted for $1 billion per year in sales; and operating expenses had fallen by more than $500 million. Hall was also able to put together a string of three consecutive profitable years. The company's sales per square foot of $233 at year-end 1999 approached Target's sales per square foot of $253, though it still trailed Wal-Mart's sales per square foot of $360. However, many consumers still found Kmart's customer service unacceptable; the company's distribution system still had many bottlenecks; shelves still lacked best-selling items; stores had too much inventory of items consumers rarely needed; and, most important, the company found itself unattractively positioned between Wal-Mart's low prices and Target's more upscale merchandising. Even though Floyd Hall had expected to serve as Kmart's CEO for only three years, he remained CEO until May 2000, when he was succeeded by former CVS executive Charles Conaway.

Charles Conaway and Kmart's Bankruptcy, June 2000–March 2002

Charles Conaway was selected as Hall's replacement in June 2000 by Kmart's board of directors, based largely on the 39-year-old Conaway's performance while president and chief operating officer of the rapidly growing drugstore chain CVS Corporation. Kmart board member James Adamson commented, "Floyd got us to Point B, now Chuck has got to get us beyond."[14] Some analysts questioned the hiring of Conaway, noting that even though he was known as an operations whiz at CVS, he had not managed a chain as large as the 2,100-store Kmart and had no experience with soft goods such as apparel. Conaway moved decisively after he was installed as Kmart's new CEO. His first official action was to replace Hall's top management team with a group of 40-ish retail veterans who became known at Kmart headquarters as "the frat boys."[15] Conaway also replaced many higher-level managers outside the corporate office with 500 outsiders from companies such as Wal-Mart, Coca-Cola, and Sears. Conaway expanded the number of district managers from 150 to 275—reducing the number of stores in each territory from 14 to 8. Conaway also expanded the number of geographic regions from six to eight and added 25 regional managers—a new level of management between district managers and senior regional vice presidents. Conaway believed that the smaller districts and additional management oversight would improve Kmart's poor customer service.

Conaway's Strategy and Execution Approaches to Revitalize Kmart

Conaway and members of Conaway's new management team crafted a strategy that addressed the discount chain's poor inventory management, muddled marketing strategy, and pricing disadvantage relative to Wal-Mart. Conaway's team tackled the company's poor image by closing 78 of the company's poorest-performing and most run-down stores, revising the company's advertising campaign to cut more than $200 million in annual advertising expenditures and eliminate its newspaper circulars used since the 1940s, improving the company's e-commerce capabilities, and improving its merchandise quality.

Conaway adopted the marketing slogan "Kmart: The authority for moms, home, and kids" and placed greater emphasis on private-label brands such as Kathy Ireland and Jaclyn Smith women's wear, Martha Stewart Everyday home collection, Sesame Street kids' wear, and Route 66 jeans in attempt to differentiate Kmart from Wal-Mart and Target. Conaway also entered into a new seven-year contract with Martha Stewart Living that called for the company to launch a new line of Martha Stewart products every six months. The original line and its extensions proved successful, with Martha Stewart products accounting for $1.5 billion in sales by year-end 2002. Analysts were less satisfied with the company tag line; many believed it failed to convey meaning to consumers and believed that the Kathy Ireland, Jaclyn Smith, Sesame Street, and Route 66 private-label brands did not come close to either Kmart's own Martha Stewart line or Target's exclusive brands such as Mossimo in terms of quality or style.

Conaway also wanted Kmart customers to be able to purchase standard and differentiated products sold in Kmart stores over the Internet. Under Conaway the company expanded its e-commerce capabilities beyond its Kmart.com website through the development of a BlueLight.com venture with Softbank. Kmart committed $55 million to the e-commerce venture, which initially began as a free Internet service for Kmart customers and evolved into a discount e-tailing site where consumers could purchase any of 100,000 items typically found in Kmart stores. Kmart eventually paid its venture partner $84 million in cash and stock to gain control of BlueLight.com.

Kmart's boldest strategies under Conaway involved a $1.7 billion investment in new information technology systems to improve Kmart's supply chain management and a Blue Light Always plan to beat Wal-Mart on price on 38,000 stock keeping units (SKUs). Kmart's Play to Win information technology initiative was designed to resolve Kmart's supply chain problems. When Conaway became the company's CEO,

Kmart's in-stock rating stood just below 90 percent, while more than 99 percent of Wal-Mart's products were always in stock. Conaway also learned that Kmart had 15,000 trailers of unsold merchandise sitting outside stores because there was no space available for the merchandise inside. In addition, Kmart's 4.39 inventory turns per year were just over one-half of Wal-Mart's 7.29 turns. The president of a retail industry consulting firm, commenting on Kmart's poor inventory management and its 15,000 trailers of overflow merchandise, said, "Trucks and trailers are supposed to move product. They are not supposed to be a warehouse on wheels."[16]

The Play to Win program was designed to improve supply chain management by keeping track of what was selling in stores, store inventory levels, warehouse inventory levels, and shipments en route to stores. Kmart contracted with i2 Technologies, a highly regarded systems designer, but had great difficulty in implementing the supply chain technology program since the software had integration problems with Kmart's existing computing systems and because of the vast amount of data to process. For example, Kmart's 2,100 stores might stock more than 70,000 items each—creating 140 million possible data points to track. Analysts claimed that Conaway's $1.7 billion plan failed, in part, because it attempted to do too much too soon, but they did commend him for eliminating $700 million in inventory, including Kmart's 15,000 trailers of overflow merchandise, during his brief stay with the company. A former Kmart executive suggested that Kmart's inventory management program also failed because, even under Conaway, point-of-sale data available through the system were ignored by Kmart's buying department, with purchasing decisions based on which vendors were willing to pay the largest slotting fees rather than what products Kmart shoppers wanted. Conaway also invested $200 million for new Internet-enabled IBM SurePOS point-of-sales systems in all 2,100 stores to speed customer checkout and built two new distribution centers to improve productivity and the flow of goods to over one-half of Kmart's stores. The company incurred a $195 restructuring charge related to the relocation of its distribution centers.

Kmart's Blue Light Always plan was developed by Conaway's most notable and influential hire, Mark Schwartz—his choice for chief operating officer. Schwarz was a former Wal-Mart executive who had been second in command of Wal-Mart's Supercenters operations at one time but who also had other responsibilities at Wal-Mart, including managing an unrelated real estate investment firm that filed for bankruptcy in 1996 and was dissolved under his leadership. Schwartz left Wal-Mart in 1998, not long after the failure of the real estate firm, to become head of Hechinger Company, a home improvement chain that was in need of a turnaround. Under Schwartz, Hechinger built up excessive inventory, ran out of cash, and filed for bankruptcy within weeks of Schwartz's departure for Big V Supermarkets, which was also looking for a turnaround. Big V also filed for bankruptcy just weeks after Schwartz left to become Kmart's chief operating officer.

Many industry analysts believed Schwartz's Blue Light Always pricing strategy, which attempted to beat Wal-Mart on price every day on 38,000 SKUs (and ultimately underprice Wal-Mart on 50,000 items), was the biggest reason for Kmart's slide into bankruptcy as compared to any of the other management gaffes. Analysts noted that no matter how much Kmart was willing to cut price, Wal-Mart, which was light-years ahead of Kmart in terms of efficiency, could cut more. Some observed that Kmart declaring a price war against Wal-Mart was comparable to Luxembourg declaring war against the United States. Similarly, they were unimpressed with the idea of revising the Blue Light Special concept. A business professor with Northwestern University's Kellogg School of Management commented, "The underlying principle behind a Blue

Light Special was 'you are going to be surprised in a positive way when you walk in the store.' You don't know what you'll see, but you will see something. It may have worked in 1965, but in 1995 or 2000 consumers are too busy, so they don't go to the store to be surprised."[17]

Kmart's Slide into Bankruptcy

Kmart's Blue Light Always pricing strategy and Schwartz's decision to build $8.3 billion worth of inventory for the Christmas shopping season led to the company's January 22, 2002, bankruptcy after Kmart had a disastrous holiday season in which sales declined by 1 percent during the month of December 2001, while Wal-Mart's sales increased by 8 percent and Target's sales increased by 0.6 percent. With sales failing to materialize, many of Kmart's suppliers went unpaid after the holiday season concluded. Kmart's food supplier, Fleming Companies, stopped its shipments of food items to Kmart stores the day before Kmart's bankruptcy after it failed to receive its weekly payment from Kmart for approximately $78 million worth of food. Although Kmart management attempted to avert bankruptcy by putting together an emergency financial package to pay its creditors and suppliers, lenders balked and a last-minute bailout in early 2002 failed to materialize.

Kmart Corporation's bankruptcy filing enabled it to restructure payments on $4.7 billion in debt and keep shipments of inventory coming from suppliers since bankruptcy courts give vendors who continue to ship goods first priority in repayment status. On the day of the bankruptcy filing, Charles Conaway commented, "After considering a wide range of alternatives, it became clear that this course of action was the only way to truly resolve the company's most challenging problems."[18] In the quarter prior to Kmart's bankruptcy filing, the company's sales per square foot reached $243—an improvement, but well below Wal-Mart's sales per square foot of $410. In addition, its selling, general, and administrative (SG&A) expenses as a percentage of sales were 22.7 percent, compared to Wal-Mart's SG&A-to-sales ratio of 17.3 percent, and its prices averaged 3.8 percent higher than Wal-Mart's pricing on comparable products despite its efforts to underprice Wal-Mart with its Blue Light Always campaign. Exhibit 3 presents Kmart's statements of operations for fiscal 1999 through fiscal 2002. Its balance sheets and cash flow statements are presented in Exhibits 4 and 5, respectively. Exhibit 6 presents a listing of Kmart's contractual obligations and other commercial commitments at fiscal year-end 2001.

Kmart's Restructuring Program and Planned Emergence from Bankruptcy, March 2002–April 2003

Five days prior to Kmart's January 22, 2002, bankruptcy filing, its board of directors promoted board member James Adamson to the position of chairman of the board, a position previously held by CEO Charles Conaway. Adamson had been a member of Kmart's board of directors since 1996 and was among those enthralled by the youthful Conaway during the selection process for Floyd Hall's replacement. Adamson was the retired chairman and CEO of Advantica Restaurant Group, which operated the Denny's, Coco's, and Carrows restaurant chains. Adamson had also held executive positions with Revco, Target, and B. Dalton Bookseller prior to joining Kmart's board.

Exhibit 3   CONSOLIDATED STATEMENT OF OPERATIONS FOR KMART CORPORATION, FISCAL 1999–2002 (DOLLARS IN MILLIONS, EXCEPT PER SHARE DATA)

	Fiscal Year Ended January			
	2002	2002	2001	2000
Sales	$30,762	$36,151	$37,028	$35,925
Cost of sales, buying, and occupancy	26,258	29,853	29,732	28,161
Gross margin	4,504	6,298	7,296	7,764
Selling, general and administrative expenses	6,544	7,588	7,366	6,569
Equity (loss) income in unconsolidated subsidiaries	34	—	(13)	44
Restructuring, impairment and other charges	739	1,091	—	—
Continuing (loss) income before interest, reorganization items, income taxes and dividends on convertible preferred securities of subsidiary trust	(2,745)	(2,381)	(83)	1,239
Interest expense, net (contractual interest for fiscal year 2001 was $352)	155	344	287	280
Reorganization items, net	386	(183)	—	—
(Benefit from) provision for income taxes	(24)	—	(148)	315
Dividends on convertible preferred securities of subsidiary trust, net of income taxes of $0, $25 and $27, respectively (contractual dividend for fiscal year 2001 was $72, net of tax)	—	70	46	50
Net (loss) income from continuing operations	(3,262)	(2,612)	(2)	594
Discontinued operations, net of income taxes	43	166	—	(230)
Net (loss) income	($ 3,219)	($ 2,446)	($ 268)	$ 364
Basic Earnings (Loss) per Common Share				
Net (loss) income from continuing operations	($6.44)	($5.29)	($0.53)	$1.21
Discontinued operations	$0.08	$0.34	—	($0.47)
Net (loss) income	($6.36)	($4.95)	($0.53)	$0.74
Diluted (Loss) Earnings per Common Share				
Net (loss) income from continuing operations	($6.44)	($5.29)	($0.53)	$1.15
Discontinued operations	$0.08	$0.34	—	($0.41)
Net (loss) income	($6.36)	($4.95)	($0.53)	$0.74
Basic weighted average shares (millions)	506.4	494.1	482.8	491.7
Diluted weighted average share (millions)	506.4	494.1	482.8	561.7

Source: 2001 Kmart Corporation revised 10K report and 2002 Kmart Corporation 10K report.

Exhibit 4   KMART'S CONSOLIDATED BALANCE SHEETS, FISCAL YEARS 2000–2002 (DOLLARS IN MILLIONS)

	As of January 29, 2003, January 30, 2002, and January 31, 2001		
	2002	**2001**	**2000**
Assets			
Current assets			
Cash and cash equivalents	$ 613	$ 1,245	$ 401
Merchandise inventories	4,825	5,796	6,350
Other current assets	664	800	925
Total current assets	6,102	7,841	7,676
Property and equipment, net	4,892	6,093	6,522
Other assets and deferred charges	244	249	617
Total assets	$11,238	$14,183	$14,815
Liabilities and Shareholders' Equity			
Current liabilities			
Long-term debt due within one year	$ —	$ —	$ 68
Accounts payable	1,248	89	2,190
Accrued payroll and other liabilities	710	420	1,691
Taxes other than income taxes	162	143	187
Total current liabilities	2,120	652	4,136
Long-term debt and notes payable	—	330	2,084
Capital lease obligations	623	857	943
Other long-term liabilities	181	132	883
Total liabilities not subject to compromise	$ 2,924	$ 1,971	$ 8,046
Liabilities subject to compromise	$ 7,969	$ 8,093	—
Company obligated mandatorily redeemable convertible preferred securities of a subsidiary trust holding solely 7¾% convertible junior subordinated debentures of Kmart (redemption value of $898 and $898, respectively)	$ 646	$ 889	$ 887
Common stock, $1 par value, 1,500,000,000 shares authorized; 503,294,515 and 486,509,736 shares issued, respectively	519	503	487
Capital in excess of par value	1,922	1,695	1,578
Retained earnings	(2,742)	1,032	3,817
Total liabilities and shareholders' equity	$11,238	$14,183	$14,815

Source: 2001 Kmart Corporation revised 10K report and 2002 Kmart Corporation 10K report.

Exhibit 5   KMART'S CONSOLIDATED STATEMENTS OF CASH FLOWS, FISCAL YEARS 2000–2002 (DOLLARS IN MILLIONS)

	Years Ended January 29, 2003, January 30, 2002, January 31, 2001, and January 26, 2000			
	2002	2001	2000	1999
Cash flows from operating activities				
Net (loss) income	($3,219)	($2,446)	($268)	$364
Adjustments to reconcile net income (loss) to net cash provided by operating activities:				
Discontinued operations	(43)	(166)	—	230
Inventory writedown	1,291	163	—	—
Restructuring, impairment and other charges	739	1,091	728	—
Reorganization items, net	386	(183)	—	—
Depreciation and amortization	737	824	777	770
Equity loss (income) in unconsolidated subsidiaries	(34)	—	13	(44)
Dividends received from Meldisco	45	51	44	38
Decrease (increase) in inventories	(168)	560	335	(544)
Increase (decrease) in accounts payable	401	1,046	(137)	169
Deferred income taxes and taxes payable	23	(55)	(204)	258
Changes in other assets	161	295	29	(127)
Changes in other liabilities	67	(23)	14	133
Cash used for store closings	(134)	(230)	(217)	(80)
Net cash provided by operating activities	252	927	1,114	1,084
Net cash used for reorganization items	135	(6)	—	—
Cash Flows from Investing Activities				
Capital expenditures	(252)	(1,385)	(1,089)	(1,277)
Investment in BlueLight.com	—	(45)	(55)	—
Acquisition of Caldor leases	—	—	—	(86)
Net cash used for investing activities	(252)	(1,430)	(1,144)	(1,363)
Cash Flows from Financing Activities				
Net borrowings on DIP credit facility	(330)	330	—	—
Proceeds from issuance of debt	—	1,494	400	300
Payments on debt	(31)	(320)	(73)	(90)
Debt issuance costs	(42)	(49)	(3)	(3)
Payments on capital lease obligations	(94)	(86)	(78)	(77)
Payments of dividends on preferred securities of subsidiary trust	—	(72)	(73)	(80)
Purchase of convertible preferred securities of subsidiary trust	—	—	(84)	—
Issuance of common shares	—	56	53	63
Purchase of common shares		—	(55)	(200)
Net cash provided by (used for) financing activities	(497)	1,353	87	(87)
Net change in cash and cash equivalents	(632)	844	57	(366)
Cash and cash equivalents, beginning of year	1,245	401	344	710
Cash and cash equivalents, end of year	$ 613	$1,245	$ 401	$ 344

Source: 2001 Kmart Corporation revised 10K report and 2002 Kmart Corporation 10K report.

Exhibit 6   KMART'S CONTRACTUAL OBLIGATIONS AND OTHER COMMERCIAL COMMITMENTS AT FISCAL YEAR-END 2001

Contractual Obligations	Payments Due by Period				
	Within 1 Year	Within 2–3 Years	Within 4–5 Years	After 5 Years	Total
Long-term debt	$1,151	$ 714	$ 728	$1,083	$ 3,676
Capital lease obligations	234	433	344	1,232	2,243
Operating leases	728	1,374	1,177	6,355	9,634
Other long-term obligations	143	248	165	90	646
Total contractual cash obligations	$2,256	$2,769	$2,414	$8,760	$16,199

Other Commercial Commitments	Amount of Commitment Expiration Per Period				
	Within 1 Year	Within 2–3 Years	Within 4–5 Years	After 5 Years	Total
Trade lines of credit	$162	$—	$—	$—	$162
Standby letters of credit	98	—	—	—	98
Guarantees	49	102	125	365	641
Total commercial commitments	$309	$102	$125	$365	$901

Source: 2001 Kmart Corporation revised 10K report.

Kmart's board named Adamson to the additional position of CEO when Charles Conaway resigned in March 2002.

Kmart's board believed that Adamson was a good choice to head up Kmart during its bankruptcy because of his retailing experience and his experience operating under bankruptcy protection. While Adamson was its chairman and CEO, Advantica filed for bankruptcy protection and successfully emerged from Chapter 11 a year later. Adamson's restructuring plan for Kmart included the following components, some of which had been initiated by Charles Conaway prior to his exit from the company:

- An announcement in March 2002 that the company would close 284 stores and eliminate 22,000 jobs before year-end. The terminations and store closings would result in a charge against earnings of $1.3 billion.

- Liquidation of $758 million in inventory in the closed stores, some of which was transferred from remaining stores.

- Reduction of annual overhead expenses by $130 million.

- Utilization of a $2 billion debtor-in-possession financing that would be used to supplement Kmart's cash flow during its reorganization.

- Development of a new advertising phrase, "The Stuff of Life." The company hoped to win customer loyalty by claiming to be the "store that understands what really matters in life."[19] The campaign was supported by an advertising budget of $20–$30 million and artistic 30-second television spots directed by filmmaker Spike Lee.

- Sale of BlueLight.com for $8.4 million to an Internet service provider. Blue-Light.com had incurred undisclosed millions in losses and sold products to fewer than 1 percent of its visitors during the fourth quarter of 2001. Kmart continued to make products available to consumers over the Internet at Kmart.com after the sale.

- Development of a prototype store that had futuristic icons, wider aisles, lower shelves, and brighter lighting. Martha Stewart Everyday, Joe Boxer, Disney, and Sesame Street products were located in dedicated sections rather than spread about the store.

- An announcement in January 2003 that the company would close an additional 316 stores and eliminate 25,000 more jobs. The store closings were expected to result in the liquidation of an additional $1.5 billion in inventory for closed and remaining stores.

Legal Worries for Kmart's Board and Former Management in Early 2003

Three days after Kmart filed for bankruptcy, an anonymous letter from a Kmart employee addressed to the Securities and Exchange Commission (SEC), Kmart's auditors (PricewaterhouseCoopers), and the company's board of directors initiated investigations into Kmart's accounting practices. The investigations were led by the SEC, the U.S. Attorney's Office for Eastern Michigan, and the company's board of directors. The letter was followed by more than a dozen additional letters from different Kmart employees, all of whom suggested that Kmart executives told finance department employees to deviate from standard accounting practices and that those executives also made misleading or deceptive statements to investors. As a result of Kmart's internal investigation, its financial statements for fiscal 1999 through the first two quarters of 2002 were restated because of the improper recording of vendor allowances that provided discounts or rebates to Kmart based on certain sales volumes of merchandise supplied by vendors. In numerous instances, Kmart recorded the discounts even though the sales volumes necessary to receive the allowances were not achieved. The audit had the effect of increasing Kmart's 2001 expenses by approximately $100 million. After Kmart had completed its audit and the letter campaign continued, James Adamson sent an e-mail to all employees asking them to end the letter campaign and report potential violations of the company's Code of Conduct through proper channels.

The letter-writing campaign also brought oversight attention to $28.9 million in retention loans granted to Charles Conaway and other top executives just days prior to Kmart's bankruptcy. The loans, which did not require a repayment, were questioned by investigators since the individual loan amounts were unusually high (e.g., Charles Conaway received a $5 million retention loan, Mark Schwartz received a $3 million loan, and a manager who had been with the company only two months received a loan for $1.75 million) and since Kmart suppliers had gone unpaid for goods shipped to and sold by Kmart. Conaway and his top management team also received generous severance packages—Conaway received severance pay of $4 million when he left the company in March 2002.

James Adamson launched a stewardship review of Kmart's outgoing management team in May 2002—agreeing to pay Conaway's severance package but suspending the severance pay of several members of Conaway's team. Kmart also suspended

$2 million in annual special retirement benefits for 20 former executives in June 2002. Some critics of Conaway questioned the veracity of Adamson's review since his own employment contract with Kmart granted him a $2.5 million "inducement payment" to take the job of Kmart's CEO and provided such perks as weekly private plane service between his residences in Detroit, New York, and Florida; limousine service in Michigan and New York; and temporary accommodations in a $320-per-night hotel near Kmart's headquarters. In addition, Adamson was the chairman of Kmart's board of directors' audit committee in 2000 and 2001, which was the period under examination for accounting irregularities.

Adamson stepped down as Kmart's CEO on January 19, 2003. Julian Day was selected to lead the company through the remaining months of bankruptcy. The investigation initiated by Kmart's board disclosed the following findings on January 27, 2003:

- Former officers were grossly derelict in performing their duties.

- Former managers failed to provide the board with important information concerning Kmart's retention loan program.

- Former senior executives authorized the purchase of $850 million in additional inventory for the Christmas 2002 shopping season that Kmart didn't need.

- In September 2001, former executives created "Project Slow It Down," in which the company avoided payments to vendors and told vendors who asked about payments that the invoices had been paid.

- Former officers hired unqualified employees and provided them with extraordinary compensation packages.

On February 27, 2003, the U.S. Justice Department filed criminal indictments against two former Kmart executives—Joseph A. Hofmeister, a divisional vice president of merchandising within Kmart's drugstore operations, and Enio Montini, a senior vice president and general merchandise manager for Kmart's drugstore division. Legal experts believed that the Justice Department had indicted the two relatively low-level managers to help gain their cooperation in investigating the actions of higher-ranking Kmart managers.

Endnotes

[1] Quoted in Kmart Corporation press release, January 19, 2003.
[2] Quoted in "Kmart's Category Approach," *Discount Merchandiser,* May 1994, p. 118.
[3] Quoted in "Antonini: On Changes in the Marketplace," *Discount Merchandiser,* December 1994, p. 12.
[4] Quoted in "The Best-Laid Plans. . . ," *Forbes,* January 3, 1994, p. 44.
[5] Quoted in "The High Cost of Second Best," *Fortune,* July 26, 1993, p. 99.
[6] Quoted in ibid.
[7] Quoted in "Kmart's Agenda for Recovery." *Discount Merchandiser,* July 1994, p. 14.
[8] Quoted in "Attention Bottom Fishers," *Financial World,* March 28, 1995, p. 31.
[9] Ibid., pp. 119–20.
[10] Quoted in "The Antonini Transcript," *Discount Store News,* April 17, 1995, p. 12.
[11] Quoted in "Kmart Is Down for the Count," *Fortune,* January 15, 1996, p. 103.
[12] Ibid., p. 102.
[13] Quoted in "Kmart: Who's in Charge Here?" *Business Week,* December 4, 1995, p. 107.
[14] Quoted in "A Kmart Special: Better Service," *Business Week,* September 4, 2000, p. 80.
[15] "Kmart's Last Chance," *Business Week,* March 11, 2002, online edition.
[16] Quoted in "Kmart Misses Mark Amid Tech Field," *Investor's Business Daily,* April 25, 2002, p. A10.
[17] Quoted in "Kmart Struggles to Escape Oblivion," *The Business,* January 27, 2002, p. 17.
[18] Quoted in "Kmart Lays Out Plans to Trim Its Size, Boost Efficiency, in Bankruptcy Filing," *The Wall Street Journal Online,* January 22, 2002.
[19] Quoted in "Kmart Pitches Family Values in New TV Spots by Spike Lee," *The Wall Street Journal Online,* February 25, 2002.

CASE 27

The Portman Ritz-Carlton Shanghai

Asia's Best Employer

Matthew Chang
International Institute for Management Development

Ellie Weldon
International Institute for Management Development

We Are Ladies and Gentlemen Serving Ladies and Gentlemen.
—Ritz-Carlton motto

We strive to find the right people for the right roles, treat them with respect, provide them with opportunities and constant teaching, but we also have great expectations.
—Mark J. DeCocinis, General Manager, The Portman Ritz-Carlton Shanghai

In an emerging market like China, the greatest challenge in establishing a first class workforce is their short-term mentality. The ongoing tug of war between professionalism and indifference requires employers to be patient with people's old habits and create an environment that will initiate and preserve lasting changes in employees.
—Michelle D. Wan, Director of Communications,
   The Portman Ritz-Carlton Shanghai

In September 2001 the Portman Ritz-Carlton Shanghai took top honors in the first regionwide survey of the Best Employers in Asia. The survey was conducted by Hewitt Associates in partnership with the *Asian Wall Street Journal* and *Far Eastern Economic Review.* More than 92,000 employees working in 355 companies took part in the survey.

The success of the Portman Ritz-Carlton in Shanghai was surprising for two reasons. First, the hotel had been open for only a short time. Second, and more important, the Shanghai labor market was notorious for high employee turnover resulting from high demand for but short supply of Westernized, English-speaking Chinese workers. As a result, the good employees had many opportunities and it was difficult to retain the best.

The Hotel Industry in Shanghai

In 1979, after 50 years of war and revolution, Deng Xiaoping announced China's new open door policy to attract Western investment to fuel China's growth. At this time, the Shanghai municipal government began an ambitious drive to reclaim its historical place as China's center of international finance and commerce and one of the world's most vibrant cities. Companies from around the world were eager to participate in

Shanghai's growth. During the 1990s over 70 percent of the Fortune Global 500 companies established a presence in Shanghai, and foreign businesspeople flocked to the city. The local government also promoted tourism and the number of foreign tourists increased.

These tourists and foreign businesspeople created a huge demand for hotels meeting international standards of quality. However, the city had only a handful of aging hotels, some dating back to colonial days and all suffering from misuse and neglect.

The Sheraton Huating Hotel, the first hotel to meet international standards, opened under Western management in 1986. By the end of 1997 there were 8 internationally recognized five-star hotels and over 20 four-star hotels in the city. Most of them were managed by major international hotel groups, and they enjoyed an average occupancy rate of 71 percent and a gross profit margin of 50 percent.

The Portman Ritz-Carlton Shanghai

Company Background

Ritz-Carlton was one of the elite names in the hotel industry. Its sterling reputation was based on its comfort, luxury and—most of all—impeccable service. The Ritz-Carlton tradition began when Swiss hotelier César Ritz, in partnership with renowned French chef Auguste Escoffier, opened the Ritz Hotel in Paris in 1898 and, later, the Carlton Hotel in London. Ritz's name became synonymous with opulence and his philosophy of service and management redefined the luxury hotel experience in Europe. When he died in 1918, his wife, Marie, continued the tradition.

In 1927 the first Ritz-Carlton hotel opened in Boston. For over 55 years, this elegant hotel was the only one operating under the Ritz-Carlton name. Then, in 1983, the Ritz-Carlton Hotel Company, LLC, was formed to manage hotels under the Ritz-Carlton service mark. Some 15 years later, the Ritz-Carlton Hotel Company was 100 percent owned by Marriott International, with headquarters in Atlanta, Georgia. The company did not own any hotels itself but managed 45 hotels worldwide, all in the "premier" segment of the hotel industry. A premier hotel offered its guests two essentials: (1) the comfort and style of the hotel's physical facilities, and (2) the quality and variety of its guest services.

The Portman Ritz-Carlton Shanghai

On January 1, 1998, the Ritz-Carlton group entered the Chinese market when it took over the operation of the Portman Shangri-La Hotel in Shanghai. The 564-room Portman Shangri-La was located in the Shanghai American Center, which was built in 1990. The principal investors in the American Center were the Portman Group, based in Atlanta, Georgia, and American International Group, the insurance giant based in New York City. When the Ritz-Carlton Group took over the management of the hotel, it was renamed the Portman Ritz-Carlton. In 1997 the Portman Shangri-La Hotel had a 75 percent occupancy rate and was profitable (specific figures were not made available).

The January 1998 Takeover

In mid-1997 general manager Mark DeCocinis had come to Shanghai with an experienced Ritz-Carlton transition team to prepare for the handover. The challenge facing the new Portman Ritz-Carlton management was daunting. There would be no shake-down period before the doors opened to the public, and the Shanghai hotel market, by then well developed, was beginning to experience a downturn precipitated by the spreading Asian financial crisis that had begun in the summer of 1997.

Looking back on the handover, DeCocinis recalled:

> It was one of the rare instances that a hotel did an instant switch. Literally at midnight on January 1, the hotel went from being a Shangri-La property to a Ritz-Carlton without any interruption of service.

Even though the Portman Shangri-La was regarded as one of Shanghai's premier hotels, DeCocinis felt that it fell far below the standards of a Ritz-Carlton hotel. First, the physical infrastructure of the hotel was lacking. DeCocinis explained:

> The property was eight years old and had experienced high occupancy rates. For whatever reason, the previous management did not reinvest in the hotel at all. Perhaps it had something to do with their new property opening across town a few months later. So we knew from the start that a major renovation was imminent and very necessary.

However, DeCocinis was not worried about this because he had the budget to bring it up to Ritz-Carlton standards. Some projects would take time, but DeCocinis also saw the opportunity to make some immediate small changes that would have a noticeable impact, such as replacing all the china used in the hotel with premium brand products.

Second, DeCocinis was worried about the level of service his staff could provide:

> The legend and strength of the Ritz-Carlton brand lie in our truly impeccable service. Our guests have certain expectations from a Ritz-Carlton property. The problem we faced was that the staff that came with the hotel did not even know that such a level of service existed.

When Ritz-Carlton took over, the Portman Shangri-La had 1,067 employees, with an average age of mid to late twenties. Although DeCocinis thought the hotel staff was too large, he and his team decided to give all of the locals working there an opportunity to find their place in the new Portman Ritz-Carlton. Ritz-Carlton did not, however, retain the expatriates working for the Shangri-La Group.

The employees had a rather diffident attitude—with more new hotels opening in the Shanghai market, there was no shortage of job opportunities for those with experience in the industry. Nevertheless, most of the local employees chose to continue working at the hotel after Ritz-Carlton took over and waited to find out what, if any, changes would come. They could always change jobs later.

Since it was clear that more experience with Ritz-Carlton standards would be required for a successful transition, veteran Ritz-Carlton managers from other Ritz-Carlton operations and from the parent Marriott Group assumed all the top management positions (i.e., division and department level managerial positions). The decision to bring in expatriates raised some concern that local employees would feel that their ability to advance was limited and that turnover would therefore increase. The non-managerial staff, the first-line supervisors and their managers were all local Chinese. (See Exhibit 1 for an outline of the Portman Ritz-Carlton Shanghai's organization structure.)

Exhibit 1   **The Portman Ritz-Carlton Shanghai Organization Structure**

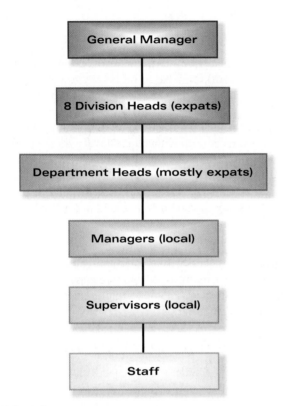

Source: Company information.

The Challenge: The Classic Foreign Employer/Chinese Employee Relationship

To succeed, DeCocinis felt he must overcome the problematic relationship with the hotel's employees that many foreign employers experienced in China. In many cases there was no cultural affinity between the foreign employer and local employees, and their values were also different. Moreover, young Chinese workers seemed to be primarily motivated by money and, with their English-language skills, they were also in demand. As a result, they changed jobs frequently, often for just a small increase in wages. A senior expatriate manager explained the prevailing mind-set:

> There was a common belief that since all local employees were motivated by the level of pay, an employer would only need to make sure they were paid adequately according to market conditions. Hence companies invested in little else, like continuous training and long-term development. The problem was made worse when the employers accepted this kind of practice. That kind of short-term mentality was the fundamental issue that contributed to the crazy job-hopping trend within foreign invested companies, including ours.

On the Road to Becoming Asia's Best Employer

Breaking the Mold: Recasting the Foreign Employer/Chinese Employee Relationship

Knowing that Ritz-Carlton had a long-term interest in China, DeCocinis saw the need to build a superior-quality workforce based on loyalty to the company grounded in a shared commitment to the highest standards of service. He was convinced that this was the only way to ensure quality and consistency in guest services, even if it meant investing money in training, which might affect the bottom line in the short term.

DeCocinis and his team came up with a three-level pyramid (Exhibit 2) to describe the essence of their business. Employee satisfaction formed the foundation, on which guest satisfaction rested. Together, they supported financial performance. The idea was that satisfied, motivated employees were necessary to achieve top-rate guest services, which in turn were necessary to establish and keep a loyal clientele and to achieve profitable financial performance over the long term.

DeCocinis was quick to point out, however:

> Happy employees don't necessarily mean the highest paid employees. We set out to show them there are many aspects to true happiness. Monetary reward is only one of them. Pride, respect, and opportunities are fantastic elements of satisfaction. They had been missing out.

Becoming Ladies and Gentlemen

When the hotel started operating under the Portman Ritz-Carlton name, DeCocinis announced to the employees that the new management's first initiative would be the complete redesign and renovation of the employee dining room. He commented:

> The state of the employee dining room was absolutely appalling. It was hard to imagine how employees could have a strong sense of self-respect in such an environment. People stayed on to see if Ritz-Carlton would be different, really different. We used the employee dining room to demonstrate our commitment to the Ritz-Carlton value: "We *are* ladies and gentlemen serving ladies and gentlemen."

With the opening of the new employee dining room, the management provided a comfortable dining facility but, more important, also created respectable and civilized surroundings that employees could be proud of.

As a senior manager commented:

> China has a sensitive problem. Many Westerners feel that there is a lack of manners and a professional attitude in modern China. For instance, people tend to speak quite loudly in public and often they rush into the elevator as soon as the door opens without letting people inside get out. This is part of an accepted daily routine, which makes it more difficult to address. Professionalism, or lack of it, is another big headache. People's attitude to their jobs often involves doing the minimum to earn the salary. That is why covering for colleagues or going the extra mile are often foreign concepts. When we took over the hotel, we were determined to change that.

**Exhibit 2   Three-Level Pyramid Representing Essence of
the Hotel's Business**

The new management team did not, however, expect to accomplish this overnight. They knew they would have to be patient with people's old habits. Such a change would have to come willingly and with practice. Some of the senior managers tried to make things easier for their staff by suggesting they incorporate good habits into the rest of their lives so that they would become automatic. Michelle Wan, director of communications, for example, encouraged her staff to answer their private telephone with the same personable and polite greeting they had been trained to use at work. She recalled:

> We were trying to leave a lasting impression on people. Our hope was to extend the civil environment beyond the workplace. Only when the employees felt accustomed to the new way of life would they truly appreciate the working environment we'd created.

Management sought to instill in their employees a sense of professionalism and pride in providing the high level of service expected at a Ritz-Carlton hotel. Professionalism began with respect from the employer but, equally, employees had to view it as an essential element of the job description, not an optional extra that earned rewards. According to DeCocinis:

> We wanted our employees to know that everyone within the organization would be treated with real and equal respect. But there would be expectations of everyone's professional conduct. Being professional means you can choose to leave if you are not satisfied with the job or company, or for any other reason. But if you choose not to leave, happy or not, you must perform your duty with full dedication.

As he explained the pyramid concept to the Portman Ritz-Carlton employees, De-Cocinis made it clear that he would always be available to them. He set up a monthly "general manager's breakfast," to which selected employees from different departments would be invited to discuss any issues that concerned them. The objective was twofold. One was to recognize promising talent and excellent performance on the job. The other was to ensure an open communication channel between staff and management so that potential problems could be dealt with as they arose and not only when they had become serious. Subjects varied from logistical problems, such as handling check-in during lobby renovation, to employee concerns, such as the comfort of the uniform. Management was open to discussion and responded quickly to employee suggestions.

Once employees could see that top management respected them, the managers thought it would be appropriate to empower the workers with trust and responsibility. The most notable action was to authorize every employee to settle a customer complaint or dissatisfaction up to $2,000 without management approval.

A senior manager acknowledged:

> This was an awesome responsibility and a tremendous source of self-respect and pride to the employees. There have been some rare cases of overcompensating the guests, but these were mostly due to inexperience. In such cases, the management team did not penalize the employees; rather we trained them and explained how to handle such situations properly. So the next time, they would do it right.

Acutely aware of the importance of employee pride, DeCocinis made a strong effort to turn the hotel into a model corporate citizen. The company often cosponsored or contributed to major charity events. And DeCocinis himself even became something of a local celebrity, with his eye-catching three-wheel motorcycle, a rare replica of the 1938 BMW R-71. Seeing their own place of work associated with noble causes and their high-profile boss roaring down the city's expressway giving local TV crews a joy ride had a positive effect on the employees. Surveys indicated that they were pleased to work for such a responsible and cool organization.

Human Investment

Although the Portman Ritz-Carlton started with a full complement of staff—indeed, with more employees than necessary—management realized that, given the expected turnover in the Shanghai job market, it would need to recruit new people. From the start, the hotel established a comprehensive human resource program with the goal of bringing suitable local recruits into the organization and providing them with continuous professional development.

During job interviews, in addition to looking at the usual technical qualifications, the Portman Ritz-Carlton also screened candidates' psychological profiles. Superior language skills and other technical training would not be enough to guarantee a job—the company also looked for sincerity, personality, and evidence of, or potential for, good teamwork. Wan explained:

> Technical capabilities can be learned on the job, but a person's drive and motivation and ability to work as a team may not. So in the hiring process, we are much more concerned about a candidate's "soft skills."

Another element of the process was DeCocinis's insistence on interviewing every candidate personally before the final decision to hire. According to him, not only did having a single decision maker ensure consistency and fairness in hiring but it also sent a message to new recruits that top management cared and would keep dialogue open with all employees. In addition, the Portman Ritz-Carlton conducted an annual employee satisfaction survey and two individual employee reviews per year, all designed to provide open feedback between management and employees.

Compensation for all employees at the Portman Ritz-Carlton Shanghai consisted of a base salary, with bonuses for both team and individual performance at year-end. In addition, employees in the top 5 percent based on performance as determined in the semiannual performance reviews received an extra bonus.

The hotel guaranteed at least 100 training hours per year for all of its employees. At junior staff levels, the emphasis was on language proficiency and information technology literacy. For middle-level managers—to counter the perception that there was a glass ceiling for local hires—training frequently included exchanges with sister properties in other countries such as Singapore or the United States. Senior managers believed that the main differentiating factor between local talent and expatriates was not competence but experience. Their long-term objective was to replace as many expatriates as possible with local hires, and they believed that the best way to achieve this was by broadening the horizons of promising locally hired middle managers.

Making Progress

By the end of 2001, four years after the Ritz-Carlton takeover, everything seemed to be moving in the right direction. DeCocinis's pyramid had yielded solid results (see Exhibit 3). The employee satisfaction rating had improved dramatically from 1998 to 2001. Over the same period, both guest satisfaction and profit growth also increased.

The company managed to improve efficiency significantly, reducing the overall number of employees to 800, from 1,067 at the beginning. DeCocinis explained:

> We never lost sight of reducing wastage in manpower. Our investment in employees has allowed us to achieve that.

The attrition rate for 2001 was 21 percent, much lower than the local industry average. The figure included regular dismissals of employees who had been given opportunities but failed to meet expectations. At the end of the year, 300 of the employees who had stayed on after the takeover in 1998 were still there. Grooming of local management talent had also begun to bear fruit—the number of expatriate managers had declined to 27, from 40 in 1998.

The net outcome of the transformation was enthusiastic reaction from international media and independent survey groups. The Portman Ritz-Carlton was awarded Best

Exhibit 3   KEY PERFORMANCE RATIOS

	1999	2000	2001
Employee satisfaction rate	70%	85%	96%
Guest satisfaction rate	91	92	96
Net profit improvement	—	18	25

Exhibit 4   MAJOR AWARDS, PORTMAN RITZ-CARLTON, SHANGHAI

1998	Best Hotel in Shanghai—Finance Asia, Institutional Investor
1999	Best Business Hotel in China—Bloomberg TV/Business Asia
2000	Best Business Hotel in China—Bloomberg TV/Business Asia
2001	Best Conference Hotel
	Best Business Hotel in China
	Best Overall Business Hotel in Asia—Bloomberg TV/Business Asia
	Best Employer in China
	Best Employer in Asia—*Asian Wall Street Journal, Far Eastern Economic Review,* and Hewitt Associates

Source: Company information.

Exhibit 5   THE TOP 20 BEST EMPLOYERS IN ASIA, 2001

Rank	Company
1.	The Portman Ritz-Carlton, Shanghai
2.	Agilent Technologies (Singapore)
3.	The Ritz-Carlton Millenia Singapore
4.	Western Digital (Malaysia)
5.	Elegant Textile Industry, Indonesia
6.	Federal Express Services (Malaysia)
7.	Tricon Restaurants International, Thailand
8.	The Ritz-Carlton, Hong Kong
9.	AMD (Thailand)
10.	Navion (Shanghai) Software Development
11.	Tenaga Nasional, Malaysia
12.	Ford Lio Ho Motor, Taiwan
13.	Intel Malaysia
14.	Four Seasons Hotel Singapore
15.	Agilent Technologies (Malaysia)
16.	Jollibee Foods, Philippines
17.	H&CB, South Korea
18.	Shanghai Hormel Foods
19.	Crown Motors, Hong Kong
20.	Hewlett-Packard Korea

Source: Survey conducted by *Asia Wall Street Journal, Far Eastern Economic Review,* and Hewitt Associates.

Hotel in Shanghai in 1998, then Best Business Hotel in China in 1999 and 2000, and ultimately Best Overall Business Hotel in Asia and Asia's Best Employer in 2001 (see Exhibits 4 and 5).

January 2002

By the end of 2001 the Portman Ritz-Carlton Shanghai could be said to be the most desirable place to stay in Shanghai. President George W. Bush, like his predecessor, Bill Clinton, stayed there in October 2001. The ensuing international exposure may have helped the hotel to achieve its highest-ever monthly occupancy rate the following month. DeCocinis was, of course, pleased with these results, but past successes do not ensure future profits, especially in a tightening market.

After the terrorist attacks on the World Trade Center in New York and the Pentagon in Washington, D.C., on September 11, 2001, international business travel saw an immediate sharp decline. For a hotel such as the Portman Ritz-Carlton, which catered mostly to business travelers, a decline in occupancy was inevitable—and it was immediate. To make matters worse, the decline in business travel happened just as the Shanghai hotel market added capacity. Before September 11, the hotel had not viewed large groups like Hilton and Sheraton as direct competitors, because the Portman Ritz-Carlton attracted a more sophisticated and demanding clientele. However, the post–September 11 decline challenged this assumption. Moreover, there was a greater threat in the form of two new direct competitors: The St. Regis had admitted its first guests in July 2001, and the first Four Seasons hotel in China was scheduled to open its doors in February 2002. From his office window, DeCocinis could see the almost-completed building just three blocks away.

But it was not only the loss of clientele that concerned DeCocinis. As a result of his own success in developing professional and service-oriented local employees, he had good reason to worry that his new competitors would aggressively recruit his staff. Although they were well paid, his competitors might offer them more. Would the job satisfaction created at the Portman Ritz-Carlton stand up to increased competitive pressures? What could DeCocinis do to make sure that it did?

Enjoying coffee served in a fine Wedgwood china cup, DeCocinis debated what to do next. Should he lower the accommodation rates, which had consistently been the highest in the city, to keep his occupancy rate up? Should he raise salaries before his competitors tried to lure his staff away? And most important of all, what could he now use to motivate his staff to keep going after such a meteoric rise to the top?

Continental Airlines in 2003
Sustaining the Turnaround

Arthur A. Thompson, Jr.
The University of Alabama

In 1994, Continental Airlines was a troubled company. While it was the fifth largest commercial airline in the United States, with revenues of $6 billion, Continental had reported a net loss every year since 1985. Strained finances had forced Continental to seek Chapter 11 bankruptcy protection in 1983 and again in 1990; it had taken the company until April 1993 to get in good enough shape to emerge from its 1990 bankruptcy filing. Since 1983, nine different CEOs had tried unsuccessfully to fix Continental, initiating numerous internal reorganizations, revitalization and turnaround efforts, and strategy shifts. During Continental's bankruptcy proceedings in 1990–93, wages and salaries had been cut and management had tried to rid the company of unions. Turnover and use of sick time were quite high; on-the-job injuries were far above the industry average. There was considerable infighting among employee groups and departments. When problems occurred, finger-pointing often overwhelmed efforts at constructive problem solving and employees ran for cover, insisting they had followed procedures. Continental's ticket agents and gate personnel spent many stressful hours dealing with dissatisfied and angry passengers—some of Continental's airport personnel, when they were off duty or on break, removed the Continental insignia from their uniforms to avoid having to answer uncomfortable questions from coworkers or customers.[1]

When Gordon Bethune agreed to become Continental's president and chief operating officer (COO) in February 1994 and take on the challenge of improving the company's operations, Continental ranked last among the 10 largest U.S. commercial airlines in on-time arrivals (the percentage of flights that arrived within 15 minutes of the scheduled time). It also had the highest number of mishandled baggage reports per 1,000 passengers and by far the highest number of complaints per 100,000 passengers. Complaints filed with the Department of Transportation by Continental passengers about various aspects of their experiences on Continental flights were 30 percent higher than the ninth-ranking airline and three times the industry average. Bethune recognized the terrible conditions that existed:

> This was a crummy place to work. The culture at Continental, after years of layoffs and wage freezes and wage cuts and broken promises, was one of backbiting, mistrust, fear, and loathing. People, to put it mildly, were not happy to come to work. They were surly to customers, surly to each other, and ashamed of their company . . .

In a company where cost-cutting was revered, departments fought one another to the death over scarce resources. In a company where management strategies—and management teams—changed overnight, employees schemed above all else to protect themselves, at the cost of their co-workers if necessary. Interdepartmental communication was almost nonexistent.

Everybody was screwing over everybody—no wonder the planes were late and the baggage was lost. The product was crummy. The fundamental reasons for that had nothing to do with flying planes correctly or being able to clean and fix them. It had to do with an environment where nobody could get their jobs done.

. . . The organization itself was so dysfunctional that it couldn't have implemented the best idea in the world.[2]

Despite his early confidence that he could rectify many of Continental's operating difficulties, Bethune soon found himself disenchanted and frustrated in his role as president and COO because Continental's CEO refused to go along with Bethune's plans to get Continental's operations on track unless the actions he wanted to initiate would also reduce costs. In late October 1994, with the company headed for another money-losing year and a looming financial crisis, Continental's board of directors determined that a change had to be made at the top. Initially, the board decided that it would give the present CEO a six-month leave of absence and let Bethune run the company from his position as president and COO. However, the CEO decided to step down immediately. Continental's board made Bethune the company's temporary CEO and asked him to present a plan for turning Continental around at the board's regularly scheduled meeting in 10 days.

Gordon Bethune's Go Forward Plan

Gordon Bethune's first act when he temporarily took over on October 24, 1994, was to prop open the doors to Continental's executive suite, which heretofore had been locked and monitored by security cameras. He wanted people to enter freely at any time rather than having to show an ID to gain admission, and he wanted to begin to change the atmosphere in the executive suite. Next, he began working on the plan he would present to the board. He requested help from Greg Brenneman, a Bain & Company vice president with expertise in turning companies around; Brenneman had been working with Continental for several months on an assortment of ways to revamp Continental's maintenance operations (which had the highest cost but the lowest dispatch reliability in the industry), and his efforts had produced some good results. Brenneman and Bethune came up with what they called the Go Forward Plan. It had four parts—a market plan to fly profitable routes, a financial plan to put the company into the black in 1995, a product plan to improve Continental's offering to customers, and a people plan to transform the company's culture. All four parts of the Go Forward Plan were to be implemented simultaneously.

The Market Plan: Fly to Win

The guiding principle behind the Fly to Win market plan was for Continental to stop doing those things that were losing money or causing the company to lose money and to concentrate on Continental's market strengths. Six strategic initiatives formed the backbone of Bethune's market plan:

1. *Substantially revising Continental's route schedule to focus on hub-and-spoke operations rather than point-to-point routes.* More flights were targeted for spoke destinations out of Continental's Newark, Houston, and Cleveland hubs that held promise of generating enough passenger traffic to generate a profit. Spoke destinations and point-to-point routes where Continental had too many flights with too few passengers and fares too low to make a profit were to be abandoned. The analysis conducted by Bethune and Brenneman revealed that the company was losing money on 18 percent of its routes, many of which were low-fare point-to-point routes for which Continental had a relatively small market share.

2. *Drastic cutbacks in the flight schedule for Continental Lite, the company's low-fare/no-frills operation that was modeled after Southwest Airlines.* Analysis indicated that about one-third of Continental Lite's routes were responsible for about 70 percent of Continental's losses. Continental Lite had been created by replacing the first-class seats with coach seats in 100 of Continental's smaller Boeing jets, painting the name Continental Lite on planes to identify the product, setting up point-to-point routes that management thought were underserved, offering a number of flights on each route, not serving meals on flights of less than two and a half hours, and flying planes from early morning to late at night to generate as much revenue per plane as feasible. But Continental Lite had failed to catch on with Continental's customer base. Bethune's diagnosis was that Continental customers were not interested in the Continental Lite product, preferring to pay full fares for full-service flights—especially on longer flights and flights spanning normal meal hours. Moreover, Continental Lite's costs were too high relative to the revenues being generated by its low-fare approach—Bethune did not believe that Continental Lite's costs could be cut far enough to make its operation profitable and, at the same time, make the Continental Lite product attractive to air travelers.

3. *Raising fares on some of Continental's routes.*

4. *Closing the company's money-losing Greensboro, North Carolina, hub.* The relatively new Greensboro hub was not generating enough traffic from the various spoke locations to justify trying to continue to win additional market share in the Southeast, where Delta and US Airways had a strong presence. (Hub operations in Denver had been abandoned several years earlier.)

5. *Eliminating Continental's big Airbus 300 planes from the fleet.* The planned flight frequency and destination cuts meant that Continental would have too much seat capacity. Taking the Airbus 300 planes out of circulation (which on many flights were only 50–60 percent full) eliminated most of Continental's excess seat capacity—and with the next-biggest planes flying these same routes at close to capacity, the revenues generated by the Airbus 300 flights were retained. Moreover, Continental's Airbus 300 aircraft were expensive to operate, required special maintenance procedures, and entailed lease payments of up to $200,000 a month. Bethune and Brenneman proposed disposing of all Airbus 300 planes in Continental's fleet, thereby removing the necessity of a special parts inventory, special facilities and people, and special procedures to manage that one particular aircraft.

6. *Launching a concerted marketing campaign to win back customers that it had lost, especially business travelers.* Continental's cost-cutting efforts in prior years had entailed reducing the commissions paid to travel agents (who at the time handled 80 percent of all flight reservations); stripping popular features from its OnePass frequent flyer program; and eliminating perks (first-class seats, upgrades, coupons for free drinks) that travel agents could offer corporate customers as inducements

to choose Continental flights. Bethune believed that such actions had alienated Continental customers, prompting many business travelers to switch much of their air travel to rival carriers. And he believed Continental's poor on-time performance and customer satisfaction ratings, along with lower commissions, had alienated travel agents, causing them to steer customers to other carriers. To try to win back the confidence and business of travel agents, Bethune proposed going hat in hand to all the major travel agents, apologizing for prior mistakes, promising that Continental's on-time performance and passenger satisfaction levels were going to improve dramatically, reestablishing higher commissions, and giving them a package of incentives they could use to induce their corporate clients to book more flights on Continental. To try to win back business travelers, Bethune planned to restore the features of the award-winning OnePass frequent flyer program that prior management had dismantled.

The Financial Plan: Fund the Future

In October 1994, Continental was strapped for cash and burdened by debt—it owed considerable money on its aircraft fleet, and it had a $2 billion debt hangover from the Chapter 11 proceedings in 1993. Bethune and Brenneman concluded that it was critical for the company's survival to have a credible financial plan for making a profit in 1995. They put together a package of proposed changes involving renegotiation of aircraft lease payments, refinancing some of Continental's debt at lower interest rates, postponing some debt repayments, and raising fares on certain routes. These moves, they projected, held a realistic chance of generating a profit of $45 million in 1995 (a substantial improvement over the $200 million in losses that Continental would likely show for 1994) and would produce sufficient cash flows for Continental to avoid another financial crisis.

The Product Plan: Make Reliability a Reality

The Make Reliability a Reality piece of Bethune's Go Forward Plan aimed at quantum improvements in Continental's on-time performance, baggage handling, and overall flying experience—doing the very things that would please customers and make them inclined to fly Continental again. The centerpiece of Bethune's product plan was to focus employees' attention on on-time performance by rewarding them with a $65 bonus each month that Continental was in the top five U.S. airlines in percentage of flights arriving on-time—as measured and reported monthly by the U.S. Department of Transportation, which considered a flight to be on time if it arrived at the gate within 15 minutes of the scheduled time.

The People Plan: Working Together

Bethune believed that the most important component of the Go Forward Plan was to radically change Continental's corporate culture. He was convinced that a successful turnaround at Continental hinged on getting Continental's employees pulling together and creating a positive work environment. Bethune explained his thinking:

> The environment was so bad that regardless of marketing strategies, financial plans, and reliability incentives, there weren't going to be any improvements in Continental's operations until we stopped treating people the way we had been

treating them and got them to start working together. You just can't be successful in any kind of business without teamwork

So part of our plan—and it was vague at this point, even though over the
long term it was by far the most important part of the plan—was to make it a
corporate goal to change how people treated each other: to find ways to measure and reward cooperation rather than infighting, to encourage and reward
trust and confidence.

Bethune's Meeting with the Board

Bethune presented the Go Forward Plan to Continental's board, indicating that it represented a joint effort with Greg Brenneman.[3] After the presentation, which was generally well received, the board deliberated whether to appoint Bethune as permanent
CEO. Board members initially indicated their preference was to establish an "office of
the chairman," with Bethune remaining as president and COO. Bethune thought that
was a mistake, arguing that the turnaround effort he proposed required the clear and
unequivocal authority of a leader who was designated CEO and enjoyed the full support of the board of directors. Many board members were unconvinced by Bethune's
plea that a strong leader/CEO was essential to implement a turnaround plan, and they
were not entirely sure that the company was in as dire straits as Bethune indicated. The
board asked Bethune to excuse himself while they reconsidered the matter. After an
hour and a half, the chairman of the board recalled Bethune to the meeting and indicated that a majority of the board had decided to appoint Bethune as CEO. Although
disappointed that the board had not enthusiastically embraced his Go Forward Plan and
then immediately and unanimously elected him as CEO, Bethune was nonetheless
gratified for the chance to try to turn Continental around.

The Implementation and Evolution of Bethune's Go Forward Plan, 1995–2001

At the outset, Bethune recognized that Continental's employees would view his actions
with suspicion and that he would therefore need to build credibility with them. He
judged that employees weren't going to rally around the Go Forward Plan without
some good reason to trust that he was different and that his administration was going
to do a far better job of really fixing what was wrong with the company than the nine
prior executive regimes. Bethune also realized that as CEO at Continental he would
need to draw on many of his prior experiences. He was a licensed airline pilot, qualified to fly Boeing 757 and 767 jets. He had an airframe and powerplant mechanic's license. He had been a maintenance facility manager at both Braniff and Western
Airlines, and a senior vice president for operations at Piedmont Airlines in the 1980s
(before Piedmont was acquired and became a part of US Airways). His operations
background at Boeing had made him familiar with the aircraft side of commercial airline business and somewhat knowledgeable about the strategies of various airlines and
the executives who ran them.

Bethune's Early Days as Continental's CEO

The same day he took over as CEO, Gordon Bethune announced the closing of the
company's Los Angeles maintenance operations, where approximately 1,800 people

were employed. With Continental moving to concentrate its flight operations at the Newark, Houston, and Cleveland hubs, a big maintenance facility in Los Angeles was no longer economic.

Bethune asked Greg Brenneman to remain as a consultant to the company and a close adviser. In May 1995 Bethune named Brenneman Continental's chief operating officer. As Continental's new COO, Brenneman played a key role in helping implement and execute the Go Forward Plan. In September 1996, Brenneman took on the additional title of president, with Bethune functioning as chairman and CEO.

After dispensing with all the security and opening the executive suite, Bethune instituted open houses for employees at the Houston headquarters on the last working day of each month. Employees were invited to tour the executive offices on the 20th floor, visit with Bethune and other executives, and help themselves to food and drinks. Casual-dress Fridays were instituted across the company for all employees except those dealing directly with customers, partly to make Continental managers and executives more approachable. Bethune mandated a no-smoking rule in all company facilities—and he extended the ban on smoking to include all North American and South American flights (over the objections of Continental's marketing people, who contended that such a ban would irritate smoking passengers). The no-smoking ban was later extended to all of Continental's European flights and then worldwide, with little apparent negative effect. At executive meetings, Bethune began sitting at the middle of the long table in the executive conference room rather than at the head. He insisted that meetings begin and end on schedule.

One of his most dramatic actions involved gathering a few Continental employees, along with some of the manuals containing the company's regulations and procedures, going out to the parking lot outside the Houston headquarters, and having the employees set fire to the manuals. Employees in the field were told that they were expected to use their best judgment to solve problems and deal with issues, rather than following the rigid procedures described in the manual. A task force of employees was created to go over the entire manual and come up with guidelines that would help employees make good decisions and take appropriate actions—the idea was that Houston headquarters was there to help but not to dictate to the nth degree. Bethune wanted the message to employees to be: "Use these guidelines, think things through, and unless you do something completely out of bounds, you don't have to worry about hearing from Houston. Houston wants you to do your job. Houston wants to leave you alone unless you need help. And believe it or not, if you need help, Houston wants to help you."[4]

As of late 1994, Continental's aircraft fleet was not painted uniformly; at the company's hubs, differently painted Continental planes were usually lined up at the gates. While in earlier years Continental had tried to create a new image with a completely new paint scheme for all its aircraft, only about half the fleet had been repainted because of executive pressures to cut costs. Believing that professional, identical-looking planes would send a message to employees and customers that Continental was running a better operation, Bethune issued an order that every one of Continental's planes was to receive a fresh paint job by July 1, 1995—there were to be no exceptions. People in Continental's fleet operations said this was too short a time frame in which to get 200 planes repainted; Bethune refused to relent:

> I did something I rarely do: I made a threat. I said, "Yes you can, and you know why?" Because I have a Beretta at home with a 15-round magazine, and if you don't get those planes painted by July 1 I'm going to come in here and empty the clip. You're wonderful people and I love you, but you're going to get those airplanes painted or I'm going to shoot every last one of you.[5]

The last Continental plane was painted on June 30, just in time to meet Bethune's deadline.

Meanwhile, Bethune and other Continental executives spread the word among employees that the Go Forward Plan was management's blueprint—there were meetings with employees at virtually every site in the company to introduce the plan and explain how it addressed all of Continental's problems. Many employees had already heard about the open houses and open-door policy, the burning of the manual, and other initiatives, but management wanted to present the plan personally and answer whatever questions employees had. The meetings did not always go smoothly; a number of employees voiced doubt and skepticism, openly expressing their mistrust of what management was telling them. One pilot told Bethune, "You're the tenth guy I've seen, and you sound good, but let me tell you, this goddamn place is broken. There ain't nobody going to fix it, including you. So it doesn't matter what you say, this place is going to fail."[6] Bethune took issue with pilot, saying in part:

> I don't know about you, but I don't know of any self-respecting pilot, regardless of what predicament the airplane is in—it's on fire, it's upside down, it's spinning around, whatever—who stops trying to fly the airplane before it hits the ground. You don't ever give up and say, screw it, it's over, I can't do anything . . . Listen, I'm the captain of this company now. This is what we are going to do. I'm flying, it's my leg. If you don't like the way I'm working, the jetway is still attached. You can step off if you want to. But I am going to fly this company where it's going.[7]

Bethune's response to the pilot mirrored his concept of what a leader did and what a leader's role was. Bethune explained further:

> My definition of a leader is pretty simple. The leader is the person who looks at the big picture and says, "Okay, everybody, go west."
>
> Now west is precisely a compass heading of 270 degrees, but anywhere from about 240 to 300 degrees is heading generally west. So if I say go west, and one person is heading out at about 295 degrees, that's okay with me . . . I don't want to precisely determine how you interpret it when I say, hey, let's go west. You see things a certain way, and what's happening in your department and what's happening to you today may affect what has to happen when I say go west.
>
> On the other hand, the guy who's going 090 degrees, which is due east, is a problem. You have to catch him and readjust his thinking so he's going the right way. If he won't be readjusted, I say no way buster: You either head west or get out of here. Maybe he needs to go to a company headed east . . .
>
> I'm not saying that everybody has to be marching in lockstep—in fact, that's exactly what we *don't* want. We want people doing their jobs with a minimum of interference from their bosses. That's why we burned the manual . . .
>
> Your real job as boss—my real job as chief executive—is to let people do their jobs. It's to assemble the right team, set the big-picture direction, communicate that, and then get out of the way . . . You have to trust people to do their jobs. That's the strongest leadership there is.[8]

At a meeting with employees in Denver in late 1995, Bethune encountered another vocal employee who reacted to his presentation of the Go Forward Plan and the turnaround actions that were under way by saying, "It sounds fine, but I still don't believe it. We've had too many new programs here and I don't believe it."[9] Bethune tried to reason with the employee, explaining why and how things were on the mend at Continental and what role the Working Together initiatives would play. The employee still did not buy what Bethune was saying, at which time Bethune told him what he told the pilot in Newark—that the jetway was still attached and that if he didn't like the direction the company was headed, maybe he should get off the plane. The employee turned and walked out the door; the audience of employees applauded his exit.

Executing the Fly to Win Market Plan

Under Bethune, Continental marketing executives began treating travel agencies as partners and worked with them closely, creating programs whereby agencies that sold a certain volume of tickets or hit other sales targets specified by Continental would be paid an incentive above the normal commission rate. Programs involving upgrades to first class and discounts for certain travel volumes were created for travel agents to use in marketing Continental to large corporations. In some cases, new destinations were added when feedback from travel agencies indicated that such destinations would be attractive to their corporate clients. Continental wanted to move its business from what Greg Brenneman called the backpack-and-flip-flop crowd to the coat-and-tie crowd or at least the Patagonia backpack crowd, believing that such travelers were usually willing to pay higher fares in order not to take chances with their comfort and convenience. To assist travel agencies in marketing Continental to business travelers, Continental sent letters to corporate CEOs, middle managers, and sales representatives who flew frequently, apologizing for the company's poor performance in past years, laying out the customer-related features of the Go Forward Plan, and asking them to give flying Continental a try. Continental executives made personal calls on the executives of companies that already were doing a lot of business with Continental to thank them for their business, and they made calls on corporate executives of companies where they thought Continental might be able to win a bigger share of the air travel budget.

To help lure Houston-area business travelers back to Continental, Gordon Bethune held a party at his house for 100 of the company's high-mileage frequent flyers—spouses were invited, too. At the party, Bethune announced that the company had made mistakes in the past and wanted another chance at proving it could be relied on to provide good service. Each attendee was presented a leather ticket case. Continental executives circulated through the crowd, thanking people for coming, asking forgiveness for past sins, and explaining what the company was doing to earn their business.

To grow the business during the 1995–2001 period, Continental gradually added more destinations from its hubs and added more flights to existing destinations. Expansion was particularly aggressive in international markets, with service being added to Hong Kong, Tokyo, Rome, Milan, Tel Aviv, several other European cities, the Caribbean, Guam, South America, Central America, and Mexico. By mid-2001, Continental had over 2,000 flights going to nearly 90 international and 130 domestic destinations; it served more international destinations than any other carrier. Guam evolved into a fourth, albeit much smaller, hub for a number of Continental flights operating in the Asia-Pacific region. Newark was the primary gateway for flights to Europe (15 cities) and the Middle East; the Houston hub was the primary gateway for flights to Mexico (20 cities), Central America (every country), and South America (6 cities). The Cleveland hub had international flights to Montreal, Toronto, San Juan, and Cancun. In 2000, Continental announced plans to expand its service to 30 European cities within the next three to five years, and it was exploring adding more destinations in the Middle East. Management believed that it could benefit from TWA's decision to cease all transatlantic services from New York—TWA had long been a force in Europe and the Middle East.

The company's website (www.continental.com) was used as an increasingly important distribution channel for marketing tickets to individuals and businesses; in 2000, Continental expanded e-ticketing to about 95 percent of its destinations. Also in 2000, Continental partnered with United, Delta, American, and Northwest to create a comprehensive travel planning website called Orbitz (www.orbitz.com), which offered airline tickets, hotel reservations, car rentals, and other services. Continental's website recorded $600 million in ticket sales in 2002, compared with $487 million in 2001 and $320 million in 2000.

Continental Express   Soon after the company decided in 1996 to phase out Continental Lite entirely, management decided to create a feeder operation for its hubs called Continental Express. Continental Express operated as a separate subsidiary with its own president. By year-end 2002, Continental Express had expanded its operations to include 950 daily flights, with regional jet service to 110 cities in the United States, Mexico, and Canada. Continental management believed that Continental Express flights allowed more frequent service to small cities than could be provided economically with larger conventional jets and contributed to higher load factors on Continental's regular jet service by feeding passengers into Continental's three major hubs to connect to regular Continental flights.

Bethune's Row 5 Test   One of the challenges Bethune faced was in deciding what constituted "better" service and "better" performance. In his view, Fly to Win meant that Continental had to fly where people wanted to go, stop doing things that lost money, find out what things customers wanted and provide them, and compete effectively against rivals. He was willing for Continental to do things that added cost, provided they added so much value that passengers were willing to pay for them and the costs could therefore be incorporated in fare prices. When Continental people came up with proposals to spend money to increase the technological sophistication of Continental planes or make other operating changes that had cost-increasing implications, Bethune insisted on applying what he called the Row 5 Test—which involved asking whether a hypothetical passenger sitting in row 5 on a Continental plane would be willing to pay 50 cents or a dollar more in order to have the proposed benefit.[10] Bethune argued, for example, that if the floors on Continental's aircraft maintenance facilities were so clean you could eat off them, then Continental was probably paying too much attention to keeping the floors clean. He wanted Continental to focus on doing the things that created value for the customer—add only those costs that added customer value. In Bethune's view, defining success and good performance in customers' terms meant clean, safe, reliable service from well-managed hubs; convenient flight schedules to places customers wanted to go; the kinds of amenities that made a customer's travel experience more pleasant; and frequent flyer benefits that represented real rewards.

Executing the Fund the Future Financial Plan

Despite Continental's having recently emerged from Chapter 11 bankruptcy proceedings in April 1993, Gordon Bethune and Greg Brenneman believed that there was substantial risk of a third bankruptcy unless the company moved decisively in late 1994 and early 1995 to get its finances in order. Aggressive implementation of Continental's initial Fund the Future plan to renegotiate aircraft lease payments, refinance some of Continental's debt at lower interest rates (saving about $25 million in annual interest payments), stretch out debt repayments on loans from 3 years to seven or eight years, and raise fares on selected routes relieved much of the near-term potential for a financial crisis. Whereas in 1994 Continental incurred $202 million in interest costs, by 1996 interest expenses had been reduced to $117 million. Three other actions helped Continental deal with its 1994–95 cash crunch:

1. When Continental determined it could not afford the new planes it had on order at Boeing and decided to cancel its order, Continental's financial predicament was such that Bethune felt compelled to telephone his close friend Ron Woodard, the president of Boeing, asking him to return Continental's $70 million nonrefundable deposit because Continental needed the cash in the worst way. Woodard suspected that Continental was in dire straits and despite his reluctance to go against company policy and refund a deposit (aircraft manufacturers used deposits to help finance initial manufacturing of planes on order), Woodard agreed to send Continental a partial $29 million refund. Bethune accepted the offer, indicating that, if possible, Boeing should wire the funds immediately; Woodard laughed but agreed to Bethune's plea.[11]

2. Excess parts inventories were sold and maintenance contracts were renegotiated.

3. Cash outlays for operating expenses were reduced by entering into code-sharing agreements with other airlines to achieve joint operating economies. Code sharing typically involved two airline partners operating a single flight to a particular destination but having that flight listed in the separate flight schedules of each partner; one of the partner's planes and crews would be used to operate flight, but both partners could book passengers on the flight to that location, share in the revenues generated, and achieve a better load factor on that flight than they might achieve operating two independent flights. Often, code-sharing partners also cooperated in other mutually beneficial ways. For instance, in Phoenix and Las Vegas, where it only had two or three flights coming in daily, Continental partnered with America West to handle the ground work on Continental's flights; in Orlando and Tampa, where Continental had a greater presence than America West, Continental personnel handled the ground work for America West's flights. Each airline thus gained the savings of not having to staff gates that were used for only a few flights a day. During the 1996–2002 period, Continental expanded its code-sharing efforts, entering into agreements with such domestic carriers as Northwest Airlines, Delta Airlines, Hawaiian Airlines, Alaska Airlines, American Eagle, and Horizon Airlines and such international carriers as Air Europa, Air France, Virgin Airways, Air China, and KLM Royal Dutch Airlines.

Upset by what he considered untrustworthy information coming from the finance department, Bethune moved to install much stronger financial systems. A new chief financial officer, Larry Kellner, was brought in to overhaul the company's financial systems and generate better information for decision-making. Under Kellner's guidance, Continental developed systems that allowed management to have dependable and regularly updated estimates of revenues, costs, profits, and cash flows; every morning by 10 A.M., executives had a report of the previous day's credit card receipts. Not long thereafter, the system was upgraded to include the capability to produce a 40-item daily forecast that included credit card receipts, fuel costs, maintenance costs, revenue per available seat mile, cost per available seat mile, profit per available seat mile per type of aircraft, profit at each hub, and profit on each route from each hub. According to Bethune, "The measurements became more and more accurate, which meant we could make better and better decisions with increasingly current numbers."[12] For instance, the

new financial systems revealed that Continental's European flights were unusually profitable; management used this information to add more European flights and to increase
the fares on some of its international routes. It also learned which routes and flights
were losing money, thus providing a basis for revising Continental's flight schedules—
employees in locations where service was discontinued (or where code sharing was implemented) were offered jobs in other parts of the company whenever possible. Kellner
also began the practice of hedging Continental's jet fuel purchases to give the company
an insurance policy against unexpected increases in fuel costs—in 1995, fuel hedges
saved Continental an estimated $3 million as fuel prices rose.

During the 1996–98 period, Continental initiated efforts to lower training and
maintenance costs by reducing the number of different types of aircraft comprising its
fleet. The company achieved its goal of having only 5 different types of aircraft by the
end of 1999, as compared to 10 in 1994. Further maintenance savings were realized as
the company took delivery on new Boeing aircraft in 1997 and 1998, reducing the average age of its fleet. New aircraft were financed by long-term borrowing and leasing
arrangements.

In July 1997, Continental launched a three-year program to bring employee wages
and salaries up to industry standards; the program was completed on schedule in July
2000. At this point, Continental launched another three-year program to bring employee benefits to industry standards by 2003; the program to improve benefits involved increases in vacations, paid holidays, increases matching contributions to
401(k) programs, and past service retirement credits for most senior employees.

Exhibit 1 provides a summary of Continental's financial and operating performance
for the 1993–2002 period. Continental had paid no dividends on its common stock and
had no current intention to do so. Starting in 1998, Continental began a stock repurchase
program under which it had purchased a total of 28.1 million shares at a cost of approximately $1.2 billion through December 2002. Throughout much of the 1998–2002
period, most of Continental's assets were pledged as collateral on its borrowings or
were otherwise encumbered; the company operated its aircraft under leasing agreements
and also had operating leases for its airport and terminal facilities—the obligations for
its leases were not included in the company's consolidated balance sheets. Going into
2003, Continental had about $1 billion in unencumbered assets, consisting mostly of
spare parts inventories and equity in its Continental Express subsidiary.

The Alliance with Northwest Airlines   In 1998, Northwest Airlines
purchased an 8.7-million-share block of Continental's common stock, sufficient to
give it voting control of Continental. This formed the basis for a long-term global alliance between Continental and Northwest that provided for each carrier to place its
flight code on a large number of flights of the other and for sharing of executive
lounges in certain airports as well as reciprocal frequent flyer benefits. The alliance
also provided for joint marketing activities, while preserving the separate identities of
the two carriers. However, the alliance soon came under fire from the U.S. Department
of Justice, which filed an antitrust suit charging that Northwest's controlling ownership
in Continental violated Section 7 of the Clayton Act and Section 1 of the Sherman Act
and had the effect of reducing actual and potential competition in various ways and in
a number of geographic markets.

Both Northwest and Continental decided to contest the lawsuit. During the
1998–2000 period, while the litigation was working itself through the court process,
Continental and Northwest proceeded to implement the terms of their alliance
agreement.

Exhibit 1   FINANCIAL AND OPERATING SUMMARY, CONTINENTAL AIRLINES, 1993–2002

	2002	2001	2000	1999	1998	1997	1995	1993
Financial Data (in millions, except for per share data)								
Operating revenues	$8,402	$8,969	$9,899	$8,639	$7,927	$7,194	$5,825	$5,767
Total operating expenses	8,714	8,825	9,170	8,024	7,226	6,478	5,440	5,786
Operating income	(312)	144	729	615	701	716	385	(19)
Net income	(451)	(95)	342	455	383	385	224	(39)[a]
Basic earnings per share	$(7.02)	$(1.72)	$5.62	$6.54	$6.34	$6.65	$4.07	$(1.17)[a]
Diluted earnings per share	$(7.02)	$(1.72)	$5.45	$6.20	$5.02	$4.99	$3.37	$(1.17)[a]
Operating Data								
Revenue passengers (000s)	41,016	44,238	46,896	45,540	43,625	41,210	37,575	38,628
Revenue passenger miles (millions)[b]	59,349	61,140	64,161	60,022	53,910	47,906	40,023	42,324
Available seat miles (millions)[c]	80,122	84,485	86,100	81,946	74,727	67,576	61,006	67,011
Passenger load factor[d]	74.1%	72.4%	74.5%	73.2%	72.1%	70.9%	65.6%	63.2%
Breakeven passenger load factor[e]	79.2%	74.9%	66.3%	64.7%	61.6%	60.1%	60.8%	63.3%
Passenger revenue per available seat mile	8.61¢	8.98¢	9.84¢	9.12¢	9.23¢	9.29¢	8.20¢	7.17¢
Total revenue per available seat mile	9.52¢	9.78¢	10.67¢	9.86¢	9.95¢	10.06¢	n.a.	n.a.
Operating cost per available seat mile	9.22¢	9.58¢	9.68¢	8.98¢	8.89¢	9.04¢	8.36¢	7.90¢
Average price per gallon of fuel	74.01¢	82.48¢	88.54¢	50.78¢	51.20¢	67.36¢	55.02¢	59.26¢
Average fare per revenue passenger	$168.25	$171.59	$180.66	$164.11	$158.02	$152.40	n.a.	n.a.
Actual aircraft in service at end of period (not including Continental Express)	366	352	371	363	363	337	309	316
Average age of jet aircraft fleet (years)	n.a.	5.2	6.7	7.4	7.6	10.7	14.4	n.a.

[a]Covers only the period April 28, 1993, through December 31, 1993, after Continental emerged from Chapter 11 bankruptcy proceedings that began in 1990; results prior to April 28 are not meaningful due to recapitalization of company and other matters pertaining to the bankruptcy proceedings.

[b]The number of scheduled miles flown by revenue passengers.

[c]The number of seats available for passengers multiplied by the number of scheduled miles those seats are flown.

[d]Revenue passenger miles divided by available seat miles.

[e]The percentage of seats that must be occupied by revenue passengers in order for the airline to break even on an income before income-tax basis, excluding nonrecurring charges, nonoperating items, and other special items.

Source: Company press release, January 15, 2003; 1999 and 2001 company 10K reports; 2001 annual report.

In January 2001, in a successful effort to end the litigation, Continental paid Northwest $450 million in cash to repurchase 6.7 million of the 8.7 million shares of Continental common stock that Northwest owned, making Continental independent of any one outside entity's control for the first time since the company had been formed. Gordon Bethune declared January 22, 2001 as Independence Day at Continental and marked the occasion by paying a $100 cash bonus to Continental's 54,300 employees around the world and holding celebrations at company facilities featuring apple pie and Coca-Cola.

However, as part of the share repurchase deal, Continental and Northwest agreed to extend until 2025 their master alliance agreement, which called for code sharing, reciprocal frequent flyer programs, shared executive lounge access, and various joint marketing agreements. At the time Continental began implementing its global alliance with Northwest Airlines in November 1998, management anticipated that the alliance would be fully implemented by the end of 2001 and would produce an increase of approximately $225 million in additional operating income for Continental. Due to implementation delays in establishing common technical platforms and jointly implementing alliances with other carriers, management subsequently revised that projection to $160 million for 2001 and projected that the full benefit would be achieved during the next few years. Due primarily to the effects on the industry of the September 11, 2001, terrorist attacks, the actual incremental contribution for 2001 was $140 million. In 2002 management was unclear whether the full projected benefit would be achieved.

Executing the Make Reliability a Reality Product Plan

Boosting On-Time Performance   Because surveys of air travelers consistently showed that on-time arrival was the single most important determinant of customer satisfaction, Bethune opted to use on-time percentage as the chief indicator of how well Continental was performing. The decision to pay employees a $65 bonus for achieving good on-time performance was the result of a company analysis showing that Continental was spending about $5 million monthly taking care of passengers who had missed connecting flights because of late incoming flights—some passengers had to be provided meals and/or housed overnight, and some had to be reticketed to the flights of other carriers. Plus, it took time on the part of ticket agents to handle all these arrangements, adding to staffing costs. Bethune determined that Continental would come out ahead if the company took half of the $5 million and gave it to employees in the form of a monthly incentive to achieve good on-time performance ($2.5 million divided by just under 40,000 Continental employees was roughly $65); Continental managers were not eligible for the $65 bonus because the company already has a performance-based bonus plan for managers.

The $65 bonus plan was announced in January 1995; that month Continental's on-time percentage was 71 percent, a ranking of 7th among the top 10 airlines—not good enough for the bonus (which required a ranking in the top 5) but better than the 61 percent on-time arrivals the prior January. In February, 80 percent of Continental's flights arrived on time, good for a fourth-place ranking; Continental cut a special $65 check and sent it to all employees (withholding taxes on the $65 bonus were taken out of the regular paychecks). In March 1995, Continental ranked first in on-time performance, with 83 percent on-time arrivals. In April, Continental was first again. Continental's on-time performance suffered in May, June, and July because pilots initiated a work slowdown as leverage in their contract negotiations then under way with the company. But following the contractual agreement with the pilots' union, Continental's on-time percentage improved to second best in the industry in August and September, third best in October, and fourth best in November.

Given these results, Bethune decided to raise the bar for paying bonuses for on-time performance. The new standard, scheduled to start in January 1996, was that Continental had to finish third or higher for employees to receive a bonus, but the bonus payment was upped to $100. When Continental came in first in on-time performance in December 1995, the month before the new $100 bonus was to go into effect, Bethune decided that all employees should be paid $100 (rather than $65) for their December 1995 performance. In 1997 Continental management began noticing that although Continental's monthly on-time percentages were at respectably high levels (sometimes at record levels) there were a number of months when the company did not rank third or higher—partly because other airlines had launched campaigns to improve their own on-time percentages. Continental adjusted the bonus requirements to either rank in the top three nationwide in on-time arrivals or have an on-time arrival percentage above 80 percent—Bethune figured that an on-time arrival percentage above 80 percent represented good performance and merited paying employees a $100 bonus even if Continental was only fourth best in a given month. The bonus standards were altered again in 2000; a $100 bonus was paid when Continental finished first in on-time performance among the major U.S. carriers, and a $65 bonus was paid when it finished second or third or had an on-time percentage above 80 percent. In 2000, Continental gave on-time bonus checks to employees 11 out of 12 months, totaling $39 million. During the 1995–2000 period, Continental paid employees a total of $157 million in on-time bonuses.

To further promote better on-time performance, Continental revised the routes of aircraft flying into airports where flights were often delayed. For example, at the congested Newark hub (where at certain times of the day it was not unusual for planes to sit on the runway for 15 to 30 minutes waiting for clearance to take off even if the weather was good) most planes departing Newark at congested times were assigned out-and-back routes between Newark and particular spoke destinations rather than, say, being routed to Washington and then on to Houston and Denver. Thus, if a particular Continental flight was regularly delayed out of Newark because of congestion, it would affect passengers traveling to the spoke destination and would hurt that routes on-time performance, but a delay leaving Newark would not spill over to create frequent delays for passengers at Washington, Houston, and Denver, resulting in three flights with poor on-time performances. Continental had on-time arrival percentages of 80.7 percent in 2001 and 83.5 percent (a record) in 2002.

Improving Baggage Handling When the on-time bonus was instituted in 1995, the number of lost bags went up at first—partly because flight crews elected not to wait on slow-arriving baggage in order to get planes away from the gates on time and help promote on-time arrivals. Continental executives elected not to institute a bonus payment for getting passengers' baggage on the planes, believing it was employees' jobs to get the bags on the planes. Bethune explained:

> We had to get the word out that if the number of baggage complaints was increasing, that wasn't going to make it. We didn't want on-time flights without bags, or without people, or with dirty aisles. On-time meant the whole system was working on time, not just part of it. So we explained this to our employees, and baggage started making it onto the planes.[13]

In the following months, Continental's baggage handling improved—during one period, Continental ranked among the top three airlines in fewest number of baggage complaints for 30 out of 31 months. Moreover, management stressed that the on-time arrival percentage was being used as a metric for measuring the reliability of the company's whole operation. They emphasized that "making reliability a reality" meant Continental's planes should not only arrive on time but also depart on time with a full supply of meals, all passengers, and all their bags.

Other Product Enhancements   To reduce the time it took Continental reservation agents to answer phone calls and handle the task of making a reservation, Continental increased its call capacity by adding more agents and upgrading its reservation systems software. Calls involving flight status and other standard questions that did not require speaking directly to a reservations agent were directed to an automated system.

In-flight services were improved according to surveys of customer preferences. Continental began serving Coca-Cola instead of Pepsi and increased the variety of beers that were available. First-class passengers were given priority baggage handling. New and tastier meals were developed, with Bethune and Brenneman personally testing and approving each of the new offerings. In-flight phones were installed in most of Continental's planes by the end of 1997. Music was played as passengers boarded planes. In 2000, Continental spent $12 million on bigger overhead bins to accommodate larger carry-on bags and provide more storage space for carry-ons.

Executing the Working Together Plan

When the rigid procedures manual was burned and replaced with general guidelines, many Continental executives feared that employees would give away the store in spending money to satisfy stranded or disgruntled passengers or to buy new airplane parts when existing ones could be repaired. But Bethune wanted employees to have more discretion and be able to use their best judgment, believing that management actions to give employees more free rein to do their jobs would build bridges of trust between management and employees. He further believed that, once the company began making money and the profit-sharing plan with employees kicked in, the vast majority of Continental employees would think twice about giving away the store. He was willing to take the risk that some employees would probably be too generous. During the 1995–2000 period, Continental paid employees $545 million in profit-sharing bonuses—the amount for 2000 (paid in February 2001) was $98 million.

To help employees better understand what was expected, the company created checklists for pilots regarding takeoffs and landings, for maintenance technicians regarding engine maintenance, for flight crews regarding proper provisioning, for crews regarding plane cleanups, and so on. The idea was that if certain jobs were broken down into a series of steps that get the job done, then it would be easier for people to do the jobs they signed on for and easier to keep them focused on the tasks at hand.

Open Communications and Teamwork   A toll-free voice-mail number directly to Bethune's office was set up for employees to use when they got particularly frustrated or felt a need to talk directly to the CEO—on a normal day, Bethune tended to get a couple of calls; on days when something unusual happened or major policy changes were announced, he might get 20 to 25 calls.[14] To make sure that employees could get help when they got into trouble or something wasn't fixed properly, an 800 line was set up for them to call whenever they encountered a technical operations problem—an operational response team was on duty seven days a week to provide assistance. There was a hotline employees could call for information about pay, benefits, and their 401(k) program. To keep employees up-to-date on company developments, there was a daily update from corporate headquarters distributed via the company intranet and e-mail, a weekly three-minute voice-mail message from Gordon Bethune giving his take on any new developments at the company, a monthly employee newsletter called *Continental Times,* and a company publication called the *Continental Quarterly* that was mailed to employees' homes. Bethune and the company's head of corporate communications decided in 1995 to install some 600 bulletin boards in employee break rooms, high-traffic hallways, and common rooms and post a daily newsletter on the same area of each bulletin board by late afternoon; in 1997, streaming LED display message boards were installed in crew break rooms and office hallways to provide employees with constantly updated breaking news, the latest daily on-time flight percentages, Continental's stock price, and airport weather reports. Bethune made a point of leveling with employees, keeping them fully informed, and giving straight answers to questions—in contrast to prior management's practice of telling employees as little as possible. The four elements of the Go Forward Plan—Fly to Win, Fund the Future, Make Reliability a Reality, and Working Together—were always discussed in the same order at employee meetings, in company publications, and on bulletin-board postings; the agenda at the biweekly management committee meetings was also structured according to the four elements of the Go Forward plan.

The monthly open houses at Houston headquarters were expanded to include employee meetings twice a year at the three hub locations and other Continental facilities with sizable workforces. Bethune wanted all Continental employees to feel like they could get to top-level executives and ask whatever questions were on their minds. One question Bethune got was from an employee at the Newark hub who asked why it made sense to give all employees a $65 bonus for good on-time performance when the jobs of many Continental employees did not directly affect on-time performance. Bethune, holding up his watch, responded, "Which part of this watch don't you think we need?"[15] The employee had no answer and sat down; Bethune believed his question about the watch made his point about the importance of teamwork, the value that each employee contributed, and why it made sense for all Continental employees to win or lose together. Bethune pushed the theme that each Continental employee was a part of what was happening at Continental, that Continental's people *were* the company, and that the Working Together Plan was about making Continental a place where people were happy to come to work. Bethune was fond of saying that he had never heard of a successful company that didn't have a good product and where people didn't enjoy coming to work. And he liked to say that running an airline was the biggest team sport in the world.

The Culture-Changing Effort In Bethune's view, the keys to changing Continental's corporate culture were for management to act differently, for the company to treat its people differently, and for management to look closely at what it was like for Continental employees to come to work every day and deliberately set out to change the things that made the work environment unpleasant or that made employees unhappy.

The manual burning, the new guidelines that gave employees more rein to do their jobs, and management's emphasis on teamwork were all deliberate steps that management took to signal employees that the Working Together initiative truly represented a new day at Continental. The final part of the Working Together plan that Continental executives implemented was to insist that Continental people treat each other with dignity and respect—the goal was for every worker to treat coworkers like a customer or family member. Bethune believed prior management had created a lot of scar tissue and mistrust that needed to be eradicated. "Dignity and Respect" became the company's slogan for 1996.

In early 1995, high-level executives ranked all managerial and supervisory employees on a scale of 1 to 4 with regard to the quality of their work and whether they were team players, with 1 being good and 4 indicating deficient work quality and/or shortcomings in people management skills. During the first nine months of 1995, executives talked to supervisors about their performance, giving them a chance to get on board and measure up to expectations. The ratings were fluid, changing as supervisors changed their behavior. In October 1995, when it became clear that the company had too many managers, especially middle managers, Continental decided to dismiss all managers and supervisors who had a 4 rating.

Within the executive ranks, there was a big but gradual turnover. Of the 61 vice presidents at Continental when Bethune took over, about half either left on their own accord for other jobs or were let go for reasons of ineffective management or failing to be team players. Some of those who departed were not happy with the direction Bethune wanted to take the company, and some were not pleased with certain aspects of the programs of change that he instituted. Bethune recruited a number of outsiders for top positions at Continental, hiring several people with whom he had worked at Piedmont Airlines and identifying others by asking trusted acquaintances. In 1998, several Delta Airlines executives told Bethune that Continental had the best management team of any airline. To retain its key executives, Continental adopted a very attractive salary and bonus package. Just as employees got monthly bonuses for on-time performance and had a performance-based profit-sharing plan that paid them up to 15 percent of pretax profits, Continental executives got bonuses based partly on Continental's overall performance and partly on the achievement of individual goals. Bethune preached teamwork among senior executives, warning them that he took a very dim view of power plays, backstabbing, jockeying for position, and departments that failed to work cooperatively with other departments.

A technique that Gordon Bethune liked to use to build trust was to reward people early and unexpectedly. In mid-1996, Continental was doing so well that it was clear the company would hit its performance targets for the whole year. Bethune decided to have bonus checks cut for 50 percent of the full 1996 bonus amounts and to give the checks to Continental's managers at the company's midyear managers' meeting. When he came in to give his luncheon address, Bethune asked the 350 executives there (who had been assigned seats) to stand and turn over their chairs—a bonus check was taped to the bottom of each chair. He told the group, "This is because you've done such an outstanding job—because Continental is going to make its plan this year. Here's the money the company owes you for that success."[16] He got a standing ovation. According to Bethune, "The managers left that meeting like it was halftime of a championship game. They had come in expecting the usual corporate rah-rah and they left with a check for half of their bonus, which they weren't expecting for another six months."[17]

Another visible action was Bethune's mandate for departments to work cooperatively, specifically in the areas of scheduling, flight operations, and aircraft maintenance. Prior to Bethune's joining Continental, marketing and scheduling personnel would work out a flight and route schedule which they thought would attract the most passengers and yield the biggest load factors; then they handed the schedule off to operations to figure out which planes to assign to fly which routes and when and where

Exhibit 2   COMPARATIVE LABOR COSTS, MAJOR U.S. AIRLINES, THIRD QUARTER 2002

Airline	Labor Cost per Available Seat Mile (in cents)
American Airlines	4.62¢
United Airlines	4.60
Delta Airlines	4.56
U.S. Airways	4.55
Alaska Air	4.32
Northwest Airlines	3.90
Continental Airlines	3.53
Southwest Airlines	2.90
America West	2.16

Source: *The Wall Street Journal*, December 10, 2002, p. B1.

maintenance on each plane would be done. Often the schedule that was drawn up created all kinds of problems and inefficiencies in flight operations and maintenance—and neither department was inclined to work with the other to resolve the difficulties. Bethune required people in marketing, scheduling, flight operations, and aircraft maintenance to form a team to arrive at a schedule that was workable from all perspectives.

Starting in 1996, Continental began a program to reward employees for perfect attendance. Employees with perfect attendance for a six-month period (either January–June or July–December) were awarded a $50 gift certificate and entered into drawings for fully equipped Eddie Bauer Ford Explorers, with the company paying all sales and gift taxes, title fees, and license fees. Since the program had been initiated, the company had given away more than 110 vehicles. For the July–December 2001 period, there were 16,207 eligible employees with perfect attendance records and Explorers were awarded to 8 employees; in 2001, Explorers were awarded to 20 employees. Continental's human resources department estimated that the perfect attendance incentives had saved the company close to $25 million.

Management believed that employee morale at Continental was the highest in the airline industry. Continental's calendar was dotted each year with company picnics, ice cream parties, barbeques, and fried chicken dinners. According to one top executive, "Three to four celebrations a year cost us $20 per employee. Compare that to our payroll and you can't find it. But those are the things people remember."[18] Voluntary turnover rates for Continental's employees were 6.7 percent in 1998, 6.1 percent in 1999, and 5.3 percent in 2000. In 2001–2002, roughly 33 percent of Continental's operating costs were for labor and 44 percent of the company's employees were represented by unions. In 2002, Continental's mechanics and related employee groups ratified a new four-year collective bargaining agreement between the company and the International Brotherhood of Teamsters by a 73 percent majority. Management operated on the principle that employee compensation and fringe benefits should be "fair to employees and fair to the company." Exhibit 2 shows comparative labor costs for the major U.S. commercial airlines during the third quarter of 2002.

At every Continental facility he visited, Bethune preached the importance of teamwork, likening the company to a watch in which each piece had to do its job to make the whole thing work and in which if even the smallest piece failed, the whole watch could fail. In 1998, Bethune wrote:

If you want to make the most sweeping statement you can about the change at Continental since I came on board, it's that now everybody's on the same team and everyone knows it. Everyone knows what the goal is and what his or her part is and how it relates to the goal. Everyone knows what the reward is for making the goal and what happens if we fail.

We're all working from the same plays, the same playbook—plays everyone's had a chance to buy into, plays the people who will be running them had a chance to help design, plays everyone believes in, plays everyone believes can win.[19]

Bethune was a firm advocate of the management principle that what gets measured is what gets managed. It was his philosophy that a company could not just run on autopilot and stay good; it had to keep getting better and better at what it did. He regularly urged Continental employees to thrash the competition. Bethune talked with every class of flight attendants at the end of their training. He was well regarded by employees. During a ceremony at which the Ford Explorer winners were presented their keys by Gordon Bethune and Greg Brenneman, one employee commented, "I started the week we went into bankruptcy 10 years ago. It is now 300 times better. What helps a lot is Gordon and Greg. Their personalities enthuse everybody. They're funny. I love listening to them speak."[20]

Exhibit 3 shows how Continental's operating costs compared with those of other major U.S. airlines during the 1995–2002 period.

Executive Changes at the Top

In May 2001, Greg Brenneman at the age of 39 resigned as Continental's president, COO, and director, electing to devote full-time to his own firm, TurnWorks, Inc., which specialized in helping start-up companies and firms going through major transitions; in announcing his resignation, Brenneman indicated he would donate $500,000 to endow two charities that helped Continental employees. Larry Kellner, formerly Continental's chief financial officer (CFO) and one of Gordon Bethune's first executive hires in early 1995, was elevated to the position of president; Kellner had the distinction in 2000 of having become the first three-time winner of the CFO Excellence Awards named annually by *CFO* magazine. C. D. McLean, former executive vice president of operations, was named Continental's chief operating officer.

Recognition and Awards

Since 1996, Continental had been the recipient of numerous awards. Continental Airlines was named Airline of the Year in 1996 and 2001 by *Air Transport World,* a leading aviation industry trade magazine; the magazine cited Continental's employee-friendly culture and said that Continental had the best labor relations of any major U.S. hub-and-spoke carrier. It also noted that Continental had "superior passenger service," especially where business travelers were concerned. OAG, publisher of *OAG Pocket Flight Guides,* in 2001 named Continental as Best Trans-Atlantic Airline and Best Airline Based in North America. J. D. Power had named Continental as tops in customer satisfaction for five of the past six years and was ranked the nation's number one airline in customer satisfaction for long-haul and short-hail flights by *Frequent Flyer* magazine in 2002. Continental was named as the second most admired U.S. airline in 2000, 2001, and 2002 by *Fortune* magazine, trailing Southwest Airlines in all three years. Continental had received numerous awards for its BusinessFirst premium cabin (from *Conde Nast Traveler, OAG, Smart*

Money, and *Entrepreneur* magazines) and for its OnePass frequent flyer program (from *InsideFlyer's* Freddie Awards). Continental had been named to the list of the 100 Best Companies to Work For in America for five years (1998–2002) and been included on *Hispanic* magazine's list of the "Corporate 100 Providing the Most Opportunities for Latinos" for five consecutive years. *Worth* magazine, in its April 2001 issue, named Gordon Bethune one of the 50 best CEOs, the third consecutive year he had appeared in *Worth's* rankings. In June 2001, *Aviation Week & Space Technology* gave Continental its highest rating for "outstanding management."

Crisis Conditions at Continental Suddenly Reappear

Going into September 2001, Continental and Continental Express were flying over 2,500 flights daily. Continental had reported 25 consecutive profitable quarters. But four days after the September 11 terrorist attacks on the World Trade Center and the Pentagon, Gordon Bethune announced that Continental Airlines would immediately reduce its long-term flight schedule by approximately 20 percent on a systemwide available-seat-mile basis and would furlough approximately 12,000 of its current 56,000 employees in connection with its flight cutbacks. On Monday, September 17, 2001, Continental announced that it would not be able to make $70 million in debt payments due that day but said it would be able to make the payments within the 10-day grace period to prevent defaulting.

Bethune indicated that even if Continental cut costs by 20 percent, the company would incur losses of $200 million per month at the presently depressed levels of passenger traffic. If passenger traffic and revenue did not snap back quickly, Bethune said, Continental might have to seek bankruptcy protection by early November. Bethune joined top executives at several other airlines in calling on the federal government to enact a major assistance package to help the airline industry cope with the sudden downturn in passenger traffic and the added costs of FAA-mandated airport security regulations regarding baggage handling; passenger screening at security checkpoints; and tighter security screening of caterers, cleaning crews, and flight crews. New security measures were expected to slow passengers moving through terminals, increase the time to process baggage and turn planes at the gates, and otherwise slow down hub operations.

Most of the flight reductions implemented by Continental in the aftermath of September 11 involved cutting the number of flights between particular locations, but the flight schedule reduction also resulted in Continental's discontinuing service to 10 cities/airports and abandoning plans to initiate service to Montego Bay and Kingston, Jamaica, as planned in late 2001. The Denver Reservations Center was closed, along with the flight attendant base in Los Angeles and several maintenance facilities. To further save on maintenance costs, Continental grounded 14 Continental Express turbo-props, all of the company's DC-10s, and 31 other aircraft.

Layoffs at Other Airlines

Meanwhile, other airlines in the United States and around the world were also hastily rearranging their flight schedules to protect their financial positions and respond to air travel reductions, figuring out how best to implement tighter security regulations, and

canceling orders or delaying deliveries of new aircraft. Many airlines had announced workforce reductions:

- American Airlines—a workforce reduction of 20,000 employees.
- United Airlines—a workforce reduction of 20,000 employees.
- US Airways—a workforce reduction of 11,000 employees and anticipated pay cuts.
- British Airways—a workforce reduction of 7,000 employees.
- America West Airlines—a workforce reduction of 2,000 employees.
- Virgin Atlantic—a workforce reduction of 1,200 employees.
- American Trans Air—a workforce reduction of 1,500 employees.
- Midwest Express—a workforce reduction of 450 employees.
- Frontier Airlines—a workforce reduction of 440 employees.
- Mesaba—undetermined furloughs and significant pay cuts.
- KLM—a workforce reduction of 10 percent.

With layoffs of 30,000 employees at Boeing and another 12,000 at Honeywell (all related to cutbacks in the production of commercial aircraft), close to 120,000 employees were affected by the flight cutbacks and cost-saving measures being initiated across the airline industry.

The Federal Government's Rescue Package

In the days following the attacks, at the urging of the Bush administration and most U.S. airline executives, Congress passed an airline bailout bill (the Air Transportation Safety and System Stabilization Act) designed to keep the U.S. airline industry solvent until travel rebounded. The act gave airlines $5 billion in direct payments (to compensate air carriers for losses resulting from the terrorist attacks) and provided for up to $10 billion in loan guarantees to assist airlines in covering negative cash flows and making debt payments even if they had weak balance sheets. Continental received $417 million in cash in the third and fourth quarters of 2001 as a result of the $5 billion emergency relief package passed by Congress. Continental viewed its ability to apply for loan guarantees as an important safety net, but its heavily leveraged status left it with few unencumbered assets to pledge in applying for government loan guarantees.

A Financial Crisis in the U.S. Airline Industry

In 2001, the major commercial airlines in the United States reported combined losses of $7.8 billion. All except Southwest Airlines reported losses for the third and fourth quarters of 2001. Continental reported a $3 million profit for the third quarter; however, except for special charges of $85 million and a federal grant of $243 million pursuant to the Air Transportation Safety and System Stabilization Act, Continental would have reported a loss of $97 million. American Airlines posted the largest quarterly operating loss in its history for the three months ending September 30. Northwest reported a third-quarter operating loss of $155 million and indicated that it incurred $250 million in operating losses during the September 11–30 period; in October 2001, despite a modest traffic rebound, Northwest indicated that it was burning through $6 to $8 million of cash a day due to fare discounts aimed at attracting traffic, fewer passengers carried, and slighter higher costs per mile. US Airways reported a third-quarter net loss of $766 million, which took into account special charges and a $331 million grant the airline received as part of the Air Transportation Safety and System Stabilization Act (ATSSSA); without the federal grant, US Airways would have lost $1.1 billion in the third quarter. United Airlines reported 2001 losses of $3 billion.

The financial crisis spilled over deep into 2002 as traffic failed to return to pre–September 11 levels. All major U.S. airlines except Southwest lost money in each of the first three quarters of 2002. During 2002, United spent close to $7 million a day more than it collected in revenues and filed for Chapter 11 bankruptcy protection in December 2002. US Airways filed for bankruptcy protection in August 2002. Losses at American Airlines totaled $2 billion for the first nine months of 2002, equal to more than $7 million a day. Combined losses of the major U.S. commercial airlines were about $11 billion in 2002, with only Southwest Airlines reporting a profit for 2002. In March 2003 analysts predicted that the major U.S. airlines would lose $7–$12 billion in 2003, depending on the length of the war in Iraq. United Airlines lost $12 million a day in January 2003.

Continental Reacts to the Crisis

On September 26, 2001, Gordon Bethune announced that he and Larry Kellner, Continental's president, would not accept any salary or bonus for the remainder of 2001.

In September 2001, Continental incurred a traffic decrease worldwide of 31.0 percent compared to September 2000, with domestic traffic being down 32.3 percent versus 29.0 percent for international flights. Traffic on Continental's flights improved during the first two weeks of October 2001, with the domestic load factor rising to 71.3 percent and the systemwide load factor increasing to 65.6 percent.

Starting in October 1, 2001, Continental began a program to award double miles to its frequent flyers for travel between October 2 and November 15; it also reduced fares for business travel on most domestic routes for the remainder of 2001. To encourage both business and leisure travel, the company began a reduced fare promotion to select destinations in Mexico, Central and South America, and Europe—passengers could save an additional 10 percent on the sale fares (and frequent flyers got an additional 1,000 bonus miles) by booking their travel at the company's website.

Continental had installed crossbar or deadbolt cockpit door restraints in all of its aircraft by October 23, ahead of the Federal Aviation Administration's targeted November deadline. Management expected to install even stronger doors in all its aircraft over the upcoming months, as manufacturers completed the production of newly designed doors with greatly enhanced cockpit security features.

Continental's full-year 2001 financial and operating results are shown in Exhibit 1. The company ended 2001 with $1.1 billion in cash and had around $1 billion in unencumbered assets that it could pledge as collateral on additional borrowing.

Continental Airlines in 2002 and 2003

During 2002, Continental reinstated 6,000 of the 12,000 positions that it had cut in late 2001 and added back about half of the capacity that it had removed in the weeks following September 11. The company took delivery of 20 of the 48 new Boeing jets originally scheduled for delivery in 2002; currently, it had no financing in place for 67 additional aircraft scheduled for delivery during 2003–2008. The company's strategy was to let its flight schedule and employment levels be driven by the market.

Also during 2002, Continental opened its new international arrivals facility at the Newark Liberty International Airport that housed customs, immigration, and other government services for arriving international passengers on Continental flights; this

Exhibit 4   ON-TIME FLIGHTS, MISHANDLED BAGGAGE, OVERSALES, AND PASSENGER
             COMPLAINTS FOR MAJOR U.S. AIRLINES, 1998–2002

Percentage of Scheduled Flights Arriving Within 15 Minutes of the Scheduled Time

Carrier	Jan.–Sept. 2002	2001	2000	1999	1998
Alaska Airlines	75.8%	69.0%	68.1%	71.0%	72.0%
America West	78.5	74.8	65.5	69.5	68.5
American	78.9	75.9	72.9	73.5	80.1
Continental*	78.7	80.7	78.1	76.6	77.3
Delta	77.5	78.0	75.3	78.0	79.6
Northwest	79.7	79.7	77.4	79.9	70.6
Southwest	82.3	81.7	75.2	80.0	80.8
TWA†		80.8	76.9	80.9	78.3
United	75.5	73.5	61.4	74.4	73.8
US Airways	78.4	78.2	72.3	71.4	78.9

Mishandled Baggage Reports per 1,000 Passengers

Carrier	Jan.–Sept. 2002	2001	2000	1999	1998
Alaska Airlines	2.68	3.00	3.48	5.75	7.27
America West	3.47	4.22	6.62	4.52	3.88
American	4.32	4.60	5.50	5.21	4.40
Continental*	3.06	4.29	5.35	4.42	4.06
Delta	3.61	4.11	4.49	4.39	4.27
Northwest	4.79	4.19	5.24	4.81	6.63
Southwest	3.54	4.77	5.00	4.22	4.53
TWA†		6.35	6.06	5.38	5.39
United	3.69	5.07	6.57	7.01	7.79
US Airways	3.01	3.86	4.76	5.08	4.09

$80 million facility was the last major milestone in $1.4 billion of customer improvements that management believed made Continental's Newark hub the premier airport facility in the New York City region. In addition, construction on Continental's new $324 million Terminal E expansion at Bush Intercontinental Airport in Houston continued; when completed, the project would add 20 gates and offer travelers a world-class facility. Also, to enhance the comfort of international passengers on long-haul flights, Continental completed installation of new BusinessFirst sleeper seats throughout its fleet of 18 Boeing 777 aircraft; the new seats featured increased seat width, a 170-degree recline from seat cushion to seat back, and six and a half feet of sleeping space in the fully extended position.

Continental launched its redesigned website in the third quarter of 2002, enabling customers to book OnePass reward travel online for the first time. The redesigned site also made it easier for customers to check fares, flight availability, and status; purchase tickets; and access OnePass frequent flyer account information.

Exhibit 4   Continued

Involuntary Denied Boardings per 10,000 Passengers Due to Oversold Flights					
Carrier	Jan.–Sept. 2002	2001	2000	1999	1998
Alaska Airlines	1.24	1.36	1.53	0.99	1.49
America West	0.21	0.38	1.27	1.38	1.12
American	0.22	0.36	0.44	0.42	0.42
Continental*	0.93	1.51	1.44	0.28	0.13
Delta	0.87	0.77	0.34	1.98	1.24
Northwest	0.53	0.45	0.43	0.20	0.33
Southwest	1.06	1.50	1.84	1.40	1.84
TWA[†]		1.83	2.76	0.88	1.69
United	0.65	0.92	1.64	0.69	0.59
US Airways	0.26	0.34	0.67	0.57	0.23

Complaints per 100,000 Passengers Boarded					
Carrier	Jan.–Sept. 2002	2001	2000	1999	1998
Alaska Airlines	1.02	1.27	2.04	1.64	0.54
America West	1.88	3.72	7.51	3.72	2.11
American	1.41	2.51	3.54	3.49	1.14
Continental*	1.46	2.23	2.84	2.62	1.02
Delta	1.51	2.16	2.01	1.81	0.79
Northwest	1.60	1.97	2.61	2.92	2.21
Southwest	0.37	0.38	0.47	0.40	0.25
TWA[†]		2.54	3.47	3.44	1.29
United	1.90	3.24	5.3	2.65	1.28
US Airways	1.24	1.87	2.59	3.13	0.84

*Figures for Continental include Continental Express flights.

[†]Acquired by American Airlines in 2001; TWA data for 2002 included in American Airlines statistics.

Source: Office of Aviation Enforcement and Proceedings, *Air Travel Consumer Report,* multiple issues.

Continental had outstanding operational performance in 2002, breaking 9 of 11 operational records during the year. For 2002, Continental reported a record on-time arrival rate of 83.5 percent and a record completion factor of 99.7 percent, going 103 days without a single flight cancellation. Exhibit 4 shows how Continental's operating performance compared with other airlines on four key measures during the 1998–2002 period.

In August 2002 Continental began implementing more than 100 changes to generate more revenues and reduce its expenses; the objective was to achieve pretax gains amounting to $80 million in 2002 and $400 million when fully implemented. These initiatives included the following:

- Removing 11 additional aircraft from the fleet (in addition to 49 that had already been grounded since September 2001) and permanently grounding the company's entire fleet of DC-10-80 leased aircraft—an action that reduced the number of different aircraft in the fleet from five to four and entailed write-offs of $52 million.

(Earlier in 2002, Continental had finalized an agreement with Boeing to defer the deliveries of aircraft on order to 2003 and beyond.)

■ Reducing its domestic capacity by 4.3 percent, to levels about 17 percent below those in August 2001. This decrease was in addition to seat-capacity reductions of about 6.5 percent that had already been implemented in 2002. However, capacity on TransAtlantic and Pacific flights was being increased by about 6 percent. By the end of 2003, management expected to reduce the number of aircraft in service from 366 to 357 and to cut the number of grounded aircraft from 25 to 15 (the company had 51 planes in storage at the end of 2001).

■ Instituting a hiring freeze, encouraging early retirements, and counting on voluntary leaves and attrition to avoid additional employee layoffs.

■ Eliminating most travel agent commissions. The company was aggressively promoting its website to passengers and urging that they make their reservations on their company's newly designed website.

■ Charging a fee of $20 on all paper tickets that were issued and rigidly enforcing all fare rules that resulted in collecting additional fares and fees from passengers. E-tickets as a percentage of total sales had climbed from 44 percent in September 1999 to 64 percent in September 2001 to 87 percent in September 2002.

■ Taking delivery of new and more fuel-efficient planes.

■ Rebidding of supplier contracts.

■ Installing the world's largest e-ticket check-in network, with more than 675 kiosks in more than 113 airports and cities. As of December 2002, 70 percent of Continental's passengers with e-tickets were using the self-service check-in kiosks, about double the percentage in 2001.

In announcing Continental's belt-tightening moves, Gordon Bethune said, "Unless market conditions improve quickly, we'll be forced to make further changes in all aspects of our operations." The company's chief financial officer indicated that the actions currently being initiated would "not be sufficient to return the company to profitability in the present environment."

Through the first three quarters of 2002, Continental had made little progress in reducing its operating costs per available seat mile—were it not for lower market prices for aircraft fuel, Continental's operating costs would have been as high in 2002 as they were in the previous year (see Exhibit 5).

The Spin-Off of Continental Express

In 2002, Continental went forward with plans to sell part of its ownership of Continental Express through an initial public offering of 10 million shares of stock and the subsequent sale of an additional 20 million shares. Continental realized $447 million from the proceeds of the stock sales; it then used $147 million of the proceeds to repay a portion of ExpressJet's debt to Continental and $150 million to fund a portion of its obligations to the Continental pension plan for its employees. The remainder was used to help cover the company's continuing negative cash flows from operations and fund Continental's ongoing capital expenditures.

Following the sale of 30 million ExpressJet shares, Continental Airlines' ownership of ExpressJet fell to about 53.1 percent. Continental Airlines did not intend to remain a stockholder of ExpressJet over the long term, instead planning to sell all or most of its remaining shares during late 2002 or 2003, subject to market conditions.

Exhibit 5   **CONTINENTAL'S OPERATING EXPENSES PER AVAILABLE SEAT MILE, NINE MONTHS ENDING SEPTEMBER 30, 2001 VERSUS 2002**

	Operating Expense per Available Seat Mile (in cents)	
	Nine Months Ending September 30, 2002	**Nine Months Ending September 30, 2001**
Wages, salaries, and related costs	3.27¢	3.21¢
Aircraft fuel	1.08	1.40
Aircraft leasing fees	0.91	0.86
Other rents, leases, and landing fees	0.69	0.57
Maintenance, materials, and repairs	0.46	0.54
Depreciation and amortization	0.49	0.46
Reservations and sales	0.42	0.48
Passenger services	0.36	0.39
Commissions	0.27	0.42
Other	1.25	1.22
Total operating expenses	9.20¢	9.55¢

Source: Company 10Q filing, September 30, 2002.

Continental Express planned to add 48 regional jets to its fleet in 2003, giving it a total of 236 jets. Passenger revenues for Continental Express in the last quarter of 2002 were 33.8 percent higher than for the same period in 2001; revenue passenger miles in 2002 were 16.6 percent higher than in 2001.

Continental's Financial Performance in 2002

Continental reported 2002 revenues of $8.4 billion, versus $8.97 billion for 2001; net losses were $451 million, versus a loss of $95 million in 2001. The company's liquidity continued to be shaky as the company reported third-quarter current assets of $2.3 billion and current liabilities of $3.0 billion. Moreover, Continental remained highly leveraged, with long-term debt and capital lease obligations of $5.1 billion and stockholders' equity of $1.4 billion as of September 30, 2002. In the third quarter of 2002, Continental received its last cash payment under the Air Transportation Safety and System Stabilization Act; total receipts under the act in 2002 were $51 million (versus $417 million in 2001).

In October 2002, Continental management had forecast that cash operating expenses would exceed revenues by an average of $1.5 million daily during the fourth quarter of 2002; counting principal payments on debt and capital expenditures, management had predicted negative cash flows averaging close to $3.0 million per day during the last three months of 2002. To bolster its cash position, Continental in December 2002 issued $200 million in five-year notes that were secured by a designated pool of spare parts and an insurance policy. But unexpected higher revenues from holiday travel allowed Continental to end 2002 with $1.34 billion in cash and short-term investments, about $200 million more than had been anticipated. Passenger revenues in the fourth quarter of 2002 were 13 percent higher than in the last quarter of 2001.

As of late 2002, Continental had 30 owned out-of-service aircraft with a fair market value of $97 million; in addition the company had 48 leased out-of-service aircraft, 2 of which had been subleased. Management was exploring sublease opportunities for the remaining 46 leased out-of-service planes.

Exhibit 6   CONTINENTAL'S FUTURE CONTRACTUAL OBLIGATIONS, 2003 AND BEYOND (IN MILLIONS)

Type of Contractual Obligation	Continental's Cash Outflows Due to Contractual Obligations					
	2003	2004	2005	2006	Later Years	Totals
Long-term debt	$ 410	$ 329	$ 563	$ 417	$ 2,209	$ 4,256
Capital lease obligations	40	38	39	41	243	446
Convertible preferred securities	—	—	—	—	250	250
Aircraft operating leases	880	843	821	715	7,089	11,271
Nonaircraft operating leases	556	616	656	656	2,259	5,132
Aircraft purchase commitments	158	641	597	397	516	3,438
Future operating lease commitments	72	116	197	202	2,986	3,591
Total	$2,116	$2,583	$2,873	$2,428	$15,552	$28,384

Source: 2001 10K report.

Exhibit 6 summarizes Continental's expected cash outflows stemming from its long-term debt, capital and operating leases, future aircraft purchase and operating lease commitments, and other contractual obligations.

As it began 2003, Continental was the world's seventh-largest airline, with more than 2,000 daily departures, 131 domestic and 93 international destinations, and the broadest global route network of any U.S. airline. According to *Conde Nast Traveler* magazine's annual survey of business travelers, Continental outperformed its U.S. rivals in premium-class comfort, reliability, and value on trans-Atlantic and trans-Pacific flights; on domestic trips, Continental's first-class service received the highest ranking among major carriers and was rated the greatest "value for cost." According to Gordon Bethune, "Our goals are simple—they are our customers' goals. We continue to deliver a high-quality product each and every day, getting our customers where they want to go, on time and with their bags, while providing preflight and inflight service that is globally recognized for consistency and excellence."

Endnotes

[1]Gordon Bethune with Scott Huler, *From Worst to First: Behind the Scenes of Continental's Remarkable Comeback* (New York: John Wiley & Sons, 1998), p. 6.
[2]Ibid., pp. 6, 14–15.
[3]Ibid., pp. 26–28.
[4]Ibid., pp. 37–38.
[5]Ibid., p. 39.
[6]Ibid., p. 41.
[7]Ibid., pp. 41–42.
[8]Ibid., pp. 42–43.
[9]Ibid., p. 142.
[10]Ibid., pp. 64–69.
[11]Ibid., pp. 84–85.
[12]Ibid., p. 88.
[13]Ibid., p. 107.
[14]Ibid., p. 115.
[15]Ibid., p. 126.
[16]Ibid., p. 241.
[17]Ibid., pp. 241–242.
[18]Quoted in "Happy Skies of Continental," *Continental*, July 2001, p. 53.
[19]Bethune, *From Worst to First,* p. 181.
[20]Quoted in "Happy Skies of Continental," p. 52.

CASE 29

Southwest Airlines
Culture, Values, and Operating Practices

Arthur A. Thompson, Jr.
The University of Alabama

John E. Gamble
The University of South Alabama

When the September 11 terrorist attacks triggered close to a 20 percent falloff in airline traffic in the fourth quarter of 2001, the commercial airline industry in the United States went into a crisis mode—companies began borrowing money to cover cash drains of $3 to $8 million daily, cutting flights, laying off employees, deferring or canceling the delivery of new aircraft on order, speculating on how much to cut fares to induce passengers to fly and on how long traffic might stay depressed, figuring out what it would take to avoid bankruptcy, and scrambling to institute a host of security measures. Roughly 100,000 of the industry's approximately 500,000 airline employees were laid off. Even after the federal government came through with emergency cash grants of over $1 billion, the major U.S. carriers lost a combined $7.8 billion in 2001, of which $3.3 billion came in the fourth quarter.

At Southwest Airlines, the crisis was dealt with far differently—no flights were cut and no employees were laid off. Because management's philosophy, for the past two decades, had been to manage Southwest in good times so that both the company and its employees could prosper through bad times, Southwest was in a strong position when the industry got hammered in the aftermath of September 11. It had the lowest operating costs of any U.S. airline, it had $1 billion in cash, and it had the strongest balance sheet and credit rating of any U.S. airline (allowing management to quickly borrow an additional $1.1 billion and give the company a buffer to pay all its bills and absorb any cash drains). Despite all the costs associated with implementing a raft of new security measures and the downturn in passenger traffic, Southwest reported a profit of $63.5 million for the fourth quarter of 2001 and a profit of $511.1 million for the full year—it was the only U.S. airline to operate in the black in either period.

And, unlike its rivals, Southwest continued to operate profitably throughout 2002 even though passenger traffic nationwide remained below levels prior to September 11. During 2002, Southwest proceeded to add almost 40 new daily flights and was able to boost its market share by about 2 percent. Southwest was profitable in 2002. Its eight biggest U.S. rivals, however, posted losses of more than $11 billion in 2002, with both US Airways and United Airlines filing for bankruptcy.

Company Background

In late 1966, Rollin King, a San Antonio, Texas, entrepreneur who owned a small commuter air service, marched into Herb Kelleher's law office with a plan to start a low-cost/low-fare airline that would shuttle passengers between San Antonio, Dallas, and Houston.[1] Over the years, King had heard many Texas businesspeople complain about the length of time that it took to drive between the three cities and the expense of flying the airlines currently serving them. His business concept for the airline was simple: Attract passengers by flying convenient schedules, get passengers to their destination on time, make sure they have a good experience, and charge fares competitive with travel by automobile. Though skeptical that King's business idea was viable, Kelleher dug into the possibilities during the next few weeks and concluded that a new airline was feasible; he agreed to handle the necessary legal work and also to invest $10,000 of his own funds in the venture.

In 1967, Kelleher filed papers to incorporate the new airline and submitted an application to the Texas Aeronautics Commission for the new company to begin serving Dallas, Houston, and San Antonio.[2] But rival airlines in Texas pulled every string they could to block the new airline from commencing operations, precipitating a contentious four-year parade of legal and regulatory proceedings. Herb Kelleher led the fight on the company's behalf, eventually prevailing in June 1971 after winning two appeals to the Texas Supreme Court and a favorable ruling from U.S. Supreme Court. Kelleher recalled, "The constant proceedings had gradually come to enrage me. There was no merit to our competitors' legal assertions. They were simply trying to use their superior economic power to squeeze us dry so we would collapse before we ever got into business. I was bound and determined to show that Southwest Airlines was going to survive and was going into operation."[3]

In January 1971, Lamar Muse was brought in as CEO to get operations under way. Muse was an aggressive and self-confident airline veteran who knew the business well and who had the entrepreneurial skills to tackle the challenges of building the airline from scratch and then competing head-on with the major carriers. Through private investors and an initial public offering of stock in June 1971, Muse raised $7 million in new capital to purchase planes and equipment and provide cash for start-up. Boeing agreed to supply three new 737s from its inventory, discounting its price from $5 million to $4 million and financing 90 percent of the $12 million deal.

Because the airline industry was in the throes of a slump in the early 1970s, Muse was able to recruit a talented senior staff that included a number of veteran executives from other carriers. He particularly sought out people who were innovative, wouldn't shirk from doing things differently or unconventionally, and were motivated by the challenge of building an airline from scratch. Muse wanted his executive team to be willing to think like mavericks and not be lulled into instituting practices at Southwest that were largely imitative of how they were done at other airlines. According to Rollin King, "It was our one opportunity to do it right. . . . We all understood that this was our opportunity to decide how to do it our way. Our philosophy was, and still is, we do whatever we have to do to get the job done."[4]

Southwest's Struggle to Gain a Market Foothold

In June 1971, Southwest initiated its first flights with a schedule that soon included 6 round-trips between Dallas and San Antonio and 12 round-trips between Houston and Dallas. The introductory $20 one-way fares to fly the Golden Triangle, well below the

$27 and $28 fares charged by rivals, attracted disappointingly small numbers of passengers—some days the total for all 18 flights would be less than 250 people. Southwest's financial resources were stretched so thin that the company bought fuel for several months on Lamar Muse's personal credit card. The company was short of ground equipment, and most of what it had was used and in worn condition. Money for parts and tools was so tight that, on occasion, company personnel got on the phone with acquaintances at rival airlines operating at the terminal and arranged to borrow what was needed. Nonetheless, morale and enthusiasm remained high; company personnel displayed can-do attitudes and adeptness at getting by on whatever resources were available.

To try to gain market visibility and drum up more passengers, Southwest decided it had to do more than just run ads in the media:

▪ Management decided to have flight hostesses dress in colorful hot pants and white knee-high boots with high heels. Recruiting ads for Southwest's first group of hostesses read, "Attention, Raquel Welch: You can have a job if you measure up." Two thousand applicants responded, and those selected for interviews were asked to come dressed in hot pants to show off their legs—the company wanted to hire long-legged beauties with sparkling personalities. Over 30 of Southwest's first graduating class of 40 flight attendants consisted of young women who were cheerleaders and majorettes in high school and thus had experience performing in front of people while skimpily dressed.

▪ A second attention-getting action was to give passengers free alcoholic beverages during daytime flights. Most passengers on these flights were business travelers. Management's thinking was that many passengers did not drink during the daytime and that with most flights being less than an hour's duration it would be cheaper to simply give the drinks away rather than collect the money.

▪ Taking a cue from being based at Dallas Love Field, Southwest began using the tag line "Now There's Somebody Else Up There Who Loves You." The routes between Houston, Dallas, and San Antonio became known as the Love Triangle. Southwest's planes were referred to as Love Birds, drinks became Love Potions, peanuts were called Love Bites, drink coupons were Love Stamps, and tickets were printed on Love Machines. The "love" campaign set the tone for Southwest's approach to its customers and company efforts to make flying Southwest an enjoyable, fun, and differentiating experience. (Later, when the company went public, it chose LUV as its stock-trading symbol.)

▪ In order to add more flights without buying more planes, the head of Southwest's ground operations came up with a plan for ground crews to off-load passengers and baggage, refuel the plane, clean the cabin, restock the galley, on-load passengers and baggage, do the necessary preflight checks and paperwork, and push away from the gate in 10 minutes. The 10-minute turn became one of Southwest's signatures during the 1970s and 1980s. (In later years, as passenger volume grew and many flights were filled to capacity, the turnaround time gradually expanded to 25 minutes—because it took more time to unload and load 125 passengers, as compared to a half-full plane with just 60–65 passengers. Even so, the 25-minute average turnaround times at Southwest in 2002 were still shorter than the 40–60-minute turnarounds typical at other major airlines.)

▪ In late November 1971, Lamar Muse came up with the idea of offering a $10 fare to passengers on the Friday-night Houston–Dallas flight. Even with no advertising, the 112-seat flight sold out. This led Muse to realize that Southwest was serving two quite distinct types of travelers in the Golden Triangle market: (1) business travelers who were more time-sensitive than price-sensitive and wanted weekday flights at times suitable for conducting business and (2) price-sensitive leisure travelers who wanted lower fares and had more flexibility about when to fly.[5] He came up with a two-tier on-peak and off-peak pricing structure in which all seats on weekday flights departing before 7 P.M. were priced at $26 and all seats on other flights were priced at $13. Passenger traffic increased significantly—and systemwide on-peak and off-peak pricing soon became standard across the whole airline industry.

■ In 1972, the company decided to move its flights in Houston from the newly opened Houston Intercontinental Airport (where it was losing money and where it took 45 minutes to get downtown) to the abandoned Houston Hobby Airport, located much closer to downtown Houston. Although Southwest was the only carrier to fly into Houston Hobby, the results were spectacular—business travelers who flew to Houston frequently from Dallas and San Antonio found the Houston Hobby location far more convenient than the Intercontinental Airport location, and passenger traffic doubled almost immediately.

■ In early 1973, in an attempt to fill empty seats on its San Antonio–Dallas flights, Southwest cut its regular $26 fare to $13 for all seats, all days, and all times. When Braniff International, at that time one of Southwest's major rivals, announced $13 fares of its own, Southwest retaliated with a two-page ad, run in the Dallas newspapers, headlining "Nobody is going to shoot Southwest Airlines out of the sky for a lousy $13" and containing copy saying Braniff was trying to run Southwest out of business. The ad announced that Southwest would not only match Braniff's $13 fare but that it would also give passengers the choice of buying a regular-priced ticket for $26 and receiving a complimentary fifth of Chivas Regal scotch, Crown Royal Canadian whiskey, or Smirnoff vodka (or, for nondrinkers, a leather ice bucket). Over 75 percent of Southwest's Dallas–Houston passengers opted for the $26 fare, although the percentage dropped as the two-month promotion wore on and corporate controllers began insisting that company employees use the $13 fare. The local and national media picked up the story of Southwest's offer, proclaiming the battle to be a David-versus-Goliath struggle in which the upstart Southwest did not stand much of a chance against the much larger and more well-established Braniff; grassroots sentiment in Texas swung to Southwest's side.

Southwest reported its first-ever annual profit in 1973.

More Legal and Regulatory Hurdles

During the rest of the 1970s, Southwest found itself embroiled in another round of legal and regulatory battles. One involved Southwest's refusal to move its flights from Dallas Love Field, located 10 minutes from downtown, out to the newly opened Dallas–Fort Worth (DFW) Regional Airport, which was 30 minutes from downtown Dallas. Local officials were furious because they were counting on fees from Southwest's flights in and out of DFW to help service the debt on the bonds issued to finance the airport's construction. Southwest's position was that it was not required to move because it had not agreed to do so, nor had it been ordered to do so, by the Texas Aeronautics Commission—moreover, the company's headquarters were located at Love Field. The courts eventually ruled Southwest's operations could remain at Love Field.

A second battle ensued when rival airlines protested Southwest's application to begin serving several smaller cities in Texas; their protest was based on arguments that these markets were already well served and that Southwest's entry would result in costly overcapacity. Southwest countered that its low fares would allow more people to fly and grow the market. Again, Southwest prevailed and its views about low fares expanding the market proved accurate. In the year before Southwest initiated service, 123,000 passengers flew from Harlingen Airport in the Rio Grande Valley to Houston, Dallas, or San Antonio; in the 11 months following Southwest's initial flights, 325,000 passengers flew to the same three cities.

Believing that Braniff and Texas International were deliberately engaging in tactics to harass Southwest's operations, Southwest convinced the U.S. government to investigate what it considered predatory tactics by its chief rivals. In February 1975, Braniff and Texas International were indicted by a federal grand jury for conspiring to put Southwest out of business—a violation of the Sherman Antitrust Act. The two airlines pleaded "no contest" to the charges, signed cease-and-desist agreements, and were fined a modest $100,000 each.

When Congress passed the Airline Deregulation Act in 1978, Southwest applied to the Civil Aeronautics Board (now the Federal Aviation Agency) to fly between Houston and New Orleans. The application was vehemently opposed by local government officials and airlines operating out of DFW because of the potential for passenger traffic to be siphoned away from that airport. The opponents solicited the aid of Fort Worth congressman Jim Wright, the majority leader of the U.S. House of Representatives, who took the matter to the floor of the House of Representatives; a rash of lobbying and maneuvering ensued. What emerged came to be known as the Wright Amendment of 1979: No airline may provide nonstop or through-plane service from Dallas Love Field to any city in any state except for locations in states bordering Texas. The amendment, which was still in effect at the start of 2003, meant that Southwest could not advertise, publish schedules or fares, or check baggage for travel from Dallas Love Field to any city it served outside Texas, Louisiana, Arkansas, Oklahoma, and New Mexico.

Battles to Survive and the Warrior Mentality

The legal, regulatory, and competitive battles that Southwest fought in its early years produced a strong esprit de corps among Southwest personnel and a drive to survive and prosper despite the odds. With newspaper and TV stories regularly reporting Southwest's difficulties, employees were fully aware that the airline's existence was constantly on the line. Had the company been forced to move from Love Field, it would most likely have gone under, an outcome that employees, Southwest's rivals, and local government officials understood well. According to Southwest's president, Colleen Barrett, the obstacles thrown in Southwest's path by competitors and local officials were instrumental in building Herb Kelleher's passion for Southwest Airlines and ingraining a combative, can-do spirit into the corporate culture:

> They would put twelve to fifteen lawyers on a case and on our side there was Herb. They almost wore him to the ground. But the more arrogant they were, the more determined Herb got that this airline was going to go into the air—and stay there.
>
> The warrior mentality, the very fight to survive, is truly what created our culture.[6]

Exhibit 1   MILESTONES AT SOUTHWEST AIRLINES, 1983–2002

1983	Three additional Boeing 737s are purchased; Southwest flies over 9.5 million passengers.
1984	Southwest is ranked first in customer satisfaction among the U.S. airlines for the fourth straight year.
1985	Service begins to St. Louis and Chicago Midway airports. Southwest names the Ronald McDonald House as its primary charity—the tie-in was the result of an effort by a Southwest pilot who lost a daughter to leukemia and who believed that Ronald McDonald Houses were a worthy way to demonstrate Southwest's community spirit.
1986	Southwest flies over 13 million passengers.
1988	Southwest becomes the first U.S. airline to win the Triple Crown (best on-time record, fewest reports of mishandled baggage, and fewest complaints per 100,000 passengers) for a single month.
1990	Revenues reach $1 billion; Southwest is the only major U.S. airline to record both an operating profit and a net profit.
1992	Southwest wins its first annual Triple Crown for best on-time record, best baggage handling, and fewest customer complaints; for the second year running, Southwest is the only major U.S. airline to record both an operating profit and a net profit.
1993	Southwest begins operations on the East Coast and wins its second annual Triple Crown; revenues exceed $2 billion, and profits exceed $100 million. For the third consecutive year, Southwest is the only major U.S. airline to record both an operating profit and a net profit.
1994	Southwest leads the industry by introducing ticketless travel in four cities; Southwest wins its third Triple Crown and acquires Morris Air, based in Salt Lake City.
1995	Ticketless travel becomes available systemwide; Southwest wins fourth consecutive Triple Crown.
1996	Service to Florida begins; Southwest wins fifth consecutive Triple Crown; Southwest and its employees contribute almost $740,000 to help support Ronald McDonald Houses, including $34,000 in cash donations from the company and $302,500 in free air travel for families staying at Ronald McDonald Houses in cities served by Southwest.
1997	Service begins to Southwest's 50th city; over 50 million people fly Southwest.
1998	Southwest is named by *Fortune* as the best company to work for in America.
1999	Service is added to three more cities.
2000	The number of passengers on Southwest flights exceeds 60 million, and revenues surpass the $5 billion mark; the company records its 28th consecutive year of profitability and ninth consecutive year of increased profits; Southwest becomes the fourth largest U.S. airline in terms of passengers carried.
2001	Southwest is profitable for the 30th consecutive year and the only U.S. airline to report a profit for 2001; a record 64.5 million passengers fly Southwest.
2002	Southwest is ranked second among companies across all industry groups, and first in the airline industry in *Fortune*'s 2002 list of America's Most Admired Companies.

The Start of the Herb Kelleher Era

When Lamar Muse resigned in 1978, Southwest's board wanted Herb Kelleher to take over as chairman and CEO. But Kelleher enjoyed practicing law and, while he agreed to become chairman of the board, he insisted that someone else be CEO. Southwest's board appointed Howard Putnam, a group vice president of marketing services at United Airlines, as Southwest's president and CEO in July 1978. Putnam asked Kelleher to become more involved in Southwest's day-to-day operations, and over the next three years Kelleher got to know many of the company's personnel and observe them in action. Putnam announced his resignation in the fall of 1981 to become president and chief operating officer at Braniff International. This time, Southwest's board succeeded in persuading Kelleher to take on the additional duties of CEO and president.

When Herb Kelleher took over in 1981, Southwest had 27 planes, $270 million in revenues, 2,100 employees, and flights to 14 cities. Over the next two decades, Southwest Airlines prospered, racking up many industry firsts and expanding geographically (see Exhibit 1). Going into 2003, Southwest was the fourth largest U.S. commercial airline in terms of passengers flown and the sixth largest in terms of revenues. It had

Exhibit 2   SUMMARY OF SOUTHWEST AIRLINES' FINANCIAL AND OPERATING PERFORMANCE, 1998–2002 (IN THOUSANDS EXCEPT PER SHARE AMOUNTS)

	2002	2001	2000	1999	1998
Financial Data					
Operating revenues	$5,521,771	$5,555,174	$5,649,560	$4,735,587	$4,163,980
Operating expenses	5,104,433	4,924,052	4,628,415	3,954,011	3,480,369
Operating income	417,338	631,122	1,021,145	781,576	683,611
Other expenses (income), net	24,656	(196,537)	3,781	7,965	(21,501)
Income before income taxes	392,682	827,659	1,017,364	773,611	705,112
Provision for income taxes	151,713	316,512	392,140	299,233	271,681
Net income	$ 240,969	$ 511,147	$625,224	$ 474,378	$ 433,431
Net income per share, basic	$0.31	$0.67	$0.84	$0.63	$0.58
Net income per share, diluted	$0.30	$0.63	$0.79	$0.59	$0.55
Cash dividends per share	$0.0180	$0.0180	$0.0147	$0.0143	$0.0126
Total assets at period-end	$8,953,750	$8,997,141	$6,669,572	$5,653,703	$4,715,996
Cash and cash equivalents at end of year	$1,815,352	$2,279,861	$522,995	$418,819	$378,511
Current assets at end of year	$2,231,960	$2,520,219	$831,536	$632,595	$574,155
Current liabilities at end of year	$1,433,828	$2,239,185	$1,298,403	$962,056	$850,653
Long-term obligations at end of year	$1,552,781	$1,327,158	$760,992	$871,717	$623,309
Stockholders' equity at end of year	$4,421,617	$4,014,053	$3,451,320	$2,835,788	$2,397,918
Operating Data					
Revenue passengers carried	63,045,988	64,446,773	63,678,261	57,500,213	52,586,400
Revenue passenger miles (000s)	45,391,903	44,493,916	42,215,162	36,479,322	31,419,110
Available seat miles (000s)	68,886,546	65,295,290	59,909,965	52,855,467	47,543,515
Load factor*	65.9%	68.1%	70.5%	69.0%	66.1%
Average passenger haul (miles)	720	690	663	634	597
Trips flown	947,331	940,426	903,754	846,823	806,822
Average passenger fare	$84.72	$83.46	$85.87	$79.35	$76.26
Passenger revenue per mile	11.77¢	12.09¢	12.95¢	12.51¢	12.76¢
Operating revenue per seat mile	8.02¢	8.51¢	9.43¢	8.96¢	8.76¢
Operating expenses per seat mile	7.41¢	7.54¢	7.73¢	7.48¢	7.32¢
Number of employees at year-end	33,705	31,580	29,274	27,653	25,844
Size of fleet at year-end†	375	355	344	312	280

*Revenue passenger miles divided by available seat miles.
†Includes leased aircraft.
Source: 2001 10K report and company press releases.

revenues in excess of $5 billion annually and 35,000 employees, and it operated 370 jets to 59 airports in 58 cities in 30 states. Southwest had been profitable every year since 1973—in an industry noted for its vulnerability to economic cycles and feast-or-famine profitability. During 1990–1994—when the airline industry had five straight money-losing years, laid off 120,000 employees, and lost a cumulative $13 billion—Southwest earned a profit every quarter of every year.

Exhibit 2 provides a five-year summary of Southwest's financial and operating performance. Exhibits 3 and 4 provide industrywide data on airline travel for the 1995–2002 period.

Exhibit 3   COMMERCIAL AIRLINE REVENUES, SCHEDULED REVENUE PASSENGER MILES,
             AND OVERALL LOAD FACTOR FOR MAJOR U.S. AIRLINE CARRIERS, 1995–2002

Year	Total Revenues	Scheduled Revenue Passenger Miles*	Operating Profit	Load Factor†
1995	$73.5 billion	509.6 billion	$4.92 billion	67.3%
1996	78.5	534.7	5.27	69.8
1997	83.5	570.0	7.52	70.8
1998	84.6	583.0	7.47	71.3
1999	89.6	616.8	6.00	71.4
2000	98.1	651.8	5.50	72.8
2001	85.4	606.7	(10.2)	70.3
2002	75.4	585.0	(9.6)	72.0

*Scheduled revenue passenger miles is the total number of miles flown by all passengers on all scheduled flights.

†Load factor is the total number of passengers boarded as a percentage of total seats available.

Source: *Airline Quarterly Financial Review, Majors*, Department of Transportation, Office of Aviation Analysis, Fourth Quarters 1995–2002.

Exhibit 4   OPERATING REVENUES OF THE MAJOR U.S. COMMERCIAL AIRLINES,
             1996–2002 (IN MILLIONS OF DOLLARS)

Airline	2002	2001	2000	1999	1998	1997	1996
American	$15,870.6	$15,638.8	$18,117.1	$16,085.5	$16,298.8	$15,855.8	$15,125.7
United[a]	13,915.6	16,087.4	19,331.3	17,966.7	17,517.5	17,335.2	16,316.7
Delta	12,410.4	13,211.2	15,320.9	14,901.4	14,629.8	14,203.9	13,317.7
Northwest	9,151.6	9,591.8	10,956.6	9,868.1	8,706.7	9,983.7	9,751.4
US Airways[b]	6,914.9	8,253.4	9,181.2	8,460.4	8,555.7	8,501.5	7,704.1
Continental	7,407.9	8,199.7	9,449.2	8,381.5	7,907.7	7,089.9	6,264.4
Southwest	5,521.8	5,555.2	5,649.6	4,735.6	4,164.0	3,817.0	3,407.4
TWA[c]	—	2,632.8	3,584.6	3,308.7	3,259.1	3,330.3	3,554.4
America West	2,021.0	2,305.5	2,309.3	2,164.0	1,983.0	1,887.1	1,751.8
Alaska	1,832.4	1,763.1	1,762.6	1,695.6	1,581.3	1,457.4	1,306.6

[a]Filed for Chapter 11 bankruptcy protection in December 2002.

[b]Filed for Chapter 11 bankruptcy protection in August 2002.

[c]Acquired by American Airlines in 2001; data for 2002 included in figures for American Airlines.

Source: *Airline Quarterly Financial Review, Majors*, Department of Transportation, Office of Aviation Analysis, Fourth Quarters 1995–2001 and Second Quarter 2002.

Herb Kelleher

Herb Kelleher majored in philosophy at Wesleyan University in Middletown, Connecticut, graduating with honors. He earned his law degree at New York University, again graduating with honors and also serving as a member of the law review. After graduation, he clerked for a New Jersey Supreme Court justice for two years and then joined a law firm in Newark. Upon marrying a woman from Texas and becoming enamored with Texas, he moved to San Antonio, where he became a successful lawyer and came to represent Rollin King's small aviation company.

When Herb Kelleher took on the role of Southwest's CEO in 1981, he made a point of visiting with maintenance personnel to check on how well the planes were running and of talking with the flight attendants. Kelleher did not do much managing from his office, preferring instead to be out among the troops as much as he could. His style was to listen, observe, and offer encouragement. Kelleher attended most graduation ceremonies of flight attendants from "Southwest University," and he often appeared to help load bags on "Black Wednesday," the busy travel day before Thanksgiving. He knew the names of thousands of Southwest employees, who held him in the highest regard. When he attended a Southwest employee function, he was swarmed like a celebrity.

Kelleher had an affinity for bold-print Hawaiian shirts, owned a tricked-out motorcycle, and made no secret of his love for drinking Wild Turkey whiskey and smoking. He loved to make jokes and engage in pranks and corporate antics, prompting some people to refer to him as the "clown prince" of the airline industry. He once appeared at a company gathering dressed in an Elvis costume and had arm-wrestled a South Carolina company executive at a public event in Dallas for rights to use "Just Plane Smart" as an advertising slogan.[7] Kelleher was well known inside and outside the company for his combativeness, particularly when it came to beating back competitors. On one occasion he reportedly told a group of veteran employees, "If someone says they're going to smack us in the face—knock them out, stomp them out, boot them in the ditch, cover them over, and move on to the next thing. That's the Southwest spirit at work."[8] On another occasion he said, "I love battles. I think it's part of the Irish in me. It's like what Patton said, 'War is hell and I love it so.' That's how I feel. I've never gotten tired of fighting."[9]

While Southwest was deliberately combative and flamboyant in some aspects of its operations, when it came to the financial side of the business Kelleher insisted on fiscal conservatism, a strong balance sheet, comparatively low levels of debt, and zealous attention to bottom-line profitability. While believing strongly in being prepared for adversity, Kelleher had an aversion to formal strategic plans, saying, "Reality is chaotic; planning is ordered and logical. The meticulous nit-picking that goes on in most strategic planning processes creates a mental straitjacket that becomes disabling in an industry where things change radically from one day to the next." Kelleher wanted Southwest managers to think ahead, have contingency plans, and be ready to act when it appeared that the future held significant risks or when new conditions suddenly appeared and demanded prompt responses.

Kelleher was a strong believer in the principle that employees—not customers—come first:

> You have to treat your employees like your customers. When you treat them right, then they will treat your outside customers right. That has been a very powerful competitive weapon for us. You've got to take the time to listen to people's ideas. If you just tell somebody no, that's an act of power and, in my opinion, an abuse of power. You don't want to constrain people in their thinking.[10]

Another indication of the importance that Kelleher placed on employees was the message he penned in 1990 and had prominently displayed in the lobby of Southwest's headquarters in Dallas:

The people of Southwest Airlines are "the creators" of what we have become—and of what we will be.

Our people transformed an idea into a legend. That legend will continue to grow only so long as it is nourished—by our people's indomitable spirit, boundless energy, immense goodwill, and burning desire to excel.

Our thanks—and our love—to the people of Southwest Airlines for creating a marvelous family and a wondrous airline.

Southwest Airlines' Strategy

From day one, Southwest had pursued a low-cost/low-price/no-frills strategy. Its signature low fares made air travel affordable to a wide segment of the U.S. population—giving substance to its tag line "The Freedom to Fly." Southwest was a shrewd practitioner of the concept of price elasticity, proving in one market after another that the revenue gains from increased ticket sales and the volume of passenger traffic would more than compensate for the revenue erosion from reduced fares. When Southwest entered the Florida market with an introductory $17 fare from Tampa to Fort Lauderdale, the number of annual passengers flying the Tampa–Fort Lauderdale route jumped 50 percent, to more than 330,000. In Manchester, New Hampshire, passenger counts went from 1.1 million in 1997, the year prior to Southwest's entry, to 3.5 million in 2000 and average one-way fares dropped from just over $300 to $129. Success in stimulating higher passenger traffic at airports across the United States via low fares and frequent flights had been dubbed the "Southwest effect" by personnel at the U.S. Department of Transportation.

The company designed its routes to stress flying between pairs of cities ranging anywhere from 150 to as much as 700 miles apart where there was high traffic potential and Southwest could offer a sizable number of flights. As a general rule, Southwest did not initiate service to an airport unless it envisioned the potential for originating at least eight flights a day there. Southwest's point-to-point route system, as opposed to the hub-and-spoke route systems of its rivals, minimized connections, delays, and total trip time—its emphasis on nonstop flights between about 350 pairs of cities allowed about 77 percent of Southwest's passengers to fly nonstop to their destination. Southwest's average aircraft trip in 2002 was 540 miles long and lasted approximately 1.5 hours. Exhibit 5 shows the cities and airports Southwest served in late 2002. Southwest was the dominant carrier at four airports (Baltimore/Washington, Las Vegas, Kansas City, and Chicago Midway) and the leading carrier in intrastate air travel in California, Texas, and Florida.

Southwest's Drive to Achieve Low Operating Costs

Southwest management fully understood that low fares necessitated zealous pursuit of low operating costs. The company had over the years instituted a number of practices to keep its costs below those of rival carriers:

- The company operated only one type of aircraft—Boeing 737s—to minimize the size of spare parts inventories, simplify the training of maintenance and repair personnel, improve the proficiency and speed with which maintenance routines could be done, and simplify the task of scheduling planes for particular flights. Further-

Exhibit 5   AIRPORTS AND CITIES SERVED BY SOUTHWEST AIRLINES, FALL 2002

Southwest's Top 10 Airports			
	Daily Departures	Number of Gates	Nonstop Cities Served
Phoenix	181	21	38
Las Vegas	171	19	42
Houston (Hobby)	141	15	24
Baltimore/Washington	139	17	33
Chicago (Midway)	130	14	29
Dallas (Love Field)	130	14	13
Oakland	123	13	19
Los Angeles	118	12	19
Nashville	86	10	28
San Diego	80	9	14

Other Airports Served by Southwest Airlines			
Albany	El Paso	Lubbock	Raleigh-Durham
Albuquerque	Fort Lauderdale	Manchester, NH	Reno/Tahoe
Amarillo	Harlingen/South Padre Island	Midland/Odessa	Sacramento
Austin	Hartford/Springfield	New Orleans	St. Louis
Birmingham	Houston (Hobby and Bush Intercontinental)	Norfolk	Salt Lake City
Boise	Indianapolis	Oklahoma City	San Antonio
Buffalo	Long Island/Islip	Omaha	San Jose
Burbank	Jackson, MS	Ontario, Canada	Seattle
Cleveland	Jacksonville	Orange County, CA	Spokane
Columbus, OH	Kansas City	Orlando	Tampa
Corpus Christi	Little Rock	Portland, OR	Tucson
Detroit (Metro)	Louisville	Providence	Tulsa
			West Palm Beach

Source: Southwest Airlines.

more, as the launch customer for Boeing's 737-300, 737-500, and 737-700 models, Southwest acquired its new aircraft at favorable prices. See Exhibit 6 for statistics on Southwest's aircraft fleet.

▪ Southwest encouraged customers to make reservations and purchase tickets at the company's website, thus bypassing the need to pay commissions to travel agents for handling the ticketing process and reducing the number of personnel needed to staff Southwest's nine reservation centers. Selling a ticket on its website cost Southwest roughly $1, versus $6–$8 for a ticket booked through a travel agent and $3–$4 for a ticket booked through its own internal reservation system. In January 2001, Southwest cut the commissions paid to travel agents to 8 percent of the price of an electronic ticket and 5 percent of the price of a paper ticket (down from 10 percent paid on both), with a commission cap of $60 for a round-trip ticket (either electronic or paper)—management estimated that the move would save the company $40 million in 2001. In 2000 about 30 percent of Southwest's revenue came from ticket sales through travel agents (versus 40 percent in 1998), and by

Exhibit 6   SOUTHWEST'S AIRCRAFT FLEET AS OF FALL 2002

Type of Aircraft	Number	Seats	Comments
Boeing 737-200	27	122	
Boeing 737-300	194	137	Southwest was Boeing's launch customer for this model
Boeing 737-500	25	122	Southwest was Boeing's launch customer for this model
Boeing 737-700	124	137	Southwest was Boeing's launch customer for this model

Other Facts

Average age of aircraft fleet—close to 9 years

Average aircraft trip length—540 miles; average duration—96 minutes

Average aircraft utilization in 2002—7.2 flights per day and about 12 hours of flight time

Fleet size—1990: 106; 1995: 224; 2000: 344; 2002: 370

Firm orders for new aircraft—2003: 21; 2004: 23; 2005: 24; 2006: 22; 2007: 25

year-end 2002 over 50 percent of ticket sales were occurring at the company's website. Ticketless travel accounted for more than 85 percent of all sales in 2002, which significantly reduced paperwork and back-office processing.

■ The company tried to steer clear of congested airports, stressing instead serving airports relatively near major metropolitan areas and in medium-sized cities. This helped produce better-than-average on-time performance and reduce the fuel costs associated with planes sitting in line on crowded taxiways or circling airports waiting for clearance to land; plus, it allowed the company to avoid paying the higher landing fees and terminal gate costs at such high-traffic airports like Atlanta's Hartsfield International, Chicago's O'Hare, Denver International, and Dallas–Fort Worth (DFW), where landing-slots were controlled and rationed to those airlines willing to pay the high fees. In several cases, Southwest was able to compete on the perimeters of several big metropolitan areas by flying into nearby airports with less congested air space. For example, Southwest drew some Boston-area passengers away from Boston's Logan International by initiating service into nearby Providence, Rhode Island, and Manchester, New Hampshire; similarly, it initiated flights into Islip, Long Island, which siphoned some passengers away from New York's LaGuardia and Kennedy International airports. Southwest's preference for less congested airports also helped minimize total travel time for passengers—driving to the airport, parking, ticketing, boarding, and flight time.

■ Southwest's point-to-point scheduling of flights was more cost-efficient than the hub-and-spoke systems used by rival airlines. Hub-and-spoke systems involved passengers on many different flights coming in from spoke locations (or perhaps another hub) to a central hub airport within a short span of time and then connecting with an outgoing flight to their destination—a spoke location or another hub. Most flights arrived and departed a hub across a two-hour window, creating big peak–valley swings in airport personnel workloads and gate utilization—airport personnel and gate areas were very busy when hub operations were in full swing and then were underutilized in the interval awaiting the next round of inbound/outbound flights. In contrast, Southwest's point-to-point routes permitted scheduling aircraft so as to minimize the time aircraft were at the gate—currently approximately 25 minutes—thereby reducing the number of aircraft and gate facilities that would otherwise be required. Furthermore, with a relatively even flow of incoming/outgoing flights and gate traffic, Southwest could staff its terminal operations to handle a fairly steady workload across a day, whereas hub-and-spoke operators had to staff their operations to serve peak-period requirements.

■ To economize on the amount of time it took terminal personnel to check passengers in and to simplify the whole task of making reservations, Southwest dispensed with the practice of assigning each passenger a reserved seat. Instead, for many years, passengers were given color-coded plastic cards with numbers on them when they checked in at the boarding gate. Passengers then boarded in groups of 30, according to the color and number on their card, sitting in whatever seat was open when they got on the plane—a procedure described by some as a "cattle call." Passengers who were particular about where they sat had to arrive at the gate early to get a low number on their boarding cards and then had to push up to the front when it was their group's turn to board. In 2002, Southwest streamlined the system further by simply printing a big, bold A, B, or C on the boarding pass when the passenger checked in at the ticket counter; passengers then boarded in groups according to the letter on their boarding pass.

■ Southwest flight attendants were responsible for cleaning up trash left by deplaning passengers and otherwise getting the plane presentable for passengers to board for the next flight. (Other carriers had cleaning crews come on board to perform this function.)

■ Southwest did not have a first-class section on any of its planes and had no fancy clubs for its frequent flyers to relax in at terminals. No meals were served on flights, even long ones; passengers were offered beverages and snacks—in 2002, Southwest provided passengers with 162.4 million packages of peanuts, 51.3 million packages of other snacks, 9.9 million alcoholic beverages, and 44.5 million cans of non-alcoholic beverages. Serving no meals made reprovisioning planes simple and quick.

■ Southwest offered passengers no baggage transfer services to other carriers—passengers with checked baggage who were connecting to other carriers to reach their destination were responsible for picking up their luggage at Southwest's baggage claim and then getting it to the check-in facilities of the connecting carrier. (Southwest booked tickets involving its own flights only; customers connecting to flights on other carriers had to book their connecting tickets through either travel agents or the connecting airline.)

■ In mid-2001 Southwest implemented use of new software that significantly decreased the time required to generate optimal crew schedules and help improve on-time performance.

■ Starting in 2001, Southwest began converting from cloth to leather seats; the team of Southwest employees who investigated the economics of the conversion concluded that an all-leather interior would be durable and easy to maintain, thus more than justifying the high initial costs.

Southwest's operating costs as a percentage of its revenues were consistently the lowest in the industry (see Exhibit 7). Exhibit 8 shows a detailed breakdown of Southwest's operating costs for the period 1995–2002.

Exhibit 7   COMPARATIVE OPERATING COST STATISTICS, MAJOR U.S. AIRLINES, 1995–SECOND QUARTER ENDING JUNE 30, 2002 (IN CENTS PER AVERAGE SEAT MILE)

Carrier	Year	Food	Salaries and Benefits	Aircraft Fuel and Oil	Commissions
American	1995	0.41¢	3.70¢	1.01¢	0.80¢
	2000	0.44	4.18	1.48	0.60
	2001	0.44	4.55	1.57	0.47
	2002*	0.40	4.97	1.33	0.35
Alaska	1995	0.31¢	2.60¢	1.07¢	0.55¢
	2000	0.29	3.53	1.76	0.38
	2001	0.31	3.81	1.45	0.35
	2002*	0.32	3.83	1.21	0.30
Continental	1995	0.22¢	2.45¢	1.11¢	0.74¢
	2000	0.28	3.30	1.62	0.54
	2001	0.27	3.44	1.39	0.37
	2002*	0.26	3.52	1.10	0.28
Delta	1995	0.26¢	3.25¢	1.11¢	0.85¢
	2000	0.27	3.73	1.27	0.42
	2001	0.28	4.10	1.20	0.36
	2002*	0.25	4.37	1.10	0.28
America West	1995	0.19¢	2.08¢	0.96¢	0.64¢
	2000	0.12	2.21	1.54	0.32
	2001	0.10	2.42	1.35	0.28
	2002*	0.06	2.36	1.09	0.19
Northwest	1995	0.28¢	3.47¢	1.24¢	0.93¢
	2000	0.29	3.65	1.80	0.61
	2001	0.27	4.15	1.73	0.45
	2002*	0.24	4.18	1.40	0.36
Southwest	**1995**	**0.02¢**	**2.56¢**	**1.01¢**	**0.39¢**
	2000	**0.03**	**2.99**	**1.38**	**0.30**
	2001	**0.03**	**3.01**	**1.29**	**0.18**
	2002*	**0.03**	**3.02**	**1.17**	**0.10**
United	1995	0.37¢	3.34¢	1.06¢	0.93¢
	2000	0.38	4.16	1.43	0.59
	2001	0.37	4.73	1.50	0.43
	2002*	0.35	4.87	1.21	0.32
US Airways	1995	0.25¢	4.93¢	1.04¢	0.90¢
	2000	0.28	5.35	1.72	0.51
	2001	0.28	5.62	1.56	0.39
	2002*	0.21	5.93	1.20	0.25

*Based on data for first six months of 2002 only.

Note: The big increases in the "other operating and maintenance expenses" category for 2001 and 2002 at several airlines (most notably United and US Airways) reflect special charges for the grounding and early retirement of aircraft and for employee severance expenses that were incurred in the aftermath of the September 11, 2001, terrorist attacks.

Source: U.S. Department of Transportation, Bureau of Transportation Statistics, Office of Airline Information, Form 41B, Form 41P, Form T100.

Landing Fees	Advertising	Other Operating and Maintenance Expenses	Total Operating Expenses	Rent and Leasing Fees
0.15¢	0.15¢	3.23¢	9.45¢	0.73¢
0.17	0.13	3.49	10.49	0.74
0.19	0.13	4.53	11.89	0.78
0.22	0.11	3.75	11.12	0.87
0.15¢	0.12¢	3.10¢	7.89¢	1.17¢
0.18	0.38	3.72	10.25	1.08
0.25	0.21	3.78	10.17	1.07
0.21	0.10	3.98	9.95	1.02
0.18¢	0.16¢	3.82¢	8.67¢	1.20¢
0.18	0.07	4.21	10.20	1.23
0.21	0.02	4.52	10.23	1.32
0.25	0.00	5.18	10.57	1.42
0.20¢	0.13¢	3.06¢	8.86¢	0.81¢
0.16	0.08	3.51	9.43	0.72
0.16	0.11	3.81	10.02	0.76
0.18	0.10	4.03	10.30	0.81
0.16¢	0.19¢	3.07¢	7.29¢	1.30¢
0.13	0.09	4.17	8.57	1.58
0.15	0.06	4.50	8.86	1.72
0.16	0.08	4.67	8.61	1.56
0.27¢	0.16¢	2.80¢	9.15¢	0.70¢
0.24	0.13	3.24	9.96	0.67
0.27	0.11	3.55	10.52	0.70
0.27	0.10	3.60	10.15	0.77
0.23¢	**0.27¢**	**2.61¢**	**7.09¢**	**0.71¢**
0.22	**0.26**	**2.55**	**7.72**	**0.55**
0.22	**0.24**	**2.51**	**7.48**	**0.54**
0.24	**0.22**	**2.58**	**7.36**	**0.55**
0.21¢	0.13¢	2.84¢	8.89¢	0.94¢
0.20	0.20	3.64	10.60	0.88
0.22	0.13	4.64	12.02	0.90
0.22	0.11	4.27	11.35	1.07
0.19¢	0.11¢	4.18¢	11.61¢	1.16¢
0.20	0.08	5.73	13.88	1.11
0.20	0.08	6.00	14.13	1.31
0.23	0.06	6.57	14.45	1.30

Exhibit 8   **TRENDS IN SOUTHWEST AIRLINE'S OPERATING EXPENSES PER AVERAGE SEAT MILE, 1995–2002**

Expense Category	2002	2001	2000	1999	1998	1997	1996	1995
Salaries, wages, and benefits	2.56¢	2.51¢	2.41¢	2.39¢	2.35¢	2.26¢	2.22¢	2.17¢
Employee retirement plans	.33	.33	.40	.36	.35	.30	.23	.23
Fuel and oil	1.11	1.18	1.34	.93	.82	1.11	1.19	1.01
Maintenance materials and repairs	.57	.61	.63	.70	.64	.58	.62	.60
Agency commissions	.08	.16	.27	.30	.33	.35	.35	.34
Aircraft rentals	.27	.29	.33	.38	.43	.45	.47	.47
Landing fees and other rentals	.50	.48	.44	.46	.45	.46	.46	.44
Depreciation	.52	.49	.47	.47	.47	.44	.45	.43
Other expenses	1.48	1.49	1.44	1.49	1.48	1.45	1.51	1.38
Total	7.41¢	7.54¢	7.73¢	7.48¢	7.32¢	7.40¢	7.50¢	7.07¢

Note: Figures in this exhibit differ slightly from those for Southwest in Exhibit 7 due to an assortment of differences in Southwest's internal accounting for its expenses and the Department of Transportation's expense category definitions and reporting for all commercial airlines.

Source: Company annual reports and 10-K reports.

Southwest's Focus on Customers and Customer Satisfaction

Southwest went all out to make sure passengers had a positive, fun flying experience. Gate personnel were cheery and witty, sometimes entertaining those in the gate area with trivia questions or contests such as "Who has the biggest hole in his or her sock?" Casually dressed flight attendants greeted passengers coming onto planes and offered friendly advice to customers looking for open seats. Flight attendants were encouraged to let their personalities show, to joke with passengers, and even to play gags. On some flights, attendants played harmonicas and sang announcements to passengers on take-off and landing. On one flight while passengers were boarding, an attendant with bunny ears popped out of an overhead bin exclaiming "Surprise!" The entertainment repertoires varied from flight crew to flight crew.

While Southwest had built up quite a reputation presenting a happy face to passengers and displaying a fun-loving attitude, the company had on occasion encouraged some of its not-so-pleasant customers to patronize other carriers. One woman who flew Southwest frequently became known as "Pen Pal" because she wrote in a complaint after almost every flight; her complaints were eventually bumped up to Herb Kelleher, who quickly penned a short note: "Dear Mrs. Crabapple, We will miss you. Love Herb."[11] Kelleher made a point of sending congratulatory notes to those employees customers singled out in complimentary letters; complaint letters were seen as learning opportunities for employees and reasons to consider making adjustments. Colleen Barrett, Southwest's president, had articulated the company's policy some years earlier:

> No Employee will ever be punished for using good judgment and good old common sense when trying to accommodate a Customer—no matter what our rules are. Let's start leaning towards our Customers again—not away from them. Let's start encouraging our line employees to be a little more flexible and to take that extra minute to accommodate special needs. Let's start encouraging our Supervisors to give our Customers the benefit of the doubt.[12]

Southwest was convinced that conveying the Southwest spirit to customers was the key to competitive advantage; as one Southwest manager put it, "Our fares can be matched; our airplanes and routes can be copied. But we pride ourselves on our customer service."[13]

Marketing and Promotion

Southwest was continually on the lookout for novel ways to tell its story, make its distinctive persona come alive, and strike a chord in the minds of air travelers. Many of its ads and billboards were deliberately unconventional and attention-getting so as to create and reinforce the company's maverick, fun-loving, and combative image. Others promoted the company's performance as "The Low-Fare Airline" or "The All-Time On-Time Airline"; still others highlighted its Triple Crown awards. Exhibit 9 provides four sample ads. One of the company's billboard campaigns touted the frequency of the company's flights with such phrases as "Austin Auften," "Phoenix Phrequently," and "L.A. A.S.A.P." Each holiday season since 1985, Southwest had run a "Christmas card" ad on TV featuring children and their families from the Ronald McDonald Houses and Southwest employees.

From time to time Southwest ran special fare promotions. To celebrate its 30th anniversary in 2001, Southwest announced special $30 one-way fares to 30 destinations from 35 cities for travel between June 25 and October 26; Southwest's car rental and hotel partners participated in the promotion, offering $30-a-day rentals, $30-off discounts, and $30-a-day hotel rooms at some locations. The 30-year celebration also included decorations in gate areas, prize giveaways, and employees playing games in the gate areas so that customers could share in the "Southwest Spirit." Along with most other airlines in 2002, Southwest featured a series of special fare promotions to stimulate ticket sales and fill up otherwise empty seats.

In 2002 Southwest began changing the look of its planes, updating its somewhat drab gold/orange/red scheme to a much fresher and brighter canyon blue/red/gold/orange scheme (see Exhibit 10).

Other Strategy Elements

Southwest's strategy included several other components:

- *A fare structure that was consistently the simplest and most straightforward of any of the major U.S. airlines.* All of Southwest's different fare options could easily be perused at the company's website, and the company's restrictions on tickets were more lenient than those of its rivals.

- *Gradual expansion into new geographic markets.* Southwest generally added one or two new cities to its route schedule annually, preferring to saturate the market for daily flights to the cities/airports it currently served before entering new markets. In selecting new cities, Southwest looked for city pairs that could generate substantial amounts of both business and leisure traffic. Management believed that lots of flights were appealing to business travelers looking for convenient flight times and the ability to catch a later flight if they unexpectedly ran late.

- *Adding flights in areas where rivals were cutting back service.* When rivals cut back flights to cities that Southwest served, Southwest often moved in with more flights of its own, believing its lower fares would attract more passengers. When Midway Airlines ceased operations in November 1990, Southwest moved in

Exhibit 9   Four Sample Southwest Ads

WE CAME. WE SAW. WE KICKED TAIL.

Make that, tails.
Head-to-head against all the major airlines in America, Southwest Airlines just won the first annual Triple Crown ever.
Number One in On-time Performance, Number One in Baggage Handling and

Number One in Customer Satisfaction for all of 1992. How can an airline that specializes in low fares deliver such a consistently high level of Customer Service? Simple. We care!
Southwest Airlines. Number One and still climbing.

SOUTHWEST AIRLINES
Just Plane Smart.

After lengthy deliberation
at the highest executive levels,
and extensive consultation
with our legal department,
we have arrived at
an official corporate response
to Northwest Airlines' claim
to be number one
in Customer Satisfaction.

"Liar, liar. Pants on fire."

SOUTHWEST AIRLINES
Just Plane Smart.
1-800-I-FLY-SWA (1-800-435-9792)

WE'D LIKE TO MATCH THEIR NEW FARES, BUT WE'D HAVE TO RAISE OURS.

No matter what the competition may come up with, Southwest Airlines' everyday low unrestricted fares are still lower than the Big Three. That's a fact that can save you a lot of money every day.
And unlike our competitors, with our low unrestricted fares, we don't charge you a penalty when your plans change. Which makes our fares the smart choice for you and your company. Always have been. Always will be.

SOUTHWEST AIRLINES
Just Plane Smart.
1-800-I-FLY-SWA
(1-800-435-9792)

CAN YOU NAME THE AIRLINE WITH LOW FARES ON EVERY SEAT OF EVERY FLIGHT, EVERYWHERE IT FLIES?

SOUTHWEST®
THE *Low Fare Airline*℠

Exhibit 10   Southwest's New Look

Old   **New**

overnight and quickly instituted flights to Chicago's Midway Airport. When American Airlines closed its hubs in Nashville and San Jose, Southwest immediately increased the number of its flights into and out of both locations. During the first half of 2002, as air traffic showed some signs of picking up, Southwest was a first-mover in adding flights on routes where rivals had cut their offerings following the September 11, 2001, terrorist attacks.

- *An attractive frequent flyer program.* Southwest's Rapid Rewards members received a free round-trip ticket, good for travel anywhere on Southwest's system for up to one year, after purchasing and flying eight round-trips. There were no restrictions on the number of free Rapid Rewards seats on a particular flight and very few blackout dates around holidays. Southwest was considered to have the most generous frequent flyer program in the industry, winning awards for best award redemption, best bonus promotion, and best customer service among all frequent flyer programs.

- *Adding longer nonstop flights to the route system.* Although over 85 percent of Southwest's flights involved actual in-air flight times of less than 90 minutes, the company was judiciously adding nonstop flights to more distant destinations at those airports where its classic low fares could generate sufficient passenger traffic to achieve high enough load factors and revenues to be profitable. Most of the flights that the company added in 2002 were longer than 750 miles.

- *Putting strong emphasis on safety, high-quality maintenance, and reliable operations.* In the 31 years it had been flying, Southwest had never had a plane crash. Southwest had one of the most extensive and thorough maintenance programs in the commercial airline industry. The company's state-of-the-art flight dispatch system helped minimize weather and operational delays.

According to Southwest management, the company's strategy of low-cost, no-frills flights and reliable, friendly service delivered "more value for less money" to customers rather than "less value for less money." Kelleher said, "Everybody values a very good service provided at a very reasonable price."[14]

Southwest's People Management Practices and Culture

Whereas the litany at many companies was that customers come first, at Southwest the operative principle was that "employees come first and customers come second." The importance placed on employees reflected management's belief that delivering superior service required employees who not only were passionate about their jobs but also knew the company was genuinely concerned for their well-being and committed to providing them with job security. Southwest's thesis was simple: Keep employees happy—then they will keep customers happy.

What Southwest management thought about the importance of Southwest's people and their role is reflected in the following excerpt from the company's 2000 annual report:

> Our people are warm, caring and compassionate, and willing to do whatever it takes to bring the Freedom to Fly to their fellow Americans. They take pride in doing well for themselves by doing good for others. They have built a unique and powerful culture that demonstrates that the only way to accomplish our mission to make air travel affordable for others, while ensuring ample profitability, job security, and plentiful Profitsharing for ourselves, is to keep our costs low and Customer Service quality high.
>
> At Southwest, our People are our greatest assets, which is why we devote so much time and energy to hiring great People with winning attitudes. Because we are well known as an excellent place to work with great career opportunities and a secure future, lots of People want to work for Southwest. . . . Once hired, we provide a nurturing and supportive work environment that gives our Employees the freedom to be creative, have fun, and make a positive difference. Although we offer competitive compensation packages, it's our Employees' sense of ownership, pride in team accomplishments, and enhanced job satisfaction that keep our Culture and Southwest Spirit alive and why we continue to produce winning seasons.

The company changed the personnel department's name to the People Department in 1989.

Recruiting, Screening, and Hiring

Southwest hired employees for attitude and trained for skills. Kelleher explained:

> We can train people to do things where skills are concerned. But there is one capability we do not have and that is to change a person's attitude. So we prefer an unskilled person with a good attitude. . . [to] a highly skilled person with a bad attitude.[15]

Management believed that delivering superior service came from having employees who genuinely believed that customers were important and that treating them warmly and courteously was the right thing to do, not from training employees to *act* like customers are important. The belief at Southwest was that superior, hospitable service and a fun-loving spirit flowed from the heart and soul of employees who themselves were fun-loving and spirited, who liked their jobs and the company they worked for, and who were also confident and empowered to do their jobs as they saw fit (rather than being governed by strict rules and procedures).

Southwest recruited employees by means of newspaper ads, career fairs, and Internet job listings; a number of candidates applied because of Southwest's *Fortune* listings as one of the best companies to work for in America and because they were impressed by their experiences as a customer on Southwest flights. Recruitment ads were designed to capture the attention of people thought to possess Southwest's "personality profile." For instance, one ad showed Herb Kelleher impersonating Elvis Presley and read as follows:

> Work In A Place Where Elvis Has Been Spotted. The qualifications? It helps to be outgoing. Maybe even a bit off center. And be prepared to stay for a while. After all, we have the lowest employee turnover rate in the industry. If this sounds good to you, just phone our jobline or send your resume. Attention Elvis.[16]

All job applications were processed through the People Department.

Screening Candidates   In hiring for jobs that involved personal contact with passengers, the company looked for people-oriented applicants who were extroverted and had a good sense of humor. It tried to identify candidates with a knack for reading people's emotions and responding in a genuinely caring, empathetic manner. Southwest wanted employees to deliver the kind of service that showed they truly enjoyed meeting people, being around passengers, and doing their job, as opposed to delivering the kind of service that came across as being forced or taught. According to Kelleher, "We are interested in people who externalize, who focus on other people, who are motivated to help other people. We are not interested in navel gazers."[17] Southwest was drawn to candidates who, in addition to having a "whistle while you work" attitude, appeared likely to exercise initiative, work harmoniously with fellow employees, and be community spirited.

Southwest did not use personality tests to screen candidates, nor did it ask candidates what they would or should do in certain hypothetical situations. Rather, the hiring staff at Southwest analyzed each job category to determine the specific behaviors, knowledge, and motivations that job holders needed and then tried to find candidates with the desired traits—a process called targeted selection. A trait common to all job categories was teamwork; a trait deemed critical for pilots and flight attendants was judgment. In exploring an applicant's aptitude for teamwork, interviewers often asked applicants to tell them about a time in a prior job when they went out of their way to help a coworker or to explain how they had handled conflict with a coworker. Another frequent question was "What was your most embarrassing moment?" Southwest believed that having applicants talk about their past behaviors provided good clues about their future behaviors.

To test for unselfishness, Southwest interviewing teams typically gave a group of potential employees ample time to prepare five-minute presentations about themselves; during the presentations, which took place in an informal conversational setting, interviewers watched the audience to see who was absorbed in polishing their own presentations and who was listening attentively, enjoying the stories being told, and applauding the efforts of the presenters. Those who were emotionally engaged in hearing the presenters and giving encouragement were deemed more apt to be team players than those who were focused on looking good themselves. All applicants for flight attendant positions were put through such a presentation exercise before an interview panel consisting of customers, experienced flight attendants, and members of the People Department. Flight attendant candidates who got through the group presentation interviews then had to complete a three-on-one interview conducted by a recruiter, a supervisor from the hiring section of the People Department, and a Southwest flight attendant; following this interview, the three-person panel tried to reach a consensus on whether to recommend or drop the candidate.

In 2002, the company reviewed 243,657 résumés and hired 5,042 new employees.

Training

Apart from the Federal Aviation Administration's mandated training for certain employees, training activities at Southwest were designed and conducted by Southwest's University for People, a part of the company's People Department. The curriculum included courses for new recruits, employees, and leadership training programs for both new and experienced managers. Leadership courses emphasized a management style based on coaching and encouraging, rather than supervising or enforcing rules and regulations. All employees who came into contact with customers, including pilots, received customer care training. There were also courses on safety, communications, stress management, career development, performance appraisal, decision making, and employee relations. From time to time supervisors and executives attended courses on corporate culture that were intended to help instill, ingrain, and nurture such cultural themes as teamwork, trust, harmony, and diversity.

Depending on the influx of new employees, orientation courses were conducted two to five times a week for between 20 and 100 new recruits. The orientation program included videos on Southwest's history, an overview of the airline industry and the competitive challenges that Southwest faced, and an introduction to Southwest's culture and management practices. One of the program's highlights was a video called the *Southwest Shuffle,* which featured hundreds of Southwest employees rapping about the fun they had on their jobs. Orientation programs at the Dallas headquarters typically included exercises designed to demonstrate the role of creativity and teamwork and a scavenger hunt in which new hires were given a time line with specific dates in Southwest's history and were asked to fill in the missing details by viewing the memorabilia decorating the corridors and getting information from people working in various offices. Much of the indoctrination of new employees into the company's culture was done by coworkers and the employee's supervisor. Southwest made active use of a one-year probationary employment period to help ensure that new employees fit in with its culture and adequately embraced the company's cultural values.

One of Southwest's supervisory training programs involved three teams; one member of each team was blindfolded and asked to throw a ball into a bucket. Unknown to the throwers, the other members on one team could say nothing about where the bucket was, members of the second team were instructed to say only "Good job" or "Keep trying," and the third group was allowed to give its thrower detailed information about where the bucket was. Not surprisingly, the third group's thrower had the most success—an outcome that was intended to demonstrate the value of good coaching on the part of supervisors and good listening on the part of supervisees.

Promotion

Approximately 80 to 90 percent of Southwest's supervisory positions were filled internally, reflecting management's belief that people who had "been there and done that" would be the ones most likely to appreciate and understand the demands that people under them were experiencing—and also most likely to enjoy the respect of their peers and higher-level managers. Employees could either apply for supervisory positions or be recommended by their present supervisor. New appointees for low-level management positions attended a three-day "Leading with Integrity" class aimed at developing leadership and communication skills. Employees being considered for managerial positions of large operations (Up and Coming Leaders) received training in every department of the company over a six-month period in which they continued to perform their current job. At the end of the six-month period, candidates were provided with 360-degree feedback from department heads, peers, and subordinates; representatives of the People Department analyzed the feedback in deciding on the specific assignment of each candidate.[18]

Compensation

Southwest's pay scales were at levels close to the industry average and its benefit packages were good relative to other airlines. According to a 1997–98 survey, Southwest's pilots earned, on average, about 10 percent above the industry average; however, they flew an average of 85 hours per month versus an industry average of 80.2 hours.

Southwest introduced a profit-sharing plan for senior employees in 1973, the first such plan in the airline industry. By the mid-1990s the plan had been extended to cover most Southwest employees. As of 2001, Southwest had 12 different stock option programs for various employee groups, a 401(k) employee savings plan that included company-matching contributions, and a profit-sharing plan that covered virtually all employees and consisted of a money purchase defined contribution plan and an employee stock purchase plan. Company contributions to employee 410(k) and profit-sharing plans totaled $167.1 million in 1998, $192.0 million in 1999, $241.5 million in 2000, $214.6 million in 2001, and $155.6 million in 2002. In recent years, these payments had represented 8 to 12 percent of base pay. Employees participating in stock purchases via payroll deduction bought 1 million shares in 2000; 1 million shares in 2001; and 1.4 million shares in 2002—at prices equal to 90 percent of the market value at each payroll period. Southwest employees owned about 10 percent of Southwest's outstanding shares and held options to buy some 138 million additional shares over the next 10 years.

Employee Relations

About 80 percent of Southwest's 35,000 employees belonged to a union, making it one of the most highly unionized U.S. airlines. The Teamsters Union represented Southwest's airline mechanics, stock clerks, and aircraft cleaners; the Transport Workers Union (TWU) represented flight attendants; Local 555 of the TWU represented baggage handlers, ground crews, and provisioning employees; and the International Association of Machinists represented the customer service and reservation employees. There was one in-house union—the Southwest Airline Pilots Association, which represented pilots. Despite having sometimes spirited disagreements over particular issues, Southwest's relationships with the unions representing its employee groups were for the most part harmonious and nonadversarial—the company had experienced only one brief strike by machinists in the early 1980s.

Management encouraged union members and negotiators to research their pressing issues and to conduct employee surveys before each contract negotiation. Southwest's contracts with the unions representing its employees were relatively free of restrictive work rules and narrow job classifications that might impede worker productivity. All of the contracts allowed any qualified employee to perform any function—thus, pilots, ticket agents, and gate personnel could help load and unload baggage when needed and flight attendants could pick up trash and make flight cabins more presentable for passengers boarding the next flight.

In 2000–2001 the company had contentious negotiations with Local 555 of the TWU (representing about 5,300 Southwest employees) over a new wage and benefits package; the previous contract had become open for renegotiation in December 1999, and a tentative agreement reached at the end of 2000 was rejected by 64 percent of the union members who voted. A memo from Kelleher to TWU representatives said, "The cost and structure of the TWU 555 negotiating committee's proposal would seriously undermine the competitive strength of Southwest Airlines; endanger our ability to grow; threaten the value of our employees' profit-sharing; require us to contract out work in order to remain competitive; and threaten our 29-year history of job security for our employees." In a union newsletter in early 2001, the president of the TWU said, "We asked for a decent living wage and benefits to support our families, and were told of how unworthy and how greedy we were." The ongoing dispute resulted in informational picket lines in March 2001 at several Southwest locations, the first picketing since 1980. Later in 2001, with the help of the National Mediation Board, Southwest and the TWU reached an agreement covering Southwest's ramp, operations, and provisioning employees.

Prior to September 11, 2001, Southwest's pilots were somewhat restive about their base pay relative to pilots at other U.S. airlines. The maximum pay for Southwest's 3,700-plus pilots (before profit-sharing bonuses) was $148,000, versus maximums of $290,000 for United's pilots; $262,000 for Delta's pilots; $206,000 for American's pilots; and $199,000 for Continental's pilots.[19] Moreover, some veteran Southwest employees were grumbling about staff shortages in certain locations (to hold down labor costs) and cracks in the company's close-knit family culture due to the influx of so many new employees over the past several years. A number of employees who had accepted lower pay because of Southwest's underdog status were said to feel entitled to "big airline" pay now that Southwest had emerged as a major U.S. carrier.[20]

The No-Layoff Policy

Southwest Airlines had never laid off or furloughed any of its employees since the company began operations in 1971. The company's no-layoff policy was seen as integral both to how the company treated its employees and to management efforts to sustain and nurture the culture. According to Kelleher,

> Nothing kills your company's culture like layoffs. Nobody has ever been furloughed here, and that is unprecedented in the airline industry. It's been a huge strength of ours. It's certainly helped negotiate our union contracts. . . . We could have furloughed at various times and been more profitable, but I always thought that was shortsighted. You want to show your people you value them and you're not going to hurt them just to get a little more money in the short term. Not furloughing people breeds loyalty. It breeds a sense of security. It breeds a sense of trust.[21]

Southwest had built up considerable goodwill with its unions over the years by avoiding layoffs.

Management Style

At Southwest, management strived to do things in a manner that would make Southwest employees proud of the company and its workforce practices. Managers were expected to spend at least one-third of their time out of the office, walking around the facilities under their supervision, observing firsthand what was going on, listening to employees and being responsive to their concerns. A former director of people development at Southwest told of a conversation he had with one of Southwest's terminal managers:

> While I was out in the field visiting one of our stations, one of our managers mentioned to me that he wanted to put up a suggestion box. I responded by saying, "Sure—why don't you put up a suggestion box right here on this wall and then admit you are a failure as a manager?" Our theory is, if you have to put up a box so people can write down their ideas and toss them in, it means you are not doing what you are supposed to be doing. You are supposed to be setting your people up to be winners. To do that, you should be there listening to them and available to them in person, not via a suggestion box. For the most part, I think we have a very good sense of this at Southwest. I think that most people employed here know that they can call any one of our vice presidents on the telephone and get heard, almost immediately.
>
> The suggestion box gives managers an out; it relinquishes their responsibility to be accessible to their people, and that's when we have gotten in trouble at Southwest—when we can no longer be responsive to our flight attendants or customer service agents, when they can't gain access to somebody who can give them resources and answers.[22]

Company executives were very approachable, insisting on being called by their first names. At new employee orientations, people were told, "We do not call the company chairman Mr. Kelleher; we call him Herb." Managers and executives had an open-door policy, actively listening to employee concerns, opinions, and suggestions for reducing costs and improving efficiency.

Employee-led initiatives were common. Southwest's pilots had been instrumental in developing new protocols for takeoffs and landings that conserved fuel. Another frontline employee had suggested not putting the company logos on trash bags, saving an estimated $250,000 annually. Rather than buy 800 computers for a new reservations center in Albuquerque, company employees determined that they could buy the parts and assemble the PCs themselves for half the price of a new PC, saving the company $1 million. It was Southwest clerks who came up with the idea of doing away with paper tickets and shifting to e-tickets.

There were only four layers of management between a frontline supervisor and the CEO. Southwest's employees enjoyed substantial authority and decision-making power. According to Kelleher:

> We've tried to create an environment where people are able to, in effect, bypass even the fairly lean structures that we have so that they don't have to convene a meeting of the sages in order to get something done. In many cases, they can just go ahead and do it on their own. They can take individual responsibility for it and know they will not be crucified if it doesn't work out. Our leanness requires people to be comfortable in making their own decisions and undertaking their own efforts.[23]

From time to time, there were candid meetings of frontline employees and managers where operating problems and issues between or among workers and departments were acknowledged, openly discussed, and resolved.[24] Informal problem avoidance and rapid problem resolution were seen as managerial virtues.

Southwest's Core Values

Two core values—LUV and fun—permeated the work environment at Southwest. LUV was much more than the company's ticker symbol or a recurring theme in Southwest's advertising campaigns. Over the years, *LUV* grew into Southwest's code word for treating individuals—fellow employees and customers—with dignity and respect and demonstrating a caring, loving attitude. The word *LUV* and red hearts commonly appeared on banners and posters at company facilities, as reminders of the compassion that was expected toward customers and other employees. Practicing the Golden Rule, internally and externally, was expected of all employees. Employees who had to struggle to live up to these expectations were subjected to considerable peer pressure and usually were asked to seek employment elsewhere if they did not soon leave of their own volition.

Fun at Southwest meant exactly what the word implies. Fun occurred throughout the company in the form of the generally entertaining behavior of employees in performing their jobs, the ongoing pranks and jokes, and frequent company-sponsored parties and celebrations. On holidays, employees were encouraged to dress in costumes. There were charity benefit games, chili cook-offs, Halloween parties, new Ronald McDonald House dedications, and other special events of one kind or another at one location or another almost every week. According to one manager, "We're kind of a big family here, and family members have fun together."

The Culture Committee

Southwest formed a Culture Committee in 1990 to promote "Positively Outrageous Service" and devise tributes, contests, and celebrations intended to nurture and perpetuate the "Southwest Spirit." The committee, chaired by Colleen Barrett, was composed of up to 100 employees representing a cross-section of departments and locations; members served a two-year term. Members, chosen for their zeal in exhibiting the Southwest Spirit and their commitment to Southwest's mission and values, functioned as cultural ambassadors, missionaries, and storytellers. The committee had four all-day meetings annually; ad hoc subcommittees, formed throughout the year, met more frequently. Over the years, the committee had sponsored and supported hundreds of ways to promote and ingrain the Southwest Spirit, with members showing up at a facility to serve pizza or ice cream to employees or to remodel and decorate an employee break room. Kelleher indicated, "We're not big on committees at Southwest, but of the committees we do have, the Culture Committee is the most important."[25]

Efforts to Nurture the Southwest Culture   Apart from the Culture Committee, Southwest reinforced its core values and culture via such efforts as a Co-Hearts mentoring program; a Day in the Field program, in which employees spent time working in another area of the company's operations; a Helping Hands program, in which volunteers from around the system traveled to work two weekend shifts at other Southwest facilities that were temporarily shorthanded or experiencing heavy workloads; and periodic Culture Exchange meetings to celebrate the Southwest Spirit and company milestones. Almost every event at Southwest was videotaped, which provided footage for creating such multipurpose videos as *Keepin' the Spirit Alive* that could be used in training courses and shown at company events all over the system. Many of the committee's activities revolved around promoting the use of red hearts and the word *LUV* to embody the spirit of Southwest employees caring about each other and Southwest's customers. The concepts of LUV and fun were spotlighted in all of the company's training manuals and videos. There was an annual "Heros of the Heart Award."

Southwest's monthly newsletter, *LUV Lines*, often spotlighted the experiences and deeds of particular employees, reprinted letters of praise from customers, and reported company celebrations of milestones. A quarterly news video, *As the Plane Turns*, was sent to all facilities to keep employees up-to-date on company happenings, provide clips of special events, and share messages from customers, employees, and executives. The company had published a book for employees describing "outrageous" acts of service. Sometimes important information was circulated to employees in "fun" packages such as Cracker Jack boxes.

Southwest executives believed that the company's growth was primarily a function of the rate at which it could hire and train people to fit into its culture and mirror the Southwest Spirit. With about 150 cities annually petitioning Southwest to initiate service to their airports, management believed that the company's growth was not constrained by a lack of market opportunities to expand into other geographic locations. About 15,000 of Southwest's 35,000 employees had been hired since 1995.

Employee Productivity

Management was convinced that the company's strategy, culture, esprit de corps, and people management practices fostered high labor productivity and contributed to Southwest's low labor costs compared to other airlines (see Exhibit 7). When a Southwest flight pulled up to the gate, ground crews, gate personnel, and flight attendants hustled to perform all the tasks requisite to turn the plane quickly—employees took pride in doing their part to achieve good on-time performance. Southwest's average turnaround times were about two-thirds the industry average. One study found that Southwest had an average of 2.2 station personnel per 1,000 passengers in 1994 versus an industry average of about 4.2.[26] According to the Air Transport Association, labor costs were the airlines' biggest cost component, accounting for 38 percent of operating costs in 2002; the average airline employee had an estimated cost of $75,200 in 2002, including pension, payroll taxes, health care, and insurance benefits. In 2000, Southwest's labor productivity compared favorably with the average of its eight biggest U.S. rivals:

Productivity Measure	Southwest	Average of Southwest's Eight Largest U.S. Rivals
Passengers enplaned per employee	2,145	1,119
Employees per plane	83.4	121.7

Awards, Recognition, and Operating Performance Comparisons

Southwest's strategy and approaches to conducting its business had resulted in numerous awards over the years. Southwest ranked number one in customer satisfaction

Exhibit 11   ON-TIME FLIGHTS, MISHANDLED BAGGAGE, OVERSALES, AND PASSENGER COMPLAINTS FOR MAJOR U.S. AIRLINES, 1998–2002

Percentage of Scheduled Flights Arriving within 15 Minutes of the Scheduled Time

Carrier	Jan.–Sept. 2002	2001	2000	1999	1998
Alaska Airlines	75.8%	69.0%	68.1%	71.0%	72.0%
America West	78.5	74.8	65.5	69.5	68.5
American	78.9	75.9	72.9	73.5	80.1
Continental	78.7	80.7	78.1	76.6	77.3
Delta	77.5	78.0	75.3	78.0	79.6
Northwest	79.7	79.7	77.4	79.9	70.6
Southwest	82.3	81.7	75.2	80.0	80.8
TWA*	—	80.8	76.9	80.9	78.3
United	75.5	73.5	61.4	74.4	73.8
US Airways	78.4	78.2	72.3	71.4	78.9

Mishandled Baggage Reports per 1,000 Passengers

Carrier	Jan.–Sept. 2002	2001	2000	1999	1998
Alaska Airlines	2.68	3.00	3.48	5.75	7.27
America West	3.47	4.22	6.62	4.52	3.88
American	4.32	4.60	5.50	5.21	4.40
Continental	3.06	4.29	5.35	4.42	4.06
Delta	3.61	4.11	4.49	4.39	4.27
Northwest	4.79	4.19	5.24	4.81	6.63
Southwest	3.54	4.77	5.00	4.22	4.53
TWA*	—	6.35	6.06	5.38	5.39
United	3.69	5.07	6.57	7.01	7.79
US Airways	3.01	3.86	4.76	5.08	4.09

among U.S. major airlines every year from 1991 though 2000. In *Fortune* magazine surveys, Southwest had been ranked as the most admired airline in the world every year since 1997. In 1998, *Fortune* named Southwest number 1 in its listing of the 100 best companies to work for in America; Southwest was ranked number 4 in 1999, number 2 in 2000, and number 4 in 2001—the company elected not to go through the screening process for the awards given out in early 2002. Southwest's website had won top awards from both *Business Week* and *PC Magazine.* In 2001, *Business Ethics* included Southwest Airlines on its "100 Best Corporate Citizens" list.

Exhibit 11 provides comparative statistics on Southwest's performance versus that of other major commercial airlines during the 1998–2002 period.

Exhibit 11   Continued

Involuntary Denied Boardings per 10,000 Passengers Due to Oversold Flights					
Carrier	Jan.–Sept. 2002	2001	2000	1999	1998
Alaska Airlines	1.24	1.36	1.53	0.99	1.49
America West	0.21	0.38	1.27	1.38	1.12
American	0.22	0.36	0.44	0.42	0.42
Continental	0.93	1.51	1.44	0.28	0.13
Delta	0.87	0.77	0.34	1.98	1.24
Northwest	0.53	0.45	0.43	0.20	0.33
Southwest	1.06	1.50	1.84	1.40	1.84
TWA*	—	1.83	2.76	0.88	1.69
United	0.65	0.92	1.64	0.69	0.59
US Airways	0.26	0.34	0.67	0.57	0.23

Complaints per 100,000 Passengers Boarded					
Carrier	Jan.–Sept. 2002	2001	2000	1999	1998
Alaska Airlines	1.02	1.27	2.04	1.64	0.54
America West	1.88	3.72	7.51	3.72	2.11
American	1.41	2.51	3.54	3.49	1.14
Continental	1.46	2.23	2.84	2.62	1.02
Delta	1.51	2.16	2.01	1.81	0.79
Northwest	1.60	1.97	2.61	2.92	2.21
Southwest	0.37	0.38	0.47	0.40	0.25
TWA*	—	2.54	3.47	3.44	1.29
United	1.90	3.24	5.3	2.65	1.28
US Airways	1.24	1.87	2.59	3.13	0.84

*Acquired by American Airlines in 2001; TWA data for 2002 included in American Airlines statistics.

Source: Office of Aviation Enforcement and Proceedings, *Air Travel Consumer Report*, multiple issues.

Southwest's New Leadership Team

In June 2001 Southwest Airlines, responding to anxious investor concerns about the company's leadership succession plans, began an orderly transfer of power and responsibilities from its longtime CEO and cofounder, Herb Kelleher, age 70, to two of his most trusted protégés. James F. Parker, 54, Southwest's general counsel, was elevated to CEO. Colleen Barrett, 56, Southwest's executive vice president of customers and self-described keeper of Southwest's pep-rally corporate culture, became president and chief operating officer. Kelleher stayed on as chairman of Southwest's board of directors and the head of the board's executive committee and continued to be in charge of strategy, expansion to new cities and aircraft scheduling, and governmental and industry affairs; his contract called for him to remain in those roles through December 2003 at an annual salary of $450,000, plus bonuses and stock options. Many observers and longtime employees did not expect Kelleher to ever fully remove himself from management of the company as long as his health held up—Kelleher had undergone treatment for prostate cancer in 1999.

James Parker

Southwest's new CEO, James Parker, had an association with Herb Kelleher going back 23 years to the time when they were colleagues at Kelleher's old law firm. Parker moved over to Southwest from the law firm in February 1986. Parker's profile inside the company as Southwest's vice president and general counsel had been relatively low, but he was Southwest's chief labor negotiator and much of the credit for Southwest's good relations with employee unions belonged to him. Prior to his appointment as CEO, Parker had been a member of the company's executive planning committee; his experiences ranged from properties and facilities to technical services team to the company's alliances with vendors and partners. Parker and Kelleher were said to think much alike, and Parker was regarded as having a good sense of humor, although he did not have as colorful and flamboyant a personality as Kelleher. Parker was seen as an honest, straight-arrow kind of person who had a strong grasp of Southwest's culture and market niche and who could be nice or tough, depending on the situation. When his appointment was announced, Parker said:

> There is going to be no change of course insofar as Southwest is concerned. We have a very experienced leadership team. We've all worked together for a long time. There will be evolutionary changes in Southwest, just as there have always been in our history. We're going to stay true to our business model of being a low-cost, low-fare airline.[27]

Colleen Barrett

Barrett began working with Kelleher as his legal secretary in 1967 and had been with Southwest since 1978. As executive vice president of customers, Barrett had a high profile among Southwest employees and spent most of her time on culture building, morale building, and customer service. She and Kelleher were regarded as Southwest's guiding lights, and some analysts said she was essentially functioning as the company's chief operating officer prior to her formal appointment. Much of the credit for the company's strong record of customer service and its strong culture belonged to Barrett.

Barrett had been the driving force behind lining the hallways at Southwest's headquarters with photos of company events and trying to create a family atmosphere at the company. Believing it was important to make employees feel cared about and important, Barrett had put together a network of contacts across the company to help her stay in touch with what was happening with employees and their families. When network members learned about events that were worthy of acknowledgment, word quickly got to Barrett—the information went into a database and an appropriate greeting card or gift was sent. Barrett had a remarkable ability to give individualized gifts that connected her to the recipient.[28]

Barrett was the first woman appointed as president and chief operating office of a major U.S. airline. In October 2001, *Fortune* included Colleen Barrett on its list of the 50 most powerful women in American business (she was ranked number 20).

Crisis Conditions Strike the Airline Industry: The Aftermath of September 11

In the days and weeks following the terrorist attacks on the World Trade Center and the Pentagon on September 11, 2001, the commercial air travel system in the United States was suddenly and unexpectedly in shambles. The unprecedented three-day shutdown of flights, the sudden erosion of passenger traffic, and strict new security measures threw major airlines into a financial crunch of huge proportions and triggered a struggle to re-vamp flight schedules and respond to sharply lower passenger travel. During the three days that flights were suspended by the Federal Aviation Administration, airlines burned through an estimated $220 million a day in cash to cover ongoing expenses.

On the first day of trading after the terrorist attacks, investor worries about almost empty flights, higher costs from added security measures, and a clouded financial fu-ture for the whole airline industry caused airline stock prices to plunge. With about $26.1 billion in debt as of 2001; billions more in capital lease obligations for planes that had been leased rather than purchased; and ongoing costs for labor, terminal facil-ities, and maintenance, U.S. commercial airlines typically had to fill close to 65 per-cent of the available seats in order to reach breakeven. For the four weeks immediately following the attacks, load factors at most airlines were in the 40–60 percent range. Most airlines responded by cutting the number of flights by about 20 percent, ground-ing the unneeded planes, and laying off employees.

Many airline executives expressed concerns about an impending liquidity crunch, rapid burns of cash on hand, and the potential for a number of carriers to end up in bankruptcy without some kind of relief from the federal government. Industry analysts speculated that losses for U.S. airlines in the wake of the terrorist attacks could reach $7 billion in 2001 and that slack demand for air travel could last well into 2002. Con-gress responded by passing a $15 billion aid package that (1) provided $5 billion in cash grants to help airlines cover losses and negative cash flows stemming from traf-fic declines and (2) allowed airlines to apply for $10 billion in loan guarantees to bol-ster their balance sheets and provide needed liquidity.

During the last three months of 2001, airlines scrambled to revise their flight schedules to better match the reduced traffic patterns. Delta, American, and TWA cut 40 percent of their international flights out of New York's Kennedy International, sus-pending all service to a number of destinations until March 2002. Late-night domestic flights and domestic flights on weak performing routes bore the brunt of the flight cut-backs. Some routes served by full-size jets were converted to commuter jet service. United Airlines announced that it would cease operating its Shuttle by United service on the West Coast, which overlapped with Southwest in such markets as Las Vegas, Oakland, and Los Angeles. US Airways announced that it would close down its low-fare MetroJet subsidiary, which operated on the East Coast and overlapped with Southwest's service in Providence and Baltimore (one of Southwest's fastest-growing locations). US Airways also announced that it would eliminate 51 of its 75 mainline jet flights from Baltimore, including all nonstop flights to Florida. Delta Airlines an-nounced that it would cut the operations of its low-fare operation, Delta Express, by 50 percent; Delta Express served three locations also served by Southwest—Orlando, Tampa, and Hartford. In Orlando, Delta Express said it would cut back from 49 daily flights to 21 (Southwest operated 52 daily nonstop flights out of Orlando to 24 cities).

Southwest's Situation

Southwest, however, continued to fly its full schedule of 2,772 flights even though its load factors for the four weeks ending October 14, 2001, were 38.5 percent, 52.4 percent, 62.5 percent, and 67.0 percent—for the period July 1, 2001, until the attacks, Southwest's load factor was 74.6 percent. The company initiated new service to Norfolk, Virginia, on October 7, as planned. Southwest's primary responses involved a temporary freeze on hiring until January 2002, deferring nonessential capital spending and nonessential operating costs, and negotiating a revised delivery schedule for the 132 Boeing 737 jets it had on order.

In January 2002, Southwest Airlines reported its 29th consecutive year of profitability, with annual net income of $511.1 million ($0.63 per diluted share), compared to 2000 net income (excluding the cumulative effect of a change in accounting principle) of $625.2 million ($0.79 per diluted share)—a decline of 18 percent. Southwest's 2001 net income included a special pretax gain of $235 million from a federal grant received pursuant to the Air Transportation Safety and System Stabilization Act and special pretax charges of $48 million arising from the terrorist attacks on September 11, 2001. Excluding the special gain, special charges, and related profit-sharing and income tax effects, the company's 2001 net income was $412.9 million, or $0.51 per diluted share.

Then in early 2002 Southwest announced that it would begin expanding its flight schedule during the February–June 2002 period; the new schedule included the addition of 21 new daily nonstop flights, many of which were on long-distance routes that Southwest had not previously served with nonstop flights. Later in 2002, Southwest announced the addition of 10 more new long-distance, nonstop flights. Many of the newly added flights were round-trip flights between points in the Northeast and Florida and Texas and between two of Southwest's most important airports, Baltimore/Washington and Chicago Midway, and points west—Las Vegas, Phoenix, Oakland, Seattle, and Los Angeles.

Chicago Midway was targeted by Southwest as a particularly lucrative place for expanded flights. Southwest's share of flight departures from Chicago (both O'Hare and Midway) was much higher in April 2002 than in April 2001:

	April 2001	April 2002
Chicago–Tampa		
Southwest	20%	27%
United	50	38
American	30	27
Chicago–Seattle		
Southwest	0	9
United	60	51
American	34	29
Chicago–Phoenix		
Southwest	9	17
United	27	22
American	27	25

*Percentages include all flights from both O'Hare and Midway; Southwest flights all were into and out of Midway.

Jim Parker, Southwest's CEO and vice chairman, said, "We are approaching growth opportunities conservatively, but we know our customers have been anxious for this new nonstop service. Although the airline is still in the recovery process, we cannot forget the wishes of our customers to continue to bring low fares and affordable travel to more people with more convenient flights." Parker indicated that Southwest's employees had been working feverishly on initiatives to make the airport experience more convenient in the new environment of heightened security.

Introductory fares for the flights on the new routes were in the range of $89–$99 each way. The fares were well below the fares on comparable flights of rival airlines. On the high-traffic Chicago–Los Angeles route, an unrestricted, fly-anytime fare or a last-minute fare (no advance purchase) on United and American ran $2,480. To try to rebuild traffic during 2002, Southwest had fare sales in January, March, April, July, August, October, and December; it had also instituted some special vacation fares to resort destinations like Las Vegas and California's Disneyland. But as 2002 drew to an end, passenger traffic on Southwest's flights (see Exhibit 2) and on those of rival airlines remained below pre–September 11 levels. In December 2002, Southwest announced another round of fare sales for January–April 2003.

Southwest's Financially Troubled Rivals

The financial picture at rival airlines was grim. Every passenger airline in the United States except Southwest lost money in 2002. US Airways filed for Chapter 11 bankruptcy in August 2002; it was trying to persuade its unions to agree to deeper wage and salary cuts in order to qualify for a $900 million federal loan and to secure $500 million in interim financing from the Retirement Systems of Alabama, which had recently purchased a 37.5 percent ownership stake. US Airways management had indicated that the company was abandoning its growth strategy and would focus instead on providing regional service with smaller jets primarily on the East Coast and in the Caribbean.

United Airlines filed for Chapter 11 bankruptcy in December 2002 and was in dire straits. United's costs per available seat mile in the third quarter of 2002 were $0.11, the highest in the industry, and its labor costs were $0.046, the second highest in the industry. While management had called on its union and nonunion employees to agree to wage and salary cuts totaling $9 billion over six years, the unions so far had pledged to give up only $5.2 billion over five years—United's employees owned 55 percent of the company's stock; however, under the bankruptcy laws, the union agreements could be declared null and void (United management was expected to take such a step if necessary to establish financial solvency). Federal officials had turned down United's request for a $1.8 billion loan, indicating the company's business plan for getting the company back on solid financial footing was unsound and contained unreasonably optimistic revenue projections. A number of observers had predicted that if United did not get its financial house in order by April 2003, the company would have to be liquidated because it would run out of cash—the company had lost nearly $4 billion in the past two years, was in default on a $920 million loan, and was bleeding millions in cash every day. Most industry observers believed that, in order to survive, United would have to scale back its operations significantly—since September 11, it had already cut its daily flights by 25 percent and laid off about 20,000 employees.

American Airlines, with the highest labor costs in the industry ($0.0462 per available seat mile), was negotiating work rule changes with its unions to try to boost labor productivity and had requested all employees to forgo any pay raise in 2003—management was trying to achieve $3–$4 billion in annual cost savings to bring American's costs more in line with those of Southwest and other lower-cost airlines. American's pilots were among the best paid in the industry and flew an average of 700 hours per year, well under the federal limit of 1,000 hours annually; they worked an average of 14 days a month. In 2002, American spent about $2.5 billion to pay for the salaries and benefits of its 10,000 pilots; the company's total payroll for its 109,000 employees was about $8.4 billion. Productivity improvements of 20 percent would save American about $500 million annually.

Endnotes

[1]Kevin and Jackie Freiberg, NUTS! *Southwest Airlines' Crazy Recipe for Business and Personal Success* (New York: Broadway Books, 1998), p.15.

[2]Ibid., pp. 16–18.

[3]Katrina Brooker, "The Chairman of the Board Looks Back," *Fortune,* May 28, 2001, p. 66.

[4]Freiberg and Freiberg, *NUTS!,* p. 41.

[5]Ibid., p. 31.

[6]Ibid., pp. 26–27.

[7]Ibid., pp. 246–47.

[8]Quoted in the *Dallas Morning News,* March 20, 2001.

[9]Quoted in Katrina Brooks, "The Chairman of the Board Looks Back," *Fortune,* May 28, 2001, p. 64.

[10]Ibid., p. 72.

[11]Freiberg and Freiberg, *NUTS!,* pp. 269–70.

[12]Ibid., p. 288.

[13]Brenda Paik Sunoo, "How Fun Flies at Southwest Airlines," *Personnel Journal* 74, no. 6 (June 1995), p. 70.

[14]Statement made in a 1993 Harvard Business School video and quoted in Roger Hallowell, "Southwest Airlines: A Case Study Linking Employee Needs Satisfaction and Organizational Capabilities to Competitive Advantage," *Human Resource Management* 35, no. 4 (Winter 1996), p. 517.

[15]Quoted in James Campbell Quick, "Crafting an Organizational Structure: Herb's Hand at Southwest Airlines," *Organizational Dynamics* 21, no. 2 (Autumn 1992), p. 51.

[16]Southwest Airlines; and Sunoo, "How Fun Flies at Southwest Airlines," pp. 64–65.

[17]Quick, "Crafting an Organizational Structure," p. 52.

[18]Sunoo, "How Fun Flies at Southwest Airlines," p. 72.

[19]Shawn Tully, "From Bad to Worse," *Fortune,* October 15, 2001, p. 124.

[20]Melanie Trottman, "Amid Crippled Rivals, Southwest Tries to Spread Its Wings," *The Wall Street Journal,* October 11, 2001, p. A10.

[21]Brooks, "The Chairman of the Board Looks Back," p. 72.

[22]Freiberg and Freiberg, *NUTS!,* p. 273.

[23]Ibid., p. 76.

[24]Hallowell, "Southwest Airlines: A Case Study," p. 524.

[25]Freiberg and Freiberg, *NUTS!,* p. 165.

[26]J. H. Gittell, "Cross-Functional Coordination and Human Resource Systems: Evidence from the Airline Industry," doctoral dissertation, Massachusetts Institute of Technology, cited in Hallowell, "Southwest Airlines: A Case Study," p. 527.

[27]Quoted in the *Seattle Times,* March 20, 2001, p. C3.

[28]Freiberg and Freiberg, *NUTS!,* p. 163.

The Collapse of Enron

Anne T. Lawrence
San Jose State University

On December 2, 2001, Enron Corporation filed for bankruptcy. The company's sudden collapse—the largest business failure in U.S. history to date—came as a shock to many. Just months earlier, *Fortune* magazine had named Enron the most innovative company in America for the sixth consecutive year. The Houston, Texas–based firm, ranked seventh on the Fortune 500, was widely considered to be the premier energy trading company in the world. At its peak in 2000, Enron employed 19,000 people and booked annual revenues in excess of $100 billion. At a meeting of executives in January 2001, chairman and CEO Kenneth Lay had said that the company's mission was no longer just to be the world's greatest energy company; rather, its mission was to become simply the world's greatest company.[1]

The pain caused by Enron's abrupt failure was widely felt. The company immediately laid off 4,000 employees, with more to follow. Thousands of Enron employees and retirees saw the value of their 401(k) retirement plans, many heavily invested in the company's stock, become worthless almost overnight. "We, the rank and file, got burned," said one retiree, who lost close to $1.3 million in savings. "I thought people had to treat us honestly and deal fairly with us. In my neck of the woods, what happened is not right."[2] Shareholders and mutual fund investors lost $70 billion in market value. Two banks—J. P. Morgan Chase and Citigroup—faced major write-downs on bad loans. Not only did Enron creditors, shareholders, and bondholders lose out, but confidence also fell across the market as investors questioned the integrity of the financial statements of other companies in which they held stock.

In the aftermath, many struggled to unravel the messy story behind Enron's collapse. Congressional committees initiated investigations, prosecutors brought criminal charges against Enron executives and their accountants for obstruction of justice and securities fraud, and institutional investors sued to recoup their losses. Some blamed Arthur Andersen, Enron's accounting firm, for certifying financial statements that had arguably wrongfully concealed the company's precarious financial situation; some blamed the board of directors for insufficient oversight. Others pointed to a go-go culture in which self-dealing by corrupt executives was condoned, or even admired, while others faulted government regulators, industry analysts, and the media for failing to uncover the company's weaknesses. It will likely take years for the courts to sort through the wreckage.

Enron Corporation

Enron Corporation was formed in 1985 through a merger of Houston Natural Gas and InterNorth of Omaha, Nebraska. The union created a mid-sized firm whose main asset was a large network of natural gas pipelines. The company's core business was distributing natural gas to utilities.

The central figure from the outset of Enron's history was Kenneth L. Lay. The son of a Baptist minister from rural Missouri, Lay trained as an economist at the University of Missouri and the University of Houston and briefly taught college-level economics. After a stint with Exxon, Lay accepted a post in the Nixon administration, serving in the Federal Energy Commission and, later, in the Interior Department as deputy undersecretary for energy. Following the Watergate scandal, Lay returned to the private sector in 1974, taking the first in a series of executive positions at various energy companies. Lay became CEO of Houston Natural Gas in 1984, and he assumed the top job at Enron in 1986, shortly after the merger. One observer described Lay as a man of "considerable charm, homespun roots, and economic expertise" who tended to play an "outside" role, leaving the day-to-day management of his company in the hands of others.[3]

A strong proponent of free markets, Lay felt that the deregulation of the 1980s presented an opportunity for the fledgling company. Historically, the U.S. energy industry had been highly regulated. Utilities were granted monopolies for specific regions, and regulators controlled the prices of electricity and natural gas. Pipeline operators could transport only their own natural gas, not that of other producers. In the 1980s, however, a series of legislative actions at both federal and state levels removed many of these restrictions. For the first time, energy producers were free to compete, buy and sell at market prices, and use each other's distribution networks. The promise of deregulation, touted by lawmakers at the time, was that competition would lead to greater efficiencies, lower prices, and better service for consumers.

Deregulation caused problems for both producers and users of energy, however, because prices for the first time became highly volatile. In the past, energy users (an industrial company or regional utility, for example) could buy extra natural gas or electricity from producers on the spot market as needed. Once prices were free to fluctuate, however, this approach became riskier for both parties. The customer did not want to be forced to buy when prices were high, and the producer did not want to be forced to sell when prices were low.

Enron moved to provide an ingenious solution: The company would leverage its large network of pipelines to set up a "gas bank" that would act as the intermediary in this transaction, reducing market risk. Enron would sign contracts with producers to buy their gas on a certain date at a certain price, and other contracts with users to sell them gas on a certain date at a certain price. Presuming that both parties were willing to pay a slight premium to insure against risk, Enron could make money on the spread. Enron had clear advantages as a market maker in natural gas: It owned pipelines that could be used to transport the product from producer to user, and it had strong institutional knowledge of how markets in the industry operated.

The idea man behind this innovation was Jeffrey Skilling. A graduate of the Harvard Business School and a partner in the consulting firm McKinsey & Company, Skilling had been brought in by Lay in the late 1980s to advise Enron on the company's response to deregulation. The gas bank, in itself, was a clever idea, but Skilling went further. He developed a series of other products, called energy derivatives, for Enron's trading partners. These products included *options,* which allowed companies to buy gas in the future at a fixed price, and *swaps,* which allowed them to trade fixed prices for floating prices and vice versa. In 1990, Skilling left McKinsey to become CEO of Enron Gas Services, as the gas bank came to be known. In 1996, he was promoted to the position of president and chief operating officer of Enron and, in February 2001, to CEO.[4]

We Make Markets

Enron's core gas services division was highly profitable, but by the mid-1990s its growth had begun to level out, as competitors entered the market and both buyers and sellers became more sophisticated and thus able to drive harder bargains. The challenge, as Skilling saw it, was to maintain Enron's growth by extending the business model that had worked so well in natural gas into a range of other commodities. As he later explained this strategy to an interviewer:

> If you have the same general [market] characteristics, all you have to do is change the units. Enron has a huge investment in capabilities that can be deployed instantly into new markets at no cost.[5]

In particular, Skilling sought to trade commodities in industries with characteristics similar to those of natural gas—ones that were undergoing deregulation, had fragmented markets, maintained dedicated distribution channels, and in which both buyers and sellers wanted flexibility.[6]

- *Electricity.* One of the most obvious markets for Enron to enter was electric power. Deregulation of electric utilities in many states—most notably California—presented an opportunity for Enron to use its trading capabilities to buy and sell contracts for electricity. Enron already owned some gas-fired power plants, and it moved to build and buy facilities designed to supply electricity during periods of peak demand. Enron also moved to expand this business internationally, especially in nations undergoing energy deregulation or privatization.

- *Water.* In 1998, Enron acquired Wessex Water in the United Kingdom and changed its name to Azurix, with the ambitious goal of operating water and wastewater businesses globally.

- *Broadband.* The company formed Enron Broadband Services in January 2000. Portland General Electric, which Enron acquired in 1997, provided the core fiber optic network for this service. The idea was to supply customers with access to bandwidth at future dates at guaranteed prices. Enron believed these contracts would appeal to customers who did not want to rely on the public Internet or build their own telecommunications networks.

- *Pulp, paper, and lumber.* Enron launched Clickpaper.com, an online market for the purchase of contracts for the delivery of wood products, and bought a newsprint company to ensure a ready source of supply.

Skilling told an interviewer from *Frontline* in March 2001: "We are looking to create open, competitive, fair markets. And in open, competitive, fair markets, prices are lower and customers get better service. . . . We are the good guys. We are on the side of the angels."[7]

By 2001, Enron was buying and selling metals, pulp and paper, specialty chemicals, bandwidth, coal, aluminum, plastics, and emissions credits, among other commodities. At the height of its power, 1,500 traders housed in Enron's office tower in Houston were trading 1,800 different products. As the *New York Times* later noted in an editorial, Enron was widely viewed as "a paragon of American ingenuity, a stodgy gas pipeline company that had reinvented itself as a high-tech clearinghouse in an ever-expanding roster of markets."[8] Reflecting the general enthusiasm, Skilling replaced his automobile vanity license plate, which had read WLEC (World's Largest Energy Company) with WMM (We Make Markets).[9]

Insisting on Results

In his 1999 letter to shareholders, Lay described the company's attitude toward its employees this way: "Individuals are empowered to do what they think is best. . . . We do, however, keep a keen eye on how prudent they are. . . . We insist on results."[10]

Enron used a recruitment process designed to hire individuals who were smart, hardworking, and intensely loyal. The company preferred to hire recent graduates. After an initial screening interview, candidates were brought to the Houston office for a "Super Saturday," during which they were individually interviewed for 50 minutes by eight interviewers, with only 10-minute breaks between interviews.

Even candidates who survived this strenuous hiring process, however, could not count on job security. Within the company, management used a "rank and yank" system in which new recruits were ranked every six months, and the 15 or 20 percent receiving the lowest scores were routinely terminated. Enron's highly competitive and results-oriented culture "created an environment," in the words of one observer, "where most employees were afraid to express their opinions or to question unethical and potentially illegal business practices."[11]

On the other hand, employees were encouraged to take initiative and were handsomely rewarded when their efforts paid off. Louise Kitchen, chief of the European gas trading unit, for example, organized a team to develop an online trading system. When it was adopted as the basis for a companywide division, Kitchen was promoted to president of Enron Online.

Executive compensation was also results-based. According to Enron's 2001 proxy statement:

> The basic philosophy behind executive compensation at Enron is to reward executive performance that creates long-term shareholder value. This pay-for-performance tenet is embedded in each aspect of an executive's total compensation package. Additionally, the philosophy is designed to promote teamwork by tying a significant portion of compensation to business unit and Enron performance.[12]

Executive compensation was primarily comprised of salary, bonus, and stock options, as shown in Exhibit 1. In addition, the company routinely loaned money to top executives, forgiving the loans if the terms of their contracts were fulfilled. Enron also awarded some executives equity stakes in various business units, which could be converted into stock or cash under certain conditions. For example, Skilling held a 5 percent stake in the retail energy unit, which he converted into $100 million worth of stock in 1998.[13]

During Enron's final years, many top executives sold significant blocs of company stock. Between October 1998 and November 2001, according to a lawsuit later filed by shareholders, Lay sold $184 million worth of Enron stock; Skilling, $71 million; and Andrew Fastow, Enron's chief financial officer, $34 million. All three men sold large blocs in late 2000 or early 2001.[14]

Exhibit 1   TOP EXECUTIVE COMPENSATION, 2000

	Base Salary	Bonus	Other	Stock Options	Total	Stock Options as % of Total
Lay	1.3	7.0	0.4	123.4	132.1	93%
Skilling	0.9	5.6	—	62.5	69.0	91%

Note: All figures are in millions of dollars, rounded to the nearest $100,000. "Stock options" represents stock options exercised and sold in 2000, *not* granted in 2000. These figures do not include the value of perquisites, such as personal use of company aircraft.

Source: Enron, SEC Schedule 14A (proxy statement), March 27, 2001, p. 18, and Dan Ackman, "Executive Compensation: Did Enron Execs Dump Shares?" Forbes.com, March 22, 2002.

Exhibit 2   ENRON CONTRIBUTIONS TO FEDERAL CANDIDATES AND PARTIES, 1990–2002

Election Cycle	Total Contri- butions	Soft Money Contri- butions	Contri- butions from PACs	Contri- butions from Individuals	% to Democrats	% to Republicans
1990	$163,250	N/A	$130,250	$33,000	42%	58%
1992	281,009	75,109	130,550	75,350	42	58
1994	520,996	136,292	189,565	195,139	42	58
1996	1,141,016	687,445	171,671	281,900	18	81
1998	1,049,942	691,950	212,643	145,349	21	79
2000	2,441,398	1,671,555	280,043	489,800	28	72
2002	353,959	304,909	32,000	17,050	6	94
Total	$5,951,570	$3,567,260	$1,146,722	$1,237,588	26%	74%

Note: Soft money contributions were not publicly disclosed until the 1991–92 election cycle. Soft money contributions were banned in 2002.

Source: Center for Responsive Politics, based on Federal Election Commission data; available online at: www.opensecrets.org/news/enron/enron_totals.asp.

Politics as Usual

Political action was an important part of Enron's overall strategy. The company's primary policy goal was to promote deregulation and reduce government oversight in the range of markets in which it traded. It maintained an office in Washington, D.C., staffed by over 100 lobbyists and also used outside lobbyists for specialized assignments. The company spent $2.1 million on lobbying in 2000 alone.[15] Enron was also a major campaign contributor. From 1994 on, Enron was the largest contributor to congressional campaigns in the energy industry, giving over $5 million to House and Senate candidates, mostly to Republicans (see Exhibit 2). In 2000, it gave $2.4 million in political contributions.

Enron CEO Kenneth Lay also had close personal ties with the Bush family. In 1992, Lay had chaired the host committee for the Republican National Convention in Houston at which George H. W. Bush was nominated to run for a second term as president. Enron donated $700,000 to George W. Bush's various campaigns between 1993 and 2001. Lay and his wife personally donated $100,000 to the younger Bush's presidential inauguration.

Over the years, Enron's efforts to influence policymaking enjoyed significant success, as illustrated by the following examples:

- *Commodities futures regulation.* The job of the Commodities Futures Trading Commission (CFTC), a federal agency, is to regulate futures contracts traded in an exchange. From 1988 to 1993, the CFTC was chaired by Wendy Gramm, an economist and wife of then-congressman Phil Gramm (Republican–Texas). In 1992, Enron petitioned the CFTC to exempt energy derivatives and swaps—such as those in which it was beginning to make a market—from government oversight. In January 1993, just days before President Clinton took office, Wendy Gramm approved the exemption. The following month, after she had left office, Gramm was invited to join Enron's board of directors. According to Enron's filings with the SEC, Gramm received somewhere between $.9 and $1.8 million in salary, fees, and stock option sales and dividends for her service on the board between 1993 and 2001.[16]

- *Securities and Exchange Commission (SEC).* In 1997, the SEC granted Enron an exemption for its foreign subsidiaries from the provisions of the Investment Company Act of 1940, a law designed to prevent abuses by utilities. The law barred companies it covered from shifting debt off their books, and barred executives of these companies from investing in affiliated partnerships. After it had failed to win the exemption it wanted from Congress in 1996, Enron hired the former director of the investment management division at the SEC as a lobbyist to take the company's case directly to his former colleagues. He was successful. The year 1997 was the last in which the SEC conducted a thorough examination of Enron's annual reports.[17]

- *Commodity Futures Modernization Act.* This law, passed by Congress in late 2000, included a special exemption for Enron that allowed the company to operate an unregulated energy trading subsidiary. Senator Phil Gramm, chair of the powerful banking committee, was instrumental in getting this provision included in the bill despite the opposition of the president's working group on financial markets. Over the years, Enron had been the largest single corporate contributor to Gramm's campaigns, with $260,000 in gifts since 1993.[18]

Reviewing the history of Enron's efforts to limit government oversight, one reporter concluded, "If the regulators in Washington were asleep, it was because the company had made their beds and turned off the lights."[19]

Off the Balance Sheet

As Enron forged ahead in the late 1990s as a market maker in a wide range of commodities, it began to assume increasing amounts of debt. Even though Skilling had touted the value of an "asset light" strategy, entry into markets for such varied commodities as water, steel, and broadband required that Enron buy significant hard assets. Enron's aggressive new business ventures required, by some estimates, on the order of $10 billion in up-front capital investments. Heavy indebtedness, however, posed a problem, because creditworthiness was critical to the company's ability to make markets in a wide range of commodities. Other parties would be unwilling to enter into contracts promising future delivery if Enron were not viewed as financially rock-solid, and the company had to maintain an investment-grade credit rating to continue to borrow money on favorable terms to fund its new ventures. A complicating factor was that several of the company's major new initiatives fell far short of expectations and some—broadband in particular—were outright failures.

Beginning in 1997, Enron entered into a series of increasingly complex financial transactions with several special purpose entities (SPEs), evidently with the intention of shifting liabilities (debt) off its books. After the bankruptcy, these transactions were investigated by a special committee of the Enron board, which released its findings in a document now known as the Powers Committee Report.

Under standard accounting rules, a company could legally exclude an SPE from its consolidated financial statements if two conditions were met: (1) An independent party had to exercise control of the SPE, and (2) this party had to own at least 3 percent of the SPE's assets. The independent party's investment had to be "at risk," that is, not guaranteed by someone else.[20] The obvious problem was that if Enron intended to burden the SPEs with debt, no truly independent party would want to invest in them.

A key figure in many of these transactions was Andrew S. Fastow. Described as a "financial whiz kid," Fastow had joined Enron Finance in 1990. He developed a close relationship with Skilling and rose quickly, becoming chief financial officer (CFO) of Enron in 1998, at age 37. Speaking of Fastow's selection, Skilling told a reporter for *CFO* magazine, "We needed someone to rethink the entire financing structure at Enron from soup to nuts. We didn't want someone stuck in the past. . . . Andy has the intelligence and youthful exuberance to think in new ways."[21]

The SPEs Enron set up in the five years leading up to its bankruptcy included the following:

- *Chewco.* In 1997, Enron created Chewco, an SPE named after the Star Wars character Chewbacca. Fastow invited a subordinate, Michael Kopper, to become the required "independent" investor in Chewco. Kopper and a friend invested $125,000 of their own funds and, with Enron providing collateral, got a $11 million loan from Barclays Bank. Between 1997 and 2000, Kopper received $2 million in management fees for his work on Chewco. In March 2001, Enron repurchased Chewco from its "investors"; Kopper and his friend received more than $10 million. The Powers Committee concluded that "our review failed to identify how these payments were determined or what, if anything, Kopper did to justify the payments."[22]

- *The LJM Partnerships.* In 1999, Enron created two partnerships known as LJM1 and LJM2 (the initials of Fastow's wife and children). Unlike Chewco, where he had delegated this role to a subordinate, Fastow himself served as general partner and invested $1 million of his own money. Enron proceeded to transfer various assets and liabilities to the LJMs in a way that benefited its bottom line. For example, in the second half of 1999, the LJM transactions generated "earnings" of $229 million for Enron (the company reported total pretax earnings of $570 million for that period).

- *Raptor Partnerships.* In 1999 and 2000, Enron established four new, even more ambitious SPEs, collectively known as the Raptor Partnerships, with such fanciful names as Talon, Timberwolf, Bobcat, and Porcupine. In a series of extremely complex financial maneuvers in the final five quarters before declaring bankruptcy, Enron conducted various transactions with and among the Raptors and between the Raptors and the LJMs that generated $1.1 billion in "earnings" for the firm. Among other actions, Enron loaned large blocs of its own stock to the Raptor partnerships in exchange for promissory notes, which were then posted to Enron's balance sheet as notes receivable.

Fastow made out handsomely on these deals. According to the Powers Committee Report, he eventually received almost $50 million for his role in the LJM partnerships and their transactions with the Raptors, in addition to his regular Enron compensation. In its review of Enron's SPE transactions, the Powers Committee Report concluded:

> These partnerships . . . were used by Enron Management to enter into transactions that it could not, or would not, do with unrelated commercial entities. Many of the most significant transactions apparently were designed to accomplish favorable financial statement results, not to achieve bonafide economic objectives or to transfer risk. . . . They allowed Enron to conceal from the market very large losses resulting from Enron's merchant investments.[23]

Manipulating Revenue

Moving liabilities off the books was one way to make the company's financial condition look better than it was. Another way was to manipulate revenue. In the period preceding its collapse, Enron used a number of accounting practices apparently aimed at inflating revenues or reducing their volatility.

- *Mark-to-market accounting.* Mark-to-market (MTM) is an accounting procedure that allows companies to book as *current earnings* their expected *future revenue* from certain assets. The Financial Accounting Standards Board (FASB), the organization that establishes generally accepted accounting principles, approved MTM in the early 1990s. Aggressively using this procedure, Enron counted projected profits from many deals in the year they were made. For example, in 2000 Enron entered into a partnership with Blockbuster to deliver movies on demand to viewers' homes over Enron's broadband network. The venture fell apart within a few months, after pilot projects in four U.S. cities failed. Nonetheless, Enron booked $110 million in profits in late 2000 and early 2001, based on the anticipated value of the partnership over 20 years.[24] In 2000, mark-to-market gains accounted for over half of Enron's reported pretax earnings.[25]

- *Sham swaps.* In the wake of its collapse, Enron was investigated by the SEC for possible sham swaps. For example, on the last day of the third quarter 2001, as the company's stock price was falling, Enron entered into an agreement with the telecommunications firm Qwest to exchange assets. Qwest and Enron agreed to buy fiber optic capacity from each other, and the two companies exchanged checks for around $112 million to complete the swap. According to the *New York Times,* "The deal enabled Enron to book a sale and avoid recording a loss on . . . assets, whose value in the open market had dropped far below the price on Enron's books."

- *Prudency accounts.* Enron traders routinely split profits from their deals into two categories—one that was added directly to the company's current financial statements, and the other that was added to a reserve fund. These so-called prudency accounts, according to Frank Partnoy, an expert in finance who testified before the U.S. Senate Committee on Governmental Affairs, functioned as "slush fund[s] that could be used to smooth out profits and losses over time." The use of prudency accounts made Enron's revenue stream appear less volatile than it actually was. Partnoy noted, "Such fraudulent practices would have thwarted the very purpose of Enron's financial statements: to give investors an accurate picture of a firm's risks."[26]

The Best Interests of the Company

The two groups most responsible for overseeing the legal and ethical integrity of the company's financial reporting were Enron's board of directors and its auditors, Arthur Andersen's Houston office. In January 2001, Enron's board was comprised of 17 members. Of the 15 outside members, many had long personal and business associations with Lay and were considered loyal supporters of his policies. Although the board included only two insiders (Lay and Skilling), other members of top management frequently attended, sitting around the edge of the boardroom.[27] The full board typically met five times a year. Members of Enron's board were unusually well compensated. In 2001, for example, each director received $381,000 in total compensation. By comparison, the average director compensation for the top 200 companies that year was $152,000; and for companies in the petroleum and pipeline industries, $160,000.[28]

The quality of the company's financial reporting was the responsibility of the audit and compliance committee. Chaired by Robert Jaedicke, professor emeritus of accounting and former dean of the Stanford Business School, the committee also included Wendy Gramm and four others.[29] The audit committee typically met for an hour or two before the regular board meetings, often for discussions with the company's professional auditors.

The board's first substantive involvement with the SPEs run by Fastow and his associates came in 1999.[30] Fastow's dual roles as both CFO and general partner of the LJM partnerships potentially violated Enron's code of ethics, which prohibited an officer from owning or participating in "any other entity which does business with . . . the company." An exception could be made if the participation was disclosed to the chairman and CEO and was judged not to "adversely affect the best interests of the company." Accordingly, in June and again in October, the board reviewed and approved the LJM partnerships and voted to suspend its code of ethics in this instance to permit Fastow to run the partnerships.

However, the board seemed sufficiently concerned that it put additional controls in place; it required both an annual board review and that the chief accounting officer and chief risk officer review all transactions with the partnerships. In October 2000, the board added additional restrictions, including provisions that Skilling personally sign off on all related approval sheets. In May 2001, an Enron attorney discovered that Skilling had not signed these documents, as the board had required, so he sent a message to the CEO that he needed to sign the papers at his convenience. Skilling never replied.[31] As for the mandated board review, the Powers Committee later concluded that although the audit committee had periodically reviewed the SPEs, "these reviews appear to have been too brief, too limited in scope, and too superficial to serve their intended function."[32]

In its oversight function, the board and its audit committee relied heavily on the professional advice of Enron's auditor, Arthur Andersen, which repeatedly told the board it was "comfortable" with the partnership transactions. Founded in 1913 and Enron's auditor since 1985, Andersen was one of the Big Five accounting firms. Since the early 1990s, Andersen's Houston office had acted both as the company's external and internal auditors, in an arrangement called an integrated audit, in which Enron subcontracted much of its "inside" work to the firm.[33] Andersen also did considerable consulting and nonauditing work for its client. All told, Enron was a very important client of the Houston office. In 2000, for example, Andersen received $25 million for audit services and $27 million for nonaudit services from Enron. Between 1997 and 2001,

Andersen received around $7 million for its accounting work on the Chewco, LJM, and Raptors transactions.

Relations between Enron and Arthur Andersen were unusually close. Many Andersen accountants had office space at Enron and easily mingled with their coworkers. "People just thought they were Enron employees," said one former Enron accountant.[34] Moreover, mobility between Andersen and its client was high; indeed, at the time of the bankruptcy, the company's chief accounting officer, Richard Causey, had formerly been in charge of Andersen's Enron audit.

Andersen's own structure gave considerable autonomy to local offices like the one in Houston. Like other big accounting firms, Andersen had a professional standards group (PSG) at its corporate headquarters whose job was to review difficult issues that arose in the field. Unlike others, however, Andersen's PSG did not have the authority to overrule its field auditors in case of disagreement. An investigation by *Business Week* showed that on four different occasions, the Enron audit team went ahead despite PSG objections to various aspects of its accounting for the Enron partnerships. Finally, Enron requested that its chief critic be removed from the PSG. Andersen headquarters complied.[35]

Later, responding to criticism of its actions as Enron auditors, Andersen simply stated that it "ignored a fundamental problem: that poor business decisions on the part of Enron executives and its board ultimately brought the company down."[36]

A Wave of Accounting Scandals

On March 5, 2001, *Fortune* magazine published a cover story, written by reporter Bethany McLean, under the title "Is Enron Overpriced?" In the article, McLean challenged the conventional wisdom that Enron stock—which had returned 89 percent to investors the previous year and was selling at 55 times earnings—was an attractive buy. Calling Enron's financial statements "nearly impenetrable," she interviewed a number of stock analysts who, although bullish on Enron stock, were unable to explain exactly how the company made money. One called the company's financial statements "a big black box."[37]

What *Fortune* did not know at the time was that the fragile structure of partnerships Enron had constructed rested on the high price of the company's stock. Much of the partnerships' assets consisted of Enron stock or loans guaranteed by Enron stock. If the share price declined too far, this would trigger a need for more financing from the company. Prior to Enron's announcement of first-quarter 2001 results, and then again prior to the second-quarter results, Andersen worked furiously to restructure the partnerships to prevent the necessity of consolidating them with Enron's books. The Powers Committee later commented that these efforts were "perceived by many within Enron as a triumph of accounting ingenuity by a group of innovative accountants. We believe that perception was mistaken. . . . [The] Raptors were little more than a highly complex accounting construct that was destined to collapse."[38]

In late July, Enron's stock slid below $47 a share—the first "trigger" price for the partnerships. On August 14, Skilling abruptly resigned as president and CEO, citing undisclosed personal reasons. Lay, who had been serving as chairman, resumed the role of CEO. In a memo to Enron employees that day, Lay assured them:

I have never felt better about the prospects for the company. All of you know that our stock price has suffered substantially over the last few months. One of my top priorities will be to restore a significant amount of the stock value we have lost as soon as possible. Our performance has never been stronger; our business model has never been more robust; our growth has never been more certain; and most importantly, we have never had a better nor deeper pool of talent throughout the company. We have the finest organization in business today. Together, we will make Enron the world's leading company.[39]

The following day, Sherron S. Watkins, an accountant and Enron vice president who worked under Fastow, wrote a memo to Lay to express her concerns about the company's accounting practices. She stated frankly:

I am incredibly nervous that we will implode in a wave of accounting scandals. My 8 years of Enron work history will be worth nothing on my résumé, the business world will consider the past successes as nothing but an elaborate accounting hoax. Skilling is resigning now for "personal reasons" but I think he wasn't having fun, looked down the road, and knew this stuff was unfixable and would rather abandon ship now than resign in shame in 2 years.

She added:

I have heard one manager . . . say, "I know it would be devastating to all of us, but I wish we would get caught. We're such a crooked company."

After a detailed review of the "questionable" accounting practices of the SPEs, Watkins recommended that Lay bring in independent legal and accounting experts to review the propriety of the partnerships and to prepare a "cleanup plan."[40]

Lay followed Watkins's advice—to a point. He brought in attorneys from Vinson & Elkins, the Houston law firm that had long been Enron's outside counsel and that had helped prepare the legal documents for the partnerships. In his instructions, Lay indicated that he saw no need to look too closely into the accounting. The lawyers interviewed Fastow, Enron's auditors, and several others, and then reported back to Lay on September 21 that although the accounting was "creative" and "aggressive," it was not "inappropriate from a technical standpoint."

Yet, despite these assurances, the partnerships were unraveling as Enron's stock price dropped (see Exhibit 3) and could no longer be supported by even the most aggressive accounting. On October 16, under pressure from its auditors, Enron announced a charge against earnings of $544 million and a reduction in shareholders' equity of $1.2 billion related to transactions with the LJM partnerships. On October 22, the SEC initiated a probe of the SPEs; Fastow was fired the following day. Then, on November 8, Enron further shocked investors by restating *all* of its financial statements back to 1997 because "three unconsolidated entities [i.e., the partnerships] should have been consolidated in the financial statements pursuant to generally accepted accounting principles." These restatements had the effect of reducing income for 1997 to 2000 by $480 million, reducing shareholders' equity by $2.1 billion, and increasing debt by $2.6 billion.[41]

Company executives frantically went searching for a white knight to purchase the company. Dynegy, another Houston-based energy trader and longtime rival, initially agreed to buy Enron for $8.9 billion on November 9. After Dynegy's CEO and board had taken a careful look at Enron's books, however, they changed their minds and withdrew the offer. The rating agencies immediately downgraded Enron to junk status, and the stock dropped below $1 a share and was delisted from the New York Stock Exchange.

Exhibit 3   Enron Stock Price and Trading Volume, 1998–2002

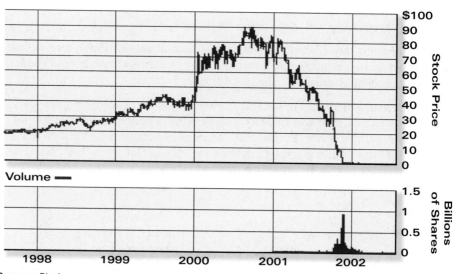

Source: Bigcharts.com.

As the company imploded, Enron tried to call in its political chits in one last Hail Mary move. Lay and other top executives placed urgent calls to commerce secretary Donald Evans, treasury secretary Paul O'Neill, and other administration officials, reportedly asking them to lean on banks to extend credit to the company. They declined to do so. Later asked why he had not helped Enron, Evans said that it would have been an "egregious abuse" to have intervened. O'Neill simply stated, "Companies come and go. . . . Part of the genius of capitalism is, people get to make good decisions or bad decisions, and they get to pay the consequence or enjoy the fruits of their decisions."[42]

Endnotes

[1]"Enron's Last Year: Web of Details Did Enron In as Warnings Went Unheeded," *New York Times,* February 10, 2002. Revenue data are from Enron's 2000 annual report.
[2]"Enron's Collapse: Audacious Climb to Success Ended in Dizzying Plunge," *New York Times,* January 13, 2002.
[3]Peter C. Fusaro and Ross M. Miller, *What Went Wrong at Enron* (New York: Wiley, 2001), p. 9.
[4]Enron's early history is described in two cases, "Enron: Entrepreneurial Energy," Harvard Business School case 700-079, and "Enron's Transformation: From Gas Pipelines to New Economy Powerhouse," Harvard Business School case 9-301-064.
[5]Darden School of Business videotape, May 25, 2001, cited in Joseph Bower and David Garvin, "Enron's Business and Strategy," unpublished paper, Harvard Business School, April 10, 2002.
[6]Mal Salter, Lynne Levesque, and Maria Ciampa, "The Rise and Fall of Enron," Harvard Business School case, pp. 12–13.
[7]"Enron's Many Strains: The Company Unravels; Enron Buffed Image Even as It Rotted from Within," *New York Times,* February 10, 2002.
[8]"The Rise and Fall of Enron" [Editorial], *New York Times,* November 2, 2001.
[9]Fusaro and Miller, *What Went Wrong at Enron,* p. 70.
[10]1999 Enron annual report.
[11]Fusaro and Miller, p. 52. Enron's "rank and yank" system is described in Malcolm Gladwell, "The Talent Myth," *The New Yorker,* September 16, 2002.
[12]Enron, SEC Schedule 14A (proxy statement), March 27, 2001, p. 15.

[13]"Enron Compensation Raised Questions," Dow Jones Newswires, March 26, 2002.

[14]Insider trading data computed by Milberg Weiss Bershad Hynes & Lerach LLP; available online at www.enronfraud.com.

[15]"The Fall of the Giant: Enron's Campaign Contributions and Lobbying," Center for Responsive Politics; available online at www.opensecrets.org.

[16]"Blind Faith: How Deregulation and Enron's Influence Over Government Looted Billions from Americans," Washington, DC: Public Citizen, December 2001.

[17]"Exemption Won in 1997 Set Stage for Enron Woes," New York Times, January 23, 2002.

[18]"Blind Faith."

[19]"Enron's Collapse: Audacious Climb to Success Ended in Dizzying Plunge," New York Times, January 13, 2002.

[20]A. Christine David, "When to Consolidate a Special Purpose Entity," California CPA, June 2002.

[21]"Andrew S. Fastow: Enron Corp.," CFO, October 1, 1999.

[22]Powers Committee Report, p. 8.

[23]Ibid., p. 4.

[24]"Show Business: A Blockbuster Deal Shows How Enron Overplayed Its Hand—Company Booked Big Profit from Pilot Video Project That Soon Fizzled Out," The Wall Street Journal, January 17, 2002; and Bryce, Pipe Dreams, pp. 281–83.

[25]"Question Mark to Market: Energy Accounting Scrutinized," CFO.com, December 4, 2001.

[26]Testimony of Professor Frank Partnoy, Senate Committee on Governmental Affairs, January 24, 2002, online at www.senate.gov/~gov_affairs/012402partnoy.htm.

[27]Jay W. Lorsch, "The Board at Enron," unpublished paper, Harvard Business School, April 10, 2002, p. 1.

[28]Pearl Meyer and Partners, 2001 Director Compensation: Boards in the Spotlight: Study of the Top 200 Corporations, 2002. Data are rounded to the nearest thousand dollars.

[29]Other members of the audit committee were John Mendelsohn, president of the M. D. Anderson Cancer Clinic; Paolo V. Ferraz Pereira, former president of the State Bank of Rio de Janeiro; John Wakeham, former British Secretary of State for Energy; and Ronnie Chan, chairman of a large property development group in Hong Kong.

[30]Earlier, the board had provided a cursory review of Chewco, but had apparently been unaware of Kopper's role.

[31]"Enron's Many Strands: The Company Unravels," New York Times, February 10, 2002.

[32]Powers Committee Report, p. 24.

[33]"Court Documents Show Andersen's Ties with Enron Were Growing in Early '90s," The Wall Street Journal, February 26, 2002.

[34]"Were Enron, Andersen Too Close to Allow Auditor to Do Its Job?" The Wall Street Journal, January 21, 2002.

[35]"Out of Control at Andersen," Business Week, April 8, 2002.

[36] "Enron's Doomed 'Triumph of Accounting,'" New York Times, February 4, 2002.

[37]"Is Enron Overpriced?" Fortune, March 5, 2001.

[38]Powers Committee Report, pp. 131–32.

[39]The full text of Lay's memo appears in Fusaro and Miller, What Went Wrong at Enron, p. 201.

[40]The full text of Watkin's memo appears in Fusaro and Miller, What Went Wrong at Enron, pp. 185–91.

[41]Based on data reported in the Powers Committee Report, p. 6.

[42]"Enron Lessons: Big Political Giving Wins Firms a Hearing, Doesn't Assure Aid," The Wall Street Journal, January 15, 2002.

Smithfield Foods

When Growing the Business Damages the Environment

LaRue T. Hosmer
The University of Alabama

Smithfield Foods was the largest hog producer and pork processor in the world, the company's fiscal 2002 output included 5.1 billion pounds of chops, roasts, ribs, loins, ground pork, bacon, hams, sausages, and sliced deli meats. Smithfield supplied both food-service wholesalers and grocery retailers, and its family of brands included some of the most popular pork brands in the world (see Exhibit 1). Smithfield Foods' fresh pork and processed meats products were sold in North America and more than 25 other global markets. The company was vertically integrated, with operations in hog farming, feed mills, packing plants, and distribution.

In 1998, Smithfield Foods began expanding into foreign markets, making acquisitions in Canada, France, and Poland. In August 1999, the company further developed its international operations through a 50-percent-owned integrated joint venture in Mexico. Management believed these acquisitions gave the company strong market positions, high-quality manufacturing facilities, and excellent growth potential in regions that had high pork consumption levels. Smithfield Foods owned and operated hog farms with about 700,000 sows in North Carolina, South Carolina, Virginia, Utah, Colorado, Texas, Oklahoma, South Dakota, Missouri, Illinois, Mexico, Brazil, and Poland. The company raised 12 million hogs in 2001, roughly 3.5 times the number of its nearest U.S. competitor. Smithfield's hog farming subsidiary, Murphy-Brown LLC, owned 700,000 U.S. sows plus an interest in another 40,000 in Mexico, Brazil, and Poland. It specialized in producing exceptionally lean hogs; the company's own special breed of SPG sows, a consistent raw material for branded Smithfield Lean Generation Pork, accounted for approximately 55 percent of the total herd.

The company was headquartered in Smithfield, Virginia, and a big fraction of the company's operations were in North Carolina—Smithfield's biggest pork processing plant was in Bladen County, North Carolina, and many of its hog farming operations were in eastern North Carolina. Smithfield's southern base provided low wages and relatively low operating costs across much of its integrated operations, factors that helped pave the way for Smithfield's competitive prices and strong growth. The company's longtime chairman and CEO, Joseph W. Luter III, continually emphasized the need to drive down costs and push up sales. In 2002, the company's sales were 6.6 times 1993 levels and net income was almost 50 times greater (see Exhibit 2). Top executives at Smithfield Foods wanted to continue the company's rapid and profitable expansion and were constantly on the lookout for opportunities to grow the company's business.

Exhibit 1   Smithfield's Family of Meat Brands and Products, 2002

Opposition to Smithfield's Expansion

Over the last decade, Smithfield Foods had met with mounting opposition to expansion of its business, particularly the hog farming aspect. The company owned or leased numerous hog production facilities, primarily in North Carolina, Utah, and Virginia, with additional hog production facilities in Colorado, South Carolina, Illinois, Texas, and Oklahoma. One of the chief pockets of opposition to Smithfield's hog farming activities came from rural residents in eastern North Carolina, where there were some 8,000 hog farms. Neighboring residents complained that commercial hog farming had essentially been imposed on them and that it entailed substantial adverse impacts in the form of low wages and environmental discharges.

Eastern North Carolina and Smithfield's Hog Farming Operations

Eastern North Carolina, essentially the area extending about 150 miles from Raleigh (the state capital) to the Atlantic coast, is a region of flat land, sandy soil, and ample rainfall. At one time it was a relatively prosperous region, with thousands of small family farms, each of which had a tobacco allotment. During the 1930s far more tobacco had been grown than was needed, and the price plummeted. One of the governmental initiatives of the Depression era was a restriction on the total amount of tobacco that could be grown, and this total amount was divided up among the existing growers by restricting each to a set percentage of the amount of their land that had been devoted to the crop during a given base year. These restrictions on growth first stabilized and latter increased the price, and the possession of an allotment almost guaranteed the financial prosperity of the farm.

The typical family farm would have 150 to 200 acres. Perhaps 15 acres would be devoted to tobacco, and the balance would be sown in corn, wheat, rye, or soybeans, or left as pasture for cattle or—more frequently—hogs. The grains grown locally would be trucked to the nearest town within the region to be milled into feed and then returned to the farm for the livestock. The cattle and hogs produced locally would be trucked to the nearest town to be sold at auction, and then slaughtered and processed at a nearby packing plant. These towns were also relatively prosperous, as the farmers

Exhibit 2   SMITHFIELD FOODS, FINANCIAL SUMMARY, 1995–2002 (DOLLARS AND SHARES IN THOUSANDS, EXCEPT PER SHARE DATA)

	Fiscal Years				
	2002	2001	1999	1997	1995
Operations					
Sales	$7,356,119	$5,899,927	$3,774,989	$3,870,611	$1,526,518
Gross profit	1,092,928	948,903	539,575	323,795	146,275
Selling, general and administrative expenses	543,952	450,965	295,610	191,225	61,723
Interest expense	94,326	88,974	40,521	26,211	14,054
Income from continuing operations before change in accounting for income taxes	196,886	223,513	94,884	44,937	31,915
Income (loss) from discontinued operations	—	—	—	—	(4,075)
Change in accounting for income taxes	—	—	—	—	—
Net income	196,886	223,513	94,884	44,937	27,840
Per Diluted Share					
Income from continuing operations before change in accounting principle for income taxes	$1.78	$2.03	$1.16	$.57	$.46
Income (loss) from discontinued operations	—	—	—	—	(.12)
Change in accounting for income taxes	—	—	—	—	—
Net income	$1.78	$2.03	$1.16	$.57	$.46
Weighted average shares outstanding	110,419	110,146	81,924	77,116	67,846
Financial Position					
Working capital	$ 798,426	$ 635,413	$ 215,865	$ 164,312	$ 60,911
Total assets	3,877,998	3,250,888	1,771,614	995,254	550,225
Long-term debt and capital lease obligations	1,387,147	1,146,223	594,241	288,486	155,047
Shareholders' equity	1,362,774	1,053,132	542,246	307,486	184,015
Financial Ratios					
Current ratio	2.11	2.01	1.46	1.51	1.35
Long-term debt to total capitalization	50.4%	52.1%	52.3%	48.4%	44.4%
Return on average shareholders' equity[a,b]	16.2%	18.4%	21.0%	15.9%	18.4%
Other Information					
Capital expenditures[c]	$171,010	$144,120	$95,447	$69,147	$90,550
Depreciation expense	139,942	124,836	63,524	35,825	19,717
Number of employees	—	34,000	33,000	17,500	9,000

[a]Computed using income from continuing operations before change in accounting principle.

[b]The fiscal 2002 computation excludes a gain on the sale of IBP, Inc. common stock and a loss as a result of a fire at a hog farm.

[c]The fiscal 2001 computation excludes gains from the sale of IBP, Inc. common stock, less related expenses, and the sale of a plant.

and their families purchased clothing and household goods at local stores and automobiles and farm machinery at local dealers.

This prosperity started downhill in the 1970s as the national campaigns against smoking led to continual reductions in the size, and consequently the profitability, of the tobacco allotments, which eventually came almost to an end. Local prosperity continued to decline in the 1980s as very large feed lots in Nebraska, Iowa, and Kansas developed a much less costly means of raising hogs prior to slaughter; the piglets spent only the first 12 to 15 months of their lives on the farms where they were bred before being brought to fenced open-air corrals where they were closely confined but fed continuously to gain weight. Farmers in eastern North Carolina had to compete against this new and far more efficient production process. Prices for the hogs raised in eastern North Carolina declined sharply, and many of the local packing plants went out of business.

Local prosperity stabilized to some extent in the 1990s, though with a greatly changed distribution of income, as Smithfield Foods introduced the concept of the factory farm. Large metal sheds with concrete floors were built, each designed to hold up to 1,000 hogs. Feeding was by means of a mechanized conveyor that carried food alongside both walls. Waste was removed by hosing it off the floors to a central trough that carried it to a storage lagoon. Temperature was controlled by huge fans at each end of each shed. Every effort was made to reduce costs. Feed grains were no longer grown, purchased, and milled locally; instead most grains were grown, purchased, and milled in the Midwest and transported to eastern North Carolina by unit feed trains, which were strings of covered hopper cars that moved as a unit, without switching, from the feed mill in Nebraska or Iowa directly to one of the company's distribution centers in North Carolina. Some feed grains were grown and purchased even more cheaply abroad, primarily in Australia and Argentina, and then carried by ship to a company-leased milling facility and distribution center in Wilmington (a port in southeastern North Carolina, near the South Carolina border).

Limited farm machinery was needed for this new method of raising hogs, given that few feed grains were grown locally, but the little that was needed was purchased by the Smithfield headquarters office directly from the manufacturer. Many farm equipment dealers within the region were forced to close. Even diesel fuel, needed for the trucks that transported the feed grains to the farms and the mature hogs to the packing plants, was purchased from the refinery, transported by railway tank cars to large storage tanks at the distribution centers, and pumped directly into the trucks. Local fuel dealers got little or none of this business. All truck purchases were arranged by bid from national dealers located in Detroit (auto companies had refused to sell outside their dealer chains, but they allegedly gave favored prices to very large dealers near their corporate headquarters) at very low prices, and all subsequent truck repairs were done at company-owned repair shops located at the company-owned distribution centers. Some truck dealers in the region were forced to close.

Executives at Smithfield Foods did not apologize for the business model that they had created. Their attitude could be summed up as follows: "This is the way the world is going and this is what the market demands. All we have done is to create a competitive system that works. Moreover, we have saved farms and brought jobs to the eastern North Carolina region through this system, and we have provided better (leaner) pork products at lower prices to our customers." Smithfield's development of a "competitive system that works" had won Joseph Luter an award as Master Entrepreneur of the Year in 2002; a Smithfield news release dated December 21, 2002, said:

Joseph W. Luter III has been named the Ernst & Young 2002 Virginia Master Entrepreneur of the Year. The Ernst & Young program recognizes entrepreneurs who have demonstrated excellence and extraordinary success in such areas as innovation, financial performance and personal commitment to their businesses and communities. . . .

Since becoming chairman and chief executive officer of Smithfield Foods, Inc. in 1975, Mr. Luter transformed the company from a small, regional meat packer with sales of $125 million and net worth of $1 million to an international concern with annual sales of $8 billion and a net worth of $1.4 billion.

Smithfield Foods did not own the farms that raised the hogs. Instead, company representatives would select a reasonably large farm, one that had been successful in the past and therefore was financially solvent now, and negotiate a contract with the owning family to raise hogs at a set price per animal. The farm family would, frequently using a loan provided through the Smithfield Corporation and a contractor licensed by the Smithfield Corporation, build the metal barns with concrete floors, feed conveyors, ventilation fans, and waste systems; connect the waste systems to storage lagoons (five to eight acres in size); construct feed bins and loading ramps; and be ready for business. Smithfield Corporation would then deliver the hogs at piglet stage, provide a constant supply of feed grains mixed with antibiotics (to prevent disease in the crowded conditions of the metal barns), and offer free veterinarian service. The responsibility of the farm family was to raise those hogs to marketable weight as quickly and as efficiently as possible. This was termed *contract farming;* it was described in the following terms in five-part investigative series that ran February 19–26, 1995, in the *Raleigh News and Observer:*

> Greg Stephens is the 1995 version of the North Carolina hog farmer. He owns no hogs. Stephens carries a mortgage on four new confinement barns that cost him $300,000 to build. The 4,000 hogs inside belong to a company called Prestage Farms, Inc. (one of the larger suppliers of Smithfield Foods). Prestage simply pays Stephens a fee to raise them. . . .
>
> This arrangement is called contract farming, and it's hardly risk-free. But for anyone wanting to break into the swine business these days, it's the only game in town. "Without a contract, there's no way I'd be raising hogs," says Stephens, "and even if I had somehow gotten in, my pockets aren't nearly deep enough to let me stay in."
>
> Welcome to corporate livestock production, the force behind the swine industry's explosive growth in North Carolina. The backbone of the new system is a network of hundreds of contractors like Stephens, the franchise owners in a system that more closely resembles a fast-food chain than traditional agriculture.
>
> Nowhere in the nation has this change been as dramatic, or as officially embraced, as in North Carolina. As a result, the hog population has more than doubled in four years, and nearly all of that growth has occurred on farms controlled by the big companies. Meanwhile, independent farmers have left the business by the thousands.

In 1998 Smithfield Foods reportedly had a two-year waiting list of farmers wishing to obtain hog farming contracts. Industry observers, however, worried about the practice of saddling hundreds of small farmers with thousands of dollars of debt. As one elected state representative said, "Why invest your capital when you can get a farmer to take the risk? Why own the farm when you can own the farmer?"[1]

The problem foreseen by industry observers was the possibility that a company could cancel its contract with only 30 days' notice, leaving the farmer with the debt and no income to repay it, or could threaten to cancel and then renew the contract only with a sharply lower price per animal. Both sudden cancellations and lower prices were said to have happened frequently in the poultry industry:

> The changes that are sweeping the swine industry today were pioneered by chicken and turkey growers in the 1960s and '70s. Total confinement housing, vertical integration, and contract farming are all standard practices in the feather world. As a result, you need only look at chickens to see where pork is headed.
>
> The poultry industry today is fully integrated—meaning a handful of companies control all phases of production—and the labor is performed by an army of contract growers, some of them decidedly unhappy. "It's sharecropping, that's what it is," said Larry Holder, a chicken farmer and president of the Contract Poultry Growers Association.

The *Raleigh News and Observer* interviewed a number of farmers with hog-growing contracts in North Carolina. One farmer with 10 years of experience growing for Carroll Farms (another large supplier of Smithfield Foods), said, "They've been nothing but good to me."[2] Greg Stephens, the farmer quoted earlier, told the *News and Observer* that in his case the biggest selling point had been his freedom from market risk: "If hog prices go south, as they did two months ago, the contact farmer is barely affected. The company that owns the pigs takes on more risk than you do."[3]

The survival of over 1,000 family farms as contract hog growers is cited as one of the major benefits of the industrialization of agriculture in eastern North Carolina. Another is the creation of new agricultural jobs. Each of the contract farms averages 7,500 animals. The owning families cannot care for all those animals, even though the hogs are closely confined and automatically fed and watered. The typical farm will employ five people from the community at wages of $7 to $8 an hour; working conditions are hard and unpleasant. Most of the people filling such jobs are untrained and poorly educated area residents.

Smithfield's two new slaughterhouses in North Carolina employed about 3,000 people. These jobs were also regarded as hard and unpleasant jobs, some of which involved killing and disemboweling the hogs. The killing was said to be painless, and much of the early processing (scraping the carcass to remove the hair, and dealing with the internal organs) was automated. One of the more labor-intensive tasks involved preparing cuts of meat for packaged sale at grocery chains. Most grocery chains, to reduce their internal costs, had eliminated the position of store butchers, opting instead to buy their fresh meats cut, wrapped, packaged, and ready for sale. The cutting at meatpacking facilities was done on a high-speed assembly line, using very sharp laser-guided knives; workers were under continual pressure to perform and were exposed to dangers of injury. Workers who became skilled at this cutting and were able to endure the stress earned $10 to $12 an hour; turnover was relatively high because of the strenuous job demands. Many of the workers at the high-volume packing plants in eastern North Carolina were immigrants from Central or South America. The jobs were described in the following terms by an undercover reporter for the *New York Times* who worked at one of the Smithfield packing plants for three weeks on what was termed the picnic line:

> One o'clock means it is getting near the end of the workday [for the first shift]. Quota has to be met, and the workload doubles. The conveyor belt always overflows with meat around 1 o'clock. So the workers redouble their pace, hacking

pork from shoulder bones with a driven single-mindedness. They stare blankly, like mules in wooden blinders, as the butchered slabs pass by.

It is called the picnic line: 18 workers lined up on both sides of a belt, carving meat from bone. Up to 16 million shoulders a year come down that line here at Smithfield Packing Co., the largest pork production plant in the world. That works out to about 32,000 per shift, 63 a minute, one every 17 seconds for each worker for eight and a half hours a day. The first time you stare down at that belt you know your body is going to give in way before the machine ever will.[4]

The vertical integration of the industry, which has resulted in very limited purchasing of feed, machinery, and fuel from local sources; the debt-laden nature of the farm contracts, which have brought concerns about the possibility of future contract cancellations or price reductions; and the low-pay/low-quality nature of the jobs that have been created at both the farms and the packing plants had all combined to create popular opposition to any planned expansion of Smithfield Foods within eastern North Carolina. A much bigger and far more intense issue, however, was the alleged impact of hog farming on the environment:

Imagine a city as big as New York suddenly grafted onto North Carolina's Coastal Plain. Double it. Now imagine that this city has no sewage treatment plants. All the wastes from 15 million inhabitants are simply flushed into open pits and sprayed onto fields.

Turn those humans into hogs, and you don't have to imagine at all. It's already here. A vast city of swine has risen practically overnight in the counties east of Interstate 95. It's a megalopolis of 7 million animals that live in metal confinement barns and produce two to four times as much waste, per hog, as the average human.

All that manure—about 9.5 million tons a year—is stored in thousands of earthen pits called lagoons, where it is decomposed and sprayed or spread on crop lands. The lagoon system is the source of most hog farm odor, but industry officials say it's a proven and effective way to keep harmful chemicals and bacteria out of water supplies. New evidence says otherwise:

■ The *News and Observer* has obtained new scientific studies showing that contaminants from hog lagoons are getting into groundwater. One N.C. State University report estimates that as many as half of existing lagoons—perhaps hundreds—are leaking badly enough to contaminate groundwater.

■ The industry also is running out of places to spread or spray the waste from lagoons. On paper, the state's biggest swine counties already are producing more phosphorous-rich manure than available land can absorb, state Agriculture Department records show.

■ Scientists are discovering that hog farms emit large amounts of ammonia gas, which returns to earth in rain. The ammonia is believed to be contributing to an explosion of algae growth that's choking many of the state's rivers and estuaries.[5]

Raising hogs is admitted even by farm families to be a messy and smelly business. Hogs eat more than other farm animals, and they excrete more. And those excretions smell far, far worse. Having 50 to 100 hogs running free in a fenced pasture is one thing. The odor is clearly noticeable, but that sharp and pungent smell is felt to be part of rural living. Having 5,000 to 10,000 hogs closely confined in metal barns, with large ventilation fans moving the air continually from each barn, and the wastes from those hogs collected in huge open-air lagoons is something else. People who live near one of the large hog farms say that, unless you've experienced it, you just can't know what it is like:

> At 11 o'clock sharp on a Sunday morning the choir marched into the sanctuary of New Brown's Chapel Baptist Church. And the stench of 4,800 hogs rolled right in with them.
>
> The odor hung oppressively in the vestibule, clinging to church robes, winter coats and fancy hats. It sent stragglers scurrying indoors from the parking lot, some holding their noses. Sherry Leveston, 4, pulled her fancy white sweater over her face as she ran. "It stinks," she cried.
>
> It was another Sunday morning in Brownsville, a Greene County North Carolina hamlet that's home to 200 people and one hog farm. Like many of its counterparts throughout the eastern portion of the state, the town hasn't been the same since the hogs moved in a couple of years ago.
>
> To some, each new gust from the south [the direction of the farm] is a reminder of serious wrongs committed for which there has been no redress. "We've basically given up," said the Rev. Charles White, pastor at New Brown's Chapel.
>
> In scores of rural neighborhoods down east [the eastern portion of North Carolina] the talk is the same. There's something new in the air, and people are furious about it.
>
> Hog odor is by far the most emotional issue facing the pork industry—and the most divisive. Growers assert their right to earn a living; neighbors say they have a right to odor-free air. Hog company officials, meanwhile, accuse activists of exaggerating the problem to stir up opposition. . . .
>
> For other residents [of Brownsville, close to New Brown's Chapel] hog odor has simply become an inescapable part of their daily routine. It's usually heaviest about 5 A.M., when Lisa Hines leaves the house for her factory job. It seeps into her car and follows her on her commute to work. It clings to her hair and clothes during the day. And it awaits her when she returns home in the afternoon.
>
> "It makes me so mad," she said. "The owner lives miles away from here, and he can go home and smell apples and cinnamon if he wants to. But we have no choice."[6]

The 7 million hogs in eastern North Carolina currently generated about 9.5 million tons of manure each year. This waste was stored in large earthen pits called lagoons. These pits were open so that sunlight would decompose the wastes and kill the harmful bacteria; the manure was then spread on farm fields as organic fertilizer. This had been the accepted means for disposing of animal wastes on small family farms for centuries. It was a method fully protected by federal, state, and local laws; a hog farmer—whether a small family or large contract farm—could not be sued for any inconveniences brought about by the hogs, unless those inconveniences were the result of clear negligence in caring for the hogs.

Exhibit 3 describes the environmental improvement projects the company had under way in 2001 and Exhibit 4 presents Smithfield Foods' environmental policy statement.

The difference now, of course, comes from the huge expansion of scale. Again, the wastes of 50 to 100 animals were easily accommodated. There was a noticeable effect on air quality, but that was felt to be a natural consequence of living in the country, and the smell came from your own farm, or that of your neighbor, or that of a person who

Exhibit 3   SMITHFIELD FOODS' ENVIRONMENTAL PROJECTS IN 2001

Environmental Project	Project Description	Project Background
Smithfield Packing Company's processing plant in Kinston, NC, began installing three cooling towers capable of recirculating more than 200,000 gallons of water daily.	"Since the cooling towers went online in February 2001, the Kinston plant has reduced its monthly groundwater use by 5 million gallons. That puts less demand on an already stressed water table, improving the quality of life for the people living here." —Bill Gill, assistant vice president, environmental affairs, Smithfield Foods.	The city's water usage had taxed the area aquifer. Smithfield's plant handles vacuum packaging, a process that requires approximately 200,000 gallons of cooling water daily. In addition to Kinston, Smithfield has implemented similar water conservation systems at facilities in Smithfield and Portsmouth, VA, and in Wilson, NC.
In 1997, Smithfield Packing Company's Tar Heel, NC, plant, the world's largest pork processing facility, introduced a state-of-the-art water treatment and reuse system.	"The plant successfully expanded production while reducing the overall need for groundwater and, in addition, decreased the volume of treated water discharged to the Cape Fear River. This waste treatment system is a model for industry. It is a typical example of our continued commitment to protect and preserve the environment." —Robert F. Urell, vice president, corporate engineering and chairman, environmental compliance committee, Smithfield Foods.	As early as 1995, Smithfield Packing began seeking a way to increase production at the Tar Heel plant without exceeding North Carolina limits on the characteristics of its wastewater and without increasing the impact on marine life in the Cape Fear River. Smithfield invested $3 million to augment existing water treatment efforts with a system that allows the plant to reuse an average of 1 million gallons daily.
In March 2001, Carroll's Foods, part of Smithfield Foods' Murphy-Brown, LLC, subsidiary, became the world's first agricultural livestock company to receive ISO 14001 certification for environmental management systems on its farms in North Carolina, South Carolina, and Virginia.	"ISO certification is the gold standard for environmental excellence. It means that Carroll's has clearly-defined methods for monitoring and measuring the environmental impact of its activities and in identifying potential problems. This should assure residents of all three states that we've really taken the lead in protecting their interests." —Don Butler, director of governmental relations and public affairs, Murphy-Brown.	As early as 1997, Carroll's began developing an environmental management system that could meet the stringent certification requirements of the Geneva-based International Organization for Standardization (www.iso.org). Sister companies Murphy Farms and Brown's of Carolina expect to receive ISO certification for their North Carolina farms by the end of 2001, with their western farming operations to be certified in 2002. Over the next 24 months, Smithfield will expand its EMS efforts and seek ISO certification for all of the company's North American meat processing operations.
John Morrell's processing facility in Sioux Falls, SD, and Smithfield Packing Company's Tar Heel, NC, plant have modified their boilers to burn methane biogas as an alternative fuel.	"We are using a cleaner-burning alternative to oil or natural gas while also reducing emissions of methane, an odorous greenhouse gas. In Sioux Falls, we recovered 125 million cubic feet of methane gas in 2000 and expect to reduce emissions by 1,400 tons annually. That has positively impacted air quality throughout the area, including Sioux Falls Park adjacent to the plant." —Dennis Dykstra, utilities engineer at the Sioux Falls plant.	In treating wastewater, both facilities use anaerobic lagoons that generate methane as a by-product. Since it opened in 1992, the Tar Heel plant has captured much of this biogas and diverted it to a recovery boiler. The plant brought a second boiler on-line in 2001. John Morrell's Sioux Falls boiler went live in 2000.

Exhibit 3   Continued

Environmental Project	Project Description	Project Background
Funded in part by a $15 million contribution from Smithfield Foods, North Carolina State University (NCSU) is investigating 18 different technologies to modify or replace current methods of swine waste disposal on hog farms.	"We could see potentially cleaner air through the reduction of methane and ammonia emissions generated by lagoons. We expect to make our final recommendation in 2003, and Smithfield Foods has agreed to apply the technologies we select, if commercially feasible, on all its company-owned farms." —Mike Williams, PhD, director of the NCSU Animal and Poultry Waste Management Center and project head.	Smithfield Foods helped pioneer two of the solutions currently under consideration—BEST (Biomass Energy Sustainable Technology) and ISSUES (Innovative Sustainable Systems Utilizing Economical Solutions). BEST, in development since 1995, removes the solids from farm wastewater for conversion into green energy such as steam or electricity. ISSUES is a series of technologies that enhance the performance of existing lagoons. NCSU has paired ISSUES with a technology that utilizes methane in a microturbine. This combined solution harvests the energy value of hog manure to create green electricity.
In August 2000, Smithfield Foods pledged $50 million ($2 million annually over 25 years) to North Carolina to aid in the state's environmental efforts. Smithfield also committed resources and manpower to help preserve the Albermarle-Pamlico estuary.	"If the state uses our contribution to purchase buffer lands and conservation easements, it would offer North Carolina's waterways additional protection from development and storm water runoff. As for this estuary, protecting its fragile ecosystem is critical because it is vital for commercial fishing." —Richard Poulson, vice president and senior advisor to the chairman, Smithfield Foods.	To date, Smithfield Foods has donated $4 million to North Carolina and is enthused about specific projects to be undertaken with this money. The Albemarle-Pamlico Sounds, the second largest estuarine complex in the United States, currently suffer from stream bank erosion, sedimentation, and nutrient loading.
Murphy Brown, Smithfield Foods' hog farming subsidiary, is finalizing plans for an integrated land management program. It will ensure the sound stewardship of all lands on more than 200 company-owned and operated farms in North Carolina.	The effects of the program will be far reaching. For example, it will conserve woodlands and ensure the continued biological diversity of wetlands and other ecologically sensitive areas. The nesting grounds of a number of species will be protected as will areas containing mature longleaf pines, mature bald cypress trees, and mature bottomland hardwoods." —Jeff Turner, vice president, environmental and government affairs, Murphy-Brown.	The land management program gives equal consideration to water quality protection, soil conservation, and wildlife habitat development. It applies equally to lands normally outside the scope of state agricultural regulation. Stewardship methods include sound irrigation, tillage, and harvesting on spray fields, timber management, and conservation easements through an appropriate agency.

Source: www.smithfieldfoods.com, December 26, 2002.

had been there for years. There was a probable effect on water quality, but farm wells were always located uphill and a substantial distance from manure piles, and it was thought that neighbors would be protected by natural filtration through the clay subsoils of the region. No one worried very much about possible public health effects of small numbers of farm animals.

The wastes from 5,000 to 10,000 animals could not be so easily accommodated, and people did worry about the possible public health effects of very large numbers of

Exhibit 4   SMITHFIELD FOODS: ENVIRONMENTAL POLICY STATEMENT, 2002

It is the corporate policy of Smithfield Foods, Inc., and its subsidiaries to conduct business in an ethical manner consistent with continual improvement in regard to protecting human health and the environment. The following management principles are adopted to ensure this policy is endorsed and implemented throughout our organization:

1. Maintaining an effective organizational and accountability structure for environmental performance;
2. Establishing policies and practices for conducting operations in compliance with environmental laws, regulations, and other organizational policies;
3. Training and motivating facility operators to conduct all activities in an environmentally responsible manner;
4. Assessing the environmental impacts of changes in operations;
5. Encouraging the operation of facilities with diligent consideration to pollution prevention and the sustainable use/reuse of energy and materials;
6. Encouraging prompt reporting of any environmentally detrimental incidents to regulators and management;
7. Providing facility operators with information relating to specific local or regional conditions, current and/or proposed environmental regulations, technologies, and stakeholder expectations;
8. Providing for environmental performance goals, assessing performance, conducting audits, and sharing appropriate performance information throughout our organization;
9. Promoting the adoption of these principles by suppliers, consultants, and others acting on behalf of the company; and
10. Documenting development, implementation, and compliance efforts associated with these principles.

Source: www.smithfieldfoods.com, December 26, 2002.

farm animals. Debilitating asthma had become a much more frequent condition among young children who lived near large hog farms, and there was concern that waste was leaking from the lagoons and contaminating the ground water. The conventional wisdom about the lagoons was that the heavier sludge was supposed to settle on the bottom and form a seal that would prevent the escape of harmful bacteria or destructive chemicals:

> As recently as two years ago, the U.S. Division of Environmental Management told state lawmakers in a briefing that lagoons effectively self-seal within months with "little or no groundwater contamination." Wendell H. Murphy, a former state senator who was also [in partnership with Smithfield Corporation] the nation's largest producer of hogs, said in an interview this month that "lagoons will seal themselves" and that "there is not one shred, not one piece of evidence anywhere in this nation that any groundwater is being contaminated by any hog lagoon."
>
> What Murphy didn't know was that a series of brand-new studies, conducted among Eastern North Carolina hog farms, showed that large numbers of lagoons are leaking, some of them severely.[7]

The *Raleigh News and Observer* had reported that researchers at North Carolina State University had dug test wells near 11 lagoons that were at least seven years old.

They found that more than half of the lagoons were leaking moderately to severely; even those lagoons that were described as leaking only moderately still produced groundwater nitrate levels up to three times the allowable limit. The researchers also found that lagoons were not the only source of groundwater contamination. They dug test wells and examined water quality in fields where hog waste had been sprayed as fertilizer, and found evidence of widespread bacterial and chemical contamination. It was felt that fully as much water contamination came from the practice of attempting to dispose of the decomposed waste through spraying on crops as from the earlier storage of decomposing waste in the lagoons. According to the *Raleigh News and Observer* reporter, too much waste was being sprayed on too few fields, even though almost all farmers in the region now accepted this natural fertilizer in lieu of buying commercial products.

The researchers from North Carolina State University, however, did not urge rural residents to rush out to buy bottled water. In most of the cases they concluded that the contaminants appeared to be migrating laterally toward the nearest ditch or stream, and they found no evidence that a private well had been contaminated. But they did find evidence that numerous streams had been contaminated, partially from leakage but primarily from spills and overflows:

> Frequently major spills are cleaned up quickly so that the public never hears about them. That's what happened in May 1995 when a 10-acre lagoon ruptured on Murphy's Farms' 8,000-hog facility in Magnolia, North Carolina. A limestone layer beneath the lagoon collapsed, sending tons of waste cascading into nearby Millers Creek in an accident that was never reported to state water-quality officials.
>
> An employee of the town's water department discovered the problem when he saw corn kernels and hog waste floating by in the creek that runs through the center of town. He alerted the company, and within hours a task force had been assembled to plug the leak.
>
> It took four days to find the source and fix the problem. But neither Magnolia town officials nor Murphy Farms executives ever notified the state about the spill.
>
> "In retrospect, maybe we should have," Wendell Murphy said, "but I would also say that to my knowledge no harm has ever come of it."
>
> Former employees of hog companies, however, told *News and Observer* reporters that spills were a common occurrence. "Hardly a week goes by," said a former manager for one of the largest hog farms in the state, "that there isn't some sort of leak or overflow. Almost any heavy rain will bring an overflow. When that happens, workers do the best they can to clean it up. After that it's just pray no one notices and keep your mouth shut," he explained.[8]

The waste lagoons could not be covered with a roof to prevent overflows associated with heavy rains, or enclosed with a building to prevent the escape of odors; They were simply too large—five to eight acres—and it was necessary to have direct sunlight to create the natural conditions that would break down the toxic chemicals and kill the harmful bacteria in the wastes. Company officials seemed to believe that there was no possible solution to the problem of the extremely bad odors; essentially they said it would just be necessary for people to learn to live with the smell, which extends up to two miles from the open lagoons and the sprayed fields. According to the *Raleigh News and Observer*,

Wendell Murphy, chairman of Murphy Family Farms [part of the Murphy Brown hog farming subsidiary of Smithfield Foods] said that while the hog industry is extremely sensitive to the odor problem, he thinks the industry's economic importance should be considered in the equation. "Should we expect the odor to never drift off the site to a neighbor's house? If so, then we're out of business. We all have to have some inconvenience once in a while for the benefits that come with it."[9]

As the *Raleigh News and Observer* reported, feelings ran high among eastern North Carolina residents in opposing further expansion of hog farming in the region:

Three weeks ago, the tiny town of Faison held a referendum of sorts on whether its residents wanted a new industrial plant, with 1,500 new jobs, built in their community. The jobs lost.

Because the industry in question was a hog-processing plant, people packed the local fire station an hour early to blast the idea. They jeered and hissed every time the county's industrial recruiter mentioned pigs or the plant. "I want to know two things," thundered one burly speaker thrusting a finger at that much smaller industrial recruiter, Woody Brinson, "How can we stop this thing, and how can we get you fired?"

The town council's eventual 3–0 vote against the proposed IBP [a subsidiary of Smithfield Foods] hog slaughterhouse may have little effect on whether the plant is built. [Zoning within rural North Carolina is controlled by the county, not the municipality, and agriculturally related zoning has always been very loosely applied, to benefit local farmers.] What was striking about this meeting, and this vote, was that both occurred in the heart of Duplin County, an economic showcase for the hog industry.

With a pigs-per-person ratio of 32-to-1, Duplin has seen big payoffs from eastern North Carolina's hog revolution in the past decade. The county's revenues from sales and property taxes have soared, and Duplin's per capital income has risen from the lowest 25 percent statewide to about the middle.

Pork production also has spawned jobs in support businesses in Duplin and neighboring counties. People in the hog business say farm odor—"the smell of money"—is a small price to pay for a big benefit. "These hog farms are putting money in people's pockets," says Woody Brinston [the county's director of industrial development]. "Duplin County is booming."

But even here, some bitterly resent the way the industry has transformed the way the countryside looks and smells. Some say that their property has gone down in value. Others note the contrasts in the economic picture. In Duplin County, just 70 miles east of the booming Research Triangle [an area located between Raleigh, Durham and Chapel Hill with a large number of advanced electronic and biotechnology firms] the population hasn't grown in 10 years. Farm jobs are dwindling despite the rise in hog production.

Daryl Walker, a newly elected Duplin County commissioner, says he hears these arguments all the time. "If this is prosperity," he says, "many of my constituents would just as soon do without it. They are scared to death that there are just going to be more and more hogs, and more and more of the problems that come with those hogs."[10]

A subsequent letter to the editor of the *Raleigh News and Observer* said:

Last Sunday, returning from a weekend at Wrightsville Beach, we stopped at an Interstate 40 rest area near Clinton. When we stepped from our car the stench brought tears to our eyes. So add to the ever-mounting environment damage the poor image our state now leaves with tourists heading towards our beautiful coast. We'll never know many big tourism bucks are now and soon will be going elsewhere.[11]

Endnotes

[1]Quoted in the five-part series by Joby Warrick and Pat Stith, "Boss Hog: North Carolina's Pork Revolution—Hog Waste Is Polluting the Ground Water," *Raleigh News and Observer*, February 19, 1995. This series, based on a seven-month investigation and run in the *News and Observer*, February 19–26, 1995, was awarded the Pulitzer Prize for Public Service Journalism in 1996.

[2]Ibid.

[3]Ibid.

[4]Charlie LeDuff, "At a Slaughterhouse, Some Things Never Die," *New York Times*, June 16, 2000, p. A1.

[5]*Raleigh News and Observer*, February 19, 1995.

[6]Joby Warrick and Pat Stith, "Boss Hog: North Carolina's Pork Revolution—Money Talks," *Raleigh News and Observer*, February 24, 1995, p. A9.

[7]Ibid.

[8]Ibid.

[9]Ibid.

[10]Joby Warrick and Pat Stith, "Boss Hog: North Carolina's Pork Revolution—Pork Barrels," *Raleigh News and Observer*, February 26, 1995.

[11]*Raleigh News and Observer*, March 4, 1995, p. A10.

Whirlpool Financial National Bank and the Sale of TV Dish Antennas in Alabama

LaRue T. Hosmer
The University of Alabama

The Whirlpool Corporation was the world's largest manufacturer of major home appliances, with a product line that included washers, dryers, ovens, stoves, refrigerators, dishwashers, freezers, trash compactors, and air conditioners. Beginning in the late 1980s and continuing to the present, Whirlpool had pursued a global strategy to become the world leader in major home appliances. Whirlpool had manufacturing plants in 13 countries and marketed its products in 170 countries under such brand names as Whirlpool, KitchenAid, Roper, Estate, Bauknecht, Ignis, Laden, Inglis, Brastemp, and Consul. Whirlpool was also the principal supplier of home appliances to Sears, Roebuck, which sold its products under the Kenmore brand name. Whirlpool's headquarters were in Benton Harbor, Michigan.

For many years Whirlpool, like many other manufacturers of "long-life" consumer products, had a customer finance subsidiary—Whirlpool Financial Corporation (WFC)—that provided financing to retailers of Whirlpool products and to consumers who purchased Whirlpool appliances on installment plans. Whirlpool's credit rating allowed it to borrow money at low market rates and then lend that money at higher commercial rates to its distributors for inventory support and to its customers for installment purchases.

Since its formation in 1957, WFC had expanded its operations to include leasing heavy equipment to highway contractors, making mortgages to mall developers, and financing so-called open-end notes that came in from independent sales agents. The sales agents with whom WFC dealt were mostly small companies or individuals who might or might not have a store location but who did most of their business by seeking out leads and selling aluminum siding, furniture, newly installed roofs, and other big-ticket household items directly to consumers. Usually such sales required little or no down payment, and the borrower agreed to make only a minimal payment each month; there were add-on penalties for missing the monthly payment. Such loans appealed to people with low income and poor credit because they enabled them to purchase products they otherwise could not afford. Frequently, the sales agents relied on telemarketing to get leads and then visited potential customers at their homes to consummate the sale, write up orders, and get the borrower's signature on the open-end note. All of these new forms of financing that WFC had entered carried higher interest rates, and

Professor Hosmer holds the Durr-Fillauer Chair in Business Ethics at The University of Alabama. Copyright © 2003 by the case author.

Exhibit 1   NOTE 3 TO WHIRLPOOL'S 1997 FINANCIAL STATEMENTS DETAILING THE DISPOSITION OF ITS WFC SUBSIDIARY

During the third quarter of 1997, the company discontinued its financing operations and adopted a plan to dispose of most of the assets of Whirlpool Financial Corporation (WFC). The company recorded a pretax gain of $70 million ($42 million after-tax) related to the transaction.

In September 1997, the company reached a definitive agreement to sell the majority of WFC's assets in a series of transactions to Transamerica Distribution Finance Corporation (TDF). During the fourth quarter of 1997, the company completed the sale of certain inventory floor planning financing assets and international factoring assets to TDF for approximately $927 million. In January 1998, the company sold to TDF additional international assets and consumer financing receivable assets for approximately $370 million. The company expects to record a pretax gain of approximately $22 million in the first quarter of 1998 related to the completion of the TDF transactions. Under an ongoing strategic partnership, TDF will continue to provide financing services to the company's trade partners and customers. In separate transactions during the fourth quarter of 1997, the company sold certain consumer financing receivables for $98 million and entered into an agreement to sell a portion of WFC's aerospace financing business for $168 million, of which $144 million was sold in the first two months of 1998.

A $36 million operating charge ($22 million after-tax) was recorded in the third quarter of 1997 to provide an additional reserve for certain retained WFC aerospace assets.

Gross financing receivables and leases at December 31, 1997 and 1996 were $331 million and $2,128 million, respectively. Unearned income, estimated residual value and allowances related to these leases were $(55) million and $(23) million, respectively. Deferred income tax liabilities relating to financing leases were $127 million and $123 million at December 31, 1997 and 1996.

Interest and discount charges are recognized in revenues using the effective yield method. Lease income is recorded in decreasing amounts over the term of the lease contract, resulting in a level rate of return on the net investment in the lease. Origination fees and related costs are deferred and amortized as yield adjustments over the life of the related receivable or lease. The allowance for losses is maintained at estimated amounts necessary to cover losses on all finance and leasing receivables based on management's assessment of various factors including loss experience and review of problem accounts.

Net losses on financing receivables and leases were $35 million (excluding operating charge), $40 million and $39 million in 1997, 1996 and 1995. Financing receivables of $109 million, $108 million and $112 million are considered impaired under Financial Accounting Standards Board Statement No. 114, "Accounting by Creditors for Impairment of a Loan" at December 31, 1997, 1996 and 1995. Specific allowances for losses on these receivables total $65 million, $29 million and $19 million at December 31, 1997, 1996 and 1995. WFC recognized $5 million, $9 million and $12 million of interest income in 1997, 1996 and 1995 on these receivables.

Source: Whirlpool's 1997 annual report.

consequently generated larger profits, than the regular inventory support loans and installment purchase contracts on appliances. The open-end notes for sales agents, being a form of credit card debt, were particularly profitable, carrying 18 to 22 percent interest rates.

Under traditional or closed-end financing, a seller was required by the Federal Truth-in-Lending Act to disclose in a simple, clear written contract the amount of the total loan, the size of the monthly payment, and the number of months to fully repay the loan. However, under credit card or open-end financing, there were far fewer disclosure requirements. The interest rate had to be stated on the contract (though it could be in small type at the bottom of the page), and the full amount of the loan had to be included. Since monthly payments were minimal, often just large enough to cover the interest, the number of months for full repayment could not be computed and did not have to be disclosed. Such lack of full disclosure had led, in many instances, to customer confusion and legal action.

In 1997, Whirlpool elected to sell the consumer finance division of its WFC subsidiary to Transamerica Distribution Finance Corporation (TDF) and form a 10-year strategic alliance whereby TDF would continue to provide financing services to Whirlpool's trade partners—Exhibit 1 presents the note to Whirlpool's financial statements in its 1997 annual report relating to the disposal of its WFC subsidiary. Exhibits

Exhibit 2   WHIRLPOOL'S CONSOLIDATED STATEMENTS OF EARNINGS, 1995–1997 (IN MILLIONS OF DOLLARS, EXCEPT PER SHARE DATA)

	1997	1996	1995
Net sales	$8,617	$8,523	$8,163
Expenses			
Cost of products sold	6,604	6,623	6,245
Selling and administrative	1,625	1,557	1,521
Intangible amortization	34	35	31
Restructuring costs	343	30	—
Total expenses	8,606	8,245	7,797
Operating profit	11	278	366
Other Income (Expense)			
Interest and sundry	(14)	(23)	(23)
Interest expense	(168)	(155)	(129)
Earnings (loss) before income taxes and other items	(171)	100	214
Income taxes (benefit)	(9)	70	90
Earnings (loss) from continuing operations before equity earnings and minority interests	(162)	30	124
Equity in affiliated companies	67	93	72
Minority interests	49	18	(1)
Earnings (loss) from continuing operations	(46)	141	195
Earnings (loss) from discontinued operations (less applicable taxes)	(11)	15	14
Gain on disposal from discontinued operations (less applicable taxes)	42	—	—
Net earnings (loss)	$(15)	$156	$209
Per share of common stock:			
Basic earnings (loss) from continuing operations	$(0.62)	$1.90	$2.64
Basic net earnings (loss)	(0.20)	2.10	2.83
Diluted earnings (loss) from continuing operations	(0.62)	1.88	2.60
Diluted net earnings (loss)	(0.20)	2.08	2.78
Cash dividends	1.36	1.36	1.36

Source: Whirlpool's 1997 annual report.

2 and 3 present Whirlpool's financial statements for the last several years in which it owned WFC. The transfer of WFC's Consumer Finance Division and its financing arm, Whirlpool Financial National Bank, was completed on January 1, 1998. The transfer of WFC's Inventory Finance Division, Latin American Finance Group, European Division, and associated corporate staff to TDF—part of the same deal—took place in the fourth quarter of 1997. The parent of TDF, Transamerica Corporation, consisted of a group of insurance, financing, and investment businesses; at the time of the acquisition, Transamerica was a Fortune 500 company with 1998 revenues of $6.4 billion and after-tax profits of $707 million.

Exhibit 3   WHIRLPOOL'S CONSOLIDATED BALANCE SHEETS, 1996–1997 (IN MILLIONS OF DOLLARS)

	1997	1996
Assets		
Current assets		
Cash and equivalents	$ 578	$ 129
Trade receivables, less allowances of $156 in 1997 and $45 in 1996	1,565	966
Financing receivables and leases, less allowances	—	1,400
Inventories	1,170	1,034
Prepaid expenses and other	191	188
Deferred income taxes	215	95
Net assets of discontinued operations	562	—
Total current assets	$4,281	$3,812
Other assets		
Investment in affiliated companies	100	513
Financing receivables and leases, less allowances	—	705
Intangibles, net	916	870
Deferred income taxes	220	152
Other	378	165
Total other assets	$1,614	$2,405
Property, plant, and equipment		
Land	92	93
Buildings	969	731
Machinery and equipment	4,201	3,015
Accumulated depreciation	(2,887)	(2,041)
Net property, plant, and equipment	2,375	1,798
Total assets	$8,270	$8,015
Liabilities and Stockholders' Equity		
Current liabilities		
Notes payable	$1,332	$2,038
Accounts payable	987	983
Employee compensation	265	226
Accrued expenses	858	624
Restructuring costs	212	32
Current maturities of long-term debt	22	119
Total current liabilities	$3,676	$4,022
Other liabilities		
Deferred income taxes	190	206
Postemployment benefits	598	563
Other liabilities	188	161
Long-term debt	1,074	955
	$2,050	$1,885
Minority interests	773	182

continued

Exhibit 3   Continued

	1997	1996
Stockholders' equity		
Common stock, $1 par value:		
250 million shares authorized	82	81
Paid-in capital	280	246
Retained earnings	1,801	1,918
Unearned restricted stock	(6)	(7)
Cumulative translation adjustments	(149)	(76)
Treasury stock—6 million shares at cost in 1997 and 1996	(237)	(236)
	1,771	1,926
Total liabilities and stockholders' equity	$8,270	$8,015

Source: Whirlpool's 1997 annual report.

Whirlpool Financial National Bank and the Financing of Satellite Dishes to Consumers

In May 1999, Whirlpool Financial National Bank was one of two defendants, along with Don Gantt, doing business as Gulf Coast Electronics, in a lawsuit filed by Barbara Carlisle and her parents, George and Velma Merriweather, in the Circuit Court of Hale County, Alabama. The plaintiffs alleged that they had been misled by the defendants concerning the terms on which they had financed the 1995 purchase of TV satellite dish antennas for their homes in rural Alabama. Gantt was the sales agent whose Gulf Coast Electronics proprietorship had sold the dish antennas to the plaintiffs. Moreover, since the sale occurred in 1995, when Whirlpool was the owner of Whirlpool Financial National Bank, Whirlpool was liable for the actions of its then subsidiary. By the time of the trial, Gantt had closed Gulf Coast Electronics, left the television dish antenna sales business, and could not be located to appear as either a defendant or a witness.[1]

In the absence of cable TV or satellite dishes, television reception tends to be poor in much of rural Alabama. The signals of the broadcasting stations in the major cities—Birmingham, Huntsville, Montgomery, and Mobile—were often weak in certain parts of the state. Moreover, low population density made it uneconomic for cable TV companies to extend their service much outside the city limits of the towns and cities they served. During the 1970s and 1980s, persons living in rural areas where cable TV service was unavailable relied on tall antennas often attached to the roof or chimney of a home, with a directional control so that the receptor could be positioned to "catch" the signals from a specific station. It was not a totally satisfactory solution; the number of channels that could be received was limited to those in nearby metropolitan areas.

In the 1990s satellite dish antennas became available. Dish antennas gave rural residents access to dozens of popular channels via rebroadcasts from satellites circling the earth. Early models of the satellite dish antennas were expensive, ranging up to $2,000 or more, but prices came down as technology improved and growing sales permitted manufacturers to achieve scale economies. Even so, many low-income families and individuals living in rural Alabama could rarely afford to make the necessary down payment to obtain traditional or closed-end installment loans from local banks or credit companies and thereby finance the purchase of a satellite dish. What was workable for some families, however, was an open-end financing arrangement. Gulf Coast Electronics—together with approximately 10 other sales agents within Alabama—used the open-end consumer financing provided by Whirlpool Financial National Bank to sell satellite dish antennas to poor customers in the rural regions of Alabama.

These sales agents generally had an office from which they would make telephone calls to sales prospects and set up appointments for a home visit. Gulf Coast Electronics employed 10 people who made calls to prospects and then went to prospects' homes to try to write up an order for a satellite dish. They apparently were paid substantial commissions, depending on the number of completed sales, and their sales techniques were said to be very aggressive. According to court records from the trial, they were trained to demonstrate the advantages of the new antenna system, quote a total price of $1,124 (which included delivery, installation, and sales tax) and then offer "nothing-down" financing from Whirlpool Financial National Bank with minimum payments of $34 a month.

In their lawsuit and at trial, the plaintiffs claimed that the sales agents working for Gulf Coast Electronics told them that payments of $34 a month for 36 months would totally pay for the antenna, delivery, and installation. According to the sales contract that was signed prior to installation, interest at the rate of 22 percent a year was to be added to the unpaid balance at the end of each month, which meant that total repayment—assuming no late charges or other penalties were added to the total—would take 60 months.

In addition to whether the terms of the sales contract had been accurately revealed was a secondary concern over the equitable nature of the full sales transaction. The total sales price, with tax and installation, for the 19-inch RCA satellite dish antenna, termed a digital satellite system (DSS), sold by Gulf Coast Electronics was $1,124.24. Apparently the same system, prior to the sales tax and without the system installation, could have been purchased at a major electronics retailer such as Radio Shack or Circuit City for about $400 in 1995. Thomas Methven, attorney for the plaintiffs, early in the trial was questioning David Carroll, a witness for the plaintiffs but a prior employee for a sales agent very similar to Gulf Coast Electronics, and the following exchange took place:

Q. Today, how much can you go to a store and buy a DSS satellite dish for?
A. $199, in some places.
Q. Back in 1995 when these victims bought theirs, how much did the same DSS satellite dishes by themselves cost in the store, not the package [tax and installation], but just the DSS [digital satellite system].
A. In '95, to the best of my recollection, as far as I remember, they were $199. I don't know what date. But at one time you could buy them for close to $400. So no more than $400.[2]

The $1,124 charged by Gulf Coast Electronics also included sales tax and installation. The sales tax would have been $32 (8 percent of $400), and installation was described as very simple. The complete DSS came with a stand, the antenna, a length of coaxial cable, and a control box. It was necessary only to position the stand close to the house, set the antenna on the stand, drill a hole through the wall of the home, connect the antenna to the control box, and then connect the box to the television set. Witnesses testified that this installation took no more than 30 minutes.

David Carroll, the witness who testified to the much lower cost of the DSS system when purchased at a retail store rather than through a sales agent, had been in charge of training for Centevision. Centevision was a sales agent similar to Gulf Coast Electronics and also sold TV antennas and financed them through Whirlpool Financial National Bank. Carroll testified that he had trained between 10 and 20 new salespeople each week for Centevision, during a period of peak demand. The following exchange took place between David Carroll and Thomas Methvin, attorney for the plaintiffs:

Q. And between the several, I believe you said two hundred or so, sales people that you trained yourself, was there a target market when you were selling these satellite dishes and home theater packages?

A. Yes, sir. We were trained to basically target the blacks, you know, any type of people living in trailers. People like that.

Tripp Haston [for the defendants]. Judge, could we have an objection for relevancy. This man worked for a company named Centevision and not Gulf Coast Electronics. He didn't train anyone from Gulf Coast Electronics, who was the merchant in this case.

Mr. Methvin [for the plaintiffs]. Judge, we think it's evidence to show not only was Gulf Coast Electronics one dealer that was doing it, but it came from the very top, that Whirlpool had lots of bad dealers. And we're going to have testimony from other witnesses that dealt with other dealers. And so that's why it's relevant.[3]

Two of the plaintiffs then testified that they had been told that payments of $34 a month would pay off the entire debt in three years. The first plaintiff, Barbara Carlisle, explained that she had not only gotten an antenna for herself but also arranged for her parents, George and Velma Merriweather, the second plaintiffs, to have one installed at their home. After paying on the debt for two years she grew concerned that the balance on her monthly statements was not going down as rapidly as she had expected and, after talking with others at her church, found that she had been misled:

Q. Mrs. Carlisle, how did it make you feel when you found out you had been flimflammed by these people?

A. It made me angry. It made me worry. I mean upset, very hurt. I got my parents involved in it, and I knew they were hurting from it. I've had headaches, sleepless nights, worrying, because I knew they were worried. And we're not rich people. We work hard for the little that we have. And we just don't deserve to be treated like that. And I think they should be punished for what they did.

Q. Mrs. Carlisle, as you sit here today, are you certain that February 1995, when you were on the phone with those individuals from Gulf Coast, that you were told your payments would be $34 a month for three years and it would be paid for?

A. I'm positive.

Q. And when you called back for your parents, are you certain that you were told that their payments would be $34 a month for three years?

A. Yes.[4]

Velma Merriweather, the second plaintiff and Barbara Carlisle's mother, also testified that she felt that she had been cheated by the company:

Q. When they told you that these people came in your house, and you trusted them because you couldn't read the papers yourselves, your husband couldn't read the papers, that you trusted to be telling you the truth. And when that lawyer told you they lied to you, were you upset?

A. I was sick, and I couldn't sleep [Velma Merriweather continued with a graphic description of her various illnesses.]

Q. You think it was right for those people—ma'am, do you know how much the satellite costs today? Did you know you can buy a satellite for less then $300 today?

A. No. I didn't know it.

Q. When those people sold you that satellite—well, let me ask you this way, how do you feel paying over a thousand and something dollars for a satellite you can buy for $300?

A. Huh, I don't feel right.

Q. You feel mad about that?

A. Sure is.

Q. You ever talk to your husband about this?

A. Yeah, I talk to him. He was just walking saying, "I'm tired of these folks doing us like this."[5]

The final witness was a senior executive in the Whirlpool National Financial Bank, Brian Chambliss. The following exchange took place between Thomas Methvin, attorney for the plaintiffs, and Chambliss:

Q. Let me just ask a question that's very simple. If what the jury has heard from this witness stand from Mr. David Carroll and several of these witnesses, from Mrs. Carlisle and the Merriweathers, if what they heard is the truth, Whirlpool is a pretty sorry company, aren't they.

Mr. Haston (attorney for the defendants): Judge, I'd object to that question as argumentative.

Mr. Methvin [attorney for the plaintiffs]. Well, let me just strike and ask it this way. [Mr. Methvin then continued the examination.]

Q. Will you stand behind what Whirlpool is selling, back them up one hundred percent? You're proud to be a part of this company?

A. Yes, I am.

Q. You're proud of what they did?

A. I'm proud to be a part of that company.

Q. Are you proud of what they did in this case?

A. I don't think we've done anything wrong.

Q. Nothing wrong. So if somebody goes into people's homes, sometimes unsophisticated people, armed with your documents, get them signed up, and they make payments to y'all and you find out they've been lied to, you say there's nothing wrong with that?

A. At this point I don't think we've done anything wrong. I think that there probably could have been a misunderstanding.

Q. Misunderstanding?

A. In what was presented to them.

Q. How about those roughly two hundred people that Mr. Carroll talked to? You reckon all two hundred of them had a misunderstanding?

Mr. Haston [attorney for the defendants]. Objection to the question as argumentative, Judge.[6]

The judge upheld the argumentative objection of Tripp Haston, attorney for the defendants. Thomas Methvin, attorney for the plaintiffs, consequently changed the direction of his questioning of Brian Chambliss, the senior executive from Whirlpool Financial National Bank:

Q. Would you agree with me that if some company was taking advantage of folks in the name of trying to make money, that would be wrong?
A. Whirlpool did nothing wrong.
Q. Right. That's not the question, sir. This lawyer [indicating Tripp Haston, for the defendants] will have a chance to ask you some questions. My question is, if a company took advantage of vulnerable people in the name of trying to make money, is that wrong?
A. Yes.
Q. How do you explain Mr. Gibson and Mrs. Atkins, how they were making their payment to Whirlpool, and Mr. Gibson can't read and Mrs. Atkins can't see because she's got diabetes or something; is that right?
A. They were taken advantage of?
Q. They were lied to about their payments. You heard them testify.
A. Did Whirlpool lie to them? Is that what you're asking?
Q. Yeah.
A. Did Whirlpool take advantage of them?
Q. Did the people in the house with the Whirlpool documents take advantage of them?
A. We don't control those people.
Q. Well, why do you give them your papers, then? Why do you make a profit off of them?
A. If they have a complaint about their financing, we evaluate that.
Q. That's not the question. The question is, if you don't control them, why do you give them the paperwork and let them go into somebody's house?
A. We looked at them as any other dealer. We have to assume—I mean, there's all kinds of dealers out there. We basically think that people are honest.
Q. Well, once you get notice through a lawsuit and stuff like that, why don't you make any changes to try to stop it?
A. We evaluate it—as I explained before, we evaluate every complaint individually. We pull all the paperwork, try and find out if there truly was validity to every complaint that we get. We get thousands and thousands of complaints a week.
Q. You get thousands of complaints a week?
A. Sure.[7]

Exhibit 4   WHIRLPOOL'S VISION STATEMENT AND CORPORATE VALUES

OUR VISION

Every Home . . . Everywhere. With Pride, Passion and Performance. We create the world's best home appliances, which make life easier and more enjoyable for all people. Our goal is a Whirlpool product in every home, everywhere. We will achieve this by creating:

Pride . . . in our work and each other

Passion . . . for creating unmatched customer loyalty for our brands

Performance . . . results that excite and reward global investors with superior returns

We bring this dream to life through the power of our unique global enterprise and our outstanding people . . . working together . . . everywhere.

OUR VALUES

- **Respect**—We do our best work when we trust one another as individuals, encourage diversity in our workplace, value the capabilities and contributions of each person, and recognize that work is but one part of a full and rewarding life.

- **Integrity**—We conduct all aspects of our business in an honorable way, recognizing there is no right way to do a wrong thing.

- **Diversity**—The broad diversity of our people and their ideas is the fundamental foundation for the future success of our company. Differences create value.

- **Teamwork**—Pride results in our working together to unleash the potential of every person. By working together we will achieve exceptional results.

Source: www.whirlpool.com, December 20, 2002.

The Jury's Verdict and Subsequent Events

At the conclusion of the trial, the jury found Whirlpool Corporation liable for the actions of its agents (Gulf Coast Electronics) in misleading the residents of rural Alabama about the terms and conditions of the sale of satellite antennas to improve television reception in the area. The jury assessed damages in the amount of $531 million. That amount was reduced upon appeal to $301 million. The two parties (attorneys for the plaintiffs and for the defendant) then settled privately out of court; the amount of that settlement has never been publicly revealed.

Whirlpool's vision statement and corporate values are presented in Exhibit 4.

Endnotes

[1]Facts as to Don Gantt's status were established in the trial transcript: *Barbara Carlisle and George & Velma Merriweather, Plaintiff,* v. *Whirlpool Financial National Bank & Don Gantt, D/B/A Gulf Coast Electronics, Defendant,* Circuit Court, Hale County, Alabama, CV-97-68 & CV-97-69, May 5–6, 1999, p. 163.
[2]Ibid., p. 48, line 17, to p. 49, line 1.
[3]Ibid., p. 30, lines 10–24.
[4]Ibid., p. 127, line 21, to p. 128, line 12.
[5]Ibid., p. 184, line 24, to p. 185, line 20.
[6]Ibid., p. 283, line 10, to p. 284, line 23.
[7]Ibid., p. 304, line 25, to p. 306, line 14.

Photo Credits

Indexes

Name

Aaron, Tommy, C–221
Adams, John, C–221
Adams, N., C–286
Adamson, James, C–459, C–472,
      C–475, C–479, C–480, C–481
Albers, Kristi, C–220
Alcorn, Al, C–232
Alexander, Marcus, 190
Alexander, Ralph, C–424, C–439
Aleyne, Alan, 96
Alfredsson, Helen, C–220
Allaire, Paul, 272
Allen, David, C–127
Allen, Paul, C–231
Alonzo, V., C–184
Amanor-Boadu, Vincent, C–134
Ames, Peter, C–32, C–33
Ames, Stephen, C–220
Anderson, Richard N., C–177
Andrews, Brad, C–221
Andrews, Donna, C–220
Antonini, Joseph, C–462, C–466
Appert, Nicolas, C–288
Applebaum, Alec, C–52
Archer, George, C–221
Arnault, Bernard, C–382 to C–409
Atkins, Luke, C–55 to C–59
Austen, I., C–286
Ayhan, Altay, C–293, C–295 to
      C–298, C–301 to C–307

Bach, Robert, C–235, C–244
Backwell, Richard, C–221
Baeb, Eddie, C–52
Baena, Marisa, C–220
Baer, Ralph, C–231, C–232
Bailey, Jeff, C–52
Baker, J. F., C–271
Baker, Peter, C–220
Ball, Edmund, C–287
Ball, Frank, C–287
Ball, George, C–287
Ball, Lucius, C–287
Ball, William, C–287
Ballesteros, Seve, C–220
Ballon, M., C–184
Barcelo, Rich, C–221
Barrett, Colleen, C–525, C–536,
      C–549, C–550

Bartlett, Christopher A., 265
Barton, David, C–134
Baser, Mehmet, C–293, C–301,
      C–303, C–307
Bateman, Ahmad, C–221
Bauer, Beth, C–220
Beem, Rich, C–220, C–227
Bell, Joseph R., C–185
Belson, Ken, C–117
Belton, Beth, C–52
Berner, Robert, C–52
Bernick, Carol Lavin, 310
Berry, Ray, C–20, C–21
Bethune, Gordon, C–492 to C–520
Bezos, Jeff, C–264
Bhide, Amar, 108, 294
Bies, Don, C–221
Birinyi, Laszlo, 36
Blair, J., C–271
Blair, Tony, C–420
Boland, Michael, C–134
Booth, Jennifer, C–247
Bossidy, Lawrence, 242, 272
Bradenberger, Adam M., 108, C–249
Brades, R., C–380
Brady, D., C–271
Brandon, David, C–164
Brennan, Edward, C–39,
      C–40, C–41
Brennan, Patrick F., C–177
Brenneman, Greg, C–493 to C–497,
      C–499, C–500, C–506, C–510
Brooker, Katrina, C–554
Brown, Alex, C–191
Brown, Suzanne C., C–164,
      C–182, C–183
Browne, Olin, C–220
Browne, Sir John, C–420, C–424,
      C–426, C–430, C–431,
      C–432, C–435, C–436,
      C–437, C–438, C–440,
      C–441, C–442
Brumback, N., C–184
Buckley, Neil, C–52
Buffett, Warren, C–358
Bull, George, C–361
Bullock, Tom, C–143
Bunch, Ashli, C–220
Bush, George W., C–491, C–559
Busnell, Nolan, C–232

Butler, Don, C–580
Butler, Nick, C–424, C–425,
      C–432, C–439
Byrne, John A., 242, 249

Calcavecchia, Mark, C–220
Callaway, Ely Reeves, Jr., C–205,
      C–206, C–208, C–218,
      C–219, C–223
Campbell, Andrew, 190
Candler, Asa, C–165
Carlisle, Barbara, C–586, C–588
Carlson, David, C–464
Carlson, Eugene, C–52
Carrington, Tim, C–52
Carroll, David, C–587, C–588
Carter, Jim, C–220
Carvajal, D., C–271
Castaldi, Richard, C–357
Cavanagh, James, C–357
Cerf, Bennett, C–269
Chadwick, Raymond, C–357,
      C–358, C–378 to C–381
Champy, James, 272
Chan, Ronnie, C–567
Chan, Timothy, C–143
Chang, Matthew, C–482
Charan, Ram, 242
Charles, Bob, C–221
Chase, Rodney, C–425, C–426,
      C–428 to C–434, C–436,
      C–438
Cheever, Eddie, C–198
Chen, TC, C–221
Chevalier, Alain, C–383,
      C–385, C–386
Choi, K. J., C–220
Chowdhury, Neel, C–117
Chronis, George T., C–235
Claar, Brian, C–221
Clark, Gary, C–220
Clark, Ken, C–52
Clark, Thomas, C–287
Cleveland, Roger, C–217
Clinton, Bill, C–491, C–560
Cohen, B., C–184
Cohen, M., C–179
Cohen, S., C–249
Colbert, Jim, C–221

Organization

Subject